‹‹

THE WISDOM OF
CATHOLICISM

THE WISDOM
OF
CATHOLICISM

<<<<<<<<<<<<<<<<<<<<<<<<<<<<<<<<<<<<<<<<<<<

EDITED, WITH AN INTRODUCTION

AND NOTES, BY

ANTON C. PEGIS

PRESIDENT, PONTIFICAL INSTITUTE OF

MEDIAEVAL STUDIES, TORONTO

<<<<<<<<<<<<<<<<<<<<<<<<<<<<<<<<<<<<<<<<<<<

THE MODERN LIBRARY
NEW YORK

THE MODERN LIBRARY

is published by RANDOM HOUSE, INC.

Manufactured in the United States of America by H. Wolff

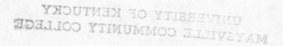

NIHIL OBSTAT

Vincent L. Kennedy, C.S.B.
Censor Deputatus

IMPRIMATUR

✠ James C. Cardinal McGuigan, D.D.
Archbishop of Toronto

March 7, 1949

To

His Eminence

JAMES C. CARDINAL McGUIGAN

Archbishop of Toronto

and

Chancellor of the Pontifical Institute

of Mediaeval Studies

To

His Eminence

JAMES C. CARDINAL McGUIGAN

Archbishop of Toronto

and

Chancellor of the Pontifical Institute

of Mediaeval Studies

ACKNOWLEDGMENTS

For the right to include the copyrighted items in this volume, the publisher is indebted to the following authors, publishers and translators:

Geoffrey Bles, Ltd., for "Who Is My Neighbour?" from *Ransoming the Time,* by Jacques Maritain.

The British Academy, London, for "St. Thomas Aquinas," by Etienne Gilson.

Cassell and Company, Ltd., for "The Cross," from *Kristin Lavransdatter,* by Sigrid Undset.

A. J. Denomy, C.S.B., for his translation of Selections from the *Pensées,* by Blaise Pascal. Copyright, 1949, by Random House, Inc.

Distributist Books for "The Restoration of Property," from *An Essay on the Restoration of Property,* by Hilaire Belloc.

Eyre & Spottiswodde, Ltd., for "The Four Last Things: Death," by St. Thomas More.

Harper and Brothers, for Book II of *The Imitation of Christ,* by Thomas à Kempis. Translated by Richard Whitford. Edward J. Klein, editor.

Harvard University Press (Loeb Classical Library) for "Address to Young Men on Reading Greek Literature," by St. Basil the Great. Translated by Roy J. Deferrari and Martin R. P. McGuire. For Books IV and V of *The Consolation of Philosophy,* by Boethius. Translated by F. H. Stewart and E. K. Rand. For "Medieval Universalism and Its Present Value," from the Harvard Tercentenary Publication: *Independence, Convergence, and Borrowing in Institutions, Thought and Art,* by Etienne Gilson.

Alfred A. Knopf, Inc., for "The Cross," from *Kristin Lavransdatter,* by Sigrid Undset. Copyright, 1926, by Alfred A. Knopf, Inc. Translated by Charles Archer and J. F. Scott.

The Macmillan Company, for "The World Inside Out," from *The Catholic Church and Conversion,* by Gilbert Keith Chesterton. Copyright, 1926, by The Macmillan Company.

Peter Nash, S. J., for his translation of *On the Ascent of the Mind to God,* by St. Robert Bellarmine. Copyright, 1949, by Random House, Inc.

J. R. O'Donnell, C.S.B., for his translation of "The Letter to Denis of Borgo-San Sepolcro," by Francis Petrarch; and *The Paraclesis,* by Desiderius Erasmus. Copyright, 1949, by Random House, Inc.

Oxford University Press, for "St. Thomas Aquinas," by Etienne Gilson. For "The Parson's Tale," from *The Canterbury Tales,* by Geoffrey Chaucer.

Pantheon Books, Inc., for "A Vision of Prayer," from *Basic Verities,* by Charles Péguy. Copyright, 1943, by Pantheon Books, Inc.

E. Allison Peers, for his translation of *The Interior Castle* (Seventh Mansion), by St. Teresa of Avila.

Anton C. Pegis, for his translations of *The Proslogion,* by St. Anselm of Canterbury; Selections from *The Ascent of the Mind to God,* by St. Bonaventure; "Wisdom, Beatitude and the Incarnation" (from the *Summa Contra Gentiles*), by St. Thomas Aquinas. Copyright, 1949, by Random House, Inc.

A. N. Peters, for "The Restoration of Property," from *An Essay on the Restoration of Property,* by Hilaire Belloc.

Routledge and Kegan Paul, Ltd., for "A Vision of Prayer," from *Basic Verities,* by Charles Péguy. Translated by Anne and Julian Green.

Dr. Ludwig Schopp, owner and editorial director of the Series *The Fathers of the Church,* for *To the Romans,* by St. Ignatius of Antioch. Translated by Gerald G. Walsh, S.J.

Charles Scribner's Sons, for "Who Is My Neighbour?" from *Ransoming the Time,* by Jacques Maritain. Translated by Harry Lorin Binsse. Copyright, 1941, by Charles Scribner's Sons.

Sheed and Ward, Inc., for a Selection from *The Satin Slipper,* by Paul Claudel. Translated by John O'Connor. For "The Failure of Liberalism," from *The Judgment of the Nations,* by Christopher Dawson.

The Society of Authors, London, for "The Failure of Liberalism," from *The Judgment of the Nations,* by Christopher Dawson.

Spiritual Book Associates, Inc., for *On the Necessity of Loving God,* by St. Bernard of Clairvaux. Translated by Terence Connolly, S.J.

PREFACE

WHEN MY PUBLISHER, Mr. Bennett Cerf, invited me to edit *The Wisdom of Catholicism,* I was fascinated by the challenge in the idea, as well as appalled by the enormity of the task that it involved. Originally, I was not even sure that it was possible. A comprehensive selection, either from the point of view of chronology or from that of subject-matter, is a sheer impossibility, even within the generous proportions of a thousand pages. On the other hand, a collection of page or half-page excerpts from hundreds of authors would be quite possible, but not worth having; for, just as "seeing Europe" does not consist in a frantic checking-off of every item in Baedeker, so meeting "the wisdom of Catholicism" does not consist in accumulating a list of names after the fashion of a directory. It has seemed to me, therefore, that the only thing worth doing in the preparation of such a volume as this is to take the history of Catholic thought in its chronological order and to select, within what is admittedly a vast literature, the enduring themes, the constant centers of interest, the great teachings and ideals, the heroic lives and eminent writings of the outstanding Catholic men and women who are the landmarks of Catholicism in history. I am sensible of the omissions from this book. I can only say that the family of Catholic writers is very large—too large to be included within the covers of any one book. Nevertheless, I should wish to argue that the selections which I have included are great monuments of Catholic writing, and that most of them are truly classical in their value and significance.

There are two omissions, however, on which some comment is necessary. Catholic writers in all ages are full of scriptural texts, and when they do not quote Scripture directly, they yet manage to echo its very language. Under such circumstances, I have thought it permissible not to include a separate section devoted to the Old and New Testaments. In the second place, I have no separate selection of Catholic poets. My reason is very simple. It seems to me that poetry in translation loses its artistic individuality; to be appreciated as poetry, it must therefore be read in the language in which it is written. The few poems which I have included are present in this volume for their doctrinal and spiritual qualities rather than for their literary form.

It is a great pleasure for me to discharge a long-standing debt and to thank the many people who have helped me in many ways in the preparation of *The Wisdom of Catholicism*. First of all, I should like to express my thanks to Etienne Gilson, who has helped me very generously in many discussions on the contents of the present book. Sincere thanks for valuable help are also due to the Reverend Louis J. Bondy, C.S.B., Superior of St. Michael's College, Toronto; to the Reverend Gerald B. Phelan, Director of The Mediaeval Institute, University of Notre Dame; and to the Reverend Vincent L. Kennedy, C.S.B., of The Pontifical Institute, Toronto. To the translators of new materials I wish to express my appreciation for their participation in the volume: to the Reverend Alexander J. Denomy, C.S.B., of The Pontifical Institute, Toronto, for his translation of Pascal; to the Reverend J. Reginald O'Donnell, C.S.B., of The Pontifical Institute, Toronto, for his translation of Petrarch and Erasmus; and to the Reverend Peter W. Nash, S.J., of the Jesuit Seminary, Toronto, for his translation of St. Robert Bellarmine. I wish to thank Dr. Ludwig Schopp, Director of the Cosmopolitan Science and Art Service Co., New York, for his assistance in securing some bibliographical material for me. For generous help during the various stages in the preparation of the manuscript of this book for the press, I must thank the Reverend Armand Maurer, C.S.B., of St. Michael's College, Toronto; Dr. Lottie Kendzierski, of Marquette University; and Mrs. George H. Newlands, of Toronto. To Mr. Bennett Cerf, I am indebted for inviting me to edit a book which has given me a great deal of pleasure along with a great deal of work. Finally, to Mr. Saxe Commins, I must express not only my thanks for the editorial wisdom and patience which he has exercised toward me, but also my apologies for many delays. If the

present book has any merits, they are due in no small part to the
help which I have received. It is to acknowledge this help that I
have set down the above names. If the present book is not better
than it is, I must take sole responsibility for that.

Toronto, Canada   A.C.P.
1 March, 1949

CONTENTS

Contents

xvii

Contents

INTRODUCTION

Per ipsam sapientiam ad immortalitatis regnum pervenitur
ST. THOMAS AQUINAS

N INTRODUCTION TO THE WRITERS REPRESENTED in this book is, in a real sense, presumptuous. They speak eloquently for themselves, and they need only to be read to prove that they are far better able than anyone else to present their work to every variety of reader. And not only are prefatory statements frequently inadequate, they are sometimes impossible. Exactly how am I to introduce the ninth and tenth books of St. Augustine's *Confessions*? Dona Prouheze's dream in Claudel's *Satin Slipper*? the reflections of God the Father in Péguy's *Vision of Prayer*? the end of Kristin's life in Sigrid Undset's *Kristin Lavransdatter*? Here are works of art which must be communicated as wholes in order to be communicated at all. For it is a fact that great artistic efforts, like human personalities, can be met, they cannot be reported.

I am not indulging, therefore, in any false humility in the presence of eminent writers when I refuse to give an introduction to them. There is no substitute for meeting them in themselves. But this is only part of the story, and of my problem. For I am not saying simply that we can be brought into contact with the genius of a great writer only by meeting it. More than this, it is a fact that the *Confessions* of St. Augustine and the *Proslogion* of St. Anselm, to choose the two most obvious examples, are religious meditations addressed, not to any particular reader, nor impersonally to all readers, but most personally to God Himself.

St. Augustine prays to God and thanks Him for turning a proud and wayward rhetorician to Himself. He bewails the desolation of those dozen years and more when he wallowed in the abyss of lust, until at length, even as in the first creation, God moved over the chaos of his passion and turned his love toward Beauty. Late, late have I loved Thee, Wisdom ever ancient and ever new! This was the cry of Augustine as he wrote the *Confessions*. How is it possible not to ruin the *Confessions* by reporting it impersonally as a spectator and in the form of a chronicle? The extraordinary gifts of Augustine as an observer of his own soul were used by him in the service of his love of God and of the dedication of his whole life to that love. Who, then, can report the prayer that was the life of Augustine?

And was it not extraordinary on the part of St. Anselm to include a proof of the existence of God in a spiritual meditation addressed to Him? As for Pascal, how is one to report those famous reasons known to the heart of man, but not to his head? For the source of the reasons that the heart has is the charity of Christ, and how can one understand them without living them?

I realize, of course, that in our own day it is extremely fashionable to speak of great books and even to prepare lists of them. Those who engage in this work often have no hesitation in uprooting a book from the world and the age in which it was written, and even from the mind of the man who wrote it. Thus understood, the great books are no more than a ghostly conversation, out of time and out of history, carried on with abstract finesse by those who are themselves no more than abstractions. The disciples of such utopian dreaming are, without any doubt, motivated by a desire to be faithful to that which is perennial in man, in his life and in his activity. Yet it is a fact that the great writers of history have not been utopians. Far from running away from history to some faraway Thule, as the price of giving expression to perennial truths, they have united themselves with remarkable fidelity to their own age in order to achieve, within its setting and circumstances, a timeless vision of man and his history. No book has been more wedded to its own world than Augustine's *City of God;* but none has been more timeless in its vision of history. Assuredly, the great writers have not been utopians; they have rather been, in the most authentic meaning of the words, reformers and deliverers.

Let me use as an example the work of Jacques Maritain in the modern world. No one can deny the timelessness of the message which Maritain has been proclaiming to his fellow men since the beginning of the twentieth century. Yet Maritain's contact with his own world is extraordinarily intimate. He has engaged in its problems, he has fought its battles with a stubborn determination, he has been sensitive to all the winds of good and evil that have been sweeping, day by day, across the Western world. In the midst of his duties as French Ambassador to the Holy See, he wrote one of his most penetrating metaphysical books. Nor is Maritain's participation in the life of the modern world some sort of external annex to the eternal truths which are at the core of his thinking. On the contrary, he has participated in the modern world as one who has wished to grasp its problems in all the immediacy of the present as well as in all the eternity of truth. Maritain's work is nothing if not timely. He has meditated on the perennial truths of Thomism, not out of history but within it; and within history he has lived, not in the thirteenth century, but in the twentieth. All this has not prevented him from seeing truth with a timeless vision and from working, with fraternal charity, toward the participation by his neighbor in that same vision. Conceivably, one might take part of Maritain's thought and ignore the rest. One might, for example, take that part of his thought which, being perennial, can suffer the violence of being disembodied. Yet that would no longer be Maritain, but rather the perennial center of his thought seen in abstraction from his whole life and work. Maritain himself, as a Catholic thinker in the twentieth century, has tried to see truth in all its eternity and to do so within the needs of the temporal order in which he has been living. He has not preached eternity against time; he has rather preached the eternalizing of time.

These remarks should not be understood as one more eulogy of

Maritain and his writings. My point has been to insist that his work
is the mirror of the world in which he lives; or rather, it is the
world in which he lives, experienced in all the demands of the
present, but seen in the timeless mirror of eternity. This is, I believe, an authentic mark of great writers and great books. The
timeless truths which they succeed in presenting are also an expression and a liberation of man's historical life. They pick up the often
obscure tendencies and problems of their world and, by the strength
of their understanding, contribute to the ordering of man's life in
the world of time. The vision of great books is universal, and yet
their substance is historically concrete. For if the author of a great
book holds up the mirror of eternity and of the eternal destiny of
man before the eyes of his contemporaries, his concern is not merely
to focus their attention upon timeless horizons; his concern is also
to permeate the restless life of their world with the light of eternity,
and in this way to enable the men of his age to experience, at their
particular moment in history, the spiritual grandeur and direction
of human nature.

And it is a fact that the eternalizing of man's life, the salvation
of the world of time in and by eternity, has been the great theme
and occupation of Catholic writers over the centuries. For them,
human history has no other substance, no other direction, no other
boundaries; and human life itself, in all its phases, individual and
social, private and public, has no other goal. How Catholic writers
have gravitated with unfailing wonder around man! How often,
too, have they not repeated the question of the Psalmist: *What is
man that Thou art mindful of him?* And they have not failed to
continue with the words of the Psalmist: *Thou hast made him a
little less than the angels, Thou hast crowned him with glory and
honor, and hast set him over the works of Thy hands* (Ps. viii, 5-7).
He is no ordinary being, this man whom God has created a little
below the angels, nor does he lead an ordinary existence. Created
with gifts of nature and grace, redeemed in his fall by the death of
the God-Man on the Cross, sustained by the sacramental life in
which he shares as a member of the Mystical Body of Christ, the
Church, the Christian man is all that St. Bernard has said of him—
a noble creature with a majestic destiny. He also verifies all that
St. Augustine saw in him—or, rather, in himself—when, after

God calmed his moral storms, he exclaimed: *Thou hast made us unto Thyself, O Lord, and our hearts are restless until they rest in Thee!* Only, because man is such a veritable wayfarer and pilgrim, living by faith and hope and love in the world of time, he has probed within the recesses of his own being in order to understand even a little of the mystery of the ways of God to him. There is, in truth, nothing else for man to do. For his very existence as a spiritual being is in itself an invitation—an invitation from God his Creator—to discover his deepest center, and to weigh the meaning of the hunger of his head and of his heart. And though Catholic thinkers have meditated on the mysteries of human existence in many ways, they have unfolded in their several ways the outlines of a common spiritual ideal, an ideal and odyssey.

What is man? He is a rational creature whose personality and liberty are a dignity which nothing in the world of time may demean. He is such a noble creature that only God is his Master; and, under God, he is asked to participate as a free man in the fulfillment of his destiny. He is the servant of truth, and only of truth; for truth is the governor of his mind, as well as the food of his growth in understanding and in love. His life as a man is for him no provincial episode destined to become part of that stale dust of history which Marcus Aurelius dreaded so much. His existence, being open in its understanding to eternity and to the source of all being, is an unfolding personal journey, *his* eternal becoming, *his* signature in the bosom of God written in the characters that are the days of his temporal pilgrimage. His life, therefore, does not pass, as the years pass; it rather becomes through time more fully and completely itself.

We must, it seems to me, recognize the deep personalism that runs through Catholic thought. It is a personalism which is at once religious and metaphysical, and which colors all the aspects of human life. For Catholic supernaturalism contains within itself not only the theme of man's salvation and redemption, but also the theme of the glorification of his nature in the Incarnation. The Incarnation does more than save man from the consequences of the fall of Adam; or rather, in redeeming man by His own death, Christ has also answered for man the question of his eternal beatitude. In the Incarnation, God has fulfilled the desire of man's nature for perfect beatitude: the tent-dweller that is the human pilgrim in history knows from Christ that he has a lasting dwelling in eternity.

That is why it is natural to all Catholics to live in a world of mystery—the mystery of the Incarnation and the Redemption, the mystery of Christ's Spouse, the Church, at once invisible and visible. Within this world, a St. Bernard, tenderly devoted to the sacred humanity of Christ, prayed and toiled, knowing, as he said, that God anticipated all his prayers. In this same world, St. Bonaventure meditated on the words of St. Matthew that only one is our Teacher, Christ. And St. Anselm, that most gentle and lovable of mediaeval monks, what is he but the very model of the Christian wayfarer, living by faith, praying for understanding and liberation, until the day when God will bring his journey to an end? And there is St. Thomas More, who, knowing very well what he could expect from Henry VIII, sealed his own fate by declaring himself to be "the King's good servant—but God's first."

There have been sinners, too, in this same Christian world, and their halting and stumbling steps have been used by God to write, with crooked lines, the mystery of their salvation—or the hope of it. Augustine certainly was not happy that he had been a sinner; but he never ceased marveling at what God had made out of a sinner. Kristin learned, at length, through a tempestuous life, that she was, after all, the Lord's anointed. And Rodrigo and Prouheze, not to mention here Evelyn Waugh's Sebastian, learn to surrender themselves to the hand of God only after they have suffered in the fires of existence. How much Prouheze had to learn from God about love, and even about her own beauty!

But the personalism of Catholic thought can be seen, not only in the reflections of a Claudel or a Péguy on the mystery of the Redemption, but also in the humanism of the Catholic ideal of man and society. Here I should like to acknowledge that my first reading of the writings of mediaeval monks was an astonishing experience; and I can report it only in a way which must surely appear astonishing to others. It seems to me that we have not noticed sufficiently the humanism of the monks of the twelfth century—St. Bernard of Clairvaux, William of Saint-Thierry, Hugh and Richard of St. Victor, to cite no others. Before the coming of

Aristotle and his major philosophical works into the Latin world, these men loved man's nature and reason. Otherworldly ascetics they may have been. Yet their otherworldliness was not a negation of human nature and its desires, but the purest of affirmations. If his cell at Clairvaux was for Bernard a veritable antechamber to heaven itself, even so, this impassioned lover of God left nothing of himself outside the doorstep of the monastery when he entered Cîteaux at the age of twenty-two—he left nothing, that is, except pride and disorder. He became a monk in order to learn how to be a man. It is literally true that the monastery was for the twelfth-century monks a school in which they learned how to grow into free and integral Christian men—free in their personal discovery of the meaning of their rational nature, in their participation in the work of liberating themselves from moral disorder, in their experience of the unfolding of their humanity in the school of the love of God. William of Saint-Thierry, a friend of St. Bernard, has even proposed that the monk is the normal man.

For, once more, what is man? The answer of Christian monasticism is an enduring one. To the Abbot of Saint-Thierry man is normally and in the very center of his being a lover of God. *Normally* does not mean here *ordinarily*. Man is not ordinarily what he ought to be. But if he will enter within himself, within his own memory, in which he is asleep in his own history; if he will push aside the accumulated storage of his life and come face to face with himself, he can verify a famous Augustinian idea: in his most secret self, man is a mind who remembers God. His life is, or should be, a fulfillment of that memory. For man's understanding and knowledge, his will and his desire, what are they in their very nature but an effort to grasp and love an unforgettable divine presence?

What a remarkable man is to be found in Abbot William! Man is most man when he loves God most perfectly; for he is then most in possession of his liberty. This is surely one of the dearest lessons of Catholic and European humanism; and it is worth remembering that the great monks of the West lived and preached this ideal of human liberty, and that they laid the foundations of Europe on it; for Europe was born, not in the fall of the Roman Empire, but in the spiritual vitality of the monasteries. What more universal and

lasting ambition has the European man had than this ideal of building a world of freedom, under God, within himself and on the
earth? The European man learned his first lessons on liberty in
the monastery, even as he first discovered himself by wearing the
habit of a monk.

The heritage of the monasteries is still the substance of the Catholic view of man and his life. The Church has proclaimed it with
all the spiritual authority at her command. From the papal encyclicals in this volume, we may learn the Church's ideal of a perennial
philosophy, of the principles of justice and charity which should
rule the economic relations of men, of the Mystical Body in which
men are united as children of God. From Maritain's essay we may
learn the spiritual fellowship of men in the kingdom of the divine
love; and from Gilson the universalism of the mediaeval notion
of man as a rational creature.

No doubt, having in the modern world allowed man to become
nothing more than an engineer in the service of nature, we have
allowed ourselves to forget this Christian heritage. Yet the heritage
is there to observe; and to observe it at the present moment may be
the only chance of survival that civilization has. For the sword
of Damocles hanging over our world is not the atom bomb; it is
the depersonalization of man. The question is not, will civilization
survive? but, what is civilization? It is, St. Augustine said many
centuries ago, man's participation in the building of the City of
God. That is the theme of Catholic wisdom. When, in the thirteenth
century, Christianity came out of the monasteries, there was a
moment in European history when the Christian conception of
man's temporal life in the world might have become a reality;
there was a moment when old Alcuin's dream of a Christian Athens,
full of the glories of nature possessed by ancient Athens, but made
much more glorious by the gifts of the Holy Spirit, could have
been established in the Western world. But, instead, Christianity
entered upon its centuries of conflict and division and disunity;
and the dream of man which had been nurtured in the devout
Christianity of the monasteries has lived as a dream of the Church
until the day it would touch men themselves with its spiritual fire.

Great Catholic writers have been touched by the mystery that is
in the depth of man's being, the mystery of his allegiance to truth

and liberty, itself rooted in the mystery of the divine love. Therein lies, in fact, their eminence. Those who read the following selections will easily realize the futility of reporting, in any editorial Introduction, the Catholic vision of man. That vision is a rich monument of prayer and meditation, of suffering and martyrdom, of repentance and thanksgiving. And I have not had the illusion that I could state in a few words what it has taken lives to build. I have rather wished, in the foregoing remarks, to record my gratitude to the great Catholic teachers of the past and of the present.

Anton C. Pegis

THE WISDOM OF CATHOLICISM

ST. IGNATIUS
of ANTIOCH

TO THE ROMANS

I am God's wheat: I am ground by the teeth of the
wild beasts that I may end as the pure bread of Christ.

IGNATIUS, disciple of the Apostles, bishop of Antioch (perhaps
from the year 69) suffered martyrdom in the Roman Coliseum at
the turn of the second century. From Smyrna, on his way to his
martyrdom, he wrote to the Christians in Rome, asking them not
to interfere with his coming death. He wants, he says, to have
the wild beasts consume him completely, so that he may end as
the pure bread of Christ. History has recorded that Ignatius received his wish in the arena of the Coliseum. The year of his
martyrdom is very likely 107.

GNATIUS THEOPHORUS TO THE CHURCH ON
which the majesty of the most high Father and
of Jesus Christ, His only Son, has had mercy; to
the Church beloved and enlightened by the faith
and charity of Jesus Christ, our God, through the
will of Him who has willed all things that exist
—the Church in the place of the country of the Romans which
holds the primacy. I salute you in the name of Jesus Christ, the
Son of the Father. You are a Church worthy of God, worthy of
honor, felicitation and praise, worthy of attaining to God, a Church
without blemish, which holds the primacy of the community of

love, obedient to Christ's law, bearing the Father's name. To you who are united, outwardly and inwardly, in the whole of His commandment and filled with grace, in union with God and with every alien stain filtered away, I wish every innocent joy in Jesus Christ, our God.

¶ 1. In answer to my prayer and beyond all I asked for, I have at last seen the faces I have longed to see. In chains as I am for Jesus Christ, I hope to salute you, if only it be His will to grant me grace to reach my goal. I shall know that the beginning is providential if, in the end, without hindrance, I am to obtain the inheritance. But I am afraid of your love; it may do me wrong. It is easy for you to have your way, but, if you do not yield to me, it will be hard for me to reach God.

¶ 2. I would have you think of pleasing God—as indeed you do—rather than men. For at no later time shall I have an opportunity like this of reaching God; nor can you ever have any better deed ascribed to you—if only you remain silent. If only you will say nothing in my behalf, I shall be a word of God. But, if your love is for my body, I shall be once more a mere voice. You can do me no greater kindness than to suffer me to be sacrificed to God while the place of sacrifice is still prepared. Thus forming yourselves into a chorus of love, you may sing to the Father in Jesus Christ that God gave the bishop of Syria the grace of being transferred from the rising to the setting sun. It is good to set, leaving the world for God, and so to rise in Him.

¶ 3. Never have you envied anyone. You have been others' teachers. I trust that what you have taught and prescribed to others may now be applied by yourselves. Beg only that I may have inward and outward strength, not only in word but in will, that I may be a Christian not merely in name but in fact. For, if I am one in fact, then I may be called one and be faithful long after I have vanished from the world. Nothing merely visible is good, for our God, Jesus Christ, is manifest the more now that He is hidden in God. Christianity is not the work of persuasion, but, whenever it is hated by the world, it is a work of power.

¶ 4. I am writing to all the Churches to tell them all that I am, with all my heart, to die for God—if only you do not prevent it. I beseech you not to indulge your benevolence at the wrong time. Please let me be thrown to the wild beasts; through them I can reach God. I am God's wheat; I am ground by the teeth of the wild beasts that I may end as the pure bread of Christ. If anything, coax the beasts on to become my sepulcher and to leave nothing of my body undevoured so that, when I am dead, I may be no bother to anyone. I shall be really a disciple of Jesus Christ if and when the world can no longer see so much as my body. Make petition, then, to the Lord for me, so that by these means I may be made a sacrifice to God. I do not command you, as Peter and Paul did. They were Apostles; I am a condemned man. They were free men; I am still a slave. Still, if I suffer, I shall be emancipated by Jesus Christ and, in my resurrection, shall be free. But now in chains I am learning to have no wishes of my own.

¶ 5. I am already battling with beasts on my journey from Syria to Rome. On land and at sea, by night and by day, I am in chains with ten leopards around me—or at least with a band of guards who grow more brutal the better they are treated. However, the wrongs they do me make me a better disciple. 'But that is not where my justification lies.' May I find my joy in the beasts that have been made ready for me. My prayer is that they will be prompt in dealing with me. I shall coax them to devour me without delay and not be afraid to touch me, as has happened in some cases. And if, when I am ready, they hold back, I shall provoke them to attack me. Pardon me, but I know what is good for me. I am now beginning to be a disciple; may nothing visible or invisible prevent me from reaching Jesus Christ. Fire and cross and battling with wild beasts, [their clawing and tearing,] the breaking of bones and mangling of members, the grinding of my whole body, the wicked torments of the devil—let them all assail me, so long as I get to Jesus Christ.

¶ 6. Neither the kingdoms of this world nor the bounds of the universe can have any use for me. I would rather die for Jesus Christ than rule the last reaches of the earth. My search is for Him who died for us; my love is for Him who rose for our salvation.

The pangs of new birth are upon me. Forgive me, brethren. Do nothing to prevent this new life. Do not desire that I should perish. Do not hand over to the world a man whose heart is fixed on God. Do not entice me with material things. Allow me to receive the pure light. When I reach it, I shall be fully a man. Allow me to be a follower of the passion of my God. Let those who hold Him in their hearts understand what urges me, realize what I am choosing, and share my feelings.

¶ 7. The prince of this world is eager to tear me to pieces, to weaken my will that is fixed on God. Let none of you who are watching the battle abet him. Come in, rather, on my side, for it is the side of God. Do not let your lips be for Jesus Christ and your heart for the world. Let envy have no place among you. And even, when I am come, if I should beseech you, pay no attention to what I say; believe, rather, what I am writing to you now. For alive as I am at this moment of writing, my longing is for death. Desire within me has been nailed to the cross and no flame of material longing is left. Only the living water speaks within me saying: Hasten to the Father. I have no taste for the food that perishes nor for the pleasures of this life. I want the Bread of God which is the Flesh of Christ, who was of the seed of David; and for drink I desire His blood which is love that cannot be destroyed.

¶ 8. I desire no longer to live a purely human life; and this desire can be fulfilled if you consent. Make this your choice, if you yourselves would be chosen. I make my petition in a few words. Please believe me; Jesus Christ will make it clear to you that I speak the truth, for He was the mouth without deceit through which the Father truly spoke. Beg for me that, through the Holy Spirit, I may not fail. I have not written to you after the manner of men, but according to the mind of God. If I die, it will prove you loved me; if I am rejected, it will be because you hated me.

¶ 9. Remember in your prayers that Church of Syria, which now, in place of me, has God for its pastor. Jesus Christ, along with your love, will be its only bishop. For myself, I am ashamed to be called one of them, for I am not worthy, being the last among them and, as it were, born out of due time. If I reach God, I shall be some one only by His mercy. My spirit salutes you—and with it the love of the Churches which welcomed me in the name of Jesus Christ. They treated me as more than a passing pilgrim; for even the communities that did not lie along the route I was taking conducted me from city to city.

¶ 10. I am writing this letter to you from Smyrna by the hands of the Ephesians, who deserve all praise. Among many others who are with me there is my dear friend Crocus. I trust you have come to know those who went ahead of me from Syria to Rome for the glory of God. Please tell them that I am not far away. All of them are worthy of God and of yourselves. You will do well to help them in every way. The date of this writing is the ninth day before the calends of September. Farewell, and persevere to the end in Jesus Christ.

ST. BASIL
the GREAT

ADDRESS *to* YOUNG MEN *on*
READING GREEK LITERATURE

✠

> It is no small advantage that a certain intimacy and
> familiarity with virtue should be engendered in the
> souls of the young, seeing that the lessons learned by
> such are likely, in the nature of the case, to be indeli-
> ble, having been deeply impressed in them by reason
> of the tenderness of their souls.

BROTHER of the no less famous Gregory of Nyssa, educated in
Caesaria, Constantinople and Athens, St. Basil the Great (330-
379) was ordained priest in 362 and elected bishop of Caesaria in
370. He has exercised considerable influence on Eastern and
Western asceticism. *The Address to Young Men,* so reminiscent
of Plato in many details, does not reveal Basil the administrator,
the fearless opponent of Arianism, the preacher, the commentator
on Genesis, the letter writer. Here we see him in the role of a
Christian teacher, steeped in the classics, who suits the mode of his
teaching to the needs and the capacities of a young audience. He
urges the young men before him to take from the writers of antiquity whatever will help their own growth in virtue, ever mindful of the ageless eternity which is their goal.

The date of the *Address* is uncertain.

I

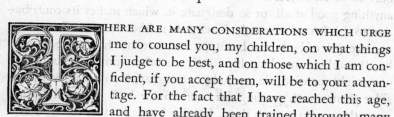

THERE ARE MANY CONSIDERATIONS WHICH URGE me to counsel you, my children, on what things I judge to be best, and on those which I am confident, if you accept them, will be to your advantage. For the fact that I have reached this age, and have already been trained through many experiences, and indeed also have shared sufficiently in the all-teaching vicissitude of both good and evil fortune, has made me conversant with human affairs, so that I can indicate the safest road, as it were, to those who are just entering upon life. Moreover, I come immediately after your parents in natural relationship to you, so that I myself entertain for you no less good-will than do your fathers; and I am sure, unless I am somewhat wrong in my judgment of you, that you do not long for your parents when your eyes rest upon me. If, then, you should receive my words with eagerness, you will belong to the second class of those praised by Hesiod; but should you not do so, I indeed should not like to say anything unpleasant, but do you of yourselves remember the verses in which he says: "Best is the man who sees of himself at once what must be done, and excellent is he too who follows what is well indicated by others, but he who is suited for neither is useless in all respects." [1]

Do not think it strange, then, if I say to you, who each day resort to teachers and hold converse with the famous men of the ancients through the words which they have left behind them, that I myself have discovered something of especial advantage to you. This it is, and naught else, that I have come to offer you as my counsel—that you should not surrender to these men once for all the rudders of your mind, as if of a ship, and follow them whithersoever they lead; rather, accepting from them only that which is useful, you should know that which ought to be overlooked. What, therefore, these things are, and how we shall distinguish them, is the lesson which I shall teach you from this point on.

[1] Hesiod, *Works and Days*, 293-297.

¶ 2. We, my children, in no wise conceive this human life of ours to be an object of value in any respect, nor do we consider anything good at all, or so designate it, which makes its contribution to this life of ours only. Therefore neither renown of ancestry, nor strength of body, nor beauty, nor stature, nor honours bestowed by all mankind, nor kingship itself, nor other human attribute that one might mention, do we judge great, nay, we do not even consider them worth praying for, nor do we look with admiration upon those who possess them, but our hopes lead us forward to a more distant time, and everything we do is by way of preparation for the other life. Whatever, therefore, contributes to that life, we say must be loved and pursued with all our strength; but what does not conduce to that must be passed over as of no account. Now just what this life is, and how and in what manner we shall live it, would take too long to discuss in view of our present purpose, and would be for the more mature to hear than for hearers of your age. After saying this much at least, I may perhaps be able to show you that if one sums up all the happiness together from the time men have first existed and collects it into one whole, he will find that it is equivalent not even to a trivial part of those other goods, but that the total of the goods of the present life is more removed in value from the least among the former goods of the other life than shadows and dreams fall short of reality. Nay, rather—that I may use a more suitable illustration—to the degree that the soul is more precious than the body in all respects, so great is the difference between the two lives. Now to that other life the Holy Scriptures lead the way, teaching us through mysteries. Yet so long as, by reason of your age, it is impossible for you to understand the depth of the meaning of these, in the meantime, by means of other analogies which are not entirely different, we give, as it were in shadows and reflections, a preliminary training to the eye of the soul, imitating those who perform their drills in military tactics, who, after they have gained experience by means of gymnastic exercises for the arms and dance-steps for the feet, enjoy when it comes to the combat the profit derived from what was done in sport. So we also must consider that a contest, the greatest of all contests, lies before us, for which we must do all things, and, in preparation for it, must strive to the best of our power, and must

associate with poets and writers of prose and orators and with all
men from whom there is any prospect of benefit with reference to
the care of our soul. Therefore, just as dyers first prepare by certain treatments whatever material is to receive the dye, and then
apply the color, whether it be purple or some other hue, so we also
in the same manner must first, if the glory of the good is to abide
with us indelible for all time, be instructed by these outside means,
and then shall understand the sacred and mystical teachings; and
like those who have become accustomed to seeing the reflection of
the sun in water, so we shall then direct our eyes to the light itself.

¶ 3. Now if there is some affinity between the two bodies of
teachings, knowledge of them should be useful to us; but if not,
at least the fact that by setting them side by side we can discover the difference between them, is of no small importance for
strengthening the position of the better. And yet with what can
you compare the two systems of education and hit upon the true
similitude? Perhaps, just as it is the proper virtue of a tree to be
laden with beautiful fruit, although it also wears like a fair raiment leaves that wave about its branches, so likewise the fruit of
the soul: the truth is primarily its fruitage, yet it is clad in the
certainly not unlovely raiment even of the wisdom drawn from
the outside,[2] which we may liken to foliage that furnishes both
protection to the fruit and an aspect not devoid of beauty. Now it
is said that even Moses, that illustrious man whose name for wisdom is greatest among all mankind, first trained his mind in the
learning of the Egyptians,[3] and then proceeded to the contemplation of Him Who is.[4] And like him, although in later times, they
say that the wise Daniel at Babylon first learned the wisdom of
the Chaldaeans and then applied himself to the divine teachings.[5]

¶ 4. But that this pagan learning is not without usefulness for
the soul has been sufficiently affirmed; yet just how you should
participate in it would be the next topic to be discussed.

First, then, as to the learning to be derived from the poets, that
I may begin with them, inasmuch as the subjects they deal with are

---

[2] *I.e.,* from the pagan literature of the Greeks.
[3] *Acts* vii, 22.   [4] *Exod.* iii, 14.   [5] *Dan.* i, 4.

of every kind, you ought not to give your attention to all they write without exception; but whenever they recount for you the deeds or words of good men, you ought to cherish and emulate these and try to be as far as possible like them; but when they treat of wicked men, you ought to avoid such imitation, stopping your ears no less than Odysseus did, according to what those same poets say, when he avoided the songs of the Sirens.[6] For familiarity with evil words is, as it were, a road leading to evil deeds. On this account, then, the soul must be watched over with all vigilance,[7] lest through the pleasure the poet's words give we may unwittingly accept something of the more evil sort, like those who take poisons along with honey. We shall not, therefore, praise the poets when they revile or mock, or when they depict men engaged in amours or drunken, or when they define happiness in terms of an over-abundant table or dissolute songs. But least of all shall we give attention to them when they narrate anything about the gods, and especially when they speak of them as being many, and these too not even in accord with one another. For in their poems brother is at feud with brother, and father with children, and the latter in turn are engaged in truceless war with their parents. But the adulteries of gods and their amours and their sexual acts in public, and especially those of Zeus, the chief and highest of all, as they themselves describe him, actions which one would blush to mention of even brute beasts—all these we shall leave to the stage-folk.

These same observations I must make concerning the writers of prose also, and especially when they fabricate tales for the entertainment of their hearers. And we shall certainly not imitate the orators in their art of lying. For neither in courts of law nor in other affairs is lying befitting to us, who have chosen the right and true way of life, and to whom refraining from litigation has been ordained in commandment.[8] But we shall take rather those passages of theirs in which they have praised virtue or condemned vice. For just as in the case of other beings enjoyment of flowers is limited to their fragrance and color, but the bees, as we see, possess the power to get honey from them as well, so it is possible here also for those who are pursuing not merely what is sweet and pleasant in such writings to store away from them some benefit also for

[6] Homer, *Odyssey,* XII, 39 ff.   [7] Cf. *Prov.* iv, 23.   [8] *I Cor.* vi, 7.

their souls. It is, therefore, in accordance with the whole similitude of the bees, that we should participate in the pagan literature. For these neither approach all flowers equally, nor in truth do they attempt to carry off entire those upon which they alight, but taking only so much of them as is suitable for their work, they suffer the rest to go untouched. We ourselves, too, if we are wise, having appropriated from this literature what is suitable to us and akin to the truth, will pass over the remainder. And just as in plucking the blooms from a rose-bed we avoid the thorns, so also in garnering from such writings whatever is useful, let us guard ourselves against what is harmful. At the very outset, therefore, we should examine each of the branches of knowledge and adapt it to our end, according to the Doric proverb, "bringing the stone to the line." [9]

¶ 5. And since it is through virtue that we must enter upon this life of ours, and since much has been uttered in praise of virtue by poets, much by historians, and much more still by philosophers, we ought especially to apply ourselves to such literature. For it is no small advantage that a certain intimacy and familiarity with virtue should be engendered in the souls of the young, seeing that the lessons learned by such are likely, in the nature of the case, to be indelible, having been deeply impressed in them by reason of the tenderness of their souls. Or what else are we to suppose Hesiod had in mind when he composed these verses which are on everybody's lips, if he were not exhorting young men to virtue?— that "rough at first and hard to travel, and full of abundant sweat and toil, is the road which leads to virtue, and steep withal." [10] Therefore it is not given to everyone to climb this road, so steep it is, nor, if one essays to climb it, easily to reach the summit. But when once one has come to the top he is able to see how smooth and beautiful, how easy and pleasant to travel it is, and more agreeable than that other road which leads to vice, which it is possible to take all at once from near at hand, as this same poet has said. For to me it seems that he has narrated these things for no other reason than to urge us on to virtue and to exhort all men to be good, and to keep us from becoming weak and cowardly in the

[9] Homer, *Odyssey*, V, 244 and 245.   [10] Hesiod, *Works and Days*, 287-292.

face of hardships and desisting before reaching the end. And assuredly, if anyone else has sung the praise of virtue in terms like Hesiod's, let us welcome his words as leading to the same end as our own.

Moreover, as I myself have heard a man say who is clever at understanding a poet's mind, all Homer's poetry is an encomium of virtue, and all he wrote, save what is accessory, bears to this end, and not least in those verses [11] in which he has portrayed the leader of the Cephallenians, after being saved from shipwreck, as naked, and the princess as having first shown him reverence at the mere sight of him (so far was he from incurring shame through merely being seen naked, since the poet has portrayed him as clothed with virtue in place of garments);—and then, furthermore, Odysseus as having been considered worthy of such high honor by the rest of the Phaeacians likewise that, disregarding the luxury in which they lived, they one and all admired and envied the hero, and none of the Phaeacians at the moment would have desired anything else more than to become Odysseus, and that too just saved from a shipwreck.[12] For in these passages, the interpreter of the poet's mind was wont to declare that Homer says in a voice that all but shouts: "You must give heed unto virtue, O men, which swims forth even with a man who has suffered shipwreck, and, on his coming naked to land, will render him more honored than the happy Phaeacians." And truly this is so. Other possessions, in fact, no more belong to their possessors than to any chance comer whatever, quickly shifting now here, now there, as in a game of dice; but virtue alone of possessions cannot be taken away, as it remains with a man whether he be living or dead. It was for this reason indeed, as it seems to me, that Solon said this with respect to the rich: "But we will not exchange with them our virtue for their wealth, since the one abides always, while riches change their owners every day." [13] And similar to these words are those of Theognis also in which he says that God, whomsoever he means indeed by this term, inclines the scale for men at one time this way, at another that way, now to be rich, but now to have nothing.[14]

And furthermore, the sophist from Ceos, Prodicus, somewhere

[11] Homer, *Odyssey*, VI, 135 ff. [12] Homer, *Odyssey*, VIII, 248 and 249.
[13] Plutarch, *Solon*, 3. [14] Theognis, *Elegies*, 157-158.

in his writings uttered a doctrine kindred to these others regarding
virtue and vice; therefore we must apply our minds to him also,
for he is not a man to be rejected. His narrative runs something
like this, so far as I recall the man's thought, since I do not know
the exact words, but only that he spoke in general to the following effect, not employing metre. When Heracles was quite a young
man and was nearly of the age at which you yourselves are now,
while he was deliberating which of the two roads he should take,
the one leading through toils to virtue, or the easiest, two women
approached him, and these were Virtue and Vice. Now at once,
although they were silent, the difference between them was evident from their appearance. For the one had been decked out for
beauty through the art of toiletry, and was overflowing with voluptuousness, and she was leading a whole swarm of pleasures in her
train; now these things she displayed, and promising still more
than these she tried to draw Heracles to her. But the other was
withered and squalid, and had an intense look, and spoke quite
differently; for she promised nothing dissolute or pleasant, but
countless sweating toils and labors and dangers through every land
and sea. But the prize to be won by these was to become a god, as
the narrative of Prodicus expressed it; and it was this second
woman that Heracles in the end followed.[15]

¶ 6. And almost all the writers who have some reputation for
wisdom have, to a greater or less degree, each to the best of his
power, discoursed in their works in praise of virtue. To these men
we must hearken and we must try to show forth their words in our
lives; for he in truth who confirms by act his devotion to wisdom,
which among others is confined to words, "he alone has understanding, but the others flit about as shadows." [16]

It seems to me that such harmony between profession and life
is very much as if a painter had made a likeness of a man of quite
wondrous beauty, and this same man should be such in reality as
the painter had portrayed him on his panels. For brilliantly to
praise virtue in public, and to make long speeches about it, but in
private to rate pleasure before temperance, and self-interest before

---

[15] Xenophon, *Memorabilia*, II, 1. 21; Cicero, *De Officiis*, I, 32.
[16] Homer, *Odyssey*, X, 495.

justice, resembles, as I would assert, those stage-folk who bring out plays and often appear as kings and potentates, although they are neither kings nor potentates, and perhaps not even free men at all. Again, a musician would not willingly consent that his lyre should be out of tune, nor a leader of a chorus that his chorus should not sing in the strictest possible harmony; but shall each individual person be at variance with himself, and shall he exhibit a life not at all in agreement with his words? But one will say, quoting Euripides,[17] "the tongue has sworn, but the mind is unsworn," and the appearance of being good will be his aim instead of being good. Yet this is the last extreme of injustice, if we are to hearken to the words of Plato—"to appear to be just without being so."[18]

¶ 7. As to the passages in literature, then, which contain admonitions of excellent things, let us accept this procedure. And since the virtuous deeds, likewise, of the men of old have been preserved for us, either through an unbroken oral tradition or through being preserved in the words of poets or writers of prose, let us not fail to derive advantage from this source also. For example, a certain fellow, a market-lounger, kept railing at Pericles,[19] but he paid no attention; and he kept it up all day long, giving Pericles a merciless dressing of abuse, but Pericles took no heed of it. Then, when it was already evening and dark, though the man was scarcely desisting, Pericles escorted him home with a light, lest his own schooling in philosophy be utterly brought to naught. Again, a certain man, having become enraged against Eucleides of Megara,[20] threatened him with death and took oath upon it; but Eucleides took a counter-oath, to the effect that verily he would appease the man and make him put aside his wrath against him. How very valuable it is that an example of this kind should be recalled to memory by a man who is on the point of being held in the grip of a fit of passion! For one must not put a simple-minded trust in the tragedy when it says "Against enemies anger arms the hand" but, on the contrary, we should not permit ourselves to be aroused to anger at all; but if this is not easy to

[17] Euripides, *Hippolytus*, 612.   [18] Plato, *Republic*, II, 361A.
[19] Plutarch, *Pericles*, 5.   [20] Plutarch, *De Frat. Am.*, VII, 907.

achieve, we should at least apply reason to our anger as a sort of curb and not allow it to be carried too far beyond bounds.

But let us bring our discussion back again to the examples of virtuous deeds. A certain man kept striking Socrates, son of Sophroniscus, full in the face, falling upon him unmercifully; yet he did not oppose, but permitted the wine-mad fellow to satiate his rage, so that his face was presently swollen and bruised from the blows. Now when the man ceased striking him, Socrates, it is said, did nothing except inscribe on his own forehead, like the name of the sculptor on a statue, "So-and-so (naming the man) made this," and only to that extent avenged himself.[21] Since these examples tend to nearly the same end as our own precepts, I maintain that it is of great value for those of your age to imitate them. For this example of Socrates is akin to that precept of ours—that to him who strikes us on the cheek, so far from avenging ourselves upon him we should offer the other cheek also.[22] And the example of Pericles or Eucleides is akin to the precept that we should submit to those who persecute us and gently suffer their anger;[23] and this other one—that we should pray for blessings for our enemies instead of cursing them. For whoever has been instructed in these examples beforehand cannot after that distrust those precepts as utterly impossible to obey. I should not pass over the example of Alexander, who, when he had taken prisoner the daughters of Darius, although it had been testified to him that they possessed a marvellous beauty, did not think it fitting even to look upon them, judging it to be disgraceful for one who had captured men to be vanquished by women.[24] Indeed, this example tends to the same purport as that well-known precept of ours—that he who looks upon a woman to enjoy her, although he does not commit adultery in act, yet in truth, because he has received the desire into his soul, is not free of guilt.[25] But as for the action of Cleinias, one of the disciples of Pythagoras, it is difficult to believe that it is by mere chance that it coincides with our own principles, and not through its imitating them designedly. What was it, then, that Cleinias did? Although it was possible by taking oath to escape a fine of three talents, he paid rather than swear, and that too though

[21] Plutarch, *De Lib. Educ.*, VI, 33.   [22] *Matt.* v, 39.   [23] *Matt.* v, 40-41.
[24] Cf. Plutarch, *De Curiositate*, VIII, 71.   [25] *Matt.* v, 28.

it would have been a true oath that he would have taken. He must have heard, it seems to me, our commandment forbidding the taking of an oath.[26]

¶ 8. But let us return again to the same subject of which we were speaking at the beginning: we ought not to take everything without exception, but only such matter as is useful. For it is disgraceful to reject foods that are harmful yet for the teachings which nourish our souls to have no concern, but to charge onward like a mountain torrent, carrying along everything it chances upon. And further, what sense or reason is there that a pilot does not heedlessly give over his ship to the winds, but steers it to harbor, or that a bowman shoots at a mark, or indeed, that any bronze-smith or worker in wood strives for the end proper to his craft, but that we should fall behind even such artisans, in respect at least to the ability to perceive our own interests? For can it be that handicraftsmen have some end in view in their work, but that there is no goal for the life of man, keeping his eye upon which that man at least, who does not intend to be wholly similar to the brute beasts, ought to do and say whatever he does or says? In that case we should really be like ships without ballast, if we had no intellect sitting at the steering-oars of the soul, being tossed up and down aimlessly through life. On the contrary, it is just as in the athletic contests, or, if you prefer, the competitions in music: there are practice exercises in preparation for those contests in which the prize offered is a crown, and no one who is training for the wrestling-match or the pancratium takes to practising on the lyre or flute. Certainly Polydamas did no such thing, but before the contest at Olympia he practised bringing speeding chariots to a stop, and by this means was wont to enhance his strength. And Milo could not be pushed away from his greased shield, but held out against the pushing no less firmly than those statues hold which are fastened to their bases with lead.[27] And, in a word, their exercises were a preparation for the games. But if they had wasted their time on the airs of Marsyas or Olympus[28] the Phrygians, abandoning the dust and the exercises of the gymnasia, would they

26 Cf. Diogenes Laertius, VIII, 22.   27 *Pausanias*, VI, 5; 14.
28 Plutarch, *De Mus.*, 5.

soon have obtained crowns or glory, or would they have escaped
incurring ridicule for their physical condition? Neither, on the
other hand, did Timotheus [29] neglect his composition of chorals
and spend his time in the wrestling-schools. For had he done so,
it would not have been possible for him so far to excel all men in
the musical art that he could arouse the passions through his vehement and severe harmony and yet, on the other hand, through his
relaxed and sensuous strains, mollify and allay them again, whenever he willed. It was by such art that once, when he was playing
the Phrygian mode to Alexander on his flute, he caused the prince,
as it is said, to leap up and rush to his arms in the midst of a banquet, and then, by relaxing the harmony, brought him back again
to his boon companions. So great is the power, in both music and
the athletic contests, produced by practice directed towards the
attainment of the end in view.

And since I have made mention of crowns and athletes, let me
add that these men, after enduring toils by the thousand, and after
increasing their strength by every possible means, after shedding
much sweat in the labors of the gymnasium, and taking many
blows at the school of the physical trainer, and choosing, not the
pleasantest fare, but that which the gymnastic masters had prescribed, and in all other ways (that I may not waste time by enu-
merating them) so passing their days that their life before the
contest might be a preparation for the contest, then, when the
moment comes, they strip for the race, undergo all hardships and
run all risks, so as to receive a crown of wild olive or of parsley
or of some such thing, all that they may win the victory and have
their name proclaimed by the herald. But as for us, before whom
are set for the life we lead prizes so marvellous in multitude and
in grandeur that they cannot be described in words, if we sleep on
both ears and live lives of abundant license, will it be possible for
us to reach out and seize them with one hand? In that event slothfulness would be of great value for living, and Sardanapalus [30]
would carry off the highest prizes of all as regards happiness, or
even Margites, who was neither a ploughman nor a digger nor
anything else useful in life, as Homer [31] said—if indeed this work

[29] Plutarch, *De Vita Alex. Or.*, II, 5.   [30] Dio Chrys., *Or.*, III, 72.
[31] Cf. Aristotle, *Nic. Eth.*, VI, 7, 1141 a15.

is really Homer's. Yet is not rather the saying of Pittacus true,[32] that "it is hard to be good"? For though we pass through many toils that are really toils, we can scarcely succeed in obtaining those goods of which, as we have already said above, no human goods can serve as an example. Therefore we ought not to idle away our time, nor for an ease that can last but a short while give up in exchange glorious hopes—that is, if we are not to be reproached and to incur retributions; I do not mean any that are inflicted here among men, although even that is no slight matter to a man of sense, but in the places of punishment, whether these are under the earth or wheresoever in the universe they may happen to be. Since, in the case of one who fails involuntarily in his duty, some degree of pardon may perhaps be granted by God; but for him who has deliberately chosen the worse course in life there is no excuse that will save him from suffering the punishment many times over.

¶ 9. What, then, shall we do? someone may ask. What else, indeed, than devote ourselves to the care of our souls, keeping all our leisure free from other things. Accordingly, we should not be slaves of the body, except so far as is strictly necessary; but our souls we should supply with all things that are best, through philosophy freeing them, as from a prison, from association with the passions of the body, and at the same time making the body likewise master of the passions, supplying the belly with what it cannot do without, but not with sweet dainties as those do who look everywhere for table-dressers and cooks and scour every land and sea, bringing tribute, as it were, to a stern master, pitiable objects because of their ceaseless activity, and suffering not a whit more tolerable pains than those who are chastised in Hades by being forced actually to card wool into a fire, fetch water in a sieve, or to pour it into a perforated jar, having labor which never ends. And to spend one's time, beyond what is necessary, on the care of the hair or on dress, is, according to the saying of Diogenes,[33] the mark of men who are either unfortunate or doing wrong. Hence, to be a dandy and get the name of being one ought, I maintain, to be considered by persons so inclined just as disgraceful as to

32 Cf. Plato, *Protag.*, 340c.　　33 Diogenes Laertius, VI, 54.

keep company with harlots or to seduce other men's wives. For
what difference should it make, at least to a man of sense, whether
he is clothed in a costly robe or wears a cheap workman's cloak,
so long as what he has on gives adequate protection against the
cold of winter and the heat of summer? And in all other matters
likewise, one ought not to be furnished out more elaborately than
need requires, nor to be more solicitous for the body than is good
for the soul. For it is no less a reproach to a man, who is truly
worthy of that appellation, to be a dandy and a pamperer of the
body than to be ignoble in his attitude towards any other vice. For
to take all manner of pains that his body may be as beautiful as
possible is not the mark of a man who either knows himself or
understands that wise precept: "That which is seen is not the man,
but there is need of a certain higher wisdom which will enable
each of us, whoever he is, to recognize himself." [34] But unless we
have purified our minds this is more impossible for us than for a
blear-eyed man to gaze at the sun.

Now purification of the soul [35]—that I may speak in general
terms and in a manner sufficient for your understanding—consists
in scorning the pleasures that arise through the senses, in not feasting the eyes on the silly exhibitions of jugglers or on the sight of
bodies which gives the spur to sensual pleasure, in not permitting
licentious songs to enter through the ears and drench your souls.
For passions sprung of lack of breeding and baseness are naturally
engendered by this kind of music. But we should cultivate that
other kind, which is better and leads to the better, through his use
of which, as they say, David, the poet of the Sacred Songs, freed
the king from his madness. [36] And it is related that Pythagoras,
too, chancing upon some drunken revellers, commanded the flute
player who led the revel to change his harmony and play to them
the Doric mode; and that thus the company came back to its senses
under the influence of the strain, so that, tearing off their garlands,
they went home ashamed. Yet others at the sound of the flute act
like Corybantes and are excited to Bacchic frenzy. [37] Such is the
difference between giving full ear to wholesome and to licentious
music. Hence, since this latter is now in vogue, you should par-

[34] Cf. Plato, *Phaedo*, 75 and 115.   [35] Cf. Plato, *Phaedo*, 82B.
[36] *I Kings* xvi, 15-23.   [37] Plato, *Crito*, 54D.

ticipate in it less than in the very basest of things. Furthermore, the mixing with the air of all manner of vapours that bring pleasure to the sense of smell, or the smearing of the body with perfumes, I am ashamed even to forbid. And what can one say about the importance of not cultivating the pleasures associated with the senses of touch and taste than that these compel those who are devoted to their pursuit to live, like animals, with all their attention centred upon the belly and the members below it?

But, in a single word, the body in every part should be despised by everyone who does not care to be buried in its pleasures, as it were in slime; or we ought to cleave to it only in so far as we obtain from it service for the pursuit of wisdom, as Plato advises,[38] speaking in a manner somewhat similar to Paul's when he admonishes us to make no provision for the body unto the arousing of concupiscences.[39] Or in what way do those differ, who are solicitous how the body may be as well off as possible, but overlook the soul, which is to make use of it as utterly worthless, from those who are much concerned about their implements but neglect the art which uses them for its work? Hence we must do quite the opposite—chastise the body and hold it in check, as we do the violent chargings of a wild beast, and by smiting with reason, as with a whip, the disturbances engendered by it in the soul, calm them to sleep; instead of relaxing every curb upon pleasure and suffering the mind to be swept headlong, like a charioteer by unmanageable horses riotously running at large. And we ought to recall Pythagoras, who, on perceiving that one of his followers was putting on superfluous flesh by exercises and heavy eating, said to him, "Pray cease making your prison-house more wretched for you to live in!" It was for this reason, in fact, that Plato also, as we are told, providing against the harmful influences of the body, deliberately occupied the pestilential region in Attica, the Academy, in order that he might prune away, as one prunes the vine of its excessive growth, the too great well-being of his body. And I myself have heard physicians say that extreme good health is even dangerous.

Since, then, such excessive concern for the body is not only unprofitable to the body itself but also a hindrance to the soul, that

---

[38] Plato, *Republic*, VI, 498B, C.   [39] St. Paul, *Rom.* xiii, 14.

it should be subject to the body and be its servant is sheer madness. Yet surely, if we should make it a practice to despise the body, we should be slow, methinks, to feel admiration for any other thing that many may possess. For to what end shall we go on employing wealth if we scorn the pleasures arising through the body? As for me, I do not see, except that it might furnish us with a sort of pleasure to keep awake at night guarding, like the dragons of mythology, buried treasures! Assuredly, however, that man who has been trained to regard such goods as a freeman should would be quite unlikely ever to choose anything base or shameful in word or deed. For that which is in excess of any need, even if it be the gold-dust of Lydia or the wealth of the gold-gathering ants, he will despise all the more the less he needs it; and "need" itself he will, of course, define in terms of the requirements of nature and not in terms of pleasure. For those who go beyond the bounds of necessity are like men who rush headlong down a slope and, being unable to bring up against any firm object, find it impossible to halt at any point their onward impetus; nay, the more they gather in to themselves the more they require that much, or even a greater amount, for the fulfilment of their desires, according to Solon son of Execestides,[40] who declares: "Of wealth no limit lies revealed to men." And we ought to use Theognis as a teacher in these matters, when he says: "I am not eager to be rich, nor do I pray for this, but may it be mine to live on little, suffering no evil." [41]

And I admire also the scorn of Diogenes for all human goods without exception, who declared himself richer than the Great King by reason of the fact that he needed less for living than the King.[42] But for us of today, it would seem, nothing will suffice except all the talents of Pythias the Mysian, and so-and-so many acres of land, and herds of cattle past numbering. But, in my opinion, we ought not to long for wealth if it be lacking, and, if we have it, we should not pride ourselves so much on its possession as on the knowledge that it is being put to good uses. For the saying of Socrates is well put. He, when a wealthy man was manifesting great pride in his riches, said that he would not admire him before he had found out by trial that he also knew how to use them.[43] Would not Pheidias and Polycleitus, one of whom made the Zeus for the Elians and the other the Hera for the Argives, if they had prided themselves greatly on the gold and the ivory in them, have been objects of derision for glorying in a wealth not their own, passing over the art which enabled them to render the gold both more pleasing and more precious; but if we suppose that human virtue is not sufficient to itself for an adornment, do we imagine that what we are doing merits a lesser shame than would have been theirs?

But, forsooth, are we to despise wealth and have contempt for the pleasures of the senses, and yet go seeking for flattery and adulation, and imitate the shiftiness and cunning of the fox of Archilochus? On the contrary, there is nothing which a prudent man must shun more carefully than living with a view to popularity and giving serious thought to the things esteemed by the multitude, instead of making sound reason his guide of life, so that, even if he must gainsay all men and fall into disrepute and incur danger for the sake of what is honourable, he will in no wise choose to swerve from what has been recognized as right. Or in what respect shall we say that a person of so unstable a character differs from the Egyptian mountebank [44] who, whenever he wished, became a plant, or a wild beast, or fire or water or anything else, if in sooth he himself is at one time to praise justice when in the presence of those who esteem that, but will at another time take quite the opposite position whenever he perceives that injustice is held in honour—as is the way of flatterers? And just as the polyp, they say, changes its color to match the ground on which it lies, so will he change his mind according to the opinions of those about him.

¶ 10. But although we Christians shall doubtless learn all these things more thoroughly in our own literature, yet for the present, at least, let us trace out a kind of rough sketch, as it were, of what virtue is according to the teaching of the pagans. For by those who make it their business to gather the benefit to be derived from each source many accretions from many sides are wont to be received, as happens to mighty rivers. Indeed we are entitled to consider

---

[43] Dio Chrys., Or., VI, 6.　　[44] Cf. Homer, Odyssey, IV, 384-386.

that the poet's saying [45] about "adding little to little" holds good
no more for increment of money than it does for increment in
respect of knowledge of any kind whatever. Bias, [46] for instance,
when he was asked by his son, who was about to depart for Egypt,
what he could do that would gratify him most, replied: "By acquiring travel-supplies for your old age," meaning by "travel-
supplies" virtue, no doubt, though the terms in which he defined
it were too narrow, seeing that he limited to human life the benefit to be derived from virtue. But as for me, if anyone should
mention the old age of Tithonus, or that of Arganthonius, or of
Methusala, whose life was the longest of any man's (for he is
said to have lived a thousand years lacking thirty), or if anyone
reckons up all the time which has elapsed since men have existed,
I shall laugh thereat as at a childish idea when I gaze towards that
long and ageless eternity whose limit the mind can in no wise
grasp any more than it can conceive an end for the immortal soul.
It is for this eternity that I would exhort you to acquire travel-
supplies, leaving no stone unturned, as the proverb has it,
wherever any benefit towards that end is likely to accrue to you.
And because this is difficult and calls for toil, let us not on this
account draw back, but recalling the words of him [47] who urged
that every man should choose the life which is in itself best, in the
expectation that through habit it will prove agreeable, we should
attempt the best things. For it would be disgraceful that we, having thrown away the present opportunity, should at some later
time attempt to summon back the past when all our vexation will
gain us nothing.

Accordingly, of the things which in my judgment are best, some
I have told you at this time, while others I shall continue to recommend to you throughout my whole life: but as for you, remembering that there are three infirmities, pray do not seem to resemble
the one which is incurable, nor to exhibit the disease of the mind,
which resembles that which those endure who are afflicted in body.
For whereas those who suffer from slight ailments go of themselves to physicians, and those who are attacked by more serious
diseases summon to their homes those who will treat them; yet

[45] Hesiod, *Works and Days*, 361-362.   [46] Cf. Diogenes Laertius, I, 88.
[47] Cf. Plutarch, *De Exilio*, VIII, 376.

those who have reached the stage of melancholy that is absolutely beyond remedy do not even admit physicians when they call. Pray do you not become afflicted in this last-named manner, characteristic of the men of the present time, by avoiding those whose reasoning faculties are sound.

ST. JOHN
CHRYSOSTOM

ON CHARITY *to the* POOR

+⁺+

Let us relieve the poverty of those that beg us, and if
they do impose upon us, let us not be over-exact about it.

ST. JOHN CHRYSOSTOM (344-407) was born in Antioch, where
he became a preacher of great renown (386-398). He died in
exile in 407, after a stormy career as Bishop of Constantinople
(398-404). The oratorical works of St. John, consisting of sermons and homilies, are his most celebrated accomplishment, and
among these the homilies on his beloved St. Paul are considered
"the best commentary ever made on the writings of the great
Apostle." [1] The homilies on the *Epistle to the Romans,* delivered
in 391, are particularly noteworthy. The following selection
notably illustrates why Chrysostom has been called the apostle of
charity and the panegyrist of almsgiving.

+⁺+

ULL OF AFFECTIONATENESS IS THE WHOLE RACE
of the saints. Wherefore also St. Paul saith, *Put*
on therefore, as the elect saints of God, bowels of
mercies, kindness, humbleness of mind.[2] You see
the strict propriety of the word, and how he
would have us continually merciful. For he does
not say, *show mercy* only, but *put it on,* that like as our garment is
always with us, so may mercy be. And he does not say merely *mercy,*

---

[1] F. Cayré, *Patrologie et histoire de la théologie,* vol. I (4th ed., Paris: Desclée
et Cie., 1945), p. 469. [2] *Coloss.* iii, 12.

but *bowels of mercies,* that we may imitate the natural affection of relations. But we do just the contrary, and if any one comes to ask a single penny of us, we insult them, abuse them, call them impostors.

Dost thou not shudder, man, and blush to call him an impostor for bread? Why even supposing he is practising imposture, he deserves to be pitied for it, because he is so pressed with famine as to put on such a character. This then is a reproach to our cruelty. For since we have not the heart to bestow with readiness, they are compelled to practise a great many arts, so as to put a cheat off upon our inhumanity, and to soften down our harshness. Now if it was gold and silver he asked of thee, then there would be some reason in thy suspicions. But if it is necessary food that he comes to thee for, why be showing wise so unseasonably, and take so over-exact an account of him, accusing him of idleness and sloth? For if we must talk in this way, it is not others, but ourselves that we ought to address.

When therefore thou art going to God to ask forgiveness for thy sins, then call these words to mind, and thou wilt know thou deservest to have these things said to thee by God, much more than the poor man by thee. And yet God hath never said such words to thee as "Stand off, since thou art an impostor, always coming to church, and hearing My laws, but when abroad, setting gold, and pleasure, and friendship, and in fact any thing above My commandments. And now thou makest thyself humble, but when thy prayers are over, thou art bold, and cruel, and inhuman. Get thee hence, therefore, and never come to Me any more." Yet this, and more than this, we deserve to have said to us; but still He never did reproach us in any such way, but is long suffering, and fulfils every thing on His own part, and gives us more than we ask for.

Calling this to mind then, let us relieve the poverty of those that beg of us, and if they do impose upon us, let us not be over exact about it. For such a salvation is it that we ourselves require, one with pardon, with kindness, with much mercy along with it. For it is not possible, it certainly is not, if our estate were searched into strictly, that we should ever be saved, but we must needs all be punished and brought to ruin. Let us not then be as bitter judges of others as we can, lest we also get a strict account demanded of us. For we have sins that are too great to plead any excuse. And therefore let us show more mercy towards those who have committed inexcusable sins, that we also may lay up for ourselves the like mercy beforehand.

And yet be as large-hearted as we may, we shall never be able to contribute such love toward man as we stand in need of at the hand of a God that loveth man. How then is it other than monstrous, when we are in need of so many things ourselves, to be over-exact with our fellow servants, and do all we can against ourselves? For thou dost not in this way so much prove him unworthy of thy liberality, as thyself of God's love toward man. For he that deals over-exactly with his fellow servant will be the more sure to find the like treatment at God's hand. Let us not speak against ourselves, but even if they come out of idleness or wilfulness, let us bestow. For we also do many sins through wilfulness, or rather we do them all through wilfulness, and yet God doth not presently call us to punishment, but gives us a set time for penance, nurturing us day by day, disciplining us, teaching us, supplying us with all other things, that we too may emulate this mercy of His.

Let us then quell this cruelty, let us cast out this brutal spirit, as benefiting thereby ourselves rather than others. For to these we give money, and bread, and clothing, but for ourselves we are laying up beforehand very great glory, and such as there is no putting into words. For we receive again our bodies incorruptible, and are glorified together and reign together with Christ. How great this is we shall see from hence—or rather there is no means of making us see it clearly now. But to start from our present blessings, and to get from them at least some kind of scanty notice of it, I will endeavor so far as I may be able to put before you what I have been speaking of. Tell me, then, if when you were grown old, and were living in poverty, and any one were to promise suddenly to make you young, and to bring you to the very prime of life, and to render you very strong, and preeminently beautiful, and were to give you the kingdom of the whole earth for a thousand years, a kingdom in a state of the deepest peace, what is there that you would not choose to do and to suffer to gain this promise? See, then, Christ promises not this, but much more than this. For the distance between old age and youth is not to be compared with

the difference of corruption and incorruption, nor that of a kingdom and poverty to that of the future glory and the present, but
the difference is that of dreams and a reality.

Or rather I have yet said nothing to the purpose, since there is
no language capable of setting before you the greatness of the
difference between things to come and things present. And as for
time, there is no place for the idea of difference. For what mode
is there for a man to compare with our present state a life that hath
no end? And as for the peace, it is as far removed from any present
peace, as peace is different from war; and for the incorruption, it
is as much better as a clear pearl is than a clod of clay. Or rather,
say as great a thing as one may, nothing can put it before you. For
were I even to compare the beauty of our bodies than to the light
of the sunbeam, or the brightest lightning, I shall not yet be saying ought that is worthy of that brilliancy. Now for such things
as these, what money so much that it were not worth the while to
give up? what bodies, or rather, what lives is it not worth one's
while to give up? At present if any one were to lead thee into the
palace, and in the presence of all were to give thee an opportunity
of conversing with the king, and make thee sit at his table, and
join in his fare, thou wouldest call thyself the happiest of men.
But when you are to go up to Heaven, and stand by the King of
the universe Himself, and to vie with angels in brightness, and to
enjoy even that unutterable glory, do you hesitate? And suppose
one must need give up property, or put off even life itself, one
ought to leap and exult, and mount on wings of pleasure. But you,
that you may get an office, as a place to pillage from, (for call a
thing of this sort gain, I cannot,) put all you have to hazard, and
after borrowing of others, will, if need be, pawn your wife and
children too without hesitation. But when the kingdom of Heaven
is set before you, that office which hath none to supersede you in
it, and God bids you take not a part of a corner of the earth, but
the whole of Heaven entirely, are you hesitating, and reluctant,
and gaping after money, and forgetful that if the parts of that
Heaven which we see are so fair and delightful, how greatly so
must the upper Heaven be, and the Heaven of Heaven?

But since we have as yet no means of seeing this with our bodily
eyes, ascend in thy thought, and standing above this Heaven, look

up unto that Heaven beyond this, into that height without a bound, into that Light surcharged with awe, into the crowds of the Angels, into the endless ranks of Archangels, into the rest of the incorporeal Powers. And then lay hold again of the image thereof we have, after coming down from above, and make a sketch of the estate of a king with us, as his men in gold armor, and his pairs of white mules proudly decked with gold, and his chariots set with jewels, and his snow-like cushions, and the spangles that flutter above the chariot, and the dragons shaped out in the silken hangings, and the shields with their gold bosses, and the straps that reach up from these to the rims of them through so many gems, and the horses with the gilded trappings and the gold bits. But when we see the king we immediately lose sight of all these. For he alone turns our eyes to him, and to the purple robe, and the diadem, and the throne, and the clasp, and the shoes, all that splendor of his appearance.

After gathering all these things together then with accuracy, then again remove your thought from these things to things above, and to that awful day in which Christ is coming. For then you will not see any pairs of mules, nor golden chariots, nor dragons and shields, but things that are big with a mighty awe, and strike such amazement that the very incorporeal Powers are astonied. For the *powers of the Heavens,* He says, *shall be shaken.*[3] Then is the whole Heaven thrown open, and the gates of those concaves unfold themselves, and the Only-begotten Son of God cometh down, not with twenty, not with a hundred men for His bodyguard, but with thousands and ten thousands of Angels and Archangels, Cherubim and Seraphim, and other Powers, and with fear and trembling shall every thing be filled, whiles the earth is bursting itself up, and the men that ever were born, from Adam's birth up to that day, are rising from the earth, and all are caught up: when Himself appears with such glory as that the moon, and the sun, and all light whatever, is cast into the shade, being outshone by that radiance.[4]

What language is to set before us that blessedness, brightness, glory? Alas! my soul. For weeping comes upon me and great groaning, as I reflect what good things we have fallen from, what

[3] *Matt.* xxiv, 29.   [4] Cf. *I Thess.* iv. 15.

blessedness we are estranged from. For estranged we are, (I am now speaking of my own case still,) unless we do some great and astonishing work; speak not then of hell to me now, for more grievous than any hell is the fall from this glory, worse than punishments unnumbered the estrangement from that lot.

But still we are gaping after this present world, and we take not thought of the devil's cunning, who by little things bereaves us of those great ones, and gives us clay that he may snatch from us gold, or rather that he may snatch Heaven from us, and showeth us a shadow that he may dispossess us of the reality, and puts phantoms before us in dreams (for such is the wealth of this world) that at day-break he may prove us the poorest of men. Laying these things to heart, late though it be, let us fly from this craft, and pass to the side of things to come. For we cannot say that we were ignorant how exposed to accidents the present life is, since things every day din in our ears, more loudly than a trumpet, the worthlessness, the ridiculousness, the shamefulness, the dangers, the pitfalls, of the present scene. What defense then shall we have to set up for pursuing things so subject to hazards, and laden with shame, with so much eagerness, and leaving things unfailing, which will make us glorious and bright, and giving our whole selves up to the thraldom of money? For the slavery to these things is worse than any bondage. And this they know who have been counted worthy to obtain their freedom from it.

That ye then may also feel this goodly liberty, burst the bonds asunder, spring out of the snare. And let there be no gold lying by in your houses, but that which is more precious than millions of money, alms and love to man, for your treasure. For this gives us boldness toward God, but the other covers us with deep shame, and causes the devil to bear hard upon us. Why then arm thy enemy, and make him stronger? Arm thy right hand against him, and transfer all the splendor of thy house into thy soul, and stow away all thy fortune in thy mind, and instead of a chest and a house, let heaven keep thy gold. And let us put all our property about our own selves; for we are much better than the walls, and more dignified than the pavement. Why then do we, to the neglect of our own selves, bestow all our attention upon those things, which when we are gone we can no longer reach, and often even while we stay here we cannot keep hold of, when we might have such riches as to be found, not in this life only, but also in that, in the easiest circumstances?

For he who carries about his farms and house and gold upon his soul, wherever he appears, appears with all this wealth. And how is this possible to be effected? one may ask. It is possible, and that with the utmost ease. For if you transfer them to Heaven by the poor man's hand, you will transfer them entire into your own soul. And if death should afterwards come upon thee, no one will take them from thee, but thou wilt depart to be rich in the next world too. This was the kind of treasure Tabitha had. Hence it was not her house that proclaimed her wealth, nor the walls, nor the stones, nor the pillars, but the bodies of widows furnished with dress, and their tears that were shed, and death that played the run-away, and life that came back again.

Let us also make unto ourselves such-like treasures, let us build up for ourselves such-like houses. In this way we shall have God for our Fellow-worker, and we ourselves shall be workers together with Him. For Himself brought the poor from not being into being, and you will prevent them, after they have been brought into life and being, from perishing with hunger and other distress, by tending them and setting them upright, and staying up the Temple of God in every quarter. And what can be equal to this in respect of utility and creditableness? Or if as yet you have not gained any clear notion of the great adornment He bestowed upon thee when He bade thee relieve poverty, consider this point with thyself.

If He had given thee so great power, that thou wert able to mend the breaches even of Heaven if it were falling, wouldest thou not think the thing an honor far too great for thee? See now He hath held thee worthy of a greater honor. For that which in His esteem is more precious than the Heaven, He hath trusted thee to repair. For of all things visible there is nothing in God's esteem equal to man. For Heaven and earth and sea did He make for him, and finds more pleasure in dwelling with him than in the Heaven. And yet we, though with a knowledge of this, bestow no attention nor forethought upon the temples of God; but leaving them in a neglected state, we provide houses splendid and large for ourselves. This is why we are devoid of all good things, and greater beggars than the poorest poor, because we pride ourselves in these houses which we cannot take away with us when we go hence, and leave those alone which we might move away along with our own selves. For the bodies of the poor after dissolution must needs rise again; and God, Who hath given this change, will bring them forth, and praise those who have taken care of them, and treat such with regard, because when they were on the point of falling to ruin at one time by starvation, at another by nakedness and cold, these repaired them by all means in their power.

But still, even with all these praises set before us, we loiter yet, and decline undertaking this honorable charge. And Christ indeed hath not where to lodge, but goeth about a stranger, and naked, and hungry, and you set up houses out of town, and baths, and terraces, and chambers without number, in thoughtless vanity; and to Christ you give not even a share of a little hut, while for daws and vultures you deck out upper chambers. What can be worse than such insanity as this? What more grievous than such madness? for madness it is in the last stage of it, or rather one has no name to suit it, use whatever one may.

Yet still if we be so minded, it is possible to beat off the disorder, tenacious as it is; and not possible only, but even easy; and not easy merely, but even easier is it to get rid of this pest than of the sufferings of the body, since the Physician is so much greater. Let us then draw Him to ourselves, and invite Him to aid us in the attempt, and let us contribute our share, good will, I mean, and energy. For He will not require any thing further, but if He can meet with this only, He will confer all that is His part. Let us then contribute our share, that in this world we may enjoy a genuine health, and may attain to the good things to come, by the grace and love towards man of our Lord Jesus Christ, with Whom be unto the Father glory, and strength, and honor, and adoration, with the Holy Ghost, forever and ever. Amen.

ST. AUGUSTINE

THE CONFESSIONS

From the end of Book VIII
to the end of Book X

> When I shall have cleaved to Thee with all of myself,
> there will be neither pain nor labor for me; and my
> life, being wholly filled with Thee, will then be alive.

ACCOMPLISHED RHETORICIAN, proud of intellect and lustful of
body, such had been St. Augustine (354-430) until 386 when the
prayers and tears of his mother Monica were answered. From
Plotinus he learned how to defeat skepticism and materialism; on
reading St. Paul, he was granted what only God could give him:
You turned me to Yourself. Baptized by St. Ambrose in the spring
of 387, Augustine was ordained priest in 391. From 396 until
his death (August 28, 430) Augustine was Bishop of Hippo.

His greatest work, it has been said, was his own life. And
others have insisted that Augustine is one of the men who have
most honored mankind. To know him is to love him. There have
been many sinners in history who have turned from their sins,
and have thanked God for this turning. But Augustine's story of
his conversion becomes in the telling not merely an act of thanksgiving, however sincere, but the humble and devout voice of a
man who cries to God, in the name of the whole creation, that
without the presence of His forming hand all creatures would
be as nothing. It is this formation by divine Wisdom that Augustine confesses, even as does the world around him, and through
his voice.

More than anything else, it is the constant sense of eternity
which gives to the *Confessions* its grandeur and its unfailing ap-

peal. The *Confessions* is the Christian story, written in the trembling prayers of Augustine, of how God gathers within the bosom of His eternity the temporal and changeful reality of man. God calls those who are temporal, Augustine has said, and he makes them eternal: *vocans temporales, faciens aeternos.*

Augustine wrote the *Confessions* about the year 400. In the pages immediately preceding the present selection, he recorded how, in Milan, he came across the books of the Platonists (*i.e.,* the *Enneads* of Plotinus). Plotinus freed Augustine from matter, but not from pride or from his body. Plotinus knew much: he looked from a distance toward heaven itself; but how much he did not know! The grace of Christ, the divine mercy, the tears of repentance, the pledge of the Holy Spirit, the chalice of the Redemption—the Platonists were unaware of all this. There was pride in Plotinus, and Augustine needed to learn humility. Having read Plotinus, Augustine had still to surrender himself humbly to God.

The following pages need no introduction. They contain the perennially fresh story of Augustine's conversion, the exalted experience at Ostia, the death of Monica. With the tenth book Augustine completes the story of his past and comes to the present.

And what a present!

[VI] 13

ND HOW THOU DIDST DELIVER ME OUT OF THE bonds of desire, wherewith I was bound most straitly to carnal concupiscence, and out of the drudgery of worldly things, I will now declare, and confess unto Thy name, *O Lord, my helper and my redeemer.*[1] Amid increasing anxiety, I was doing my wonted business, and daily sighing unto Thee. I attended Thy Church, whenever free from the business under the burden of which I groaned. Alypius was with me, now after the third sitting released from his law business, and awaiting to whom to sell his counsel, as I sold the skill of speaking, if indeed teach-

---

[1] *Ps.* xviii, 15.

ing can impart it. Nebridius had now, in consideration of our friendship, consented to teach under Verecundus, a citizen and a grammarian of Milan, and a very intimate friend of us all; who urgently desired, and by the right of friendship challenged from our company, such faithful aid as he greatly needed. Nebridius then was not drawn to this by any desire of advantage, (for he might have made much more of his learning had he so willed,) but as a most kind and gentle friend, he would not be wanting to a good office, and slight our request. But he acted herein very discreetly, shunning to become known to personages great according to this world, avoiding the distraction of mind thence ensuing, and desiring to have it free and at leisure, as many hours as might be, to seek, or read, or hear something concerning wisdom.

14. Upon a day then, Nebridius being absent, (I recollect not why,) lo, there came to see me and Alypius, one Pontitianus, our countryman so far as being an African, in high office in the Emperor's court. What he would with us, I know not, but we sat down to converse, and it happened that upon a table for some game, before us, he observed a book, took, opened it, and contrary to his expectation, found it the Apostle Paul; for he had thought it some of those books, which I was wearing myself in teaching. Whereat smiling, and looking at me, he expressed his joy and wonder, that he had on a sudden found this book, and this only before my eyes. For he was a Christian, and baptized, and often bowed himself before Thee our God in the Church, in frequent and continued prayers. When then I had told him, that I bestowed very great pains upon those Scriptures, a conversation arose (suggested by his account) on Antony the Egyptian Monk: whose name was in high reputation among Thy servants, though to that hour unknown to us. Which when he discovered, he dwelt the more upon that subject, informing and wondering at our ignorance of one so eminent. But we stood amazed, hearing Thy wonderful works most fully attested, in times so recent, and almost in our own, wrought in the true Faith and Church Catholic. We all wondered; we, that they were so great, and he, that they had not reached us.

15. Thence his discourse turned to the flocks in the Monasteries, and their holy ways, a sweet smelling savour unto Thee,

and the fruitful deserts of the wilderness, whereof we knew nothing. And there was a Monastery at Milan, full of good brethren,
without the city walls, under the fostering care of Ambrose, and
we knew it not. He went on with his discourse, and we listened in
intent silence. He told us then how one afternoon at Triers, when
the Emperor was taken up with the Circensian games, he and three
others, his companions, went out to walk in gardens near the city
walls, and there as they happened to walk in pairs, one went apart
with him, and the other two wandered by themselves; and these,
in their wanderings, lighted upon a certain cottage, inhabited by
certain of thy servants, *poor in spirit, of whom is the kingdom of
heaven,*[2] and there they found a little book, containing the life of
Antony. This one of them began to read, admire, and kindle at it,
and as he read, to meditate on taking up such a life, and giving
over his secular service to serve Thee. And these two were of those
whom they style agents for the public affairs. Then suddenly, filled
with an holy love, and a sober shame, in anger with himself he
cast his eyes upon his friend, saying, "Tell me, I pray thee, what
would we attain by all these labours of ours? what aim we at? what
serve we for? Can our hopes in court rise higher than to be the
Emperor's favourites? and in this, what is there not brittle, and
full of perils? and by how many perils arrive we at a greater peril?
And when arrive we thither? But a friend of God, if I wish it, I
become now at once." So spake he. And in pain with the travail
of a new life, he turned his eyes again upon the book, and read
on, and was changed inwardly, where Thou sawest, and his mind
was stripped of the world, as soon appeared. For as he read, and
rolled up and down the waves of his heart, he stormed at himself
a while, then discerned, and determined on a better course; and
now being Thine, said to his friend, "Now have I broken loose
from those our hopes, and am resolved to serve God; and this,
from this hour, in this place, I begin upon. If thou likest not to
imitate me, oppose not." The other answered, he would cleave to
him, to partake so glorious a reward, so glorious a service. Thus
both being now Thine, were *building* the *tower* at the necessary
cost, the forsaking all that they had, and following Thee.[3] Then
Pontitianus and the other with him, that had walked in other parts

[2] *Matt.* v, 3.   [3] *Luke* xiv, 24 ff.

of the garden, came in search of them to the same place; and finding them, reminded them to return, for the day was now far spent.
But they relating their resolution and purpose, and how that will
was begun, and settled in them, begged them, if they would not
join, not to molest them. But the others, though nothing altered
from their former selves, did yet bewail themselves, (as he
affirmed,) and piously congratulated them, recommending themselves to their prayers; and so, with hearts lingering on the earth,
went away to the palace. But the other two, fixing their heart on
heaven, remained in the cottage. And both had affianced brides,
who when they heard hereof, also dedicated their virginity unto
God.

[VII] 16. Such was the story of Pontitianus; but Thou, O Lord,
while he was speaking, didst turn me round towards myself, taking me from behind my back, where I had placed me, unwilling
to observe myself; and setting me before my face, that I might see
how foul I was, how crooked and defiled, bespotted and ulcerous.
And I beheld and stood aghast; and whither to flee from myself
I found not. And if I sought to turn mine eye from off myself, he
went on with his relation, and Thou again didst set me over against
myself, and thrustedst me before my eyes, that *I might find out
mine iniquity, and hate it*.[4] I had known it, but made as though I
saw it not, winked at it, and forgot it.

17. But now, the more ardently I loved those, whose healthful
affections I heard of, that they had resigned themselves wholly to
Thee to be cured, the more did I abhor myself, when compared
with them. For many of my years (some twelve) had now run out
with me since my nineteenth, when, upon the reading of Cicero's
Hortensius, I was stirred to an earnest love of wisdom; and still
I was deferring to reject mere earthly felicity, and give myself to
search out that, whereof not the finding only, but the very search,
was to be preferred to the treasures and kingdoms of the world,
though already found, and to the pleasures of the body, though
spread around me at my will. But I wretched, most wretched, in
the very commencement of my early youth, had begged chastity
of Thee, and said, "Give me chastity and continency, only not
yet." For I feared lest Thou shouldest hear me soon, and soon cure

[4] *Ps*. xxxv, 3.

me of the disease of concupiscence, which I wished to have satisfied, rather than extinguished. And I had wandered through
crooked ways in a sacrilegious superstition, not indeed assured
thereof, but as preferring it to the others which I did not seek
religiously, but opposed maliciously.

18. And I had thought, that I therefore deferred from day
to day to reject the hopes of this world, and follow Thee only,
because there did not appear aught certain, whither to direct my
course. And now was the day come wherein I was to be laid bare
to myself, and my conscience was to upbraid me. "Where art thou
now, my tongue? Thou saidst, that for an uncertain truth thou
likedst not to cast off the baggage of vanity; now, it is certain, and
yet that burthen still oppresseth thee, while they who neither have
so worn themselves out with seeking it, nor for ten years and more
have been thinking thereon, have had their shoulders lightened,
and received wings to fly away." Thus was I gnawed within, and
exceedingly confounded with an horrible shame, while Pontitianus
was so speaking. And he having brought to a close his tale and
the business he came for, went his way; and I into myself. What
said I not against myself? with what scourges of condemnation
lashed I not my soul, that it might follow me, striving to go after
Thee! Yet it drew back; refused, but excused not itself. All arguments were spent and confuted; there remained a mute shrinking;
and she feared, as she would death, to be restrained from the flux
of that custom, whereby she was wasting to death.

[VIII] 19. Then in this great contention of my inward dwelling,
which I had strongly raised against my soul, in *the chamber* of my
heart,[5] troubled in mind and countenance, I turned upon Alypius.
"What ails us?" I exclaim: "what is it? what heardest thou? The
unlearned start up and *take heaven by force,*[6] and we with our
learning, and without heart, lo, where we wallow in flesh and
blood! Are we ashamed to follow, because others are gone before,
and not ashamed not even to follow?" Some such words I uttered,
and my fever of mind tore me away from him, while he, gazing
on me in astonishment, kept silence. For it was not my wonted
tone; and my forehead, cheeks, eyes, colour, tone of voice, spake
my mind more than the words I uttered. A little garden there was

[5] *Isa.* xxvi, 20; *Matt.* vi, 6.   [6] *Matt.* xi, 12.

to our lodging, which we had the use of, as of the whole house; for the master of the house, our host, was not living there. Thither had the tumult of my breast hurried me, where no man might hinder the hot contention wherein I had engaged with myself, until it should end as Thou knewest, I knew not. Only I was healthfully distracted and dying, to live; knowing what evil thing I was, and not knowing what good thing I was shortly to become. I retired then into the garden, and Alypius, on my steps. For his presence did not lessen my privacy; or how could he forsake me so disturbed? We sat down as far removed as might be from the house. I was troubled in spirit, most vehemently indignant that I entered not into Thy will and covenant, O my God, which *all my bones cried out* unto me to enter, and praised it to the skies. And therein we enter not by ships, or chariots, or feet, no, move not so far as I had come from the house to that place where we were sitting. For, not to go only, but to go in thither was nothing else but to will to go, but to will resolutely and thoroughly; not to turn and toss, this way and that, a maimed and half-divided will, struggling, with one part sinking as another rose.

20. Lastly, in the very fever of my irresoluteness, I made with my body many such motions as men sometimes would, but cannot, if either they have not the limbs, or these be bound with bands, weakened with infirmity, or any other way hindered. Thus, if I tore my hair, beat my forehead, if locking my fingers I clasped my knee; I willed, I did it. But I might have willed, and not done it, if the power of motion in my limbs had not obeyed. So many things then I did, when "to will" was not in itself "to be able;" and I did not what both I longed incomparably more to do, and which soon after, when I should will, I should be able to do; because soon after, when I should will, I should will thoroughly. For in these things the ability was one with the will, and to will was to do; and yet was it not done: and more easily did my body obey the weakest willing of my soul, in moving its limbs at its nod, than the soul obeyed itself to accomplish in the will alone this its momentous will.

[IX] 21. Whence is this monstrousness? and to what end? Let Thy mercy gleam that I may ask, if so be the secret penalties of men, and those darkest pangs of the sons of Adam, may perhaps answer me. Whence is this monstrousness? and to what end? The mind commands the body, and it obeys instantly; the mind commands itself, and is resisted. The mind commands the hand to be moved; and such readiness is there, that command is scarce distinct from obedience. Yet the mind is mind, the hand is body. The mind commands the mind, its own self, to will, and yet it doth not. Whence this monstrousness? and to what end? It commands itself, I say, to will, and would not command, unless it willed, and what it commands is not done. But it willeth not entirely: therefore doth it not command entirely. For so far forth it commandeth, as it willeth: and, so far forth is the thing commanded, not done, as it willeth not. For the will commandeth that there be a will; not another, but itself. But it doth not command entirely, therefore what it commandeth, is not. For were the will entire, it would not even command it to be, because it would already be. It is therefore no monstrousness partly to will, partly to nill, but a disease of the mind, that it doth not wholly rise, by truth up-borne, borne down by custom. And therefore are there two wills, for that one of them is not entire: and what the one lacketh, the other hath.

[x] 22. *Let them perish from Thy presence,*[7] O God, as perish *vain talkers, and seducers* of the soul: [8] who [9] observing that in deliberating there were two wills, affirm that there are two minds in us of two kinds, one good, the other evil. Themselves are truly evil, when they hold these evil things; and themselves shall become good, when they hold the truth, and assent unto the truth, that Thy Apostle may say to them, *Ye were sometimes darkness, but now light in the Lord.*[10] But they, wishing to be light, not *in the Lord,* but in themselves, imagining the nature of the soul to be that which God is, are made more gross darkness through a dreadful arrogancy; for that they *went back farther from Thee, the true Light that enlightened every man that cometh into the world.*[11] Take heed what you say, and blush for shame: *draw near unto Him and be enlightened, and your faces shall not be ashamed.*[12] Myself when I was deliberating upon serving the Lord my God now, as I had long purposed, it was I who willed, I who nilled, I, I myself. I neither willed entirely, nor nilled entirely. Therefore was I at

[7] *Ps.* lxvii, 2.　　[8] *Titus* i, 10.　　[9] The Manichaeans.　　[10] *Ephes.* v, 8.
[11] *Jo.* i, 9.　　[12] *Ps.* xxxiii, 6.

strife with myself, and rent asunder by myself. And this rent befel me against my will, and yet indicated, not the presence of another mind, but the punishment of my own. *Therefore it was no more I that wrought it, but sin that dwelt in me;* [13] the punishment of a sin more freely committed, in that I was a son of Adam.

23. For if there be so many contrary natures, as there be conflicting wills, there shall now be not two only, but many. If a man deliberate, whether he should go to their conventicle, or to the theatre, these Manichees cry out, Behold, here are two natures: one good, draws this way; another bad, draws back that way. For whence else is this hesitation between conflicting wills? But I say, that both be bad: that which draws to them, as that which draws back to the theatre. But they believe not that will to be other than good, which draws to them. What then if one of us should deliberate, and amid the strife of his two wills be in a strait, whether he should go to the theatre, or to our church? would not these Manichees also be in a strait what to answer? For either they must confess, (which they fain would not,) that the will which leads to our church is good, as well as theirs, who have received and are held by the mysteries of theirs: or they must suppose two evil natures, and two evil souls conflicting in one man, and it will not be true, which they say, that there is one good and another bad; or they must be converted to the truth, and no more deny, that where one deliberates, one soul fluctuates between contrary wills.

24. Let them no more say then, when they perceive two conflicting wills in one man, that the conflict is between two contrary souls, of two contrary substances, from two contrary principles, one good, and the other bad. For Thou, O true God, dost disprove, check, and convict them; as when, both wills being bad, one deliberates, whether he should kill a man by poison, or by the sword; whether he should seize this or that estate of another's, when he cannot both; whether he should purchase pleasure by luxury, or keep his money by covetousness; whether he go to the circus, or the theatre, if both be open on one day; or, thirdly, to rob another's house, if he have the opportunity; or, fourthly, to commit adultery, if at the same time he have the means thereof also; all these meeting together in the same juncture of time, and all being

[13] *Rom.* vii, 17.

equally desired, which cannot at one time be acted: for they rend
the mind amid four, or even (amid the vast variety of things desired) more, conflicting wills, nor do they yet allege that there are
so many divers substances. So also in wills which are good. For I
ask them, is it good to take pleasure in reading the Apostle? or
good to take pleasure in a sober Psalm? or good to discourse on
the Gospel? They will answer to each, "It is good." What then if
all give equal pleasure, and all at once? Do not divers wills distract the mind, while he deliberates, which he should rather
choose? yet are they all good, and are at variance till one be chosen,
whither the one entire will may be borne, which before was divided into many. Thus also, when, above, eternity delights us, and
the pleasure of temporal good holds us down below, it is the same
soul which willeth not this or that with an entire will; and therefore is rent asunder with grievous perplexities, while out of truth
it sets this first, but out of habit sets not that aside.

[XI] 25. Thus soul-sick was I, and tormented, accusing myself
much more severely than my wont, rolling and turning me in my
chain, till that were wholly broken, whereby I now was but just,
but still was, held. And Thou, O Lord, pressedst upon me in my
inward parts by a severe mercy, redoubling the lashes of fear and
shame, lest I should again give way, and not bursting that same
slight remaining tie, it should recover strength, and bind me the
faster. For I said within myself, "Be it done now, be it done now."
And as I spake, I all but enacted it. I all but did it, and did it not:
yet sunk not back to my former state, but kept my stand hard by,
and took breath. And I essayed again, and wanted somewhat less
of it, and somewhat less, and all but touched and laid hold of it;
and yet came not at it, nor touched, nor laid hold of it: hesitating
to die to death and to live to life: and the worse whereto I was
inured, prevailed more with me than the better, whereto I was
unused: and the very moment wherein I was to become other than
I was, the nearer it approached me, the greater horror did it strike
into me; yet did it not strike me back, nor turned me away, but
held me in suspense.

26. The very toys of toys, and vanities of vanities, my ancient
mistresses, still held me; they plucked my fleshly garment, and
whispered softly, "Dost thou cast us off? and from that moment

shall we no more be with thee for ever? and from that moment
shall not this or that be lawful for thee for ever?" And what was
it which they suggested in that I said, "this or that," what did they
suggest, O my God? Let Thy mercy turn it away from the soul of
Thy servant. What defilements did they suggest! what shame! And
now I much less than half heard them, and not openly shewing
themselves and contradicting me, but muttering as it were behind
my back, and privily plucking me, as I was departing, but to look
back on them. Yet they did retard me, so that I hesitated to burst
and shake myself free from them, and to spring over whither I
was called; a violent habit saying to me, "Thinkest thou, thou
canst live without them?"

27. But now it spake very faintly. For on that side whither
I had set my face, and whither I trembled to go, there appeared
unto me the chaste dignity of Continence, serene, yet not relaxedly
gay, honestly alluring me to come, and doubt not; and stretching
forth to receive and embrace me, her holy hands full of multitudes
of good examples. There were so many young men and maidens
here, a multitude of youth and every age, grave widows and aged
virgins; and Continence herself in all, not barren, but a *fruitful
mother of children* of joys, by Thee her Husband, O Lord. And
she smiled on me with a persuasive mockery, as would she say,
"Canst not thou what these youths, what these maidens can? or
can they either in themselves, and not rather in the Lord their
God? The Lord their God gave me unto them. Why standest thou
in thyself, and so standest not? Cast thyself upon Him, fear not
He will not withdraw Himself that thou shouldest fall; cast thyself fearlessly upon Him, He will receive, and will heal thee."
And I blushed exceedingly, for that I yet heard the muttering of
those toys, and hung in suspense. And she again seemed to say,
"Stop thine ears against *those* thy unclean *members on the earth,
that they may be mortified. They tell thee of delights, but not as
doth the law of the Lord thy God."* [14] This controversy in my heart
was self against self only. But Alypius sitting close by my side, in
silence waited the issue of my unwonted emotion.

[XII] 28. But when a deep consideration had from the secret
bottom of my soul drawn together and heaped up all my misery

[14] *Coloss.* iii, 5; *Ps.* cxvii, 85.

in the sight of my heart; there arose a mighty storm, bringing a mighty shower of tears. Which that I might pour forth wholly, in its natural expressions, I rose from Alypius: solitude was suggested to me as fitter for the business of weeping; so I retired so far that even his presence could not be a burthen to me. Thus was it then with me, and he perceived something of it; for something I suppose I had spoken, wherein the tones of my voice appeared choked with weeping, and so had risen up. He then remained where we were sitting, most extremely astonished. I cast myself down I know not how, under a certain fig-tree, giving full vent to my tears; and the floods of mine eyes gushed out, an *acceptable sacrifice to Thee.* And, not indeed in these words, yet to this purpose, spake I much unto Thee: *And Thou, O Lord, how long? how long, Lord, wilt Thou be angry, for ever? Remember not our former iniquities,*[15] for I felt that I was held by them. I sent up these sorrowful words: How long? how long, "tomorrow, and tomorrow?" Why not now? why not is there this hour an end to my uncleanness?

29. So was I speaking, and weeping in the most bitter contrition of my heart, when, lo! I heard from a neighbouring house a voice, as of boy or girl, I know not, chanting, and oft repeating, "Take up and read; Take up and read." Instantly, my countenance altered, I began to think most intently, whether children were wont in any kind of play to sing such words: nor could I remember ever to have heard the like. So checking the torrent of my tears, I arose; interpreting it to be no other than a command from God, to open the book, and read the first chapter I should find. For I had heard of Antony, that coming in during the reading of the Gospel, he received the admonition, as if what was being read was spoken to him; *Go, sell all that thou hast, and give to the poor, and thou shalt have treasure in heaven, and come and follow me.*[16] And by such oracle he was forthwith converted unto Thee. Eagerly then I returned to the place where Alypius was sitting; for there had I laid the volume of the Apostle, when I arose thence. I seized, opened, and in silence read that section, on which my eyes first fell: *Not in rioting and drunkenness, not in chambering*

---

[15] *Ps.* vi. 4: lxxviii, 5; 8.   [16] *Matt.* xix, 21.

and wantonness, not in strife and envying: but put ye on the Lord Jesus Christ, and make not provision for the flesh, in concupis-cence.[17] No further would I read; nor needed I: for instantly at the end of this sentence, by a light as it were of serenity infused into my heart, all the darkness of doubt vanished away.

30. Then putting my finger between, or some other mark, I shut the volume, and with a calmed countenance made it known to Alypius. And what was wrought in him, which I knew not, he thus shewed me. He asked to see what I had read: I shewed him; and he looked even further than I had read, and I knew not what followed. This followed, *him that is weak in the faith, receive;* [18] which he applied to himself, and disclosed to me. And by this admonition was he strengthened; and by a good resolution and purpose, and most corresponding to his character, wherein he did always very far differ from me, for the better, without any turbu-lent delay he joined me. Thence we go in to my mother; we tell her; she rejoiceth: we relate in order how it took place; she leaps for joy, and triumpheth, and blesseth Thee, *Who art able to do above that which we ask or think;* [19] for she perceived that Thou hadst given her more for me, than she was wont to beg by her pitiful and most sorrowful groanings. For Thou convertedst me unto Thyself, so that I sought neither wife, nor any hope of this world, standing in that rule of faith, where Thou hadst shewed me unto her in a vision, so many years before. And Thou didst *convert her mourning into joy,*[20] much more plentiful than she had desired, and in a much more precious and purer way than she erst required, by having grandchildren of my body.

BOOK NINE

Augustine determines to devote his life to God, and to abandon his profession of Rhetoric, quietly however; retires to the country to prepare himself to receive the grace of Baptism, and is baptized

[17] *Rom.* xiii, 13-14. [18] *Rom.* xiv, 1. [19] *Ephes.* iii, 20.
[20] *Ps.* xxix, 12.

*with Alypius, and his son Adeodatus. At Ostia, in his way to
Africa, his mother Monica dies, in her fifty-sixth year, the thirty-
third of Augustine. Her life and character.*

[I] 1. *O Lord, I am Thy servant; I am Thy servant, and the son
of Thy handmaid: Thou hast broken my bonds in sunder. I will
offer to Thee the sacrifice of praise.*¹ Let my heart and my tongue
praise Thee; yea let *all my bones say, O Lord, who is like unto
Thee?* ² Let them say, and answer Thou me, and *say unto my soul,
I am thy salvation.* Who am I, and what am I? What evil have not
been either my deeds, or if not my deeds, my words, or if not my
words, my will? But Thou, O Lord, art good and merciful, and
Thy right hand had respect unto the depth of my death, and from
the bottom of my heart emptied that abyss of corruption. And this
Thy whole gift was, to nill what I willed, and to will what Thou
willedst. But where through all those years, and out of what low
and deep recess was my free-will called forth in a moment,
whereby to submit my neck to Thy *easy yoke,* and my shoulders
unto Thy *light burthen, O Christ Jesus, my Helper and my Redeemer?* ³ How sweet did it at once become to me, to want the
sweetnesses of those toys! and what I feared to be parted from,
was now a joy to part with. For Thou didst cast them forth from
me, Thou true and highest sweetness. Thou castest them forth, and
for them enteredst in Thyself, sweeter than all pleasure, though
not to flesh and blood; brighter than all light, but more hidden
than all depths, higher than all honour, but not to the high in their
own conceits. Now was my soul free from the biting cares of can-
vassing and getting, and weltering in filth, and scratching off the
itch of lust. And my infant tongue spake freely to Thee, my brightness, and my riches, and my health, the Lord my God.

[II] 2. And I resolved in Thy sight, not tumultuously to tear, but
gently to withdraw, the service of my tongue from the marts of
lip-labour: that the young, no students in Thy law, nor in Thy
peace, but in lying dotages and law-skirmishes, should no longer
buy at my mouth arms for their madness. And very seasonably, it
now wanted but very few days unto the Vacation of the Vintage,
and I resolved to endure them, then in a regular way to take my

¹ *Ps.* cxv, 16; 17.   ² *Ps.* xxxiv, 10.   ³ *Matt.* xi, 30: *Ps.* xvii, 15.

leave, and having been purchased by Thee, no more to return for sale. Our purpose then was known to Thee; but to men, other than our own friends, was it not known. For we had agreed among ourselves not to let it out abroad to any: although to us, now ascending from the *valley of tears,* and singing that *song of degrees,* Thou hadst given *sharp arrows,* and *destroying coals* against the *subtle tongue,*[4] which as though advising for us, would thwart, and would out of love devour us, as it doth its meat.

3. Thou hadst pierced our hearts with Thy charity, and we carried Thy words as it were fixed in our entrails: and the examples of Thy servants, whom for black Thou hadst made bright, and for dead, alive, being piled together in the receptacle of our thoughts, kindled and burned up that our heavy torpor, that we should not sink down to the abyss; and they fired us so vehemently, that all the blasts of *subtle tongues* from gainsayers might only inflame us the more fiercely, not extinguish us. Nevertheless, because for *Thy Name's* sake which Thou hast *hallowed* throughout the earth, this our vow and purpose might also find some to commend it, it seemed like ostentation not to wait for the vacation now so near, but to quit beforehand a public profession, which was before the eyes of all; so that all looking on this act of mine, and observing how near was the time of vintage which I wished to anticipate, would talk much of me, as if I had desired to appear some great one. And what end had it served me, that people should repute and dispute upon my purpose, and that *our good should be evil spoken of?* [5]

4. Moreover, it had at first troubled me, that in this very summer my lungs began to give way, amid too great literary labour, and to breathe deeply with difficulty, and by the pain in my chest to shew that they were injured, and to refuse any full or lengthened speaking; this had troubled me, for it almost constrained me, of necessity, to lay down that burthen of teaching, or, if I could be cured and recover, at least to intermit it. But when the full wish for leisure, that I might see *how that Thou art the Lord,*[6] arose, and was fixed in me, my God, Thou knowest, I began even to rejoice that I had this secondary, and that no feigned, excuse, which might something moderate the offense

[4] *Ps.* lxxxiii, 7; cxix, 3-4.   [5] *Rom.* xiv, 16.   [6] *Ps.* xlv, 11.

taken by those who, for their sons' sake, wished me never to have the freedom of Thy sons. Full then of such joy, I endured till that interval of time were run; it may have been some twenty days, yet they were endured manfully; endured, for the covetousness which aforetime bore a part of this heavy business, had left ne, and I remained alone, and had been overwhelmed, had not patience taken its place. Perchance, some of Thy servants, my brethren, may say, that I sinned in this, that with a heart fully set on Thy service, I suffered myself to sit even one hour in the chair of lies. Nor would I be contentious. But hast not Thou, O most merciful Lord, pardoned and remitted this sin also, with my other most horrible and deadly sins, in the holy water?

[III] 5. Verecundus was worn down with care about this our blessedness, for that being held back by bonds, whereby he was most straitly bound, he saw that he should be severed from us. For himself was not yet a Christian, his wife one of the faithful; and yet hereby, more rigidly than by any other chain, was he let and hindered from the journey which we had now essayed. For he would not, he said, be a Christian on any other terms than on those he could not. However, he offered us courteously to remain at his country-house, so long as we should stay there. Thou, O Lord, shalt reward him *in the resurrection of the just,*[7] seeing thou hast already given him *the lot* of the righteous.[8] For although, in our absence, being now at Rome, he was seized with bodily sickness, and therein being made a Christian, and one of the faithful, he departed this life; yet *hadst Thou mercy not on him only, but on us also:*[9] lest remembering the exceeding kindness of our friend towards us, yet unable to number him among Thy flock, we should be agonized with intolerable sorrow. Thanks unto Thee, our God, we are Thine: Thy suggestions and consolations tell us, Faithful in promises, Thou now requitest Verecundus for his country-house of Cassciacum, where from the fever of the world we reposed in Thee, with the eternal freshness of Thy Paradise: for that Thou hast forgiven him his sins upon earth, in that rich mountain, that mountain which yieldeth milk, Thine own mountain.

6. He then had at that time sorrow, but Nebridius joy. For

[7] *Luke* xiv, 14.   [8] *Ps.* cxxiv, 3.   [9] *Phil.* ii, 27.

although he also, not being yet a Christian, had fallen into the pit of that most pernicious error, believing the flesh of Thy Son to be a phantom: yet emerging thence, he believed as we did; not as yet indued with any Sacraments of Thy Church, but a most ardent searcher out of truth. Whom, not long after our conversion and regeneration by Thy Baptism, being also a faithful member of the Church Catholic, and serving Thee in perfect chastity and continence amongst his people in Africa, his whole house having through him first been made Christian, didst Thou release from the flesh; and now he lives in Abraham's bosom. Whatever that be, which is signified by that bosom, there lives my Nebridius, my sweet friend, and Thy child, O Lord, adopted of a freed man; there he liveth. For what other place is there for such a soul? There he liveth, whereof he asked much of me, a poor inexperienced man. Now lays he not his ear to my mouth, but his spiritual mouth unto Thy fountain, and drinketh as much as he can receive, wisdom in proportion to his thirst, endlessly happy. Nor do I think that he is so inebriated therewith, as to forget me; seeing Thou, Lord, Whom he drinketh, art mindful of us. So were we then, comforting Verecundus, who sorrowed, as far as friendship permitted, that our conversion was of such sort; and exhorting him to become faithful, according to his measure, namely, of a married estate; and awaiting Nebridius to follow us, which, being so near, he was all but doing: and so, lo! those days rolled by at length; for long and many they seemed, for the love I bare to the easeful liberty, that I might sing to Thee from my inmost marrow, *My heart hath said unto Thee, I have sought Thy face: Thy face, Lord, will I seek.*[10]

[IV] 7. Now was the day come, wherein I was in deed to be freed of my Rhetoric Professorship, whereof in thought I was already freed. And it was done. Thou didst rescue my tongue, whence Thou hadst before rescued my heart. And I blessed Thee, rejoicing; retiring with all mine to the villa. What I there did in writing, which was now enlisted in Thy service, though still, in this breathing-time as it were, panting from the school of pride, my books may witness,[11] as well what I debated with others,

10 *Ps.* xxvi, 8.
11 *I.e., Against the Academics, On the Happy Life, On Order.*

as what with myself alone, before Thee: what with Nebridius, who was absent, my epistles bear witness. And when shall I have time to rehearse all Thy great benefits towards us at that time, especially when hasting on to yet greater mercies? For my remembrance recalls me, and pleasant is it to me, O Lord, to confess to Thee, by what inward goads Thou tamedst me; and how Thou hast evened me, *lowering the mountains and hills of my high imaginations, straightening my crookedness, and smoothing my rough ways;* [12] and how Thou also subduedst the brother of my heart, Alypius, unto the Name of Thy Only Begotten, our Lord and Saviour Jesus Christ, which he would not at first vouchsafe to have inserted in our writings. For rather would he have them savour of the lofty *cedars* of the Schools, which *the Lord* hath now *broken down,* [13] than of the wholesome herbs of the Church, the antidote against serpents.

8. Oh in what accents spake I unto Thee, my God, when I read the Psalms of David, those faithful songs, and sounds of devotion, which allow of no swelling spirit, as yet a Catechumen, and a novice in Thy real love, resting in that villa, with Alypius, a Catechumen, my mother cleaving to us, in female garb with masculine faith, with the tranquillity of age, motherly love, Christian piety. Oh, what accents did I utter unto Thee in those Psalms, and how was I by them kindled towards Thee, and on fire to rehearse them, if possible, through the whole world, against the pride of mankind. And yet they are sung through the whole world, nor can *any hide himself from Thy heat.* [14] With what vehement and bitter sorrow was I angered at the Manichees! and again I pitied them, for that they knew not those Sacraments, those medicines, and were mad against the antidote, which might have recovered them of their madness. How I would they had then been somewhere near me, and without my knowing that they were there, could have beheld my countenance, and heard my words, when I read the fourth Psalm in that time of my rest, and how that Psalm wrought upon me, *When I called, the God of my righteousness heard me; in tribulation Thou enlargedst me. Have mercy upon me, O Lord, and hear my prayer.* [15] Would

---

[12] Cf. *Isa.* xl, 3; *Luke* iii, 5.   [13] *Ps.* xxviii, 5.   [14] *Ps.* xviii, 7.
[15] *Ps.* iv, 1-2.

that what I uttered on these words, they could hear, without my knowing whether they heard, lest they should think I spake it for their sakes! Because in truth neither should I speak the same things, nor in the same way, if I perceived that they heard and saw me; nor if I spake them would they so receive them, as when I spake by and for myself before Thee, out of the natural feelings of my soul.

9. I trembled for fear, and again kindled with hope, and with rejoicing in Thy mercy, O Father; and all issued forth both by mine eyes and voice, when Thy good Spirit turning unto us, said, *O ye sons of men, how long slow of heart? why do ye love vanity, and seek after leasing?* [16] For I had *loved vanity, and sought after leasing. And Thou, O Lord,* hadst already *magnified Thy Holy One, raising Him from the dead, and setting Him at Thy right hand,* whence *from on high* He should *send* His *promise, the Comforter, the Spirit of truth.* [17] And He had already sent Him, but I knew it not; He had sent Him, because He was now magnified, rising again from the dead, and ascending into heaven. For till then, *the Spirit was not yet given, because Jesus was not yet glorified.* [18] And the prophet cries out, *How long, slow of heart? why do ye love vanity, and seek after leasing? Know this, that the Lord hath magnified his Holy One.* He cries out, *How long?* He cries out, *Know this:* and I so long, not knowing, *loved vanity, and sought after leasing:* and therefore I heard and trembled, because it was spoken unto such as I remembered myself to have been. For in those phantoms which I had held for truths, was there *vanity and leasing;* and I spake aloud many things earnestly and forcibly, in the bitterness of my remembrance. Which would they had heard, who yet *love vanity and seek after leasing!* They would perchance have been troubled, and have vomited it up; and *Thou wouldest hear them when they cried unto Thee;* for by a true death in the flesh did He die for us, who now *intercedeth unto Thee for us.* [19]

10. I further read, *Be angry, and sin not.* [20] And how was I moved, O my God, who had now learned to be angry at myself for things past, that I might not sin in time to come! Yea, to be

[16] *Ps.* iv, 3.   [17] *Ephes.* 1, 20; *Luke* xxiv, 49; *Jo.* xiv, 16-17.
[18] *Jo.* vii, 39.   [19] *Rom.* viii. 34.   [20] *Ephes.* iv, 26.

justly angry; for that it was not another nature of a people of darkness which sinned for me, as they say who are not angry at themselves, and *treasure up* wrath *against the day of* wrath, *and of the revelation of Thy just judgment*.[21] Nor were my *good things* now without, nor sought with the eyes of flesh in that earthly sun; for they that would have joy from without soon become vain, and waste themselves on the things seen, and temporal, and in their famished thoughts do lick their very shadows. Oh that they were wearied out with their famine, and said, *Who will shew us good things?* And we would say, and they hear, *The light of Thy countenance is sealed upon us*.[22] For we are not *that light which enlighteneth every man,* but we are enlightened by Thee; that *having been sometimes darkness, we may be light in Thee*.[23] Oh that they could see the eternal Internal, which having tasted, I was grieved that I could not shew It them, so long as they brought me their heart in their eyes, roving abroad from Thee, while they said, *Who will shew us good things?* For there, where I was *angry* within myself *in my chamber,* where I was inwardly pricked, where I had sacrificed, slaying my old man and commencing the purpose of a new life, *putting my trust in Thee,*—there hadst Thou begun to grow sweet unto me, and *hadst put gladness in my heart.* And I cried out, as I read this outwardly, finding it inwardly. Nor would I be multiplied with worldly goods; wasting away time, and wasted by time; whereas I had in Thy eternal Simple Essence other *corn, and wine, and oil*.[24]

11. And with a loud cry of my heart I cried out in the next verse, O *in peace,* O for *The Self-Same!* O what said he, *I will lay me down and sleep,* for who shall hinder us, when *cometh to pass that saying which is written, Death is swallowed up in victory?*[25] And Thou surpassingly art the Self-same, Who *art not changed;* and in Thee is rest which forgetteth all toil, for there is none other with Thee, nor are we to seek those many other things, which are not what Thou art: but Thou, Lord, *alone* hast *made me dwell in hope.* I read, and kindled; nor found I what to do to those deaf and dead, of whom myself had been, a pestilent

---

[21] *Rom.* ii, 5.   [22] *Ps.* iv, 6-7.   [23] *Jo.* i, 9; *Ephes.* v, 8.   [24] *Ps.* iv, 6-8.
[25] *Ps.* iv, 9; *I Cor.* xv, 54.

person, a bitter and a blind bawler against those writings, which are honied with the honey of heaven, and lightsome with Thine own light: and I was consumed with zeal at the enemies of this Scripture.

12. When shall I recall all which passed in those holy-days? Yet neither have I forgotten, nor will I pass over the severity of Thy scourge, and the wonderful swiftness of Thy mercy. Thou didst then torment me with pain in my teeth; which when it had come to such height, that I could not speak, it came into my heart to desire all my friends present to pray for me to Thee, the God of all manner of health. And this I wrote on wax, and gave it them to read. Presently so soon as with humble devotion we had bowed our knees, that pain went away. But what pain? or how went it away? I was affrighted, O my Lord, my God; for from infancy I had never experienced the like. And the power of Thy Nod was deeply conveyed to me, and rejoicing in faith, I praised Thy Name. And that faith suffered me not to be at ease about my past sins, which were not yet forgiven me by Thy baptism.

[v] 13. The vintage-vacation ended, I gave notice to the Milanese to provide their scholars with another master to sell words to them; for that I had both made choice to serve Thee, and through my difficulty of breathing and pain in my chest, was not equal to the Professorship. And by letters I signified to Thy Prelate, the holy man Ambrose, my former errors and present desires, begging his advice what of Thy Scriptures I had best read, to become readier and fitter for receiving so great grace. He recommended Isaiah the Prophet: I believe, because he above the rest is a more clear fore-shewer of the Gospel and of the calling of the Gentiles. But I, not understanding the first lesson in him, and imagining the whole to be like it, laid it by, to be resumed when better practised in our Lord's own words.

[vi] 14. Thence, when the time was come, wherein I was to give in my name, we left the country and returned to Milan. It pleased Alypius also to be with me born again in Thee, being already clothed with the humility befitting Thy Sacraments; and a most valiant tamer of the body, so as, with unwonted venture, to wear the frozen ground of Italy with his bare feet. We joined with us the boy Adeodatus, born after the flesh, of my sin. Excellently

hadst Thou made him. He was not quite fifteen, and in wit surpassed many grave and learned men. I confess unto Thee Thy gifts,
O Lord my God, Creator of all, and abundantly able to reform
our deformities: for I had no part in that boy, but the sin. For
that we brought him up in Thy discipline, it was Thou, none else,
had inspired us with it. I confess unto Thee Thy gifts. There is a
book of ours entitled *The Teacher;* it is a dialogue between him
and me. Thou knowest, that all there ascribed to the person conversing with me were his ideas, in his sixteenth year. Much besides,
and yet more admirable, I found in him. That talent struck awe
into me. And who but Thou could be the workmaster of such
wonders? Soon didst Thou take his life from the earth: and I now
remember him without anxiety, fearing nothing for his childhood
or youth, or his whole self. Him we joined with us, our contemporary in grace, to be brought up in Thy discipline; and we
were baptized, and anxiety for our past life vanished from us.
Nor was I sated in those days with the wondrous sweetness of considering the depth of Thy counsels concerning the salvation of
mankind. How did I weep, in Thy Hymns and Canticles, touched
to the quick by the voices of Thy sweet-attuned Church! The voices
flowed into mine ears, and the Truth distilled into my heart, whence
the affections of my devotion overflowed, and tears ran down, and
happy was I therein.

[VII] 15. Not long had the Church of Milan begun to use this
kind of consolation and exhortation, the brethren zealously
joining with harmony of voice and hearts. For it was a year, or
not much more, that Justina, mother to the Emperor Valentinian,
a child, persecuted Thy servant Ambrose, in favour of her heresy,
to which she was seduced by the Arians. The devout people kept
watch in the Church, ready to die with their Bishop Thy servant.
There my mother Thy handmaid, bearing a chief part of those
anxieties and watchings, lived for prayer. We, yet unwarmed by
the heat of Thy Spirit, still were stirred up by the sight of the
amazed and disquieted city. Then it was first instituted that after
the manner of the Eastern Churches, Hymns and Psalms should
be sung, lest the people should wax faint through the tediousness
of sorrow: and from that day to this the custom is retained, divers,

yea, almost all Thy congregations, throughout other parts of the world, following herein.

16. Then didst Thou by a vision discover to Thy forenamed Bishop, where the bodies of Gervasius and Protasius the martyrs lay hid, (whom Thou hadst in Thy secret treasury stored uncorrupted so many years,) whence Thou mightest seasonably produce them to repress the fury of a woman, but an Empress. For when they were discovered and dug up, and with due honour translated to the Ambrosian Basilica, not only they who were vexed with unclean spirits (the devils confessing themselves) were cured, but a certain man, who had for many years been blind, a citizen, and well known to the city, asking and hearing the reason of the people's confused joy, sprang forth, desiring his guide to lead him thither. Led thither, he begged to be allowed to touch with his handkerchief the bier of Thy *saints, whose death is precious in Thy sight.*[26] Which when he had done, and put to his eyes, they were forthwith opened. Thence did the fame spread, thence Thy praises glowed, shone; thence the mind of that enemy, though not turned to the soundness of believing, was yet turned back from her fury of persecuting. Thanks to Thee, O my God. Whence and whither hast Thou thus led my remembrance, that I should confess these things also unto Thee? which great though they be, I had passed by in forgetfulness. And yet then, when *the odour of Thy ointments was so fragrant,* did we not *run after Thee.*[27] Therefore did I more weep among the singing of Thy Hymns, formerly sighing after Thee, and at length breathing in Thee, as far as the breath may enter into this our house of grass.

[VIII] 17. Thou *that makest men to dwell of one mind in one house,*[28] didst join with us Euodius also, a young man of our own city. Who, being an officer of Court, was before us converted to Thee and baptized: and quitting his secular warfare, girded himself to Thine. We were together, about to dwell together in our devout purpose. We sought where we might serve Thee most usefully, and were together returning to Africa: whitherward being as far as Ostia, my mother departed this life. Much I omit, as hastening much. Receive my confessions and thanksgivings, O

[26] *Ps.* cxv, 15.   [27] *Cant.* i, 2-3.   [28] *Ps.* lxvii, 7.

my God, for innumerable things whereof I am silent. But I will
not omit whatsoever my soul would bring forth concerning that
Thy handmaid, who brought me forth, both in the flesh, that I
might be born to this temporal light, and in heart, that I might
be born to Light eternal. Not her gifts, but Thine in her, would
I speak of; for neither did she make nor educate herself. Thou
createdst her; nor did her father and mother know what a one
should come from them. And the sceptre of Thy Christ, the
discipline of Thine only Son, in a Christian house, a good member
of Thy Church, educated her in Thy fear. Yet for her good discipline, was she wont to command not so much her mother's diligence, as that of a certain decrepit maid-servant, who had carried
her father when a child, as little ones used to be carried at the
backs of elder girls. For which reason, and for her great age, and
excellent conversation, was she, in that Christian family, well respected by its heads. Whence also the charge of her master's
daughters was entrusted to her, to which she gave diligent heed,
restraining them earnestly, when necessary, with a holy severity,
and teaching them with a grave discretion. For, except at those
hours wherein they were most temperately fed at their parents'
table, she would not suffer them, though parched with thirst, to
drink even water; preventing an evil custom and adding this
wholesome advice; "Ye drink water now, because you have not
wine in your power; but when you come to be married, and be
made mistresses of cellars and cupboards, you will scorn water,
but the custom of drinking will abide." By this method of instruction, and the authority she had, she refrained the greediness
of childhood, and moulded their very thirst to such an excellent
moderation, that what they should not, that they would not.

18. And yet (as Thy handmaid told me her son) there had
crept upon her a love of wine. For when (as the manner was)
she, as though a sober maiden, was bidden by her parents to draw
wine out of the hogshead, holding the vessel under the opening,
before she poured the wine into the flagon, she sipped a little
with the tip of her lips; for more her instinctive feelings refused.
For this she did, not out of any desire of drink, but out of the
exuberance of youth, whereby it boils over in mirthful freaks,
which in youthful spirits are wont to be kept under by the gravity

of their elders. And thus by adding to that little, daily littles, (*for whoso despiseth little things, shall fall by little and little*,²⁹) she had fallen into such a habit, as greedily to drink off her little cup brim-full almost of wine. Where was then that discreet old woman, and that her earnest countermanding? Would aught avail against a secret disease, if Thy healing hand, O Lord, watched not over us? Father, mother, and governors absent, Thou present, who createdst, who callest, who also by those set over us, workest something towards the salvation of our souls, what didst Thou then, O my God? how didst Thou cure her? how heal her? didst Thou not out of another soul bring forth a hard and a sharp taunt, like a lancet out of Thy secret store, and with one touch remove all that foul stuff? For a maid-servant with whom she used to go to the cellar, falling to words (as it happens) with her little mistress, when alone with her, taunted her with this fault, with most bitter insult, calling her wine-bibber. With which taunt she, stung to the quick, saw the foulness of her fault, and instantly condemned and forsook it. As flattering friends pervert, so reproachful enemies mostly correct. Yet not what by them Thou doest, but what themselves purposed, dost Thou repay them. For she in her anger sought to vex her young mistress, not to amend her; and did it in private, either for that the time and place of the quarrel so found them; or lest herself also should have anger, for discovering it thus late. But Thou, Lord, Governor of all in heaven and earth, who turnest to Thy purposes the deepest currents, and the ruled turbulence of the tide of times, didst by the very unhealthiness of one soul, heal another; lest any, when he observes this, should ascribe it to his own power, even when another, whom he wished to be reformed, is reformed through words of his.

[IX] 19. Brought up thus modestly and soberly, and made subject rather by Thee to her parents, than by her parents to Thee, so soon as she was of marriageable age, being bestowed upon a husband, she served him as her lord; and did her diligence to win him unto Thee, preaching Thee unto him by her conversation; by which Thou ornamentedst her, making her reverently amiable, and admirable unto her husband. And she so endured the wrong-

²⁹ *Ecclus.* xix, 1.

ing of her bed, as never to have any quarrel with her husband
thereon. For she looked for Thy mercy upon him, that believing
in Thee, he might be made chaste. But besides this, he was fervid,
as in his affections, so in anger: but she had learnt, not to resist
an angry husband, not in deed only, but not even in word. Only
when he was smoothed and tranquil, and in a temper to receive
it, she would give an account of her actions, if haply he had
overhastily taken offence. In a word, while many matrons, who
had milder husbands, yet bore even in their faces marks of shame,
would in familiar talk blame their husbands' lives, she would
blame their tongues, giving them, as in jest, earnest advice; "That
from the time they heard the marriage writings read to them,
they should account them as indentures, whereby they were made
servants; and so, remembering their condition, ought not to set
themselves up against their lords." And when they, knowing what
a choleric husband she endured, marvelled, that it had never been
heard, nor by any token perceived, that Patricius had beaten his
wife, or that there had been any domestic difference between
them, even for one day, and confidentially asking the reason, she
taught them her practice above mentioned. Those wives who observed it found the good, and returned thanks; those who observed
it not, found no relief, and suffered.

20. Her mother-in-law also, at first by whisperings of evil
servants incensed against her, she so overcame by observance and
persevering endurance and meekness, that she of her own accord
discovered to her son the meddling tongues, whereby the domestic
peace betwixt her and her daughter-in-law had been disturbed,
asking him to correct them. Then, when in compliance with his
mother, and for the well-ordering of the family, and the harmony
of its members, he had with stripes corrected those discovered, at
her will who had discovered them, she promised the like reward
to any who, to please her, should speak ill of her daughter-in-law
to her: and, none now venturing, they lived together with a remarkable sweetness of mutual kindness.

21. This great gift also Thou bestowedst, O my God, my
mercy, upon that good handmaid of Thine, in whose womb Thou
createdst me, that between any disagreeing and discordant parties
where she was able, she shewed herself such a peacemaker, that

hearing on both sides most bitter things, such as swelling and in-digested choler uses to break out into, when the crudities of en-mities are breathed out in sour discourses to a present friend against an absent enemy, she never would disclose aught of the one unto the other, but what might tend to their reconcilement. A small good this might appear to me, did I not to my grief know numberless persons, who through some horrible and wide-spreading contagion of sin, not only disclose to persons mutually angered things said in anger, but add withal things never spoken, whereas to humane humanity, it ought to seem a light thing, not to foment or increase ill will by ill words, unless one study withal by good words to quench it. Such was she, Thyself, her most in-ward Instructor, teaching her in the school of the heart.

22. Finally, her own husband, towards the very end of his earthly life, did she gain unto Thee; nor had she to complain of that in him as a believer, which before he was a believer she had borne from him. She was also the servant of thy servants; whosoever of them knew her, did in her much praise and honour and love Thee; for that through the witness of the fruits of a holy conversation they perceived Thy presence in her heart. For she had been *the wife of one man,* had *requited her parents, had governed her house* piously, *was well reported of for good works, had brought up children,* so often *travailing in birth of them,* as she saw them swerving from Thee.[30] Lastly, of all of us Thy servants, O Lord, (whom on occasion of Thy own gift Thou sufferest to speak,) us, who before her sleeping in Thee lived united together, having received the grace of Thy baptism, did she so take care of, as though she had been mother of us all; so served us, as though she had been child to us all.

[x] 23. The day now approaching whereon she was to depart this life, (which day Thou well knewest, we knew not,) it came to pass, Thyself, as I believe, by Thy secret ways so ordering it, that she and I stood alone, leaning in a certain window, which looked into the garden of the house where we now lay, at Ostia; where removed from the din of men, we were recruiting from the fatigues of a long journey, for the voyage. We were discoursing then together, alone, very sweetly; and *forgetting those things*

[30] *I Tim.* v, 4; 9; 10; 14; *Gal.* iv, 19.

*which are behind, and reaching forth unto those things which
are before,*[31] we were enquiring between ourselves in the presence
of the Truth, which Thou art, of what sort the eternal life of
the saints was to be, *which eye hath not seen, nor ear heard, nor
hath it entered into the heart of man.*[32] But yet we gasped with the
mouth of our heart, after those heavenly streams of Thy fountain,
the fountain of life, which is *with Thee;*[33] that being bedewed
thence according to our capacity, we might in some sort meditate
upon so high a mystery.

24. And when our discourse was brought to that point, that
the very highest delight of the earthly senses, in the very purest
material light, was, in respect of the sweetness of that life, not
only not worthy of comparison, but not even of mention; we
raising up ourselves with a more glowing affection towards the
"Self-same," did by degrees pass through all things bodily, even
the very heaven, whence sun and moon and stars shine upon the
earth; yea, we were soaring higher yet, by inward musing, and
discourse, and admiring of Thy works; and we came to our own
minds, and went beyond them, that we might arrive at that region of never-failing plenty, where *Thou feedest Israel*[34] for
ever with the food of truth, and where life is the *Wisdom by
whom all* these *things are made,* and what have been, and what
shall be, and she is not made, but is, as she hath been, and so
shall she be ever; yea rather, to "have been," and "hereafter to
be," are not in her, but only "to be," seeing she is eternal. For to
"have been," and to "be hereafter," are not eternal. And while
we were discoursing and panting after her, we slightly touched
on her with the whole effort of our heart; and we sighed, and
there we leave bound *the first fruits of the Spirit;*[35] and returned
to vocal expressions of our mouth, where the word spoken has
beginning and end. And what is like unto Thy Word, our Lord,
who *endureth in Himself* without becoming old, and *maketh all
things new?*[36]

25. We were saying then: If to any the tumult of the flesh were
hushed, hushed the images of earth, and waters, and air, hushed
also the poles of heaven, yea the very soul be hushed to herself,

[31] *Phil.* iii, 13.   [32] *I Cor.* ii, 9.   [33] *Ps.* xxxv, 10.   [34] *Ps.* lxxix, 6.
[35] *Rom.* viii, 23.   [36] *Wis.* vii, 27.

and by not thinking on self surmount self, hushed all dreams and imaginary revelations, every tongue and every sign, and whatsoever exists only in transition, since if any could hear, all these say, *We made not ourselves, but He made us that abideth for ever* —If then having uttered this, they too should be hushed, having roused only our ears to Him who made them, and He alone speak, not by them, but by Himself, that we may hear His Word, not through any tongue of flesh, nor Angel's voice, nor sound of thunder, nor in the dark riddle of a similitude, but, might hear Whom in these things we love, might hear His Very Self without these, (as we two now strained ourselves, and in swift thought touched on that Eternal Wisdom, which abideth over all;)— could this be continued on, and other visions of kind far unlike be withdrawn, and this one ravish, and absorb, and wrap up its beholder amid these inward joys, so that life might be for ever like that one moment of understanding which now we sighed after; were not this, *Enter into thy Master's joy?* [37] And when shall that be? When *we shall all rise again,* though we *shall not all be changed?* [38]

26. Such things was I speaking, and even if not in this very manner, and these same words, yet, Lord, Thou knowest, that in that day when we were speaking of these things, and this world with all its delights became, as we spake, contemptible to us, my mother said, "Son, for mine own part I have no further delight in any thing in this life. What I do here any longer, and to what end I am here, I know not, now that my hopes in this world are accomplished. One thing there was, for which I desired to linger for a while in this life, that I might see thee a Catholic Christian before I died. My God hath done this for me more abundantly, that I should now see thee withal, despising earthly happiness, become His servant: what do I here?"

[XI] 27. What answer I made her unto these things, I remember not. For scarce five days after, or not much more, she fell sick of a fever; and in that sickness one day she fell into a swoon, and was for a while withdrawn from these visible things. We hastened round her; but she was soon brought back to her senses; and looking on me and my brother standing by her, said to us enquiringly,

[37] *Matt.* xxv. 21. [38] *I Cor.* xv. 51.

"Where was I?" And then looking fixedly on us, with grief amazed; "Here," saith she, "shall you bury your mother." I held my peace and refrained weeping; but my brother spake something, wishing for her, as the happier lot, that she might die, not in a strange place, but in her own land. Whereat, she with anxious look, checking him with her eyes, for that he still *savoured such things,* and then looking upon me; "Behold," saith she, "what he saith:" and soon after to us both, "Lay," she saith, "this body any where; let not the care for that any way disquiet you: this only I request, that you would remember me at the Lord's altar, wherever you be." And having delivered this sentiment in what words she could, she held her peace, being exercised by her growing sickness.

27. But I, considering Thy gifts, Thou unseen God, which Thou instillest into the hearts of Thy faithful ones, whence wondrous fruits do spring, did rejoice and give thanks to Thee, recalling what I before knew, how careful and anxious she had ever been, as to her place of burial, which she had provided and prepared for herself by the body of her husband. For because they had lived in great harmony together, she also wished (so little can the human mind embrace things divine) to have this addition to that happiness, and to have it remembered among men, that after her pilgrimage beyond the seas, what was earthly of this united pair had been permitted to be united beneath the same earth. But when this emptiness had through the fulness of Thy goodness begun to cease in her heart, I knew not, and rejoiced admiring what she had so disclosed to me; though indeed in that our discourse also in the window, when she said, "What do I here any longer?" there appeared no desire of dying in her own country. I heard afterwards also, that when we were now at Ostia, she with a mother's confidence, when I was absent, one day discoursed with certain of my friends about the contempt of this life, and the blessing of death: and when they were amazed at such courage which Thou hadst given to a woman, and asked, "Whether she were not afraid to leave her body so far from her own city?" she replied, "Nothing is far to God; nor was it to be feared lest at the end of the world, He should not recognize whence He were to raise me up." On the ninth day then of her sickness, and the

fifty-sixth year of her age, and the three and thirtieth of mine, was that religious and holy soul freed from the body.

[XII] 29. I closed her eyes; and there flowed withal a mighty sorrow into my heart, which was overflowing into tears; mine eyes at the same time, by the violent command of my mind, drank up their fountain wholly dry; and woe was me in such a strife! But when she breathed her last, the boy Adeodatus burst out into a loud lament; then, checked by us all, held his peace. In like manner also a childish feeling in me, which was, through my heart's youthful voice, finding its vent in weeping, was checked and silenced. For we thought it not fitting to solemnize that funeral with tearful lament, and groanings: for thereby do they for the most part express grief for the departed, as though unhappy, or altogether dead; whereas she was neither unhappy in her death, nor altogether dead. Of this, we were assured on good grounds, the testimony of her good conversation and her *faith unfeigned*.[39]

30. What then was it which did grievously pain me within, but a fresh wound wrought through the sudden wrench of that most sweet and dear custom of living together? I joyed indeed in her testimony, when, in that her last sickness, mingling her endearments with my acts of duty, she called me "dutiful," and mentioned, with great affection of love, that she never had heard any harsh or reproachful sound uttered by my mouth against her. But yet, O my God, Who madest us, what comparison is there betwixt that honour that I paid to her, and her slavery for me? Being then forsaken of so great comfort in her, my soul was wounded, and that life rent asunder as it were, which, of hers and mine together, had been made but one.

31. The boy then being stilled from weeping, Euodius took up the Psalter, and began to sing, our whole house answering him, the Psalm, *I will sing of mercy and judgment to Thee, O Lord*.[40] But hearing what we were doing, many brethren and religious women came together; and whilst they (whose office it was) made ready for the burial, as the manner is, I (in a part of the house, where I might properly), together with those who thought not fit to leave me, discoursed upon something fitting the time; and

[39] *I Tim.* i, 5.   [40] *Ps.* c.

by this balm of truth, assuaged that torment, known to Thee, they unknowing and listening intently, and conceiving me to be without all sense of sorrow. But in Thy ears, where none of them heard, I blamed the weakness of my feelings, and refrained my flood of grief, which gave way a little unto me; but again came, as with a tide, yet not so as to burst out into tears, nor to a change of countenance; still I knew what I was keeping down in my heart. And being very much displeased, that these human things had such power over me, which in the due order and appoint of our natural condition, must needs come to pass, with a new grief I grieved for my grief, and was thus worn by a double sorrow.

32. And behold, the corpse was carried to the burial; we went and returned without tears. For neither in those prayers which we poured forth unto Thee, when the sacrifice of our ransom was offered for her, when now the corpse was by the grave's side, as the manner there is, previous to its being laid therein, did I weep even during those prayers; yet was I the whole day in secret heavily sad, and with troubled mind prayed Thee, as I could, to heal my sorrow, yet Thou didst not; impressing, I believe, upon my memory by this one instance, how strong is the bond of all habit, even upon a soul, which now feeds upon no deceiving Word. It seemed also good to me to go and bathe, having heard that the bath had its name (balneum) from the Greek βαλανεῖον, for that it drives sadness from the mind. And this also I confess unto Thy mercy, *Father of the fatherless,*[41] that I bathed, and was the same as before I bathed. For the bitterness of sorrow could not exude out of my heart. Then I slept, and woke up again, and found my grief not a little softened; and as I was alone in my bed, I remembered those true verses of Thy Ambrose. For Thou art the

> Maker of all, the Lord,
>   And Ruler of the height,
> Who, robing day in light, hast poured
>   Soft slumbers o'er the night,
> That to our limbs the power
>   Of toil may be renew'd,

[41] *Ps.* lxvii, 6.

And hearts be rais'd that sink and cower,
And sorrows be subdu'd.

33. And then by little and little I recovered my former thoughts
of Thy handmaid, her holy conversation towards Thee, her holy
tenderness and observance towards us, whereof I was suddenly
deprived: and I was minded to weep in Thy sight, for her and
for myself, in her behalf and in my own. And I gave way to the
tears which I before restrained, to overflow as much as they desired; reposing my heart upon them; and it found rest in them,
for it was in Thy ears, not in those of man, who would have
scornfully interpreted my weeping. And now, Lord, in writing
I confess it unto Thee. Read it, who will, and interpret it, how
he will: and if he finds sin therein, that I wept my mother for a
small portion of an hour, (the mother who for the time was dead
to mine eyes, who had for many years wept for me, that I might
live in Thine eyes,) let him not deride me; but rather, if he be
one of large charity, let him weep himself for my sins unto Thee,
the Father of all the brethren of Thy Christ.

[XIII] 34. But now, with a heart cured of that wound, wherein
it might seem blameworthy for an earthly feeling, I pour out unto
Thee, our God, in behalf of that Thy handmaid, a far different
kind of tears, flowing from a spirit shaken by the thoughts of the
dangers of every soul *that dieth in Adam.*[42] And although she,
having been quickened in Christ, even before her release from
the flesh, had lived to the praise of Thy name for her faith and
conversation; yet dare I not say that from what time Thou re-
generatedst her by baptism, no word issued from her mouth
against Thy Commandment. Thy Son, the Truth, hath said, *Whosoever shall say unto his brother, Thou fool, shall be in danger of
hell fire.*[43] And woe be even unto the commendable life of men,
if, laying aside mercy, Thou shouldest examine it. But because
Thou art not extreme in inquiring after sins, we confidently hope
to find some place with Thee. But whosoever reckons up his real
merits to Thee, what reckons he up to Thee, but Thine own gifts?
O that men would know themselves to be men; *and that he that
glorieth, would glory in the Lord.*[44]

[42] *I Cor.* xv, 22.   [43] *Matt.* v, 22.   [44] *II Cor.* x, 17.

35. I therefore, O my Praise and my Life, God of my heart, laying aside for a while her good deeds, for which I give thanks to Thee with joy, do now beseech Thee for the sins of my mother. Hearken unto me, I entreat Thee, by the Medicine of our wounds, Who hung upon the tree, and now *sitting at Thy right hand maketh intercession to Thee for us.*[45] I know that she dealt mercifully, and from her heart *forgave her debtors their debts; do Thou also forgive her debts,*[46] whatever she may have contracted in so many years, since the water of salvation. Forgive her, Lord, forgive, I beseech Thee; *enter not into judgment with her. Let Thy mercy be exalted above Thy justice,* since Thy words are true, and *Thou hast promised mercy unto the merciful;* which Thou gavest them to be, *who wilt have mercy on whom Thou wilt have mercy; and wilt have compassion, on whom Thou hast had compassion.*[47]

36. And, I believe, Thou hast already done what I ask; but *accept, O Lord, the free-will offerings of my mouth.*[48] For she, the day of her dissolution now at hand, took no thought to have her body sumptuously wound up, or embalmed with spices; nor desired she a choice monument, or to be buried in her own land. These things she enjoined us not; but desired only to have her name commemorated at Thy Altar, which she had served without intermission of one day: whence she knew that holy sacrifice to be dispensed, by which the *hand-writing that was against us, is blotted out;*[49] through which the enemy was triumphed over, who summing up our offenses, and seeking what to lay to our charge, *found nothing in Him,*[50] in Whom we conquer. Who shall restore to Him the innocent blood? Who repay Him the price wherewith He bought us, and so take us from Him? Unto the Sacrament of which our ransom, Thy handmaid bound her soul by the bond of faith. Let none sever her from Thy protection: let neither *the lion nor the dragon*[51] interpose himself by force or fraud. For she will not answer that she owes nothing, lest she be convicted and seized by the crafty accuser: but she will answer, that *her sins are forgiven*[52] her by Him, to Whom none can repay that price, which He, Who owed nothing, paid for us.

[45] *Rom.* viii, 34.   [46] *Matt.* xviii, 35; vi, 12.
[47] *Ps.* cxlii, 2; *Jas.* ii, 13; *Matt.* v, 7; *Rom.* ix, 15.   [48] *Ps.* cxviii, 108
[49] *Coloss.* ii, 14.   [50] *Jo.* xiv, 30.   [51] *Ps.* xc, 13.   [52] *Matt.* ix, 2.

37. May she rest then in peace with the husband, before and after whom she had never any; whom she obeyed, *with patience bringing forth fruit* [53] unto Thee, that she might win him also unto Thee. And inspire, O Lord my God, inspire Thy servants my brethren, Thy sons my masters, whom with voice, and heart, and pen I serve, that so many as shall read these confessions, may at Thy Altar remember Monica Thy handmaid, with Patricius, her sometimes husband, by whose bodies Thou broughtest me into this life, how, I know not. May they with devout affection remember my parents in this transitory light, my brethren under Thee our Father in our Catholic Mother, and my fellow citizens in that eternal Jerusalem, which Thy pilgrim people sigheth after from their Exodus, even unto their return thither. That so, my mother's last request of me, may through my confessions, more than through my prayers, be, through the prayers of many, more abundantly fulfilled to her.

✛

BOOK TEN

Having in the former books spoken of himself before his receiving the grace of Baptism, in this Augustine confesses what he then was. But first, he enquires by what faculty we can know God at all, whence he enlarges on the mysterious character of the memory, wherein God, being made known, dwells, but which could not discover Him. Then he examines his own trials under the triple division of temptation, "lust of the flesh, lust of the eyes, and pride;" what Christian continence prescribes as to each. On Christ the Only Mediator, who heals and will heal all infirmities.

[I] 1. Let me know Thee, O Lord, who knowest me: *let me know Thee, as I am known.* [1] Power of my soul, enter into it, and fit it for Thee, that Thou mayest have and hold it *without spot or wrinkle.* [2] This is my hope, *therefore do I speak;* [3] and in this hope do I rejoice, when I rejoice healthfully. Other things of this life

---

[53] *Luke* viii, 15.　　[1] *I Cor.* xiii, 12.　　[2] *Ephes.* v, 27.　　[3] *Ps.* cxv, 10.

are the less to be sorrowed for, the more they are sorrowed for;
and the more to be sorrowed for, the less men sorrow for them.
For behold, Thou *lovest the truth,* and *he that doth it, cometh to
the light.*[4] This would I do in my heart before Thee in confession:
and in my writing, before many witnesses.

[II] 2. And from Thee, O Lord, *unto whose eyes*[5] the abyss of
man's conscience is naked, what could be hidden in me though I
would not confess it? For I should hide Thee from me, not me
from Thee. But now, for that my groaning is witness, that I am
displeased with myself, Thou shinest out, and art pleasing, and
beloved, and longed for; that I may be ashamed of myself, and
renounce myself, and choose Thee, and neither please Thee, nor
myself, but in Thee. To Thee therefore, O Lord, am I open, whatever I am; and with what fruit I confess unto Thee, I have said.
Nor do I it with words and sounds of the flesh, but with the words
of my soul, and the cry of the thought which Thy ear knoweth.
For when I am evil, then to confess to Thee, is nothing else than
to be displeased with myself; but when holy, nothing else than not
to ascribe it to myself: because Thou, O Lord, *blessest the godly,*
but first Thou *justifieth him when ungodly.*[6] My confession then,
O my God, in Thy sight, is made silently, and not silently. For in
sound, it is silent; in affection, it cries aloud. For neither do I utter
any thing right unto men, which Thou hast not before heard from
me; nor dost Thou hear any such thing from me, which Thou hast
not first said unto me.

[III] 3. What then have I to do with men, that they should hear
my confessions; as if they could *heal all my infirmities?*[7] A race,
curious to know the lives of others, slothful to amend their own.
Why seek they to hear from me what I am; who will not hear
from Thee what themselves are? And how know they, when from
myself they hear of myself, whether I say true; seeing *no man
knows what is in man, but the spirit of man which is in him?*[8]
But if they hear from Thee of themselves, they cannot say, "The
Lord lieth." For what is it to hear from Thee of themselves, but
to know themselves? and who knoweth and saith, "It is false,"
unless himself lieth? But because *charity believeth all things,*[9]

[4] *Ps.* i, 8; *Jo.* iii, 21.   [5] *Heb.* iv, 13.   [6] *Ps.* v, 13; *Rom.* iv, 5.
[7] *Ps.* cii, 3.   [8] *I Cor.* ii, 11.   [9] *I Cor.* xiii, 7.

(that is, among those whom knitting unto itself it maketh one,) I also, O Lord, will in such wise confess unto Thee, that men may hear, to whom I cannot demonstrate whether I confess truly; yet they believe me, whose ears charity openeth unto me.

4. But do Thou, my inmost Physician, make plain unto me, what fruit I may reap by doing it. For the confessions of my past sins, which Thou hast *forgiven and covered,*[10] that Thou mightest bless me in Thee, changing my soul by Faith and Thy Sacrament, when read and heard, stir up the heart, that it sleep not in despair and say, "I cannot," but awake in the love of Thy mercy and the sweetness of Thy grace, whereby, whoso *is weak, is strong,* when by it he became conscious of his own weakness. And the good delight to hear of the past evils of such as are now freed from them, not because they are evils, but because they have been and are not. With what fruit then, O Lord my God, to Whom my conscience daily confesseth, trusting more in the hope of Thy mercy than in their own innocency, with what fruit, I pray, do I by this book, confess to men also in Thy presence, what I now am, not what I have been? For that other fruit I have seen and spoken of. But what I now am, at the very time of making these confessions, divers desire to know, who have or have not known me, who have heard from me or of me; but their ear is not at my heart, where I am, whatever I am. They wish then to hear me confess what I am within; whither neither their eye, nor ear, nor understanding, can reach; they wish it, as ready to believe—but will they know? For charity, whereby they are good, telleth them, that in my confessions I lie not; and she in them, believeth me.

[IV] 5. But for what fruit would they hear this? do they desire to joy with me, when they hear how near, by Thy gift, I approach unto Thee? and to pray for me, when they shall hear how much I am held back by my own weight? To such will I discover myself. For it is no mean fruit, O Lord my God, *that by many thanks should be given* to Thee *on our behalf,*[11] and Thou be by many intreated for us. Let the brotherly mind love in me, what Thou teachest is to be loved, and lament in me, what Thou teachest is to be lamented. Let a brotherly, not a stranger, mind, not that of the *strange children, whose mouth talketh of vanity, and their*

[10] *Ps.* xxxi, 1.   [11] *II Cor.* i, 11

right hand is a right hand of iniquity,[12] but that brotherly mind which when it approveth, rejoiceth for me, and when it disapproveth me, is sorry for me; because whether it approveth or disapproveth, it loveth me. To such will I discover myself: they will breathe freely at my good deeds, sigh for my ill. My good deeds are Thine appointments, and Thy gifts; my evil ones, are my offenses, and Thy judgments. Let them breathe freely at the one, sigh at the other; and let hymns and weeping go up into Thy sight, out of the hearts of my brethren, Thy *censers.*[13] And do Thou, O Lord, be pleased with the incense of Thy holy temple, *have mercy upon me according to Thy great mercy for Thine own name's sake;* [14] and no ways forsaking what Thou hast begun, perfect my imperfections.

6. This is the fruit of my confessions of what I am, not of what I have been, to confess this, not before Thee only, in a secret *exultation with trembling,*[15] and a secret sorrow with hope; but in the ears also of the believing sons of men, sharers of my joy, and partners in my mortality, my fellow citizens, and fellow pilgrims, who are gone before, or are to follow on, companions of my way. These are Thy servants, my brethren, whom Thou willest to be Thy sons; my masters whom Thou commandest me to serve, if I would live with Thee, of Thee. But this Thy Word, were little did it only command by speaking, and not go before in performing. This then I do in deed and word, this I do *under Thy wings;* in over great peril, were not my soul subdued unto Thee under Thy wings, and my infirmity known unto Thee. I am a little one, but my Father ever liveth, and my Guardian is *sufficient for me.*[16] For He is the same who begat me, and defends me: and Thou Thyself art all my good; Thou, Almighty, Who are with me, yea, before I am with Thee. To such then whom Thou commandest me to serve will I discover, not what I have been, but what I now am, and what I yet am. *But neither do I judge myself.*[17] Thus therefore I would be heard.

[v] 7. For *Thou, Lord, dost judge me:* because, although *no man knoweth the things of a man, but the spirit of a man which is in him,* yet is there something of man, which neither *the spirit of*

---

[12] *Ps.* cxliii. 11. [13] *Apoc.* viii, 3. [14] *Ps.* 1, 3. [15] *Ps.* ii, 11.
[16] *II Cor.* xii, 9. [17] *I Cor.* iv, 3.

man that is in him, itself *knoweth.*[18] But Thou, Lord, knowest all of him, Who hast made him. Yet I, though in Thy sight I despise myself, and account myself *dust and ashes;* yet know I something of Thee, which I know not of myself. And truly, *now we see through a glass darkly,* not *face to face* as yet.[19] So long therefore as *I be absent from Thee,*[20] I am more present with myself than with Thee; and yet know I Thee that Thou art in no ways passible; but I, what temptations I can resist, what I cannot, I know not. And there is hope, because *Thou art faithful, Who wilt not suffer us to be tempted above that we are able; but wilt with the temptation also make a way to escape, that we may be able to bear it.*[21] I will confess then what I know of myself, I will confess also what I know not of myself. And that because what I do know of myself, I know by Thy shining upon me; and what I know not of myself, so long know I not it, until *my darkness be made as the noon-day in Thy countenance.*[22]

[VI] 8. Not with doubting, but with assured consciousness, do I love Thee, Lord. Thou hast stricken my heart with Thy word, and I loved Thee. Yea also *heaven, and earth, and all that therein is,* behold, on every side they bid me love Thee; nor cease to say so unto all, *that they may be without excuse.*[23] But more deeply *wilt Thou have mercy on whom Thou wilt have mercy, and wilt have compassion on whom Thou hast had compassion:*[24] else in deaf ears do the heaven and the earth speak Thy praises. But what do I love, when I love Thee? not beauty of bodies, nor the fair harmony of time, nor the brightness of the light, so gladsome to our eyes, nor sweet melodies of varied songs, nor the fragrant smell of flowers, and ointments, and spices, not manna and honey, not limbs acceptable to embracements of flesh. None of these I love, when I love my God; and yet I love a kind of light, and melody, and fragrance, and meat, and embracement, when I love my God, the light, melody, fragrance, meat, embracement of my inner man: where there shineth unto my soul, what space cannot contain, and there soundeth, what time beareth not away, and there smelleth, what breathing disperseth not, and there tasteth, what eating di-

---

[18] *I Cor.* iv, 4; ii, 11.   [19] *I Cor.* xiii, 12.   [20] *II Cor.* v, 6.
[21] *I Cor.* x, 13.   [22] *Isa.* lviii. 10.   [23] *Rom.* i, 20.   [24] *Rom.* ix, 15.

minisheth not, and there clingeth, what satiety divorceth not. This is it which I love, when I love my God.

9. And what is this? I asked the earth, and it answered me, "I am not He;" and whatsoever are in it, confessed the same. I asked the sea and the deeps, and the living creeping things, and they answered, "We are not thy God, seek above us." I asked the moving air; and the whole air with his inhabitants answered, "Anaximenes was deceived, I am not God." I asked the heavens, sun, moon, stars, "Nor (say they) are we the God whom thou seekest." And I replied unto all the things which encompass the door of my flesh; "Ye have told me of my God, that ye are not He; tell me something of Him." And they cried out with a loud voice, "He made us." My questioning them, was my thoughts on them: and their form of beauty gave the answer. And I turned myself unto myself, and said to myself, "Who art thou?" And I answered, "A man." And behold, in me there present themselves to me soul, and body, one without, the other within. By which of these ought I to seek my God? I had sought Him in the body from earth to heaven, so far as I could send messengers, the beams of mine eyes. But the better is the inner, for to it as presiding and judging, all the bodily messengers reported the answers of heaven and earth, and all things therein, who said, "We are not God, but He made us." These things did my inner man know by the ministry of the outer: I the inner, knew them; I, the mind, through the senses of my body. I asked the whole frame of the world about my God; and it answered me, "I am not He, but He made me."

10. Is not this corporeal figure apparent to all whose senses are perfect? why then speaks it not the same to all? Animals small and great see it, but they cannot ask it: because no reason is set over their senses to judge on what they report. But men can ask, so that *the invisible things of God are clearly seen, being understood by the things that are made;* [25] but by love of them, they are made subject unto them: and subjects cannot judge. Nor yet do the creatures answer such as ask, unless they can judge: nor yet do they change their voice, (i.e. their appearance,) if one man only sees, another seeing asks, so as to appear one way to this man, another way to that; but appearing the same way to both, it is dumb to

[25] *Rom.* i. 20.

this, speaks to that; yea rather it speaks to all; but they only understand, who compare its voice received from without, with the truth within. For truth saieth unto me, "Neither heaven, nor earth, nor any other body is thy God." This, their very nature saith to him that seeth them; "They are a mass; a mass is less in a part thereof, than in the whole." Now to thee I speak, O my soul, thou art my better part: for thou quickenest the mass of my body, giving it life, which no body can give to a body: but thy God is even unto thee the Life of thy life.

[VII] 11. What then do I love, when I love my God? who is He above the head of my soul? By my very soul will I ascend to Him. I will pass beyond that power whereby I am united to my body, and fill its whole frame with life. Nor can I by that power find my God; for so *horse and mule that have no understanding,*[26] might find Him; seeing it is the same power, whereby even their bodies live. But another power there is, not that only whereby I animate, but that too whereby I imbue with sense my flesh, which the Lord hath framed for me: commanding the eye not to hear, and the ear not to see; but the eye, that through it I should see, and the ear, that through it I should hear; and to the other senses severally, what is to each their own peculiar seats and offices; which, being divers, I the one mind, do through them enact. I will pass beyond this power of mine also; for this also have the horse and mule, for they also perceive through the body.

[VIII] 12. I will pass then beyond this power of my nature also, rising by degrees unto Him, who made me. And I come to the fields and spacious palaces of my memory, where are the treasures of innumerable images, brought into it from things of all sorts perceived by the senses. There is stored up, whatsoever besides we think, either by enlarging or diminishing, or any other way varying those things which the sense hath come to; and whatever else hath been committed and laid up, which forgetfulness hath not yet swallowed up and buried. When I enter there, I require what I will, to be brought forth, and something instantly comes; others must be longer sought after, which are fetched, as it were, out of some inner receptacle; others rush out in troops, and while one thing is desired and required, they start forth, as who should say,

[26] *Ps.* xxxi. 9.

"Is it perchance I?" These I drive away with the hand of my heart, from the face of my remembrance; until what I wished for be unveiled, and appear in sight, out of its secret place. Other things come up readily, in unbroken order, as they are called for; those in front making way for the following; and as they make way, they are hidden from sight, ready to come when I will. All which takes place, when I repeat a thing by heart.

13. There are all things preserved distinctly and under general heads, each having entered by its own avenue: as light, and all colours and forms of bodies, by the eyes; by the ears all sorts of sounds; all smells by the avenue of the nostrils; all tastes by the mouth; and by the sensation of the whole body, what is hard or soft; hot or cold; smooth or rugged; heavy or light; either outwardly or inwardly to the body. All these doth that great harbour of the memory receive in her numberless secret and inexpressible windings, to be forthcoming, and brought out at need; each entering in by his own gate, and there laid up. Nor yet do the things themselves enter in; only the images of the things perceived, are there in readiness, for thought to recall. Which images, how they are formed, who can tell, though it doth plainly appear by which sense each hath been brought in and stored up? For even while I dwell in darkness and silence, in my memory I can produce colours, if I will, and discern betwixt black and white, and what others I will: nor yet do sounds break in, and disturb the image drawn in by my eyes, which I am reviewing, though they also are there, lying dormant, and laid up, as it were, apart. For these too I call for, and forthwith they appear. And though my tongue be still, and my throat mute, so can I sing as much as I will; nor do those images of colours, which notwithstanding be there, intrude themselves and interrupt, when another store is called for, which flowed in by the ears. So the other things, piled in and up by the other senses, I recall at my pleasure. Yea, I discern the breath of lilies from violets, though smelling nothing; and I prefer honey to sweet wine, smooth before rugged, at the time neither tasting, nor handling, but remembering only.

14. These things do I within, in that vast court of my memory. For there are present with me, heaven, earth, sea, and whatever I could think on therein, besides what I have forgotten. There also

meet I with myself, and recall myself, and when, where, and what I have done, and under what feelings. There be all which I remember, either on my own experience, or others' credit. Out of the same store do I myself with the past continually combine fresh and fresh likenesses of things, which I have experienced, or, from what I have experienced, have believed: and thence again infer future actions, events and hopes, and all these again I reflect on, as present. "I will do this or that," say I to myself, in that great receptacle of my mind, stored with the images of things so many and so great, "and this or that will follow." "O that this or that might be!" "God avert this or that!" So speak I to myself: and when I speak, the images of all I speak of are present, out of the same treasury of memory; nor would I speak of any thereof, were the images wanting.

15. Great is this force of memory, excessive great, O my God; a large and boundless chamber! who ever sounded the bottom thereof? yet is this a power of mine, and belongs unto my nature; nor do I myself comprehend all that I am. Therefore is the mind too strait to contain itself. And where should that be, which it containeth not of itself? Is it without it, and not within? how then doth it not comprehend itself? A wonderful admiration surprises me, amazement seizes me upon this. And men go abroad to admire the heights of mountains, the mighty billows of the sea, the broad tides of rivers, the compass of the ocean, and the circuits of the stars, and pass themselves by; nor wonder, that when I spake of all these things, I did not see them with mine eyes, yet could not have spoken of them, unless I then actually saw the mountains, billows, rivers, stars, which I had seen, and that ocean which I believe to be, inwardly in my memory, and that, with the same vast spaces between, as if I saw them abroad. Yet did not I by seeing draw them into myself, when with mine eyes I beheld them; nor are they themselves with me, but their images only. And I know by what sense of the body, each was impressed upon me.

[IX] 16. Yet not these alone does the unmeasurable capacity of my memory retain. Here also is all, learnt of the liberal sciences and as yet unforgotten; removed as it were to some inner place, which is yet no place: nor are they the images thereof, but the things themselves. For, what is literature, what the art of disputing, how many kinds of questions there be, whatsoever of these I know, in such manner exists in my memory, as that I have not taken in the image, and left out the thing, or that it should have sounded and passed away like a voice fixed on the ear by that impress, whereby it might be recalled, as if it sounded, when it no longer sounded; or as a smell while it passes, and evaporates into air affects the sense of smell, whence it conveys into the memory an image of itself, which remembering, we renew, or as meat, which verily in the belly hath now no taste, and yet in the memory still in a manner tasteth; or as any thing which the body by touch perceiveth, and which when removed from us, the memory still conceives. For those things are not transmitted into the memory, but their images only are with an admirable swiftness caught up, and stored as it were in wondrous cabinets, and thence wonderfully by the act of remembering, brought forth.

[x] 17. But now when I hear that there be three kinds of questions, "Whether the thing be? what it is? of what kind it is?" I do indeed hold the images of the sounds, of which those words be composed, and that those sounds, with a noise passed through the air, and now are not. But the things themselves which are signified by those sounds, I never reached with any sense of my body, nor even discerned them otherwise than in my mind; yet in my memory have I laid up not their images, but themselves. Which how they entered into me, let them say if they can; for I have gone over all the avenues of my flesh, but cannot find by which they entered. For the eyes say, "if those images were coloured, we reported of them." The ears say, "if they sound, we gave knowledge of them." The nostrils say, "if they smell, they passed by us." The taste says, "unless they have a savour, ask me not." The touch says, "if it have not size, I handled it not; if I handled it not, I gave no notice of it." Whence and how entered these things into my memory? I know not how. For when I learned them, I gave not credit to another man's mind, but recognized them in mine; and approving them for true, I commended them to it, laying them up as it were, whence I might bring them forth when I willed. In my heart then they were, even before I learned them, but in my memory they were not. Where then? or wherefore, when they were spoken, did I acknowledge them, and said, "So is it, it is true,"

unless that they were already in the memory, but so thrown back and buried as it were in deeper recesses, that had not the sugges- tion of another drawn them forth, I had perchance been unable to conceive of them?

[XI] 18. Wherefore we find, that to learn these things whereof we imbibe not the images by our senses, but perceive within by themselves, without images, as they are, is nothing else, but by conception to receive, and by marking to take heed that those things which the memory did before contain at random and un- arranged, be laid up at hand as it were in that same memory, where before they lay unknown, scattered and neglected, and so readily occur to the mind familiarized to them. And how many things of this kind does my memory bear which have been already found out, and as I said, placed as it were at hand, which we are said to have learned and come to know; which were I for some short space of time to cease to call to mind, they are again so buried, and glide back, as it were, into the deeper recesses, that they must again, as if new, be thought out thence, for other abode they have none: but they must be drawn together again, that they may be known; that is to say, they must as it were be collected together from their dispersion: whence the word "cogitation" is derived. For *cogo* (collect) and *cogito* (re-collect) have the same relation to each other as *ago* and *agito, facio* and *factito*. But the mind hath appro- priated to itself this word (cogitation), so that, not what is "col- lected" any how, but what is "re-collected," i.e. brought together, in the mind, is properly said to be cogitated, or thought upon.

[XII] 19. The memory containeth also reasons and laws innu- merable of numbers and dimensions, none of which hath any bod- ily sense impressed; seeing they have neither colour, nor sound, nor taste, nor smell, nor touch. I have heard the sound of the words whereby when discussed they are denoted: but the sounds are other than the things. For the sounds are other in Greek than in Latin: but the things are neither Greek, nor Latin, nor any other language. I have seen the lines of architects, the very finest, like a spider's thread; but those are still different, they are not the images of those lines, which the eye of flesh shewed me: he knoweth them, whosoever without any conception whatsoever of a body, recognizes them within himself. I have perceived also the numbers of the things with which we number all the senses of my body; but those numbers wherewith we number, are different, nor are they the images of these, and therefore they indeed are. Let him who seeth them not, deride me for saying these things, and I will pity him, while he derides me.

[XIII] 20. All these things I remember, and how I learnt them I remember. Many things also most falsely objected against them have I heard, and remember; which though they be false, yet is it not false that I remember them; and I remember also that I have discerned betwixt those truths and these falsehoods objected to them. And I perceive, that the present discerning of these things is different from remembering that I oftentimes discerned them, when I often thought upon them. I both remember then to have often understood these things; and what I now discern and understand, I lay up in my memory, that hereafter I may remember that I understood it now. So then I remember also to have remembered; as, if hereafter I shall call to remembrance, that I have now been able to remember these things, by the force of memory shall I call it to remembrance.

[XIV] 21. The same memory contains also the affections of my mind, not in the same manner that my mind itself contains them, when it feels them; but far otherwise, according to a power of its own. For without rejoicing I remember myself to have joyed; and without sorrow do I recollect my past sorrow. And that I once feared, I review without fear; and without desire call to mind a past desire. Sometimes, on the contrary, with joy do I remember my fore-past sorrow, and with sorrow, joy. Which is not wonderful, as to the body; for mind is one thing, body another. If I therefore with joy remember some past pain of body, it is not so wonderful. But now seeing this very memory itself is mind, (for when we give a thing in charge, to be kept in memory, we say, "See that you keep it in mind;" and when we forget, we say, "It did not come to my mind," and, "It slipped out of my mind," calling the memory itself the mind;) this being so, how is it, that when with joy I remember my past sorrow, the mind hath joy, the memory hath sorrow; the mind upon the joyfulness which is in it, is joyful, yet the memory upon the sadness which is in it, is not sad? Does the memory perchance not belong to the mind? Who will say so?

The memory then is, as it were, the belly of the mind, and joy and sadness, like sweet and bitter food; which, when committed to the memory, are, as it were, passed into the belly, where they may be stowed, but cannot taste. Ridiculous it is to imagine these to be alike; and yet are they not utterly unlike.

22. But, behold, out of my memory I bring it, when I say there be four perturbations of the mind, desire, joy, fear, sorrow; and whatsoever I can dispute thereon, by dividing each into its subordinate species, and by defining it, in my memory find I what to say, and thence do I bring it: yet am I not disturbed by any of these perturbations, when by calling them to mind, I remember them; yea, and before I recalled and brought them back, they were there; and therefore could they, by recollection, thence be brought. Perchance, then, as meat is by chewing the cud brought up out of the belly, so by recollection these out of the memory. Why then does not the disputer, thus recollecting, taste in the mouth of his musing the sweetness of joy, or the bitterness of sorrow? Is the comparison unlike in this, because not in all respects like? For who would willingly speak thereof, if so oft as we name grief or fear, we should be compelled to be sad or fearful? And yet could we not speak of them, did we not find in our memory, not only the sounds of the names according to the images impressed by the senses of the body, but notions of the very things themselves which we never received by any avenue of the body, but which the mind itself perceiving by the experience of its own passions, committed to the memory, or the memory of itself retained, without being committed unto it.

[xv] 23. But whether by images or no, who can readily say? Thus, I name a stone, I name the sun, the things themselves not being present to my senses, but their images to my memory. I name a bodily pain, yet it is not present with me, when nothing aches: yet unless its image were present to my memory, I should not know what to say thereof, nor in discoursing discern pain from pleasure. I name bodily health; being sound in body, the thing itself is present with me; yet, unless its image also were present in my memory, I could by no means recall what the sound of this name should signify. Nor would the sick, when health were named, recognize what were spoken, unless the same image were by the force of

memory retained, although the thing itself were absent from the body. I name numbers whereby we number; and not their images, but themselves are present in my memory. I name the image of the sun, and that image is present in my memory. For I recall not the image of its image, but the image itself is present to me, calling it to mind. I name memory, and I recognize what I name. And where do I recognize it, but in the memory itself? Is it also present to itself by its image, and not by itself?

[XVI] 24. What, when I name forgetfulness, and withal recognize what I name? whence should I recognize it, did I not remember it? I speak not of the sound of the name, but of the thing which it signifies: which if I had forgotten, I could not recognize what that sound signifies. When then I remember memory, memory itself is, through itself, present with itself: but when I remember forgetfulness, there are present both memory and forgetfulness; memory whereby I remember, forgetfulness which I remember. But what is forgetfulness, but the privation of memory? How then is it present that I remember it, since when present I cannot remember? But if what we remember we hold it in memory, yet, unless we did remember forgetfulness, we could never at the hearing of the name, recognize the thing thereby signified, then forgetfulness is retained by memory. Present then it is, that we forget not, and being so, we forget. It is to be understood from this, that forgetfulness, when we remember it, is not present to the memory by itself, but by its image: because if it were present by itself, it would not cause us to remember, but to forget. Who now shall search out this? who shall comprehend how it is?

25. Lord, I, truly, toil therein, yea and toil in myself; I am become a heavy soil requiring over-much *sweat of the brow*. For we are not now searching out the regions of heaven, or measuring the distances of the stars, or enquiring the balancings of the earth. It is I myself who remember, I the mind. It is not so wonderful, if what I myself am not, be far from me. But what is nearer to me than myself? And lo, the force of mine own memory is not understood by me; though I cannot so much as name myself without it. For what shall I say, when it is clear to me that I remember forgetfulness? Shall I say that that is not in my memory, which I remember? or shall I say that forgetfulness is for this purpose in my

memory, that I might not forget? Both were most absurd. What third way is there? How can I say that the image of forgetfulness is retained by my memory, not forgetfulness itself, when I remember it? How could I say this either, seeing that when the image of any thing is impressed on the memory, the thing itself must needs be first present, whence that image may be impressed? For thus do I remember Carthage, thus all places where I have been, thus men's faces whom I have seen, and things reported by the other senses; thus the health or sickness of the body. For when these things were present, my memory received from them images, which, being present with me, I might look on and bring back in my mind, when I remembered them in their absence. If then this forgetfulness is retained in the memory through its image, not through itself, then plainly, itself was once present, that its image might be taken. But when it was present, how did it write its image in the memory, seeing that forgetfulness by its presence effaces even what it finds already noted? And yet, in whatever way, although that way be past conceiving and explaining, yet certain am I that I remember forgetfulness itself also, whereby what we remember is effaced.

[XVII] 26. Great is the power of memory, a fearful thing, O my God, a deep and boundless manifoldness; and this thing is the mind, and this am I myself. What am I then, O my God? What nature am I? A life various and manifold, and exceeding immense. Behold in the plains, and caves, and caverns of my memory, innumerable and innumerably full of innumerable kinds of things, either through images, as all bodies; or by actual presence, as the arts; or by certain notions or impressions, as the affections of the mind, which, even when the mind doth not feel, the memory retaineth, while yet whatsoever is in the memory, is also in the mind —over all these do I run, I fly; I dive on this side and on that, as far as I can, and there is no end. So great is the force of memory, so great the force of life, even in the mortal life of man. What shall I do then, O Thou my true life, my God? I will pass even beyond this power of mine which is called memory: yea, I will pass beyond it, that I may approach unto Thee, O sweet Light. What sayest Thou to me? See, I am mounting up through my mind towards Thee who abidest above me. Yea I now will pass beyond

this power of mine which is called memory, desirous to arrive at
Thee, whence Thou mayest be arrived at; and to cleave unto Thee,
whence one may cleave unto Thee. For even beasts and birds have
memory; else could they not return to their dens and nests, nor
many other things they are used unto: nor indeed could they be
used to any thing, but by memory. I will pass then beyond memory also, that I may arrive at Him who hath separated me from the
four-footed beasts and made me wiser than the fowls of the air,
I will pass beyond memory also, and where shall I find Thee, Thou
truly good and certain sweetness? And where shall I find Thee?
If I find Thee without my memory, then do I not retain Thee in
my memory. And how shall I find Thee, if I remember Thee not?
[xviii] 27. For the woman that had lost her groat,[27] and sought
it with a light; unless she had remembered it, she had never found
it. For when it was found, whence should she know whether it
were the same, unless she remembered it? I remember to have
sought and found many a thing; and this I thereby know, that
when I was seeking any of them, and was asked, "Is this it?" "Is
that it?" so long said I "No," until that were offered me which I
sought. Which had I not remembered (what ever it were) though
it were offered me, yet should I not find it, because I could not
recognize it. And so it ever is, when we seek and find any lost
thing. Notwithstanding, when any thing is by chance lost from the
sight, not from the memory, (as any visible body,) yet its image
is still retained within, and it is sought until it be restored to sight;
and when it is found, it is recognized by the image which is within:
nor do we say that we have found what was lost, unless we recognize it; nor can we recognize it, unless we remember it. But this
was lost to the eyes, but retained in the memory.
[xix] 28. But what when the memory itself loses any thing, as
falls out when we forget and seek that we may recollect? Where
in the end do we search, but in the memory itself? and there, if
one thing be perchance offered instead of another, we reject it,
until what we seek meets us; and when it doth, we say, "This is
it;" which we should not unless we recognized it, nor recognize
it unless we remembered it. Certainly then we had forgotten it.
Or, had not the whole escaped us, but by the part whereof we had

[27] *Luke* xv, 8.

hold, was the lost part sought for; in that the memory felt that it did not carry on together all which it was wont, and maimed, as it were, by the curtailment of its ancient habit, demanded the restoration of what it missed? For instance, if we see or think of some one known to us, and having forgotten his name, try to recover it; whatever else occurs, connects itself not therewith; because it was not wont to be thought upon together with him, and therefore is rejected, until that present itself, whereon the knowledge reposes equably as its wonted object. And whence does that present itself, but out of the memory itself? for even when we recognize it, on being reminded by another, it is thence it comes. For we do not believe it as something new, but, upon recollection, allow what was named to be right. But were it utterly blotted out of the mind, we should not remember it, even when reminded. For we have not as yet utterly forgotten that, which we remember ourselves to have forgotten. What then we have utterly forgotten, though lost, we cannot even seek after.

[XX] 29. How then do I seek Thee, O Lord? For when I seek Thee, my God, I seek a happy life. *I will seek Thee, that my soul may live.*[28] For my body liveth by my soul; and my soul by Thee. How then do I seek a happy life, seeing I have it not, until I can say, where I ought to say it, "It is enough"? How seek I it? By remembrance, as though I had forgotten it, remembering that I had forgotten it? Or, desiring to learn it as a thing unknown, either never having known, or so forgotten it, as not even to remember that I had forgotten it? Is not a happy life what all will, and no one altogether wills it not? Where have they known it, that they so will it? where seen it, that they so love it? Truly we have it, how, I know not. Yea, there is another way, wherein when one hath it, then is he happy; and there are, who are blessed, in hope. These have it in a lower kind, than they who have it in very deed; yet are they better off than such as are happy neither in deed, nor in hope. Yet even these, had they it not in some sort, would not so will to be happy, which that they do will, is most certain. They have known it then, I know not how, and so have it by some sort of knowledge, what, I know not, and am perplexed whether it be in the memory, which if it be, then we have been happy once:

28 *Amos* v, 4.

whether all severally, or in that man who first sinned, *in whom also we all died,*[29] and from whom we are all born with misery, I now enquire not; but only, whether the happy life be in the memory? For neither should we love it, did we not know it. We hear the name, and we all confess that we desire the thing; for we are not delighted with the mere sound. For when a Greek hears it in Latin, he is not delighted, not knowing what is spoken; but we Latins are delighted, as would he too, if he heard it in Greek; because the thing itself is neither Greek nor Latin, which Greeks and Latins, and men of all other tongues, long for so earnestly. Known therefore it is to all, for could they with one voice be asked, "would they be happy?" they would answer without doubt, "they would." And this could not be, unless the thing itself whereof it is the name, were retained in their memory.

[XXI] 30. But is it so, as one remembers Carthage who hath seen it? No. For a happy life is not seen with the eye, because it is not a body. As we remember numbers then? No. For these, he that hath in his knowledge, seeks not further to attain unto; but a happy life, we have in our knowledge, and therefore love it, and yet still desire to attain it, that we may be happy. As we remember eloquence then? No. For although upon hearing this name also, some call to mind the thing, who still are not yet eloquent, and many who desire to be so, whence it appears that it is in their knowledge; yet these have by their bodily senses observed others to be eloquent, and been delighted, and desire to be the like; (though indeed they would not be delighted but for some inward knowledge thereof, nor wish to be the like, unless they were thus delighted;) whereas a happy life, we do by no bodily sense experience in others. As then we remember joy? Perchance; for my joy I remember, even when sad, as a happy life, when unhappy; nor did I ever with bodily sense see, hear, smell, taste, or touch my joy; but I experienced it in my mind, when I rejoiced; and the knowledge of it clave to my memory, so that I can recall it with disgust sometimes, at others with longing, according to the nature of the things, wherein I remember myself to have joyed. For even from foul things have I been immersed in a sort of joy; which now recalling, I detest and execrate; otherwhiles in good and

---

[29] *I Cor.* xv. 22.

honest things, which I recall with longing, although perchance no longer present; and therefore with sadness I recall former joy.

31. Where then and when did I experience my happy life, that I should remember, and love, and long for it? Nor is it I alone, or some few besides, but we all would fain be happy; which, unless by some certain knowledge we knew, we should not with so certain a will desire. But how is this, that if two men be asked whether they would go to the wars, one, perchance, would answer that he would, the other, that he would not; but if they were asked, whether they would be happy, both would instantly without any doubting say they would; and for no other reason would the one go to the wars, and the other not, but to be happy. Is it perchance, that as one looks for his joy in this thing, another in that, all agree in their desire of being happy, as they would, (if they were asked,) that they wished to have joy, and this joy they call a happy life? Although then one obtains this joy by one means, another by another, all have one end, which they strive to attain, namely, joy. Which being a thing, which all must say they have experienced, it is therefore found in the memory, and recognized whenever the name of a happy life is mentioned.

[XXII] 32. Far be it, Lord, far be it from the heart of Thy servant who here confesseth unto Thee, far be it, that, be the joy what it may, I should therefore think myself happy. For there is a *joy* which is *not* given *to the ungodly*,[30] but to those who love Thee for Thine own sake, whose joy Thou Thyself art. And this is the happy life, to rejoice to Thee, of Thee, for Thee; this is it, and there is no other. For they who think there is another, pursue some other and not the true joy. Yet is not their will turned away from some semblance of joy.

[XXIII] 33. It is not certain then that all wish to be happy, inasmuch as they who wish not to joy in Thee, which is the only happy life, do not truly desire the happy life. Or do all men desire this, but *because the flesh lusteth against the Spirit, and the Spirit against the flesh, that they do not do what they would,*[31] they fall upon that which they can, and are content therewith; because, what they are not able to do, they do not will so strongly, as would suffice to make them able? For I ask any one, had he rather joy

---

[30] *Isa.* xlviii, 22.   [31] *Gal.* v, 17.

in truth, or in falsehood? They will as little hesitate to say, "in the truth," as to say, "that they desire to be happy;" for a happy life is joy in the truth: for this is a joying in Thee, Who art *the Truth,* O God *my light, health of my countenance, my God.*[32] This is the happy life which all desire; this life which alone is happy, all desire; to joy in the truth all desire. I have met with many that would deceive; who would be deceived, no one. Where then did they know this happy life, save where they knew the truth also? For they love it also, since they would not be deceived. And when they love a happy life, which is no other than joying in the truth, then also do they love the truth; which yet they would not love, were there not some notice of it in their memory. Why then joy they not in it? why are they not happy? because they are more strongly taken up with other things which have more power to make them miserable, than that which they so faintly remember to make them happy. For there is yet a little light in men; let them walk, let them *walk, that the darkness overtake them not.*[33]

34. But why doth "truth generate hatred," [34] and the *man of thine,*[35] preaching the truth, become an enemy to them? whereas a happy life is loved, which is nothing else but joying in the truth; unless that truth is in that kind loved, that they who love any thing else, would gladly have that which they love to be the truth; and because they would not be deceived, would not be convinced that they are so? Therefore do they hate the truth, for that thing's sake, which they love instead of the truth. They love truth when she enlightens, they hate her when she reproves. For since they would not be deceived, and would deceive, they love her, when she discovers herself unto them, and hate her, when she discovers them. Whence she shall so repay them, that they who would not be made manifest by her, she both against their will makes manifest, and herself becometh not manifest unto them. Thus, thus, yea thus doth the mind of man, thus blind and sick, foul and ill-favoured, wish to be hidden, but that aught should be hidden from it, it wills not. But the contrary is requited it, that itself should not be hidden from the Truth; but the Truth is hid from it. Yet even thus miserable, it had rather joy in truths than in falsehoods. Happy

32 *Jo.* xiv, 6; *Ps.* xxvi, 1; xli, 2.   33 *Jo.* xii, 35.
34 Terence, *Andria,* I, 1, 41.   35 *Jo.* viii, 40.

then will it be, when, no distraction interposing, it shall joy in that only Truth, by Whom all things are true.

[XXIV] 35. See what a space I have gone over in my memory seeking Thee, O Lord; and I have not found Thee, without it. Nor have I found any thing concerning Thee, but what I have kept in memory, ever since I learnt Thee. For since I learnt Thee, I have not forgotten Thee. For where I found Truth, there found I my God, the Truth Itself; which since I learnt, I have not forgotten. Since then I learned Thee, Thou residest in my memory; and there do I find Thee, when I call Thee to remembrance, and delight in Thee. These be my holy delights, which Thou hast given me in Thy mercy, having regard to my poverty.

[XXV] 36. But where in my memory residest Thou, O Lord, where residest Thou there? what manner of lodging hast Thou framed for Thee? what manner of sanctuary hast Thou builded for Thee? Thou hast given this honour to my memory, to reside in it; but in what quarter of it Thou residest, that am I considering. For in thinking on Thee, I passed beyond such parts of it, as the beasts also have, for I found Thee not there among the images of corporeal things: and I came to those parts to which I committed the affections of my mind, nor found Thee there. And I entered into the very seat of my mind, (which it hath in my memory, inasmuch as the mind remembers itself also,) neither wert Thou there: for as Thou art not a corporeal image, nor the affection of a living being; (as when we rejoice, condole, desire, fear, remember, forget, or the like;) so neither art Thou the mind itself; because Thou art the Lord God of the mind; and all these are changed, but Thou remainest unchangeable over all, and yet hast vouchsafed to dwell in my memory, since I learnt Thee. And why seek I now, in what place thereof Thou dwellest, as if there were places therein? Sure I am, that in it Thou dwellest, since I have remembered Thee, ever since I learnt Thee, and there I find Thee, when I call Thee to remembrance.

[XXVI] 37. Where then did I find Thee, that I might learn Thee? For in my memory Thou wert not, before I learned Thee. Where then did I find Thee, that I might learn Thee, but in Thee above me? Place there is none; *we go backward and forward,*[36] and there

36 *Job* xxiii. 8.

is no place. Every where, O Truth, dost Thou give audience to all
who ask counsel of Thee, and at once answerest all, though on
manifold matters they ask Thy counsel. Clearly dost Thou answer,
though all do not clearly hear. All consult Thee on what they will,
though they hear not always what they will. He is Thy best servant,
who looks not so much to hear that from Thee, which himself
willeth; as rather to will that, which from Thee he heareth.

[XXVII] 38. Too late loved I Thee, O Thou Beauty of ancient
days, yet ever new! too late I loved Thee! And behold, Thou wert
within, and I abroad, and there I searched for Thee; deformed I,
plunging amid those fair forms, which Thou hadst made. Thou
wert with me, but I was not with Thee. Things held me far from
Thee, which, unless they were in Thee, were not at all. Thou
calledst, and shoutedst, and burstest my deafness. Thou flashedst,
shonest, and scatteredst my blindness. Thou breathedst odours,
and *I drew in breath* and *pant for Thee*. I tasted, and *hunger and
thirst*. Thou touchedst me, and I burned for Thy peace.

[XXVIII] 39. When I shall with my whole self cleave to Thee,
I shall no where have sorrow, or labour; and my life shall wholly
live, as wholly full of Thee. But now since whom Thou fillest,
Thou liftest up, because I am not full of Thee I am a burthen to
myself. Lamentable joys strive with joyous sorrows: and on which
side is the victory, I know not. Woe is me! Lord, have pity on me.
My evil sorrows strive with my good joys; and on which side is
the victory, I know not. Woe is me! Lord, have pity on me. Woe
is me! lo! I hide not my wounds; Thou art the Physician, I the
sick; Thou merciful, I miserable. *Is not the life of man upon earth
all trial?* [37] Who wishes for troubles and difficulties? Thou commandest them to be endured, not to be loved. No man loves what
he endures, though he love to endure. For though he rejoices
that he endures, he had rather there were nothing for him to endure. In adversity, I long for prosperity, in prosperity I fear adversity. What middle place is there betwixt these two, where *the
life of man is* not *all trial?* Woe to the prosperities of the world,
once and again, through fear of adversity, and corruption of joy!
Woe to the adversities of the world, once and again, and the third
time, from the longing for prosperity, and because adversity itself

[37] *Job.* vii, 1.

is a hard thing, and lest it shatter endurance. Is not the *life of man upon earth all trial,* without any interval?

[XXIX] 40. And all my hope is no where but in Thy exceeding great mercy. Give what Thou enjoinest, and enjoin what Thou wilt. Thou enjoinest us continence; and *when I knew,* saith one, *that no man can be continent, unless God give it, this also was a part of wisdom to know whose gift she is.*[38] By continence verily, are we bound up and brought back into One, whence we were dissipated into many. For too little doth he love Thee, who loves any thing with Thee, which he loveth not for Thee. O love, who ever burnest and never consumest! O charity, my God! kindle me. Thou enjoinest continence: give me what Thou enjoinest, and enjoin what Thou wilt.

[XXX] 41. Verily Thou enjoinest me continence from the *lust of the flesh, the lust of the eyes, and the ambition of the world.*[39] Thou enjoinest continence from concubinage; and, for wedlock itself, Thou has counselled something better than what Thou hast permitted. And since Thou gavest it, it was done, even before I became a dispenser of Thy Sacrament. But there yet live in my memory (whereof I have much spoken) the images of such things, as my ill custom there fixed; which haunt me, strengthless when I am awake: but in sleep, not only so as to give pleasure, but even to obtain assent, and what is very like reality. Yea, so far prevails the illusion of the image, in my soul and in my flesh, that, when asleep, false visions persuade to that which, when waking, the true cannot. Am I not then myself, O Lord my God? And yet there is so much difference betwixt myself and myself, within that moment wherein I pass from waking to sleeping, or return from sleeping to waking! Where is reason then, which, awake, resisteth such suggestions? And should the things themselves be urged on it, it remaineth unshaken. Is it clasped up with the eyes? is it lulled asleep with the senses of the body? And whence is it that often even in sleep we resist, and mindful of our purpose, and abiding most chastely in it, yield no assent to such enticements? And yet so much difference there is, that when it happeneth otherwise, upon waking we return to peace of conscience: and by

[38] *Wis.* viii, 21.   [39] *I John* ii, 16.

this very difference discover that we did not, what yet we be sorry that in some way it was done in us.

42. Art Thou not mighty, God Almighty, so as to *heal all the diseases of my soul,*[40] and by Thy more abundant grace to quench even the impure motions of my sleep? Thou wilt increase, Lord, Thy gifts more and more in me, that my soul may follow me to Thee, disentangled from the bird-lime of concupiscence; that it rebel not against itself, and even in dreams not only not, through images of sense, commit those debasing corruptions, even to pollution of the flesh, but not even to consent unto them. For that nothing of this sort should have, over the pure affections even of a sleeper, the very least influence, not even such as a thought would restrain,—to work this, not only during life, but even at my present age, is not hard for the Almighty, Who art *able to do above all that we ask or think.*[41] But what I yet am in this kind of my evil, have I confessed unto my good Lord; *rejoicing with trembling,* in that which Thou hast given me, and bemoaning that wherein I am still imperfect; hoping, that Thou wilt perfect Thy mercies in me, even to perfect peace, which my outward and inward man shall have with Thee, when *death shall be swallowed up in victory.*[42]

[XXXI] 43. There is another *evil of the day,* which I would were *sufficient for it.*[43] For by eating and drinking we repair the daily decays of our body, until Thou *destroy both belly and meat,*[44] when Thou shalt slay my emptiness with a wonderful fulness, and *clothe this incorruptible with* an eternal *incorruption.*[45] But now the necessity is sweet unto me, against which sweetness I fight, that I be not taken captive; and carry on a daily war by fastings; often *bringing my body into subjection,*[46] and my pains are removed by pleasure. For hunger and thirst are in a manner pains; they burn and kill like a fever, unless the medicine of nourishments come to our aid. Which since it is at hand through the consolations of Thy gifts, with which land, and water, and air serve our weakness, our calamity is termed gratification.

44. This hast Thou taught me, that I should set myself to take food as physic. But while I am passing from the discomfort of

[40] *Ps.* cii, 3.   [41] *Ephes.* iii, 20.   [42] *I Cor.* xv, 54.   [43] *Matt.* vi, 34.
[44] *I Cor.* vi, 13.   [45] *I Cor.* xv, 53.   [46] *I Cor.* ix, 27.

emptiness to the content of replenishing, in the very passage the snare of concupiscence besets me. For that passing is pleasure, nor is there any other way to pass thither, whither we needs must pass. And health being the cause of eating and drinking, there joineth itself as an attendant a dangerous pleasure, which mostly endeavours to go before it, so that I may for her sake do what I say I do, or wish to do, for health's sake. Nor have each the same measure; for what is enough for health is too little for pleasure. And oft it is uncertain, whether it be the necessary care of the body which is yet asking for sustenance, or whether a voluptuous deceivableness of greediness is proffering its services. In this uncertainty the unhappy soul rejoiceth, and therein prepares an excuse to shield itself, glad that it appeareth not what sufficeth for the moderation of health, that under the cloak of health, it may disguise the matter of gratification. These temptations I daily endeavour to resist, and I call on Thy right hand, and to Thee do I refer my perplexities; because I have as yet no settled counsel herein.

45. I hear the voice of my God commanding, *Let not your hearts be overcharged with surfeiting and drunkenness.*[47] Drunkenness is far from me; Thou wilt have mercy that it come not near me. But full-feeding sometimes creepeth upon Thy servant; Thou wilt have mercy, that it may be far from me. For *no one can be continent unless Thou give it.*[48] Many things Thou givest us, praying for them; and what good soever we have received before we prayed, from Thee we received it; yea to the end we might afterwards know this, did we before receive it. Drunkard was I never, but drunkards have I known made sober by Thee. From Thee then it was that they who never were such, should not so be, as from Thee it was that they who have been, should not ever so be; and from Thee it was that both might know from Whom it was. I heard another voice of Thine, *Go not after thy lusts, and from thy pleasure turn away.*[49] Yea by Thy favour have I heard that which I have much loved; *neither if we eat, shall we abound; neither if we eat not, shall we lack;*[50] which is to say, neither shall the one make me plenteous, nor the other miserable. I heard also another, *for I have learned in whatsoever state I am, there-*

[47] *Luke* xxi, 34.   [48] *Wis.* viii, 21.   [49] *Ecclus.* xviii, 30.   [50] *I Cor.* viii, 8.

with to be content; I know how to abound, and how to suffer
need. I can do all things through Christ that strengtheneth me.[51]
Behold a soldier of the heavenly camp, not the dust which we are.
But *remember*, Lord, *that we are dust*, and that of *dust thou hast*
made man; and he *was lost and is found.*[52] Nor could he of himself do this, because he whom I so loved, saying this through the
in-breathing of Thy inspiration, was of the same dust. *I can do*
all things (saith he) *through Him that strengtheneth me.*
Strengthen me, that *I can*. Give what Thou enjoinest, and enjoin
what Thou wilt. He confesses to have received, and when *he*
glorieth, in the Lord he glorieth.[53] Another have I heard begging
that he might receive, *Take from me* (saith he) *the desires of the*
belly; [54] whence it appeareth, O my holy God, that Thou givest,
when that is done which Thou commandest to be done.

46. Thou hast taught me, good Father, that *to the pure, all*
things are pure; but that *it is evil unto the man that eateth with*
offense; [55] and, that *every creature of Thine is good, and nothing*
to be refused, which is received with thanksgiving; [56] and that
meat commendeth us not to God; and, that *no man should judge*
us in meat or drink; [57] and, that *he which eateth, let him not*
despise him that eateth not; and let not him that eateth not, judge
him that eateth.[58] These things have I learned, thanks be to Thee,
praise to Thee, my God, my Master, knocking at my ears, enlightening my heart; deliver me out of all temptation. I fear not
uncleanness of meat, but the uncleanness of lusting. I know, that
Noah was permitted to eat all kind of flesh that was good for
food; [59] that Elijah was fed with flesh; [60] that John, endued with
an admirable abstinence, was not polluted by feeding on living
creatures, locusts.[61] I know also that Esau was deceived by lusting
for lentiles; [62] and that David blamed himself for desiring a
draught of water; [63] and that our King was tempted, not concerning flesh, but bread.[64] And therefore the people in the wilderness
also deserved to be reproved, not for desiring flesh, but because,
in the desire of food, they murmured against the Lord.[65]

[51] *Phil.* iv, 11-13.　　[52] *Ps.* cii, 14; *Gen.* iii, 19; *Luke* xv, 32.
[53] *I Cor.* i, 30-31.　　[54] *Ecclus.* xxiii, 6.　　[55] *Titus* i, 15; *Rom.* xiv, 20.
[56] *I Tim.* iv, 4.　　[57] *I Cor.* viii, 8; *Coloss.* ii, 16.　　[58] *Rom.* xiv, 3.
[59] *Gen.* ix, 3.　　[60] *III Kings* xvii, 6.　　[61] *Matt.* iii, 4.　　[62] *Gen.* xxv, 30-34.
[63] *II Kings* xxiii, 15-17.　　[64] *Matt.* iv, 3.　　[65] *Num.* xi.

47. Placed then amid these temptations, I strive daily against concupiscence in eating and drinking. For it is not of such nature, that I can settle on cutting it off once for all, and never touching it afterward, as I could of concubinage. The bridle of the throat then is to be held attempered between slackness and stiffness. And who is he, O Lord, who is not somewhit transported beyond the limits of necessity? whoever he is, he is a great one; let him make Thy Name great. But I am not such, for *I am a sinful man.*[66] Yet do I too magnify Thy name; and *He maketh intercession to Thee for my sins, who hath overcome the world;* [67] numbering me among the *weak members* of *His body;* [68] because *thine eyes have seen* that of Him which is *imperfect, and in Thy book shall all be written.*[69]

[XXXII] 48. With the allurements of smells, I am not much concerned. When absent, I do not miss them; when present, I do not refuse them; yet ever ready to be without them. So I seem to myself; perchance I am deceived. For that also is a mournful darkness, whereby my abilities within me are hidden from me; so that my mind making enquiry into herself of her own powers, ventures not readily to believe herself; because even what is in it, is mostly hidden, unless experience reveal it. And no one ought to be secure in that life, the whole whereof is called *a trial,*[70] that he who hath been capable, of worse to be made better, may not likewise of better be made worse. Our only hope, only confidence, only assured promise, is Thy mercy.

[XXXIII] 49. The delights of the ear had more firmly entangled and subdued me; but Thou didst loosen, and free me. Now, in those melodies which Thy words breathe soul into, when sung with a sweet and attuned voice, I do a little repose; yet not so as to be held thereby, but that I can disengage myself when I will. But with the words which are their life and whereby they find admission into me, themselves seek in my affections a place of some estimation, and I can scarcely assign them one suitable. For at one time I seem to myself to give them more honour than is seemly, feeling our minds to be more holily and fervently raised unto a flame of devotion, by the holy words themselves when thus sung,

[66] *Luke* v, 8.   [67] *Rom.* viii, 34; *Jo.* xvi, 33.   [68] *I Cor.* xii. 22.
[69] *Ps.* cxxxviii, 16.   [70] *Job* vii, 1.

than when not; and that the several affections of our spirit, by a sweet variety, have their own proper measures in the voice and singing, by some hidden correspondence wherewith they are stirred up. But this contentment of the flesh, to which the soul must not be given over to be enervated, doth oft beguile me, the sense not so waiting upon reason, as patiently to follow her; but having been admitted merely for her sake, it strives even to run before her, and lead her. Thus in these things I unawares sin, but afterwards am aware of it.

50. At other times, shunning over-anxiously this very deception, I err in too great strictness; and sometimes to that degree, as to wish the whole melody of sweet music which is used to David's Psalter, banished from my ears, and the Church's too; and that mode seems to me safer, which I remember to have been often told me of Athanasius Bishop of Alexandria, who made the reader of the psalm utter it with so slight inflection of voice, that it was nearer speaking than singing. Yet again, when I remember the tears I shed at the Psalmody of Thy Church, in the beginning of my recovered faith; and how at this time, I am moved, not with the singing, but with the things sung, when they are sung with a clear voice and modulation most suitable, I acknowledge the great use of this institution. Thus I fluctuate between peril of pleasure, and approved wholesomeness; inclined the rather (though not as pronouncing an irrevocable opinion) to approve of the usage of singing in the church; that so by the delight of the ears, the weaker minds may rise to the feeling of devotion. Yet when it befalls me to be more moved with the voice than the words sung, I confess to have sinned penally, and then had rather not hear music. See now my state; weep with me, and weep for me, ye, who so regulate your feelings within, as that good action ensues. For you who do not act, these things touch not you. But Thou, O Lord my God, hearken; behold, and see, and *have mercy, and heal me,* Thou, in whose presence I have become a problem to myself; and *that is my infirmity.*[71]

[XXXIV] 51. There remains the pleasure of these eyes of my flesh, on which to make my confessions in the hearing of the

---

[71] *Ps.* vi, 3; cii, 2-5.

ears of Thy temple, those brotherly and devout ears; and so to conclude the temptations of the *lust of the flesh,* which yet assail me,
*groaning earnestly, and desiring to be clothed upon with my house
from heaven.*[72] The eyes love fair and varied forms, and bright
and soft colours. Let not these occupy my soul; let God rather
occupy it, *who made these* things, *very good* [73] indeed, yet is He
my good, not they. And these affect me, waking, the whole day,
nor is any rest given me from them, as there is from musical, sometimes, in silence, from all voices. For this queen of colours, the
light, bathing all which we behold, wherever I am through the
day, gliding by me in varied forms, soothes me when engaged on
other things, and not observing it. And so strongly doth it en-
twine itself, that if it be suddenly withdrawn, it is with longing
sought for, and if absent long, saddeneth the mind.

52. O Thou Light, which Tobias saw, when, these eyes closed,
he taught his son the way of life; [74] and himself went before with
the feet of charity, never swerving. Or which Isaac saw, when his
fleshly *eyes being heavy* [75] and closed by old age, it was vouchsafed him, not, knowingly to bless his sons, but by blessing to
know them. Or which Jacob saw, when he also, blind through
great age, with illumined heart, in the persons of his sons shed
light on the different races of the future people, in them fore-
signified; and laid his hands,[76] mystically crossed, upon his grandchildren by Joseph, not as their father by his outward eye corrected
them, but as himself inwardly discerned. This is the light, it is
one, and all are one, who see and love it. But that corporeal light
whereof I spake, it seasoneth the life of this world for her blind
lovers, with an enticing and dangerous sweetness. But they who
know how to praise Thee for it, "O All-creating Lord," [77] take
it up in Thy hymns, and are not taken up with it in their sleep.
Such would I be. These seductions of the eyes I resist, lest my
feet wherewith I walk upon Thy way be ensnared; and I lift up
mine invisible eyes to Thee, that Thou wouldest *pluck my feet
out of the snare.*[78] Thou dost ever and anon pluck them out, for
they are ensnared. Thou ceasest not to pluck them out, while I

[72] *II Cor.* v, 2.   [73] *Gen.* i, 31.   [74] *Tobias,* iv.   [75] *Gen.* xxvii, 1.
[76] *Gen.* xlviii, 13 ff.   [77] Cf. *Confessions,* IX, 12.32 (above, p. 66).
[78] *Ps.* xxiv, 15.

often entangle myself in the snares on all sides laid; because *Thou that keepest Israel shalt neither slumber nor sleep.*[79]

53. What innumerable toys, made by divers arts and manufactures, in our apparel, shoes, utensils and all sort of works, in pictures also and divers images, and these far exceeding all necessary and moderate use and all pious meaning, have men added to tempt their own eyes withal; outwardly following what themselves make, inwardly forsaking Him by whom themselves were made, and destroying that which themselves have been made! But I, my God and my Glory, do hence also sing a hymn to Thee, and do consecrate praise to Him who consecrateth me, because those beautiful patterns which through men's souls are conveyed into their cunning hands, come from that Beauty, Which is above our souls, Which my soul day and night sigheth after. But the framers and followers of the outward beauties, derive thence the rule of judging of them, but not of using them. And He is there, though they perceive Him not, that so they might not wander, but *keep their strength for Thee,*[80] and not scatter it abroad upon pleasureable wearinesses. And I, though I speak and see this, entangle my steps with these outward beauties; but Thou pluckest me out, O Lord, Thou pluckest me out; *because Thy loving-kindness is before my eyes.*[81] For I am taken miserably, and Thou pluckest me out mercifully; sometimes not perceiving it, when I had but lightly lighted upon them; otherwhiles with pain, because I had stuck fast in them.

[xxxv] 54. To this is added, another form of temptation more manifoldly dangerous. For besides that concupiscence of the flesh which consisteth in the delight of all senses and pleasures, wherein its slaves, who *go far from Thee,* waste and *perish,*[82] the soul hath, through the same senses of the body, a certain vain and curious desire, veiled under the title of knowledge and learning, not of delighting in the flesh, but of making experiments through the flesh. The seat whereof being in the appetite of knowledge, and sight being the sense chiefly used for attaining knowledge, it is in Divine language called, *The lust of the eyes.*[83] For, to see, belongeth properly to the eyes; yet we use this word of the other

[79] *Ps.* cxx, 4.   [80] *Ps.* lviii, 10.   [81] *Ps.* xxv, 3.   [82] *Ps.* lxxii, 27.
[83] *I John* ii, 16.

senses also, when we employ them in seeking knowledge. For we do not say, hark how it flashes, or smell how it glows, or taste how it shines, or feel how it gleams; for all these are said to be seen. And yet we say not only, see how it shineth, which the eyes alone can perceive; but also, see how it soundeth, see how it smelleth, see how it tasteth, see how hard it is. And so the general experience of the senses, as was said, is called *The lust of the eyes,* because the office of seeing, wherein the eyes hold the prerogative, the other senses by way of similitude take to themselves, when they make search after any knowledge.

55. But by this may more evidently be discerned, wherein pleasure and wherein curiosity is the object of the senses; for pleasure seeketh objects beautiful, melodious, fragrant, savoury, soft; but curiosity, for trial's sake, the contrary as well, not for the sake of suffering annoyance, but out of the lust of making trial and knowing them. For what pleasure hath it, to see in a mangled carcase what will make you shudder? and yet if it be lying near, they flock thither, to be made sad, and to turn pale. Even in sleep they are afraid to see it. As if when awake, any one forced them to see it, or any report of its beauty drew them thither! Thus also in the other senses, which it were long to go through. From this disease of curiosity, are all those strange sights exhibited in the theatre. Hence men go on to search out the hidden powers of nature, (which is besides our end,) which to know profits not, and wherein men desire nothing but to know. Hence also, if with that same end of perverted knowledge magical arts be enquired by. Hence also in religion itself, is God tempted, when signs and wonders are demanded of Him, not desired for any good end, but merely to make trial of.

56. In this so vast wilderness, full of snares and dangers, behold many of them I have cut off, and thrust out of my heart, as Thou hast given me, O God of my salvation. And yet when dare I say, since so many things of this kind buzz on all sides about our daily life—when dare I say, that nothing of this sort engages my attention, or causes in me an idle interest? True, the theatres do not now carry me away, nor care I to know the courses of the stars, nor did my soul ever consult ghosts departed; all sacrilegious mysteries I detest. From Thee, O Lord my God, to whom I owe

humble and single-hearted service, by what artifices and suggestions
doth the enemy deal with me to desire some sign! But I beseech thee
by our King, and by our pure and holy country, Jerusalem, that as
any consenting thereto is far from me, so may it ever be further and
further. But when I pray Thee for the salvation of any, my end
and intention is far different. Thou givest and wilt give me to
follow Thee willingly, doing what Thou *wilt*.[84]

57. Notwithstanding, in how many most petty and contemptible
things is our curiosity daily tempted, and how often we give way,
who can recount? How often do we begin, as if we were tolerating
people telling vain stories, lest we offend the weak; then by degrees
we take interest therein! I go not now to the circus to see a dog
coursing a hare; but in the field, if passing, that coursing peradventure will distract me even from some weighty thought, and draw
me after it: not that I turn aside the body of my beast, yet still
incline my mind thither. And unless Thou, having made me see my
infirmity, didst speedily admonish me either through the sight
itself, by some contemplation to rise towards Thee, or altogether
to despise and pass it by, I dully stand fixed therein. What, when
sitting at home, a lizard catching flies, or a spider entangling them
rushing into her nets, oft-times takes my attention? Is the thing
different, because they are but small creatures? I go on from them
to praise Thee the wonderful Creator and Orderer of all, but this
does not first draw my attention. It is one thing to rise quickly, another not to fall. And of such things is my life full; and my one
hope is Thy wonderful great mercy. For when our heart becomes
the receptacle of such things, and is over-charged with throngs of
this abundant vanity, then are our prayers also thereby often interrupted and distracted, and whilst in Thy presence we direct the
voice of our heart to Thine ears, this so great concern is broken
off, by the rushing in of I know not what idle thoughts. Shall we
then account this also among things of slight concernment, or
shall aught bring us back to hope, save Thy complete mercy,
since Thou hast begun to change us?

[XXXVI] 58. And Thou knowest how far Thou hast already
changed me, who first healedst me of the lust of vindicating myself, that so Thou mightest *forgive all* the rest of my *iniquities*,

[84] *Jo.* xxi, 22.

and heal all my infirmities, and redeem my life from corruption, and crown me with mercy and pity, and satisfy my desire with good things: [85] who didst curb my pride with Thy fear, and tame my neck to Thy *yoke.*[86] And now I bear it and it is *light* unto me, because so hast Thou promised, and hast made it; and verily so it was, and I knew it not, when I feared to take it.

59. But, O Lord, Thou alone Lord without pride, because Thou art the only true Lord, who hast no lord; hath this third kind of temptation also ceased from me, or can it cease through this whole life? To wish, namely, to be feared and loved of men, for no other end, but that we may have a joy therein which is no joy? A miserable life this, and a foul boastfulness! Hence especially it comes, that men do neither purely love, nor fear Thee. And therefore *dost Thou resist the proud, and givest grace to the humble:* [87] yea, Thou thunderest down upon the ambitions of the world, and *the foundations of the mountains tremble.*[88] Because now certain offices of human society make it necessary to be loved and feared of men, the adversary of our true blessedness layeth hard at us, every where spreading his snares of "well-done, well-done;" that greedily catching at them, we may be taken unawares, and sever our joy from Thy truth, and set it in the deceivingness of men; and be pleased at being loved and feared, not for Thy sake, but in Thy stead: and thus having been made like him, he may have them for his own, not in the bonds of charity, but in the bonds of punishment: who purposed to *set his throne in the north,*[89] that dark and chilled they might serve him, pervertedly and crookedly imitating Thee. But we, O Lord, behold we are Thy *little flock;* [90] possess us as Thine, stretch Thy wings over us, and let us fly under them. Be Thou our glory; let us be loved for Thee, and Thy word feared in us. Who would be praised of men, when Thou blamest, will not be defended of men, when Thou judgest; nor delivered, when Thou condemnest. But when —not *the sinner is praised in the desires of his soul,* nor he *blessed who doth ungodlily,*[91] but—a man is praised for some gift which Thou hast given him, and he rejoices more at the praise for himself than that he hath the gift for which he is

[85] *Ps.* cii, 2-5.   [86] *Matt.* xi, 30.   [87] *Jas.* iv, 6.   [88] *Ps.* xvii, 8.
[89] *Isa.* xiv, 13-14.   [90] *Luke* xii, 32.   [91] *Ps.* ix, 24.

praised, he also is praised, while Thou dispraisest; and better is he who praised than he who is praised. For the one took pleasure in the gift of God in man; the other was better pleased with the gift of man, than of God.

[XXXVII] 60. By these temptations we are assailed daily, O Lord; without ceasing are we assailed. Our daily *furnace* [92] is the tongue of men. And in this way also Thou commandest us continence. Give what Thou enjoinest, and enjoin what Thou wilt. Thou knowest on this matter the groans of my heart, and the floods of mine eyes. For I cannot learn how far I am more cleansed from this plague, and I much fear my *secret sins,*[93] which Thine eyes know, mine do not. For in other kinds of temptations I have some sort of means of examining myself; in this, scarce any. For, in refraining my mind from the pleasures of the flesh, and idle curiosity, I see how much I have attained to, when I do without them; foregoing, or not having them. For then I ask myself how much more or less troublesome it is to me, not to have them? Then, riches, which are desired, that they may serve to some one or two or all of the three concupiscences,[94] if the soul cannot discern, whether, when it hath them, it despiseth them, they may be cast aside, that so it may prove itself. But to be without praise, and therein essay our powers, must we live ill, yea so abandonedly and atrociously, that no one should know without detesting us? What greater madness can be said, or thought of? But if praise useth and ought to accompany a good life and good works, we ought as little to forego its company, as good life itself. Yet I know not, whether I can well or ill be without any thing, unless it be absent.

61. What then do I confess unto Thee in this kind of temptation, O Lord? What, but that I am delighted with praise, but with truth itself, more than with praise? For were it proposed to me, whether I would, being phrenzied in error on all things, be praised by all men, or being consistent and most settled in the truth be blamed by all, I see which I should choose. Yet fain would I, that the approbation of another should not even increase my joy for any good in me. Yet I own, it doth increase it, and not so only, but dispraise doth diminish it. And when I am troubled at

[92] *Prov.* xxvii, 21.   [93] *Ps.* xviii, 13.   [94] *1 John* ii, 16.

this my misery, an excuse occurs to me, which of what value it is, Thou God knowest, for it leaves me uncertain. For since Thou hast commanded us not continency alone, that is, from what things to refrain our love, but righteousness also, that is, whereon to bestow it, and hast willed us to love not Thee only, but our neighbour also; often, when pleased with intelligent praise, I seem to myself to be pleased with the proficiency or towardliness of my neighbour, or to be grieved for evil in him, when I hear him dispraise either what he understands not, or is good. For sometimes I am grieved at my own praise, either when those things be praised in me, in which I mislike myself, or even lesser and slight goods are more esteemed, than they ought. But again how know I whether I am therefore thus affected, because I would not have him who praiseth me, differ from me about myself; not as being influenced by concern for him, but because those same good things which please me in myself, please me more when they please another also? For some how I am not praised when my judgment of myself is not praised; forasmuch as either those things are praised, which displease me; or those more, which please me less. Am I then doubtful of myself in this matter?

62. Behold, in Thee, O Truth, I see, that I ought not to be moved at my own praises; for my own sake, but for the good of my neighbour. And whether it be so with me, I know not. For herein I know less of myself, than of Thee. I beseech now, O my God, discover to me myself also, that I may confess unto my brethren, who are to pray for me, wherein I find myself maimed. Let me examine myself again more diligently. If in my praise I am moved with the good of my neighbour, why am I less moved if another be unjustly dispraised than if it be myself? Why am I more stung by reproach cast upon myself, than at that cast upon another, with the same injustice, before me? Know I not this also? or is it at last that I *deceive myself*,[95] and do not the truth before Thee in my heart and tongue? This madness put far from me, O Lord, lest mine own mouth be to me the *sinner's oil to make fat my head*.[96] *I am poor and needy;*[97] yet best, while in hidden groanings I displease myself, and seek Thy mercy, until

[95] *Gal.* vi, 3; *I John* i, 8.   [96] *Ps.* cxl, 5.   [97] *Ps.* cviii, 22.

what is lacking in my defective state be renewed and perfected, on to that peace which the eye of the proud knoweth not.

[XXXVIII] 63. Yet the word, which cometh out of the mouth, and deeds known to men, bring with them a most dangerous temptation through the love of praise: which, to establish a certain excellency of our own, solicits and collects men's suffrages. It tempts, even when it is reproved by myself in myself, on the very ground that it is reproved; and often glories more vainly of the very contempt of vain-glory; and so it is no longer contempt of vain-glory, whereof it glories; for it doth not contemn when it glorieth.

[XXXIX] 64. Within also, within is another evil, arising out of a like temptation; whereby men become vain, pleasing themselves in themselves, though they please not, or displease, or care not to please others. But pleasing themselves, they much displease Thee, not only taking pleasure in things not good, as if good, but in Thy good things, as though their own; or even if as thine, yet as though for their own merits; or even if as though from Thy grace, yet not with brotherly rejoicing, but envying that grace to others. In all these and the like perils and travails, Thou seest the trembling of my heart; and I rather feel my wounds to be cured by Thee, than not inflicted by me.

[XL] 65. Where hast Thou not walked with me, O Truth, teaching me what to beware, and what to desire; when I referred to Thee what I could discover here below, and consulted Thee? With my outward senses, as I might, I surveyed the world, and observed the life, which my body hath from me, and these my senses. Thence entered I the recesses of my memory, those manifold and spacious chambers, wonderfully furnished with innumerable stores; and I considered, and stood aghast; being able to discern nothing of these things without Thee, and finding none of them to be Thee. Nor was I myself, who found out these things, who went over them all, and laboured to distinguish and to value every thing according to its dignity, taking some things upon the report of my senses, questioning about others which I felt to be mingled with myself, numbering and distinguishing the reporters themselves, and in the large treasure-house of my memory, revolving some things, storing up others. drawing out others. Nor yet was

I myself when I did this, *i.e.*, that my power whereby I did it, neither was it Thou, for Thou art the abiding light, which I consulted concerning all these, whether they were, what they were, and how to be valued; and I heard Thee directing and commanding me; and this I often do, this delights me, and as far as I may be freed from necessary duties, unto this pleasure have I recourse. Nor in all these which I run over consulting Thee, can I find any safe place for my soul, but in Thee; whither my scattered members may be gathered, and nothing of me depart from Thee. And sometimes Thou admittest me to an affection, very unusual, in my inmost soul; rising to a strange sweetness, which if it were perfected in me, I know not what in it would not belong to the life to come. But through my miserable encumbrances I sink down again into these lower things, and am swept back by former custom, and am held, and greatly weep, but am greatly held. So much doth the burthen of a bad custom weigh us down. Here I can stay, but would not; there I would, but cannot; both ways, miserable.

[XLI] 66. Thus then have I considered the sicknesses of my sins in that threefold concupiscence, and have called Thy right hand to my help. For with a wounded heart have I beheld Thy brightness, and stricken back I said, "who can attain thither? *I am cast away from the sight of Thine eyes.*" [98] Thou art the Truth who presidest over all, but I through my covetousness, would not indeed forego Thee, but would with Thee possess a lie; as no man would in such wise speak falsely, as himself to be ignorant of the truth. So then I lost Thee, because Thou vouchsafest not to be possessed with a lie.

[XLII] 67. Whom could I find to reconcile me to Thee? was I to have recourse to Angels? by what prayers? by what sacraments? Many endeavouring to return unto Thee, and of themselves unable, have, as I hear, tried this, and fallen into the desire of curious visions, and been accounted worthy to be deluded. For they, being high minded, sought Thee by the pride of learning, swelling out rather, than smiting upon, their breasts, and so by the agreement of their heart, drew unto themselves the *princes of the air,* [99] the fellow-conspirators of their pride, by whom, through magical influences, they were deceived, seeking a mediator, by whom they

[98] *Ps.* xxx, 23.   [99] *Ephes.* ii, 2.

might be purged, and there was none. For the devil it was, *trans-forming himself into an Angel of light.*[100] And it much enticed proud flesh, that he had no body of flesh. For they were mortal, and sinners; but Thou, Lord, to whom they proudly sought to be reconciled, art immortal, and without sin. But a mediator between God and man, must have something like to God, something like to men; lest being in both like to man, he should be far from God: or if in both like God, too unlike man: and so not be a mediator. That deceitful mediator then, by whom in Thy secret judgments pride deserved to be deluded, hath one thing in common with man, that is sin; another, he would seem to have in common with God; and not being clothed with the mortality of flesh, would vaunt himself to be immortal. But since *the wages of sin is death,*[101] this hath he in common with men, that with them he should be condemned to death.

[XLIII] 68. But the true Mediator, Whom in Thy secret mercy Thou hast shewed to the humble, and sentest, that by His example also they might learn that same humility, that *Mediator between God and man, the Man Christ Jesus,*[102] appeared betwixt mortal sinners and the immortal Just One; mortal with men, just with God: that because the wages of righteousness is life and peace, He might by a righteousness conjoined with God make void that death of sinners, now made righteous, which He willed to have in common with them. Hence He was shewed forth to holy men of old; that so they, through faith in His Passion to come, as we through faith of it passed, might be saved. For as Man, He was a Mediator; but as the Word, not in the middle between God and man, because equal to God, and God with God, and together one God.

69. How hast Thou loved us, good Father, who *sparedst not Thine only Son, but deliveredst Him up for us ungodly!*[103] How hast Thou loved us, for whom, *He that thought it no robbery to be equal with Thee, was made subject even to the death of the cross,*[104] He alone *free among the dead, having power to lay down His life, and power to take it again:*[105] for us to Thee both Victor and Victim, and therefore Victor, because the Victim; for us to

---

100 *II Cor.* xi, 14.   101 *Rom.* vi, 23.   102 *I Tim.* ii, 5.
103 *Rom.* viii, 32.   104 *Phil.* ii, 6; 8.   105 *Ps.* lxxxvii, 6; *Jo.* x, 18.

Thee Priest and Sacrifice, and therefore Priest because the Sacrifice; making us to Thee, of servants, sons, by being born of Thee, and serving us. Well then is my hope strong in Him, that Thou *wilt heal all my infirmities,* by Him Who *sitteth at Thy right hand and maketh intercession for us;* [106] else should I despair. For many and great are my infirmities, many they are, and great; but Thy medicine is mightier. We might imagine that Thy Word was far from any union with man, and despair of ourselves, unless He had been *made flesh and dwelt among us.*[107]

70. Affrighted with my sins and the burthen of my misery, I had cast in my heart, and had purposed to *flee to the wilderness:* [108] But Thou forbaddest me, and strengthenedst me, saying, *Therefore Christ died for all, that they which live may now no longer live unto themselves, but unto Him that died for them.* [109] See, Lord, I *cast my care upon Thee,* that I may live, and *consider wondrous things out of Thy law.*[110] Thou knowest my unskilfulness, and my infirmities; teach me, and heal me. He Thine only Son, *in Whom are hid all the treasures of wisdom and knowledge,*[111] hath redeemed me with His blood. *Let not the proud speak evil of me;* [112] because I meditate on my ransom, and eat and drink, and communicate it; and *poor,* desired to be *satisfied* from Him, amongst those that *eat and are satisfied, and they shall praise the Lord who seek Him.*[113]

[106] *Ps.* cii, 3; *Rom.* viii, 34.   [107] *Jo.* i, 14.   [108] *Ps.* liv, 8.
[109] *II Cor.* v, 15.   [110] *Ps.* liv, 23; cxviii, 18.   [111] *Coloss.* ii, 3.
[112] *Ps.* cxviii, 122.   [113] *Ps.* xxi, 27.

ST. AUGUSTINE

THE CITY of GOD

Glorious things are said of thee, O City of God
(*Ps.* lxxxvi, 3)

BEGUN AS A DEFENSE of Christianity against the charge that it was responsible for the fall of the Roman Empire, the *City of God* (written in 413-426) is one of the great monuments of Western thought. It contains not only a long examination of the history and institutions of pagan Rome, but also the justly famous exposition of the two cities—Jerusalem, the City of God, ruled by Christ, and Babylon, the City of Worldliness (if I may so translate the phrase *secundum saeculum*), ruled by the devil. The division between the two cities is one of loves; it is not a political division. Book XIX deals with the ends of the two cities. To the confusion and this-worldliness of ancient philosophy Augustine opposes an optimistic Christian otherworldliness. The same beatitude which is the hoped-for destiny of Augustine in the *Confessions* will likewise be the final reward of the elect at the hands of Christ.

BOOK NINETEEN

ARGUMENT

In this book the end of the two cities, the earthly and the heavenly, is discussed. Augustine reviews the opinions of the philosophers regarding the supreme good, and their vain efforts to make for them-

selves a happiness in this life; and, while he refutes these, he takes occasion to show what the peace and happiness belonging to the heavenly city, or the people of Christ, are both now and hereafter.

CHAPTER I

That Varro has made out that two hundred and eighty-eight different sects of philosophy might be formed by the various opinions regarding the supreme good.

A S I SEE THAT I HAVE STILL TO DISCUSS THE FIT destinies of the two cities, the earthly and the heavenly, I must first explain, so far as the limits of this work allow me, the reasonings by which men have attempted to make for themselves a happiness in this unhappy life, in order that it may be evident, not only from divine authority, but also from such reasons as can be adduced to unbelievers, how the empty dreams of the philosophers differ from the hope which God gives to us, and from the substantial fulfillment of it which He will give us as our blessedness. Philosophers have expressed a great variety of diverse opinions regarding the ends of goods and of evils, and this question they have eagerly canvassed, that they might, if possible, discover what makes a man happy. For the end of our good is that for the sake of which other things are to be desired, while it is to be desired for its own sake; and the end of evil is that on account of which other things are to be shunned, while it is avoided on its own account. Thus, by the *end of good,* we at present mean, not that by which good is destroyed, so that it no longer exists, but that by which it is finished, so that it becomes complete; and by the *end of evil* we mean, not that which abolishes it, but that which completes its development. These two ends, therefore, are the supreme good and the supreme evil; and, as I have said, those who have in this vain life professed the study of wisdom have been at great pains to discover these ends, and to obtain the supreme good and avoid the supreme evil in this life. And although they erred in a variety of ways, yet natural insight has not deterred them from wandering from the truth so far that they have not placed the su-

preme good and evil, some in the soul, some in the body, and some
in both. From this tripartite distribution of the sects of philosophy,
Marcus Varro, in his book *De Philosophia,*[1] has drawn so large a
variety of opinions, that, by a subtle and minute analysis of distinctions, he numbers without difficulty as many as 288 sects—not
that these have actually existed, but sects which are possible.

   To illustrate briefly what he means, I must begin with his own
introductory statement in the above-mentioned book, that there are
four things which men desire, as it were by nature without a master,
without the help of any instruction, without industry or the art of
living, which is called virtue, and which is certainly learned:[2] either
pleasure, which is an agreeable stirring of the bodily sense; or repose, which excludes every bodily inconvenience; or both these,
which Epicurus calls by the one name, pleasure; or the primary objects of nature,[3] which comprehend the things already named and
other things, either bodily, such as health and safety and integrity
of the members, or spiritual, such as the greater and lesser mental
gifts that are found in men. Now these four things—pleasure, repose, the two combined, and the primary objects of nature—exist in
us in such sort that we must either desire virtue on their account, or
them for the sake of virtue, or both for their own sake; and consequently there arise from this distinction twelve sects, for each is
by this consideration tripled. I will illustrate this in one instance,
and, having done so, it will not be difficult to understand the others.
According, then, as bodily pleasure is subjected, preferred, or united
to virtue, there are three sects. It is subjected to virtue when it is
chosen as subservient to virtue. Thus it is a duty of virtue to live for
one's country, and for its sake to beget children, neither of which
can be done without bodily pleasure. For there is pleasure in eating
and drinking, pleasure also in sexual intercourse. But when it is preferred to virtue, it is desired for its own sake, and virtue is chosen
only for its sake, and to effect nothing else than the attainment or
preservation of bodily pleasure. And this, indeed, is to make life
hideous; for where virtue is the slave of pleasure it no longer deserves the name of virtue. Yet even this disgraceful distortion has
found some philosophers to patronize and defend it. Then virtue is

---

[1] Not extant.   [2] Alluding to the vexed question whether virtue could be taught.
[3] The *prima naturae,* or τὰ πρῶτα κατὰ φύσιν of the Stoics.

united to pleasure when neither is desired for the other's sake, but both for their own. And therefore, as pleasure, according as it is subjected, preferred, or united to virtue, makes three sects, so also do repose, pleasure and repose combined, and the prime natural blessings, make their three sects each. For as men's opinions vary, and these four things are sometimes subjected, sometimes preferred, and sometimes united to virtue, there are produced twelve sects. But this number again is doubled by the addition of one difference, viz., the social life; for whoever attaches himself to any of these sects does so either for his own sake alone, or for the sake of a companion, for whom he ought to wish what he desires for himself. And thus there will be twelve of those who think some one of these opinions should be held for their own sakes, and other twelve who decide that they ought to follow this or that philosophy not for their own sakes only, but also for the sake of others whose good they desire as their own. These twenty-four sects again are doubled, and become forty-eight by adding a difference taken from the New Academy. For each of these four and twenty sects can hold and defend their opinion as certain, as the Stoics defended the position that the supreme good of man consisted solely in virtue; or they can be held as probable, but not certain, as the New Academics did. There are, therefore, twenty-four who hold their philosophy as certainly true, other twenty-four who hold their opinions as probable, but not certain. Again, as each person who attaches himself to any of these sects may adopt the mode of life either of the Cynics or of the other philosophers, this distinction will double the number, and so make ninety-six sects. Then, lastly, as each of these sects may be adhered to either by men who love a life of ease, as those who have through choice or necessity addicted themselves to study, or by men who love a busy life, as those who, while philosophizing, have been much occupied with state affairs and public business, or by men who choose a mixed life, in imitation of those who have apportioned their time partly to erudite leisure, partly to necessary business: by these differences the number of the sects is tripled, and becomes 288.

I have thus, as briefly and lucidly as I could, given in my own words the opinions which Varro expresses in his book. But how he refutes all the rest of these sects, and chooses one, the Old

Academy, instituted by Plato, and continuing to Polemo, the fourth teacher of that school of philosophy which held that their system was certain; and how on this ground he distinguishes it from the New Academy,[4] which began with Polemo's successor Arcesilaus, and held that all things are uncertain; and how he seeks to establish that the Old Academy was as free from error as from doubt—all this, I say, were too long to enter upon in detail, and yet I must not altogether pass it by in silence. Varro then rejects, as a first step, all those differences which have multiplied the number of sects; and the ground on which he does so is that they are not differences about the supreme good. He maintains that in philosophy a sect is created only by its having an opinion of its own different from other schools on the point of the ends-in-chief. For man has no other reason for philosophizing than that he may be happy; but that which makes him happy is itself the supreme good. In other words, the supreme good is the reason of philosophizing; and therefore that cannot be called a sect of philosophy which pursues no way of its own towards the supreme good. Thus, when it is asked whether a wise man will adopt the social life, and desire and be interested in the supreme good of his friend as in his own, or will, on the contrary, do all that he does merely for his own sake, there is no question here about the supreme good, but only about the propriety of associating or not associating a friend in its participation: whether the wise man will do this not for his own sake, but for the sake of his friend in whose good he delights as in his own. So, too, when it is asked whether all things about which philosophy is concerned are to be considered uncertain, as by the New Academy, or certain, as the other philosophers maintain, the question here is not what end should be pursued, but whether or not we are to believe in the substantial existence of that end; or, to put it more plainly, whether he who pursues the supreme good must maintain that it is a true good, or only that it appears to him to be true, though possibly it may be delusive—both pursuing one and the same good. The distinction, too, which is founded on the dress and manners of the Cynics, does not touch the question of the chief good, but only the question whether he who pursues that good which seems to himself true should live as do the Cynics. There were, in fact, men who, though

4 Frequently called the Middle Academy; the New beginning with Carneades.

they pursued different things as the supreme good, some choosing pleasure, others virtue, yet adopted that mode of life which gave the Cynics their name. Thus, whatever it is which distinguishes the Cynics from other philosophers, this has no bearing on the choice and pursuit of that good which constitutes happiness. For if it had any such bearing, then the same habits of life would necessitate the pursuit of the same chief good, and diverse habits would necessitate the pursuit of different ends.

CHAPTER II

How Varro, by removing all the differences which do not form sects, but are merely secondary questions, reaches three definitions of the Chief Good, of which we must choose one.

THE SAME may be said of those three kinds of life, the life of studious leisure and search after truth, the life of easy engagement in affairs, and the life in which both these are mingled. When it is asked, which of these should be adopted, this involves no controversy about the end of good, but inquires which of these three puts a man in the best position for finding and retaining the supreme good. For this good, as soon as a man finds it, makes him happy; but lettered leisure, or public business, or the alternation of these, does not necessarily constitute happiness. Many, in fact, find it possible to adopt one or other of these modes of life, and yet to miss what makes a man happy. The question, therefore, regarding the supreme good and the supreme evil, and which distinguishes sects of philosophy, is one; and these questions concerning the social life, the doubt of the Academy, the dress and food of the Cynics, the three modes of life—the active, the contemplative, and the mixed —these are different questions, into none of which the question of the chief good enters. And therefore, as Marcus Varro multiplied the sects to the number of 288 (or whatever larger number he chose) by introducing these four differences derived from the social life, the New Academy, the Cynics, and the threefold form of life, so, by removing these differences as having no bearing on the supreme good, and as therefore not constituting what can properly be called sects, he returns to those twelve schools which concern them-

selves with inquiring what that good is which makes man happy,
and he shows that one of these is true, the rest false. In other words,
he dismisses the distinction founded on the threefold mode of life,
and so decreases the whole number by two-thirds, reducing the sects
to ninety-six. Then, putting aside the Cynic peculiarities, the number decreases by a half, to forty-eight. Taking away next the distinction occasioned by the hesitancy of the New Academy, the number
is again halved, and reduced to twenty-four. Treating in a similar
way the diversity introduced by the consideration of the social life,
there are left but twelve, which this difference had doubled to
twenty-four. Regarding these twelve, no reason can be assigned why
they should not be called sects. For in them the sole inquiry is regarding the supreme good and the ultimate evil—that is to say,
regarding the supreme good, for this being found, the opposite evil
is thereby found. Now, to make these twelve sects, he multiplies by
three these four things—pleasure, repose, pleasure and repose combined, and the primary objects of nature which Varro calls *primi-
genia*. For as these four things are sometimes subordinated to virtue,
so that they seem to be desired not for their own sake, but for virtue's sake; sometimes preferred to it, so that virtue seems to be
necessary not on its own account, but in order to attain these things;
sometimes joined with it, so that both they and virtue are desired
for their own sakes—we must multiply the four by three, and thus
we get twelve sects. But from those four things Varro eliminates
three—pleasure, repose, pleasure and repose combined—not because he thinks these are not worthy of the place assigned them, but
because they are included in the primary objects of nature. And
what need is there, at any rate, to make a threefold division out of
these two ends, pleasure and repose, taking them first severally and
then conjunctly, since both they, and many other things besides, are
comprehended in the primary objects of nature? Which of the three
remaining sects must be chosen? This is the question that Varro
dwells upon. For whether one of these three or some other be
chosen, reason forbids that more than one be true. This we shall
afterwards see; but meanwhile let us explain as briefly and distinctly
as we can how Varro makes his selection from these three, that is,
from the sects which severally hold that the primary objects of nature are to be desired for virtue's sake, that virtue is to be desired

for their sake, and that virtue and these objects are to be desired each for their own sake.

Which of the three leading opinions regarding the chief good should be preferred, according to Varro, who follows Antiochus and the Old Academy.

WHICH OF THESE three is true and to be adopted he attempts to show in the following manner. As it is the supreme good, not of a tree, or of a beast, or of a god, but of man, that philosophy is in quest of, he thinks that, first of all, we must define man. He is of opinion that there are two parts in human nature, body and soul, and makes no doubt that of these two the soul is the better and by far the more worthy part. But whether the soul alone is the man, so that the body holds the same relation to it as a horse to the horseman, this he thinks has to be ascertained. The horseman is not a horse and a man, but only a man, yet he is called a horseman, because he is in some relation to the horse. Again, is the body alone the man, having a relation to the soul such as the cup has to the drink? For it is not the cup and the drink it contains which are called the cup, but the cup alone; yet it is so called because it is made to hold the drink. Or, lastly, is it neither the soul alone nor the body alone, but both together, which are man, the body and the soul being each a part, but the whole man being both together, as we call two horses yoked together a pair, of which pair the near and the off horse is each a part, but we do not call either of them, no matter how connected with the other, a pair, but only both together? Of these three alternatives, then, Varro chooses the third, that man is neither the body alone, nor soul alone, but both together. And therefore the highest good, in which lies the happiness of man, is composed of goods of both kinds, both bodily and spiritual. And consequently he thinks that the primary objects of nature are to be sought for their own sake, and that virtue, which is the art of living, and can be communicated by instruction, is the most excellent of spiritual goods. This virtue, then, or art of regulating life, when it has received these primary objects of nature which existed independ-

ently of it, and prior to any instruction, seeks them all, and itself
also, for its own sake; and it uses them, as it also uses itself, that
from them all it may derive profit and enjoyment, greater or less,
according as they are themselves greater or less; and while it takes
pleasure in all of them, it despises the less that it may obtain or
retain the greater when occasion demands. Now, of all goods, spiritual or bodily, there is none at all to compare with virtue. For virtue makes a good use both of itself and of all other goods in which
lies man's happiness; and where it is absent, no matter how many
good things a man has, they are not for his good, and consequently
should not be called good things while they belong to one who
makes them useless by using them badly. The life of man, then, is
called happy when it enjoys virtue and these other spiritual and
bodily good things without which virtue is impossible. It is called
happier if it enjoys some or many other good things which are not
essential to virtue; and happiest of all, if it lacks not one of the good
things which pertain to the body and the soul. For life is not the
same thing as virtue, since not every life, but a wisely regulated
life, is virtue; and yet, while there can be life of some kind without
virtue, there cannot be virtue without life. This I might apply to
memory and reason, and such mental faculties; for these exist prior
to instruction, and without them there cannot be any instruction,
and consequently no virtue, since virtue is learned. But bodily advantages, such as swiftness of foot, beauty, or strength, are not essential
to virtue, neither is virtue essential to them, and yet they are good
things; and, according to our philosophers, even these advantages
are desired by virtue for its own sake, and are used and enjoyed by
it in a becoming manner.

They say that this happy life is also social, and loves the advantages of its friends as its own, and for their sake wishes for them
what it desires for itself, whether these friends live in the same
family, as a wife, children, domestics; or in the locality where one's
home is, as the citizens of the same town; or in the world at large,
as the nations bound in common human brotherhood; or in the universe itself, comprehended in the heavens and the earth, as those
whom they call gods, and provide as friends for the wise man, and
whom we more familiarly call angels. Moreover, they say that, regarding the supreme good and evil, there is no room for doubt, and

that they therefore differ from the New Academy in this respect, and they are not concerned whether a philosopher pursues those ends which they think true in the Cynic dress and manner of life or in some other. And, lastly, in regard to the three modes of life, the contemplative, the active, and the composite, they declare in favor of the third. That these were the opinions and doctrines of the Old Academy, Varro asserts on the authority of Antiochus, Cicero's master and his own, though Cicero makes him out to have been more frequently in accordance with the Stoics than with the Old Academy. But of what importance is this to us, who ought to judge the matter on its own merits, rather than to consider elaborately what different men have thought about it?

CHAPTER IV

What the Christians believe regarding the supreme good and evil, in opposition to the philosophers, who have maintained that the supreme good is in themselves.

IF, THEN, we be asked what the city of God has to say upon these points, and, in the first place, what its opinion regarding the supreme good and evil is, it will reply that life eternal is the supreme good, death eternal the supreme evil, and that to obtain the one and escape the other we must live rightly. And thus it is written, *The just lives by faith,*[5] for we do not as yet see our good, and must therefore live by faith; neither have we in ourselves power to live rightly, but can do so only if He who has given us faith to believe in His help do help us when we believe and pray. As for those who have supposed that the sovereign good and evil are to be found in this life, and have placed it either in the soul or the body, or in both, or, to speak more explicitly, either in pleasure or in virtue, or in both; in repose or in virtue, or in both; in pleasure and repose, or in virtue, or in all combined; in the primary objects of nature, or in virtue, or in both—all these have, with a marvelous shallowness, sought to find their blessedness in this life and in themselves. Contempt has been poured upon such ideas by the Truth, saying by the prophet, *The Lord knoweth the thoughts of men* (or, as the

[5] *Hab.* ii. 4.

Apostle Paul cites the passage, *The Lord knoweth the thoughts of the wise) that they are vain.*[6]

For what flood of eloquence can suffice to detail the miseries of this life? Cicero, in the *Consolation* on the death of his daughter, has spent all his ability in lamentation; but how inadequate was even his ability here? For when, where, how, in this life can these primary objects of nature be possessed so that they may not be assailed by unforeseen accidents? Is the body of the wise man exempt from any pain which may dispel pleasure, from any disquietude which may banish repose? The amputation or decay of the members of the body puts an end to its integrity, deformity blights its beauty, weakness its health, lassitude its vigour, sleepiness or sluggishness its activity—and which of these is it that may not assail the flesh of the wise man? Comely and fitting attitudes and movements of the body are numbered among the prime natural blessings; but what if some sickness makes the members tremble? what if a man suffers from curvature of the spine to such an extent that his hands reach the ground, and he goes upon all-fours like a quadruped? Does not this destroy all beauty and grace in the body, whether at rest or in motion? What shall I say of the fundamental blessings of the soul, sense and intellect, of which the one is given for the perception, and the other for the comprehension of truth? But what kind of sense is it that remains when a man becomes deaf and blind? where are reason and intellect when disease makes a man delirious? We can scarcely, or not at all, refrain from tears, when we think of or see the actions and words of such phrenetic persons, and consider how different from and even opposed to their own sober judgment and ordinary conduct their present demeanor is. And what shall I say of those who suffer from demoniacal possession? Where is their own intelligence hidden and buried while the malignant spirit is using their body and soul according to his own will? And who is quite sure that no such thing can happen to the wise man in this life? Then, as to the perception of truth, what can we hope for even in this way while in the body, as we read in the true book of Wisdom, *The corruptible body weigheth down the soul, and the earthly tabernacle presseth down the mind that museth upon many things?*[7] And eagerness, or desire of action, if this is the right meaning to

[6] *Ps.* xci. 11, and *I Cor.* iii. 20.   [7] *Wis.* ix. 15.

put upon the Greek ὁρμή, is also reckoned among the primary advantages of nature; and yet is it not this which produces those pitiable movements of the insane, and those actions which we shudder to see, when sense is deceived and reason deranged?

In fine, virtue itself, which is not among the primary objects of nature, but succeeds to them as the result of learning, though it holds the highest place among human good things, what is its occupation save to wage perpetual war with vices—not those that are outside of us, but within; not other men's, but our own—a war which is waged especially by that virtue which the Greeks call σωφροσύνη, and we temperance [8] and which bridles carnal lusts, and prevents them from winning the consent of the spirit to wicked deeds? For we must not fancy that there is no vice in us, when, as the Apostle says, *The flesh lusteth against the spirit;* [9] for to this vice there is a contrary virtue, when, as the same writer says, *the spirit lusteth against the flesh. For these two,* he says, *are contrary one to the other, so that you do not do the things which you would.* But what is it we wish to do when we seek to attain the supreme good, unless that the flesh should cease to lust against the spirit, and that there be no vice in us against which the spirit may lust? And as we cannot attain to this in the present life, however ardently we desire it, let us by God's help accomplish at least this, to preserve the soul from succumbing and yielding to the flesh that lusts against it, and to refuse our consent to the perpetration of sin. Far be it from us, then, to fancy that while we are still engaged in this intestine war, we have already found the happiness which we seek to reach by victory. And who is there so wise that he has no conflict at all to maintain against his vices?

What shall I say of that virtue which is called prudence? Is not all its vigilance spent in the discernment of good from evil things, so that no mistake may be admitted about what we should desire and what avoid? And thus it is itself a proof that we are in the midst of evils, or that evils are in us; for it teaches us that it is an evil to consent to sin, and a good to refuse this consent. And yet this evil, to which prudence teaches and temperance enables us not to consent, is removed from this life neither by prudence nor by temperance. And justice, whose office it is to render to every man his due,

[8] Cicero, *Tusc. Quaest.* iii. 8.   [9] *Gal.* v. 17.

whereby there is in man himself a certain just order of nature, so that the soul is subjected to God, and the flesh to the soul, and consequently both soul and flesh to God—does not this virtue demonstrate that it is as yet rather labouring towards its end than resting in its finished work? For the soul is so much the less subjected to God as it is less occupied with the thought of God; and the flesh is so much the less subjected to the spirit as it lusts more vehemently against the spirit. So long, therefore, as we are beset by this weakness, this plague, this disease, how shall we dare to say that we are safe? and if not safe, then how can we be already enjoying our final beatitude? Then that virtue which goes by the name of fortitude is the plainest proof of the ills of life, for it is these ills which it is compelled to bear patiently. And this holds good, no matter though the ripest wisdom co-exists with it. And I am at a loss to understand how the Stoic philosophers can presume to say that these are no ills, though at the same time they allow the wise man to commit suicide and pass out of this life if they become so grievous that he cannot or ought not to endure them. But such is the stupid pride of these men who fancy that the supreme good can be found in this life, and that they can become happy by their own resources, that their wise man, or at least the man whom they fancifully depict as such, is always happy, even though he become blind, deaf, dumb, mutilated, racked with pains, or suffer any conceivable calamity such as may compel him to make away with himself; and they are not ashamed to call the life that is beset with these evils happy. O happy life, which seeks the aid of death to end it! If it is happy, let the wise man remain in it; but if these ills drive him out of it, in what sense is it happy? Or how can they say that these are not evils which conquer the virtue of fortitude, and force it not only to yield, but so to rave that it in one breath calls life happy and recommends it to be given up? For who is so blind as not to see that if it were happy it would not be fled from? And if they say we should flee from it on account of the infirmities that beset it, why then do they not lower their pride and acknowledge that it is miserable? Was it, I would ask, fortitude or weakness which prompted Cato to kill himself? for he would not have done so had he not been too weak to endure Caesar's victory. Where, then, is his fortitude? It has yielded, it has succumbed, it has been so thoroughly overcome as to abandon, forsake, flee this happy life. Or was it no longer happy? Then it was miserable. How, then, were these not evils which made life miserable, and a thing to be escaped from?

And therefore those who admit that these are evils, as the Peripatetics do, and the Old Academy, the sect which Varro advocates, express a more intelligible doctrine; but theirs also is a surprising mistake, for they contend that this is a happy life which is beset by these evils, even though they be so great that he who endures them should commit suicide to escape them. "Pains and anguish of body," says Varro, "are evils, and so much the worse in proportion to their severity; and to escape them you must quit this life." What life, I pray? This life, he says, which is oppressed by such evils. Then it is happy in the midst of these very evils on account of which you say we must quit it? Or do you call it happy because you are at liberty to escape these evils by death? What, then, if by some secret judgment of God you were held fast and not permitted to die, nor suffered to live without these evils? In that case, at least, you would say that such a life was miserable. It is soon relinquished, no doubt, but this does not make it not miserable; for were it eternal, you yourself would pronounce it miserable. Its brevity, therefore, does not clear it of misery; neither ought it to be called happiness because it is a brief misery. Certainly there is a mighty force in these evils which compel a man—according to them, even a wise man—to cease to be a man that he may escape them, though they say, and say truly, that it is as it were the first and strongest demand of nature that a man cherish himself, and naturally therefore avoid death, and should so stand his own friend as to wish and vehemently aim at continuing to exist as a living creature, and subsisting in this union of soul and body. There is a mighty force in these evils to overcome this natural instinct by which death is by every means and with all a man's efforts avoided, and to overcome it so completely that what was avoided is desired, sought after, and if it cannot in any other way be obtained, is inflicted by the man on himself. There is a mighty force in these evils which make fortitude a homicide—if, indeed, that is to be called fortitude which is so thoroughly overcome by these evils, that it not only cannot preserve by patience the man whom it undertook to govern and defend, but is itself obliged to kill him. The wise man, I admit, ought to bear death with patience, but when it is inflicted by another. If, then, as these men maintain, he is obliged to inflict it on himself, certainly it must be owned that the ills which compel him to this are not only evils, but intolerable evils. The life, then, which is either subject to accidents, or environed with evils so considerable and grievous, could never have been called happy, if the men who give it this name had condescended to yield to the truth, and to be conquered by valid arguments, when they inquired after the happy life, as they yield to unhappiness, and are overcome by overwhelming evils, when they put themselves to death, and if they had not fancied that the supreme good was to be found in this mortal life; for the very virtues of this life, which are certainly its best and most useful possessions, are all the more telling proofs of its miseries in proportion as they are helpful against the violence of its dangers, toils, and woes. For if these are true virtues—and such cannot exist save in those who have true piety—they do not profess to be able to deliver the men who possess them from all miseries; for true virtues tell no such lies, but they profess that by the hope of the future world this life, which is miserably involved in the many and great evils of this world, is happy as it is also safe. For if not yet safe, how could it be happy? And therefore the Apostle Paul, speaking not of men without prudence, temperance, fortitude, and justice, but of those whose lives were regulated by true piety, and whose virtues were therefore true, says, *For we are saved by hope: now hope which is seen is not hope; for what a man seeth, why doth he yet hope for? But if we hope for that we see not, then do we with patience wait for it.*[10] As, therefore, we are saved, so we are made happy by hope. And as we do not as yet possess a present, but look for a future salvation, so is it with our happiness, and this "with patience;" for we are encompassed with evils, which we ought patiently to endure, until we come to the ineffable enjoyment of unmixed good; for there shall be no longer anything to endure. Salvation, such as it shall be in the world to come, shall itself be our final happiness. And this happiness these philosophers refuse to believe in, because they do not see it, and attempt to fabricate for themselves a happiness in this life, based upon a virtue which is as deceitful as it is proud.

[10] *Rom.* viii. 24.

CHAPTER V

Of the social life, which, though most desirable, is frequently disturbed by many distresses.

WE GIVE a much more unlimited approval to their idea that the life of the wise man must be social. For how could the city of God (concerning which we are already writing no less than the nineteenth book of this work) either take a beginning or be developed, or attain its proper destiny, if the life of the saints were not a social life? But who can enumerate all the great grievances with which human society abounds in the misery of this mortal state? Who can weigh them? Hear how one of their comic writers makes one of his characters express the common feelings of all men in this matter: "I am married; this is one misery. Children are born to me; they are additional cares." [11] What shall I say of the miseries of love which Terence also recounts—"slights, suspicions, quarrels, war today, peace tomorrow?" [12] Is not human life full of such things? Do they not often occur even in honorable friendships? On all hands we experience these slights, suspicions, quarrels, war, all of which are undoubted evils; while, on the other hand, peace is a doubtful good, because we do not know the heart of our friend, and though we did know it to-day, we should be as ignorant of what it might be to-morrow. Who ought to be, or who are more friendly than those who live in the same family? And yet who can rely even upon this friendship, seeing that secret treachery has often broken it up, and produced enmity as bitter as the amity was sweet, or seemed sweet by the most perfect dissimulation? It is on this account that the words of Cicero so move the heart of every one, and provoke a sigh: "There are no snares more dangerous than those which lurk under the guise of duty or the name of relationship. For the man who is your declared foe you can easily baffle by precaution; but this hidden, intestine, and domestic danger not merely exists, but overwhelms you before you can foresee and examine it." [13] It is also to this that allusion is made by the divine saying, *A man's foes are those of his own household,*[14]—words which one cannot hear without pain; for though a man have sufficient fortitude to endure

[11] Terence, *Adelph.* v. 4.   [12] *Eunuch,* i. 1.   [13] *In Verrem,* ii. 1. 15.
[14] *Matt.* x. 36.

it with equanimity, and sufficient sagacity to baffle the malice of a
pretended friend, yet if he himself is a good man, he cannot but be
greatly pained at the discovery of the perfidy of wicked men,
whether they have always been wicked and merely feigned goodness, or have fallen from a better to a malicious disposition. If,
then, home, the natural refuge from the ills of life, is itself not
safe, what shall we say of the city, which, as it is larger, is so much
the more filled with lawsuits civil and criminal, and is never free
from the fear, if sometimes from the actual outbreak, of disturbing
and bloody insurrections and civil wars?

CHAPTER VI

Of the error of human judgments when the truth is hidden.

WHAT SHALL I SAY of these judgments which men pronounce on
men, and which are necessary in communities, whatever outward
peace they enjoy? Melancholy and lamentable judgments they are,
since the judges are men who cannot discern the consciences of
those at their bar, and are therefore frequently compelled to put
innocent witnesses to the torture to ascertain the truth regarding
the crimes of other men. What shall I say of torture applied to the
accused himself? He is tortured to discover whether he is guilty,
so that, though innocent, he suffers most undoubted punishment
for crime that is still doubtful, not because it is proved that he committed it, but because it is not ascertained that he did not commit
it. Thus the ignorance of the judge frequently involves an innocent
person in suffering. And what is still more unendurable—a thing,
indeed, to be bewailed, and, if that were possible, watered with
fountains of tears—is this, that when the judge puts the accused
to the question, that he may not unwittingly put an innocent man
to death, the result of this lamentable ignorance is that this very
person, whom he tortured that he might not condemn him if innocent, is condemned to death both tortured and innocent. For if he
has chosen, in obedience to the philosophical instructions to the
wise man, to quit this life rather than endure any longer such tortures, he declares that he has committed the crime which in fact
he has not committed. And when he has been condemned and put

to death, the judge is still in ignorance whether he has put to
death an innocent or a guilty person, though he put the accused to
the torture for the very purpose of saving himself from condemn-
ing the innocent; and consequently he has both tortured an innocent
man to discover his innocence, and has put him to death without
discovering it. If such darkness shrouds social life, will a wise judge
take his seat on the bench or no? Beyond question he will. For human society, which he thinks it a wickedness to abandon, constrains
him and compels him to this duty. And he thinks it no wickedness
that innocent witnesses are tortured regarding the crimes of which
other men are accused; or that the accused are put to the torture, so
that they are often overcome with anguish, and, though innocent,
make false confessions regarding themselves, and are punished; or
that, though they be not condemned to die, they often die during,
or in consequence of, the torture; or that sometimes the accusers,
who perhaps have been prompted by a desire to benefit society by
bringing criminals to justice, are themselves condemned through
the ignorance of the judge, because they are unable to prove the
truth of their accusations though they are true, and because the
witnesses lie, and the accused endures the torture without being
moved to confession. These numerous and important evils he does
not consider sins; for the wise judge does these things, not with
any intention of doing harm, but because his ignorance compels
him, and because human society claims him as a judge. But though
we therefore acquit the judge of malice, we must none the less condemn human life as miserable. And if he is compelled to torture
and punish the innocent because his office and his ignorance con-
strain him, is he a happy as well as a guiltless man? Surely it were
proof of more profound considerateness and finer feeling were
he to recognize the misery of these necessities, and shrink from his
own implication in that misery; and had he any piety about him,
he would cry to God *from my necessities deliver Thou me.*[15]

[15] *Ps.* xxiv. 17.

CHAPTER VII

*Of the diversity of languages, by which the intercourse of men is
prevented; and of the misery of wars, even of those called just.*

AFTER THE STATE or city comes the world, the third circle of human society—the first being the house, and the second the city.
And the world, as it is larger, so it is fuller of dangers, as the
greater sea is the more dangerous. And here, in the first place, man
is separated from man by the difference of languages. For if two
men, each ignorant of the other's language, meet, and are not compelled to pass, but, on the contrary, to remain in company, dumb
animals, though of different species, would more easily hold intercourse than they, human beings though they be. For their common
nature is no help to friendliness when they are prevented by diversity of language from conveying their sentiments to one another; so that a man would more readily hold intercourse with his
dog than with a foreigner. But the imperial city has endeavored to
impose on subject nations not only her yoke, but her language, as a
bond of peace, so that interpreters, far from being scarce, are numberless. This is true; but how many great wars, how much slaughter
and bloodshed, have provided this unity! And though these are
past, the end of these miseries has not yet come. For though there
have never been wanting, nor are yet wanting, hostile nations beyond the empire, against whom wars have been and are waged, yet,
supposing there were no such nations, the very extent of the empire itself has produced wars of a more obnoxious description—
social and civil wars—and with these the whole race has been agitated, either by the actual conflict or the fear of a renewed outbreak.
If I attempted to give an adequate description of these manifold
disasters, these stern and lasting necessities, though I am quite unequal to the task, what limit could I set? But, say they, the wise
man will wage just wars. As if he would not all the rather lament
the necessity of just wars, if he remembers that he is a man; for if
they were not just he would not wage them, and would therefore
be delivered from all wars. For it is the wrong-doing of the opposing party which compels the wise man to wage just wars; and this
wrong-doing, even though it gave rise to no war, would still be
matter of grief to man because it is man's wrong-doing. Let every

one, then, who thinks with pain on all these great evils, so horrible, so ruthless, acknowledge that this is misery. And if any one either endures or thinks of them without mental pain, this is a more miserable plight still, for he thinks himself happy because he has lost human feeling.

CHAPTER VIII

That the friendship of good men cannot be securely rested in, so long as the dangers of this life force us to be anxious.

IN OUR PRESENT WRETCHED condition we frequently mistake a friend for an enemy, and an enemy for a friend. And if we escape this pitiable blindness, is not the unfeigned confidence and mutual love of true and good friends our one solace in human society, filled as it is with misunderstandings and calamities? And yet the more friends we have, and the more widely they are scattered, the more numerous are our fears that some portion of the vast masses of the disasters of life may light upon them. For we are not only anxious lest they suffer from famine, war, disease, captivity, or the inconceivable horrors of slavery, but we are also affected with the much more painful dread that their friendship may be changed into perfidy, malice, and injustice. And when these contingencies actually occur—as they do the more frequently the more friends we have, and the more widely they are scattered—and when they come to our knowledge, who but the man who has experienced it can tell with what pangs the heart is torn? We would, in fact, prefer to hear that they were dead, although we could not without anguish hear of even this. For if their life has solaced us with the charms of friendship, can it be that their death should affect us with no sadness? He who will have none of this sadness must, if possible, have no friendly intercourse. Let him interdict or extinguish friendly affection; let him burst with ruthless insensibility the bonds of every human relationship; or let him contrive so to use them that no sweetness shall distil into his spirit. But if this is utterly impossible, how shall we contrive to feel no bitterness in the death of those whose life has been sweet to us? Hence arises that grief which affects the tender heart like a wound or a bruise, and which is healed by the application of kindly consolation. For though the

:ure is affected all the more easily and rapidly the better condition
the soul is in, we must not on this account suppose that there is
nothing at all to heal. Although, then, our present life is afflicted
sometimes in a milder, sometimes in a more painful degree, by the
death of those very dear to us, and especially of useful public men,
yet we would prefer to hear that such men were dead rather than to
hear or perceive that they had fallen from the faith, or from virtue—
in other words, that they were spiritually dead. Of this vast material
for misery the earth is full, and therefore it is written, *Is not human
life upon earth a trial?* [16] And with the same reference the Lord
says, *Woe to the world because of offenses!* [17] and again, *Because
iniquity abounded, the love of many shall wax cold.* [18] And hence
we enjoy some gratification when our good friends die; for though
their death leaves us in sorrow, we have the consolatory assurance
that they are beyond the ills by which in this life even the best of
men are broken down or corrupted, or are in danger of both results.

CHAPTER IX

*Of the friendship of the holy angels, which men cannot be sure of in
this life, owing to the deceit of the demons who hold in bondage
the worshippers of a plurality of gods.*

THE PHILOSOPHERS who wished us to have the gods for our friends
rank the friendship of the holy angels in the fourth circle of society,
advancing now from the three circles of society on earth to the universe, and embracing heaven itself. And in this friendship we have
indeed no fear that the angels will grieve us by their death or deteri-
oration. But as we cannot mingle with them as familiarly as with
men (which itself is one of the grievances of this life), and as Satan,
as we read,[19] sometimes transforms himself into an angel of light,
to tempt those whom it is necessary to discipline, or just to deceive,
there is great need of God's mercy to preserve us from making
friends of demons in disguise, while we fancy we have good angels
for our friends; for the astuteness and deceitfulness of these wicked
spirits is equalled by their hurtfulness. And is this not a great misery
of human life, that we are involved in such ignorance as, but for

16 *Job* vii. 1.   17 *Matt.* xvii. 7.   18 *Matt.* xxiv. 12.   19 *II Cor.* xi. 14.

God's mercy, makes us a prey to these demons? And it is very certain that the philosophers of the godless city, who have maintained that the gods were their friends, had fallen a prey to the malignant demons who rule that city, and whose eternal punishment is to be shared by it. For the nature of these beings is sufficiently evinced by the sacred or rather sacrilegious observances which form their worship, and by the filthy games in which their crimes are celebrated, and which they themselves originated and exacted from their worshippers as a fit propitiation.

CHAPTER X

The reward prepared for the saints after they have endured the trial of this life.

BUT NOT even the saints and faithful worshippers of the one true and most high God are safe from the manifold temptations and deceits of the demons. For in this abode of weakness, and in these wicked days, this state of anxiety has also its use, stimulating us to seek with keener longing for that security where peace is complete and unassailable. There we shall enjoy the gifts of nature, that is to say, all that God the Creator of all natures has bestowed upon ours—gifts not only good, but eternal—not only of the spirit, healed now by wisdom, but also of the body renewed by the resurrection. There the virtues shall no longer be struggling against any vice or evil, but shall enjoy the reward of victory, the eternal peace which no adversary shall disturb. This is the final blessedness, this the ultimate consummation, the unending end. Here, indeed, we are said to be blessed when we have such peace as can be enjoyed in a good life; but such blessedness is mere misery compared to that final felicity. When we mortals possess such peace as this mortal life can afford, virtue, if we are living rightly, makes a right use of the advantages of this peaceful condition; and when we have it not, virtue makes a good use even of the evils a man suffers. But this is true virtue, when it refers all the advantages it makes a good use of, and all that it does in making good use of good and evil things, and itself also, to that end in which we shall enjoy the best and greatest peace possible.

CHAPTER XI

Of the happiness of the eternal peace, which constitutes the end or true perfection of the saints.

AND THUS we may say of peace, as we have said of eternal life, that it is the end of our good; and the rather because the Psalmist says of the city of God, the subject of this labourious work, *Praise the Lord, O Jerusalem; praise thy God, O Zion: for He hath strengthened the bars of thy gates; He hath blessed thy children within thee; who hath made thy borders peace.*[20] For when the bars of her gates shall be strengthened, none shall go in or come out from her; consequently we ought to understand the peace of her borders as that final peace we are wishing to declare. For even the mystical name of the city itself, that is, *Jerusalem,* means, as I have already said, "Vision of Peace." But as the word peace is employed in connection with things in this world in which certainly life eternal has no place, we have preferred to call the end or supreme good of this city life eternal rather than peace. Of this end the Apostle says, *But now, being freed from sin, and become servants to God, ye have your fruit unto holiness, and the end life eternal.*[21] But, on the other hand, as those who are not familiar with Scripture may suppose that the life of the wicked is eternal life, either because of the immortality of the soul, which some of the philosophers even have recognized, or because of the endless punishment of the wicked, which forms a part of our faith, and which seems impossible unless the wicked live for ever, it may therefore be advisable, in order that every one may readily understand what we mean, to say that the end or supreme good of this city is either peace in eternal life, or eternal life in peace. For peace is a good so great, that even in this earthly and mortal life there is no word we hear with such pleasure, nothing we desire with such zest, or find to be more thoroughly gratifying. So that if we dwell for a little longer on this subject, we shall not, in my opinion, be wearisome to our readers, who will attend both for the sake of understanding what is the end of this city of which we speak, and for the sake of the sweetness of peace which is dear to all.

[20] *Ps.* cxlvii. 12-14.   [21] *Rom.* vi. 22.

That even the fierceness of war and all the disquietude of man make towards this one end of peace, which every nature desires.

WHOEVER gives even moderate attention to human affairs and to our common nature, will recognize that if there is no man who does not wish to be joyful, neither is there any one who does not wish to have peace. For even they who make war desire nothing but victory —desire, that is to say, to attain to peace with glory. For what else is victory than the conquest of those who resist us? and when this is done there is peace. It is therefore with the desire for peace that wars are waged, even by those who take pleasure in exercising their warlike nature in command and battle. And hence it is obvious that peace is the end sought for by war. For every man seeks peace by waging war, but no man seeks war by making peace. For even they who intentionally interrupt the peace in which they are living have no hatred of peace, but only wish it changed into a peace that suits them better. They do not, therefore, wish to have no peace, but only one more to their mind. And in the case of sedition, when men have separated themselves from the community, they yet do not effect what they wish, unless they maintain some kind of peace with their fellow-conspirators. And therefore even robbers take care to maintain peace with their comrades, that they may with greater effect and greater safety invade the peace of other men. And if an individual happen to be of such unrivalled strength, and to be so jealous of partnership, that he trusts himself with no comrades, but makes his own plots, and commits depredations and murders on his own account, yet he maintains some shadow of peace with such persons as he is unable to kill, and from whom he wishes to conceal his deeds. In his own home, too, he makes it his aim to be at peace with his wife and children, and any other members of his household; for unquestionably their prompt obedience to his every look is a source of pleasure to him. And if this be not rendered, he is angry, he chides and punishes; and even by this storm he secures the calm peace of his own home, as occasion demands. For he sees that peace cannot be maintained unless all the members of the same domestic circle be subject to one head, such as he himself is in his own house. And therefore if a city or nation offered to submit itself to him, to serve him in the same style as he had made his household serve him, he would no longer lurk in a brigand's hiding-places, but lift his head in open day as a king, though the same coveteousness and wickedness should remain in him. And thus all men desire to have peace with their own circle whom they wish to govern as suits themselves. For even those whom they make war against they wish to make their own, and impose on them the laws of their own peace.

But let us suppose a man such as poetry and mythology speak of—a man so insociable and savage as to be called rather a semi-man than a man.[22] Although, then, his kingdom was the solitude of a dreary cave, and he himself was so singularly bad-hearted that he was named Κακός, which is the Greek word for *bad;* though he had no wife to soothe him with endearing talk, no children to play with, no sons to do his bidding, no friend to enliven him with intercourse, not even his father Vulcan (though in one respect he was happier than his father, not having begotten a monster like himself); although he gave to no man, but took as he wished whatever he could, from whomsoever he could, when he could; yet in that solitary den, the floor of which, as Virgil [23] says, was always reeking with recent slaughter, there was nothing else than peace sought, a peace in which no one should molest him, or disquiet him with any assault or alarm. With his own body he desired to be at peace, and he was satisfied only in proportion as he had this peace. For he ruled his members, and they obeyed him; and for the sake of pacifying his mortal nature, which rebelled when it needed anything, and of allaying the sedition of hunger which threatened to banish the soul from the body, he made forays, slew, and devoured, but used the ferocity and savageness he displayed in these actions only for the preservation of his own life's peace. So that, had he been willing to make with other men the same peace which he made with himself in his own cave, he would neither have been called bad, nor a monster, nor a semi-man. Or if the appearance of his body and his vomiting smoky fires frightened men from having any dealings with him, perhaps his fierce ways arose not from a desire to do mischief, but from the necessity of finding a living. But he may

[22] He refers to the giant Cacus.   [23] *Aeneid,* viii. 195.

have had no existence, or, at least, he was not such as the poets fancifully describe him, for they had to exalt Hercules, and did so at the expense of Cacus. It is better, then, to believe that such a man or semi-man never existed, and that this, in common with many other fancies of the poets, is mere fiction. For the most savage animals (and he is said to have been almost a wild beast) encompass their own species with a ring of protecting peace. They cohabit, beget, produce, suckle, and bring up their young, though very many of them are not gregarious, but solitary—not like sheep, deer, pigeons, starlings, bees, but such as lions, foxes, eagles, bats. For what tigress does not gently purr over her cubs, and lay aside her ferocity to fondle them? What kite, solitary as he is when circling over his prey, does not seek a mate, build a nest, hatch the eggs, bring up the young birds, and maintain with the mother of his family as peaceful a domestic alliance as he can? How much more powerfully do the laws of man's nature move him to hold fellowship and maintain peace with all men so far as in him lies, since even wicked men wage war to maintain the peace of their own circle, and wish that, if possible, all men belonged to them, that all men and things might serve but one head, and might, either through love or fear, yield themselves to peace with him! It is thus that pride in its perversity apes God. It abhors equality with other men under Him; but, instead of His rule, it seeks to impose a rule of its own upon its equals. It abhors, that is to say, the just peace of God, and loves its own unjust peace; but it cannot help loving peace of one kind or other. For there is no vice so clean contrary to nature that it obliterates even the faintest traces of nature.

He, then, who prefers what is right to what is wrong, and what is well-ordered to what is perverted, sees that the peace of unjust men is not worthy to be called peace in comparison with the peace of the just. And yet even what is perverted must of necessity be in harmony with, and in dependence on, and in some part of the order of things, for otherwise it would have no existence at all. Suppose a man hangs with his head downwards, this is certainly a perverted attitude of body and arrangement of its members; for that which nature requires to be above is beneath, and *vice versa*. This perversity disturbs the peace of the body, and is therefore painful. Nevertheless the spirit is at peace with its body, and labours for its preservation, and hence the suffering; but if it is banished from the body by its pains, then, so long as the bodily framework holds together, there is in the remains a kind of peace among the members, and hence the body remains suspended. And inasmuch as the earthly body tends towards the earth, and rests on the bond by which it is suspended, it tends thus to its natural peace, and the voice of its own weight demands a place for it to rest; and though now lifeless and without feeling, it does not fall from the peace that is natural to its place in creation, whether it already has it, or is tending towards it. For if you apply embalming preparations to prevent the bodily frame from mouldering and dissolving, a kind of peace still unites part to part, and keeps the whole body in a suitable place on the earth—in other words, in a place that is at peace with the body. If, on the other hand, the body receive no such care, but be left to the natural course, it is disturbed by exhalations that do not harmonize with one another, and that offend our senses; for it is this which is perceived in putrefaction until it is assimilated to the elements of the world, and particle by particle enters into peace with them. Yet throughout this process the laws of the most high Creator and Governor are strictly observed, for it is by Him the peace of the universe is administered. For although minute animals are produced from the carcass of a larger animal, all these little atoms, by the law of the same Creator, serve the animals they belong to in peace. And although the flesh of dead animals be eaten by others, no matter where it be carried, nor what it be brought into contact with, nor what it be converted and changed into, it still is ruled by the same laws which pervade all things for the conservation of every mortal race, and which bring things that fit one another into harmony.

CHAPTER XIII

Of the universal peace which the law of nature preserves through all disturbances, and by which every one reaches his desert in a way regulated by the just judge.

THE PEACE of the body then consists in the duly proportioned arrangement of its parts. The peace of the irrational soul is the harmonious repose of the appetites, and that of the rational soul the harmony of knowledge and action. The peace of body and soul is the well-ordered and harmonious life and health of the living creature. Peace between mortal man and God is obedience, ordered within faith, to eternal law. Peace between man and man is well-ordered concord. Domestic peace is the well-ordered concord between those of the family who rule and those who obey. Civil peace is a similar concord among the citizens. The peace of the celestial city is the perfectly ordered and harmonious enjoyment of God, and of one another in God. The peace of all things is the tranquillity of order. Order is the distribution which allots things equal and unequal, each to its own place. And hence, though the miserable, in so far as they are such, do certainly not enjoy peace, but are severed from that tranquillity of order in which there is no disturbance, nevertheless, inasmuch as they are deservedly and justly miserable, they are by their very misery connected with order. They are not, indeed, conjoined with the blessed, but they are disjoined from them by the law of order. And though they are disquieted, their circumstances are notwithstanding adjusted to them, and consequently they have some tranquillity of order, and therefore some peace. But they are wretched because, although not wholly miserable, they are not in that place where any mixture of misery is impossible. They would, however, be more wretched if they had not that peace which arises from being in harmony with the natural order of things. When they suffer, their peace is in so far disturbed; but their peace continues in so far as they do not suffer, and in so far as their nature continues to exist. As, then, there may be life without pain, while there cannot be pain without some kind of life, so there may be peace without war, but there cannot be war without some kind of peace, because war supposes the existence of some natures to wage it, and these natures cannot exist without peace of one kind or other.

And therefore there is a nature in which evil does not or even cannot exist; but there cannot be a nature in which there is no good. Hence not even the nature of the devil himself is evil, in so far as it is nature, but it made evil by being perverted. Thus he did not abide in the truth,[24] but could not escape the judgment of the Truth; he did not abide in the tranquillity of order, but did not therefore

[24] *Jo.* VIII. 44.

escape the power of the Ordainer. The good imparted by God to his nature did not screen him from the justice of God by which order was preserved in his punishment; neither did God punish the good which He had created, but the evil which the devil had committed. God did not take back all He had imparted to his nature, but something He took and something He left, that there might remain enough to be sensible of the loss of what was taken. And this very sensibility to pain is evidence of the good which has been taken away and the good which has been left. For, were nothing good left, there could be no pain on account of the good which had been lost. For he who sins is still worse if he rejoices in his loss of righteousness. But he who is in pain, if he derives no benefit from it, mourns at least the loss of health. And as righteousness and health are both good things, and as the loss of any good thing is matter of grief, not of joy—if, at least, there is no compensation, as spiritual righteousness may compensate for the loss of bodily health—certainly it is more suitable for a wicked man to grieve in punishment than to rejoice in his fault. As, then, the joy of a sinner who has abandoned what is good is evidence of a bad will, so his grief for the good he has lost when he is punished is evidence of a good nature. For he who laments the peace his nature has lost is stirred to do so by some relics of peace which make his nature friendly to itself. And it is very just that in the final punishment the wicked and godless should in anguish bewail the loss of the natural advantages they enjoyed, and should perceive that they were most justly taken from them by that God whose benign liberality they had despised. God, then, the most wise Creator and most just Ordainer of all natures, who placed the human race upon earth as its greatest ornament, imparted to men some good things adapted to this life, to wit, temporal peace, such as we can enjoy in this life from health and safety and human fellowship, and all things needful for the preservation and recovery of this peace, such as the objects which are accommodated to our outward senses, light, night, the air, and waters suitable for us, and everything the body requires to sustain, shelter, heal, or beautify it: and all under this most equitable condition, that every man who made a good use of these advantages suited to the peace of this mortal condition, should receive ampler and better blessings, namely, the peace of immortality, accompanied by glory and honour in an endless life made fit for the enjoyment of God and of one another in God; but that he who used the present blessings badly should both lose them and should not receive the others.

CHAPTER XIV

Of the order and law which obtain in heaven and earth, whereby it comes to pass that human society is served by those who rule it.

THE WHOLE USE, then, of things temporal has a reference to this result of earthly peace in the earthly community, while in the city of God it is connected with eternal peace. And therefore, if we were irrational animals, we should desire nothing beyond the proper arrangement of the parts of the body and the satisfaction of the appetites—nothing, therefore, but bodily comfort and abundance of pleasures, that the peace of the body might contribute to the peace of the soul. For if bodily peace be wanting, a bar is put to the peace even of the irrational soul, since it cannot obtain the gratification of its appetites. And these two together help out the mutual peace of soul and body, the peace of harmonious life and health. For as animals, by shunning pain, show that they love bodily peace, and, by pursuing pleasure to gratify their appetites, show that they love peace of soul, so their shrinking from death is a sufficient indication of their intense love of that peace which binds soul and body in close alliance. But, as man has a rational soul, he subordinates all this which he has in common with the beasts to the peace of his rational soul, that his intellect may have free play and may regulate his actions, and that he may thus enjoy the well-ordered harmony of knowledge and action which constitutes, as we have said, the peace of the rational soul. And for this purpose he must desire to be neither molested by pain, nor disturbed by desire, nor extinguished by death, that he may arrive at some useful knowledge by which he may regulate his life and manners. But, owing to the liability of the human mind to fall into mistakes, this very pursuit of knowledge may be a snare to him unless he has a divine Master, whom he may obey without misgiving, and who may at the same time give him such help as to preserve his own freedom. And because, so long as he is in this mortal body, he is a stranger to God, he walks by faith, not by sight; and he therefore refers all peace, bodily or spiritual or both, to that peace which mortal man has with the immortal God, so that he exhibits the well-ordered obedience of faith to eternal law. But as this divine Master inculcates two precepts—the love of God and the love of our neighbour—in which precepts a man finds three things he has to love—God, himself, and his neighbour—and as he who loves God does not err in loving himself, it follows that he must endeavour to get his neighbour to love God, since he is ordered to love his neighbour as himself. He ought to make this endeavour in behalf of his wife, his children, his household, all within his reach, even as he would wish his neighbour to do the same for him if he needed it; and consequently he will be at peace, or in well-ordered concord, with all men, as far as in him lies. And this is the order of this concord, that a man, in the first place, injure no one, and, in the second, do good to every one he can reach. Primarily, therefore, his own household are his care, for the law of nature and of society gives him readier access to them and greater opportunity of serving them. And hence the Apostle says, *Now, if any provide not for his own, and specially for those of his own house, he hath denied the faith, and is worse than an infidel.*[25] This is the origin of domestic peace, or the well-ordered concord of those in the family who rule and those who obey. For they who care for the rest rule—the husband the wife, the parents the children, the masters the servants; and they who are cared for obey—the women their husbands, the children their parents, the servants their masters. But in the family of the just man who lives by faith and is as yet a pilgrim journeying on to the celestial city, even those who rule serve those whom they seem to command; for they rule not from a love of power, but from a sense of the duty they owe to others—not because they are proud of authority, but because they love mercy.

CHAPTER XV

Of the liberty proper to man's nature, and the servitude introduced by sin—a servitude in which the man whose will is wicked is the

[25] *I Tim.* v. 8.

slave of his own lust. though he is free so far as regards other men.

THIS IS PRESCRIBED by the order of nature: it is thus that God has created man. For *let them*, He says, *have dominion over the fish of the sea, and over the fowl of the air, and over every creeping thing which creepeth on the earth.*[26] He did not intend that His rational creature, who was made in His image, should have dominion over anything but the irrational creation—not man over man, but man over the beasts. And hence the righteous men in primitive times were made shepherds of cattle rather than kings of men, God intending thus to teach us what the relative position of the creatures is, and what the desert of sin; for it is with justice, we believe, that the condition of slavery is the result of sin. And this is why we do not find the word "slave" in any part of Scripture until righteous Noah branded the sin of his son with this name. It is a name, therefore, introduced by sin and not by nature. The origin of the Latin word for slave is supposed to be found in the circumstance that those who by the law of war were liable to be killed were sometimes preserved by their victors, and were hence called servants. And these circumstances could never have arisen save through sin. For even when we wage a just war, our adversaries must be sinning; and every victory, even though gained by wicked men, is a result of the first judgment of God, who humbles the vanquished either for the sake of removing or of punishing their sins. Witness that man of God, Daniel, who, when he was in captivity, confessed to God his own sins and the sins of his people, and declares with pious grief that these were the cause of the captivity.[27] The prime cause, then, of slavery is sin, which brings man under the dominion of his fellow—that which does not happen save by the judgment of God, with whom is no unrighteousness, and who knows how to award fit punishments to every variety of offence. But our Master in heaven says, *Every one who doeth sin is the servant of sin.*[28] And thus there are many wicked masters who have religious men as their slaves, and who are yet themselves in bondage; *for of whom a man is overcome, of the same is he brought in bondage.*[29] And beyond question it is a happier thing to be the slave of a man than of a lust; for even this very lust of ruling, to mention no others,

[26] *Gen.* i. 26. [27] *Dan.* ix. [28] *Jo.* viii. 34. [29] *II Pet.* ii. 19.

lays waste men's hearts with the most ruthless dominion. Moreover, when men are subjected to one another in a peaceful order, the lowly position does as much good to the servant as the proud position does harm to the master. But by nature, as God first created us, no one is the slave either of man or of sin. This servitude is, however, penal, and is appointed by that law which enjoins the preservation of the natural order and forbids its disturbance; for if nothing had been done in violation of that law, there would have been nothing to restrain by penal servitude. And therefore the Apostle admonishes slaves to be subject to their masters, and to serve them heartily and with good-will, so that, if they cannot be freed by their masters, they may themselves make their slavery in some sort free, by serving not in crafty fear, but in faithful love, until all unrighteousness pass away, and all principality and every human power be brought to nothing, and God be all in all.

CHAPTER XVI

Of equitable rule.

AND THEREFORE, although our righteous fathers[30] had slaves, and administered their domestic affairs so as to distinguish between the condition of slaves and the heirship of sons in regard to the blessings of this life, yet in regard to the worship of God, in whom we hope for eternal blessings, they took an equally loving concern for all the members of their household. And this is so much in accordance with the natural order, that the head of the household was called *paterfamilias*; and this name has been so generally accepted, that even those whose rule is unrighteous are glad to apply it to themselves. But those who are true fathers of their households desire and endeavor that all the members of their household, equally with their own children, should worship and win God, and should come to that heavenly home in which the duty of ruling men is no longer necessary, because the duty of caring for their everlasting happiness has also ceased; but, until they reach that home, masters ought to feel their position of authority a greater burden than servants their service. And if any member of the family interrupts the domestic peace by disobedience, he is corrected either by word or

30 The patriarchs.

blow, or some kind of just and legitimate punishment, such as society permits, that he may himself be the better for it, and be readjusted to the family harmony from which he had dislocated himself. For as it is not benevolent to give a man help at the expense of some greater benefit he might receive, so it is not innocent to spare a man at the risk of his falling into graver sin. To be innocent, we must not only do harm to no man, but also restrain him from sin or punish his sin, so that either the man himself who is punished may profit by his experience, or others be warned by his example. Since, then, the house ought to be the beginning or element of the city, and every beginning bears reference to some end of its own kind, and every element to the integrity of the whole of which it is an element, it follows plainly enough that domestic peace has a relation to civic peace—in other words, that the well-ordered concord of domestic obedience and domestic rule has a relation to the well-ordered concord of civic obedience and civic rule. And therefore it follows, further, that the father of the family ought to frame his domestic rule in accordance with the law of the city, so that the household may be in harmony with the civic order.

CHAPTER XVII

What produces peace, and what discord, between the heavenly and earthly cities.

BUT THE FAMILIES which do not live by faith seek their peace in the earthly advantages of this life; while the families which live by faith look for those eternal blessings which are promised, and use as pilgrims such advantages of time and of earth as do not fascinate and divert them from God, but rather aid them to endure with greater ease, and to keep down the number of those burdens of the corruptible body which weigh upon the soul. Thus the things necessary for this mortal life are used by both kinds of men and families alike, but each has its own peculiar and widely different aim in using them. The earthly city, which does not live by faith, seeks an earthly peace, and the end it proposes, in the well-ordered concord of civic obedience and rule, is the combination of men's wills to attain the things which are helpful to this life. The heavenly city, or rather the part of it which sojourns on earth and lives by faith, makes use of this peace only because it must, until this mortal condition which necessitates it shall pass away. Consequently, so long as it lives like a captive and a stranger in the earthly city, though it has already received the promise of redemption, and the gift of the Spirit as the earnest of it, it makes no scruple to obey the laws of the earthly city, whereby the things necessary for the maintenance of this mortal life are administered; and thus, as this life is common to both cities, so there is a harmony between them in regard to what belongs to it. But, as the earthly city has had some philosophers whose doctrine is condemned by the divine teaching, and who, being deceived either by their own conjectures or by demons, supposed that many gods must be invited to take an interest in human affairs, and assigned to each a separate function and a separate department —to one the body, to another the soul; and in the body itself, to one the head, to another the neck, and each of the other members to one of the gods; and in like manner, in the soul, to one god the natural capacity was assigned, to another education, to another anger, to another lust; and so the various affairs of life were assigned —cattle to one, corn to another, wine to another, oil to another, the woods to another, money to another, navigation to another, wars and victories to another, marriages to another, births and fecundity to another, and other things to other gods: and as the celestial city, on the other hand, knew that one God only was to be worshipped, and that to Him alone was due that service which the Greeks call λατρεία, and which can be given only to a god, it has come to pass that the two cities could not have common laws of religion, and that the heavenly city has been compelled in this matter to dissent, and to become obnoxious to those who think differently, and to stand the brunt of their anger and hatred and persecutions, except in so far as the minds of their enemies have been alarmed by the multitude of the Christians and quelled by the manifest protection of God accorded to them. This heavenly city, then, while it sojourns on earth, calls citizens out of all nations, and gathers together a society of pilgrims of all languages, not scrupling about diversities in the manners, laws, and institutions whereby earthly peace is secured and maintained, but recognizing that, however various these are, they all tend to one and the same end of earthly peace. It therefore is so far from rescinding and abolishing these diversities, that it even preserves and adopts them, so long only as no hindrance to the worship of the one supreme and true God is thus introduced. Even the heavenly city, therefore, while in its state of pilgrimage, avails itself of the peace of earth, and, so far as it can without injuring faith and godliness, desires and maintains a common agreement among men regarding the acquisition of the necessaries of life, and makes this earthly peace bear upon the peace of heaven; for this alone can be truly called and esteemed the peace of the reasonable creatures, consisting as it does in the perfectly ordered and harmonious enjoyment of God and of one another in God. When we shall have reached that peace, this mortal life shall give place to one that is eternal, and our body shall be no more this animal body which by its corruption weighs down the soul, but a spiritual body feeling no want, and in all its members subjected to the will. In its pilgrim state the heavenly city possesses this peace by faith; and by this faith it lives righteously when it refers to the attainment of that peace every good action towards God and man; for the life of the city is a social life.

CHAPTER XVIII

How different the uncertainty of the New Academy is from the certainty of the Christian Faith.

As REGARDS the uncertainty about everything which Varro alleges to be the differentiating characteristic of the New Academy, the city of God thoroughly detests such doubt as madness. Regarding matters which it apprehends by the mind and reason it has most absolute certainty, although its knowledge is limited because of the corruptible body pressing down the mind, for, as the Apostle says, *we know in part.*[31] It believes also the evidence of the senses which the mind uses by aid of the body; for if one who trusts his senses is sometimes deceived, he is more wretchedly deceived who fancies he should never trust them. It believes also the Holy Scriptures, Old and New, which we call canonical, and which are the source of the faith by which the just lives [32] and by which we walk without doubting whilst we are absent from the Lord.[33] So long as this faith remains inviolate and firm, we may without blame enter-

[31] *I Cor.* xiii. 9.　　[32] *Hab.* ii. 4.　　[33] *II Cor.* v. 6.

tain doubts regarding some things which we have neither perceived by sense nor by reason, and which have not been revealed to us by the canonical Scriptures, nor come to our knowledge through witnesses whom it is absurd to disbelieve.

CHAPTER XIX
Of the dress and habits of the Christian people.

IT IS A MATTER of no moment in the city of God whether he who adopts the faith that brings men to God adopts it in one dress and manner of life or another, so long only as he lives in conformity with the commandments of God. And hence, when philosophers themselves become Christians, they are compelled, indeed, to abandon their erroneous doctrines, but not their dress and mode of living, which are no obstacle to religion. So that we make no account of that distinction of sects which Varro adduced in connection with the Cynic school, provided always nothing indecent or self-indulgent is retained. As to these three modes of life, the contemplative, the active, and the composite, although, so long as a man's faith is preserved, he may choose any of them without detriment to his eternal interests, yet he must never overlook the claims of truth and duty. No man has a right to lead such a life of contemplation as to forget in his own ease the service due to his neighbour; nor has any man a right to be so immersed in active life as to neglect the contemplation of God. The charm of leisure must not be indolent vacancy of mind, but the investigation or discovery of truth, that thus every man may make solid attainments without grudging that others do the same. And, in active life, it is not the honours or power of this life we should covet, since all things under the sun are vanity, but we should aim at using our position and influence, if these have been honourably attained, for the welfare of those who are under us, in the way we have already explained. [34] It is to this the Apostle refers when he says, *He that desireth the episcopate desireth a good work.*[35] He wished to show that the episcopate is the title of a work, not of an honour. It is a Greek word, and signifies that he who governs superintends or takes care of those whom

[34] Ch. 6.   [35] *I Tim. iii. 1.*

he governs: for ἐπί means *over*, and σκοπεῖν, *to see*; therefore επίσκοπεῖν means "to oversee." [36] So that he who loves to govern rather than to do good is no bishop. Accordingly no one is prohibited from the search after truth, for in this leisure may most laudably be spent; but it is unseemly to covet the high position requisite for governing the people, even though that position be held and that government be administered in a seemly manner. And therefore holy leisure is longed for by the love of truth; but it is the necessity of love to undertake requisite business. If no one imposes this burden upon us, we are free to sift and contemplate truth; but if it be laid upon us, we are necessitated for love's sake to undertake it. And yet not even in this case are we obliged wholly to relinquish the sweets of contemplation; for were these to be withdrawn, the burden might prove more than we could bear.

CHAPTER XX

That the saints are in this life blessed in hope.

SINCE, then, the supreme good of the city of God is perfect and eternal peace, not such as mortals pass into and out of by birth and death, but the peace of freedom from all evil, in which the immortals ever abide, who can deny that that future life is most blessed, or that, in comparison with it, this life which now we live is most wretched, be it filled with all blessings of body and soul and external things? And yet, if any man uses this life with a reference to that other which he ardently loves and confidently hopes for, he may well be called even now blessed, though not in reality so much as in hope. But the actual possession of the happiness of this life, without the hope of what is beyond, is but a false happiness and profound misery. For the true blessings of the soul are not now enjoyed; for that is no true wisdom which does not direct all its prudent observations, manly actions, virtuous self-restraint, and just arrangements, to that end in which God shall be all and all in a secure eternity and perfect peace.

[36] Augustine's words are: ἐπί, *quippe, super:* σκοπός, *vero, intentio est: ergo* ἐπισκοπεῖν, *si velimus, latine superintendere possumus dicere.*

CHAPTER XXI

*Whether there ever was a Roman Republic answering to the defi-
nitions of Scipio in Cicero's dialogue.*

THIS, then, is the place where I should fulfill the promise gave in
the second book of this work,[37] and explain, as briefly and clearly
as possible, that if we are to accept the definitions laid down by
Scipio in Cicero's *De Republica,* there never was a Roman republic;
for he briefly defines a republic as the weal of the people. And if
this definition be true, there never was a Roman republic, for the
people's weal was never attained among the Romans. For the people, according to his definition, is an assemblage associated by a
common acknowledgment of right and by a community of interests.
And what he means by a common acknowledgment of right he explains at large, showing that a republic cannot be administered
without justice. Where, therefore, there is no true justice there can
be no right. For that which is done by right is justly done, and what
is unjustly done cannot be done by right. For the unjust inventions
of men are neither to be considered nor spoken of as rights; for even
they themselves say that right is that which flows from the fountain
of justice, and deny the definition which is commonly given by
those who misconceive the matter, that right is that which is useful
to the stronger party. Thus, where there is not true justice there can
be no assemblage of men associated by a common acknowledgment
of right, and therefore there can be no people, as defined by Scipio
or Cicero; and if no people, then no weal of the people, but only
of some promiscuous multitude unworthy of the name of people.
Consequently, if the republic is the weal of the people, and there
is no people if it be not associated by a common acknowledgment
of right, and if there is no right where there is no justice, then most
certainly it follows that there is no republic where there is no justice.
Further, justice is that virtue which gives every one his due. Where,
then, is the justice of man, when he deserts the true God and yields
himself to impure demons? Is this to give every one his due? Or is
he who keeps back a piece of ground from the purchaser, and gives
it to a man who has no right to it, unjust, while he who keeps back
[37] Ch. 21.

himself from the God who made him, and serves wicked spirits, is just?

This same book, *De Republica,* advocates the cause of justice against injustice with great force and keenness. The pleading for injustice against justice was first heard, and it was asserted that without injustice a republic could neither increase nor even subsist, for it was laid down as an absolutely unassailable position that it is unjust for some men to rule and some to serve; and yet the imperial city to which the republic belongs cannot rule her provinces without having recourse to this injustice. It was replied in behalf of justice, that this ruling of the provinces is just, because servitude may be advantageous to the provincials, and is so when rightly administered—that is to say, when lawless men are prevented from doing harm. And further, as they became worse and worse so long as they were free, they will improve by subjection. To confirm this reasoning, there is added an eminent example drawn from nature: for "why," it is asked, "does God rule man, the soul the body, the reason the passions and other vicious parts of the soul?" This example leaves no doubt that, to some, servitude is useful; and, indeed, to serve God is useful to all. And it is when the soul serves God that it exercises a right control over the body; and in the soul itself the reason must be subject to God if it is to govern as it ought the passions and other vices. Hence, when a man does not serve God, what justice can we ascribe to him, since in this case his soul cannot exercise a just control over the body, nor his reason over his vices? And if there is no justice in such an individual, certainly there can be none in a community composed of such persons. Here, therefore, there is not that common acknowledgment of right which makes an assemblage of men a people whose affairs we call a republic. And why need I speak of the advantageousness, the common participation in which, according to the definition, makes a people? For although, if you choose to regard the matter attentively, you will see that there is nothing advantageous to those who live godlessly, as every one lives who does not serve God but demons, whose wickedness you may measure by their desire to receive the worship of men though they are most impure spirits, yet what I have said of the common acknowledgment of right is enough to demonstrate that, according to the above definition, there can be no people, and

therefore no republic, where there is no justice. For if they assert
that in their republic the Romans did not serve unclean spirits, but
good and holy gods, must we therefore again reply to this evasion,
though already we have said enough, and more than enough, to
expose it? He must be an uncommonly stupid, or a shamelessly
contentious person, who has read through the foregoing books to
this point, and can yet question whether the Romans served wicked
and impure demons. But, not to speak of their character, it is written in the law of the true God, *He that sacrificeth unto any god
save unto the Lord only, he shall be utterly destroyed.*[38] He, therefore, who uttered so menacing a commandment decreed that no
worship should be given either to good or bad gods.

CHAPTER XXII

*Whether the God whom the Christians serve is the true God to
whom alone sacrifice ought to be paid.*

BUT IT MAY BE replied, Who is this God, or what proof is there
that He alone is worthy to receive sacrifice from the Romans? One
must be very blind to be still asking who this God is. He is the God
whose prophets predicted the things we see accomplished. He is
the God from whom Abraham received the assurance, *In thy seed
shall all nations be blessed.*[39] That this was fulfilled in Christ,
who according to the flesh sprang from that seed, is recognized,
whether they will or no, even by those who have continued to be
the enemies of this name. He is the God whose divine Spirit spake
by the men whose predictions I cited in the preceding books, and
which are fulfilled in the Church which has extended over all the
world. This is the God whom Varro, the most learned of the Romans, supposed to be Jupiter, though he knows not what he says;
yet I think it right to note the circumstance that a man of such
learning was unable to suppose that this God had no existence or
was contemptible, but believed Him to be the same as the supreme
God. In fine, He is the God whom Porphyry, the most learned of
the philosophers, though the bitterest enemy of the Christians, confesses to be a great God, even according to the oracles of those
whom he esteems gods.

[38] *Exod.* xxii. 20.   [39] *Gen.* xxii. 18.

Porphyry's account of the responses given by the oracles of the Gods concerning Christ.

FOR in his book called ἐκ λογίων φιλοσοφίας, in which he collects and comments upon the responses which he pretends were uttered by the gods concerning divine things, he says—I give his own words as they have been translated from the Greek: "To one who inquired what god he should propitiate in order to recall his wife from Christianity, Apollo replied in the following verses." Then the following words are given as those of Apollo: "You will probably find it easier to write lasting characters on the water, or lightly fly like a bird through the air, than to restore right feeling in your impious wife once she has polluted herself. Let her remain as she pleases in her foolish deception, and sing false laments to her dead God, who was condemned by right-minded judges, and perished ignominiously by a violent death." Then after these verses of Apollo (which we have given in a Latin version that does not preserve the metrical form), he goes on to say: "In these verses Apollo exposed the incurable corruption of the Christians, saying that the Jews, rather than the Christians, recognized God." See how he misrepresents Christ, giving the Jews the preference to the Christians in the recognition of God. This was his explanation of Apollo's verses, in which he says that Christ was put to death by right-minded or just judges—in other words, that He deserved to die. I leave the responsibility of this oracle regarding Christ on the lying interpreter of Apollo, or on this philosopher who believed it or possibly himself invented it; as to its agreement with Porphyry's opinions or with other oracles, we shall in a little have something to say. In this passage, however, he says that the Jews, as the interpreters of God, judged justly in pronouncing Christ to be worthy of the most shameful death. He should have listened, then, to this God of the Jews to whom he bears this testimony, when that God says, *He that sacrificeth to any other god save to the Lord alone shall be utterly destroyed.* But let us come to still plainer expressions, and hear how great a God Porphyry thinks the God of the Jews is. Apollo, he says, when asked whether word, *i.e.,* reason, or law is the better

thing, replied in the following verses. Then he gives the verses of
Apollo, from which I select the following as sufficient: "God, the
Generator, and the King prior to all things, before whom heaven
and earth, and the sea, and the hidden places of hell tremble, and
the deities themselves are afraid, for their law is the Father whom
the holy Hebrews honour." In this oracle of his god Apollo, Porphyry avowed that the God of the Hebrews is so great that the
deities themselves are afraid before Him. I am surprised, therefore,
that when God said, He that sacrificeth to other gods shall be utterly
destroyed, Porphyry himself was not afraid lest he should be destroyed for sacrificing to other gods.

This philosopher, however, has also some good to say of Christ,
oblivious, as it were, of that contumely of his of which we have just
been speaking; or as if his gods spoke evil of Christ only while
asleep, and recognized Him to be good, and gave Him His deserved
praise, when they awoke. For, as if he were about to proclaim some
marvellous thing passing belief, he says, "What we are going to
say will certainly take some by surprise. For the gods have declared
that Christ was very pious, and has become immortal, and that they
cherish his memory: that the Christians, however, are polluted, contaminated, and involved in error. And many other such things," he
says, "do the gods say against the Christians." Then he gives speci-
mens of the accusations made, as he says, by the gods against them,
and then goes on: "But to some who asked Hecate whether Christ
were a God, she replied, You know the condition of the disembodied immortal soul, and that if it has been severed from wisdom
it always errs. The soul you refer to is that of a man foremost in
piety: they worship it because they mistake the truth." To this so-
called oracular response he adds the following words of his own:
"Of this very pious man, then, Hecate said that the soul, like the
souls of other good men, was after death dowered with immortality,
and that the Christians through ignorance worship it. And to those
who ask why he was condemned to die, the oracle of the goddess
replied, The body, indeed, is always exposed to torments, but the
souls of the pious abide in heaven. And the soul you inquire about
has been the fatal cause of error to other souls which were not fated
to receive the gifts of the gods, and to have the knowledge of immortal Jove. Such souls are therefore hated by the gods; for they

who were fated not to receive the gifts of the gods, and not to know God, were fated to be involved in error by means of him you speak of. He himself, however, was good, and heaven has been opened to him as to other good men. You are not, then, to speak evil of him, but to pity the folly of men: and through him men's danger is imminent."

Who is so foolish as not to see that these oracles were either composed by a clever man with a strong animus against the Christians, or were uttered as responses by impure demons with a similar design—that is to say, in order that their praise of Christ may win credence for their vituperation of Christians; and that thus they may, if possible, close the way of eternal salvation, which is identical with Christianity? For they believe that they are by no means counterworking their own hurtful craft by promoting belief in Christ, so long as their calumniation of Christians is also accepted; for they thus secure that even the man who thinks well of Christ declines to become a Christian, and is therefore not delivered from their own rule by the Christ he praises. Besides, their praise of Christ is so contrived that whosoever believes in Him as thus represented will not be a true Christian but a Photinian heretic, recognizing only the humanity, and not also the divinity of Christ, and will thus be precluded from salvation and from deliverance out of the meshes of these devilish lies. For our part, we are no better pleased with Hecate's praises of Christ than with Apollo's calumniation of Him. Apollo says that Christ was put to death by right-minded judges, implying that He was unrighteous. Hecate says that He was a most pious man, but no more. The intention of both is the same, to prevent men from becoming Christians, because if this be secured, men shall never be rescued from their power. But it is incumbent on our philosopher, or rather on those who believe in these pretended oracles against the Christians, first of all, if they can, to bring Apollo and Hecate to the same mind regarding Christ, so that either both may condemn or both praise Him. And even if they succeeded in this, we for our part would notwithstanding repudiate the testimony of demons, whether favorable or adverse to Christ. But when our adversaries find a god and goddess of their own at variance about Christ, the one praising, the other vituperating

Him, they can certainly give no credence, if they have any judgment, to mere men who blaspheme the Christians.

When Porphyry or Hecate praises Christ, and adds that He gave Himself to the Christians as a fatal gift, that they might be involved in error, he exposes, as he thinks, the causes of this error. But before I cite his words to that purpose, I would ask, If Christ did thus give Himself to the Christians to involve them in error, did He do so willingly, or against His will? If willingly, how is He righteous? If against His will, how is He blessed? However, let us hear the causes of this error. "There are," he says, "in a certain place very small earthly spirits, subject to the power of evil demons. The wise men of the Hebrews, among whom was this Jesus, as you have heard from the oracles of Apollo cited above, turned religious persons from these very wicked demons and minor spirits, and taught them rather to worship the celestial gods, and especially to adore God the Father. This," he said, "the gods enjoin; and we have already shown how they admonish the soul to turn to God, and command it to worship Him. But the ignorant and the ungodly, who are not destined to receive favours from the gods, nor to know the immortal Jupiter, not listening to the gods and their messages, have turned away from all gods, and have not only refused to hate, but have venerated the prohibited demons. Professing to worship God, they refuse to do those things by which alone God is worshipped. For God, indeed, being the Father of all, is in need of nothing; but for us it is good to adore Him by means of justice, chastity, and other virtues, and thus to make life itself a prayer to Him, by inquiring into and imitating His nature. For inquiry," says he, "purifies and imitation deifies us, by moving us nearer to Him." He is right in so far as he proclaims God the Father, and the conduct by which we should worship Him. Of such precepts the prophetic books of the Hebrews are full, when they praise or blame the life of the saints. But in speaking of the Christians he is in error, and calumniates them as much as is desired by the demons whom he takes for gods, as if it were difficult for any man to recollect the disgraceful and shameful actions which used to be done in the theatres and temples to please the gods, and to compare with these things what is heard in our churches, and what is offered to the true God, and from this comparison to conclude where character is edified, and where it is ruined. But who but a diabolical spirit has told or suggested to this man so manifest and vain a lie, as that the Christians reverenced rather than hated the demons, whose worship the Hebrews prohibited? But that God, whom the Hebrew sages worshipped, forbids sacrifice to be offered even to the holy angels of heaven and divine powers, whom we, in this our pilgrimage, venerate and love as our most blessed fellow-citizens. For in the law which God gave to His Hebrew people He utters this menace, as in a voice of thunder: *He that sacrificeth unto any god, save unto the Lord only, he shall be utterly destroyed.*[40] And that no one might suppose that this prohibition extends only to the very wicked demons and earthly spirits, whom this philosopher calls very small and inferior——for even these are in the Scripture called gods, not of the Hebrews, but of the nations, as the Septuagint translators have shown in the psalm where it is said, *For all the gods of the nations are demons,*[41]——that no one might suppose, I say, that sacrifice to these demons was prohibited, but that sacrifice might be offered to all or some of the celestials, it was immediately added, "save unto the Lord alone," that is, only to the Lord, lest by chance in the phrase *Domino solo* some one may believe that the Lord is the Sun, to whom he thinks sacrifice should be made. That it is not to be thus understood is easily discoverable in the Greek version. The God of the Hebrews, then, to whom this renowned philosopher bears this signal testimony, gave to His Hebrew people a law, composed in the Hebrew language, and not obscure and unknown, but published now in every nation, and in this law it is written, *He that sacrificeth unto any god, save unto the Lord only, he shall be utterly destroyed.* What need is there to seek further proofs in the law or the prophets of this same thing? *Seek,* we need not say, for the passages are neither few nor difficult to find; but what need to collect and apply to my argument the proofs which are thickly sown and obvious, and by which it appears clear as day that sacrifice may be paid to none but the supreme and true God? Here is one brief but decided, even menacing, and certainly true utterance of that God whom the wisest of our adversaries so highly extol. Let this be listened to, feared, fulfilled, that there may be no disobedient soul cut off. *He that sacrifices,* He

[40] *Exod.* xxii. 20.   [41] *Ps.* xcvi. 5.

says, not because He needs anything, but because it behooves us to be His possession. Hence the Psalmist in the Hebrew Scriptures sings, *I have said to the Lord, Thou art my God, for Thou needest not my good.*[42] For we ourselves, who are His own city, are His most noble and worthy sacrifice, and it is this mystery we celebrate in our sacrifices, which are well known to the faithful, as we have explained in the preceding books. For through the prophets the oracles of God declared that the sacrifices which the Jews offered as a shadow of that which was to be would cease, and that the nations, from the rising to the setting of the sun, would offer one sacrifice. From these oracles, which we now see accomplished, we have made such selections as seemed suitable to our purpose in this work. And therefore, where there is not this righteousness whereby the one supreme God rules the obedient city according to His grace, so that it sacrifices to none but Him, and whereby, in all the citizens of this obedient city, the soul consequently rules the body and reason the vices in the rightful order, so that, as the individual just man, so also the community and people of the just, live by faith, which works by love, that love whereby man loves God as He ought to be loved, and his neighbour as himself—there, I say, there is not an assemblage associated by a common acknowledgment of right, and by a community of interests. But if there is not this, there is not a people, if our definition be true, and therefore there is no republic; for where there is no people there can be no republic.

CHAPTER XXIV

The definition which must be given of a people and a republic, in order to vindicate the assumption of these titles by the Romans and by other kingdoms.

BUT IF WE DISCARD this definition of a people, and, assuming another, say that a people is an assemblage of reasonable beings bound together by a common agreement as to the objects of their love, then, in order to discover the character of any people, we have only to observe what it loves. Yet whatever it loves, if only it is an assemblage of reasonable beings and not of beasts, and is bound

[42] *Ps.* xvi. 2.

together by an agreement as to the objects of love, it is reasonably called a people; and it will be a superior people in proportion as it is bound together by higher interests, inferior in proportion as it is bound together by lower. According to this definition of ours, the Roman people is a people, and its weal is without doubt a commonwealth or republic. But what its tastes were in its early and subsequent days, and how it declined into sanguinary seditions and then to social and civil wars, and so burst asunder or rotted off the bond of concord in which the health of a people consists, history shows, and in the preceding books I have related at large. And yet I would not on this account say either that it was not a people, or that its administration was not a republic, so long as there remains an assemblage of reasonable beings bound together by a common agreement as to the objects of love. But what I say of this people and of this republic I must be understood to think and say of the Athenians or any Greek state, of the Egyptians, of the early Assyrian Babylon, and of every other nation, great or small, which had a public government. For, in general, the city of the ungodly, which did not obey the command of God that it should offer no sacrifice save to Him alone, and which, therefore, could not give to the soul its proper command over the body, nor to the reason its just authority over the vices, is void of true justice.

CHAPTER XXV

That where there is no true religion there are no true virtues.

FOR though the soul may seem to rule the body admirably, and the reason the vices, if the soul and reason do not themselves obey God, as God has commanded them to serve Him, they have no proper authority over the body and the vices. For what kind of mistress of the body and the vices can that mind be which is ignorant of the true God, and which, instead of being subject to His authority, is prostituted to the corrupting influences of the most vicious demons? It is for this reason that the virtues which it seems to itself to possess, and by which it restrains the body and the vices that it may obtain and keep what it desires, are rather vices than virtues so long as there is no reference to God in the matter.

For although some suppose that virtues which have a reference only to themselves, and are desired only on their own account, are yet true and genuine virtues, the fact is that even then they are inflated with pride, and are therefore to be reckoned vices rather than virtues. For as that which gives life to the flesh is not derived from flesh, but is above it, so that which gives blessed life to man is not derived from man, but is something above him; and what I say of man is true of every celestial power and virtue whatsoever.

CHAPTER XXVI

Of the peace which is enjoyed by the people that are alienated from God, and the use made of it by the people of God in the time of its pilgrimage.

WHEREFORE, as the life of the flesh is the soul, so the blessed life of man is God, of whom the sacred writings of the Hebrews say, *Blessed is the people whose God is the Lord.*[43] Miserable, therefore, is the people which is alienated from God. Yet even this people has a peace of its own which is not to be lightly esteemed, though, indeed, it shall not in the end enjoy it, because it makes no good use of it before the end. But it is our interest that it enjoy this peace meanwhile in this life; for as long as the two cities are commingled, we also enjoy the peace of Babylon. For from Babylon the people of God is so freed that it meanwhile sojourns in its company. And therefore the Apostle also admonished the Church to pray for kings and those in authority, assigning as the reason, *that we may live a quiet and tranquil life in all godliness and love.*[44] And the prophet Jeremiah, when predicting the captivity that was to befall the ancient people of God, and giving them the divine command to go obediently to Babylonia, and thus serve their God, counselled them also to pray for Babylonia, saying, *In the peace thereof shall ye have peace,*[45]—the temporal peace which the good and the wicked together enjoy.

[43] *Ps.* cxliii. 15.   [44] *I Tim.* ii. 2.   [45] *Jer.* xxix. 7.

CHAPTER XXVII

*That the peace of those who serve God cannot in this mortal life be
apprehended in its perfection.*

BUT THE PEACE which is peculiar to ourselves we enjoy now with
God by faith, and shall hereafter enjoy eternally with Him by sight.
But the peace which we enjoy in this life, whether common to all
or peculiar to ourselves, is rather the solace of our misery than the
positive enjoyment of felicity. Our very righteousness, too, though
true in so far as it has respect to the true good, is yet in this life
of such a kind that it consists rather in the remission of sins than
in the perfecting of virtues. Witness the prayer of the whole city
of God in its pilgrim state, for it cries to God by the mouth of all
its members, *Forgive us our debts as we forgive our debtors.*[46]
And this prayer is efficacious not for those whose faith is without
works and is dead,[47] but for those whose faith worketh by love.[48]
For as reason, though subjected to God, is yet pressed down by the
corruptible body,[49] so long as it is in this mortal condition, it
has not perfect authority over vice, and therefore this prayer is
needed by the righteous. For though it exercises authority, the vices
do not submit without a struggle. For however well one maintains the conflict, and however thoroughly he has subdued these
enemies, there steals in some evil thing, which, if it do not find
ready expression in act, slips out by the lips, or insinuates itself
into the thought; and therefore his peace is not full so long as
he is at war with his vices. For it is a perilous conflict he wages
with those that resist, and his victory over those that are defeated is
not secure, but full of anxiety and effort. Amidst these temptations,
therefore, of all which it has been summarily said in the divine
oracles, *is not human life upon earth a temptation?*[50] who but
a proud man can presume that he so lives that he has no need to
say to God, *Forgive us our debts?* And such a man is not great,
but swollen and puffed up with vanity, and is justly resisted by
Him who abundantly gives grace to the humble. Whence it is
said, *God resisteth the proud, but giveth grace to the humble.*[51]
In this, then, consists the righteousness of a man, that he submit

[46] *Matt.* vi. 12.   [47] *Jas.* ii. 17.   [48] *Gal.* v. 6.   [49] *Wis.* ix. 15.
[50] *Job* vii. 1.   [51] *Jas.* iv. 6; *I Pet.* v. 5.

himself to God, his body to his soul, and his vices, even when they rebel, to his reason, which either defeats or at least resists them; and also that he beg from God the grace of merit, and the pardon of his sins, and that he render to God thanks for all the blessings he receives. But, in that final peace to which all our righteousness has reference, and for the sake of which it is maintained, as our nature shall enjoy a sound immortality and incorruption, and shall have no more vices, and as we shall experience no resistance either from ourselves or from others, it will not be necessary that reason should rule vices which no longer exist, but God shall rule the man, and the soul shall rule the body, with a sweetness and facility suitable to the felicity of a life which is done with bondage. And this condition shall there be eternal, and we shall be assured of its eternity; and thus the peace of this blessedness and the blessedness of this peace shall be the supreme good.

CHAPTER XXVIII
The end of the wicked.

BUT, on the other hand, they who do not belong to this city of God shall inherit eternal misery, which is also called the second death, because the soul shall then be separated from God its life, and therefore cannot be said to live, and the body shall be subjected to eternal pains. And consequently this second death shall be the more severe, because no death shall terminate it. But war being contrary to peace, as misery to happiness, and life to death, it is not without reason asked what kind of war can be found in the end of the wicked answering to the peace which is declared to be the end of the righteous? The person who puts this question has only to observe what it is in war that is hurtful and destructive, and he shall see that it is nothing else than the mutual opposition and conflict of things. And can he conceive a more grievous and bitter war than that in which the will is so opposed to passion, and passion to the will, that their hostility can never be terminated by the victory of either, and in which the violence of pain so conflicts with the nature of the body, that neither yields to the other? For in this life, when this conflict has arisen, either pain conquers and death expels the feeling of it, or nature conquers and health expels the pain. But in the world to come the pain continues that it may torment, and the nature endures that it may be sensible of it; and neither ceases to exist, lest punishment also should cease. Now, as it is through the last judgment that men pass to these ends, the good to the supreme good, the evil to the supreme evil, I will treat of this judgment in the following book.

BOETHIUS

THE CONSOLATION *of* PHILOSOPHY

Good men are always powerful, and evil men
of no strength.

BOETHIUS (?480-524/6) was born of the old and illustrious
Anician family, and served as consul under Theodoric in 510.
On the occasion of defending another senator against a trumped-up
charge of treason, Boethius suffered the same fate: he was imprisoned, tortured and put to death. A Christian, a man of great
sincerity and probity, Boethius cherished a grandiose ideal. He
wished to translate Plato and Aristotle into Latin and to reconcile
their philosophies. Whether this ambitious dream was no more
than an illusion is still an earnestly debated question. What is
certain is that Boethius, called the last Roman and the first
Scholastic, helped in a decisive way to enkindle and to transmit
the light of philosophical learning to the whole Middle Ages.
His translations of Porphyry and of the logical works of Aristotle,
accompanied by his commentaries and his own logical writings,
were the only philosophical tool known to Western writers for
centuries. His *Theological Tractates* gave to the mediaeval Latin
world many of its technical terms and formulas, and were the
basis of extremely important commentaries by the great theologians

of the twelfth and thirteenth centuries. The much-read *Consolation of Philosophy,* to whose popularity scores of manuscripts are a witness, was written by Boethius in prison. And what can a man in prison, facing the prospect of death, do save to face also the question which is one of the last frontiers of human life, namely, the search for beatitude? The *Consolation* is a dialogue between a miserable and exiled Boethius (his disposition improves with the discussion) and Lady Philosophy. The first question, in view of Boethius' fate, naturally is: is this world ruled by chance and fortuitously, or is it governed by a rational principle, God? While the third book of the *Consolation,* which is an impassioned defense and eulogy of true beatitude, is considered the central piece of the whole work, yet it is in books four and five that Boethius turns to his basic questions: the reconciliation of the divine providence with the existence of evil, and the demonstration of the harmony between the divine omniscience and human liberty.

+*+

THE FOURTH BOOK

I

HEN PHILOSOPHY HAD SUNG THESE VERSES WITH a soft and sweet voice, observing due dignity and gravity in her countenance and gesture, I, not having altogether forgotten my inward grief, interrupted her speech which she was about to continue, and said: "O thou who bringest us to see true light, those things which hitherto thou hast treated of have manifestly appeared both to be divine when contemplated apart, and invincible when supported by thy reason, and what thou hast uttered, though the force of grief had made me forget it of late, yet heretofore I was not altogether ignorant of it. But this is the chiefest cause of my sorrow, that since the governor of all things

is so good, there can either be any evil at all, or that it pass unpunished. Which alone I beseech thee consider, how much admiration it deserveth. But there is another greater than this; for wickedness bearing rule and sway, virtue is not only without reward, but
lieth also trodden under the wicked's feet, and is punished instead
of vice. That which things should be done in the kingdom of God,
who knoweth all things, can do all things, but will do only that
which is good, no man can sufficiently admire nor complain."

To which she answered: "It were indeed infinitely strange, and
surpassing all monsters, if, as thou conceivest, in the best-ordered
house of so great an householder the vilest vessels were made account of and the precious neglected; but it is not so. For if those
things which were a little before concluded be kept unviolated,
thou shalt by His help, of whose kingdom we speak, know that
the good are always powerful, and the evil always abject and weak,
and that vices are never without punishment, nor virtue without
reward, and that the good are always prosperous, and the evil unfortunate, and many things of that sort, which will take away all
cause of complaint, and give thee firm and solid strength. And
since by my means thou hast already seen the form of true blessedness, and known where it is placed, running over all those things
which I think necessary to rehearse, I will show thee the way which
will carry thee home. And I will also fasten wings upon thy mind,
with which she may rouse herself, that, all perturbation being
driven away, thou mayest return safely into thy country by my
direction, by my path, and with my wings.

I

"For I have swift and nimble wings which will ascend
            the lofty skies,
    With which when thy quick mind is clad, it will the
            loathéd earth despise,
    And go beyond the airy globe, and watery clouds
            behind thee leave,
    Passing the fire which scorching heat doth from the
            heavens' swift course receive,

Until it reach the starry house, and get to tread
bright Phoebus' ways,

Following the chilly sire's path,[1] companion of his
flashing rays,

And trace the circle of the stars which in the night
to us appear,

And having stayed there long enough go on beyond
the farthest sphere,

Sitting upon the highest orb partaker of the glorious
light,

Where the great King his sceptre holds, and the
world's reins doth guide aright,

And, firm in his swift chariot, doth everything in
order set.

Unto this seat when thou art brought, thy country,
which thou didst forget,

Thou then wilt challenge to thyself, saying: 'This is
the glorious land

Where I was born, and in this soil my feet for evermore shall stand.

Whence if thou pleasest to behold the earthly night
which thou hast left,

Those tyrants which the people fear will seem of
their true home bereft.' "

I I[2]

"Oh!" quoth I. "How great things dost thou promise! And I
doubt not but thou canst perform them, wherefore stay me not
now that thou hast stirred up my desires." "First then," quoth she,
"that good men are always powerful, and evil men of no strength,
thou mayest easily know, the one is proved by the other. For since
that good and evil are contraries, if it be convinced that goodness
is potent, the weakness of evil will be also manifest; and contrariwise if we discern the frailty of evil, we must needs acknowledge

[1] Cf. "frigida Saturni sese quo stella receptet," Virg. *Georg.* i. 336.
[2] The whole of this and of the following chapter is a paraphrase of Plato's *Gorgias.*

the firmness of goodness. But that our opinions may be more certainly embraced, I will take both ways, confirming my propositions, sometime from one part, sometime from another.

There be two things by which all human actions are affected, will and power, of which if either be wanting, there can nothing be performed. For if there want will, no man taketh anything in hand against his will, and if there be not power, the will is in vain. So that, if thou seest any willing to obtain that which he doth not obtain, thou canst not doubt but that he wanted power to obtain what he would." "It is manifest," quoth I, "and can by no means be denied." "And wilt thou doubt that he could, whom thou seest bring to pass what he desired?" "No." "But every man is mighty in that which he can do, and weak in that which he cannot do." "I confess it," quoth I. "Dost thou remember then," quoth she, "that it was inferred by our former discourses that all the intentions of man's will doth hasten to happiness, though their courses be divers?" "I remember," quoth I, "that that also was proved." "Dost thou also call to mind that blessedness is goodness itself, and consequently when blessedness is sought after, goodness must of course be desired?" "I call it not to mind, for I have it already fixed in my memory." "Wherefore all men both good and bad without difference of intentions endeavour to obtain goodness." "It followeth," quoth I. "But it is certain that men are made good by the obtaining of goodness." "It is so." "Wherefore good men obtain what they desire." "So it seemeth." "And if evil men did obtain the goodness they desire, they could not be evil." "It is true." "Wherefore since they both desire goodness, but the one obtaineth it and the other not, there is no doubt but that good men are powerful, and the evil weak." "Whosoever doubteth of this," quoth I, "he neither considereth the nature of things, nor the consequence of thy reasons." "Again," quoth she, "if there be two to whom the same thing is proposed according to nature, and the one of them bringeth it perfectly to pass with his natural function, but the other cannot exercise that natural function but after another manner than is agreeable to nature, and doth not perform that which he had proposed, but imitateth the other who performeth it: which of these two wilt thou judge to be more powerful?" "Though I conjecture," quoth I, "at thy meaning, yet I desire to hear it more plainly."

"Wilt thou deny," quoth she, "that the motion of walking is agreeable to the nature of men?" "No," quoth I. "And makest thou any doubt that the function of it doth naturally belong to the feet?" "There is no doubt of this neither," quoth I. "Wherefore if one that can go upon his feet doth walk, and another who hath not this natural function of his feet endeavoureth to walk by creeping upon his hands, which of these two is deservedly to be esteemed the stronger?" "Infer the rest," quoth I, "for no man doubteth but that he which can use that natural function is stronger than he which cannot." "But," quoth she, "the good seek to obtain the chiefest good, which is equally proposed to bad and good, by the natural function of virtues, but the evil endeavour to obtain the same by divers concupiscences, which are not the natural function of obtaining goodness. Thinkest thou otherwise?" "No," quoth I, "for it is manifest what followeth. For by the force of that which I have already granted, it is necessary that good men are powerful and evil men weak."

"Thou runnest before rightly," quoth she, "and it is (as physicians are wont to hope) a token of an erected and resisting nature. Wherefore, since I see thee most apt and willing to comprehend, I will therefore heap up many reasons together. For consider the great weakness of vicious men, who cannot come so far as their natural intention leadeth and almost compelleth them. And what if they were destitute of this so great and almost invincible help of the direction of nature? Ponder likewise the immense impotency of wicked men. For they are no light or trifling rewards[3] which they desire, and cannot obtain: but they fail in the very sum and top of things: neither can the poor wretches compass that which they only labour for nights and days: in which thing the forces of the good eminently appear. For as thou wouldst judge him to be most able to walk who going on foot could come as far as there were any place to go in: so must thou of force judge him most powerful who obtaineth the end of all that can be desired, beyond which there is nothing. Hence that which is opposite also followeth, that the same men are wicked and destitute of all forces. For why do they follow vices, forsaking virtues? By ignorance of that which is good? But what is more devoid of strength than blind ignorance?

[3] Cf. Virgil, *Aen.* xii. 764.

Or do they know what they should embrace, but passion driveth them headlong the contrary way? So also intemperance makes them frail, since they cannot strive against vice. Or do they wittingly and willingly forsake goodness, and decline to vices? But in this sort they leave not only to be powerful, but even to be at all. For they which leave the common end of all things which are, leave also being. Which may perhaps seem strange to some, that we should say that evil men are not at all, who are the greatest part of men: but yet it is so. For I deny not that evil men are evil, but withal I say that purely and simply they are not.

For as thou mayest call a carcase a dead man, but not simply a man, so I confess that the vicious are evil, but I absolutely cannot grant that they are. For that is which retaineth order, and keepeth nature, but that which faileth from this leaveth also to be that which is in his own nature. But thou wilt say that evil men can do many things, neither will I deny it, but this their power proceedeth not from forces but from weakness. For they can do evil, which they could not do if they could have remained in the performance of that which is good. Which possibility declareth more evidently that they can do nothing. For if, as we concluded a little before, evil is nothing, since they can only do evil, it is manifest that the wicked can do nothing." "It is most manifest." "And that thou mayest understand what the force of this power is we determined a little before that there is nothing more powerful than the Sovereign Goodness." "It is true," quoth I. "But He can not do evil." "No." "Is there any then," quoth she, "that think that men can do all things?" "No man, except he be mad, thinketh so." "But yet men can do evil." "I would to God they could not," quoth I. "Since therefore he that can only do good, can do all things, and they who can do evil, cannot do all things, it is manifest that they which can do evil are less potent. Moreover, we have proved that all power is to be accounted among those things which are to be wished for, and that all such things have reference to goodness, as to the very height of their nature. But the possibility of committing wickedness cannot have reference to goodness. Wherefore it is not to be wished for. Yet all power is to be wished for; and consequently it is manifest, possibility of evil is no power. By all which the power of the good and the undoubted infirmity of evil appeareth. And it is manifest that the sentence of Plato is true: that only wise men can do that which they desire, and that the wicked men practise indeed what they list, but cannot perform what they would. For they do what they list, thinking to obtain the good which they desire by those things which cause them delight; but they obtain it not, because shameful action cannot arrive to happiness.

I I

The kings whom we behold
In highest glory placed,
And with rich purple graced,
Compassed with soldiers bold;
Whose countenance shows fierce threats,
Who with rash fury chide,
If any strip the pride
From their vainglorious feats;
He'll see them close oppressed
Within by galling chains.
For filthy lust there reigns
And poisoneth their breast,
Wrath often them perplexeth
Raising their minds like waves,
Sorrow their power enslaves
And sliding hope them vexeth.
So many tyrants still
Dwelling in one poor heart,
Except they first depart
She cannot have her will.

I I I

Seest thou then in what mire wickedness wallows, and how clearly honesty shineth? By which it is manifest that the good are never without rewards, nor the evil without punishments. For in all things that are done that for which anything is done may deservedly seem the reward of that action, as to him that runneth a race, the crown for which he runneth is proposed as a reward. But we have showed that blessedness is the selfsame goodness for which all things are done. Wherefore this goodness is proposed as a common reward for all human actions, and this cannot be separated from those who are good. For he shall not rightly be any longer called good, who wanteth goodness; wherefore virtuous manners are not left without their due rewards. And how much so ever the evil do rage, yet the wise man's crown will not fade nor wither. For others' wickedness depriveth not virtuous minds of their proper glory. But if he should rejoice at anything which he hath from others, either he who gave it, or any other might take it away. But because every man's virtue is the cause of it, then only he shall want his reward when he leaveth to be virtuous. Lastly, since every reward is therefore desired because it is thought to be good, who can judge him to be devoid of reward, which hath goodness for his possession? But what reward hath he? The most beautiful and the greatest that can be. For remember that *corollarium* [4] which I presented thee with a little before, as with a rare and precious jewel, and infer thus: Since that goodness itself is happiness, it is manifest that all good men even by being good are made happy. But we agreed that happy men are gods. Wherefore the reward of good men, which no time can waste, no man's power diminish, no man's wickedness obscure, is to become gods. Which things being so, no wise man can any way doubt of the inseparable punishment of the evil. For since goodness and evil, punishment and reward, are opposite the one to the other, those things which we see fall out in the reward of goodness must needs be answerable in a contrary manner in the punishment of evil. Wherefore as to honest men honesty itself is a reward, so to the wicked their very wickedness is a punishment. And he that is punished doubteth not but that he is afflicted with the evil. Wherefore if they would truly consider their own estate, can they think themselves free from punishment, whom wickedness, the worst of all evils, doth not only touch but strongly infect? But weigh the punishment which accompanieth the wicked, by comparing it to the reward of the virtuous. For thou learnedst not long before that whatsoever is at all is one, and that unity is goodness, by which it followeth that whatsoever is must also be good. And in this manner, whatsoever falleth from goodness ceaseth to be, by which it followeth that evil men leave to be that

[4] Cf. above, Book IV, 1.

which they were, but the shape of men, which they still retain, showeth them to have been men: wherefore by embracing wickedness they have lost the nature of men. But since virtue alone can exalt us above men, wickedness must needs cast those under the desert of men, which it hath bereaved of that condition. Wherefore thou canst not account him a man whom thou seest transformed by vices. Is the violent extorter of other men's goods carried away with his covetous desire? Thou mayest liken him to a wolf. Is the angry and unquiet man always contending and brawling? Thou mayest compare him to a dog. Doth the treacherous fellow rejoice that he hath deceived others with his hidden frauds? Let him be accounted no better than a fox. Doth the outrageous fret and fume? Let him be thought to have a lion's mind. Is the fearful and timorous afraid without cause? Let him be esteemed like to hares and deer. Is the slow and stupid always idle? He liveth an ass's life. Doth the light and unconstant change his courses? He is nothing different from the birds. Is he drowned in filthy and unclean lusts? He is entangled in the pleasure of a stinking sow. So that he who, leaving virtue, ceaseth to be a man, since he cannot be partaker of the divine condition, is turned into a beast.

I I I

The sails which wise Ulysses bore,
And ships which in the seas long time did stray
The eastern wind drave to that shore
Where the fair Goddess Lady Circe lay,
Daughter by birth to Phoebus bright,
Who with enchanted cups and charms did stay
Her guests, deceived with their delight
And into sundry figures them did change,
Being most skilful in the might
And secret force of herbs and simples strange;
Some like to savage boars, and some
Like lions fierce, which daily use to range
Through Libya,[5] in tooth and claw become.

---

[5] Literally "Marmaric," *i.e.* properly, the region between Egypt and the great Syrtis; generally, African, cf. Lucan iii. 293.

Others are changed to the shape and guise
Of ravenous wolves, and waxing dumb
Use howling in the stead of manly cries.
Others like to the tiger rove [6]
Which in the scorched Indian desert lies.
And though the wingèd son of Jove [7]
From these bewitchèd cups' delightful taste
To keep the famous captain strove,
Yet them the greedy mariners embraced
With much desire, till turned to swine
Instead of bread they fed on oaken mast.
Ruined in voice and form, no sign
Remains to them of any human grace;
Only their minds unchanged repine
To see their bodies in such ugly case.
O feeble hand and idle art
Which, though it could the outward limbs deface,
Yet had no force to change the heart.
For all the force of men given by God's arm
Lies hidden in their inmost part.
The poisons therefore which within them swarm
More deeply pierce, and with more might,
For to the body though they do no harm,
Yet on the soul they work their spite."

I V

Then said I, "I confess and perceive that thou affirmest not without cause that the vicious, though they keep the outward shape of
men, are in their inward state of mind changed into brute beasts.
But I would have had them whose cruel and wicked heart rageth to
the harm of the good, restrained from executing their malice."
"They are restrained," quoth she, "as shall be proved in convenient
place. But yet if this liberty which they seem to have be taken away,
their punishment also is in great part released. For (which perhaps
to some may seem incredible) evil men must necessarily be more

[6] Literally, "rove tame round the house."
[7] *i.e.* Mercury who was born in Arcadia; cf. Virg. *Aen.* viii. 129-138.

unhappy when they have brought to pass their purposes than if they could not obtain what they desire. For if it be a miserable thing to desire that which is evil, it is more miserable to be able to perform it without which the miserable will could not have any effect. Wherefore since everyone of these hath their peculiar misery, they must of force be oppressed with a threefold wretchedness, whom thou seest desire, be able, and perform wickedness." "I grant it," quoth I, "but earnestly wish that they may soon be delivered from this misery, having lost the power to perform their malice." "They will lose it," quoth she, "sooner than perhaps either thou wouldst, or they themselves suppose. For in the short compass of this life there is nothing so late that any one, least of all an immortal soul, should think it long in coming; so that the great hope and highest attempts of the wicked are many times made frustrate with a sudden and unexpected end, which in truth maketh their misery to be in some measure.

For if wickedness make men miserable, the longer one is wicked, the more miserable he must needs be; and I should judge them the most unhappy men that may be, if death at least did not end their malice. For if we have concluded truly of the misery of wickedness, it is manifest that the wretchedness which is everlasting must of force be infinite." "A strange illation," quoth I, "and hard to be granted; but I see that those things which were granted before agree very well with these." "Thou thinkest aright," quoth she, "but he that findeth difficulty to yield to the conclusion must either show that something which is presupposed is false, or that the combination of the propositions makes not a necessary conclusion; otherwise, granting that which went before, he hath no reason to doubt of the inference. For this also which I will conclude now will seem no less strange, and yet followeth as necessarily out of those things which are already assumed." "What?" quoth I. "That wicked men," quoth she, "are more happy being punished than if they escaped the hands of justice. Neither do I now go about to show that which may come into every man's mind, that evil customs are corrected by chastisement, and are reduced to virtue by the terror of punishment, and that others may take example to avoid evil, but in another manner also I think vicious men that go unpunished to be more miserable, although we take no account of correction and

pay no regard to example." "And what other manner shall this be,"
quoth I, "besides these?" "Have we not granted," quoth she, "that
the good are happy, and the evil miserable?" "We have," quoth I.
"If then," quoth she, "something that is good be added to one's
misery, is he not happier than another whose misery is desolate and
solitary, without any participation of goodness?" "So it seemeth,"
quoth I. "What if there be some other evil annexed to this miserable
man who is deprived of all goodness, besides those which make
him miserable, is he not to be accounted much more unhappy than
he whose misery is lightened by partaking of goodness?" "Why
not?" quoth I. "But it is manifest that it is just that the wicked be
punished, and unjust that they should go unpunished." "Who can
deny that?" "But neither will any man deny this," quoth she, "that
whatsoever is just, is good, and contrariwise, that whatsoever is
unjust, is evil." "Certainly," I answered. "Then the wicked have
some good annexed when they are punished, to wit, the punishment
itself, which by reason of justice is good, and when they are not
punished, they have a further evil, the very impunity which thou
hast deservedly granted to be an evil because of its injustice." "I
cannot deny it." "Wherefore the vicious are far more unhappy by
escaping punishment unjustly, than by being justly punished."
"This followeth," quoth I, "out of that which hath been concluded
before.

But I pray thee, leavest thou no punishments for the souls after
the death of the body?" "And those great too," quoth she. "Some
of which I think to be executed as sharp punishments, and others
as merciful purgations.[8] But I purpose not now to treat of those.
But we have hitherto laboured that thou shouldest perceive the
power of the wicked, which to thee seemed intolerable, to be none
at all, and that thou shouldest see, that those whom thou com-
plainedst went unpunished, do never escape without punishment
for their wickedness. And that thou shouldest learn that the licence
which thou wishedst might soon end, is not long, and yet the longer
the more miserable, and most unhappy if it were everlasting. Besides, that the wicked are more wretched being permitted to escape
with unjust impunity, than being punished with just severity. Out

[8] See discussion of this passage in *Boethius, An Essay*, H. F. Stewart (1891), pp.
98 ff.

of which it followeth that they are then more grievously punished, when they are thought to go scot-free."

"When I consider thy reasons," quoth I, "I think nothing can be said more truly. But if I return to the judgments of men, who is there that will think them worthy to be believed or so much as heard?" "It is true," quoth she, "for they cannot lift up their eyes accustomed to darkness, to behold the light of manifest truth, and they are like those birds whose sight is quickened by the night, and dimmed by the day. For while they look upon, not the order of things, but their own affections, they think that licence and impunity to sin is happy. But see what the eternal law establisheth. If thou apply thy mind to the better, thou needest no judge to reward thee: thou hast joined thyself to the more excellent things. If thou declinest to that which is worse, never expect any other to punish thee: thou has put thyself in a miserable estate; as if by turns thou lookest down to the miry ground, and up to heaven, setting aside all outward causes, by the very law of sight thou seemest sometime to be in the dirt, and sometime present to the stars. But the common sort considereth not these things. What then? Shall we join ourselves to them whom we have proved to be like beasts? What if one having altogether lost his sight should likewise forget that he ever had any, and should think that he wanted nothing which belongeth to human perfection: should we likewise think them blind, that see as well as they saw before? For they will not grant that neither, which may be proved by as forcible reasons, that they are more unhappy that do injury than they which suffer it." "I would," quoth I, "hear these reasons." "Deniest thou," quoth she, "that every wicked man deserveth punishment?" "No." "And it is many ways clear that the vicious are miserable?" "It is true," quoth I. "If then," quoth she, "thou wert to examine this cause, whom wouldest thou appoint to be punished, him that did or that suffered wrong?" "I doubt not," quoth I, "but that I would satisfy him that suffered with the sorrow of him that did it." "The offerer of the injury then would seem to thee more miserable than the receiver?" "It followeth," quoth I. "Hence therefore, and for other causes grounded upon that principle that dishonesty of itself maketh men miserable, it appeareth that the injury which is offered any man is not the receiver's but the doer's misery." "But now-a-days,"

quoth she, "orators take the contrary course. For they endeavour to
draw the judges to commiseration of them who have suffered any
grievous afflictions; whereas pity is more justly due to the causers
thereof, who should be brought, not by angry, but rather by favourable and compassionate accusers to judgment, as it were sick men
to a physician, that their diseases and faults might be taken away
by punishments; by which means the defenders' labour would either
wholly cease, or if they had rather do their clients some good, they
would change their defence into accusations. And the wicked themselves, if they could behold virtue abandoned by them, through
some little rift, and perceive that they might be delivered from the
filth of sin by the affliction of punishments, obtaining virtue in exchange, they would not esteem of torments, and would refuse the
assistance of their defenders, and wholly resign themselves to their
accusers and judges. By which means it cometh to pass, that in wise
men there is no place for hatred. For who but a very fool would
hate the good? And to hate the wicked were against reason. For as
faintness is a disease of the body, so is vice a sickness of the mind.
Wherefore, since we judge those that have corporal infirmities to be
rather worthy of compassion than of hatred, much more are they to
be pitied, and not abhorred, whose minds are oppressed with wickedness, the greatest malady that may be.

I V

Why should we strive to die so many ways,
    And slay ourselves with our own hands?
    If we seek death, she ready stands,
She willing comes, her chariot never stays.
Those against whom the wild beasts arméd be,
    Against themselves with weapons rage.[9]
    Do they such wars unjustly wage,
Because their lives and manners disagree,
And so themselves with mutual weapons kill?
    Alas, but this revenge is small.
    Wouldst thou give due desert to all?
Love then the good, and pity thou the ill."

[9] Literally, "Men whom serpent, lion, tiger, bear, and boar attack with tooth, yet
attack each other with the sword."

V

I see," quoth I, "what felicity or misery is placed in the deserts of honest and dishonest men. But I consider that there is somewhat good or evil even in this popular fortune. For no wise man had rather live in banishment, poverty, and ignominy, than prosper in his own country, being rich, respected, and powerful. For in this manner is the office of wisdom performed with more credit and renown, when the governors' happiness is participated by the people about them; so chiefly because prisons, death, and other torments of legal punishments are rather due to pernicious subjects, for whom they were also ordained. Wherefore I much marvel why these things are thus turned upside down, and the punishments of wickedness oppress the good, while evil men obtain the rewards of the good. And I desire to know of thee what may seem to be the reason of so unjust confusion. For I would marvel less if I thought that all things were disordered by casual events. Now God being the Governor, my astonishment is increased. For since that He distributeth oftentimes that which is pleasant to the good, and that which is distasteful to the bad, and contrariwise adversity to the good, and prosperity to the evil, unless we find out the cause hereof, what difference may there seem to be betwixt this and accidental chances?" "It is no marvel," quoth she, "if anything be thought temerarious and confused, when we know not the order it hath. But although thou beest ignorant of the causes why things be so disposed, yet because the world hath a governor, doubt not but all things are well done.

V

Who knows not how the stars near to the poles do slide,
  And how Boötes his slow wain doth guide,
And why he sets so late, and doth so early rise,
  May wonder at the courses of the skies.
If when the moon is full her horns seem pale to sight,
  Infested with the darkness of the night,
And stars from which all grace she with her brightness took,
  Now show themselves, while she doth dimly look.

A public error straight through vulgar minds doth pass,
　　And they with many strokes beat upon brass.[10]
None wonders why the winds upon the waters blow,
　　Nor why hot Phoebus' beams dissolve the snow.
These easy are to know, the other hidden lie.
　　And therefore more our hearts they terrify.
All strange events which time to light more seldom brings,
　　And the vain people count as sudden things,
If we our clouded minds from ignorance could free,
　　No longer would by us admired be."

VI

"It is true," quoth I, "but since it is thy profession to explicate
the causes of hidden things, and to unfold the reasons which are
covered with darkness, I beseech thee vouchsafe to declare what
conclusion thou drawest from these things, for this miracle troubleth me above all others." Then she smiling a little said: "Thou
invitest me to a matter which is most hardly found out, and can
scarcely be sufficiently declared; for it is such that, one doubt being
taken away, innumerable others, like the heads of Hydra, succeed,
neither will they have any end unless a man repress them with the
most lively fire of his mind. For in this matter are wont to be handled these questions: of the simplicity of Providence; of the course
of Fate; of sudden chances; of God's knowledge and predestination,
and of free will; which how weighty they are, thou thyself discerneth. But because it is part of thy cure to know these things also,
though the time be short, yet we will endeavour to touch them
briefly. But if the sweetness of verse delight thee, thou must forbear
this pleasure for a while, until I propose unto thee some few arguments." "As it pleaseth thee," quoth I.

Then taking as it were a new beginning, she discoursed in this
manner: "The generation of all things, and all the proceedings of
mutable natures, and whatsoever is moved in any sort, take their
causes, order, and forms from the stability of the Divine mind.
This, placed in the castle of its own simplicity, hath determined

---

10 See Tylor's *Primitive Culture*, pp. 296 ff. Cf. "carmina uel caelo possunt deducere
lunam," Virg. *Ecl.* viii. 69, and Juvenal, *Sat.* vi. 440 *sq.*

manifold ways for doing things; which ways being considered in the purity of God's understanding, are named Providence, but being referred to those things which He moveth and disposeth, they are by the ancients called Fate. The diversity of which will easily appear if we weigh the force of both. For Providence is the very Divine reason itself, seated in the highest Prince, which disposeth all things. But Fate is a disposition inherent in changeable things, by which Providence connecteth all things in their due order. For Providence embraceth all things together, though diverse, though infinite; but Fate putteth every particular thing into motion being distributed by places, forms, and time; so that this unfolding of temporal order being united into the foresight of God's mind is Providence, and the same uniting, being digested and unfolded in time, is called Fate. Which although they be diverse yet the one dependeth on the other. For fatal order proceedeth from the simplicity of Providence. For as a workman conceiving the form of anything in his mind taketh his work in hand, and executeth by order of time that which he had simply and in a moment foreseen, so God by His Providence disposeth whatsoever is to be done with simplicity and stability, and by Fate effecteth by manifold ways and in the order of time those very things which He disposeth. Wherefore, whether Fate be exercised by the subordination of certain Divine spirits to Providence, or this fatal web be woven by a soul or by the service of all nature, or by the heavenly motions of the stars, by angelical virtue, or by diabolical industry, or by some or all of these, that certainly is manifest that Providence is an immovable and simple form of those things which are to be done, and Fate a movable connexion and temporal order of those things which the Divine simplicity hath disposed to be done. So that all that is under Fate is also subject to Providence, to which also Fate itself obeyeth. But some things which are placed under Providence are above the course of Fate. And they are those things which nigh to the first Divinity, being stable and fixed, exceed the order of fatal mobility. For as of orbs which turn about the same centre, the inmost draweth nigh to the simplicity of the midst, and is as it were the hinge of the rest, which are placed without it, about which they are turned, and the outmost, wheeled with a greater compass, by how much it departeth from the middle indivisibility of the centre, is so much the more extended into larger spaces, but that which is joined and coupled to that middle approacheth to simplicity, and ceaseth to spread and flow abroad, in like manner that which departeth farthest from the first mind is involved more deeply in the meshes of Fate, and everything is so much the freer from Fate, by how much it draweth nigh to the hinge of all things. And if it sticketh to the stability of the Sovereign mind, free from motion, it surpasseth also the necessity of Fate. Wherefore in what sort discourse of reason is compared to pure understanding, that which is produced to that which is, time to eternity, a circle to the centre, such is the course of movable Fate to the stable simplicity of Providence. That course moveth the heaven and stars, tempereth the elements one with another, and transformeth them by mutual changing. The same reneweth all rising and dying things by like proceeding of fruits and seeds. This comprehendeth also the actions and fortunes of men by an unloosable connexion of causes, which since it proceeds from the principles of immovable Providence, the causes also must needs be immutable. For in this manner things are best governed, if the simplicity which remaineth in the Divine mind produceth an inflexible order of causes, and this order restraineth with its own immutability things otherwise mutable, and which would have a confused course. Whereof it ensueth that though all things seem confused and disordered to you, who are not able to consider this order, notwithstanding all things are disposed by their own proper measure directing them to good. For there is nothing which is done for the love of evil, even by the wicked themselves: whom, as hath been abundantly proved, lewd error carrieth away while they are seeking after that which is good, so far is it that order proceeding from the hinge of the Sovereign Goodness should avert any from his first beginning.

But, thou wilt say, what more unjust confusion can there be than that both adversity and prosperity should happen to the good, and in like manner both desired and hateful things to the wicked? But are men so completely wise that whomsoever they judge wicked or honest must needs be so? How then are their censures contrary one to another, so that to divers the same men seem worthy of reward and punishment! But let us grant that some are able to discern the good from the evil. Can they therefore behold, as is wont to be said

of bodies, that inward complexion of souls? For he that knoweth
not the cause may marvel in like manner why some sound bodies
agree better with sweet things and other with tart; and why some
sick men are healed with gentle and some with sharper physic. But
to a physician who knoweth the manner and temper both of health
and sickness this is nothing strange. Now, what is the health of
souls but virtue? What sickness have they but vices? And who either
conserveth goodness or expelleth evils, but God the Ruler and Governor of men's minds? Who beholding from His high turret of
providence seeth what is fitting for everyone, and applieth that
which He knoweth to be most convenient. Here ariseth that strange
wonder of fatal order, to wit that He that knoweth what is best,
doth that which the ignorant admire. For to touch briefly some few
things of the divine depth, which human reason is able to attain,
he whom thou thinketh most just and most observant of equity,
seemeth otherwise in the eyes of Providence which knoweth all.
And our disciple Lucan noteth that the cause of conquerers pleased
the gods, and that of the conquered, Cato.[11] Wherefore whatsoever
thou seest done here against thy expectation is right order in the
things themselves, but a perverse confusion in thy opinion. But let
there be one so well conditioned that God and men approve and
praise him; yet perhaps he is so weak a minded man, that if he falleth into adversity, he will forsake his innocency, which was not
able to keep him in prosperity. Wherefore God's wise dispensation
spareth him that adversity might make worse, lest he should suffer
to whom difficulties are dangerous. There is another complete in
all virtues, a saint and nigh to God; Providence judgeth it a sacri-
lege to lay affliction on him, insomuch that she permitteth him not
to be troubled so much as with corporal sickness. For as one that
excelleth me saith 'the body of an holy man is builded of pure
ether.'[12] It happeneth often also that the chief command is given
to good men, that wickedness, which otherwise would overflow all,
may be kept down. She mixeth for others sour and sweet according
to the disposition of their souls; she troubles some lest they should
fall to dissolution by long prosperity, others are vexed with hardships, that they may confirm the forces of their mind with the use
and exercise of patience. Some are too much afraid of that which

11 *Pharsal.* i. 126.   12 Source unknown.

they are able to bear. Others make less account than there is cause of that which they cannot endure. All these she affrayeth with afflictions that they make trial of themselves. Many have bought the renown of this world with a glorious death. Some, overcoming all torments, have showed by their example that virtues cannot be conquered by miseries, which things how well and orderly they are done, and how much to their good upon whom they are seen to fall, there can be no doubt. For that sometime grievous, sometime pleasant things befall in like manner the wicked, proceedeth from the same causes. And as for adversity no man marvelleth because all think they deserve ill. Whose punishments do both terrify others from the like courses, and move them to amend themselves. And their prosperity is a great argument to the good, what they ought to judge of this happiness which they see oftentimes bestowed upon the wicked. In which thing also is to be considered that peradventure some have so headlong and untoward a disposition, that poverty would rather make him worse; whose disease is cured by Providence, with giving him store of money. Another, knowing his own guilty conscience, and comparing his character with his own estate, is afraid lest the loss of that should be grievous unto him, the use of which is pleasant. Wherefore he resolveth to change his customs, and whiles he feareth to lose his prosperity, he forsaketh wickedness. The increase of honour undeservedly obtained hath thrown some headlong into their deserved destruction. Others are permitted to have authority to punish others, that they may exercise the good and punish the bad. For as there is no league between virtuous and wicked men, so neither can the wicked agree among themselves. Why not? Since they disagree within themselves by reason of their vices which tear their conscience, so that they many times do that which afterwards they wish undone. From whence that highest Providence often worketh that wonderful miracle, that evil men make those which are evil good. For some, considering the injustice done them by most wicked men, inflamed with hatred of evildoers have returned to the practice of virtue, procuring to be contrary to them whom they hate. For it is only a divine strength to which even evil things are good, when, by using them in due sort, it draweth some good effect out of them. For a certain order embraceth all things, so that even that which departeth from the order appointed to it, though it falleth into another, yet that is order also, lest confused rashness should bear any sway in the kingdom of Providence. 'But it is hard for me to rehearse all this as if I were a God.' [13] For it is impossible for any man either to comprehend by his wit or to explicate in speech all the frame of God's work. Be it sufficient that we have seen thus much, that God, the author of all natures, directeth and disposeth all things to goodness, and while He endeavoureth to retain in His own likeness those things which He hath produced, He banisheth all evil from the bounds of His commonwealth, by the course of fatal necessity. So that if thou considerest the disposition of Providence, thou wilt perceive that evil, which is thought so to abound upon earth, hath no place left for it at all. But I see that long since burdened with so weighty a question, and wearied with my long discourse, thou expectest the delight of verses; wherefore take a draught, that, being refreshed, thou mayest be able to go forward.

V I

If thou would'st see
God's laws with purest mind,
Thy sight on heaven must fixéd be,
Whose settled course the stars in peace doth bind.
The sun's bright fire
Stops not his sister's team,
Nor doth the northern bear desire
Within the ocean's wave to hide her beam.
Though she behold
The other stars there couching,
Yet she uncessantly is rolled
About high heaven, the ocean never touching.
The evening light
With certain course doth show
The coming of the shady night,
And Lucifer before the day doth go.
This mutual love
Courses eternal makes,
And from the starry spheres above

All cause of war and dangerous discord takes.
This sweet consent
In equal bands doth tie
The nature of each element,
So that the moist things yield unto the dry.
The piercing cold
With flames doth friendship keep,
The trembling fire the highest place doth hold,
And the gross earth sinks down into the deep.
The flowery year
Breathes odours in the spring
The scorching summer corn doth bear,
The autumn fruit from laden trees doth bring.
The falling rain
Doth winter's moisture give.
These rules thus nourish and maintain
All creatures which we see on earth to live.
And when they die,
These bring them to their end,
While their Creator sits on high,
Whose hand the reins of the whole world doth bend.
He as their King
Rules them with lordly might.
From Him they rise, flourish, and spring,
He as their law and judge decides their right.
Those things whose course
Most swiftly glides away
His might doth often backward force,
And suddenly their wandering motion stay.
Unless His strength
Their violence should bound,
And them which else would run at length,
Should bring within the compass of a round,
That firm decree
Which now doth all adorn
Would soon destroyed and broken be,
Things being far from their beginning borne.
This powerful love

Is common unto all,
Which for desire of good do move
Back to the springs from whence they first did fall.
No worldly thing
Can a continuance have
Unless love back again it bring
Unto the cause which first the essence gave.

VII

Perceiveth thou now what followeth of all that we have hitherto
said?" "What?" quoth I. "That," quoth she, "all manner of fortune is good." "How can that be?" quoth I. "Be attentive," quoth
she, "since that all fortune, be it pleasing or unpleasing, is directed
to the reward or exercise of the good, and to the punishment and
direction of the wicked, it is manifest it is all good, since all is just
or profitable." "Thy reason is very true," quoth I, "and if I consider Providence and Fate, which thou didst explicate a little before,
thy opinion is well grounded. But if thou pleasest let us account
it among those which thou not long since supposest incredible."
"Why?" quoth she. "Because men commonly use to say and repeat
that some have ill fortune." "Shall we," quoth she, "frame our
speech to the vulgar phrase, lest we seem to have as it were forsaken the use of human conversation?" "As it pleaseth thee," quoth
I. "Dost thou not think then that that is good which is profitable?"
"Yes," quoth I. "But that fortune which either exerciseth or correcteth is profitable?" "It is true," quoth I. "It is good then?" "Why
not?" "But this is the estate of them who being either virtuous
strive with adversity, or forsaking vices betake themselves to the
way of virtue." "I cannot deny it," quoth I. "Now, what sayest
thou to that pleasing fortune which is given in reward to the good,
doth the common people account it bad?" "No, but judgeth it
exceeding good, as it is indeed." "And what of the other which,
being unpleasing, restraineth the evil with just punishment, doth
not the people think it good?" "Nay," quoth I, "they think it the
most miserable that can be." "Look then," quoth she, "how, following the people's opinion, we have concluded a very incredible
matter." "What?" quoth I. "For it followeth," quoth she, "out of

that which is granted, that all their fortune, whatsoever it be, who are either in the possession or increase or entrance of virtue, is good: and theirs, which remain in vices, the worst that may be." "This," quoth I, "is true, though none dare say so." "Wherefore," quoth she, "a wise man must be no more troubled when he is assaulted with adversity, than a valiant captain dismayed at the sound of an alarum. For difficulties are the matter by which the one must extend his glory, and the other increase his wisdom. For which cause virtue is so called, because it hath sufficient strength to overcome adversity.[14] For you, that are proficients in virtue, are not come hither to be dissolute with dainties or to languish in pleasures. You skirmish fiercely with any fortune, lest either affliction oppress you or prosperity corrupt you. Stay yourselves strongly in the mean! For whatsoever cometh either short, or goeth beyond, may well contemn felicity, but will never obtain any reward of labour. For it is placed in your power to frame to yourselves what fortune you please. For all that seemeth unsavoury either exerciseth or correcteth or punisheth."

V I I

Revengeful Atreus' son did ten whole years employ
In wars, till he his brother's loss repaid with ransacked Troy.
    He setting forth the fleet of Greece upon the seas,
And knowing well that only blood the angry winds would please,
    Forgot a father's part, and with his cruel knife
Unto the gods did sacrifice his dearest daughter's life.
    Ulysses wailed the loss of his most faithful men,
Whom Polyphemus did devour enclosèd in his den
    But when his hands by sleight had made the Cyclops blind,
Most pleasant joy instead of former tears possessed his mind.
    Hercules famous is for his laborious toil,
Who tamed the Centaurs and did take the dreadful lion's spoil.
    He the Stymphalian birds with piercing arrows strook,
And from the watchful dragon's care the golden apples took.[15]
    He in a threefold chain the hellish porter led,

[14] Boethius shows his independence in adopting for *uirtus* a different etymology from that given by Cicero, viz. *uir* (cf. 2 *Tuscul.* xviii.).
[15] Literally, "his left hand weighted with the golden metal."

And with their cruel master's flesh the savage horses fed.
He did th' increasing heads of poisonous Hydra burn,
And breaking Achelous' horns, did make him back return.[16]
He on the Libyan sands did proud Antaeus kill,
And with the mighty Cacus' blood Euander's wrath fulfil.
That world-uplifting back the boar's white foam did fleck.
To hold on high the sphere of heaven with never bending neck.
Of all his many toils the last was, and most hard,
And for this last and greatest toil the heaven was his reward.
You gallant men pursue this way of high renown,
Why yield you? Overcome the earth, and you the stars shall crown."

THE FIFTH BOOK

I

HAVING SAID THUS, she began to turn her speech to treat and explicate certain other questions, when I interrupted her, saying: "Thy exhortation is very good, and well-seeming thy authority. But I find it true by experience, as thou affirmedst, that the question of Providence is entangled with many other. For I desire to know whether thou thinkest chance to be anything at all, and what it is."
"I make haste," quoth she, "to perform my promise, and to show thee the way by which thou mayest return to thy country. But these other questions, though they be very profitable, yet they are somewhat from our purpose, and it is to be feared lest being wearied with digressions thou beest not able to finish thy direct journey."
"There is no fear of that," quoth I, "for it will be a great ease to me to understand those things in which I take great delight, and withal, when thy disputation is fenced in on every side with sure conviction, there can be no doubt made of anything thou shalt infer." "I will," quoth she, "do as thou wouldst me have," and withal began in this manner. "If any shall define chance to be an

[16] Lit. "The river Achelous dishonoured in his brow (by the loss of his horns) buried his shame-stricken face in his banks."

event produced by a confused motion, and without connexion of causes, I affirm that there is no such thing, and that chance is only an empty voice that hath beneath it no real signification. For what place can confusion have, since God disposeth all things in due order? For it is a true sentence that of nothing cometh nothing, which none of the ancients denied, though they held not that principle of the efficient cause, but of the material subject, laying it down as in a manner the ground of all their reasonings concerning nature. But if anything proceedeth from no causes, that will seem to have come from nothing, which if it cannot be, neither is it possible there should be any such chance as is defined a little before." "What then," quoth I, "is there nothing that can rightly be called chance or fortune? Or is there something, though unknown to the common sort, to which these names agree?" "My Aristotle," quoth she, "in his *Books of Nature* [17] declared this point briefly and very near the truth." "How?" quoth I. "When," quoth she, "anything is done for some certain cause, and some other thing happeneth for other reasons than that which was intended, this is called chance; as if one digging his ground with intention to till it, findeth an hidden treasure. This is thought to have fallen thus out by fortune, but it is not of nothing, for it hath peculiar causes whose unexpected and not foreseen concourse seemeth to have brought forth a chance. For unless the husbandman had digged up his ground, and unless the other had hidden his money in that place, the treasure had not been found. These are therefore the causes of this fortunate accident, which proceedeth from the meeting and concourse of causes, and not from the intention of the doer. For neither he that hid the gold nor he that tilled his ground had any intention that the money should be found, but, as I said, it followed and concurred that this man should dig up in the place where the other hid. Wherefore, we may define chance thus: That it is an unexpected event of concurring causes in those things which are done to some end and purpose. Now the cause why causes so concur and meet so together, is that order proceeding with inevitable connexion, which, descending from the fountain of Providence, disposeth all things in their places and times.

[17] *Phys.* ii. 4.

I

In the Achaemenian rocks, where Parthians with their darts
In their dissembled flight do wound their enemies,
Tigris from the same head doth with Euphrates rise,
And forthwith they themselves divide in several parts;
But if they join again, and them one channel bound,
Bringing together all that both their waves do bear;
The ships and trees, whose roots they from the bank do tear,
Will meet, and they their floods will mingle and confound,
Yet run this wandering course in places which are low,
And in these sliding streams a settled law remains.[18]
So fortune, though it seems to run with careless reins,
Yet hath it certain rule, and doth in order flow."

I I

"I observe it," quoth I, "and I acknowledge it to be as thou
sayest. But in this rank of coherent causes, have we any free-will,
or doth the fatal chain fasten also the motions of men's minds?"
"We have," quoth she, "for there can be no reasonable nature,
unless it be endued with free-will. For that which naturally hath
the use of reason hath also judgment by which it can discern of
everything by itself, wherefore of itself it distinguisheth betwixt
those things which are to be avoided, and those which are to be
desired. Now every one seeketh for that which he thinketh is to be
desired, and escheweth that which in his judgment is to be avoided.
Wherefore, they which have reason in themselves have freedom to
will and nill. But yet I consider not this equal in all. For the supreme and divine substances have both a perspicuous judgment and
an uncorrupted will, and an effectual power to obtain their desires.
But the minds of men must needs be more free when they conserve
themselves in the contemplation of God, and less when they come
to their bodies, and yet less when they are bound with earthly fetters. But their greatest bondage is when, giving themselves to vices,
they lose possession of their own reason. For, having cast their eyes
from the light of the sovereign truth to inferior obscurities, forth-

18 Lit. "Yet all these (apparently) random happenings are governed by the shelving
ground and the flowing course of the stream as it runs."

with they are blinded with the cloud of ignorance, molested with
hurtful affections, by yielding and consenting to which they increase
the bondage which they laid upon themselves, and are, after a certain manner, captives by their own freedom. Which notwithstanding that foresight of Providence which beholdeth all things from
eternity, foreseeth, and by predestination disposeth of everything
by their merits.

I I

Sweet Homer [19] sings the praise
Of Phoebus clear and bright,
And yet his strongest rays
Cannot with feeble light
Cast through the secret ways
Of earth and seas his sight,
Though 'all lies open to his eyes.' [20]
But He who did this world devise—
The earth's vast depths unseen
From his sight are not free,
No clouds can stand between,
He at one time doth see
What are, and what have been,
And what shall after be.
Whom, since he only vieweth all,
You rightly the true Sun may call."

I I I

Then I complained that I was now in a greater confusion and
more doubtful difficulty than before. "What is that?" quoth she,
"for I already conjecture what it is that troubleth thee." "It seemeth," quoth I, "to be altogether impossible and repugnant that God
foreseeth all things, and that there should be any free-will. For if
God beholdeth all things and cannot be deceived, that must of
necessity follow which His providence foreseeth to be to come.
Wherefore, if from eternity he doth not only foreknow the deeds

[19] Cf. *Il.* iv. 277, *Od.* xii. 323.
[20] This line renders the Greek with which Boethius begins the poem, adapting
Homer's phrase "all surveying, all o'erhearing."

of men, but also their counsels and wills, there can be no free-will; for there is not any other deed or will, but those which the divine providence, that cannot be deceived, hath foreseen. For if things can be drawn aside to any other end than was foreknown, there will not be any firm knowledge of that which is to come, but rather an uncertain opinion, which in my opinion were impious to believe of God. Neither do I allow of that reason with which some suppose that they can dissolve the difficulty of this question. For they say that nothing is therefore to come to pass because Providence did foresee it, but rather contrariwise, because it shall be, it could not be unknown to Providence, and in this manner the necessity passes over to the other side. For it is not necessary, they argue, that those things should happen which are foreseen, but it is necessary that those things should be foreseen that are to come—as though our problem were this, which of them is the cause of a thing, the fore-knowledge of the necessity of things to come, or the necessity of the foreknowledge of things to come, and we were not trying to prove that, howsoever these causes be ordered, the event of the things which are foreknown is necessary, even though the fore-knowledge seemeth not to confer necessity of being upon the things themselves. For if any man sitteth the opinion which thinketh so must needs be true, and again on the other side, if the opinion that one sitteth be true, he must needs sit. Wherefore, there is necessity in both, in the one of sitting and in the other of truth. But one sitteth not because the opinion is true, but rather this is true because one hath taken his seat. So that though the cause of truth proceedeth from one part, yet there is a common necessity in both.

And the like is to be inferred of Providence and future things. For even though they be foreseen because they shall be, yet they do not come to pass because they are foreseen, notwithstanding it is necessary that either things to come be foreseen by God, or that things foreseen do fall out, which alone is sufficient to overthrow free-will. But see how preposterous it is that the event of temporal things should be said to be the cause of the everlasting foreknowl-edge! And what else is it to think that God doth therefore foresee future things, because they are to happen, than to affirm that those things which happened long since, are the cause of that sovereign providence? Furthermore, as when I know anything to be, it must needs be; so when I know that anything shall be, it must needs be to come. And so it followeth that the event of a thing foreknown cannot be avoided. Finally, if any man thinketh otherwise than the thing is, that is not only no knowledge, but it is a deceitful opinion far from the truth of knowledge; wherefore, if anything is to be in such sort that the event of it is not certain or necessary, how can that be foreknown that it shall happen? For as knowledge is without mixture of falsity, so that which is conceived by it cannot be otherwise than it is conceived. For this is the cause why knowledge is without deceit, because everything must needs be so as the knowledge apprehendeth it to be. What then? How doth God foreknow that these uncertain things shall be? For if He judgeth that those things shall happen inevitably, which it is possible shall not happen, He is deceived, which is not only impious to think, but also to speak. But if He supposeth that they shall happen in such sort as they are, so that He knoweth that they may equally be done and not be done, what foreknowledge is this which comprehendeth no certain or stable thing? Or in what is this better than that ridiculous prophecy of Tiresias "Whatsoever I say shall either be or not be" [21] ? or in what shall the divine providence exceed human opinion, if, as men, God judgeth those things to be uncertain the event of which is doubtful? But if nothing can be uncertain to that most certain fountain of all things, the occurrence of those things is certain, which He doth certainly know shall be. Wherefore there is no freedom in human counsels and actions, which the divine mind, foreseeing all things without error or falsehood, tieth and bindeth to one event. Which once admitted, it is evident what ruin of human affairs will ensue. For in vain are rewards and punishments proposed to good and evil, which no free and voluntary motion of their minds hath deserved. And that will seem most unjust which is now judged most just, that either the wicked should be punished or the good rewarded, since their own will leadeth them to neither, but they are compelled by the certain necessity of that which is to come. By which means virtues and vices shall be nothing, but rather there will follow a mixed confusion of all deserts. And—than which there can be nothing invented more impious—since that all order of things proceedeth

[21] Hor. *Sat.* ii. 5. 59.

from Providence, and human counsels can do nothing, it followeth that our vices also shall be referred to the author of goodness. Wherefore there is no means left to hope or pray for anything, since an unflexible course connecteth all things that can be desired! Wherefore that only traffic betwixt God and men of hope and prayer shall be taken away: if indeed by the price of just humility we deserve the unestimable benefit of God's grace; for this is the only manner by which it seemeth that men may talk with God, and by the very manner of supplication be joined to that inaccessible light before they obtain anything; which if by the admitting the necessity of future things, they be thought to have no force, by what shall we be united and cleave to that Sovereign Prince of all things? Wherefore mankind must needs (as thou saidest in thy verse a little before), being separated and severed from its source, fail and fall away.

III

What cause of discord breaks the bands of love?
What God between two truths such wars doth move?
That things which severally well settled be
Yet joined in one will never friendly prove?
Or in true things can we no discord see,
Because all certainties do still agree?
But our dull soul, covered with members blind,
Knows not the secret laws which things do bind,
By the drowned light of her oppressed fire.
Why then, the hidden notes of things to find,
Doth she with such a love of truth desire?
If she knows that which she doth so require,
Why wisheth she known things to know again?
If she knows not, why strives she with blind pain?
Who after things unknown will strive to go?
Or will such ignorant pursuit maintain?
How shall she find them out? Or having so,
How shall she then their forms and natures know?
Because this soul the highest mind did view,
Must we needs say that it all nature knew?

Now she, though clouds of flesh do her debar,
Forgets not all that was her ancient due,
But in her mind some general motions are,
Though not the skill of things particular.
He that seeks truth in neither course doth fall;
Not knowing all, nor ignorant of all,
He marketh general things which he retains,
And matters seen on high doth back recall,
And things forgotten to his mind regains,
And joins them to that part which there remains."

I V

"This," quoth she, "is an ancient complaint of providence, vehemently pursued by Marcus Tullius in his *Distribution of Divina-
tion*,[22] and a thing which thou thyself hast made great and long
search after. But hitherto none of you have used sufficient diligence
and vigour in the explication thereof. The cause of which obscurity
is for that the motion of human discourse cannot attain to the
simplicity of the divine knowledge, which if by any means we
could conceive, there would not remain any doubt at all; which I
will endeavour to make manifest and plain when I have first ex-
plicated that which moveth thee. For I demand why thou thinkest
their solution unsufficient, who think that free-will is not hindered
by foreknowledge, because they suppose that foreknowledge is not
the cause of any necessity in things to come. For fetchest thou any
proof for the necessity of future things from any other principle,
but only from this, that those things which are foreknown cannot
choose but happen? Wherefore if foreknowledge imposeth no
necessity upon future events, which thou didst grant not long before, why should voluntary actions be tied to any certain success?
For example's sake, that thou mayest see what will follow, let us
suppose that there were no providence or foresight at all. Would
those things which proceed from free-will be compelled to any
necessity by this means?" "No." "Again, let us grant it to be, but
that it imposeth no necessity upon anything; no doubt the same
freedom of will will remain whole and absolute.

[22] *De diuin.* ii.

But thou wilt say, even though foreknowledge be not a necessity for things to happen, yet it is a sign that they shall necessarily come to pass. Wherefore now, even if there had been no foreknowledge, the events of future things would have been necessary. For all signs only show what is, but cause not that which they design. And consequently it must first be proved that all things fall out by necessity, that it may appear that foreknowledge is a sign of this necessity. For otherwise, if there be no necessity, neither can foreknowledge be the sign of that which is not. Besides it is manifest that every firm proof must be drawn from intrinsical and necessary causes and not from signs and other farfetched arguments. But how is it possible those things should not happen which are foreseen to be to come! As though we did believe that those things will not be which providence hath foreknown and do not rather judge that although they happen, yet by their own nature they had no necessity of being, which thou mayest easily gather hence. For we see many things with our eyes while they are in doing, as those things which the coachmen do while they drive and turn their coaches and in like manner other things. Now doth necessity compel any of these things to be done in this sort?" "No. For in vain should art labour if all things were moved by compulsion." "Wherefore, as these things are without necessity when they are in doing, so likewise they are to come without necessity before they be done. And consequently there are some things to come whose event is free from all necessity. For I suppose no man will say that those things which are done now were not to come before they were done. Wherefore these things even being foreseen come freely to effect. For as the knowledge of things present causeth no necessity in things which are in doing, so neither the foreknowledge in things to come. But thou wilt say: This is the question, whether there can be any foreknowledge of those things whose events are not necessary. For these things seem opposite, and thou thinkest that, if future things be foreseen, there followeth necessity, if there be no necessity, that they that are not foreknown, and that nothing can be perfectly known unless it be certain. But if uncertain events be foreseen as certain, it is manifest that this is the obscurity of opinion and not the truth of knowledge. For thou thinkest it to be far from the integrity of knowledge to judge otherwise than the thing is. The cause of which error is because thou thinkest that all that is known is known only by the force and nature of the things themselves, which is altogether otherwise. For all that is known is not comprehended according to the force which it hath in itself, but rather according to the faculty of them which know it. For to explicate it with a brief example: the sight and the feeling do diversely discern the same roundness of a die. The sight standing aloof beholdeth it altogether by his beams; but the feeling united and joined to the orb, being moved about the compass of it, comprehendeth the roundness by parts. Likewise sense, imagination, reason and understanding do diversely behold a man. For sense looketh upon his form as it is placed in matter or subject, the imagination discerneth it alone without matter, reason passeth beyond this also and considereth universally the species or kind which is in particulars. The eye of the understanding is higher yet. For surpassing the compass of the whole world it beholdeth with the clear eye of the mind that simple form in itself.

In which that is chiefly to be considered, that the superior force of comprehending embraceth the inferior; but the inferior can by no means attain to the superior; for the sense hath no force out of matter, neither doth the imagination conceive universal species, nor is reason capable of the simple form, but the understanding, as it were looking downward, having conceived that form, discerneth of all things which are under it, but in that sort in which it apprehendeth that form which can be known by none of the other. For it knoweth the universality of reason, and the figure of imagination, and the materiality of sense, neither using reason, nor imagination, nor senses, but as it were formally beholding all things with that one twinkling of the mind. Likewise reason, when it considereth any universality, comprehendeth both imagination and sensible things without the use of either imagination or senses. For she defineth the universality of her conceit thus: Man is a reasonable, two-footed, living creature, which being an universal knowledge, no man is ignorant that it is an imaginable and sensible thing, which she considereth by a reasonable conceiving and not by imagination or sense. Imagination also, although it began by the senses of seeing and forming figures, yet when sense is absent it beholdeth sensible things, not after a sensible, but after an imag-

inary manner of knowledge. Seest thou now how all these in knowing do rather use their own force and faculty than the force of those
things which are known? Nor undeservedly; for since all judgment
is the act of him who judgeth, it is necessary that every one should
perfect his operation by his own power and not by the force of
any other.

IV

Cloudy old prophets of the Porch [23] once taught
That sense and shape presented to the thought
　　From outward objects their impression take.
As when upon a paper smooth and plain
On which as yet no marks of ink have lain
　　We with a nimble pen do letters make.
But if our minds to nothing can apply
Their proper motions, but do patient lie
　　Subject to forms which do from bodies flow,
As a glass renders empty [24] shapes of things,
Who then can show from whence that motion springs
　　By force of which the mind all things doth know?
Or by what skill are several things espied?
And being known what power doth them divide,
　　And thus divided doth again unite,
And with a various journey oft aspires
To highest things, and oft again retires
　　To basest, nothing being out of sight,
And when she back unto herself doth move,
Doth all the falsehoods by the truth reprove?
　　This vigour needs must be an active cause,
And with more powerful forces must be deckt,
Than that which from those forms, that do reflect
　　From outward matter, all her virtue draws.

[23] The Porch, *i.e.* the Painted Porch (στοὰ ποικίλη) at Athens, the great hall
adorned with frescoes of the battle of Marathon, which served as lecture-room to
Zeno, the founder of the Stoic sect.
[24] Cf.　Quin potius noscas rerum simulacra uagari
　　　　Multa modis multis nulla ui cassaque sensu.
"But rather you are to know that idols of things wander about many in number in
many ways, of no force, powerless to excite sense."—Lucr. iv. 127, 128 (trans.
Munro).

And yet in living bodies passion's might
Doth go before, whose office is to incite,
    And the first motions in the mind to make.
As when the light unto our eyes appears,
Or some loud voice is sounded in our ears,
    Then doth the strength of the dull mind awake
Those phantasies which she retains within;
She stirreth up such notions to begin,
    Whose objects with their natures best agree,
And thus applying them to outward things,
She joins the external shapes which thence she brings
    With forms which in herself included be.

V

And if in sentient bodies, although the qualities of outward objects do move the organs of sense, and the passion of the body
goeth before the vigour of the active mind, provoking her action
to itself and exciting the inward forms which before lay quiet; if,
I say, in perceiving these corporal objects the mind taketh not her
impression from passion, but by her own force judgeth of the
passion itself, which is objected to the body; how much more do
those powers exercise the action of their mind and not only follow the outward objects in their judgment, which are free from
all affections of the body? Wherefore in this sort have diverse and
different substances knowledges of many kinds. For only sense
destitute of all other means of knowledge is in those living creatures
which are unmovable, as some shell-fish and other which stick to
stones and so are nourished; and imagination in movable beasts
who seem to have some power to covet and fly. But reason belongeth only to mankind, as understanding to things divine. So
that that knowledge is most excellent which of itself doth not only
know her own object, but also those which belong to others. What
then, if sense and imagination repugn to discourse and reason,
affirming that universality to be nothing which reason thinketh herself to see? For that cannot be universal, they argue, which is
either sensible or imaginable; wherefore either the judgment of
reason must be true and nothing at all sensible, or because they

know that many things are subject to the senses and imagination, the conceit of reason is vain, which considereth that which is sensible and singular as if it were universal. Moreover if reason should answer that she beholdeth in her universality all that which is sensible or imaginable, but they cannot aspire to the knowledge of universality, because their knowledge cannot surpass corporal figures and shapes, and that we must give more credit to the firmer and more perfect judgment about the knowledge of things, in this contention should not we, who have the power of discoursing as well as of imagination and sense, rather take reason's part? The very like happeneth when human reason doth not think that the divine understanding doth behold future things otherwise than she herself doth. For thus thou arguest: If any things seem not to have certain and necessary events, they cannot be certainly foreknown to be to come. Wherefore there is no foreknowledge of these things, and if we think that there is any, there shall be nothing which happeneth not of necessity. If, therefore, as we are endued with reason, we could likewise have the judgment proper to the divine mind, as we have judged that imagination and sense must yield to reason, so likewise we would think it most reasonable and just that human reason should submit herself to the divine mind. Wherefore let us be lifted up as much as we can to that height of the highest mind; for there reason shall see that which she cannot behold in herself. And that is, how a certain and definite foreknowledge seeth even those things which have no certain issue, and that this is no opinion, but rather the simplicity of the highest knowledge enclosed within no bounds.

V

What several figures things that live upon the earth
  do keep!
Some have their bodies stretched in length by
  which the dust they sweep
And do continual furrows make while on their
  breasts they creep.
Some lightly soaring up on high with wings the
  wind do smite

And through the longest airy space pass with an
    easy flight.
Some by their paces to imprint the ground with
    steps delight,
Which through the pleasant fields do pass or to the
    woods do go,
Whose several forms though to our eyes they do a
    difference show,
Yet by their looks cast down on earth their senses
    heavy grow.
Men only with more stately shape to higher objects
    rise,
Who with erected bodies stand and do the earth
    despise.
These figures warn (if baser thoughts blind not
    thine earthly eyes)
That thou who with an upright face dost look upon
    the sky,
Shouldst also raise thy mind aloft, lest while thou
    bearest high
Thine earthly head, thy soul opprest beneath thy
    body lie.

V I

Seeing, therefore, as hath been showed, all that is known is not
comprehended by its own nature but by the power of him which
comprehendeth it, let us see now, as much as we may, what is the
state of the divine substance that we may also know what His
knowledge is. Wherefore it is the common judgment of all that
live by reason that God is everlasting, and therefore let us consider what eternity is. For this declareth unto us both the divine
nature and knowledge. Eternity therefore is a perfect possession
altogether of an endless life, which is more manifest by the comparison of temporal things, for whatsoever liveth in time, that
being present proceedeth from times past to times to come, and
there is nothing placed in time which can embrace all the space of
its life at once. But it hath not yet attained to-morrow and hath
lost yesterday. And you live no more in this day's life than in that

movable and transitory moment. Wherefore, whatsoever suffereth the condition of time, although, as Aristotle thought of the world, it never began nor were ever to end, and its life did endure with infinite time, yet it is not such that it ought to be called everlasting. For it doth not comprehend and embrace all the space of its life together, though that life be infinite, but it hath not the future time which is yet to come. That then which comprehendeth and possesseth the whole fulness of an endless life together, to which neither any part to come is absent, nor of that which is past hath escaped, is worthy to be accounted everlasting, and this is necessary, that being no possession in itself, it may always be present to itself, and have an infinity of movable time present to it. Wherefore they are deceived who, hearing that Plato thought that this world had neither beginning of time nor should ever have any end, think that by this means the created world should be coeternal with the Creator. For it is one thing to be carried through an endless life, which Plato attributed to the world, another thing to embrace the whole presence of an endless life together, which is manifestly proper to the divine mind. Neither ought God to seem more ancient than the things created, by the quantity of time, but rather by the simplicity of His divine nature. For that infinite motion of temporal things imitateth the present state of the unmovable life, and since it cannot express nor equal it, it falleth from immobility to motion, and from the simplicity of presence, it decreaseth to an infinite quantity of future and past, and since it cannot possess together all the fulness of its life, by never leaving to be in some sort, it seemeth to emulate in part that which it cannot fully obtain and express, tying itself to this small presence of this short and swift moment, which because it carrieth a certain image of that abiding presence, whosoever hath it, seemeth to be. But because it could not stay it undertook an infinite journey of time, and so it came to pass that it continued that life by going whose plenitude it could not comprehend by staying. Wherefore, if we will give things their right names, following Plato, let us say that God is everlasting and the world perpetual. Wherefore, since every judgment comprehendeth those things which are subject unto it, according to its own nature, and God hath always an everlasting and present state, His knowledge also surpassing all motions of time, remaineth in the sim-

plicity of His presence, and comprehending the infinite spaces of
that which is past and to come, considereth all things in His simple
knowledge as though they were now in doing. So that, if thou wilt
weigh His foreknowledge with which He discerneth all things,
thou wilt more rightly esteem it to be the knowledge of a never
fading instant than a foreknowledge as of a thing to come. For
which cause it is not called praevidence or foresight, but rather
providence, because, placed far from inferior things, it overlooketh
all things, as it were, from the highest top of things. Why, therefore,
wilt thou have those things necessary which are illustrated by the
divine light, since that not even men make not those things necessary which they see? For doth thy sight impose any necessity upon
those things which thou seest present?" "No." "But the present
instant of men may well be compared to that of God in this: that
as you see some things in your temporal instant, so He beholdeth
all things in His eternal present. Wherefore this divine foreknowledge doth not change the nature and propriety of things, and it
beholdeth them such in His presence as they will after come to be,
neither doth He confound the judgment of things, and with one
sight of His mind He discerneth as well those things which shall
happen necessarily as otherwise. As you, when at one time you see
a man walking upon the earth and the sun rising in heaven, although they be both seen at once, yet you discern and judge that
the one is voluntary, and the other necessary, so likewise the divine
sight beholding all things disturbeth not the quality of things which
to Him are present, but in respect of time are yet to come. And so
this is not an opinion but rather a knowledge grounded upon truth,
when He knoweth that such a thing shall be, which likewise He is
not ignorant that it hath no necessity of being. Here if thou sayest
that cannot choose but happen which God seeth shall happen, and
that which cannot choose but happen, must be of necessity, and so
tiest me to this name of necessity, I will grant that it is a most
solid truth, but whereof scarce any but a contemplator of divinity is
capable. For I will answer that the same thing is necessary when
it is referred to the Divine knowledge; but when it is weighed in
its own nature that it seemeth altogether free and absolute. For
there be two necessities: the one simple, as that it is necessary for
all men to be mortal; the other conditional, as if thou knowest that

any man walketh, he must needs walk. For what a man knoweth cannot be otherwise than it is known. But this conditional draweth not with it that simple or absolute necessity. For this is not caused by the nature of the thing, but by the adding a condition. For no necessity maketh him to go that goeth of his own accord, although it be necessary that he goeth while he goeth. In like manner, if providence seeth anything present, that must needs be, although it hath no necessity of nature. But God beholdeth those future things, which proceed from free-will, present. These things, therefore, being referred to the divine sight are necessary by the condition of the divine knowledge, and, considered by themselves, they lose not absolute freedom of their own nature. Wherefore doubt-less all those things came to pass which God foreknoweth shall come, but some of them proceed from free-will, which though they come to pass, yet do not, by coming into being, lose, since before they came to pass, they might also not have happened. But what importeth it that they are not necessary, since that by reason of the condition of the divine knowledge they come to pass in all respects as if they were necessary? It hath the same import as those things which I proposed a little before—the sun rising and the man going. While they are in doing, they cannot choose but be in doing; yet one of them was necessarily to be before it was, and the other not. Likewise those things which God hath present, will have doubtless a being, but some of them proceed from the necessity of things, other from the power of the doers. And therefore we said not without cause that these, if they be referred to God's knowl-edge, are necessary; and if they be considered by themselves, they are free from the bonds of necessity. As whatsoever is manifest to senses, if thou referrest it to reason, is universal; if thou considerest the things themselves, it is singular or particular. But thou wilt say, 'If it is in my power to change my purpose, shall I frustrate providence if I chance to alter those things which she foreknoweth?' I answer that thou mayest indeed change thy purpose, but because the truth of providence, being present, seeth that thou canst do so, and whether thou wilt do so or no, and what thou purposest anew, thou canst not avoid the divine foreknowledge, even as thou canst not avoid the sight of an eye which is present, although thou turnest thyself to divers actions by thy free-will.

But yet thou wilt inquire whether God's knowledge shall be changed by thy disposition, so that when thou wilt now one thing, and now another, it should also seem to have divers knowledges. No. For God's sight preventeth all that is to come and recalleth and draweth it to the presence of His own knowledge; neither doth He vary, as thou imaginest, now knowing one thing and now another, but in one instant without moving preventeth and comprehendeth thy mutations. Which presence of comprehending and seeing all things, God hath not by the event of future things but by His own simplicity. By which that doubt is also resolved which thou didst put a little before, that it is an unworthy thing that our future actions should be said to cause the knowledge of God. For this force of the divine knowledge comprehending all things with a present notion appointeth to everything its measure and receiveth nothing from ensuing accidents. All which being so, the free-will of mortal men remaineth unviolated, neither are the laws unjust which propose punishments and rewards to our wills, which are free from all necessity. There remaineth also a beholder of all things which is God, who foreseeth all things, and the eternity of His vision, which is always present, concurreth with the future quality of our actions, distributing rewards to the good and punishments to the evil. Neither do we in vain put our hope in God or pray to Him; for if we do this well and as we ought, we shall not lose our labour or be without effect. Wherefore fly vices, embrace virtues, possess your minds with worthy hopes, offer up humble prayers to your highest Prince. There is, if you will not dissemble, a great necessity of doing well imposed upon you, since you live in the sight of your Judge, who beholdeth all things."

ST. ANSELM
of CANTERBURY

THE PROSLOGION

> Teach me to seek You, and reveal Yourself to me in
> my search; because neither can I seek You unless You
> teach me, nor can I find You unless You reveal Your-
> self to me.

PRIOR AND ABBOT of the Benedictine monastery of Bec in Nor-
mandy, Archbishop of Canterbury, opponent of Roscelin in
theology and of the English kings on the question of investitures,
Anselm (1033-1109) dedicated his entire life to the pursuit of
God which he had begun in the mountains of his native Aosta in
Northern Italy. He entered Bec in 1060, and was named archbishop in 1093. Delicate and sensitive in spirit, Anselm is not
an extensive writer. He has composed treatises on the existence
of God, the motives of the Incarnation, the reconciliation of the
divine foreknowledge and human liberty, truth, sin and rectitude.
The *Proslogion,* celebrated for its argument for the existence of
God, was written by Anselm at Bec in answer to the request of his
monks who found the earlier *Monologion* too complicated. The
Proslogion aims at being an example of *faith seeking understanding.* Its second chapter has been responsible for a whole library
of philosophical controversy. The controversy was begun in Anselm's own day by an aged monk named Gaunilo, and has num-

bered great thinkers among its defenders as well as among its opponents.

But the second chapter should not be separated from the rest of the *Proslogion*. Though the sons of Eve are under the cloud of original sin, and though Anselm's littleness cannot encompass the immensity of God, yet the divine light shines through upon Anselm's mind. And this is Anselm's constant wonder, as well as the central theme of his speculations. Hugh of St. Victor, who owes much to him, was destined in the next century to crystallize the Anselmian experience in the following formula: God has so related Himself to man that man can neither comprehend Him nor ignore Him. This is the Anselmian message.

INTRODUCTION

 OME TIME AGO, IN ANSWER TO THE URGENT prayers of some of my brethren, I published a short tract as a sort of example of meditating on the basis of faith. That tract was written in the person of one who sets out to investigate, by means of silent reasoning within himself, what he does not know. However, that work was woven and linked together by many arguments. That is why I began to ask myself whether it might not be possible to find a single argument, needing only itself as proof and demonstration, which would be equal to the task of showing that God truly exists, that He is the highest good, needing no other being but needful to the existence and the well-being of all other things, as well as showing whatever else we believe of the divine being. I spent a great deal of diligent thought on this problem, and at times it seemed to me that I had the solution within my grasp, while at other times what I was looking for was totally beyond the vision of my mind. Finally, in despair, I made up my mind to give up investigating a thing which it was impossible to find. And so I wanted to drive the whole affair completely from my mind in order to free it from a vain occupation

for those matters in which it might make some progress. It was then, however, in the midst of my refusal and opposition that the proof began to insert itself into my mind with a certain insistence. In any case, one day when I was particularly tired as the result of opposing its insistent demands, the proof of which I had despaired so made itself known within the turmoil of my thought, that I eagerly embraced the very notion which I had been carefully resisting.

I thought, consequently, that if I were to write the proof which I rejoiced in finding, it might give pleasure to those reading it. I have written the following tract on this matter, as well as on some other connected points, in the person of one trying to raise his mind to the contemplation of God and seeking to understand what he believes. Now it did not seem to me that this tractate or the one which I mentioned before is worthy to bear the name of book or author. At the same time, I did not think that they should be sent forth without some title by means of which to invite the readers into whose hands they fell. I therefore gave each work a title. The former was to be called "an example of meditating on the basis of faith," the latter, "faith seeking understanding". But after both works had often been copied under these titles, I was urged to sign my name to them by many persons, and especially by Hugh, the most reverend Archbishop of Lyons, Papal Legate to France, who advised me to do this in the name of the authority of his office. And that this might be done all the more fittingly, I called the former work *Monologion*, that is to say, a soliloquy, while this present work I called *Proslogion*, that is to say, an allocution.

CHAPTER I

An Arousing of the Mind to the Contemplation of God

COME now, little man! flee for awhile from your tasks, hide yourself for a little space from the turmoil of your thoughts. Come, cast aside your burdensome cares, and put aside your laborious pursuits. For a little while give your time to God, and rest in Him for a little while. Enter into the inner chamber of your mind, shut out all things save God and whatever may aid you in seeking God;

and having barred the door of your chamber, seek Him. Speak now, O my heart, O my whole heart, speak now and say to your God: *My face hath sought thee: Thy face, O Lord, will I still seek* (*Ps.* xxvi, 8).

And do You, O Lord my God, do You teach my heart where and how it shall seek You, where and how it may find You. If You are not here, Lord, where, since You are absent, shall I seek You? But if You are everywhere, why then, since You are present, do I not see You? Surely it is *light inaccessible* that You inhabit (*I Tim.* vi, 16). And yet where is inaccessible light, and how shall I approach a light that cannot be approached? Or who shall lead and direct me to it that I may see You in it? What is more, in what signs and appearances shall I seek You? I have never seen You, O Lord my God, nor have I knowledge of Your face. Most high God, what shall he do, what shall he do, this exile who is so far away from You? What shall this servant of Yours do, tormented as he is in his love of You, yet cast far away from Your face (*Ps.* i, 13)? He longs to see You, and Your face is too far away from him. He desires to approach You, and Your dwelling place is unapproachable. He desires to find You and he does not know where You are. He strives to seek You out, and he does not know Your appearance. Lord, You are my God, and You are my Lord, and I have never seen You. You have made me and You have remade me, and whatever I possess You have given to me,—and yet I have still to see You. And finally I have been made in order that I may see You, and I have still to do that for which I was made.

O how miserable is the lot of man when he has lost that for which he was made! O that Fall, how cruel and terrible it was! Alas, what man has lost and what he has found! What departed from him and what has remained! He lost the beatitude for which he was made, and he found the misery for which he was not made. There departed from him that without which there is no happiness; there remained that which by itself is wretched. *Then* man ate the bread of angels, for which he now hungers; *now* he eats the bread of sorrows which then he did not taste. Alas the common grief of men, alas the universal lament of the sons of Adam. He lived in abundance, we sigh with hunger. He lived in plenty, and we live by begging. He was a happy possessor and he became a wretched deserter; we are unhappy beggars and wretched children of desires. And alas for us, we remain empty! Why, since he could easily do it, why did he not guard for us that whose absence we should miss so much, why did he thus take away from us the light and cover us with darkness? Why, why, did he take life from us and inflict death on us? Poor wretches that we are! For consider whence we have been driven, whence and also whither! Consider from what a height we have been hurled, and to what a depth! We have been driven from our country into exile, and from the vision of God into this blindness of ours. We have been driven from the joyousness of immortality to the bitterness and the awfulness of death. Woeful change! From how great a good to how great an evil! What a grievous loss, what a grievous sorrow, what complete grief!

But alas for me, alas for this poor wretch who is one of the wretched sons of Eve far away from God! What did I set out to find, and what did I reach? Whither was I going and where did I arrive? What did I pine to possess, and amidst what possessions do I grieve now? I sought after good things, and behold trouble (*Jerem.* xiv, 19). I set out to reach God, and I stumbled into myself. I sought repose within my secret self, and I found confusion and grief in the innermost center of my being. I wanted to smile, out of the very joy of my mind, and I am compelled to cry out *with the groaning of my heart* (Ps. xxxvii, 9). I hoped for joyousness, and behold I have found a vale of sighs.

But Thou, O Lord, how long? (Ps. vi, 4). *How long, O Lord, wilt Thou forget me unto the end? How long dost Thou turn away Thy face from me?* (Ps. xii, 1). When will You think of us again and hear us? When will You illumine our eyes and show us Your face? When will You restore Yourself to us? Call us to mind again, Lord, hear us, illumine us, show us Yourself. Restore Yourself to us, that we may abound, for without You we are deep in wretchedness. Have pity upon our striving and our effort to reach you, for without You our efforts are nothing. Call us, and aid us. I beg You to do so, Lord, that my sighs may not end in despair but that my hopes may be given new life. Lord, my heart has been made bitter by its own desolation: I beg You, sweeten it by Your own consolation. Lord, I set out as a hungry man to seek You: I beseech You let me not end with my hunger for You unbroken. I came to You hungry: let me not depart unfed. I came, a poor man, to one Who is rich, a wretch to one Who is compassionate: let me not return empty and despised. And if, *before I eat, I sigh (Job* iii, 24), grant that at least after my sighs I shall eat. Lord, being bowed over, I can see only downward: raise me, that I may direct my gaze upward. *For my iniquities are gone over my head,* and they engulf me; *and as a heavy burden are become heavy upon me* (Ps. xxxvii, 5). Save me Lord, take my burden from me, and *let not the pit shut her mouth upon me* (Ps. lxviii, 16). Grant that I may receive Your light—even from a distance, even in the depths. Teach me to seek You, and reveal Yourself to me in my search; because neither can I seek You unless You teach me, nor can I find You unless You reveal Yourself to me. Let me seek You by desire, let me desire You in my search. Let me find You by love, let me love You in finding You.

I confess and give thanks Lord that You have created in me this Your image, so that I may remember You, that I may think of You, that I may love You. But Your image has been so worn away by the continued corruption of vices, it has been so clouded by the smoke of sins, that it cannot do what it was made to do, except You renew and reform it. I am not seeking, Lord, to penetrate Your heights, for I do not in any way consider my understanding equal to it; but I desire only a little understanding of the truth which my heart believes and loves. For I seek not to understand that I may believe, but I believe that I may understand. For I believe even this, that unless I believe, I shall not understand.

CHAPTER II
That there is truly a God

THEREFORE, Lord, You who give understanding to faith, grant me that I may come to understand (as much as You think best) that You exist, as we believe, and that You are what we believe You to be. Now, we believe You to be a being than which none greater can be thought.

Or is it possible that such a being does not exist, since *the fool* has said in his heart: there is no God (Ps. xiii, 1)? And yet when that very fool hears what I am saying, namely, a-being-than-which-none-greater-can-be-thought, he understands what he hears, and what he understands is in his understanding—even if he does not understand that such a being exists. For it is one thing for a being to be in the understanding, and another thing to understand that a being exists. When a painter thinks over in advance what he is going to make, this is in his understanding; but he understands that what he has not made does not yet exist. However, when he has painted it, he both has in his understanding what he has made and he also understands that it exists.

Even the fool, therefore, is made to admit that there is something in his understanding than which nothing greater can be thought. For when he hears this, he understands it, and whatever is understood is in the understanding.

But, evidently, that than which a greater cannot be thought cannot be solely in the understanding. For if it is solely in the understanding, it can be thought to be also in reality; and this is greater. If, therefore, that than which a greater cannot be thought is solely in the understanding, then that than which a greater cannot be thought is the very thing than which a greater can be thought. But this is clearly impossible.

Therefore, it is indubitably true that something than which a greater cannot be thought exists both in the understanding and in reality.

CHAPTER III

That God cannot be thought not to exist

AND THIS being exists so truly, that it cannot even be thought not to exist. Assuredly, it is possible to think of something which cannot be thought not to be; and this is greater than that which can be thought not to be. Hence the conclusion: if that than which a greater cannot be thought can be thought not to be, then that than which a greater cannot be thought is not that than which a greater cannot be thought: which is impossible. There therefore truly exists a being than which a greater cannot be thought; and this is so true, that it cannot even be thought not to be. And You are this being,

O Lord our God. So truly, therefore, do You exist, O Lord my God, that You cannot even be thought not to exist. And rightly so. For if there were a mind which could think of something better than You, then the creature would rise above the Creator and subject Him to its judgment: which is most absurd. Indeed, it is possible to think of every being, other than You, as non-existing. You alone, therefore, of all beings have existence most truly and supremely, for no other being has existence so truly—which means that all other beings have existence in a lesser way. Why, then, did the fool say in his heart, *there is no God* (Ps. xiii, 1), when it is so immediately evident to a reasoning mind that of all beings You exist supremely? Why, indeed, unless because he was an empty-headed fool?

CHAPTER IV

How it was that the Fool said in his Heart what cannot be thought

BUT how was it that the fool said in his heart something which could not be thought? And how was it that he was unable to think what he said in his heart? For, to say something in one's heart and to think are one and the same thing. But if he truly thought, indeed, because he truly thought, since he said it in his heart, and because he did not say it in his heart, since he could not think it, it follows that to say something in one's heart or to think has more than one meaning. In one way, we think of a thing when we think of the word signifying it; in a second way, we think of a thing when the very reality which the thing is is understood. It is therefore in the first sense that God can be thought not to be, while in the second sense it is impossible. For no one who understands the reality that God is can think that God does not exist, in spite of the fact that he may say these words in his heart either without any significance whatever, or with some quite extraneous significance. For God is that than which a greater cannot be thought. Now he who understands this well, understands that this very reality so exists that even in thought it cannot not exist. He, therefore, who understands that God exists in this way cannot think that God does not exist.

I thank You, good Lord, I thank You because, through Your

illumination I now so understand that which, through Your generous gift, I formerly believed, that, were I to refuse to believe that You exist, I should be unable not to understand it to be true.

CHAPTER V

That God is whatever it is better to be than not to be; and that He, alone existing through Himself, makes all other things from nothing

O LORD GOD, than whom nothing greater can be thought, what, therefore, are You? What are You save that which, highest reality of all, alone existing through itself, has made all other things from nothing? For that which is not this highest reality is lesser than what can be thought not to be. But this cannot be thought of You. What good, then, is lacking to the highest good, through which every good has its existence? You are, therefore, just, truthful, blessed, and whatever it is better to be than not to be. And clearly, it is better to be just than not to be just, to be blessed than not to be blessed.

CHAPTER VI

How God is Sensible although He is not a Body

HOWEVER, since it is better to be than not to be sensible, omnipotent, compassionate, impassible, how is it that You are sensible, if You are not a body? or how are You omnipotent, if You are not able to do all things? or how are You, at one and the same time, compassionate and impassible?

For if only bodies are sensible, since the senses are concerned with bodies and reside in a body, how is it that You are sensible when You are not a body, but rather the highest of spirits, superior to a body? But if to sense is the same thing as to know, or if it exists only for the purpose of knowing (for he who senses knows according to a way that is proper to the senses: for example, through sight he knows colors, and through taste he knows flavors), it is not unbefitting to say that that which in a way knows, in a way senses. Hence it is, Lord, though You are not a body, that You are in a true sense supremely sensible: this means, not that You have knowledge through a corporeal sense as does an animal, but that You know all things in a supreme way.

CHAPTER VII

How God is Omnipotent, although there are many Things that He cannot do

FURTHERMORE: how are You omnipotent, if You cannot do all things? You cannot be corrupted, You cannot lie, You cannot make that which is true to be false, You cannot make that which has been done not to have been done, and so forth. Hence, if You cannot do these things, how can You do all things? Or is it that to be able to do these things is not power but powerlessness? For he who can do these things is able to do what is not advantageous to him and what he should not do. And the more he can do things of this sort, the more does the power of adversity and perversity ascend over him and the more does his power wane against them. He, therefore, who can do these things can do them, not through power, but through powerlessness. For such a man is not said to be able to do something because he himself can do it, but because his powerlessness enables something else to have power against him. He may, indeed, be said to be able in an improper manner of speaking, which often happens. We sometimes use "to exist" in the place of "not to exist," "to do" in the place of "not to do" or in the place of "to do nothing." Here is a frequent example. When a man denies that something exists, we say to him, "it *is* as you say that it is"; although it would seem to be more appropriate if we were to say, "it is not, as you say that it is not." In the same way, we say, "this man is sitting down, just as that man is doing"; or, "this man is resting just as that man is doing." Yet, in fact, to sit down is a not-doing and to rest is to do nothing. In the same way, therefore, when a man is said to have the power of doing or of receiving what is not to his advantage or what he should not, powerlessness is what is understood by power. For the more a man possesses this power, the more powerful are adversity and perversity against him, and the more powerless is he against them. That is why, O Lord,

God, You are the more truly omnipotent because You can do nothing through powerlessness and nothing is powerful against You.

CHAPTER VIII

How God is Compassionate though Impassible

BUT again: how are You at once compassionate and impassible? For if You are impassible, You do not join in the suffering of others; and if You do not join in such suffering, Your heart is not sorrowful out of compassion for the wretched—and this is to be compassionate. But if You are not compassionate, whence the great consolation of those who are wretched? How, then, is it that You both are and are not compassionate, Lord? How is it, except because you are compassionate according to us, but not according to Your being. You are compassionate according to our sense, and not according to Yours. For when Your mind dwells on our wretchedness, we sense the effect of Your compassion, but You do not sense our affliction. You are, therefore, both compassionate, since You save the wretched and spare Your sinners, and not compassionate, because You are not afflicted by any share in our misery.

CHAPTER IX

How He Who is wholly Just and supremely Just spares the Wicked, and that He has Compassion for the Wicked justly

YET how is it that You spare the wicked if You are wholly just and supremely just? For how does he who is just, wholly and supremely, do something which is unjust? Or what justice is it to give eternal life to one who deserves eternal death? What enables You then, O good God, to be good to the good and to the wicked? And, what enables You to save the wicked, if this is not just and if You do not do what is not just? Or, because of the incomprehensibility of Your goodness, does this lie hidden in the inaccessible light in which You dwell (cf. *I Tim.* vi, 16)? In the most exalted and most secret recesses of Your goodness there is truly to be found the fountainhead whence flows forth the river of Your compassion.

For though You are wholly and supremely just, nevertheless You are merciful even towards the wicked because You are wholly supremely good. For You would be less good than You are if You were to be merciful to no one who is wicked. For he who is good both to the good and to the wicked is better than he who is good only to the good. And better is he who is good both by punishing and sparing the wicked than is he who is good only by punishing them. The reason, therefore, why You are compassionate is because You are wholly and supremely good. And though perhaps we might come to see why You return goodness to the good and evils to the wicked, here surely is something completely marvellous: why do You, wholly just that You are and in need of nothing, give of the goods that You possess to those who are wicked and guilty in Your sight? O the majesty of Your goodness, O God! I have a glimpse of the source of Your compassion, but only a glimpse. I perceive whence the river of that compassion flows forth, but I do not see the source whence it takes its origin. For it belongs to the fulness of Your goodness that You show mercy to sinners; and the reason for this mercy lies hidden in the majesty of Your goodness. What is more, although out of Your goodness You repay the good with goodness and the wicked with evil, yet the very nature of justice seems to demand this. But when You repay the wicked with goodness! *then* we know that He Who is supremely good willed to do this, and we marvel at why He Who is supremely just could have willed it.

O compassion, from what abundant sweetness and sweet abundance do you flow forth to us! O limitless goodness of God! with what affection are You to be loved by sinners! For the just You save since justice is with them, but You free sinners though justice condemns them. The just deserved aid, the wicked opposed it. The just You save by acknowledging the goods You have given them, the wicked you save by pardoning the wickedness that you hate. O limitless goodness which thus surpasses every intellect, grant that that compassion which comes forth from Your great abundance may come down over me! Let the compassion which flows forth from You flow to me! Spare me through Your mercy, that You may not be avenged against me through Your justice. For though it is difficult to understand how Your mercy is not separated from Your justice, yet we must believe that it in no wise is opposed to justice, for it flows forth from goodness, which is nothing without justice, indeed, which has perfect concord with justice. For if You are compassionate because You are supremely good, and if You are supremely good only because You are supremely just, truly therefore are You compassionate because You are supremely just. Help me, just and compassionate God, whose light I am seeking, help me to understand what I am saying: *Truly, therefore, are You compassionate because You are just.*

Does this mean that we know Your compassion from Your justice? Is it, then, because of Your justice that You spare the wicked? If it is thus, Lord, if it is thus, teach me how this is so. Or is it because it is just for You to be so good that You cannot be understood as being better, and for you to act so powerfully that You cannot be thought as being more powerful in operation? For what is more just than this? Certainly, what is happening would not happen if You were good only by repayment and not by sparing, and if You made good only those who were not good and not also those who were wicked. In this way, consequently, it is just that You spare the wicked and that You make good those who are wicked. Finally, what is done unjustly ought not to be done; and what ought not to be done is done unjustly. If, therefore, it is unjustly that You have compassion for the wicked, You ought not to have compassion for them; and if You ought not to have compassion for them, You do so unjustly. Hence, if to say this sort of thing is impious, it is permissible to believe that Your compassion for the wicked is just.

CHAPTER X

How God justly punishes and justly spares the Wicked

YET it is also just that You should punish the wicked. For what is more just than that those who are good should receive what is good and those who are wicked should receive evils? How, then, is it just that You should punish the wicked, and just that You should spare them? Or do You, in one way, punish the wicked justly, and, in another way, justly spare those who are wicked? For when You punish the wicked, it is just, since it befits their merits; but when You spare the wicked, it is just, not because it befits their merits, but because it is befitting (*condecens*) to Your goodness. For when You spare the wicked, You are as just, according to Yourself but not according to us, as You are compassionate, according to us but not according to Yourself. For in saving us, whom You might justly destroy, You are as compassionate as You are just. You are compassionate, not because You sense our affliction but because we sense the effect of Your compassion; and You are just, not because You return to us our due, but because You do what befits You Who are supremely good. Thus it is that, without contradiction, You punish justly and justly spare.

CHAPTER XI

How "all the ways of the Lord are mercy and truth" (Ps. xxiv, 10), *and yet how "the Lord is just in all His ways"* (Ps. cxliv, 17).

BUT is there any reason why it is not also just, in a way befitting You, Lord, that You should punish the wicked? It is certainly just that You should be so just that You cannot be thought to be more just. Now this would not at all be the case if You only returned what was good to the good and did not return evils to the wicked. For he who repays the merits of both the good and the wicked is more just than he who repays the merits of only the good. So it is just in a way befitting You, O just and merciful God, both when You punish and when You spare. Truly, therefore, *all the ways of the Lord are mercy and truth* (Ps. xxiv, 10), and yet *the Lord is just in all His ways* (Ps. cxliv, 17). And this is so without any contradiction, because those whom You wish to punish, it is not just for them to be saved, and those whom You wish to spare, it is not just for them to be damned For that alone is just which You will, and unjust that which You will not. Thus it is, then, that Your compassion is born of Your justice; for it is just that You be so good as to be good also in sparing those whom You spare. And perhaps this is why He Who is supremely just can will what is good for the wicked. But if we can somehow grasp why You can will to save the wicked, it is certainly beyond the comprehension of all reason why, among sinners of like wickedness, through Your supreme goodness You rather save these, whereas through Your supreme justice You rather damn those than these.

Truly, then, You are sensible, omnipotent, compassionate and impassible, even as You are living, wise, good, blessed, eternal, and whatever it is better to be than not to be.

CHAPTER XII

That God is the very Life by which He lives

BUT, clearly, whatever You are You are through Yourself and not through another. You are therefore the very life by which You live, the very wisdom by which You are wise, and the very goodness by which You are good both to the good and to the wicked. And the same is true of Your other attributes.

CHAPTER XIII

That God alone is Limitless and Eternal, although other Spiritual Beings are said to be Limitless and Eternal

WHATEVER is in any way enclosed by place or time is less than that which no law of place or time delimits. And since there is no being greater than You, no place or time confines You; rather, You are everywhere and always. And since this can be said only of You, You alone are limitless and eternal. Yet if this is so, how is it that other spiritual beings are also said to be limitless and eternal? Now You alone are said to be eternal because, alone of all beings You neither cease to be nor begin to be. But how are You alone limitless? Or is a created spirit limited when compared with You, but unlimited when compared with a body? Certainly, that being is absolutely limited which, once it is found somewhere wholly, it cannot at the same time be found somewhere else. Now this, as we are aware, is true only of bodies. On the other hand, that being is limitless which is, at once, wholly everywhere; and this is true only of You. Now that being is, at one and the same time, limited and limitless which, existing in some place wholly, can at the same time be wholly in some other place, though not everywhere. And this is true of created spirits. For if the soul were not wholly in the individual members of its body, it would not sense wholly in each one of them.

You, therefore, Lord, are alone both limitless and eternal. Yet it is also true that other spiritual beings are limitless and eternal.

CHAPTER XIV

How and why it is that God is both seen and not seen by those who seek Him

O MY soul have you found what you were seeking? You were seeking God, and you found Him to be a certain highest being of all, than whom a greater cannot be thought. You found that this being is life itself, light, wisdom, goodness, eternal blessedness and blessed eternity; and you found that this being exists everywhere and always. For if you have not found your God, how is it that He is what you have found, and how is it that you have understood Him with such certain truth and such true certitude? But if you have found Him, why is it that you do not sense what you have found? Why is it, Lord God, that my soul does not sense you if my soul has found You? Or has it not found Him whom it has found to be light and truth? For how could it understand this except by seeing light and truth? Or could it understand anything whatever about You except through Your light and Your truth (*Ps.* xlii, 3)? If, therefore, my soul saw light and truth, it saw You. If it did not see You, it did not see light and truth. Or is it truth and light that my soul saw, and yet did not come to see You because it saw You only to some extent, but did not see You as You are (*I John* iii, 2)?

O my Lord God, You who have formed and reformed me, answer the desire of my soul. Tell my soul what You are other than what it has seen, that it may have a pure vision of what it desires. It strains forward to see more, and it sees nothing beyond what it sees except darkness. Or rather it does not see darkness because there is no darkness in You (*I John* i, 5). But it sees that it cannot see more because of its own darkness. Why, Lord, why is this? Is the eye of my soul darkened by its weakness, or is it blinded by the brilliance of Your light? Yes it is both darkened in itself and blinded by You. In very truth it is obscured by its own smallness and it is overpowered by Your immensity. Truly it is confined by its own littleness and it is overwhelmed by Your fulness. For how great is that light from which shines forth every truth that illumines the rational mind! How ample is that truth in which is to be found everything that is true, and outside which there is to be found only the nothing and the false! And how immense is that reality which by one glance can see everything that was made and which can see by whom and through whom and how all things were made from nothing. What pureness, what simplicity, what certitude, and what brilliance there is there! Indeed it is more than any creature can understand.

CHAPTER XV

That God is greater than can be thought

THEREFORE Lord not only are You that than which a greater cannot be thought, but You are also something greater than can be thought. For since such a being can be thought to exist, if You are not this being, then something greater than You can be thought— which is impossible.

CHAPTER XVI

That this is the Inaccessible Light in which He dwells

TRULY, Lord, this is the inaccessible light in which You dwell. For there is nothing else to penetrate it in order to see You there. Rightly, therefore, do I not see it, since it is too excessive for me; and yet whatever I see, I see through it, much as an eye that is weak sees through the light of the sun whatever it sees, although it is unable to see that light in the sun itself. My intellect is not equal to the vision of that light. It shines too brightly and my intellect cannot grasp it, nor does the eye of my soul suffer for too long to direct its gaze upon it. It is blinded by its brilliance, it is overpowered by its amplitude, it is overwhelmed by its immensity, it is confounded by its greatness. O supreme and inaccessible light, O complete and blessed truth, how far are You from me who am yet so near to You! How removed are You from my sight, when I am so present to Yours! You are wholly present everywhere, and I do not see You. In You I move and have my being (*Acts* xvii, 28), and yet I cannot approach You. You are within me and around me, and yet I do not sense You.

CHAPTER XVII

That in His own Ineffable Way God possesses Harmony, Fragrance, Sweetness, Softness and Beauty

YOU continue, Lord, to hide away from my soul in Your light and in Your blessedness, and so my soul still tarries in the darkness and in its own wretchedness. For it looks for Your beauty, and does not see it. It strains its ear, and it does not hear Your harmony. It scents Your odor, and does not find it. It tastes, and does not recognize Your savor. It feels, and does not sense Your softness. For You possess these characteristics, O Lord God, in Your own ineffable way, seeing that You gave them to Your creatures in their own sensible way. But the senses of my soul, as the result of the ancient weakness of sin, have become hardened and stupefied and obstructed.

CHAPTER XVIII

That there are no Parts in God or in the Eternity which He is

ONCE more behold confusion! Once more sorrow and grief confront one who is seeking joy and gladness. For my soul hoped to reach fulfillment; and behold it is once again overwhelmed by its need. I sought after food, and behold I hunger all the more. I strove to rise to the light of God, and I fell back into my own darkness. And not only did I fall into it, but, what is more, I feel that I am enclosed within it. I fell before my mother conceived me. In truth, I was conceived in that darkness, and I was born with its covering. For we all fell in him in whom we all sinned (*Rom.* v, 12). In him we all suffered our loss who easily held and shamefully lost for himself and for us that which we do not know when we wish to seek after it. And when we seek after it we do not find it, and when we find it it is not what we are seeking. Help me, in the name of Your goodness, help me, Lord. *My face hath sought Thee: Thy face, O Lord, will I still seek. Turn not away Thy face from me* (Ps. xxvi, 8-9). Raise me from myself to You. Cleanse, heal, sharpen and illumine the eye of my mind that it may behold You. Let my soul gather its powers once more, and with its whole understanding once more strive towards You, O Lord.

What are You, Lord, what are You? What shall my heart understand You to be? You are, in truth, life and wisdom and truth and goodness and blessedness and eternity; You are every true good. Now these are many things, and my narrow understanding cannot see them all together in one glance, in order to delight in them all together. How, then, O Lord, how are You all these things? Are they parts of You? Or are You rather wholly each one of these? For that which is joined together of parts is not absolutely one; it is in a way many and other than itself, and it can be broken into its parts either actually or by the understanding. Now all this is foreign to You, than Whom nothing better can be thought. Therefore, Lord, You do not have any parts, nor are You many. But You are so one and the same with Yourself that there is nothing in which You are unlike Yourself. Indeed, You are unity itself, divisible by no intellect. Life and wisdom and the other characteristics, therefore, are not parts of You; but all of them are one, and each one of them is wholly what You are and what all the others are.

Since, therefore, there are no parts either in You or in the eternity which You are, there is no part of You or of Your eternity anywhere or at any time; but You are wholly everywhere, and Your eternity is always whole.

CHAPTER XIX

That God is not in Place or in Time, but All Things are in Him

BUT if You were and are and will be through Your eternity, and if to have been is not to be in the future, and to be is not to have been or to be in the future, how is Your eternity always whole? Or is Your eternity such that no part of it is past so as no longer to exist nor any part of it future and as yet nonexisting? Therefore You *were* not yesterday, nor *will* You be tomorrow; but yesterday and today and tomorrow You *are*. Nay, rather, neither yesterday nor today nor tomorrow are You; but You are absolutely outside all time. For yesterday and today and tomorrow are nothing other than parts of time. You, however, though nothing can be without You, yet You are not in place or in time, but all things are in You. For nothing contains You, but You contain all things.

CHAPTER XX

That God is before and beyond even All Eternal Things

YOU, therefore, fill and embrace all things. You are before and beyond all things. You are before all things because, before they came to be, You are (*Ps.* lxxxix, 2). But how are You beyond all things? For how are You beyond the things which will not have an end? Is it because these things cannot in any way be without You, while You are in no way less even if they return to nothingness? It is thus, then, that You are in a way beyond them. Are You beyond them also because they can be thought to have an end, whereas this is impossible for You? For in this way they do have an end in a certain way, whereas You do not at all have one. And, clearly, that which in no way has an end is beyond that which in a way is limited. And is this, too, the way in which You transcend even all eternal things? For Your eternity, and theirs, is wholly present to You, although they do not have that part of their eternity which is to come, just as they no longer have that part which is past. Thus, certainly, are You always beyond all things, since You are always present in Your eternity, and since that to which they have not as yet arrived is always present to You.

CHAPTER XXI

Whether this is the Saeculum Saeculi *or the* Saecula Saeculorum

Is THIS the *saeculum saeculi* (the age of the age) or *saecula saeculorum* (the ages of the ages)? For just as an age of time contains all things temporal, so Your eternity contains even the very ages of time. Now this eternity is a *saeculum* (an age) because of its indivisible unity, but it is *saecula* (ages), because of its interminable immensity. And though You are so great, O Lord, that all things are full of You and are in You, yet You are so without all interval of time, that there is neither a middle nor a half nor any part at all in You.

CHAPTER XXII

That God alone is What He is and Who He is

YOU alone, therefore, O Lord, are what You are, and You alone are Who You are. For when a thing is different in itself as a whole and in its part, and if it contains something mutable within it, it is not entirely what it is. So, too, in the case of that which rose from non-being and which can be thought not to be and which returns to non-being unless it subsists through something else; and the same applies to that which has a past that no longer exists and a future that does not yet exist:—such things do not exist properly and absolutely. But You are what You are, for whatever You are at any time or in any way, that You are wholly and always. Furthermore, You are He Who properly and absolutely You are; for neither do You have a past or a future, but only a present, nor can You be thought not to be at any time. And You are life and light and wisdom and blessedness and eternity and many such goods, and yet You are only the one and highest good. You are absolutely self-sufficient, You are in need of nothing, and You are He Whom all things need in order that they may be and have well-being.

CHAPTER XXIII

That this Good is equally the Father and the Son and the Holy Spirit; and that it is One Necessary Being, entirely and wholly and solely Good

THIS good is You, O God the Father, it is Your Word, it is Your Son. Furthermore there cannot be any other than what You are, or anything greater or lesser than You, in the Word by which You speak Yourself. For Your Word is as true as You are truthful, and therefore it is very truth itself even as You are, and not another truth than You. And You are so simple that there cannot be born of You anything other than what You are. This is the Love which is one and common to You and to Your Son, that is, the Holy Spirit, proceeding from both of You. For this same Love is not unequal to You and to Your Son, for You love Yourself and Him, and He loves You and Himself, as much as You and He are. And that which is not unequal to You and to Him is not other than You and than He; nor can there proceed from the highest simplicity that which is other than the being from which it proceeds. What each of the Persons is, this the whole Trinity is together, Father, Son and Holy Spirit. For each Person is not other than the supremely simple unity and the supremely one simplicity which can neither be multiplied nor diversified. *But one thing is necessary* (*Luke* x, 42). And this one necessary being is that in which there is every good; or rather it is entirely and uniquely and wholly and solely good.

C H A P T E R   X X I V

Of what Nature and how great is this Good? A Conjecture

COME now, arouse and raise your whole understanding, O my soul, and give as much thought as you can to what sort of good this is and how great it is. For if particular goods are enjoyable, consider with great care how enjoyable is that good which contains the joy of all goods. Consider the good which contains not such a joy as we have experienced in created things, but as different from it as the Creator differs from the creature. For if life that is created is good, how good is the life that creates? If the salvation we have received is enjoyable, how enjoyable is the salvation that is the source of all salvation? If the wisdom that is based on the knowledge of created things is lovable, how lovable is the wisdom which created all things out of nothing? And finally, if the delights that we get from enjoyable things are many and great, what and how great is the delight that is in Him Who made the things that are enjoyable?

CHAPTER XXV

The Goods that belong to those who enjoy this Good, and their Greatness

HE WHO shall enjoy this good, what will he possess, what will he not possess! Certainly he will possess whatever he wills and he will not possess whatever he does not will. For he will find there the goods of his body and of his soul, such *that eye hath not seen, nor ear heard, neither hath it entered into the heart of man* (*1 Cor.* ii, 9).

Why, then, do you wander over the whole creation, little man, seeking the goods of your soul and of your body? Love the one good in which there is every good, and that suffices. Desire the simple good which contains every good, and that is enough. For what do you love, O my flesh, and what do you desire, O soul? There, there is to be found whatever you both love, whatever you both desire.

Does beauty delight you? *Then shall the just shine as the sun* (*Matt.* xiii, 43). Does the swiftness and the strength and the agility of a body whose movement is irresistible delight you? They will be like the angels of God, for *it is sown a natural body, it shall rise a spiritual body* (*1 Cor.* xv, 44), that is to say, in power, not in nature. Do you love a long and healthful life? There will be a healthful eternity and eternal health, *for the just shall live forever* (*Wis.* v, 16) and *the health* [Douay, *salvation*] *of the just is from the Lord* (*Ps.* xxxvi, 39). Do you love abundance? There will be abundance for your hunger when the glory of God shall appear (*Ps.* xvi, 15). Do you want to drink until you have satisfied your thirst? *They shall be inebriated with the plenty of Thy house* (*Ps.* xxxv, 9).

If it is melody you love, there the choirs of angels will sing harmoniously without end in the presence of God. Do you wish some pleasure which is not impure but pure? *Thou shalt make them drink of the torrent of Thy pleasure* (*ibid.*). If you desire wisdom, the very wisdom of God will show itself to the blessed. Is it friendship? They shall love God more than they love themselves, and they shall love one another as themselves; and God shall love them more than they love themselves, for it is through Him that they love Him and themselves and one another, while He loves Himself and them through Himself. Is it peace? In heaven they shall all have but one will, for there they shall have only the will of God. Is it power? They shall be all powerful over their own wills, as God is over His. For just as God will be able to do through Himself whatever He wills, so they will be able to do through Him whatever they will; for just as they will will only what He wills, so He will will whatever they will—and His will cannot remain un-fulfilled.

Do you want preferment and wealth? God will place His *good and faithful servants over many things* (*Matt.* xxv, 21, 23). Indeed, *they shall be called the children of God* (*and Gods*) (*Matt.* v, 9), and they shall be; and where the Son of God shall be, they shall be also, *heirs indeed of God, and joint heirs with Christ* (*Rom.* viii, 17). Do you want true security? In truth, they will be as certain that these goods, or rather this good will never and in no way be lacking to them as they will be certain that they will not lose it of their own accord; just as they will be certain, too, that the God Who loves them will not take this good away from them against their wills, nor that anything more powerful than God will separate God and them against His will and theirs.

Where there is such and so great a good, what and how great must be the joy? O heart of man, heart full of needs, heart expert in suffering, indeed, engulfed by suffering, how much would you rejoice if you abounded in all these goods? Ask your most secret self if it can grasp its own joy in the possession of such a beatitude. Certainly, if someone else whom you loved as yourself were to possess the same beatitude, your joy would be doubled; for you would rejoice no less for him than for yourself. If, therefore, two or three or even many more were to possess this same beatitude, you would rejoice for each one as much as for yourself, if you loved each one as yourself. Therefore, in that perfect love of char-ity of countless blessed angels and men, in which no one will love another less than himself, each will rejoice in the same way for each other as for himself. If, therefore, the heart of man will hardly con-tain its own joy in its possession of so great a good, how will it contain so many and such great joys? And indeed, since one will rejoice over the good of another as much as each one loves another, just as in that perfect blessedness each one will love God incomparably more than himself and all others with him, so he will rejoice incomparably more over the blessedness of God than over his own and all others with him.

Now if the blessed will so love God with their whole heart, their whole mind and their whole soul that nevertheless their whole heart and mind and soul will not be equal to the dignity of this love, they will certainly so rejoice with their whole heart, their whole mind and their whole soul that their whole heart and mind and soul will not be equal to the fulness of their joy.

CHAPTER XXVI

Is this the Perfect Joy, promised by Our Lord?

O MY God and my Lord, my hope and joy of my heart, say to my soul whether this is the joy of which You say to us through Your Son: *Ask and you shall receive, that your joy may be full (Jo.* xvi, 24). For I have found a joy which is full and more than full. Indeed, when the heart and the mind and the soul and the whole of man is filled with that joy, there will still remain joy beyond measure. The whole of that joy will not therefore enter into those who rejoice; rather those who rejoice will enter wholly into that joy.

Speak, Lord, and say to Your servant within his very heart whether this is the joy into which will enter the servants of Yours who will enter *into the joy of thy Lord (Matt.* xxv, 21). Surely that joy in which Your elect shall rejoice *eye hath not seen, nor ear heard, neither hath it entered into the heart of man (I Cor.* ii, 9). Therefore, Lord, I have not yet said or thought how great shall be the joy of Your blessing. Assuredly, they shall rejoice as much as they shall love, and they shall love as much as they shall know. But how much, Lord, will they know You then, and how much will they love You? Truly, *eye hath not seen, nor ear heard, neither hath it entered into the heart of man (ibid.)* in the present life how much they will know and love You in that life.

I pray, O God, that I shall know You and love You and rejoice in You. And if I cannot do this to the full in the present life, at least may I progress from day to day until that day of fulness shall come. Let the knowledge of You progress in me now, and there become full. Let the love of You grow and there be full, so that my joy may be here great in its hope and there full in its reality.

Lord, through Your Son You command, or rather You counsel us to seek and You promise us that we shall receive, so that our joy may be full. Lord, I seek what You counsel through our wonderful Counsellor. May I receive what You promise through Your Truth, that my joy may be full. O God of truth, I seek that I may receive, so that my joy may be full. Till then, let my mind meditate on it, and let my tongue speak of it, let my heart love it, and let the words of my mouth be about it. Let my soul hunger for it, my flesh thirst for it, my whole being desire it, until I shall enter into the joy of my Lord, the Triune God, *blessed forever.* Amen (Rom. i, 25).

ST. BERNARD
of CLAIRVAUX

ON THE NECESSITY of
LOVING GOD

+‡+

> The reason for loving God is God Himself; the measure of loving God is to love Him beyond measure.

THE RELIGIOUS VOCATION of St. Bernard is extraordinary to behold even after eight hundred years. Born in 1090, he entered the Cistercian monastery at Citeaux in 1112—bringing some thirty others with him. His abbot, St. Stephen Harding, sent him to found the monastery of Clairvaux in 1115. From there, as it has been said with understandable hyperbole, Bernard ruled the Church! Who did not feel his influence? Abelard and Gilbert de la Porrée can testify to Bernard's energy and zeal. He wrote letters, sermons (particularly celebrated are those on the *Canticle*), treatises on humility, on grace and liberty, on the theology (Bernard says the *fool*-ology) of Peter Abelard. He wrote a manual for the examination of conscience, the treatise *On Consideration,* for his former monk, Pope Eugenius III. Bernard died in 1153.

Behind this incessant activity is the great soul of a monk who makes his own the old words of St. Martin of Tours: *I desire rest, but I do not spurn toil. Thy will be done.* Bernard cannot give enough to God. For God loved him first, in creating and redeeming him. God even anticipates and precedes all his prayers. How much, then, should he love this God?

Such is the question of the following treatise, written in 1126.

PREFACE

To the Illustrious Lord Aimeric, Cardinal-Deacon and Chancellor of the Church of Rome, Bernard, Abbot of Clairvaux, wishes Life unto the Lord and Death in Him

OU WERE ACCUSTOMED TO ASK PRAYERS OF ME and not questions, and indeed I feel certain that I am equipped for neither. My professed vocation, it is true, imposes the former obligation upon me even if my way of acting does not; but in regard to the latter obligation (to speak the truth) I see that in me those qualifications are lacking which seem especially necessary to meet it—diligence and natural talent. Nevertheless it is pleasing, I admit, that in return for things of the body you ask those of the spirit, although, to be sure, it would have been better if you had gone to one richer than I am. But since it is customary among the learned and unlearned alike to make excuses of this sort, and it is not easily known whether the excuse is really prompted by ignorance or by modesty unless the performance of the task enjoined makes it clear, accept of my poverty what I have, lest by keeping silence I should be looked upon as a philosopher. I do not, however, pledge myself to answer all your questions. To that, only, which you ask concerning the love of God I shall make answer as He Himself suggests. For, this tastes sweeter and is imparted more confidently and is heard with greater profit. Reserve the other questions for the more diligent.

CHAPTER I

Why and how God should be loved

YOU wish, therefore, to hear from me why and how God should be loved? And I: the reason for loving God is God Himself; the measure of loving God is to love Him beyond measure. Is this enough? It is, perchance, but only for one who is wise. But if *to the unwise I am debtor* (*Rom.* i, 14) where enough has been said to the wise I must also, as usual, administer to the needs of others.

And so out of consideration for those who are slower to understand, I shall consider it no burden to repeat what I have said, more fully rather than more profoundly. There is a twofold reason, I should say, why God should be loved for His own sake: because nothing can be more justly, nothing more profitably loved. Indeed when the question is asked why God should be loved it may have one of two meanings. For the question may arise from the fact that a person does not clearly see what particularly constitutes the basis of his inquiry: whether it is God's title to our love or our own advantage in loving Him. To be sure, I would give the same answer to both of these questions: I find no other worthy reason for loving Him except Himself. And first let us examine the question of God's title to our love. A very special title to it is His Who gave Himself to us despite the fact that we were so undeserving. For, what better than Himself could even He have given? If, then, in asking the reason why we should love God we seek to know His title to our love, it is chiefly this: *because He hath first loved us* (I John iv, 10). He it is Who is clearly deserving of being loved in return, especially if one considers Who He is that loved, who they are whom He loved and how much He loved them. And Who is He? Is He not the One to whom every spirit bears witness: *Thou art my God, for Thou hast no need of my goods* (Ps. xv, 2)? And the true love of this Sovereign One lies in this, that it does not seek its own interests. But to whom is such unmixed love shown? *When we were enemies,* it is said, *we were reconciled to God* (Rom. v, 10). God, therefore, has loved His enemies and that, *gratis.* But how much? As much as Saint John says: *God so loved the world as to give His only begotten Son* (Jo. iii, 16). And Saint Paul adds: *He spared not even His own Son, but delivered Him up for us all* (Rom. viii, 32). That very Son says of Himself: *Greater love than this no man hath, that a man lay down his life for his friends* (Jo. xv, 13). Thus has the Just deserved from the ungodly, the Greatest from the least, the All-powerful from the weak. But some one may say: Yes, thus has He deserved of mankind, but of the Angels, not so. That is true, because the Angels had no need of it. Moreover, He who succored men in so great a necessity preserved the Angels from it, and He who by His love for men brought it about that they should no longer remain such as they were, the Same with equal love bestowed upon the Angels the grace of never becoming such as men once were.

CHAPTER II

How greatly God deserves to be loved by Man because of His gifts of Body and Soul. How these are to be known and kept without wrong to Him who gave them

THOSE to whom what I have said is plain will also, I think, plainly see why God should be loved: that is, whence He deserves to be loved. But if unbelievers blind themselves to these truths God is still ready to confound their ingratitude with His numberless benefits conferred for man's advantage and manifest to human sense. Who else, forsooth, supplies food to everyone who eats, light to everyone who sees, breath to everyone who breathes? But it is foolish to strive to enumerate what I have just spoken of as innumerable. It is enough, by way of example, to have mentioned the chief ones—bread, sun and air. The chief ones, I mean, not because they are superior but because they are more necessary since they pertain to the body. Let man seek his higher goods—dignity, knowledge and virtue—in that higher part of him which excels self, that is, in the soul. By man's dignity I mean his free will in which it is surely given him not only to excel other creatures but also to rule over all other [visible] living things. By knowledge I mean that by which he recognizes that his dignity is within himself but not from himself. By virtue I mean that by which he ardently seeks Him from Whom he has his being and valiantly holds fast to Him when found.

Thus every one of these three goods presents a two-fold aspect. Accordingly, human dignity appears not only as the prerogative of man naturally considered, but as the basis of his power of dominion which determines the fear which he commands in every other living creature on the face of the earth. Knowledge will likewise be of a double nature if we perceive that this same dignity as well as any other good that is in us dwells within us but is not from ourselves. Lastly, virtue, too, will be recognized as two-fold if it leads us to seek after Him to Whom we owe our existence and when we have found Him, makes us cling to Him so that we shall never again be separated from Him. And so dignity without knowledge is of no avail; nay, it is even a hindrance if virtue be lacking, as the reasoning that follows makes clear. What glory can one have in possessing what he does not know that he possesses? Furthermore, to know what you have while not knowing that it does not come from yourself, begets glory but not in the sight of God (*Rom.* iv, 2). And to him who glories in himself the Apostle says: *What hast thou that thou hast not received? And if thou hast received, why dost thou glory as if thou hadst not received it (I Cor.* iv, 7)? He does not say simply, *Why dost thou glory?* but he adds, *as if thou hadst not received it,* as if to declare that not he is blameworthy who glories in what he has, but he who glories in it as though he had not received it. Not without reason *vain* glory is the name given to glory of this sort for it lacks the solid foundation of truth. Indeed the Apostle draws a distinction between this and true glory when he says: *He that glorieth, may glory in the Lord (I Cor.* i, 31). That is, in truth. For the Lord is truth.

It is necessary, therefore, that you know both what you are, and that you are not such of yourself, lest you be altogether boastful [*i.e.,* without any limitation], or vainly so [*i.e.,* without any foundation in truth]. Finally it is said: *If thou know not thyself, . . . go forth and follow after the steps of the flocks . . . of thy companions (Cant.* i, 6-7). This is in truth what happens. When man fashioned in honor does not perceive the honor that is his, he is, by reason of such ignorance, justly likened to the beasts of the field that share his present corruption and mortality. It happens, therefore, that a creature distinguished by the gift of reason, through not knowing itself begins to be herded with the droves of unthinking beasts. While ignorant of his own peculiar glory which is from within he is carried away by his own curiosity, determined upon fashioning himself conformably to things purely sensible and becomes one with the rest of visible creatures because he thinks that he has received nothing beyond the rest of them. And so we must be especially on our guard against this ignorance by which, perchance, we think of ourselves as being less than we really are. But no less, indeed much more, must we avoid that other ignorance by which we attribute to ourselves more than we possess. This is what happens when we deceive ourselves into thinking that any good whatever that we have comes from ourselves (*Gal.* vi, 3). But besides both these kinds of ignorance you must shun and abhor that sort of presumption by which knowingly and of set purpose you may, perchance, dare to seek your own glory in goods that are not yours. Thus you would not fear to rob Another of the honor which comes from a good which you well know is in no way attributable to yourself. The former ignorance has no glory at all: the latter has, but not in God's sight. But this third evil, because it is now knowingly committed, usurps what belongs to God Himself. By comparison with that latter ignorance, this presumption is clearly more grievous and more dangerous in this, that in ignorance God is not known, but in presumption He is contemned. It is worse and more detestable than the former because while the former puts us in a class with the beasts of the field, this latter makes us the fellows of demons. Assuredly it is pride and the greatest offense of all to use the gifts we have received as if they were part of our very selves, and after having accepted favors to usurp the glory of the Bestower.

Thus it is that with these two, dignity and knowledge, there is also need of virtue which is the fruit of both. For it is through virtue that He is sought after and retained Who, as Author and Giver of all things, is deservedly glorified in everything. Otherwise, knowing and not doing what is worthy of him, a man *shall be beaten with many stripes* (*Luke* xii, 47). Why? Because *he would not understand that he might do well* (*Ps.* xxxv, 4); rather, *he hath devised iniquity on his bed* (*ibid.* 5), while as a wicked servant he strives to arrogate to himself, nay, even to destroy the glory due his gracious Lord from those goods which, by the gift of intelligence, he knows for certain he has not of himself. It is evident, therefore, that dignity is altogether useless without knowledge, and knowledge without virtue is sinful. But the man of virtue to whom neither knowledge can be sinful nor dignity unfruitful, lifts up his voice to God and frankly confesses: *Not to us, O Lord, not to us, but to Thy name give glory* (*Ps.* cxiii, 9). That is: We attribute to ourselves, O Lord, neither any knowledge nor any dignity; but to Thy name from Whom all proceeds do we impute all.

But we have wandered rather far from our purpose while engaged in showing that those also who do not know Christ are sufficiently admonished by the natural law through the goods of body and soul which they perceive are theirs. How much they, too, should love God for God's own sake! For, to repeat briefly what has been said on this point, what unbeliever does not know that the necessities to which allusion has already been made—whence he derives life, whereby he sees, whereby he breathes—are administered to his body in this mortal life by no other than by Him *Who giveth food to all flesh* (Ps. cxxxv, 25), *Who maketh His sun to rise upon the good and the bad, and raineth upon the just and the unjust* (Matt. v, 45)? What man is there, even though he be ungodly, who can think that the human dignity with which his soul is resplendent is attributable to any other than to Him Who says in *Genesis: Let us make man to Our image and likeness* (i, 26)? Who can deem any other the Bestower of knowledge save Him *that teacheth man knowledge* (Ps. xciii, 10)? Who, again, can think that the gift of virtue has been bestowed in the past or hope for it to be given in the future, save from the hand, likewise, of the Lord of Hosts? God, then, deserves to be loved for His own sake even by the unbeliever who, although he knows not Christ, yet knows himself. Hence there is no excuse even for an unbeliever if he does not love the Lord his God with his whole heart, with his whole soul, and with all his strength (cf. *Deut.* vi, 5). For, that innate sense of justice which reason is not ignorant of, cries out to him from within that he is bound with his whole self to love Him to Whom, he is not unaware, he owes all that he is. But it is difficult, nay impossible, for anyone with his powers of free will to render wholly to God's will the things he once received from God, and not rather to twist them according to his own will and retain them as his own, according as it is written: *all seek the things that are their own* (Phil. ii, 21); and again: *the imagination and thought of man's heart are prone to evil* (Gen. viii, 21).

CHAPTER III

How many incentives Christians have, more than unbelievers, for loving God

THE faithful, on the other hand, know well how complete is their need of Jesus and of Him crucified. While embracing in wonder *the charity* revealed in Him *which surpasseth all knowledge* (*Ephes.* iii, 19), they are filled with shame at not paying back even the very little which they are themselves, in return for love and condescension so great. Easily, therefore, do they grow in love who know that they themselves are more loved: for he to whom less has been given loves less (cf. *Luke* vii, 47). The Jew or the Pagan, to be sure, can never be urged on by such spurs of love as the Church feels who says: I am wounded with charity; and again: *Stay me up with flowers; compass me about with apples: because I languish with love* (*Cant.* ii, 5). She sees *King Solomon in the diadem wherewith his mother crowned him* (*ibid.* iii, 11); she sees the Only-begotten of the Father *bearing His own cross* (*Jo.* xix, 17); she sees the Lord of Majesty struck and spat upon; she sees the Author of life and glory held fast with nails, pierced with a lance, overwhelmed with reproaches, finally laying down that precious Life of His for His friends. She sees all this and the sword of love pierces her soul the more and she says: *Stay me up with flowers, compass me about with apples: because I languish with love* (*Cant.* ii, 5). These *apples,* to be sure, are the pomegranates which the bride, led into the garden of her Beloved, plucks from the tree of life; they have borrowed their own peculiar savour from the Great of Heaven, their color from the Blood of Christ. She [the Church] then sees death itself struck dead and the Author of death led in triumph. She sees captivity led captive (cf. *Ephes.* iv, 8) from under the earth to earth, from earth to heaven, *that in the name of Jesus every knee should bow of those that are in heaven, on earth and under the earth* (*Phil.* ii, 10). She perceives that the earth which under the ancient curse had brought forth thorns and thistles (cf. *Gen.* iii, 18), has sprung into blossom again at the grace of a new benediction. And in all this recalling that verse: *And my flesh hath flourished again, and with my will I will give praise to Him* (*Ps.* xxvii, 7), she longs to add to the fruits of the Passion which she had plucked from the tree of the cross, some of the flowers of the resurrection whose fragrance especially allures the Beloved to visit her again and again.

At last she exclaims: *Behold Thou art fair, my Beloved, and comely; our bed is decked with flowers* (*Cant.* i, 15). In showing Him the bridal-couch she frankly makes known what she desires;

and when she speaks of it as *decked with flowers,* she reveals whence she presumes to obtain the gratification of her desires. For it is not from her own merits but from the flowers gathered in a field which God has blessed (cf. *Gen.* xxvii, 27). Christ Who willed to be conceived and reared in Nazareth finds His delight in flowers. The heavenly Bridegroom rejoices in such fragrance and freely enters often into the bridal-chamber of the heart which He has found filled with fruits of this sort and strewn with flowers. For where He perceives that the grace of His Passion or the glory of His Resurrection is pondered as the subject of diligent meditation, there straightway He is present with eagerness and joy. Know well that the memorials of the Passion are as the fruits of the past year and of all times past under the domination of sin and death, now at last in the fulness of time beginning to appear. But the signs of the Resurrection, mark you, are the new flowers of the season that follows and blooms forth, a new summer, under the influence of grace. Of these flowers the general resurrection which is to come will in the end of time bring forth the fruit which will remain forever. For, it is said, *winter is now past; the rain is over and gone. The flowers have appeared in our land* (*Cant.* ii, 11-12); which means that summer has returned with Him, Who, released from the coldness of death, was restored to the mild Spring of a new life. *Behold,* He says, *I make all things new* (*Apoc.* xxi, 5). He whose flesh was sown in death, bursts into blossom again in the resurrection, at the sweet odor whereof in the field of our valley, withered things straightway grow green once more, things that were cold grow warm again, and the dead pulse anew with life.

Because of the freshness of these flowers and fruits and because of the beauty of the field giving forth the sweetest fragrance, the Father Himself so delights in the Son that He says: *Behold the smell of my son is as the smell of a plentiful field which the Lord hath blessed* (*Gen.* xxvii, 27). Plentiful indeed, *of whose fulness we have all received* (*Jo.* i, 16). But the bride, on terms of greater intimacy, gathers flowers and plucks fruit therefrom, with which to deck the innermost chamber of her own conscience so that the little bed of her heart may give forth sweet odors to the Bridegroom at His coming. For if we wish to have Christ as a frequent guest, we must ever have our hearts fortified with unfailing testimonies both of His mercy in dying and of His power in rising from the dead. This is what David meant when he said: *These two things have I heard, that power belongeth to God, and mercy to Thee, O Lord* (*Ps.* lxi, 12-13). The testimonies concerning both of these truths have become credible in the highest degree (cf. *Ps.* xcii, 5), for Christ died for our sins and rose from the dead for our justification and ascended for our protection and sent the Spirit for our consolation and will one day return for the consummation [of our souls' salvation]. Surely in death He showed mercy; power, in rising from the dead; and both in all the rest [of His life's mysteries].

These are the apples, these the flowers with which the bride prays that meanwhile she may be encompassed and sustained; feeling, I believe, that the power of love within her can in a measure become lukewarm and languid if it be not continually fostered by such helps, until, brought at last into the bridal-chamber she is caught in the long-desired embrace and exclaims: *His left hand is under my head, and His right hand shall embrace me* (*Cant.* ii, 6). Then she will feel and judge how all the evidences of love which at His former coming she had received as if from the left hand of the Beloved are to be disdained in comparison with the surpassing sweetness of the right hand's embrace, and in time to come to be regarded as of a lower degree. She will feel what she has heard: *It is the spirit that quickeneth: the flesh profiteth nothing* (*Jo.* vi, 64). She will know from experience what she had known from hearsay: *my spirit is sweet above honey, and my inheritance above honey and honeycomb* (*Ecclus.* xxiv, 27). In regard to what follows: *My memory is unto everlasting generations* (*ibid.* 28), this means that as long as the present age is seen to abide, in which a generation comes and a generation goes, the consolation which flows from the memory will not be lacking to the elect to whom, as yet, the full satisfaction of the presence [of the Bridegroom] is not granted. Hence it is written: *They shall publish the memory of the abundance of Thy sweetness* (*Ps.* cxliv, 7). There can be no doubt that *they* are those of whom it had been said a little before: *Generation and generation shall praise Thy works* (*ibid.* 4). Memory, therefore, in a generation of time; presence, in the kingdom of heaven. By this latter the company of the elect already taken up into heaven is glorified: by the former, meanwhile, the generation of wayfarers is consoled.

CHAPTER IV

*Who they are who find consolation in the remembrance of God:
and who are more capable of loving Him*

BUT it is important to consider what generation it is that finds comfort in the remembrance of God. Not *a perverse and exasperating generation* (*Ps.* lxxvii, 8), to which it is said: *Woe to you that are rich: for you have your consolation* (*Luke* vi, 24); but such as can say with truth: *My soul refused to be comforted* (*Ps.* lxxvi, 3). It is indeed right that those who do not find their delight in things present should here rejoice in the remembrance of things to come, and the remembrance of eternity should prove a source of delight to those who disdain to derive consolation from any of the things that pass away. And this is the generation of those who seek the Lord, seeking not *the things that are their own* (*Phil.* ii, 21), but *the face of the God of Jacob* (*Ps.* xxiii, 6). To those, therefore, who seek and sigh for the vision of God there is present, meanwhile, a sweet remembrance which, however, does not afford them complete satisfaction but makes them hunger the more for that which will satisfy them fully. To this, indeed, He Who is their Food bears witness in His own regard when He speaks thus: *They that eat Me, shall yet hunger* (*Ecclus.* xxiv, 29); and he who is fed says, *I shall be satisfied when Thy glory shall appear* (*Ps.* xvi, 15). Yet, *blessed are they,* even now, *that hunger and thirst after justice, for,* one day, *they,* and not others, *shall have their fill* (*Matt.* v, 6). Woe to thee, *a wicked and perverse generation* (*Deut.* xxxii, 5)! Woe to thee, a people foolish and unwise who both loathes the remembrance of Him, and is terrified at the thought of His coming! Deservedly indeed, for neither now would you be delivered *from the snare of the hunters* (*Ps.* xc, 3), since *they that will become rich* in this world, *fall into . . . the snare of the devil* (*I Tim.* vi, 9); nor will you then be able to be *delivered . . . from the sharp word* (*Ps.* xc, 3). O sharp word, O hard saying! *Depart from Me ye cursed into everlasting fire* (*Matt.* xxv, 41). Much harder, indeed, and sharper than that word which in the Church is repeated every day in remembrance of the Passion: *He that eateth My flesh and drinketh My blood, hath everlasting life* (*Jo.* vi, 55). That is, he who recalls to mind My death and after My example mortifies his *members which are upon the earth* (*Col.* iii, 5), shall have life everlasting; that is, if you suffer with Him now you shall reign with Him hereafter (cf., *Rom.* viii, 17; *II Tim.* ii, 12). And nevertheless, a very great number in these days also [as of old], recoiling from His voice, going back and walking no more with Him (cf. *Jo.* vi, 67), answers not by word but by deed: *This saying is hard, and who can hear it?* And so, *A generation that set not their heart aright: and whose spirit was not faithful to God* (*Ps.* lxxvii, 8), but rather trusting *in the uncertainty of riches* (*I Tim.* vi, 17), is weighed down at hearing even *the word of the cross* (*I Cor.* i, 18), and looks upon any reminder of the Passion as burdensome. But in His presence how will that generation ever bear the weight of that other word: *Depart from Me, you cursed, into everlasting fire which was prepared for the devil and his angels* (*Matt.* xxv, 41). Assuredly *on whomsoever* this stone *shall fall, it shall grind him to powder* (*Matt.* xxi, 44). But *the generation of the righteous shall be blessed* (*Ps.* cxi, 2): they who with the Apostle, *whether absent or present* (*II Cor.* v, 9), labor to please God. In the end they shall hear: *Come, ye blessed of My Father, possess you the kingdom prepared for you from the foundation of the world* (*Matt.* xxv, 34). Then that *generation that set not their heart aright* (*Ps.* lxxvii, 8), will too late, alas, come to know how sweet was the yoke of Christ (cf. *Matt.* xi, 30), in comparison with their anguish, and how light was His burden from which, in pride, they withdrew their stiff necks as from the weight bitter and crushing (cf. *Deut.* xxxi, 27). You cannot, O wretched slaves of Mammon (cf. *Matt.* vi, 24), you cannot at the same time glory *in the cross of Our Lord Jesus Christ* (*Gal.* vi, 14), and place your trust in great hoards of money (cf. *I Tim.* vi, 17; *Ecclus.* xxxi, 8); you cannot go after gold and also experience how sweet is the Lord (cf. *Ps.* xxxiii, 9). Hence He Whom you do not know in remembrance, as sweet, will prove bitter, no doubt, in His presence.

The faithful soul, on the other hand, longs eagerly for the presence [of God] and reposes sweetly in the remembrance [of Him], and until she is capable of *beholding the glory of the Lord with open face* (*II Cor.* iii, 18), she glories in the ignominy of the Cross (cf. *Gal.* vi, 14). Thus, truly, thus does the bride and dove of Christ (cf. *Cant.* v, 2) find rest meanwhile and sleep *among the midst of lots* (*Ps.* lxvii, 14), having chosen for the present in remembrance of the abundance of Thy sweetness, Lord Jesus (cf. *Ps.* cxliv, 7), *wings . . . covered with silver* (*Ps.* lxvii, 14), that is, the whiteness of innocence and purity; and hoping, besides, to be filled with joy at Thy countenance (cf. *Ps.* xv, 11) where, also, *the hinder parts of her back* will be covered *with the paleness of gold* (*Ps.* lxvii, 14). When with joy she has been brought into *the brightness of the saints* (*Ps.* cix, 3), she will be more completely illumined by the light of Wisdom. With good reason, therefore, does she glory even now and say: *His left hand is under my head, and His right hand shall embrace me* (*Cant.* ii, 6); reflecting that in His left hand is the remembrance of that love than which there is no greater, by which He laid down His life for His friends (cf. *Jo.* xv, 13); but in His right hand is the Beatific Vision which He has promised His friends and the joy [that flows] from the presence of His Majesty. Justly is that vision of God (cf. *I John* iii, 2), that vision that makes us like unto God (cf. *II Cor.* iii, 18), that inconceivable delight of the Divine presence, justly is it ascribed to the right hand concerning which it is joyously sung: *at Thy right hand are delights even to the end* (*Ps.* xv, 11). Justly is it the left hand in which is placed that wonderful love which we have recalled to mind and which is ever to be remembered, for, *until iniquity pass away* (*Ps.* lvi, 2), it is upon this hand that the bride shall lay her head and rest.

Justly, therefore, is the left hand of the Bridegroom under the head of the bride. Leaning back, it is upon it that she rests her head, that is, the intention of her mind, lest it should be inclined and bent toward fleshly and worldly desires: *For the corruptible body is a load upon the soul, and the earthly habitation presseth down the mind that museth upon many things* (*Wis.* ix, 15). For when we come to consider it, what else is effected by compassion so great and so undeserved, by love so gratuitous and hence so amply proved, by esteem so unexpected, by meekness so invincible, by sweetness so wonderful? What, I ask, will all these effect when they are diligently pondered save that they will marvelously draw to themselves the soul of him who ponders them freed from every unworthy love; they will powerfully affect that soul and make it despise, as compared with themselves, whatever one cannot make the object of his desire save by contemning them? Surely, then, the bride runs eagerly to the odor of their ointments (cf. *Cant.* i, 3), loves ardently; and so loved, she seems to herself to love very little even when she has wholly bound herself first in love. Not without cause. For, if a grain of dust (cf. *Isa.* xl, 15) will have brought together its whole self to return the love of another, and that other, the Divine Majesty itself preceding it in love, is seen wholly bent upon its salvation—what that is great can recompense a love so great shown by One who is Himself great? Finally, *God so loved the world, as to give His only Begotten Son* (*Jo.* iii, 16). This, beyond doubt, is said of the Father. Again: *He hath delivered His soul unto death* (*Isa.* liii, 12); and there is no doubt that this is spoken of the Son. And it is said of the Holy Spirit: *But the Paraclete, the Holy Spirit, whom the Father will send in My name, He will teach you all things, and bring all things to your mind, whatsoever I shall have said to you* (*Jo.* xiv, 26). God therefore loves and loves with His whole Self because the whole Trinity loves, if, indeed, *whole* can be said of the Infinite and Incomprehensible, or of what is simple.

CHAPTER V

To what degree the obligation of love is binding, especially upon Christians

ONE who beholds these truths, I believe, realizes fully why God should be loved, that is by what title He deserves to be loved. But the unbeliever, not having the Son, consequently has neither the Father nor the Holy Spirit (cf. *I John* v, 12). For *he who honoreth not the Son, honoreth not the Father Who hath sent Him* (*Jo.* v, 23), nor the Holy Spirit Whom He sent (cf. *ibid.* xvi, 7). It is therefore no wonder if he has less love for Him Whom he knows less. Nevertheless even the unbeliever is not unaware of the fact that he owes all that he is to Him Whom he recognizes as the

Author of his whole being. What of me, then? For I hold my God not only as the gratuitous Bestower of my life, most bountiful in His providence, a devoted Consoler, a solicitous Ruler, but also a most abundant Redeemer as well, an eternal Conserver, Enricher, Glorifier. As it is written: *with Him (there is) plentiful redemption* (Ps. cxxix, 7); and again: *(Christ) entered once into the holies, having obtained eternal redemption* (Heb. ix, 12). Concerning His conservation: *(The Lord) will not forsake His saints: they shall be preserved forever* (Ps. xxxvi, 28); and concerning His enriching: *good measure and pressed down and shaken together and running over shall they give into your bosom* (Luke vi, 38). And again: *eye hath not seen, nor ear heard, neither hath it entered into the heart of man, what things God hath prepared for them that love Him* (I Cor. ii, 9). And concerning His giving of glory: *we look for the Saviour, our Lord Jesus Christ, Who will reform the body of our lowness, make like to the Body of His glory* (Phil. iii, 20-21); and this: *the sufferings of this time are not worthy to be compared with the glory to come, that shall be revealed in us* (Rom. viii, 18); and again: *For that which is at present momentary and light of our tribulation, worketh for us above measure exceedingly an eternal weight of glory, while we look not at the things which are seen, but at the things which are not seen* (II Cor. iv, 17-18).

What shall I render to the Lord for all these things (Ps. cxv, 12)? Reason as well as natural justice impels the unbeliever to surrender his whole self to Him from Whom he has received all that he is, and reminds him that he is bound to love Him with his whole self. To me, surely, faith reveals that He should be loved the more by as much as I understand that He is to be esteemed above myself. For to me, He is the Bestower not only of myself but even of His very Self as well. Finally (when the Psalmist asked, *what shall I render,* etc.) the time of the Faith had not yet come, God had not yet become known in the Flesh, died upon the cross, come forth from the tomb, returned to the Father. Not as yet, I say, had He commended His great charity towards us (cf. *Rom.* v, 8)—that charity concerning which we have already spoken much —at the time when it was already commanded man to *love the Lord his God with his whole heart, with his whole soul, with his whole strength* (*Deut.* vi, 5), that is with all that he is with all that he knows, and with every power that he has. And yet God is not unjust in claiming as His own the work of His hands and His gifts (cf. *Heb.* vi, 10). For why should not a thing which has been made, love its Maker since it has the power of doing so? And why should it not do so as much as it can, since it has no power at all except as a gift from Him? In addition to this, the fact that it was made out of nothing, and that, gratuitously and in this present state of dignity, this fact makes the debt of love clearer and makes what is demanded of it appear more just. Moreover, how great do we consider that increase of His benefaction when He preserved *men and beasts* (*Ps.* xxxv, 7), whereby God has multiplied His mercy (cf. *ibid.* 8)! We, I say, who *changed our glory into the likeness of a calf that eateth grass* (*Ps.* cv, 20), were by sinning *compared to senseless beasts* (*Ps.* xlvii, 13). If I owe my whole self for being made, what more shall I give now in return for being re-made, and re-made in such wise? For I was not re-made as easily as I was made, if, indeed, it is written not only of me but of every thing that was made: *He spoke, and they were made* (*Ps.* cxlviii, 5). But, in truth, He Who made me so great, and that, by speaking once only, in remaking me surely spoke many times and worked wonders and endured hardships; and not only hardships but things unworthy, even. *What shall I render to the Lord, for all the things that He hath rendered to me* (*Ps.* cxv, 12)? In the first work He gave me myself; in the second, Himself: and when He gave me Himself, He restored me to myself again. Given, therefore, and restored, I owe myself in return for myself and I owe it as a two-fold debt. What shall I render to God in return for Himself? For even if I were able to give myself back a thousand times, what am I in comparison with God?

CHAPTER VI

A brief recapitulation and summary of what has been said

HERE first see in what measure, yes, how beyond measure God has deserved to be loved by us; He who (if I may repeat in a few words what has been said) first loved us Himself (cf. *I John* iv,

19)—He so great, yet He loved us greatly and *gratis;* we, so small and [sinners] such as we are (cf. *Rom.* v, 8). Notice! I remember what I said in the beginning, that the measure of loving God is to love Him beyond measure. And since love which has God as its object, has as its object the Immeasurable and Unlimited (for God is both Immeasurable and Unlimited), what, I ask, ought to be the limit or measure of our love? What of the fact that our love itself is not given as a free gift but as the payment of a debt? Immeasurableness, therefore, loves, Eternity loves, *the charity . . . which surpasseth all knowledge* (*Ephes.* iii, 19) loves, God loves of Whose *greatness there is no end* (*Ps.* cxliv, 3), of Whose wisdom there is no measure, Whose *peace . . . surpasseth all understanding* (*Phil.* iv, 7):—and do we love Him in turn so much and no more? *I will love thee, O Lord, my strength . . . my firmament, my refuge, and my deliverer* (*Ps.* xvii, 2-3); and I shall finally possess whatever can be said to be desirable and lovable. My God, my Help, I shall love You according to Your gift to me, and according to my measure, which is less, to be sure, than justice demands but clearly not less than I am able to give; for although I cannot give as much as I owe, nor yet can I give beyond what I am able. I shall be able to give more when You deign to give me more: but never according to Your worth. *Thy eyes did see my imperfect being* (*Ps.* cxxxviii, 16); but nevertheless, *in Thy book all shall be written* (*ibid.*) they who do what they are able to do, although they are not able to do what they ought to do. It is clear enough, as far as I can judge, both how God should be loved and by what desert of His own. By *what* desert of His, I say, for to whom can its *greatness* be clearly manifest? Who can say? Who can know?

CHAPTER VII

Not without fruit and reward, is God loved, and earthly things cannot satisfy the longing of the human heart

Now let us see with what advantage to ourselves God is to be loved. But how little is our insight into this compared with what it really is! Nevertheless one ought not to remain silent about what is seen, even though it is not seen entirely as it is. Above, when *it* was asked why and how God should be loved, I said that the question *why* can be understood in two ways, so that it seems equally to ask, either by what desert of His or for what advantage of ours God should be loved. And since something has been said on the subject of God's desert—not in a manner worthy of Him, but according to the power given me—it remains that I should speak of the reward, according as it lies in my power.

For not without reward is God loved although He should be loved without thought of the reward. True charity cannot be unprofitable nor is it, however, mercenary; certainly it *seeketh not its own* (*I Cor.* xiii, 5). It is a matter of affection, not a contract: it neither gains nor is gained by a compact. It exerts its influence freely and makes one free. True love finds satisfaction in itself. It has its reward but it is the object it loves. For whatever you seem to love because of something else, you clearly love that to which the end of love ultimately attains and not that by which it attains it. Paul does not preach the Gospel in order that he may eat but he eats in order that he may preach the Gospel: because he loves, not food, but the Gospel (cf. *I Cor.* ix, 14-18). True love asks no reward but deserves one. It is when a man has not yet learned to love that a reward is set before him; it is due one who loves; it is awarded to him who perseveres. Finally, in urging things of a lower order, it is the unwilling that we invite with promises or rewards, and not the willing. For who is there who thinks that a man should be rewarded in order that he may do what he freely desires? No one, for instance, pays a hungry man to eat, or a thirsty man to drink, or a mother to give milk to the child of her womb (cf. *Isa.* xlix, 15). Or who thinks that a man ought to be induced by a price or an entreaty to fence in his own vine, to dig about his own tree, or to erect the structure of his own home? How much less does the soul that loves God seek anything besides God as the reward of her love! If she seeks anything else, it is clearly something else and not God that she loves.

It is natural to everyone who uses his reason to desire always, according to his judgment and intention, what is more capable of satisfying him and to be content with nothing which is wanting in what he considers preferable. For he who has a good-looking wife, for instance, gazes with wanton eye and mind upon one more beautiful, and he who is dressed in costly attire desires something more costly, and one possessing much wealth envies the man who is wealthier. You may see those already abounding in farms and property, still, day by day adding field to field and with unlimited avarice extending their boundaries. You may see those, too, who dwell in the houses of kings and in spacious palaces, nevertheless joining house to house and with restless curiosity building up, tearing down, turning everything upside down. What do we see if not men elevated by honors? What do we see such men doing if not, with insatiable ambition straining more and more with all their might, toward higher things? And of all these there is no end because there is nothing found in these things that is uniquely the highest or best. And what wonder is it if that which is not able to find rest anywhere short of the highest or best should not be really satisfied by things lower and worse? But this is foolish and utterly mad always to be striving after those things which never, I do not say satisfy, but do not even moderate one's appetite, while whatever of such things you may chance to have, you none the less long for what you have not and ever restless pant after whatever may be wanting. Thus it happens that a vagabond mind running hither and thither among the varying and false delights of the world is tired out, not satisfied, by its vain exertion; while, starved, it counts as little whatever it gulps down as compared with what remains to be devoured and ever it craves the things removed from it, not less anxiously than it joyfully has and holds those that are at hand. For who is there who can gain the whole world? And although a man were to cling fearfully to the little which he has gained through his labor, he has no certainty as to when he will lose it to his grief; but he is certain that at some time or other he will lose it (cf. *Ecclus.* v, 14). Thus a perverted will strains eagerly after a direct short-cut to the *best* and hurries on to that whereby it may be filled. Yea, in truth, by such tortuous routes as these does vanity amuse itself, does iniquity deceive itself. So if you would attain to the fulfilment of what you wish for, that is if you would lay hold upon that which, once grasped, leaves no more to be desired—what is the necessity of putting the rest to the test? You run along by-paths and you will die long before you attain the object of your desires along this circuitous route.

Thus, then, *the wicked walk round about* (Ps. xi, 9), desiring in a natural way that whereby they may put an end to desire, and foolishly rejecting the means by which they might approach their true end, God: by *the end* I mean not *consumption* but consummation. Wherefore they make haste not to be consummated in a blessed end but to be consumed with empty toil—they who find their delight in the appearance of things rather than in the Author of them, they who would run through everything to find out by experience concerning every individual thing before they trouble themselves about attaining to the Lord of the universe Himself. And indeed, they might reach their goal if at some time or other they might be made possessors of what they wish for, to wit, that one might possess everything except the Cause of all things. For by the very law of his own cupidity, according to which in all other matters he is accustomed to hunger for what he has not rather than for what he has, and to loathe what he has because of what he has not; presently having obtained and having disdained everything in heaven and upon the earth, man would beyond the shadow of a doubt run at last to Him Who alone is lacking to him, the God of all. There henceforth, he would find rest; for as no rest holds him, short of that goal, so no unrest touches him, when he attains it. He would for certain say: *it is good for me to adhere to my God* (Ps. lxxii, 28). He would say: *For what have I in heaven? and besides Thee what do I desire upon earth* (*ibid.* 25)? and in similar strain: *Thou art the God of my heart, and the God that is my portion forever* (*ibid.* 26). Thus, therefore (as has been said), any greedy man might ultimately attain to what is best if he could really attain the object short of the best, which he desires, before he reached *the* Best.

Truly, this is made absolutely impossible because man's life is too short, his powers too weak, the number of his fellows too vast. Hence, they, assuredly, sweat along an endless road with futile toil who, while they wish to get whatever they want, cannot attain to the end of all things desirable. And would that they wished to attain to an intellectual grasp of all things, and not to an experimental knowledge of them! This, indeed, they could easily do and not in vain. For, the mind, as much quicker than bodily sense as it is more penetrating, has been given for this, that in all things it should precede sense, and that there is nothing that sense may dare to touch which the mind, preceding it, has not first ratified as useful. Hence, I believe, the saying: *prove all things; hold fast that which is good* (I Thess. v, 21); to the end, that is to say, that the former [the mind] may so oversee the latter [sense] that it may not attain its desire save only in accordance with the judgment of the former. Otherwise you will not *ascend into the mountain of the Lord,* nor *stand in His holy place* (Ps. xxiii, 3), because you have taken your soul in vain (cf. *ibid.* 4), that is, your rational soul, while like the beasts of the field you follow sense, while your reason remains unconcerned and offers no resistance in anything. Those therefore whose steps reason does not precede, run, but off the path (cf. *Isa.,* lix, 8), and thus despising the counsel of the Apostle, do not *so run that* they *may obtain* (I Cor. ix, 24). For when will they obtain Him Whom they refused to obtain save after all things else? It is a crooked road and an endless maze, to wish to attain all things before God.

But not so the just man. Hearing, of course, the blame of the many tarrying in the maze (for many there are who eagerly pursue the broad way that leads to death) (cf. *Matt.* vii, 13), he chooses for himself the king's highway, *neither turning to the right hand nor to the left* (cf. *Num.* xx, 17; xxi, 22). Finally the prophet bears witness to this: *The way of the just is right, the path of the just is right to walk in* (Isa. xxvi, 7). These are they who by a salutary short way (cf. II Kings xviii, 23) are careful to avoid the roundabout way, dangerous and fruitless, and choose the shortened and shortening word (cf. *Rom.* ix, 28), not to desire everything they see but rather to *sell what they have, and give to the poor* (Matt. xix, 21). Clearly, *Blessed are the poor in spirit: for theirs is the kingdom of heaven* (Matt. v, 3). All indeed run (cf. I Cor. ix, 24); but there is a distinction made among the runners. *For the Lord knoweth the way of the just: and the way of the wicked shall perish* (Ps. i, 6). Therefore, *Better is a little to the just, than the great riches of the wicked* (Ps. xxxvi, 16), since indeed, as the wise man says and the fool finds out from experience, *A covetous man shall not be satisfied with money* (Eccles. v, 9); but *they that hunger and thirst after justice . . . shall have their fill* (Matt. v, 6).

If indeed justice is the life-giving and natural food of the spirit that makes use of reason, money to be sure no more lessens the hunger of the mind than air does that of the body. If then you should happen to see a starved man with mouth opened in the wind drinking in the air with puffed-out cheeks as if to satisfy his hunger thereby, would you not believe him mad? Thus it is not less madness if you think that a rational spirit is not more puffed up than satisfied by any bodily things whatever. For, what have bodies to do with spirits? Neither can bodies, surely, find refreshment in things spiritual nor can spirits find refreshment in bodily things. *Bless the Lord, O my soul . . . who satisfieth thy desire with good things* (*Ps.* cii, 1, 5). He satisfies us with good things, He incites us to good, He preserves us in good, He prevents, He sustains, He fulfills. It is He Who makes you desire; He is what you desire.

I said above: The cause of loving God is God. I spoke the truth, for He is both the efficient and final Cause. It is He Who gives the occasion, it is He Who creates the affection, He Who consummates the desire. It is He Who wrought, or rather, *exists* in order that He might be loved; He, it is hoped, will be so fruitfully loved as not to be loved in vain. His love makes our love ready and rewards it. He goes before more graciously than any other, He is repaid more justly, He is awaited more sweetly. He *is rich unto all who call upon Him* (*Rom.* x, 12); still He has nothing better than Himself to give. He gave Himself to merit for us, He retains Himself to be our reward, He offers Himself as the food of saintly souls, He gives Himself as the price of the redemption of those in captivity. You are *good, O Lord, to the soul that seeketh* You (*Lament.* iii, 25): what, then, to one who finds? But in this is the wonder that no one can seek You save him who first has found You. Therefore You wish to be found in order that You may be sought, to be sought in order that You may be found. You can, indeed, be sought and found but not prevented. For although we say, *in the morning my prayer shall prevent thee* (*Ps.* lxxxvii, 14); there can be no doubt, however, that every prayer is lukewarm which inspiration has not prevented.

We must now state whence our love has its beginning, since we have already told where it has its consummation.

CHAPTER VIII

*The first degree of love, whereby a man loves himself for his own
sake*

LOVE is a natural affection, one of four. They are well known; there
is no need of mentioning them by name.[1] It would therefore be just
that what is natural should serve its own Author before all others.
Hence the first commandment is called the greatest: *Thou shalt love
The Lord thy God,* etc. (*Matt.* xxii, 37). But since nature is rather
weak and feeble, it is impelled, by the necessity to preserve itself,
to serve itself first. It is carnal love by which before all other things
man loves himself for his own sake. For as yet he is aware
only of himself. As it is written: *first . . . that which is natural
[animale]; afterwards that which is spiritual* (*I Cor.* xv, 46).
Nor is it imposed by any command, but implanted in nature;
for who *ever hated his own flesh* (*Ephes.* v, 29)? But truly if
this love, as is its wont, begins to be too precipitate or too lavish
and is not at all satisfied with the river-bed of necessity, overflowing
rather widely it will be seen to invade the fields of pleasure. At
once its overflow is held in check by the commandment that opposes itself to it: *Thou shalt love thy neighbor as thyself* (*Matt.*
xxii, 39). It happens, very justly indeed, that the sharer in nature
should not be excluded from a part in grace as well, especially in
that grace which is inborn in nature itself. If a man finds it a
burden, I do not say to relieve his brother in matters of necessity
but to administer to his pleasures, let him restrain his own unless he
wishes to be a transgressor. Let him be as indulgent as he likes to
himself, so long as he is mindful to show the same degree of indulgence to his neighbor. The bridle of temperance is put upon
you, O man, out of the law of life and of discipline lest you should
go after your concupiscences and perish; lest in the goods of nature
you become a slave to your soul's enemy, that is, to lust. How much
more justly and honorably do you give such things to your fellow-
sharer, that is, your neighbor rather than to your enemy! And if
indeed, according to the advice of the wise man, you turn away
from your own pleasures (cf. *Ecclus.* xviii, 30), and according to

[1] Love, fear, joy and sorrow.

the teaching of the Apostle, content with food and raiment (cf. *I Tim.* vi, 8), you find it no burden to withhold your love for a little while *from carnal desires which war against the soul* (I Peter ii, 11); surely, I think, what you take away from your soul's enemy you will find no burden to bestow upon the sharer of your nature. Your love will then be both temperate and just if what is taken from your own pleasures is not denied to your brother's needs. Thus carnal love is made neighborly when it is extended to the common good.

But if, while you are sharing what you have with your neighbor, even the necessities of life should, perchance, be lacking to you, what will you do? What indeed, unless with all confidence you should *ask* of Him *Who giveth to all men abundantly, and upbraideth not* (*Jas.* i, 5); Who *openest thy hand, and fillest with blessing every living creature* (*Ps.* cxliv, 16)? There is no doubt, surely, that He who is not absent in the midst of plenty will gladly be present in the time of need. He says, at length: *seek ye first the kingdom of God and His justice, and all these things shall be added to you* (*Luke* xii, 31). He promises that He will of His own accord give whatever is necessary to him who restricts himself in superfluities and loves his neighbor. This surely, is to seek first the kingdom of God and to implore help against the tyranny of sin, that you prefer to bear the yoke of modesty and restraint rather than endure that sin should reign in your mortal body. But this, too, is part of the righteousness in question, not to possess the gift of nature independently of him whose common nature you share.

Nevertheless, in order that to love one's neighbor may be a matter of perfect justice, it is imperative that it be referred to God as its cause. Otherwise how can he love his neighbor without alloy who does not love him in God? He surely cannot love in God who does not love God. God must be loved first, in order that one's neighbor, too, may be loved in God. God, therefore, Who makes all else that is good, makes Himself to be loved. And He does it as follows. He Who fashioned nature, it is He Who shields it from harm as well. For it was so fashioned that it should have as a necessary Protector, Him whom it had as Maker, in order that what could not have come into being save through Him, should not be able to subsist at all without Him. And lest the creature might not know this about itself and consequently (which God forbid) in its pride arrogate to itself the benefits it had received from its Creator, the same Maker, in His high and salutary counsel wills that man should be harassed with troubles; so that when man has failed and God has come to his assistance, while man is being delivered by God, God, as is fitting, may be honored by man. For this is what He says: *call upon Me in the day of trouble: I will deliver thee, and thou shalt glorify Me* (Ps. xlix, 15). Thus it comes to pass in this wise that animal and carnal man, who knew how to love no one except himself, may begin even for his own sake to love God too, because in Him beyond a shadow of doubt, as he has often learned from experience, he can do all things—those, to be sure, which it is good to be able to do—and without Him he can do nothing.

CHAPTER IX

The second and third degrees of love

AND so now he loves God, but still for his own sake, not for Himself. It is, however, a sort of prudence to know what you are able to do by yourself, what with God's help, and to preserve yourself guiltless for Him who keeps you unharmed. But if tribulation assails you again and again, and on this account there occurs an oft-repeated turning towards God; and as often, there follows deliverance obtained from God, is it not true that even though the breast were of steel or the heart of stone in one so many times rescued, it must of necessity be softened at the grace of the Rescuer so that man might love God not merely for his own sake but for God Himself.

From the occasion that arises from frequent needs it is necessary that man should frequently, in repeated petition, go to God Who in such petition is tasted, and it is by tasting that it is proved how sweet is the Lord (cf. Ps. xxxiii, 9). Thus it happens that when once His sweetness has been tasted, it draws us to the pure love of God more than our need impels. Just as in the case of the Samaritans who said, speaking to the woman who had announced that the Lord was come: *We now believe, not for thy saying: for we ourselves have heard Him, and know that this is indeed the Saviour of*

the world (*Jo.* iv, 42), similarly I say, we too, following their
example, speaking to our flesh may justly say: We now love God,
not for your necessity; for we ourselves have tasted and know how
sweet is the Lord. For it is true that a need of the flesh is a sort of
speech, and the benefits which it knows from experience it proclaims in transports of joy. And so for one who feels thus, it will
not now be hard to fulfil the commandment in regard to loving his
neighbor. For he truly loves God and in this way also loves the
things which are God's. He loves purely and it is no burden for the
pure to be obedient to a command; rather, *purifying* his heart, as it
is written, *in* the obedience of *charity* (*I Peter* i, 22). He loves
justly and gladly embraces a just command. This love is deservedly
acceptable because it is unselfish. It is pure because it is paid neither
by word nor tongue, but by deed and truth (cf. *I John* iii, 18). It
is just, since it is paid back as it is received. For he who loves thus
undoubtedly loves in no other wise than he is loved; seeking, in
his turn, not the things that are his own but the things are Jesus
Christ's (cf. *Phil.* ii, 21), just as He sought the things that are ours,
or rather ourselves, and not His own. It is thus He loves who says:
Give praise to the Lord, for He is good (*Ps.* cxvii, 1). He who
gives praise to the Lord not because He is good to him but because
He is good, he truly loves God for God and not for his own sake.
It is not thus that he loves of whom it is said: *he will praise thee
when thou shalt do well to him* (*Ps.* xlviii, 19). This is the third
degree of love by which God is now loved for His very self.

CHAPTER X

*The fourth degree of love, when a man does not love even himself
except for the sake of God*

HAPPY IS HE who has deserved to attain as high as the fourth degree where a man does not love even himself except for the sake of
God. *Thy justice, (O God) is as the mountains of God* (*Ps.* xxxv,
7). This love is a mountain and the high mountain of God. In
truth, *a curdled mountain, a fat mountain* (*Ps.* lxvii, 16). *Who
shall ascend into the mountain of the Lord* (*Ps.* xxiii, 3): *Who
will give me wings like a dove, and I will fly and be at rest* (*Ps.*

lɪv, 7)? This place is in peace: and this abode in Sion (*Ps.* lxxv, 3). *Woe is me, that my sojourning is prolonged* (*Ps.* cxix, 5)! Flesh and blood, vessel of clay, when will your earthly dwelling place compass this? When will the mind experience such an affection as this so that inebriated with divine love, forgetful of self, and become in its own eyes like *a vessel that is destroyed* (*Ps.* xxx, 13), the whole of it may continue on to God and being joined to God, become one spirit with Him (cf. *I Cor.* vi, 17), and say: *For Thee my flesh and my heart hath fainted away: thou art the God of my heart, and the God that is my portion forever* (*Ps.* lxxii, 26)? Blessed and holy, I would say, is he to whom it has been given to experience such a thing in this mortal life at rare intervals or even once, and this suddenly and scarcely for the space of a single moment. In a certain manner to lose yourself as though you were not (cf. *Gal.* ii, 20), and to be utterly unconscious of yourself and to be emptied of yourself and, as it were, brought to nothing, this pertains to heavenly conversation, not to human affection. And if indeed, anyone among mortals is suddenly from time to time (as has been said) even for the space of a moment admitted to this, straightway the wicked world grows envious, the evil of the day throws everything into confusion (cf. *Matt.* vi, 34), the body of death becomes a burden, the necessity of the flesh causes unrest, the fainting away of corruption (cf. *Ps.* lxxii, 26) offers no support, and what is more vehement than these, fraternal charity calls one back. Alas! he is forced to return to himself, to fall back upon his own, and in his wretchedness to cry out: *Lord, I suffer violence, answer Thou for me* (*Isa.* xxxviii, 14); and this: *Unhappy man that I am, who shall deliver me from the body of this death* (*Rom.* vii, 24)?

Since however, Scripture says God *hath made all things for Himself* (*Prov.* xvi, 4), it will certainly come to pass that the creature will at one time or other conform itself to its Author and be of one mind with Him. We ought therefore be transformed into this same disposition of soul, so that as God has willed that everything should be for Himself, so we too may deliberately desire neither ourselves nor any other thing to have been in the past, or to be in the future, unless it be equally for His sake, to wit, for His sole will, not for our own pleasure. A need allayed, or good fortune received will not delight us so much as that His will is seen perfectly fulfilled in us and by us; which, too, is what we daily ask in prayer when we say: *Thy will be done on earth as it is in heaven (Matt. vi, 10)*. O love, holy and chaste! O sweet and pleasing affection! O pure and undefiled intention of the will! the more surely undefiled and purer, as there is now mixed with it nothing of its own; so much the sweeter and more pleasing, as its every feeling is wholly divine. To be thus affected is to become deified. Just as a little drop of water mixed with a lot of wine seems entirely to lose its own identity, while it takes on the taste of wine and its color; just as iron, heated and glowing, looks very much like fire, having divested itself of its original and characteristic appearance; and just as air flooded with the light of the sun is transformed into the same splendor of light so that it appears not so much lighted up as to be light itself:—so it will inevitably happen that in the saints every human affection will then, in some ineffable manner, melt away from self and be entirely transfused into the will of God. Otherwise how will God ... *be all in all (I Cor. xv, 28)*, if in man there is left anything at all of man himself? The substance, indeed, will remain, but in another *form,* another glory, and another power. When will this be? Who will see this? Who will possess it? *When shall I come and appear before the face of God (Ps. xlii, 3)*? O Lord, my God, *My heart hath said to Thee: my face hath sought Thee: Thy face, O Lord, will I still seek (Ps. xxvi, 8)*. Will I, do You think, see Your holy temple?

As for me, I think that it will not have come to pass with perfect fulfilment that: *Thou shalt love the Lord thy God with thy whole heart, and with thy whole soul, and with thy whole strength (Deut. vi, 5)*, until the heart itself is no longer compelled to think about the body, and the soul ceases to have to attend to quickening the body and to providing it with sense-life, and the body's strength freed from vexations is made strong in the power that is of God. For it is impossible wholly to concentrate all these upon God and to hold them fixed upon the Divine Countenance so long as it is necessary for them, absorbed and dissipated, to be subject to this frail and wretched body. And so, in a spiritual and immortal body (cf. *Deut. vi, 5*), in a body perfect, calm and acceptable, and in all things subject to the spirit, let the soul hope to *apprehend* the fourth degree of love, or, rather, to be *apprehended* in it (cf. *Phil.* iii, 12-13); for, in truth, it is within the power of God to give it to whomsoever He wishes, not for human diligence to procure by its own efforts. Then, I say, she will easily come into the possession of the highest degree, when, without the slightest delay, as she hastens most eagerly into the joy of her Lord (cf. *Matt.* xxv, 21, 23), no allurement of the flesh will now retard her progress, no vexation destroy her peace. Do we think, however, that the holy martyrs actually attained to this grace, even in part, while still detained in those victorious bodies of theirs? Great power of love, certainly, had caught up their souls, within, and thus they had strength so to expose their bodies, without, and contemn their tortures. But, assuredly, the sense of most bitter pain could not but disturb their calm, although it had no power to destroy their peace.

But what of souls already separated from their bodies? We believe that they are completely immersed in that sea of eternal light and of eternity overflowing with light.

CHAPTER XI

This perfection of love is not possible of attainment even by the souls of the blessed separated from their bodies, before the resurrection

BUT if (as is not denied) they would fain have received their bodies or, certainly, long and hope to receive them, it is clear beyond a shadow of doubt that they are not yet completely changed from their former selves, for admittedly there is still something which they regard as their own, to which at least in small measure their attention returns. Therefore, until *death is swallowed up in victory* (*I Cor.* xv, 54), and until the very moment when perpetual light invades the boundaries of night on every side and holds them, until the heavenly glory shines forth even in bodies, until that moment souls cannot altogether set themselves aside as of no account and become united with God, since even then they are surely bound to their bodies, if not by life or sense, certainly by a natural affection, so that without them they have neither the desire nor the power to attain their consummation. And so, before the restoration of their bodies there will not be that complete self-abandonment on the part of souls, which is their perfect and highest state; nor would the spirit now seek again for the fellowship of the flesh if it could attain to its perfect consummation without it. In truth, not without progress for the soul is the body laid down or taken up again. *Precious,* indeed, *in the sight of the Lord is the death of His saints* (Ps. cxv, 15). But if death is precious, what is life, and *that* life? Nor is it any wonder if the body, now glorified, seems to confer something upon the spirit, since even when weak and mortal it is manifest that it was of no little help to it. O how truly did he speak who said: *to them that love God, all things work together unto good* (Rom. viii, 28). To the soul that loves God the body avails in its weakness, it avails in its death, it avails in its restoration: in the first instance, forsooth, for the fruit of penitence; in the second, for rest; in the last, for consummation. Rightly she does not wish to be made perfect without that which she feels helps her to what is good for her in every state.

Clearly a good and faithful companion to a good spirit is the flesh which if it is a burden, is a source of delight; or, certainly is a source of delight and hardly a burden at all. The first state is full of toil but abounding in fruit; the second is one of complete repose but in no wise wearisome; the third abounds in glory, as well. Listen to the Bridegroom in the Canticle inviting his followers to this three-fold progress: *Eat,* He says, *O friends, and drink, and be inebriated, my dearly beloved* (Cant. v, 1). Those still toiling in the body He calls to food; those who have laid down the body and are enjoying complete repose, He invites to drink; those who again take their bodies up He urges even to inebriation, and these He calls His most beloved ones because they most abound in charity. For, in the case of all others whom He calls not *most beloved,* but *friends,* there is a difference. As a result, those, to be sure, who groan, still weighed down in the flesh (cf. *II Cor.* v, 4), are held dear in return for the love that they have. But those who are already freed from the fetters of the flesh are dearer according as they are made more ready and become less encumbered for loving. Rightly, then, beyond both others are they called *most beloved* and are so, who having now received a second garment in bodies which they have resumed with glory, are borne along in the love of God more freely and more swiftly according as there is nothing of their own left in them to cause them the slightest solicitude or to retard their progress. This distinction neither of the other states can claim, since in the first the body is carried along with labor; and in the second it is awaited not without a certain desire for something that is missing.

First, then, the faithful soul eats her bread but alas! in the sweat of her brow (cf. *Gen.* iii, 19). Still, in fact, remaining in the flesh she still walks by faith (*II Cor.* v, 7), which, to be sure, must be reduced to action through love because if it be not expressed in works it is dead (*James*, ii, 17). This very work itself is food, as the Lord says: *My meat is to do the will of My Father* (*Jo.* iv, 34). Henceforth, having divested herself of the flesh she no longer eats the bread of sorrow but it is allowed her to drink more abundantly, as if after meat, of the wine of love not unmixed however, but as is read in the *Canticle* as spoken by the Bridegroom: *I have drunk my wine with my milk* (*Cant.* v, 1). For the soul even then, mixes with the wine of divine love the sweetness of natural affection with which she longs to resume her body and that, glorified. She is exalted, therefore, having already drunk of the wine of holy charity but clearly not as yet to the point of inebriation; for, in the meanwhile, the admixture of this milk tempers that ardor. Finally, inebriation is wont to upset the mind and to render it altogether forgetful of itself. But she has not entirely forgotten self who still dwells upon her own body that is to be raised from the dead. But when this has been attained which alone was lacking, what is there now that hinders her from leaving self, in a way, wholly to go to God to become completely unlike herself, to the degree in which it is granted her to be made most like unto God? Then, at last, admitted to the cup of wisdom concerning which it is read: *my chalice which inebriateth me, how goodly it is* (*Ps.* xxii, 5)!—what wonder is it if now she becomes inebriated with the plenty of the house of God (cf. *Ps.* xxxv, 9), when, vexed with no anxiety for what is her own and free from care, she drinks that wine pure and new, with Christ in the kingdom of His Father (cf. *Matt.* xxvi, 29).

Wisdom, in truth, gives a triple banquet and from a single love she supplies the fare,—she herself feeding those who labor, she herself giving drink to those who rest, she herself inebriating those who reign as kings (cf. *Matt.* xix, 28). But just as in a banquet for the body food is served before drink, since nature prescribes such an order, so too here. First, indeed, before death we *eat the labors of our hands* (Ps. cxxvii, 2), with labor masticating what is to be swallowed. But after death, in the spiritual life, we drink, clarifying what is perceived by a very pleasing sort of facility. Finally, our bodies living once again in immortal life, we become inebriated, abounding in wondrous plenty. This is the meaning of what the Spouse says in the *Canticle: Eat, O friends, and drink, and be inebriated, my dearly beloved* (v, 1). Eat before death, drink after death, become inebriated after the resurrection. Justly now are they most beloved who are inebriated with love, and justly are they inebriated who have deserved to be brought into the wedding-feast of the Lamb (cf. *Apoc.* xix, 9), eating and drinking at His table in His kingdom (cf. *Luke* xxii, 30), when He now presents *to Himself a glorious church, not having spot or wrinkle, or any such thing* (*Ephes.* v, 27). Then straightway He inebriates His most beloved, then does He *make them drink of the torrent of His pleasures* (Ps. xxxv, 9); since, indeed, in that closest and purest embrace of Bridegroom and bride, *the stream of the river maketh the city of God joyful* (Ps. xlv, 5). This I think is nothing else than the Son of God Who *passing will minister unto them* as He Himself promised (cf. *Luke* xii, 37), so that from this source *the just feast and rejoice before God: and be delighted with gladness* (Ps. lxvii, 4). Hence that satiety without weariness; hence that longing never satisfied yet never knowing want; hence, finally, that inebriation without drunkenness, filled with truth, not with strong drink, not drenched with wine, but on fire with God.

Thus that fourth degree of love is now possessed forever when God alone is loved in the highest possible degree; because, now, we do not even love ourselves save for His sake, so that He Himself is the reward of those who love Him, the reward eternal of those who love for all eternity.

CHAPTER XII

Charity, as treated in a letter to the Carthusians

I REMEMBER well that a while ago I wrote a letter to the holy Carthusian brethren and in it, among other matters, I discussed these very grades of love. But, perchance, I there said other things though not foreign to the matter, on the subject of charity, and for this reason certain of those remarks I do not consider it useless to append also to this discourse, especially since it is easier to transcribe what has already been written than to write something new.[2] That, I say, is true and genuine charity and must be admitted as proceeding entirely from *a pure heart, a good conscience and a faith unfeigned (I Tim.* i, 5), by which we love the good of our neighbor equally with our own. For he who loves only what is his, or loves it more, stands convicted of loving good unchastely, since he loves for his own and not for His sake. And such a one cannot obey the prophet who says: *Give praise to the Lord for He is good (Ps.* cxvii, 1). He gives praise, to be sure, because, perhaps, He is good to him but not because He is good in Himself. Therefore let him understand that it is against him that that reproach was directed by the same prophet: *he will praise thee when thou shalt do well to him (Ps.* xlviii, 19). There is a man who gives praise to the Lord because He is powerful, and there is a man who gives praise to Him because He is good to him, and, again there is a man who gives praise to Him because He is simply good. The first is a servant and fears for himself; the second, a hireling, desires things for his own sake; the third, a son, gives honor to the Father. And so he who is afraid and he who desires things for his own sake, both act for themselves. Only the charity which is found in a son, *seeketh not her own (I Cor.* xiii, 5). For this reason I think that it was of charity that it was said: *The law of the Lord is unspotted, converting souls (Ps.* xviii, 8); for it is she alone which is strong enough to *convert* a soul from love of self and of the world, and direct it to God. For neither fear nor love of one's self converts the soul. At times they change an expression of countenance or an external act, but affection, never. Even a servant, to be sure, sometimes does the work of God but because he does not do it freely he is known still to remain in his hardness. Even the hireling does the work of God but because he does not do it without recompense he is convicted of being led by his own cupidity. Truly,

---

[2] Cf. St. Bernard, *Epist.* xi, 3 (PL 182, 109).

where there is something of one's own there is peculiarity [3]; where there is peculiarity, there is a [private] corner; and where there is a *corner* there without doubt there is dirt and mouldiness. And so, let that very fear by which he is restrained be his law for the servant; let his cupidity by which he, too, is circumscribed be the hireling's law, since by it he *is tempted . . . being drawn away and allured* (*Jas.* i, 14). But neither one of these two can be unspotted, or can convert souls. But charity converts souls whom she makes free agents.

Again, I would call her unspotted because she has accustomed herself to retain for herself nothing of her own. Certainly, in the case of one who has nothing of his own, all that he has is assuredly God's, but what is God's cannot be unclean. Therefore the unspotted law of the Lord is charity, which seeks not what is useful for itself but what is of use to many. For it is called the law of the Lord either because He Himself lives by it or because no one possesses it except as a gift from Him. Nor let it seem absurd that I have said that even God lives by law, since I said by no other law save charity. What in that supreme and blessed Trinity preserves that supreme and ineffable unity, save charity? Charity is the law, the law of the Lord, which in a certain way holds the Trinity together in unity and binds it *in the bond of peace* (*Ephes.* iv, 3). Let no one think, however, that I am here taking charity as a quality or as a sort of accident (otherwise I should be saying, which Heaven forbid, that there is in God something which is not God), but as the very divine substance; and this, surely, is neither a new nor an unusual expression, for John says: *God is charity* (*I John* iv, 8). Therefore charity is rightly called both God and the gift of God. And so charity gives charity, the substantial gives what is an accident. Where it means the Giver it is the name of a substance, where it means the gift it is the name of a quality. This is the eternal law, the creative and governing law of the universe. Indeed, *all things have been made by her in measure, and number and weight* (*Wis.* xi, 21), and nothing is left without a law: for even the Law of

---

[3] Peculiarity: St. Bernard's fifth degree of pride: cf. *De Gradibus Humilitatis,* xiv; ed. W. W. Williams, *Select Treatises of St. Bernard of Clairvaux* (Cambridge: University Press, 1926), pp. 136 ff.

all is not without a Law, not however any other than Itself; and though It did not create Itself by this Law, yet It rules Itself by It.

CHAPTER XIII

The law of self-will and cupidity: the law of servants and hirelings

BUT the servant and the hireling have a law, not from the Lord, but which they themselves have made for themselves:—the former by not loving God; the latter by loving something else, more. They have, I say, a law, not the Lord's but their own; nevertheless it is subject to the law which is the Lord's. And indeed each one of them could make a law for himself, but he could not withdraw it from the unchangeable order of the eternal law. Then, I should say, each one made a law unto himself when he preferred his own will to the universal and eternal law, perversely wishing to imitate the Creator, so that just as He is a law unto Himself and this of His own right, so, man also would rule himself and make his own will his own law. Heavy and insupportable yoke upon all the children of Adam alas! bending down our necks and bowing our heads, so that our *life hath drawn nigh to hell* (Ps. lxxxvii, 4). *Unhappy man that I am, who shall deliver me from the body of this death* (Rom. vii, 24)? by which, surely, I am pressed down and almost crushed so that *unless the Lord had been my Helper, my soul had almost dwelt in hell* (Ps. xciii, 17). Weighed down under this burden was he groaning who said: *Why hast Thou set me opposite to Thee, and I am become burdensome to myself* (Job vii, 20)? Where he said, *I am become burdensome to myself,* he shows that he himself was a law unto himself and that no other had done this save himself for himself. But his first remarks when he spoke to God (*Thou hast set me opposite to Thee*) indicated, nevertheless, that he had not escaped the law of God. This, to be sure, pertained to the eternal and just law of God, that he who would refuse to be ruled sweetly by God should be ruled by himself in a state of bondage, and he who of his own accord cast off the sweet yoke and light burden of charity (cf. *Matt.* xi, 30) should unwillingly carry the insupportable burden of his own will. Thus in a wonderful and just way the eternal law both set its fugitive opposite to Himself and kept him subject, for while he did not elude the law of justice which judges according to every man's deserts, he did not, however, remain with God in His light, in His rest, in His glory, but was subject to His power and excluded from His felicity. O Lord my God, *why dost Thou not remove my sin, and why dost Thou not take away my iniquity (Job* vii, 21)? So that, having cast away the heavy load of my own will I may breathe under the light burden of charity, that now I may not be encompassed with servile fear nor seduced by mercenary cupidity, but that I may be led by Thy spirit, the spirit of liberty by which Thy sons are led. And may it give testimony to my spirit that I am one of Thy sons (cf. *Rom.* viii, 14-16) since the same law is mine as is Thine, and as Thou art so may I also be in this world. These, indeed, are they who do what the Apostle says: *Owe no man anything, but love one another (Rom.* xiii, 8); without any doubt as God is, so too are they in this world. They are neither servants nor hirelings, but sons.

CHAPTER XIV

The law governing the charity of sons

THUS neither are sons without law unless perchance someone should think otherwise because of this which has been written: *the law is not made for the just (I Tim.* i, 9). But it ought to be known that the law promulgated in fear by a spirit of servitude is one thing; it is quite another, given in sweetness by a spirit of liberty (cf. *Rom.* viii, 15). Sons are neither constrained to be under the former, nor do they suffer themselves to be without the latter. Do you wish to hear why the law is not given for the just? *You have not received,* he says, *the spirit of bondage again in fear (ibid.).* Do you wish to hear how, nevertheless, they are not without the law of charity? *But you have received,* he adds, *the spirit of adoption of sons (ibid.).* Then, hear the just man confessing both how he is not under the law nor yet without law. *I became,* he says, . . . *to them that are under the law, as if I were under the law (whereas myself was not under the law),* . . . *To them that were without the law, as if I were without the law, (whereas I was not without the law of God, but was in the law of Christ)*

(*I Cor.* ix, 20-21). Hence it is not rightly said that the just have no law, or that the just are without the law, but *the law is not made for the just* (*I Tim.* i, 9); that is, it is not imposed upon them as upon unwilling subjects but it is given them as to willing subjects, with a freedom equal to the sweetness with which it is breathed into them. Hence, also, the Lord says beautifully: *Take up My yoke upon you* (*Matt.* xi, 29); as if He would say: I do not place it upon the unwilling, but you, if you are willing, take it up; otherwise you will find not rest but labor for your souls.

The law of charity, therefore, is good and sweet. It is not only lightly and sweetly borne but renders the laws even of servants and hirelings bearable and light. It does not destroy these laws, to be sure, but it brings about their fulfilment in accordance with Our Lord's words when He said: *I am not come to destroy (the law) but to fulfil it* (*Matt.* v, 17). It modifies the one, it puts order into the other, and it lightens both of them. Never will charity be without fear, but chaste fear; never will it be without cupidity, but kept within bounds. Charity, therefore, perfects the law of the servant when it imparts devotion, and that of the hireling when it orders his cupidity. When devotion is mingled with fear it does not annihilate it, but rather purifies it. Dread of punshment, only, is taken away, without which fear cannot exist so long as it is servile; and this fear is pure and filial, *enduring for ever and ever* (*Ps.* xviii, 10). For the text which reads, *perfect charity casteth out fear* (*I John* iv, 18), is to be understood of a dread of punishment which (as we have said) is never wanting to servile fear. In saying this, we used that sort of speech in which, often, the cause is put for the effect. As for cupidity, it is then kept within bounds by the charity which is joined to it, when evil is completely rejected, better things are preferred to the good, nor are good things desired save for the sake of those which are better. When the complete fulfilment of this will have been attained through God's grace, the body and every good that pertains to the body will be loved only for the sake of the soul, the soul for the sake of God, but God for His own sake.

CHAPTER XV

The four degrees of love, and the happy state of the heavenly country

NEVERTHELESS, because we are carnal (cf. *Rom.* vii, 14) and are born of the concupiscence of the flesh (cf. *I John* ii, 16), it follows as a necessary consequence that our cupidity, or our love should have its source in the flesh. But if it is directed by a right order, advancing by its several degrees under the guidance of grace, it will at last be consummated by the spirit because: *that was not first which is spiritual, but that which is natural* [*animale*]; *afterwards that which is spiritual* (*I Cor.* xv, 46). It is necessary that we first bear *the image of the earthly,* and after that *the image of the heavenly* (*I Cor.* xv, 49). First, therefore, man loves himself for his own sake; for, he is flesh and he can have no taste for anything except for what he is. And when he sees that he cannot subsist by himself, he begins to seek God through faith as something, as it were, necessary for him (cf. *Heb.* xi, 6), and to love Him. Thus he loves God according to the second degree, but for his own sake, not for Himself. But when on account of his own necessity he has begun to worship and come to Him again and again by meditating, by reading, by prayer and by obedience, little by little God becomes known to him through experience, in a sort of familiarity, and consequently He grows sweet; and thus by tasting how sweet is the Lord (cf. *Ps.* xxxiii, 9) he passes to the third degree so that he loves God now, not for his own sake but for Himself. Now in this degree he remains for a very long time and I know not if the fourth degree is attained in its perfection by any man in this life so that, in other words, a man loves himself only for the sake of God. If there are any who have experience of this let them declare it; to me, I confess, it seems impossible. But it will be so, beyond a doubt, when the good and faithful servant has been brought into the joy of his Lord (cf. *Matt.* xxv, 21) and *inebriated with the plenty of God's house* (cf. *Ps.* xxxv, 9). For, forgetful of himself in a wonderful way, as it were, and as though entirely falling away from self he will advance wholly into God, and thereafter being joined to Him he will be one spirit with Him (cf. *I Cor.* vi, 17). I am of the opinion that this is what the prophet meant when he said: *I will enter into the powers of the Lord: O Lord I will be mindful of Thy justice alone* (*Ps.* lxx, 16). He felt, certainly, that when he entered into the spiritual powers of the Lord, he would have laid aside self in all that concerns the infirmities of the flesh; so that now he would have to give no thought to the flesh, but living entirely in the spirit, he would be mindful of the justice of the Lord alone.

Then, for certain, the several individual members of Christ will be able to say, everyone concerning himself, what Paul said of the Head: *And if we have known Christ according to the flesh, but now we know Him so no longer* (*II Cor.* v, 16). No one, there, will know himself according to the flesh because flesh and blood shall not possess the kingdom of God (cf. *I Cor.* xv, 50). Not that the substance of flesh will not be there, but that every carnal necessity will be absent and the love of the flesh will be absorbed in the love of the spirit, and human affections, weak as they now are, shall be changed into those which are divine. Then the net of charity which now, drawn through this great and vast sea does not cease to gather together fish of every kind, when brought at last to the shore, casting forth the bad, will retain only the good (cf. *Matt.* xiii, 47-48). Indeed in this life the net of charity includes fish of every kind within its vast folds, where, fashioning itself to suit all according to the time (cf. *I Cor.* ix, 19) and taking over the good and evil fortunes of all and, in a sense, making them its own, it is wont not only to *rejoice with them that rejoice,* but also *to weep with them that weep* (*Rom.* xii, 15). But when it shall have reached the shore, casting away as bad fishes everything that it suffered in sadness, it will retain those only which can give it pleasure and be to it a source of gladness. For can it be that Paul, for instance, will then be weak with the weak or be on fire for those who are scandalized (cf. *II Cor.* xi, 29), where scandals and weakness will be far away? Or will he, surely, mourn for those who have not done penance (cf. *ibid.* xii, 21), where it is certain there will be no one either sinning or doing penance? Far be it from us to think that he will lament over those who are to be condemned to everlasting fire together with the devil and his angels (cf. *Matt.* xxv, 41), and weep for them in that *City* which *the stream of the river maketh . . . joyful* (Ps. xlv, 5), and whose gates *the Lord loveth . . . above all the tabernacles of Jacob* (Ps. lxxxvi, 2). For in the tabernacles, although the joy of victory is sometimes felt, there is, nevertheless, the anxiety of combat and often danger to life itself; but in that native land no suffering or sadness will be allowed to enter in, even as it is sung thereof: *The dwelling in thee is as it were of all rejoicing* (Ps. lxxxvi, 7); and again: *everlasting joy shall be unto them* (Isa. lxi, 7). Finally, how shall one be mindful of mercy where the justice of God alone will be remembered (cf. Ps. lxx, 16)? Just so, where there will no longer be place for misery or occasion for pity, surely there can be no feeling of compassion.

The end of the book on the Necessity of Loving God.

ANONYMOUS

JESU DULCIS MEMORIA

✝✝✝

If the memory is so sweet, what will the presence be?
ST. BERNARD

THIS TENDER HYMN, so filled with the memory of Christ and with the longing for His return, has been attributed to St. Bernard—and with good reason: his mystical doctrine is its model and its source. The cell of St. Bernard at Clairvaux was full of memories of Christ—and expectations. Yet the author of the *Jesu dulcis memoria* is not St. Bernard. The recent monumental edition of the Latin text goes to show that the author, still unknown, was an English Cistercian who wrote the hymn at the turn of the thirteenth century.[1]

✝✝✝

I

JESU! the very thought of Thee
    With sweetness fills my breast;
But sweeter far thy face to see,
    And in thy presence rest.

Nor voice can sing, nor heart can frame,
    Nor can the memory find,
A sweeter sound than thy blest name,
    O Saviour of mankind!

[1] André Wilmart, OSB, *Le "Jubilus" sur le nom de Jesus dit de saint Bernard* (Ephemerides Liturgicae, LVII, 1-4, 1943).

O hope of every contrite heart,
O joy of all the meek,
To those who fall, how kind Thou art!
How good to those who seek!

But what to those who find? ah! this
Nor tongue nor pen can show:
The love of Jesus, what it is,
None but his lovers know.

Jesu! our only joy be Thou,
As Thou our prize wilt be;
Jesu! be Thou our glory now,
And through eternity.

II

O Jesu! King most wonderful!
Thou Conqueror renown'd!
Thou Sweetness most ineffable!
In whom all joys are found!

When once Thou visitest the heart,
Then truth begins to shine;
Then earthly vanities depart;
Then kindles love divine.

O Jesu! Light of all below!
Thou Fount of life and fire!
Surpassing all the joys we know,
And all we can desire.
May every heart confess thy name,
And ever Thee adore;
And seeking Thee itself inflame,
To seek Thee more and more.
Thee may our tongues for ever bless;
Thee may we love alone;
And ever in our lives express
The image of thine own.

III

O Jesu! Thou the beauty art
　　Of angel worlds above;
Thy name is music to the heart,
　　Enchanting it with love.

Celestial sweetness unalloy'd!
　　Who eat Thee hunger still;
Who drink of Thee still feel a void,
　　Which nought but Thou can fill.

O my sweet Jesu! hear the sighs
　　Which unto Thee I send;
To Thee mine inmost spirit cries,
　　My being's hope and end!

Stay with us, Lord, and with thy light
　　Illume the soul's abyss;
Scatter the darkness of our night,
　　And fill the world with bliss.

O Jesu! spotless Virgin flower!
　　Our life and joy! to Thee
Be praise, beatitude, and power,
　　Through all eternity.

ST. BONAVENTURE

THE ASCENT *of the* MIND *to* GOD

(*Itinerarium Mentis in Deum*)

In everything, be it a thing sensed or a thing known,
God Himself is hidden within.

ITALIAN BY BIRTH (1221), St. Bonaventure entered the Franciscan Order (perhaps in 1243), after completing his course in the
Faculty of Arts of the University of Paris. His actual admission to
the University as a Master was delayed until 1257. But early the
same year, he had been elected General of the Order. He was made
Archbishop of York in 1268, and Cardinal of Albano in 1273.
He died July 15, 1274. His early works include commentaries on
St. Luke and Peter Lombard. The Augustinian direction of his
thought, as well as its devout texture, can be seen from a series of
questions he has discussed on the knowledge of Christ, on the
Trinity, and on evangelical perfection. The *Breviloquium* (before
1257) is an important summary of Christian doctrine according
to St. Bonaventure.

The famous *Ascent of the Mind to God,* written in 1259 (*i.e.,*
thirty-three years after the death of St. Francis), represents St.
Bonaventure at his distinctive best. In the face of the growing
Aristotelianism after the middle of the century, he reasserted zeal-

ously the doctrines of St. Augustine. He distrusted the philosophers, and the Parisian Averroists were at least an excuse for this distrust. That St. Bonaventure's distrust was exaggerated is true. It is no less true that the *Ascent*, written in the spirit of the school of St. Victor, contains an aspect of Christian thought that is as rich as it is traditional. There have been Christian thinkers, such as Richard of St. Victor, who have looked out upon the world neither for knowledge nor for information. They have wanted, not to journey across the world in order finally to discover God; for what need was there to seek to discover a God Who was so hard to avoid? From the world, therefore, they sought aid in admiring God, in devoutly increasing their admiration, until the religious song which was their whole life would soar to the cherished Jerusalem. St. Bonaventure is one of their company, and an illustrious one. The Seraph who had visited Francis on top of Mt. Alverno, some two years before his death, and taught him, not the martyrdom for which Francis longed, but the total devotion of his mind —the same Seraph stands at the beginning of the *Ascent*.

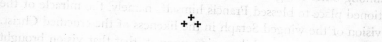

PROLOGUE

I

N THE BEGINNING I CALL UPON THE FIRST BEginning from Whom descend all illuminations as *from the Father of lights* from Whom is *every best gift and every perfect gift*.[1] This is the eternal Father upon Whom I shall call through His Son, our Lord Jesus Christ, that, through the intercession of the most holy Virgin Mary, the Mother of God and of our Lord Jesus Christ, and the intercession of blessed Francis our leader and our father, He may give *enlightened eyes* [2] to our minds *to direct our feet in the way of* that *peace* [3] *which surpasseth all understanding*.[4]

This is the peace which our Lord preached and gave. Our father

[1] *Jas.* i, 17. [2] *Ephes.* i, 18. [3] *Luke* i, 79. [4] *Phil.* iv, 7.

Francis reasserted that preaching. He proclaimed peace at the beginning and at the end in all his preaching; in his every greeting there was a message of desire for peace; and in all his contemplation he yearned for an ecstatic peace, as a citizen of that heavenly Jerusalem. Of this peace, that man of peace, who was *peaceable with them that hated peace,*[5] says: *Pray ye for the things that are for the peace of Jerusalem.*[6] For he knew that the throne of Solomon rested only in peace, since it is written: *His place is in peace: and his abode in Sion.*[7]

¶ 2. And so, following the example of the most blessed father Francis, I was seeking that peace with a breathless soul,—I a sinner who, though all unworthy, am the seventh to succeed as Minister-General of the brothers in the place of the blessed father after his death. It was then that, thirty-three years after the saint's death, at a divine command, I stopped at Mt. Alverno as at a quiet place out of the desire to seek peace of soul. While there, in the course of going through some mental elevations to God, there came to me among other things that miracle which happened in the aforementioned place to blessed Francis himself, namely, the miracle of the vision of the winged Seraph in the likeness of the crucified Christ. I immediately saw, while gazing upon it, that that vision brought out the elevation of father Francis himself in contemplation and the way by which that elevation is reached.

¶3. For by those six wings we may rightly understand the elevations of the six illuminations by which the soul is disposed, as by certain grades or steps, to reach peace through the ecstatic excesses of Christian wisdom. Now the way is only through the most burning love of the Crucified, which so transformed Paul into Christ when he was *caught up to the third heaven*[8] that he said: *with Christ I am nailed to the Cross; and I live, now not I, but Christ liveth in me.*[9] This most burning love likewise so absorbed the mind of Francis, that his mind revealed itself in its flesh, as he carried the most sacred stigmata of the Passion in his body for two years before his death.

[5] *Ps.* cxix, 7.   [6] *Ps.* cxii, 6.   [7] *Ps.* lxxv, 3.   [8] *II Cor.* xii, 2.
[9] *Gal.* iv, 19-20.

The image of the six Seraphic wings, therefore, suggests the six graded illuminations which begin with creatures and lead us to God Whom no one rightly reaches except through the Crucified. For *he that entereth not by the door into the sheepfold, but climbeth up another way, the same is a thief and a robber.*[10] But *if any man enter in through* this door, *he shall go in and go out, and shall find pastures.*[11] That is why John says in the *Apocalypse: Blessed are they that wash their robes in the blood of the Lamb: that they may have a right to the tree of life, and may enter in by the gate into the city.*[12] This is as much as to say that there is no entering the heavenly Jerusalem through contemplation unless it be through the blood of the Lamb as through a door. For one is not disposed in any way towards the divine contemplations which lead to excesses of soul except unless one be with Daniel a *man of desires.*[13] Now desires are kindled in us in two ways, namely, through the cry of prayer which makes one roar with *the groaning of the heart,*[14] and through the brightness of speculation by which the soul turns itself most directly and most strenuously to the rays of light.

¶ 4. And so I first invite the reader to the groaning of prayer through the crucified Christ through Whose blood we are purged of the uncleanness of sins; and I invite him first to prayer lest perchance he believe that it is enough for him to have reading without holiness, speculation without devotion, investigation without admiration, circumspection without exaltation, industry without piety, knowledge without charity, understanding without humility, study without divine grace, a mirror without divinely inspired wisdom.

To those who have been met by grace, therefore, the humble and the pious, those who have compunction and those who are devout, those who are anointed with the oil of gladness and those who love divine wisdom and who are afire with a desire for it, those who wish to give themselves to magnifying, admiring and even tasting God,—to these I propose the following speculations, with the contention that the mirror that is offered to us from the outside means little or nothing unless the mirror of our mind has been cleansed and polished.

[10] *Jo.* x, 1.   [11] *Jo.* x, 9.   [12] *Apoc.* xxii, 14.   [13] *Dan.* ix, 23.
[14] *Ps.* xxxvii, 9.

Exercise yourself, therefore, O man of God, on the prodding goad of conscience before you raise your eyes to the rays of wisdom reflected in wisdom's mirrors, lest, from the very vision of the rays, you might possibly fall into a deeper pit of darkness.

¶ 5. It seemed good to me to divide the tractate into seven chapters, giving the titles in advance for the easier understanding of the things that are to be said. I ask, furthermore, that you weigh the writer's intention rather than his execution, the meaning of his words rather than his unpolished language, the truth rather than the charm, the training of affection rather than the instruction of the intellect. To this end, the development of these speculations should not be run over perfunctorily; it should be mulled over very slowly.

CHAPTER V

The Contemplation of the Divine Unity by Way of Its Primary Name Which is Being

I

IT IS POSSIBLE to contemplate God not only outside us and within us, but also above us. Outside us we contemplate Him through His vestige, within us through His image and above us through the light which is sealed on our minds.[15] This light is the light of the Eternal Truth since "our very mind is immediately formed by Truth itself." [16] Those who have been trained in the first mode of contemplation have already entered into the court before the Tabernacle; those who have been trained in the second have entered into the Holy Places; but those who have been trained in the third enter with the High Priest into the Holy of Holies, where above the ark are the Cherubim of glory overshadowing the Propitiatory. By these Cherubim we understand the two modes or grades of contemplating the invisible and eternal things of God. One of them is turned to what belongs to the divine essence, while the other is turned to what is appropriated to the Divine Persons.

15 *Ps.* iv, 7.
16 St. Augustine, *De Diversis Quaestionibus LXXXIII*, q. 51, nos. 2, 4 (PL 40, 32-33, 33-34); Pseudo-Augustine, *De Spiritu et Anima*, ch. 11 (PL 40, 786).

¶ 2. The first mode primarily and principally fixes the sight on being itself, declaring that *He who is* is the first name of God.[17] The second mode fixes the sight on the good itself, declaring that this is the first name of God. The first looks most to the Old Testament, which preaches especially the unity of the divine essence. Hence was it said to Moses: *I am who am.* The second looks to the New Testament, which determines the plurality of the Divine Persons, baptizing *in the name of the Father and of the Son and of the Holy Ghost.*[18] That is why our master Christ, wishing to raise to evangelical perfection a youth who had observed the Law, attributes to God principally and distinctively the name of goodness. *None, He said, is good but God alone.*[19] That is why Damascene, who follows Moses, says that *He who is* is the first name of God; while Dionysius, who follows Christ, says that the Good is the first name of God.[20]

¶ 3. He, therefore, who wishes to contemplate the invisible things of God with reference to the unity of His essence must first fix his sight on being itself; and he should see that being itself is in itself so certain that it cannot be thought not to be: for the most pure being itself is found only in the complete avoidance of non-being, just as *nothing* is found in the complete avoidance of being. Just as, therefore, every *nothing* has no part of being or of its conditions, so, contrariwise, being itself has no part of non-being, neither actually nor potentially, neither in reality nor according to our judgment. But since non-being is the privation of being, it does not strike the intellect except through being. Being, however, does not strike the intellect through anything else, for everything that is grasped by the intellect is grasped either as a non-being or as a being in potency or as a being in act. Hence if a non-being cannot be grasped except through a being, and if a being in potency cannot be grasped except through a being in act; if, furthermore, being is the name of the pure act of what is being:—it follows that being is that which first falls in the intellect, and this being is that which is pure act. But this being is not a particular being, which is a lim-

[17] Cf. *Exod.* III, 14.   [18] *Matt.* XXVIII, 19.   [19] *Luke* XVIII, 19.
[20] St. John Damascene, *De Fide Orthodoxa*, I, 9 (PG 94, 836); Pseudo-Dionysius, *De Divinis Nominibus*, III, 1; IV, 1 (PG 3, 680; 693).

ited being, since it is mixed with potency; nor is it an analogous being because it is least possessed of actuality, since it least exists. It remains, therefore, that this being is the divine being.

¶ 4. Strange, therefore, is the blindness of the intellect which does not observe the being that it sees before all others and without which it cannot know anything. As the eye, intent upon the various differences of colors, does not see the light through which it sees other things, and, if it does see, it does not notice, so the eye of our mind, intent upon beings that are particular and universal, does not notice the being that is beyond every genus, even though this is what first comes to the mind and even though the mind sees other beings through it. Hence it is most truly apparent that "as the eye of the bat is disposed towards the light, so the eye of our mind is disposed towards the most evident things in nature." [21] For having become accustomed to opaqueness in beings and to the phantasms of sensible things, the eye of our mind seems to itself to be seeing nothing when it sees the light itself of the highest being. It does not understand that this very darkness is the highest illumination of our mind, in the same way as, when the eye sees pure light, it seems to itself to see nothing.

¶ 5. Behold, therefore, if you can, this most pure being, and what you find is that it cannot be thought as derived from another. That is why it is necessarily thought as in every way prime, since it can be neither from nothing nor from something. For, after all, what being is through itself if being itself is not through itself or of itself? The most pure being also presents itself to you as completely lacking in non-being; it has thus no beginning nor end, but is eternal. It likewise presents itself as possessing in every way only that which is being itself; it is therefore not composed with anything, but is rather most simple. Furthermore, it contains nothing of possibility, since every possible being is in some way possessed of some non-being; it is therefore supremely actual. It is in no way subject to lack, and is thus most perfect. Finally, it has nothing of diversity, and thus presents itself to you as supremely one.

The being, therefore, which is pure and simple and absolute is

21 Aristotle, *Metaph.*, Iα, I, 993b 9.

the being that is primary, eternal, most simple, most actual, mos' perfect and supremely one.

¶ 6. What is more, these conclusions are so certain that he whc has an understanding of being cannot think their opposite; and one of them necessarily implies the other. For, because being itself is unqualifiedly being, therefore it is unqualifiedly prime; and because it is unqualifiedly prime, therefore it has not been made by another, nor could it be made by itself: it is therefore eternal. Again, because it is prime and eternal, it is therefore not composed of other things and is consequently most simple. Furthermore, as prime, eternal and most simple, it has nothing of possibility mixed with act and is thus most actual. Moreover, as prime, eternal, most simple and most actual, it is therefore most perfect; for such a being lacks absolutely nothing, nor can any addition be made to it. As prime, eternal, most simple, most actual and most perfect, it is as a consequence supremely one. For what is said by unrestricted superabundance is said in comparison with all things. "For it is impossible that that which is said unqualifiedly by superabundance should belong to any but one being alone." [22] Hence, if *God* is the name of the being that is primary, eternal, most simple, most actual and most perfect, such a being cannot be thought not to be, nor can it be thought to be other than one. Therefore: *Hear, O Israel, thy God is one God*.[23] If you behold this in pure simplicity of mind, you will be covered somewhat by the illumination of the Eternal Light.

¶ 7. But there is matter here to rouse you to admiration. For being itself is first and last, it is eternal and most present, it is simplest and greatest, it is most actual and most immutable, it is most perfect and boundless, it is supremely one and yet all-perfect. If you wonder at these things with a pure mind, you will be covered with a greater light as you take the further step and see that the pure being is last because it is first. For since it is first, it accomplishes all things for itself; and hence it necessarily is the last end, the beginning and the consummation, the *Alpha* and the *Omega*. It is most present because it is eternal. For, being eternal, it does not come from another nor does it fall away from itself, nor yet

[22] Aristotle, *Topics*, V, 5, 134b 24.   [23] Cf. *Deut.* vi, 4.

does it proceed from one thing to another: it has therefore neither a past being nor a future being, but only a being that is present. It is greatest because it is most simple. For, being most simple in its essence, it is therefore greatest in power, since power is the more infinite according as it is more unified.[24] It is most immutable because it is most actual. For it is pure act by being most actual; and every such being acquires nothing new, loses nothing of what it possesses, and consequently cannot change. It is boundless because it is most perfect. For since it is most perfect, nothing can be thought more perfect than it, more noble or of higher dignity, and consequently nothing greater. Now every such being is boundless. It is all-perfect because it is supremely one. For that which is supremely one is the universal source of all multitude. It is consequently the universal efficient, exemplary and final cause of all things, as "the cause of being, the principle of understanding and the order of living."[25] Pure being is therefore all-perfect, not as being the essence of all things, but as the most supremely excellent and most universal cause of all essences, whose power is supremely boundless and multiple in its efficacy because it is supremely unified in its essence.

¶ 8. Let us return again to our beginning and say that because the most pure and absolute being (that is, the being that is unqualifiedly being) is first and last, it is for this reason the beginning and the consummating end of all things. As eternal and most present, it consequently encompasses and penetrates all durations, as though being at once their center and their circumference. Because it is most simple and most great, it is therefore as a whole within all things and as a whole outside them. It is therefore "an intelligible sphere whose center is everywhere and whose circumference is nowhere."[26] Because it is most perfect and boundless, it is within all things, but not included in them, it is outside all things, but not excluded, it is above all things, but not upraised, it is below all things but not beneath them. Furthermore, by being supremely one

24 *Liber de Causis,* Prop. 17; ed. R. Steele, *Opera hactenus inedita Rogeri Baconi,* Fasc. XII, Oxford: Clarendon Press, 1935, p. 175.
25 St. Augustine, *De Civit. Dei,* VIII, 4 (PL 41, 228-229).
26 Alain of Lille, *Theolog. Regulae,* Reg. VII (PL 210, 627).

and all-perfect it is *all in all*,[27] though all things be many and it is only one. And this is so because all power, all exemplarity and all communicability exists in it according to the simplest unity, the clearest truth and the purest goodness. Hence it is that *of Him, and by Him, and in Him are all things*.[28] For God is all-powerful, all-knowing and all-good; and to see such a good perfectly is to be happy, as it was said to Moses: *I will show thee all good*.[29]

CHAPTER VI

The Contemplation of the Most Blessed Trinity in Its Name, which *is the* Good

I

HAVING considered what belongs to the essence of God, we must now raise the eye of the understanding to the vision of the most Blessed Trinity, so that the second Cherub may take his place opposite the first. Now just as being itself is the root source of our vision of what belongs to the divine essence as well as the name through which other things are known, so the Good itself is the principal foundation of our contemplation of the divine emanation.

¶ 2. Do you, therefore, see and observe that that is best which is unqualifiedly that than which a greater cannot be thought. Furthermore, it is such that it cannot be rightly thought not to be, since to be is in every way better than not to be; and it is such that it cannot be thought rightly without being thought as trine and one. For "the good is said to be diffusive of itself," [30] and the highest good therefore is supremely diffusive of itself. But such a supreme diffusion cannot take place unless it be actual and intrinsic, substantial and hypostatic, natural and voluntary, free and necessary, unfailing and perfect. Unless, therefore, there were eternally in the highest good an actual and consubstantial production, and this of a hypostasis of equal dignity (such as is the case with one who produces by way of generation and spiration), so that it be the

---

[27] *I Cor.* xv, 28.   [28] *Rom.* xi, 36.   [29] *Exod.* xxxiii, 19.
[30] Pseudo-Dionysius, *De Cael. Hier.*, IV, 1 (PG 3, 120); *De Div. Nom.*, IV, 1 (PG 3, 693).

production of an eternal principle eternally co-principiating, so that, furthermore, there would be one loved and one loved mutually, one generated and one spirated, that is, the Father, the Son and the Holy Spirit,—unless this were so, the highest good would in no way be highest because it would not supremely diffuse itself. For the diffusion of the divine goodness in time, in the world of creatures, is only a center or a point in comparison with the immensity of the eternal goodness. That is why a greater diffusion than it can be thought, that, namely, in which He who diffuses communicates to another His whole substance and nature. The highest good, therefore, would not be the highest good if it could, either in reality or in our understanding of it, lack these things.

Hence, if you are able to see with the eye of your mind the purity of the goodness which is the pure act of the Principle lovingly loving with a love which is free and owing and mixed of both [31] (which act is a plenary diffusion according to the mode of nature and will, a diffusion in the manner of the Word in which all things are spoken and in the manner of the Gift in which all other gifts are given),—if you are able to do this, then you can see, through the supreme communicability of the good, that the Trinity of Father, Son and Holy Spirit must be. In the Trinity it is necessary that there be supreme communicability because of supreme goodness, supreme consubstantiality because of supreme communicability, supreme configurability because of supreme consubstantiality. And as a result of these there must be supreme co-equality and hence supreme co-eternity; and as a result there must also be supreme mutual intimacy, by which one Person is necessarily in another according to a supreme circumincession, and one works with another according to the complete indivision of the substance and power and operation of the Blessed Trinity Itself.

¶ 3. Yet when you contemplate these things, see to it that you do not think that you are comprehending the incomprehensible. For here are six further characteristics to consider in the Divine Trinity which will drive the eye of the mind to gaping admiration. For in the Trinity there is supreme communicability together with a distinction of Persons, supreme consubstantiality with a plurality of

31 Cf. Richard of St. Victor, *De Trinitate*, V, 16 (PL 196, 961).

hypostases, supreme configurability with distinct personality, supreme co-equality with order, supreme co-eternity with emanation, supreme mutual intimacy with the mission of Persons. Who is there who does not rise in admiration in the presence of such wonders?

Even so, we understand most certainly that all these things are in the Blessed Trinity if we raise our eyes to the all-excelling Goodness. For if there is in this Goodness the highest communication and a true diffusion, then there is there true origination and true distinction. Furthermore, since it is the whole, and not a part, which is communicated, therefore that which is given (the whole of it) is the very thing which is possessed; so that He who proceeds and He who produces are both distinguished by their personal properties and are one in essence. And because they are distinguished by properties, they therefore have personal properties, plurality of hypostases, an emanation of origin and an order, not of posteriority, but of origin, a mission which is not that of local change but of free inspiration, by reason of the authority of the One Producing, possessed by the Sender in relation to Him Who is sent. Moreover, because the divine Persons are substantially one, there must therefore be among them unity in essence and form and dignity and eternity and existence and incircumscribability.

Therefore, as you consider these things one by one, you have wherewith to contemplate the truth. When you compare them with one another, you have wherewith to be raised in the highest admiration. And so, that your mind may rise through admiration to an admiring contemplation these are proposed together for your consideration.

¶ 4. For the Cherubim themselves, who looked towards one another, point this out. Nor is there wanting mystery in the fact that they looked towards one another, *their faces being turned toward the Propitiatory.*[32] Hence is verified what Our Lord says in John: *this is eternal life, that they may know thee, the only true God, and Jesus Christ, whom thou hast sent.*[33] For we must admire the characteristics of the divine essence and the divine Persons not only in themselves, but also in relation to the most wonderful union of God and man in the unity of the person of Christ.

[32] *Exod.* xxv, 20.   [33] *Jo.* xvii, 3.

¶ 5. Are you the Cherub contemplating what belongs to the essence of God? And do you wonder that the divine being is at once first and last, eternal and most present, most simple and greatest or uncircumscribed, everywhere as a whole and nowhere comprehended, most actual and never moved, most perfect and having nothing superfluous or missing, and yet boundless and unlimitedly infinite, supremely one and yet all-perfect, as possessing all things in Himself—all power, all truth, all goodness? If you wonder at these attributes of the divine essence, turn to the Propitiatory and wonder that in it the First Principle is joined with the last, God is joined with man who was formed on the sixth day, the eternal is joined with temporal man, born of a Virgin in the fullness of time, the most simple is joined with the supremely composite, the most actual is joined with the supremely subject to corruption and death, the most perfect and boundless is joined to a mite, the supremely one and all-perfect is joined to the individual that is composite and distinct from all others, that is, to the man Jesus Christ.

Perhaps you are the other Cherub, contemplating the properties of the divine Persons. And perhaps you wonder that communicability can exist with personal propriety, consubstantiality with plurality, configurability with personality, co-equality with order, co-eternity with emanation, mutual intimacy with mission (for the Son is sent by the Father, and the Holy Spirit by both, and yet the Holy Spirit always remains with them and never departs from them). If you are thus the second Cherub, then turn to the Propitiatory and wonder that in Christ there is found a personal union with a trinity of substances and a duality of natures; there is found complete agreement of judgment with a plurality of wills; there is found together a predication of God and man with a plurality of properties; there is found co-adoration with a plurality of ranks; there is found co-elevation over all things with a plurality of dignities; and there is found co-domination with a plurality of powers.

¶ 6. In this contemplation there is a perfect illumination of the mind when, as on the sixth day, it sees man made to the image of God. For if an *image* is an expressive likeness, when our mind contemplates in Christ the Son of God, Who is by nature the image of the invisible God, our human nature so wonderfully exalted, so ineffably united:—when our mind has this contemplation and sees in one the first and the last, the highest and the lowest, the circumference and the center, the *Alpha* and *Omega,* the caused and the cause, the creator and the creature, the book, namely, that is written both within and without, then it has reached a certain perfect reality, so that it can with God arrive at the perfection of its illuminations in the sixth grade as on the sixth day. Nor does anything further remain except the day of rest, on which, through an excess of mind, the sight of the human mind rests *from all the work which it has done.*[34]

CHAPTER VII

On the Mystical Excess of Mind, in which, when by Excess Love Completely Passes to God, Repose is given to the Intellect

I

THE MIND, therefore, goes over these six contemplations as the six steps of the throne of the true Solomon, and by them it reaches the peace in which he who is truly a man of peace reposes in a mind that is at peace as in an inner Jerusalem; it also goes over them as the six wings of the Cherub, by means of which the mind of the true contemplative, filled with the illumination of heavenly wisdom, is able to be led upward; and it also uses them as the six first days of creation, in which the mind must exercise itself so that it might finally reach the Sabbath of rest.

And after our mind, through these contemplations, has seen God outside itself through and in His vestiges, within itself through and in His image, and above itself through the likeness of the divine light shining over us and in the divine light itself (so far as this is possible according to the state of this life and the exercise of our mind); and when at length in the sixth grade of contemplation the mind reaches the point of seeing in the first and highest principle and in the mediator of God and men, Jesus Christ, those things whose like can in no wise be found among creatures and which transcend every power of the human intellect:—when the human mind has reached this point, there remains for it to transcend these

[34] Cf. *Gen.* ii, 2.

things in contemplation and to leave behind not only this world of sense but also itself. In this crossing Christ is *the way* and *the door, the ladder* and *the conveyance* as *the Propitiatory placed above the ark of God* and *the mystery hidden from eternity*.[35]

¶ 2. He who looks upon the Propitiatory with the full turning of his face, and through faith, hope and charity, through devotion, admiration, exaltation, appreciation, praise and jubilation sees Christ hanging upon the Cross, such a one celebrates with Him the Pasch, that is, the Passover, so that through the rod of the Cross he may pass over the Red Sea, from Egypt entering the desert where he may taste the *hidden manna* and may rest with Christ in a sepulchre as though externally dead, yet withal feeling, so far as is possible according to the state of the present life, what was said on the Cross to the thief who adhered to Christ: *This day thou shalt be with me in paradise*.[36]

¶ 3. This was shown likewise to the Blessed Francis when in the excess of contemplation on the mountaintop (where I went over in my mind the words that I am writing here) there appeared to him the six-winged Seraph affixed to a cross, as I and many others have heard, in the same place, from the companion who was with him. There Francis crossed to God in an excess of contemplation, and he was made an example of perfect contemplation even as formerly he had been an example of action, like another Jacob and Israel, so that through Francis God might invite all truly spiritual men to such a crossing and excess of mind by example rather than by word.

¶ 4. That this transport may be perfect, it is necessary that all intellectual operations be abandoned within it, and that the peak of the affections be as a whole transferred and redirected towards God. This is, however, something mystical and most secret, *which no man knoweth but he that receiveth it;*[37] and only he receives it who desires it, and only he desires it whom the fire of the Holy Spirit, sent by Christ to the earth, inflames to his very marrow. That is why

---

[35] *Jo.* xiv, 6; x, 7; *Exod.* xxv, 20; *Ephes.* iii, 9.
[36] *Luke* xxiii, 43.   [37] *Apoc.* ii, 17.

the Apostle says that this mystical wisdom is revealed by the Holy Spirit.[38]

¶ 5. But since to this end nature avails nothing and industry very little, very little should be granted to inquiry and much to devotion, little to outward speech and much to interior joy, little to the spoken and written word and the whole to the gift of God, that is, to the Holy Spirit, little or nothing to the creature and the whole to the creative essence, the Father and the Son and the Holy Spirit, addressing the Trinity in the words of Dionysius as follows: "O super-essential Trinity, super-God, and super-good Director of the divine wisdom of Christians, direct us towards the supremely unknown and supremely bright and sublime peak of mystical knowledge. There the new and absolute and incorruptible mysteries of theology are hidden according to the super-brilliant darkness of a secretly teaching silence, a darkness that supremely illumines an obscurity that is most manifest, in which everything is revealed, and which completely fulfills unseeing intellects with the splendors of unseen supreme goods." These are Dionysius' words to God; but let us join Dionysius in the words which he addresses to the friend to whom this treatise is written: "But thou, O friend, in a constantly strengthened effort towards mystical visions, do thou desert the senses and intellectual operations, sensible things and invisible things, every non-being and being, and, unaware of thyself, be restored, as far as is possible, to the unity who is above all essence and knowledge. And abandoning all things and freed from all things, do thou ascend to the super-essential ray of the divine darkness by means of an ecstasy of a pure mind which is entirely freed and delivered from thyself and from all other things." [39]

¶ 6. If you should inquire how these things may be, direct your question towards grace, not towards instruction, towards desire, not towards understanding, towards the groaning of prayer, not the inquiry of reading, towards the Spouse, not the teacher, towards God, not man, towards darkness, not brightness; not towards the light, but towards that fire that completely inflames and leads to

[38] *I Cor.* ii, 10.
[39] Pseudo-Dionysius, *De Mystica Theol.*, I, 1 (*via* Eriugena, PL., 122, 1171-1173).

God by transporting devotions and most burning desires. For this *fire* is God, and His *furnace is in Jerusalem*;[40] and Christ enkindles this furnace in the heat of his most burning passion, a heat which is perceived by him alone who says: *My soul chooseth hanging, and my bones death.*[41] And it is he who loves this death who can see God; for the indubitable truth is this: *Man shall not see me and live.*[42]

Let us, therefore, die and go forth into the darkness. Let us still our cares and our desires and our imaginings. Let us go with Christ crucified *from this world to the Father,*[43] so that, when we have seen the Father, we may say with Philip; *It is enough for us,*[44] and we may hear with Paul: *My grace is sufficient for thee;*[45] and so that we may exult with David and say: *My flesh and my heart hath fainted away: thou art the God of my heart, and the God that is my portion forever.*[46] *Blessed be the Lord forever, and let all the people say: so be it, so be it.*[47] Amen.

[40] *Isa.* xxxi, 9. [41] *Job* vii, 15. [42] *Exod.* xxxiii, 20. [43] *Jo.* xiii, 1.
[44] *Jo.* xiv, 8. [45] *II Cor.* xii, 9. [46] *Ps.* lxxii, 26. [47] *Ps.* cv, 48.

ST. THOMAS AQUINAS

WISDOM, BEATITUDE
and the INCARNATION
(from the *Summa Contra Gentiles*)

+‡+

> In the name of the divine mercy I have the confidence
> to embark upon the work of a wise man, even though
> this may surpass my powers, and I have set myself the
> task of making known, as far as my limited powers
> will allow, the truth which the Catholic Faith pro-
> fesses, and of setting aside the errors that are opposed
> to it. To use the words of Hilary: *I am aware that I
> owe this to God as the chief duty of my life, that my
> every word and sense speak of Him.*

BORN EARLY IN 1225, St. Thomas entered upon his early studies
in the University of Naples. From there he went to Paris in 1245.
During 1248-1252, he studied under St. Albert the Great in
Cologne. He taught in Paris (1257-1259), at the Papal Curia in
Italy (1259-1268), and again in Paris during stormy days (1269-
1272). In 1272 he was asked by his Order to found a house of
studies in Naples. He died March 7, 1274, at the Cistercian monastery of Fossanuova, on his way to the Council of Lyons. Canonized by Pope John XXII (July 18, 1323), St. Thomas has received
extraordinary commendation from the Church, including the honor
of being her *Common Doctor.*

The writings of St. Thomas are a landmark in the history of
Western thought. To discover the reason and nature of man in
the integrity and autonomy of its specific constitution; to defend
the human in man without isolating it from God, as did the

Averroists, and without violating its creaturely dignity, as the
Augustinians tended to do; to serve with calm order and justice
the unity of truth at a moment when others either destroyed or
despaired of it; to insist upon the humanism of the Incarnation,
upon the mystery of a divine love which, in generous response to
the deepest desires of man's rational nature, freely raises man to
a life with God which man could not have expected but which,
once given, answers beyond measure to man's search for beatitude:
—such accomplishments, achieved with firmness and charity, St.
Thomas can lay claim to in his discussions on faith and on the
power of God; in his *Summa Contra Gentiles* (about 1260) and
in his *Summa Theologica* (1266-1272), a work which stands as
an unrivaled classic in Catholic theology. To these works we must
add his commentaries on Aristotle and Boethius, as well as a
number of short treatises (e.g., *On Being and Essence, On Separate Substances*) that are masterpieces of philosophical analysis.

Yet St. Thomas remains primarily and eminently a student of
divine wisdom, meditating on the marvels of the ways of God
to man.

I

The author's intention in the present work[1]

MONG ALL HUMAN PURSUITS, THE PURSUIT OF
wisdom is more perfect, more noble, more useful
and more full of joy.

It is more perfect because, in so far as a man
gives himself to the pursuit of wisdom, so far
does he even now have some share in true beati-
tude. And so a wise man has said: Blessed is the man that shall
continue in wisdom (*Ecclus.* xiv, 22).

It is more noble because through this pursuit man especially approaches to a likeness to God Who *made all things in wisdom* (*Ps.
ciii, 24*). And since likeness is the cause of love, the pursuit of
wisdom especially joins man to God in friendship. That is why it

[1] *Summa Contra Gentiles*, I, c. 2.

is said of wisdom that *she is an infinite treasure to men! which they that use become the friends of God* (*Wis.* vii, 14).

It is more useful because through wisdom we arrive at the kingdom of immortality. For the desire of wisdom bringeth to the everlasting kingdom (*Wis.* vi, 21).

It is more full of joy because *her conversation hath no bitterness, nor her company any tediousness, but joy and gladness* (*Wis.* viii, 16).

And so, in the name of the divine mercy I have the confidence to embark upon the work of a wise man, even though this may surpass my powers, and I have set myself the task of making known, as far as my limited powers will allow, the truth which the Catholic faith professes, and of setting aside the errors that are opposed to it. To use the words of Hilary: *I am aware that I owe this to God as the chief duty of my life, that my every word and sense may speak of Him.*[2]

To proceed against individual errors, however, is a difficult business, and this for two reasons. In the first place, it is difficult because the sacrilegious remarks of individual men who have erred are not so well known to us so that we may use what they say as the basis of proceeding to a refutation of their errors. This is, indeed, the method which the ancient Doctors of the Church used in the refutation of the errors of the gentiles. For they could know the positions taken by the gentiles since they themselves had been gentiles, or at least had lived among the gentiles and had been instructed in their teaching. In the second place, it is difficult because some of them, such as the Mohammedans and the pagans, do not agree with us in accepting the authority of any Scripture, by which they might be convinced of their error. Thus, against the Jews we are able to argue by means of the Old Testament, while against heretics we are able to argue by means of the New Testament. But the Mohammedans and the pagans accept neither the one nor the other. We must therefore have recourse to the natural reason, to which all men are forced to give their assent. However, it is true, in divine matters the natural reason has its failings.

Now while we are investigating some given truth, we shall also show what errors are set aside by it; and we shall likewise show

2 St. Hilary, *De Trinitate*, I, 37 (PL 10, 48).

how the truth that we come to know by demonstration is in accord
with the Christian religion.

I I

On the way in which divine truth is to be made known [3]

THE WAY of making truth known is not always the same. For as
the Philosopher has very well said, *it belongs to an educated man
to seek such certitude in each thing as the nature of that thing
allows.*[4] The remark is also quoted by Boethius.[5] But since such is
the case, we must first show what way is open to us in order that
we may make known the truth which is our object.

There is a twofold mode of truth in what we profess about God.
Some truths about God exceed all the ability of the human reason.
Such is the truth that God is triune. But there are some truths which
the natural reason itself is able to reach. Such are that God exists,
that He is one, and the like. In fact, such truths about God have
been proved demonstratively by the philosophers, guided by the
natural light of reason.

That there are truths about God which totally surpass man's ability appears with the greatest evidence. Since, indeed, the principle of
all knowledge which the reason perceives about any being is the
understanding of the very substance of that being (for according
to Aristotle *what a thing is* is the principle of demonstration),[6]
it follows that the way in which we know the substance of a thing
determines the way in which we know what belongs to it. Hence,
if the human intellect comprehends the substance of some thing,
e.g., that of a stone or of a triangle, no intelligible characteristic
belonging to that thing surpasses the grasp of the human reason.
But this is not what happens to us in relation to God. For the human intellect is not able to reach a comprehension of the divine
substance through its own natural power. For according to its manner of knowing in the present life, the intellect depends on the
sense for the origin of knowledge; and so those things which do
not fall under the senses cannot be grasped by the human intellect

[3] *Summa Contra Gentiles*, I, c. 3.
[4] Aristotle, *Nicomachean Ethics*, I, 3 (1094 b 24).
[5] Boethius, *De Trinitate*, II (PL 64, 1250).
[6] Aristotle, *Posterior Analytics*, II, 3 (90 b 31).

except in so far as the knowledge of them is gathered from sensible things. Now sensible things cannot lead the human intellect to the point of seeing in them the nature of the divine substance; for sensible things are effects which fall short of the power of their cause. Yet, beginning with sensible things, our intellect is led to the point of knowing about God that He exists, and other such characteristics which must be attributed to the First Principle. There are, consequently, some intelligible truths about God which are open to the human reason; but there are others which absolutely surpass its power.

We may easily reach the same conclusion from the gradation of intellects. Consider the case of two persons of whom one has a more penetrating grasp of a thing by means of his intellect than does the other. He who has the superior intellect understands many things which the other one cannot grasp at all. Such is the case with a very simple person who has absolutely no comprehension of the subtle speculations of philosophy. But the intellect of an angel surpasses the human intellect much more than the intellect of the greatest philosopher surpasses the intellect of the most uncultivated simple person; for the distance between the best philosopher and a simple person is contained within the limits of the human species, which the angelic intellect surpasses. For the angel knows God on the basis of a more noble effect than does man; and this by as much as the substance of an angel, through which the angel in his natural knowledge is led to the knowledge of God, is nobler than sensible things and even than the soul itself, through which the human intellect mounts to the knowledge of God. Now, the divine intellect surpasses the angelic intellect much more than the angelic surpasses the human. For the divine intellect is in its capacity equal to its substance, and therefore it knows fully what it is, including all its intelligible attributes. But by his natural knowledge the angel does not know the nature of God, since the substance itself of the angel, through which he is led to the knowledge of God, is an effect that is not equal to the power of its cause. Hence, the angel is not able, by means of his natural knowledge, to grasp all the things which God understands in Himself; nor is the human reason sufficient to grasp all the things which the angel understands through his own natural power. Just as, therefore, it would be the height of folly for a simple person to assert that what a philosopher proposes is false on the ground that he himself cannot understand it, so (and even more so) it is the acme of stupidity for a man to judge as false what is divinely revealed through the ministry of the angels simply because it cannot be investigated by reason.

The same thing appears quite clearly from the defect which we experience every day in our knowledge of things. We do not know a great many of the properties of sensible things, and in most cases we are not able to discover fully the natures of those properties which we apprehend by the sense. Much more is it the case, therefore, that the human reason is not equal to the task of investigating all the intelligible characteristics of that most excellent substance.

The remark of Aristotle likewise agrees with his conclusion. He says that *our intellect is related to the prime beings, which are most evident in their nature, as the eye of an owl is related to the sun.*[7]

Sacred Scripture also gives testimony to this truth. We read in *Job: Peradventure thou wilt comprehend the steps of God, and wilt find out the Almighty perfectly* (xi, 7)? And again: *Behold, God is great, exceeding our knowledge* (*Job* xxxvi, 26). And St. Paul: *We know in part* (*I Cor.* xiii, 9).

We should not therefore immediately reject as false, following the opinion of the Manicheans and many unbelievers, everything that is said about God even though it cannot be investigated by reason.

III

That the truth about God to which the natural reason reaches is fittingly proposed to men for belief [8]

SINCE, therefore, there exists a twofold truth concerning the divine being, one to which the inquiry of the reason can reach, the other which surpasses the whole ability of the human reason, it is fitting that both of these truths be proposed to man divinely for belief. This point must first be shown concerning that truth which is open to the inquiry of the reason; or otherwise it might perhaps seem to someone that, since such a truth can be known by the reason, it was

[7] Aristotle, *Metaphysics*, I, 1 (993 b 9).
[8] *Summa Contra Gentiles*, I, c. 4.

pointless to give it to men through a supernatural inspiration as an object of belief.

Yet if this truth were left solely as a matter of inquiry for the human reason, there would follow three awkward consequences.

The first is that few men would possess the knowledge of God. For there are three reasons why most men are cut off from the fruit of diligent inquiry which is the discovery of truth. Some do not have the physical disposition for such work. As a result, there are many who are naturally not fitted for knowledge; and so, however much they try, they would be unable to reach the highest level of human knowledge which consists in knowing God. Others are cut off from pursuing this truth by the necessities imposed upon them by their daily lives. For some men must devote themselves to taking care of temporal matters. Now such men would not be able to give so much time to the leisure of contemplative inquiry as to reach the highest peak at which human investigation can arrive, namely, the knowledge of God. Finally, there are some who are cut off by indolence. In order to know the things which the reason can investigate concerning God, a knowledge of many things must already be possessed. For all of philosophy is directed towards the knowledge of God, and that is why metaphysics, whose occupation aims at divine things, is the last part of philosophy to be learned. This means that we are able to arrive at the inquiry concerning the aforementioned truth only on the basis of a great deal of labor spent in study. Now those who wish to undergo such a labor for the mere love of knowledge are few, even though God has inserted into the minds of men a natural appetite for knowledge.

The second awkward effect is that those who would come to discover the above-mentioned truth would barely reach it after a great deal of time. The reasons are several. There is the profundity of this truth, which the human intellect is made capable of grasping by natural inquiry only after a long training. Then, there are many things which must be presupposed, as we have said. There is also the fact that, in youth, when the soul is swayed by the various movements of the passions, it is not in a suitable state for the knowledge of such lofty truth. On the contrary, *one becomes wise and knowing in repose,* as it is said in the *Physics.*[9] The result is

[9] Aristotle, *Physics*, VII, 3 (247 b 9).

this. If the only way open to us for the knowledge of God were solely that of the reason, the human race would remain in the blackest shadows of ignorance. For then the knowledge of God, which especially renders men perfect and good, would come to be possessed only by a few, and these few would require a great deal of time in order to reach it.

The third awkward effect is this. The inquiry of the human reason for the most part has falsity present within it, and this is due partly to the weakness of our intellect in judgment, and partly to the interference of images. The result is that many, remaining ignorant of the power of demonstration, would hold in doubt those things which have been most truly demonstrated. This would be particularly the case since they see that, among those who are reputed to be wise men, each one teaches his own brand of doctrine. Furthermore, with the many truths which are demonstrated, there sometimes mingles something that is false, which is not demonstrated but rather asserted on the basis of some probable or sophistical argument, which yet has the credit of being a demonstration. That is why it was necessary that the unshakeable certitude and pure truth concerning divine things should be presented to men by way of faith.

Beneficially, therefore, did the divine mercy provide that it should instruct us to hold by faith even those truths which the human reason is able to investigate. In this way, all men would easily be able to have a share in the knowledge of God, and this without uncertainty and error.

Hence it is written: *Henceforward you walk not as also the gentiles walk in the vanity of their mind, having their understanding darkened* (Ephes. iv, 17-18). And again: *All thy children shall be taught of the Lord* (Isa. liv, 13).

I V

That the truths which the human reason is not able to investigate are fittingly proposed to men for belief [10]

NOW PERHAPS some will think that men should not be asked to believe what the reason is not adequate to investigate, since the

[10] *Summa Contra Gentiles,* I, c. 5.

divine wisdom provides in the case of each thing according to the mode of its nature. We must therefore prove that it is necessary for man to receive from God as objects of belief even those truths which are above the human reason.

No one tends with desire and zeal towards something which is not already known to him. But, as we shall show later on in this work, men are ordained by the divine providence towards a higher good than human fragility can experience in the present life.[11] That is why it was necessary for the human mind to be called to something higher than the human reason here and now can reach, so that it might thus learn to desire something and with zeal tend towards something which surpasses the whole state of the present life. This characteristic belongs especially to the Christian religion which in a unique way promises spiritual and eternal goods. And so there are many things proposed to men in it which transcend human sense. The Old Law, on the other hand, whose promises were of a temporal character, contained very few proposals which transcended the grasp of the human reason. Following this same direction, the philosophers themselves, in order that they might lead men from the pleasures of sensible things to virtue, were concerned to show that there were in existence other goods of a higher nature than the things of sense, and that those who gave themselves to the virtues of the active and contemplative lives would find much sweeter enjoyment in the taste of these higher goods.

It is also necessary that such truth be proposed to men for belief in order to have a truer knowledge of God. For then only do we know God truly when we believe Him to be above everything that it is possible for man to think about Him; for, as we have shown,[12] the divine substance surpasses the knowledge of which man is naturally capable. Hence, by the fact that some things about God are proposed to man which surpass his reason, there is strengthened in man the opinion that God is something above what man can think.

Another benefit which comes from the revelation to men of truths that exceed the reason is the curbing of presumption, which is the mother of error. For there are some who have such a presumptuous opinion of their own ability that they deem themselves able to measure the nature of everything; I mean to say, that, in

[11] Cf. *op. cit.*, III, c. 48.   [12] Cf. *op. cit.*, I, c. 3.

their estimation, everything is true that seems to them so, and everything is false that does not. So that the human mind, therefore, might be freed from this presumption and come to a humble inquiry after truth, it was necessary that some things should be proposed to man by God which would completely surpass his intellect.

A still further benefit may also be seen in what Aristotle says in the *Ethics*.[13] There was a certain Simonides who exhorted people to set aside the knowledge of divine things and to apply their talents to human occupations. He said that *he who is a man should know human things, and he who is mortal things that are mortal.* Against Simonides Aristotle says that *man should draw himself towards what is immortal and divine as much as he can.* And so he says in the *De Animalibus* that, although what we know of the higher substances is very little, yet that little is loved and desired more than all the knowledge that we have about less noble substances.[14] He also says in the *De Caelo et Mundo* that when questions about the heavenly bodies can be given a brief and imperfect solution, he who hears this experiences intense joy.[15] From all these considerations it is clear that even the most imperfect knowledge about the most noble realities brings the greatest perfection to the soul. Therefore, although the human reason cannot grasp fully the truths which are above it, yet, if it somehow holds these truths at least by faith, it acquires great perfection for itself.

Therefore it is written: *For many things are shewn to thee above the understanding of men* (*Ecclus.* iii, 25). Again: *So the things that are of God no man knoweth but the Spirit of God. But to us God hath revealed them by His Spirit* (*I Cor.* ii, 11, 10).

V

That to give assent to the truths of faith is not foolishness even though they are above reason [16]

THOSE who place their faith in this truth, however, *for which the human reason offers no experimental evidence,*[17] do not believe

---

[13] Aristotle, *Nic. Eth.*, X, 7 (1177 b 31).
[14] Aristotle, *De Partibus Animalium,* I, 5 (644 b 32).
[15] Aristotle, *De Caelo et Mundo,* II, 12 (291 b 26).
[16] *Summa Contra Gentiles,* I, c. 6.
[17] St. Gregory, *Hom. in Evangelia,* II, hom. 26, 1 (PL 76, 1197).

foolishly, as though *following artificial fables* (*II Peter* i, 16). For these *secrets of divine Wisdom* (*Job* xi, 6) the divine wisdom itself, which knows all things to the full, has deigned to reveal to men. It reveals its own presence, as well as the truth of its teaching and inspiration, by fitting arguments; and in order to confirm those truths which exceed natural knowledge, it gives visible manifestation to works that surpass the ability of all nature. Thus, there are the wonderful cures of illnesses, there is the raising of the dead, and the more wonderful immutation in the heavenly bodies; and what is more wonderful, there is the inspiration given to human minds, so that simple and untutored persons, filled with the gift of the Holy Spirit, come to possess instantaneously the highest wisdom and the readiest eloquence. When these arguments were examined, through the efficacy of the above-mentioned proof, and not the violent assault of arms nor the promise of pleasures, and (what is most wonderful of all) in the midst of the tyranny of the persecutors, an innumerable throng of people, both simple and most learned, flocked to the Christian faith. In this faith there are truths preached which surpass every human intellect; the pleasures of the flesh are curbed; it is taught that the things of the world should be spurned. Now for the minds of mortal men to assent to these things is the greatest of miracles, just as it is a manifest work of divine inspiration that, spurning visible things, men should seek only what is invisible. Now that this has happened neither unexpectedly nor by chance, but as a result of the disposition of God, is clear from the fact that through many pronouncements of the ancient prophets God had foretold that He would do this. The books of these prophets are held in veneration among us Christians, since they give witness to our faith.

The manner of this confirmation is touched on by St. Paul. *Which* [that is, human salvation] *having begun to be declared by the Lord, was confirmed unto us by them that heard Him: God also bearing them witness by signs, and wonders, and divers miracles, and distributions of the Holy Ghost* (*Heb.* ii, 3-4).

This wonderful conversion of the world to the Christian faith is the clearest witness of the signs given in the past; so that it is not necessary that they should be further repeated, since they appear most clearly in their effect. For it would be truly more wonder-

ful than all signs if the world had been led by simple and lowly
men to believe such lofty truths, to accomplish such difficult actions
and to have such high hopes. Yet it is also a fact that, even in our
own time, God does not cease to work miracles through His saints
for the confirmation of the faith.

On the other hand, those who founded sects committed to erroneous doctrines proceeded in a way that is opposite to this. The
point is clear in the case of Mohammed. He seduced the people by
promises of carnal pleasures to which the concupiscence of the
flesh goads us. His teaching also contained precepts which were in
conformity with his promises, and he gave free reign to carnal
pleasure. In all this, as is not unexpected, he was obeyed by carnal
men. As for proofs of the truth of his doctrine, he brought forward
only such as could be grasped by the natural ability of anyone with
a very modest wisdom. Indeed, the truths which he taught he
mingled with many fables and with doctrines of the greatest falsity.
He did not bring forth any signs produced in a supernatural way,
which alone fittingly witness to divine inspiration; for a visible action which can be only divine reveals an invisibly inspired teacher
of truth. On the contrary, Mohammed said that he was sent in the
power of his arms—which are signs not lacking even to robbers and
tyrants. What is more, no wise men, men trained in things divine
and human, believed in him from the beginning. Those who believed in him were brutal men and desert wanderers, utterly ignorant of all divine teaching, through whose numbers Mohammed
forced others to become his followers by the violence of his arms.
What is more, no divine pronouncements on the part of preceding
prophets offer him any witness. On the contrary, he perverts almost
all the testimonies of the Old and New Testaments by making them
into fabrications of his own, as can be seen by anyone who examines
his teaching. It was therefore a shrewd decision on his part to forbid his followers to read the Old and New Testaments, lest these
books convict him of falsity. It is thus clear that those who placed
any faith in his words believed foolishly.

V I

That the truth of reason is not opposed to the truth of the Christian faith [18]

Now although the truth of the Christian faith which we have discussed surpasses the capacity of the reason, nevertheless that truth which the human reason is naturally endowed to know cannot be opposed to the truth of the Christian faith. For that with which the human reason is naturally endowed is clearly most true; so much so, that it is impossible for us to think of such truths as false. Nor is it permissible to believe as false that which we hold by faith, since this is confirmed in a way which is so clearly divine. Since, therefore, only the false is opposed to the true, as is clearly evident from an examination of their definitions, it is impossible that the truth of faith should be opposed to those principles which the human reason knows by nature.

Furthermore, that which is introduced into the soul of the student by the teacher is contained within the knowledge of the teacher—unless his teaching is fictitious, which it is improper to say of God. Now the knowledge of the principles which are known to us by nature has been implanted in us by God; for God is the Author of our nature. These principles therefore are also contained by the divine wisdom. Hence whatever is opposed to them is opposed to the divine wisdom, and cannot therefore come from God. Hence that which we hold by faith as divinely revealed cannot be opposed to our natural knowledge.

Again. In the presence of opposed arguments our intellect is chained, so that it cannot proceed to the knowledge of the truth. If therefore opposed knowledges were implanted in us by God, our intellect would be hindered from knowing truth by this very fact. Now such an effect cannot come from God.

And again. What is natural cannot change as long as nature does not. Now it is impossible that opposed opinions should exist in the same knowing subject at the same time. No opinion or belief, therefore, is implanted in man by God which is opposed to man's natural knowledge.

[18] *Summa Contra Gentiles*, I, c. 7

Therefore the Apostle says: *The word is nigh thee, even in thy mouth and in thy heart. This is the word of faith, which we preach* (*Rom.* x, 8). But because it overcomes reason, there are some who think that it is opposed to it: which is impossible.

The authority of St. Augustine agrees with this. He writes as follows: *That which truth will reveal cannot in any way be opposed to the sacred books of the Old and the New Testament.*[19]

From this we may evidently gather the following conclusion: whatever arguments are brought forward against the doctrines of faith are conclusions incorrectly derived from the first principles imbedded in nature, which are evident of themselves. Such conclusions do not have the force of demonstration; they are arguments which are either probable or sophistical. And so there exists the possibility to answer them.

V I I

How the human reason is related to the Truth of Faith [20]

THERE is also a further consideration. Sensible things, from which the human reason takes the origin of its knowledge, retain within themselves some sort of trace of a likeness to God. This is so imperfect, however, that it is absolutely inadequate to manifest the substance of God. For effects bear within themselves, in their own way, the likeness of their causes, since an agent produces its like; yet an effect does not always reach to the full likeness of its cause. Now the human reason is related to the knowledge of the truth of faith (a truth which can be most evident only to those who see the divine substance) in such a way that it can gather certain likenesses of it, which are yet not sufficient so that the truth of faith may be comprehended as being understood demonstratively or through itself. Yet it is useful for the human reason to exercise itself in such arguments, however weak they may be, provided only that there be present no presumption to comprehend or to demonstrate. For to be able to see something of the highest realities even by an argument which is thin and weak is, as our previous remarks indicate, a cause of the greatest joy.

[19] St. Augustine, *De Genesi ad Litteram,* II, c. 18 (PL 34, 280).
[20] *Summa Contra Gentiles,* I. c. 8.

The testimony of Hilary agrees with this. Speaking of this same truth, he writes as follows in his *De Trinitate: Enter these truths by believing, press forward, persevere. And though I may know that you will not arrive at an end, yet I will congratulate you in your progress. For though he who pursues the infinite with reverence will never finally reach the end, yet he will always progress by going forward. But do not intrude yourself into the divine secret, do not, presuming to comprehend the peak of intelligence, plunge yourself into the mystery of the eternal Nativity; rather, understand that these things are incomprehensible.*[21]

VIII

That the end of every intellectual substance is to understand God [22]

ALL CREATURES, including those that are without an intellect, are directed to God as to their final end. Now, all things reach their end in so far as they come to possess some likeness of it. Intellectual creatures reach their end in an even more special way, that is to say, by having an understanding of the end through their own operation. Now given that all this is true, it follows that the end of the intellectual creature is to understand God.

For, as we have shown,[23] God is the ultimate end of each and every thing. Each thing, therefore, tends as much as possible to be joined to God as to its ultimate end. Now a thing is joined more intimately to God by the fact of reaching His very substance in some way; and this takes place when a being knows something concerning the divine substance, rather than when it reaches some likeness of It. An intellectual substance, therefore, tends to the knowledge of God as to its ultimate end.

Furthermore, the proper operation of each thing is its end, for it is its second perfection. That is why, when a thing is well-disposed towards its proper operation, it is said to be virtuous and good. Now to understand is the proper operation of an intellectual substance. It is therefore its end. Hence, that which is most perfect in this operation is the ultimate end of the intellectual substance. This applies particularly to those operations, such as understanding and

[21] St. Hilary, *De Trin.*, II, 10, 11 (PL 10, 58, 59).
[22] *Summa Contra Gentiles*, III, c. 25.   [23] *Op. cit.*, III, c. 17.

sensing, which are not directed to external works. Now since these operations are specified by their objects, by which they are likewise known, any such operation is all the more perfect according as its object is more perfect. Consequently, to understand the most perfect intelligible object, God, is the greatest perfection in the genus of the operation *understanding*. To know God, therefore, by understanding Him is the final end of an intellectual substance.

At this point the following objection might be proposed. It might be urged that, while the ultimate end of an intellectual substance was to be found in the understanding of a highest intelligible, yet the highest intelligible of this or that intellectual substance is not the intelligible which is absolutely highest. On the contrary, the higher an intellectual substance, the more elevated is its highest intelligible object. And so (the argument would run) perhaps the highest created intellectual substance has as its highest intelligible object the absolutely best intelligible; and so its felicity will consist in understanding God. But the felicity of any given lesser intellectual substance will consist in understanding some lesser intelligible, which yet is the highest of those known by that intellectual substance. As concerns the human intellect especially, it does not seem that this intellect can understand the absolutely highest intelligible, since it is weak; for it is related to the work of knowing the greatest intelligible *as the eye of an owl is related to the sun*.[24]

But it is quite clear that the end of every intellectual substance, including the lowest, is to understand God. For we have already shown that God is the ultimate end towards which all beings tend.[25] And although the human intellect is lowest in the order of intellectual substances, yet it is higher than all beings lacking an intellect. And since a more noble substance does not have an inferior end, the human intellect itself will have as its end God Himself. Now every being possessing intelligence reaches its highest end, as we have shown, by understanding it. The human intellect, therefore, reaches to God as to its end by understanding Him.

Again, just as beings that lack an intellect tend towards God as their end by assimilating themselves to Him, so intellectual substances, as we have seen, tend towards God by knowing Him. Now

24 Aristotle, *Metaph.*, I, 1 (993 b 9).   25 *Summa Contra Gentiles*, III, c. 17.

although beings that are devoid of intellect tend to the likeness of more immediate causes, yet the intention of their nature does not stop there but, as we have said, it has for its end to be assimilated to the highest good,[26] even though such beings are able to reach this assimilation in a most imperfect way. However little, therefore, the human intellect can grasp of the knowledge of God, this will be its ultimate end, in preference to a full knowledge of lesser intelligible objects.

Then, too, each thing especially desires its ultimate end. Now the human intellect has a greater desire and love of the knowledge of divine things, as well as delight in it, however little it can perceive divine things, than it has of the full knowledge open to it about the lowest realities. So the ultimate end of man is, in whatever way possible, to understand God.

Another argument is this. Each thing tends to the divine likeness as to its proper end. Hence, that through which each thing is especially assimilated to God is its ultimate end. Now the intellectual creature is especially assimilated to God according to its intellectual nature; for this likeness the intellectual creature possesses over and above all the other creatures, which are included within it. But in the order of such assimilation to God there is a greater assimilation when there is actual understanding than when the understanding is habitual or potential; for, as we showed in the First Book, God always has actual understanding.[27] And in its actual understanding, the intellectual creature is especially assimilated to God according as it understands God Himself; for, as we have likewise proved in the First Book, God in understanding Himself understands all other things.[28] To understand God, therefore, is the ultimate end of every intellectual substance.

There is the further consideration that what is lovable for the sake of something else exists for the sake of that which is lovable only for its own sake. For we cannot proceed to infinity in the appetite of nature, since the desire of nature would then be frustrated, because the infinite cannot possibly be traversed. Now all the practical sciences, arts and powers, are lovable only for the sake of something else; for their end is, not knowledge, but action. But the speculative sciences are lovable for their own sake, for their end is the very

[26] *Op. cit.,* III, c. 19.   [27] *Op. cit.,* I, c. 56.   [28] *Op. cit.,* I, c. 49.

act of knowing. Nor, in the whole domain of human affairs, can there be found any action which is not directed to another end, save speculative contemplation. For the very actions of play, which seem to take place without an end, have a due end, namely, that after becoming in a manner refreshed in mind through them, we may afterwards be all the stronger for serious occupation. Were this not so, and play were sought for its own sake, we should always have to be playing—which is an awkward conclusion. Let us say then that the practical arts are directed to the speculative, and, likewise, that all human operation is directed to the speculation of the intellect as to its end. Now in all sciences and arts that are mutually ordered, the last end appears to belong to that one which holds the rule and the primacy over the others. Thus, the art of piloting a ship, to which the ship's end or purpose pertains (which end is the use to which the ship is put), has the primacy and rulership with respect to the art of making a ship. Now this is the relation of first philosophy to the other speculative sciences. For they receive their principles from it, as well as direction against those who deny their principles; whereas first philosophy itself is entirely directed to the knowledge of God as to its ultimate end. That is why it is called a *divine science*.[29] Hence, the knowledge of God is the ultimate end of all human knowledge and operation.

Again. In all agents and movers that are mutually ordered, it is necessary that the end of the first agent and mover be the ultimate end of all of them. Thus, the end of the general of an army is the end of all those who fight under him. Now among all the parts which constitute man, the intellect is found to be the ruling mover. For the intellect moves the appetite by proposing to it its object; the intellectual appetite, that is to say, the will, moves the sensitive appetites, namely, the irascible and the concupiscible powers (which is why we do not obey concupiscence without the presence of the command of the will); and the sensitive appetite, when the will has given its consent, then moves the body. The end of the intellect is thus what is the end of all human action. *But the end and good of the intellect is truth*,[30] and consequently its ultimate end is the First Truth. The ultimate end of the whole man, therefore, of all

29 Aristotle, *Metaph.*, I, 10 (983 a 6).
30 Aristotle, *Nic. Eth.*, VI, 2 (1139 a 26).

his operations and desires, is to know the First Truth, namely, God.

There are further arguments. All men possess by nature the desire to know the causes of the things which they seek. In fact, it was because they wondered at the things which they saw, whose causes remained hidden, that men first began to philosophize. But when they found the causes, they were at peace. But human inquiry does not stop until it reaches the First Cause. *Then,* as Aristotle says, *do we judge that we know a thing fully when we know the First Cause.*[31] Man, therefore, naturally desires to know the First Cause as his ultimate end. Now the First Cause of all things is God. To know God, therefore, is the ultimate end of man.

But when, furthermore, we know any given effect, we naturally desire to know its cause. Now the human intellect knows universal being; it therefore has a natural desire to know its cause, which, as we have proved in the Second Book, is God alone.[32] But the final end has not been reached until natural desire has been set at rest. Not any intellectual knowledge, therefore, is sufficient for the human felicity which is the ultimate end, unless the knowledge of God be present which terminates natural desire as its ultimate end. The ultimate end of man is, consequently, the very knowledge of God.

There is the additional argument that a body, which tends to its proper place with a natural appetite, is moved more intensely and swiftly the nearer it is to its end. And so Aristotle proves that natural rectilinear motion cannot be infinite because it would not increase as it proceeded.[33] Now that whose tendency increases in intensity as it proceeds, is not moved to infinity but rather tends towards something fixed. We find this to be the case in the desire to know. For the more things a man knows, the greater is the desire with which he wants to know. Man's natural desire in knowing, therefore, tends to some fixed end; and this end cannot be other than the most noble knowable object, namely, God. The knowledge of God, therefore, is man's ultimate end.

Now the ultimate end of man, as well as of any other intellectual substance, is called *felicity* or *beatitude;* for it is this that every intellectual substance desires as its ultimate end and for its own sake.

---

[31] Aristotle, *Metaph.,* I, 10 (983 a 24).   [32] *Summa Contra Gentiles,* II, c. 15.
[33] Aristotle, *De Caelo et Mundo,* I, 8 (277 a 28).

Hence, the ultimate beatitude and felicity of every intellectual substance is to know God.

Hence St. Matthew says, *blessed are the clean of heart, for they shall see God* (v, 8); and St. John says, *now this is eternal life, that they may know Thee, the only true God* (xvii, 3).

The view of Aristotle, in the last book of the *Ethics,* harmonizes with this judgment. He there says that man's highest felicity is *speculation, and this in relation to the highest object of speculation.*[34]

IX

That man's ultimate felicity consists in the contemplation of God[35]

IT IS therefore clear that man's ultimate felicity is not to be found in those external things which are called the goods of fortune. It is not to be found in the goods of the body; it is not to be found in the goods of the soul, so far as this refers to the sensitive part of the soul. It is not to be found in the goods of the soul, so far as this refers to its intellectual part in its occupation with the operation of the moral virtues; nor is it to be found in those intellectual virtues which pertain to action, namely, art and prudence.[36] If such is the case, it therefore remains that man's highest felicity resides in the contemplation of truth.

For this operation of man is alone proper to him: none of the other animals in any way communicates in it.

This operation, likewise, is directed to nothing else as to its end; for the contemplation of truth is sought for its own sake.

Through this operation man is joined to the beings that are above him by being like them; for, among man's operations, this is the one which is to be found in God and in the separate substances.

This is the operation by which man reaches to those beings that are above him, by knowing them in whatever way possible.

For this operation man is particularly self-sufficient, since he has little need of the aid of external things for it.

What is more, all other human operations seem to be directed to

[34] Aristotle, *Nic. Eth.,* X, 7 (1177 a 12).   [35] *Summa Contra Gentiles,* III, c. 37.
[36] *Op. cit.,* III, cc. 35, 36.

this operation as to their end. For the perfection of contemplation requires soundness of body, to which are directed all the artificial things that are necessary for life. Contemplation also requires for its perfection freedom from the disturbances of the passions: this freedom is reached through the moral virtues and through prudence; and it requires freedom from external disturbances: to this the whole regimen of life in society is directed. In this way a proper consideration of all human functions would show that they serve the contemplation of truth.

Now it is not possible that man's highest felicity should consist in that contemplation of truth which is according to the understanding of first principles. For such a contemplation is most imperfect, as well as most universal, containing a knowledge of things only in a potential way. It is furthermore the beginning of man's pursuit, belonging to man by nature, and not as the result of the pursuit of truth. Nor, again, is man's highest felicity to be found in that contemplation which belongs to the sciences of very lowly things; for, felicity ought to consist in an operation of intellect in relation to the most noble intelligible object. It remains, therefore, that the highest felicity of man is to be found in the contemplation of wisdom, according to the consideration of divine things.

From this we also see in an inductive way something which was proved by means of arguments above, namely, that man's highest felicity consists only in the contemplation of God.[37]

X

That man's highest felicity is not to be found in this life [38]

MAN'S HIGHEST FELICITY, consequently, does not consist in that knowledge of God according to which He is known in common by all men, or by men for the most part, in terms of a certain imprecise appreciation of His existence. Nor, again, does this felicity consist in that knowledge of God by which He is known in a demonstrative way within the speculative sciences. Furthermore we have shown that it does not consist in that knowledge of God by which God is known through faith. What is more, it is not possible for man in

[37] *Op. cit.,* III, c. 25.   [38] *Op. cit.,* III, c. 48.

this life to reach to a higher knowledge of God, so as to know Him through His essence; nor, as we have shown, is it possible that man should come to know the other spiritual substances, so that he might know God through them as through a medium nearer to Him. Yet, as we have already shown, it is necessary that man's highest felicity should be found in some knowledge of God.[39] Now given that all this is true, it follows that it is impossible for man's highest felicity to be found in this life.

Furthermore, man's highest end terminates his natural appetite, with the result that, once this end is possessed, nothing else is sought. For if man continues to be moved towards something else, he does not yet possess the end in which to rest. Now this cannot be achieved in the present life. For the more a man adds to his understanding, so much the more is the desire to understand increased in him, for this desire is part of his nature—unless there should be a man who knows all things. Now this has never happened to anyone in the present life if he is no more than a man, nor can it happen; for in this life, as we have shown, we are not able to know separate substances, which are most intelligible.[40] It is not possible, therefore, for man's highest felicity to be found in this life.

There is also the consideration that whatever is moved to an end desires by nature to be established in that end and to rest in it. That is why a body does not depart from the place which moves it naturally except through a violent motion which is contrary to its appetite. Now felicity is the final end, which man desires naturally. It is therefore a natural desire in man that he should be established in felicity. Hence, unless man were to acquire, along with felicity, an immovable establishment in it, he is not yet blessed, since his natural desire is not yet at rest. When, therefore, anyone reaches the possession of felicity, he will reach both stability and rest. That is why all are agreed in considering it to be part of the notion of felicity that it requires stability within its nature. And so the Philosopher says in the *Ethics* that *we do not judge the blessed man to be a sort of chameleon.*[41] Now in the present life there is no fixed stability to be found. For it can happen to any-

[39] *Op. cit.,* III, c. 37.   [40] *Op. cit.,* III, c. 45.
[41] Aristotle, *Nic. Eth.,* I, 10 (1100 b 4).

one, however blessed he may be called, that infirmities and bad fortune may befall him, by which he is prevented from exercising that operation, whatever it be, in which felicity resides. It is not therefore possible that man's highest felicity should be found in this life.

Then, too, it seems unfitting and unreasonable that a thing should take a great deal of time to come into existence, and yet endure in existence for only a very short time; for it would follow from this that nature would be deprived of its end for the greater part of time. And so we see that animals which live for a short time likewise have a short time in which to reach their maturity. Now if man's felicity be found in perfect operation according to perfect virtue, whether intellectual or moral, it is impossible for felicity to come to man except after a very long time. This is especially evident in the domain of speculative knowledge in which, as we have seen, the highest felicity of man is found; [42] for in the domain of the speculative sciences, man is scarcely able to reach maturity at such an advanced age, he generally has very little of his life left before him. Man's highest felicity therefore cannot be located in the present life.

Again. Everyone agrees that felicity is a certain perfect good, or otherwise it would not give repose to the appetite. But a good is perfect when it has absolutely no admixture of evil; just as that is perfectly white which is absolutely unmixed with black. Now, in the state of the present life, it is absolutely impossible for man to be free of evils. There are not only bodily evils, such as hunger, thirst, heat and cold, and other similar evils, but there are also the evils of the soul. For there is no man who, at some time or other, is not disturbed by disordered passion; who does not, at some time, forsake the mean in which virtue consists, either by excess or defect; who is not deceived in some matters, or at least does not know what he desires to know, or has a faltering judgment on matters on which he would wish to have certitude. There is therefore no one who in this life is blessed.

Man, furthermore, naturally flees death, and is saddened over it; and he flees it not only when he feels its presence, but also whenever he again thinks about it. Now in this life man cannot bring

[42] *Summa Contra Gentiles,* III, c. 37.

it about that he should not die. It is therefore impossible that in this life man should be blessed.

Man's highest felicity does not consist in habit but in operation, for habits exist for the sake of operations. But in the present life it is impossible for man to carry on any given operation continuously. And so, again, it is impossible that man should be entirely blessed in this life.

The more a thing is desired and loved, furthermore, the more the loss of that thing brings a greater grief and sadness. Now felicity is something that we most desire and love. Now, if man's highest felicity is to be found in the present life, it is certain that man would lose it, at least by death. What is more, it is not certain that this felicity will last until death. For any person in this life might be the victim of diseases by which he is entirely impeded from the operation of virtue: such are madness and other similar illnesses, which impede the use of reason. A felicity such as that of the present life, therefore, naturally has sadness joined to it; it will therefore not be a felicity which is perfect.

Now it might be argued that felicity is the good of an intellectual nature, and that perfect and true felicity belongs to those beings in which intellectual nature is found in its perfection, that is, in intellectual substances. In man, however, intellectual nature is found in an imperfect way, by a certain participation. For men cannot reach a full understanding of truth except through a certain movement of inquiry. Furthermore, as is clear from what we have said, men are totally helpless in relation to those beings which are in their nature most intelligible. From this it follows that men cannot possess felicity according to its perfect nature; they rather participate in some part of it, even in the present life.

This, let me add, seems to have been the opinion of Aristotle concerning felicity. When, in the *Ethics,* he is inquiring whether the slings of fortune take away felicity, after showing that felicity is to be found among the works of virtue (which works seem to be especially permanent in the present life), he concludes that those who possess such a perfection in this life are happy *as men* —as though to say by this that they did not reach felicity absolutely, but in a human way.[43]

43 Aristotle, *Nic. Eth.,* I, 10 (1101 a 18).

It remains now to show that this Aristotelian answer does not remove the arguments which I gave above. For though man is below separate substances according to the order of nature, he is yet above irrational creatures. He, therefore, reaches his final end in a more perfect way than these creatures do. Now they reach their final end so perfectly that they seek nothing further. That which is heavy rests when it has reached its natural place. So too, when animals enjoy the pleasures of sense, their natural desire is in repose. All the more strongly, therefore, should man's natural desire find repose when man has reached his final end. But this cannot happen in the present life. Man, therefore, as we have shown, does not reach felicity, according as it is his proper end, in this life. He must therefore reach it after this life.

Again. It is impossible that natural desire should be futile, *for nature does nothing in vain.*[44] Now the desire of nature would be futile if it could never be fulfilled. The natural desire of man, therefore, can be fulfilled,—but not in this life, as has been shown. It must therefore be fulfilled after this life; which means that man's highest felicity is to be found after this life.

Furthermore, so long as a thing is in motion towards perfection, it has not yet reached its ultimate end. But as concerns the knowledge of truth, all men are always disposed as in motion to their perfection and as tending to it; for those who come after add certain things to those which have been discovered by their predecessors, as Aristotle likewise says in the *Metaphysics.*[45] In relation to the knowledge of truth, therefore, the condition of men is not as though they were in possession of their last end. Since, therefore, the highest felicity of man in this life seems to consist in the speculation through which he is seeking the knowledge of truth, as Aristotle himself proves in the *Ethics,*[46] we cannot possibly say that man comes into the possession of his ultimate end in the present life.

There is also the argument that what is in potency aims at issuing in act. So long, therefore, as it is not wholly produced in act, it has not reached its final end. Now our intellect is in potency to the

[44] Aristotle, *De Caelo et Mundo*, II, 11 (291 b 14).
[45] Aristotle, *Metaph.*, I, 1 (993 a 12).
[46] Aristotle, *Nic. Eth.*, X, 7 (1177 a 12).

knowledge of the forms of all things, and it is reduced to act when it knows some one form in things. Therefore, the human intellect will not be wholly in act, nor in its ultimate end save when it knows all things—at least, all these material things. Now man cannot accomplish this through the speculative sciences, by which we know truth in the present life. Man's highest felicity, consequently, cannot possibly be found in the present life.

For these and such reasons, Alexander and Averroes held that the highest felicity of man does not consist in that human knowledge which is by way of the speculative sciences; they held that it rather takes place through the contact of the intellect with a separate substance, a contact which they believed to be possible for man in this life.[47] On the other hand, since Aristotle saw that no other knowledge is possible to man in this life except that which is to be had through the speculative sciences, he held that man does not reach perfect felicity, but a merely human one.

From this we can see very well how great a difficulty beset on all sides the noble genius of these men. From these difficulties we shall be freed if, in accord with the proofs already given, we posit that man can reach true felicity after this life, since the human soul is immortal. In that state, the soul will know according to the manner of the separate substances, as was shown in the Second Book of this work.[48]

To conclude, the highest felicity of man will be found in that knowledge of God which the human mind has after this life, according to the manner in which separate substances know God. That is why Our Lord promises us a reward in heaven (*Matt.* v, 12). He says, too, that the saints *shall be as the angels* (*Matt.* xxii, 30), who *in heaven always see the face of God,* as it is said in Matthew (xviii, 10).

X I

That it was befitting for God to become Incarnate [49]

IF ONE were to consider the mystery of the Incarnation with diligence and reverence, he would find in it a depth of wisdom such as exceeds human knowledge. For, as St. Paul says, *the foolishness of*

---

[47] Cf. *Summa Contra Gentiles,* III, cc. 32, 43.
[48] *Op. cit.,* II, c. 81.   [49] *Op. cit.,* IV, c. 54.

God is wiser than men (*I Cor.* i, 25). So it is that when a man meditates on this mystery with reverence, he sees in it aspects that are ever increasingly wonderful.

In the first place, it is to be observed that the Incarnation of God was a most powerful aid to man in his journey towards beatitude. For we have shown in the Third Book of this work that the perfect beatitude of man is to be found in the immediate vision of God.[50] Now, because of the immense distance between the natures of God and man, someone might possibly think that man could never reach the state in which the human intellect would be immediately united to the divine essence in the way in which an intellect is united to its intelligible object. And so a man, chained by his very despair, might lose heart in his search for beatitude. By the fact, however, that God wished to join human nature to Himself in person, He gave to men a most clear demonstration that man can be joined to God through his intellect, having an immediate vision of Him. It was most befitting, therefore, that God should assume human nature in order to raise man's hope of beatitude. That is why, after the Incarnation of Christ, men began to aspire more and more to a heavenly beatitude. As Christ Himself says, *I am come that they may have life, and may have it more abundantly* (*Jo.* x, 10).

At the same time, the Incarnation removes from man's path the things which impede his acquisition of beatitude. For, as we have already shown, man's perfect beatitude consists in nothing else than the enjoyment of God; and from this it necessarily follows that whoever is attached to anything below God as his last end is prevented from participating in true beatitude. Now, by not knowing the dignity of his nature, a man could be misled and cling to the things which are below God as though they were his end. This is why some persons, looking upon themselves according to the corporeal and sentient nature which they have in common with other animals, seek after a certain animal beatitude in corporeal things and in the pleasures of the flesh. On the other hand, there are others who, observing that some creatures are in some respects more excellent than are human beings, have confined themselves to the worship of such creatures. And so they worship the world and its parts, impressed by the magnitude of quantity and the enduringness

[50] *Op. cit.,* III. c. 48.

of time. Or they worship spiritual substances such as angels and demons, because they are found to surpass man both in the immortality and power of his intellect; and this they have done in the conviction that, since such beings are above man, man's beatitude is to be sought in them. Now it is true that in respect of certain conditions man is inferior to some other creatures; and it is also true that in some respects he has a likeness to the lowest of creatures. Nevertheless, from the point of view of the end to which man is directed, no being surpasses man save God alone, in Whom alone man's perfect beatitude is to be found.

This dignity of man, therefore—the dignity, namely, that he is to receive beatitude through the immediate vision of God—is most fittingly shown forth by God by the fact that He Himself has assumed human nature. And so, the achievement of the Incarnation of God is that a great part of men, putting aside the worship of angels, demons and of creatures of whatever sort, and spurning as well the pleasures of the flesh and all corporeal things, have devoted themselves to the worship of God alone, in Whom alone they expect to find the fullness of their beatitude. This is the warning of the Apostle: *Seek the things that are above, where Christ is sitting at the right hand of God: mind the things that are above, not the things that are upon the earth* (*Coloss.* iii, 1-2).

But there is more. Man's perfect beatitude, as we have shown in the Third Book, consists in such a knowledge of God as exceeds the ability of every created intellect. Hence man had to have a foretaste of that knowledge, by which to direct himself to the fullness of the knowledge that gives blessedness. This takes place through faith, as we have shown in the Third Book.[51] Now the knowledge by which man is directed to his final end must be a knowledge of the greatest certitude, since it is the principle or reason for all the things which are directed towards the final end. In the same way, the principles which are known to us by nature are of the greatest certitude. Now there are two ways in which we can have such a most certain knowledge of a thing. We can have it when the knowledge in question is self-evident, as is the case with the first principles of demonstration; or we can have it in the case of that knowledge which is reduced to what is self-evident; for example, the conclusion of a

[51] In a now deleted chapter of the Third Book.

demonstration is a knowledge of the greatest certainty. Now what we are asked to hold by faith about God cannot be self-evident to man, since it surpasses the ability of the human intellect. It had therefore to be made known to man by Him to Whom it is self-evident. And although what they have held about God on faith is in a way self-evident to those who see the divine essence, nevertheless, for the possession of a most certain knowledge it was necessary to make a resolution to the First Cause of this knowledge, namely, God, to Whom such a knowledge is by nature self-evident, and by Whom it is made known to all. So, too, the certitude of demonstrative knowledge comes only when there is a resolution to the first and indemonstrable principles. If man, therefore, was to reach a perfect certitude concerning the truth of faith, he had to be taught by God Himself made man, so that man might receive the divine teaching in a human way. And this is what is said in the Gospel of John: *No man hath seen God at any time: the only begotten Son Who is in the bosom of the Father, He hath declared Him* (i, 18). Our Lord Himself says: *For this was I born, and for this came I into the world, that I should give testimony to the truth* (Jo. xvii, 37). That is why we find that after the Incarnation of Christ men have received a clearer and a surer teaching in the knowledge of God. As Isaias says, *the earth is filled with the knowledge of the Lord* (xi, 9).

Furthermore, since man's perfect beatitude is to be found in the enjoyment of God, it was necessary that man's love should be disposed towards the desire of the enjoyment of God. In the same way, as we see, man possesses by nature the desire of beatitude. Now the desire to enjoy a certain thing arises as the result of the love of that thing. It was therefore necessary that man, on his journey to perfect beatitude, should be led to the love of God. Now nothing so leads us to the love of some being as the experience of the love of that being for us. But God's love for men could not be shown more effectively than by the fact that God wished to be joined to man in person. For it belongs to the nature of love that it should join him who loves with what he loves, as much as possible. And so it was necessary to man, on his way to perfect beatitude, that God should become man.

There is also the fact that, since friendship consists in a certain equality, when beings are most unequal they cannot be joined in friendship. Hence, so that the friendship between man and God should be all the more intimate, it was helpful to man that God should become man, for by very nature man is a friend to man. In this wise, *by seeing God visibly, we are caught up to the love of what is invisible.*[52]

Then, too, beatitude is clearly the reward of virtue. Hence it is necessary that those who tend to beatitude should be disposed according to virtue. Now we are aroused to virtue by word and example; and a person's example and word lead to virtue all the more efficaciously according as there is a more unshakeable opinion of his goodness. But we cannot have an infallible opinion concerning the goodness of any holy man, for even the holiest men are found to fall short in some respects. In order that man might be strengthened in virtue, therefore, it was necessary for him to receive both teaching and examples in virtue from a God become man. That is why Our Lord Himself says: *For I have given you an example, that as I have done to you, so you do also* (Jo. xiii, 15).

Again, just as virtues dispose a man towards beatitude, so sins turn him away from it. Now sin, which is the opposite of virtue, places a hindrance in the way of beatitude not only by introducing into the soul a certain disorderliness, in which respect it leads the soul away from the order of its due end, but also by offending God, from Whom we expect beatitude as a reward, in so far as God exercises care over human actions, and in so far as sin is opposed to the divine charity. We have set this point forth at greater length in the Third Book.[53] And furthermore, man, being aware of this offense against God, loses the confidence of approaching God—a confidence which he must have in order to acquire beatitude. The human race, therefore, abounding as it does in sin, must have some remedy against sin. But this remedy can be applied only by God, Who can both move the will of man towards good, so as to lead it back to its due order, and remit the offense committed against Him (for an offense is not remitted except by Him against Whom it is committed). In order to be freed of the awareness of his past offenses, therefore, man must have a knowledge of the remission of

---

52 Preface of the Mass of the Nativity.
53 In a now deleted chapter of the Third Book.

his offenses by God. Now he cannot know this with certainty unless his knowledge of it comes from God. It was therefore befitting, as well as helpful to the human race in its acquisition of beatitude, that God should become man. In this way, man would acquire the remission of his sins by God, and he would have the certitude of this remission through the Man-God. And so Our Lord Himself has said: *But that you may know that the Son of man hath power on earth to forgive sins* . . . (*Matt.* ix, 6). And St. Paul says that *the blood of Christ* . . . [shall] *cleanse our conscience from dead works, to serve the living God* (*Heb.* ix, 14).

A final argument. The tradition of the Church teaches us that the whole human race is infected by sin. Now it belongs to the order of the divine justice, as is clear from what we have already said, that sin cannot be remitted by God without satisfaction.[54] Now, no holy man could give satisfaction for the sin of the whole human race, since any given holy man is less than the totality of the human race. In order that the human race might be freed from the sin which was common to it, it was therefore necessary that someone give satisfaction who was both a man (to whom it belonged to give satisfaction) and something more than a man, so that his merit might be sufficient to give satisfaction for the sin of the whole human race. But as concerns the order of beatitude, nothing is greater than man save God alone; for though the angels are higher than man according to the condition of their nature, they are not higher according to the order of the end, for they will be beatified by the same order. Hence, that man might come to possess beatitude, it was necessary for him that God should become man in order to take away the sin of the human race. And this is, indeed, what John the Baptist has said of Christ: *Behold the Lamb of God, behold Him Who taketh away the sin of the world* (*Jo.* i, 29). And the Apostle says: *Therefore, as by the offense of one, unto all men to condemnation, so also by the justice of one unto all men to justification of life* (*Rom.* v, 18).

Such, therefore, and others like them, are the arguments by which one can understand that it was not unbefitting to the divine goodness that God should become man, but that it was rather most helpful to the salvation of man.

[54] *Summa Contra Gentiles.* III, c. 158.

DANTE ALIGHIERI

PARADISO

(from *The Divine Comedy*)

✠
✠

> Already my desire and will were rolled—even as a
> wheel that moveth equally—by the Love that moves
> the sun and the other stars.

DANTE WAS BORN in Florence in 1265. In 1292 he wrote the
Vita Nuova which recounts his love for Beatrice, whom he first
met in 1274. He spent the greater part of his life in political
banishment, and died in 1321. In his tract *On Monarchy* (about
1311), he wrote a passionate defense of the independence of the
Empire, though in subordination to the Church and her spiritual
mission. *The Divine Comedy* (written during the first two decades
of the fourteenth century) is a poetic masterpiece that defies summary. Everyone knows that the poem, perhaps originally conceived
as a eulogy of Beatrice, is Dante's journey through hell and purgatory and heaven, through time and eternity, from the icy depths
of hell to the vision of that God whose love moves the sun and
the other stars. Let the reader be prepared to live in an exalted
realm as he follows the rich and intricate symbolism, the cosmic
journeys and spiritual flights of the man who (as Dante said of
himself) wrote down the lessons that love recorded in his heart.

CANTO I

Subject matter and invocation. The sun is in the equinoctial point. It is midday at Purgatory and midnight at Jerusalem, when Dante sees Beatrice gazing at the sun and instinctively imitates her gesture, looking away from her and straight at the sun. The light glows as though God had made a second sun, and Dante now turns once more to Beatrice who is gazing heavenward. As he looks his human nature is transmuted to the quality of heaven and he knows not whether he is still in the flesh or no. They pass through the sphere of fire and hear the harmonies of heaven, but Dante is bewildered because he knows not that they have left the earth, and when enlightened by Beatrice he is still perplexed to know how he can rise, counter to gravitation. Beatrice, pitying the delirium of his earthly mind, explains to him the law of universal (material and spiritual) gravitation. All things seek their true place, and in the orderly movement thereto, and rest therein, consists the likeness of the universe to God. Man's place is God, and to rise to him is therefore natural to man. It is departing from him that (like fire darting downwards) is the anomaly that needs to be explained.

THE ALL-MOVER'S GLORY PENETRATES THROUGH the universe, and regloweth in one region more, and less in another.

In that heaven which most receiveth of his light, have I been; and have seen things which whoso descendeth from up there hath not knowledge nor power to re-tell:

because, as it draweth nigh to its desire, our intellect sinketh so deep, that memory cannot go back upon the track.

Nathless, whatever of the holy realm I had the power to treasure in my memory, shall now be matter of my song.

O good Apollo, for the crowning task, make me a so-fashioned vessel of thy worth, as thou demandest for the grant of thy beloved laurel.

Up till here one peak of Parnassus hath sufficed me; but now, with both the two, needs must I enter this last wrestling-ground.

Into my bosom enter thou, and so breathe as when thou drewest Marsyas from out what sheathed his limbs.

O divine Virtue, if thou dost so far lend thyself to me, that I make manifest the shadow of the blessed realm imprinted on my brain,

thou shalt see me come to thy chosen tree and crown me, then, with the leaves of which the matter and thou shalt make me worthy.

So few times, Father, is there gathered of it, for triumph or of Cæsar or of poet,—fault and shame of human wills,—

that the Peneian frond should bring forth gladness in the joyous Delphic deity, when it sets any athirst for itself.

A mighty flame followeth a tiny spark; perchance, after me, shall prayer with better voices be so offered that Cirrha may respond.

The lantern of the universe riseth unto mortals through divers straits; but from that which joineth four circles in three crosses he issueth with more propitious course, and united with a more propitious star, and doth temper and stamp the mundane wax more after his own mood.

Almost this strait had made morning on that side and evening on this; and there that hemisphere all was aglow, and the other region darkling;

when I beheld Beatrice turned on her left side and gazing on the sun. Never did eagle so fix himself thereon.

And even as the second ray doth ever issue from the first, and rise back upward (like as a pilgrim whose will is to return);

so from her gesture, poured through the eyes into my imagination, did mine own take shape; and I fixed mine eyes upon the sun, transcending our wont.

Much is granted there which is not granted here to our powers, in virtue of the place made as proper to the human race.

I not long endured him, nor yet so little but that I saw him sparkle all around, like iron issuing molten from the furnace.

And, of a sudden, meseemed that day was added unto day, as though he who hath the power, had adorned heaven with a second sun.

Beatrice was standing with her eyes all fixed upon the eternal wheels, and I fixed my sight, removed from there above, on her.

Gazing on her such I became within, as was Glaucus, tasting of the grass that made him the sea-fellow of the other gods.

To pass beyond humanity may not be told in words, wherefore let the example satisfy him for whom grace reserveth the experience.

If I was only that of me which thou didst new-create, O Love who rulest heaven, thou knowest, who with thy light didst lift me up.

When the wheel which thou, by being longed for, makest eternal, drew unto itself my mind with the harmony which thou dost temper and distinguish,

so much of heaven then seemed to me enkindled with the sun's flame, that rain nor river ever made a lake so wide distended.

The newness of the sound and the great light kindled in me a longing for their cause, ne'er felt before so keenly.

Whence she who saw me even as I saw myself, to still my agitated mind, opened her lips, e'er I mine to ask;

and she began: "Thou thyself makest thyself dense with false imagining, and so thou seest not what thou wouldst see, if thou hadst cast it off.

Thou art not upon earth, as thou believest; but lightning, fleeing its proper site, ne'er darted as dost thou who are returning thither."

If I was stripped of my first perplexity by the brief smile-enwrapped discourse, I was the more enmeshed within another;

and I said: "Content already and at rest from a great marvelling, now am I in amaze how I transcend these lightsome bodies."

Whereon she, after a sigh of pity, turned her eyes toward me with that look a mother casts on her delirious child;

and began: "All things whatsoever observe a mutual order; and this is the form that maketh the universe like unto God.

Herein the exalted creatures trace the impress of the Eternal Worth, which is the goal whereto was made the norm now spoken of.

In the order of which I speak all things incline, by diverse lots, more near and less unto their principle;

wherefore they move to diverse ports o'er the great sea of being, and each one with instinct given it to bear it on.

This beareth the fire toward the moon; this is the mover in the hearts of things that die; this doth draw the earth together and unite it.

Nor only the creatures that lack intelligence doth this bow shoot, but those that have both intellect and love.

The Providence that doth assort all this, doth with its light make ever still the heaven wherein whirleth that one that hath the greatest speed;

and thither now, as to the appointed site, the power of that bowstring beareth us which directeth to a joyful mark whatso it doth discharge.

True is it, that as the form often accordeth not with the intention of the art, because that the material is dull to answer;

so from this course sometimes departeth the creature that hath power, thus thrust, to swerve to-ward some other part,

(even as fire may be seen to dart down from the cloud) if its first rush be wrenched aside to earth by false seeming pleasure.

Thou shouldst no more wonder, if I deem aright, at thine uprising, than at a river dropping down from a lofty mountain to the base.

Marvel were it in thee if, bereft of all impediment, thou hadst settled down below; even as were stillness on the earth in a living flame." Thereon toward Heaven she turned back her gaze.

CANTO II

Warning and promise to the reader, who shall see stranger tilth than when Jason sowed the dragon's teeth. They reach the moon and inconceivably penetrate into her substance without cleaving it, even as deity penetrated into humanity in Christ; which mystery shall in heaven be seen as axiomatic truth. Dante, dimly aware of the inadequacy of his science, questions Beatrice as to the dark patches on the moon which he had thought were due to rarity of substance. She explains that if such rarity pierced right through the moon in the dark parts, the sun would shine through them when eclipsed; and if not, the dense matter behind the rare would cast back the sun's light; and describes to him an experiment by which he may satisfy himself that in that case the light reflected from the dense matter at the surface and from that in the interior of the moon would be equally bright. She then explains that Dante has

*gone wrong and accepted a scientifically inadequate explanation,
because he has not understood that all heavenly phenomena are
direct utterances of God and of his Angels. The undivided power
of God, differentiated through the various heavenly bodies and
agencies, shines in the diverse quality and brightness of the fixed
stars, of the planets and of the parts of the moon, as the vital principle manifests itself diversely in the several members of the body,
and as joy beams through the pupil of the eye.*

O YE who in your little skiff longing to hear, have followed on
my keel that singeth on its way,

turn to revisit your own shores; commit you not to the open sea;
for perchance, losing me, ye would be left astray.

The water which I take was never coursed before; Minerva
bloweth, Apollo guideth me, and the nine Muses point me to the
Bears.

Ye other few, who timely have lift up your necks for bread of
angels whereby life is here sustained but where from none cometh
away sated,

ye may indeed commit your vessel to the deep keeping my fur-
row, in advance of the water that is falling back to the level.

The glorious ones who fared to Colchis not so marvelled as shall
ye, when Jason turned ox-plough-man in their sight.

The thirst, born with us and ne'er failing, for the godlike realm
bore us swift almost as ye see the heaven.

Beatrice was gazing upward, and I on her; and perchance in
such space as an arrow stays and flies and is discharged from the
nocking point,

I saw me arrived where a wondrous thing drew my sight to it;
and therefore she from whom my doing might not be hidden

turning to me as much in joy as beauty, "Direct thy mind to
God in gratitude," she said, "who hath united us with the first
star."

Meseemed a cloud enveloped us, shining, dense, firm and polished, like diamond smitten by the sun.

Within itself the eternal pearl received us, as water doth receive
a ray of light, though still itself uncleft.

If I was body,—and if here we conceive not how one dimension could support another, which must be, if body into body creep,—

The more should longing enkindle us to see that Essence wherein we behold how our own nature and God unified themselves.

There what we hold by faith shall be beheld, not demonstrated, but self-known in fashion of the initial truth which man believeth.

I answered: "Lady, devoutly as I most may, do I thank him who hath removed me from the mortal world.

But tell me what those dusky marks upon this body, which down there on earth make folk to tell the tale of Cain?"

She smiled a little, and then: "And if," she said, "the opinion of mortals goeth wrong, where the key of sense doth not unlock,

truly the shafts of wonder should no longer pierce thee; since even when the senses give the lead thou see'st reason hath wings too short.

But tell me what thou, of thyself, thinkest concerning it?" And I: "That which to us appeareth diverse in this high region, I hold to be produced by bodies rare and dense."

And she: "Verily, thou shalt see thy thought plunged deep in falsity, if well thou hearken to the argument which I shall make against it.

The eighth sphere revealeth many lights to you, the which in quality, as eke in quantity, may be observed of diverse countenance.

If rare and dense alone produced this thing, one only virtue, more or less or equally distributed, were in them all.

Diverse virtues must needs be fruits of formal principles, the which, save only one, would have no leave to be, upon thy reasoning.

Again, were rarity cause of that duskiness whereof thou makest question, either in some certain part, right through, thus stinted of its matter

were this planet; or, like as a body doth dispose the fat and lean, would it alternate pages in its volume.

Were the first true, 'twould be revealed in the eclipses of the sun, by the light shining through it, as it doth when hurled on aught else rare.

This is not; wherefore we have to see what of the other case, and if it chance that I make vain this also, thy thought will be refuted.

If it be that this rare matter goeth not throughout, needs must there be a limit, from which its contrary doth intercept its passing on;

and thence that other's ray were so cast back, as colour doth return from glass which hideth lead behind it.

Now thou wilt urge that the ray here is darkened rather than in other parts, because here it is recast from further back.

From this plea experiment may disentangle thee, (if thou wilt make the proof) which ever is the spring of the rivers of your arts.

Three mirrors thou shalt take, and set two equally remote from thee; and let the third further removed strike on thine eyes between the other two.

Turning to them, have a light set behind thy back, enkindling the three mirrors, and, backsmitten by them all, coming again to thee.

Whereas in size the more distant show shall not have so great stretch, yet thou there shalt see it needs must shine as brightly as the others.

Now,—as at the stroke of the warm rays the substrate of the snow is stripped both of the colour and of the coldness which it had,—

thee, so left stripped in thine intellect, would I inform with light so living, it shall tremble as thou lookest on it.

Within the heaven of the divine peace whirleth a body, in whose virtue lieth the being of all that it containeth.

The heaven next following, which hath so many things to show, parteth this being amid diverse essences, which it distinguisheth and doth contain;

the other circling bodies by various differentiatings, dispose the distinct powers they have within themselves, unto their end and to their fertilizings.

These organs of the universe go, as thou seest now, from grade to grade; for from above do they receive, and downward do they work.

Now mark well how I thread this pass to the truth for which

thou longest, that thou thereafter mayest know to keep the ford alone.

The movement and the virtue of the sacred wheelings, as the hammer's art from the smith, must needs be an effluence from the blessed movers;

and the heaven which so many lights make beautiful, from the deep mind which rolleth it, taketh the image and thereof maketh the seal.

And as the soul within your dust, through members differing and conformed to divers powers, doth diffuse itself,

so doth the Intelligence deploy its goodness, multiplied through the stars, revolving still on its own unity.

Diverse virtue maketh diverse alloy with the precious body which it quickeneth, wherein, as life in you, it is upbound.

By cause of the glad nature whence it floweth, the mingled virtue shineth through the body, as gladness doth through living pupil.

Thence cometh what seems different 'twixt light and light, and not from dense and rare; this is the formal principle that produceth, conformably to its own excellence, the turbid and the clear."

CANTO III

As Dante is about to speak he sees the faint outlines of human features and taking them for reflections looks behind him but sees nothing. Beatrice smiles at his taking the most real existences he has ever yet beheld for mere semblances, tells him why they are there and bids him address them. Dante learns from Piccarda that each soul in heaven rejoices in the whole order of which it is part, and therefore desires no higher place than is assigned to it, for such desire would violate the law of love, and therefore the harmony of heaven, and with it the joy of the unduly aspiring soul itself. He further learns Piccarda's history and that of Constance. After which the souls disappear and Dante's eyes return to Beatrice.

THAT SUN which first warmed my bosom with love had thus unveiled for me, by proof and refutation, fair truth's sweet aspect;

and I, to confess me corrected and assured, in measure as was meet, sloped up my head to speak.

But there appeared to me a sight which so straitly held me to itself, to look upon it, that I bethought me not of my confession.

In such guise as, from glasses transparent and polished, or from waters clear and tranquil, not so deep that the bottom is darkened,

come back the notes of our faces, so faint that a pearl on a white brow cometh not slowlier upon our pupils;

so did I behold many a countenance, eager to speak; wherefore I fell into the counter error of that which kindled love between the man and fountain.

No sooner was I aware of them, than, thinking them reflected images, I turned round my eyes to see of whom they were;

and I saw naught, and turned them forward again straight on the light of my sweet guide, whose sacred eyes glowed as she smiled.

"Wonder not that I smile," she said, "in presence of thy child-like thought, since it trusts not its foot upon the truth,

but turneth thee after its wont, to vacancy. True substances are they which thou beholdest, relegated here for failure of their vows.

Wherefore speak with them, and listen and believe; for the true light which satisfieth them, suffereth them not to turn their feet aside from it."

And I to the shade who seemed most to long for converse turned me and began, as one whom too great longing doth confound:

"O well-created spirit, who in the rays of eternal life dost feel the sweetness which, save tasted, may ne'er be understood;

it were acceptable to me, wouldst thou content me with thy name and with your lot." Whereat she, eager and with smiling eyes:

"Our love doth no more bar the gate to a just wish, than doth that love which would have all its court like to itself.

In the world I was a virgin sister; and if thy memory be rightly searched, my greater beauty will not hide me from thee,

but thou wilt know me again for Piccarda, who, placed here with these other blessed ones, am blessed in the sphere that moveth slowest.

Our affections, which are aflame only in the pleasure of the Holy Spirit, rejoice to be informed after his order.

And this lot, which seemeth so far down, therefore is given us because our vows were slighted, and on some certain side were not filled in."

Whereon I to her: "In your wondrous aspects a divine somewhat regloweth that doth transmute you from conceits of former times.

Wherefore I lagged in calling thee to mind; now what thou tellest me giveth such help that more articulately I retrace thee.

But tell me, ye whose blessedness is here, do you desire a more lofty place, to see more, or to make yourselves more dear?"

With those other shades first she smiled a little, then answered me so joyous that she seemed to burn in love's first flame:

"Brother, the quality of love stilleth our will, and maketh us long only for what we have, and giveth us no other thirst.

Did we desire to be more aloft, our longings were discordant from his will who here assorteth us,

and for that, thou wilt see, there is no room within these circles, if of necessity we have our being here in love, and if thou think again what is love's nature.

Nay, 'tis the essence of this blessed being to hold ourselves within the divine will, whereby our own wills are themselves made one.

So that our being thus, from threshold unto threshold throughout the realm, is a joy to all the realm as to the king, who draweth our wills to what he willeth;

and his will is our peace; it is that sea to which all moves that it createth and that nature maketh."

Clear was it then to me how everywhere in heaven is Paradise, e'en though the grace of the chief Good doth not rain there after one only fashion.

But even as it chanceth, should one food sate us while for another the appetite remaineth, that returning thanks for that, we ask for this;

so with gesture and with word did I, to learn from her what was that web through which she had not drawn the shuttle to the end.

"Perfected life and high desert enheaveneth a lady more aloft," she said, "by whose rule down in your world there are who clothe and veil themselves, that they, even till death, may wake and sleep with that Spouse who accepteth every vow that love hath made conform with his good pleasure.

From the world, to follow her, I fled while yet a girl, and in her habit I enclosed myself, and promised the way of her company.

Thereafter men more used to ill than good tore me away from the sweet cloister; and God doth know what my life then became.

And this other splendour who revealeth herself to thee on my right side, and who kindleth herself with all the light of our sphere,

doth understand of her that which I tell of me. She was a sister, and from her head was taken in like manner the shadow of the sacred veil.

Yet, turned back as she was into the world, against her pleasure and against good usage, from her heart's veil never was she loosened.

This is the light of the great Constance, who, from the second blast of Suabia, conceived the third and final might."

Thus did she speak to me, and then began to sing *Ave Maria,* and vanished as she sang, like to a heavy thing through the deep water.

My sight, which followed her far as it might, when it had lost her turned to the target of a greater longing,

and bent itself all upon Beatrice; but she so flashed upon my look, that at the first my sight endured it not; and this made me the slower with my questioning.

CANTO IV

Piccarda has left Dante entangled in two perplexities. Why are the nuns shorn of what had else been the full measure of their glory because they were torn against their will from the cloister? And if the inconstant moon is the abode of such as have left their vows unfulfilled, was Plato right after all in saying that men's souls come down from the planets connatural with them, and return thereto? This latter speculation might lead to dangerous heresy, and Beatrice hastens to explain that the souls who come to meet

*Dante in the several spheres all have their permanent abiding place
with God and the Angels in the Empyrean. Their meeting places
with Dante are but symbolical of their spiritual state. But Plato
may have had in mind the divine influences that, through the
agency of the planets, act upon men's dispositions and produce
good or ill effects which should be credited to them rather than to
the human will. And indeed it was a confused perception of these
divine influences that led men into idolatry. The other difficulty is
removed by a distinction between what we wish to do and what,
under pressure, we consent to do; for if we consent we cannot plead
violence in excuse, although we have done what we did not wish
to do. More questions are started in Dante's mind, for only in the
all-embracing truth of God can the human mind find that restful
possession which its nature promises it. Short of that each newly
acquired truth leads on to further questions. Beatrice, who had
sighed at Dante's previous bewildered questions, smiles approval
now, for he asks her a question as to vows which has some spiritual
import.*

BETWEEN TWO FOODS, distant and appetizing in like measure, death
by starvation would ensue ere a free man put either to his teeth.

So would a lamb stand still between two cravings of fierce wolves,
in equipoise of dread; so would a dog stand still between two hinds.

Wherefore, if I held my peace I blame me not, (thrust in like
measure either way by my perplexities) since 'twas necessity, nor
yet commend me.

I held my peace, but my desire was painted on my face, and my
questioning with it, in warmer colours far than if set out by speech.

And Beatrice took the part that Daniel took when he lifted
Nebuchadnezzar out of the wrath that had made him unjustly cruel,

and she said: "Yea, but I see how this desire and that so draweth
thee, that thy eagerness entangleth its own self, and therefore
breathes not forth.

Thou arguest: *If the right will endureth, by what justice can
another's violence sheer me the measure of desert?*

And further matter of perplexity is given thee by the semblance
of the souls returning to the stars, as Plato's doctrine hath it.

These are the questions which weigh equally upon thy will; and therefore I will first treat that which hath the most of gall.

He of the Seraphim who most doth sink himself in God, Moses, Samuel, and that John whichso thou choose to take, not Mary's self,

in any other heaven hold their seats than these spirits who but now appeared to thee, nor have they to their being more nor fewer years.

But all make beauteous the first circle, and share sweet life, with difference, by feeling more and less the eternal breath.

They have here revealed themselves, not that this sphere is given them, but to make sign of the celestial one that hath the least ascent.

Needs must such speech address your faculty, which only from the sense-reported thing doth apprehend, what it then proceedeth to make fit matter for the intellect.

And therefore doth the Scripture condescend to your capacity, assigning foot and hand to God, with other meaning:

and Holy Church doth represent to you with human aspect Gabriel and Michael, and him too who made Tobit sound again.

That which Timæus argueth of the souls is not the like of what may here be seen, for seemingly he thinketh as he saith.

He saith the soul returneth to its star, believing it cleft thence when nature gave it as a form.

Although perchance his meaning is of other guise than the word soundeth, and may have a not-to-be-derided purport.

If he meaneth that the honour and the blame of their influence return unto these wheels, perchance his bow smiteth a certain truth.

This principle misunderstood erst wrenched aside the whole world almost, so that it rushed astray to call upon the names of Jove and Mercury and Mars.

The other perplexity which troubleth thee hath less poison, because its malice could not lead thee away from me elsewhere.

For our justice to appear unjust in mortal eyes is argument of faith, and not of heretic iniquity.

But since your wit hath power to pierce unto this truth, e'en as thou wishest I will satisfy thee.

If *violence* is when he who suffereth doth naught contribute to what forceth him, then these souls had not the excuse of it:

for if the will willeth not, it cannot be crushed, but doth as nature doeth in the flame, though violence wrench it aside a thousand times.

For should it bend itself, or much or little, it doth abet the force; and so did these, since they had power to return to the sacred place.

If their will had remained intact, like that which held Lawrence upon the grid, and made Mucius stern against his own right hand,

it would have thrust them back upon the path whence they were drawn, so soon as they were loose; but such sound will is all too rare.

Now by these words, if thou hast gleaned them as thou should'st, the argument which would have troubled thee more times than this, is rendered void.

But now across thy path another strait confronts thine eyes, through which ere thou should'st win thy way alone, thou should'st be weary.

I have set it in my mind for sure, that no blessed soul may lie because hard by the Primal Truth it ever doth abide;

and then thou mightest hear from Piccarda that her devotion to the veil Constance still held, so that here she seemeth me to contradict.

Many a time ere now, my brother, hath it come to pass that to flee peril things were done, against the grain, that were unmeet to do;

so did Alcmæon, moved by his father's prayer, slay his own mother, and not to sacrifice his filial piety became an impious son.

At this point, I would have thee think, violence receiveth mixture from the will, and they so work that the offenses may not plead excuse.

The absolute will consenteth not to the ill, but yet consenteth in so far as it doth fear, should it draw back, to fall into a worse annoy.

Wherefore, when Piccarda expresseth this, she meaneth it of the absolute will, and I of the other; so that we both speak truth together."

Such the rippling of the sacred stream which issued from the Spring whence all truth down-floweth; and being such, it set at peace one and the other longing.

"O love of the primal Lover, O divine one," said I then, "whose speech o'erfloweth me and warmeth, so that more and more it quickeneth me, my love hath no such depth as to suffice to render grace for grace; but may he who seeth it, and hath the power, answer thereto.

Now do I see that never can our intellect be sated, unless that Truth shine on it, beyond which no truth hath range.

Therein it resteth as a wild beast in his den so soon as it hath reached it; and reach it may; else were all longing futile.

Wherefore there springeth, like a shoot, questioning at the foot of truth; which is a thing that trusteth us towards the summit, on from ridge to ridge.

This doth invite me and giveth me assurance, with reverence, lady, to make question to thee as to another truth which is dark to me.

I would know if man can satisfy you so for broken vows, with other goods, as not to weigh too short upon your balance."

Beatrice looked on me with eyes filled so divine with sparks of love, that my vanquished power turned away, and I became as lost with eyes downcast.

CANTO V

Beatrice, rejoicing in Dante's progress, explains the supreme gift of Free Will, shared by angels and men and by no other creature. Hence may be deduced the supreme significance of vows, wherein this Free Will, by its own act, sacrifices itself. Wherefore there can be nothing so august as to form a fitting substitute, nor any use of the once consecrated thing so hallowed as to excuse the breaking of the vow. And yet Holy Church grants dispensations. The explanation lies in the distinction between the content of the vow (the specific thing consecrated) and the act of vowing. The vow must in every case be kept, but he who has made it, may, under due authority, sometimes substitute for the specific content of the vow some other, worth half as much again; which last condition precludes any substitute for the complete self-dedication of monastic vows. And he who makes a vow such as God cannot sanction, has in that act already done evil; to keep such a vow is only to deepen his guilt; and, kept or broken, it brings his religion into contempt. Dante's further questioning is cut short by their ascent to Mercury, which grows brighter at their presence. Here, in the star that scarce asserts itself, but is lost to mortals in the sun's rays, are the once ambitious

*souls, that now rejoice in the access of fresh objects of love. They
approach Dante, and one of them, with lofty gratulations, offers
himself as the vehicle of divine enlightenment. Dante questions
him as to his history and the place assigned to him in heaven;
whereon the spirit (Justinian) so glows with joy that his outward
form is lost in light.*

"IF I FLAME on thee in the warmth of love, beyond the measure
witnessed upon earth, and so vanquish the power of thine eyes,

marvel not; for this proceedeth from perfect vision, which, as it
apprehendeth, so doth advance its foot in the apprehended good.

Well do I note how in thine intellect already doth reglow the
eternal light, which only seen doth ever kindle love;

and if aught else seduce your love, naught is it save some vestige
of this light, ill understood, that shineth through therein.

Thou wouldst know whether with other service reckoning may
be paid for broken vow, so great as to secure the soul from process."

So Beatrice began this chant, and, as one who interrupteth not
his speech, continued thus the sacred progress:

"The greatest gift God of his largess made at the creation, and
the most conformed to his own excellence, and which he most
prizeth,

was the will's liberty, wherewith creatures intelligent, both all
and only, were and are endowed.

Now will appear to thee (if thence thou draw due inference)
the high worth of the vow, if so made that God consent when thou
consentest;

for in establishing the compact between God and man, the victim
is made from out this treasure, such as I pronounce it, and made by
its own act.

What may be rendered, then, as restoration? If thou think to
make good use of that which thou hadst consecrated, thou wouldst
do good works from evil gains.

Thou art now assured as to the greater point; but since Holy
Church granteth herein dispensations, which seemeth counter to
the truth I have unfolded to thee,

it behoves thee still to sit a while at table, because the stubborn
food which thou hast taken demandeth further aid for thy digestion.

Open thy mind to that which I unfold to thee, and fix it there within; for to have understood without retaining maketh not knowledge.

Two things pertain to the essence of this sacrifice: first, that whereof it is composed, and then the compact's self.

This last can ne'er be cancelled save by being kept; and concerning this it is that the discourse above is so precise;

therefore it was imperative upon the Hebrews to offer sacrifice in any case, though the thing offered might sometimes be changed, as thou shouldst know.

The other thing, which hath been unfolded to thee as the matter, may in sooth be such that there is no offence if it be interchanged with other matter.

But let none shift the load upon his shoulder at his own judgment, without the turn both of the white and of the yellow key

and let him hold all changing to be folly, unless the thing remitted be contained in that assumed in four to six proportion.

Wherefore what thing soe'er weigheth so heavy in virtue of its worth as to turn every scale, can never be made good by any other outlay.

Let mortals never take the vow in sport; be loyal, and in doing this not squint-eyed; like as with Jephthah in his firstling vow;

whom it had more become to say: *I did amiss,* than keep it and do worse; and in like folly mayst thou track the great chief of the Greeks,

wherefore Iphigenia wept that her face was fair, and made simple and sage to weep for her, hearing of such a rite.

Ye Christians, be more sedate in moving, not like a feather unto every wind; nor think that every water cleanseth you.

Ye have the Old and the New Testament and the shepherd of the Church to guide you; let this suffice you, unto your salvation.

If sorry greed proclaim aught else to you, be men, not senseless sheep, lest the Jew in your midst should scoff at you.

Do not ye as the lamb who leaves his mother's milk, silly and wanton, fighting with himself for his disport."

Thus Beatrice to me, as I write; then turned her all in longing to that part where the world quickeneth most.

Her ceasing and her transmuted semblance enjoined silence on my eager wit, which already had new questionings before it.

And even as an arrow which smiteth the targe ere the cord be still, so fled we to the second realm.

There I beheld my Lady so glad, when to the light of this heaven she committed her, that the planet's self became the brighter for it.

And if the star was changed and laughed, what then did I, who of my very nature am subjected unto change through every guise!

As in a fish-pool still and clear, the fishes draw to aught that so droppeth from without as to make them deem it somewhat they may feed on,

so did I see more than a thousand splendours draw towards us, and in each one was heard:

Lo! one who shall increase our loves.

And as each one came up to us, the shade appeared full filled with joy, by the bright glow that issued forth of it.

Think, reader, if what I now begin proceeded not, how thou would'st feel an anguished dearth of knowing more,

and by thyself thou shalt perceive how it was in my longing to hear from these concerning their estate, soon as they were revealed unto my eyes.

"O happy-born, to whom grace concedeth to look upon the Thrones of the eternal triumph ere thou abandonest thy time of warfare,

by the light that rangeth through all heaven are we enkindled; and therefore if thou desire to draw light from us, sate thee at thine own will."

Thus by one of those devout spirits was said to me, and by Beatrice: "Speak, speak securely, and believe as thou would'st deities."

"Verily, I see how thou dost nestle in thine own light, and that thou dost draw it through thine eyes, because they sparkle as thou smilest;

But I know nor who thou art, nor why, O worthy soul, thou art graded in this sphere, which veileth it to mortals in another's rays."

This I said, turned towards the light which first had spoken to me; whereat it glowed far brighter yet than what it was before.

Like as the sun which hideth him by excess of light when the heat hath gnawed away the tempering of the thick vapours, so by access of joy the sacred figure hid him in his own rays, and thus enclosed, answered me in such fashion as chanteth the following chant.

CANTO VI

Note that Justinian, the Lawgiver, is the spokesman of the Roman Empire, whereby is indicated that the true significance of the empire lies in its imposing and fostering the arts of peace. Justinian tells how Constantine removed the seat of Empire east from Rome to Byzantium, reversing the progress of Æneas who went from Troy to Rome, and how he, Justinian, came to the throne two hundred years later. He was a believer in the divine but not in the human nature of Christ, till converted by Agapetus to the truth which he now sees as clearly as logicians see the axiomatic law of contradictories. After his conversion God inspired him with the project of codifying the Roman Law, and he resigned the conduct of war to Belisarius. He goes on to rebuke the Guelf and Ghibelline factions by showing the august nature of the Roman Empire. In his exposition we note that the key of self-sacrifice is at once struck in the name of Pallas, the Etruscan-Greek volunteer who died for the Trojan cause, and is maintained till it leads up to the great struggles with Carthage and the East, and against internal factiousness; the founding of the Empire under Julius and Augustus and the establishment of universal peace; the great act of Redemption for which all was a preparation, and the subsequent fall of Jerusalem; and the Empire's championship of the Church which had been born under its protection. It is equally wicked, therefore, to think of opposing the Empire or of turning it to factious purposes. The story of Rome has been told in the star adorned by those souls whose virtuous deeds had in them some taint of worldly ambition or anxiety for good repute, but who are now free from all envious desire to have a greater reward, and rejoice rather in the harmony of which their estate is part. Here too is the lowly Romeo who was so disinterested but so sensitive concerning his reputation.

"AFTER CONSTANTINE had wheeled back the eagle, counter to the course of heaven which it had followed in train of the ancient wight who took Lavinia, a hundred and a hundred years and more the bird of God abode on Europe's limit, neighbouring the mountains whence he first had issued;

and there he governed the world beneath the shadow of his sacred wings from hand to hand till by succeeding change he came to mine.

Cæsar I was, and am Justinian who, by will of the Primal Love which now I feel, withdrew from out the Laws excess and inefficiency;

and ere I fixed my mind upon the work, one nature, and no more, I held to be in Christ, and with such faith was I content;

but the blessed Agapetus, who was high pastor, to the faith without alloy directed me by his discourse.

Him I believed, and now the content of his faith I see as clear as thou dost see that every contradiction is both false and true.

So soon as with the Church I moved my feet, God of his grace it pleased to inspire me with the high task, and all to it I gave me;

and to my Belisarius committed arms; to whom heaven's righthand was so conjoined it was a signal I should rest me from them.

Now here already is my answer's close to thy first question; but its conditions force me to go on to some addition.

That thou mayst see with how good right against the sacred standard doth proceed both he who doth annex it to himself and he who doth oppose him to it,

see how great virtue hath made it worthy of reverence, beginning from the hour when Pallas died to give it sway.

Thou knowest that it made its sojourn in Alba for three hundred years and more, until the close, when three with three yet fought for it.

And thou knowest what it wrought from the Sabine women's wrong unto Lucretia's woe, through seven kings, conquering around the neighbour folk.

Thou knowest what it wrought, borne by the chosen Romans against Brennus, against Pyrrhus and against the rest, princes and governments;

whence Torquatus and Quinctius, named from his neglected locks, the Decii and the Fabii, drew the fame which I rejoice in thus embalming.

It cast down the pride of the Arabs that followed Hannibal across the Alpine rocks, whence, Po, thou glidest.

Under it, Scipio and Pompey triumphed, yet in their youth, and bitter did it seem unto those hills beneath which thou wast born.

Then, nigh the time when all heaven willed to bring the world to its own serene mood, Cæsar, at Rome's behest, laid hold of it;

and what it wrought from Var to Rhine knoweth Isère and Arar, knoweth Seine and every valley by which Rhone is filled.

What it then wrought when he issued forth of Ravenna, and sprang the Rubicon, was of such flight that neither tongue nor pen might follow it.

Towards Spain it wheeled the host, then towards Durazzo, and so smote Pharsalia that to hot Nile was felt the woe.

Antandros and Simois, whence it first came, it saw once more, and saw the spot where Hector lieth couched; and then (alas for Ptolemy!) ruffled itself again;

thereafter swooped in lightning upon Juba, then wheeled towards your west, where it heard the Pompeian trumpet.

For what it wrought with the succeeding marshal Brutus and Cassius howl in hell; and Modena and Perugia it made doleful.

Yet doth wail for it the wretched Cleopatra, who, as she fled before it, caught from the viper sudden and black death.

With him it coursed unto the Red Sea shore, with him it set the world in so deep peace that Janus saw his temple barred upon him.

But what the ensign that doth make me speak had done before, what it was yet to do throughout the mortal realm subject unto it,

becometh small and dusky to behold, if it be looked upon in the third Cæsar's hand with clear eye and pure heart;

for the living justice that inspireth me, granted it, in his hand of whom I speak, the glory of wreaking vengeance for his wrath.

Now find a marvel in the double thing I tell thee! Thereafter, under Titus, to wreak vengeance on the vengeance on the ancient sin it rushed.

And when the Lombard tooth bit into Holy Church, under its wings did Charlemagne victorious succour her.

Now mayst thou judge of such as I accused but now, and of their sins, which are the cause of all your ills.

The one opposeth to the public standard the yellow lilies, and the other doth annex it to a faction, so that 'tis hard to see which most offendeth.

Ply, ply the Ghibellines their arts under some other standard; for this he ever followeth ill who cleaveth justice from it;

and let not that new Charles down beat it with his Guelfs, but let him fear talons that have ripped its fell from mightier lion.

Many a time ere now have children wailed for father's fault, and let him not suppose God will change arms for those his lilies.

This little star adorneth her with good spirits who were active that honour and that fame might come to them;

and when hereon desire, thus swerving, leaneth, needs must the rays of the true love mount upward with less life.

But in the commeasuring of our rewards to our desert is part of our joy, because we see them neither less nor more.

Whereby the living justice so sweeteneth our affection that it may ne'er be warped to any malice.

Divers voices upon earth make sweet harmony, and so the divers seats in our life render sweet harmony amongst these wheels.

And within the present pearl shineth the light of Romeo, whose beauteous and great work was so ill answered.

But the Provençals who wrought against him have not the laugh; wherefore he taketh an ill path who maketh of another's good work his own loss.

Four daughters, and each one a queen, had Raymond Berengar; and this was wrought for him by Romeo, a lowly and an alien man;

then words uttered askance moved him to demand account of this just man, who gave him five and seven for every ten;

then took his way in poverty and age; and might the world know the heart he had within him, begging his life by crust and crust, much as it praiseth, it would praise him more."

CANTO VII

In significant connection with the Empire comes the treatment of the Redemption, the chief theological discourse in the Paradiso. Justinian and the other spirits vanish with hymns of triumph. Dante would fain ask a question, but when he raises his head to speak, he is overcome by awe, and bends it down again. Beatrice reads his

*thoughts, and bids him give good heed to her discourse. After
man's fall, the Word of God united to himself in his own person
the once pure now contaminated human nature. That human nature
bore on the cross the just penalty of its sin, but that divine Person
suffered by the same act the supremest outrage. At the act of justice
God rejoiced and heaven opened. At the outrage the Jews exulted
and the earth trembled; and vengeance fell upon Jerusalem. But
why this method of redemption? Only those who love can understand the answer. God's love ungrudgingly reveals itself, and whatever it creates without intermediary is immortal, free, and god-like.
Such was man till made unlike God by sin, and so disfranchised
only to be reinstated by a free pardon, or by full atonement. But
man cannot humble himself below what he is entitled to, as much
as he had striven to exalt himself above it; and therefore he cannot
make atonement. So God must reinstate man; and since "all the
ways of the Lord are mercy and truth," God proceedeth both by the
way of mercy, and by the way of truth or justice, since by the incarnation man was made capable of reinstating himself. Beatrice further explains that the elements and their compounds are made not
direct by God, but by angels, who also draw the life of animal and
plant out of compound matter that has the potentiality of such life
in it; whereas first matter, the angels, and the heavens are direct
creations of God; and so were the bodies of Adam and Eve, which
were therefore immortal, save for sin; as are therefore the bodies
of the redeemed who are restored to all the privileges of unfallen
man.*

"HOSANNAH! Holy God of Sabaoth! making lustrous by thy
brightness from above the blessed fires of these kingdoms!"

So, revolving to its own note, I saw that being sing, on whom the
twin lights double one another:

and it and the others entered on their dance, and like most rapid
sparks, veiled them from me by sudden distance.

I, hesitating, said, "Speak to her, speak to her," within myself,
"speak to her," I said, "to my lady who slaketh my thirst with the
sweet drops";

but that reverence which all o'ermastereth me, though but by Be
or Ice, again down-bowed me, as a man who slumbers.

Short time Beatrice left me thus; and began, casting the ray upon me of a smile such as would make one blessed though in the flame:

"According to my thought that cannot err, how just vengeance justly was avenged, hath set thee pondering;

but I will speedily release thy mind; and do thou hearken, for my words shall make thee gift of an august pronouncement.

Because he not endured for his own good a rein upon the power that wills, that man who ne-er was born, as he condemned himself, condemned his total offspring;

wherefore the human race lay sick down there for many an age, in great error, till it pleased the Word of God to descend

where he joined that nature which had gone astray from its Creator to himself, in person, by sole act of his eternal Love.

Now turn thy sight to what I now discourse: This nature, so united to its Maker, as it was when created was unalloyed and good;

but by its own self had it been exiled from Paradise, because it swerved from the way of truth, and from its proper life.

As for the penalty, then, inflicted by the cross,—if it be measured by the Nature taken on, never did any other bite as justly;

and, in like manner, ne'er was any so outrageous if we look to the Person who endured it, in whom this nature was contracted.

So from one act issued effects apart; God and the Jews rejoiced in one same death; thereat shuddered the earth and heaven opened.

No more, now, should it seem hard saying to thee that just vengeance was afterward avenged by a just court.

But now I see thy mind from thought to thought entangled in a knot, from which, with great desire, it release awaiteth.

Thou sayest, *Yea, what I hear I understand; but why God willed for our redemption this only mode, is hidden from me.*

This decree, my brother, is buried from the eyes of every one whose wit is not matured within love's flame.

But since this target much is aimed at, and discerned but little, I will declare why such mode was more worthy.

The divine excellence, which spurns all envy from it, burning within itself shooteth such sparkles out as to display the eternal beauties.

That which distilleth from it without mean, thereafter hath no end; because its imprint may not be removed when it hath stamped the seal.

That which down raineth from it without mean, is all free, because not subject to the power of changing things.

It is more close conformed to it, therefore more pleasing to it; for the sacred glow that rayeth over everything, in that most like itself is the most living.

All these points of vantage hath the human creature, and should one fail, needs must it fall from its nobility.

Sin only is the thing that doth disfranchise it, and maketh it unlike to the highest good, so that its light the less doth brighten it;

and to its dignity it ne'er may come again, except it fill again where fault hath made a void, against the ill delight setting just penalty.

Your nature, when it sinned in its totality in its first seed, from these dignities, even as from Paradise, was parted;

nor might they be recovered, if thou look right keenly, by any way save passing one or the other of these fords:

either that God, of his sole courtesy, should have remitted; or that man should of himself have given satisfaction for his folly.

Fix now thine eye within the abyss of the eternal counsel, as close attached as e'er thou mayest to my discourse.

Man had not power, within his own boundaries, ever to render satisfaction; since he might not go in humbleness by after-obedience so deep down

as in disobedience he had framed to exalt himself on high; and this the cause why from the power to render satisfaction by himself man was shut off.

Wherefore needs must God with his own ways reinstate man in his unmaimed life, I mean with one way or with both the two.

But because the doer's deed is the more gracious the more it doth present us of the heart's goodness whence it issued,

the divine Goodness which doth stamp the world, deigned to proceed on all his ways to lift you up again;

nor between the last night and the first day was, nor shall be, so lofty and august a progress made on one or on the other;

for more generous was God in giving of himself to make man

able to uplift himself again, than had he only of himself granted remission;

and all other modes fell short of justice, except the Son of God had humbled him to become flesh.

Now, to fulfil for thee every desire, I go back to explain a certain passage, that thou may'st there discern e'en as do I.

Thou sayest: *I see the water, I see the fire, the air, the earth, and all their combinations meet their dissolution and endure but little;*

and yet these things were creatures, so that if that which I have said to thee be true, they ought to be secure against corruption.

The Angels, brother, and the unsullied country in which thou art, may be declared to be created, even as they are, in their entire being;

but the elements which thou hast named and all the things compounded of them, have by created virtue been informed.

Created was the matter which they hold, created was the informing virtue in these stars which sweep around them.

The life of every brute and of the plants is drawn from compounds having potency, by the ray and movement of the sacred lights.

But your life is breathed without mean by the supreme beneficence who maketh it enamoured of itself, so that thereafter it doth ever long for it.

And hence thou further may'st infer your resurrection, if thou think again how was the making of the human flesh then when the first parents both of them were formed."

CANTO VIII

The planet Venus and ancient idolatry. All angels, heavens and blessed spirits, from the Seraphim nearest God outwards, are twined in one concerted cosmic dance; this dance the spirits in Venus leave to minister to Dante, singing Hosannah *as they come; and one of them declares their kinship of movement and of love with the celestial Beings to whom he had once addressed his love hymn. Dante, with Beatrice's sanction, asks who the spirit is, and he with a flash of joy reveals himself as Dante's friend, Carlo Martello, once heir to the lordship of Provence and the kingdom of*

Naples, and actual king of Hungary, though Sicily had revolted from his house in consequence of that ill government against which his brother, Robert of Naples, mean offspring of a generous sire, would do well to take warning. Dante's joy in meeting his friend is increased by the knowledge that it is seen as clearly by that friend as by himself, and further, by the thought that it is in God that it is thus discerned. He asks him how it is that degenerate children can spring from noble parents. Carlo explains that for every natural attribute of any being there is provision of a corresponding good, and that since God is perfect and has made his ministers perfect for their offices, it follows that there is a fit place for everything and every one, for which place it is designed and at which it is aimed. The social relations of man demand diversity of gift, which diversity is provided for by the action of the heavens on human natures, but without regard to descent, so that natural heredity is overruled by celestial influences. Whereas we in assigning a man's place to him give heed only to hereditary position or such-like irrelevancies instead of studying his natural gift. Hence general confusion and incompetency.

THE WORLD was wont to think in its peril that the fair Cyprian rayed down mad love, rolled in the third epicycle;

wherefore not only to her did they do honour of sacrifice and votive cry, those ancient folk in the ancient error,

but Dione did they honour, and Cupid, the one as her mother, the other as her son, and told how he had sat in Dido's lap;

and from her from whom I take my start, they took the name of the star which courts the sun, now from the nape, now from the brow.

I had no sense of rising into her, but my Lady gave me full faith that I was there, because I saw her grow more beautiful.

And as we see a spark within a flame, and as a voice within a voice may be distinguished, if one stayeth firm, and the other cometh and goeth;

so in that light itself I perceived other torches moving in a circle more and less swift, after the measure, I suppose, of their eternal vision.

From a chill cloud there ne'er descended blasts, or visible or no, so rapidly as not to seem hindered and lagging

to whoso should have seen those lights divine advance towards us, quitting the circling that hath its first beginning in the exalted Seraphim.

And within those who most in front appeared, *Hosannah* sounded in such wise that never since have I been free from longing to re-hear it.

Then one drew himself more nigh to us, and alone began: "All we are ready at thy will, that thou mayst have thy joy of us.

We roll with those celestial Princes in one circle and in one circling and in one thirst, to whom thou from the world didst sometime say:

Ye who by understanding give the third heaven motion, and so full of love are we that, to pleasure thee, a space of quiet shall be no less sweet to us."

When mine eyes had been raised in reverence to my Lady, and she had satisfied them with herself and given them assurance,

they turned them back to the light which so largely had made proffer of itself, and, "Say who ye be," was my word, with great affection stamped.

Ah! how I saw it wax in quantity and kind at the new joy which, when I spoke, was added to its joys!

Thus changed, it said to me: "The world held me below but little space; had it been more much ill shall be that had not been.

My joy holdeth me concealed from thee, raying around me, and hideth me like to a creature swathed in its own silk.

Much didst thou love me, and thou hadst good cause; for had I stayed below I had shown thee a further growth of love than the mere leaves.

That left bank which is bathed by Rhone after it hath mingled with Sorgue, me for its timely lord awaited;

so did that corner of Ausonia, down from where Tronto and Verde discharge into the sea, citied by Bari, Gaeta and Catona.

Upon my brow already glowed the crown of the land the Danube watereth after it hath left its German banks;

and fair Trinacria which darkeneth between Pachynus and Pelorus, o'er the gulf tormented most by Eurus, (not for Typheus, but for sulphur that ariseth there) would yet have looked to have its kings, sprung through me from Charles and Rudolf,

had not ill lordship, which doth ever cut the heart of subject peoples, moved Palermo to shriek out: *Die! die!*

And had my brother seen it in good time, he would already flee the greedy poverty of Catalonia, lest it should work him ill;

and of a truth provision needs be made by him or by another, lest on his bark already laden heavier load be laid.

His nature,—mean descendant from a generous forebear,—were in need of soldiery who should not give their care to storing in the chest."

"Sire, in that I believe the lofty joy which thy discourse poureth into me, there where every good hath end and hath beginning

is seen by thee even as I see it, 'tis more grateful to me; and this too I hold dear, that thou discernest it looking on God.

Thou hast rejoiced me, now enlighten me; for in speaking thou hast moved me to question how from sweet seed may come forth bitter."

Thus I to him; and he to me: "If I can show a certain truth to thee, thou wilt get before thine eyes the thing thou askest just as thou hast it now behind thy back.

The Good which doth revolve and satisfy the whole realm thou art climbing, maketh its providence become a virtuous power in these great bodies;

and not only is provision made for the diverse-natured creatures, by the mind that is perfection in itself, but for their weal too, co-related with them.

Wherefore whate'er this bow dischargeth doth alight disposed to a provided end, even as a thing directed to its mark.

Were this not so, the heaven thou art traversing would so bring its effects to being, that they would be not works of art, but ruins;

and this may not be, if the intellects which move these stars be not defective, and defective, too, that primal one which failed to perfect them.

Wouldst thou that this truth be more illuminated?" And I: "Not so, for I see 'tis impossible that nature, in the needful, should fall short."

Whence he again: "Now, say, would it be worse for man on earth were he no citizen?" "Yea," I replied, "and here I ask no reason."

"And may that be, except men live below diversely and with diverse offices? No, if your master write the truth for you."

Up to this point he came deduction-wise; then the conclusion: "Therefore must needs the roots of your effects be diverse;

wherefore is one born Solon and one Xerxes, one Melchizedek, and one the man who, soaring through the welkin, lost his son.

That which in circling hath its nature, and is the seal upon the mortal wax, plieth aright its art, but maketh not distinction between one or other tenement.

Wherefore it cometh that Esau severeth himself in seed from Jacob, and Quirinus cometh of so base father that he is assigned to Mars.

The begotten nature would ever take a course like its begetters, did not divine provision overrule.

Now that which was behind thee is before; but that thou mayst know that I delight in thee, I will have a corollary wrap thee round.

Ever doth nature, if she find fortune unharmonious with herself, like any other seed out of its proper region, make an ill essay.

And if the world down there took heed to the foundation nature layeth, and followed it, it would have satisfaction in its folk.

But ye wrench to a religious order him born to gird the sword, and make a king of him who should be for discourse; wherefore your track runneth abroad the road."

CANTO IX

Charles, after a note of warning, turns again to God, whom we so impiously neglect. Cunizza approaches; she describes the site of Romano whence she and the tyrant Ezzelin, her brother, sprang. She tells how her past sins no longer trouble her. She speaks of the fair fame on earth of the troubadour Folco, and laments that no such fame is now sought by her countrymen of Venetia; whose woes she predicts and whose crimes she denounces; and then seeming no longer to heed Dante drops again into her place in the cosmic dance. Folco now flashes brighter in Dante's sight, and at his entreaty diverts his voice from its place in the universal song (which, like the universal dance, takes its note from the Seraphim) to minister to his special need. He indicates his birthplace of Marseilles. He tells of his amorous youth but shows how in heaven there is no repentance, because the sin is only seen or remembered as the occasion of the act of God by which the fallen one was uplifted again into his true element: and it is on this divine power and grace that the soul's whole thought and love are centred. He points out to Dante the light of Rahab, speaks of this heaven as just within the range of the cone of the earth's shadow, thereby indicating that the place of these souls in heaven is, in part, determined by the earthly sin that is now no longer in their minds; refers to Rahab's help given to Joshua in conquering the Holy Land, and denounces the Pope for his indifference to its recovery. It is devil-planted Florence that corrupts the world, both shepherd and flock, by her florins. But vengeance shall not lag.

WHEN THY CHARLES, fair Clemence, had enlightened me, he told me of the frauds his seed was destined to encounter;

but added: "Hold thy peace, and let the years revolve"; so that I can say naught, save that wailing well-deserved shall track your wrongs.

And already the life of that sacred light had turned to the sun that filleth it, as to the good ample for all things.

Ah! souls deceived, ah! creatures impious, who from such good wry-twist your hearts, squaring your temples unto vanity!

And lo, another of those splendours drew him towards me, and signified his will to pleasure me, by brightening outwardly.

Beatrice's eyes, fixed on me as before, of dear assent to my desire assured me.

"Nay! make swift counterpoise unto my will," I said, "thou blessed spirit, and give proof that I can cast reflection upon thee of what I think."

Whereat the light which was new to me, from out its depth, wherein it first was singing, went on as one rejoicing to do well:

"In that region of the depraved Italian land which sitteth 'twixt Rialto and the springs of Brenta and Piave, riseth a hill, lifted to no great height, whence erst came down a firebrand that made a dire assault upon the country.

Out of one root spring I with it; Cunizza was I called, and here I glow because the light of this star overcame me.

But joyously I grant myself indulgence for the occasion of my lot, nor doth it grieve me, which would seem, mayhap, hard saying to your common herd.

Of this shining and dear gem of our heaven, which most doth neighbour me, great fame remaineth, and ere it shall perish

this centenary year shall be five times repeated. See if a man should make himself excel, so that the first life leave another after!

And of this thinketh not the present crowd that Tagliamento and Adige enclose; the which, though smitten, yet repenteth not.

But soon shall come to pass that Padua at the pool shall change the water that doth bathe Vicenza, because the folk are stubborn against duty.

And where Sile meets Cagnano, one holdeth sway and goeth with uplifted head to catch whom even now the net is being woven.

A wail shall yet arise from Feltro for the trespass of its impious pastor, which shall be so foul that for the like none ever entered Malta.

Too ample were the charger which should receive Ferrara's blood, and weary who should weigh it ounce by ounce,

which this obliging priest shall give to prove himself a partisan; and such-like gifts shall suit the country's way of life.

Aloft are mirrors,—ye name them Thrones,—whence God in judgment shineth upon us so that these words approve themselves to us."

Here she was silent, and to me her semblance was of one who turneth him to other heeding, judging as by the wheel whereto she gave herself, like as she was before.

The other joy, noted already to me as a thing illustrious, shone in my sight like a fine ruby that the sun should strike.

By joy up there brightness is won, just as a smile on earth; but down below darkeneth the shade externally as the mind saddeneth.

"God seeth all, and into him thy seeing sinketh," said I, "blessed spirit, so that no wish may steal itself from thee.

Then wherefore doth thy voice, which gladdeneth Heaven ceaselessly,—together with the singing of those Flames devout, which make themselves a cowl with the six wings,—

not satisfy my longings? Not till now had I awaited thy demand, were I in thee even as thou art in me."

"The greatest valley in which water stretcheth," then began his words, "forth from that sea which garlandeth the earth,

betwixt opposing shores, against the sun, goeth so far that it meridian maketh of what was first horizon.

Of this valley was I a shoresman, midway 'twixt the Ebro and the Macra, which, with short course, parteth the Genoese and Tuscan.

Almost alike for sunset and for sunrise the site of Bougiah and of the place I spring from, which with its blood once made the harbour warm.

Folco they called me to whom my name was known, and this heaven is stamped by me, as I was stamped by it;

for Belus' daughter, wronging alike Sichæus and Creüsa, did not more burn than I, so long as it consorted with my locks;

nor yet the Rhodopeian maid who was deluded by Demophoön, neither Alcides when he had shut Iole in his heart.

Yet here we not repent, but smile; not at the sin, which cometh not again to mind, but at the Worth that ordered and provided.

Here gaze we on the Art that beautifieth its so great effect, and here discern the Good which bringeth back the world below unto the world above.

But that thou mayst bear away full satisfied all the desires born within this sphere, needs must I yet proceed.

Thou wouldst know who is within that light which here by me so sparkleth as the sun's ray in pure water.

Now know that there within hath Rahab peace; and when she joined our order, it stamped itself with her in the highest grade.

By this heaven,—touched by the shadow's point which your world casteth,—ere other soul was she uptaken from Christ's triumph.

And soothly it beseemed to leave her as a trophy, in some heaven, of the lofty victory which was achieved with the one and the other palm;

because she favoured Joshua's first glory in the Holy Land, which little toucheth the Papal memory.

Thy city,—of his planting who first turned his shoulders on his Maker, and from whose envy hath such wailing sprung,—

maketh and spreadeth that accursed flower which hath set sheep and lambs astray, for it hath turned the shepherd to a wolf.

Therefore it is the Gospel and great Doctors are deserted, and only the Decretals are so studied, as may be seen upon their margins.

Thereon the Pope and Cardinals are intent; ne'er wend their thoughts to Nazareth, where Gabriel spread his wings.

But Vatican, and the other parts elect of Rome, the cemetery of the soldiery that followed Peter, shall soon be freed from the adultery.''

CANTO X

God as self-existence contemplating himself as manifested, in that love which in either aspect he breathes forth, made all objects of intelligence or sense with that order which speaks of him to all beholders. Let the reader, then, look upon the equinoctial point, which so clearly displays that art of God which he himself ever contemplates, in love. Let him reflect how the influences of the sun and planets—the seasons and other alternations—would be effective over a smaller part of the earth if the inclination of the ecliptic were less, and would be too violent in their contrasts if it were greater. If the reader will not give himself time to work out these and other such hints, weary listlessness instead of enjoyment will be the fruit of his study, for the author cannot pause to elaborate them for him. The sun is in the spring equinoctial point and Dante is with him. Standing out against the sun by their very brightness are spirits rejoicing in the vision of the relation of the Father to the Son and to the Holy Spirit. Beatrice calls on Dante to thank the sun of the angels; and he thereon so concentrates his thought on God as to forget Beatrice; in pleasure whereat she smiles so beauteously as to shatter the undivided unity of his mind; which thus broken up distributes itself amongst the wondrous objects that claim it. Twelve spirits surround Dante and Beatrice, as with a crown, and thrice circle them, uttering music that may not be conceived on earth;

then pause, while one of them, Thomas Aquinas, declares that since the divine grace has kindled in Dante such true love as must ever increase itself by the mere act of loving, and has revealed to him that heavenly bliss to which he who has once known it must ever return, it follows that every blessed soul must freely love to do him pleasure; whereon he tells him who are the other flames; whereon the wheel of lights again begins to revolve with ineffable music.

GAZING upon his Son with the Love which the one and the other eternally breathes forth, the primal and ineffable Worth,

made whatsoever circleth through mind or space with so great order that whoso looketh on it may not be without some taste of him.

Then, reader, raise with me thy sight to the exalted wheels, directed to that part where the one movement smiteth on the other;

and amorously there begin to gaze upon that Master's art, who within himself so loveth it, that never doth he part his eye from it.

See how thence offbrancheth the oblique circle that beareth the planets, to satisfy the world that calleth on them;

and were their pathway not inclined, much virtue in the heaven were in vain, and dead were almost every potency on earth;

and if, from the straight course, or more or less remote were the departure, much were lacking to the cosmic order below and eke above.

Now stay thee, reader, on thy bench, back thinking on this foretaste, wouldst thou have good joyance ere that thou be weary.

I have set before thee; now feed thou thyself, for that matter whereof I have made me scribe, now wresteth to itself my total care.

The greatest minister of Nature, who with the worth of heaven stampeth the world, and with his light measureth the time for us,

united with that part now called to mind, was circling on the spirals whereon he doth present him ever earlier.

And I was with him; but of my ascent I was no more aware than is a man, ere his first thought, aware that it is coming.

'Tis Beatrice who leadeth thus from good to better, so instantly that her act doth not expatiate through time.

How shining in itself must that needs be which in the sun, whereinto I had entered, itself revealeth not by hue, but light!

Though I should summon genius, art, tradition, ne'er could I so express it as to make it imaged; but it may be believed—and let men long to see it.

And if our fantasies are low for such an exaltation, it is no marvel, for never was there eye that could transcend the sun.

Such, there, was the fourth household of the exalted Father who ever satisfieth it, showing how he doth breathe, and how beget.

And Beatrice began: "Give thanks, give thanks to the sun of the Angels, who of his grace hath to this sun of sense exalted thee."

Never was heart of mortal so disposed unto devotion, and so keen to give itself to God with all its will,

as to those words was I; and so wholly was my love committed unto him, it eclipsed Beatrice in oblivion.

Her it displeased not; but she so smiled thereat, the splendour of her laughing eyes parted my erst united mind amongst things multiform

Then saw I many a glow, living and conquering, make of us a centre, and of themselves a crown; sweeter in voice than shining in appearance.

Thus girt we sometimes see Latona's daughter, when the air is so impregnated as to retain the thread that makes her zone.

In the court of heaven, whence I have returned, are many gems so dear and beauteous that from that realm they may not be withdrawn,

and the song of these lights was of such; he who doth not so wing himself that he may fly up there, must look for news thence from the dumb.

When, so singing, those burning suns had circled round us thrice, like stars neighbouring the fixed poles,

they seemed as ladies, not from the dance released, but pausing, silent, listening till they catch the notes renewed.

And within one I heard begin: "Since the ray of grace,—whereat true love is kindled, and then doth grow, by loving, multifold—doth so glow in thee as to conduct thee up upon that stairway, which, save to reascend, no one descendeth,

whoso refused his vial's wine to quench thy thirst, were no more free than water that should flow not to the sea.

Thou wouldst know with what plants this garland is enflowered, which amorously doth circle round the beauteous lady who strengtheneth thee for heaven.

I was of the lambs of the sacred flock that Dominic leadeth upon the way where is good fattening if there be no straying.

This, who most neighboureth me upon the right, brother and master was to me, and he was Albert of Cologne, I Thomas of Aquino.

If in like manner thou wouldst be assured of all the rest, take way with thy sight after my words, circling above along the blessed wreath.

This next flaming issueth from the smile of Gratian, who gave such aid to the one and the other forum, as is acceptable in Paradise.

The other who doth next adorn our choir, was that Peter who, with the poor widow, offered his treasure unto Holy Church.

The fifth light, which amongst us is most fair, doth breathe from such a love that all the world down there thirsteth to know the news of it;

within there is the lofty mind, to which a wisdom so profound was granted, that, if the truth be true, no second ever rose to such full vision.

Next look upon that taper's light, which, in the flesh below, saw deepest into the angelic nature and its ministry.

In the next little light laugheth that pleader for the Christian times, with whose discourse Augustine fortified him.

Now if thou drawest thy mind's eye from light to light, following my praises, already for the eighth thou art athirst.

In seeing every good therein rejoiceth the sainted soul, which unmasketh the deceitful world to whoso giveth it good hearing.

The body whence it was chased forth, lieth down below in Cieldauro, and itself from martyrdom and exile came unto this peace.

See flaming next the glowing breath of Isidor, of Bede, and of Richard, who, in contemplating, was more than man.

The one from which thy glance returneth unto me, is the light of a spirit who, in weighty thoughts, him seemed went all too slowly to his death;

it is the light eternal of Sigier who, lecturing in the *Vicus Straminis,* syllogized truths that brought him into hate."

Then as the horologue, that calleth us, what hour the spouse of God riseth to sing her matins to her spouse that he may love her,

wherein one part drawing and thrusting other, giveth a chiming sound of so sweet note, that the well-ordered spirit with love swelleth;

so did I see the glorious wheel revolve and render voice to voice in harmony and sweetness that may not be known except where joy maketh itself eternal.

CANTO XI

Contrast between earth and heaven. Thomas, reading Dante's thoughts, renews his discourse in order to remove certain difficulties. Providence raised up Francis and Dominic to succour the Church. From Assisi Francis rose sun-like, even as the sun in which Doctor and Poet are now discoursing rises to mortals from Ganges or elsewhere according to the place of their abode. His marriage with poverty. The founding and confirming of his order. He preaches to the Soldan, receives the stigmata, and dies commending his bride to his disciples. If he was such, what must Dominic have been, seeing that he was worthy to be his colleague. But almost all his followers are degenerate.

INSENSATE care of mortals! Oh how false the arguments which make thee downward beat thy wings!

One was following after law, and one aphorisms, one was pursuing priesthood, and one dominion by violence or by quibbles,

and another plunder, and another civil business, and one, tangled in the pleasures of the flesh, was moiling, and one abandoned him to ease;

the whilst, from all these things released, with Beatrice up in heaven thus gloriously was I received.

When each had come again to that point of the circle whereat he was before, he stayed him, as the taper in its stand.

And within that light which first had spoken to me I heard smiling begin, as it grew brighter:

"Even as I glow with its ray, so, gazing into the Eternal Light, I apprehend whence thou dost take occasion for thy thoughts.

Thou questionest and wouldst fain discern, in such open and dispread discourse as may be level to thine understanding, my utterance

wherein I said but now: *Where is good fattening,* and wherein I said: *No second ever rose;* and here we need to make precise distinction.

The providence which governeth the world,—with counsel wherein every creature's gaze must stay, defeated, e'er it reach the bottom,—

in order that the spouse of him, who with loud cries espoused her with the blessed blood, might go toward her delight,

secure within herself and faithfuller to him, two Princes did ordain on her behalf, who on this side and that should be for guides.

The one was all seraphic in his ardour, the other by his wisdom was on earth a splendour of cherubic light.

Of one will I discourse, because of both the two he speaketh who doth either praise, which so he will; for to one end their works.

Between Tupino and the stream that drops from the hill chosen by the blessed Ubaldo, a fertile slope hangs from a lofty mount,

wherefrom Perugia feeleth cold and heat through Porta Sole, and behind it waileth Nocera, for the heavy yoke, and Gualdo.

From this slope, where most it breaks the steepness of decline, was born into the world a sun, even as is this some whiles from Ganges.

Wherefore who speaketh of that place, let him not say *Assisi,* 'twere to speak short, but *Orient,* would he name it right.

Not yet was he far distant from his rising when he began to make the earth to feel from his great power a certain strengthening;

for in his youth for such a lady did he rush into war against his father, to whom, as unto death, not one unbars the gate of his good pleasure;

and in the spiritual court that had rule over him, and in his father's presence he was united to her, and then from day to day loved her more strongly.

She, reft of her first husband, a thousand and a hundred years and more, despised, obscure, even till him stood without invitation.

And nought availed her the report that she was found unterrified together with Amyclas, when sounded that man's voice, who struck all the world with terror;

and nought availed her to have been so constant and undaunted, that she, when Mary stayed below, mounted the cross with Christ.

But, lest I should proceed too covertly, Francis and Poverty as these two lovers now accept in speech outspread.

Their harmony and joyous semblance, made love and wonder and tender looks the cause of sacred thoughts;

so that the venerable Bernard first cast off his sandals and ran to follow so great peace, and as he ran him thought him all too slow.

Oh wealth unrecognized, oh fertile good! Unsandals him Egidius, unsandals him Sylvester, following the spouse, so doth the bride delight.

Thence took his way, this father and this master, together with his lady, and with the household already binding on the humble cord;

nor abjectness of heart weighed down his brow, that he was Pietro Bernadone's son, nor that he seemed so marvelous despised.

But royally his stern intent to Innocent revealed he, and from him had the first imprint upon his Order.

When the poor folk increased, after his track whose marvellous life were better sung in heaven's glory,

then was the holy will of this chief shepherd circled with a second crown by Honorius at the eternal inspiration.

And when, in thirst of martyrdom, in the proud presence of the Soldan, he preached Christ and his followers;

and because he found the folk too crude against conversion,— not to stay in vain,—returned to gather fruit from the Italian herbage;

then on the harsh rock between Tiber and Arno, from Christ did he receive that final imprint which his limbs two years carried.

When it pleased him who for such good ordained him, to draw him up to his reward which he had earned in making himself lowly,

to his brethren; as to his right heirs, his dearest lady he commended, and bade that they should love her faithfully;

and from her bosom the illustrious soul willed to depart, turning to its own realm, and for its body would no other bier.

Think now what he was, who was a worthy colleague to maintain the bark of Peter in deep sea towards the right sign!

And such was our patriarch; wherefore who followeth him as he commandeth, thou must perceive, loadeth him with good wares.

But his flock hath grown so greedy for new viands, it may not be but that through divers glades it strayeth;

and the more his sheep distant and wandering depart from him, the emptier of milk they return foldwards.

There are of them, indeed, who fear the loss and cleave close to the shepherd, but they are so few that little cloth doth furnish forth their cowls.

Now if my words have not been faint, if thy listening hath been attent, if thou call back to mind what I have said,

in part thy will must now be satisfied, for thou shalt see the plant from which they whittle, and thou shalt see the rebuke that is intended in: *Where is good fattening if there be no straying.*"

CANTO XII

A second circle of lights encloses the first and—with music whereof our sweetest strains are but as the reflection—the two, like the parallels of a double rainbow, circle Dante and Beatrice, first moving and then at rest. Like the needle of the compass to the north star so Dante is swept round to one of the new-come lights at the sound of its voice. It is Bonaventura, the Franciscan, who undertakes the encomium of Dominic, just as Thomas, the Dominican, had pronounced that of Francis. Dominic's zeal for true learning and against heresy. If he was such, what must his colleague have been? But his disciples are ruined by the extremes of the strict and lax schools of observance. Bonaventura names himself and the other lights that circle with him.

SOON AS the blessed flame had taken up the final word to speak, began the sacred millstone to revolve,

and in its rolling had not turned full round ere a second, circling, embraced it and struck motion to its motion and song to its song;

song which so far surpasseth our Muses, our Sirens, in those sweet tubes, as the first splendour that which it back throweth.

As sweep o'er the thin mist two bows, parallel and like in colour, when Juno maketh behest to her handmaiden,

the one without born from the one within—in fashion of the speech of that wandering nymph whom love consumed as the sun doth the vapours,—

making folk here on earth foreknow, in virtue of the compact that God made with Noah, that the world never shall be drowned again;

so of those sempiternal roses revolved around us the two garlands, and so the outmost answered to the other.

Soon as the dance and high great festival,—alike of song and flashing light with light, gladsome and benign,—

accordant at a point of time and act of will had stilled them, like to the eyes which at the pleasure that moveth them must needs be closed and lifted in accord,

from out the heart of one of the new lights there moved a voice which made me seem the needle to the star in turning me to where it was;

and it began: "the love which maketh me beautiful draweth me to discourse of the other chief, on whose account such fair utterance is made to us concerning mine.

Meet is it that wherever is the one the other be led in, that, as they warred together, so may their glory shine in union.

Christ's army, which it cost so dear to re-equip, was following the standard, laggard, fearsome and thin-ranked;

when the Emperor who ever reigneth took counsel for his soldiery that was in peril, of his grace only, not that it was worthy;

and, as hath been said, came to the succour of his spouse with two champions, at whose doing, at whose saying, the straggling squadron gathered itself again.

To-wards that part where sweet Zephyr riseth to open the new leaves, wherewith Europe seeth herself reclad, not far off from the smiting of the waves, behind the which, be, cause of their long stretch, the sun sometimes hideth himself from all,

the fortune-favoured Calahorra sitteth under protection of the mighty shield, whereon submits the lion, and subdueth.

Therewithin was born the amorous frere of the Christian faith, the sacred athlete, benignant to his own and cruel to his foes;

and, so soon as created, his mind was so replete with living virtue, that in his mother's womb he made her prophetess.

When the espousals were complete at the sacred font, betwixt him and the faith, where they gave dower of mutual salvation,

the lady who for him gave the assent saw in her sleep the marvellous fruit destined to issue from him and from his heirs;

and that he might in very construing be what he was, a spirit from up here moved them to call him by the possessive adjective of him whose he all was.

Dominic was he named; and I speak of him as of the husbandman whom Christ chose for his orchard, to bring aid to it.

Well did he show himself a messenger and a familiar of Christ, for the first love made manifest in him was to the first counsel that Christ gave.

Many a time, silent and awake, was he found on the floor, by her who nursed him, as who should say, *It was for this I came.*

Oh father his, Felice in good sooth! Oh mother his, Giovanna in good sooth, if the word means, translated, what they say!

Not for the world for whose sake now men toil after him of Ostia and Thaddeus, but for love of the true manna,

in short season he became a mighty teacher, such that he set him to go round the vineyard, which soon turneth gray if the vinedresser be to blame;

and from the seat which erst was more benign to the just poor— not in itself, but in him who sitteth on it, and degenerateth—

not to dispense or two or three for six, not for the fortune of the next vacancy, not for the tithes belonging to God's poor,

he made demand; but for leave against the erring world to fight for that seed wherefrom these four and twenty plants ensheaf thee.

Then with teaching and with will together, with the apostolic office he moved forth, like a torrent that a deep vein out-presseth, and his rush smote amongst the stumps of heresy most livingly where the resistances were grossest.

From him then diverse streamlets sprung, whereby the Catholic orchard is so watered that its shrubs have the fuller life.

If such was the one wheel of the chariot wherein Holy Church defended her, and won in open field her civil strife,

clear enough should be to thee the excellence of that other, concerning whom, ere my coming, Thomas was so courteous.

But the track which the highest part of its circumference took hath been so abandoned, that there now is mould where once was crust.

His household, who marched straight with feet in his footprints, hath turned so round, that the toe striketh on the heel's imprint;

and soon shall sight be had of the harvest of the ill-culture, when the tare shall wail that the chest is reft from it.

I well allow that whoso should search leaf after leaf through our volume, might yet find a page where he might read: *I am as I was wont;*

but not from Casale, nor from Acquasparta shall he be, whence come such to our Scripture that the one shirketh, the other draweth it yet tighter.

I am the life of Bonaventura of Bagnoregio, who in the great offices did ever place behind the left-hand care.

Illuminato and Augustine are here, who were of the first unshod poor brethren, that with the cord made themselves friends to God.

Hugh of St. Victor is here with them, and Pietro Mangiadore, and Pietro Ispano, who giveth light below in twelve booklets;

Nathan the prophet, the metropolitan Chrysostom, and Anselm, and that Donatus who deigned to set his hand to the first art;

Rabanus is here, and there shineth at my side the Calabrian abbot Joachim, dowed with prophetic spirit.

To emulous speech of so great paladin moved me the enkindled courtesy of brother Thomas and his well-judged discourse, and moved this company with me."

The four and twenty brightest stars of heaven, ranged in two crowns, will give a feeble image of the two circles that swept round Dante and his guide. They sing of the Three Persons in the one nature of God and of the two natures in the one Person of Christ. Then they pause again, and Thomas once more speaks. He reads Dante's perplexity: "Did not both Adam and Christ possess all human knowledge in perfection? How then can it be that none ever rose to equal Solomon's wisdom?" Behold the answer: All mortal and immortal things are but a reflection of the divine Idea—i.e., of the loving self-utterance of the Divine Power—which remains one in itself while it is broken into countless manifestations. But the imprinting influences of heaven and the imprinted matter of earth are not always in equally propitious habit, and hence individual diversities of excellence. But matter was perfectly disposed and the heaven was in supreme excellence of power when Adam was created and when the Virgin conceived. Therefore Dante's initial supposition is true. But there is no contradiction; for Solomon desired not astronomical, nor logical, nor metaphysical, nor geometrical, but regal wisdom. Of all who ever rose to kingly rule (which Adam and Christ did not) none had such wisdom as Solomon. Let Dante take warning from this discussion and observe extremest caution in making unqualified deductions however obvious they may appear; for when once we are committed our own vanity prevents us from retreating and we had better not have thought about a problem than so thought as to fortify ourselves against the truth. Philosophy and Theology alike furnish sad examples. And seeming-obvious moral judgments may be as hasty and false as intellectual ones.

LET HIM IMAGINE, who would grasp rightly what I now beheld (and let him hold the image while I speak, like a firm rock),

fifteen of those stars that, in sundry regions, quicken the heaven with such brightness as to pierce all the knitted air,

let him imagine that wain for which the bosom of our heaven sufficeth night and day, so that it faileth not to the wain-pole's sweep, let him imagine the mouth of that horn which starteth from the axle round which the primal circling goeth,

all to have made of themselves two signs in heaven, such as Minos' daughter made when she felt the chill of death;

and one to have its rays within the other, and both the two to turn them in such fashion that one should take the lead, and the other follow;

and he shall have as though the shade of the real constellation and the twofold dance which circled round the point whereat I was;

for it as far transcendeth our use as doth transcend the movement of Chiana the motion of that heaven which all the rest surpasseth.

There did they sing, not Bacchus, and not Pæan, but three Persons in the divine nature, and it and the human nature in one Person.

The song and wheeling had fulfilled their measure, and to us turned their heed those sacred torches, rejoicing as they passed from charge to charge.

Then 'mid the harmonious divinities silence was broken by the light wherein the wondrous life of the poor man of God had been rehearsed to me,

which said: "Since the one sheaf is thrashed, and its seed stored already, to beat out the other sweet love inviteth me.

Thou holdest that into the breast wherefrom the rib was drawn to form the beauteous cheek for whose palate all the world doth pay,

and into that which, thrust by the lance, made satisfaction both for past and future, such as to turn the scale against all trespass,

such light as human nature may receive was all infused by that same Worth which made the one and the other.

And so thou wonderest at what I said above, when I declared the good enclosed in the fifth light ne'er to have had a second.

Now ope thine eyes to what I answer thee, and thou shalt see what thou believest and what I say, strike on the truth as centre in the circle.

That which dieth not, and that which can die, is nought save the reglow of that Idea which our Sire, in Loving, doth beget;

for that living Light which so outgoeth from its Source that it departeth not therefrom, nor from the Love that maketh three with them,

doth, of its goodness, focus its own raying, as though reflected, in nine existences, eternally abiding one.

Thence it descendeth to the remotest potencies, down, from act to act, becoming such as maketh now mere brief contingencies;

by which contingencies I understand the generated things which are produced from seed, or seedless, by the moving heaven.

The wax of these, and that which mouldeth it, standeth not in one mode, and therefore, 'neath the ideal stamp, is more and less transparent;

whence cometh, that one same tree in kind better and worse doth fruit; and ye are born with diverse genius.

Were the wax exactly moulded, and were the heaven in its supremest virtue, the light of the signet would be all apparent;

but nature ever furnisheth it faulty, doing as doth the artist who hath the knack of the art and a trembling hand.

Wherefore if the warm Love, if the clear Vision, of the primal Power dispose and stamp, entire perfection is acquired there.

Thus was the clay made worthy once of the full animal perfection; and thus the Virgin was impregnated.

Wherefore I sanction thine opinion that human nature never was, nor shall be, such as in those two persons.

Now, should I proceed no further, 'how then was he without a peer?' were the beginning of thy words.

But, that what now appeareth not may be apparent, think who he was, and what the cause which moved him—when he was bidden: 'Choose,'—to make demand.

I have not spoken so but that thou mayst perceive he was a king, who chose such wit that as a king he might be adequate;

not to know the number in which exist the mover spirits here above, nor if a necessary and a contingent premise can ever give a necessary conclusion;

nor whether we must grant a *primum motum;* nor whether in a semi-circle can be constructed a triangle that shall have no right angle.

Wherefore, (if this and all that I have said thou note) that insight without peer whereon the arrow of my intention smiteth, is regal prudence.

And if to *rose* thou turn discerning eyes, thou shalt see that it hath respect only to kings, the which are many and the good ones few.

Thus qualified do thou accept my saying; and so it may consist with what thou holdest of the first father and of our delight.

And let this ever be lead to thy feet, to make thee move slow, like a weary man; both to the yea and nay thou seest not;

for he is right low down amongst the fools who maketh affirmation or negation without distinction between case and case;

wherefore it chanceth many times swift-formed opinion leaneth the wrong way, and then conceit bindeth the intellect.

Far worse than vainly doth he leave the shore, since he returneth not as he puts forth, who fisheth for the truth and hath not the art;

and of this to the world are open proofs, Parmenides, Melissus, Bryson, and the host who still were going, but they knew not whither.

So did Sabellius and Arius, and those fools who were as swords unto the Scripture, in making the straight countenances crooked.

Let not folk yet be too secure in judgment, as who should count the ears upon the field ere they be ripe;

for I have seen first all the winter through the thorn display itself hard and forbidding and then upon its summit bear the rose;

and I have seen ere now a ship fare straight and swift over the sea through her entire course, and perish at the last, entering the harbour mouth.

Let not Dame Bertha or Squire Martin think, if they perceive one steal and one make offering, they therefore see them as in the divine counsel; for the one yet may rise and the other fall."

CANTO XIV

As vibrations pass outward and inward in a vessel filled with water, when disturbed by a blow, so the speech of the blessed spirits passed from Thomas in the circumference to Beatrice in the centre, and then back from her to the circumference. Dante has now become accustomed to the spirit world freed from those limitations of cor-

poreal sense-organs of which he is himself still conscious, and the perplexity is diffusing itself within him, though not yet precipitated into definite thought, as to how it can be that the resurrection of the body shall not reimpose limitations and weariness upon the now emancipated souls, making the very glory of heaven painful. Or will that glory be then tempered? Beatrice requests an answer for this yet unspoken and even unthought demand; and when all have sung a hymn of praise, Solomon tells how human nature includes body and soul, and therefore the disembodied soul is less complete than the whole person when the soul shall be reclad with the glorified body. When more complete it will be more pleasing to God, and will so receive more of his grace (above its merit, though not given without relation thereto), and will thus see him more adequately and therefore love him more warmly and therein have greater joy, expressed in more dazzling brightness. But the organs of sense will be incapable of pain or weariness; no excess of delight will be beyond their joyous grasp. The souls quiver in response to the reference to the resurrection. A third circle shows itself, first in dubious faintness then with a sudden flash, at the very moment when Dante and his guide pass into the red-glowing Mars. A cross gleams white athwart the red planet, whereon Christ flashes in such fashion as tongue may not tell. Souls in light move and pass upon the limbs of the cross, uttering divine melody and singing hymns of victory but half comprehended by Dante, yet more entrancing than aught that he had hitherto experienced; experienced hitherto, but he had not yet looked upon the beloved eyes of his guide in this fifth heaven, and therefore he must not be taken, by implication, to place the heavenly song above the ever-deepening beauty of Beatrice's eyes.

FROM CENTRE to circumference and again from circumference to centre vibrates the water in a rounded vessel according as 'tis smitten from without or from within.

Into my mind this thought dropped sudden, just as the glorious life of Thomas held its peace,

because of the resemblance that sprang from his discourse, and then from Beatrice's, whom to begin thus after him it pleased:

"This man hath need, and telleth it you not, neither with voice, nor as yet with his thought, to track another truth unto its root.

Tell if the light wherewith your being blossometh, eternally will cleave to you as now,

and if it doth remain, tell how, when ye grow visible again, it may not grieve your vision."

As by access of gladness thrust and drawn, at once all they who circle in the dance uplift their voice and gladden their gestures,

so at the eager and devoted prayer the sacred circles showed new joy in their revolving and their wondrous note.

Whoso lamenteth that we here must die to live up yonder seeth not here the refreshment of the eternal shower.

That One and Two and Three who ever liveth and reigneth ever in Three and Two and One, not circumscribed, but all circumscribing,

three times was hymned by each one of those spirits with such melody as were a fit reward to any merit.

And I heard in the divinest light of the smaller circle an unassuming voice, perchance such as the Angel's unto Mary,

answering: "As long as the festival of Paradise shall be, so long our love shall cast round us the rays of such a garment.

Its brightness shall keep pace with our ardour, our ardour with our vision, and that shall be as great as it hath grace beyond its proper worth.

Whenas the garment of the glorified and sainted flesh shall be resumed, our person shall be more acceptable by being all complete.

Whereby shall grow that which the highest Good giveth to us of unearned light, light which enableth us him to see;

wherefore the vision must needs wax, and wax the ardour which is kindled by it, and wax the ray which goeth forth from it.

But like the coal which giveth forth the flame, and by its living glow o'ercometh it, so that its own appearance is maintained,

so shall this glow which doth already swathe us, be conquered in appearance by the flesh which yet and yet the earth o'ercovereth;

nor shall such light have power to baffle us, for the organs of the body shall be strong to all that may delight us."

So swift and eager to cry *Amen,* meseemed, was the one and the other chorus, that verily they showed desire for their dead bodies;

not only, as I take it, for themselves, but for their mothers and their fathers and the others who were dear, ere they became eternal flames.

And lo! around, of lustre equable, upsprings a shining beyond what was there, in fashion of a brightening horizon.

And as, at the first rise of evening, new things-to-see begin to show in heaven, so that the sight doth, yet doth not, seem real;

I there began to perceive new-come existences making a circle out beyond the other two circumferences.

Oh very sparkling of the Holy Breath! how sudden and how glowing it became before my eyes, which, vanquished, might not bear it!

But Beatrice showed herself to me so beauteous and smiling, it must be left amongst those sights that followed not my memory.

Therefrom my eyes regained their power to uplift them, and I saw me transported, only with my Lady, to more exalted weal.

Surely did I perceive that I was more uplifted by the enkindled smile of the star which seemed to me more ruddy than his wont.

With all the heart, and in that tongue which is one unto all, to God I made burnt sacrifice such as befitted this new-given grace;

and not yet from my bosom was drawn out the ardour of the sacrifice before I knew the prayer had been accepted and propitious;

for with such shining, and so ruddy, within two rays, splendours appeared to me, that I exclaimed: "O God! who thus dost glorify them!"

As, pricked out with less and greater lights, between the poles of the universe the Milky Way so gleameth white as to set very sages questioning,

so did those rays, star-decked, make in the depth of Mars the venerable sign which crossing quadrant lines make in a circle.

Here my memory doth outrun my wit, for that cross so flashed forth Christ I may not find example worthy.

But whoso taketh his cross and followeth Christ shall yet forgive me what I leave unsaid, when he shall see Christ lighten in that glow.

From horn to horn, from summit unto base, were moving lights that sparkled mightily in meeting one another and in passing.

So we see here, straight, twisted, swift, or slow, changing appearance, long or short, the motes of bodies

moving through the ray which doth sometimes streak the shade, which folk with skill and art contrive for their defense.

And as viol and harp tuned in harmony of many cords, make sweet chiming to one by whom the notes are not apprehended,

so from the lights that there appeared to me was gathered on the cross a strain that rapt me albeit I followed not the hymn.

Well I discerned it was of lofty praise, for there came to me "Rise thou up and conquer," as to who understandeth not, but heareth.

And so was I enamoured there, that up till then there had been naught that me had bound with so sweet chains.

Perchance my saying may appear too bold, as slighting the delight of those fair eyes, gazing in which my longing hath repose.

But he who doth advise him how the living signets of all beauty have ever more effect in higher region, and that I there had not yet turned to them,

may find excuse from my own accusation, brought that I may excuse it; and may see that I speak truth; for the sacred joy is not excluded here, which as it mounteth groweth more unalloyed.

CANTO XV

The souls of the warriors of God upon the cross of Mars cease their hymn, that Dante may converse with one of their number, who shoots like a falling star from his place and, approaching Dante with such joy as Anchises showed to Æneas in the Elysian Fields, greets him as his offspring and as the recipient of unique grace, the twice-received (now and at his death) of heaven. Dante, giving heed to him and (now first in this higher sphere) looking on Beatrice, is smitten with twofold marvel. The spirit, after rapturous words beyond the scope of the Poet's comprehension, gives thanks to God, tells Dante how eager yet how sweet has been his longing for his arrival, foreread in the heavens; confirms his thought that the spirits see all things in God, as the true mathematician sees all numbers in the conception of unity; but bids him none the less

The Paradiso

speak out his questions, though already known to him, in God, with their appointed answers. Dante, unlike the souls in glory, has no utterance adequate to show forth his thanks. The spirit, in answer to his question, reveals himself as his great-great-grandfather, the father of Alighieri from whom the Poet's family name is derived. He describes the ancient Florence, confined within the walls to which the Badia was adjacent, and dwells upon the simple ways of her citizens. In such a city was he born, baptized and married. Thence he followed Conrad in his crusade, was knighted, was slain, and arose to the peace of heaven.

THE BENIGN WILL—wherein distilleth ever the love that hath the right perfume, as doth, in the grudging will, cupidity—

imposed silence on that sweet lyre and stilled the sacred strings, which the right hand of heaven looseneth and stretcheth.

How shall those beings unto righteous prayers be deaf, who, to excite in me the will to make my prayer to them, agreed in silence?

Right is it he should grieve without a limit, who, for the love of what endureth not, eternally doth strip him of this love.

As through the tranquil and pure skies darteth, from time to time, a sudden flame setting a-moving eyes that erst were steady,

seeming a star that changeth place, save that from where it kindleth no star is lost, and that itself endureth but a little;

such from the horn that stretcheth to the right unto that cross's foot, darted a star of the constellation that is there a-glow;

nor did the gem depart from off its riband, but coursed along the radial line, like fire burning behind alabaster.

With such-like tenderness Anchises' shade proffered itself, if our greatest Muse deserveth credit, when in Elysium he perceived his son.

"Oh blood of mine! oh grace of God poured o'er thee! to whom, was ever twice, as unto thee, heaven's gate thrown open?"

So spake that light; wherefore I gave my heed to him. Then I turned back my sight unto my Lady, and on this side and that I was bemazed;

for in her eyes was blazing such a smile, I thought with mine I had touched the bottom both of my grace and of my Paradise.

Then—joyous both to hearing and to sight—the spirit added things to his beginning I understood not, so profound his speech;

neither of choice hid he himself from me, but of necessity, for above the target of mortals his thought took its place.

And when the bow of ardent love was so tempered that his discourse descended towards the target of our intellect;

the first I understood was, "Blessed be thou, thou Three and One, who art so greatly courteous in my seed."

And followed on: "A dear long-cherished hunger, drawn from the reading of the mighty volume wherein not changeth ever white nor black,

thou hast assuaged, my son, within this light, wherein I speak to thee; thanks unto her who for the lofty flight clad thee with wings.

Thou deemest that to me thy thought hath way e'en from the primal Thought, as ray forth from the monad, rightly known, the pentad and the hexad;

and therefore, who I be, or why I seem to thee more gladsome than another in this festive throng thou makest not demand.

Rightly thou deemest; for less and great in this life gaze on the mirror whereon, or ere thou thinkest, thou dost outspread thy thought.

But that the sacred love, wherein I watch with sight unintermitted, and which setteth me athirst with a sweet longing, may be fulfilled the better,

secure and bold and joyous let thy voice sound forth the will, sound forth the longing, whereto my answer already is decreed."

I turned to Beatrice, and she heard ere that I spoke, and granted me a signal that made the wings of my desire increase.

Then I thus began: "Love and intelligence, soon as the prime equality appeared to you, became of equal poise to each of you,

because the sun which lightened you and warmed with heat and brightness hath such equality that illustrations all fall short of it.

But unto mortals, will and instrument, for reason manifest to you, unequally are feathered in their wings.

Wherefore I, a mortal, feel the stress of this unequalness, and therefore only with my heart give thanks for the paternal greeting.

But I may and do entreat thee, living topaz, who dost be-gem this precious jewel, that thou assuage me with thy name."

"Oh leaf of mine, in whom I took delight, only expecting thee, I was thy taproot," such opening in his answer made he me.

Then said: "He from whom thy kindred hath its name, and who a hundred years and more hath circled round the Mount on the first terrace,

was son to me, and thy grandfather's father; meet it is, that with thy works thou shouldst abate his long-stretched toil for him.

Florence, within the ancient circling wherefrom she still receiveth tierce and nones, abode in peace, sober and chaste.

There was no chain or coronet, nor dames decked out, nor girdle that should set folk more agaze than she who wore it.

As yet the daughter's birth struck not the father with dismay; for wedding day and dowry evaded not the measure on this side and on that.

There were no mansions empty of the household; Sardanapalus had not yet arrived to show what may be done within the chamber.

Not yet was Montemalo overpassed by your Uccellatoio, which, as it hath been passed in the uprising, shall be in the fall.

Bellincion Berti have I seen no girt with bone and leather, and his dame come from her mirror with unpainted face;

I have seen him of the Nerlo, and him of the Vecchio, content with the skin jerkin and nought over it, and their dames at the spindle and the flax.

O happy they, each one of them secure of her burial place, and none yet deserted in her couch because of France.

The one kept watch in minding of the cradle, and soothing spake that speech which first delighteth fathers and mothers;

another, as she drew its locks from the distaff, would tell her household about the Trojans, and Fiesole, and Rome.

Then a Cianghella, or a Lapo Salterello, would have been as great a marvel as now would Cincinnatus or Cornelia.

To so reposeful and so fair a life among the citizens, to so faithful cityhood, to so sweet abode,

Mary—with deep wailings summoned—gave me; and, in your ancient Baptistery, at once a Christian I became and Cacciaguida.

Moronto was my brother and Eliseo; my wife came to me from Po valley, and from her was thy surname derived.

Then followed I the Emperor Conrad, who girt me with his knighthood, so much by valiant work did I advance me in his grace.

In his train I marched against the infamy of that Law whose people doth usurp, shame to the pastors, what is yours by right.

There by that foul folk was I unswathed of the deceitful world, whose love befouleth many a soul, and came from martyrdom unto this peace."

CANTO XVI

In profound reverence for his ancestor, and not without a sense of his own derived dignity, Dante addresses the spirit with the ceremonious plural ye, said to have originated in Rome, though no longer in use there; and hereon Beatrice (only moderately interested in Florentine antiquities, and so standing a little apart, but keenly alert to all that may affect the moral or spiritual weal of her charge) checks his rising vanity with a warning smile. Dante, full of such lofty joy as would on earth strain the mind to bursting, questions Cacciaguida as to ancient Florence, whereon he, in the speech of an earlier day, tells the date of his birth and the place where his forebears dwelt, declining, in enigmatical terms, to say more of them. The population of military age was then but a fifth of what it had since become, and the narrow limits of the territory of Florence kept the blood of her citizens pure. Would that it were so yet! But lust of power, the confusion resulting from Papal ambition, and the fatal quarrel between the Buondelmonti and Amidei, have ruined all, and have given unwieldly bulk to Florence while polluting her blood. Then follows a dirge on the great families of ancient Florence, introduced by tragic reflections on the tide-like instability of all earthly things. Many of these families are mentioned by name, others are indicated by their characteristics or their blazon. Count Hugo ennobled the six families that bear his coat of arms, with various differences, though Giano della Bella had since joined the people. The Gualterotti and Importuni were already in Florence, but the Buondelmonti were not yet—would that they had never been!—their neighbours. The Amidei and their associates were held in honour. Alas that Buondelmonte broke his marriage word with them, and gave rise to all the internal strife of Florence. How much ill had been avoided if God had plunged him into the Ema as he rode into Florence. But it was fated that she should make her sacrifice to that torso of Mars, at whose feet he was slain.

AH PUNY blood-nobility of ours! If thou makest folk glory in thee here below, where our affections sicken,

it shall be marvel to me never more; for there, where appetite is unwarped, I mean in heaven, I gloried me therein.

Yet verily thou art a mantle that soon shrinketh, so that, if day by day there be nought added, time goeth round with the shears,

With that *ye* that Rome was first to allow wherein her household doth least persevere, my words began again;

whereon Beatrice, who was a little sundered from us, smiled, and seemed to me like her who coughed at the first trespass writ of Guinivere.

I began: "Ye are my father, ye give me full boldness to speak, ye so uplift me, that I am more than I.

By so many streams my mind is filled with gladness, it giveth itself joy that it can bear it and yet not be rent.

Tell me, then, dear stock from which I spring, what was your ancestry, and what the years recorded in your boyhood.

Tell me of the sheepfold of St. John, how great it then was, and who were the folk worthy of loftiest seats in it."

As a coal quickeneth into flame at the wind's breathing, so did I see that light glow forth at my caressing words;

and even as to my sight it grew more beauteous, so with a voice more sweet and gentle, but not in this our modern dialect,

he said: "From the day on which *Ave* was uttered, to the birth wherein my mother, now sainted, unburdened her of me with whom she was laden,

five hundred, fifty, and thirty times did this flame return to his own Lion to rekindle him beneath his feet.

My forebears and myself were born in the spot where he who runneth in your annual games doth first encounter the last sesto.

About my ancestors let it suffice so much to hear; of who they were and whence they hither came silence were comelier than discourse.

At that time all who were there, between Mars and the Baptist, capable of arms, were but the fifth of the now living ones.

But the citizenship, contaminated now from Campi, from Certaldo and from Fighine, saw itself pure down to the humblest artisan.

Oh, how much better were it for these folk of whom I speak to be your neighbours, and to have your boundary at Galluzzo and at Trespiano,

than to have them within, and bear the stench of the hind of Aguglion, and of him of Signa, who still for jobbery hath his eye alert!

Had the race, which goeth most degenerate on earth, not been to Cæsar as a stepmother, but, as a mother to her son, benign,

one who is now a Florentine and changeth coin and wares, had been dispatched to Simifonte, where his own grandfather went round a-begging.

Still would Montemurlo pertain unto the Conti, still were the Cerchi in Acone parish, and perchance in Valdigreve were still the Buondelmonti.

Ever was mingling of persons the source of the city's woes, as piled on food is of the body's.

And a blind bull falleth more presently than a blind lamb, and many a time cutteth one sword better and more than five.

If thou regard Luni and Urbisaglia, how they have perished, and how are following them Chiusi and Sinigaglia;

it shall not seem a novel or hard thing to hear how families undo themselves, since even cities have their term.

Your affairs all have their death, even as have ye; but in such an one as long endureth, it escapeth note because your lives are short.

And as the rolling of the lunar heaven covereth and layeth bare the shores incessantly, so fortune doth to Florence;

wherefore it should appear no wondrous thing which I shall tell of the exalted Florentines whose fame lieth concealed by time.

I have seen the Ughi, seen the Catellini, Filippi, Greci, Ormanni, and Alberichi, illustrious citizens, already in decline;

I have seen, even as great as ancient, with him of the Sannella, him of the Arca, and Soldanieri and Ardinghi and Bostichi.

Over the gate which is now laden with new felony of so great weight, that soon 'twill be the wrecking of the bark,

were the Ravignani, whence descendeth the County Guy, and whoso since hath taken lofty Bellincione's name.

The Della Pressa knew already how to govern, and Galigaio in his mansion already had the hilt and pummel gilt.

Great already were the Vair column, Sacchetti, Giuochi, Fifanti, and Barucci; and Galli, and they who blush red for the bushel.

The stock whence the Calfucci sprang was great already, and already drawn to curule office were Sizii and Arrigucci.

Oh, how great have I seen those now undone by their pride! And the balls of gold adorned Florence in all her mighty feats.

So did their fathers who, whene'er your church is vacant, stand guzzling in consistory.

The outrageous tribe that playeth dragon after whoso fleeth, and to whoso showeth tooth—or purse—is quiet as a lamb,

was coming up already, but from humble folk, so that it pleased not Ubertin Donato when his father-in-law made him their relative.

Already Caponsacco had come down from Fiesole into the market-place; and good citizens already were Giuda and Infangato.

I will tell a thing incredible but true: the little circuit was entered by a gate named after them of Pera.

Each one who beareth aught of the fair arms of the great baron whose name and worth the festival of Thomas keepeth living,

from him derived knighthood and privilege; though he who fringeth it around hath joined him now unto the people.

Already there were Gaulterotti and Importuni; and still were Borgo a more quiet spot, if from new neighbours they were still afasting.

The house from which your wailing sprang, because of the just anger which hath slain you and placed a term upon your joyous life,

was honoured, it and its associates. Oh Buondelmonte, how ill didst thou flee its nuptials at the prompting of another!

Joyous had many been who now are sad, had God committed thee unto the Ema the first time that thou camest to the city.

But to that mutilated stone which guardeth the bridge 'twas meet that Florence should give a victim in her last time of peace.

With these folk, and with others with them, did I see Florence in such full repose, she had not cause for wailing;

with these folk I saw her people so glorious and so just, ne'er was the lily on the shaft reversed, nor yet by faction dyed vermilion."

CANTO XVII

As Phaëton came to Clymene to have his doubts resolved, so, encouraged by Beatrice, did Dante turn to Cacciaguida to learn from him the meaning of all the dark hints as to his future lot which he had heard in the three realms. Cacciaguida, not in oracular ambiguities but in plain speech, tells how contingency is but relative to material and human limitations (though free will is an absolute reality), and therefore he already sees, as a harmonious part of the blessed whole, the future that as a fragment of Dante's experience shall be so bitter. Florence shall accuse him of that treachery of which herself is guilty, and shall do it as at the instigation of the Pope. Slandered, exiled, and in penury, he must go his way, in evil company, till he isolates himself from all, and is justified in so doing by the event. His first refuge shall be in the court of the Scaliger who will anticipate all his requests by granting them, and with whom he shall find the now youthful hero who shall give proof of his worth before Henry VII's mission, and shall at last do deeds which even they who see them shall not credit. He further bids Dante not envy the wrong-doers, whose downfall he shall long outlive, and in answer to the timid suggestions of prudence urges him to reveal to the world the whole content of his vision.

As CAME to Clymene, to have assurance as to that which he had heard uttered against himself, he who still maketh fathers grudging to their sons;

such was I; and such was I felt both by Beatrice and by the sacred lamp which had already, for my sake, changed its position.

Wherefore my Lady: "Let forth the heat of thy desire," she said, "that it may issue, struck aright with the internal stamp;

not that our knowledge may increase by thy discourse, but that thou mayst learn to tell thy thirst, that men may mingle for thee."

"Dear turf, wherein I root me, who art so high uplifted that even as earthly minds perceive that two obtuse angles may not find room in one triangle,

so thou dost see contingent things, or ere themselves exist, gazing upon the point whereto all times are present;

whilst I was companioned by Virgil along the mount which cureth souls, and down-going through the world defunct,

heavy words were said to me anent my future life; albeit I feel me squarely set against the blows of fortune;

wherefore my will were well content to hear what the disaster drawing nigh to me; for the arrow seen before cometh less rudely."

So spake I unto that same light which had before addressed me, and, as Beatrice willed, was my wish confessed.

In no dark sayings, such as limed the foolish folk of old, before the Lamb of God who taketh sins away, was slain,

but in clear words, and with precise discourse, answered that love paternal, hidden and revealed by his own smile:

"Contingency, which beyond the sheet of your material stretcheth not, is all limned in the eternal aspect;

albeit it deriveth not necessity from this, no more than doth the ship that droppeth down the stream from the sight wherein she doth reflect herself.

Thence, as cometh to the ear sweet harmony from an organ, cometh to my sight the time that is in store for thee.

As Hippolytus was severed from Athens by machination of his cruel and perfidious stepmother, so must thou needs sever thee from Florence.

So it is willed, so already plotted, and so shall be accomplished soon, by him who pondereth upon it in the place where Christ, day in day out, is put to sale.

The blame shall cleave unto the injured side in fame, as is the wont; but vengeance shall bear witness to the truth which doth dispense it.

Thou shalt abandon everything beloved most dearly; this is the arrow which the bow of exile shall first shoot.

Thou shalt make trial of how salt doth taste another's bread, and how hard the path to descend and mount upon another's stair.

And that which most shall weigh thy shoulders down, shall be the vicious and ill company with which thou shalt fall down into this vale,

for all ungrateful, all mad and impious shall they become against thee; but, soon after, their temples and not thine shall redden for it.

Of their brutishness their progress shall make proof, so that it shall be for thy fair fame to have made a party for thyself.

Thy first refuge and first hostelry shall be the courtesy of the great Lombard, who on the ladder beareth the sacred bird,

for he shall cast so benign regard on thee that of doing and demanding, that shall be first betwixt you two, which betwixt others most doth lag.

With him shalt thou see the one who so at his birth stamped by this strong star, that notable shall be his deeds.

Not yet have folk taken due note of him, because of his young age, for only nine years have these wheels rolled round him.

But ere the Gascon have deceived the lofty Henry, sparkles of his virtue shall appear in carelessness of silver and of toils.

His deeds munificent shall yet be known so that concerning them his very foes shall not be able to keep silent tongues.

Look to him and to his benefits; by him shall many folk be changed, altering state, the wealthy and the beggars;

and thou shalt bear it written in thy mind of him, but shalt not tell it";—and he told me things past the belief even of who shall see them.

Then he added: "Son, these are the notes on what hath been said to thee; behold the snares that behind but few circlings are hidden.

Yet would I not have thee envious of thy neighbours, since thy life shall be prolonged far beyond falling of the penalty upon their perfidies."

When by his silence the sacred soul showed he had finished setting of the woof across the warp I had held out in readiness to him,

I began, as he who longeth in doubt for counsel from one who seeth and willeth straight, and loveth:

"Well do I see, my father, how time cometh spurring toward me to give me such a buffet as is heaviest to whoso most abandoneth himself;

wherefore with foresight it were well to arm me, that if the dearest place be reft from me, I lose not all the rest by reason of my songs.

Down in the world endlessly bitter, and along the mount from whose fair summit my Lady's eyes uplifted me,

and after, through the heaven from light to light, I have learnt that which if I tell again, will have strong-bitter flavour unto many;

and if to truth I am a shrinking friend, I fear to lose life amongst those who shall call this time ancient."

The light wherein was smiling my treasure which I there had found, first coruscated as at the sun's rays doth a golden mirror;

then answered: "Conscience darkened, or by its own or by another's shame, will in truth feel thy utterance grating.

But none the less, every lie set aside, make thy entire vision manifest, and let them scratch wherever is the scab;

for if thy voice be grievous at first taste, yet vital nutriment shall it leave thereafter when digested.

This cry of thine shall do as doth the wind, which smiteth most upon the loftiest summits; and this shall be no little argument of honour.

Therefore have been displayed to thee, in these wheels, upon the mount, and in the dolorous vale, only souls known to fame;

for the soul of him who heareth resteth not nor fixeth faith by an example which hath its root unknown and hidden, nor other unconspicuous argument."

CANTO XVIII

Dante, pondering Cacciaguida's revelation, is roused from his reverie by the consoling words and by the beauty of Beatrice who directs him once again to the spirit of his ancestors; who names to him some of the warrior saints that shoot, as he speaks, along the cross; and who then himself joins in their hymn. Dante turns again to Beatrice and sees, by her yet greater beauty, that they have risen into a higher heaven. Then as he looks again upon the star he sees that the white glowing Jupiter has replaced the ruddy Mars. The spirits here form themselves into successive letters and spell out the opening words of the book of Wisdom "Love righteousness ye that be judges of the earth." Then other spirits gather upon the crest of

the last letter, twine round its limbs and insensibly form it into an
eagle, the symbol of Roman law and justice. From this star, then,
proceeds our justice. Oh that the divine mind whence it draws its
power would once more, in wrath, cleanse the mercenary temple
which pollutes its rays! Oh that the chivalry of heaven would pray
for the misled world! As for the Pope who makes a traffic of his
awful power to grant or withhold Communion, let him think of
Peter and Paul! But he will plead that John Baptist, whose image
is stamped upon the golden florins, has absorbed all his thoughts.

ALREADY was that blessed mirror rejoicing only in his own discourse, and I was tasting mine, tempering with the sweet the bitter;

and that Lady, who was leading me to God, said: "Change thy
thought; think that I am nigh to him who every wrong unloadeth."

I turned me to the lovesome sound of my comfort, and what
love I then beheld within the sacred eyes, I here attempt not;

not because merely I distrust my speech, but for my memory
which may not re-ascend so far above itself unless another guide it.

So much anent this point may I re-tell, that as I gazed upon her
my affection was freed from every other longing,

whilst the eternal joy which rayed direct on Beatrice was satisfying me with its derived aspect from the fair face.

O'ercoming me with the light of a smile, she said to me: "Turn
thee, and hearken, for not only in my eyes is Paradise."

As here sometimes we read the affection in the countenance, if
it be so great that all the mind is taken up by it,

so in the flaming of the sacred glow to which I turned me, I
recognized the will in him yet further somewhat to discourse with
me.

He began: "In this fifth range of the tree which liveth from the
summit, and ever beareth fruit, and never sheddeth leaf,

are spirits blessed, who below, ere they came unto heaven, were
of a great name, so that every Muse would be enriched by them.

Wherefore gaze upon the horns of the cross; he whom I shall
name shall there do the act which in a cloud its swift flame doth."

I saw a light drawn along the cross at the naming of Joshua, as
it was done; nor was the word known to me ere the fact.

And at the name of the lofty Maccabee I saw another move, wheeling, and gladness was the lash unto the top.

Thus for Charlemagne and for Orlando two more were followed by my keen regard, as the eye followeth its falcon flying.

Then drew my sight along that cross William and Rinoardo and the duke Godfrey, and Robert Guiscard.

Thereon amongst the other lights, moving and mingling, the soul which had discoursed to me showed me his artist quality among heaven's singers.

I turned to my right side to see in Beatrice my duty, whether by speech or gesture indicated,

and I saw her eyes so clear, so joyous, that her semblance surpassed all former usage and the last.

And as by feeling more delight in doing well, man from day to day perceiveth that his virtue gaineth ground;

so did I perceive that my circling round together with the heaven had increased its arc, seeing this miracle yet more adorned.

And such change as cometh in short passage of time over a fair dame, when her countenance unburdeneth shame's burden,

was presented to my eyes, when I turned me, because of the white glow of the temperate sixth star which had received me into it.

I saw in that torch of Jove the sparkling of the love which was therein signalling to my eyes our speech.

And as birds, risen from the bank, as though rejoicing together o'er their pasture, make themselves now a round, now a long, flock,

so within the lights the sacred creatures flying sang, and in their shapings made themselves now D, now I, now L.

First singing to their note they moved, then as they made themselves one of these signs, a little space would stay and hold their peace.

O goddess Pegasæan, who givest glory unto genius, and renderest it long life, as with thy aid doth it to cities and to realms,

make me bright with thyself, that I may throw into relief their figures as I have them in conception; let thy might show in these brief verses.

They displayed them then in five times seven vowels and consonants, and I took note of the members, even as they appeared in utterance to me.

Diligite justitiam, were the first verb and substantive of all the picturing; *qui judicatis terram* were the last.

Then ordered in the M of the fifth word they stayed so that Jove seemed silver in that place, pricked out with gold;

and I saw descending other lights where was the M's peak, and there still them; singing, I take it, the good that moveth them unto himself.

Then, as at the smiting of burnt brands there rise innumerable sparks, wherefrom the foolish ones use to draw augury,

meseemed there rose thence more than thousand lights, and mounted some much, some little, even as the sun which kindleth them, ordained them;

and when each one had stilled it in its place, an eagle's head and neck I saw presented by that pricked-out fire.

He who there painteth hath not one to guide him, but he himself doth guide, and from him cometh to the mind that power which is form unto the nests;

the other blessedness, which at first seemed content to twine the M with lilies, by a slight motion followed the imprint.

O sweet star, what quality and magnitude of gems made plain to me that our justice is the effect of the heaven thou dost engem!

Wherefore I pray the mind wherein thy motion and thy power hath beginning, to look upon the place whence issueth the smoke that vitiates thy ray;

so that once more the wrath be kindled against the buying and the selling in the temple which made its walls of miracles and martyrdoms.

O soldiery of heaven, whom I look upon, pray for them who have all gone astray on earth, following the ill example.

Erst 'twas the wont to make war with swords; now it is made by withholding, now here, now there, the bread the tender father bars from none;

but thou, who but to cancel, dost record, reflect that Peter and Paul who died for the vineyard thou layest waste, are living yet.

Though thou indeed mayst urge: "I have so fixed my longing on him who lived a solitary, and by tripping steps was drawn to martyrdom, that I know not the fisherman nor Paul."

CANTO XIX

The just Kings, who compose the eagle of Jupiter, speak as one person, just as many brands give out one warmth, so indicating that the work of all righteous governors is one and the same, the voice of all of them being the one voice of justice. In the heaven of justice, there rises in Dante's mind a passion of hope that he may find the solution of the problem, which so long has tortured him, as to the exclusion of the virtuous heathen from heaven, so contrary in seeming to God's justice. The divine eagle first responds with a burst of triumphant joy, then tells how God's wisdom is in excess of all that the whole creation expresses; and since Lucifer himself, the highest of created things, could not see all (and fell because he would not wait for the full measure of light God would have given him), it follows far more that lesser minds cannot so see but that God sees unutterably deeper. Wherefore our sight must needs be lost in the depths of divine justice, which God's eye alone can pierce. But our very idea of justice is from God, and this thought must quiet Dante's protest as to the exclusion of the virtuous heathen. Who is he that he should judge? There were matter enough for the human mind to boggle at, had we not the authority of Scripture for our guidance and did we not know that the Will of God is itself the perfect standard of goodness and of justice, not to be called to account by any other standard. As the little stork (the symbol of obedient docility) looks up, when fed, to the parent bird that wheels over the nest, so Dante gazes on the eagle; which sings a hymn as far above our understanding as God's judgments are; and then, while reasserting without qualification that belief in Christ is the sole means of access to heaven, yet declares that many heathen will be far nearer Christ on the judgment day than many who call upon his name; whereon follows a long denunciation, in detail, of contemporary Christian monarchs.

WITH OUTSTRETCHED WINGS appeared before me the fair image which those enwoven souls, rejoicing in their sweet fruition, made.

Each one appeared as a ruby whereon the sun's ray should burn, enkindled so as to re-cast it on mine eyes.

And that which I must now retrace, nor ever voice conveyed, nor ink did write, nor ere by fantasy was comprehended;

for I saw and eke I heard the beak discourse and utter in its voice both *i* and *Mine,* when in conception it was *We* and *Our.*

And it began: "In that I was just and duteous am I here exalted to this glory which suffereth not itself to be surpassed by longing;

and upon earth have I left a memory, so fashioned that there the evil folk commend it, though they follow not the tale."

So do we feel one glow from many coals as from those many loves there issued forth one only sound out of that image.

Whereon straightway I: "O perpetual flowers of the eternal gladness, ye who make all your odours seem to me but one,

solve, as ye breathe, the great fast which long hath held me hungering, because on earth I found no food for it.

Well do I know that if the divine justice maketh any other realm of heaven its mirror, yours apprehendeth it without a veil.

Ye know how eager I prepare me to hearken; ye know what is that question which hath been to me a fast of so long date."

As the falcon issuing from the hood shaketh head and clappeth wings, showing his will and making himself beauteous,

such did I see that ensign which was woven of the praises of divine grace, with songs such as be known to whoso up there rejoiceth.

Then it began: "He who rolled the compass round the limit of the universe, and within it marked out so much both hidden and revealed,

could not so stamp his worth on all the universe but that his word remained in infinite excess.

And this is certified by that first proud being, who was the summit of all creation, because he would not wait for light, falling unripe;

and hence it is apparent that each lesser nature is a receptacle too scant for that good which hath not end, and itself measureth with itself.

Wherefore our sight, which needs must be one of the rays of that mind whereby all things are filled,

cannot of its nature have so great power but that its principle should discern far beyond that which unto it appeareth.

Wherefore in the eternal justice such sight as your world doth receive, like the eye in the ocean, is absorbed;

for, albeit it can see the bottom by the shore, in the open sea it seeth it not, and none the less 'tis there, but the depth it hath concealeth it.

There is no light unless from that serene which never is disturbed, else it is darkness or shadow of the flesh or else its poison.

Enough is opened to thee now the labyrinth which hid from thee the living justice of which thou hast made question so incessantly;

for thou didst say: 'A man is born upon the bank of Indus and there is none to tell of Christ, nor none to read, nor none to write;

and all his volitions and his deeds are good so far as human reason seeth, sinless in life or in discourse.

He dieth unbaptized and without faith; where is that justice which condemneth him? where is his fault, in that he not believes?'

Now what art thou who wouldst sit upon the seat to judge at a thousand miles away with the short sight that carries but a span?

Truly to him who goeth subtly to work with me, were not the Scripture over you, there were marvellous ground for questioning.

O animals of earth, minds gross! the primal Will, good in itself, never departed from its own self which is the highest good.

All is just which doth harmonize with it; no created good draweth it to itself, but it by raying forth giveth rise to it."

As right above her nest the stork sweepeth when she hath fed her brood, and as the one which she hath fed looketh up to her;

so did (and so did I uplift my brow) the blessed image, which plied its wings driven by so many counsels.

Wheeling it sang, and said: "As are my notes to thee who understandest them not, such is the eternal judgment to you mortals."

When those glowing flames of the Holy Spirit were stilled, yet in the ensign which gained the Romans reverence from all the world,

it began again: "To this realm ne'er rose one who believed not in Christ, neither before nor after he was nailed unto the tree.

But see, many cry Christ, Christ, who at the judgment shall be far less near to him than such as know not Christ;

and such Christians the Ethiop shall condemn when the two colleges shall dispart, the one for ever rich, the other stripped.

What may the Persians say unto your kings when they shall see that volume opened wherein are their dispraises all recorded?

There shall be seen amidst the deeds of Albert that one which soon shall move its wing to make the realm of Prague a desert.

There shall be seen the woe which he is bringing on the Seine by making false the coinage, who by the wild boar's stroke shall die.

There shall be seen the pride which maketh athirst and doth the Scot and Englishman so madden they may not abide within their proper bound.

The lechery shall be seen and life effeminate of him of Spain, and him of Bohemia, who knew not ever worthiness, nor willed it.

For the cripple of Jerusalem shall be seen marked with an I, his excellence, where an M shall mark the countercharge.

The avarice and baseness shall be seen of him who hath in ward the Isle of Fire where Anchises ended his long life;

and to give to understand how great his paltriness, his record shall be kept in stunted letters which shall note much in little space.

And plain to all shall be revealed the foul deeds of his uncle and his brother which have made so choice a family, and two crowns, cuckold.

And he of Portugal and he of Norway there shall be known, and he of Rascia, who in ill hour saw the coin of Venice.

O happy Hungary, if she suffereth herself to be mauled no more! And happy Navarre, were she to arm herself with the mount that fringeth her!

And all should hold that 'tis in pledge of this that Nicosia and Famagosta already wail and shriek by reason of their beast, who doth not part him from beside the others."

CANTO XX

As when the one light of the sun disappears, the heaven is straightway rekindled by many stars, so when the one voice of the eagle ceased the many beings that composed it, shining yet more brightly, burst into an angelic chime of many notes, which was followed by a murmuring as of falling waters, gathering once more in the neck of the eagle into a single voice. The eagle declares that the six lights which form its pupil and eyebrow are the greatest of all, and goes on to enumerate them, using, in most cases, rich and pregnant cir-

cumlocution, but expressly naming Ripheus the Trojan, that there
may be no room to misconceive a statement so incredible as that he
(as well as Trajan, the heathen emperor, already indicated by a
paraphrase not to be misunderstood) is in heaven. Then once more
the eagle bursts into rapturous song, and when it pauses, Dante,
though he knows that the spirits read his inmost thoughts as we on
earth see colour through a sheet of glass, yet can not restrain the
utterance of his amazement at the presence of these two heathen;
whereon the eagle declares that both of them died in the true faith,
Ripheus in Christ to come and Trajan in Christ come; and so ex-
plains the former case as to suggest that revelations may have been
vouchsafed to other righteous Pagans. So little do men fathom the
divine counsels! Nay, the redeemed souls, as they look on God,
know not yet who shall be the saved; and in this very limitation of
their knowledge they rejoice, for it is a point of conscious contact
with the will of God. Thus, as the souls of Trajan and Ripheus
glint responsive to the eagle's discourse, Dante receives sweet solace
partly from the thought that he knows not, after all, how many of
the supposed heathen are in truth saved, and partly from the spec-
tacle of the souls in bliss rejoicing in the limitations of their knowl-
edge no less than in its conquests.

WHEN HE who doth illumine all the world descendeth so from our
hemisphere that day on every side is done away,

the heaven which before is kindled by him only, now straightway
maketh itself reappear by many lights wherein the one regloweth.

And this act of heaven came to my mind when the ensign of the
world and of its leaders within its blessed beak was silent;

because all those living lights, far brightlier shining, began songs
which from my memory must slip and fall.

O sweet love, smile-bemantled, how glowing didst thou seem in
those flute holes breathed on only by sacred ponderings!

When the dear and shining stones, whereby I saw the sixth
heaven gemmed, had imposed silence on the angelic chimes,

meseemed to hear the murmuring of a river which droppeth
clear from rock to rock and showeth the abundance of its source.

And as the sound taketh its form in the lute-neck, or at the opening of the pipes the wind that entereth,

so, delay of expectation done away, that murmuring of the eagle rose up through its neck as it were hollow;

there it became a voice and issued thence, out from its beak, in form of words, such as the heart awaited, whereon I wrote them.

"That part in me which seeth and which doth endure the sun in mortal eagles," it began to me, "must now fixedly be gazed upon,

for of the fires wherefromout I make my figure, those with which the eye sparkleth in my head, of all their ranks are chief.

He who shineth midmost, as the pupil, was the singer of the Holy Spirit who bore the ark from city unto city;

now knoweth he the merit of his song, in so far as 'twas the effect of his own counsel, by the remuneration like unto it.

Of the five who make the eyebrow's arch, he who doth neighbour closest on the beak consoled the widow for her son;

now knoweth he how dear it costs Christ not to follow, by his experience of this sweet life and of the opposite.

And he who followeth on the circumference whereof I tell, upon the upper arch, death did delay by his true penitence;

now knoweth he that the eternal judgment is not transmuted when a worthy prayer giveth unto to-morrow upon earth what was to-day's.

The next who followeth, with the laws and me, with good intention that bore evil fruit, to give place to the pastor, made himself a Greek;

now knoweth he that the ill deduced from his good deed hurteth not him though the world be destroyed thereby.

And him thou seest on the down-sloping arch was William, whom that land deploreth which weepeth for that Charles and Frederick live;

now knoweth he how heaven is enamoured of the righteous king, and by the semblance of his glow he maketh it yet seen.

Who would believe, down in the erring world, the Trojan Ripheus in this circle to be the fifth of the holy lights?

now knoweth he right much of the divine grace that the world hath no power to see, albeit his sight discerneth not the bottom."

Like to the lark who soareth in the air, first singing and then silent, content with the last sweetness that doth sate her, so seemed to me the image of the imprint of the eternal pleasure, by longing for whom each thing becometh what it is.

And albeit there I was to my questioning like glass unto the colour which it clothes, yet would it not endure to bide its time in silence;

but from my mouth: "What things are these?" it thrust by force of its own weight, whereat I saw great glee of coruscation.

Then straightway, with its eye more kindled, the blessed ensign answered me, that it might not hold me in suspense of wonder:

"I see that thou believest these things because I tell them thee, but the how thou seest not; so that, although believed, yet are they hidden.

Thou art as he who doth apprehend the thing by name, but may not see its quidity unless another bring it forth to light.

The kingdom of heaven suffereth violence from warm love and living hope which conquereth the divine will;

not in fashion wherein man subdueth man, but conquereth it because it willeth to be conquered, and, conquered, with its own benignity doth conquer.

The first life of the eyebrow and the fifth set thee a-marvelling, because thou seest the region of the angels painted with them.

From their bodies they issued not, as thou supposest, Gentiles, but Christians in established faith, in the feet that—to the one— should suffer, and—to the other—had already suffered.

For the one from hell,—where none returneth ever to right will, came back unto its bones, and this was the reward of living hope;

the living hope which put might into the prayers made unto God to raise him up, that his will might have power to be moved.

The glorious soul, whereof is the discourse, returning to the flesh where it abode short space, believed in him who had the power to aid it;

and believing kindled into so great flame of very love, that at the second death it was worthy to come unto this mirth.

The other, by that grace which welleth from so deep a fountain that never creature thrust eye down to its first wave,

set all his love below on righteousness, wherefore from grace to grace God opened his eye to our redemption yet to come;

whereat he believed therein, and thenceforth endured not the mire of paganism, and reproved the folk perverse concerning it.

Those three dames stood as baptism for him, whom thou didst see at the right wheel, more than a thousand years before baptizing.

O predestination, how far withdrawn is thy root from such vision as sees not the first cause entire!

And ye mortals, hold yourselves straitly back from judging; for we who see God, know not as yet all the elect;

and sweet to us is such defect because our good in this good is refined, that what God willeth we too will."

So by this divine image to clear my curtailed vision was given me sweet medicine.

And as on a good singer a good harpist maketh the quivering of the chord attend, wherein the song gaineth more pleasantness,

so whilst he spake I mind me that I saw the two blessed lights, just as the beating of the eyes concordeth, making their flames to quiver to the words.

CANTO XXI

Beatrice and Dante have risen to Saturn, now in the constellation of Leo, and there Beatrice smiles not (lest her beauty should shatter Dante's mortal senses as Jove's undisguised presence burned Semele to ashes) but bids him gaze upon that which shall be revealed to him. The joy it gives him to obey her behests is compensations even for the withdrawal of his eyes from her countenance, whereon they feasted; and he sees the golden Jacob's ladder stretch up from Saturn; while a throng of splendours descends, as though all heaven had been emptied, and splashes in light upon a certain step of the ladder. Dante addresses the light that arrests itself nearest to him, first with silent thought, then, when Beatrice gives him leave, with open speech; and asks why he more than others has approached him, and why the harmony of heaven is no longer heard. The spirit answers that Dante's senses are not yet sufficiently inured to bear the divine music in this higher sphere; and that he has approached to welcome him not because he has greater love than others, but because the divine love, to which all eagerly respond, has assigned that office to him. Dante though satisfied by the answer within its limits, yet pushes his demand further and asks why God assigned

*this office just to his interlocutor and no other. Hereon the spirit
whirls and glows, rapt into such immediate and intense communion
with God as to see his very essence, and yet declares that neither
he nor the highest of the Seraphim sees the answer to this question,
which lies unfathomably deep in the being of God. Let Dante warn
the world, with its smoke-dimmed faculties, not to presume henceforth to attempt a problem which even in heaven is insoluble.
Appalled by this reply, Dante now bashfully requests to know who
it is that has thus checked his presumptuous enquiry, and he learns
that it is Peter Damiani, who called himself Peter the Sinner, and
who had dwelt in the now degenerate convent of Fonte Avellana,
and in that of S. Maria in Pomposa. In connection with his reception, shortly before his death, of the Cardinal's hat he denounces
the pomp and obesity of the Church dignitaries, whereupon there
comes whirling down a throng of flames that group themselves
round him and raise a cry which so stuns Dante that he understands
not what it says.*

ALREADY were mine eyes fixed on my Lady's countenance again,
and my mind with them, from all other intent removed;

and she smiled not, but: "Were I to smile," she began, "thou
wouldst be such as was Semele, when she turned to ashes;

for my beauty, which, along the steps of the eternal palace kindleth more, as thou hast seen, the higher the ascent,

were it not tempered, so doth glow as that thy mortal power, at
its flash, would be like foliage that the thunder shattereth.

We have arisen to the seventh splendour, which, underneath the
bosom of the glowing Lion, downrayeth now mingling with its
power.

Fix thy mind after thine eyes, and make of them mirrors to the
figure which in this mirror shall be shown unto thee."

Whoso should know what was the pasture of my sight in the
blessed aspect when I changed me to another care,

would recognize how much it was my joy to be obedient to my
heavenly guide, weighing the one against the other side.

Within the crystal which doth bear the name, circling the world,
of its illustrious leader, beneath whom every wickedness lay dead,

coloured like gold which doth re-cast the ray, I saw a ladder erected upward so far that my sight might not follow it.

I saw, moreover, descend upon the steps so many splendours that methought every light which shineth in the heaven had been thence poured down.

And as, after their nature's way, the daws at the beginning of the day set out in company to warm their chilled feathers;

then some go off without return, others come again to whence they started, and others make a wheeling sojourn;

such fashion, meseemed, was in that sparkling which came in company, soon as it smote upon a certain step,

and the one which abode nighest to us became so bright that in my thought I said: "I do perceive the love which thou art signalling unto me.

But she from whom I wait the how and when of speech and silence, pauses, and therefore I, counter to my desire, do well not to demand."

Whereat she, who saw my silence in his sight who seeth all, said to me: "Loose thy warm desire."

And I began: "My merit maketh me not worthy of thy response, but for her sake who granteth me to make request,

O blessed life, who abidest hidden in thy gladness, make known to me the cause which so nigh to me hath placed thee;

and say, wherefore in this wheel the sweet symphony of Paradise keepeth silence, which below throughout the others soundeth so devoutly."

"Thou hast the hearing, as the sight, of mortals," he answered me; "wherefore here is no song for that same reason for which Beatrice hath not smiled.

Down by the steps of the sacred ladder I so far descended only to do thee joyance with speech and with the light which mantleth me;

nor was it greater love that made me swifter; for more and so much love up there doth burn, as the flashing maketh plain to thee;

but the deep love which holdeth us prompt servants of the counsel which governeth the world, maketh assignment here as thou observest."

"Yea, I perceive, O sacred lamp," said I, "how free love in this court sufficeth to make follow the eternal providence;

but this it is, which seemeth me hard to discern: Wherefore thou alone amongst thy consorts wast predestined to this office."

Nor had I come to the last word, ere the light made his mid point a centre, and whirled himself like to a swift millstone.

Then answered the love that was therein: "The divine light doth focus it on me, piercing into that wherein I am embowelled;

the power whereof, conjoined unto my sight, uplifteth me above myself so far that I perceive the supreme essence whence it is milked.

Thence cometh the joy wherewith I flame; for to my sight, even as it is clear, the brightness of the flame do I equate.

But that soul in heaven which is most illuminated, that Seraph who hath his eye most fixed on God, had given no satisfaction to thy question;

because so far within the abyss of the eternal statute lieth the thing thou askest, that from all created vision it is cut off.

And to the mortal world, when thou returnest, take this report, that it presume not more to move its feet to-ward so great a goal.

The mind which shineth here, on earth doth smoke, and therefore think how it should have power there below, which it hath not even though heaven take it to itself."

Such limits did his words impose on me, I left the question, and restrained me to demanding humbly who himself was.

" 'Twixt the two shores of Italy crags arise, and not far distant from thy fatherland, so high the thunders sound far lower down,

and make a hump whose name is Catria, 'neath which a hermitage is consecrate, which erst was given only unto prayer."

So he began to me again the third discourse, and then continuing, said: "There in God's service I became so rooted

that only with olive-juice viands I lightly traversed heat and cold, satisfied in thoughts contemplative.

That cloister erst bore ample fruit unto these heavens, and is now become so futile, that ere long needs must it be revealed.

I, Peter of Damian, was in that same place; and I, Peter the Sinner, was in the house of Our Lady on the Adriatic shore.

Little of mortal life was left to me when I was called and drawn unto the hat which doth but change from bad receptacle to worse.

Cephas came, and the great vessel of the Holy Spirit came, lean and unshod, taking their food from every hostelry.

Now the modern pastors must needs be buttressed on this side and on that, and have one to lead them on, so heavy are they, and one to hoist behind.

With their mantles they o'erspread their palfreys, so that two beasts travel beneath one hide; O patience, that so much endureth!"

At this voice I saw more flames from step to step descend and whirl, and every whirl made them more beauteous.

Around this one they came and stayed themselves and raised a cry of so deep sound that here it may not find similitude; nor did I understand it, so vanquished me the thunder.

CANTO XXII

Beatrice soothes and reassures Dante in his terror, and tells him of the divine vengeance, invoked in the cry he has heard. She bids him look again upon the lights of Saturn; and the brightest amongst them then advances to him, encourages him to trust in the affection of the spirits that surround him, and answers his question without awaiting its utterance. He is Benedict, of Monte Cassino fame, and he is surrounded by other contemplative saints. Encouraged by his words to fling all restraint aside, Dante asks if he may see him in his undisguised form of glory; and he replies that this lofty desire shall be fulfilled in the Empyrean where all desires have their perfect fulfilment, because there is no temporal succession there but eternal fulness. Contemplation alone can lead to this timeless and spaceless life, whence the Jacob's ladder, that Dante's human eye cannot follow to its summit, is planted upon the star of abstinence and contemplation, and reaches to the heaven which Jacob saw it touch. But now none mounts this ladder, for all the monastic orders are degenerate. Yet God has ere now wrought greater wonders than the renewal of their spirit would be. Therefore there is yet hope. Hereon Benedict returns to his company, and they all are swept whirling back to the highest heaven, while Beatrice by her glance raises Dante instantaneously into his natal sign of Gemini, to the influences of which the Poet now appeals for aid in his recording

*task. Beatrice bids him, as he draws near to the final glory, and ere
he meets the triumphant hosts in this eighth sphere, to strengthen
and rejoice his heart by gathering together his heavenly experiences
up to this point and realizing how far he has left earth behind. He
looks down through all the seven spheres, sees the clear side of the
moon and all the related movements and positions of the heavenly
bodies, sees the little earth for which we fight so fiercely stretched
out before him so that he can trace the rivers right down from the
watersheds to the seashore. Then he turns again to Beatrice's eyes.*

Oppressed with stupor to my guide I turned, as doth a little child
who hath recourse ever where most he hath his confidence;

and she, like a mother who succoureth quick her pale and gasp-
ing child, with her own voice which still disposeth him aright,

said to me: "Knowest thou not thou art in heaven? and knowest
thou not heaven is all holy, and that which here is done cometh of
righteous zeal?

How the song had transmuted thee, and I in smiling, now mayst
thou think since the cry hath so moved thee;

wherein, hadst thou understood their prayers, already would be
known to thee the vengeance which thou shalt see ere that thou die.

The sword from here above cleaveth not in haste nor tardy, save
to his deeming who in longing or in fear awaiteth it.

But turn thee now to others; for many illustrious spirits shalt
thou see, if thou again dost lead thy look accordant to my speaking."

As was her pleasure directed I mine eyes, and saw an hundred
spherelets, which together were made more beauteous by their
mutual rays.

I stood as one repressing in himself the prick of his desire, who
doth not frame to ask, so feareth he to exceed.

And the greatest and most shining of these pearls came forward
to make my will content concerning him.

Then there within I heard: "Didst thou see, as I, the love which
burneth amongst us, thy thoughts had been expressed;

but, lest thou by waiting lag from the lofty goal, I will make
answer only to the thought of which thou art thus circumspect.

That mount, upon whose slope Cassino lieth, was erst thronged
on its summit by the folk deceived and ill-disposed.

And I am he who first bore up there his name, who brought to earth that truth which doth lift us so high;

and so great grace shone o'er me, that I drew the places round about back from the impious cult which did seduce the world.

These other flames were all contemplatives kindled by that warmth which giveth birth to the holy flowers and fruits.

Here is Maccarius, here is Romoaldus, here are my brothers who within the cloisters stayed their feet and kept sound their heart."

And I to him: "The love thou showest, speaking with me, and the propitious semblance which I perceive and note in all your glows,

hath so outstretched my confidence as the sun doth the rose when it openeth to its utmost power;

wherefore, I pray thee, and do thou, father, give me assurance whether I may receive so great grace as to behold thee with uncovered image."

Whereat he: "Brother, thy high desire shall be fulfilled in the last sphere, where all the rest have their fulfilment, and mine too.

There perfect, ripe, and whole is each desire; in it alone is every part there where it ever was,

for it is not in space, nor hath it poles; and our ladder even to it goeth, wherefore it thus doth steal it from thy sight.

Right up to there the patriarch Jacob saw it stretch its upper part, when it was seen by him so with angels laden.

But to ascend it now none severeth his feet from earth, and my rule abideth there for wasting of the parchments.

The walls which were wont to be a house of prayer, have become dens, and the hoods are sacks full of foul meal.

But heavy usury is not exacted so counter to God's pleasure as that fruit which doth so madden the monks' hearts.

For what the Church holdeth in her keeping, all pertaineth to the folk that make petition in God's name; not unto kindred, or other filthier thing.

The flesh of mortals is so blandishing that down on earth good beginning sufficeth not for all the space from the upspringing of the oak to acorn-bearing.

Peter began his gathering without gold or silver, and I mine with prayers and fast, and Francis his in humbleness.

And if thou scan the beginning of each one, and scan again whither it hath gone astray, thou shalt see the white turned dusky.

But Jordan back returning, and the sea fleeing when God willed, are more wondrous sights than were the rescue here."

So spake he to me, and then gathered him to his assembly; and the assembly drew close; then like a whirlwind was all gathered upward.

The sweet Lady thrust me after them, only with a sign, up by that ladder, so did her power overcome my nature;

nor ever here below, where we mount and descend by nature's law, was so swift motion as might compare unto my wing.

O reader, by my hopes of turning back to that devout triumph, for the which I many a time bewail my sins, and smite upon my breast,

thou hadst not drawn back and plunged thy finger in the flame in so short space as that wherein I saw the sign that followeth the Bull, and was within it.

O stars of glory, O light impregnated with mighty power, from which I recognize all, whatsoe'er it be, my genius;

with you was rising, and hiding him with you, he who is father of each mortal life, when I first felt the air of Tuscany;

and then when grace was bestowed on me to enter the lofty wheel that rolleth you, your region was assigned to me.

To you devoutly now my soul doth breathe, to gain the power for the hard passage that doth draw her to it.

"Thou art so nigh to the supreme weal," began Beatrice, "that thou shouldst have thine eyes clear and keen.

And therefore, ere thou further wend thereinto, look down and see how great a universe I have already put beneath thy feet;

so that thy heart, rejoicing to its utmost, may be presented to the throng triumphant which cometh glad through this sphered ether."

With my sight I turned back through all and every of the seven spheres, and saw this globe such that I smiled at its sorry semblance;

and that counsel I approve as best which holdeth it for least; and he whose thoughts are turned elsewhither may be called truly upright.

I saw the daughter of Latona kindled without that shade which erst gave me cause to deem her rare and dense.

The aspect of thy son, Hyperion, I there endured, and saw how Maia and Dione move about and near him.

Next appeared to me the tempering of Jove between his father and his son; and there was clear to me the varying they make in their position.

And all the seven were displayed to me, how great they are and swift, and how distant each from other in repair.

The thrashing-floor which maketh us wax so fierce, as I rolled with the eternal Twins, was all revealed to me from ridge to river-mouth; then to the beauteous eyes mine eyes again I turned.

CANTO XXIII

Beatrice turns towards Cancer, the region of the summer Solstice, from Gemini where the Poet and his guide are placed; and her intent look wakes the eagerness of expectancy in him. Ere long he sees heaven lighted by the approach of the triumphant hosts of Christ, the whole harvest of the heavenly husbandry; and outshining all is Christ, whose person pierces the swathings of his glory with blinding light; whereupon, as lightning dilating in the womb of a cloud bursts forth, having no space within, so Dante's mind bursts its own limits and loses itself. . . . Beatrice recalls him as from a forgotten dream, and his sight strengthened by the vision of Christ, is now able to endure her smile. What he then saw he needs must leave untold, albeit what he is forcing himself, line by line, to record proclaims that he yields to no shrinking desire to spare himself. At Beatrice's bidding he mans himself again to look upon the garden of Christ, the Virgin rose and the Apostolic lilies; but Christ himself, in tenderness to the pilgrim's powers, has withdrawn above and shines down upon his chosen ones, himself unseen. Gabriel descends and crowns the virgin who then rises through the Primum Mobile far out of sight, while the saints reach up tenderly after her with their flames. Oh, what wealth of glory is in these sainted souls who on earth chose and spread the true riches that wax not old. There Peter triumphs in the victory of Christ, with the ancient and the modern assembly for whom his key has unlocked heaven.

As THE BIRD amidst the loved foliage who hath brooded on the nest of her sweet offspring through the night which hideth things from us,

who, to look upon their longed-for aspect and to find the food wherewith to feed them, wherein her heavy toils are pleasant to her,

foreruns the time, upon the open spray, and with glowing love awaiteth the sun, fixedly gazing for the dawn to rise;

so was my Lady standing, erect and eager, turned toward the region beneath which the sun showeth least speed;

so that, as I looked on her in her suspense and longing, I became like him who, desiring, would fain have other than he hath, and payeth him with hope.

But short the space 'twixt one and the other *when*, of fixing my attent I mean, and of seeing the heaven grow brilliant more and more.

And Beatrice said: "Behold the hosts of Christ's triumph, and all the fruit gathered by the circling of these spheres."

Meseemed her countenance was all a-glow, and her eyes so full of gladness, that I must needs pass it unconstrued by.

As in the calm full moons Trivia smileth amongst the eternal nymphs who paint the heaven in each recess,

I saw, thousands of lamps surmounting, one sun which all and each enkindled, as doth our own the things we see above;

and through the living light outglowed the shining substance so bright upon my vision that it endured it not.

O Beatrice, sweet guide and dear! She said to me: "That which o'ercometh thee is power against which nought hath defence.

Therein is the wisdom and the might which oped the pathways betwixt heaven and earth, for which there erst had been so long desire."

Even as fire is unbarred from the cloud, because it so dilateth that it hath not space within, and counter to its nature dasheth down to earth,

so my mind, grown greater 'mid these feasts, forth issued from itself, and what it then became knoweth not to recall. . . .

"Open thine eyes and look on what I am; thou hast seen things by which thou art made mighty to sustain my smile."

I was as one who cometh to himself from a forgotten vision, and doth strive in vain to bring it back unto his mind,

when I heard this proffer, worthy of so great gratitude, as never to be blotted from the book that doth record the past.

If now there were to sound all of those tongues which Polyhymnia with her sisters made richest with their sweetest milk,

it would not mount, in aiding me, unto the thousandth of the truth, hymning the sacred smile, and how deep-clear it made the sacred aspect.

And therefore, figuring Paradise, needs must the sacred poem make a leap, as who should find his pathway intercepted.

But whoso thinketh of the weighty theme and of the mortal shoulder which hath charged itself therewith, will think no blame if under it it trembleth.

It is no voyage for a little bark, that which my daring keel cleaveth as it goeth, nor for a helmsman who doth spare himself.

"Wherefore doth my face so enamour thee that thou turnest thee not to the fair garden which flowereth beneath the rays of Christ?

There is the Rose wherein the Word Divine made itself flesh; there are the Lilies at whose odour the good path was taken."

So Beatrice: and I, who to her counsels was all eager, again surrendered me to the conflict of the feeble brows.

As under the sun's ray, which issueth pure through a broken cloud, ere now mine eyes have seen a meadow full of flowers, when themselves covered by the shade;

so beheld I many a throng of splendours, glowed on from above by ardent rays, beholding not the source whence came the glowings.

O benign power which dost so imprint them! thou hadst thyself uplifted to yield place there for mine eyes that lacked in power.

The name of the beauteous flower which I ever invoke, morning and evening, drew all my mind together to look upon the greatest flame.

And when on both mine eyes had been depicted the quality and greatness of the living star which conquereth up there, e'en as down here it conquered,

from within the heaven descended a torch circle-formed, in fashion of a crown, and girt her and wheeled round her.

Whatever melody soundeth sweetest here below, and most doth draw the soul unto itself, would seem a rent cloud thundering,

compared unto the sound of that lyre whereby was crowned the beauteous sapphire by which the brightest heaven is ensapphired.

"I am the angelic love who circles the lofty gladness that doth breathe from out the womb which was the hostelry of our desire;

and I will circle, Lady of heaven, until thou followest thy son, and dost make yet more divine the supreme sphere in that thou enterest it."

Thus the circling melody impressed itself, and all the other lights made sound the name of Mary.

The royal mantel of all the swathings of the universe which most doth burn and most is quickened in the breath and in the ways of God,

above us had its inner shore so distant that its appearance, there where I was, not yet appeared to me.

Therefore mine eyes had not power to follow the crowned flame as she ascended after her own offspring.

And as the infant who toward his mother stretcheth up his arms when he hath had the milk, because his mind flameth forth even into outward gesture; so each one of these glowings up-stretched with its flame, so that the deep love which they had for Mary was made plain to me.

Then they stayed there within my sight, singing *O Queen of heaven* so sweetly that ne'er hath parted from me the delight.

Oh how great the wealth crammed in those most rich chests, which here on earth were goodly acres for the seeding!

Here they have life and joy even in that treasure which was earned in weeping in the exile of Babylon, where gold was scorned.

Here triumphs under the lofty Son of God and Mary, in his victory, together with the ancient and new council, he who doth hold the keys of so great glory.

CANTO XXIV

Beatrice appeals to the saints in the starry heaven to give Dante to drink from the heavenly table to which they have been summoned. The divine grace which gives him a foretaste of their feast is their

*warrant, his immeasurable longing is his claim, and their unbroken
enjoyment of that knowledge which he desires makes it easy for
them to give. The saints respond joyously to her appeal and in
groups of circling lights reveal their varying measures of ecstasy.
Peter comes out from the brightest group in answer to Beatrice's
prayer. She addresses him as the representative of that Faith by
which he himself once walked upon the sea, and to which heaven
owes all its citizens; and urges him to test Dante as to Faith. Dante
prepares himself, as for examination, and Peter questions him.
Dante founds his confession upon the definition in the Epistle to
the Hebrews. Faith is the substance or foundation upon which hope
is reared, and the basis of the argument by which the reality of unseen things is established. His own faith is unquestioning. It is
based on Scripture which is authenticated by miracle. And if one
should question the miracles he must face the yet greater miracle
of the spread of Christianity without miracle. Peter further demands to hear the positive content of Dante's faith and the specific
warrant for it. Dante declares his faith in God, defined first in Aristotelian phrase as the unmoved mover whom the heaven loves and
longs for, and then as three Persons in one Essence. For the first
belief proofs are drawn from the* Physics *and* Metaphysics *as well
as from Scripture, for the second from Scripture alone. All else
is secondary. Peter signifies his delight in Dante's confession by
circling him thrice.*

"O FELLOWSHIP elect to the great supper of the blessed Lamb, who
feedeth you in such fashion that your desire ever is fulfilled;

if by the grace of God this man foretasteth of that which falleth
from your table ere death prescribe the time to him,

give heed to his unmeasured yearning and bedew him somewhat:
ye drink ever of the fountain whence floweth that on which his
thought is fixed."

Thus Beatrice: and those glad souls made themselves spheres
upon fixed poles, outflaming mightily like unto comets.

And even as wheels in harmony of clock-work so turn that the
first, to whoso noteth it, seemeth still, and the last to fly,

so did these carols with their differing whirl, or swift or slow,
make me deem of their riches.

From the one I noted of most beauty, I saw issue a so blissful flame it left none there of greater brightness;

and thrice round Beatrice did it sweep with so divine a song, my fantasy repeateth it not to me;

wherefore my pen leapeth, and I write it not; for such folds our imagination, not only our speech, is too vivid colouring.

"O holy sister mine, who thus dost pray to us devoutly, by thy glowing love, thou dost unloosen me from this fair sphere."

The breath that thus discoursed, as I have written down, was turned unto my Lady by that blessed flame so soon as it had stayed.

And she: "O light eternal of that great man to whom our Lord gave up the keys he brought down of this wondrous joy,

test this man here on the points both light and grave, as it doth please thee, anent the faith whereby thou once didst walk upon the sea.

Whether he loveth well and well hopeth and believeth is not hidden from thee, for thou hast thy vision there where everything is seen depicted.

But since this realm hath made its citizens by the true faith, 'tis well that, for the glorifying of it, it should chance him to speak thereof."

Even as the bachelor armeth himself and speaketh not until the master setteth forth the question, to sanction it, but not determine it:

so did I arm myself with every reason whilst she was speaking, that I might be ready for such examiner and such profession.

"Good Christian, speak, and manifest thyself; what thing is faith?" Whereat I lifted up my brow upon that light whence breathed forth this word;

then turned me to Beatrice, and she made eager indication to me that I should pour the water forth from my inward fountain.

"May the grace that granteth me to confess me," I began, "to the veteran fore-fighter, make my thought find expression!"

And I followed on: "As wrote for us, O father, the veracious pen of thy dear brother, who, with thee, set Rome on the good track;

faith is the substance of things hoped for, and argument of things which are not seen; and this I take to be its quiddity."

Then heard I: "Rightly dost thou deem, if well thou understandest wherefore he placed it amongst the substances, and then amongst the arguments."

And I thereon: "The deep things which grant me here the largess to appear before me, are from the eyes of them below so hidden

that their existence is there only in belief, whereon is built the lofty hope; and so of *substance* it embraceth the intention;

and from this belief needs must we syllogize without further sight; therefore it includes the intention of *argument*."

Then heard I: "If all that is acquired down below by teaching were so understood, there were no room left for the wit of sophist."

Thus was breathed forth from that enkindled love; then did it add: "Right well hath now been traversed this coin's alloy and weight;

but tell me if thou hast it in thy purse." Whereupon I: "Yea, so bright and round I have it that for me is no *perhaps* in its impression."

Then issued from the deep light that was glowing there: "This dear gem on which all virtue is up-built,

whence came it to thee?" And I: "The ample shower of the Holy Spirit which is poured over the old and over the new parchments,

is syllogism that hath brought it to so sharp conclusion for me, that, compared to it, all demonstration seemeth blunt to me."

Then heard I: "That old and that new proposition which bringeth thee to such conclusion, wherefore dost hold it for divine discourse?"

And I: "The proof which doth unfold the truth to me lieth in the works that followed, for which nature ne'er heated iron yet, nor hammered anvil."

The answer came to me: "Say, who assureth thee that these works were? The very script that would attest itself, no other, sweareth it to thee."

"If the world turned to Christianity," I said, "without miracles, this one is such that the others are not the hundredth of it;

for thou didst enter poor and hungry upon the battlefield to sow the good plant which was erst a vine, but now has grown a thorn."

This ended, the high holy court made *God we praise* ring through the spheres, in melody such as up there is sung.

And that baron who so from branch to branch, examining, had drawn me now, that we were nigh unto the utmost leaves,

began again: "The grace which holdeth amorous converse with thy mind hath oped thy mouth till now as it behoved to open;

so that I sanction that which forth emerged; but now behoveth thee to utter what it is thou dost believe, and whence it offered it to thy believing."

"O holy father, thou spirit who now seest that which of old thou didst so believe that thou didst overcome more youthful feet drawing anigh the sepulchre,"

I began, "thou wouldst have me here make plain the form of my eager belief, and dost also ask the cause of it;

whereto I answer: I believe in one God, sole and eternal, who moveth all the heaven, himself unmoved, with love and with desire.

And for such belief I have not only proofs physic and metaphysic, but it is given me likewise by the truth which hence doth rain

through Moses, through the Prophets and through the Psalms, through the Gospel and through you who wrote when the glowing Spirit had made you fosterers.

And I believe in three eternal Persons, and I believe them one Essence, so One and so Trine as to comport at once with *are* and *is*.

With the profound divine state whereof I speak, my mind is stamped more times than once by evangelic teaching.

This the beginning is; this is the spark which then dilates into a living flame, and like a star in heaven shineth in me."

Like as the master who heareth what doth please him, and thereupon embraceth the servant, rejoicing at the news, so soon as he is silent;

so, blessing me as it sang, three times circled me, so soon as I was silent, the apostolic light at whose command I had discoursed; so did I please him in my utterance.

CANTO XXV

It was the Faith that gained Dante the high privilege of the apostolic benediction. Therefore if his poem should ever melt the heart of the Florentines he will take the poet's crown at that same font whereat he was received into the Faith. St. James now joins St.

*Peter. When we read of the three chosen disciples to whom Jesus
reveals more than to the others we are to take Peter as representing
faith, James hope, and John love; and therefore Beatrice urges
James to test Dante as to Hope. James questions him. Beatrice herself declares on his behalf that he possesses in fullest measure the
virtue of hope, and that it is on that very ground that he has been
allowed to anticipate death in his vision of divine things. As to the
nature of Hope and its source he shall answer for himself. Dante
defines hope with exclusive reference to the future life, and derives
it from Scripture. James, whose own hope, which followed him
even to death, is now swallowed up in victory, still loves the virtue
he once practised, and demands to hear the content of Dante's
hope, and its source. Dante declares that Isaiah and John tell him
of the double garments of the blessed, and that this symbol indicates to him the resurrection of the body as well as the immortality
of the soul as the substantive content of his hope. A light as bright
as the sun now joins Peter and James, and is declared by Beatrice
to be the Apostle John. Dante strains his sight to see John's body,
but is blinded by the glory, and is told that his body is dust, and
awaits the general resurrection; Jesus and Mary alone of human
beings having arisen with their bodies to heaven. Then of a sudden
the harmony is stilled, and the blinded Dante turns in vain to look
upon Beatrice.*

SHOULD IT E'ER come to pass that the sacred poem to which both
heaven and earth so have set hand, that it hath made me lean
through many a year,

should overcome the cruelty which doth bar me forth from the
fair sheepfold wherein I used to sleep, a lamb, foe to the wolves
which war upon it;

with changed voice now, and with changed fleece shall I return,
a poet, and at the font of my baptism shall I assume the chaplet;

because into the Faith which maketh souls known of God, 'twas
there I entered; and afterward Peter, for its sake, circled thus my
brow.

Thereafter moved a light toward us from out that sphere whence
issued forth the first fruits of his vicars left by Christ.

And my Lady, full of gladness, said to me, "Look! look! behold the Baron for whose sake, down below, they seek Galicia."

As when a dove taketh his place near his companion, and the one poureth out his love for the other, circling round and murmuring,

so did I see one great chieftain glorious received by the other, praising the food which there above doth feast them.

But when the greeting was fulfilled, silent before me each one fixed himself, so kindled that it subdued my countenance.

Smiling then Beatrice said: "Illustrious life, by whom the generosity of our court was chronicled,

make hope be sounded in this height; thou knowest that all those times thou figurest it when Jesus gave more light unto the three."

"Uplift thy head, and see thou reassure thee, for whatso cometh from the mortal world up hither, behoves it ripen in our rays."

Such exhortation from the second flame came to me; whereat I lifted up mine eyes unto the mountains, which had before downbowed them with excess of weight.

"Since of his grace our Emperor willeth that ere thy death thou be confronted with his Counts in his most secret hall;

that, having seen the truth of this court, thou mayst thereby strengthen in thyself and mo' the hope that upon earth enamoureth folk of good;

say what thing it is, and how thy mind is therewith enflowered, and say whence unto thee it cometh"; so followed on the second light.

And that tender one who guided the feathers of my wings to so lofty flight, thus foreran me in answer:

"Church militant hath not a child richer in hope, as is written in the sun who o'errayeth all our host;

therefore was it granted him to come from Egypt to Jerusalem, to look on her, e'er the prescribed limit of his soldiery.

Those two other points—asked not that thou mayst learn, but that he may bear back word how much this virtue is held in pleasure by thee.—

to him I leave; for they will not be hard, nor boastful matter, to him; so let him thereto answer, and may the grace of God concede this to him."

As the pupil who followeth the teacher, eager and glad, in that wherein he is expert, in order that his excellence may be revealed;

"Hope," said I, "is a certain expectation of future glory, the product of divine grace and precedent merit.

From many stars cometh this light to me; but he first distilled it into my heart who was the supreme singer of the supreme leader.

Let them hope in thee, in his divine song he saith, *who know thy name;* and who knoweth it not, having my faith?

Thou then didst drop it on me with his dropping, in thine Epistle, so that I am full and pour again your shower upon others."

Whilst I was speaking, within the living bosom of that flame trembled a flash sudden and dense like unto lightning.

Then breathed forth: "The love whence I am still aflame toward that virtue which followed me even to the palm and issuing from the field,

willeth that I breath on thee who dost delight thee in her; and further, 'tis my pleasure that thou tell the thing which hope doth promise thee."

And I: "The new and the ancient scriptures set down the symbol, which again doth point me to the thing itself. Of the souls which God hath made his friends

Isaiah saith that each one shall be clad with double garb in its own land, and its own land is this sweet life.

And more worked out by far, doth thy brother, where he treateth of the white robes, set forth this revelation to us."

And, close upon the ending of these words, first rang above us, *Let them hope in thee,* whereunto all the carols answered;

then, from amongst themselves, a light flashed out, in fashion such that if the Crab contained a crystal like it winter would have a month of one unbroken day.

And as doth rise and go her way and enter on the dance a joyous virgin, only to do honour to the bride, and not for any failing,

so did I see the illumined splendour join the other two, who were wheeling round in such guise as their burning love befitted.

There it launched itself into their music and their words; and my Lady held her look upon them just like a bride, silent and unmoving.

"This is he who lay upon the breast of our Pelican, and this was he chosen from upon the cross for the great office."

My Lady thus; but no more after than before her words moved she her eyes from their fixed intent.

As who doth gaze and strain to see the sun eclipsed a space, who by looking grows bereft of sight;

so did I to this last flame till a word came: "Wherefore dost dazzle thee to see that which hath here no place?

Earth in the earth my body is, and there it shall be, with the rest, until our number equalleth the eternal purpose.

With the two robes in the blessed cloister are the two lights alone which rose; and this thou shalt take back into your world."

At this voice the flamed circle stilled itself, together with the sweet interlacing made by the sound of the three-fold breath,

as, to avert or weariness or peril, the oars till now submitten upon the water, all pause at a whistle's sound.

Ah! how was I stirred in my mind, turning to look on Beatrice, for that I might not see her, albeit I was nigh to her and in the world of bliss!

CANTO XXVI

The Apostle John reassures Dante as to his lost sight, which Beatrice will restore to him as Ananias restored his to Paul; and invites him to discourse meanwhile of Love; and first to tell him what is the supreme object on which his soul's affection is fixed. Dante, resignedly awaiting Beatrice's succour, declares that he is still burning in that same flame which she brought into his heart, and that God is the beginning and end of that and of all his other loves. Moved by the Apostle to declare more at large the justification of his love Dante answers that, since good as good must be loved, to know God is of necessity to love Him, and goes on to declare how Aristotle and the Scriptures have made this truth level to his capacity. When questioned as to other reasons for loving God Dante perceives that he is expected to supplement his account of the supreme love of God, as god in Himself, by a statement of the accessory gratitude to God as good to us, and enumerates the creation of the world, his own creation, the redemption and the hope of heaven. He adds that all creatures share his love in pro-

portion as they share the good which is supreme in the Creator. A hymn of praise is raised, and Dante's sight is restored to him; whereon he is bewildered by Beatrice's greater beauty and then by the presence of a fourth flame, wherein he learns the soul of Adam to abide. Overwhelmed at first, then moved to eagerness that will not brook delay, by finding himself face to face with the human being who has had such unique experience and who holds the answer to questions that have so long tantalized the world, Dante reads the answering affection of the first father in the swaying undulations of the light that clothes him and receives the answer to his unspoken questions, as to chronology, the language of Eden, the length of the period of innocence and the nature of the sin that cost the world so dear.

WHILST I WAS in suspense concerning my quenched sight, I was made heedful by a breath that issued from the glowing flame which quenched it,

saying: "Until thou hast again the sense of sight thou hast consumed on me, 'tis well thou compensate it by discourse.

Begin then, and declare whereon thy mind is focussed; and assure thee that thy sight within thee is confounded, not destroyed;

because the lady who through this divine region doth conduct thee hath in her look the power that was in Ananis' hand."

I said: "At her good pleasure, soon or late, let succour come to the eyes which were the gates when she did enter with the fire wherewith I ever burn.

The good which satisfieth this court is Alpha and Omega of all the scripture which love readeth to me with light or heavy stress."

That same voice which had removed my terror at the sudden dazzlement, set my concern again upon discourse,

and said: "Yea, through a closer sieve thou needs must strain; needs must thou tell me what it was that aimed thy bow at such a targe."

And I: "By philosophic arguments and by authority which downcometh hence, such love must needs stamp itself on me;

for good, as good, so far as understood, kindleth love, and so much more by how much more of excellence it graspeth in itself.

Therefore to the Essence which hath such privilege that whatsoever good he found outside of it is nought else save a light of its own ray,

more than to any other must the mind needs move, in love, of whoso doth discern the truth whereon this proof is founded.

And this same truth is made level to my intellect by him who doth reveal to me the primal love of all the eternal beings.

It is made level to me by the voice of that veracious author who saith to Moses speaking of himself: *I will cause thee to see all worth.*

It is made level to me by thee also, where thou openest the lofty proclamation which doth herald upon earth the secrets of this place above all other declaration."

And I heard: "As urged by human intellect and by authorities concordant with it, of thy loves keep for God the sovereign one.

But tell me yet if thou feel other cords draw thee towards him, so that thou utter forth with how many teeth this love doth grip thee."

Not hidden was the sacred purpose of Christ's eagle, but rather I perceived whither he will to lead on my profession.

Wherefore I began again: "All those toothgrips which have power to make the heart turn unto God co-work upon my love;

for the being of the world and my own being, the death that he sustained that I might live, and that which each believer hopeth, as do I,

together with the aforesaid living consciousness, have drawn me from the sea of the perverted and placed me on the shore of the right love.

The leaves wherewith all the garden of the eternal Gardener is leafed, I love in measure of the good that hath been proffered to them from him."

Soon as I held my peace a sweetest song rang through the Heaven, and my Lady with the rest cried: "Holy, Holy, Holy!"

And as at a keen light one wakeneth from slumber by reason of the vessel spirit which runneth to meet the glow that pierceth tunic after tunic,

and he thus awakened confoundeth what he seeth, so undiscerning his sudden vigil until reflection cometh to its succour;

so from mine eyes did Beatrice dissipate every scale with the ray of hers that might cast their glow more than a thousand miles;

whence better than before I saw thereafter, and as one stupefied, made question as to a fourth light which I perceived with us.

And my Lady: "Within those rays holdeth amorous converse with its maker the first soul that the first Power e'er created."

As the spray which bendeth down its head as the wind passeth over, and doth then uplift itself by its own power which doth raise it up,

did I, whilst she was speaking, all bemazed; and then was re-assured by a desire to speak, wherewith I was a-burning;

and I began: "O fruit, who wast alone produced mature, O ancient father who hast both daughter and daughter-in-law in every bride;

devoutly as I may do I implore thee that thou speak to me; thou seest my will, and to hear thee the sooner I not utter it."

Sometimes an animal swayeth beneath a covering so that its impulse must needs be apparent, since what envelopeth it followeth its movements;

and in like manner that first soul made appear through its covering with what elation it advanced to do me pleasure.

And from it breathed: "Though not set forth to me by thee, I better do discern thy will than thou the thing which is most certain to thee,

because I see it in the veracious Mirror which doth make himself reflector of all other things, and nought doth make itself reflector unto him.

Thou wouldst know how long the time since God placed me in the uplifted garden wherein she there prepared thee for so long a stair,

and how long the delight endured unto my eyes, and the true cause of the great indignation, and the idiom which I used and which myself composed.

Now know, my son, that not the tasting of the tree was in itself the cause of so great exile, but only the transgressing of the mark.

From that place whence thy Lady dispatched Virgil, four thousand three hundred and two revolutions of the sun went out my longing for this gathering;

and I beheld him course through all the lights of his path nine hundred times and thirty whilst I abode on earth.

The tongue I spoke was all quenched long ere the work that ne'er might be completed was undertaken by the folk of Nimrod;

for never yet did product of the reason maintain itself for ever, because of human preference which doth change in sequence with the heaven.

That man should speak is nature's doing; but thus or thus nature permitteth to you as best seemeth you.

Ere I descended to the infernal anguish, *I* was the name on earth of that supreme good whence cometh the gladness that doth swathe me;

El was he called thereafter; and this is fitting, for the use of mortals is as the leaf upon the branch which goeth and another followeth.

On the mount which most doth rise from out the wave was I, with life pure and disgraced, from the first hour to that which followeth, when the sun changeth quadrant, next on the sixth hour."

CANTO XXVII

The Poet's ear and eye drink for a space of the glory of Paradise and afterwards, amid deep silence, first the light of Peter glows red with indignation, as he denounced the doings of Pope Boniface VIII; then all heaven is suffused with the same glow and Beatrice's cheek flushes as at a tale of shame, while Peter pursues his denunciation, including Clement the Gascon and John of Cahors in its sweep and then promises redress and bids Dante bear the news to earth. The triumphant spirits, like flashes of flame, rain upwards into the higher heaven, and Beatrice bids Dante look down upon the earth. Dante is in Gemini and the Sun in Aries, with Taurus between, and therefore the half of the earth illuminated by the sun does not correspond with the half that the Seer commands. He sees the earth as we see the moon when she is past the full. The illuminated portion stretches from far west of Gibraltar to the shore of the Levant; and the darkened portion stretches further east. Turning back with renewed longing to Beatrice Dante sees her yet more beautiful and rises with her to the Primum Mo-

*bile. Beatrice expounds to him how time and space take their source
and measure from this sphere, and have no relevancy to aught that
lies beyond it. It is girt (how, God only understandeth) not by
space but by the Divine light and love. Then, with deep yearning,
Beatrice turns her thoughts back to the besotted world wherein
faith and innocence find refuge only in the hearts and lives of infants, and where humanity blackens from its birth. And all this not
because of any inherent degeneracy but because there is none to
rule. But ere the hundredth of a day by which the Julian exceeds
the Solar year shall by its accumulations have made January cease
to be a Winter month! the course shall be reversed.*

ALL PARADISE took up the strain, "To the Father, to the Son, to
the Holy Spirit, glory!" so that the sweet song intoxicated me.

Meseemed I was beholding a smile of the universe; wherefore
my intoxication entered both by hearing and by sight.

O joy! O gladness unspeakable! O life compact of love and
peace! O wealth secure that hath no longing!

Before my eyes the four torches stood enkindled, and the one
which had first approached me began to grow more living;

and such became in semblance as would Jupiter if he and Mars
were birds and should exchange their plumage.

The providence which there assigneth function and office had
imposed silence on the blessed choir on every side,

when I heard: "If I transform my hue, marvel thou not; for, as
I speak, thou shalt see all of these transform it too.

He who usurpeth upon earth my place, my place, my place,
which in the presence of the Son of God is vacant,

hath made my burial-ground a conduit for that blood and filth,
whereby the apostate one who fell from here above, is soothed
down there below."

With that colour which painteth a cloud at even or at morn by
the opposing sun, did I then see all heaven o'erfused;

and as a modest dame who remaineth sure of herself, yet at
another's fault, though only hearing it, feeleth all timid,

so Beatrice changed her semblance; and such, I take it, was the
eclipse in heaven when the supreme Might suffered.

Then his discourse proceeded, with voice so far transmuted from itself, that his semblance had not altered more:

"The spouse of Christ was not reared upon my blood, and that of Linus and of Cletus, that she might then be used for gain of gold;

but 'twas for gain of this glad life that Sixtus and Pius, Calixtus and Urban shed their blood after many a tear.

It was not our purpose that on the right hand of our successors one part of the Christian folk should sit, and one part on the other;

nor that the keys given in grant to me should become the ensign on a standard waging war on the baptized;

nor that I should become the head upon the seal to sold and lying privileges, whereat I often blush and shoot forth flames.

In garb of pastors ravening wolves are seen from here above in all the pastures. Succour of God! oh wherefore liest thou prone?

Cahorsines and Gascons make ready to drink our blood. Oh fair beginning, to what vile ending must thou fall!

But the lofty Providence, which with Scipio defended the glory of the world for Rome, will soon bring succour, as I deem.

And thou, my son, who, for thy mortal weight, shalt return below once more, open thy mouth and hide thou not the thing which I not hide."

As our atmosphere raineth down in flakes the frozen vapours when the horn of the heavenly Goat is touched by the sun;

so did I see the ether adorn itself and rain upward the flakes of the triumphal flashes, which had made sojourn there with us.

My sight was following their semblance, and followed till the medium, by excess, deprived it of the power to pierce more far.

Whereat the Lady, who saw me now absolved from straining upward, said to me: "Down plunge thy sight and see how thou hast rolled."

From the hour at which I had before looked down, I saw that I had moved through the whole arc which the first Climate makes from middle unto end;

so that I saw beyond Cadiz the mad way which Ulysses took, and on this side, hard by, the shore whereon Europa made herself a sweet burden.

And further had the site of this thrashing-floor been unfolded to me, save that the sun was in advance beneath my feet, served by a Sign and more from me.

My enamoured mind, which held amorous converse ever with my Lady, burned more than ever to bring back my eyes to her;

and whatsoever food nature or art e'er made, to catch the eyes and so possess the mind, be it in human flesh, be it in pictures,

if all united, would seem nought towards the divine delight which glowed upon me when that I turned me to her smiling face.

And the power of which that look made largess to me, from the fair nest of Leda plucked me forth, and into the swiftest heaven thrust me.

Its parts most living and exalted are so uniform that I know not to tell which Beatrice chose for my position.

But she, who saw my longing, smiling began—so glad that God seemed joying in her countenance—

"The nature of the universe which stilleth the centre and moveth all the rest around, hence doth begin as from its starting point.

And this heaven hath no other *where* than the divine mind wherein is kindled the love which rolleth it and the power which it sheddeth.

Light and love grasp it in one circle, as doth it the others, and this engirdment he only who doth gird it understandeth.

Its movement by no other is marked out; but by it all the rest are measured, as ten by half and fifth.

And how Time in this same vessel hath its roots, and in the rest its leaves, may now be manifest to thee.

O greed, who so dost abase mortals below thee, that not one hath power to draw his eyes forth from thy waves!

'Tis true the will in men hath vigour yet; but the continuous drench turneth true plum fruits into cankered tubers.

Faith and innocence are found only in little children; then each of them fleeth away before the cheeks are covered.

Many a still lisping child observeth fast, who after, when his tongue is free, devoureth every food in every month;

and many a lisping child loveth and hearkeneth to his mother, who after, when his speech is full, longeth to see her buried.

So blackeneth at the first aspect the white skin of his **fair** daughter who bringeth morn and leaveth evening.

And thou, lest thou make marvel at it, reflect that there is none
to govern upon earth, wherefore the human household so strayeth
from the path.

But, ere that January be all unwintered by that hundredth part
neglected upon earth, so shall these upper circles roar

that the fated season so long awaited shall turn round the poops
where are the prows, so that the fleet shall have straight course; and
true fruit shall follow on the flower."

CANTO XXVIII

*After Beatrice's discourse Dante, gazing upon her eyes, is suddenly
aware of the reflection in them of a thing which was not in his sight
or thought, and on turning to see what it may be he perceives a
point of intensest light with nine concentric circles wheeling around
it; swift and bright in proportion to their nearness to the point.
Beatrice, quoting Aristotle's praise concerning God, declares that
Heaven and all Nature hang upon that point, and bids Dante note
the burning love that quickens the movement of the inmost circle.
Thereon Dante at once perceives that the nine circles represent the
Intelligences or angelic orders connected with the nine revolving
heavens, but cannot see why the outmost, swiftest, widest sweeping
and most divine heaven should correspond with the inmost and
smallest angelic circle. Beatrice explains that the divine substance
of the heavens being uniform that heaven which is materially greatest has in it the most of excellence; but it is the excellence, not the
size, that is essential. In like manner swiftness and brightness are
the measure of the excellence of the angelic circles, and therefore
the inmost of them which is swiftest and brightest represents those
intelligences that love and know most; and the spiritual correspondence is complete between the two diverse spatial presentations.
Thus the relativity of space-conceptions is suggested. God may be
conceived as the spaceless centre of the universe just as well as
the all-embracer. Dante, now enlightened, sees the circles shoot out
countless sparks that follow them in their whirling; and hears them
all sing Hosanna; while Beatrice further explains how the swift joy
of the angels is proportioned to their sight, their sight to their merit,
won by grace and by exercise of will; whereas love is not the foun-*

dation but the inevitable consequence of knowledge. She has ex-
plained the three hierarchies and nine orders of the Angels, as
Dionysius (enlightened by his own intense passion of contemplation,
and instructed by Paul who had been rapt to heaven) had set them
forth. Gregory, having departed from the scheme of Dionysius,
smiled at his own error when he beheld this heaven.

WHEN, counter to the present life of wretched mortals the truth had been revealed by her who doth emparadise my mind;

as in the mirror a taper's flame, kindled behind a man, is seen of him or ere itself be in his sight or thought,

and he turneth back to see whether the glass speak truth to him, and seeth it accordant with it as song-words to their measure;

so doth my memory recall it chanced to me, gazing upon the beauteous eyes whence love had made the noose to capture me;

and when I turned, and mine own were smitten by what appeareth in that volume whene'er upon its circling the eye is rightly fixed,

a point I saw which rayed forth light so keen, needs must the vision that it flameth on be closed because of its strong poignancy;

and whatever star from here appeareth smallest, were seen a moon neighboured with it, as star with star is neighboured.

Perhaps as close as the halo seemeth to gird the luminary that doth paint it, whenso the vapour which supporteth it is thickest,

at such interval around the point there wheeled a circle of fire so rapidly it had surpassed the motion which doth swiftest gird the universe;

and this was by a second girt around, that by a third, and the third by a fourth, by a fifth the fourth, then by a sixth the fifth.

Thereafter followed the seventh, already in its stretch so far outspread that were the messenger of Juno made complete, it were too strait to hold it.

And so the eighth and ninth; and each one moved slower according as in number it was more remote from unity;

and that one had the clearest flame, from which the pure spark was least distant; because, I take it, it sinketh deepest into the truth thereof.

My Lady, who beheld me in toil of deep suspense, said: "From that point doth hang heaven and all nature.

Look on that circle which is most conjoint thereto, and know its movement is so swift by reason of the enkindled love whereby 'tis pierced."

And I to her: "Were the universe disposed in the order I behold in these wheelings, then were I satisfied with what is set before me.

But in the universe of sense we may see the circlings more divine as from the centre they are more removed.

Wherefore, if it behoveth my desire to find its goal in this wondrous and angelic temple which hath only love and light for boundary,

needs must I further hear wherefore the copy and the pattern go not in one fashion; for, for myself, I gaze on it in vain."

"And if for such a knot thy fingers are not able, no marvel is it; so hard hath it become by never being tried."

So my Lady; and then said: "Take that which I shall tell thee, wouldst thou be satisfied, and ply thy wit around it.

The corporeal circles are ample or strait according to the more or less of the virtue which spreadeth over all their parts.

Greater excellence hath purpose to work greater weal; and greater weal is comprehended in the greater body if that the parts be equally consummate.

Therefore the one which sweepeth with it all the rest of the universe, correspondeth to the circle that most loveth and most knoweth.

Wherefore, if thou draw thy measure round the virtue, not the semblance of the substances which appear to thee in circles,

thou wilt see a wondrous congruence of greater unto more and smaller unto less in every heaven to its intelligence."

As the hemisphere of air becometh shining and serene when Boreas bloweth from his gentler cheek,

whereby is purged and is resolved the film which erst obscured it, so that the heaven laugheth with the beauties of its every district;

so did I, when my Lady had made provision to me of her clear-shining answer; and like a star in heaven the truth was seen.

And when her words stayed, no otherwise doth iron shoot forth sparkles, when it boileth, than did the circles sparkle.

And every spark followed their blaze; and their numbers were such as ran to thousands beyond the duplication of the chessboard.

From choir to choir I heard Hosanna sung to that fixed point which holdeth and shall ever hold them to the *where,* in which they have been ever;

and she who saw the questioning thoughts within my mind, said: "The first circles have revealed to thee the Seraphs and the Cherubs.

So swift they follow their withies that they may liken them unto the point as most they may; and they may in measure as they are sublime in vision.

Those other loves which course around them are named Thrones of the divine aspect, because they brought to its completion the first ternary.

And thou shouldst know that all have their delight in measure as their sight sinketh more deep into the truth wherein every intellect is stilled.

Hence may be seen how the being blessed is founded on the act that seeth, not that which loveth, which after followeth;

and the measure of sight is the merit which grace begetteth and the righteous will; and thus from rank to rank the progress goeth.

The second ternary which thus flowereth in this eternal spring which nightly Aries doth not despoil,

unceasingly unwintereth Hosanna with three melodies which sound in the three orders of gladness, whereof it is three-plied.

In that hierarchy are tne three divinities, first Dominations, and then Virtues; the third order is of Powers.

Then in the two last-save-one up-leapings, Principalities and Archangels whirl; the last consisteth all of Angelic sports.

These orders all gaze upward, and downward have such conquering might that toward God all are drawn and all draw.

And Dionysius with such yearning set himself to contemplate these orders that he named them and distinguished them as I.

But Gregory afterward departed from him, wherefore so soon as he opened his eye in this heaven he smiled at his own self.

And if so hidden truth was uttered forth by mortal upon earth, I would not have thee marvel; for he who saw it here above revealed it to him, with much beside of truth about these circles."

Beatrice gazes for a moment upon that point of light wherein every where is here and every when is now, and therein reads the questions Dante would fain have her answer. It was not to acquire any good for himself, but that his reflected light might itself have the joy of conscious existence, that God, in his timeless eternity, uttered himself as love in created beings, themselves capable of loving. It is vain to ask what God was doing before the creation, for Time has no relevance except within the range of creation; nor was the first creation itself successive, or temporal at all; for pure form or act (the angels) pure matter or potentiality (the materia prima) and inseparably united act and potentiality (the material heavens) issued into simultaneous being. Jerome was wrong (as Scripture and reason testify) in thinking that the angels were created long before the heavens over which it is the office of certain of them to preside. Dante now knows where the angels were created (in God's eternity) and when (contemporaneously with Time and with the Heavens) and how (all loving); but has yet to learn how soon certain fell (ere one might count twenty) and why (because of Satan's pride), and how the less presumptuous ones recognized the source of their swift and wide range of understanding, and so received grace (the acceptance of which was itself a merit), and were confirmed. This instruction were enough, did not the prevalence of erroneous teaching (honest and dishonest) make it needful to add that the angels, ever rejoicing in the direct contemplation of God, see all things always, and therefore exercise no changing stress of attention, and therefore need no power of memory, since their thought never having lost immediate hold of aught needs not to recall aught. Beatrice goes on to denounce the vain and flippant teaching by which the faithful are deluded, and especially the unauthorized pardonings; and finally, returning to the subject of the angels, explains that though in number they surpass the power of human language or conception, yet each has his own specific quality of insight and of resultant love. Such is the wonder of the divine love which breaks itself upon such countless mirrors, yet remains ever one.

WHEN both the two children of Latona, covered by the Ram and by the Scales, make the horizon their girdle at one same moment,

as long as from the point when the zenith balanceth the scale, till one and other from that belt unbalanceth itself, changing its hemisphere,

so long, with a smile traced on her countenance, did Beatrice hold her peace, gazing fixedly on the point which had o'ermastered me;

then she began: "I tell, not ask, that which thou fain wouldst hear; for I have seen it where every *where* and every *when* is focussed.

Not to have gain of any good unto himself, which may not be, but that his splendour might, as it glowed, declare, *I am*.

In his eternity beyond time, beyond all other comprehension, as was his pleasure, the eternal love revealed him in new loves.

Nor did he lie, as slumbering, before; for nor before nor after was the process of God's outflowing over these waters.

Form and matter, united and in purity, issued into being which had no flaw, as from a three-stringed bow three arrows;

and as in glass, in amber, or in crystal, a ray so gloweth that from its coming to its pervading all, there is no interval;

so the threefold effect of its Lord rayed out all at once into its being, without distinction of beginning.

Co-created was order and co-woven with the substances, and those were the summit in the universe wherein pure act was produced.

Pure potentiality held the lowest place; in the midst power twisted such a withy with act as shall ne'er be unwithied.

Jerome wrote to you of a long stretch of ages wherein the Angels were created ere aught else of the universe was made;

but the truth I tell is writ on many a page of the writers of the Holy Spirit, and thou shalt be aware of it if well thou look;

and also reason seeth it some little, which would not grant that the movers should so long abide without their perfecting.

Now dost thou know where and when these Loves were chosen and how, so that three flames are quenched already in thy longing.

Nor should one, counting, come so soon to twenty as did a part of the Angels disturb the substrate of your elements.

The rest abode and began this art which thou perceivest, with so great delight that from circling round they ne'er depart.

The beginning of the fall was the accursed pride of him whom thou didst see constrained by all the weights of the universe.

Those whom thou seest here were modest to acknowledge themselves derived from that same Excellence which made them swift to so great understanding;

wherefore their vision was exalted with grace illuminating and with their merit, so that they have their will full and established.

And I would not have thee doubt, but be assured that 'tis a merit to receive the grace by laying the affection open to it.

Now, as concerns this consistory much mayst thou contemplate (if my words have been upgathered) with no other aid.

But since on earth in your school 'tis said in lectures that the angelic nature is such as understandeth and remembereth and willeth,

I will speak on, that thou mayst see in purity the truth that down there is confounded by the equivocations of such like discourse.

These substances, since first they gathered joy from the face of God, have never turned their vision from it wherefrom nought is concealed;

wherefore their sight is never intercepted by a fresh object, and so behoveth not to call aught back to memory because thought hath been cleft.

Wherefore they dream, down there, though sleeping not; thinking or thinking not, they speak the truth; but more in one than other is the fault and shame.

Ye below tread not on one path when ye philosophize, so far doth love of show, and the thought it begets transport you.

Yet even this with lesser indignation is endured here above than when divine Scripture is thrust behind or wrenched aside.

They think not how great the cost of blood to sow it in the world, and how he pleaseth who humbly keepeth by its side.

Each one straineth his wit to make a show and plieth his inventions; and these are handled by the preachers, and the Gospel left in silence.

One saith the moon drew herself back when Christ suffered, and interposed herself that the sun's light spread not itself below;

and others, that the light concealed itself of its own self; wherefore that same eclipse responded to the Spaniards and the Indians as to the Jews.

Florence hath not so many Lapos and Bindos as the fables of such fashion that yearly are proclaimed from the pulpit on this side and on that;

so that the sheep, who know not aught, return from their pasture fed with wind, and not to see their loss doth not excuse them.

Christ said not to his first assembly: *Go and preach trifles to the world;*—but gave to them the true foundation;

that, and that only, sounded on their lips; wherefore for their battle to kindle faith they made both shield and lance out of the Gospel.

Now they go forth with jests and with grimaces to preach, and if loud laughter rise, the hood inflates and no more is required.

But such a bird is nestling in the hood-tail that if the crowd should see it, they would see what pardon they are trusting in;

wherefore such folly hath increased on earth that without proof of any testimony the folk would jump with any promise.

Whereby Antonio fatteneth his swine, and others too, more swinish far than they, paying with money that hath no imprint.

But since we have digressed enough, turn back thine eyes now to the true path, so that our journey may contract with our time.

This nature ranketh so wide in number that ne'er was speech nor thought of mortal that advanced so far:

and if thou look at that which is revealed by Daniel, thou shalt see that in his thousands determinate number is lost to sight.

The primal light which doth o'erray it all, is received by it in so many ways as are the splendours wherewithal it paireth.

Wherefore, since affection followeth on the act that doth conceive, the sweetness of love in diverse fashion boileth or is warm in them.

See now the height and breadth of the eternal worth, since it

hath made itself so many mirrors wherein it breaketh, remaining
in itself one as before."

*When it is dawn with us and noon six thousand miles to the East
of us, and the shadow of the earth cast by the sun is level with the
plane of our horizon, the stars one by one disappear. And in like
manner the angelic rings that seemed to enclose the all-enclosing
divine point gradually disappeared; whereon Dante turned to
Beatrice and saw her of such transcendent beauty that like every
artist who has reached the extreme limit of his skill he must leave
this excess unchronicled. Beatrice tells him that they have now
issued forth from the heaven that compasses all space into the
heaven of light, love, joy, which is not a thing of space, and where
he shall behold the angels, and shall see the elect in the forms they
will wear after the resurrection. A blinding flash of light enwraps
the Poet, and his sight then becomes such that naught can vanquish
it; whereon he sees (first in symbolic form, as by the stream of
Time; then in their true shapes, as gathering round the circle of
Eternity) the things of heaven. The light of God, striking upon the
Primum Mobile, is reflected up upon the ranks of the blest, to
whom it gives power to look upon God himself. Dante, in this region, where far and near have no relevancy, gazes upon the saints
and Beatrice bids him rejoice in their number; and then directs his
sight to one of the few places yet vacant. It is appointed for the
emperor Henry who shall strive to set Italy straight, but shall be
thwarted by the blinding greed of the Italians and the hypocrisy of
Pope Clement, whose fearful fate Beatrice proclaims.*

PERCHANCE six thousand miles away from us blazeth the noon,
and this world already slopeth its shadow as to a level couch,

when the midst of heaven deep above us, beginneth to grow such
that here and there a star loseth power to shine down to this floor;

and as the brightest handmaid of the Sun advanceth, so doth
the heaven close up sight after sight even till the most fair.

Not otherwise the triumph which ever sporteth round the point which vanquished me, seeming embraced by that which it embraceth,

little by little quenched itself from my sight; wherefore my seeing nought, and love, constrained me to turn with mine eyes to Beatrice.

If that which up till here is said of her were all compressed into one act of praise 'twould be too slight to serve this present turn.

The beauty I beheld transcendeth measure, not only past our reach, but surely I believe that only he who made it enjoyeth it complete.

At this pass I yield me vanquished more than e'er yet was overborne by his theme's thrust comic or tragic poet.

For as the Sun in sight that most trembleth, so the remembrance of the sweet smile sheareth my memory of its very self.

From the first day when in this life I saw her face, until this sight, my song hath ne'er been cut off from the track;

but now needs must my tracking cease from following her beauty further forth in poesy, as at his utmost reach must every artist.

Such as I leave her for a mightier proclamation than of my trumpet, which draweth its arduous subject to a close,

with alert leader's voice and gesture, did she again begin: "We have issued forth from the greatest body into the heaven which is pure light,

light intellectual full-charged with love, love of true good full-charged with gladness, gladness which transcendeth every sweetness.

Here shalt thou see the one and the other soldiery of Paradise, and the one in those aspects which thou shalt see at the last judgment."

As a sudden flash of lightning which so shattereth the visual spirits as to rob the eye of power to realize e'en strongest objects;

so there shone around me a living light, leaving me swathed in such a web of its glow that naught appeared to me.

"Ever doth the love which stilleth heaven, receive into itself with such like salutation, duly to fit the taper for its flame."

So soon as these brief words came into me I felt me to surmount my proper power;

and kindled me with such new-given sight that there is no such brightness unalloyed that mine eyes might not hold their own with it.

And I saw a light, in river form, glow tawny betwixt banks painted with marvellous spring.

From out this river issued living sparks, and dropped on every side into the blossoms, like rubies set in gold.

Then as inebriated with the odours they plunged themselves again into the marvellous swirl, and as one entered issued forth another.

"The lofty wish that now doth burn and press thee to have more knowledge of the things thou seest, pleaseth me more the more it swelleth.

But of this water needs thou first must drink, ere so great thirst in thee be slaked." So spoke mine eyes' sun unto me;

then added: "The river and the topaz-gems that enter and go forth, and the smiling of the grasses are the shadowy prefaces of their reality.

Not that such things are harsh as in themselves; but on thy side is the defect, in that thy sight not yet exalteth it so high."

Never doth child so sudden rush with face turned to the milk, if he awake far later than his wont,

as then did I, to make yet better mirrors of mine eyes, down bending to the wave which floweth that we may better us.

And no sooner drank of it mine eye-lids' rim than into roundness seemed to change its length.

Then—as folk under masks seem other than before, if they do off the semblance not their own wherein they hid them,—

so changed before me into ampler joyance the flowers and the sparks, so that I saw both the two courts of heaven manifested.

O splendour of God whereby I saw the lofty triumph of the truthful realm, give me the power to tell how I beheld it.

A light there is up yonder which maketh the Creator visible unto the creature, who only in beholding him hath its own peace;

and it so far outstretcheth circle-wise that its circumference would be too loose a girdle for the sun.

All its appearance is composed of rays reflected from the top of the First Moved, which draweth thence its life and potency.

And as a hill-side reflect itself in water at its foot, as if to look upon its own adornment when it is rich in grasses and in flowers,

so, mounting o'er the light, around, around, casting reflection in more than thousand ranks I saw all that of us hath won return up yonder.

And if the lowest step gathereth so large a light within itself, what then the amplitude of the rose's outmost petals?

My sight in the breadth and height lost itself not, but grasped the scope and nature of that joyance.

Near and far addeth not nor subtracteth there, for where God governeth without medium the law of nature hath no relevance.

Within the yellow of the eternal rose, which doth expand, rank upon rank, and reeketh perfume of praise unto the Sun that maketh spring for ever,

me—as who doth hold his peace yet fain would speak—Beatrice drew, and said: "Behold how great the white-robed concourse!

See how large our city sweepeth! See our thrones so filled that but few folk are now awaited there.

On that great seat where thou dost fix thine eyes, for the crown's sake already placed above it, ere at this wedding feast thyself do sup,

shall sit the soul (on earth 't will be imperial), of the lofty Henry who shall come to straighten Italy ere she be ready for it.

The blind greed which bewitcheth you hath made you like the little child who dieth of hunger and chaseth off his nurse;

and he who then presideth in the court of things divine shall be such an one as, openly and covertly, shall not tread the same path with him.

But short space thereafter shall he be endured of God in the sacred office; for he shall be thrust down where Simon Magus is for his desert, and lower down shall force him of Anagna."

CANTO XXXI

The redeemed are seen, rank above rank, as the petals of the divine rose; and the angels flying between them and God minister peace and ardour to them, for passion is here peaceful and peace passionate. Nor does this angelic multitude intercept the piercing light of God nor the piercing sight of the redeemed. The realm, whose joy no longer needs the stimulus supplied by the fear of losing it or the effort to retain it, centres its look and love on the triune God. Oh! that he would look down on the storm-tossed earth; from the most evil quarter of which Dante coming to that region is smitten dumb by the contrast. Mutely gazing, as the pilgrim at the shrine of his pilgrimage, thinking to tell again what he has seen, Dante after a time turns to question Beatrice, but finds her gone. Bernard, the type of contemplation, or immediate vision, has come at Beatrice's request, to bring Dante to the goal of his desire, by directing his eyes to that actual vision of divine things in their true forms for which her patient instructions have prepared him. And he first directs his sight to Beatrice herself in her place of glory. To her he pours out his gratitude, while imploring her further protection and praying that he may live and die worthy of her love; whereon she smiles upon him and then turns to God in whom alone is true and abiding union of human souls. Dante now learns who his guide is and gazes with awe-struck wonder on the features of the saint who had seen God while yet on earth; then, at his prompting, he looks above and sees the glory of Mary like the glory of the dawn, flaming amongst countless angels—each one having his own specific beauty of light and gesture—and gladdening all the saints.

IN FORM, then, of a white rose displayed itself to me that sacred soldiery which in his blood Christ made his spouse;

but the other, which as it flieth seeth and doth sing his glory who enamoureth it, and the excellence which hath made it what it is,

like to a swarm of bees which doth one while plunge into the flowers and another while wend back to where its toil is turned to sweetness,

ever descended into the great flower adorned with so many leaves, and reascended thence to where its love doth ceaseless make sojourn.

They had their faces all of living flame, and wings of gold, and the rest so white that never snow reacheth such limit.

When they descended into the flower, from rank to rank they proffered of the peace and of the ardour which they acquired as they fanned their sides,

nor did the interposing of so great a flying multitude, betwixt the flower and that which was above, impede the vision nor the splendour;

for the divine light so penetrateth through the universe, in measure of its worthiness, that nought hath power to oppose it.

This realm, secure and gladsome, thronged with ancient folk and new, had look and love all turned unto one mark.

O threefold light, which in a single star, glinting upon their sight doth so content them, look down upon our storm!

If the Barbarians coming from such region as every day is spanned by Helice, wheeling with her son towards whom she yearneth,

on seeing Rome and her mighty works—what time the Lateran transcended mortal things—were stupefied;

what then of me, who to the divine from the human, to the eternal from time had passed, and from Florence to a people just and sane,

with what stupor must I needs be filled! verily, what with it and what with joy, my will was to hear nought and to be dumb myself.

As the pilgrim who doth draw fresh life in the temple of his vow as he gazeth, and already hopeth to tell again how it be placed,

so, traversing the living light, I led mine eyes along the ranks, now up, now down, and now round circling.

I saw countenances suasive of love, adorned by another's light and their own smile, and gestures graced with every dignity.

The general form of Paradise my glance had already taken in, in its entirety, and on no part as yet had my sight paused;

and I turned me with rekindled will to question my Lady concerning things whereanent my mind was in suspense.

One thing I purposed, and another answered me; I thought to see Beatrice, and I saw an elder clad like the folk in glory.

His eyes and cheeks were overpoured with benign gladness, in kindly gesture as befits a tender father.

And: "Where is she?" all sudden I exclaimed; whereunto he: "To bring thy desire to its goal Beatrice moved me from my place; and if thou look up to the circle third from the highest rank, thou shalt re-behold her, on the throne her merits have assigned to her."

Without answering I lifted up mine eyes and saw her, making to herself a crown as she reflected from her the eternal rays.

From that region which thundereth most high, no mortal eye is so far distant, though plunged most deep within the sea,

as there from Beatrice was my sight; but that wrought not upon me, for her image descended not to me mingled with any medium.

"O Lady, in whom my hope hath vigour, and who for my salvation didst endure to leave in Hell thy footprints;

of all the things which I have seen I recognize the grace and might, by thy power and by thine excellence.

Thou hast drawn me from a slave to liberty by all those paths, by all those methods by which thou hadst the power so to do.

Preserve thy munificence in me, so that my soul which thou hast made sound, may unloose it from the body, pleasing unto thee.

So did I pray; and she, so distant as she seemed, smiled and looked on me, then turned her to the eternal fountain.

And the holy elder said: "That thou mayest consummate thy journey perfectly—whereto prayer and holy love dispatched me,—

fly with thine eyes throughout this garden; for gazing on it will equip thy glance better to mount through the divine ray.

And the Queen of heaven for whom I am all burning with love, will grant us every grace, because I am her faithful Bernard."

As is he who perchance from Croatia cometh to look on our Veronica and because of ancient fame is sated not,

but saith in thought, so long as it be shown; "My Lord Jesus Christ, true God, and was this, then, the fashion of thy semblance?"

such was I, gazing upon the living love of him who in this world by contemplation tasted of that peace.

"Son of grace! this joyous being," he began, "will not become known to thee by holding thine eyes only here down at the base;

but look upon the circles even to the remotest, until thou seest enthroned the Queen to whom this realm is subject and devoted."

I lifted up mine eyes, and as at morn the oriental regions of the horizon overcome that where the sun declineth,

so, as from the valley rising to the mountain; with mine eyes I saw a region at the boundary surpass all the remaining ridge in light.

And as with us that place where we await the chariot pole that

Phaëton guided ill, is most aglow, and on this side and on that the light is shorn away;

so was that pacific oriflamme quickened in the midst, on either side in equal measure tempering its flame.

And at that mid point, with out-stretched wings, I saw more than a thousand Angels making festival, each one distinct in glow and art.

I saw there, smiling to their sports and to their songs, a beauty which was gladness in the eyes of all the other saints.

And had I equal wealth in speech as in conception, yet dared I not attempt the smallest part of her delightsomeness.

Bernard, when he saw mine eyes fixed and eager towards the glowing source of his own glow, turned his eyes to her, with so much love that he made mine more ardent to regaze.

CANTO XXXII

Beginning with Mary, Bernard indicates to Dante the great distinctions of heaven. Cleaving the rose downwards into two halves run the lines that part those who looked forward to Christ about to come from those who looked back upon him after he had come. Mary who had faith in Christ before he was conceived ranks as a Hebrew, and John Baptist who, when still in the womb, greeted him and afterwards proclaimed him as already come, ranks as a Christian. The two aspects of the faith embrace equal numbers of saints, the one tale being already full and the other near upon it. Midway across the cleaving lines runs the circle that divides the infants who died ere they had exercised free choice, and who were saved by the faith and the due observances of their parents, from those whose own acts of faith or merit have contributed to their salvation. The children are ranked in accordance with the abysmal but just and orderly judgments of God in the assignment of primal endowment. Dante then gazes in transport upon the face of Mary and sees the rejoicing Gabriel exult before her. He looks upon other great denizens of heaven, and is then bidden to turn again in prayer to Mary that after this so great preparation he may receive from her the final grace to enable him to lift his eyes right upon the Primal Love.

WITH HIS LOVE fixed on his Delight, that contemplating saint took the free office of the teacher on him, and began these sacred words:

"The wound which Mary closed and anointed, she who is so beauteous at her feet opened and thrust.

In the order which the third rank maketh sitteth below her, Rachael with Beatrice, even as thou seest.

Sarah, Rebecca, Judith, and her from whom, third in descent, the singer came who for grief at his sin cried out *have pity on me!*

these mayst thou see from rank to rank descending; even as I, naming their proper names, go down the rose petal by petal.

And down from the seventh onward, even as thereto, follow Hebrew dames, disparting all the flower's locks;

because, accordant with the way faith looked to Christ, these are the partition-wall whereat the sacred steps are parted.

On this side, wherein the flower is mature in all its petals, are seated who believe in Christ to come.

On the other side, where they are broke by empty seats, abide in semi-circles such as had their sight turned towards Christ come.

And as on the one side the glorious seat of the Lady of heaven and the other seats below it make so great partition,

so, over against her, doth the seat of that great John who ever holy endured the desert and the martyr death and thereafter Hell for two years' space;

and beneath him the making of such severance hath been assigned to Francis, Benedict and Augustine, and others down to here from circle unto circle.

Now marvel at the deep divine provision; for either aspect of the faith, in equal measure shall fill full this garden.

And know that, downward from the rank which in mid line cleaveth the two divisions, in virtue of no merit of their own they have their seats,

but by another's, under fixed conditions; for these are spirits all released ere they had exercised true choice.

Well mayst thou perceive it by their faces, and also their child voices if thou look aright and if thou listen.

Now thou art perplexed, and in perplexity thou keepest silence; but I will loose the hard knot for thee wherein thy subtle thoughts are binding thee.

Within this kingdom's amplitude no chance point may have place, no more than sadness may nor thirst, nor hunger;

because established by eternal law is whatsoe'er thou seest, so that the correspondence is exact between the ring and finger.

Wherefore this swift-sped folk to the true life is here, not without cause, more or less excellent in mutual order.

The King through whom this realm resteth in so great love and in so great delight that never will hath daring for aught more,

as he createth all minds in his own glad sight, doth at his pleasure with grace endow them diversely; and here let the effect suffice.

And this, express and clear, is noted unto you in Holy Writ, anent those twins whose wrath was stirred within their mother's womb.

Wherefore accordant to the colour of the locks of such grace, needs must the lofty light enchaplet them after their worth.

Wherefore, without reward for their own ways, they are placed in different ranks, differing only in their primal keenness.

Thus, in the new-born ages the parents' faith alone sufficed, with innocence, to secure salvation;

when the first ages were complete male children behoved to gather power to their innocent wings by circumcision.

But when the time of grace had come, then without perfect baptism of Christ such innocence was held back there below.

Look now upon the face which is most likened unto Christ; for its brightness, and no other, hath power to fit thee to see Christ."

I saw rain down upon that face such joyance (borne on the sacred minds created for flying through that lofty region),

that all which I had seen before held me not in suspense of so great marvelling, nor showed me so great semblance of God.

And that Love which first descended to her, singing: *Hail, Mary, full of grace* now spread his wings before her.

The divine canticle was answered from every side by the blest Court, so that every face thereby gathered serenity.

"O holy Father, who for my sake acceptest being here below, leaving the sweet place wherein thou sittest by eternal lot,

what is that angel who with such delight looketh our Queen in the eyes, enamoured so he seemeth all aflame?"

So did I turn again unto his teaching who drew beauty from Mary, as from the sun the morning star.

And he to me, "Exultancy and winsomeness as much as there may be in angel or in soul, is all in him; and we would have it so,

for he it is who brought down the palm to Mary, when the Son of God willed to load him with our burden.

But come now with thine eyes even as I shall traverse in discourse, and note the great patricians of this most just and pious empire.

Those two who sit up there, most blest by being nearest to the Empress, are as two roots of this our rose.

He who neighboureth her upon the left is that Father because of whose audacious tasting the human race tasteth such bitterness.

On the right, look upon that ancient Father of Holy Church to whom Christ commended the keys of this lovesome flower.

And he who, ere he died, saw all the grievous seasons of that fair spouse who with the lance and with the nails was won,

sitteth by his side; and by the other resteth that leader under whom was fed by manna the folk ungrateful, fickle and mutinous.

Over against Peter see Anna sit, so satisfied to gaze upon her daughter that she removeth not her eyes to sing Hosanna.

And o'er against the greatest of housefathers sitteth Lucy who moved thy Lady when thou wert stooping down thy brows to thy destruction.

But since the time that doth entrance thee fleeth, here let us make a stop, like to the careful tailor who to the cloth he hath cutteth the garment;

and let us turn our eyes to the Primal Love, so that gazing toward him thou mayst pierce as far as may be into his shining.

But—lest perchance thou backward fall as thou dost ply thy wings, thinking to forward thee,—by prayer behoveth grace to be acquired,

grace from her who hath power to aid thee; and do thou follow me with such affection that from my words thy heart be severed not." And he began this holy prayer.

CANTO XXXIII

The final goal of divine Providence, the mysteries of the incarnation and the redemption, the contrast between earthly hope and heavenly fruition, the whole order of the spiritual universe epitomized in the Poet's journey, the crowning grace still awaiting him, the need of yet further purging away of mortal dross if he is to receive it, the high obligation that will rest upon his life hereafter, the sustaining grace that will be needed to enable him to meet it by keeping his affections true to so great a vision, and the intense sympathy with which all the saints enter into his aspiration and plead for the fulfilment of the utmost grace to him as a part of their own bliss,—all this, with the praises of the Virgin, etherialized into the very perfume of devotion, rises in Bernard's prayer to Mary. Mary answers the prayer by looking into the light of God, thereby to gain Bernard's petition for Dante; and Dante, anticipating Bernard's permission, with the passion of his longing already assuaged by the peace of now assured fruition, looks right into the deep light. Memory cannot hold the experience that then was his, though it retains the sweetness that was born of it. But as he gropes for the recovery of some fragment of his vision, he feels in the throb of an ampler joy the assurance that he is touching on the truth as he records his belief that he saw the whole essence of the universe, all beings and all their attributes and all their relations, no longer as scattered and imperfect fragments, but as one perfect whole, and that whole naught else than one single flame of love. So keen is the light of that flame that it would shrivel up the sight if it should turn aside. But that may not be, since good, which is the object of all volition, is whole and perfect in it, and only fragmentary and imperfect away from it, so that a free will cannot by its nature turn away; and the sight is ever strengthened that turns right into it. As when we look upon a picture or a script, glorious but at first imperfectly mastered by us, and as our eyes slowly adjust themselves, the details rise and assert themselves and take their places, and all the while that the impression changes and deepens the thing that we look upon changes not nor even seems to change, but only we to see it clearer, so Dante's kindling vision reads deeper and deeper into the unchanging glory of the triune Deity, till his mind fastens itself upon the contemplation of the union (in the second Person) of the circle of Deity and the featured countenance of humanity—the unconditioned self-completeness of God that reverent thought asserts and the character and features which the heart demands and which its experience proclaims,—but his powers fail to grapple with the contradiction till the reconciliation is brought home to him in a flash of exalted insight. Then the vision passes away and may not be recalled, but already all jarring protest and opposition to the divine order has given way in the seer's heart to oneness of wish and will with God, who himself is love.

"VIRGIN MOTHER, daughter of thy son, lowly and uplifted more than any creature, fixed goal of the eternal counsel,

thou art she who didst human nature so ennoble that its own Maker scorned not to become its making.

In thy womb was lit again the love under whose warmth in the eternal peace this flower hath thus unfolded.

Here art thou unto us the meridian torch of love and there below with mortals art a living spring of hope.

Lady, thou art so great and hast such worth, that if there be who would have grace yet betaketh not himself to thee, his longing seeketh to fly without wings.

Thy kindliness not only succoureth whoso requesteth, but doth oftentimes freely forerun request.

In thee is tenderness, in thee is pity, in thee munificence, in thee united whatever in created being is of excellence.

Now he who from the deepest pool of the universe even to here hath seen the spirit lives one after one

imploreth thee, of grace, for so much power as to be able to uplift his eyes more high towards final bliss;

and I, who never burned for my own vision more than I do for his, proffer thee all my prayers and pray they be not scant

that thou do scatter for him every cloud of his mortality with prayers of thine, so that the joy supreme may be unfolded to him.

And further do I pray thee, Queen who canst all that thou wilt, that thou keep sound for him, after so great a vision, his affections.

Let thy protection vanquish human ferments; see Beatrice, with how many Saints, for my prayers folding hands."

Those eyes, of God beloved and venerated, fixed upon him who prayed, showed us how greatly devout prayers please her.

Then to the eternal light they bent themselves, wherein we may not ween that any creature's eye findeth its way so clear.

And I, who to the goal of all my longings was drawing nigh, even as was meet the ardour of the yearning quenched within me.

Bernard gave me the sign and smiled to me that I should look on high, but I already of myself was such as he would have me;

because my sight, becoming purged, now more and more was entering through the ray of the deep light which in itself is true.

Thence forward was my vision mightier than our discourse, which faileth at such sight, and faileth memory at so great outrage.

As is he who dreaming seeth, and when the dream is gone the passion stamped remaineth, and naught else cometh to the mind again;

even such am I; for almost wholly faileth me my vision, yet doth the sweetness that was born of it still drop within my heart.

So doth the snow unstamp it to the sun, so to the wind on the light leaves was lost the Sybil's wisdom.

O light supreme who so far dost uplift thee o'er mortal thoughts, re-lend unto my mind a little of what then thou didst seem,

and give my tongue such power that it may leave only a single sparkle of thy glory unto the folk to come;

for by returning to my memory somewhat, and by a little sounding in these verses, more of thy victory will be conceived.

I hold that by the keenness of the living ray which I endured I had been lost, had mine eyes turned aside from it.

And so I was the bolder, as I mind me, so long to sustain it as to unite my glance with the Worth infinite.

O grace abounding, wherein I presumed to fix my look on the eternal light so long that I consumed my sight thereon!

Within its depths I saw ingathered, bound by love in one volume, the scattered leaves of all the universe;

substance and accidents and their relations, as though together fused, after such fashion that what I tell of is one simple flame.

The universal form of this complex I think that I beheld, because more largely, as I say this, I feel that I rejoice.

A single moment maketh a deeper lethargy for me than twenty

and five centuries have wrought on the emprise that erst threw Neptune in amaze at Argo's shadow.

Thus all suspended did my mind gaze fixed, immovable, intent, ever enkindled by its gazing.

Such at that light doth man become that to turn thence to any other sight could not by possibility be ever yielded.

For the good, which is the object of the will, is therein wholly gathered, and outside it that same thing is defective which therein is perfect.

Now shall my speech fall farther short even of what I can remember than an infant's who still bathes his tongue at breast.

Not that more than a single semblance was in the living light whereon I looked, which ever is such as it was before;

but by the sight that gathered strength in me one sole appearance even as I changed worked on my gaze.

In the profound and shining being of the deep light appeared to me three circles, of three colours and one magnitude;

one by the second as Iris by Iris seemed reflected, and the third seemed a fire breathed equally from one and from the other.

Oh but how scant the utterance, and how faint, to my conceit! and it, to what I saw, is such that it sufficeth not to call it little.

O Light eternal who only in thyself abidest, only thyself dost understand, and to thyself, self-understood self-understanding, turnest love and smiling!

That circling which appeared in thee to be conceived as a reflected light, by mine eyes scanned some little,

in itself, of its own colour, seemed to be painted with our effigy, and thereat my sight was all committed to it.

As the geometer who all sets himself to measure the circle and who findeth not, think as he may, the principle he lacketh;

such was I at this new-seen spectacle; I would perceive how the image consorteth with the circle, and how it settleth there;

but not for this were my proper wings, save that my mind was smitten by a flash wherein its will came to it.

To the high fantasy here power failed; but already my desire and will were rolled—even as a wheel that moveth equally—by the Love that moves the sun and the other stars.

FRANCIS PETRARCH

to DENIS *of* BORGO-SAN SEPOLCRO *of the* ORDER *of* St. AUGUSTINE *Professor of* SACRED SCRIPTURE CONCERNING HIS OWN CARES[1]

> What I was wont to love, now I do not love; I lie:
> I do love, but more moderately. Behold, once more I
> lie: I do love, but with more shame and sadness. Now
> finally I have spoken the truth.

ON APRIL 6, 1327, when he was twenty-three years old, Petrarch (1304-1374) first met Laura. She became for him the muse of his poetry; and if in life she was never more to him than a muse, he loved her with a passion and a lust that were to embark him on a long moral struggle until he found peace some sixteen years later. When he wrote the present letter in 1336, he had been reading the *Confessions* of St. Augustine for some three years. In St. Augustine's moral storms he saw his own. The vision of Laura had begun in Petrarch's soul a brilliant literary career; St. Augustine taught him not only that simple devotion to Christ which was to set him against the novelties of the dialectical theologians, but also the return to Christ from the wilderness of immorality. On the top of Mount Ventoux with his brother Gherardo, Petrarch opened the *Confessions of St. Augustine* and then went on to recall the words of St. Paul, "Not in revelling . . ." There was

[1] *Familiarium Rerum,* IV, 1. Francesco Petrarca, *Le Familiari,* ed. Vittorio Rossi, I (Florence, 1933), pp. 153-161.

no doubt in Petrarch's mind that it was God Who, through Augustine, directed him to the reading of Paul, even as He had directed Augustine. And Petrarch slowly began to put on the Lord Jesus interiorly, even as he proclaimed Him exteriorly against the philosophizing theologians and the Aristotelians.

ODAY I CLIMBED THE HIGHEST MOUNTAIN OF this district, which is not unsuitably called *Ventoux*,[2] induced by the sole desire of seeing the extraordinary height of the place. For many years I had had this excursion in mind. For from childhood, as you know, by the fate which rules the affairs of men I have spent my time in these places; and this mountain, visible for a great distance from all sides, is almost constantly in view. Finally the impulse seized me long and last to do what I was today doing, especially since, while reading, there chanced to occur to me the spot in Livy's Roman History [3] where King Philip of Macedon—he who waged war against the Roman People—made the ascent of Mount Haemus in Thessaly,[4] from whose top he believed the report that two seas could be seen, the Adriatic and the Euxine. On whether he believed truly or falsely, I have not sufficient information, both because the mountain is far from our territory and the disagreement of writers makes it doubtful. Not to run over the whole list, Pomponius Mela the cosmographer unhesitatingly states it to be true; [5] Titus Livy thinks it false. For myself, if a test of that mountain were as easy as this one, I should not suffer for long any doubts. But to get back to the present mountain and leave off the former, what was not blameworthy in a king advanced in years seemed excusable in a youthful private citizen.

But strange to say, in thinking over a companion, scarcely any of my friends seemed wholly acceptable; so rare indeed, even among dear friends, is there that perfect agreement of every desire and habit. This one was too lazy, that one too observant; one too slow

[2] *Ventosa* = windy.   [3] Bk. I, c. 21, 2.
[4] This is evidently a mistake. It should be Thrace.
[5] *De Chorographia*, Bk. II, c. 17.

of foot, another too agile; one too gloomy, another too cheerful; finally one was too silly, another more sagacious than I should have liked. The reticence of one, the volubility of another, the weight and obesity of one and the lankness and languor of another held me back. The cold indifference of this one, the excited attention of the other discouraged me. And these things, although burdensome, are tolerable at home—for Charity suffers all things and friendship refuses no burden; these same things actually while on a journey become too irksome. And so my discerning mind, desirous of upright pleasure, circumspectly weighed each and every circumstance, without any injury to friendship, and quietly condemned whatever it saw could be an annoyance on the intended trip. And what do you suppose? I finally turned to my own household for help and made known the design to my one and only brother, younger than I, whom you know well. There is nothing which he could have heard with greater pleasure, happy because he held in my regard the place of friend as well as brother. On the set day we left home and came by evening to Malaucène; the place is in the foothills facing the mountain on the north. After having spent one day there, today, along with our respective servants, we climbed the mountain, not without a good deal of difficulty, for it was a steep and almost inaccessible mass of rocky earth. But it has been well said by the Poet: [6] "Persistent toil overcomes all." The travellers enjoyed a long day, balmy weather, energy of mind, strength and agility of body, as well as what belongs to these categories. Our sole obstacle was the nature of the place. On the mountain slopes we came upon a shepherd, advanced in years, who profusely tried to restrain us from the climb. He told us that fifty years before he himself, from a like impulse of youthful enthusiasm, had climbed to the very top and had brought back nothing but regrets and labour, a body and clothes torn by rocks and brambles; and that no one of the district had either before that time or afterwards been heard to have attempted a like experience. While he was giving voice to all this, our desire increased because of the dissuasion, since the youthful mind is skeptical of advisers. And so when the old man saw that his attempts were to no avail, he went along with us a bit and pointed out with his finger the difficult

[6] Virgil. *Georgics,* I, 145.

mountain path, all the while giving us much advice over and over again, still lamenting after we had left him behind. We left with him whatever clothes or effects that might be a hindrance on the journey, girded ourselves simply for the excursion alone and joyfully made the ascent. But as usually happens, fatigue followed hard upon our mighty effort. Consequently not far from there we stopped on a rock. Setting out hence once again we carried on, but more slowly. I especially tread along the mountain path at a more moderate gait. My brother, however, sought the heights by a shorter route through the ridges of the mountain itself. I, being softer, turned towards the lower sections, and replied to him, when he shouted and pointed out to me a straighter path, that I was looking for the easier approach on the other side and that I had no fear of the longer route by which it was possible to walk along more level ground. I made this pretence of an excuse for my laziness, and when the others were already on the heights, I wandered through the valley, since no easier approach opened up from any other direction. The distance increased and my useless toil grew more arduous.

Meanwhile, overcome with fatigue, I began to regret the fruitless wandering and fully decided to head for the heights. And when tired and worried I caught sight of my brother, who was refreshed by a considerable rest, we walked along for some time side by side. When we had scarcely left that hill, lo and behold I forgot the former tortuous route and went again down to the lower ground and, once more pursuing the long and easy expanse of the way, I wandered through the valleys and fell into serious difficulty. Obviously I kept putting off the trial of the ascent; but the nature of things is not taken away by the contrivances of man, nor does it ever come about that anything bodily reach the top by descending. Why go through the many details? In the space of a few hours this happened three or four times to me already disgusted, while my brother laughed at me.

Thus often mocked I sat down in a valley. There passing from the corporeal to the incorporeal in fleeting meditation I addressed myself in these or like words: "Be sure that what you have experienced today in the ascent of this mountain happens to you and to many others on their path to the blessed life. The reason this is not so readily seen by men is because the motions of the body are apparent, of the soul, however, invisible and hidden. To be sure, the life which they call blessed is seated on a lofty place, and a narrow path, it is said, leads to it.[7] Likewise there are many hills in evidence and we must march from virtue to virtue with noble strides. On the top is the end of all men and the goal of the route towards which our pilgrimage is aimed. Thither all wish to go, but, as Ovid [8] says: 'To wish is not enough, you must desire to take possession of the thing.' Certainly, unless in this as in many another thing you are deceived, you not only wish, but also desire. What then holds you back? Doubtlessly nothing but the evener and easier route, as it appears on the surface, through the basest pleasures of earth. Nonetheless when you have wandered a good deal, it is necessary either that you climb the heights of the blessed life carrying the weight of a wrongfully deferred labour or sink down inertly in the valley of your sins. And if there, which I tremble to forbode, the darkness of the shadow of death [9] come upon you, you will spend an eternal night in perpetual torments."

Strange to say, these thoughts buoyed me up in both body and soul for what was yet to come. And would indeed I might likewise travel in soul that route, for which I sigh day and night, as I travelled with bodily feet today's route, once I had overcome the difficulties. And I know not whether it ought to be easier by far for the immortal soul to bring about in the flicker of an eye and without any local motion what must be executed through the medium of a frail and sickly body laden with the heavy burden of its members.

The tallest hill of all is the one which the woodsmen call "The Little Son". I know not why unless it is, as in so many other cases, by way of antiphrasis, for indeed it seems to be the father of all the surrounding mountains. There is a small flat surface on top of that mountain, where finally tired out we rested. And since you have heard the cares which arose in the bosom of him who made the ascent, listen also, father, to what came after. And I ask one thing of you: give an hour of your time to read about what I did on that one day.

First of all, exhilarated by the unaccustomed lightness of the air

7 *Matt.* vii, 14.   8 *Ex Ponto* III, 1, 35.   9 *Ps.* c, 10-14.

and the more extensive view, I stood as one amazed. I looked back; the clouds were beneath my feet; already Athos and Olympus are become less incredible to me as I see upon a mountain of lesser fame what I had heard and read of them. Next I focus my eyes in the direction of Italy whither my heart is more inclined. The very Alps, cold and snow-capped (through which that barbarous enemy of the Roman Name crossed, breaking through the rocks with vinegar, if we believe the report) seemed very near to me, even though they are afar off. I confess I sighed for the Italian sky, visible to my soul rather than my eyes, and an incalculable desire to see once more my friend and fatherland came over me. And yet I blamed the softness of an affection not yet grown manly, although in both cases the excuse would not be without the support of great witnesses in either event.

Then a new thought took possession of my soul and transported me from the realm of place to that of time. For I said to myself: "Today the tenth year has rolled by since you completed your boyhood studies and left Bologna. And O immortal God, O changeless Wisdom! How many changes in your way of life has this intervening period not witnessed? I pass over innumerable things, for I am not yet in the harbour so that I can recall in security passed storms. Perhaps the time will come when I can run over all the things in the order in which they happened, repeating that saying of your Augustine: [10] 'I like to recall the foulness which I have perpetrated and my carnal corruptions, not because I love them, but that I may love Thee, my God.' In fact for me there still remained much that was uncertain and many difficulties. What I was wont to love, now I do not love; I lie: I do love, but more moderately. Behold once more I lie: I do love, but with more shame and sadness. Now finally I have spoken the truth. For thus it is: I love, but what I would not love, what I would hate. Nonetheless I love, but unwillingly, forced, sorrowful and lamenting, and I dejectedly experience in myself the sentiment of that famous verse: [11] 'I shall hate if I can; if not, I shall love unwillingly.' Three years had not yet passed me by, from the time that that distorted and evil will, which possessed me entirely, and which reigned unopposedly in the confines of my heart, began to have a rebellious and contrary desire.

[10] *Conf.* II, i, i.   [11] Ovid, *De Arte Amandi*, III, ii, 35.

And between these, now for a long time, a distressful and dubious battle has raged within the domain of my thoughts over the sway of the two men."

Thus was I absorbed in thought about the past ten years and I directed my attention from hence to the times that lay ahead of me and besought myself: "If perchance it were to happen that you prolonged this fleeting life through another ten years and were to make proportionate progress in virtue as in the last two years and have left behind the former contumacy through the conflict of the new against the old will, could you not then, although not certainly, but at least hopefully, meet death at your fortieth year, and with equanimity forget about that remnant of life in fleeting old age?" These and like thoughts, father, kept running through my bosom. I rejoiced at my progress, I wept over my imperfection and commiserated the common vagaries of human conduct. Somehow I forgot whither I had come and why, until setting aside my cares for which another place would be more suitable, I looked about and saw what I had come to see. Admonished that the time to leave was close at hand, as already the sun was setting, I turned around towards the west. The top of the Pyrenees, the boundary line between France and Spain, cannot be seen from that point, not because of any intervening obstacle that I know, but by the weakness alone of mortal vision. At the right were clearly visible, though several days' journey distant, the mountains of the province of Lyons; at the left the Bay of Marseilles which beats against the shores of Aigues Mortes. The Rhone itself lay under our eyes.

And while I was wondering at these things individually, and was enjoying the earthly objects and lifting my soul up after the example of my body, it seemed fitting for me to look up the book of Augustine's *Confessions* which you had given me as a token of affection, and which I keep in my possession, always at hand, as a memorial of the author and giver. It is a handy little work, small in size, but of immeasurable sweetness. I opened it with the intention of reading whatever turned up. For what could turn up except what is pious and devout? By chance the tenth book of that work presented itself. My brother stood by with attentive ears expecting to hear me read something from Augustine. I call God to witness and him who was present to what was written where I first fixed my eyes: [12] "And men go forth to admire the heights of mountains and the mighty billows of the sea, the broad tides of rivers and the compass of the ocean, the orbit of the stars, and forget themselves." I confess I was amazed. I asked my brother, who was eager to hear, not to bother me, and I closed the book. I was angry with myself because even now I was admiring what is of the earth, I, who already ought to have learned from the pagan philosophers that only the mind is worthy of wonder, in comparison with which noble thing nothing else is great.

Then, indeed, satisfied that I had seen enough of the mountain, I turned my interior eyes upon myself and from that hour on no one heard me speak until we reached the bottom. That text made me quite aware of an unmentioned business. I could not make myself think that it happened to me by chance, but rather whatever I read there I considered as spoken to myself and no one else. I recalled that Augustine himself once supposed the same thing about himself, when, as he himself relates,[13] there first occurred to him while reading the text of the Apostle: *Not in revelling and in drunkenness, not in lust and wantonness, not in quarrels and rivalries. Rather arm yourselves with the Lord Jesus Christ; spend no more thought on nature and nature's appetites.*[14] And this had already happened to Anthony, when he heard the section of the Gospel read: *If thou hast a mind to be perfect, go home and sell all that belongs to thee; give it to the poor, and so the treasure thou hast shall be in heaven; then come back and follow me,*[15] as if this text of Scripture had been written for himself, as his biographer Athanasius tells us, he took to himself the Lord's command.[16] And just as Anthony, upon hearing these words, sought nothing else, and as Augustine, when he read that text, looked no further, so also did I myself stop reading with the few words I have mentioned above. In silence I turned over in my mind thoughts about the lack of counsel among mortals, who, neglecting their most noble endowment, and seeking without what is to be found within, are distracted by the multiplicity of things and dissipated by empty show. I was in wonder at the nobility of the mind, if it has not willingly deviated from its pristine beginnings, and turned what

---

[12] *Conf.* X, 8, 15. [13] *Conf.* VIII, 12, 29. [14] *Rom.* xiii, 13.
[15] *Matt.* xix, 21. [16] *Patrologia Graeca*, 26, 842 B-C.

God gave it as an honour into dishonour. How often on that day, think you, did I not on the return journey look back upon the peak of the mountain! In comparison with the loftiness of human contemplation, unless one is mired in earthly corruptions, its height appeared to be scarcely a cubit in height. A thought kept occurring to me at every step. If one were not slow to undergo so much sweat and toil to bring the body closer to the heavens, what cross, what prison, what rock should terrify the mind from approaching God and from trampling underfoot the puffed-up heights of insolence and mortal fate? There also kept occurring to me this thought: to how many will it happen that they will not turn from this path either through fear of difficulties or through love of comfort? O how happy is he, if anywhere there is such a one as the Poet had in mind: "Happy is he who has been able to learn the causes of things and subdues all fears and implacable fate and the noise of greedy hell beneath his feet." [17] And how zealously we should strive, not to seek a higher spot on earth, but to keep our desires, enticed by earthly allurements, beneath our feet. Amid these emotions of my agitated breast and quite unconscious of the stony path, late at night I wandered back to the little rustic hospice whence I had gone forth before dawn; the full moon gave us acceptable assistance as we went along.

Meanwhile, when the servants were busy preparing the meal, I went off alone to a secluded part of the house to write this hurriedly and on the spur of the moment, lest perhaps, if I put it off, my intention of writing would weaken, my dispositions changing with the change of place. See then, my very dear father, that I want nothing in me to be hidden from your eyes, I who not only disclose to you my whole life, but so minutely make manifest my individual thoughts. And for these thoughts I beg your prayers, that long and last, unstable and fickle as they are, they may sometime stand fast, and after much tossing about may they turn to the one, true, certain and enduring good. Fare thee well.

Malaucène, April 26, 1336 [?]

[17] Virgil, *Georgics*, II, 490.

FRANÇOIS VILLON

THE BALLADE *to* OUR LADY

Dame du ciel, Regente terrienne

> But all mine undeserving may not mar
> Such mercies as thy sovereign mercies are.

HIS OWN NAME was François de Montcorbier, but Villon took that of the priest who brought him up, Guillaume de Villon. He was born in Paris in 1431, and disappears from history in 1463. Our knowledge of him, as it has been said, is based on the university and police records of the time. Villon was a gifted poet, who in his most vagabond moments retained a haunting awareness of death. Where, he asks in a famous ballade, where are the snows of yesteryear? Yet the grimness of death is lost in the faith and the hope expressed in the following tender ballade, written by Villon for his mother.

LADY OF HEAVEN AND EARTH, AND THEREWITHAL,
Crowned Empress of the nether clefts of Hell,
I, thy poor Christian, on thy name do call,
Commending me to thee, with thee to dwell,
Albeit in nought I be commendable.
But all mine undeserving may not mar
Such mercies as thy sovereign mercies are;
Without the which (as true words testify)
No soul can reach thy Heaven so fair and far.
Even in this faith I choose to live and die.

Unto thy Son say thou that I am His,
And to me graceless make Him gracious.
Sad Mary of Egypt lacked not of that bliss,
Nor yet the sorrowful clerk Theophilus,
Whose bitter sins were set aside even thus
Though to the Fiend his bounden service was.
Oh help me, lest in vain for me should pass
(Sweet Virgin that shalt have no loss thereby)
The blessed Host and sacring of the Mass.
Even in this faith I choose to live and die.

A pitiful poor woman, shrunk and old,
I am, and nothing learn'd in letter-lore:
Within my parish-cloister I behold
A painted Heaven where harps and lutes adore,
And eke a Hell whose damned folk seethe full sore:
One bringeth fear, the other joy to me.
That joy, great Goddess, make thou mine to be—
Thou of whom all must ask it, even as I;
And that which faith desires, that let it see.
For in this faith I choose to live and die.

ENVOY

O excellent Virgin Princess! Thou didst bear
King Jesus, our most excellent Comforter,
Who even of this our weakness craved a share
And for our sake stooped to us from on high,
Offering to death His young life sweet and fair.
Such as He is, Our Lord, I Him declare
And in this faith I choose to live and die.

GEOFFREY CHAUCER

THE PARSON'S TALE

(from *The Canterbury Tales*)

For soothly, oure swete lord Jesu Crist hath spared
us so debonairly in our folies, that if he ne hadde pitee
of mannes soule, a sory song we mighten alle singe.

CHAUCER WAS BORN in London in 1340. From his early days he
was engaged in commissions for the King on the continent. He
died in 1400. *The Canterbury Tales,* written in the last decade of
the fourteenth century, has been compared with the *Divine Comedy.* There can be little doubt that Chaucer does not have the exalted and almost apocalyptic vision of Dante. Yet there is also no
doubt that Chaucer wrote of humanity, its saints and its sinners, its
virtues and its vices, its vanities and its vulgarities, with optimism
and sympathy, perspective and understanding. *The Canterbury
Tales* is no journey through human history, or to hell and heaven;
there is no Virgil, no Beatrice, no St. Bernard in it. The scene is
an Inn, and the characters are an assorted lot of men and women,
seen in midpassage, on a pilgrimage to Canterbury. They are
Christian wayfarers, their Redeemer is Christ, and from the lovable Parson they learn "Christes lore," how "there are many spiritual ways that lead man to our Lord Jesus Christ, and to the Kingdom of glory." Of these there is one which admirably meets the
needs of the man or woman "who has strayed from the straight

way to the heavenly Jerusalem." This "very noble way" is Repentance.

And now the company of twenty-nine people, who trooped into the Inn where Chaucer had stopped on the way to Canterbury, receive a lesson on contrition.

✠

HERE FOLLOWETH THE PROLOGE OF THE PERSONES TALE

BY THAT the maunciple hadde his tale al ended,
The sonne fro the south lyne was descended
So lowe, that he nas nat, to my sighte,
Degreës nyne and twenty as in highte.
Foure of the clokke it was tho, as I gesse:
For eleven foot, or litel more or lesse,
My shadwe was at thilke tyme, as there.
Of swich feet as my lengthe parted were
In six feet equal of proporcioun.
Ther-with the mones exaltacioun,
I mene Libra, alwey gan ascende,
As we were entringe at a thropes ende;
For which our host, as he was wont to gye,
As in this caas, our joly companye,
Seyde in this wyse, 'lordings everichoon,
Now lakketh us no tales mo than oon.
Fulfild is my sentence and my decree;
I trowe that we han herd of ech degree.
Almost fulfild is al myn ordinaunce;
I prey to god, so yeve him right good chaunce,
That telleth this tale to us lustily.
Sir preest,' quod he, 'artow a vicary?
Or art a person? sey sooth, by thy fey!
Be what thou be, ne breke thou nat our pley;
For every man, save thou, hath told his tale.
Unbokel, and shewe us what is in thy male;

For trewely, me thinketh, by thy chere,
Thou sholdest knitte up wel a greet matere.
Tel us a tale anon, for cokkes bones!'
        This Persone him answerde, al at ones,
'Thou getest fable noon y-told for me;
For Paul, that wryteth unto Timothee,
Repreveth hem that weyven soothfastnesse,
And tellen fables and swich wrecchednesse.
Why sholde I sowen draf out of my fest,
Whan I may sowen whete, if that me lest?
For which I seye, if that yow list to here
Moralitee and vertuous matere,
And thanne that ye wol yeve me audience,
I wol ful fayn, at Cristes reverence,
Do yow plesaunce leefful, as I can.
But trusteth wel, I am a Southren man,
I can nat geste—rum, ram, ruf—by lettre,
Ne, god wot, rym holde I but litel bettre;
And therfor, if yow list, I wol nat glose.
I wol yow telle a mery tale in prose
To knitte up al this feeste, and make an ende.
And Jesu, for his grace, wit me sende
To shewe yow the wey, in this viage,
Of thilke parfit glorious pilgrimage
That highte Jerusalem celestial.
And, if ye vouche-sauf, anon I shal
Biginne upon my tale, for whiche I preye
Telle your avys, I can no bettre seye.
But nathelees, this meditacioun
I putte it ay under correccioun
Of clerkes, for I am nat textuel;
I take but the sentens, trusteth wel.
Therfor I make protestacioun
That I wol stonde to correccioun.'
        Up-on this word we han assented sone,
For, as us semed, it was for to done,
To enden in som vertuous sentence,
And for to yeve him space and audience;

And bede our host he sholde to him seye,
That alle we to telle his tale him preye.
　　Our host hadde the wordes for us alle:—
'Sir preest,' quod he, 'now fayre yow bifalle?
Sey what yow list, and we wol gladly here'—
And with that word he seyde in this manere—
'Telleth,' quod he, 'your meditacioun.
But hasteth yow, the sonne wol adoun;
Beth fructuous, and that in litel space,
And to do wel god sende yow his grace!'

Explicit prohemium

HERE BEGINNETH THE PERSONES TALE

Jer. 6°. State super vias et videte et interrogate de viis antiquis, que sit via bona; et ambulate in ea, et inuenietis refrigerium animabus vestris, &c.

¶ 1. Our swete lord god of hevene, that no man wol perisse, but wole that we comen alle to the knoweleche of him, and to the blisful lyf that is perdurable, amonesteth us by the prophete Jeremie, that seith in this wyse: 'stondeth upon the weyes, and seeth and axeth of olde pathes (that is to seyn, of olde sentences) which is the goode wey; and walketh in that wey, and ye shul finde refresshinge for your soules,' &c. Manye been the weyes espirituels that leden folk to oure Lord Jesu Crist, and to the regne of glorie. Of whiche weyes, ther is a ful noble wey and a ful covenable, which may nat faile to man ne to womman, that thurgh sinne hath misgoon fro the righte wey of Jerusalem celestial; and this wey is cleped Penitence, of which man sholde gladly herknen and enquere with al his herte; to witen what is Penitence, and whennes it is cleped Penitence, and in how manye maneres been the accions or werkinges of Penitence, and how manye spyces ther ben of Penitence, and whiche thinges apertenen and bihoven to Penitence, and whiche thinges destourben Penitence.

¶ 2. Seint Ambrose seith, that 'Penitence is the pleyninge of man for the gilt that he hath doon, and na-more to do anything for which him oghte to pleyne.' And som doctour seith: 'Penitence is the waymentinge of man, that sorweth for his sinne and peyneth himself for he hath misdoon.' Penitence, with certeyne circumstances, is verray repentance of a man that halt him-self in sorwe and other peyne for hise giltes. And for he shal be verray penitent, he shal first biwailen the sinnes that he hath doon, and stidefastly purposen in his herte to have shrift of mouthe, and to doon satisfaccioun, and never to doon thing for which him oghte more to biwayle or to compleyne, and to continue in goode werkes: or elles his repentance may nat availle. For as seith seint Isidre: 'he is a japer and a gabber, and no verray repentant, that eftsoone doth thing, for which him oghte repente.' Wepinge, and not for to stinte to doon sinne, may nat avaylle. But nathelees, men shal hope that every tyme that man falleth, be it never so ofte, that he may arise thurgh Penitence, if he have grace: but certeinly it is greet doute. For as seith Seint Gregorie: 'unnethe aryseth he out of sinne, that is charged with the charge of yvel usage.' And therfore repentant folk, that stinte for to sinne, and forlete sinne er that sinne forlete hem, holy chirche holdeth hem siker of hir savacioun. And he that sinneth, and verraily repenteth him in his laste ende, holy chirche yet hopeth his savacioun, by the grete mercy of oure lord Jesu Crist, for his repentaunce; but tak the siker way.

¶ 3. And now, sith I have declared yow what thing is Penitence, now shul ye understonde that ther been three accions of Penitence. The firste accion of Penitence is, that a man be baptized after that he hath sinned. Seint Augustin seith: 'but he be penitent for his olde sinful lyf, he may nat biginne the newe clene lif.' For certes, if he be baptized withouten penitence of his olde gilt, he receiveth the mark of baptisme, but nat the grace ne the remission of his sinnes, til he have repentance verray. Another defaute is this, that men doon deedly sinne after that they han received baptisme. The thridde defaute is, that men fallen in venial sinnes after hir baptisme, fro day to day. Ther-of seith Seint Augustin, that 'penitence of goode and humble folk is the penitence of every day.'

¶ 4. The spyces of Penitence been three. That oon of hem is solempne, another is commune, and the thridde is privee. Thilke penance that is solempne, is in two maneres; as to be put out of holy
chirche in lente, for slaughtre of children, and swich maner thing.
Another is, whan a man hath sinned openly, of which sinne the fame
is openly spoken in the contree; and thanne holy chirche by jugement
destreineth him for to do open penaunce. Commune penaunce is that
preestes enjoinen men comunly in certeyn caas; as for to goon,
peraventure, naked in pilgrimages, or barefoot. Privee penaunce is
thilke that men doon alday for privee sinnes, of which we shryve us
prively and receyve privee penaunce.

¶ 5. Now shaltow understande what is bihovely and necessarie to
verray parfit Penitence. And this stant on three thinges: Contricioun
of herte, Confessioun of Mouth, and Satisfaccioun. For which seith
Seint John Crisostom: 'Penitence destreyneth a man to accepte
benignely every peyne that him is enjoyned, with contricion of
herte, and shrift of mouth, with satisfaccioun; and in werkinge of
alle maner humilitee.' And this is fruitful Penitence agayn three
thinges in whiche we wratthe oure lord Jesu Crist: this is to seyn,
by delyt in thinkinge, by recchelesnesse in spekinge, and by wikked
sinful werkinge. And agayns thise wikked giltes is Penitence, that
may be lykned un-to a tree.

¶ 6. The rote of this tree is Contricion, that hydeth him in the
herte of him that is verray repentant, right as the rote of a tree
hydeth him in the erthe. Of the rote of Contricion springeth a
stalke, that bereth braunches and leves of Confession, and fruit of
Satisfaccion. For which Crist seith in his gospel: 'dooth digne
fruit of Penitence'; for by this fruit may men knowe this tree, and
nat by the rote that is hid in the herte of man, ne by the braunches
ne by the leves of Confession. And therefore oure Lord Jesu Crist
seith thus: 'by the fruit of hem ye shul knowen hem.' Of this rote
eek springeth a seed of grace, the which seed is moder of siker-
nesse, and this seed is egre and hoot. The grace of this seed
springeth of god, thurgh remembrance of the day of dome and on
the peynes of helle. Of this matere seith Salomon, that 'in the
drede of god man forleteth his sinne.' The hete of this seed is the
love of god, and the desiring of the joye perdurable. This hete
draweth the herte of a man to god, and dooth him haten his sinne.

For soothly, ther is no-thing that savoureth so wel to a child as the milk of his norice, ne no-thing is to him mere abhominable than thilke milk whan it is medled with other mete. Right so the sinful man that loveth his sinne, him semeth that it is to him most swete of anything; but fro that tyme that he loveth sadly our Lord Jesu Crist, and desireth the lif perdurable, ther nis to him no-thing more abhominable. For soothly, the lawe of god is the love of god; for which David the prophete seith: 'I have loved thy lawe and hated wikkednesse and hate'; he that loveth god kepeth his lawe and his word. This tree saugh the prophete Daniel in spirit, up-on the avision of the king Nabugodonosor, whan he conseiled him to do penitence. Penaunce is the tree of lyf to hem that it receiven, and he that holdeth him in verray penitence is blessed; after the sentence of Salomon.

¶ 7. In this Penitence or Contricion man shal understonde foure thinges, that is to seyn, what is Contricion: and whiche been the causes that moeven a man to Contricion: and how he sholde be contrit: and what Contricion availleth to the soule. Thanne is it thus: that Contricion is the verray sorwe that a man receiveth in his herte for his sinnes, with sad purpos to shryve him, and to do penaunce, and nevermore to do sinne. And this sorwe shal been in this manere, as seith seint Bernard: 'it shal been hevy and grevous, and ful sharpe and poinant in herte.' First, for man hath agilt his lord and his creatour; and more sharpe and poinant, for he hath agilt his fader celestial; and yet more sharpe and poinant, for he hath wrathed and agilt him that boghte him; which with his precious blood hath delivered us fro the bondes of sinne, and fro the crueltee of the devel and fro the peynes of helle.

¶ 8. The causes that oghte moeve a man to Contricion been six. First, a man shal remembre him of hise sinnes; but loke he that thilke remembrance ne be to him no delyt by no wey, but greet shame and sorwe for his gilt. For Job seith: 'sinful men doon werkes worthy of Confession.' And therfore seith Ezechie: 'I wol remembre me alle the yeres of my lyf, in bitternesse of myn herte.' And god seith in the Apocalips: 'remembreth yow fro whennes that ye been falle'; for biforn that tyme that ye sinned, ye were the children of god, and limes of the regne of god; but for your sinne ye been woxen thral and foul, and members of the feend,

hate of aungels, sclaundre of holy chirche, and fode of the false
serpent; perpetuel matere of the fyr of helle. And yet more foul
and abhominable, for ye trespassen so ofte tyme, as doth the hound
that retourneth to eten his spewing. And yet be ye fouler for your
longe continuing in sinne and your sinful usage, for which ye be
roten in your sinne, as a beest in his dong. Swiche manere of
thoghtes maken a man to have shame of his sinne, and no delyt,
as god seith by the prophete Ezechiel: 'ye shal remembre yow of
youre weyes, and they shuln displese yow.' Sothly, sinnes been the
weyes that leden folk to helle.

¶ 9. The seconde cause that oghte make a man to have desdeyn of
sinne is this: that, as seith seint Peter, 'who-so that doth sinne is
thral of sinne'; and sinne put a man in greet thraldom. And therfore seith the prophete Ezechiel: 'I wente sorweful in desdayn of
my-self.' And certes, wel oghte a man have desdayn of sinne, and
withdrawe him from that thraldom and vileinye. And lo, what
seith Seneca in this matere. He seith thus: 'though I wiste that
neither god ne man ne sholde nevere knowe it, yet wolde I have
desdayn for to do sinne.' And the same Seneca also seith: 'I am
born to gretter thinges than to be thral to my body, or than for to
maken of my body a thral.' Ne a fouler thral may no man ne
womman maken of his body, than for to yeven his body to sinne.
Al were it the fouleste cherl, or the fouleste womman that liveth,
and leest of value, yet is he thanne more foule and more in servitute.
Evere fro the hyer degree that man falleth, the more is he thral,
and more to god and to the world vile and abhominable. O gode
god, wel oghte man have desdayn of sinne; sith that, thurgh sinne,
ther he was free, now is he maked bonde. And therfore seyth Seint
Augustin: 'if thou hast desdayn of thy servant, if he agilte or
sinne, have thou thanne desdayn that thou thy-self sholdest do
sinne.' Take reward of thy value, that thou ne be to foul to thy-self.
Allas! wel oghten they thanne have desdayn to been servauntz and
thralles to sinne, and sore been ashamed of hem-self, that god of
his endelees goodnesse hath set hem in heigh estaat, or yeven
hem wit, strengthe of body, hele, beautee, prosperitee, and boghte
hem fro the deeth with his herte blood, that they so unkindely,
agayns his gentilesse, quyten him so vileinsly, to slaughtre of hir
owene soules. O god, ye wommen that been of so greet beautee,

remembreth yow of the proverbe of Salomon, that seith: 'he lykneth a fair womman, that is a fool of hir body, lyk to a ring of gold that were in the groyn of a sowe.' For right as a sowe wroteth in everich ordure, so wroteth she hir beautee in the stink- inge ordure of sinne.

¶10. The thridde cause that oghte moeve a man to Contricion, is drede of the day of dome, and of the horrible peynes of helle. For as seint Jerome seith: 'at every tyme that me remembreth of the day of dome, I quake; for whan I ete or drinke, or what-so that I do, evere semeth me that the trompe sowneth in myn ere: riseth up, ye that been dede, and cometh to the jugement.' O gode god, muchel oghte a man to drede swich a jugement, 'ther-as we shullen been alle,' as seint Poul seith, 'biforn the sete of oure lord Jesu Crist'; wher-as he shal make a general congregacion, wher-as no man may been absent. For certes, there availeth noon essoyne ne excusacion. And nat only that oure defautes shullen be juged, but eek that alle oure werkes shullen openly be knowe. And as seith Seint Bernard: 'ther ne shal no pledinge availle, ne no sleighte; we shullen yeven rekeninge of everich ydel word.' Ther shul we han a juge that may nat been deceived ne corrupt. And why? For, certes, alle our thoghtes been discovered as to him; ne for preyere ne for mede he shal nat been corrupt. And therfore seith Salomon: 'the wratthe of god ne wol nat spare no wight, for preyere ne for yifte'; and therfore, at the day of doom, ther nis noon hope to escape. Wherfore, as seith Seint Anselm: 'ful greet angwissh shul the sinful folk have at that tyme; ther shal the sterne and wrothe juge sitte above, and under him the horrible put of helle open to destroyen him that moot biknowen hise sinnes, whiche sinnes openly been shewed biforn god and biforn every creature. And on the left syde, mo develes than herte may bithinke, for to harie and drawe the sinful soules to the pyne of helle. And with-inne the hertes of folk shal be the bytinge conscience, and with-oute-forth shal be the world al brenninge. Whider shal thanne the wrecched sinful man flee to hyden him? Certes, he may nat hyden him; he moste come forth and shewen him.' For certes, as seith Seint Jerome: 'the erthe shal casten him out of him, and the see also; and the eyr also, that shal be ful of thonder-clappes and lightninges.' Now sothly, who-so wel remembreth him of thise thinges, I gesse that his sinne shal nat turne him in-to delyt, but to greet sorwe, for drede of the peyne of helle. And therfore seith Job to god: 'suffre, lord, that I may a whyle biwaille and wepe, er I go with-oute returning to the derke lond, covered with the derk-nesse of deeth; to the lond of misese and of derknesse, wher-as is the shadwe of deeth; wher-as ther is noon ordre or ordinance, but grisly drede that evere shal laste.' Lo, here may ye seen that Job preyde respyt a whyle, to biwepe and waille his trespas; for soothly oon day of respyt is bettre than al the tresor of the world. And for-as-muche as a man may acquiten him-self biforn god by penitence in this world, and nat by tresor, therfore sholde he preye to god to yeve him respyt a whyle, to biwepe and biwaillen his trespas. For certes, al the sorwe that a man mighte make fro the beginning of the world, nis but a litel thing at regard of the sorwe of helle. The cause why that Job clepeth helle 'the lond of derknesse'; understondeth that he clepeth it 'londe' or erthe, for it is stable, and nevere shal faille; 'derk,' for he that is in helle hath defaute of light material. For certes, the derke light, that shal come out of the fyr that evere shal brenne, shal turne him al to peyne that is in helle; for it sheweth him to the horrible develes that him tormenten. 'Covered with the derknesse of deeth': that is to seyn, that he that is in helle shal have defaute of the sighte of god; for certes, the sighte of god is the lyf perdurable. 'The derknesse of deeth' been the sinnes that the wrecched man hath doon, which that destourben him to see the face of god; right as doth a derk cloude bitwixe us and the sonne. 'Lond of misese': by-cause that ther been three maneres of defautes, agayn three thinges that folk of this world han in this present lyf, that is to seyn, honours, delyces, and richesses. Agayns honour, have they in helle shame and confusion. For wel ye woot that men clepen 'honour' the reverence that man doth to man; but in helle is noon honour ne reverence. For certes, na-more reverence shal be doon there to a king than to a knave. For which god seith by the prophete Jeremye: 'thilke folk that me despysen shul been in despyt.' 'Honour' is eek cleped greet lordshipe; ther shal no man serven other but of harm and torment. 'Honour' is eek cleped greet dignitee and heighnesse; but in helle shul they been al for-troden of develes. And god seith: 'the horrible develes shulle goon and comen up-on the hevedes of the dampned folk.' And this is for-as-muche as, the hyer that they were in this present lyf, the more shulle they been abated and defouled in helle. Agayns the richesses of this world, shul they han misese of poverte; and this poverte shal been in foure thinges: in defaute of tresor, of which that David seith: 'the riche folk, that embraceden and oneden al hir herte to tresor of this world, shul slepe in the slepinge of deeth; and no-thing ne shul they finden in hir handes of al hir tresor.' And more-over, the miseise of helle shal been in defaute of mete and drinke. For god seith thus by Moyses: 'they shul been wasted with hunger, and the briddes of helle shul devouren hem with bitter deeth, and the galle of the dragon shal been hir drinke, and the venim of the dragon hir morsels.' And forther-over, hir miseise shal been in defaute of clothing: for they shulle be naked in body as of clothing, save the fyr in which they brenne and othere filthes; and naked shul they been of soule, of alle manere vertues, which that is the clothing of the soule. Where been thanne the gaye robes and the softe shetes and the smale shertes? Lo, what seith god of hem by the prophete Isaye: 'that under hem shul been strawed motthes, and hir covertures shulle been of wormes of helle.' And forther-over, hir miseise shal been in defaute of freendes; for he nis nat povre that hath goode freendes, but there is no freend; for neither god ne no creature shal been frend to hem, and everich of hem shal haten other with deedly hate. 'The sones and the doghtren shullen rebellen agayns fader and mooder, and kinrede agayns kinrede, and chydon and despysen everich of hem other,' bothe day and night, as god seith by the prophete Michias. And the lovinge children, that whylom lovedon so fleshly everich other, wolden everich of hem aeten other if they mighte. For how sholden they love hem togidre in the peyne of helle, whan they hated ech of hem other in the prosperitee of this lyf? For truste wel, hir fleshly love was deedly hate; as seith the prophete David: 'who-so that loveth wikkednesse he hateth his soul.' And who-so hateth his owene soule, certes, he may love noon other wight in no manere. And therefore, in helle is no solas ne no frendshipe, but evere the more fleshly kinredes that been in helle, the more cursinges, the more chydings, and the more dedly hate ther is among hem. And forther-over, they shul have defaute of alle manere delyces; for certes, delyces been after the appetytes of the fyve wittes, as sighte,

heringe, smellinge, savoringe, and touchinge. But in helle hir
sighte shal be ful of derknesse and of smoke, and therfore ful of
teres; and hir heringe, ful of way mentinge and of grintinge of
teeth, as seith Jesu Crist; hir nosethirles shullen be ful of stinkinge
stink. And as seith Isaye the prophete: 'hir savoring shal be ful of
bitter galle.' And touchinge of al hir body, y-covered with 'fyr that
nevere shal quenche, and with wormes that nevere shul dyen,' as
god seith by the mouth of Isaye. And for-as-muche as they shul
nat wene that they may dyen for peyne, and by hir deeth flee fro
peyne, that may they understonden by the word of Job, that seith:
'ther-as is the shadwe of deeth.' Certes, a shadwe hath the lyknesse
of the thing of which it is shadwe, but shadwe is nat the same
thing of which it is shadwe. Right so fareth the peyne of helle; it
is lyk deeth for the horrible anguissh, and why? For it peyneth hem
evere, as though they sholde dye anon; but certes they shal nat
dye. For as seith Seint Gregorie: 'to wrecche caytives shal be deeth
with-oute deeth, and ende with-outen ende, and defaute with-oute
failinge. For hir deeth shal alwey liven, and hir ende shal everemo
biginne, and hir defaute shal nat faille.' And therfore seith Seint
John the Evangelist: 'they shullen folwe deeth, and they shul nat
finde him; and they shul desyren to dye, and deeth shal flee fro
hem.' And eek Job seith: that 'in helle is noon ordre of rule.' And
al-be-it so that god hath creat alle thinges in right ordre, and nothing with-outen ordre, but alle thinges been ordeyned and nom-
bred; yet nathelees they that been dampned been no-thing in ordre,
ne holden noon ordre. For the erthe ne shal bere hem no fruit.
For, as the prophete David seith: 'god shal destroye the fruit of the
erthe as fro hem'; ne water ne shal yeve hem no moisture; ne the eyr
no refresshing, ne fyr no light. For as seith seint Basilie: 'the
brenninge of the fyr of this world shal god yeven in helle to hem
that been dampned; but the light and the cleernesse shal be yeven
in hevene to hise children'; right as the gode man yeveth flesh to
hise children, and bones to his houndes. And for they shullen have
noon hope to escape, seith seint Job atte laste: that 'ther shal horrour and grisly drede dwellen with-outen ende.' Horrour is alwey
drede of harm that is to come, and this drede shal evere dwelle in
the hertes of hem that been dampned. And therefore han they lorn
al hir hope, for sevene causes. First, for god that is hir juge shal

be withouten mercy to hem; ne they may nat plese him, ne noon of hise halwes; ne they ne may yeve no-thing for hir raunson; ne they have no vois to speke to him; ne they may nat flee fro peyne; ne they have no goodnesse in hem, that they mowe shewe to de-livere hem fro peyne. And therfore seith Salomon: 'the wikked man dyeth; and whan he is deed, he shal have noon hope to escape fro peyne.' Who-so thanne wolde wel understande these peynes, and bithinke him weel that he hath deserved thilke peynes for his sinnes, certes, he sholde have more talent to syken and to wepe than for to signen and to pleye. For as that seith Salomon: 'who-so that hadde the science to knowe the peynes that been establissed and ordeyned for sinne, he wolde make sorwe.' 'Thilke science,' as seith seint Augustin, 'maketh a man to waymenten in his herte.'

¶ 11. The fourthe point, that oghte maken a man to have con-tricion, is the sorweful remembrance of the good that he hath left to doon here in erthe; and eek the good that he hath lorn. Soothly, the gode werkes that he hath left, outher they been the gode werkes that he wroghte er he fel in-to deedly sinne, or elles the gode werkes that he wroghte while he lay in sinne. Soothly, the gode werkes, that he dide biforn that he fil in sinne, been al mortified and astoned and dulled by the ofte sinning. The othere gode werkes, that he wroghte whyl he lay in deedly sinne, they been outrely dede as to the lyf perdurable in hevene. Thanne thilke gode werkes that been mortified by ofte sinning, whiche gode werkes he dide whyl he was in charitee, ne mowe nevere quiken agayn with-outen verray penitence. And ther-of seith god, by the mouth of Ezechiel: that 'if the rightful man returne agayn from his rightwisnesse and werke wikkednesse, shal he live?' Nay; for alle the gode werkes that he hath wroght ne shul nevere been in remembrance; for he shal dyen in his sinne. And up-on thilke chapitre seith seint Gregorie thus: 'that we shulle understonde this principally; that whan we doon deedly sinne, it is for noght thanne to rehercen or drawen in-to memorie the gode werkes that we han wroght biforn.' For certes, in the werkinge of the deedly sinne, ther is no trust to no good werk that we han doon biforn; that is to seyn, as for to have therby the lyf perdurable in hevene. But nathelees, the gode werkes quiken agayn, and comen agayn, and helpen, and availlen to have the lyf perdurable in hevene, whan we han con-

tricion. But soothly, the gode werkes that men doon whyl they been
in deedly sinne, for-as-muche as they were doon in deedly sinne,
they may nevere quiken agayn. For certes, thing that nevere hadde
lyf may nevere quikene; and nathelees, al-be-it that they ne availle
noght to han the lyf perdurable, yet availlen they to abregge of the
peyne of helle, or elles to geten temporal richesse, or elles that god
wole the rather enlumine and lightne the herte of the sinful man to
have repentance; and eek they availlen for to usen a man to doon
gode werkes, that the feend have the lasse power of his soule. And
thus the curteis lord Jesu Crist wole that no good werk be lost; for in
somwhat it shal availle. But for-as-muche as the gode werkes that
men doon whyl they been in good lyf, been al mortified by sinne
folwinge; and eek, sith that alle the gode werkes that men doon
whyl they been in deedly synne, been outrely dede as for to hav
the lyf perdurable; wel may that man, that no good werke ne dooth,
singe thilke newe Frenshe song: '*Jay tout perdu mon temps et mon
labour.*' For certes, sinne bireveth a man bothe goodnesse of nature
and eek the goodnesse of grace. For soothly, the grace of the holy
goost fareth lyk fyr, that may nat been ydel; for fyr faileth anoon
as it forleteth his wirkinge, and right so grace fayleth anoon as it
forleteth his werkinge. Than leseth the sinful man the goodnesse of
glorie, that only is bihight to gode men that labouren and werken.
Wel may he be sory thanne, that oweth al his lif to god as longe as
he hath lived, and eek as longe as he shal live, that no goodnesse ne
hath to paye with his dette to god, to whom he oweth al his lyf.
For trust wel, 'he shal yeven acountes,' as seith seint Bernard, 'of
alle the godes that han be yeven him in this present lyf, and how
he hath hem despended; in so muche that ther shal nat perisse an
heer of his heed, ne a moment of an houre ne shal nat perisse of his
tyme, that he ne shal yeve of it a rekening.'

¶ 12. The fifthe thing that oghte moeve a man to contricion, is
remembrance of the passion that oure lord Jesu Crist suffred for
oure sinnes. For, as seith seint Bernard: 'whyl that I live, I shal
have remembrance of the travailles that oure lord Crist suffred in
preching; his werinesse in travailling, hise temptacions whan he
fasted, hise longe wakinges whan he preyde, hise teres whan that
he weep for pitee of good peple; the wo and the shame and the filthe
that men seyden to him; of the foule spitting than men spitte in

his face, of the buffettes that men yaven him, of the foule mowes, and of the repreves that men to him seyden; of the nayles with whiche he was nailed to the croys, and of al the remenant of his passion that he suffred for my sinnes, and no-thing for his gilt.' And ye shul understonde, that in mannes sinne is every manere of ordre or ordinance turned up-so-doun. For it is sooth, that god, and reson, and sensualitee, and the body of man been so ordeyned, that everich of thise foure thinges sholde have lordshipe over that other; as thus: god sholde have lordshipe over reson, and reson over sensualitee, and sensualitee over the body of man. But sothly, whan man sinneth, al this ordre or ordinance is turned up-so-doun. And therfore thanne, for-as-muche as the reson of man ne wol nat be subget ne obeisant to god, that is his lord by right, therfore leseth it the lordshipe that it sholde have over sensualitee, and eek over the body of man. And why? For sensualitee rebelleth thanne agayns reson; and by that wey leseth reson the lordshipe over sensualitee and over the body. For right as reson is rebel to god, right so is bothe sensualitee rebel to reson and the body also. And certes, this disordinance and this rebellion oure lord Jesu Crist aboghte up-on his precious body ful dere, and herkneth in which wyse. For-as-muche thanne as reson is rebel to god, therfore is man worthy to have sorwe and to be deed. This suffred oure lord Jesu Crist for man, after that he hadde be bitraysed of his disciple, and distreyned and bounde, 'so that his blood brast out at every nail of hise handes,' as seith seint Augustin. And forther-over, for-as-muchel as reson of man ne wol nat daunte sensualitee whan it may, therfore is man worthy to have shame; and this suffred oure lord Jesu Crist for man, whan they spetten in his visage. And forther-over, for-as-muchel thanne as the caitif body of man is rebel bothe to reson and to sensualitee, therfore it is worthy the deeth. And this suffred oure lord Jesu Crist for man up-on the croys, where-as ther was no part of his body free, with-outen greet peyne and bitter passion. And al this suffred Jesu Crist, than nevere forfeted. And therfore resonably may be seyd of Jesu in this manere: 'to muchel am I peyned for the thinges that I never deserved, and to muche defouled for shendshipe that man is worthy to have.' And therfore may the sinful man wel seye, as seith seint Bernard: 'acursed be the bitternesse of my sinne, for which ther moste be suffred so muchel bitternesse.' For certes, after the diverse discordances of oure wikkednesses, was the passion of Jesu Crist ordeyned in diverse thinges, as thus. Certes, sinful mannes soule is bitraysed of the devel by coveitise of temporel prosperitee, and scorned by deceite whan he cheseth fleshly delyces; and yet is it tormented by impacience of adversitee, and bispet by servage and subjeccion of sinne; and atte laste it is slayn fynally. For this disordinaunce of sinful man was Jesu Crist first bitraysed, and after that was he bounde, that cam for to unbynden us of sinne and peyne. Thanne was he biscorned, that only sholde han been honoured in alle thinges and of alle thinges. Thanne was his visage, that oghte be desired to be seyn of al man-kinde, in which visage aungels desyren to looke, vileynsly bispet. Thanne was he scourged that no-thing hadde agilt; and fynally, thanne was he crucified and slayn. Thanne was acompliced the word of Isaye: 'he was wounded for oure misdedes, and defouled for oure felonies.' Now sith that Jesu Crist took up-on him-self the peyne of alle oure wikkednesses, muchel oghte sinful man wepen and biwayle, that for hise sinnes goddes sone of heven sholde al this peyne endure.

¶ 13. The sixte thing that oghte moeve a man to contricion, is the hope of three thynges; that is to seyn, foryifnesse of sinne, and the yifte of grace wel for to do, and the glorie of hevene, with which god shal guerdone a man for hise gode dedes. And for-as-muche as Jesu Crist yeveth us thise yiftes of his largesse and of his sovereyn bountee, therfore is he cleped *Jesus Nazarenus rex Judeorum.* Jesus is to seyn 'saveour' or 'salvacion,' on whom men shul hope to have foryifnesse of sinnes, which that is proprely salvacion of sinnes. And therfore seyde the aungel to Joseph: 'thou shalt clepen his name Jesus, that shal saven his peple of hir sinnes.' And heer-of seith seint Peter: 'ther is noon other name under hevene that is yeve to any man, by which a man may be saved, but only Jesus.' *Nazarenus* is as muche for to seye as 'florisshinge,' in which a man shal hope, that he that yeveth him remission of sinnes shal yeve him eek grace wel for to do. For in the flour is hope of fruit in tyme cominge; and in foryifnesse of sinnes hope of grace wel for to do. 'I was atte dore of thyn herte,' seith Jesus, 'and cleped for to entre; he that openeth to me shal have foryifnesse of sinne. I wol entre in-to him by my grace, and soupe with him,' by the goode werkes that he shal doon; whiche werkes been the foode

of god; 'and he shal soupe with me,' by the grete joye that I shal
yeven him. Thus shal man hope, for hise werkes of penaunce, that
god shall yeven him his regne; as he bihoteth him in the gospel.

¶ 14. Now shal a man understonde, in which manere shal been his
contricion. I seye, that it shal been universal and total; this is to
seyn, a man shal be verray repentant for alle hise sinnes that he
hath doon in delyt of his thoght; for delyt is ful perilous. For ther
been two manere of consentinges; that oon of hem is cleped consentinge of affeccion, whan a man is moeved to do sinne, and
delyteth him longe for to thinke on that sinne; and his reson
aperceyveth it wel, that it is sinne agayns the lawe of god, and yet
his reson refreyneth nat his foul delyt or talent, though he see wel
apertly that it is agayns the reverence of god; al-though his reson
ne consente noght to doon that sinne in dede, yet seyn somme
doctours that swich delyt that dwelleth longe, it is ful perilous, al
be it nevere so lite. And also a man sholde sorwe, namely, for al
that evere he hath desired agayn the lawe of god with perfit consentinge of his reson; for ther-of is no doute, that it is deedly sinne
in consentinge. For certes, ther is no deedly sinne, that it nas first
in mannes thought, and after that in his delyt; and so forth in-to
consentinge and in-to dede. Wherfore I seye, that many men ne
repenten hem nevere of swiche thoghtes and delytes, ne nevere
shryven hem of it, but only of the dede of grete sinnes outward.
Wherfore I seye, that swiche wikked delytes and wikked thoghtes
been subtile bigyleres of hem that shullen be dampned. More-over,
man oghte to sorwe for hise wikkede wordes as wel as for hise
wikkede dedes; for certes, the repentance of a singuler sinne, and
nat repente of all hise othere sinnes, or elles repenten him of alle
hise other sinnes, and nat of a singular sinne, may nat availle. For
certes, god almighty is al good; and ther-fore he foryeveth al, or
elles right noght. And heer-of seith seint Augustin: 'I woot certeinly that god is enemy to everich sinnere'; and how thanne? He
that observeth o sinne, shal he have foryifnesse of the remenaunt
of hise othere sinnes? Nay. And forther-over, contricion sholde be
wonder sorweful and anguissous, and therfore yeveth him god
pleynly his mercy; and therfore, whan my soule was anguissous
with-inne me, I hadde remembrance of god that my preyere mighte
come to him. Forther-over, contricion moste be continuel, and that

man have stedfast purpos to shryven him, and for to amenden him of his lyf. For soothly, whyl contricion lasteth, man may evere have hope of foryifnesse; and of this comth hate of sinne, that destroyeth sinne bothe in himself, and eek in other folk, at his power. For which seith David: 'ye that loven god hateth wikkednesse.' For trusteth wel, to love god is for to love that he loveth, and hate that he hateth.

¶ 15. The laste thing that man shal understonde in contricion is this; wher-of avayleth contricion. I seye, that som tyme contricion delivereth a man fro sinne; of which that David seith: 'I seye,' quod David, that is to seyn, 'I purposed fermely to shryve me; and thow, Lord, relesedest my sinne.' And right so as contricion availleth noght, with-outen sad purpos of shrifte, if man have oportunitee, right so litel worth is shrifte or satisfaccion with-outen contricion. And more-over, contricion destroyeth the prison of helle, and maketh wayk and feble alle the strengthes of the develes, and restoreth the yiftes of the holy goost and of alle gode vertues; and it clenseth the soule of sinne, and deliverth the soule fro the peyne of helle, and fro the companye of the devel, and fro the servage of sinne, and restoreth it to alle godes espirituels, and to the companye and communion of holy chirche. And fortherover, it maketh him that whylom was sone of ire to be sone of grace; and alle thise thinges been preved by holy writ. And therfore, he that wolde sette his entente to thise thinges, he were ful wys; for soothly, he ne sholde nat thanne in all his lyf have corage to sinne, but yeven his body and al his herte to the service of Jesu Crist, and ther-of doon him homage. For soothly, oure swete lord Jesu Crist hath spared us so debonairly in our folies, that if he ne hadde pitee of mannes soule, a sory sang we mighten alle singe.

Explicit prima pars Penitentie

THOMAS À KEMPIS

THE IMITATION *of* CHRIST

> Learn to despise outward things, and give thyself to
> inward things, and thou shalt see the kingdom of God
> come into thy soul.

THE AUTHORSHIP of *The Imitation of Christ,* no doubt the most
famous devotional work of the end of the Middle Ages, remains
to this day an unsettled question, although the balance of evidence
and scholarly opinion still favors Thomas à Kempis (1379-1471).
Born at Kempen, Thomas began his education at Deventer, where
Gerrit Groot (1340-1384) and his friend and pupil Florens
Radewyns (1350-1400) had founded the Brethren of the Common Life in 1375. In 1399, Thomas entered the monastery St.
Agnes of the Canons Regular of St. Augustine at Windesheim, and
was ordained priest in 1413.

That the piety and devotion of the *Imitation* is opposed to the
curiosity and the syllogisms of the philosophers should be clear
to the most casual reader. I should rather feel compunction, à
Kempis has written, than know its definition. Yet the devotion of
the *Imitation* goes back to St. Augustine and St. Bernard, to St.
Anselm and St. Francis; and though, in his biography of Groot,
à Kempis has given us the spiritual sources of the devout life at
Deventer and Windesheim, we could scarcely miss the traditional
Christian signature of the single-minded allegiance to Christ in
the *Imitation.* There are, to be sure, those who speak of the *new*
or *modern* devotion of the *Imitation.* But it is a fact that the call

to the interior life, which is the theme of the second book of the *Imitation,* was already old when Guido the Carthusian wrote his *Meditations* at the beginning of the twelfth century. Centuries before, St. Augustine, who knew at least something of the interior man, looked back to St. Paul's *inward man.*

Let us say that the message of the *Imitation* is new because it is perennially Christian; in which sense it is as old as Christianity.

BOOK TWO

Admonitions drawing to the inner life

CHAPTER I
Of inward conversation

HE KINGDOM OF GOD IS WITHIN YOU, SAITH Christ our Saviour. Turn thee therefore with all thy heart to God and forsake this wretched world, and thy soul shall find great inward rest. Learn to despise outward things and give thyself to inward things, and thou shalt see the kingdom of God come into thy soul.

The kingdom of God is peace and joy in the Holy Ghost that is not granted to wicked people. Our Lord Jesus Christ will come to thee and will show to thee his consolations if thou wilt make ready for him withinforth a dwelling place. All that he desireth in thee is withinforth, and there is his pleasure to be. There are betwixt almighty God and a devout soul many ghostly visitings, sweet inward speaking, great gifts of grace, many consolations, much heavenly peace, and wondrous familiarity of the blessed presence of God.

Therefore, thou faithful soul, prepare thy heart to Christ thy spouse, that he may come to thee and dwell in thee, for he saith himself: Whoso loveth me shall keep my commandment, and my Father and I and the Holy Ghost shall come to him and we shall make in him our dwelling-place.

Give therefore to Christ free entrance into thy heart and keep out all things that withstand his entrance. When thou hast him thou art rich enough, and he only shall suffice to thee. Then he shall be thy provider and defender, and thy faithful helper in every necessity, so that thou shalt not need to put thy trust in any other without him.

Man is soon changed and lightly falleth away, but Christ abideth for ever and standeth strongly with his lover unto the end. There is no great trust to be put in man, that is but mortal and frail, though he be right much profitable and much beloved unto thee; nor any great heaviness to be taken though he sometimes turn and be against thee. For they that this day be with thee, tomorrow may happen to be against thee, and may oft turn as doth the wind.

Put thy full trust therefore in God. Let him be thy love and dread above all things, and he will answer for thee and will do for thee in all things as shall be most needful and most expedient for thee. Thou hast here no place of long abiding, for wheresoever thou be come thou art but a stranger and a pilgrim and never shalt thou find perfect rest till thou be fully joined to God. Why dost thou look to have rest here since this is not thy resting place? Thy full rest must be in heavenly things, and all earthly things thou must behold as things transitory and shortly passing away. And be well ware thou cleave not overmuch to them lest thou be taken with love of them and in the end perish thereby.

Let thy thought be always upward to God and direct thy prayers to Christ continually. If thou may not for frailty of thyself always occupy thy mind in contemplation of the Godhead, be then occupied with mind of his Passion and in his blessed wounds make thee a dwelling-place. And if thou flee devoutly to the wound of Christ's side and to the marks of his Passion thou shalt feel great comfort in every trouble. Thou shalt little heed though thou be openly despised in the world, and what evil words soever be spoken of thee shall little grieve thee.

Our Master, Christ, was despised of men in the world, and in his most need was forsaken of his acquaintance and friends, and left among shames and rebukes. He was content to suffer wrongs and be naught set by of the world, and we will not that any person do us wrong or dispraise our deeds. Christ had many adversaries and revilers, and we would have all to be our friends and lovers. How should thy patience be crowned in heaven if none adversity should befall to thee in earth? If thou wilt suffer none adversity how mayst thou be the friend of Christ? It behoveth thee to suffer with Christ and for Christ, if thou wilt reign with Christ.

Truly, if thou hadst once entered into the bloody wounds of Jesus and hadst there tasted a little of his love, thou shouldst care nothing for likings or mislikings of the world, but rather thou shouldst have great joy when wrongs and reproofs were done unto thee; for perfect love of God maketh a man perfectly to despise himself. The true inward lover of God that is free from all inordinate affections may anon turn himself freely to God, and in spirit lift himself up in contemplation and fruitfully rest him in Christ.

He to whom all things be esteemed as they be, and not as they be taken and thought to be by worldly people, is very wise and is rather taught of God than of man. And he that can inwardly lift his mind upward to God and can little regard outward things needeth not to seek for time or place to go to prayers, or to do other good deeds or virtuous works. For the spiritual man may soon gather himself together and fix his mind in God because he never suffereth it to be fully occupied in outward things. Therefore his outward labours and his worldly occupations, necessary for the time, hinder him but little; for, as they come, so he applieth himself to them and referreth them always to the will of God. Moreover, a man that is well ordered in his soul heedeth little the unkind demeanour of worldly people nor yet their proud behaviour. As much as a man loveth any worldly thing more than it should be beloved, so much his mind is hindered from the true ordinate love that he should have to God.

If thou were well purged from all inordinate affections, then whatsoever should befall to thee should turn to thy ghostly profit and to the great increasing of grace and virtue in thy soul. The cause why so many things displease thee and trouble thee, is that thou art not yet perfectly dead to the world nor fully severed from the love of earthly things, and nothing so much defileth the soul as an unclean love to creatures.

If thou forsake to be comforted by worldly things, thou mayst behold more perfectly heavenly things, and thou shalt then sing continually lauds and praisings to God with great joy and inward gladness of heart: the which grant thee and me, the blessed Trinity.

CHAPTER II

Of a meek knowing of our own defaults

REGARD NOT MUCH who is with thee nor who is against thee, but be this thy greatest study, that God may be with thee in everything that thou dost. Have a good conscience and he shall well defend thee, and whomsoever he will help and defend there may no malice hinder nor grieve. If thou can be still and suffer awhile thou shalt without doubt see the help of God come in thy need. He knoweth the time and place how to deliver thee, and therefore thou must resign thyself wholly to him. It pertaineth to him to help and to deliver from all confusion.

Nevertheless it is oft times much profitable to us for the more sure keeping of meekness, that other men know our defaults and reprove us of them. When a man meeketh himself for his offences he easily pleaseth others and reconcileth himself to them that he hath offended. The meek man almighty God defendeth and comforteth; to him he inclineth himself and sendeth him great plenty of his grace. To the meek man also he showeth his secrets and lovingly he draweth him to himself; and after his oppression he lifteth him up to glory. The meek man, when he hath suffered confusion and reproof, is in good peace, for he trusteth in God and not in the world. Moreover, if thou wilt come to the highness of perfection, think not thyself to have anything profited in virtue till thou can feel meekly in thy heart that thou hast less meekness and less virtue than any other hath.

CHAPTER III

How good it is for a man to be peaceful

FIRST put thyself in peace, and then thou mayst the better pacify others. A peaceful man and a patient, profiteth more to himself, and to others also, than a man well-learned that is unpeaceful. A man that is passionate turneth oft times good into evil and lightly believeth the worse part, but a good peaceful man turneth all things to the best and hath suspicion to no man.

He that is not content is oft troubled with many suspicions, and neither is he quiet himself nor yet suffereth he others to be quiet. He speaketh oft times what he should not speak and he omitteth to speak that which were more expedient to be spoken; he considereth greatly what others be bounden to do but to that which he is bounden to himself he is full negligent.

Have therefore first a zeal and a respect to thyself and to thine own soul, and then thou mayst the more rightwisely and with the more due order of charity, have zeal towards thy neighbour's. Thou art anon ready to excuse thine own defaults, but thou wilt not hear the excuses of thy brethren. Truly, it were more charitable and more profitable to thee that thou shouldst accuse thyself and excuse thy brother; for if thou wilt be borne, bear others. Behold how far thou art yet from the perfect meekness and charity of Christian people, who can not be angry with any but with themselves.

It is no great thing to be well conversant with good men and with tractable men, for that naturally pleaseth all people; and all men gladly have peace with them and most love them that follow their liking. But to live peaceably with evil men and with froward men that lack good manners and be untaught, and that be also contrarious unto us, is a great grace, and a manly deed and much to be praised; for it can not be done but through great ghostly strength. Some persons can be quiet themselves and also can live quietly with others; and some can not be quiet themselves, nor yet suffer others to be quiet: they be grievous to others, but they be more grievous to themselves. And some can keep themselves in good peace and can also bring others to live in peace.

Nevertheless all our peace while we be in this mortal life, standeth more in meek suffering of troubles and of things that be contrarious unto us, than in not feeling them; for no man may live here without some trouble. Therefore he that can best suffer shall have most peace; and he is the very true overcomer of himself, he is the lord of the world, the friend of Christ, and the true inheritor of the kingdom of heaven.

CHAPTER IV

Of a pure mind and a simple intent

MAN is borne up from earthly things with two wings, that is to say, with plainness and cleanness: plainness is in the intent, and cleanness is in the love. The good, true, and plain intent looketh towards God, but the clean love taketh assay and tasteth his sweetness. If thou be free from all inordinate love, there shall no good deed hinder thee, but thou shalt therewith increase in the way of perfection. If thou intend well and seek nothing but God and the profit of thine own soul and of thy neighbour's, thou shalt have great inward liberty of mind. And if thy heart be straight with God, then every creature shall be to thee a mirror of life and a book of holy doctrine, for there is no creature so little nor so vile but that it showeth and representeth the goodness of God.

If thou were withinforth in thy soul pure and clean, thou shouldst then, without letting, take all things to the best. A clean heart pierceth both heaven and hell. Such as a man is in his conscience inwardly, such he showeth to be by his outward conversation. If there be any true joy in this world, that hath a man of a clean conscience. And if there be anywhere tribulation or anguish, an evil conscience knoweth it best. For as iron put into the fire is cleansed from rust and is made all clean and pure, right so a man turning himself wholly to God is purged from slothfulness and suddenly is changed into a new man.

When a man beginneth to wax dull and slow to ghostly business then a little labour feareth him greatly, and then he taketh gladly outward comforts of the world and of the flesh; but when he beginneth perfectly to overcome himself and to walk strongly in the way of God, then he regardeth those labours but little that before he thought were right grievous and insupportable unto him.

CHAPTER V

Of the knowing of ourselves

WE MAY not trust much in ourselves nor in our own wit, for oft times through our presumption we lack grace, and right little light of true understanding is in us. Many times what we have we lose through our negligence; and yet we see not, nor will we see, how blind we are. Oft times we do evil and in defence thereof we do much worse; and sometimes we be moved with passion and we think it is of a zeal to God. We can anon reprove small defaults in our neighbours, but our own defaults, that be much greater, we will not see. We feel anon and ponder greatly what we suffer of others, but what others suffer of us we will not consider. He that would well and rightwisely judge his own defaults should not so rigorously judge the defaults of his neighbours.

A man that is inwardly turned to God taketh heed of himself before all others, and he that can well take heed of himself can easily be still of other men's deeds. Thou shalt never be a spiritual man and a devout follower of Christ, unless thou can keep thee from meddling in other men's deeds and can especially take heed of thine own. If thou take heed wholly to God and to thyself, the defaults that thou seest in others shall little move thee. Where art thou when thou art not present to thyself? And when thou hast all run about and much hast considered other men's works, what hast thou profited thereby if thou have forgotten thyself? If thou wilt therefore have peace in thy soul and be perfectly united to God in blessed love, set apart all other men's deeds and only set thyself and thine own deeds before the eye of thy soul; and if thou seest anything amiss in thyself, shortly reform it.

Thou shalt much profit in grace if thou keep thee free from all temporal cares, and it shall hinder thee greatly if thou set price by any temporal thing. Therefore let nothing be in thy sight high, nothing great, nothing liking nor acceptable to thee, unless it be purely God, or of God. Think all comforts vain that come to thee by any creature. He that loveth God, and his own soul for God, despiseth all other love; for he seeth well that God alone, who is eternal and incomprehensible, and fulfilleth all things with his goodness, is the whole solace and comfort of the soul; and that he is the very true gladness of heart, and none other but only he.

CHAPTER VI

Of the gladness of a clean conscience

THE GLORY of a good man is the witness of God that he hath a good conscience; have therefore a good conscience and thou shalt always have gladness. A good conscience may bear many wrongs and is ever merry and glad in adversities, but an evil conscience is always fearful and unquiet. Thou shalt rest thee sweetly and blessedly if thine own heart reprove thee not.

Be never glad but when thou hast done well. Evil men have never perfect gladness nor feel inward peace, for our Lord saith there is no peace to wicked people. And though they say: We be in good peace, there shall no evil come to us! Lo, who may grieve us or hurt us? believe them not; for suddenly the wrath of God shall fall upon them, unless they amend, and all that they have done shall turn to naught, and whatsoever they would have done shall be undone.

It is no grievous thing to a fervent lover of God to joy in tribulation, for all his joy and glory is in the cross of our Lord Jesus Christ. It is a short glory that is given by man, and commonly some heaviness followeth shortly after. The joy and gladness of good men is in their own conscience. The joy of rightwise men is in God and of God, and their joy is in virtue and in good life. He that desireth the very perfect joy, that is everlasting, setteth little price by temporal joy; and he that seeketh any worldly joy, or doth not in his heart fully despise it, showeth himself openly to love but little the joy of heaven.

He hath great tranquillity and peace of heart that neither regardeth praises nor dispraises, and he shall soon be pacified and content that hath a good conscience. Thou art not the better because thou art praised, nor the worse because thou art dispraised, for as thou art, thou art; and whatsoever be said of thee, thou art no better than almighty God, who is the searcher of man's heart, will witness thee to be. If thou behold well what thou art inwardly, thou shalt not care much what the world speaketh of thee outwardly. Man seeth the face but God beholdeth the heart; man beholdeth the deed but God beholdeth the intent of the deed. It is a great token of a meek heart, that a man ever shall do well and yet think himself to have done but little. And it is a great sign of cleanness of life and of an inward trust in God, when a man taketh not his comfort of any creature. When a man seeketh no outward witness for himself, it appeareth that he hath wholly committed himself to God. Also after the words of Saint Paul, he that commendeth himself is not justified, but he whom God commendeth. He that hath his mind always lifted up to God and is not bounden with any inordinate affection withoutforth, is in the degree and in the state of a holy and blessed man.

CHAPTER VII

Of the love of Jesus above all things

BLESSED is he that knoweth how good it is to love Jesus, and for his sake to despise himself. It behoveth the lover of Jesus to forsake all other love besides him, for he will be loved only, above all other. The love of creatures is deceivable and failing, but the love of Jesus is faithful and always abiding. He that cleaveth to any creature must of necessity fail as doth the creature, but he that cleaveth abidingly to Jesus shall be made stable in him for ever.

Love him, therefore, and hold him thy friend; for when all others forsake thee he will not forsake thee nor suffer thee finally to perish. Thou must of necessity be departed from thy friends and from all man's company whether thou wilt or not; and therefore, keep thee with thy Lord Jesus, living and dying. Commit thee to his fidelity and he will be with thee and help thee when all others forsake thee. Thy beloved is of such nature that he will not admit any other love, for he will have alone the love of thy heart and will sit therein as a king in his proper throne. If thou couldst well avoid from thee the love of creatures, he would always abide with thee and never would he forsake thee.

Thou shalt in manner find it all as lost, whatsoever trust thou hast put in any manner of thing besides Jesus. Put not thy trust therefore in such a thing as is but a quill, full of wind; or as a hollow stick, which is not able to sustain thee nor to help thee, but in thy most need will deceive thee; for man is but as grass, and all his glory is as a flower in the field which suddenly vanisheth away.

If thou take heed only to the outward appearance thou shalt soon be deceived, and if thou seek thy comfort in anything but in Jesus thou shalt feel thereby great spiritual loss. If thou seek in all things thy Lord Jesus, thou shalt truly find him; and if thou seek thyself, thou shalt find thyself. And that shall be to thine own great loss; for truly a man is more grievous and more hurtful to himself if he seek not Christ than is all the world, and more than all his adversaries may be.

CHAPTER VIII

Of the familiar friendship of Jesus

WHEN our Lord Jesus is present all things are liking and nothing seemeth hard to do for his love; but when he is absent all things that are done for his love are painful and hard. When Jesus speaketh not to the soul there is no faithful consolation, but if he speak but one word only, the soul feeleth great inward comfort. Did not Mary Magdalen rise soon from weeping when Martha showed her that her Master, Christ, was nigh and called her? Yes, truly. O that is an happy hour when Jesus calleth us from weeping to joy of spirit!

Remember how dry and how undevout thou art without Jesus; and how unwise, how vain, and how unlearned thou art when thou desirest anything besides Jesus. Truly that desire is more hurtful to thee than if thou hadst lost all the world. What may this world give thee but through the help of Jesus? To be without Jesus is a pain of hell, and to be with him is a pleasant paradise. If Jesus be with thee there may no enemy grieve thee. He that findeth Jesus, findeth a great treasure that is best above all other treasures; and he that loseth him hath lost more than all the world. He is most poor that liveth without Jesus, and he is most rich that is with Jesus. It is great wisdom to be well conversant with him, and to keep him is right great wisdom. Be meek and peaceful, and Jesus shall be with thee; be devout and quiet and he will abide with thee.

Thou mayst anon drive away thy Lord Jesus and lose his grace, if thou apply thyself to outward things; and if through negligence of thyself thou lose him, what friend shalt thou then have? Without a friend thou mayst not long endure, and if Jesus be not thy friend before all others, thou shalt be very heavy and desolate and be left without all perfect friendship; therefore thou dost not wisely if thou trust or joy in any other thing besides him. We should rather choose to have all the world against us than to offend God; and therefore, of all that be to thee lief and dear, let thy Lord Jesus be to thee most lief and dear, and most beloved to thee above all others. And let all others be beloved for him and he only for himself.

Jesus is only to be beloved for himself, for he only is proved good and faithful before all other friends. In him and for him, both enemies and friends are to be beloved; and before all things we ought meekly, with all diligence, to pray to him, that he may be beloved and honoured of all his creatures. Never covet to be singularly loved or commended, for that belongeth only to God, who hath none like unto him. And desire not that anything be occupied with thee in thy heart, nor that thou be occupied with love of any created thing; but that thy Lord Jesus may be in thee, and in every good man and woman.

Be pure and clean withinforth without hindrance of any creature, as nigh as thou can, for it behoveth thee to have a right clean and a pure heart to Jesus, if thou wilt know and feel how sweet he is. And verily thou mayst not come to that purity unless thou be prevented and drawn through his grace; and unless, all other things set apart, thou be inwardly knit and joined to him.

When the grace of God cometh to a man, then is he made mighty and strong to do everything that belongeth to virtue; and when grace withdraweth, then is he made weak and feeble to do any good deed, and is in manner as if he were left only to pain and punishments. And if it happen so with thee, yet despair not overmuch therefore and leave not thy good deeds undone, but stand always strongly after the will of God, and turn all things that shall come to thee to the laud and praising of his name. For after winter cometh summer, and after the night cometh the day, and after a great tempest showeth again right clear and pleasant weather.

CHAPTER IX

Of the wanting of all solace and comfort

IT IS no great thing to despise man's comfort when the comfort of God is present. But it is a great thing, and that a right great thing, that a man should be so strong in spirit that he may bear the wanting of them both; and for the love of God and to his honour should have a ready will to bear, as it were, a desolation of spirit, and yet in nothing to seek himself nor his own merits.

What proof of virtue is it, if a man be merry and devout in God when grace cometh and visiteth the soul, for that hour is desired of every creature? He rideth right safely whom the grace of God beareth and supporteth; and what marvel is it, if he feel no burden that is borne up by him that is almighty, and led by the sovereign guide who is God himself? We be always glad to have solace and consolation; but we would have no tribulation, and we will not lightly cast from us the false love of ourselves. The blessed martyr, Saint Laurence, through the love of God, mightily overcame the love of the world and of himself. He despised all that was liking and delectable in the world; and Sixtus the Pope, whom he most loved, he suffered meekly to be taken from him. So through the love of God he overcame the love of man, and instead of man's comfort he chose rather to follow the will of God. Do thou in like wise, and learn to forsake some necessary and some well-beloved friend for the love of God. Take it not grievously when thou art left or forsaken by thy friend, for of necessity it behoveth worldly friends to be dissevered.

It behoveth a man to fight long, and mightily to strive with himself, or ever he shall learn fully to overcome himself, and freely and readily set all his desires in God. When a man loveth himself and much trusteth to himself, he falleth anon to man's comforts. But the very true lover of Christ and the diligent follower of virtue falleth not so lightly to them; he seeketh little such sensible sweetness and bodily delights, but rather is glad to suffer great hard labours and pain for the love of Christ.

Nevertheless, when ghostly comfort is sent to thee of God, take it meekly and give thanks meekly for it. But know for certain that it is of the great goodness of God that it is sent to thee, and not of thy deserving. And look thou be not lifted up therefor unto pride, nor that thou joy much thereof, nor presume vainly therein, but rather that thou be the more meek for so noble a gift, and the more watchful and fearful in all thy works; for that time will pass away, and the time of temptation will shortly follow after. When comfort is withdrawn, despair not therefore, but meekly and patiently abide the visitation of God, for he is able and of power to give thee more grace and more ghostly comfort than thou hadst first.

Such alteration of grace is no new thing, and no strange thing to them that have had experience in the way of God; for in great saints and in holy prophets was many times found like alteration, wherefore the prophet David saith: *Ego dixi in abundancia mea non movebor in aeternum.* That is to say, when David had abundance of ghostly comfort he said to our Lord that he trusted he should never be removed from such comfort. But after, when grace withdrew, he said: *Avertisti faciem tuam a me et factus sum conturbatus*; that is, O Lord, thou hast withdrawn thy ghostly comforts from me and I am left in great trouble and heaviness. Yet nevertheless he despaired not therefor, but prayed heartily unto our Lord, and said: *Ad te domine, clamabo, et ad Deum meum deprecabor*; that is, I shall busily cry to thee, Lord, and I shall meekly pray to thee for grace and comfort. And anon he had the effect of his prayer, as he witnesseth himself, saying thus: *Audivit Dominus et misertus est mei, Dominus factus est adiutor meus*; that is, Our Lord hath heard my prayer, and hath had mercy on me, and hath now again sent me his help and ghostly comfort. And therefore he saith afterwards: Lord, thou hast turned my sorrow into joy, and thou hast encompassed me with heavenly gladness.

If almighty God hath thus done with holy saints, it is not for us, weak and feeble persons, to despair, though we sometimes have fervour of spirit, and be sometimes left cold and void of devotion. The Holy Ghost cometh and goeth after his pleasure, and therefore Job saith: Lord, thou graciously visitest thy lover in the morrowtide, that is to say, in the time of comfort; and suddenly thou provest him in withdrawing such comforts from him.

Wherein then may I trust, or in whom may I have any confidence, but only in the great endless grace and mercy of God? For the company of good men and the fellowship of devout brethren and faithful friends, the having of holy books or of devout treatises, the hearing of sweet songs or of devout hymns, may little avail, and bring forth but little comfort to the soul when we are left to our own frailty and poverty. And when we be so left there is no better remedy than patience, with a whole resigning of our own will to the will of God.

I never found yet any religious person so perfect but that he had sometimes absenting of grace or some minishing of fervour; and there was never yet any saint so highly rapt but that, first or last, he had some temptation. He is not worthy to have the high gift of contemplation that hath not suffered for God some tribulation. The temptations going before were wont to be a soothfast token of heavenly comfort shortly coming after. And to them that be found stable in their temptations great consolation is promised by our Lord; and therefore he saith thus: He that overcometh, I shall give him to eat of the tree of life.

Heavenly comfort is sometimes given to a man that he may be more strong to suffer adversities, but temptation followeth after, that he be not lifted up unto pride and think that he is worthy such consolation. The ghostly enemy sleepeth not and the flesh is not yet fully mortified; and therefore thou shalt never cease to prepare thyself to ghostly battle, for thou hast enemies on every side that ever will be ready to assail thee and to hinder thy good purpose all that they can.

CHAPTER X

Of yielding thanks to God for his manifold graces

WHY seekest thou rest here, since thou art born to labour? Dispose thyself to patience rather than to comforts; to bear the cross of penance rather than to have gladness. What temporal man would not gladly have spiritual comforts if he might always keep them? For spiritual comforts exceed far all worldly delights and all bodily pleasures. All worldly delights be either foul or vain; but ghostly delights are only jocund and honest, brought forth by virtues and sent of God into a clean soul. But such comforts no man may have when he would, for the time of temptation tarrieth not long.

The false liberty of will and the overmuch trust that we have in ourselves be much contrary to the heavenly visitations. Our Lord doth well in sending such comforts, but we do not well when we yield not all thanks therefore to him again. The greatest cause why the gifts of grace may not lightly come to us, is that we be ungrateful to the giver and yield not thanks to him from whom all goodness cometh. Grace is always given to them that be ready to yield thanks for it again, and therefore it is wont to be given to the meek man and to be taken from the proud man.

I would none of that consolation that should take from me compunction! I would none of that contemplation that should lift my soul into presumption! Every high thing in sight of man is not holy, every desire is not clean and pure, every sweet thing is not good; all that is lief and dear to man is not always pleasant to God. We shall therefore gladly take such gifts as make us the more ready to forsake ourselves and our own will. He that knoweth the comforts that come through the gift of grace and knoweth also how sharp and painful the absenting of grace is, shall not dare think that any goodness cometh of himself; but he shall openly confess that of himself he is right poor and naked of all virtue. Yield therefore to God that which is his, and to thyself that which is thine; that is, thank God for his manifold graces and blame thyself for thine offences. Hold in thee always a sure ground and a sure foundation of meekness, and then the highness of virtue shall shortly be given unto thee; for the high tower of virtue may not long stand unless it be borne up with the low foundation of meekness.

They that be greatest in heaven be least in their own sight; and the more glorious they be, the meeker they are in themselves, full of truth and of heavenly joy, not desirous of any vainglory or praising of man. Also they that be fully stabled and confirmed in God may in no wise be lifted up into pride. They that ascribe all goodness to God seek no glory nor vain praisings in the world. They covet only to joy and to be glorified in God, and desire in heart that he may be honoured, lauded, and praised, above all things, both in himself and in all his saints; and that is always the thing that perfect men most desire to bring about.

Be thou loving and thankful to God for the least benefit that he giveth thee, and then thou shalt be the better prepared and the more worthy to receive of him greater benefits. Think the least gift that he giveth is great; and the most despisable things take as special gifts and as great tokens of love. For if the dignity of the giver be well considered, no gift that he giveth shall seem little. It is no little thing that is given of God, for though he send pain and sorrow we should take them gladly and thankfully, since all that he suffereth to come unto us is for our ghostly health. If a man desire to hold the grace of God, let him be kind and thankful for such grace as he hath received, and patient when it is withdrawn; let him pray devoutly that it may shortly come again, and then let him be meek and humble in spirit, so that he lose it not through his presumption and pride of heart.

C H A P T E R   X I

Of the small number of the lovers of the cross

JESUS hath many lovers of his kingdom of heaven, but he hath few bearers of his cross. Many desire his consolation, but few desire his tribulation. He findeth many fellows at eating and drinking, but he findeth few that will be with him in his abstinence and fasting. All men would joy with Christ, but few will anything suffer for Christ. Many follow him to the breaking of his bread for their bodily refection, but few will follow him to drink a draught of the chalice of his Passion. Many honour his miracles, but few will follow the shame of his cross and of his other ignominies. Many love Jesus as long as no adversity falleth to them, and can praise him and bless him when they receive any benefit of him; but if Jesus a little withdraweth from them and a little forsaketh them, anon they fall to some great grudging, or to over-great dejection, or into open desperation.

But they that love Jesus purely for himself and not for their own profit or commodity, bless him as heartily in temptation and tribulation, and in all other adversities, as they do in time of consolation. And if he never sent them consolation yet would they always laud him and praise him. O how much more may the love of Jesus do to the help of a soul if it be pure and clean, not mixed with any inordinate love to itself? May not they, then, that ever look for worldly comforts and for worldly consolations be called worldly merchants and worldly lovers rather than lovers of God? Do they not openly show by their deeds that they rather love themselves than God? Yes truly. O where may be found any that will serve God freely and purely without looking for some reward for it again? And where may be found any so spiritual that he is clearly delivered and bereft from love of himself, truly poor in spirit, and wholly avoided from love of creatures? I trow none such can be found, unless it be far hence and in far countries.

If a man give all his substance for God, yet he is naught; and if he do great penance for his sins, yet he is but little; and if he have great wisdom and knowledge, yet he is far from virtue. And if he have great virtue and burning devotion, yet much wanteth him, and that is especially one thing which is most necessary to him. What is that? That, all things forsaken, and himself also forsaken, he go clearly out from himself and keep nothing to himself of any private love. And when he hath done all that he ought to do, that he feel in himself as he had nothing done; that he think it but little that some other might think great, and that he believe himself truly, as he is, an unprofitable servant. For the author of truth, our Saviour Christ, saith: When ye have done all that is commanded you to do, yet say that ye be but unprofitable servants. Then he that can thus do, may well be called poor in spirit and naked of private love, and he may well say with the prophet David: I am one with God, and am poor and meek in heart. There is none more rich, none more free, none of more power, than he that can forsake himself and all passing things, and that truly can hold himself to be lowest and vilest of all.

CHAPTER XII

Of the way of the cross and how profitable patience is in adversity

THE WORDS of our Saviour be thought very hard and grievous when he saith thus: Forsake thyself, take the cross, and follow me. But it shall be much more grievous to hear these words at the last judgment: Go ye from me, ye cursed people, into the fire that ever shall last. But those that now gladly hear and follow the words of

Christ, whereby he counselleth them to follow him, shall not then need to dread for hearing those words of everlasting damnation. The sign of the cross shall appear in heaven when our Lord shall come to judge the world, and the servants of the cross, who conformed themselves here in this life to Christ crucified on the cross, shall go to Christ their judge with great faith and trust in him.

Why dost thou then dread to take this cross since it is the very way to the kingdom of heaven, and none but that? In the cross is health, in the cross is life, in the cross is defence from our enemies, in the cross is infusion of heavenly sweetness; in the cross is the strength of mind, the joy of spirit, the highness of virtue, and the full perfection of all holiness; and there is no health of soul nor hope of everlasting life but through virtue of the cross. Take therefore thy cross and follow Jesus, and thou shalt go in to the life everlasting. He hath gone before thee bearing his cross, and died for thee upon the cross, that thou shouldst in like wise bear with him the cross of penance and of tribulation; and that thou shouldst be ready likewise for his love to suffer death, if need require, as he hath done for thee. If thou die with him, thou shalt live with him; and if thou be fellow with him in pain, thou shalt be with him in glory.

Behold then how in the cross standeth all, and how in dying to the world lieth all our health; and that there is no other way to life and true inward peace but the way of the cross, and of daily mortifying of the body to the spirit. Go whither thou wilt, and seek what thee list, and thou shalt never find, above thee or beneath thee, within thee or without thee, a more high, a more excellent, nor a more sure way to Christ than the way of the holy cross.

Dispose everything after thy will and yet thou shalt find that thou must of necessity somewhat suffer, either with thy will or against thy will, and so thou shalt always find the cross; for either thou shalt feel pain in thy body, or in thy soul thou shalt have trouble of spirit. Thou shalt be sometimes as if thou were forsaken of God. Sometimes thou shalt be vexed with thy neighbour; and what is yet more painful, thou shalt sometimes be grievous to thyself. And thou shalt find no means to be delivered, but that it behoveth thee to suffer till it shall please almighty God of his goodness otherwise to dispose for thee; for he desireth thou shalt learn to suffer tribulation without consolation, so that thou mayst thereby learn wholly to submit thyself to him, and by tribulation to be made more meek than thou were first. No man feeleth the Passion of Christ so effectuously as he that feeleth like pain as Christ did.

This cross is always ready, and everywhere it abideth thee. And thou mayst not flee it nor fully escape it wherever thou be come; for wheresoever thou be come thou shalt bear thyself about with thee, and so thou shalt always find thyself. Turn thee where thou wilt, above thee and beneath thee, within thee and without thee, and thou shalt find this cross on every side, so that it shall be necessary for thee that thou always keep thee in patience; and this it behoveth thee to do if thou wilt have inward peace and deserve the perpetual crown in heaven.

If thou wilt gladly bear this cross, it shall bear thee; and it shall bring thee to the end that thou desirest, where thou shalt never after have anything to suffer. But if thou bear this cross against thy will, thou makest a great burden to thyself and it will be the more grievous to thee, and yet it behoveth thee to bear it. And if it happen thee to put away one cross, that is to say, one tribulation, yet surely another will come, and haply more grievous than the first was.

Trowest thou to escape that which never yet any mortal man might escape? What saint in this world hath been without his cross and without some trouble? Truly our Lord Jesus was not one hour without some sorrow and pain as long as he lived here, for it behoved him to suffer death, and to rise again, and so to enter into his glory. And how is it then that thou seekest any other way to heaven than this plain high way of the cross? All the life of Christ was cross and martyrdom, and seekest thou pleasure and joy? Thou errest greatly if thou seek any other thing than to suffer, for all this mortal life is full of miseries and is all beset about and marked with crosses. And the more highly that a man profiteth in spirit the more painful crosses shall he find, for by the soothfastness of Christ's love, wherein he daily increaseth, daily appeareth unto him more and more the pain of this exile.

Nevertheless, a man thus vexed with pain is not left wholly without all comfort, for he seeth well that great fruit and high reward shall grow unto him by the bearing of his cross. And when a man freely submitteth himself to such tribulation, then all the burden of tribulation is suddenly turned into a great trust of heavenly solace. The more the flesh is punished with tribulation, the more is the soul strengthened daily by inward consolation. And sometimes the soul shall feel such comfort in adversities, that for love and desire to be conformed to Christ crucified, it would not be without sorrow and trouble; for the more that it may suffer for his love here, the more acceptable shall it be to him in the life to come. But this working is not in the power of man unless through the grace of God; that is to say, that a frail man should take and love adversities that his bodily kind so much abhorreth and fleeth.

It is not in the power of man gladly to bear the cross, to love the cross, to chastise the body and to make it submissive to the will of the spirit; to flee honours gladly, to sustain reproofs, to despise himself and to covet to be despised; patiently to suffer adversities with all displeasures thereof, and not to desire any manner of profit in this world. If thou trust in thyself thou shalt never bring this matter about; but if thou trust in God, he shall send thee strength from heaven, and the world and the flesh shall be made subject to thee. Yea, and if thou be strongly armed with faith and be marked with the cross of Christ as his household servant, thou shalt not need to fear thy ghostly enemy for he shall also be made subject to thee so that he shall have no power against thee.

Purpose thyself as a true faithful servant of God, to bear manfully the cross of thy Lord Jesus, who for thy love was crucified upon the cross. Prepare thyself to suffer all manner of adversities and discommodities in this wretched life, for so shall it be with thee wheresoever thou hide thee, and there is no remedy to escape, but thou must keep thyself always in patience. If thou desire to be a dear and a well-beloved friend of Christ, drink effectuously with him a draught of the chalice of his tribulation. As for consolations, commit them to his will, that he order them as he knoweth most expedient for thee; but as for thyself, and as much as in thee is, dispose thee to suffer. And when tribulations come, take them as special consolations, saying with the apostle thus: The passions of this world be not worthy of themselves to bring us to the glory that is ordained for us in the life to come. And that is true, though one man alone might suffer as much as all men do suffer.

When thou comest to that degree of patience that tribulation is sweet to thee, and for the love of God is savoury and pleasant in thy sight, then mayst thou trust that it is well with thee and that thou art in good estate; for thou hast found paradise on earth. But as long as it is grievous to thee to suffer and thou seekest to flee, so long it is not well with thee and so long thou art not in the perfect way of patience. If thou couldst bring thyself to that estate that thou shouldst be at, that is, to suffer gladly for God, and to die fully to the world, then it should shortly be better with thee and thou shouldst find great peace.

Yet although thou were rapt with Paul into the third heaven, thou shouldst not therefore be sure without all adversity; for our Saviour, speaking of Saint Paul after he had been rapt into heaven, said thus of him: I shall show him how many things he shall suffer for me. To suffer, therefore, remaineth to thee if thou wilt love thy Lord Jesus and serve him perpetually. Would to God that thou wert worthy to suffer somewhat for his love! O how great joy should it be to thee to suffer for him! What gladness to all the saints of heaven, and how great edifying to thy neighbour! All men commend patience, and yet few men will suffer. Rightwisely oughtest thou, that sufferest much more for the world to suffer some little thing for God.

Know this for certain, that after this bodily death thou shalt yet live, and the more that thou canst die to thyself here, the more thou beginnest to live to God. No man is worthy to receive the heavenly rewards, unless he have first learned to bear adversities for the love of Christ; for nothing is more acceptable to God or more profitable to man in this world than to be glad to suffer for Christ, insomuch that if it were put in thy election, thou shouldst rather choose adversity than prosperity, for then, by the patient suffering thereof, thou shouldst be the more like to Christ and the more conformed to all his saints. Our merit and our perfection of life standeth not in consolations and sweetness, but rather in suffering of great grievous adversities and tribulations.

If there had been any nearer or better way for the health of man's soul than to suffer, our Lord Jesus would have showed it by words and by examples. But for there was not, therefore he openly exhorted his disciples that followed him, and all others that desired to follow him, to forsake their own will and to take the cross of penance and follow him, saying thus: Whoso will come after me let him forsake his own will, take the cross, and follow me. Therefore, all things searched and read, be this the final conclusion: that by many tribulations it behoveth us to enter into the kingdom of heaven; to the which bring us, our Lord Jesus.

ST. THOMAS MORE

THE FOUR LAST THINGS

DEATH

A treatise (unfinished) upon these words
of Holy Scripture

Memorare novissima, et in aeternum non peccabis
"Remember the last things, and thou shalt never sin."
ECCLUS. 7

> What availeth it to know that there is a God, which
> thou not only believest by faith but also knowest by
> reason, what availeth that thou knowest Him, if thou
> think little of Him?

HUMANIST, lawyer, heroic Christian and happy martyr, such was Sir Thomas More, whom Pope Pius XI canonized in 1935. He was born in 1478, and died on the block in 1535. He held important offices under Henry VIII, but was driven to retirement in 1532 when he showed himself unwilling to approve Henry's divorce from Catherine of Aragon. And when he refused to abandon his faith in the supremacy of the Pope, he was imprisoned in the Tower of London and beheaded, shortly after the execution of St. John Fisher. A distinguished man of letters, friend of Erasmus and other humanists, More had an irresistible, merry innocence and a deep faith, as his letters to his daughter Margaret reveal. The famous *Utopia* was written in Latin in 1516 and was translated into English in 1551. The present selection is taken from an unfinished work written by More some ten years before he fell out of kingly favor. Here are earnest words on the certainty of death.

Made about the year of our Lord 1522, by Sir Thomas More then knight, and one of the Privy Council of King Henry VIII, and also Under-Treasurer of England.

F THERE WERE ANY QUESTION AMONG MEN whether the words of holy Scripture or the doctrine of any secular author were of greater force and effect to the weal and profit of man's soul (though we should let pass so many short and weighty words spoken by the mouth of our Saviour Christ Himself, to Whose heavenly wisdom the wit of none earthly creature can be comparable) yet this only text written by the wise man in the seventh chapter of Ecclesiasticus is such that it containeth more fruitful advice and counsel to the forming and framing of man's manners in virtue and avoiding of sin, than many whole and great volumes of the best of old philosophers or any other that ever wrote in secular literature.

Long would it be to take the best of their words and compare it with these words of holy Writ. Let us consider the fruit and profit of this in itself: which thing, well advised and pondered, shall well declare that of none whole volume of secular literature shall arise so very fruitful doctrine. For what would a man give for a sure medicine that were of such strength that it should all his life keep from sickness, namely [1] if he might by the avoiding of sickness be sure to continue his life one hundred years? So is it now that these words giveth us all a sure medicine (if we forsloth [2] not the receiving) by which we shall keep from sickness, not the body, which none health may long keep from death (for die we must in

[1] especially.   [2] postpone.

few years, live we never so long), but the soul, which here preserved from the sickness of sin, shall after this eternally live in
joy and be preserved from the deadly life of everlasting pain.

The physician sendeth his bill to the apothecary, and therein
writeth sometimes a costly receipt of many strange herbs and roots,
fetched out of far countries, long-lain drugs, all the strength worn
out, and some none such to be got. But this physician sendeth his
bill to thyself, no strange thing therein, nothing costly to buy,
nothing far to fetch, but to be gathered all times of the year in the
garden of thine own soul.

Let us hear, then, what wholesome receipt this is. "Remember,"
saith this bill, "thy last things, and thou shalt never sin in this
world." Here is first a short medicine containing only four herbs,
common and well known, that is to wit, death, doom, pain, and
joy.

This short medicine is of a marvellous force, able to keep us all
our life from sin. The physician cannot give no one medicine to
every man to keep him from sickness, but to divers men divers, by
reason of the diversity of divers complexions. This medicine serveth
every man. The physician doth but guess and conjecture that his
receipt shall do good: but this medicine is undoubtedly sure.

How happeth it, then, thou wilt haply say, that so few be preserved from sin, if every man have so sure a medicine, so ready at
hand? For folk fare commonly as he doth that goeth forth fasting
among sick folk for sloth, rather than he will take a little treacle [3]
before.

Thou wilt say, peradventure, that some part of this medicine is
very bitter and painful to receive. Surely there can be nothing so
bitter but wisdom would brook it for so great a profit? But yet this
medicine, though thou make a sour face at it, is not so bitter as
thou makest for.[4] For well thou wottest, he biddeth thee not to
take neither death, nor doom, nor pain, but only to remember them,
and yet the joy of heaven therewith to temper them withal. Now if
a man be so dainty stomached that going where contagion is he
would grudge to take a little treacle, yet were he very nicely wanton if he might not at the leastwise take a little vinegar and rose
water in his handkercher.

[3] a prophylactic.   [4] pretend.

Yet wot I well that many one will say that the bare remembrance of death alone, if a man consider it and advise it well, were able to bereave a man of all the pleasure of his life. How much more, then, should his life be painful and grievous if, to the remembrance and consideration of death, a man should add and set to, the deep imagination of the dreadful doom of God, and bitter pains of purgatory or hell, of which every one passeth and exceedeth many deaths. These are the sage saws of such as make this world their heaven, and their lust their God.

Now see the blindness of us worldly folk, how precisely we presume to shoot our foolish bolt, in those matters most in which we least can skill.[5] For I little doubt but that among four thousand taken out at adventure, we shall not find four score but they shall boldly affirm it for a thing too painful, busily to remember these four last things. And yet durst I lay a wager that of those four thousand ye shall not find fourteen that hath deeply thought on them four times in all their days.

If men would vouchsafe to put in proof and experience the operation and working of this medicine, the remembrance of these four last things, they should find therein, not the pleasure of their life lost, but so great a pleasure grow thereby that they never felt the like before nor would have supposed that ever they should have felt any such. For it is to be known that, like as we be made of two far divers and unlike substances, the body and the soul, so we be apt and able to receive two diverse and unlike pleasures, the one carnal and fleshly, the other ghostly and spiritual. And like as the soul excelleth the body, so doth the sweetness of spiritual pleasure far pass and excel the gross and filthy pleasure of all fleshly delight, which is of truth no very true pleasure, but a false counterfeit image of pleasure. And the cause why men be so mad thereon is only for ignorance and lack of knowledge of the other,—as those that lack insight of precious stones hold themselves as well content and satisfied with a beryl or crystal well counterfeited, as with a right natural diamond. But he that by good use and experience hath in his eye the right mark and very true lustre of the diamond, rejecteth anon and listeth not to look upon the counterfeit, be it never so well handled, never so craftily polished. And trust it well

[5] have least knowledge.

that, in likewise, if men would well accustom themselves in the taste of spiritual pleasure and of that sweet feeling that virtuous people have of the good hope of heaven, they should shortly set at naught, and at length abhor, the foul delight and filthy liking that riseth of sensual and fleshly pleasure, which is never so pleasantly spiced with delight and liking but that it bringeth therewith such a grudge and grief of conscience that it maketh the stomach wamble [6] and fare as it would vomit. And that notwithstanding, such is our blind custom that we persevere therein without care or cure of the better, as a sow content with draff,[7] dirt and mire careth neither for better meat nor better bed.

Think not that everything is pleasant that men for madness laugh at. For thou shalt in Bedlam see one laugh at the knocking of his own head against a post, and yet there is little pleasure therein. But ye think peradventure this example as mad as the mad man, and as little to the purpose. I am content ye so think. But what will ye say if ye see men that are taken and reputed wise laugh more madly than he? Shall ye not see such laugh at their own craft, when they have, as they think, wilfully done their neighbour wrong? Now whoso seeth not that his laughter is more mad than the laughter of the mad man, I hold him madder than they both. For the mad man laughed when he had done himself but little hurt, by a knock of his head to the post. This other sage fool laugheth at the casting of his own soul into the fire of hell, for which he hath cause to weep all his life. And it cannot be but the grudge and fear thereof followeth his laughter, and secret sorrow marreth all such outward mirth. For the heart of a wicked wretch is like a stormy sea that cannot rest,[8] except a man be fallen down into the dungeon of wretchedness, and the door shut over his head. For when a sinner is once fallen down into the depth, he waxeth a desperate wretch and setteth all at naught, and he is in the worst kind of all, and farthest from all recovery. For like as in the body his sickness is most incurable that is sick and feeleth it not, but weeneth himself whole (for he that is in that case is commonly mad), so he that by a mischievous custom of sin perceiveth no fault in his evil deed nor hath no remorse thereof, hath lost the natural light of reason and the spiritual light of faith, which two lights

[6] uneasy.   [7] refuse, hogwash.   [8] *Isa.* lvii, 20.

of knowledge and understanding quenched, what remaineth in him more than the bodily senses and sensual wits common to man and brute beasts?

Now albeit so that the fleshly and worldly pleasure is of truth not pleasant but bitter, and the spiritual pleasure is of truth so sweet that the sweetness thereof many times darkeneth [9] and diminisheth the feeling of bodily pain, by reason whereof good virtuous folk feel more pleasure in the sorrow of their sins and affliction of their penance than wretches feel in the fulfilling of their foul delight, and credible is it that the inward spiritual pleasure and comfort which many of the old holy martyrs had in the hope of heaven darkened [10] and in manner overwhelmed the bodily pains of their torment,—yet this notwithstanding like as a sick man feeleth no sweetness in sugar, and some women with child have such fond lust that they had liefer eat tar than treacle and rather pitch than marmalade, and some whole people love tallow better than butter, and Iceland loveth no butter till it be long barrelled, so we gross carnal people, having our taste infected by the sickness of sin and filthy custom of fleshly delight that we list not once prove what manner of sweetness good and virtuous folk feel and perceive in spiritual pleasure. And the cause is why? Because we cannot perceive the one, but if we forbear the other. For like as the ground that is all forgrown [11] with nettles, briars, and other evil weeds, can bring forth no corn till they be weeded out, so can our soul have no place for the good corn of spiritual pleasure as long as it is overgrown with the barren weeds of carnal delectation. For the pulling out of which weeds by the root, there is not a more meet instrument than the remembrance of the four last things, which as they shall pull out these weeds of fleshly voluptuousness, so shall they not fail to plant in their places, not only wholesome virtues, but also marvellous ghostly pleasure and spiritual gladness, which in every good soul riseth of the love of God, and hope of heaven, and inward liking that the godly spirit taketh in the diligent labour of good and virtuous business.

I would not so long tarry in this point nor make so many words of the pleasure that men may find by the receipt of this medicine, were it not that I well perceive the world so set upon the seeking

[9] deadens.   [10] deadens.   [11] overgrows.

of pleasure, that they set by pleasure much more than by profit. And therefore, to the intent that ye may perceive that it is not a fantasy found [12] of mine own head, that the abandoning and refusing of carnal pleasure and the ensuing of labour, travail, penance and bodily pain, shall bring therewith to a Christian man, not only in the world that is coming but also in this present life, very sweetness, comfort, pleasure, and gladness, I shall prove it to be true by their testimony and witness whose authority, speaking of their own experience, there will, I ween, none honest man mistrust.

Lo, the holy doctor, Saint Austin, exhorting penitents and repentant sinners to sorrow for their offences, saith unto them: "Sorrow," saith this holy man, "and be glad of thy sorrow." In vain should he bid him be glad of his sorrow, if man in sorrow could not be glad. But this holy father showeth by this counsel, not only that a man may be joyful and glad for all his sorrow, but also that he may be and hath cause to be glad because of his sorrow.

Long were it to rehearse the places that prove this point among the holy doctors of Christ's Church; but we will, instead of them all, allege you the words of Him that is doctor of them all, our Saviour Jesu Christ. He saith that the way to heaven is straight and aspre [13] or painful.[14] And therefore He saith that few folk find it out or walk therein. And yet saith He for all that, *My yoke is easy and my burden light*.[15] How could these two sayings stand together, were it not that as the labour, travail, and affliction of the body is painful and sharp to the flesh, so the comfort and gladness that the soul conceiveth thereof, rising into the love of our Lord and hope of His glory to come, so tempereth and overmastereth the bitterness of the grief, that it maketh the very labour easy, the sourness very sweet, and the very pain pleasant?

Will ye see the example? Look upon His holy apostles,—when they were taken and scourged with whips for Christ's sake, did it grieve them, think ye? Imagine yourself in the same case, and I think ye will think yea. Now see, then, for all the pain of their flesh, what joy and pleasure they conceived in their soul. The holy Scripture saith [16] that they rejoiced and joyed that God had accounted them worthy for Christ's sake, not only to be scourged, but

---

[12] contrived, invented.   [13] sharp.   [14] *Matt.* vii, 14.   [15] *Matt.* xi, 30.
[16] *Acts* v, 41.

also—which would be far greater grief to an honest man than the pain itself—to be scourged with despite and shame, so that the more their pain was, the more was their joy. For as the holy doctor, Saint Chrysostom, saith, though pain be grievous for the nature of the affliction, yet is it pleasant by the alacrity and quick mind of them that willingly suffer it. And therefore, though the nature of the torments make great grief and pain, yet the prompt and willing mind of them that were scourged passed and overcame the nature of the thing, that is to wit, mastering the outward fleshly pain with inward spiritual pleasure. And surely this is so true that it may stand for a very certain token that a penitent beginneth to profit and grow in grace and favour of God when he feeleth a pleasure and quickness in his labour and pain taken in prayer, almsdeeds, pilgrimage, fasting, discipline, tribulation, affliction, and such other spiritual exercise, by which the soul willingly worketh with the body by their own punishment to purge and rub out the rusty, cankered spots that sin hath defiled them with in the sight of God, and to leave the fewer to be burned out in the fire of purgatory. And whensoever, as I say, that a man feeleth in this pain a pleasure, he hath a token of great grace and that his penance is pleasant to God, for, as the holy Scripture saith, our Lord loveth a glad giver.[17] And on the other side, whereas one doth such spiritual business with a dulness of spirit and weariness of mind, he doth twice as much and thereby taketh four times as much pain, since his bodily pain is relieved with no spiritual rejoice nor comfort. I will not say that his labour is lost, but I dare be bold to say that he profiteth much less with much more pain. For certain it is that the best souls and they that have best travailed in spiritual business, find most comfort therein.[18] And therefore if they most pleased God that in the bodily pain of their penance took less spiritual pleasure, it should thereof follow that the farther a man proceeded in the perfection of spiritual exercise, in the worse case he were. Which can in no wise be so, since that we see the holy apostles and other holy men and women, the better that they were, the more pleasure they perceived in their fleshly afflictions, either

[17] *II Cor.* ix, 7.
[18] Cf. *Dialogue Concerning Tyndale*, II, 8 (*The English Works of Sir Thomas More;* Vol. II, p. 151).

put unto them by God, or taken by themselves for God's sake.

Therefore let every man by the labour of his mind and help of prayer, enforce himself in all tribulation and affliction, labour pain and travail, without spot of pride or ascribing any praise to himself, to conceive a delight and pleasure in such spiritual exercise and thereby to rise in the love of our Lord, with an hope of heaven, contempt of the world, and longing to be with God. To the attaining of which mind, by the putting away of the malicious pleasures of the devil, the filthy pleasures of the flesh, and the vain pleasures of the world, which once excluded there is place made and clean purged to receive the very sweet and pure pleasure of the spirit,—there is not any one thing lightly, as I have said, more accommodated nor more effectual than this thing I have begun with and taken in hand to entreat, that is to wit, the remembrance of the four last things, which is, as the Scripture saith, so effectual that if a man remember it well, he shall never sin.

Thou wilt haply say that it is not enough that a man do none evil, but he must also do good. This is very truth that ye say. But first, if there be but these two steps to heaven, he that getteth him on the one is half up. And over that, whoso doth none evil, it will be very hard but he must needs do good, since man's mind is never idle but occupied commonly either with good or evil.

And therefore, when folk have few words and use much musing, likewise as among many words all be not always well and wisely set, so, when the tongue lieth still, if the mind be not occupied well it were less evil, save for worldly rebuke, to blabber on trifles somewhat sottishly, than while they seem sage in keeping silence, secretly peradventure the meanwhile to fantasy with themselves filthy sinful devices, whereof their tongues, if they were set on babbling, could not for shame utter and speak the like.

I say not this for that I would have folks fall to babbling, well wotting that, as the Scripture saith, in many words lacketh not sin [19]—but that I would have folk in their silence take good heed that their minds be occupied with good thoughts, for unoccupied be they never. For if ever the mind were empty, it would be empty when the body sleepeth. But if it were then all empty, we should have no dreams. Then, if the fantasies leave us not sleeping, it is

[19] *Prov.* x, 19.

not likely that ever they leave us waking. Wherefore, as I say, let us keep our minds occupied with good thoughts, or else the devil will fill them with evil.

And surely everything hath his mean. There is, as Scripture saith, time to speak and time to keep thy tongue.[20] Whensoever the communication is naught [21] and ungodly, it is better to hold thy tongue and think on some better thing the while, than to give ear thereto and underpin [22] the tale. And yet better were it than holding of thy tongue, properly to speak, and with some good grace and pleasant fashion to break into some better matter; by which thy speech and talking, thou shalt not only profit thyself as thou shouldst have done by thy well minded silence, but also amend the whole audience, which is a thing far better and of much more merit. Howbeit, if thou can find no proper means to break the tale, then, except thy bare authority suffice to command silence, it were peradventure good, rather to keep a good silence thyself, than blunder forth rudely and irritate them to anger, which shall haply therefor not let [23] to talk on, but speak much the more, lest they should seem to leave at thy commandment. And better were it for the while to let one wanton word pass uncontrolled, than give occasion of twain. But if the communication be good, then is it better not only to give ear thereto, but also first well and prudently to devise with thyself upon the same, and then moderately and in good manner, if thou find aught to the purpose, speak thereto and say thy mind therein. So shall it appear to the presence,[24] that your mind was well occupied the while and your thought not wandering forty miles thence while your body was there; as it often happeth that the very face showeth the mind walking a pilgrimage, in such wise that, not without some note and reproach of such vagrant mind, other folk suddenly say to them: "A penny for your thoughts." Which manner of wandering mind in company may percase be the more excusable sometimes by some chargeable business of the party, but surely it is never taken for wisdom nor good manners.

But now to return to my purpose, since the remembrance of these four last things is of such force and efficacy that it is able always to keep us from sin, and since we can never be long void of both,

[20] *Eccles.* iii, 7.   [21] the talk is evil.   [22] support.   [23] refrain.
[24] those present.

it must thereof ensue that we shall consequently do good; and thereof must it needs follow that this only lesson well learned and busily put in ure [25] must needs lead us to heaven.

Yet will ye peradventure say that ye know these four things well enough, and if the knowledge thereof had so great effect as the Scripture speaketh of, there should not be so many naught [26] as there be. For what Christian man is he, that hath wit and discretion, but he hath heard and, having any faith, believeth these four last things, of which the first, that is to say, death, we need no faith to believe, we know it by daily proof and experience?

I say not nay, but that we know them either by faith or experience,—and yet not so very thoroughly as we might, peradventure, and hereafter undoubtedly shall. Which if we knew once thoroughly, and so feelingly perceived as we might, percase, and namely as we surely shall, there would be little doubt but the least of all the four would well keep us from sin. For as for yet, though we have heard of the doom, yet were we never at it: though we have heard of hell, yet came we never in it; though we have heard of heaven, yet came we never to it; and though we daily see men die, and thereby know the death, yet ourselves never felt it. For if we knew these things thoroughly, the least of all four were, as I said, enough to keep us from sin.

Howbeit, the foresaid words of Scripture biddeth thee not know the four last things, but remember thy four last things, and then, he saith, thou shall never sin.

Many things know we that we seldom think on: and in the things of the soul, the knowledge without the remembrance little profiteth. What availeth it to know that there is a God, which thou not only believest by faith but also knowest by reason, what availeth that thou knowest Him, if thou think little of Him? The busy minding of thy four last things, and the deep consideration thereof, is the thing that shall keep thee from sin. And if thou put it in essay and make a proof, thou shalt well find, by that thou shalt have no lust to sin for the time that thou deeply thinkest on them, that if our frailty could endure never to remit or slacken in the deep devising of them, we should never have delight or pleasure in any sinful thing.

[25] into practice.　[26] evil.

For the proof whereof, let us first begin at the remembrance of the first of these four last, which is undoubtedly far the least of the four, and thereby shall we make a proof what marvellous effect may grow by the diligent remembrance of all four, towards the avoiding of all the trains,[27] darts, sleights, enticings and assaults of the three mortal enemies, the devil, the world and our own flesh. THE REMEMBRANCE OF DEATH. What profit and commodity cometh unto man's soul by the meditation of death is not only marked of [28] the chosen people of God, but also of such as were the best sort among gentiles and paynims. For some of the old famous philosophers, when they were demanded what faculty philosophy was, answered that it was the meditation or exercise of death. For like as death maketh a severance of the body and the soul, when they by course of nature must needs depart asunder, so (said they) doth the study of philosophy labour to sever the soul from the love and affections of the body while they be together. Now if this be the whole study and labour of philosophy, as the best philosophers said that it is, then may we within short time be well learned in philosophy. For nothing is there that may more effectually withdraw the soul from the wretched affections of the body than may the remembrance of death,—if we do not remember it hoverly,[29] as one heareth a word and let it pass by his ear, without any receiving of the sentence [30] into his heart. But if we not only hear this word "death," but also let sink into our hearts the very fantasy and deep imagination thereof, we shall perceive thereby that we were never so greatly moved by the beholding of the Dance of Death pictured in Paul's, as we shall feel ourselves stirred and altered by the feeling of that imagination in our hearts. And no marvel. For those pictures express only the loathly figure of our dead bony bodies, bitten away the flesh; which though it be ugly to behold, yet neither the light thereof, nor the sight of all the dead heads in the charnel house, nor the apparition of a very ghost, is half so grisly as the deep conceived fantasy of death in his nature, by the lively imagination graven in thine own heart. For there seest thou, not one plain grievous sight of the bare bones hanging by the sinews, but thou seest (if thou fantasy thine own death, for so art thou by this counsel advised), thou seest, I say, thyself, if thou die

[27] schemes, plots.   [28] observed in.   [29] inattentively.   [30] meaning.

no worse death, yet leastwise lying in thy bed, thy head shooting, thy back aching, thy veins beating, thine heart panting, thy throat rattling, thy flesh trembling, thy mouth gaping, thy nose sharping, thy legs cooling, thy fingers fumbling, thy breath shortening, all thy strength fainting, thy life vanishing, and thy death drawing on.

If thou couldst now call to thy remembrance some of those sicknesses that have most grieved thee and tormented thee in thy days, as every man hath felt some, and then findest thou that some one disease in some one part of thy body, as percase the stone or the strangury, have put thee to thine own mind to no less torment than thou shouldst have felt if one had put up a knife into the same place, and wouldst, as thee then seemed, have been content with such a change,—think what it will be then when thou shalt feel so many such pains in every part of thy body, breaking thy veins and thy life strings, with like pain and grief as thou as many knives as thy body might receive should everywhere enter and meet in the midst. A stroke of a staff, a cut of a knife, the flesh singed with fire, the pain of sundrt sickness, many men have essayed in themselves; and they have not yet, somewhat have heard by them that felt it. But what manner dolour and pain, what manner of grievous pangs, what intolerable torment, the silly creature feeleth in the dissolution and severance of the soul from the body, never was there body that yet could tell the tale.

Some conjecture and token of this point we have of the bitter passion and piteous departing of our Saviour Jesu Christ, of Whom we nothing read that ever He cried for any pain, neither for the whips and rods beating His blessed body nor the sharp thorns pricking His holy head, or the great, long nails piercing His precious hands and feet. But when the point approached in which His sacred soul should depart out of His blessed body, at that point He cried loud once or twice to His Father in heaven, into Whose mighty and merciful hands, at the extreme point, with a great loud cry He gave up the ghost.[31] Now if that death was so painful and ragious to our Saviour Christ, Whose joy and comfort of His godhead, if He would have suffered it, might in such wise have redounded into His soul, and so forth into His body, that it should not only have supped up all His pain, but also have transformed His holy body into a

[31] *Matt.* xxvii, 50; *Mark* xv, 37; *Luke* xxiii, 46.

glorious form and made it impossible,—what intolerable torment will death be then to us miserable wretches, of which the more part among the pangs of our passage shall have yet so painful twitches of our own conscience that the fear of hell, the dread of the devil, and sorrow at our heart at the sight of our sins, shall pass and exceed the deadly pains of our body.

Other things are there which will peradventure seem no great matter to them that feel them not, but unto him that shall lie in that case, they shall be tedious out of all measure.

Have ye not ere this, in a sore sickness, felt it very grievous to have folk babble to you, and namely [32] such things as ye should answer to, when it was pain to speak? Think ye not now that it will be a gentle pleasure, when we lie dying, all our body in pain, all our mind in trouble, our soul in sorrow, our heart all in dread while our life walketh awayward, while our death draweth toward, while the devil is busy about us, while we lack stomach and strength to bear any one of so manifold heinous troubles, will it not be, as I was about to say, a pleasant thing to see before thine eyes and hear at thine ear a rabble of fleshly friends, or rather of flesh flies, skipping about thy bed and thy sick body, like ravens about thy corpse, now almost carrion, crying to thee on every side, "What shall I have? What shall I have?" Then shall come thy children and cry for their parts; then shall come thy sweet wife, and where in thine health haply she spake thee not one sweet word in six weeks, now shall she call thee sweet husband and weep with much work and ask thee what shall she have; then shall thine executors ask for the keys, and ask what money is owing thee, ask what substance thou hast, and ask where thy money lieth. And while thou liest in that case, their words shall be so tedious that thou wilt wish all that they ask for upon a red fire, so thou mightest lie one half-hour in rest.

Now is there one thing which a little I touched before, I wot not whether more painful or more perilous,—the marvellous intent business and solicitation of our ghostly enemy the devil, not only in one fashion present, but surely never absent from him that draweth towards death. For since that of his pestilent envy conceived from the beginning of man's creation, by which he lay in wait to take our first mother, Eve, in a train, and thereby drawing our

[32] especially.

former father, Adam, into the breach of God's behest, found the
means not without the grievous increase of his own damnation, to
deprive us of paradise and bereave us our immortality, making us
into subjection not only of temporal death but also of his eternal
tormentry, were we not by the great bounty of God and Christ's
painful passion, restored to the possibility of everlasting life, he
never ceased since to run about like a ramping lion,[33] looking whom
he might devour,—it can be no doubt but he most busily travaileth
in that behalf at the time that he perceiveth us about to depart hence.
For well he knoweth that then he either winneth a man for ever, or
for ever loseth him; for have he him never so fast afore, yet if he
break from him then he can after his death never get him again. Well
he may, peradventure, have him as his gaoler in his prison of purgatory for the time of his punition temporal; but as he would have
him for his perpetual slave, shall he never have him after, how sure
soever he had him afore, if he get from him at the time of his death.
For so lost he suddenly the thief that hung on the right hand of
Christ. And on the other side, if he catch a man fast at the time of
his death, he is sure to keep him for ever. For as the Scripture saith,
Wheresoever the stone [34] *falleth, there shall it abide.*[35] And since
he knoweth this for very surety and is of malice so venomous and
envious that he had liefer double his own pain than suffer us to escape from pain, he, when we draw to death, doth his uttermost endeavour to bring us to damnation, never ceasing to minister, by subtle
and incogitable [36] means, first unlawful longing to live and horror
to go gladly to God at His calling.

Then giveth he some false glade [37] of escaping that sickness, and
thereby putteth in our mind a love yet and cleaving to the world,
keeping of our goods, loathsomeness of shrift, sloth towards good
works. And if we be so far gone that we see we cannot recover,
then he casteth in our minds presumption and security of salvation
as a thing well won by our own works, of which, if we have any
done well, he casteth them into our minds with over great liking
and thereby withdraweth us from the haste of doing any more, as
a thing that either needeth not or may be done by our executors.
And instead of sorrow for our sins and care of heaven, he putteth

[33] *Ps.* xxi, 14; *I Peter* v, 8.   [34] rather, tree.   [35] *Eccles.* xi, 3.
[36] incalculable.   [37] opening.

us in mind of provision for some honourable burying,—so many torches, so many tapers, so many black gowns, so many merry mourners laughing under black hoods, and a gay hearse, with the delight of goodly and honourable funerals: in which the foolish sick man is sometimes occupied as though he thought that he should stand in a window and see how worshipfully he shall be brought to church.

And thus inveigleth he them that either be good, or but meetly [38] bad.

But as for those that he hath known for special wretches, whose whole life hath in effect been all bestowed in his service, whom he hath brought into great and horrible sins by the horror whereof he hath kept them from confession, these folk at their end he handleth in another fashion. For into their minds he bringeth their shameful sins by heap, and by the abominable sight thereof draweth them into desperation. For the aggrieving whereof our Lord, after their deserving, suffereth him to show himself to them for their more discomfort in some fearful figure and terrible likeness, by the beholding whereof they conceive, sometimes despair of their salvation and yield themselves as captives quick, beginning their hell in this world, as hath appeared by the words and wretched behaviour of many that of a shameful, sinful life have died and departed with heavy desperate death. Now death being such as I have described, or rather much more horrible than any man can describe, it is not to be doubted but if we busily remembered the terror and grief thereof, it must needs be so bitter to the fleshly mind that it could not fail to take away the vain delight of all worldly vanities. But the thing that letteth us to consider death in his kind, and to take great profit that would arise of the remembrance thereof is that for by the hope of long life, we look upon death either so far off that we see him not at all, or but a slight and uncertain sight, as a man may see a thing so far off that he wotteth not whether it be a bush or a beast. And surely so fare we by death, looking thereat afar off through a great long space of as many years as we hope to live,— and those we imagine many, and perilously and foolishly beguile ourselves. For likewise as wives would their husbands should ween by the example of Sarah that there were no woman so old but she

[38] moderately.

might have a child, so is there none old man so old but that, as
Tully [39] saith, he trusteth to live one year yet. And as for young
folk, they look not how many be dead in their own days younger
than themselves, but who is the oldest man in the town, and upon
his years they make their reckoning,—where the wiser way were
to reckon that a young man may die soon, and an old man cannot
live long, but within a little while die the one may, the other must.
And with this reckoning shall they look upon death much nearer
hand, and better perceive him in his own likeness, and thereby take
the more fruit of the remembrance and make themselves the more
ready thereto.

Thou wouldst somewhat remember death the more effectually,
and look upon him somewhat the more nearly, if thou knewest thyself sick, and specially of any perilous sickness that would make an
end of thee though thou feltest yet little pain. For commonly when
we be sick then begin we to know ourselves, then pain bringeth us
home,[40] then we think how merry a thing it were to be praying in
health, which we cannot now do for grief. Then care we little for
our gay gear, then desire we no delicate dainties; and as for Lady
Lechery, then abhor we to think on. And then we think in ourselves that if ever we recover and mend in body, we will amend in
soul, leave all vices and be virtuously occupied the remnant of our
life. Insomuch that very true we find the words of the epistle that
the well-learned man, Plinius Secundus, after his sickness wrote
unto his friend, wherein after the description of men's fantasies in
their disease, he closeth up his letter in this wise: "Look," saith
he, "all the good counsel and precepts that all the philosophers and
wise men in this world give us for instruction of virtuous living,
all that can I compendiously give to myself and thee in few words:
no more, lo, but let us be such when we be whole, as we think we
will be when we be sick."

Now then if thou be ever sick, and ever sick of a perilous sickness, wouldst thou not, if thou knewest thyself in such case, have
better remembrance of death than thou hast? It would be hard,
peradventure, to make thee believe thyself sick while thou feelest
no harm, and yet is that no sure knowledge of health. Trow ye
not that many a man is infected with the great sickness a good while

[39] Cicero.   [40] brings things home to us.

ere he perceive it, and the body sore corrupt within ere he feel the grief? How many men have there been that have gone about with God's marks on their body, never perceiving themselves to be sick, but as merry as ever they were in their lives, till other men gave them warning how near they were their deaths? And therefore never reckon thyself whole, though thou feel no grief.

But thou wilt haply say, "Be it that I cannot surely reckon myself whole, yet ye show me not why I should reckon myself sick." Thou sayest right well, and that shall I show thee now. Tell me, if one were in case that he must be fain once or twice a day to swaddle and plaster his leg and else he could not keep his life, wouldst thou reckon his leg sick or whole? I ween ye will agree that his leg is not well at ease, nor the owner neither. Now if ye felt your belly in such case that ye must be fain all day to tend it with warm clothes [41] or else ye were not able to abide the pain, would ye reckon your belly sick or whole? I ween ye would reckon your belly not in good quart.[42] If thou shouldst see one in such case that he could not hold up his head, that he could not stand on his feet, that he should be fain to lie down along and there lie speechless as a dead stock an hour or two every day, wouldst thou not say that he were perilously sick and had good cause to remember death, when he lieth every day in such case as though he were dead already?

Now then I pray thee consider me that all our bodies be ever in such case so tender of themselves that except we lapped them continually with warm clothes, we were not able to live one winter week. Consider that our bodies have so sore a sickness and such a continual consumption in themselves that the strongest were not able to endure and continue ten days together, were it not that once or twice a day we be fain to take medicines inward to clout them up withal and keep them as long as we can. For what is our meat and drink but medicines against hunger and thirst, that give us warning of that we daily lose by our inward consumption? And of that consumption shall we die in conclusion, for all the medicines that we use, though never other sickness came at us.

Consider also that all our swaddling and tending with warm clothes and daily medicines, yet can our bodies not bear themselves

41 hot compresses.   42 health, condition.

but that almost half our time ever in twenty-four hours we be fain to fall in a swoon which we call sleep, and there lie like dead stocks by a long space ere we come to ourselves again: insomuch that among all wise men of old it is agreed that sleep is the very image of death.

Now thou wilt peradventure say that this is but a fantasy. For though we call this hunger sickness and meat a medicine, yet men know well enough what very [43] sickness is and what very medicines be, and thereby we know well enough that they be none.

If thou think this, then would I wit of thee what thou callest a sickness. Is not that a sickness that will make an end of thee if it be not helped? If that be so, then I suppose thou bearest ever thy sickness with thee,—for very sure art thou that it will make an end of thee if thou be not helped.

What callest thou, then, a medicine? Is it not such a thing as either applied outwardly to thy body, or received inward, shall preserve thee against that sore or sickness that else would put thee or some part of thee in peril? What can be, then, more properly and more verily a medicine than is our meat and drink, by which is resisted the peril and undoubted death that else should in so few days follow, by the inward sickness of our own nature continually consuming us within? For as for that ye reckon that we know which be sickness, that is but a custom of calling, by which we call no sickness by that name but such as be casual and come and go. For that that is common to all men, and never from any man, because we reckon it natural, we give it not the name of sickness, but we name sickness a passion [44] that cometh seldomer and, as we reckon, against nature, whereas the conflict of the divers qualified elements tempered in our body, continually labouring each to vanquish other and thereby to dissolve the whole, though it be as sore against the continuance of our nature and as sore laboureth to the dissolution of the whole body as other sickness do, yet we neither call it sickness, nor the meat that resisteth it we call no medicine, and that for none other cause but for the continual familiarity that we have therewith.

But now consider, if it were so that one whole country were born all lepers, which is a sickness rather foul and perilous than painful, or all an whole country born with the falling sickness, so that never

[43] real.   [44] suffering.

any of them had ever in their lives known or heard either themselves or any other void of those diseases, trow ye this, then, that
they would ever have reckoned them for sickness? Nay surely, but
they would have counted for sickness the colic and the stone and
such other like as come and go. But as for their leprosy and falling
evil, they would never account it other than we account hunger or
sleep. For as for that thy hunger doth thee pleasure when it is fed,
so doth sometimes the itch of a sore leg when thou clawest about
the brinks.[45]

And thus mayest thou surely see that all our whole life is but a
sickness never curable, but as an incurable canker, with continual
swaddling and plastering blotched up to live as long as we may, and
in conclusion undoubtedly to die of the same sickness, and though
there never came other. So that, if you consider this well, thou
mayest look upon death, not as a stranger, but as a nigh neighbour.
For as the flame is next the smoke, so is death next an incurable
sickness; and such is all our life.

And yet if this move you little, but that ye think for all this that
death is far from you, I will go somewhat nearer you. Thou reckon-
est every man near his death when he is dying. Then if thyself be
now already dying, how canst thou reckon thyself far from death?
Some man saith merrily to his fellow, "Be merry, man,—thou shalt
never die as long as thou livest." And albeit he seem to say true,
yet saith he more than he can make good. For if that were true, I
could make him much merrier, for then he should never die. Ye
will peradventure marvel of this, but it is easy to prove. For I think
ye will grant me that there is no time after that a man hath once
life, but he is either alive or dead. Then will there no man say
that one can die either before he get life or after that he hath lost
it, and so hath he no time left to die in but while he hath life.
Wherefore, if we neither die before our life nor when we be dead
already, needs must it follow that we never die but while we live.

It is not all one to die and to be dead. Truth it is that we be never
dead while we live; and it is, meseemeth, as true, not only that we
die while we live, but also that we die all the while we live. What
thing is dying? Is it any other thing than the passage and going out
of this present life?

[45] edges.

Now tell me, then, if thou wert going out of an house, whether art thou going out only when thy foot is on the uttermost inch of the threshold, thy body half out of the door, or else when thou beginnest to set the first foot forward to go out, in what place of the house soever ye stand when ye buskle [46] forward? I would say that ye be going out of the house from the first foot ye set forward to go forth. No man will think other, as I suppose, but all is one reason in going hence and coming hither. Now if one were coming hither to this town, he were not only coming hither while he were entering in at the gate, but all the way also from whence he came hitherward. Nor, in likewise, in going hence from this town,—a man is not only going from this town while he hath his body in the gate going outward, but also while he setteth his foot out of his host's house to go forward. And therefore, if a man met him by the way, far yet within the town, and asked him whither he were going, he should truly answer that he were going out of the town, all were the town so long that he had ten miles to go ere he came at the gate.

And surely, methinketh that in likewise a man is not only dying, that is to say, going in his way out of this life, while he lieth drawing on, but also all the while that he is going towards his end,—which is by all the whole time of his life, since the first moment in which he began to live, until the last moment of his life, or rather the first in which he is fully dead.

Now if this be thus, as meseemeth that reason proveth, a man is always dying from afore his birth, and every hour of our age, as it passeth by, cutteth his own length out of our life and maketh it shorter by so much, and our death so much the nearer. Which measuring of time and diminishing of life, with approaching towards death, is nothing else but from our beginning to our ending, one continual dying: so that wake we, sleep we, eat we, drink we, mourn we, sing we, in what wise soever live we, all the same while die we. So that we never ought to look towards death as a thing far off, considering that although he made no haste towards us, yet we never cease ourselves to make haste towards him.

Now if thou think this reason but a sophistical subtlety, and thinkest while thou art a young man thou mayest for all this think

[46] start.

thy death far off, that is to wit, as far as thou hast by likelihood of nature many years to live, then will I put thee an homely example, not very pleasant, but none the less very true and very fit for the matter.

If there were two, both condemned to death, both carried out at once towards execution; of which two, the one were sure that the place of his execution were within one mile, the other twenty miles off, yea an hundred, and ye will, he that were in the cart to be carried an hundred miles would not take much more pleasure than his fellow in the length of his way, notwithstanding that it were an hundred times as long as his fellow's and that he had thereby a hundred times as long to live, being sure and out of all question to die at the end.

Reckon me now yourself a young man in your best lust, twenty years of age, if ye will. Let there be another, ninety. Both must ye die, both be ye in the cart carrying forward. His gallows and death standeth within ten miles at the farthest, and yours within eighty. I see not why ye should reckon much less of your death than he, though your way be longer, since ye be sure ye shall never cease riding till ye come at it. And this is true, although ye were sure that the place of your execution stood so far beyond his. But what if there were to the place of your execution two ways, of which the one were four score miles farther about than your fellow's, the other nearer by five miles than his; and when ye were put in the cart, had warning of both; and though ye were showed that it were likely that ye should be carried the longer way, yet it might hap ye should go the shorter, and whether ye were carried the one or the other, ye should never know till ye come to the place: I trow ye could not in this case make much longer of your life than of your fellow's.

Now in this case are we all. For our Lord hath not indented [47] with us of the time.[48] He hath appointed what we may not pass, but not how soon we shall go, nor where, not in what wise. And therefore if thou wilt consider how little cause thou hast to reckon thy death so far off by reason of thy youth, reckon how many as young as thou have been drowned in the selfsame waters in which thou rowest. And thus shalt thou well see that thou hast no cause to look upon

[47] entered into an agreement.   [48] Job xiv, 13.

thy death as a thing far off, but a thing undoubtedly nigh thee, and ever walking with thee. By which, not a false imagination but a very true contemplation, thou shalt behold him and advise [49] him such as he is, and thereby take occasion to flee vain pleasures of the flesh that keep out the very [50] pleasures of the soul.

[49] mark, heed, consider.　　　　[50] true.

DESIDERIUS ERASMUS

THE PARACLESIS

An Exhortation to the Study of Christian Philosophy

> The pure and genuine Philosophy of Christ cannot be
> drawn more happily than from the Gospels and from
> the Epistles of the Apostles.

BORN IN ROTTERDAM, Erasmus (1466-1536) received his early education at the famous monastic school of the Brethren of the Common Life organized at Deventer by Gerrit Groot. In his biography of Groot, Thomas à Kempis had written: Let the basis of your study and the mirror of your life be, first, the Gospel of Christ, because *there* is the life of Christ; then, the lives and the discourses of the Fathers; then, the Epistles of Paul, the canonic epistles and the Acts of the Apostles; then the devout books— Bernard, Anselm, Augustine.[1] This is the old and familiar world of the Fathers and the Benedictine monks, and it was to become Erasmus' ideal. He was ordained priest in 1492, went to Paris, and then, in 1499, to England. Under Colet's influence, he dreamed of returning to the "ancient and true theology," in opposition to the scholastics whom they both heartily disliked. In the face of the labyrinths of "this new race of theologians," Erasmus, who is for many the great figure of the Renaissance, wished to return to the philosophy whose center and substance is Christ, and to become a

---

[1] Thomas à Kempis, *Vita M. Gerardi Magni*, xviii, 11 (*Opera Omnia*, 2nd ed., Antwerp, 1607, vol. iii, p. 785).

soldier of Christ, a *miles Christi.* The *Paraclesis,* published in 1516, as an appendix to his edition of the New Testament, reveals an Erasmus who loved classical letters more than Aristotelian philosophy, but who loved Christ incomparably more than both.

HE FAMOUS LACTANTIUS FIRMIANUS, DEAR reader, whose language Jerome especially admired, wished above all, when he was about to take up the defence of the Christian religion against the pagans, for an eloquence approaching that of Cicero; he considered it improper, I think, to have desired an equal eloquence. But I, to be sure, if there be any profit in such wishes, so long as I am urging all men to the holy and salutary study of Christian Philosophy and sounding as it were its trumpet, desire from my heart that there be given me an eloquence far different from Cicero's; if less flowery than his, certainly much more effectual.

If only such a power of speech ever happened to anyone, as the fables of the ancient poets not unreasonably ascribed to Mercury! For he, as if with magic rod and heavenly lute induced sleep, whenever he wished and likewise snatched it away again, all the while driving whom he willed into hell and calling them forth again. Or as was assigned to Amphion and Orpheus, the first of whom is supposed to have moved solid rocks, the second to have transported oaks and ash with the lute. Or as the Gauls attributed to Ogmius, who led all mortals, whithersoever he willed, by chains fixed into their ears from his tongue. Or as Antiquity, fond of fables, imputed to Marsias. Or, not to spend too much time on fables, certainly, as Alcibiades ascribed to Socrates, and the Ancient Comedy to Pericles; an eloquence which not only soothed the ears with a quickly vanishing pleasure, but which left clinging darts in the minds of the hearers; an eloquence which lays hold of, which transforms, which sends away a different hearer than it received. We read that the noble musician, Timothy, was wont to arouse Alexander the Great to a zest for war to the tune of Dorian measures. And formerly there were not lacking those who thought nothing more efficacious than conjurations, which the Greeks call incantations. But if ever there was any such incantation, if there be any power in harmony which possesses a true quality of inspiration, if there be any Delphic power to affect, I should like to ask it for the present task, to persuade with a most salutary eloquence upon everyone the one thing among all. Rather it is to be desired that Christ Himself, whose case is being pleaded, so tune the strings of our lute, that this lay may deeply touch and move the hearts of all.

To achieve this work there is no need of the argumentation or apostrophes of the rhetoricians. In what we are preparing nothing presents itself with greater certitude than the truth, and the more simple its expression, the more efficacious it is. First of all, however, I do not want to reopen that complaint, not altogether new, but alas too just, (and I know whether ever juster than in these times when with feverish minds men apply themselves to studies, each to his own), that this one Philosophy of Christ is laughed at by many, even Christians, neglected by many, studied by a few, albeit coldly, not to say insincerely. But in all the other disciplines, which human endeavour has set forth, nothing is so hidden and obscure which the discernment of genius has not investigated, nothing so difficult which persistent toil has not conquered. But how does it happen that we, as many of us as profess by our very surname the Name of Christ, do not embrace this one Philosophy with suitable minds?

Platonists, Pythagoreans, Academicians, Stoics, Cynics, Peripatetics, all both know well and commit to memory the doctrines of their sect. For these doctrines they do battle, ready to die rather than desert the defence of their founder. But why do not we with greater reason offer such minds to our Founder and Head, Christ? Who would not think it most unseemly for anyone professing the philosophy of Aristotle not to know what he thought about the causes of lightning, about prime matter, about the infinite? And these things, when known, do not make him happy, nor when unknown, make him unhappy. And we, consecrated in so many ways to Christ, and by so many sacraments bound to Him, do we not think it shameful and unseemly to be ignorant of His doctrines, which offer a most sure happiness to all? But what avails it here to exaggerate the case for the sake of argument—this is a kind of folly,—to want to compare Christ with Zeno or Aristotle, and His doctrine with their (to put it mildly) petty precepts? Let them add to their heart's content supplementary fabrications for the leaders of their sect, certainly He alone, who came forth from Heaven, is Teacher; He alone has been able to teach what is certain, since He is Eternal Wisdom. He, the One Author of the salvation of men, alone has taught what is salutary; He alone is the full and complete guarantee for whatever He has ever taught; He alone can bestow what He has promised.

If anything is done by the Chaldaeans or the Egyptians, for the very reason we are the more avid to know it because it has been brought from a foreign land, and part of its value is to have come from afar. And oftentimes we are so distressfully disturbed by the midnight vigils of some insignificant man, (let me not call him an imposter), not only fruitlessly, but at a great expenditure of time. I should not like to add anything more serious, and yet the very fact of having accomplished nothing is most serious. But how does it happen that an eagerness of this kind does not likewise thrill Christian souls, convinced as they are of the facts of the case, that this Doctrine came not from Egypt nor Syria, but from Heaven itself? Why do we not all reflect thus within ourselves? It must be a new and marvellous kind of Philosophy since, to transmit it to men, He Who was God became man; He Who was immortal became mortal; He Who was in the bosom of the Father came down upon earth. Whatever it is, it must be great and in no way trivial since its wonderful Author, after so many families of outstanding philosophers, after so many renowned prophets, came to teach It.

Why do we not now learn, examine and analyze Its each and every tenet with dutiful care? Especially since it is possible to draw from these few Books, as from crystal fountains, this kind of wisdom, so extraordinary that once and for all it rendered foolish the wisdom of this world. It is possible to draw this wisdom with much less ado (not to add and with how much more profit) than to draw the teaching of Aristotle from so many thorny volumes and from the immense and contradictory expositions of the commentators. Here there is no necessity to enter in, instructed in many troublesome disciplines. It is simple and a ready provision for everyone on the Journey; only bring a pious and ready mind and above all one endowed with a simple and pure Faith. Be but docile and you have already made much progress in this Philosophy. It possesses in abundance the Spirit, the Teacher who gives Himself to no one more willingly than to simple souls. The disciplines of the former (Aristotelian doctrine), in addition to promising a false beatitude, upset the minds of many, to wit, by the very difficulty of their tenets. This Philosophy accommodates Itself to all; adapts Itself to children, moderates Itself to their stature, nourishes them with milk; it sustains, fosters, supports, and does all things, until we grow up in Christ.

And again, It is not kept from the least thus that It may be admired by the great. Nay rather the further you have made progress in Its riches, the more are you moved by Its majesty. For the little, It is little; for the great, It is superlatively great. It rejects no age, no sex, no fortune, no condition. The sun is not as common and present to all men here on earth as the teaching of Christ. It in no way restricts anyone, unless he restrict himself by contemning himself. I am in serious disagreement with those who do not wish the Divine Letters to be read by the ignorant when they have been translated into the vulgar tongue, as if either Christ taught what is so involved that it can scarcely be understood by a handful of theologians; or as if the defence of the Christian religion were founded on the fact that It be unknown. Perhaps it is tolerable that the secrets of kings be hidden; but Christ wishes His Mysteries to be broadcast as far as possible.

I should like all women of low estate to read the Gospels; let them read the Pauline Epistles. And would that these were translated into every tongue of every people, to be read not only by the Scots and Irish, but also by Turks and Saracens. Certainly however the first step is knowledge. Grant that many do laugh; but something will be gained. Would that the farmer recite something from this source while at the ploughhandles; would that the weaver chant something from therein while at the shuttle; that the traveller relieve the monotony of his journey with such narratives. Let the sayings of all Christians be from this source; for as are our daily conversations, so are we. Let each one follow what he can; let each one express what he is able. Let him who is in second place not

envy him who is in first; let him who is first encourage him wh
follows; let him not despair. Why do we restrict a profession, con
mon to all, to a few? For it is incongruous that the dogmas alone b
relegated to those few who are today commonly called theologiar
or monks, since Baptism, in which there is the first profession o
Christian Philosophy, is equally common to all Christians, and sinc
all the other Sacraments, and finally the reward of immortality be
long equally to all. And these very ones, although they represent
very small proportion of those bearing the name of Christian, thes
very ones, I say, I should like to practice in greater measure th
lessons to which they have listened.

I fear, however, that there can be found among theologians thos
who depart a good deal from their title, that is, who speak o
earthly, not divine, things. And among monks who profess th
poverty of Christ and contempt of the world, rather will you fin
worldliness. As far as I am concerned he is truly a theologian wh
teaches, not by artfully constructed syllogisms, but by love, by h
very countenance, by his life itself that riches are to be spurnec
that the Christian ought not place his trust in the bulwarks of th
world, but rather depend on Heaven; that there should be no re
taliation for an injury; that we should bless those who curse, de
serve well of the undeserving; that all good men are to be love
and cherished as if members of the same body; that evil men are t
be put up with, if they cannot be corrected; that they, who are shor
of their goods, despoiled of their possessions, who mourn, ai
blessed and not to be pited; that for the pious, death is to be de
sired as merely a passage to immortality. If anyone, I say, fille
with the Spirit of Christ, teach, preach, inculcate and exhort i
these things and their like, if he invite and animate towards thes
he it is, in a word, who is the true theologian, even if he be
ditchdigger or a weaver. If anyone show forth these things in h
very life, he it is who is the great teacher. As to how the ange
know, perchance some one else, even a non-Christian, will gi
a more subtle explanation; but to persuade anyone of the fact tha
freed from all sin, we should lead an angelic life here below,
the office of the Christian theologian. But if anyone object tha
these things are dull and doltish I shall reply to him only, tha
Christ above all taught these things; the Apostles inculcate ther

these things, dull if you will, have been set before us by so many true Christians, and by the trials of so many martyrs. This Philosophy, I say, illiterate as it seems to them, has drawn within its laws the mightiest princes of the world, so many kingdoms, so many peoples, a thing which no power of tyrants, no erudition of philosophers, could do. I am not really against the idea that secular wisdom be spoken of among the accomplished, if it seems fitting. But to be sure, the rank and file of Christians consoles itself in this Name; because the Apostles certainly did not teach those subtleties; let others search out whether they knew them. If princes were to rule, I say, with this simple Philosophy, if priests were to inculcate it in their sermons, if schoolmasters were to instil it into their boys, rather than those learned things drawn from the sources of Aristotle and Averroes, Christendom would not be shaken with almost perpetual wars on every side. Everything would not be so fired with such an unhealthy zeal for gathering riches by fair means and foul; sacred as well as secular affairs would not be everywhere adin with so many litigations. Finally, we should not differ from those, who do not profess the Philosophy of Christ, by title alone and ceremonies.

Indeed in the hands of these three classes of men is the task of either restoring or furthering the Christian religion: princes and their vicegerents, the magistrates, bishops and their vicars the priest, and those who instruct those early wholly tractable years. And if, when they forget about their own preoccupations, it should happen that these three classes would heartily agree together in Christ, doubtless in not so many years you would see a true and, as Paul says,[2] a sincere Christian gradually come forth, one who would renew the Philosophy of Christ, not by ceremonies alone and decrees, but by his very heart and whole life. By these arms the enemies of the Christian name would be brought over to the Faith of Christ much more quickly than by threats or armaments. Nothing is more powerful than truth itself to assemble all our defences. He is not a Platonist who has not read the works of Plato. But is he a theologian, in any wise Christian, who has not read the Word of Christ? *He who has any love for Me,* He says, *is true to my words.*[3] He Himself has established this mark.

[2] II Cor. viii, 8.   [3] Jo. xiv. 22

If then we are really Christians at heart, if we truly believe that He was sent from Heaven to teach us those things which the wisdom of the philosophers could not, if indeed we expect from Him what no princes, however rich, can give, why is anything more important in our eyes than His Words? Why does anything appear learned which is at variance with His Decrees? Why do we take the same, and I almost said more, liberty with these adorable Words than secular commentators take with the laws of Caesar and the books of the physicians, just as if we were dealing with some trifling thing? Thus whatever has come to our mind we comment, distort and render intricate; we adjust the heavenly dogmas to our life like the Lydian rule; and avoiding in every way the appearance of a meagre knowledge we draw upon whatever is to the point in secular literature, and, I am loath to say it, we corrupt what is paramount in Christian Philosophy. And what cannot be denied is that we restrict the very thing which Christ wished to be most common. This kind of Philosophy finds Itself in the affections rather than in syllogisms; It is a life rather than a disputation; an inspiration rather than learning; a transformation rather than reasoning. It has happened to few to be learned; but to no one is it not permitted to be a Christian, to no one is it not granted to be pious; to no one is it not allowed to be a theologian. What is particularly natural comes easily into the souls of all. But what is the Philosophy of Christ, which He Himself calls a rebirth, other than the restoration of a well-founded nature?

Although no one has in fact taught these things more distinctly, more efficaciously than Christ, nonetheless it is possible to find in pagan books many things which are in accord with His Doctrine. Never was there philosophical sect so gross as that which taught that money makes man happy; none so shameless as that which placed the good of man in vulgar honours or pleasures. The Stoics deemed none wise except the good man; they considered nothing really good or upright except true virtue; nothing abhorrent or evil save turpitude alone. In Plato [4] Socrates taught in many ways that injury should not be repaid with injury; likewise since the soul is immortal, that they are not to be pitied who depart hence into a

[4] *Crito* 49 C; *Abol.* 35 A ff; *Phaedo* 81 A ff.

happier life in the confidence of a life well lived. In addition he
taught that the soul must be completely freed from the affections of
the body and turned to those things which truly are, though we do
not experience them. Aristotle wrote in the *Politics* [5] that nothing,
save virtue alone, can be so sweet to us which is not in some way
contemned. For this reason even Epicurus admits that nothing in
life can be pleasant for man unless the soul be conscious of no evil
done, whence true pleasure springs forth as from a fountain. [6] Why
have not a few manifested a small part of this Doctrine, especially
Socrates, Diogenes and Epictetus? But since Christ taught and
manifested those same things so much more fully, is it not somewhat of a wonder that they are either ignored or neglected or even
ridiculed by Christians? If there are things which are close to Christianity we follow the former, the Latter being outmoded. If these
alone are the things which can make a true Christian, why do we
in like manner consider them as more obsolete and abrogated than
the Books of Moses? The first thing is to know what He taught,
the next to manifest it.

I do not think that anyone should consider himself a Christian
for the reason that he carries on, with thorny and complicated subtlety of words, disputations about instants, relations, quiddities and
formalities, but rather if he holds fast to and expresses what Christ
taught and manifested. This is not because I condemn the zeal of
those who have exercised the force of their talents, not unpraise-
worthily, in disputations of this kind, for I wish to offend no one,
but because I think and unless I am mistaken, truly think that the
pure and genuine Philosophy of Christ cannot be drawn more happily than from the Gospels and the Epistles of the Apostles. And
I think that if he piously and prayerfully rather than argumenta-
tively meditate upon These and if he be eager to be transformed
rather than armed, he will certainly find that there is nothing which
pertains to the happiness of man, nothing which more readily fits
every phase of this life, which has not been transmitted, discussed
and set forth in these Writings.

Suppose we wish to know something, why does another author
please us more than Christ? If we are seeking a way of life, why
is another example preferable to the Archetype Himself, Christ?

[5] Bk. 7, 1323 b 7 ff.   [6] Cf. Diogenes Laertius, X, 138 ff.

Or if we desire some ointment for the painful passions of the soul, why do we think there is a more ready remedy elsewhere? Or if we wish to arouse a lethargic and sluggish soul by reading, I ask you, where will you find sparks as alive and efficacious? If we wish to withdraw the soul from the cares of this life, why do other delights please us more? Why do we stubbornly prefer to learn the Wisdom of Christ from human literature rather than from Christ Himself Who has promised to be with us always to the consummation of the world,[7] and who gives this Wisdom especially in these Letters in which even now He lives, breathes, speaks for us, and, I might add, more efficaciously than when He was among men? The Jews saw and heard less than you see and hear in the Gospel, provided only you apply the eyes and ears by which He can be seen and heard.

How, I ask, does this fit the facts? We keep, fondle and carry about letters written by a dear friend; we read and reread them; and there are so many thousand Christians, and even though they are otherwise learned, not once in their whole life have they read the Gospels and the books of the Apostles. Mohametans cling to their teachings; Jews from childhood, even today, study their Moses. Why do we not give as much to Christ? Those who make profession in the Order of Benedict keep, learn and imbibe a Rule written for the ignorant by a man, himself quite ignorant. Those who are of the Order of Augustine know well the Rule of their founder. Franciscans worship and cherish the traditions of Francis and wherever on earth they betake themselves, they carry these about with them and do not believe themselves safe unless that little book is at their bosom. Why do they attribute more to their Rule, written as it was by a man, than the whole body of Christians to their Rule which Christ gave to all, one that all have equally professed in Baptism, and finally one than which there is none holier, take any number you wish? And would that, as Paul has written, the Law be not a glory to Moses above the glory of the Gospel to come.[8]

Thus may the Gospels and thus may the Apostolic Letters be held as sacred for all Christians so that these human things may not appear holier than Those. Let others grant to Albert, to Alexander,

[7] *Matt.* xxviii, 20.   [8] *II Cor.* iii, 7-8.

to Thomas, to Giles, to Richard, to Ockham anything they wish. As far as I am concerned, each one is quite free to do so; I should not like to detract from anyone's glory or to quarrel with the long established studies of men. If they wish, let those studies be as learned, as subtle, as angelic as you will, the Latter must be admitted to be the most certain. Paul wishes to discern the spirits of the Prophets; [9] Augustine, while reading all books with discernment, demands no more for his own.[10] And albeit I do not follow these Letters, nevertheless I adore them. No school of theologians, rather the Heavenly Father Himself by the testimony of the divine voice has approved this Author, and that twice: first in His Baptism at the Jordan, and secondly on Mount Thabor at the Transfiguration: *This*, He said, *is my beloved Son in whom I am well pleased; hear ye Him*.[11]

To be sure He is the one and only Teacher; be His disciples. In his studies let each one cling to his heart's content to his own founder; these words have been spoken of Christ alone without restriction. On Him first did the dove descend in confirmation of the Father's testimony. Shortly afterwards testimony of His Spirit was given by Peter, whom The Supreme Shepherd commissioned once, twice and a third time to feed His sheep,[12] to feed them doubtless with the food of Christian doctrine. It was, as it were, reborn in Paul, whom He Himself called an instrument of election and an outstanding herald of His Name.[13] What John drew from the sacrosanct fountain of His bosom, he expressed in his own writings. What is there like it, I ask, in Scotus? I should not like what I have said to appear as an intended contumely. What is there like it in Thomas? Although I admire the genius of the former, I am in veneration of His holiness. Why do we not all find our speculation in such great authors as John and Paul? Wherefore do we not carry These about in our bosom, have Them always in our hands? Why do we not diligently seek, search and examine These? Why is a greater portion of our life given to Averroes than to the Gospels? Why is almost a whole lifetime wasted in the ordinances of men and in contradictory opinions? Even grant, if you so desire, that they are of the loftiest theologians. But cer-

[9] Perhaps *I John* iv, 1. [10] *Ep.* 143, 2 (PL 33, 586).
[11] *Matt.* xvii, 5; *Luke* ix, 35; *Mark* i. 11. [12] *Jo.* xxi, 17 ff. [13] *Acts* ix, 15.

tainly let there be an apprenticeship in These of the sometime great theologian.

If we have given our oath from our heart, as many of us as have given our oath in the Words of Christ at Baptism, are soon imbued with the teachings of Christ in the midst of parental embraces and the persuasions of nurses. For what that rude little vessel of our mind first takes in, is deeply rooted and clings tenaciously. It first stammers the Name of Christ; from His Gospels its early years are formed. I wish above all that Christ be so taught that He be beloved of boys. Then let them be so busied in these Studies until with silent increase they grow into manhood in Christ. The writings of others are such that not a few regret the energy expended upon them, and frequently it comes to pass that they, who throughout their whole life fight unto death to defend their principles, in death desert the sect of their founder. But happy is he whom death seized while intent upon these Writings. Let us all thirst after These with all our heart; let us embrace Them; let us continually be occupied with and fondle These. In fine when studies turn to moral questions let us pine for Them, let us be transformed in Them. He who cannot follow them, (but who cannot, if only he wish?), at least let him adore these Letters as the repository of the divine Bosom.

If anyone should point out a footprint made by the feet of Christ, how we Christians should bow in reverence; how we should adore. But why do we not venerate His living, breathing image in these Books? If anyone were to place on exhibition Christ's cloak, whither should we not travel on earth to be permitted to kiss it? But suppose you present all His goods, there will be nothing which represents Christ more clearly and truly than the Gospels. For the love of Christ we decorate a wooden and stone statue with gems and gold. Why rather do we not sign these Gospels with gold and jewels, as if there were anything more precious than These, which make Christ much more present to us than any little images? What else does an image express but the shape of the body, if indeed it does express anything? But the Gospels bring to you the living image of that sacrosanct mind, Christ Himself, speaking, healing, dying, rising. In a word They make Him so present that you would see less were He before your eyes.

ST. TERESA
of AVILA

THE INTERIOR CASTLE

SEVENTH MANSION
In which there are Four Chapters

> We always find that those who walked closest to Christ
> our Lord were those who had to bear the greatest trials.

BORN IN AVILA (1515) of a noble Castilian family, as a child
Teresa would play a game which already foretold her later life:
she built convents. In 1535 she joined the Carmelites and began
her famous reform in 1562. She was a courageous and zealous
reformer, a wise and practical administrator. Above all, she was
a saint who knew divine things, not from books, but from having
suffered them. Among her works, which are written in a direct
and almost conversational style, full of homely metaphors, are the
Autobiography (1562-1565), the *Relations* (a spiritual diary begun
in 1560), *The Way of Perfection* (about 1565) and *The Interior
Castle* (1577). Written at the request of her superior and confessor, this last work is an exposition of the degrees of prayer. The
interior castle is the soul itself. Teresa died in 1581.

CHAPTER I

*Treats of great favours which God bestows on the souls that have
attained entrance to the Seventh Mansion. Describes how in the*

author's opinion there is some difference between the soul and the
spirit, although both are one. There are notable things in this
chapter.

OU WILL THINK, SISTERS, THAT SO MUCH HAS been said about this spiritual road that there cannot possibly be any more to say. It would be a great mistake to think that; just as the greatness of God is without limit, even so are His works. Who will ever come to an end of recounting His mercies and wonders? It is impossible that any should do so; do not be surprised, therefore, at what has been said and at what will be said now, for it is only a fraction of the things that still remain to be related about God. Great is the mercy that He shows us in communicating these things in such a way that we may come to learn of them; for the more we know of His communion with creatures, the more we shall praise His greatness, and we shall strive not to despise a soul in which the Lord takes such delight. Each of us possesses a soul, but we do not prize our souls as creatures made in God's image deserve and so we do not understand the great secrets which they contain. If it be His Majesty's will, may it please Him to guide my pen, and give me to understand how I may tell you some of the many things which there are to be said and which God reveals to every soul that He brings into this Mansion. Earnestly have I besought His Majesty, since He knows my intention is that His mercies be not hidden, to the greater praise and glory of His name.

I am hopeful, sisters, that, not for my sake but for your sakes, He will grant me this favour, so that you may understand how important it is that no fault of yours should hinder the celebration of His Spiritual Marriage with your souls, which, as you will see, brings with it so many blessings. O great God! Surely a creature as miserable as I must tremble to treat of anything so far beyond what I deserve to understand. And indeed I have been in a state of great confusion and have wondered if it will not be better for me in a few words to bring my account of this Mansion to an end. I am so much afraid it will be thought that my knowledge of it comes from experience, and this makes me very much ashamed; for, knowing myself as I do for what I am, such a thought is terrible. On the other hand, whatever your judgment about it may be, it has seemed to me that this shame is due to temptation and weakness. Let the whole world cry out upon me, so long as God is praised and understood a little better. At all events I may perhaps be dead when this comes to be seen. Blessed be He Who lives and shall live for ever. Amen.

When Our Lord is pleased to have pity upon this soul, which suffers and has suffered so much out of desire for Him, and which He has not taken spiritually to be His bride, He brings her into this Mansion of His, which is the seventh, before consummating the Spiritual Marriage. For He must needs have an abiding-place in the soul, just as He has one in Heaven, where His Majesty alone dwells: so let us call this a second Heaven. It is very important, sisters, that we should not think of the soul as of something dark. It must seem dark to most of us, as we cannot see it, for we forget that there is not only a light which we can see, but also an interior light, and so we think that within our soul there is some kind of darkness. Of the soul that is not in grace, I grant you, that is true—not, however, from any defect in the Sun of Justice, Who is within it and is giving it being, but because, as I think I said in describing the first Mansion, this soul is not capable of receiving the light.[1] A certain person came to see that these unhappy souls are, as it were, in a dark prison, with their feet and hands bound so that they can do no good thing which will help them to win merit; they are both blind and dumb. We do well to take pity on them, realizing that there was a time when we were ourselves like them and that the Lord may have mercy on them also.

Let us take especial care, sisters, to pray to Him for them, and not be negligent. To pray for those who are in mortal sin is the best kind of almsgiving—a much better thing than it would be to loose a Christian whom we saw with his hands tied behind him, bound with a stout chain, made fast to a post and dying of hunger, not for lack of food, since he has beside him the most delicious things to eat, but because he cannot take them and put them into his mouth

---

[1] *Interior Castle,* I Mansion, ch. 2; in *The Complete Works of Saint Teresa of Jesus,* translated and edited by E. A. Peers (3 vols., New York: Sheed & Ward, 1946), vol. II, pp. 210-211.

although he is weary to death and actually knows that he is on the point of dying, and not merely a death of the body, but one which is eternal. Would it not be extremely cruel to stand looking at such a man and not give him this food to eat? And supposing you could loose his chains by means of your prayers? You see now what I mean. For the love of God, I beg you always to remember such souls when you pray.

However, it is not of these that we are now speaking, but of those who, by God's mercy, have done penance for their sins and are in grace. We must not think of souls like theirs as mean and insignificant; for each is an interior world, wherein are the many and beauteous Mansions that you have seen; it is reasonable that this should be so, since within each soul there is a mansion for God. Now, when His Majesty is pleased to grant the soul the aforementioned favour of this Divine Marriage, He first of all brings it into His own Mansion. And His Majesty is pleased that it should not be as on other occasions, when He has granted it raptures, in which I certainly think it is united with Him, as it is in the above-mentioned Prayer of Union,[2] although the soul does not feel called to enter into its own centre, as here in this Mansion, but is affected only in its higher part. Actually it matters little what happens: whatever it does, the Lord unites it with Himself, but He makes it blind and dumb, as He made Saint Paul at his conversion (*Acts* ix, 8), and so prevents it from having any sense of how or in what way that favour comes which it is enjoying; the great delight of which the soul is then conscious is the realization of its nearness to God. But when He unites it with Him, it understands nothing; the faculties are all lost.

But in this Mansion everything is different. Our good God now desires to remove the scales from the eyes of the soul (*Acts,* ix, 18), so that it may see and understand something of the favour which He is granting it, although He is doing this in a strange manner. It is brought into this Mansion by means of an intellectual vision, in which, by a representation of the truth in a particular way, the Most Holy Trinity reveals Itself, in all three Persons. First of all the spirit becomes enkindled and is illumined, as it were, by a cloud of the greatest brightness. It sees these three Persons, individually,

[2] *Interior Castle,* V Mansion, ch. 2; ed. E. A. Peers, vol. II, p. 254.

and yet, by a wonderful kind of knowledge which is given to it, the soul realizes that most certainly and truly all these three Persons are one Substance and one Power and one Knowledge and one God alone; so that what we hold by faith the soul may be said here to grasp by sight, although nothing is seen by the eyes, either of the body or of the soul, for it is no imaginary vision. Here all three Persons communicate Themselves to the soul and speak to the soul and explain to it those words which the Gospel attributes to the Lord—namely, that He and the Father and the Holy Spirit will come to dwell with the soul which loves Him and keeps his commandments (*Jo.* xiv, 23).

Oh, God help me! What a difference there is between hearing and believing these words and being led in this way to realize how true they are! Each day this soul wonders more, for she feels that they have never left her, and perceives quite clearly, in the way I have described, that They are in the interior of her heart—in the most interior place of all and in its greatest depths. So although, not being a learned person, she cannot say how this is, she feels within herself this Divine companionship.

This may lead you to think that such a person will not remain in possession of her senses but will be so completely absorbed that she will be able to fix her mind upon nothing. But no: in all that belongs to the service of God she is more alert than before; and, when not otherwise occupied, she rests in that happy companionship. Unless her soul fails God, He will never fail, I believe, to give her the most certain assurance of His Presence. She has great confidence that God will not leave her, and that, having granted her this favour, He will not allow her to lose it. For this belief the soul has good reason, though all the time she is walking more carefully than ever, so that she may displease Him in nothing.

This Presence is not of course always realized so fully—I mean so clearly—as it is when it first comes, or on certain other occasions when God grants the soul this consolation; if it were, it would be impossible for the soul to think of anything else, or even to live among men. But although the light which accompanies it may not be so clear, the soul is always aware that it is experiencing this companionship. We might compare the soul to a person who is with others in a very bright room; and then suppose that the shutters are closed so that the people are all in darkness. The light by which they can be seen has been taken away, and, until it comes back, we shall be unable to see them, yet we are none the less aware that they are there. It may be asked if, when the light returns, and this person looks for them again, she will be able to see them. To do this is not in her power; it depends on when Our Lord is pleased that the shutters of the understanding shall be opened. Great is the mercy which He grants the soul in never going away from her and in willing that she shall understand this so clearly.

It seems that the Divine Majesty, by means of this wonderful companionship, is desirous of preparing the soul for yet more. For clearly she will be greatly assisted to go onward in perfection and to lose the fear which previously she sometimes had of the other favours that were granted to her, as has been said above. The person already referred to found herself better in every way; however numerous were her trials and business worries, the essential part of her soul seemed never to move from that dwelling-place. So in a sense she felt that her soul was divided; and when she was going through great trials, shortly after God had granted her this favour, she complained of her soul, just as Martha complained of Mary (*Luke* x, 40). Sometimes she would say that it was doing nothing but enjoy itself in that quietness, while she herself was left with all her trials and occupations so that she could not keep it company.

You will think this absurd, daughters, but it is what actually happens. Although of course the soul is not really divided, what I have said is not fancy, but a very common experience. As I was saying, it is possible to make observations concerning interior matters and in this way we know that there is some kind of difference, and a very definite one, between the soul and the spirit, although they are both one. So subtle is the division perceptible between them that sometimes the operation of the one seems as different from that of the other as are the respective joys that the Lord is pleased to give them. It seems to me, too, that the soul is a different thing from the faculties and that they are not all one and the same. There are so many and such subtle things in the interior life that it would be presumptuous for me to begin to expound them. But we shall see everything in the life to come if the Lord, of His mercy, grants us the favour of bringing us to the place where we shall understand these secrets.

Continues the same subject. Describes the difference between spiritual union and spiritual marriage. Explains this by subtle comparisons.

LET US now come to treat of the Divine and Spiritual Marriage, although this great favour cannot be fulfilled perfectly in us during our lifetime, for if we were to withdraw ourselves from God this great blessing would be lost. When granting this favour for the first time, His Majesty is pleased to reveal Himself to the soul through an imaginary vision of His most sacred Humanity, so that it may clearly understand what is taking place and not be ignorant of the fact that it is receiving so sovereign a gift. To other people the experience will come in a different way. To the person of whom we have been speaking the Lord revealed Himself one day, when she had just received Communion, in great splendour and beauty and majesty, as He did after His resurrection, and told her that it was time she took upon her His affairs as if they were her own and that He would take her affairs upon Himself; and He added other words which are easier to understand than to repeat.[3]

This, you will think, was nothing new, since on other occasions the Lord had revealed Himself to that soul in this way. But it was so different that it left her quite confused and dismayed: for one reason, because this vision came with great force; for another, because of the words which He spoke to her; and also because, in the interior of her soul, where He revealed Himself to her, she had never seen any visions but this. For you must understand that there is the greatest difference between all the other visions we have mentioned and those belonging to this Mansion, and there is the same difference between the Spiritual Betrothal and the Spiritual Marriage as there is between two betrothed persons and two who are united so that they cannot be separated any more.

As I have already said, one makes these comparisons because

[3] Cf. *Relations*, XXXV; ed. E. A. Peers, vol. I, pp. 351-352.

there are no other appropriate ones, yet it must be realized that the Betrothal has no more to do with the body than if the soul were not in the body, and were nothing but spirit. Between the Spiritual Marriage and the body there is even less connection, for this secret union takes place in the deepest centre of the soul, which must be where God Himself dwells, and I do not think there is any need of a door by which to enter it. I say there is no need of a door because all that has so far been described seems to have come through the medium of the senses and faculties and this appearance of the Humanity of the Lord must do so too. But what passes in the union of the Spiritual Marriage is very different. The Lord appears in the centre of the soul, not through an imaginary, but through an intellectual vision (although this is a subtler one than that already mentioned), just as He appeared to the Apostles, without entering through the door, when He said to them: *Pax vobis* (*Jo.* xx, 19, 21). This instantaneous communication of God to the soul is so great a secret and so sublime a favour, and such delight is felt by the soul, that I do not know with what to compare it, beyond saying that the Lord is pleased to manifest to the soul at that moment the glory that is in Heaven, in a sublimer manner than is possible through any vision or spiritual consolation. It is impossible to say more than that, as far as one can understand, the soul (I mean the spirit of this soul) is made one with God, Who, being likewise a Spirit, has been pleased to reveal the love that He has for us by showing to certain persons the extent of that love, so that we may praise His greatness. For He has been pleased to unite Himself with His creature in such a way that they have become like two who cannot be separated from one another: even so He will not separate Himself from her.

The Spiritual Betrothal is different: here the two persons are frequently separated, as is the case with union, for, although by union is meant the joining of two things into one, each of the two, as is a matter of common observation, can be separated and remain a thing by itself. This favour of the Lord passes quickly and afterwards the soul is deprived of that companionship—I mean so far as it can understand. In this other favour of the Lord it is not so: the soul remains all the time in that centre with its God. We might say that union is as if the ends of two wax candles were joined so that the light they give is one: the wicks and the wax and the light are all one; yet afterwards the one candle can be perfectly well separated from the other and the candles become two again, or the wick may be withdrawn from the wax. But here it is like rain falling from the heavens into a river or a spring; there is nothing but water there and it is impossible to divide or separate the water belonging to the river from that which fell from the heavens. Or it is as if a tiny streamlet enters the sea, from which it will find no way of separating itself, or as if in a room there were two large windows through which the light streamed in: it enters in different places but it all becomes one.

Perhaps when St. Paul says: *He who is joined to God becomes one spirit with Him* (I Cor. vi, 17), he is referring to this sovereign Marriage, which presupposes the entrance of His Majesty into the soul by union. And he also says: *Mihi vivere Christus est, mori lucrum (Phil.* i, 21). This, I think, the soul may say here, for it is here that the little butterfly to which we have referred dies, and with the greatest joy, because Christ is now its life.[4]

This, with the passage of time, becomes more evident through its effects; for the soul clearly understands, by certain secret aspirations, that it is endowed with life by God. Very often these aspirations are so vehement that what they teach cannot possibly be doubted: though they cannot be described, the soul experiences them very forcibly. One can only say that this feeling is produced at times by certain delectable words which, it seems, the soul cannot help uttering, such as: "O life of my life, and sustenance that sustaineth me!" and things of that kind. For from those Divine breasts, where it seems that God is ever sustaining the soul, flow streams of milk, which solace all who dwell in the Castle; it seems that it is the Lord's will for them to enjoy all that the soul enjoys, so that, from time to time, there should flow from this mighty river, in which this tiny little spring is swallowed up, a stream of this water, to sustain those who in bodily matters have to serve the Bridegroom and the bride. And just as a person suddenly plunged into such water would become aware of it, and, however unobservant he might be, could not fail to become so, the same thing may be said, with even greater confidence, of these operations to which I refer.

[4] *Interior Castle,* V Mansion, ch. 2; ed. E. A. Peers, vol. II, pp. 255 ff.

For just as a great stream of water could never fall on us without having an origin somewhere, as I have said, just so it becomes evident that there is someone in the interior of the soul who sends forth these arrows and thus gives life to this life, and that there is a sun whence this great light proceeds, which is transmitted to the faculties in the interior part of the soul. The soul, as I have said, neither moves from that centre nor loses its peace, for He Who gave His peace to the Apostles when they were all together (*Jo.* xx, 19, 21) can give peace to the soul.

It has occurred to me that this salutation of the Lord must mean much more than the mere words suggest, as must also His telling the glorious Magdalen to go in peace (*Luke*, vii, 50); for the words of the Lord are like acts wrought in us, and so they must have produced some effect in those who were already prepared to put away from them everything corporeal and to leave the soul in a state of pure spirituality, so that it might be joined with Uncreated Spirit in this celestial union. For it is quite certain that, when we empty ourselves of all that is creature and rid ourselves of it for the love of God, that same Lord will fill our souls with Himself. Thus, one day, when Jesus Christ was praying for His Apostles (I do not know where this occurs [cf. *Jo.* xvii, 21]), He asked that they might become one with the Father and with Him, even as Jesus Christ our Lord is in the Father and the Father is in Him. I do not know what greater love there can be than this. And we shall none of us fail to be included here, for His Majesty went on to say: *Not for them alone do I pray, but also for all who believe in Me* (*Jo.* xvii, 20); and again: *I am in them* (*Jo.* xvii, 23).

Oh, God help me! How true are these words and how well the soul understands them, for in this state it can actually see their truth for itself. And how well we should all understand them were it not for our own fault! The words of Jesus Christ our King and Lord cannot fail; but, because we ourselves fail by not preparing ourselves and departing from all that can shut out this light, we do not see ourselves in this mirror into which we are gazing and in which our image is engraved.[5]

Let us now return to what we were saying. When Our Lord brings the soul into this Mansion of His, which is the centre of the

[5] Cf. *Poems*, VIII; ed. E. A. Peers, vol. III, pp. 287-288.

soul itself (for they say that the empyrean heaven, where Our Lord is, does not move like the other heavens), it seems, on entering, to be subject to none of the usual movements of the faculties and the imagination, which injure it and take away its peace. I may seem to be giving the impression that, when the soul reaches the state in which God grants it this favour, it is sure of its salvation and free from the risk of backsliding. But that is not my meaning, and whenever I treat of this matter and say that the soul seems to be in safety I should be understood as meaning for so long as the Divine Majesty holds it thus by the hand and it does not offend Him. At all events, I know for certain that, even when it finds itself in this state, and even if the state has lasted for years, it does not consider itself safe, but goes on its way with much greater misgiving than before and refrains more carefully from committing the smallest offence against God. It is also strongly desirous of serving Him, as will be explained later on, and is habitually afflicted and confused when it sees how little it is able to do and how great is the extent of its obligations, which is no small cross to it and a very grievous penance; for the harder the penance which this soul performs, the greater is its delight. Its real penance comes when God takes away its health and strength so that it can no longer perform any. I have described elsewhere the great distress which this brings, but it is much greater here. This must be due to the nature of the ground in which the soul is planted, for a tree planted by the streams of water is fresher and gives more fruit (*Ps. i, 3*), so how can we marvel at the desires of this soul, since its spirit is verily made one with the celestial water of which we have been speaking?

Returning to what I was saying, it must not be thought that the faculties and senses and passions are always in this state of peace, though the soul itself is. In the other Mansions there are always times of conflict and trial and weariness, but they are not of such a kind as to rob the soul of its peace and stability—at least, not as a rule. This "centre" of our soul, or "spirit," is something so difficult to describe, and indeed to believe, that I think, sisters, as I am so bad at explaining myself, I will not subject you to the temptation of disbelieving what I say, for it is difficult to understand how the soul can have trials and afflictions and yet be in peace. I want to put before you one or two comparisons: God grant they may be of some value, but, if they are not, I know that what I have said is the truth.

A king is living in His palace: many wars are waged in his kingdom and many other distressing things happen there, but he remains where he is despite them all. So it is here: although in the other Mansions there are many disturbances and poisonous creatures, and the noise of all this can be heard, nobody enters this Mansion and forces the soul to leave it; and, although the things which the soul hears cause it some distress, they are not of a kind to disturb it or to take away its peace, for the passions are already vanquished, and thus are afraid to enter there because to do so would only exhaust them further. Our whole body may be in pain, yet if our head is sound the fact that the body is in pain will not cause it to ache as well. These comparisons make me smile and I do not like them at all, but I know no others. Think what you will; what I have said is the truth.

CHAPTER III

Treats of the striking effects produced by this prayer aforementioned. It is necessary to observe and remember the effects it produces, for the difference between them and those already described is remarkable.

As WE ARE SAYING, then, this little butterfly has now died, full of joy at having found rest, and within her lives Christ. Let us see what her new life is like, and how different it is from her earlier one, for it is by the effects which result from this prayer that we shall know if what has been said is true. As far as I can understand, the effects are these.

First, there is a self-forgetfulness which is so complete that it really seems as though the soul no longer existed, because it is such that she has neither knowledge nor remembrance that there is either heaven or life or honour for her, so entirely is she employed in seeking the honour of God. It appears that the words which His Majesty addressed to her have produced their effect—namely, that she must take care of His business and He will take care of hers. And thus, happen what may, she does not mind in the least, but lives in so strange a state of forgetfulness that, as I say, she seems no longer to exist, and has no desire to exist—no, absolutely none —save when she realizes that she can do something to advance the glory and honour of God, for which she would gladly lay down her life.

Do not understand by this, daughters, that she neglects to eat and sleep (though having to do this is no little torment to her), or to do anything which is made incumbent upon her by her profession. We are talking of interior matters: as regards exterior ones there is little to be said. Her great grief is to see that all she can do of her own strength is as nothing. Anything that she is capable of doing and knows to be of service to Our Lord she would not fail to do for any reason upon earth.

The second effect produced is a great desire to suffer, but this is not of such a kind as to disturb the soul, as it did previously. So extreme is her longing for the will of God to be done in her that whatever His Majesty does she considers to be for the best: if He wills that she should suffer, well and good; if not, she does not worry herself to death as she did before.

When these souls are persecuted again, they have a great interior joy, and much more peace than in the state described above. They bear no enmity to those who ill-treat them, or desire to do so. Indeed they conceive a special love for them, so that, if they see them in some trouble, they are deeply grieved and would do anything possible to relieve them; they love to commend them to God, and they would rejoice at not being given some of the favours which His Majesty bestows upon them if their enemies might have them instead and thus be prevented from offending Our Lord.

What surprises me most is this. You have already seen what trials and afflictions these souls have suffered because of their desire to die and thus to enjoy Our Lord. They have now an equally strong desire to serve Him, and to sing His praise, and to help some soul if they can. So what they desire now is not merely not to die but to live for a great many years and to suffer the severest trials, if by so doing they can become the means whereby the Lord is praised, even in the smallest thing. If they knew for certain that, on leaving the body, they would have fruition of God, their attitude would not be affected, nor is it altered when they think of the glory which belongs to the saints, for they do not desire as yet to attain this.

Their conception of glory is of being able in some way to help the Crucified, especially when they see how often people offend Him and how few there are who really care about His honour and are detached from everything else.

True, they sometimes forget this, turn with tender longing to the thought of enjoying God and desire to escape from this exile, especially when they see how little they are doing to serve Him. But then they turn back and look within themselves and remember that they have Him with them continually; and they are content with this and offer His Majesty their will to live as the most costly oblation they can give Him. They are no more afraid of death than they would be of a gentle rapture. The explanation of this is that it is He Who gave the soul those earlier desires, accompanied by such excessive torment, that now gives it these others. May He be blessed and praised for ever.

In short, the desires of these souls are no longer for consolations or favours, for they have with them the Lord Himself and it is His Majesty Who now lives in them. His life, of course, was nothing but a continual torment and so He is making our life the same, at least as far as our desires go. In other respects, He treats us as weaklings, though He has ample fortitude to give us when He sees that we need it. These souls have a marked detachment from everything and a desire to be always either alone or busy with something that is to some soul's advantage. They have no aridities or interior trials but a remembrance of Our Lord and a tender love for Him, so that they would like never to be doing anything but giving Him praise. When the soul is negligent, the Lord Himself awakens it in the way that has been described, so that it sees quite clearly that this impulse, or whatever it is called, proceeds from the interior of the soul, as we said when discussing these impulses. It is now felt very gently, but it proceeds neither from the thought nor from the memory, nor can it be supposed that the soul has had any part in it. This is so usual and occurs so frequently that it has been observed with special care: just as the flames of a fire, however great, never travel downwards, but always upwards, so here it is evident that this interior movement proceeds from the centre of the soul and awakens the faculties.

Really, were there nothing else to be gained from this way of prayer but our realization of God's special care for us in His communing with us and of the way He keeps begging us to dwell with Him (for He seems to be doing nothing less), I believe that all trials would be well endured if they led to the enjoyment of these gentle yet penetrating touches of His love. This, sisters, you will have experienced, for I think that, when the soul reaches the Prayer of Union, the Lord begins to exercise this care over us if we do not neglect the keeping of His commandments. When this experience comes to you, remember that it belongs to this innermost Mansion, where God dwells in our souls, and give Him fervent praise, for it is He who sends it to you, like a message, or a letter, written very lovingly and in such a way that He would have you alone be able to understand what He has written and what He is asking of you in it. On no account must you fail to answer His Majesty, even if you are busy with exterior affairs and engaged in conversation. It may often happen that Our Lord will be pleased to bestow this secret favour upon you in public; as your reply must needs be an interior one, it will be very easy for you to do what I say and make an act of love or exclaim with Saint Paul: *Lord, what wilt Thou have me to do?* (*Acts* ix, 6). Then He will show you many ways of pleasing Him. For now is the accepted time: He seems indeed to be listening to us and this delicate touch almost always prepares the soul to be able to do, with a resolute will, what He has commanded it.

The difference between this Mansion and the rest has already been explained. There are hardly any of the periods of aridity or interior disturbance in it which at one time or another have occurred in all the rest, but the soul is almost always in tranquillity. It is not afraid that this sublime favour may be counterfeited by the devil but retains the unwavering certainty that it comes from God. For, as has been said, the senses and faculties have no part in this: His Majesty has revealed Himself to the soul and taken it with Him into a place where, as I believe, the devil will not enter, because the Lord will not allow him to do so; and all the favours which the Lord grants the soul here, as I have said, come quite independently of the acts of the soul itself, apart from that of its having committed itself wholly to God.

So tranquilly and noiselessly does the Lord teach the soul in this state and do it good that I am reminded of the building of Solomon's temple, during which no noise could be heard; just so, in this temple of God, in this Mansion of His, He and the soul alone have fruition of each other in the deepest silence. There is no reason now for the understanding to stir, or to seek out anything, for the Lord Who created the soul is now pleased to calm it and would have it look, as it were, through a little chink, at what is passing. Now and then it loses sight of it and is unable to see anything; but this is only for a very brief time. The faculties, I think, are not lost here; it is merely that they do not work but seem to be dazed.

And I am quite dazed myself when I observe that, on reaching this state, the soul has no more raptures (accompanied, that is to say, by the suspension of the senses), save very occasionally and even then it has not the same transports and flights of the spirit. These raptures, too, happen only rarely, and hardly ever in public as they very often did before. Nor have they any connection, as they had before, with great occasions of devotion; if we see a devotional image or hear a sermon, it is almost as if we had heard nothing, and it is the same with music. Previously, the poor little butterfly was always so worried that everything frightened her and made her fly away. But it is not so now, whether because she has found her rest, or because the soul has seen so much in this Mansion that it can be frightened at nothing, or because it no longer has that solitude which it was wont to have, now that it is enjoying such companionship. Well, sisters, I do not know what the reason may be, but, when the Lord begins to reveal the contents of this Mansion and brings souls into it, they lose the great weakness which was such a trial to them and of which previously they could not rid themselves. Perhaps the reason is that the Lord has so greatly strengthened and dilated and equipped the soul, or it may be that, for reasons which His Majesty alone knows, He was anxious to make a public revelation of His secret dealings with such souls, for His judgments surpass all that we can imagine here on earth.

These effects God bestows, together with all those other good effects already described in the above-mentioned degrees of prayer, when the soul approaches Him, and He also gives the soul that kiss for which the Bride besought Him; for I understand it to be in this

Mansion that that petition is fulfilled. Here to this wounded hart are given waters in abundance. Here the soul delights in the tabernacle of God (*Apoc.* xxi, 3). Here the dove sent out by Noe to see if the storm is over finds the olive-branch (*Gen.* viii, 8-9)— the sign that it has discovered firm ground amidst the waters and storms of this world.

Oh, Jesus! If only one knew how many things there are in Scripture which describe this peace of the soul! My God, since Thou seest how needful it is for us, do Thou inspire Christians to desire to seek it; take it not, by Thy mercy, from those to whom Thou hast given it, and who, until Thou give them true peace and take them where peace will never end, must always live in fear. I say "true" peace, not because I think this peace is not true, but because in this life war might always begin again if we were to withdraw from God.

And what will be the feeling of these souls when they realize that they might lack so great a blessing? The thought makes them walk the more warily and endeavour to bring strength out of their weakness, so as not to be responsible for losing any opportunity which might offer itself to them of pleasing God better. The more they are favoured by God, the more timorous and fearful do they become concerning themselves, and as they have learned more about their own wretchedness by comparing it with His greatness and their sins are now so much more serious to them, they often go about, like the Publican, without daring to lift up their eyes (*Luke* xviii, 13). At other times, they long to reach the end of their lives so as to be in safety, though they are soon anxious again to live longer so that they may serve Him because of the love which they bear Him, as has been said, and they trust all that concerns themselves to His mercy. Sometimes the many favours they receive leave them overwhelmed, and afraid lest they be like an overladen ship sinking to the bottom of the sea.

I assure you, sisters, that they have no lack of crosses, but these do not unsettle them or deprive them of their peace. The few storms pass quickly, like waves of the sea, and fair weather returns, and then the Presence of the Lord which they have within them makes them forget everything. May He be for ever blessed and praised by all His creatures. Amen.

CHAPTER IV

Concludes by describing what appears to be Our Lord's aim in granting the soul such great favours and says how necessary it is for Martha and Mary to walk in each other's company. This chapter is very profitable.

YOU MUST not take it, sisters, that the effects which I have described as occurring in these souls are invariably present all the time; it is for this reason that, whenever I have remembered to do so, I have referred to them as being present "habitually." Sometimes Our Lord leaves such souls to their own nature, and when that happens, all the poisonous things in the environs and mansions of this castle seem to come together to avenge themselves on them for the time during which they have not been able to have them in their power.

It is true that this lasts only for a short time—for a single day, or a little longer, at the most—and in the course of the ensuing turmoil, which as a rule is the result of some chance happening, it becomes clear what the soul is gaining from the good Companion Who is with it. For the Lord gives it great determinaton, so that it will on no account turn aside from His service and from its own good resolutions. On the contrary, these resolutions seem to increase, and so the soul will not make the slightest move which may deflect it from its resolve. This, as I say, happens rarely, but Our Lord's will is for the soul not to forget what it is—for one reason, so that it may always be humble; for another, so that it may the better realize what it owes to His Majesty and what a great favour it is receiving, and may praise Him.

Do not, of course, for one moment imagine that, because these souls have such vehement desires and are so determined not to commit a single imperfection for anything in the world, they do not in fact commit many imperfections, and even sins. Not intentionally, it is true, for the Lord will give such persons very special aid as to this: I am referring to venial sins, for from mortal sins, as far as they know, they are free, though they are not completely proof against them; and the thought that they may commit some without knowing it will cause them no small agony. It also distresses them to see so many souls being lost; and, although on the one hand they have great hopes of not being among them, yet, when they remember some whom the Scriptures describe as having been favoured of the Lord—like Solomon, who enjoyed such converse with His Majesty (*III Kings* xi)—they cannot, as I have said, but be afraid. And let whichever of you feels surest of herself fear most, for, says David, *Blessed is the man that feareth God* (*Ps.* cxi, 1). May His Majesty always protect us; let us beseech Him to do so, that we may not offend Him; this is the greatest security that we can have. May He be for ever praised. Amen.

It will be a good thing, sisters, if I tell you why it is that the Lord grants so many favours in this world. Although you will have learned this from the effects they produce, if you have observed them, I will speak about it further here, so that none of you shall think that He does it simply to give these souls pleasure. That would be to make a great error. For His Majesty can do nothing greater for us than grant us a life which is an imitation of that lived by His Beloved Son. I feel certain, therefore, that these favours are given us to strengthen our weakness, as I have sometimes said here, so that we may be able to imitate Him in His great sufferings.

We always find that those who walked closest to Christ Our Lord were those who had to bear the greatest trials. Consider the trials suffered by His glorious Mother and by the glorious Apostles. How do you suppose Saint Paul could endure such terrible trials? We can see in his life the effects of genuine visions and of contemplation coming from Our Lord and not from human imagination or from the deceit of the devil. Do you imagine that he shut himself up with his visions so as to enjoy those Divine favours and pursue no other occupation? You know very well that, so far as we can learn, he took not a day's rest, nor can he have rested by night, since it was then that he had to earn his living (*I Thess.* ii, 9). I am very fond of the story of how, when Saint Peter was fleeing from prison, Our Lord appeared to him and told him to go back to Rome and be crucified. We never recite the Office on his festival, in which this story is found, without my deriving a special consolation from it. How did Saint Peter feel after receiving this favour from the Lord?

And what did he do? He went straight to his death; and the Lord showed him no small mercy in providing someone to kill him.

Oh, my sisters, how little one should think about resting, and how little one should care about honours, and how far one ought to be from wishing to be esteemed in the very least if the Lord makes His special abode in the soul. For if the soul is much with Him, as it is right it should be, it will very seldom think of itself; its whole thought will be concentrated upon finding ways to please Him and upon showing Him how it loves Him. This, my daughters, is the aim of prayer: this is the purpose of the Spiritual Marriage, of which are born good works and good works alone.

Such works, as I have told you, are the sign of every genuine favour and of everything else that comes from God. It will profit me little if I am alone and deeply recollected, and make acts of love to Our Lord and plan and promise to work wonders in His service, and then, as soon as I leave my retreat and some occasion presents itself, I do just the opposite. I was wrong when I said it will profit me little, for anyone who is with God must profit greatly, and, although after making these resolutions we may be too weak to carry them out, His Majesty will sometimes grant us grace to do so, even at great cost to ourselves, as often happens. For, when He sees a very timorous soul, He sends it, much against its own will, some very sore trial the bearing of which does it a great deal of good; and later, when the soul becomes aware of this, it loses its fear and offers itself to Him the more readily. What I meant was that the profit is small by comparison with the far greater profit which comes from conformity between our deeds on the one hand and our resolutions and the words we use on the other. Anyone who cannot achieve everything at once must progress little by little. If she wishes to find help in prayer, she must learn to subdue her own will and in these little nooks of ours there will be very many occasions when you can do this.

Reflect carefully on this, for it is so important that I can hardly lay too much stress on it. Fix your eyes on the Crucified and nothing else will be of much importance to you. If His Majesty revealed His love to us by doing and suffering such amazing things, how can you expect to please Him by words alone? Do you know when people really become spiritual? It is when they become the slaves of

God and are branded with His sign, which is the sign of the Cross, in token that they have given Him their freedom. Then He can sell them as slaves to the whole world, as He Himself was sold, and if He does this He will be doing them no wrong but showing them no slight favour. Unless they resolve to do this, they need not expect to make great progress. For the foundation of this whole edifice, as I have said, is humility, and, if you have not true humility, the Lord will not wish it to reach any great height: in fact, it is for your own good that it should not; if it did, it would fall to the ground. Therefore, sisters, if you wish to lay good foundations, each of you must try to be the least of all, and the slave of God, and must seek a way and means to please and serve all your companions. If you do that, it will be of more value to you than to them and your foundation will be so firmly laid that your Castle will not fall.

I repeat that if you have this in view you must not build upon foundations of prayer and contemplation alone, for, unless you strive after the virtues and practise them, you will never grow to be more than dwarfs. God grant that nothing worse than this may happen—for, as you know, anyone who fails to go forward begins to go back, and love, I believe, can never be content to stay for long where it is.

You may think that I am speaking about beginners, and that later on one may rest: but, as I have already told you, the only repose that these souls enjoy is of an interior kind; of outward repose they get less and less, and they have no wish to get more. What is the purpose, do you suppose, of these inspirations—or, more correctly, of these aspirations—which I have described, and of these messages which are sent by the soul from its innermost centre to the folk outside the Castle and to the Mansions which are outside that in which it is itself dwelling? Is it to send them to sleep? No, no, no. The soul, where it now is, is fighting harder to keep the faculties and senses and every thing to do with the body from being idle than it did when it suffered with them. For it did not then understand what great gain can be derived from trials, which may indeed have been means whereby God has brought it to this state, nor did it realize how the companionship which it now enjoys would give it much greater strength than it ever had before. For if, as David says, with the holy we shall be holy (*Ps.* xvii, 26), it cannot be doubted that, if we are made one with the Strong, we shall gain strength through the most sovereign union of spirit with Spirit, and we shall appreciate the strength of the saints which enabled them to suffer and die.

It is quite certain that, with the strength it has gained, the soul comes to the help of all who are in the Castle, and, indeed, succours the body itself. Often the body appears to feel nothing, but the strength derived from the vigour gained by the soul after it has drunk of the wine from this cellar, where its Spouse has brought it and which He will not allow it to leave, overflows into the weak body, just as on the earthly plane the food which is introduced into the stomach gives strength to the head and to the whole body. In this life, then, the soul has a very bad time, for, however much it accomplishes, it is strong enough inwardly to attempt much more and this causes such strife within it that nothing it can do seems to it of any importance. This must be the reason for the great penances done by many saints, especially by the glorious Magdalen, who had been brought up in such luxury all her life long; there was also that hunger for the honour of his God suffered by our father Elias (*III Kings* xix, 10); and the zeal of Saint Dominic and Saint Francis for bringing souls to God, so that He might be praised. I assure you that, forgetful as they were of themselves, they must have endured no little suffering.

This, my sisters, I should like us to strive to attain: we should desire and engage in prayer, not for our enjoyment, but for the sake of acquiring this strength which fits us for service. Let us not try to walk along an untrodden path, or at the best we shall waste our time: it would certainly be a novel idea to think of receiving these favours from God through any other means than those used by Him and by all His saints. Let us not even consider such a thing: believe me, Martha and Mary must work together when they offer the Lord lodging, and must have Him ever with them, and they must not entertain Him badly and give Him nothing to eat. And how can Mary give Him anything, seated as she is at His feet, unless her sister helps her? His food consists in our bringing Him souls, in every possible way, so that they may be saved and may praise Him for ever.

You will reply to me by making two observations. The first, that

Mary was said to have chosen the better part (*Luke* x, 42)—and she had already done the work of Martha and shown her love for the Lord by washing His feet and wiping them with her hair (*Luke* vii, 37-38). And do you think it would be a trifling mortification to a woman in her position to go through those streets—perhaps alone, for her fervour was such that she cared nothing how she went —to enter a house that she had never entered before and then to have to put up with uncharitable talk from the Pharisee (*Luke* vii, 39) and from very many other people, all of which she was forced to endure? What a sight it must have been in the town to see such a woman as she had been making this change in her life! Such wicked people,[6] as we know, would only need to see that she was friendly with the Lord, Whom they so bitterly hated, to call to mind the life which she had lived and to realize that she now wanted to become holy, for she would of course at once have changed her style of dress and everything else. Think how we gossip about people far less notorious than she and then imagine what she must have suffered. I assure you, sisters, that that better part came to her only after sore trials and great mortification—even to see her Master so much hated must have been an intolerable trial to her. And how many such trials did she not endure later, after the Lord's death! I think myself that the reason she was not granted martyrdom was that she had already undergone it through witnessing the Lord's death. The later years of her life, too, during which she was absent from Him, would have been years of terrible torment; so she was not always enjoying the delights of contemplation at the Lord's feet.

The other thing you may say is that you are unable to lead souls to God, and have no means of doing so; that you would gladly do this, but, being unable to teach and preach like the Apostles, you do not know how. That is an objection which I have often answered in writing, though I am not sure if I have done so in discussing this Castle. But, as it is a thing which I think must occur to you, in view of the desires which the Lord implants in you, I will not omit to speak of it here. I told you elsewhere that the devil sometimes puts

[6] *Tan mala gente* (Silverio, IV, p. 206). I have departed from Mr. Peers' translation of these words (vol. II, pp. 348-349). Cf. William Thomas Walsh in *Thought*, XXII, 86 (Sept., 1947), p. 508.

ambitious desires into our hearts, so that, instead of setting our hand to the work which lies nearest to us, and thus serving Our Lord in ways within our power, we may rest content with having desired the impossible. Apart from praying for people, by which you can do a great deal for them, do not try to help everybody, but limit yourselves to your own companions; your work will then be all the more effective because you have the greater obligation to do it. Do you imagine it is a small advantage that you should have so much humility and mortification, and should be the servants of all and show such great charity towards all, and such fervent love for the Lord that it resembles a fire kindling all their souls, while you constantly awaken their zeal by your other virtues? This would indeed be a great service to the Lord and one very pleasing to Him. By your doing things which you really can do, His Majesty will know that you would like to do many more, and thus He will reward you exactly as if you had won many souls for Him.

"But we shall not be converting anyone," you will say, "for all our sisters are good already." What has that to do with it? If they become still better, their praises will be more pleasing to the Lord, and their prayers of greater value to their neighbours. In a word, my sisters, I will end by saying that we must not build towers without foundations, and that the Lord does not look so much at the magnitude of anything we do as at the love with which we do it. If we accomplish what we can, His Majesty will see to it that we become able to do more each day. We must not begin by growing weary; but during the whole of this short life, which for any one of you may be shorter than you think, we must offer the Lord whatever interior and exterior sacrifice we are able to give Him, and His Majesty will unite it with that which He offered to the Father for us upon the Cross, so that it may have the value won for it by our will, even though our actions in themselves may be trivial.

May it please His Majesty, my sisters and daughters, to bring us all to meet where we may praise Him and to give me grace to do some of the things of which I have told you, through the merits of His Son, Who liveth and reigneth for ever, Amen. As I say this to you, I am full of shame and by the same Lord I beg you not to forget this poor miserable creature in your prayers.

JHS

ALTHOUGH when I began to write what I have set down here it was with great reluctance, as I said at the beginning, I am very glad I did so now that it is finished, and I think my labour has been well spent, though I confess it has cost me very little. And considering how strictly you are cloistered, my sisters, how few opportunities you have of recreation and how insufficient in number are your houses, I think it will be a great consolation for you, in some of your convents, to take your delight in this Interior Castle, for you can enter it and walk about in it at any time without asking leave from your superiors.

It is true that, however strong you may think yourselves, you cannot enter all the Mansions by your own efforts; the Lord of the Castle Himself must admit you to them. So, if you meet with any resistance, I advise you not to make any effort to get in, for if you do you will displease Him so much that He will never admit you. He is a great Lover of humility. If you consider yourselves unworthy of entering even the third Mansion, He will more quickly give you the will to reach the fifth, and thenceforward you may serve Him by going to these Mansions again and again, till He brings you into the Mansion which He reserves as His own and which you will never leave, except when you are called away by the prioress, whose wishes this great Lord is pleased that you should observe as if they were His own. And even if, at her command, you are often outside these Mansions, He will always keep the door open against your return. Once you have been shown how to enjoy this Castle, you will find rest in everything, even in the things which most try you, and you will cherish a hope of returning to it which nobody can take from you.

Although I have spoken here only of seven Mansions, yet in each there are comprised many more, both above and below and around, with lovely gardens and fountains and things so delectable that you will want to lose yourselves in praise of the great God Who created it in His image and likeness. If you find anything good in this book which helps you to learn to know Him better, you can be quite sure that it is His Majesty Who has said it, and if you find anything bad, that it has been said by me.

By the earnest desire that I have to be of some use in helping you to serve this my God and Lord, I beg you, in my own name, whenever you read this, to give great praise to His Majesty and beg Him to multiply His Church and to give light to the Lutherans and to pardon my sins and set me free from Purgatory, where perhaps, by the mercy of God, I shall be when this is given you to read, if, after being revised by learned men, it is ever published. And if there is any error in it, that is due to my lack of understanding, for in all things I submit to what is held by the Holy Roman Catholic Church, in which I live, and protest and promise that I will both live and die. Praised and blessed for ever be God our Lord. Amen, Amen.

The writing of this was finished in the convent of Saint Joseph of Ávila, in the year one thousand five hundred and seventy seven, on the vigil of Saint Andrew, to the glory of God, Who liveth and reigneth for ever and ever. Amen.

ST. JOHN
of the CROSS

THE ASCENT of MOUNT CARMEL

Without other light or guide
Save that which in my heart was burning.

THE SHORT LIFE of St. John of the Cross (1542-1591) is remark-able for its intensity and occupation. He studied theology in Sala-manca (1564-1568), was ordained in 1567, and from that time onward dedicated himself to the cause of St. Teresa, the reform of the Carmelites. In December of 1577 began his imprisonment at the hands of those who opposed the reform. This imprisonment was, physically and spiritually, a dark night; but it was followed by the great works of his life: *The Ascent of Mount Carmel, The Dark Night of the Soul, The Living Flame of Love* and *The Spiritual Canticle* (1579-1584). The dark night is the closing of one's life to its normal and earthly occupations, and begins with the purification of the life of sense in man.

ARGUMENT

The following stanzas are a summary of the doctrine contained in this book of the Ascent of Mount Carmel. They also describe how we are to ascend to the summit of it, that is, to the high estate of perfection, called here union of the soul with God. I place all the stanzas together, because what I have to say is founded upon them.

*Thus the whole substance of my book may be comprehended at
once. I shall also transcribe each stanza again, and each line separately, as the nature of my work requires.*

STANZAS

I

In an obscure night,
With anxious love inflamed,
O, happy lot!
Forth unobserved I went,
My house being now at rest.

II

In darkness and obscurity,
By the secret ladder, disguised,
O, happy lot!
In darkness and concealment,
My house being now at rest.

III

In that happy night,
In secret, seen of none,
Seeing nought myself,
Without other light or guide
Save that which in my heart was burning,

IV

That light guided me
More surely than the noonday sun
To the place where He was waiting for me,
Whom I knew well,
And where none but He appeared.

V

O, guiding night;
O, night more lovely than the dawn;
O, night that hast united

The Lover with His beloved,
And changed her into her Love.

VI

On my flowery bosom,
Kept whole for Him alone,
He reposed and slept;
I kept Him, and the waving
Of the cedars fanned Him

VII

Then His hair floated in the breeze
That blew from the turret;
He struck me on the neck
With His gentle hand,
And all sensation left me.

VIII

I continued in oblivion lost,
My head was resting on my Love;
I fainted away, abandoned,
And, amid the lilies forgotten,
Threw all my cares away.

PROLOGUE

HE DARK NIGHT, THROUGH WHICH THE SOUL
passes, on its way to the Divine light of the per-
fect union of the love of God—so far as it is in
this life possible—requires for its explanation
greater experience and light of knowledge than I
possess. For so great are the trials, and so pro-
found the darkness, spiritual as well as corporal, which souls must
endure, if they will attain to perfection, that no human knowledge
can comprehend them, nor experience describe them. He only who
has passed through them can know them, but even he cannot ex-

plain them. Therefore, while touching but slightly on the subject of this dark night, I trust neither to experience nor to knowledge, for both may mislead me; but solely to the Holy Scriptures, under the teaching of which I cannot err, because he who speaks therein is the Holy Ghost. Nevertheless, I accept the aid of experience and knowledge, and if through ignorance I should err, it is not my intention to depart from the sound doctrine of our holy mother the Catholic Church. I resign myself absolutely to her light, and bow down before her decisions, and moreover to the better judgment herein of private men, be they who they may.

It is not any personal fitness which I recognize in myself that has led me to undertake this work, so high and so difficult, but solely my trust in our Lord, Who, I hope, will enable me to speak on account of the great necessities of many souls. Many persons begin to walk in the way of virtue—our Lord longing to lead them into the obscure night that they may travel onwards into the Divine union—but make no progress; sometimes because they will not enter upon this night, or suffer Him to lead them into it; and sometimes also because they do not understand their own state and are destitute of fit and wise directors who may guide them to the summit of the mount. How miserable it is to see many souls, to whom God has given grace to advance—and who, had they taken courage, would have reached perfection—remain satisfied with narrow-minded views of God's dealings, through want of will or through ignorance, or because there is not one to direct their steps, and to teach them how to go onwards from the beginning. And in the end, when our Lord has compassion on them, and leads them on in spite of these hindrances, they arrive late, with much difficulty, and less merit, because they have not submitted themselves to His ways, nor suffered Him to plant their feet on the pure and certain road of union. Though it is true that God, Who conducts them, can do so without these helps, still, because they do not yield themselves up to Him, they make less progress on the road, resisting their Guide; and they merit less because they do not submit their will, whereby their sufferings are increased. There are souls who, instead of abandoning themselves to the care and protection of God, hinder Him rather by their indiscreet behaviour, or resist Him like little children who, when their mothers would carry them in their arms, struggle and cry that they may be allowed to walk. These souls make no progress, or if they do, it is comparable only to the walking of an infant child.

So, then—that men may know, beginners as well as those who have made some progress, how to resign themselves into the hands of God when it is His pleasure to lead them—I purpose, by His help, to furnish some directions, so that they may understand the matter for themselves, or at least submit to the guidance of God. Some confessors and spiritual directors, because they have no perception or experience of these ways, are a hindrance and an evil, rather than a help to such souls: they are like the builders of Babel; who, when required to furnish certain materials, furnished others of the very different sort, because they knew not the language of those around them, and thus the building was stopped. *Come ye therefore,* saith God, *let us go down and there confound their tongue, that they may not understand one another's speech. And so the Lord scattered them.*[1]

It is a hard and miserable thing for souls when they cannot comprehend their own state, nor meet with any one who can. For when God leads any one along the highest road of obscure contemplation and aridity, such an one will think himself lost; and in this darkness and affliction, temptation and distress, some will be sure to tell him, like the comforters of Job [2], that his sufferings are the effects of melancholy, or disordered health, or of natural temperament, or, it may be, some secret sin for which God has abandoned him. Yea, they will decide that he is, or that he has been, exceedingly wicked, seeing that he is thus afflicted. Some also will say that he is going backwards, because he finds no consolation or pleasure, as before, in the things of God. Thus they multiply the sorrows of this poor soul, for his greatest trial is the knowledge of his own misery, when it seems to him clearer than light that he is full of evil and sin, because God enables him, as I shall hereafter explain, to see this in the obscure night of contemplation. And so, when he meets with those who tell him, in accordance with his own impressions, that his troubles arise out of his own sins, his grief and misery are infinitely increased and rendered more bitter than death.

Such confessors as these, not satisfied with considering all his

[1] *Gen.* xi, 7, 8.   [2] *Job* iv.

sorrows to flow from past sins, compel him to retrace his whole life, and to make frequent general confessions, putting him on the rack anew. They do not understand that this is not the time for such acts, but that it is now the day of God's purgation; and when they ought to leave him alone, comforting him, indeed, and encouraging him to bear his trials patiently until God shall be pleased to deliver him; for until then, notwithstanding all they may say or do, there can be no relief.

I have to treat this matter hereafter, and how the soul is to be guided, and how the confessor is to conduct himself with regard to his penitent, and what are the signs whereby we may ascertain whether this be a state of purgation, and if it be, whether of sense or of spirit—this is the obscure night—and whether or not it be the effect of melancholy or any other imperfection of body or soul. For there are persons who will think, or their confessors for them, that God is leading them along the road of the obscure night, of spiritual purgation, and yet, perhaps, all is nothing but imperfection of sense and spirit; and others also who will think they do not pray when they pray much, and, on the other hand, there are others who think they pray much when they do not in reality pray scarcely at all.

There are some—and it is sad to see them—who toil and labour, wearying themselves, and yet go backwards, because they make the fruit which is profitable to consist in that which profits not, but which is rather a hindrance; and others who, in rest and quietness, make great advancement. Others also there are who turn the graces and the gifts of God, given them for their advancement, into embarrassments and stumbling-blocks on this road.

Those who travel on this road will meet with many occasions of joy and sorrow, hope and pain, some of which are the result of the spirit of perfection, others of imperfections. I shall endeavour, by God's help, to speak of all, so that everyone who shall read my book may, in some degree, see the road he takes, and that which he ought to take, if he wishes to ascend to the summit of this mount.

As my book treats of the obscure night in which the soul journeys on to God, let no one be surprised if he finds it also somewhat obscure. It will be so, certainly, at first, but as the reader advances he will understand it better, for one part of it will throw light on another. If it be read a second time it will become more intelligible, and the doctrine it contains will appear the more certain. But if still there should be any to whom it shall seem hard, let them ascribe it to my ignorance and poor style, for the matter of it is in itself good and most necessary.

But after all I believe that, if I had written it in a more perfect manner, many would not appreciate it, because its contents are not those moralities and soothing matters which those spiritual persons run after who desire to draw near to God in pleasant ways, but a solid and substantial doctrine suited to all, if they seek to advance to that detachment of spirit which is here described. My principal object, however, is not to address myself to all, but only to certain persons of our holy religion of Mount Carmel, who by the grace of God are on the pathway of this mount. It is at their request I have undertaken my task. They, indeed, already detached from the things of this life, will the better understand this doctrine of detachment of spirit.

BOOK ONE

The Nature of the Obscure Night, the Necessity of Passing through it in Order to Attain to the Divine Union: and Specially the Obscure Night of Sense and Desire, with the Evils which these Inflict on the Soul

CHAPTER I

Two kinds of this night, corresponding with the division of the soul into higher and lower

STANZA I

In an obscure night,
With anxious love inflamed,
O, happy lot!
Forth unobserved I went,
My house being now at rest.

THIS stanza describes the happy state of the soul at its departure from all things, from the appetites and imperfections of our sensual nature to which all are subject because of our disobedience to reason. I mean that, in order to reach perfection, the soul has to pass, ordinarily, through two kinds of night, which spiritual writers call purgations, or purifications of the soul, and which I have called night, because in the one as well as in the other the soul travels, as it were, by night, in darkness.

The first is the night, or purgation of the sensual part of the soul, treated of in this first stanza, and described in the first part of this work. The second is the night of the spiritual part, of which the second stanza speaks, and which I shall discuss in the second part of my work, so far as it relates to the soul's activity therein, and in the third and fourth part, so far as it relates to its passive condition in it.

The meaning of the stanza then is, that the soul went forth, led of God, through love of Him only, and with that love inflamed, into the obscure night, which is the privation of, and purgation from, all sensual desires, in all external things; all the pleasures of the flesh, and all the satisfactions of the will. This is wrought in this purgation of the will, and for this reason is it said that the soul departed, its house, that is the sensual part, being at rest—all the desires being at rest and asleep, and the soul asleep to them; for there is no departing from the pains and vexations of desire till it be mortified and put to sleep.

The happy lot of the soul, then, is this unobserved departure, when no carnal desire or aught else was able to detain it. And also in that this departure took place by night, which is the privation of all desire wrought by God, a condition which is as night to the soul. The happy lot of the soul, then, consists in being led by God into this night from which so great a blessing results, but into which it could not have entered of itself, because no one is able in his own strength to empty his heart of all desires, so as to draw near unto God. This is the meaning of the stanza. I now proceed to explain each line of it separately, and to discuss the subject of this book.

CHAPTER II

The nature and cause of the obscure night

"IN AN obscure night." The journey of the soul to the Divine union is called night for three reasons. The first is derived from the point from which the soul sets out, the privation of the desire of all pleasure in all the things of this world, by an entire detachment therefrom. This is as night for every desire and sense of man. The second, from the road by which it travels; that is faith, for faith is obscure, like night, to the intellect. The third, from the goal to which it tends, God, incomprehensible and infinite, Who in this life is as night to the soul. We must pass through these three nights if we are to attain to the Divine union with God.

They are foreshadowed in Holy Scripture by the nights which were to elapse, according to the command of the angel, between the betrothal and the marriage of the younger Tobias. *When thou shalt take her,* said the angel, *go into the chamber, and for three days keep thyself continent from her.*[1] On the first night, he was to burn the liver of the fish in the fire, which is the heart whose affections are set on the things of this world, and which, if it will enter on the road that leadeth unto God, must be burned up, and purified of all created things in the fire of this love. This purgation drives away the evil spirit who has dominion over our soul, because of our attachment to those pleasures which flow from temporal and corporeal things.

The second night, said the angel, *thou shalt be admitted into the society of the Holy Patriarchs,* the fathers of the faith. The soul having passed the first night, which is the privation of all sensible things, enters immediately into the second night, alone in pure faith, and by it alone directed: for faith is not subject to sense.

The third night, said the angel, *thou shalt obtain a blessing—* that is, God, Who, in the second night of faith, communicates Himself so secretly and so intimately to the soul. This is another night, inasmuch as this communication is more obscure than the others, as I shall presently explain. When this night is over, which is the accomplishment of the communication of God in spirit, ordinarily

[1] *Tob.* vi, 18.

effected when the soul is in great darkness, the union with the bride, which is the Wisdom of God, immediately ensues. The angel adds also, saying to Tobias, *When the third night is passed, thou shalt take the virgin with the fear of the Lord.* This fear is then perfect when it is also the love of God, and it is made perfect when the soul is by love transformed in God.

I shall speak of these three causes separately, that they may be the better understood, first reminding the reader that the three nights are but one divided into three parts. The first, which is that of the senses, may be likened to the commencement of night when material objects begin to be invisible. The second, of faith, may be compared to midnight, which is utter darkness. The third resembles the close of night, which is God, when the dawn of day is at hand.

CHAPTER III

The first cause, the privation of desire

THE PRIVATION of all pleasure to the desire in all things is here called night. For as night is nothing else but the absence of light, and, consequently, of visible objects, whereby the faculty of vision remains in darkness unemployed, so the mortification of the desires is as night to the soul. For when the soul denies itself those pleasures which outward things furnish to the desire, it is as it were in darkness, without occupation. As the faculty of vision is nourished by light and fed by visible objects, and ceases to be so fed when the light is withdrawn, so the soul by means of the desire feeds on those things which, corresponding with its powers, give it pleasure; but when the desire is mortified, it derives no more pleasure from them, and thus, so far as the desire is concerned, the soul abides in darkness, without occupation.

This may be illustrated in the case of all the faculties of the soul. When the soul denies itself the pleasure arising from all that gratifies the ear, it remains, so far as the faculty of hearing is concerned, in darkness, without occupation; and when it denies itself in all that is pleasing to the eye, it remains in darkness, so far as it relates to the faculty of sight. The same may be said of the other senses, so that he who shall deny himself all satisfaction derivable from external objects, mortifying the desire thereof, may be said to be in a state which is as night, and this is nothing else but an entire detachment from all things.

Philosophers say that the soul is a blank when first infused into the body, without knowledge of any kind whatever, and incapable of receiving knowledge, in the course of nature, in any other way than through the senses. Thus, while in the body, the soul is like a man imprisoned in darkness, who has no knowledge of what passes without beyond what he can learn by looking through the window of his cell, and who if he did not so look could in no other way learn anything at all. Thus, then, the soul cannot naturally know anything beyond what reaches it through the senses, which are the windows of its cell. If, then, the impressions and communications of sense be neglected and denied, we may well say that the soul is in darkness and empty, because according to this opinion there is no other natural way for knowledge or light to enter in. It is true, indeed, that we cannot help hearing, seeing, smelling, tasting and touching, but this is of no moment, and does not trouble the soul, when the objects of sense are repelled, any more than if we neither heard nor saw; for he who shuts his eyes is as much in darkness as a blind man who cannot see. This is the meaning of the Psalmist when he said, *I am poor and in labours from my youth.*[1] He says that he is poor, though it is certain he was rich; because he had not set his mind upon riches, he was really like a poor man. But if he had been really poor, yet not in spirit, he would not have been truly poor, for his soul would have been rich, full of desires.

I call this detachment the night of the soul, for I am not speaking here of the absence of things—for absence is not detachment, if the desire of them remain—but of that detachment which consists in suppressing desire, and avoiding pleasure; it is this that sets the soul free, even though possession may be still retained. The things of this world neither occupy nor injure the soul, because they do not enter within, but rather the will and desire of them which abide within it. This is the night of the sensual part of the soul. And now I proceed to explain how the soul is to depart from its house in the obscure night of sense, in order to be united with God.

[1] *Ps.* lxxxvii, 16.

CHAPTER IV

*The necessity of passing truly through the obscure night of sense,
which is the mortification of the desire*

THE SOUL must of necessity—if we would attain to the Divine union of God—pass through the obscure night of mortification of the
desires, and self-denial in all things. The reason is that all the love
we bestow on creatures is in the eyes of God mere darkness, and
that while we are involved therein, the soul is incapable of being
enlightened and possessed by the pure and simple light of God, unless we first cast it away. Light hath no fellowship with darkness,
for as St. John saith, *The light shineth in darkness, and the darkness did not comprehend it.*[1] Two contrary qualities, as the philosophers say, cannot co-exist in the same subject. Darkness, which is
the love of creatures, and light, which is God, are contrary to one
another, for *What fellowship hath light with darkness?*[2] The light
of the Divine union cannot, therefore, dwell in the soul if these
affections are not cast away.

The affection and attachment which the soul feels for the creature
renders the soul its equal and its like, and the greater the affection
the greater will be the likeness. Love begets a likeness between the
lover and the object of his love, and so the Psalmist, speaking of
those who set their heart upon idols, says, *Let them that make them
become like unto them, and all such as trust in them.*[3] Thus, he
then who loves the creature becomes vile as that creature itself, and
in one sense even viler, for love not only levels, but subjects also
the lover to the object of his love.

He, therefore, who loveth anything beside God renders his soul
incapable of the Divine union and transformation in God, for the
vileness of the creature is much less capable of the dignity of the
Creator than darkness is of light. All things in heaven and earth
are nothing in comparison with God. *I beheld the earth,* saith he,
*and lo, it was void and nothing, and the heavens, and there was no
light in them.*[4] The earth *void and nothing* signifies that the
earth and all it contains are nothing, and the heavens without light,
that all the lights of heaven, in comparison with God, are perfect

[1] *John* i, 5.   [2] *II Cor.* vi, 14.   [3] *Ps.* cxiii, 8.   [4] *Jerem.* iv, 23.

darkness. Thus all created things, with the affections bestowed upon them, are nothing, because they are a hindrance, and the privation of our transformation in God, just as darkness is nothing, and less than nothing, being the absence of light. And as he who is in darkness comprehends not the light, so the soul whose affections are given to the creature shall never comprehend God. Until our soul is purged of these affections we shall not possess God in this life in the pure transformation of love, nor in the life to come in the beatific vision. To make this more clear I shall enter into some particulars.

The whole creation, compared with the infinite Being of God, is nothing; and so the soul whose affections are set on created things is nothing, and even less than nothing before God, because love begets equality and likeness, and even inferiority to the object beloved. Such a soul, therefore, cannot by any possibility be united to the infinite Being of God, because that which is not can have no communion with that which is. All the beauty of the creation, in comparison with the infinite Beauty of God, is supreme deformity, for *favour is deceitful and beauty is vain,*[5] and so the soul whose affections are set on the beauty of any created thing whatever shows before God nothing but deformity, and can never be transformed in Beauty, which is God, because deformity cannot attain unto beauty. All the grace and comeliness of creation, compared with the Grace of God, is supreme disgrace and supreme disfavour, and that soul, therefore, which is captivated by the grace and comeliness of created things is in the eyes of God in disfavour and disgrace, incapable of the infinite grace and beauty, for that which is ill-favoured is far removed from that which is infinitely gracious.

All the goodness of the whole world together, in comparison with the infinite Goodness of God, is wickedness rather than goodness, for *none is good but God alone,*[6] and that soul is, therefore, wicked before God, whose affections are set on the things of this world. And as wickedness can have no fellowship with goodness, so that soul cannot be united in perfect union with God, who is the supreme Goodness.

All the wisdom of the world, and all human cunning, compared with the infinite Wisdom of God, is simple and supreme ignorance,

[5] *Prov.* xxxi, 30.   [6] *Luke* xviii, 19.

for the wisdom of this world is foolishness with God.[7] He,
therefore, who shall labour to attain to union with the Wisdom of
God, in reliance on his own wisdom and skill, is supremely ignorant, and infinitely distant therefrom: for ignorance knoweth not
what wisdom is. They who consider themselves gifted with knowledge are in the eyes of God most ignorant: *professing themselves
to be wise, they become fools.*[8] They alone attain to the Divine
Wisdom who, like children and ignorant ones, lay aside their own
wisdom, and serve God in love. This is the wisdom to which the
Apostle refers, saying, *Let no man deceive himself; if any man
among you seem to be wise in this world, let him become a fool
that he may be wise. For the wisdom of this world is foolishness
with God.*[9] Ignorance, therefore, and not knowledge, becomes
that soul which strives after union with the Wisdom of God.

All the liberty and power of the world, compared with the Power
and Liberty of the Spirit of God, is but supreme slavery, wretchedness, and captivity; and so he who loves superiority and dignities,
and the indulgence of his desires, stands before God, not as a son
who is free, but as a person of mean condition, the slave of his
passions, because he submits not to the holy teaching, which saith,
He that is the greater among you, let him become as the younger.[10]
Such an one will never attain to the true liberty of spirit attainable
in the Divine union, because slavery has no fellowship with liberty,
liberty dwelleth not in a heart subject to desires, for that heart is
in captivity, but in that which is free, the heart of a son. It was for
this reason that Sara said unto Abraham: *Cast out this bond-woman
and her son, for the son of the bond-woman shall not be heir with
my son Isaac.*[11]

All the sweetness and all the pleasures which all the things of
this world furnish to the will are, in comparison with the sweetness
and pleasure which is God, supreme pain, torment, and bitterness.
He, therefore, who shall set his heart upon them is, in the eyes of
God, worthy of pain, torment, and bitterness, and can never attain
to those delights with which the Divine union abounds.

All the riches and glory of the whole creation compared with the
true riches, which is God, is supreme poverty and meanness, and

---

[7] *I Cor.* iii, 19.   [8] *Rom.* i, 22.   [9] *I Cor.* iii, 18, 19.   [10] *Luke* xxii, 26.
[11] *Gen.* xxi, 10.

he who sets his heart upon them is, in God's sight, supremely poor and mean, and can never attain to the blessed estate of riches and glory, which is the transformation of the soul in God; for that which is mean and poor is infinitely distant from that which is supremely rich and glorious.

For this cause, then, the Divine Wisdom bewails men; namely, because they make themselves loathsome, mean, wretched and poor, through their love for that which is beautiful, rich, and noble in the eyes of the world. *O ye men, to you I call, and my voice is to the sons of men. O little ones, understand subtlety, and ye unwise take notice. Hear, for I will speak of great things . . . With me are riches and glory, glorious riches and justice. For my fruit is better than gold and the precious stone, and my blossoms than choice silver. I walk in the way of justice, in the midst of the paths of judgment, that I may enrich them that love me, and may fill their treasures.*[12] Here God addresses Himself to those who set their affections on the things of this world; He calls them little ones, because they make themselves little, like the object of their love. He bids them 'understand subtlety', and 'take notice', because He is speaking of great things, and not of little things, such as they are. He tells them that great riches and glory, objects of their love, are with Him and in Him, and not where they think they shall find them. *Glorious riches and justice* are with wisdom. For though the things of this world may seem to men to be something, yet let them take notice, the things of God are more. The fruit of wisdom is better than gold and precious stones, and that which wisdom produces in the soul is preferable to the choice silver which men covet. This is applicable to every kind of affection to which we are liable in this life.

CHAPTER V

Continuation of the same subject. Proofs from Scripture

I HAVE now explained how great is the distance between created things and God, and how souls which set their affections thereon are equally distant from Him, because—as I have said—love begets

[12] *Prov.* viii, 4-6, 18-21.

equality and likeness. This was well understood by St. Augustine when, considering his own inclination towards the creature, he thus spoke unto God: "Miserable man that I am, what fellowship hath my perverseness with Thy uprightness? Thou art truly good, I wicked; Thou full of compassion, I impious; Thou holy, I miserable; Thou just, I unjust; Thou art light, I am blind; Thou art life, and I am dead; Thou art medicine, I am sick; Thou supreme truth, and I utter vanity." [1]

It is, therefore, supreme ignorance for any one to think that he can ever attain to the high estate of union with God before he casts away from him the desire of natural things, and of supernatural also, so far as it concerns self-love, because the distance between them and the state of perfection is the very greatest. For Christ our Lord hath said, *Every one of you that doth not renounce all that he possesseth, cannot be my disciple.* [2] The doctrine of Christ which He came into the world to teach, is contempt of all things, that we may thereby have power to receive the reward of the Spirit of God. For he who does not withdraw himself from the things of the world, is not qualified to receive the Spirit of God in the pure transformation.

This truth is foreshadowed in the book of *Exodus,* [3] where we read that God did not give the manna to the people of Israel till the corn they had brought from Egypt had failed them, for the bread of angels is not given to, neither is it meant for, that palate which is pleased with the bread of man. He who feeds on strange meats, and is delighted therewith, not only disqualifies himself for the reception of the Holy Ghost, but also provokes God to anger exceedingly, as all do who, while they seek spiritual food, are not content with God only, but intermingle therewith carnal and earthly satisfaction. This appears from the same history, where it is said that the people cried, *Who will give us flesh to eat?* [4] They were not satisfied with food so pure, for they desired and demanded the flesh of beasts. God was grievously offended because they would mingle flesh, so vile and coarse, with the pure and heavenly bread which, though always the same, had in it *the sweetness of every taste,* [5] for while *their meat was in their mouth the*

[1] *Soliloquia,* c. ii.   [2] *Luke* xiv, 33.   [3] *Exod.* xvi, 4.   [4] *Num.* xi, 4.
[5] *Wis.* xvi, 20.

wrath of God came upon them, and He slew the fat ones amongst them, and brought down the chosen men of Israel.[6] God regarded it as an evil wish to desire other food when He was giving them the bread of heaven.

Oh, would that spiritual persons knew how they are losing the good things of the Spirit, abundantly furnished, because they will not raise up their desires above trifles, and how they might have the sweetness of all things in the pure food of the Spirit if they would only forego them. But as they will not, so they shall not have such sweetness. The people of Israel perceived not the sweetness of every taste in the manna, though it was there, because they would not limit their desires to it alone. The sweetness and strength of the manna was not for them, not because it was not there, but because they longed for other meats beside it. He who loves any other thing with God makes light of Him, because he puts into the balance with Him that which is infinitely beneath Him. We know by experience that the will, when set on a particular object, magnifies it above all others, if it has no pleasure in them, though they may be of greater importance than what it desires. And if it should desire two things together, it does wrong to the chief of the two, because it establishes an unjust equality between them. There is nothing in the whole world to be compared with God; and, therefore, he who loves anything together with Him, wrongs Him. And if this be true, what does he do who loves anything more than God?

This truth is set before us in the book of *Exodus.* When God commanded Moses to go up into Mount Sinai, He bade him go up alone; the children of Israel were to remain below, and even the cattle were not to feed in sight of the mountain. *Thou shalt stand with Me on the top of the mount. Let no man go up with thee, and let not any man be seen throughout all the mount: neither let the oxen nor the sheep feed over against it.*[7] He, therefore, that will go up into the mount of perfection and hold communion with God, must not only abandon everything, but restrain even his desires, the sheep and the cattle from feeding in sight of the mount—that is, upon anything which is not simply God, in Whom, in the estate of perfection, every desire must cease. This journey or ascent must therefore be a perpetual struggle with

[6] *Ps.* lxxvii, 30, 31.   [7] *Exod.* xxxiv, 2, 3.

our desires to make them cease, and the more earnest we are the sooner shall we reach the summit. But until the desires cease we can never reach it, notwithstanding our many virtues, for virtue is not perfectly acquired before our souls are empty, detached, and purified from all desire.

Of this truth we have a lively figure in the history of the patriarch Jacob. When he was on his way to Bethel to build an altar for sacrifice unto God, he commanded his household the observance of three things: the casting away of strange gods, self-purification, and the changing of their garments. *Jacob having called together all his household, said, Cast away the strange gods that are among you, and be cleansed and change your garments.*[8] He, therefore, who will ascend to the mount of perfection, to build an altar there, whereon to offer unto God the sacrifice of pure love, praise, and adoration, must first of all perfectly fulfil the three commandments of Jacob. He must cast away the strange gods, the earthly affections and attachments. He must purify himself from the impressions which the desires have made on the soul, in the obscure night of sense, denying them and doing penance for their past indulgence, and, in the third place, he must change his garments. This God himself will do during the observance of the first two commandments; He will change them from old into new, by infusing into the soul a new understanding of God in God, the human understanding being set aside, and a new love of God in God, the will being detached from its old desires and human satisfactions, by bringing the soul into a state of new knowledge and of deep delight, all other knowledge and old imaginings being cast away; and, finally, by causing that which is of the old man to cease, which is our natural aptitudes, and investing us with a new supernatural aptitude corresponding with the powers of the soul, so that all that is human in the action of the soul may become divine. This is the object gained in the estate of union, in which the soul is nothing else but an altar of God whereon the sacrifice of praise and love is offered, and where He alone dwells.

This is the reason why, under the old law, the altar of sacrifice was to be hollow within. *Thou shalt not make it solid, but empty and hollow in the inside.*[9] It is the will of God that the soul

8 *Gen.* xxxv, 2.   9 *Exod.* xxvii, 8.

should be empty of all created things, so that it may become a fitting altar of His Majesty. He would not endure strange fires on the altar, nor that His own should fail. *Nadab and Abiu, the sons of Aaron, taking their censers, put fire therein, and incense on it, offering before the Lord strange fire: which was not commanded them, and fire coming out from the Lord destroyed them, and they died before the Lord.*[10] Because Nadab and Abiu, sons of Aaron the high priest, offered strange fire on the altar, God in His anger slew them before it. That soul, therefore, which would become a fitting altar, must not be without the love of God, nor mingle therewith any other and strange love. God will never dwell there where aught is present beside Himself. Thus, when the Philistines took the ark of God and brought it into the temple of Dagon, their idol was thrown to the ground, and at last broken to pieces.[11]

One desire only doth God allow, and suffer, in His presence, that of perfectly observing His law, and of carrying the cross of Christ. We do not know that He commanded anything except the book of the law, to be laid up with the ark where the manna was preserved—*Take this book, and put it in the side of the ark of the covenant of the Lord your God* [12]—and the rod of Aaron, type of the cross. *Take back the rod of Aaron into the tabernacle of the testimony.*[13] That soul which has no other aim than the perfect observance of the law of God, and the carrying of the cross of Christ, will be a true ark containing the true manna, which is God.

CHAPTER VI

Two great evils of the desires: negative and positive. Proofs from Scripture

To MAKE this matter clear, it is advisable here to explain how the desires inflict these two great evils on the soul. These evils are, the privation of the Spirit of God, and the fatigue, torture, darkness, defilement, and weakness of that soul which indulges them. *My people have done two evils,* saith God, *They have forsaken Me, the fountain of living water, and have digged to themselves cis-*

---

[10] *Levit.* x, 1, 2.   [11] *I Kings* v, 1-5.   [12] *Deut.* xxxi, 26; *Exod.* xvi, 33.
[13] *Num.* xvii, 10.

terns, broken cisterns, that can hold no water.[1] These two evils flow from one single act of desire; for it is clear that the instant we set our affections upon any one created thing, our capacity for union with God is diminished in proportion to the intensity of that act of affection. For, as I said before, [2] two contrary qualities cannot coexist in the same subject; the love of God and the love of the creature are contrary, the one to the other, and so cannot dwell together in the same heart. What connection is there between the creature and the Creator? Between the sensual and the spiritual? The seen and the unseen? The temporal and the eternal? Between the heavenly food, pure and spiritual, and the food of the flesh, simply sensual? Between the poverty of Christ and selfish attachments? As in natural generation, no new form results without the corruption of the one previously existing—for this obstructs the former by reason of the contrariety between them—so while our souls are under the dominion of the sensual and animal spirit, the pure and heavenly spirit can never enter within them.

This explains those words of our Lord, *It is not good to take the bread of children and to cast it to the dogs,*[3] and *Give not that which is holy to dogs.*[4] Our Lord compares those who, renouncing all earthly desires, prepare themselves in simplicity for the graces of the Holy Ghost, with children, and those who satisfy their desires in earthly things, with dogs: children are admitted to the Father's table, and nourished by the Spirit, but only the crumbs which fall from it are given to the dogs. All created things are but the crumbs which fall from the table of God. Thus they who go about feeding on the creature are rightly called dogs; the children's bread is withheld from such, because they will not rise from the crumbs of the creature to the table of the uncreated Spirit of their Father. These are always hungry like dogs, and justly so, because crumbs excite the appetite rather than appease hunger. These are they of whom it is written, *They shall suffer hunger like dogs; and shall go round about the city—and shall murmur if they be not filled.*[5] They who gratify their desires are always morose and discontented, like hungry persons: for what is there in common between the hunger which the creature occasions, and the fulness which proceeds from the

[1] *Jerem.* ii, 13.   [2] Ch. **IV**.   [3] *Matt.* xv, 26.   [4] *Ib.* vii, 6.
[5] *Ps.* lviii, 15, 16

Spirit of God? The fulness of God cannot enter into the soul before we drive away the hunger of desire, for two contrary qualities, such as hunger and fulness, cannot dwell together in the same subject. We may see from this how much greater is the work of God in purifying the soul from these contrarieties, than it was when He first created it out of nothing. For these rebellious desires and opposing affections seem to resist God more than nothing: that which is not, cannot resist His Majesty, but not so the love of the creature. Let this suffice for the first great evil which desires inflict on the soul, namely, resistance to the Spirit of God.

Let us now proceed to the second, which is manifold in its operations. The desires fatigue, torment, darken, defile and weaken the soul. Of these five forms of evil, I shall discuss each separately. As to the first, it is evident that the desires weary the soul, because they resemble little children, restless and dissatisfied, who always begging of their mother, now one thing, now another, are never content. As one given to covetousness fatigues himself digging for gold, so the soul wearies itself in the pursuit of those things which the desires demand, and though we may obtain them, yet the end is weariness, because we are never satisfied. We have recourse to broken cisterns, which can hold no water to quench our thirst, as it is written, *Faint with thirst and his soul is empty.*[6] The soul which yields to its desires, is weary and faint, like one ill of a burning fever, never at rest, and whose thirst increases while the fever lasts. It is written in the book of Job, *When he shall be filled, he shall be straightened, he shall burn, and every sorrow shall fall upon him.*[7] Thus is it with the soul, wearied and afflicted by the desires: they wound it, agitate and disturb it, as wind does water, harassing it, so that it can never repose on anything or in any place.

Of such souls is it written, *The wicked are like the raging sea which cannot rest.*[8] The heart of the wicked is like the raging sea, and he is wicked who does not subdue his desires. That soul which seeks to satisfy them wearies and torments itself, and is like one who, in the pains of hunger, opens his mouth to be filled with the wind, and who, instead of being satisfied therewith, becomes still more hungry, for wind is not his meat and drink. Of such it

[6] *Isa.* xxix, 8.   [7] *Job* xx, 22.   [8] *Isa.* lvii, 20.

is written, *In the desire of his heart, he snuffed up the wind of his love,*[9] and again warning the soul against the increasing dryness towards which it tends: *Keep thy foot,* that is thy thoughts, *from being bare, and thy throat from thirst,*[10]—that is, thy will from the gratification of the desire which is the occasion of greater dryness. As the ambitious man is wearied in the day of disappointed expectations, so the soul with its desires and their fulfilment, for they make it more empty and hungry than it was before. The desires are, as it is commonly said, like fire which burns when supplied with fuel, but which, when the fuel is consumed, immediately dies away. In truth, the desire is in a much worse condition: the fire is quenched when the fuel fails, but the desire ceases not with the matter on which it fed while it raged, even though that be utterly consumed; for instead of ceasing, like fire when the fuel is burnt out, the desire pines away in weariness, for hunger is increased, and food diminished.

A soul in this condition is thus described by the prophet, *He shall turn to the right hand, and shall be hungry, and shall eat on the left hand, and shall not be filled.*[11] They who mortify not their desires are justly punished with hunger when they 'turn to the right hand', that is, when they swerve from the way of God; for they do not deserve the fulness of His sweet Spirit, and justly also shall they *not be filled,* when they *eat on the left hand,* that is, when they satisfy their desire with created things; for then abandoning that which can alone satisfy them they feed on that which is the source of greater hunger. Thus, then, is it clear that the desires weary and fatigue the soul.

CHAPTER VII

The desires torment the soul. Proofs and Illustrations

THE SECOND positive evil which the desires inflict is a certain torment and affliction of soul, so that he who suffers therefrom is like one in torture, bound with chains, finding no rest until released. *The cords of my sins,* that is, my desires, saith the Psalmist, *have encompassed me.*[1] As a man who lies naked amid thorns and

[9] *Jerem.* ii, 24.   [10] *Jerem.* ii, 25.   [11] *Isa.* ix, 20.   [1] *Ps.* cxviii, 61.

briars, so is the soul in the power of its desires; for they pierce, torture and tear it painfully, as it is written, *They surrounded me like bees, and they burned like fire among thorns.*[2] The desires, which are as thorns, increase the fire of affliction and trouble. As the husbandman, greedy of the harvest, goads the oxen at the plough, so concupiscence goads the soul harnessed to its desires, till it shall obtain its will. Such was the desire of Dalila to know the secret of the strength of Samson; she *pressed him—giving him no time to rest,* so that *his soul fainted away, and was wearied even unto death.*[3]

The desire tortures the soul in proportion to its intensity, so that the pain equals the desires, and the more numerous the desires the greater the pain: for the words which the apostle heard are fulfilled even in this life. *As much as she hath glorified herself, and lived in delicacies, so much torment and sorrow give ye to her.*[4] As he is tormented who falls into the hands of his enemies, so is the soul carried away by its desires. This truth is foreshadowed in the history of Samson, who was once so strong and free, the judge of Israel. But when he had fallen into the hands of his enemies, they robbed him of his great strength, plucked out his eyes, imprisoned him in a mill, and *made him grind,* torturing and afflicting him. So is it with the soul, whose enemies, its own desires, live and triumph: their first act is to weaken and blind the soul, then to torment it, imprisoning it in the mill of concupiscence, and the cords that bind it are its own desires themselves.

God, therefore, compassionating those who, with so much toil and cost, go about to satisfy the hunger and thirst of their desires in created things, thus speaks to them by the mouth of His prophet: *all you that thirst* and desire *come to the waters, and you that have no money,* self-will, *make haste, buy and eat, come, buy wine and milk,* peace and spiritual sweetness, *without money* of self-will, *and without price,* without that labour which your desires demand. *Why do you spend money* of self-will *for that which is not bread,* that is, the Spirit of God, and the *labour* of your desires *for that which doth not satisfy you? Hearken diligently unto Me and eat that which is good,* and which you desire, *and your soul shall be delighted in fatness.*[5] We attain to this fatness when we

[2] *Ps.* cxvii, 12. [3] *Judges* xvi, 16. [4] *Apoc.* xviii, 7. [5] *Isa.* lv, 1, 2.

abandon all created satisfactions, for pain and sorrow flow from the creature, and refreshment from the Spirit of God.

Come to Me, saith our Lord, *all you that labour and are burdened, and I will refresh you.*[6] All you who are tormented and afflicted, labouring beneath the burden of anxiety and desire, cast it aside, by coming unto Me, and I will refresh you; and your souls shall find that rest of which your desires rob you, for they *as a heavy burden are become heavy upon Me.*[7]

CHAPTER VIII

The desires darken the soul. Proofs and Illustrations

THE THIRD EVIL which the desires inflict is darkness and blindness of soul. For as vapours darken the air, and hide the light of the sun, or as stained mirror cannot clearly receive an image, or as muddy water cannot distinctly reflect his face who looks into it, so the soul, stained by its desires, is intellectually blind, so that neither the understanding itself nor the sun of natural reason, nor that of the supernatural wisdom of God, can inform and enlighten it. To this the Psalmist referred when he said, *My iniquities have overtaken me, and I was not able to see.*[1] And thus, while the soul is intellectually blind, the will becomes torpid, the memory fails, and every lawful function is disordered. These faculties depend on the intellect, and it is therefore clear that, when the intellect is embarrassed, they must all be thrown into confusion and disorder. *My soul,* saith the Psalmist, *is troubled exceedingly,*[2] that is, all my faculties are in disorder; for, as I have said, the intellect in this state cannot receive the illumination of the Divine Wisdom, just as the obscured air cannot reflect the brightness of the sun. The will cannot embrace God in pure love, just as the stained mirror cannot represent an object placed before it. The memory overclouded by desires cannot calmly dwell on the Image of God, just as muddy water cannot reflect the face of him who looks into it.

The desire also blinds and darkens the soul, for the desire, as such, is blind and unreasonable, and reason is that which ever guides the soul aright in its several acts. Hence it is that the soul

[6] *Matt.* xi, 28. [7] *Ps.* xxxviii, 5. [1] *Ps.* xxxix, 13. [2] *Ps.* vi, 4.

become blind whenever the desires guide it, because it is as if one who saw were led by one who saw not: the result being the same as if both were blind. This is what our Lord referred to when He said, *If the blind lead the blind, both fall into the pit.*[3] Eyes are of little service to the moth, whose desire for the beauty of the light leads it dazzled into the midst of the flame. He who gives the rein to his desires may be likened to the fish dazzled by the light which the fishermen throw over the water, that the nets may not be seen: in this case, light serves but to increase the obscurity.

This is the meaning of the Psalmist when he said, *Fire hath fallen upon them, and they have not seen the sun,*[4] for the desire is like fire, warming with its heat, and dazzling with its light, and the effect of the desire in the soul is, that it enkindles concupiscence, and dazzles the intellect, so that it cannot see. The cause of this dazzling obscurity is, the interposition of another light between the object and the eye, whereon the eye rests, so as to see nothing beyond. Thus the desire comes so close to the soul, and within the range of its vision, that we are dazzled, and satisfied with the light it gives, and so it hides from us the clear light of the intellect, which we do not, and never shall see, until the glare of the desire shall have ceased.

This renders so deplorable their case who burden themselves with indiscreet penances, and other imprudent methods of devotion—voluntary certainly—on which they rely, thinking such alone, without mortifying their desires in other matters, to be sufficient to lead them on to the union of the Divine Wisdom. But this can never be, if the desires be not diligently mortified. If these persons bestowed but half their labour on this, they would make greater progress in a month than they can now make in many years, if they persevere in their present ways. As it is necessary to till the earth that it may bring forth fruit—for otherwise nothing will grow therein but weeds—so also is it necessary to mortify our desires, if we are to make progress towards perfection. Without mortification, I say it boldly, we shall make no progress whatever in the knowledge of God and of ourselves, notwithstanding all our efforts, any more than the seed will grow which is thrown away on uncultivated ground. Neither can the darkness and ignorance of our souls be

[3] *Matt.* xv, 14.   [4] *Ps.* lvii, 9.

removed, if the desires are not extinguished: for they are like a mote or cataract in the natural eye, obstructing the vision, until it be taken away.

The Psalmist, considering the blindness of those souls which are under the power of their desires, the impossibility of their clearly beholding the truth, and the greatness of God's anger with them, said, *Before your thorns could know the briar, He swalloweth them up, as alive, in His wrath.*[5] Before your thorns, your desires, harden and grow into a thicket, shutting out the sight of God, as the thread of life is frequently broken in the midst thereof, so will God swallow them up in His anger. Those persons in whom their desires live, and hinder the knowledge of God, God will swallow up in His wrath, either in the next life, or in the purifying pains of Purgatory, or in this, in afflictions and sufferings, sent to detach them from their desires, or in the mortification of those very desires voluntarily undergone. God doeth this to take away the false light of desire between Himself and us, which dazzles us, and hinders us from knowing Him; and that, the intellect becoming clear, the ravage of desire may be repaired.

Oh that men knew how great a blessing, that of the Divine Light, this their blindness, the result of their desires, robs them of, and how great the evils they daily fall into, because they do not mortify them. We are not to rely on a clear intellect, or on the gifts received from God, and then imagine that any affections or desires we may indulge in will not blind us, nor cause us to fall into a worse state, little by little. Who would have thought that a man of perfect wisdom, filled with the gifts of God, as Solomon was, could have fallen away in his old age into such blindness and torpor of the will, as to build altars to idols and worship them? His affection for his wives, and his negligence in controlling his desires and the satisfactions of his heart, were alone sufficient to reduce him to this. So he tells us himself, saying, *Whatsoever my eyes desired, I refused them not, and I withheld not my heart from enjoying every pleasure.*[6] Such was the effect upon Solomon of unbridled desires, and their gratification, though at first he was cautious; they soon blinded his understanding, and at last put out the light of wisdom within him, so that in his old age he forsook God. And if unmorti-

[5] *Ps.* lvii, 10.   [6] *Eccles.* ii, 10.

fied desires could produce such a disaster in the case of Solomon, who knew so well the difference between good and evil, what shall they not produce in us who are so ignorant? We are like the people of Ninive, of whom God said, *They know not how to distinguish between their right hand and their left,*⁷ since, at every step, we take good for evil, and evil for good; and this is as it were natural to us. What, then, must it be when our desires are added to our natural blindness, but that which the prophet bewailed, speaking of those who love to follow after their desires: *We have groped for the wall, and like the blind, we have groped as if we had no eyes, we have stumbled at noon as if in darkness.*⁸

CHAPTER IX

The desires pollute the soul. Proofs from Scripture

THE FOURTH EVIL which the desires inflict on the soul is that they pollute and defile it, as it is written, *He that toucheth pitch shall be defiled with it.*¹ He, then, toucheth pitch who satisfies the desires of the will in any created thing. Observe here that the wise man compareth the creature with pitch: for there is a greater distance between the excellence of the soul and the noblest creature than there is between the glittering diamond or fine gold and pitch. As a diamond or a piece of gold, if placed, heated, in contact with pitch becomes foul and stained in proportion to the heat, so the soul inflamed by the desire it may entertain for the creature, draws corruption therefrom and defilement. And there is a greater difference between the soul and all other created corporeal things than there is between the most pellucid water and the foulest mud. So, then, as such water mingled with mud becomes foul, so the soul whose affections are set on created things becomes polluted; for then it resembles them. As soot defiles the most beautiful face, so the unruly desires of the soul, if indulged in, defile and pollute that soul, which is in itself the most beautiful and perfect image of God.

The prophet Jeremias, bewailing the ravages of corruption produced by these unruly desires, first of all describes the beauty of the soul and then its defilement: *Her Nazarites were whiter than*

---

⁷ *Jo.* iv, 11.   ⁸ *Isa.* lix, 10.   ¹ *Eccles.* xiii, 1.

*snow, purer than milk, more ruddy than the old ivory, fairer than
the sapphire; their face is now made blacker than coals, and they
are not known in the streets.*[2] The hair of the Nazarites signify
the thoughts and affections of the soul, which, ordered according
to the law of God, that is referred all to Him, are whiter than snow,
purer than milk, more ruddy than the old ivory, fairer than the
sapphire. The whole physical creation in all its beauty and magnificence is signified by these four things, and higher than all is the
soul of man and its operations—that is, the Nazarites with their
long hair—which, when ordered, not according to the commandments of God, that is, when occupied with created things, is now
made blacker than coals. All this and far greater ruin befalls the
soul's beauty from the indulgence of unruly desires.

So, then, if my object were to describe the foul and corrupt condition to which the desires reduce the soul, I should not be able to
find anything so full of cobwebs and worms, not even corruption
itself, wherewith to compare it. For though the disordered soul in
its natural substance be as perfect as God has made it, its reasonable
substance is foul, filthy, and dark, overladen with all these evils and
even more. Even one unruly desire—as I shall hereafter explain—
though not a mortal sin, sullies and deforms the soul, and indisposes it for the perfect union with God, until it be cast away. What,
then, must be the corruption of that soul which is wholly disordered, which has abandoned itself to the sway of its desires, and
how far removed from the purity of God! No language can describe, no understanding can comprehend, the diverse impurities
which diverse desires produce in the soul.

If, indeed, any description of this could be given, so that men
might understand it, it would be a matter for wonder and for great
pity: for each desire, according to its nature and intensity, deposits
the filth and sediment of corruption and uncleanness in the soul,
everyone in its own way. For as the soul of the just man, in one
single perfection, which is the justice thereof, possesses innumerable most rich gifts, and many virtues of exceeding beauty, every
one of them lovely, different from each other according to the multitude and variety of the acts of the love of God; so the disordered
soul in the same way, according to the multitude of the desires, the

[2] *Lament.* iv, 7, 8.

object of which are created things, contracts a miserable diversity of vileness and impurity, with which these desires pollute it.

These diverse pollutions are described by the prophet Ezechiel, when God showed him the interior of the temple with its walls painted round about with the likenesses of creeping things, and all abominable and unclean beasts: *I went in,* saith the prophet, *and saw, and behold every form of creeping things, and of living creatures, the abomination and all the idols of the house of Israel were painted on the wall round about.*[3] When the prophet had seen this, God said to him, *Surely thou seest, O son of man, what the ancients of the house of Israel do in the dark, everyone in private in his chamber. Turn thee again; thou shalt see greater abominations.* The prophet turned, and *behold women sat there mourning for Adonis. Turn thee again,* said God to the prophet *and thou shalt see greater abominations than these.* And then the prophet saw *at the door of the temple of the Lord, between the porch and the altar, five and twenty men having their backs to the temple of the Lord.*[4]

The various creeping things and unclean beasts painted on the walls of the temple within are the thoughts and conceptions of the intellect derived from the vile things of earth and of other created things, which, because contrary to those that are eternal, defile the temple of the soul; and the soul by means thereof, embarrasses the intellect, which is its first court. The women in the second court, *mourning for Adonis,* are the desires of the will, the second faculty of the soul; these weep, as it were, when they covet that on which the will is bent, that is, the unclean things painted on the understanding. The men in the third court are the fancies and imaginations resulting from created objects which the third faculty of the soul, the memory, preserves and dwells on. These had their backs to the temple of the Lord: for when the faculties of the soul have been completely occupied with any object of earth, the soul itself may be said to have turned its back upon God's temple, which is right reason, and which tolerates nothing that is in opposition to God.

Let this suffice for the present to give us some insight into the foul disorder which desires engender in the soul. For were I to

[3] *Ezech.* viii, 10.   [4] *Ezech.* viii, 14, 16.

treat separately of the impediment to the Divine union which these imperfections and their varieties occasion; of that of venial sin, which is much greater than that of imperfections, and of its varieties; and also of mortal sin, which is complete defilement, and of its various forms, I should never come to an end. What I say—and it is to the purpose—is, that every single desire, though it be but the slightest imperfection, darkens the soul, and hinders its perfect union with God.

C H A P T E R   X

*The desires make the soul lukewarm, and enfeeble virtue. Proofs
and Illustrations*

THE FIFTH EVIL inflicted on the soul by its desires is lukewarmness and feebleness, so that it has no strength to follow after virtue nor to persevere therein. As the strength of desire is diminished when it is applied to many objects, instead of being concentrated upon one, and the more numerous the objects embraced, the less is the energy with which each is sought, so, philosophers say, is it with virtue, which is more vigorous when united than when it is dispersed. It is, therefore, clear that if the desire of the will be directed to other objects than virtue it must be most ineffectual in the pursuit thereof. The soul whose will is divided among trifles, is like water which never rises, because it has an outlet below, and is therefore profitless. Thus it was that the patriarch Jacob compared Ruben his son to *water poured out,* because he had given way to his desires in a certain sin: *Thou art poured out as water, grow thou not;* [1] that is, because thou art poured out as water in thy desires thou shalt not grow in virtues. As boiling water left uncovered quickly loses its heat, and as aromatic spices exposed to the air gradually lose their fragrance and the strength of their perfume, so the soul not recollected in the love of God alone loses the heat and vigour of virtue. This truth was well understood by the Psalmist when he said, *I will keep my strength to Thee,* [2] that is, I will concentrate the strength of my affections on Thee alone.

The desires enfeeble the soul, for they are like the little twigs and suckers which grow on a tree, sapping its strength so that it

[1] *Gen.* xlix, 4.   [2] *Ps.* lviii, 10.

shall not be so fruitful. Of such souls our Saviour says: *Woe unto them that are with child, and that give suck in those days.*[3] This signifies the desires, which, if not cut off, will continually lessen the strength of the soul, and grow to be its ruin, like the suckers on a tree. Our Lord, therefore, warns us, saying, *Let your loins be girt.*[4] The loins are the desires; they are also like leeches sucking the blood from the veins, for so the wise man calls them, saying, *The horse leech hath two daughters,* the desires, *that say, bring, bring.*[5]

It is, therefore, evident that the desires bring no good at all to the soul, but rather deprive it of what it has, and if we do not mortify them, they will not rest until they have done what the young vipers are said to do to their mother: these, as they grow in the womb, devour the entrails of their mother, and kill her, preserving their own life at the cost of hers. Thus the unmortified desires grow and devour the soul, killing the life of God within it. They alone live in that soul, because that soul has not destroyed them first. This it is that made the wise man pray: *Take from me the greediness of the belly.*[6]

But even if the desires do not issue in this great calamity, it is lamentable to see how they torture the poor soul in which they dwell—how hateful to itself they render it, how profitless to its neighbours, how dull and slothful in the things of God. There are no corrupt humours which can so bow down a sick man, enfeeble him in his gait, and make him loathe his proper food, as the desire of the creature bows down the soul in sadness, and indisposes it for the practice of virtue. And, in general, the reason why many souls have no love or inclination for virtue is, that they entertain affections and desires which are not innocent nor directed towards our Lord God.

CHAPTER XI

The necessity of freedom from all desires, however slight, for the Divine union

IT SEEMS reasonable here for the reader to ask, whether it be necessary to mortify completely every desire, small and great, before perfection can be reached, or whether it will be enough to have morti-

[3] *Matt.* xxiv, 19.   [4] *Luke* xii, 35.   [5] *Prov.* xxx, 15.   [6] *Eccles.* xxiii, 6.

fied some of them, overlooking others—at least those which seem of less moment—because it is a matter most difficult to attain to such pureness and detachment, as to have no affection for anything remaining in the will.

To this I reply: in the first place, it is true that all the desires are not equally hurtful, neither do they perplex the soul in the same degree. I am speaking of those which are voluntary: for the natural desires, when we do not consent to them, and when they do not pass beyond the first movements, do but slightly or not at all stand in the way of union. By natural and first movements I mean all those in which the natural will had no share, either before or after they arose: for to banish and mortify these completely is, in this life, impossible. The hindrance which these create is not such as to prevent the Divine union, though they may not be wholly mortified; they may remain in our nature, and yet the soul in its spiritual part may be most free from them. For it will sometimes happen that the soul enjoys the profound union of quiet in the will, while these remain in the sensual portion of man's nature, but having no communication with the spiritual portion occupied in prayer.

But all the other voluntary desires, whether mortal sins, which are the most grievous, or venial sins, which are less so, or imperfections only, which are still less so, must be banished away, and the soul which would attain to perfect union must be delivered from them all, however slight they may be. The reason is this: the estate of Divine union consists in the total transformation of the will into the will of God, in such a way that every movement of the will shall be always the movement of the will of God only. This is the reason why, in this state, two wills are said to be one—my will and God's will—so that the will of God is also that of the soul. But if the soul then cleaves to any imperfection, contrary to the will of God, His will is not done, for the soul wills that which God wills not. It is clear, therefore, that if the soul is to be united in love and will with God, every desire of the will must first of all be cast away, however slight it may be; that is, we must not deliberately and knowingly assent with the will to any imperfection, and we must have such power over it, and such liberty, as to reject every such desire the moment we are aware of it. I say knowingly, for without deliberation and a clear perception of what we are doing, or because it is not wholly in our power, we may easily give way to imperfections and venial sins, and to those natural desires of which I have just spoken. It is of such sins as these, not so entirely voluntary, that it is written: *A just man shall fall seven times, and shall rise again.*[1]

But as to those voluntary and perfectly deliberate desires, how slight soever their objects may be, any one of them, not overcome, is sufficient to prevent this union. I am speaking of the unmortified habit thereof, because certain acts occasionally have not so much power, for the habit of them is not settled; still we must get rid of them, for they, too, proceed from habitual imperfection. Some habits of voluntary imperfections, so far as they are never perfectly overcome, impede not only the Divine union but our progress towards perfection.

These habitual imperfections are, for instance, much talking, certain attachments, which we never resolve to break through— such as to individuals, to a book or a cell, to a particular food, to certain society, the satisfaction of one's taste, science, news, and such things. Every one of these imperfections, if the soul is attached and habituated to them, results in such serious injuries to our growth and progress in perfection. Yea, even if we fall daily into many other imperfections greater than these, provided they are not the result of the habitual indulgence of any evil inclination, we should not be so much hindered in our spiritual course as we are by this selfish attachment of the soul to particular objects; for while the soul entertains it, it is useless to hope that we can ever attain to perfection, even though the object of our attachment be but of the slightest importance possible.

Does it make any difference whether a bird be held by a slender thread or by a rope, while the bird is bound and cannot fly till the cord that holds it is broken? It is true that a slender thread is more easily broken, still, notwithstanding, if it is not broken the bird cannot fly. This is the state of a soul with particular attachments: it never can attain to the liberty of the Divine union, whatever virtues it may possess. Desires and attachments affect the soul as the remora is said to affect a ship; that is but a little fish, yet when it adheres to the vessel it effectually prevents its progress.

[1] *Prov.* xxiv, 16.

How sad it is to see certain souls, like vessels richly freighted, full of good works, of spiritual exercises, virtues and gifts of God, which, because they have not the courage to break with certain tastes, attachments, or affections—these are all one—never reach the haven of perfect union. And yet it would cost them but a single vigorous flight to break the thread of their attachment or to shake off the remora of desire. It is a matter of deep regret, when God has given them strength to burst other and stronger bonds—those of vanity and sins—merely because they will not detach themselves from trifles, which God has left for them to break away from for love of Him, and which are no more than a single thread—that they should for this neglect their own advancement and the attainment of so great a blessing. And what is still more deplorable, because of such attachments, not only do they not advance, but, so far as perfection is concerned, they fall back, losing in some measure what they had already gained with so much labour. For it is well known that on the spiritual road not to go on overcoming self is to go backwards, and not to increase our gain is to lose.

This is what our Lord would teach us when He says, *He that gathereth not with me scattereth.*[2] He who will neglect to repair the vessel that is but slightly cracked, will at last lose all the liquid it may hold; for *he that contemneth small things shall fall by little and little:*[3] and *of one spark cometh a great fire.*[4] One imperfection is enough to beget another, and this other, others again. We shall never see a soul, negligent in overcoming a single desire, which has not also many other desires arising out of the weakness and imperfection from which the first proceeds. There have been many persons who, by the grace of God, had made great progress in detachment and freedom, and yet because they gave way, under the pretence of some good—as of society and friendship—to petty attachments, have thereby lost the spirit and sweetness of God, holy solitude, and cheerfulness, and have injured the integrity of their spiritual exercises, so as to be unable to stop before all was gone. All this has befallen them because they did not root out the principle of pleasure and of the sensual desires, keeping themselves in solitude for God.

We must ever walk on this road so as to reach the end; that is,

2 *Matt.* xii. 30.   3 *Eccles.* xix. 1.   4 *Ibid.* xi. 34.

in the constant repression of our desires, and not in their indulgence: and if we do not perfectly repress them we shall never perfectly reach the end As wood can never be transformed into fire if but one degree of heat necessary for that end be wanting, so the soul that has but one imperfection can never be perfectly transformed in God, as I shall hereafter explain when speaking of the Night of Faith. The soul has but one will; and if this will be occupied or embarrassed, it is not free, perfect, solitary, and pure, as it ought to be for this Divine transformation. This truth is foreshadowed in the Book of Judges, where we read that an angel of the Lord came to the children of Israel and told them that, because they had not destroyed the inhabitants of the land, but had made a league with some of them, those, therefore, would be left among them as their enemies, and an occasion to them of their fall and destruction: *Wherefore I would not destroy them from before your face, that you may have enemies, and their gods may be your ruin.*[5]

God is just in thus dealing with those souls whom He has led forth out of the Egypt of this world, for whom he has slain the giants of their sins, and whose enemies he has destroyed, which are the occasions of sin which they meet with in the world, and all this for the sole purpose of their entrance into the promised land of the Divine union. He is just, I say, in thus dealing with them, when he sees them form friendships, and become confederate with the heathen, which are their imperfections; when they do not mortify themselves wholly, but are negligent and slothful in their lives: for this, then, He becomes angry with them, and suffers them to fall through their desires from bad to worse.

This truth is also shadowed forth in the command of God to Josue when the children of Israel were about to enter into the land of promise. The city of Jericho was to be utterly destroyed and all that was within, man and woman, young and old, together with the cattle; and the people were not to take, nor even to touch any of the spoil thereof.[6] He, therefore, that will enter into the Divine union must put to death all that lives in his soul, whether small or great, many or few; he must abstain from all desire thereof, and be completely detached therefrom, as if neither existed for the other.

St. Paul, also writing to the Corinthians, says the same thing:

[5] *Judges* ii, 3.   [6] *Josue* vi, 18, 21.

This therefore I say, brethren, the time is short: it remaineth, that they also who have wives be as if they had none, and they that weep, as though they wept not, and they that rejoice as if they rejoiced not, and they that buy as though they possessed not, and they that use this world as if they used it not.[7] The apostle teaches here that we must be detached in spirit from the world if we would walk so as to attain unto God.

CHAPTER XII

The nature of those desires which suffice to injure the soul

I MIGHT have entered at greater length on the night of sense according to the extent of evil which the desires occasion, not only in the way described, but in many others as well, but this is enough for my purpose, because it is now clear why the mortification of them is called night, and how necessary it is to enter into this night in order to draw near unto God.

One thing only remains for discussion before I speak of the way by which this night is entered upon, and so conclude this book—namely, a doubt which might be suggested to the reader by the matter in hand. It might be asked, in the first place, whether any desire be enough to produce in the soul these positive and negative evils of which I have spoken, and, in the second place, whether any desire, however slight, and of whatever kind, be enough to produce all these evils together, or whether each desire produces a distinct evil, as one desire weariness, another pain, and another darkness.

To this I reply as follows: In the first place, if we are speaking of the negative evil, which consists in the soul's being deprived of God, it is only those voluntary desires which are the matter of mortal sin that can, and do, result in this: for these rob the soul in this life of grace, and in the next of glory, which is the fruition of God. And in the second place that all these desires, those which are the matter of mortal sin, and those voluntary desires, which are matter of venial sin, and those which are imperfections, are, every one of them, enough to inflict on the soul the positive evils. These evils, though in one sense negative, are here called positive, because they

[7] *I Cor.* vii, 29-31.

correspond to a turning towards the creature, as the negative evils correspond to a turning away from God.

There is, however, this difference: those desires which are matter of mortal sin produce complete blindness, pain, impureness, and weakness. But those other desires, matter of venial sin, or known imperfection, do not produce these evils in this perfect and supreme degree, seeing that they do not cast the soul out of the state of grace: for the loss of grace is concurrent with their dominion over the soul, because their life consists in the death of grace. Still they occasion somewhat of these evils, though but remissly, proportional to that weakness and remissness which they generate in the soul; so that the particular desire which most weakens the soul is most fruitful in pain, blindness, and impureness. But it is to be remarked that, though every desire generates all these evils, which we here call positive, there are some which chiefly and directly produce particular evils, and other evils incidentally. For though it is true that one sensual desire produces all these evils, yet its chief and proper fruit is the defilement of soul and body. Though one avaricious desire also produces all these evils, yet its principal and direct result is trouble. Though one vainglorious desire, precisely like the rest, produces all these evils, yet its chief and immediate effect is darkness and blindness. And, though one gluttonous desire issues in the same evils, yet still its primary direct result is weakness in those things that pertain to virtue. The same may be said of all other desires.

The reason why any act of voluntary desire produces all these evils in the soul together, is that contrariety which subsists directly between it and those acts of virtue which result in opposite effects. As an act of virtue produces and generates in the soul sweetness, peace, consolation, light, pureness, and fortitude together, so an unruly desire begets pain, fatigue, weariness, blindness, and weakness. All virtues increase by the practice of each; so also vices thrive and grow, and their effects are magnified in the soul in the same way. Though all these evils are not visible then when the desire is gratified, because the satisfaction thereof furnishes at the time no opportunity for them, yet afterwards the evil results become clearly visible. For the desire, when it is fulfilled, is sweet, and appears good, but afterwards the effects thereof are found to be bitter, which is the experience of everyone who has suffered himself to be led away thereby. I am not ignorant, however, that there are some so blind and so insensible as not to feel this: they do not walk in the ways of God, and therefore see not that which hinders their drawing near unto Him.

I am not speaking here of those other natural desires which are involuntary, nor of thoughts which do not go beyond the first movements, nor of other temptations to which we consent not, because none of these produce any of the evils I describe. Though a person liable to these trials may imagine that the passion and disturbance thus occasioned darken and defile his soul, in reality it is not so— yea, rather the contrary effects are sometimes the result of them. Because, in proportion to the resistance offered, such an one gains strength, pureness, light, consolation, and many other good things, according to the words of our Lord to St. Paul: *Virtue is made perfect in infirmity.*[1] But voluntary desires produce these and more evils. For this cause the chief solicitude of spiritual directors is to mortify the desires of their penitents, and to make them deny themselves in all that is pleasing to them, so as to deliver them from so great misery.

CHAPTER XIII

How the soul enters by faith into the night of sense

IT NOW remains for me to give some directions by which the soul may be able to enter on this night of sense. Ordinarily, the soul enters in two ways on this night: one is the active way, the other is passive. The active way is that by which the soul is able to make, and does make, efforts of its own to enter in, assisted by divine grace. Of this I shall speak in the instructions that follow. The passive way is that in which the soul doeth nothing as of itself, neither does it make therein any efforts of its own; but it is God who works in it, giving special aids, and the soul is, as it were, patient, freely consenting thereto. Of this I shall speak when treating of the obscure night, when I shall have to describe those who are beginners. And as I shall have then to give many counsels to such with reference to the many imperfections to which they are

[1] *II Cor.* xii, 9.

liable on this road, I shall not enlarge on that question now. Besides, this is not the place to do so, for I am now concerned only with the reasons why this journey is called night, with the nature and divisions of the same. But as it seems a defect, and not so profitable as it should be, to abstain here from furnishing some help or instructions proper for this night of the desires, I have determined to lay down the brief instruction following. I shall adopt the same course at the conclusion of each of these divisions or causes of this night, of which by the help of our Lord I undertake to speak.

These instructions for the subduing of our desires are, in my opinion, though brief and few, as profitable and effectual as they are brief. He who will reduce them to practice will need none others, for they include everything.

1. Be continually careful and earnest in imitating Christ in everything, conforming thyself to His life: for this end thou must meditate thereon, that thou mayest know how to imitate it, and conduct thyself in all things as He would have done Himself.

2. To do this well, every satisfaction offered to the senses, which is not for God's honour and glory, must be renounced and rejected for the love of Jesus Christ, who in this life had, and sought, no other pleasure than doing the will of His Father, which was His meat,[1] as He tells us Himself. For instance, if the pleasure of listening to anything which tends not to the service of God presents itself, seek not that pleasure, neither give ear to what is said. If thou art offered the sight, pleasurable in itself, of things which do not tend to God's honour, seek not that pleasure, and abstain from that sight. Do the same also in conversation and every other commerce of society. Practise the same mortification with respect to the other senses, as far as possible; and if it be not possible, it will be enough not to seek the pleasure that is offered. Thus the mortification of the senses and the absence of all pleasure must be striven after, so that the soul may be as in darkness. The practice of this counsel will bring with it great profit in a short time.

In order to mortify and calm the four natural passions of joy, hope, fear, and grief, from the concord and tranquility of which result these and other great advantages, the following instructions are a perfect means of great merit and the source of great virtues:

[1] *Io.* iv, 34.

Strive always, not after that which is most easy, but that which is most difficult.

Not after that which is most pleasant, but that which is most unpleasant.

Not after that which giveth pleasure, but after that which giveth none.

Not after that which is consoling, but that which is afflictive.

Not after that which ministers repose, but after that which ministers labour.

Not after great things, but after little things.

Not after that which is elevated and precious, but after that which is vile and despised.

Strive not to desire anything, but rather nothing.

Seek not after that which is better, but that which is worse, and desire to be detached from all things, empty and poor for Christ's sake. This state is to be embraced with a perfect heart, and the will must conform thereto. Because if our heart be truly engaged herein, we shall in a short time attain to great joy and consolation, doing our work orderly with discretion.

These instructions, well acted upon, are sufficient for our entrance on the night of sense. But still, out of the abundance of the matter, I will give another method of devotion, which teaches us how to mortify truly the desire of honour, from which so many others proceed.

1. Do those things which bring thee into contempt, and desire that others also may do them.

2. Speak disparagingly of thyself, and contrive that others may do so too.

3. Think humbly and contemptuously of thyself, and desire that others may do so also.

I think it fitting, in conclusion, to insert here certain instructions for ascending to the summit of Mount Carmel, which is the high estate of union. Though the doctrine they contain is spiritual and interior, it relates also to the spirit of imperfection in sensible and exterior things, which may be met in the two roads on either side of the way of perfection. We shall, therefore, take these sentences in this sense, namely, as referring to sensible things, and afterwards, in the second division of the night, we shall take them as referring to that which is spiritual.

1. That thou mayest have pleasure in everything, seek pleasure in nothing.

2. That thou mayest know everything, seek to know nothing.

3. That thou mayest possess all things, seek to possess nothing.

4. That thou mayest be everything, seek to be nothing.

5. That thou mayest attain to that of which thou hast no present perception, thou must walk there where thou hast no perception.

6. That thou mayest attain to that thou knowest not, thou must go through that thou knowest not.

7. That thou mayest attain to that thou possessest not, thou must go through that thou possessest not.

8. That thou mayest attain to that which thou art not, thou must go through that which thou art not.

Instructions how not to impede the All

1. When thou dwellest upon anything, thou hast ceased to cast thyself upon the All.

2. Because in order to arrive from all to the All, thou hast to deny thyself wholly in all.

3. And when thou comest to attain the All, thou must keep it without desiring anything.

4. Because if thou wilt keep anything with the All, thou hast not thy treasure simply in God.

In detachment the spirit finds quiet and repose, for coveting nothing, nothing wearies it by elation, and nothing oppresses it by dejection, because it stands in the centre of its own humility; for as soon as it covets anything it is immediately fatigued thereby.

ST. ROBERT
BELLARMINE, S. J.

ON *the* ASCENT *of the*
MIND *to* GOD

How securely, O my soul, mayest not thou rest in the
bosom of so mighty a Father, even in the deepest darkness!

BORN IN 1542, Bellarmine became a Jesuit in 1560 and taught
at Louvain and Rome (1569-1576). His activity during the next
decade is best illustrated by the title of the work which he published (1586) and which is considered his masterpiece: *Disputations on the Controversies of the Christian Faith against the
Heretics of our Day*. He was created Cardinal in 1599, and died
in 1621. Indefatigable apologist, addressing himself to Protestants
on questions of faith, the Church, sacraments and grace, Bellarmine also wrote shorter ascetical and devotional works.

THE THIRTEENTH
STEP

From the Consideration of His Practical
Wisdom

E ARE NOW TO CONSIDER THE PRACTICAL WISDOM
of God. Like His speculative wisdom, which we
have already discussed, this practical or effective
wisdom has its own *breadth, length, height and
depth*.[1] Its "breadth" we learn from creation,
its "length" from the conservation of creatures,
its "height" from the work of redemption, and its "depth" from
providence and predestination. Let us begin with creation.

[1] *Ephes.* iii, 18.

God has *made all things in wisdom,* as the Psalms say,[2] *and he poured her out upon all his works,* as Ecclesiasticus writes.[3] Just as the creation of all things from nothing teaches us the might of the Mastercraftsman, so the consummate skill discernible in each and every product reveals the wisdom of the Creator: for He has ordered all things *in measure, and number, and weight,* as the Wise Man says.[4] This is the seasoning (*sapor*) with which God has seasoned all things, and through which we can realize how savoury (*sapida*) is the divine Wisdom (*sapientia*), and how lovable and desirable.

There are two reasons why all creatures are endowed with a determined measure, number and weight. The first is that thus they might be distinguished from God, Who is without measure, since He is immense; without number, for He is supremely one and simple; and without weight, as He surpasses in worth and value all price and evaluation. The second reason is that creatures might be both beautiful and good, as Moses has so truly said: *And God saw all the things that he had made, and they were very good.*[5] Hence the proportions of each thing exactly fit the end for which it was made. These proportions cannot be increased or diminished without deforming the creature, impairing its efficiency and lessening its worth. *He hath made all good things in their time,*[6] says Ecclesiastes, and *we cannot add any thing, nor take away from those things which God has made that he may be feared.*[7] That is why God has endowed the firmament with the most generous proportions, since it has to embrace all lower things within its expanse. That is why He gave the atmosphere a lesser extent than the firmament, though a greater extent than that of the earth and its seas, for these latter, which together make up one globe, are entirely surrounded by the atmosphere. God gave the elephant the largest bodily proportions, so that it could carry the heaviest burdens and even howdahs filled with men. He made the horse a little smaller, just large enough in fact for carrying one rider. The birds He made small enough to hang nests in the branches of trees. And the bees and ants He made very tiny to fit them for concealment in ant-hills, beehives and holes in the ground.

[2] *Ps.* ciii, 24.   [3] *Ecclus.* i, 10.   [4] *Wis.* xi, 21.   [5] *Gen.* i, 31.
[6] *Eccles.* iii, 11.   [7] *Eccles.* iii, 14.

We can say the same thing about number. God created one sun, since one is enough for lighting up the whole earth and making daylight with its brilliance. Likewise He made one moon, for one suffices to illumine the night. But He willed that there be many stars, so that, in the absence of the sun and the moon, as at the time of an eclipse, they might rout the darkness from every quarter.

It is not only in general that God has so fixed the number of parts that no additions or subtractions may be made. Thus He has given to man two eyes, two ears, two hands, two feet, one nose, one mouth, one chest and one head: the result is something very beautiful and well-proportioned. But upset that order, apportion to any man one eye, two noses, one ear, two mouths, one hand and one foot, two trunks and two heads: you would find nothing more disgusting or more useless.

Finally, God has bestowed on each thing a weight, that is, the worth that its nature requires. By "weight" or "value" we mean the qualities that make goods valuable; for everything is perfected by the number of its parts (none must be missing), its measure (or proper proportion of the parts), and the internal and external qualities, such as the outward healthy glow of the skin and the inner powers that are both necessary and useful for any activity.

But particularly worthy of admiration is the degree of power which God has given even to the tiniest of His creatures. His might He seems to have willed to show forth in the larger creatures, but in the small, His wisdom. Who indeed would suspect the power latent in the grain of mustard-seed, which is the smallest of all seeds, so small that the eye can barely see it, and yet within that seed is hidden a tree so large that the birds of the air dwell in the branches thereof, as Truth Himself has said in the Gospel.[8] This is not peculiar to the mustard-seed: it is the common property of all seeds, for in them are hidden virtually the roots, trunks, branches, leaves, flowers and fruit of the mightiest trees. If personal observation did not force this fact on us, it would surely be difficult to persuade anybody that so large an agglomeration of disparate objects could come forth from so tiny a seed. Who also would imagine that ants, gnats, fleas, and other minute insects have feet that move with lightning-like rapidity, a head, heart, internal and external senses,

[8] *Matt.* xiii, 31.

and even, in their own imperfect fashion, prudence and judgment? Who would dream that these insects, despite their infinitesimally tiny size, have the power to pierce and perforate living flesh? Gnats, for example, are not only a nuisance to men, but even terrify lions and elephants.

God, therefore, is great, and great is His wisdom in the greatest as in the smallest. Long ago that famous prince of doctors,[9] though a heathen, admired the skill of God in constructing the human hand, and burst forth in praise of the Creator. And thou, O Christian, what oughtest not thou to do, since thou knowest of a certainty that not only the bodies of men and of all breathing things, but even the firmament and the stars and the angels and the immortal minds of men have been created with incredible wisdom by that same infinitely wise Creator?

The "length" of God's practical wisdom is patent in the conservation of creatures, even as its "breadth" we have seen to be evident in the fact of creation. Hence in the conservation and duration of created things, especially the corruptible, we may see the great and admirable wisdom of God.

In the first place reflection on the manner in which God gives nourishment and growth to herbs, plants, animals and our own bodies for their maximum preservation can only leave one stupefied with amazement and admiration at the wisdom of God. For with earth and water He feeds the flowers and the trees, and makes the nourishing sap flow from the roots to the trunk, and from the trunk to the branches and the leaves until fruit is brought forth and the cycle is completed. And this fits admirably into a general and well thought out plan. For God uses fruit and vegetables and meat to feed the animals and man himself. And He has so arranged matters that the nourishment, which we take into our bodies, penetrates to every part, both internal and external, with almost incredible ease and agreeableness.

God acts like a learned and sympathetic doctor, who knows how to mix drugs in such a way that the medicine is not only easily absorbed but even to the patient's liking. For food is assuredly a medicine: if we mortals did not take it at frequent intervals we would die. But our most thoughtful and wise doctor, God Himself,

[9] Avicenna.

has made food pleasant to eat. Why, He has afforded enough varieties of food for even the most fastidious. Then, by means of various reactions in mouth, stomach, liver and heart He changes our food into a juice thin and subtle enough to course painlessly and endlessly throughout every vein, capillary and pore of the body until it penetrates every part of our flesh and bones and nerves, and all this without our feeling anything of the process and even during our sleep.

When philosophers see these marvels they admire the ingenuity and artfulness of nature. But how can they speak of ingenuity in inanimate things that are bereft of sense and reason? They should admire not the ingenuity of nature but the wisdom of the Creator, for He made nature and discovered the way to accomplish all these wonders. Recall what the Wisdom of God says to us in the Gospel: *Consider the lilies of the field how they grow: they labour not, nor do they spin* [10] yet God clothes them. It is God, and not the ingenuity of nature, who makes the lilies grow, and as it were clothes them with beauty. The same is true of the nourishment and growth of all living things. Saint Paul is a witness to this, when he says: *Neither he that planteth is anything, nor he that watereth, but God that giveth the increase.* [11]

If the wisdom of God is to be thought wonderful in the way He feeds and nourishes and keeps the plants and animals alive, think, if thou art able, O my soul, of the manner in which God nourishes the minds of angels and men in the life that is eternal. On earth we are fed with terrestrial food, fashioned by divine Wisdom. In heaven Wisdom Itself is the food and drink of those who live for ever. How blessed art thou if thou fathomest the meaning of these words: *God will be all in all.* [12] If thou didst but understand what it means that God is the greatest and infinite good, the food of all the Saints, their friend, their life, their all, thou wouldst assuredly find the things of this life wearisome, and wouldst relish and seek only those that are above. But let us proceed to the other considerations.

Akin to the miraculous is the way God preserves and propagates the life of mortal beings by endowing even the smallest of things with a continuous, tireless and nigh ageless motion. Men go to great

[10] *Matt.* vi, 28.   [11] *I Cor.* iii, 8.   [12] Cf. *I Cor.* xv, 28.

pains to construct a clock whose weights will make the wheels run for twenty-four hours. Think how extraordinary is God's wisdom in making the nutritive power of animals and plants operate ceaselessly for a lifetime, and in causing lungs and arteries to work without stopping for seventy years and more. The ability to take in nourishment and to breathe must go on from the first moment of life till the last. This is as true of the octogenarian as of those who, before the Flood, lived until they were nine hundred years old. Their lungs and arteries, despite their delicacy, had to be in constant motion, without let-up or rest, during all those years. If anybody feels no sense of wonder at these things and cannot see therein the wisdom of God, he must be totally devoid of the light of wisdom.

Furthermore, the wisdom of God could dispense with the labour of men and animals, of the sun and all secondary causes, and could produce and conserve herbs and trees as food ready prepared for every living being. But it so happens that He has willed to use the services of secondary causes, such as the work and toil of men and animals, to keep us from wasting away in idleness and to make us develop all our powers.

God has also willed that some men be rich and others poor that all might have the occasion of practising virtue and being united by the bonds of charity. This is done when the rich show liberality and mercy, and the poor, patience and humility. The wealthy need the labour of the poor for the tilling of the fields, the pasturing of the flocks, and the manufacture of vital commodities. On the other hand the poor need the labour of the wealthy, since from the latter come the money and the tools for making clothes, growing food, etc.

There is no reason why the poor should complain of the dispositions of divine wisdom. For God, Who knows all things and loves everyone, has given each man what He foresees is more useful for obtaining everlasting life. He acts like our doctors who sometimes prescribe strict diets and bloodletting, and at other times wine and meat and a pleasant regime. Assuredly most of the poor attain everlasting life. Were they wealthy they would perish eternally. But the rich too can be saved, provided they make it their business to be rich in good works and to give freely and gladly what they have received from their common Lord solely for the purpose of sharing with others and not for selfish hording.

Yet it cannot be denied that poverty and not riches is the surer, clearer and easier way to eternal life. Our divine Master does not deceive us in saying: *Amen, I say to you that a rich man shall hardly enter into the kingdom of heaven.*[13] And again: *Blessed are ye poor: for yours is the kingdom of God,*[14] and *Woe to you that are rich: for you have your consolation.*[15] Nor does the Apostle mislead us when he says in his first epistle to Timothy: *For they that will become rich fall into temptation and into the snare of the devil and into many unprofitable and hurtful desires, which drown men into destruction and perdition.*[16] And this teaching both our Lord and St. Paul confirmed by the example of their lives. For our Lord says of Himself: *The foxes have holes, and the birds of the air nests, but the Son of Man hath not where to lay His head.*[17] And St. Paul says of himself and his fellow Apostles: *Even until this hour we both hunger and thirst and are naked, and buffeted and have no fixed abode,*[18] that is, we have no fixed abode of our own. It cannot be doubted that the Wisdom of God and His Son and the disciple of Wisdom chose the safest and clearest route to life. But since *the number of fools is infinite,*[19] few choose this life of their own accord: most shun it strenuously and heartily.

A last consideration whereby we may discern the "length" of divine wisdom is the fact that this wisdom, being itself eternal, has given all things the most lively instinct for self-preservation and for prolonging life or their very being as much as possible. We see how the knowledge of imminent danger to life affects men. They move heaven and earth and spare no effort to save themselves. We know how every living creature will fight with unexpected strength against more powerful foes. Even a burning lamp will flare up two or three times more brightly just before it goes out, as though it were gathering all its forces to do battle with extinction. See how drops of water, hanging from a branch or a rock, form themselves into tight globules, and stay that way as long as they can, for dispersion means annihilation. And, we observe, heavy things will rise and light things fall to prevent their being cut off by a vacuum from the preserving influence of other bodies.

[13] *Matt.* xix, 23.   [14] *Luke* vi, 20.   [15] *Luke* vi, 24.   [16] *I Tim.* vi, 9.
[17] *Luke* ix, 58.   [18] *I Cor.* iv, 11.   [19] *Eccles.* i. 15.

But most wonderful of all is the incredibly strong affection for their offspring which God, with a view to the propagation of the species, has bestowed on all parents. Consider how the hen makes itself ill for the sake of its chickens, and how, despite its weakness and feebleness, will fight to the bitter end against hawks, dogs and foxes. And it is common knowledge what toil and trouble women gladly undergo in bearing and raising children. This is all according to God's wise counsel, for He imprinted on all living beings, even on the most ferocious of wild beasts, an intense love for their offspring, in order to encourage propagation, which is, in a manner, the shadow of eternity. Think of the multitude of animals whose destruction men seek to encompass. Some we kill for food, for example, rabbits, wild boars, thrushes, quails, partridges, and every kind of fish; others, for our own protection, e.g. wolves and foxes. Many species, such as snakes and the like, would have disappeared long ago had not the wisdom of God provided for their preservation and propagation through this parental affection.

If it is natural that such a burning love for this present brief life, full as it is of tribulation, be present in all living beings, how great should not be our love for the blessed life of eternity! O the blindness and stupidity of mankind! All things fight, even beyond their strength, for this short life, which is but the shadow of eternity. Yet for everlasting life and supreme happiness man, who is able to reason, will not deign to labour, I will not say beyond his power, but even as much as in him lies. All things by natural instinct shun temporal death as the worst of evils. Yet man, a rational being, and taught by divine faith, will not shun everlasting death even to the extent to which he is wont to fly from temporal death. Ecclesiastes has spoken well and truly: *The number of fools is infinite.*[20] And truthfully has Truth declared in the Gospel: *How narrow is the gate and strait is the way that leadeth to life, and few there are that find it.*[21]

We now come to the "height" of God's wisdom, which is discernible in the work of redemption. I could never sate myself, says St. Augustine, with the wonderful sweetness of contemplating the loftiness of Thy counsels for the salvation of mankind. It was highest wisdom, indeed, to remedy by the ignominy of the

[20] *Eccles.* I, 15.   [21] *Matt.* xvii, 14.

Cross all those evils which the devil, in his craftiness, had accomplished through the sin of the first man, and so to remedy them that the masterpiece was more beautiful after it was restored than before it needed restoration.[22]

Four evils were born of the sin of the first man. The insult to God offered by the pride and disobedience of Adam. The punishment of the first man and of the entire human race, which consisted in forfeiting the grace of God and everlasting happiness. The sorrow caused the Angels at the sight of the insult to God and the unhappiness of men. And, finally, the glee of the devil and all wicked spirits who rejoiced at the downfall they had caused man and at his slavery to themselves. All these evils did the wisdom of God permit and turn to greater good by the mystery of the Cross. It is not without reason that the Church sings, "O happy fault, that merited so great a redeemer." [23] If a tailor, for example, had the skill to repair an ugly tear in a brand-new expensive suit in such a way as to make the suit better fitting and of higher quality, one could rightly say that it was a happy tear that occasioned such elegance.

Now the first man, thanks to the insidious craftiness of the devil, became puffed up with pride and put on the airs of equality with God. By his disobedience and lies he robbed God, as it were, of the honour due to Him. But the second Adam, Christ, the very Wisdom of God, *humbled himself, becoming obedient unto death*,[24] and restored to God far greater honour than that which was taken away by the pride and disobedience of the first Adam. For Adam was simply a man, and had he obeyed God it would have been in a relatively simple matter. There was nothing particularly difficult in abstaining from the fruit of one forbidden tree, when there were thousands of other fine trees. The sin of our first parents was all the more grave because the obedience demanded was so easy and required practically no effort. But Christ, Who was both God and man, humbled Himself to obey His Father in what was most difficult and arduous, that is in dying a painful, ignominious death on the Cross.

Moreover, if we consider the personal worth of Christ, and the

[22] *Cf.* St. Paul, *Rom.* v, 17.   [23] Office, Blessing of Candle, Holy Saturday.
[24] *Phil.* ii. 8.

depths of His humiliation and obedience, we cannot conceive anything more meritorious and redounding to God's honour than the
humble obedience of Christ. Most truly did our Lord say in
the Gospel: *I have glorified Thee on earth.*[25] For indeed in the
presence of the Angels of God and of the holy souls of the prophets
and others to whom the redemption was revealed, Jesus Christ
glorified God the Father with an ineffable glory. If at the birth of
Christ the Angels, seeing the lowliness of the crib, sang *Glory to
God in the highest,*[26] with what incomparably greater joy must
they not have sung this same praise at the humiliation of the Cross.

Had man not sinned, he would have obtained, at most, equality
with the Angels. Now, however, because of the redemption, which
is in Christ Jesus, mankind has been blessed with the exaltation,
above all the Angels, of one man who should sit at the right hand
of God and be the head and lord of both Angels and men. For thus
did the Apostle Peter write of Christ in his first epistle: *being
gone into heaven, the angels and powers and virtues being made
subject to him.*[27] And his fellow-apostle St. Paul wrote to the
Philippians: *For which cause, God also hath exalted him and hath
given him a name which is above all names, that in the name of
Jesus every knee should bow, of those that are in heaven, on earth
and under the earth.*[28] And so the Son has ineffably glorified the
Father by the humiliation of His passion, and the Father in a like
ineffable manner has glorified the Son by exalting Him to His
right hand. This glory has redounded to that of the whole human
race. It would be most ungrateful of us not to acknowledge this
immense benefit and to thank God for it. But that is not all. Not
only Christ, Who is God and Man, but also His mother has been
exalted above all the choirs of Angels. Yet she is not divine but
only human. Hence, this great addition of glory, over and above
that which would have been ours had the first man not sinned, gives
us the right to exclaim: O happy fault, that has merited so great
a Redeemer.

Furthermore, the Angels, saddened though they were by the
utter ruin of their younger brother in the fall of the first man, were
filled with exceeding great joy at the superabundant redemption
wrought by Christ. If *there shall be joy before the angels of God*

[25] *Jo.* 17, 4.   [26] *Luke* ii, 14.   [27] *I Peter* iii, 22.   [28] *Phil.* ii, 8-9.

upon one sinner doing penance,[29] we can certainly believe that their joy was boundless when they beheld Christ fully satisfying the justice of God on behalf of the human race and opening the kingdom of heaven by the key of His Cross.

We do not need to fear that the holy Angels took it ill to see the Man-Christ and the most blessed Virgin exalted above them by God. The Angels harbour no rancour or jealousy: within them there flames the truest charity. Charity envieth not, is not puffed up, is not saddened at another's good fortune, but rejoices and is glad as though others' blessings were its own.[30] In this spirit the Church sings, "Mary is assumed into heaven and the Angels rejoice." [31] She does not say that the Angels grieve but that they rejoice to see the Virgin-Mother of God raised in heaven above the choirs of Angels. For they know well that this was done with perfect justice by Him Who acts only with the greatest wisdom and justice. Their wills are so closely united to the will of God by the unbreakable bonds of their love that whatever pleases God pleases them and can in no way displease them.

The devil, on the other hand, exulted for a time over the slavery and ruin which he brought about for the first man. But now his sadness at the victory of Christ the Man is all the more bitter because of that previous exultation. For the victory of Christ has made it possible not only for men, such as Adam was, but even for little children and women to mock the devil and triumph over him. It would have been no disgrace for the devil to be vanquished by Adam in the Garden of Paradise, for Adam at that time was free from ignorance and weakness and was armed with that original justice which so subjected his lower powers to the superior that they could not rebel before the mind itself rebelled. But now how ashamed the devil must feel to be overcome by mortal, wayfaring man, who is so liable to error and concupiscence. It is the grace of Christ which thus binds the devil. It is the grace of Christ which enables countless thousands to set up trophies of chastity, patience, humility, and charity, despite the well-aimed fiery darts of diabolical temptation and persecution.

And here especially we must admire the "height" of the wisdom of God. For God saw that, against the wiles of the devil, man would

29 *Luke* xv, 10.   30 Cf. *I Cor.* xiii, 4.   31 Offertory, Mass of the Assumption.

need to hold in contempt worldly wealth, the desires of the flesh, earthly glory and the suchlike, for these are nothing but snares of the devil with which he buries his captives in deepest ruin. What did the wisdom of God devise to make all these things bitter to man and to give him a taste for chastity, poverty, humility, patience, and contempt of the world? He Himself, taking on the form of a slave, came down from heaven to be the remedy that man in his sickness needed, a most bitter and awesome medicine, which He made sweet and pleasant by His example.

See how Christ's example has made many prefer fasting to feasting; poverty to riches; virginity to marriage; martyrdom to a comfortable life; obedience to governing; contempt to honours; lowliness to public recognition; humiliation to fame. How could anyone at the sight of God in human form, full of wisdom and grace, Who can neither deceive nor be deceived, so poor, lowly, patient, pure and, more amazing still, fixed to a cross for our salvation, willingly pouring out His blood for us, dying because of His burning love for us, how could anyone, I say, seeing all this not be moved with a great longing to imitate Him?

Such was the supreme and wondrous inventiveness of the wisdom of God. Of this ingenuity Isaias said: *Make his works (adinventiones) known among the people.*[32] Yet it is a fact that this loftiest wisdom of God still seems stupidity not only to the wise of this world, as the Apostle says in his first epistle to the Corinthians,[33] but also to the carnal-minded who, despite their belief in Christ, refuse to follow in His footsteps. These latter the Apostle calls enemies of the Cross of Christ.[34]

But do thou, my soul, occupy thyself with drawing honey from the rock and oil from granite, that is, wisdom from foolishness, the wisdom of God from the folly of the Cross. Consider carefully and well Who it is Who hangs on the Cross, and why He hangs there. When thou hast found Him to be the one *Who sitteth upon the Cherubim,*[35] yea, *Who sitteth at the right hand of Majesty on high,*[36] thou willst easily understand that He hangs there on the Cross not for His own sins, nor through powerlessness, nor even through the might of others, but voluntarily because of His

[32] *Isa.* xii, 4.　　[33] Cf. *I Cor.* i, 18-28.　　[34] *Phil.* iii, 18.
[35] *IV Kings* xix, 15.　　[36] *Heb.* i, 3.

consuming desire to satisfy divine justice for the sins of the whole world, to honour and glorify His Father, and to ensure the eternal salvation of the elect. As the Apostle says, His purpose was *that he might present it to himself a glorious church, not having spot or wrinkle.*[37] Finally we can say He did all this for love of thee, since indeed He *hath loved us and hath delivered himself for us, an oblation and a sacrifice to God for an odour of sweetness.*[38] When thou shalt have discovered these mighty truths, acknowledge with heartfelt love the generosity of so great a benefactor, strive to imitate Him, begin to thirst eagerly for the glory of God, the salvation of men, and, above all, for the beauty and glory of the Church and thine own eternal salvation. Begin to thirst for a perfect hatred of iniquity, for purity of heart, and perfect justice. In time thou mayst begin to thirst for a share in the Cross of thy Lord and to glory in trials and tribulations, that hereafter thou mayst gloriously partake in His resurrection with all the just and not be ignominiously punished with the damned.

It now remains for us to consider the "depth" of God's practical wisdom, which consists in His providence, in predestination and the Judgment. For it is written: *Thy judgments are a great deep.*[39] First we can gather that the divine providence is worthy of all admiration from the fact that all things are under His immediate governance and are directed by Him to their proper ends. *He hath equally care of all,* says the Wise Man,[40] that is, with no exceptions God looks after everything, so that not even a sparrow falls to the ground without the providence of God, as our Saviour says.[41]

If you could count all the things that are in the whole universe you might have some slight idea of the vastness of God's wisdom that rules and directs each and every single thing. The Holy Father can rule the entire Christian world with a providence that is general, but not with a special providence that would extend to each Christian: he has to call on a host of bishops to help carry the burden of government. So too a king can govern many provinces with a general but not with a special providence that would be concerned with each citizen: for this purpose he has to employ an army of consuls, governors, and judges. But God cares for each just as well as He

[37] *Ephes.* v, 27.   [38] *Ephes.* v, 2.   [39] *Ps.* xxxv, 7.   [40] *Wis.* vi, 8.
[41] *Matt.* x, 29.

cares for all. A sparrow is not forgotten by God. The hairs of our heads are numbered,[42] and if any of these are not to perish, God's providence must be ever watchful over us. The young ravens may be abandoned by their parents, but not by God.

How securely, O my soul, mayst not thou rest in the bosom of so mighty a Father, even in the deepest darkness! No matter if thou be surrounded by ravenous lions and dragons and be in the midst of innumerable legions of evil spirits, hold all the more fast to Him with true love, holy fear, unshakable confidence and firm faith.

God's providence extends far beyond the circle of existent things. *He reaches from end to end mightily, and ordereth all things sweetly.*[43] For God is called *the king of ages,*[44] because from eternity He has fixed the order of the centuries, and the successions of kingdoms, and the changing fortunes of the years. Nothing new or unforeseen or unlooked for can occur as far as God is concerned. *For the thoughts of mortal men are fearful,* as the Wise Man says, *and our counsels uncertain,*[45] since all we know of the future is fallible conjecture. But God's knowledge of the future is no less certain than that of the past and the present. Before the constitution of the world He had fixed in His own mind the disposition and order of all things. Hence Mother Church publicly and with assurance sings of the infallibility of God's providence in disposing things.[46]

Because, however, the designs of God's providence are deeply hidden and His judgments as great deeps, it happens that some, seeing that all the evils, which men do, go unpunished rashly conclude that human affairs are not governed by God's providence or even that all crimes are committed because God so wills. "Both errors are impious," says St. Augustine, "especially the latter." [47] Those who precipitately rush into these errors do so because they look only at a part of God's providence: instead of waiting for the solution that will be given at the Last Judgment, they prematurely pass judgment and so err most grievously. That is why the Apostle cries out in his first epistle to the Corinthians: *Therefore, judge not before the time: until the Lord come, who both will bring to*

---

[42] Cf. *Matt.* x, 29.   [43] *Wis.* viii, 1.   [44] *I Tim.* i, 17.   [45] *Wis.* ix, 14.
[46] Cf. Breviary hymns for Sext and None.
[47] *De Ordine,* I, c. 1 (PL 32, 978).

light the hidden things of darkness and will make manifest the counsels of the hearts.[48]

St. Augustine clarifies this point with a remarkable comparison. Suppose, he says, that in a mosiac pavement you could see only one tile at a time, you would blame the artist for his ignorance of composition and design.[49] This is bound to happen when only a tiny segment of a work and not a major portion is scrutinized. But if you were to take in the whole mosaic with all its parts and the harmony thereof, you could not but praise both the work and the artist. In the same way many, seeing the ignorant prosper and the just oppressed, and being ignorant of the way God will requite the iniquity of the wicked and the long-suffering of the just, burst forth into blasphemies. They side either with those who said to Job: God *walketh about the poles of heaven; and he doth not consider our things,*[50] or with those who, according to the prophet Malachi, say: *Every one that doth evil is good in the sight of the Lord and such please him?* [51]

St. Augustine also made frequent use of the comparison of a poem.[52] Suppose someone, hearing only the beginning, middle or end of an epic poem, were to say it was a poor poem, he would be foolishly jumping to conclusions. He should wait until every syllable has been uttered and passed away. Then, if the poem is not to his fancy, he may criticize. Also guilty of indecent haste are they who most stupidly dare to berate the providence of God before the whole plan of providence has been unfolded.

And so, my soul, if thou art wise, make it thy concern, as far as thou art able, to prevent evils from coming to pass. God demands this of thee. But why He should permit evils, leave that to His judgment, which, though it be hidden, cannot be unjust.

Although the designs of God's providence in the governance of human affairs are a deep mystery, deeper still and beyond all compare is the plan of predestination and eternal reprobation. For it is impossible for us in each particular case to search out the reason why God fills many of the wicked with good things and leaves their sins unpunished in this life, while allowing many innocent people

---

[48] *I Cor.* iv, 5.   [49] *De Ordine*, I, c. 1 (PL 32, 979).
[50] *Job* xxii, 14.   [51] *Mal.* ii, 17.   [52] Cf. above, p. 66.

to be oppressed with want, unjustly treated, beaten, and even killed. We can, however, with some probability assign a general reason.

For God often sees to it that the wicked abound with temporal goods as a reward for any morally good deeds they may do, since He is not to give them eternal life. Or perhaps it is that His temporal benefits may entice them from their sins and lead them to hope and long for eternal benefits. Sometimes He does not punish their sins in this life, as He will punish them sufficiently in hell. On the other hand He allows the just to be afflicted with want, disgrace and all manner of tribulation, in order to purge them in this life from their lighter offences, and to lay up for them a more glorious and splendid crown in heaven as recompense for their patience, humility and other merits.

Who can say why God should have loved Jacob, and hated Esau, even before they did any good or evil? [53] St. Paul in his epistle to the Romans marveled at this; for there were twin brothers, born of the same mother and father, and yet God in His predestination loved one and in His reprobation hated the other. It might be objected that God foresaw the future good works of one and the future misdeeds of the other. But the Apostle forestalls this objection by saying that this was done *that the purpose of God according to election might stand*.[54] He supports this view with the words of God to Moses: *I will have mercy on whom I will have mercy. And I will shew mercy to whom I will shew mercy*.[55]

It is astonishing that anyone should persevere in doing good for a long period, and yet fail and perish at the end of his life, as did Judas the traitor. It is also awe-inspiring to see a man persevering in evildoing for a long time and yet, at the hour of death, changing and escaping immediately to Paradise, as did the Good Thief. Perhaps you will say that Judas betrayed Christ, and the thief confessed. That is true, but could not Christ have looked on Judas as He looked on Peter? Could He not have inspired Judas with that efficacious grace which not even the hardest of hearts refuses? Could not Christ have given the gifts of faith and penance to both thieves crucified with Him, just as He had given them to one, or again have left both to die in their sins, as He in fact allowed one? Who can

[53] Cf. *Mal.* i, 2, and *Rom.* ix, 11.   [54] *Rom.* ix, 11.
[55] *Exod.* xxxiii, 19, cited in *Rom.* ix, 15.

explain why God should take some to Himself before evil could corrupt their souls, as the Wise Man says of Henoch,[56] or not take others and allow them to be corrupted and finish their days evilly? What can we say of those vast countries, some of which were called early, others later to the faith, without which no one can be saved? For *he that doth not believe is already judged.*[57] And as the Apostle says: *For whosoever shall call upon the name of the Lord shall be saved. How then shall they call on him in whom they have not believed? Or how shall they believe him of whom they have not heard? And how shall they hear without a preacher? And how shall they preach unless they be sent?* [58]

These are the deepest and most profound secrets which the Father has placed in the depths of His wisdom, which the Apostle does not reveal but only wonders at, saying: *O the depths of the riches of the wisdom and of the knowledge of God. How incomprehensible are his judgments, and how unsearchable his ways! For who hath known the mind of the Lord? Or who hath been his counsellor?* [59] This alone we may know that God does no evil, and that on the Last Day no one will be denied the right to say with all justice: Thou art just, O Lord, and right is Thy judgment. This secret is useful for all of us, since it does not allow the wicked to despair of salvation nor the upright to be presumptuous. It means that good men need never lose heart over the conversion of the wicked, but should pray for all and strive for the salvation of all. On the other hand, it has the effect also of preventing even the holiest from becoming careless, for no one knows what tomorrow will bring, but all must work out their salvation in fear and trembling.[60]

Consider all these things, O my soul, and strive by good works to ensure thy vocation and election, as the Apostle Peter warns thee in his second epistle.[61] The Apostle John teaches us what are meant by the good works that work our vocation when he says: *My children, let us not love in word nor in tongue, but in deed and in truth.*[62] For charity is that with which no man is damned, and without which no one is saved. Charity is shown through good works, as, for example, when any one, not through the hope of temporal reward or because of any inordinate affection for creatures,

---

[56] *Ecclus.* xliv, 16, and *Rom.* xi, 5.　　[57] *Jo.* iii, 18.　　[58] *Rom.* x, 13-15.
[59] *Rom.* xi, 33-4.　　[60] Cf. *Phil.* ii, 12.　　[61] *II Pet.* i, 10.　　[62] *I John* iii, 18.

but out of a pure personal love for God and his neighbour gives alms to the poor or forgives wrongs done by enemies. And it is not enough to begin well, but *he that shall persevere to the end, he shall be saved.*[63] That is why the Apostle says we must apply ourselves to the work of salvation most earnestly and diligently.

If there is any probable indication of the divine election, it is that a man is more mindful of his salvation than of anything else and does not cease to pray God for the gift of true repentance, true humility, perfect charity and perseverance to the end, and is not satisfied with prayer alone, but, as our Lord has warned us, with his whole strength seeks and searches for the kingdom of God and His justice.[64]

[63] *Matt.* xxiv, 13.   [64] Cf. *Matt.* vi, 33.

On the Ascent of the Mind to God

BLAISE PASCAL

PENSÉES

(Selections)

✛

The God of Abraham, the God of Isaac, the God of
Jacob, the God of the Christians, is a God of love and
solace, a God Who fills the soul and the heart of those
whom He possesses, a God Who impresses on them
interiorly a sense of their own wretchedness and His
own infinite mercy.

BLAISE PASCAL (1623-1662) was at once a gifted student of mathematics and physics and a remarkably devout man. He came into early contact with the religious ideas of the Jansenists (1646), he had a brief so-called worldly period, and then on that night of November 23, 1654, he had the fiery experience of the divine presence in his soul, recorded in the *Mémorial*. In 1656 appeared the celebrated and controversial *Provincial Letters*. The *Pensées* is a fragmentary work, projected as a defense of Christianity, which was not published until 1670.

There are in the *Pensées* flashing intuitions, deeply Augustinian in origin, about the greatness of the thinking reed that is man—the greatness and the instability. That is why this thinking reed must recognize the majesty of God and its own wretchedness without God. The famous conflict between the head and the heart in Pascal is not so much a conflict as an insistence that Christian life and love offer an experimental evidence which is at once richer than the abstract arguments of Cartesian-minded philosophers and impervious to their criticism. The heart is schooled by living, and its lessons come from the divine charity.

I I

First Part
The wretchedness of man without God

Second Part
The happiness of man with God

In other words:

First Part
That nature is corrupted. [Proven] by nature itself

Second Part
That there is a Repairer. [Proven] by Scripture

rder – I MIGHT HAVE, INDEED, PROCEEDED IN THIS discourse in an order such as the following: to portray the vanity of all kinds of conditions of life, show the vanity of common-place lives, and then the vanity of philosophical lives, Pyrrhonic and Stoic; but such an order would not be kept. I know something about it, and how few people do understand it. No human science can observe it. Saint Thomas did not observe it. Mathematics keep it, but it is useless because of its profundity.

Preface to the First Part – To speak of those who have treated of the knowledge of oneself; of Charron's divisions which vex and weary; of Montaigne's confusion; that he had fully sensed the want of a [correct] method, that he avoided it by jumping from one subject to another, that he strove for gentility.

What a stupid scheme to portray himself! and that not merely incidentally and contrary to his maxims, as may happen to anyone to err, but by way of his very own maxims and by an intent that was primary and principle. For to utter stupidities haphazardly and because of weakness is a commonplace evil; but to do so intentionally is insufferable, and to utter such as these . . .

Montaigne's shortcomings are great. Lewd words; that is bad in spite of Miss de Gournay. Gullible, *sightless people.* Ignorant, *squaring the circle, a greater world.* His opinions on suicide, on death. He instils a heedlessness of salvation, *unawed and unrepentant*. Since his book was not written to induce to religion, he was not bound to it: nevertheless, there is always the obligation of not deterring from it. His rather licentious and lewd opinions on certain hazards of life may be excused, but one cannot excuse his completely pagan opinions on death. For a man must renounce religion altogether if he does not wish, at least, to die like a Christian. Throughout his book, he thinks only of dying in a base and effeminate manner.

It is not in Montaigne but in myself that I find everything that I see in him.

What there is of good in Montaigne can be acquired only with difficulty. What there is of evil, I mean exclusive of morals, could have been corrected instantaneously if he had been warned that he talked too much nonsense and that he spoke too much of himself.

One has to know oneself: even though that would be of no assistance in discovering the true, it is, at least, of help in regulating one's life and there is nothing more fitting.

Vanity of the Sciences – In time of affliction, the science of exterior things will not console me for my ignorance of morality; but the science of morals will ever console me for my ignorance of exterior sciences.

Men are not taught to be upright men, and they are taught everything else; and they never pride themselves in knowing something of the rest as much as they do in being upright men. They pride themselves only in knowing the single thing that they do not learn.

Two infinites, the mean — When one reads too swiftly or too leisurely, one understands nothing.

Nature cannot . . . [Nature has fixed us so exactly in the middle that if we shift one point of the scales, we shift the other too. *Je fesons, zoa trekei*. This leads me to believe that there are

springs in our heads that are so adjusted that he who touches one
touches also its contrary.]

Too much and too little wine: do not give him any, and he cannot
discover the truth; give him too much, and the result is the same.

Man's disproportion – [This is where natural learning leads us.
If it is not true, then there is no truth in man; if it is true, then man
finds in it great grounds for humiliation, compelled as he is to demean himself in one way or another. And since he cannot exist
without believing it, before he concerns himself with further inquiries into nature, I hope he will consider nature earnestly and
leisurely, that he will examine himself too and, conscious of the
proportion that he has] . . . Let man, then, examine nature as a
whole in its lofty and full majesty; let him banish from his sight
the mean objects that surround him. Let him contemplate this
dazzling luminary set as an eternal lamp to illumine the universe;
let the earth appear to him as a dot in comparison to the immense
circumference that this luminary describes, and let him marvel at
the fact that this same vast circumference is but a very small dot
compared to that described by the stars which revolve in the firmament. But if our sight stops there, let our imagination go further.
It will grow weary with imagining sooner than nature with providing. All this visible world is but a minute point in nature's ample
bosom. No motion comes close to it. In vain do we swell our imaginings, beyond imaginable spaces, we produce but atoms in comparison to the reality of things. It is a sphere whose center is
everywhere, whose circumference nowhere.[1] Finally, the fact that
our imagination gets lost in this thought is the greatest sign of God's
omnipotence.

Once he recovers his senses, let man consider what he is in comparison to what is; let him look upon himself as lost in this remote
patch of nature, and from this little prison cell where he is lodged,
I mean the universe, let him learn to value the earth, kingdoms,
cities and himself at their true worth. What is a man in the infinite?

But to introduce him to another wonder just as startling, let him
investigate the daintiest things he knows. In the littleness of its

[1] Cf. above, p. 280.

body, let a mite present him parts that are incomparably smaller, legs with their joints, veins in its legs, blood in its veins, humors in this blood, drops in its humors, vapors in these drops; and dividing still further these latter, let him exhaust himself in these imaginings and let the last object to which he can arrive be now that of our discourse; he will think perhaps that here is the extreme minuteness in nature. I want to show him therein a further abyss. I want to picture for him not only the visible universe but also the vastness that can be imagined in nature, within the enclosure of this epitome of an atom. Let him see therein an infinity of universes each with its own firmament, its planets, its earth, in the same proportion as in the visible world; in this earth, [are] animals and finally mites in which he will meet again with what the first have proffered; and discovering again in these first the same things endlessly and perpetually, let him lose himself in these wonders as marvellous in their littleness as the others are in their immensity. For who will not be amazed that our body, a little while ago imperceptible in the universe which in turn is imperceptible in the bosom of the all, should be now a colossus, a world, or rather an all, compared to the nothingness to which we cannot reach?

Who examines himself in this fashion will grow frightened of himself, and, feeling himself suspended between the two abysses of nothingness and the infinite in this mass given to him by nature, he will tremble at the sight of these wonders; and I think that as his curiosity changes to admiration he will become more and more disposed to contemplate them in silence rather than to inquire into them with presumption.

For, in fine, what is man in nature? a nothing compared to the infinite, an all compared to nothing, a mean between nothing and everything. Infinitely removed from understanding the extremes, as far as he is concerned the end of things and their beginning are invincibly hidden in an impenetrable secret, identically incapable as he is of seeing the nothingness from which he is drawn as the infinite wherein he is engulfed.

What shall he do, then, if not discover some semblance of the mean of things in his endless despair of knowing either their beginning or their end? All things are sprung from nothingness and are carried along even to the infinite. Who shall follow these astounding proceedings? The author of these marvels can comprehend them. Anyone else cannot.

For want of having meditated on these infinites, men are prompted to investigate foolhardily into nature as if they had some proportion to it. Strange that they have wished to understand the principles of things and thence to reach a knowledge of every thing through an arrogance that is as infinite as their object in view! For there is no doubt that one cannot form this plan without a presumption and without a capacity as infinite as nature.

When one is well-informed, one understands that, because nature has imprinted its image and that of its author on all things, these depend almost all of them on its double infinity. Thus it is that we see that all sciences are infinite in the extent of their inquiries: For who questions but that geometry, for instance, has an infinity of infinities of propositions to expound? They are just as infinite in the multitude and delicacy of their principles: For who does not see that those proposed as final do not find support in themselves but are supported by others which, having others in turn for their support, do not admit of such ultimates? But we deal with such ultimates which appear to reason just as we do material things, where we declare a point invisible that beyond which our senses perceive nothing, even though it be divisible infinitely and by its very nature.

Of these two infinites in science, that of magnitude is much more observable and that is the reason why it has happened to few to lay claim to a knowledge of all things. "I am going to speak about everything," Democritus used to say.

But infinity in minuteness is much less visible. Philosophers have much preferred impudently to claim to attain it, and that is where they have all come to grief. That is what has given rise to these quite current titles: *Principles of Things, Principles of Philosophy,* and to similar ones that are, in fact, as pompous—though less in appearance—as this one that is so obvious: *De omni scibili.*

One feels that he is naturally much more able to get at the center of things than to take in their circumference; the visible expanse of the world visibly goes beyond us; but because we go beyond little things, we believe that we are more capable of mastering them.

And yet no less capacity is needed to reach nothingness than the all; capacity needs to be infinite for both, and it seems to me that whoever has understood the ultimate principles of things can also attain a knowledge of the infinite. One depends on the other and one leads to the other. These extremes meet and combine by dint of receding from each other and meet again in God and in God alone.

Let us then understand what is our capacity; we are something and we are not everything; what we have of being deprives us of the knowledge of first principles, which arise from nothingness; and the little we have of being conceals from us the sight of the infinite.

In the order of intelligible things our intelligence holds the same rank as our body does in the vastness of nature.

Limited in every mode, this state which holds the mean between two extremes exists in all our powers. Our senses perceive nothing that is extreme; too much sound deafens us, too much light dazzles us, too much distance and too much proximity impedes sight, too much verbosity and too much brevity in speech beclouds it, too much truth daunts us (I know people who cannot understand that, if you subtract four from zero, the result is zero), first principles are too obvious for us, too much pleasure bores us, too much consonance displeases us in music; and too many favors done us are sources of irritation: we want to have the means to reciprocate over and above our debts: *Beneficia eo usque laeta sunt dum videntur exsolvi posse; ubi multum antevenere, pro gratia odium redditur.*[2] We feel neither extreme heat nor extreme cold. Excessive qualities are injurious to us and are not perceptible; we do not perceive them, we endure them. Too much youth and too much age hinder our minds as do too much and too little education; in fine, extremes are for us as if they did not exist and as if we do not exist in regard to them; they escape us, or we them.

That is our true state; that is what makes us incapable of knowing with certitude and of not knowing completely. We float on a vast mean, always uncertain and wavering, driven from end to end. Whatever be the goal we hope to cleave to and there be secure, it gives way and leaves us; and if we pursue it, it escapes our grasp, slips away and flees us in eternal flight. Nothing stops for us. That

2 *Tacitus. Ann.*, IV, 18.

is the state that is natural to us and yet the most contrary to our inclinations; we burn with desire to find some stable site and a last steady base on which to erect a tower which will rise to the infinite, but our whole foundation crumbles and the earth opens up to its very depths.

Let us not look, then, for certainty and stability. Our reason is always deceived by the inconstancy of appearances, nothing can fix the finite between the two infinites which enclose and evade it.

Once that is well understood, I think that we will be at peace, each in the state wherein nature has placed him. Since this mean which has fallen to our lot is always distant from the extremes, what does it matter if one has a bit more understanding of things? If he has, it will be from a bit higher that he will grasp them. Is he not always infinitely distant from his end, and is not the duration of our life equally infinitely removed from eternity, even though it last ten years longer?

In comparison to these infinites, all finites are equal; and I do not see any reason for fixing one's imagination on one rather than the other. The mere comparison that we make of ourselves to the finite is painful to us.

If man studied himself first of all, he would see how incapable he is of going beyond. How can it be that one part know the whole? But perhaps he will aspire to know those parts at least with which he has a proportion. But all parts of the world have such an affinity and such a connection one with the other that I think it impossible to know one without the other and without the whole.

Man, for example, has a relationship to everything he knows. He needs space to contain him, time in which to exist, movement to live, elements to fashion him, heat and food to nurture him, air to breathe; he sees light, he perceives bodies; in short, everything falls under his ambiance. To know man, it is necessary to know how it is that he needs air to live; and to know air, how it is that it has this relation to man's life, etc. Fire does not exist without air; therefore, to know one, it is necessary to know the other. Thus, since all things are caused and themselves causes, supported and supporting, mediate and immediate, and since all things sustain each other by a natural and imperceptible bond binding things that are most distant and diverse, I maintain that it is impossible to have knowledge of the parts without knowing the whole, just as it is to know the whole without a specific knowledge of the parts.

[The eternity of things in itself or in God must also astonish our brief duration. The fixed and constant immobility of nature in comparison to the continual flux that takes place in us must have the same effect.]

What crowns our powerlessness to know things is that they are simple in themselves and that we are composed of two contrary natures and of two different genera, of soul and of body. Because it is impossible that the part that reasons in us be other than spiritual; and however much one were to allege that we are merely corporeal, that very thing would exclude us the more from the knowledge of things since there is nothing so unthinkable as to say that matter knows itself; it is not possible for us to know how it would know itself.

And so if we are simply material, we can know nothing at all, and if we are composed of spirit and matter, we cannot have perfect knowledge of simple things, be they spiritual or corporeal.

Whence arises that nearly all philosophers jumble their ideas of things and speak of corporeal things in a spiritual way and of spiritual things corporeally. For they say unhesitatingly that bodies tend downwards, that they yearn for their center, that they fly their destruction, that they fear the void, that it [*i.e.,* nature] has inclinations, sympathies, antipathies—things that belong only to spirits. And speaking of spiritual things, they think of them as in a place and attribute to them movement from place to place— things which belong only to bodies.

Instead of accepting the ideas of those pure things, we color them with our own characteristics and impress on all simple things that we contemplate our own composite being.

Seeing us fashion all things of spirit and body, who would not imagine but that mixture would be very understandable to us? Yet that is the thing we understand least. Man is to himself the most amazing thing in nature; for he cannot imagine what a body is and still less what a spirit is, and least of all how a body can be united to a spirit. That is the zenith of his difficulties, and yet it is his own proper being: *Modus quo corporibus adhaerent spiritus comprehendi ab hominibus non potest et hoc tamen homo est.*[3]

Finally, to complete the proof of our weakness, I shall conclude with these two considerations. . . .

I cannot forgive Descartes. He would have been quite willing, throughout his philosophy, to be able to get along without God; but he could not help making Him give an impetus to put the world in motion; after that, he has nothing more to do with God.

I V

The heart has its reasons which reason does not know at all; that is evident in a thousand things. I say that the heart loves universal being naturally and itself naturally in the measure that it surrenders itself to it; and it hardens itself against one or the other as it chooses. You have rejected one and kept the other; is it through reason that you love yourself?

It is the heart that senses God, and not the reason. That is what faith is, God perceptible to the heart and not to reason.

Faith is a gift of God; do not believe that we say that it is a gift of reason. Other religions do not say that of their faith; they provided reasoning only to attain it but it does not lead them there nevertheless.

How far it is from the knowledge of God to a love of Him!

Heart, instinct, principles.

We know truth not only by reason but also by the heart. It is in this latter way that we know first principles and it is in vain that reasoning which has no part in them tries to oppose them. The skeptics who have that as their sole object labor in vain to that end. We know that we are not dreaming; however powerless we are to prove it by reason, our inability proves nothing but the weakness

[3] St. Augustine, *De Civit. Dei,* XXI, 10 1 (PL 41, 725).

of our reason, not the incertitude of all our knowledge, as they maintain it does. Because the knowledge of first principles as, for instance, the existence of space, time, movement, numbers, [is] as certain as any of those that our reasoning affords. And it is on this knowledge of the heart and instinct that reason must lean and must base all its discourse. (The heart senses that there are three dimensions in space and that numbers are infinite; and then reason proves that there are no two numbers squared of which one is double the other. Principles are sensed, propositions are proven; and the whole with certitude although by different ways.) And it is just as futile and ridiculous for reason to demand of the heart proofs of its first principles, so that it might be willing to consent to them, as it would be ridiculous for the heart to demand of reason a sentiment of all the propositions it proves, so that it might be willing to accept them.

This powerlessness then cannot but serve to humble reason which would wish to be judge of everything; but it cannot serve at all to combat our certitude, as though reason only were capable of teaching us. Would to God, on the contrary, that we never needed it and that we knew all things by instinct and feeling! But nature has refused us this boon; on the contrary, it has given us but too little knowledge of this kind; all the rest can be acquired only by reasoning.

And that is why those to whom God has given religion by perception of the heart are completely happy and quite legitimately convinced. But to those who have it not, we can give it only by reasoning until such a time as God grants it to them by the perception of their heart, without which faith is but human and useless for salvation.

Order. Against an objection that Scripture has no order. The heart has its order; the mind has its own which is by way of principle and demonstration: the heart has another. It cannot be proven that one ought to be loved by setting down in order the causes of love: that would be absurd.

Jesus Christ, Saint Paul use the order of charity, not of the mind; because they wanted to inflame, not to teach. The same with Saint Augustine. This order consists principally in digressing on each point, a digression which is referred to the end in view in order to prove it nevertheless.

Do not be astonished to see simple folk believe without reasoning. God gives them love of Him and hatred of themselves. He inclines their hearts to believe. One will never believe with a profitable faith and sincerely unless God inclines his heart; and one will believe the moment He inclines it. And that is what David knew so well: *inclina cor meum, Deus, in. . . .*[4]

Religion is adapted to all sorts of minds. The first kind stop at its mere institution; and that religion is such that its very institution is enough to prove its truth. Others reach right to the Apostles. The more educated go back to the beginning of the world. Angels see it better still and from further off.

Those who believe without having read the Testaments do so because they have a very holy interior disposition and because what they hear of our religion is consistent with it. They feel that a God made them; they desire to love only God; and they wish to hate but themselves. They feel they have no strength of themselves; that they are powerless to go to God; and that, if God does not come to them, they can have no communication with Him. And they hear in our religion that God alone must be loved and only ourselves hated; but since we are corrupted and incapable of God, God became man to unite Himself to us. Nothing more is needed to convince men who have this disposition in their hearts and who have this knowledge of their duty and of their incapacity.

Those whom we see to be Christians with no knowledge of prophecies and of demonstration pass judgment on them nevertheless as well as those who have this knowledge. They judge them by their hearts just as the others judge them by their minds. It is God Himself Who disposes them to believe; and so they are convinced quite efficaciously.

I grant that one of these Christians who believe without proofs will perhaps not have the means to convince an unbeliever who will admit as much of himself. But those who know the proofs of religion will prove without difficulty that this believer is truly inspired by God although unable to prove it himself.

[4] *Ps.* cxviii, 36.

Since God said in His prophecies (which are prophecies beyond doubt) that in the kingdom of Jesus Christ He would pour out His spirit upon the nations, and that the sons and daughters and children of the Church would prophesy, there is no doubt that the spirit of God is upon the former and not upon the others.

Instead of complaining that God has hidden Himself, give thanks that He has revealed Himself so much. And give thanks again that He has not revealed Himself to the haughty wise, unworthy to know a God so holy. Two kinds of persons know: those who have a heart that has been humbled, and who love humility, whatever grade of mind they may have, high or low; or those who have sufficient intelligence to see the truth, however much they may be opposed to it.

Proof. 1. The Christian religion, by its institution, established by itself so strongly, so meekly, while so contrary to nature. 2. The holiness, the greatness and humility of a Christian soul. 3. The marvels of Holy Scripture. 4. Jesus Christ, in particular. 5. The Apostles, in particular. 6. Moses and the Prophets, in particular. 7. The Jewish people. 8. The prophecies. 9. Perpetuity: no religion is perpetual. 10. Doctrine, which gives an account of everything. 11. The holiness of this law. 12. By the conduct of the world.

It is unquestionable that after this one may not refuse, considering what life is and what this religion is, to obey the inclination to follow after it, if it comes to us in our hearts; and it is certain that there is no occasion for making fun of those who do follow it.

V I

Thinking is the cause of man's greatness.

Man is but a reed, the slightest thing in nature; but he is a thinking reed. The whole universe need not take up arms to overwhelm him: a vapor, a drop of water, is enough to kill him. But, even though the universe were to crush him, man would be still nobler than what kills him, because he is aware that he is dying and aware of the advantage that the universe has over him; the universe knows nothing of it.

Our whole dignity, then, consists in thinking. It is in it that we must rise again and not in space and time which we are ever unable to fill. Let us strive, then, to think well: behold the principle of morality.

Thinking reed.—It is not in space and time that I am to look for my dignity, but in the ordering of my thinking. I shall possess no more through owning lands; by space, the universe contains me and engulfs me as a speck; by thinking, I contain it.

Thinking.—Man's whole dignity consists in thinking. But what is this thinking? How stupid it is!

Thinking is, therefore, an admirable and peerless thing by its nature. It required some strange defects to make it despicable; but it has so many such that nothing is more absurd. How great it is by its nature; how mean because of its defects!

The mind of this sovereign judge of the world is not so independent that it is not liable to be disturbed by the first hubbub that takes place about it. It needs not the roar of a cannon to hinder its thoughts: it needs but the noise of a weather-vane or a pulley. Do not be surprised if it does not reason so very well at the moment: a fly is buzzing about its ears; that is enough to make it incapable of good direction. If you want it to be able to discover the truth, then drive away that beast that holds its reason in check and distracts this mighty intelligence that rules cities and kingdoms. The droll god that it is! *O ridicolosissimo eroe.*

Man's nobility is great from the fact that he is aware that he is wretched. A tree is not aware that it is wretched.

To be aware, therefore, of one's self as wretched is to be wretched; but to know that one is wretched is the measure of greatness.

All those miseries prove his greatness. They are the miseries of a nobleman, of a deposed king.

One is not wretched without the consciousness [of it]: a crumbling house is not so. Man only is wretched. *Ego vir videns.*[5]

[5] *Lament.* iii, 1.

Greatness of man.—We have such a lofty conception of man's soul that we cannot bear to be despised, and not to be esteemed by a soul; and the entire happiness of men consists in this esteem.

Glory.—Beasts do not honor one another. A horse does not respect its mate. Not but there is no rivalry between them on the race-track, but that is of no moment; for, when in the stable, the heaviest and most ill-favored does not yield its oats to the other because of that fact, as men are wont to expect others to do to them. Their virtue is gratified of itself.

Greatness of man even in his lusts, because out of it he has contrived to draw forth an admirable code and to frame a picture of charity.

Greatness.—Considerations of consequences underscore man's greatness because he has drawn forth so noble an order out of concupiscence.

Man's greatest meanness is his pursuit of glory, but that very thing is the greatest indication of his excellence; for, whatever he possesses upon earth, whatever of health and essential comfort he may have, he is not satisfied unless he is esteemed of men. He values man's reason so highly that, whatever advantage he may have on earth, if he is not set favorably in man's reason, he is not happy. That is the fairest spot in the world, nothing can divert him from this longing, and it is the most ineffaceable characteristic of the human heart.

And those who despise men the most and equate them to beasts nevertheless want to be admired and believed by them, and they contradict themselves by their own feeling; their nature, stronger than everything, convinces them of man's greatness more forcibly than their reason does of his meanness.

Contradiction.—Pride, counterbalancing all wretchedness; either man conceals his miseries; or, if he does lay them bare, he takes pride in the knowledge of them.

Pride counterbalances and takes away all miseries. It is a strange monster and a frenzy that is quite apparent. Down he falls from his place, and he looks for it anxiously! That is what all men do. Let us see who will find it.

When malevolence has reason on its side, it becomes proud and makes a display of reason in all its splendor. When severity or stern choice has not succeeded in [attaining] the true good and when a return to the following of nature is necessary, it becomes proud because of this conversion.

Evil is easy [of access], there is an infinity of it; the good practically unique. But a certain kind of evil is as difficult to find as what is called good, and often, under that token, this particular evil is passed off as good. An extraordinary nobility of soul is likewise needed to attain it as well as the good.

The greatness of man.—Man's greatness is so obvious that it springs even from his wretchedness. For that which in the case of beasts is nature we call wretchedness in man. Therefore, since his nature nowadays is like that of the beasts, we recognize that he has fallen from a better nature which was peculiar to him in former times.

For who feels miserable at not being king except a deposed king? Was Paulus Aemilius thought miserable at being consul no longer? On the contrary, everybody thought he was fortunate to have been one, since his condition in life was not to have been one for ever. But Perseus was considered so wretched at being king no longer that it was thought queer that he endured living, just because his condition in life was to be such for ever.[6] Who feels wretched because he has but one mouth? and who will not feel wretched at having but one eye? Probably it has never occurred to any one to grieve because he has not three eyes, but he is inconsolable at not having any.

Perseus, King of Macedonia, Paulus Aemilius.—Perseus was upbraided because he did not kill himself.

[6] Cicero, *Tusc. Disp.* V, 40.

Notwithstanding the sight of all our miseries, which affect us, which hold us by the throat, we possess an instinct which we cannot suppress, which raises us up.

Man's interior war between his reason and his passions.
If he had only reason without passions . . .
If he had only passions without reason . . .
But since he has both, he cannot exist without strife, unable to be at peace with the one except by waging war against the other. Thus he is always divided, and at odds with himself.

This interior war of reason against the passions has brought it about that those who have yearned for peace have split into two camps. Some wished to renounce their passions and to become gods; others wanted to renounce their reason and to become brute beasts. (Des Barreaux). But neither have been able to do so. And reason abides forever complaining of the vileness and injustice of the passions and disquietening the peace of those who abandon themselves to her; and the passions are ever alive in those who want to renounce them.

Men are fools so of necessity that not to be a fool is simply to be one by another manner of folly.

Man's nature is viewed in two ways: one according to his end and then he is great and matchless; the other according to multitude, the same way that one judges a horse's nature or that of a dog, individually, from seeing it race, *et animum arcendi;* and then man is abject and base. These are the two ways that cause him to be judged differently and which have made philosophers wrangle so much.

For one denies the supposition of the other. One says: "He is not born towards this end, because all his actions contradict it"; the other says: "He departs from his end when he performs these base deeds".

To P.R. Greatness and Wretchedness.—Since wretchedness is inferred from greatness and greatness from wretchedness, some have deduced all the more concerning wretchedness that they were able to use greatness as proof, while others deduced greatness much more forcibly because they had inferred it from wretchedness itself; and so everything that some could say only served as an argument for the others to infer wretchedness, since the fact that one has fallen from so high is simply to be more wretched; the others, quite the contrary. They have attacked each other in a vicious circle, since it is certain that in the measure that men are enlightened, they discover both greatness and wretchedness in man. In a word, man knows that he is wretched; therefore is he wretched since he is so; but he is very great because he knows it.

This two-fold characteristic of man is so obvious that there are some who thought we had two souls. A simple subject seemed to them incapable of suchlike and sudden changes from unbridled presumption to horrible despondency of heart.

It is dangerous to show man overmuch how equal he is to beasts without showing him his greatness. It is dangerous furthermore to show him his greatness without his wretchedness. It is still more dangerous to allow him to be ignorant of one and the other. But it is very profitable to picture both to him.

Man must not believe that he is all one with beasts, or with angels, nor must he be in ignorance of them both; but he must know both.

I shall not allow him to rely on himself or on another, so that being without foundation and resting place . . .

If he exalts himself, I humble him; if he humbles himself, I exalt him; and I contradict him continually until he understands that he is an unfathomable monster.

I blame equally both those who advocate praising man, and those who advocate blaming him as well, and those who take sides for their own amusement; and I can countenance only those who make their quest in tears.

It is good to be wearied and exhausted by the vain quest of the true good so as to stretch forth one's arms to the liberator.

Contradictions. After showing the meanness and greatness of man.—Let man now reckon his worth. Let him love himself because he has within him a nature capable of good; but let him not love for that reason the meannesses that are present there. Let him despise himself because this capacity is void; but let him not therefore despise this natural capacity. Let him hate himself, let him love himself; he has within him the capacity to know truth and to be happy; but there is not truth within him either lasting or satisfying.

I should, therefore, like to incite man to a longing to find it, and, delivered from his passions, to be ready to follow it wherever he shall come upon it, knowing how much his knowledge is clouded by his passions. I should like him to hate in himself the concupiscence that influences him of itself, so that it may not blind him in making his choice and that it may not obstruct him after he has chosen.

All these contradictions which seemed to me to avert me most from the knowledge of religion are really what has rather led me to the true one.

V I I

Only the Christian religion makes men *lovable and happy* at the same time. In genteelness, we cannot be lovable and happy together.

Preface.—The metaphysical proofs of God are so foreign to men's reasoning and so intricate that they make but little impression; and though this may be of use to certain ones, it would serve but for the very instant that they see the demonstration. But an hour afterwards, they are afraid that they have made a mistake.

Quod curiositate cognoverunt superbia amiserunt.[7]

This is the product of the knowledge of God gotten without Jesus Christ: to have communication, without a Mediator, with

[7] St. Augustine, *Serm.* CXLI, ii, 2 (PL 38, 777).

the God known without a Mediator. Whereas those who have come to a knowledge of God by means of a Mediator know their wretchedness.

The God of Christians is a God Who makes the soul perceive that He is its unique good; that all its repose is in Him, that it shall feel joy only in loving Him; and Who makes it, at the same time, detest the obstacles that hold it back and prevent it from loving God with all its strength. Self-love and concupiscence, which obstruct it, are intolerable to it. This God brings home to it that it has a root of self-love which is fatal to it and that He alone can cure it.

Jesus Christ simply taught men that they loved themselves, that they were slaves, blind, sick, wretched and sinners; that it was necessary that He deliver them, enlighten them, make them blessed and heal them; that this would be brought about by hatred of oneself and by following Him through His suffering and the death of the Cross.

Without Jesus Christ, men must be in vice and wretchedness; with Jesus Christ, man is free from vice and wretchedness. In Him is all our virtue and all our happiness. Outside Him, there is only vice, wretchedness, error, darkness, death, despair.

We know God only through Jesus Christ. Without this Mediator, all communication with Him is removed; through Jesus Christ, we know God. All those who claimed to know God and to prove Him without Jesus Christ have had but ineffectual proofs. But to prove Jesus Christ we have the prophecies, which are solid and tangible proofs. And since the prophecies were accomplished and proven true by event, they testify to the certitude of these truths, and likewise to the proof of the divinity of Jesus Christ. In Him, and by Him, therefore, we know God. Otherwise and without the Scriptures, without original sin, without a necessary Mediator, promised and come, one cannot prove God positively nor teach either true doctrine or true morality. But through Jesus Christ and in Jesus Christ one does prove God and one does teach morality and doctrine. Jesus Christ is, therefore, the veritable God of men.

But, at the same time, we know our wretchedness, for that God is none other than the Repairer of our wretchedness. Thus we can know God well only by knowing our iniquities. Therefore those who have known God without knowing their wretchedness have not glorified Him but have thereby glorified themselves. *Quia . . . non cognovit per sapientiam . . . placuit Deo per stultitiam praedicationis salvos facere.*[8]

Not only do we know God only through Jesus Christ, but we know ourselves only through Jesus Christ. We know life and death only through Jesus Christ. Apart from Jesus Christ, we do not know what our life is, our death, God or ourselves.

Thus, without the Scriptures which have Jesus Christ as their sole object, we know nothing and see but darkness and confusion in the nature of God and in nature itself.

It is not only impossible but futile to know God without Jesus Christ. They have not forsaken Him but have drawn near to Him; they have not humbled themselves but . . .

Quo quisquam optimus est, pessimus, si hoc ipsum, quod optimum sit, adscibat sibi.[9]

I love poverty, because He loved it. I love wealth because it provides the means of helping the needy. I keep faith with every one, I do not return evil to those who do evil to me; but I desire for them a condition like to my own wherein no evil or good is received at the hands of men. I try to be just, honest, sincere and faithful to all men; I feel an affection for those to whom God has united me more intimately; but whether I be alone or in the sight of men, in all my actions I have God before me Who is to judge them and to whom I have consecrated them all.

Such are my feelings, and every day of my life I bless my Redeemer Who has placed them within me and Who of a man full of weakness, wretchedness, lust, pride and ambition has formed *a*

---

[8] *I Cor.* i, 21.　　　[9] St. Bernard, *In Cant. Cant.,* LXXXIV, 2 (PL 183, 1185).

man free from all these evils by virtue of His grace, to which be all the glory thereof, since of myself I have but wretchedness and error.

Dignior plagis quam osculis non timeo quia amo.[10]

The Tomb of Jesus Christ.—Jesus Christ was dead, but visible, on the Cross. He is dead and hidden in the tomb.

Jesus Christ was buried only by saints.

Jesus Christ did no miracles in the tomb.

Only saints enter therein.

It is there, not on the Cross, that Jesus Christ assumes a new life.

It is the last mystery of the Passion and Redemption.

Jesus Christ had nowhere to rest on earth except in the tomb.

His enemies stopped tormenting Him only in the tomb.

The Mystery of Jesus—In His passion, Jesus undergoes the sufferings that men cause Him; but in His agony, He endures the anguish He gives Himself: *turbare semtipsum.*[11] It is the torture of a hand that is not human but omnipotent because one must be omnipotent to bear it.

Jesus seeks some comfort, at least from His three dearest friends, and they are asleep; He entreats them to watch a little with Him, and they desert Him with complete heedlessness, possessed of so little compassion that it did not even prevent them from sleeping a while. And thus Jesus was abandoned alone to the wrath of God.

Jesus is alone on earth, not only alone to experience and partake of His sufferings but even to know it: Heaven and He alone share in this knowledge.

Jesus is in a garden, not in a garden of delight like the first Adam, wherein he caused the ruin of himself and the whole human race, but in a garden of torments wherein He delivered Himself and the whole human race.

He suffers this pain and desertion in the horror of the night.

I think that Jesus never complained but this once; but at that time He complains as if no longer able to curb His excessive grief: *My soul is sorrowful even unto death.*[12]

[10] St. Bernard, *Ibid.* 6 (PL 183, 1186). [11] *Jo.* xxi, 23. [12] *Mark* xiv, 34.

Jesus seeks the companionship and comfort of men. That is unique in His whole life, I think. But He receives none, because His disciples are sleeping.

Jesus will be in agony until the end of the world; we must not sleep during that time.

In the midst of this universal abandonment, and that by His friends chosen to watch with Him, Jesus, finding them asleep, grows angry because of the danger to which they expose, not Him, but themselves; and He admonishes them of their own salvation and of their own interest with a heartfelt tenderness for them in the midst of their ingratitude, and warns them that the spirit is willing but the flesh weak.

Finding them still sleeping, not restrained therefrom by any consideration for Him or for themselves, Jesus has the kindness not to awaken them but leaves them to their rest.

Jesus prays in uncertainty as to His Father's will, and fears death; but, having known it, He goes forward to offer Himself to it: *Eamus. Processit* (Joannes).

Jesus entreated men, but His prayer was not heard by them.

While His disciples slept, Jesus effected their salvation. He did it for each of them just as they slept, both in their nothingness before their birth, as well as in their sins after their birth.

He prays but once that the chalice pass away and nevertheless submissively, and twice that it may come if it must.

Jesus weary.

Seeing all His friends asleep and all His enemies watching, Jesus delivers Himself wholly to His Father.

In Judas, Jesus does not behold his enmity, but the order of God Whom He loves, and He confesses it since He calls him friend.

Jesus tears Himself away from His disciples to enter upon His agony; we must tear ourselves away from our closest and dearest ones to imitate Him.

When Jesus is in the midst of His agony and His greatest pains, let us pray the longer.

We implore the mercy of God, not that He may leave us in peace in the midst of our vices, but that He deliver us from them.

If God were to give us masters from His hands, oh! how necessary would it be to obey them cheerfully! Necessity and events follow each other infallibly.

"Take comfort, thou wouldst not be looking for Me, if thou hadst not found Me.

"I thought of thee during my agony, I shed many a drop of blood for thee.

"To imagine whether thou wouldst really do such and such an absent deed, is to tempt Me rather than to try thyself; I shall accomplish it in thee if it comes to pass.

"Let thyself be guided by My rules: see how I have rightly guided the Virgin and the saints who have allowed Me to act in them.

"The Father loves all that I do.

"Dost thou desire that it cost Me ever of the blood of My humanity, without your shedding tears?

"Thy conversion is My affair; fear not and pray confidently as though for Me.

"I am present to thee by My word in the Scriptures, by My spirit and by inspiration in the Church, by My power in priests, by My prayers among the faithful.

"Physicians will not heal thee because thou shalt die at length. But it is I who heal and make the body immortal.

"Suffer bodily chains and servitude; at the present time I deliver thee only from spiritual servitude.

"I am more thy friend than anyone else. For I have done more for thee than they have, and they would not endure what I have suffered at thy hands; and they would not die for thee in the time of thy infidelities and cruelties as I have done, and as I am ready to do and do in my elect and in the Blessed Eucharist.

"If thou didst know thy sins, thou wouldst lose heart."

—I shall do so then, Lord, for at Thy word I believe in their malice.

"No, because I, from whom thou dost learn so, can heal thee of them, and the fact that I have told thee so is a sign that I desire to heal thee. Accordingly as thou dost atone for them, thou shalt know them and it shall be said to thee: 'Behold thy sins are forgiven thee'. Do penance, therefore, for thy secret sins and for the hidden malice of those thou knowest."

—Lord, I give Thee my all.

"I love thee more ardently than thou hast loved thy defilement, *ut immundus pro luto.*

"To Me be the glory thereof and not to thee, thou worm and earth.

"Question thy director, when My very words are an occasion of evil to thee, and an occasion of vain glory and curiosity."

—I see the depths of my pride, curiosity, lust. There is no conformity of myself to God, nor to Jesus Christ the Righteous. But He was made sin for sake of me; all Thy scourgings have fallen upon Him. He is more loathsome than I, and, far from abominating me, He considers Himself honored that I go to Him and succor Him.

But He has healed Himself, and still more so will He heal me.

I must add my wounds to His, and unite myself to Him, and He will save me while He saves Himself. But I must not add any more in the future.

Eritis sicut dii scientes bonum et malum.[13] Everyone plays god when he sits in judgment: "That is good or evil", and when he mourns or rejoices too much at the turn of events.

Do little things as though they were important because of the majesty of Jesus Christ Who does them in us, and Who lives our life; do the important as though they were little and easy because of His omnipotence.

I think that Jesus Christ permits only His wound to be touched after His resurrection; *Noli me tangere.*[14] We must unite ourselves only to His sufferings.

He gave Himself in communion as mortal man at the Last Supper, as risen from the dead to the disciples of Emmaus, as ascended into heaven to the entire Church.

"Do not compare thyself to others, but to Me. If thou dost not find Me within those to whom thou dost compare thyself, thou art comparing thyself to an odious person. If thou dost find Me in them, compare thyself to them. But with what wilt thou compare thyself therein? will it be thyself or Me in thee? If it be thyself, it

[13] *Gen.* ii, 5.   [14] *Jo.* xx, 17.

is with an odious person. If it be I, thou art comparing Me to Myself. For I am God in all things.

"I speak to thee and counsel thee often, because thy director cannot speak to thee; for I do not desire thee to be lacking a director.

"And perhaps I do so at his prayers, and so he directs thee without thy seeing him. Thou wouldst not search for Me if thou didst not possess Me.

"Do not, then, be troubled."

VIII

They revile what they do not know. The Christian religion consists in two points: it is equally important for men to know them and it is equally dangerous to be ignorant of them; and it is due equally to the mercy of God to have given indications of both.

And yet they assume grounds for deciding that one of these points does not exist from what ought to cause them to infer the other. The sages who said that there was but one God were persecuted, the Jews were hated, the Christians still more so. They saw by the light of natural wisdom that, if there is a true religion on earth, the disposition of all things ought to tend towards it as to its center.

The whole course of things ought to have as its object the foundation and greatness of religion; men ought to have within themselves ideas consistent with what it teaches us; and, finally, so much ought it to be the object and center to which all things tend that he who knows its principles may also account not only for the complete nature of man in particular but also for the entire course of the world in general.

And on these grounds, they take occasion to blaspheme against the Christian religion, because they know it badly. They imagine that it consists simply in the adoration of a God considered as great, powerful and eternal: this is, properly speaking, deism, almost as far removed from the Christian religion as atheism, which is completely contrary to it. And thence they conclude that this religion is not true, because they do not see that all things concur to prove this point, namely, that God does not manifest Himself to men with all the clarity of which He is capable.

Conclude as they will against deism, they will prove nothing against the Christian religion which consists properly in the mystery of the Redeemer, Who, uniting in Himself two natures, human and divine, has withdrawn men from the corruption of sin to reconcile them to God in His divine person.

It teaches men simultaneously, then, these two truths: both that there is a God of Whom men are capable, and that there exists a corruption in their nature which makes them unworthy of Him. It is equally important for men to know both of these points; it is equally dangerous for man to know God without knowing his own wretchedness and to know his wretchedness without knowing the Redeemer Who can heal him of it. Knowledge of but a single one of these produces either the pride of the philosophers who have known God but not their wretchedness or the despair of the atheists who know their wretchedness without Redeemer.

And so, just as it belongs equally to man's necessity to know these two points, so also it belongs no less to God's mercy to make them known to us. The Christian religion accomplishes this; it is in this that it consists.

Let us examine the disposition of the world from that point of view, and let us see whether all things do not tend towards proving the two principal points of this religion: Jesus Christ is the object of all things and the center to which all things tend. Who knows Him, knows the reason of all things.

Those who fall into error do so simply because they fail to see one of these two things. We can indeed know God fully without a knowledge of our wretchedness and our wretchedness without God; but we cannot know Jesus Christ without knowing at one and the same time both God and our wretchedness.

And that is the reason why I shall not undertake here to prove by natural arguments either the existence of God, or the Trinity, or the immortality of the soul or any thing of like nature; not only because I should not feel clever enough to find in nature wherewith to convince hardened atheists, but also because that knowledge, without Jesus Christ, is futile and fruitless. Even though a man were to be fully satisfied that the proportions of numbers are truths immaterial, eternal and dependent on a first truth in which they subsist and which is called God, I should not consider him much advanced towards his own salvation.

The God of the Christians is not a God Who is merely the author of geometrical truths and of the disposition of the elements; that is the position of the pagans and epicureans. He is not simply a God Who exercises His Providence on the life and goods of men to confer a prosperous succession of years on those who adore Him; that is the portion of the Jews. But the God of Abraham, the God of Isaac, the God of Jacob, the God of the Christians, is a God of love and solace, a God Who fills the soul and the heart of those whom He possesses, a God Who impresses on them interiorly a sense of their wretchedness and His own infinite mercy; a God Who desires to unite Himself to their inmost soul; Who fills that soul with humility, joy, trust and love; Who renders them incapable of any other end than Himself.

All who seek God outside Jesus Christ, and who halt in nature, either find no light to satisfy them, or they happen to contrive a method of knowing God and of serving Him without a Mediator, and thereby fall either into atheism or deism, two things almost equally loathsome to the Christian religion.

Without Jesus Christ, the world would not subsist; for it would be necessary either that it be destroyed or that it be as it were a hell.

If the world existed to teach man about God, His divinity would shine forth therein on all sides in an unquestionable way; but, since it exists only through Jesus Christ and for Jesus Christ, and to apprise men of their corruption and redemption, everything shows forth in it the proofs of these two truths.

What appears therein testifies neither to a complete exclusion nor to a manifest presence of divinity, but to the presence of a hidden God. Everything declares forth this characteristic.

Shall that sole person who knows nature know it simply to be wretched? shall that sole person who has knowledge of it be the sole wretch?

It should not be that he sees nothing whatsoever; he must not see, moreover, enough of it for him to believe that he possesses it; but he must see enough of it to know that he has lost it, because, to know that it is lost, one must see and not see; and that is exactly the state wherein nature has placed him.

Whatever course he may take, I shall not leave him at rest . . .

It is true then that everything apprises man of his condition, but the fact must be clearly understood: because it is not true that everything reveals God and it is not true that everything veils God. But it is at once true that He conceals Himself from those who tempt Him and that He reveals Himself to those who seek Him; for men are at once unworthy of God and capable of God; unworthy because of their corruption, and capable by their first nature.

What shall we infer from all our obscurities if not our unworthiness?

If nothing belonging to God had ever appeared, this eternal privation would be equivocal and might be referred to the want of all divinity as well as to the unworthiness of man to know it. But the fact that He does appear, at times, and not continually, removes the equivocation. If He appears but once, He exists eternally; and so from this we can infer only that there is a God and that men are unworthy of Him.

We understand neither the glorious state of Adam, nor the nature of his sin, nor the transmission of it that has been realized in us. These are matters that took place in a state of a nature wholly different from ours, and that surpass the state of our present capacity.

The knowledge of all this is futile as a means of setting ourselves free of it; and all that it matters for us to know is that we are wretched, corrupted, separated from God, but redeemed by Jesus Christ; and of this we have admirable proofs on earth.

Thus the two proofs of corruption and redemption are verified by the impious who live in indifference to religion and by the Jews who are its irreconcilable enemies.

There are two ways of proving the truths of our religion: one by the power of reason, the other by the authority of the one speaking.

No use is made of the latter but only of the former. We do not say: "We must believe that because the Scripture which says it is divine"; but we do say that we must believe because of such and such a reason, which are but weak arguments since reason is pliable in every direction.

There is nothing on earth that does not show forth either the wretchedness of man or the mercy of God, either the powerlessness of man without God or the power of man with God.

To see that they are condemned by their own reason with which they have aspired to condemn the Christian religion will be one of the mortifications of the damned.

Prophecies, even miracles and the proofs of our religion are not of such a nature that they can be said to be absolutely convincing. But they are also such that it cannot be said that to believe them is to go contrary to reason. Thus there is evidence and obscurity, to enlighten some and to becloud others. But the evidence is such that it surpasses or at least equals the evidence of the contrary. The result is that reason is not able to determine not to follow it; and thus it can be only lust and malice of heart. In this way there is sufficient evidence to condemn and not enough to convince; so that it seems that, in those who do pursue it, it is grace and not reason which is the cause of their pursuit; and in those who avoid it, it is lust and not reason which is the cause of their evasion.

Vere discipuli, vere Israelita, vere liberi, vere cibus.

Recognize, therefore, the truth of religion in the very obscurity of religion, in the little light that we have of it, in the indifference that we have to know it.

We understand the works of God not at all unless we take it as a principle that He has willed to blind some and to enlighten others.

That God willed to hide Himself. — If there were but one religion, God would be very manifest in it. The same, if there were martyrs only in our religion.

Since God has thus concealed Himself, every religion that does not proclaim that God is hidden is not true; and every religion that does not account for that fact is not instructive. Ours does all this: *Vere tu es Deus absconditus.*[15]

[15] *Isa.* xlv, 15.

If there were no obscurity, man would not be conscious at all of his corruption; if there were no light, man would have no hope of a remedy. Thus, it is not only right but profitable for us that God be partly concealed and partly revealed, since it is equally dangerous for man to know God without a knowledge of his wretchedness and to know his wretchedness without a knowledge of God.

This religion, which is so great in miracles, saints, holy, spotless, blameless people; learned and great witnesses; martyrs; constituted kings (David); Isaias, prince of the blood—which is so great in science, after it has displayed all its miracles and all its wisdom, it condemns all that and declares that it possesses neither wisdom nor signs but the Cross and folly.

For those who by these signs and this wisdom have deserved your confidence and have proven their character to you, declare to you that nothing of all this can change us and make us capable of knowing and loving God but the virtue of the folly of the Cross, without wisdom and without signs, and not at all the signs without this virtue. So our religion is folly considered in its effective cause and wise considered in the wisdom which leads to it.

JOHN HENRY CARDINAL NEWMAN

APOLOGIA PRO VITA SUA

+‡+

> I believe the whole revealed dogma as taught by the
> Apostles, as committed by the Apostles to the Church,
> and as declared by the Church to me.

BORN in London (1801), Newman studied at Oxford, where he
was fellow and tutor of Oriel College. His genius is almost universal, and in many ways he dominates English thought in the
nineteenth century. Student of the ancients and the Fathers, controversialist and preacher, Newman has a spiritual delicacy that
is reminiscent of St. Anselm. In 1841, with *Tract 90,* he came to
a major cross-road, which marked the beginning of his journey
from Anglicanism to Catholicism. He was received into the Catholic
Church on October 8, 1845, was ordained priest some two years
later, and spent his life in the Oratory that he founded in 1848
near Birmingham. In 1879 Pope Leo XIII made him a cardinal.
Newman died on August 11, 1890.

His was a full and apostolic life. The *Essay on the Development
of Christian Doctrine* was written in 1843. The *Apologia Pro Vita
Sua* belongs to the year 1864. Occasioned by some famous barbed
remarks of Charles Kingsley, the *Apologia* is one of Newman's
greatest works. *The Grammar of Assent* (1870) is an introduction
to the reasonableness of Catholic belief, while the equally well-
known *Idea of a University* (1873) is a much-discussed plan for
a liberal arts college. Nor is this all, for I have said nothing of

Newman as a student of Christian history, as a man of letters and as a poet.

The present selection from the *Apologia* records Newman's beliefs and opinions after he had answered the great questions on the nature and role of the Church as the custodian of the divine revelation.

v [v i i]

Position of My Mind since 1845

ROM THE TIME THAT I BECAME A CATHOLIC OF course I have no further history of my religious opinions to narrate. In saying this, I do not mean to say that my mind has been idle, or that I have given up thinking on theological subjects; but that I have had no variations to record, and have had no anxiety of heart whatever. I have been in perfect peace and contentment; I never have had one doubt. I was not conscious to myself, on my conversion, of any change, intellectual or moral, wrought in my mind. I was not conscious of firmer faith in the fundamental truths of Revelation, or of more self-command; I had not more fervour; but it was like coming into port after a rough sea; and my happiness on that score remains to this day without interruption.

Nor had I any trouble about receiving those additional articles, which are not found in the Anglican Creed. Some of them I believed already, but not any one of them was a trial to me. I made a profession of them upon my reception with the greatest ease, and I have the same ease in believing them now. I am far of course from denying that every article of the Christian Creed, whether as held by Catholics or by Protestants, is beset with intellectual difficulties;

and it is simple fact, that, for myself, I cannot answer those difficulties. Many persons are very sensitive of the difficulties of Religion; I am as sensitive of them as any one; but I have never been
able to see a connexion between apprehending those difficulties,
however keenly, and multiplying them to any extent, and on the
other hand doubting the doctrines to which they are attached. Ten
thousand difficulties do not make one doubt, as I understand the
subject; difficulty and doubt are incommensurate. There of course
may be difficulties in the evidence; but I am speaking of difficulties
intrinsic to the doctrines themselves, or to their relations with each
other. A man may be annoyed that he cannot work out a mathematical problem, of which the answer is or is not given to him,
without doubting that it admits of an answer, or that a certain particular answer is the true one. Of all points of faith, the being of a
God is, to my own apprehension, encompassed with most difficulty,
and yet borne in upon our minds with most power.

People say that the doctrine of Transubstantiation is difficult to
believe; I did not believe the doctrine till I was a Catholic. I had
no difficulty in believing it, as soon as I believed that the Catholic
Roman Church was the oracle of God, and that she had declared
this doctrine to be part of the original revelation. It is difficult, impossible, to imagine, I grant;—but how is it difficult to believe?
Yet Macaulay thought it so difficult to believe, that he had need of
a believer in it of talents as eminent as Sir Thomas More, before he
could bring himself to conceive that the Catholics of an enlightened age could resist "the overwhelming force of the argument
against it." "Sir Thomas More," he says, "is one of the choice speci-
mens of wisdom and virtue; and the doctrine of Transubstantiation
is a kind of proof charge. A faith which stands that test, will stand
any test." But for myself, I cannot indeed prove it, I cannot tell
how it is; but I say, "Why should it not be? What's to hinder it?
What do I know of substance or matter? just as much as the greatest
philosophers, and that is nothing at all";—so much is this the case,
that there is a rising school of philosophy now, which considers
phenomena to constitute the whole of our knowledge in physics.
The Catholic doctrine leaves phenomena alone. It does not say that
the phenomena go; on the contrary, it says that they remain; nor
does it say that the same phenomena are in several places at once.

It deals with what no one on earth knows any thing about, the material substances themselves. And, in like manner, of that majestic Article of the Anglican as well as of the Catholic Creed,—the doctrine of the Trinity in Unity. What do I know of the Essence of the Divine Being? I know that my abstract idea of three is simply incompatible with my idea of one; but when I come to the question of concrete fact, I have no means of proving that there is not a sense in which one and three can equally be predicated of the Incommunicable God.

But I am going to take upon myself the responsibility of more than the mere Creed of the Church; as the parties accusing me are determined I shall do. They say, that now, in that I am a Catholic, though I may not have offences of my own against honesty to answer for, yet, at least, I am answerable for the offences of others, of my co-religionists, of my brother priests, of the Church herself. I am quite willing to accept the responsibility; and, as I have been able, as I trust, by means of a few words, to dissipate, in the minds of all those who do not begin with disbelieving me, the suspicion with which so many Protestants start, in forming their judgment of Catholics, viz. that our Creed is actually set up in inevitable superstition and hypocrisy, as the original sin of Catholicism; so now I will proceed, as before, identifying myself with the Church and vindicating it,—not of course denying the enormous mass of sin and error which exists of necessity in that world-wide multiform Communion,—but going to the proof of this one point, that its system is in no sense dishonest, and that therefore the upholders and teachers of that system, as such, have a claim to be acquitted in their own persons of that odious imputation.

Starting then with the being of a God (which, as I have said, is as certain to me as the certainty of my own existence, though when I try to put the grounds of that certainty into logical shape I find a difficulty in doing so in mood and figure to my satisfaction,) look out of myself into the world of men, and there I see a sight which fills me with unspeakable distress. The world seems simply to give the lie to that great truth, of which my whole being is so full; and the effect upon me is, in consequence, as a matter of necessity, as confusing as if it denied that I am in existence myself. If I looked into a mirror, and did not see my face, I should have the sort of feeling which actually comes upon me, when I look into this living busy world, and see no reflexion of its Creator. This is, to me, one of those great difficulties of this absolute primary truth, to which I referred just now. Were it not for this voice, speaking so clearly in my conscience and my heart, I should be an atheist, or a pantheist, or a polytheist when I looked into the world. I am speaking for myself only; and I am far from denying the real force of the arguments in proof of a God, drawn from the general facts of human society and the course of history, but these do not warm me or enlighten me; they do not take away the winter of my desolation, or make the buds unfold and the leaves grow within me, and my moral being rejoice. The sight of the world is nothing else than the prophet's scroll, full of *lamentations, and mourning, and woe.*

To consider the world in its length and breadth, its various history, the many races of man, their starts, their fortunes, their mutual alienation, their conflicts; and then their ways, habits, governments, forms of worship; their enterprises, their aimless courses, their random achievements and acquirements, the impotent conclusion of long-standing facts, the tokens so faint and broken of a superintending design, the blind evolution of what turn out to be great powers or truths, the progress of things, as if from unreasoning elements, not towards final causes, the greatness and littleness of man, his far-reaching aims, his short duration, the curtain hung over his futurity, the disappointments of life, the defeat of good, the success of evil, physical pain, mental anguish, the prevalence and intensity of sin, the pervading idolatries, the corruptions, the dreary hopeless irreligion, that condition of the whole race, so fearfully yet exactly described in the Apostle's words, *having no hope and without God in the world,*—all this is a vision to dizzy and appal; and inflicts upon the mind the sense of a profound mystery, which is absolutely beyond human solution.

What shall be said to this heart-piercing, reason-bewildering fact? I can only answer, that either there is no Creator, or this living society of men is in a true sense discarded from His presence. Did I see a boy of good make and mind, with the tokens on him of a refined nature, cast upon the world without provision, unable to say whence he came, his birth-place or his family connexions, I should conclude that there was some mystery connected with his history, and that he was one, of whom, from one cause or other, his parents were ashamed. Thus only should I be able to account for the contrast between the promise and the condition of his being. And so I argue about the world;—*if* there be a God, *since* there is a God, the human race is implicated in some terrible aboriginal calamity. It is out of joint with the purposes of its Creator. This is a fact, a fact as true as the fact of its existence; and thus the doctrine of what is theologically called original sin becomes to me almost as certain as that the world exists, and as the existence of God.

And now, supposing it were the blessed and loving will of the Creator to interfere in this anarchical condition of things, what are we to suppose would be the methods which might be necessarily or naturally involved in His purpose of mercy? Since the world is in so abnormal a state, surely it would be no surprise to me, if the interposition were of necessity equally extraordinary—or what is called miraculous. But that subject does not directly come into the scope of my present remarks. Miracles as evidence, involve a process of reason, or an argument; and of course I am thinking of some mode of interference which does not immediately run into argument. I am rather asking what must be the face-to-face antagonist, by which to withstand and baffle the fierce energy of passion and the all-corroding, all-dissolving skepticism of the intellect in religious inquiries? I have no intention at all of denying, that truth is the real object of our reason, and that, if it does not attain to truth, either the premiss or the process is in fault; but I am not speaking here of right reason, but of reason as it acts in fact and concretely in fallen man. I know that even the unaided reason, when correctly exercised, leads to a belief in God, in the immortality of the soul, and in a future retribution; but I am considering the faculty of reason actually and historically; and in this point of view, I do not think I am wrong in saying that its tendency is towards a simple unbelief in matters of religion. No truth, however sacred, can stand against it, in the long run; and hence it is that in the pagan world, when our Lord came, the last traces of the religious knowledge of former times were all but disappearing from those portions of the world in which the intellect had been active and had had a career.

And in these latter days, in like manner, outside the Catholic Church things are tending,—with far greater rapidity than in that old time from the circumstance of the age,—to atheism in one shape or other. What a scene, what a prospect, does the whole of Europe present at this day! and not only Europe, but every government and every civilization through the world, which is under the influence of the European mind! Especially, for it most concerns us, how sorrowful, in the view of religion, even taken in its most elementary, most attenuated form, is the spectacle presented to us by the educated intellect of England, France, and Germany! Lovers of their country and of their race, religious men, external to the Catholic Church, have attempted various expedients to arrest fierce wilful human nature in its onward course, and to bring it into subjection. The necessity of some form of religion for the interests of humanity, has been generally acknowledged: but where was the concrete representative of things invisible, which would have the force and the toughness necessary to be a breakwater against the deluge? Three centuries ago the establishment of religion, material, legal and social, was generally adopted as the best expedient for the purpose, in those countries which separated from the Catholic Church; and for a long time it was successful; but now the crevices of those establishments are admitting the enemy. Thirty years ago, education was relied upon: ten years ago there was a hope that wars would cease for ever, under the influence of commercial enterprise and the reign of the useful and fine arts; but will any one venture to say that there is any thing anywhere on this earth, which will afford a fulcrum for us, whereby to keep the earth from moving onwards?

The judgment, which experience passes whether on establishments or on education, as a means of maintaining religious truth in this anarchical world, must be extended even to Scripture, though Scripture be divine. Experience proves surely that the Bible does not answer a purpose for which it was never intended. It may be accidentally the means of the conversion of individuals; but a book, after all, cannot make a stand against the wild living intellect of man, and in this day it begins to testify, as regards its own structure and contents, to the power of that universal solvent, which is so successfully acting upon religious establishments.

Supposing then it to be the Will of the Creator to interfere in human affairs, and to make provisions for retaining in the world a knowledge of Himself, so definite and distinct as to be proof against the energy of human skepticism, in such a case,—I am far from saying that there was no other way,—but there is nothing to surprise the mind, if He should think fit to introduce a power into the world, invested with the prerogative of infallibility in religious matters. Such a provision would be a direct, immediate, active, and prompt means of withstanding the difficulty; it would be an instrument suited to the need; and, when I find that this is the very claim of the Catholic Church, not only do I feel no difficulty in admitting the idea, but there is a fitness in it, which recommends it to my mind. And thus I am brought to speak of the Church's infallibility, as a provision, adapted by the mercy of the Creator, to preserve religion in the world, and to restrain that freedom of thought, which of course in itself is one of the greatest of our natural gifts, and to rescue it from its own suicidal excesses. And let it be observed that, neither here nor in what follows, shall I have occasion to speak directly of Revelation in its subject-matter, but in reference to the sanction which it gives to truths which may be known independently of it,—as it bears upon the defence of natural religion. I say, that a power, possessed of infallibility in religious teaching, is happily adapted to be a working instrument, in the course of human affairs, for smiting hard and throwing back the immense energy of the aggressive, capricious, untrustworthy intellect:—and in saying this, as in the other things that I have to say, it must still be recollected that I am all along bearing in mind my main purpose, which is a defence of myself.

I am defending myself here from a plausible charge brought against Catholics, as will be seen better as I proceed. The charge is this:—that I, as a Catholic, not only make profession to hold doctrines which I cannot possibly believe in my heart, but that I also believe in the existence of a power on earth, which at its own will imposes upon men any new set of *credenda,* when it pleases, by a claim to infallibility; in consequence, that my own thoughts are not my own property; that I cannot tell that to-morrow I may not have to give up what I hold to-day, and that the necessary effect of such a condition of mind must be a degrading bondage, or a bitter inward rebellion relieving itself in secret infidelity, or the necessity of ignoring the whole subject of religion in a sort of disgust, and of mechanically saying every thing that the Church says, and leaving to others the defence of it. As then I have above spoken of the relation of my mind towards the Catholic Creed, so now I shall speak of the attitude which it takes up in the view of the Church's infallibility.

And first, the initial doctrine of the infallible teacher must be an emphatic protest against the existing state of mankind. Man had rebelled against his Maker. It was this that caused the divine interposition: and to proclaim it must be the first act of the divinely-accredited messenger. The Church must denounce rebellion as of all possible evils the greatest. She must have no terms with it; if she would be true to her Master, she must ban and anathematize it. This is the meaning of a statement of mine, which has furnished matter for one of those special accusations to which I am at present replying: I have, however, no fault at all to confess in regard to it; I have nothing to withdraw, and in consequence I here deliberately repeat it. I said, "The Catholic Church holds it better for the sun and moon to drop from heaven, for the earth to fail, and for all the many millions on it to die of starvation in extremest agony, as far as temporal affliction goes, than that one soul, I will not say, should be lost, but should commit one single venial sin, should tell one wilful untruth, or should steal one poor farthing without excuse." I think the principle here enunciated to be the mere preamble in the formal credentials of the Catholic Church, as an Act of Parliament might begin with a *"Whereas."* It is because of the intensity of the evil which has possession of mankind, that a suitable antagonist has been provided against it; and the initial act of that divinely-commissioned power is of course to deliver her challenge and to defy the enemy. Such a preamble then gives a meaning to her position in the world, and an interpretation to her whole course of teaching and action.

In like manner she has ever put forth, with most energetic distinctness, those other great elementary truths, which either are an explanation of her mission or give a character to her work. She does not teach that human nature is irreclaimable, else wherefore should she be sent? not, that it is to be shattered and reversed, but to be extricated, purified, and restored; not, that it is a mere mass of hopeiess evil, but that it has the promise upon it of great things, and even now, in its present state of disorder and excess, has a virtue and a praise proper to itself. But in the next place she knows and she preaches that such a restoration, as she aims at effecting in it, must be brought about, not simply through certain outward provisions of preaching and teaching, even though they be her own, but from an inward spiritual power or grace imparted directly from above, and of which she is the channel. She has it in charge to rescue human nature from its misery, but not simply by restoring it on its own level, but by lifting it up to a higher level than its own. She recognizes in it real moral excellence though degraded, but she cannot set it free from earth except by exalting it towards heaven. It was for this end that a renovating grace was put into her hands; and therefore from the nature of the gift, as well as from the reasonableness of the case, she goes on, as a further point, to insist, that all true conversion must begin with the first springs of thought, and to teach that each individual man must be in his own person one whole and perfect temple of God, while he is also one of the living stones which build up a visible religious community. And thus the distinctions between nature and grace, and between outward and inward religion, become two further articles in what I have called the preamble of her divine commission.

Such truths as these she vigorously reiterates, and pertinaciously inflicts upon mankind; as to such she observes no half-measures, no economical reserve, no delicacy or prudence. "Ye must be born again," is the simple, direct form of words which she uses after her Divine Master: "your whole nature must be reborn; your passions, and your affections, and your aims, and your conscience, and your will, must all be bathed in a new element, and reconsecrated to your Maker,—and, the last not the least, your intellect." It was for repeating these points of her teaching in my own way, that certain passages of one of my Volumes have been brought into the general accusation which has been made against any religious opinions. The writer has said that I was demented if I believed, and unprincipled if I did not believe, in my own statement, that a lazy, ragged, filthy, story-telling beggar woman, if chaste, sober, cheerful, and religious, had a prospect of heaven, such as was absolutely closed to an accomplished statesman, or lawyer, or noble, be he ever so just, upright, generous, honourable, and conscientious, unless he had also some portion of the divine Christian graces;—yet I should have thought myself defended from criticism by the words which our Lord used to the chief priests, *The publicans and harlots go into the kingdom of God before you.* And I was subjected again to the same alternative of imputations, for having ventured to say that consent to an unchaste wish was indefinitely more heinous than any lie viewed apart from its causes, its motives, and its consequences: though a lie, viewed under the limitation of these conditions, is a random utterance, an almost outward act, not directly from the heart, however disgraceful and despicable it may be, however prejudicial to the social contract, however deserving of public reprobation; whereas, we have the express words of our Lord to the doctrine that "whoso looketh on a woman to lust after her, hath committed adultery with her already in his heart." On the strength of these texts, I have surely as much right to believe in these doctrines which have caused so much surprise, as to believe in original sin, or that there is a supernatural revelation, or that a Divine Person suffered, or that punishment is eternal.

Passing now from what I have called the preamble of that grant of power, which is made to the Church, to that power itself, Infallibility, I premise two brief remarks:—1. on the one hand, I am not here determining any thing about the essential seat of that power, because that is a question doctrinal, not historical and practical; 2. nor, on the other hand, am I extending the direct subject-matter, over which that power of Infallibility has jurisdiction, beyond religious opinion:—and now as to the power itself.

This power, viewed in its fullness, is as tremendous as the giant evil which has called for it. It claims, when brought into exercise but in the legitimate manner, for otherwise of course it is but quiescent, to know for certain the very meaning of every portion of that Divine Message in detail, which was committed by our Lord to His Apostles. It claims to know its own limits, and to decide what it can determine absolutely and what it cannot. It claims, moreover, to have a hold upon statements not directly religious, so far as this,—to determine whether they indirectly relate to religion, and, according to its own definitive judgment, to pronounce whether or not, in a particular case, they are simply consistent with revealed truth. It claims to decide magisterially, whether as within its own province or not, that such and such statements are or are not prejudicial to the *Depositum* of faith, in their spirit or in their consequences, and to allow them, or condemn and forbid them, accordingly. It claims to impose silence at will on any matters, or controversies, of doctrine, which on its own *ipse dixit,* it pronounces to be dangerous, or inexpedient, or inopportune. It claims that, whatever may be the judgment of Catholics upon such acts, these acts should be received by them with those outward marks of reverence, submission, and loyalty, which Englishmen, for instance, pay to the presence of their sovereign, without expressing any criticism on them on the ground that in their matter they are inexpedient, or in their manner violent or harsh. And lastly, it claims to have the right of inflicting spiritual punishment, of cutting off from the ordinary channels of the divine life, and of simply excommunicating, those who refuse to submit themselves to its formal declarations. Such is the infallibility lodged in the Catholic Church, viewed in the concrete, as clothed and surrounded by the appendages of its high sovereignty: it is, to repeat what I said above, a supereminent prodigious power sent upon earth to encounter and master a giant evil.

And now, having thus described it, I profess my own absolute submission to its claim. I believe the whole revealed dogma as taught by the Apostles, as committed by the Apostles to the Church, and as declared by the Church to me. I receive it, as it is infallibly interpreted by the authority to whom it is thus committed, and (implicitly) as it shall be, in like manner, further interpreted by that same authority till the end of time. I submit, moreover, to the universally received traditions of the Church, in which lies the matter of those new dogmatic definitions which are from time to time made, and which in all times are the clothing and the illustration of the Catholic dogma as already defined. And I submit myself to those other decisions of the Holy See, theological or not, through the organs which it has itself appointed, which, waiving the question of their infallibility, on the lowest ground come to me with a claim to be accepted and obeyed. Also, I consider that, gradually and in the course of ages, Catholic inquiry has taken certain definite shapes, and has thrown itself into the form of a science, with a method and a phraseology of its own, under the intellectual handling of great minds, such as St. Athanasius, St. Augustine, and St. Thomas; and I feel no temptation at all to break in pieces the great legacy of thought thus committed to us for these latter days.

All this being considered as the profession which I make *ex animo,* as for myself, so also on the part of the Catholic body, as far as I know it, it will at first sight be said that the restless intellect of our common humanity is utterly weighed down, to the repression of all independent effort and action whatever, so that, if this is to be the mode of bringing it into order, it is brought into order only to be destroyed. But this is far from the result, far from what I conceive to be the intention of that high Providence who has provided a great remedy for a great evil,—far from borne out by the history of the conflict between Infallibility and Reason in the past, and the prospect of it in the future. The energy of the human intellect "does from opposition grow;" it thrives and is joyous, with a tough elastic strength, under the terrible blows of the divinely-fashioned weapon, and is never so much itself as when it has lately been overthrown. It is the custom with Protestant writers to consider that, whereas there are two great principles in action in the history of religion, Authority and Private Judgment, they have all the Private Judgment to themselves, and we have the full inheritance and the superincumbent oppression of Authority. But this is not so; it is the vast Catholic body itself, and it only, which affords an arena for both combatants in that awful, never-dying duel. It is necessary for the very life of religion, viewed in its large operations and its history, that the warfare should be incessantly carried on. Every exercise of Infallibility is brought out into act by an intense and varied operation of the Reason, both as its ally and as its opponent, and provokes again, when it has done its work, a reaction of Reason against it; and, as in a civil polity the State exists and endures by means of the rivalry and collision, the encroachments and defeats of its constituent parts, so in like manner Catholic Christendom is no simple exhibition of religious absolutism, but presents a continuous picture of Authority and Private Judgment alternately advancing and retreating as the ebb and flow of the tide;— it is a vast assemblage of human beings with wilful intellects and wild passions, brought together into one by the beauty and the

Majesty of a Superhuman Power,—into what may be called a large reformatory or training-school, not as if into a hospital or into a prison, not in order to be sent to bed, not to be buried alive, but (if I may change my metaphor) brought together as if into some moral factory, for the melting, refining, and moulding, by an incessant, noisy process, of the raw material of human nature, so excellent, so dangerous, so capable of divine purposes.

St. Paul says in one place that his Apostolical power is given him to edification, and not to destruction. There can be no better account of the Infallibility of the Church. It is a supply for a need, and it does not go beyond that need. Its object is, and its effect also, not to enfeeble the freedom or vigour of human thought in religious speculation, but to resist and control its extravagance. What have been its great works? All of them in the distinct province of theology:—to put down Arianism, Eutychianism, Pelagianism, Manichaeism, Lutheranism, Jansenism. Such is the broad result of its action in the past;—and now as to the securities which are given us that so it ever will act in time to come.

First, Infallibility cannot act outside of a definite circle of thought, and it must in all its decisions, or *definitions,* as they are called, profess to be keeping within it. The great truths of the moral law, of natural religion, and of Apostolical faith, are both its boundary and its foundation. It must not go beyond them, and it must ever appeal to them. Both its subject-matter, and its articles in that subject-matter, are fixed. And it must ever profess to be guided by Scripture and by tradition. It must refer to the particular Apostolic truth which it is enforcing, or (what is called) *defining.* Nothing, then, can be presented to me, in time to come, as part of the faith, but what I ought already to have received, and hitherto have been kept from receiving, (if so,) merely because it has not been brought home to me. Nothing can be imposed upon me different in kind from what I hold already,—much less contrary to it. The new truth which is promulgated, if it is to be called new, must be at least homogeneous, cognate, implicit, viewed relatively to the old truth. It must be what I may even have guessed, or wished, to be included in the Apostolic revelation; and at least it will be of such a character, that my thoughts readily concur in it or coalesce with it, as soon as I hear it. Perhaps I and others actually have always believed it, and the only question which is now decided in my behalf, is, that I have henceforth the satisfaction of having to believe, that I have only been holding all along what the Apostles held before me.

Let me take the doctrine which Protestants consider our greatest difficulty, that of the Immaculate Conception. Here I entreat the reader to recollect my main drift, which is this. I have no difficulty in receiving the doctrine; and that, because it so intimately harmonizes with that circle of recognised dogmatic truths, into which it has been recently received;—but if I have no difficulty, why may not another have no difficulty also? why may not a hundred? a thousand? Now I am sure that Catholics in general have not any intellectual difficulty at all on the subject of the Immaculate Conception; and that there is no reason why they should. Priests have no difficulty. You tell me that they *ought* to have a difficulty;—but they have not. Be large-minded enough to believe, that men may reason and feel very differently from yourselves; how is it that men, when left to themselves, fall into such various forms of religion, except that there are various types of mind among them, very distinct from each other? From my testimony then about myself, if you believe it, judge of others also who are Catholics: we do not find the difficulties which you do in the doctrines which we hold; we have no intellectual difficulty in that doctrine in particular, which you call a novelty of this day. We priests need not be hypocrites, though we be called upon to believe in the Immaculate Conception. To that large class of minds, who believe in Christianity after our manner,—in the particular temper, spirit, and light (whatever word is used), in which Catholics believe it,—there is no burden at all in holding that the Blessed Virgin was conceived without original sin; indeed, it is a simple fact to say, that Catholics have not come to believe it because it is defined, but that it was defined because they believed it.

So far from the definition in 1854 being a tyrannical infliction on the Catholic world, it was received everywhere on its promulgation with the greatest enthusiasm.

It was in consequence of the unanimous petition, presented from all parts of the Church to the Holy See, in behalf of an *ex cathedrâ* declaration that the doctrine was Apostolic, that it was declared so to be. I never heard of one Catholic having difficulties in receiving the doctrine, whose faith on other grounds, was not already suspicious. Of course there were grave and good men, who were made anxious by the doubt whether it could be formally proved to be Apostolical either by Scripture or tradition, and who accordingly, though believing it themselves, did not see how it could be defined by authority and imposed upon all Catholics as a matter of faith; but this is another matter. The point in question is, whether the doctrine is a burden. I believe it to be none. So far from it being so, I sincerely think that St. Bernard and St. Thomas, who scrupled at it in their day, had they lived into this, would have rejoiced to accept it for its own sake. Their difficulty, as I view it, consisted in matters of words, ideas, and arguments. They thought the doctrine inconsistent with other doctrines; and those who defended it in that age had not that precision in their view of it, which has been attained by means of the long disputes of the centuries which followed. And in this want of precision lay the difference of opinion, and the controversy.

Now the instance which I have been taking suggests another remark; the number of those (so called) new doctrines will not oppress us, if it takes eight centuries to promulgate even one of them. Such is about the length of time through which the preparation has been carried on for the definition of the Immaculate Conception. This of course is an extraordinary case: but it is difficult to say what is ordinary, considering how few are the formal occasions on which the voice of Infallibility has been solemnly lifted up. It is to the Pope in Ecumenical Council that we look, as to the normal seat of Infallibility: now there have been only eighteen such Councils since Christianity was,—an average of one to a century,—and of these Councils some passed no doctrinal decree at all, others were employed on only one, and many of them were concerned with only elementary points of the Creed. The Council of Trent embraced a large field of doctrine certainly; but I should apply to its Canons a remark contained in that University Sermon of mine, which has been so ignorantly criticized in the Pamphlet which has been the occasion of this Volume;—I there have said that the various verses of the Athanasian Creed are only repetitions in various shapes of one and the same idea; and in like manner, the Tridentine Decrees are not isolated from each other, but are occupied in bringing out in detail, by a number of separate declarations, as if into bodily form, a few necessary truths. I should make the same remark on the various theological censures, promulgated by Popes, which the Church has received, and on their dogmatic decisions generally. I own that at first sight those decisions seem from their number to be a greater burden on the faith of individuals than are the Canons of Councils; still I do not believe that in matter of fact they are so at all, and I give this reason for it:—it is not that a Catholic, layman or priest, is indifferent to the subject, or, from a sort of reckless-ness, will accept any thing that is placed before him, or is willing, like a lawyer, to speak according to his brief, but that in such con-demnations the Holy See is engaged, for the most part, in repu-diating one or two great lines of error, such as Lutheranism or Jansenism, principally ethical not doctrinal, which are divergent from the Catholic mind, and that it is but expressing what any good Catholic, of fair abilities, though unlearned, would say him-self, from common and sound sense, if the matter could be put before him.

Now I will go on in fairness to say what I think *is* the great trial to the Reason, when confronted with that august prerogative of the Catholic Church, of which I have been speaking. I enlarged just now upon the concrete shape and circumstances, under which pure infallible authority presents itself to the Catholic. That authority has the prerogative of an indirect jurisdiction of sub-ject-matters which lie beyond its own proper limits, and it most reasonably has such a jurisdiction. It could not act in its own prov-ince, unless it had a right to act out of it. It could not properly defend religious truth, without claiming for that truth what may be called *pomaeria*; or, to take another illustration, without acting as we act, as a nation, in claiming as our own, not only the land on which we live, but what are called British waters. The Catholic Church claims, not only to judge infallibly on religious questions, but to animadvert on opinions in secular matters which bear upon religion, on matters of philosophy, of science, of literature, of his-tory, and it demands our submission to her claim. It claims to cen-sure books, to silence authors, and to forbid discussions. In this province, taken as a whole, it does not so much speak doctrinally, as enforce measures of discipline. It must of course be obeyed without a word, and perhaps in process of time it will tacitly recede from its own injunctions. In such cases the question of faith does not come in at all; for what is matter of faith is true for all times, and never can be unsaid. Nor does it at all follow, because there is a gift of infallibility in the Catholic Church, that therefore the parties who are in possession of it are in all their proceedings infallible. "O, it is excellent," says the poet, "to have a giant's strength, but tyrannous, to use it like a giant." I think history supplies us with instances in the Church, where legitimate power has been harshly used. To make such admission is no more than saying that the divine treasure, in the words of the Apostle, is "in earthen vessels"; nor does it follow that the substance of the acts of the ruling power is not right and expedient, because its manner may have been faulty. Such high authorities act by means of instruments; we know how such instruments claim for themselves the name of their principals, who thus get the credits of faults which really are not theirs. But granting all this to an extent greater than can with any show of reason be imputed to the ruling power in the Church, what difficulty is there in the fact of this want of prudence or moderation more than can be urged, with far greater justice, against Protestant communities and institutions? What is there in it to make us hypocrites, if it has not that effect upon Protestants? We are called upon, not to profess any thing, but to submit and be silent, as Protestant Churchmen have before now obeyed the royal command to abstain from certain theological questions. Such injunctions as I have been contemplating are laid merely upon our actions, not upon our thoughts. How, for instance, does it tend to make a man a hypocrite, to be forbidden to publish a libel? his thoughts are as free as before: authoritative prohibitions may tease and irritate, but they have no bearing whatever upon the exercise of reason.

So much at first sight; but I will go on to say further, that, in spite of all that the most hostile critic may urge about the encroachments or severities of high ecclesiastics, in times past, in the use of their power, I think that the event has shown after all, that they were mainly in the right, and that those whom they were hard upon were mainly in the wrong. I love, for instance, the name of Origen: I will not listen to the notion that so great a soul was lost; but I

am quite sure that, in the contest between his doctrine and followers and the ecclesiastical power, his opponents were right, and he
was wrong. Yet who can speak with patience of his enemy and
the enemy of St. John Chrysostom, that Theophilus, bishop of
Alexandria? who can admire or revere Pope Vigilius? And here
another consideration presents itself to my thoughts. In reading
ecclesiastical history, when I was an Anglican, it used to be forcibly
brought home to me, how the initial error of what afterwards
became heresy was the urging forward some truth against the prohibition of authority at an unseasonable time. There is a time for
every thing, and many a man desires a reformation of an abuse, or
the fuller development of a doctrine, or the adoption of a particular
policy, but forgets to ask himself whether the right time for it is
come: and, knowing that there is no one who will be doing anything towards its accomplishment in his own lifetime unless he
does it himself, he will not listen to the voice of authority, and he
spoils a good work in his own century, in order that another man,
as yet unborn, may not have the opportunity of bringing it happily
to perfection in the next. He may seem to the world to be nothing
else than a bold champion for the truth and a martyr to free opinion, when he is just one of those persons whom the competent
authority ought to silence; and, though the case may not fall within
that subject-matter in which that authority is infallible, or the formal conditions of the exercise of that gift may be wanting, it is
clearly the duty of authority to act vigorously in the case. Yet its act
will go down to posterity as an instance of a tyrannical interference
with private judgment, and of the silencing of a reformer, and of
a base love of corruption or error; and it will show still less to
advantage, if the ruling power happens in its proceedings to evince
any defect of prudence or consideration. And all those who take the
part of that ruling authority will be considered as time-servers, or
indifferent to the cause of uprightness and truth; while, on the
other hand, the said authority may be accidentally supported by
a violent ultra party, which exalts opinions into dogmas, and has
it principally at heart to destroy every school of thought but its own.

Such a state of things may be provoking and discouraging at the
time, in the case of two classes of persons; of moderate men who
wish to make differences in religious opinion as little as they fairly

can be made; and of such as keenly perceive, and are honestly eager to remedy, existing evils,—evils, of which divines in this or that foreign country know nothing at all, and which even at home, where they exist, it is not every one who has the means of estimating. This is a state of things both of past time and of the present. We live in a wonderful age; the enlargement of the circle of secular knowledge just now is simply a bewilderment, and the more so, because it has the promise of continuing, and that with greater rapidity and more signal results. Now these discoveries, certain or probable, have in matter of fact an indirect bearing upon religious opinions, and the question arises how are the respective claims of revelation and of natural science to be adjusted. Few minds in earnest can remain at ease without some sort of rational grounds for their religious belief; to reconcile theory and fact is almost an instinct of the mind. When then a flood of facts, ascertained or suspected, comes pouring in upon us, with a multitude of others in prospect, all believers in Revelation, be they Catholic or not, are aroused to consider their bearing upon themselves, both for the honour of God, and from tenderness for those many souls who, in consequence of the confident tone of the schools of secular knowledge, are in danger of being led away into a bottomless liberalism of thought.

I am not going to criticize here that vast body of men, in the mass, who at this time would profess to be liberals in religion; and who look towards the discoveries of the age, certain or in progress, as their informants, direct or indirect, as to what they shall think about the unseen and the future. The Liberalism which gives colour to society now, is very different from that character of thought which bore the name thirty or forty years ago. Now it is scarcely a party; it is the educated lay world. When I was young, I knew the word first as giving name to a periodical, set up by Lord Byron and others. Now, as then, I have no sympathy with the philosophy of Byron. Afterwards, Liberalism was the badge of a theological school, of a dry and repulsive character, not very dangerous in itself, though dangerous as opening the door to evils which it did not itself either anticipate or comprehend. At present it is nothing else than that deep, plausible skepticism, of which I spoke above, as

being the development of human reason, as practically exercised
by the natural man.

The Liberal religionists of this day are a very mixed body, and
therefore I am not intending to speak against them. There may be,
and doubtless is, in the hearts of some or many of them a real an-
tipathy or anger against revealed truth, which it is distressing to
think of. Again: in many men of science or literature there may be
an animosity arising from almost a personal feeling; it being a
matter of party, a point of honour, the excitement of a game, or a
satisfaction to the soreness or annoyance occasioned by the acrimony
or narrowness of apologists for religion, to prove that Christianity
or that Scripture is untrustworthy. Many scientific and literary men,
on the other hand, go on, I am confident, in a straightforward impartial way, in their own province and on their own line of thought,
without any disturbance from religious difficulties in themselves,
or any wish at all to give pain to others by the result of their investigations. It would ill become me, as if I were afraid of truth of
any kind, to blame those who pursue secular facts, by means of the
reason which God has given them, to their logical conclusions: or
to be angry with science, because religion is bound in duty to take
cognizance of its teaching. But putting these particular classes of
men aside, as having no special call on the sympathy of the Catholic, of course he does most deeply enter into the feelings of a
fourth and large class of men, in the educated portions of society,
of religious and sincere minds, who are simply perplexed,—frightened or rendered desperate, as the case may be,—by the utter confusion into which late discoveries or speculations have thrown their
most elementary ideas of religion. Who does not feel for such men?
who can have one unkind thought of them? I take up in their
behalf St. Augustine's beautiful words, "Illi in vos saeviant," etc.
Let them be fierce with you who have no experience of the difficulty
with which error is discriminated from truth, and the way of life is
found amid the illusions of the world. How many a Catholic has in
his thoughts followed such men, many of them so good, so true,
so noble! how often has the wish risen in his heart that some one
from among his own people should come forward as the champion
of revealed truth against its opponents! Various persons, Catholic
and Protestant, have asked me to do so myself; but I had several

strong difficulties in the way. One of the greatest is this, that at the moment it is so difficult to say precisely what it is that is to be encountered and overthrown. I am far from denying that scientific knowledge is really growing, but it is by fits and starts; hypotheses rise and fall; it is difficult to anticipate which of them will keep their ground, and what the state of knowledge in relation to them will be from year to year. In this condition of things, it has seemed to me to be very undignified for a Catholic to commit himself to the work of chasing what might turn out to be phantoms, and, in behalf of some special objections, to be ingenious in devising a theory, which, before it was completed, might have to give place to some theory newer still, from the fact that those former objections had already come to naught under the uprisings of others. It seemed to be especially a time, in which Christians had a call to be patient, in which they had no other way of helping those who were alarmed, than that of exhorting them to have a little faith and fortitude, and to "beware," as the poet says, "of dangerous steps." This seemed so clear to me, the more I thought of the matter, as to make me surmise, that, if I attempted what had so little promise in it, I should find that the highest Catholic authority was against the attempt, and that I should have spent my time and my thought, in doing what either it would be imprudent to bring before the public at all, or what, did I do so, would only complicate matters further which were already complicated, without my interference, more than enough. And I interpret recent acts of that authority as fulfilling my expectation; I interpret them as tying the hands of a controversialist, such as I should be, and teaching us that true wisdom, which Moses inculcated on his people, when the Egyptians were pursuing them, "Fear ye not, stand still; the Lord shall fight for you, and ye shall hold your peace." And so far from finding a difficulty in obeying in this case, I have cause to be thankful and to rejoice to have so clear a direction in a matter of difficulty.

But if we would ascertain with correctness the real course of a principle, we must look at it at a certain distance, and as history represents it to us. Nothing carried on by human instruments, but has its irregularities, and affords ground for criticism, when minutely scrutinized in matters of detail. I have been speaking of that aspect of the action of an infallible authority, which is most open to invidious criticism from those who view it from without; I have tried to be fair, in estimating what can be said to its disadvantage, as witnessed at a particular time in the Catholic Church, and now I wish its adversaries to be equally fair in their judgment upon its historical character. Can, then, the infallible authority, with any show of reason, be said in fact to have destroyed the energy of the Catholic intellect? Let it be observed, I have not here to speak of any conflict which ecclesiastical authority has had with science, for this simple reason, that conflict there has been none; and that, because the secular sciences, as they now exist, are a novelty in the world, and there has been no time yet for a history of relations between theology and these new methods of knowledge, and indeed the Church may be said to have kept clear of them, as is proved by the constantly cited case of Galileo. Here "exceptio probat regulam": for it is the one stock argument. Again, I have not to speak of any relations of the Church to the new sciences, because my simple question all along has been whether the assumption of infallibility by the proper authority is adapted to make me a hypocrite, and till that authority passes decrees on pure physical subjects and calls on me to subscribe them, (which it will never do, because it has not the power,) it has no tendency to interfere by any of its acts with my private judgment on these points. The simple question is, whether authority has so acted upon the reason of individuals, that they can have no opinion of their own, and have but an alternative of slavish superstition or secret rebellion of heart; and I think the whole history of theology puts an absolute negative upon such a supposition.

It is hardly necessary to argue out so plain a point. It is individuals, and not the Holy See, that have taken the initiative, and given the lead to the Catholic mind, in theological inquiry. Indeed, it is one of the reproaches urged against the Roman Church, that it has originated nothing, and has only served as a sort of *remora* or brake in the development of doctrine. And it is an objection which I really embrace as a truth; for such I conceive to be the main purpose of its extraordinary gift. It is said, and truly, that the Church of Rome possessed no great mind in the whole period of persecution. Afterwards for a long while, it has not a single doctor to show; St. Leo, its first, is the teacher of one point of doctrine; St. Gregory, who stands at the very extremity of the first age of the Church, has no place in dogma or philosophy. The great luminary of the western world is, as we know, St. Augustine; he, no infallible teacher, has formed the intellect of Christian Europe; indeed to the African Church generally we must look for the best early exposition of Latin ideas. Moreover, of the African divines, the first in order of time, and not the least influential, is the strong-minded and heterodox Tertullian. Nor is the Eastern intellect, as such, without its share in the formation of the Latin teaching. The free thought of Origen is visible in the writings of the Western Doctors, Hilary and Ambrose; and the independent mind of Jerome has enriched his own vigorous commentaries on Scripture, from the stores of the scarcely orthodox Eusebius. Heretical questionings have been transmuted by the living power of the church into salutary truths. The case is the same as regards the Ecumenical Councils. Authority in its most imposing exhibition, grave Bishops, laden with the traditions and rivalries of particular nations or places, have been guided in their decisions by the commanding genius of individuals, sometimes young and of inferior rank. Not that uninspired intellect overruled the super-human gift which was committed to the Council, which would be a self-contradictory assertion, but that in that process of inquiry and deliberation, which ended in an infallible enunciation, individual reason was paramount. Thus Malchion, a mere presbyter, was the instrument of the great Council of Antioch in the third century in meeting and refuting, for the assembled Fathers, the heretical Patriarch of that see. Parallel to this instance is the influence, so well known, of a young deacon, St. Athanasius, with the 318 Fathers at Nicaea. In mediaeval times we read of St. Anselm at Bari, as the champion of the Council there held, against the Greeks. At Trent, the writings of St. Bonaventura, and, what is more to the point, the address of a Priest and theologian, Salmeron, had a critical effect on some of the definitions of dogma. In some of these cases the influence might be partly moral, but in others it was that of a discursive knowledge of ecclesiastical writers, a scientific acquaintance with theology, and a force of thought in the treatment of doctrine.

There are of course intellectual habits which theology does not tend to form, as for instance the experimental, and again the philosophical; but that is because it *is* theology, not because of the gift of infallibility. But, as far as this goes, I think it could be shown that physical science on the other hand, or again mathematical, affords but an imperfect training for the intellect. I do not see then how any objection about the narrowness of theology comes into our question, which simply is, whether the belief in an infallible authority destroys the independence of the mind; and I consider that the whole history of the Church, and especially the history of the theological schools, gives a negative to the accusation. There never was a time when the intellect of the educated class was more active, or rather more restless, than in the middle ages. And then again all through Church history from the first, how slow is authority in interfering! Perhaps a local teacher, or a doctor in some local school, hazards a proposition, and a controversy ensues. It smoulders or burns in one place, no one interposing; Rome simply lets it alone. Then it comes before a Bishop; or some priest, or some professor in some other seat of learning takes it up; and then there is a second stage of it. Then it comes before a University, and it may be condemned by the theological faculty. So the controversy proceeds year after year, and Rome is still silent. An appeal perhaps is next made to a seat of authority inferior to Rome; and then at last after a long while it comes before the supreme power. Meanwhile, the question has been ventilated and turned over and over again, and viewed on every side of it, and authority is called upon to pronounce a decision, which has already been arrived at by reason. But even then, perhaps the supreme authority hesitates to do so, and nothing is determined on the point for years: or so generally and vaguely, that the whole controversy has to be gone through again, before it is ultimately determined. It is manifest how a mode of proceeding, such as this, tends not only to the liberty, but to the courage, of the individual theologian or controversialist. Many a man has ideas, which he hopes are true, and useful for his day, but he is not confident about them, and wishes to have them discussed. He is willing, or rather would be thankful, to give them up, if they can be proved to be erroneous or dangerous, and by means of controversy he obtains his end. He is answered, and he yields; or on the contrary he finds that he is considered safe. He would not dare to do this, if he knew an authority, which was supreme and final, was watching every word he said, and made signs of assent or dissent to each sentence, as he uttered it. Then indeed he would be fighting, as the Persian soldiers, under the lash, and the freedom of his intellect might truly be said to be beaten out of him. But this has not been so:—I do not mean to say that, when controversies run high, in schools or even in small portions of the Church, an interposition may not advisably take place; and again, questions may be of that urgent nature, that an appeal must, as a matter of duty, be made at once to the highest authority in the Church; but if we look into the history of controversy, we shall find, I think, the general run of things to be such as I have represented it. Zosimus treated Pelagius and Caelestius with extreme forbearance; St. Gregory VII was equally indulgent with Berengarius:—by reason of the very power of the Popes they have commonly been slow and moderate in their use of it.

And here again is a further shelter for the legitimate exercise of the reason:—the multitude of nations which are within the fold of the Church will be found to have acted for its protection, against any narrowness, on the supposition of narrowness, in the various authorities at Rome, with whom lies the practical decision of controverted questions. How have the Greek traditions been respected and provided for in the later Ecumenical Councils, in spite of the countries that held them being in a state of schism! There are important points of doctrine which have been (humanly speaking) exempted from the infallible sentence, by the tenderness with which its instruments, in framing it, have treated the opinions of particular places. Then, again, such national influences have a providential effect in moderating the bias which the local influences of Italy may exert upon the See of St. Peter. It stands to reason that, as the Gallican Church has in it a French element, so Rome must have in it an element of Italy; and it is no prejudice to the zeal and devotion with which we submit ourselves to the Holy See to admit this plainly. It seems to me, as I have been saying, that Catholicity is not only one of the notes of the Church, but, according to the divine purposes, one of its securities. I think it would be a very serious evil, which Divine Mercy avert! that the Church should be contracted in Europe within the range of particular nationalities. It is a great idea to introduce Latin civilization into America, and to improve the Cath-

olics there by the energy of French devotedness; but I trust that all
European races will ever have a place in the Church, and assuredly
I think that the loss of the English, not to say the German element,
in its composition has been a most serious misfortune. And certainly, if there is one consideration more than another which should
make us English grateful to Pius the Ninth, it is that, by giving us
a Church of our own, he has prepared the way for our own habits
of mind, our own manner of reasoning, our own tastes, and our
own virtues, finding a place and thereby a sanctification, in the
Catholic Church.

There is only one other subject, which I think it necessary to
introduce here, as bearing upon the vague suspicions which are
attached in this country to the Catholic Priesthood. It is one of
which my accusers have before now said much,—the charge of
reserve and economy. They found it in no slight degree on what I
have said on the subject in my History of the Arians, and in a note
upon one of my Sermons in which I refer to it. The principle of
Reserve is also advocated by an admirable writer in two numbers
of the *Tracts for the Times,* and of these I was the Editor.

Now, as to the Economy itself, it is founded upon the words of
our Lord, "Cast not your pearls before swine"; and it was observed
by the early Christians, more or less, in their intercourse with the
heathen populations among whom they lived. In the midst of the
abominable idolatries and impurities of that fearful time, the Rule
of the Economy was an imperative duty. But that rule, at least as I
have explained and recommended it, in anything that I have written, did not go beyond (1) the concealing the truth when we could
do so without deceit, (2) stating it only partially, and (3) representing it under the nearest form possible to a learner or inquirer,
when he could not possibly understand it exactly. I conceive that
to draw Angels with wings is an instance of the third of these economical modes; and to avoid the question, "Do Christians believe
in a Trinity?" by answering, "They believe in only one God,"
would be an instance of the second. As to the first, it is hardly an
Economy, but comes under what is called the *Disciplina Arcani.*
The second and third economical modes Clement calls *lying;* meaning that a partial truth is in some sense a lie. as is also a represent-

ative truth. And this, I think, is about the long and the short of the ground of the accusation which has been so violently urged against me, as being a patron of the Economy.

Of late years I have come to think, as I believe most writers do, that Clement meant more than I have said. I used to think he used the word "lie" as an hyperbole, but I now believe that he, as other early Fathers, thought that, under certain circumstances, it was lawful to tell a lie. This doctrine I never maintained, though I used to think, as I do now, that the theory of the subject is surrounded with considerable difficulty; and it is not strange that I should say so, considering that great English writers declare without hesitation that in certain extreme cases, as to save life, honour, or even property, a lie is allowable. And thus I am brought to the direct question of truth, and of the truthfulness of Catholic priests generally in their dealings with the world, as bearing on the general question of their honesty, and of their internal belief in their religious professions.

It would answer no purpose, and it would be departing from the line of writing which I have been observing all along, if I entered into any formal discussion on this question; what I shall do here, as I have done in the foregoing pages, is to give my own testimony on the matter in question, and there to leave it. Now first I will say, that, when I became a Catholic, nothing struck me more at once than the English out-spoken manner of the Priests. It was the same at Oscott, at Old Hall Green, at Ushaw; there was nothing of that smoothness, or mannerism, which is commonly imputed to them, and they were more natural and unaffected than many an Anglican clergyman. The many years, which have passed since, have only confirmed my first impressions. I have ever found it in the priests of this Diocese; did I wish to point out a straightforward Englishman, I should instance the Bishop, who has, to our great benefit, for so many years presided over it.

And next, I was struck, when I had more opportunity of judging of the Priests, by the simple faith in the Catholic Creed and system, of which they always gave evidence, and which they never seemed to feel, in any sense at all, to be a burden. And now that I have been in the Church nineteen years, I cannot recollect hearing of a single instance in England of an infidel priest. Of course there are men from time to time, who leave the Catholic Church for another religion, but I am speaking of cases when a man keeps a fair outside to the world and is a hollow hypocrite in his heart.

I wonder that the self-devotion of our priests does not strike a Protestant in this point of view. What do they gain by professing a Creed, in which, if their enemies are to be credited, they really do not believe? What is their reward for committing themselves to a life of self-restraint and toil, and perhaps to a premature and miserable death? The Irish fever cut off between Liverpool and Leeds thirty priests and more, young men in the flower of their days, old men who seemed entitled to some quiet time after their long toil. There was a bishop cut off in the North; but what had a man of his ecclesiastical rank to do with the drudgery and danger of sick calls, except that Christian faith and charity constrained him? Priests volunteered for the dangerous service. It was the same with them on the first coming of the cholera, that mysterious awe-inspiring infliction. If they did not heartily believe in the Creed of the Church, then I will say that the remark of the Apostle had its fullest illustration:—*If in this life only we have hope in Christ, we are of all men most miserable.* What could support a set of hypocrites in the presence of a deadly disorder, one of them following another in long order up the forlorn hope, and one after another perishing? And such, I may say, in its substance is every Mission-Priest's life. He is ever ready to sacrifice himself for his people. Night and day, sick or well himself, in all weathers, off he is, on the news of a sick call. The fact of a parishioner dying without the Sacraments through his fault is terrible to him; why terrible, if he has not a deep absolute faith, which he acts upon with a free service? Protestants admire this, when they see it; but they do not seem to see as clearly, that it excludes the very notion of hypocrisy.

Sometimes, when they reflect upon it, it leads them to remark on the wonderful discipline of the Catholic priesthood; they say that no Church has so well ordered a clergy, and that in that respect it surpasses their own; they wish they could have such exact discipline among themselves. But is it an excellence which can be purchased? is it a phenomenon which depends on nothing else than itself, or is it an effect which has a cause? You cannot buy devotion at a price.

"It hath never been heard of in the land of Chanaan, neither hath it been seen in Theman. The children of Agar, the merchants of Meran, none of these have known its way." What then is that wonderful charm, which makes a thousand men act all in one way, and infuses a prompt obedience to rule, as if they were under some stern military compulsion? How difficult to find an answer, unless you will allow the obvious one, that they believe intensely what they profess!

I cannot think what it can be, in a day like this, which keeps up the prejudice of this Protestant country against us, unless it be the vague charges which are drawn from our books of Moral Theology; and with a short notice of the work in particular which by our accusers is especially thrown into our teeth, I shall bring these observations to a close.

St. Alfonso Liguori, then, it cannot be denied, lays down that an equivocation, (that is, a play upon words, in which one sense is taken by the speaker, and another sense intended by him for the hearer,) is allowable, if there is a just cause, that is, in an extraordinary case, and may even be confirmed by an oath. I shall give my opinion on this point as plainly as any Protestant can wish; and therefore I avow at once that in this department of morality, much as I admire the high points of the Italian character, I like the English rule of conduct better; but, in saying so, I am not, as will shortly be seen, saying any thing disrespectful to St. Alfonso, who was a lover of truth, and whose intercession I trust I shall not lose, though, on the matter under consideration, I follow other guidance in preference to his.

Now I make this remark first:—great English authors, Jeremy Taylor, Milton, Paley, Johnson, men of very different schools of thought, distinctly say, that under certain extraordinary circumstances it is allowable to tell a lie. Taylor says: "To tell a lie for charity, to save a man's life, the life of a friend, of a husband, of a prince, of a useful and a public person, hath not only been done at all times, but commended by great and wise and good men. Who would not save his father's life, at the charge of a harmless lie, from persecutors or tyrants?" Again, Milton says: "What man in his senses would deny, that there are those whom we have the best grounds for considering that we ought to deceive,—as boys, mad-men, the sick, the intoxicated, enemies, men in error, thieves? I would ask, by which of the commandments is a lie forbidden? You will say, by the ninth. If then my lie does not injure my neighbour, certainly it is not forbidden by this commandment." Paley says: "There are falsehoods, which are not lies, that is, which are not criminal." Johnson: "The general rule is, that truth should never be violated; there must, however, be some exceptions. If, for in-stance a murderer should ask you which way a man is gone."

Now, I am not using these instances as an *argumentum ad homi-nem*; but the purpose to which I put them is thus:—

1. First, I have set down the distinct statements of Taylor, Mil-ton, Paley, and Johnson:—now, would any one give ever so little weight to these statements, in forming a real estimate of the veracity of the writers, if they now were alive? Were a man, who is so fierce with St. Alfonso, to meet Paley or Johnson tomorrow in society, would he look upon him as a liar, a knave, as dishonest and untrust-worthy? I am sure he would not. Why then does he not deal out the same measure to Catholic priests? If a copy of Scavini, which speaks of equivocation as being in a just cause allowable, be found in a student's room at Oscott, not Scavini himself, but even the unhappy student, who has what a Protestant calls a bad book in his possession, is judged to be for life unworthy of credit. Are all Prot-estant text-books, which are used at the University, immaculate? Is it necessary to take for gospel every word of Aristotle's *Ethics*, or every assertion of Hey or Burnett on the Articles? Are text-books the ultimate authority, or rather are they not manuals in the hands of a lecturer, and the groundwork of his remarks? But, again, let us suppose, not the case of a student, or of a professor, but of Scavini himself, or of St. Alfonso; now here again I ask, since you would not scruple in holding Paley for an honest man, in spite of his defence of lying, why do you scruple at holding St. Alfonso honest? I am perfectly sure that you would not scruple at Paley personally; you might not agree with him, but you would not go further than to call him a bold thinker: then why should St. Alfonso's person be odious to you, as well as his doctrine?

Now I wish to tell you why you are not afraid of Paley; because, you would say, when he advocated lying, he was taking *extreme* or *special cases.* You would have no fear of a man who you knew had shot a burglar dead in his own house, because you knew you are *not* a burglar: so you would not think that Paley had a habit of telling lies in society, because in the case of a cruel alternative he thought it the lesser evil to tell a lie. Then why do you show such suspicion of a Catholic theologian, who speaks of certain extraordinary cases in which an equivocation in a penitent cannot be visited by his confessor as if it were a sin? for this is the exact point of the question.

But again, why does Paley, why does Jeremy Taylor when no practical matter is actually before him, lay down a maxim about the lawfulness of lying, which will startle most readers? The reason is plain. He is forming a theory of morals, and he must treat every question in turn as it comes. And this is just what St. Alfonso or Scavini is doing. You only try your hand yourself at a treatise on the rules of morality, and you will see how difficult the work is. What is the *definition* of a lie? Can you give a better than that it is a sin against justice, as Taylor and Paley consider it? but, if so, how can it be a sin at all, if your neighbour is not injured? If you do not like this definition, take another; and then, by means of that, perhaps you will be defending St. Alfonso's equivocation. However, this is what I insist upon; that St. Alfonso, as Paley, is considering the different portions of a large subject, and he must, on the subject of lying, give his judgment though on that subject it is difficult to form any judgment which is satisfactory.

But further still: you must not suppose that a philosopher or moralist uses in his own case the licence which his theory itself would allow him. A man in his own person is guided by his own conscience; but in drawing out a system of rules he is obliged to go by logic, and follow the exact deduction of conclusion from conclusion, and must be sure that the whole system is coherent and one. You hear of even immoral or irreligious books being written by men of decent character; there is a late writer who says that David Hume's sceptical works are not at all the picture of the man. A priest might write a treatise which was really lax on the subject of lying, which might come under the condemnation of the Holy See, as some treatises on that score have already been condemned, and yet in his own person be a rigorist. And, in fact, it is notorious from

St. Alfonso's Life, that he who has the repute of being so lax a moralist, had one of the most scrupulous and anxious of consciences himself. Nay, further than this, he was originally in the Law, and on one occasion he was betrayed into the commission of what seemed like a deceit, though it was an accident; and that was the very occasion of his leaving the profession and embracing the religious life.

The account of this remarkable occurrence is told us in his Life:—

"Notwithstanding he had carefully examined over and over the details of the process, he was completely mistaken regarding the sense of one document, which constituted the right of the adverse party. The advocate of the Grand Duke perceived the mistake, but he allowed Alfonso to continue his eloquent address to the end without interruption; as soon, however, as he had finished, he rose, and said with cutting coolness, 'Sir, the case is not exactly what you suppose it to be; if you will review the process, and examine this paper attentively, you will find there precisely the contrary of all you have advanced.' 'Willingly,' replied Alfonso, without hesitating; 'the decision depends on this question—whether the fief were granted under the law of Lombardy, or under the French Law.' The paper being examined, it was found that the Grand Duke's advocate was in the right. 'Yes,' said Alfonso, holding the paper in his hand, 'I am wrong, I have been mistaken.' A discovery so unexpected, and the fear of being accused of unfair dealing filled him with consternation, and covered him with confusion, so much so, that every one saw his emotion. It was in vain that the President Caravita, who loved him, and knew his integrity, tried to console him, by telling him that such mistakes were not uncommon, even among the first men at the bar. Alfonso would listen to nothing, but, overwhelmed with confusion, his head sunk on his breast, he said to himself, 'World, I know you now; courts of law, never shall you see me again!' And turning his back on the assembly, he withdrew to his own house, incessantly repeating to himself, 'World, I know you now.' What annoyed him most was, that having studied and re-studied the process during a whole month, without having discovered this important flaw, he could not understand how it had escaped his observation."

And this is the man, so easily scared at the very shadow of trickery, who is so flippantly pronounced to be a patron of lying.

But, in truth, a Catholic theologian has objects in view which men in general little compass; he is not thinking of himself, but of a multitude of souls, sick souls, sinful souls, carried away by sin, full of evil, and he is trying with all his might to rescue them from their miserable state; and, in order to save them from more heinous sins, he tries, to the full extent that his conscience will allow him to go, to shut his eyes to such sins, as are, though sins, yet lighter in character or degree. He knows perfectly well that, if he is as strict as he would wish to be, he shall be able to do nothing at all with the run of men; so he is as indulgent with them as ever he can be. Let it not be for an instant supposed, that I allow of the maxim of doing evil that good may come; but, keeping clear of this, there is a way of winning men from greater sins by winking for the time at the less, or at mere improprieties or faults; and this is the key to the difficulty which Catholic books of moral theology so often cause to the Protestant. They are intended for the Confessor, and Protestants view them as intended for the Preacher.

2. And I observe upon Taylor, Milton, and Paley thus: What would a Protestant clergyman say to me, if I accused him of teaching that a lie was allowable; and if, when he asked for my proof, I said in reply that such was the doctrine of Taylor and Milton? Why, he would sharply retort, "I am not bound by Taylor or Milton"; and if I went on urging that "Taylor was one of his authorities," he would answer that Taylor was a great writer, but great writers were not therefore infallible. This is pretty much the answer which I make, when I am considered in this matter a disciple of St. Alfonso.

I plainly and positively state, and without any reserve, that I do not at all follow this holy and charitable man in this portion of his teaching. There are various schools of opinion allowed in the Church: and on this point I follow others. I follow Cardinal Gerdil, and Natalis Alexander, nay, St. Augustine. I will quote one passage from Natalis Alexander:—"They certainly lie, who utter the words of an oath, without the will to swear or bind themselves: or who make use of mental reservations and *equivocations* in swearing, since they signify by words what they have not in mind, contrary to the end for which language was instituted, viz. as signs of ideas. Or they mean something else than the words signify in themselves and the common custom of speech." And, to take an instance: I do not believe any priest in England would dream of saying, "My friend is not here"; meaning, "He is not in my pocket or under my shoe." Nor should any consideration make me say so myself. I do not think St. Alfonso would in his own case have said so; and he would have been as much shocked at Taylor and Paley, as Protestants are at him.

And now, if Protestants wish to know what our real teaching is, as on other subjects, so on that of lying, let them look not at our books of casuistry, but at our catechisms. Works on pathology do not give the best insight into the form and the harmony of the human frame; and as it is with the body, so is it with the mind. The Catechism of the Council of Trent was drawn up for the express purpose of providing preachers with subjects for their Sermons; and, as my whole work has been a defence of myself, I may here say that I rarely preach a Sermon, but I go to this beautiful and complete Catechism to get both my matter and my doctrine. There we find the following notices about the duty of Veracity:—

" 'Thou shalt not bear false witness,' etc.: let attention be drawn to two laws contained in this commandment:—the one, forbidding false witness; the other bidding, that removing all pretence and deceits, we should measure our words and deeds by simple truth, as the Apostle admonished the Ephesians of that duty in these words: *Doing truth in charity, let us grow in Him through all things.*

"To deceive by a lie in joke or for the sake of compliment, though to no one there accrues loss or gain in consequence, nevertheless is altogether unworthy: for thus the Apostle admonishes, 'Putting aside lying, speak ye truth.' For therein is great danger of lapsing into frequent and more serious lying, and from lies in joke men gain the habit of lying, whence they gain the character of not being truthful. And thence again, in order to gain credence to their words, they find it necessary to make a practice of swearing.

"Nothing is more necessary [for us] than truth of testimony, in those things, which we neither know ourselves, nor can allowably be ignorant of, on which point there is extant that maxim of St. Augustine's; Whoso conceals the truth, and whoso puts forth a lie, each is guilty; the one because he is not willing to do a service, the other because he has a wish to do a mischief.

"It is lawful at times to be silent about the truth, but out of a court of law; for in court, when a witness is interrogated by the judge according to law, the truth is wholly to be brought out.

"Witnesses, however, must beware, lest, from overconfidence in their memory, they affirm for certain, what they have not verified.

"In order that the faithful may with more good will avoid the sin of lying, the Parish Priest shall set before them the extreme misery and turpitude of this wickedness. For, in holy writ, the devil is called the father of a lie; for, in that he did not remain in Truth, he is a liar, and the father of a lie. He will add, with the view of ridding men of so great a crime, the evils which follow upon lying; and, whereas they are innumerable, he will point out [at least] the sources and the general heads of these mischiefs and calamities, viz. 1. How great is God's displeasure and how great His hatred of a man who is insincere and a liar. 2. What little security there is that a man who is specially hated by God may not be visited by the heaviest punishments. 3. What more unclean and foul, as St. James says, than . . . that a fountain by the same jet should send out sweet water and bitter? 4. For that tongue, which just now praised God, next, as far as in it lies, dishonours Him by lying. 5. In consequence, liars are shut out from the possession of heavenly beatitude. 6. That too is the worst evil of lying, that that disease of the mind is generally incurable.

"Moreover, there is this harm too, and one of vast extent, and touching men generally, that by insincerity and lying faith and truth are lost, which are the firmest bonds of human society, and, when they are lost, supreme confusion follows in life, so that men seem in nothing to differ from devils.

"Lastly, the Parish Priest will set those right who excuse their insincerity and allege the example of wise men who, they say, are used to lie for an occasion. He will tell them, what is most true, that the wisdom of the flesh is death. He will exhort his hearers to trust in God, when they are in difficulties and straits, nor to have recourse to the expedient of a lie.

"They who throw the blame of their own lie on those who have already by a lie deceived them, are to be taught that men must not revenge themselves, nor make up for one evil by another." . . .

There is much more in the Catechism to the same effect, and it is of universal obligation; whereas the decision of a particular author in morals need not be accepted by any one.

To one other authority I appeal on this subject, which commands from me attention of a special kind, for it is the teaching of a Father. It will serve to bring my work to a conclusion.

"St. Philip," says the Roman Oratorian who wrote his Life, "had a particular dislike of affectation both in himself and others, in speaking, in dressing, or in anything else.

"He avoided all ceremony which savoured of worldly compliment, and always showed himself a great stickler for Christian simplicity in every thing; so that, when he had to deal with men of worldly prudence, he did not very readily accommodate himself to them.

"And he avoided, as much as possible, having anything to do with *two-faced persons,* who did not go simply and straightforwardly to work in their transactions.

"*As for liars, he could not endure them,* and he was *continually reminding* his spiritual children, *to avoid them as they would a pestilence.*"

These are the principles on which I have acted before I was a Catholic; these are the principles which, I trust, will be my stay and guidance to the end.

I have closed this history of myself with St. Philip's name upon St. Philip's feast-day; and, having done so, to whom can I more suitably offer it, as a memorial of affection and gratitude, than to St. Philip's sons, my dearest brothers of this House, the Priests of the Birmingham Oratory, AMBROSE ST. JOHN, HENRY AUSTIN MILLS, HENRY BITTLESTON, EDWARD CASWALL, WILLIAM PAINE NEVILLE, and HENRY IGNATIUS DUDLEY RYDER, who have been so faithful to me; who have been so sensitive of my needs; who have been so indulgent to my failings; who have carried me through so many trials; who have grudged no sacrifice, if I asked for it; who have been so cheerful under discouragements of my causing; who have done so many good works, and let me have the credit of them;—with whom I have lived so long, with whom I hope to die.

And to you especially, dear AMBROSE ST. JOHN; whom God gave me, when He took every one else away; who are the link between my old life and my new; who have now for twenty-one years been so devoted to me, so patient, so zealous, so tender; who have let me lean so hard upon you; who have watched me so narrowly; who have never thought of yourself, if I was in question.

And in you I gather up and bear in memory those familiar affectionate companions and counsellors, who in Oxford were given to me, one after another, to be my daily solace and relief; and all those others, of great name and high example, who were my thorough friends, and showed me true attachment in times long past; and also those many younger men, whether I knew them or not, who have never been disloyal to me by word or deed; and of all these, thus various in their relations to me, those more especially who have since joined the Catholic Church.

And I earnestly pray for this whole company, with a hope against hope, that all of us, who once were so united, and so happy in our union, may even now be brought at length, by the Power of the Divine Will, into One Fold and under One Shepherd.

May 26, 1864
In Festo Corp. Christ.

CHARLES
PÉGUY

A VISION *of* PRAYER
(from *Basic Verities*)

+ + +

We know well enough how a father judges!

THE short life of Péguy (1873-1914) is a veritable mystery. A fiery revolutionary, a socialist and an atheist at twenty, Péguy professed his return to the Catholic Church in 1908—but he did not go to Mass until August 15, 1914, some twenty days before he died as a soldier at the battle of the Marne. Did Péguy return to the Sacraments at that Mass of the Assumption of the Blessed Virgin? We do not know; yet, however wrong and misguided his reasoning may have been, we can scarcely doubt the genuineness of the faith of the man who wrote *The Mystery of the Charity of St. Joan of Arc, The Porch of the Mystery of the Second Virtue, The Mystery of the Holy Innocents,* and *Eve* (1910-1913). His life was an anguished struggle, full of hope in God's love, yet also beset with intellectual blindness. Out of loyalty to his wife, who was not a Catholic and did not wish their children to be baptized, Péguy lived as a believer and a rebel. This was a perplexing mystery to his friends—to Dom Baillet and Maritain. Nor is it for us to judge Péguy. What is certain is that his life, like his works, is a prolonged

685

meditation on man's salvation. And though it be true that he wrote many of the *Cahiers de la Quinzaine,* which he founded in 1900, with a furious pen, it is also true that the pages of his plays are full of prayers written with tears and with faith, and with Christian vision.

The world of Péguy is the world of the theological virtues, the peasant St. Joan is his constant heroine, the poor are his brothers, man's hope in God's love is his theme, and a language that is built by progressive repetition into a chant is his poetic vehicle.

GOD SPEAKS:

 AM THEIR father, says God. *Our Father who art in Heaven.* My son told them often enough that I was their father.
I am their judge. My son told them so. I am also their father.
I am especially their father.
Well, I am their father. He who is a father is above all a father.
Our Father who art in Heaven. He who has once been a father can be nothing else but a father.
They are my son's brothers; they are my children; I am their father.
Our Father who art in Heaven, my son taught them that prayer.
Sic ergo vos orabitis. After this manner therefore pray ye.
Our Father who art in Heaven, he knew well what he was doing that day, my son who loved them so.
Who lived among them, who was like one of them.
Who went as they did, who spoke as they did, who lived as they did.
Who suffered.
Who suffered as they did, who died as they did.
And who loved them so, having known them.
Who brought back to heaven a certain taste for man, a certain taste for the earth.
My son who loved them so, who loves them eternally in heaven.

He knew very well what he was doing that day, my son who loved
   them so.

When he put that barrier between them and me, *Our Father who
   art in Heaven,* those three or four words.

That barrier which my anger and perhaps my justice will never pass.

Blessed is the man who goes to sleep under the protection of that
   outpost, the outpost of those three or four words.

Those words that move ahead of every prayer like the hands of the
   suppliant in front of his face.

Those three or four words that conquer me, the unconquerable.

And which they cause to go before their distress like two joined
   and invincible hands.

Those three or four words which move forward like a beautiful
   cutwater fronting a lowly ship.

Cutting the flood of my anger.

And when the cutwater has passed, the ship passes, and back of
   them the whole fleet.

That, actually, is the way I see them, says God;

During my eternity, eternally, says God.

Because of that invention of my Son's, thus must I eternally see
   them.

(And judge them. How do you expect me to judge them now.
   After that.)

Our Father who art in Heaven, my son knew exactly what to do

In order to tie the arms of my justice and untie the arms of my
   mercy.

(I do not mention my anger, which has never been anything but
   my justice.

And sometimes my charity.)

And now I must judge them like a father. As if a father were any
   good as a judge. *A certain man had two sons.*

As if he were capable of judging. *A certain man had two sons.* We
   know well enough how a father judges. There is a famous
   example of that.

We know well enough how the father judged the son who had
   gone away and came back.

The father wept even more than the son.

That is the story my son has been telling them. My son gave them
The secret of judgment itself.
And now this is how they seem to me; this is how I see them;
This is how I am obliged to see them.
Just as the wake of a beautiful ship grows wider and wider until
      it disappears and loses itself,
But begins with a point, which is the point of the ship itself.
So the huge wake of sinners grows wider and wider until it dis-
      appears and loses itself
But it begins with a point, which is the point of the ship itself, and
      it is that point which comes towards me,
Which is turned towards me.
It begins with a point, which is the point of the ship itself.
And the ship is my own son, laden with all the sins of the world.
And the point of the ship is the two joined hands of my son.
And before the look of my anger and the look of my justice
They have all hidden behind him.
And all of that huge cortège of prayers, all of that huge wake grows
      wider and wider until it disappears and loses itself.
But it begins with a point and it is that point which is turned
      towards me.
Which advances towards me.
And that point is those three or four words: *Our Father who art
      in Heaven;* verily my son knew what he was doing.
And every prayer comes up to me hidden behind those three or four
      words.—
Our Father who art in Heaven.—And behind (these words) widens
      until it disappears and loses itself
The wake of innumerable prayers
As they are spoken in their text for innumerable days
By innumerable men,
(By simple men, his brothers).
Morning prayers, evening prayers;
(Prayers said on all other occasions);
On so many other occasions during innumerable days;
Prayers for noon and for the whole day;
Prayers of monks for all hours of the day,
And for the hours of the night;

Laymen's prayers and clerics' prayers
As they were said innumerable times
For innumerable days.
(He spoke like them, he spoke with them, he spoke as one of
them.)
All of that huge fleet of prayers laden with the sins of the world.
All of that huge fleet of prayers and penances attacks me
Having the spear you wot of,
Advances towards me having the spear you wot of.
It is a fleet of freighters, *classis oneraria*.
And a fleet of the line,
A combat fleet.
Like a beautiful fleet of yore, like a fleet of triremes
Advancing to attack the king.
And what do you expect me to do: I am attacked
And in that fleet, in that innumerable fleet
Each *Our Father* is like a high riding ship
Having itself its own spear, *Our Father who art in Heaven*
Turned towards me, and coming behind this selfsame spear.
Our Father who art in Heaven, not so smart after all. Of course,
when a man says that, he can get behind what he has said.
When he has said those three or four words.
And behind those beautiful high riding ships, the *Hail Marys*
Advance like innocent galleys, like virginal biremes.
Like flat-bottomed boats which do not offend the humility of the
sea.
Which do not offend the rule, which follow, humble and faithful
in their submissiveness on the surface of the water.
Our Father who art in Heaven. Of course when a man begins like
that.
When he says those three or four words to me.
When he begins by making those three or four words move ahead
of him.
After that he can go on, he can tell me what he pleases.
Because, you understand, I am disarmed.
And my son knew it well.
My son who loved those men so very much.
Who had acquired a taste for them, and for the earth, and all that

And in this innumerable fleet I clearly distinguish three great innumerable fleets.

(I am God, I see well).

And this is what I see in that huge wake which begins with that
point and which little by little loses itself on the horizon
of my gaze.

They are all one behind the other, even those which are outside the
wake,

Towards my left hand and towards my right hand.

At the head of all of them comes the innumerable fleet of *Our
Fathers*

Cutting and defying the flood of my anger.

Powerfully seated on three rows of oars.

(That is the way I am attacked. I ask you. Is it fair? Is it just?)

(No, it is not just, because all this has to do with the reign of my
Mercy)

So, all these sinners and all these saints, walking together behind
my son.

And behind the joined hands of my son,

And they themselves with joined hands as if they were my son.

Well then, my sons. Well then each one a son like my son.

First comes the heavy fleet of *Our Fathers,* an innumerable fleet.

And in that formation they attack me. I suppose you have understood.

*The kingdom of heaven suffereth violence, and the violent take it
by force.* They know it well. My son told them everything.
Regnum coeli, the kingdom of heaven. Or *regnum coe-
lorum,* the kingdom of heavens.

Regnum coeli vim patitur. Et violenti rapiunt illud. Or *rapient.*
The kingdom of heaven suffereth violence. And the violent
take it by force. Or will take it by force.

How do you expect me to defend myself? My son told them everything. And not only did he do that. But he put himself at
their head. And they are like a great fleet of yore, like an
innumerable fleet attacking the great king.—

From the high point of my promontory,
The promontory of my justice,

And from the seat of my anger,
And from the chair of my jurisprudence,
In cathedra jurisprudentiae,
From the throne of my eternal greatness
I see coming up towards me, from the far horizon I see coming
This fleet which attacks me,
The triangular fleet,
Pointing towards me the spear you wot of.—
And in that innumerable fleet I discover three fleets equally innumerable.
And the first is in front, to attack me with greatest vigor. The high riding fleet,
The ships of powerful hull,
Armored like hoplites,
That is, like soldiers heavily armed.
And they move invincibly ahead, borne on their triple rows of oars.
And the first row of oars is:
Hallowed be thy name,
Thy name;

And the second row of oars is:
Thy kingdom come,
Thy kingdom;

And the third row of oars is the words insurmountable among all words,
Thy will be done on earth as it is in heaven,
Thy will.
Sanctificetur nomen
Tuum.
Adveniat regnum
Tuum.
Fiat voluntas
Tua
Sicut in coelo et in terra.

And such is the fleet of *Our Fathers,* stalwart and more innumerable than the stars in heaven. And behind it I see the second

fleet, and it is an innumerable fleet, for it is the white sailed
fleet, the innumerable fleet of *Hail Marys*.

And it is a fleet of biremes. And the first row of oars is:

Ave Maria, gratia plena;

And the second row of oars is:

Sancta Maria, mater Dei.

And all those Hail Marys, and all those prayers of the Virgin and
the noble *Salve Regina* are white caravels, humbly resting
under their sails on the surface of the water; like white
doves which one might take with the hand.

Now those sweet doves (resting) under their wings,

Those white familiar doves, those doves in one's hand,

Those humble doves lying on the surface of the hand,

Those doves accustomed to one's hand,

Those caravels vested with sails,

Of all ships are the most opportune,

That is, the ships which present themselves with greatest directness
in front of the port.

Such is the second fleet, the prayers of the Virgin. And the third
fleet is made up of the other innumerable prayers.

All of them. Those which are said at mass and at vespers. And at
benediction.

And the prayers of the monks which mark all the hours of the day.
And the hours of the night.

And the *Benedicite* which is said before sitting down to meals.

Before a nice smoking soup-tureen.

All those prayers, all of them. And none are left.

Now I see the fourth fleet. I see the invisible fleet. And it is made
up of all the prayers which are not even said, the words that
are not even spoken.

But I hear them. Those obscure impulses of the heart, the obscure
and good impulses, the secret good impulses.

Which unconsciously soar up, which are born and unconsciously
ascend towards me.

And he in whose breast they originate is not even aware of them.
He doesn't know about them, he is only the originator.

But I collect them, says God, and I count them and weigh them.
Because I am the secret judge.

Such are, says God, these three innumerable fleets. And the fourth.
These three visible fleets and this fourth invisible one.
These secret prayers originating in a heart, these secret prayers of
the heart. These secret impulses.
And being thus assailed with such effrontery, assailed with prayers
and with tears,
Directly assailed, assailed right in the face
After that I am expected to condemn them. How easy that is!
I am expected to judge them. We know well enough how all those
judgments end up and all those sentences.
A certain man had two sons. It always ends with embraces.
(And the father crying even more than anyone else).
And with that tenderness which is, which I shall always put above
the Virtues themselves.
Because with its sister Purity it proceeds directly from the Virgin.

POPE LEO XIII

Encyclical Letter

ON *the* RESTORATION *of* CHRISTIAN PHILOSOPHY

(*Aeterni Patris*)

> Every word of wisdom, every useful thing by whomso-
> ever discovered or planned, ought to be received with
> a willing and grateful mind.

THE three following encyclicals were issued, respectively, in 1879, 1931 and 1943.

The first of these is a famous exposition by Pope Leo XIII of Christian philosophy, of its genesis and particularly of the honored place of St. Thomas Aquinas within it. This Encyclical has given a tremendous impetus to the study of mediaeval philosophy in the modern world, and especially to the study of Thomism in the authentic writings of St. Thomas.

Forty years after the publication of the Encyclical *Rerum Novarum* in 1891, and in celebration of the event, Pope Pius XI issued a remarkably forceful and energetic statement on the economic rights of the working man, as well as on his spiritual dignity as a free human person. This Encyclical of Pius XI is rightly considered as the charter of labor in society today. We have scarcely caught up with the daring program of *Quadragesimo Anno*.

It will be recalled with what loftiness of judgment and depth of compassion Pope Pius XII spoke to all mankind during the

Second World War. In the Encyclical *On the Mystical Body of Christ,* he has given authoritative expression to the deepest principles of the unity of all men as members of the Body of Christ. These principles stand as the lasting pillars of the Catholic conception of human society, of the Church, and of Christ her Head.

The pontificate of Leo XIII (1810-1903) began in 1878; that of Pius XI (1857-1939) in 1922; that of Pius XII (1876-   ) in 1939.

HE ONLY-BEGOTTEN SON OF THE ETERNAL Father, who came on earth to bring salvation and the light of divine wisdom to men, conferred a great and wonderful blessing on the world when, about to ascend again into heaven, He commanded the apostles to go and teach all nations,[1] and left the Church which He had founded to be the common and supreme teacher of the peoples. For men, whom the truth had set free, were to be preserved by the truth; nor would the fruits of heavenly doctrines, by which salvation comes to men, have long remained had not the Lord Christ appointed an unfailing authority for the instruction of the faithful. And the Church built upon the promises of its own divine Author, whose charity it imitated, so faithfully followed out His commands that its constant aim and chief wish was this: to teach true religion and contend forever against errors. To this end assuredly have tended the incessant labors of individual bishops; to this end also the published laws and decrees of Councils, and especially the constant watchfulness of the Roman Pontiffs, to whom, as successors of the blessed Peter in the primacy of the apostles, belongs the right and office of teaching and confirming their brethren in the faith. Since, then, according to the warning of the Apostle, the minds of Christ's faithful are apt to be deceived and the integrity of the faith to be corrupted among men *by philosophy and vain deceit,*[2] the supreme pastors of the

[1] *Matt.* xxviii, 19.   [2] *Coloss.* ii. 8.

Church have always thought it their duty to advance, by every means in their power, science truly so called, and at the same time to provide with special care that all studies should accord with the Catholic faith, especially philosophy, on which a right apprehension of the other sciences in great part depends. Indeed, Venerable Brethren, on this very subject among others, We briefly admonished you in Our first Encyclical Letter; but now, both by reason of the gravity of the subject and the condition of the time, we are again compelled to speak to you on the mode of taking up the study of philosophy which shall respond most fitly to the true faith, and at the same time be most consonant with the dignity of human knowledge.

Whoso turns his attention to the bitter strifes of these days and seeks a reason for the troubles that vex public and private life, must come to the conclusion that a fruitful cause of the evils which now afflict, as well as of those which threaten us, lies in this: that false conclusions concerning divine and human things, which originated in the schools of philosophy, have crept into all the orders of the State, and have been accepted by the common consent of the masses. For since it is in the very nature of man to follow the guide of reason in his actions, if his intellect sins at all his will soon follows; and thus it happens that looseness of intellectual opinion influences human actions and perverts them. Whereas, on the other hand, if men be of sound mind and take their stand on true and solid principles, there will result a vast amount of benefits for the public and private good. We do not, indeed, attribute such force and authority to philosophy as to esteem it equal to the task of combating and rooting out all errors; for, when the Christian religion was first constituted, it came upon earth to restore it to its primeval dignity by the admirable light of faith, diffused not by persuasive words of human wisdom, but in the manifestation of spirit and of power; [3] so also at the present time we look above all things to the powerful help of Almighty God to bring back to a right understanding the minds of men and dispel the darkness of error. But the natural helps with which the grace of the divine wisdom, strongly and sweetly disposing all things, has supplied the human race are neither to be despised nor neglected, chief among which

[3] I Cor. ii, 4.

is evidently the right use of philosophy. For not in vain did God set the light of reason in the human mind; and so far is the super-added light of faith from extinguishing or lessening the power of the intelligence that it completes it rather, and by adding to its strength renders it capable of greater things.

Therefore divine Providence itself requires that in calling back the peoples to the paths of faith and salvation advantage should be taken of human science also—an approved and wise practice which history testifies was observed by the most illustrious Fathers of the Church. They, indeed, were wont neither to belittle nor under-value the part that reason had to play, as is summed up by the great Augustine when he attributes to this science "that by which the most wholesome faith is begotten, . . . is nourished, defended, and made strong." [4]

In the first place, philosophy, if rightly made use of by the wise, in a certain way tends to smooth and fortify the road to true faith, and to prepare the souls of its disciples for the fit reception of revelation; for which reason it is well called by ancient writers sometimes a stepping-stone to the Christian faith,[5] sometimes the prelude and help of Christianity,[6] sometimes the Gospel teacher.[7] And assuredly the God of all goodness, in all that pertains to divine things, has not only manifested by the light of faith those truths which human intelligence could not attain of itself, but others also not altogether unattainable by reason, that by the help of divine authority they may be made known to all at once and without any admixture of error. Hence it is that certain truths which were either divinely proposed for belief, or were bound by the closest chains to the doctrine of faith, were discovered by pagan sages with noth-ing but their natural reason to guide them, were demonstrated and proved by becoming arguments. *For,* as the Apostle says, *the in-visible things of Him, from the creation of the world, are clearly seen, being understood by the things that are made: His eternal power also and divinity;* [8] and the Gentiles who have not the law show, nevertheless, the work of the law written in their hearts.[9]

[4] *De Trin.,* xiv, 1, 3 (PL 42, 1037).
[5] Clem. Alex., *Strom.,* I, 16; VII, 3 (PG 8, 795; 9, 426).
[6] Origen, *Epistola ad Gregorium* (PG 11, 87-91).
[7] Clem. Alex., *Strom.,* I, 5 (PG 8, 718-719).
[8] *Rom.* i, 20.   [9] *Ibid.* ii, 14, 15.

But it is most fitting to turn these truths, which have been discovered by the pagan sages even, to the use and purposes of revealed doctrine, in order to show that both human wisdom and the
very testimony of our adversaries serve to support the Christian
faith—a method which is not of recent introduction, but of established use, and has often been adopted by the holy Fathers of the
Church. For instance, those venerable men, the witnesses and guard-
ians of religious traditions, recognize a certain form and figure
of this in the action of the Hebrews, who, when about to depart
out of Egypt, were commanded to take with them the gold and silver
vessels and precious robes of the Egyptians, that by a change of use
the things might be dedicated to the service of the true God which
had formerly been the instruments of ignoble and superstitious
rites. Gregory of Neocaesarea [10] praises Origen expressly because,
with singular dexterity, as one snatches weapons from the enemy,
he turned to the defence of Christian wisdom and to the destruction
of superstition many arguments drawn from the writings of the
pagans. And both Gregory of Nazianzus [11] and Gregory of Nyssa [12]
praise and commend a like mode of disputation in Basil the Great;
while Jerome especially commends it in Quadratus, a disciple of
the apostles, in Aristides, Justin, Irenaeus, and very many others.[13]
Augustine says: "Do we not see Cyprian, that mildest of doctors
and most blessed of martyrs, going out of Egypt laden with gold
and silver and vestments? And Lactantius also and Victorinus,
Optatus and Hilary? And, not to speak of the living, how many
Greeks have done likewise?" [14] But if natural reason first sowed
this rich field of doctrine before it was rendered fruitful by the
power of Christ, it must assuredly become more prolific after the
grace of the Saviour has renewed and added to the native faculties
of the human mind. And who does not see that a plain and easy
road is opened up to faith by such a method of philosophic study?

But the advantage to be derived from such a school of philosophy
is not to be confined within these limits. The foolishness of those
men is gravely reproved in the words of divine wisdom who by these
good things that are seen could not understand Him that is, neither

---

[10] *Orat. paneg. ad Origen,* 14 (PG 10, 1094).   [11] *Carm.* i, Iamb. 3.
[12] *Vita Moysis* (PG 44, 359).   [13] *Epist. ad Magnum,* 4 (PL 22, 667).
[14] *De Doctr. Christ.,* I, ii, 40 (PL 34, 63).

by attending to the works could have acknowledged who was the workman.[15] In the first place, then, this great and noble fruit is gathered from human reason, that it demonstrates that God *is*; *for by the greatness of the beauty, and of the creature, the Creator of them may be seen so as to be known thereby.*[16] Again, it shows God to excel in the height of all perfections, in infinite wisdom before which nothing lies hidden, and in absolute justice which no depraved affection could possibly shake; and that God, therefore, is not only true but truth itself, which can neither deceive nor be deceived. Whence it clearly follows that human reason finds the fullest faith and authority united in the word of God. In like manner reason declares that the doctrine of the Gospel has even from its very beginning been made manifest by certain wonderful signs, the established proofs, as it were, of unshaken truth; and that all, therefore, who set faith in the Gospel do not believe rashly as though following cunningly devised fables,[17] but, by a most reasonable consent, subject their intelligence and judgment to an authority which is divine. And of no less importance is it that reason most clearly sets forth that the Church instituted by Christ (as laid down in the Vatican Synod), on account of its wonderful spread, its marvellous sanctity, and its inexhaustible fecundity in all places, as well as of its Catholic unity and unshaken stability, is in itself a great and perpetual motive of belief and an irrefragable testimony of its own divine mission.[18]

Its solid foundations having been thus laid, a perpetual and varied service is further required of philosophy, in order that sacred theology may receive and assume the nature, form, and genius of a true science. For in this, the most noble of studies, it is of the greatest necessity to bind together, as it were, in one body the many and various parts of the heavenly doctrines, that, each being allotted to its own proper place and derived from its own proper principles, the whole may join together in a complete union; in order, in fine, that all and each part may be strengthened by its own and the others' invincible arguments. Nor is that more accurate or fuller knowledge of the things that are believed, and somewhat more lucid understanding, as far as it can go, of the very mysteries

---

[15] *Wis.* xiii, 1.   [16] *Ibid.* xiii, 5.   [17] *II Peter* i, 16.
[18] *Const. Dogm. de Fid. Cath.,* c. 3.

of faith which Augustine and the other Fathers commended and strove to reach, and which the Vatican Synod itself [19] declared to be most fruitful, to be passed over in silence or belittled. Those will certainly more fully and more easily attain that knowledge and understanding who to integrity of life and love of faith join a mind rounded and finished by philosophic studies, as the same Vatican Synod teaches that the knowledge of such sacred dogmas ought to be sought as well from analogy of the things that are naturally known as from the connection of those mysteries one with another and with the final end of man.[20]

Lastly, the duty of religiously defending the truths divinely delivered, and of resisting those who dare oppose them, pertains to philosophic pursuits. Wherefore it is the glory of philosophy to be esteemed as the bulwark of faith and the strong defence of religion. As Clement of Alexandria testifies, the doctrine of the Saviour is indeed perfect in itself and wanteth naught, since it is the power and wisdom of God. And the assistance of Greek philosophy maketh not the truth more powerful; but in as much as it weakens the contrary arguments of the sophists and repels the veiled attacks against the truth, it has been fitly called the hedge and fence of the vine.[21] For as the enemies of the Catholic name, when about to attack religion, are in the habit of borrowing their weapons from the arguments of philosophers, so the defenders of sacred science draw many arguments from the store of philosophy which may serve to uphold revealed dogmas. Nor is the triumph of the Christian faith a small one in using human reason to repel powerfully and speedily the attacks of its adversaries by the hostile arms which human reason itself supplied. Which species of religious strife St. Jerome, writing to Magnus, notices as having been adopted by the Apostle of the Gentiles himself: Paul, the leader of the Christian army skilfully turns even a chance inscription into an argument for the faith; for he had learned from the true David to wrest the sword from the hands of the enemy and to cut off the head of the boastful Goliath with his own weapon.[22] Moreover, the Church herself not only urges, but even commands, Christian teachers to seek help from philosophy. For the fifth Council of the Lateran, after it had decided

[19] *Const. cit.*, c. 4. [20] *Loc. cit.* [21] *Strom.*, I, 20 (PG 8, 818).
[22] *Epist. ad Magnum*, 2 (PL 22, 666).

that "every assertion contrary to the truth of revealed faith is altogether false, for the reason that it contradicts, however slightly, the truth," [23] advises teachers of philosophy to pay close attention to the exposition of fallacious arguments; since, as Augustine testifies, "if reason is turned against the authority of sacred Scripture, no matter how specious it may seem, it errs in the likeness of truth; for true it cannot be." [24]

But in order that philosophy may be found equal to the gathering of those precious fruits which we have indicated, it behooves it above all things never to turn aside from that path which the Fathers have entered upon from a venerable antiquity, and which the Vatican Council solemnly and authoritatively approved. As it is evident that very many truths of the supernatural order which are far beyond the reach of the keenest intellect must be accepted, human reason, conscious of its own infirmity, dare not pretend to what is beyond it, nor deny those truths, nor measure them by its own standard, nor interpret them at will; but receive them rather with a full and humble faith, and esteem it the highest honor to be allowed to wait upon heavenly doctrines like a handmaid and attendant, and by God's goodness attain to them in any way whatsoever. But in the case of such doctrines as the human intelligence may perceive, it is equally just that philosophy should make use of its own method, principles, and arguments—not indeed in such fashion as to seem rashly to withdraw from the divine authority. But since it is established that those things which become known by revelation have the force of certain truth, and that those things which war against faith war equally against right reason, the Catholic philosopher will know that he violates at once faith and the laws of reason if he accepts any conclusion which he understands to be opposed to revealed doctrine.

We know that there are some who, in their overestimate of the human faculties, maintain that as soon as man's intellect becomes subject to divine authority it falls from its native dignity, and, hampered by the yoke of this species of slavery, is much retarded and hindered in its progress towards the supreme truth and excellence. Such an idea is most false and deceptive, and its final result is

[23] Bulla *Apostolici regiminis.*
[24] *Epist. 143 (al. 7), ad Marcelin.,* 7 (PL 33, 589).

to induce foolish and ungrateful men wilfully to repudiate the most sublime truths, and reject the divine gift of faith, from which the fountains of all good things flow out upon civil society. For the human mind, being confined within certain limits, and those narrow enough, is exposed to many errors and is ignorant of many things; whereas the Christian faith, reposing on the authority of God, is the unfailing mistress of truth, whom whoso followeth he will be neither immeshed in the snares of error nor tossed hither and thither on the waves of fluctuating opinion. Those, therefore, who to the study of philosophy unite obedience to the Christian faith are philosophers indeed; for the splendor of the divine truths, received into the mind, helps the understanding, and not only detracts in nowise from its dignity, but adds greatly to its nobility, keenness, and stability. For surely that is a worthy and most useful exercise of reason when men give their minds to disproving those things which are repugnant to faith and proving the things which conform to faith. In the first case they cut the ground from under the feet of error and expose the viciousness of the arguments on which error rests; while in the second case they make themselves masters of weighty reasons for the sound demonstration of truth and the satisfactory instruction of any reasonable person. Whoever denies that such study and practice tend to add to the resources and expand the faculties of the mind must necessarily and absurdly hold that the mind gains nothing from discriminating between the true and the false. Justly, therefore, does the Vatican Council commemorate in these words the great benefits which faith has conferred upon reason: *Faith frees and saves reason from error, and endows it with manifold knowledge.*[25] A wise man, therefore, would not accuse faith and look upon it as opposed to reason and natural truths, but would rather offer heartfelt thanks to God, and sincerely rejoice that, in the density of ignorance and in the flood-tide of error, holy faith, like a friendly star, shines down upon his path and points out to him the fair gate of truth beyond all danger of wandering.

If, Venerable Brethren, you open the history of philosophy, you will find all We have just said proved by experience. The philosophers of old who lacked the gift of faith, yet were esteemed so wise, fell into many appalling errors. You know how often among some

[25] *Const. Dogm. de Fid. Cath.*, c. 4.

truths they taught false and incongruous things; what vague and doubtful opinions they held concerning the nature of the Divinity, the first origin of things, the government of the world, the divine knowledge of the future, the cause and principle of evil, the ultimate end of man, eternal beatitude, concerning virtue and vice, and other matters, a true and certain knowledge of which is most necessary to the human race; while, on the other hand, the early Fathers and Doctors of the Church, who well understood that, according to the divine plan, the restorer of human science is Christ, who is the power and the wisdom of God,[26] *and in whom are hid all the treasures of wisdom and knowledge,*[27] took up and investigated the books of the ancient philosophers, and compared their teachings with the doctrines of revelation, and, carefully sifting them, they cherished what was true and wise in them and amended or rejected all else. For as the all-seeing God against the cruelty of tyrants raised up mighty martyrs to the defence of the Church, men prodigal of their great lives, in like manner to false philosophers and heretics he opposed men of great wisdom, to defend, even by the aid of human reason, the treasure of revealed truths. Thus from the very first ages of the Church, Catholic doctrine has encountered a multitude of most bitter adversaries, who, deriding the Christian dogmas and institutions, maintained that there were many gods, that the material world never had a beginning or cause, and that the course of events was one of blind and fatal necessity, not regulated by the will of divine Providence.

But the learned men whom We call apologists speedily encountered these teachers of foolish doctrine, and, under the guidance of faith, found arguments in human wisdom also to prove that one God, who stands pre-eminent in every kind of perfection, is to be worshipped; that all things were created from nothing by His omnipotent power; that by His wisdom they flourish and serve each their own special purposes. Among these St. Justin Martyr claims the chief place. After having tried the most celebrated academies of the Greeks, he saw clearly, as he himself confesses, that he could only draw truths in their fulness from the doctrines of revelation. These he embraced with all the ardor of his soul, purged of calumny, courageously and fully defended before the Roman emperors, and

[26] *I Cor.* i, 24. [27] *Coloss.* ii, 3.

reconciled with them not a few of the sayings of the Greek philosophers.

Quadratus also and Aristides, Hermias and Athenagoras, stood nobly forth in that time. Nor did Irenaeus, the invincible martyr and bishop of Lyons, win less glory in the same cause when, forcibly refuting the perverse opinions of the Orientals, the work of the Gnostics, scattered broadcast over the territories of the Roman Empire, he explained (according to Jerome) the origin of each heresy and in what philosophic source it took its rise.[28] But who knows not the disputations of Clement of Alexandria, which the same Jerome thus honorably commemorates: "What is there in them that is not learned, and what that is not of the very heart of philosophy?" [29] He himself, indeed, with marvellous versatility treated of many things of the greatest utility for preparing a history of philosophy, for the exercise of the dialectic art, and for showing the agreement between reason and faith. After him came Origen, who graced the chair of the school of Alexandria, and was most learned in the teachings of the Greeks and Orientals. He published many volumes, involving great labor, which were wonderfully adapted to explain the divine writings and illustrate the sacred dogmas; which, though, as they now stand, not altogether free from error, contain nevertheless a wealth of knowledge tending to the growth and advance of natural truths. Tertullian opposes heretics with the authority of the sacred writings; with the philosophers he changes his fence and disputes philosophically; but so learnedly and accurately did he confute them that he made bold to say, "Neither in science nor in schooling are we equals, as you imagine." [30] Arnobius also, in his works against the pagans, and Lactantius in the divine *Institutions* especially, with equal eloquence and strength strenuously strive to move men to accept the dogmas and precepts of Catholic wisdom, not by philosophic juggling, after the fashion of the academics, but vanquishing them partly by their own arms, and partly by arguments drawn from the mutual contentions of the philosophers.[31] But the writings on the human soul, the divine attributes, and other questions of mighty moment which the great Athanasius and Chrysostom, the prince of orators, have left behind them are,

---

[28] *Epist. ad Magnum,* 4 (PL 22, 667).   [29] *Loc. cit.*
[30] *Apologet.* 46 (PL 1, 573).   [31] *Inst.* vii, 7 (PL 6, 759).

by common consent, so supremely excellent that it seems scarcely anything could be added to their subtlety and fulness. And, not to cover too wide a range, we add to the number of the great men of whom mention has been made the names of Basil the Great and of the two Gregories, who, on going forth from Athens, that home of all learning, thoroughly equipped with all the harness of philosophy, turned the wealth of knowledge which each had gathered up in a course of zealous study to the work of refuting heretics and preparing Christians.

But Augustine would seem to have wrested the palm from all. Of a most powerful genius and thoroughly saturated with sacred and profane learning, with the loftiest faith and with equal knowledge, he combated most vigorously all the errors of his age. What height of philosophy did he not reach? What region of it did he not diligently explore, either in expounding the loftiest mysteries of the faith to the faithful, or defending them against the fell onslaught of adversaries, or again when, in demolishing the fables of the academics or the Manichaeans, he laid the safe foundations and sure structure of human science, or followed up the reason, origin, and causes of the evils that afflict man? How subtly he reasoned on the angels, the soul, the human mind, the will and free choice, on religion and the life of the blessed, on time and eternity, and even on the very nature of changeable bodies! Afterwards, in the East, John Damascene, treading in the footsteps of Basil and of Gregory Nazianzen, and in the West Boethius and Anselm, following the doctrines of Augustine, added largely to the patrimony of philosophy.

Later on the doctors of the middle ages, who are called Scholastics, addressed themselves to a great work—that of diligently collecting and sifting and storing up, as it were, in one place, for the use and convenience of posterity, the rich and fertile harvests of Christian learning scattered abroad in the voluminous works of the holy Fathers. And with regard, Venerable Brethren, to the origin, drift, and excellence of this scholastic learning, it may be well here to speak more fully in the words of one of the wisest of Our predecessors, Sixtus V.: "By the divine favor of Him who alone gives the spirit of science, and wisdom, and understanding, and who through all ages, as there may be need, enriches His Church with new blessings and strengthens it with new safeguards, there was founded by Our Fathers, men of eminent wisdom, the scholastic theology, which two glorious doctors in particular, the angelic St. Thomas and the seraphic St. Bonaventure, illustrious teachers of this faculty, . . . with surpassing genius, by unwearied diligence, and at the cost of long labors and vigils, set in order and beautified, and, when skilfully arranged and clearly explained in a variety of ways, handed down to posterity.

"And, indeed, the knowledge and use of so salutary a science, which flows from the fertilizing founts of the sacred writings, the Sovereign Pontiffs, the holy Fathers and the councils, must always be of the greatest assistance to the Church, whether with the view of really and soundly understanding and interpreting the Scriptures, or more safely and to better purpose reading and explaining the Fathers, or for exposing and refuting the various errors and heresies; and in these late days, when those dangerous times described by the Apostle are already upon us, when the blasphemers, the proud, and the seducers go from bad to worse, erring themselves and causing others to err, there is surely a very great need of confirming the dogmas of the Catholic faith and confuting heresies."

Although these words seem to bear reference solely to scholastic theology, nevertheless they may plainly be accepted as equally true of philosophy and its praises. For the noble endowments which make the scholastic theology so formidable to the enemies of truth —to wit, as the same pontiff adds, "that ready and close coherence of cause and effect, that order and array as of a disciplined army in battle, those clear definitions and distinctions, that strength of argument and those keen discussions, by which light is distinguished from darkness, the true from the false, expose and strip naked, as it were, the falsehoods of heretics wrapped around by a cloud of subterfuges and fallacies" [32]—those noble and admirable endowments, We say, are only to be found in a right use of that philosophy which the scholastic teachers have been accustomed carefully and prudently to make use of even in theological disputations. Moreover, since it is the proper and special office of the scholastic theologians to bind together by the fastest chain human and divine science, surely the theology in which they excelled would not have

[32] Bulla *Triumphantis* an. 1588.

gained such honor and commendation among men if they had made use of a lame and imperfect or vain philosophy.

Among the scholastic doctors, the chief and master of all towers Thomas Aquinas, who, as Cajetan observes, because "he most venerated the ancient doctors of the Church, in a certain way seems to have inherited the intellect of all." [33] The doctrines of those illustrious men, like the scattered members of a body, Thomas collected together and cemented, distributed in wonderful order, and so increased with important additions that he is rightly esteemed the special bulwark and glory of the Catholic faith. With his spirit at once humble and swift, his memory ready and tenacious, his life spotless throughout, a lover of truth for its own sake, richly endowed with human and divine science, like the sun he heated the world with the ardor of his virtues and filled it with the splendor of his teaching. Philosophy has no part which he did not touch finely at once and thoroughly; on the laws of reasoning, on God and incorporeal substances, on man and other sensible things, on human actions and their principles, he reasoned in such a manner that in him there is wanting neither a full array of questions, nor an apt disposal of the various parts, nor the best method of proceeding, nor soundness of principles or strength of argument, nor clearness and elegance of style, nor a facility for explaining what is abstruse.

Moreover, the Angelic Doctor pushed his philosophic conclusions into the reasons and principles of the things which are most comprehensive and contain in their bosom, so to say, the seeds of almost infinite truths, to be unfolded in good time by later masters and with a goodly yield. And as he also used this philosophic method in the refutation of error, he won this title to distinction for himself: that single-handed he victoriously combated the errors of former times, and supplied invincible arms to put those to rout which might in after-times spring up. Again, clearly distinguishing, as is fitting, reason from faith, while happily associating the one with the other, he both preserved the rights and had regard for the dignity of each; so much so, indeed, that reason, borne on the wings of Thomas to its human height, can scarcely rise higher, while faith could scarcely expect more or stronger aids from reason than those which she has already obtained through Thomas.

[33] *In 2m. 2ae.*, q. 148, a. 4; Leonine ed. Vol. X, n. 6, p. 174.

For these reasons learned men, in former ages especially, of the highest repute in theology and philosophy, after mastering with infinite pains the immortal works of Thomas, gave themselves up not so much to be instructed in his angelic wisdom as to be nourished upon it. It is known that nearly all the founders and framers of laws of the religious orders commanded their associates to study and religiously adhere to the teachings of St. Thomas, fearful lest any of them should swerve even in the slightest degree from the footsteps of so great a man. To say nothing of the family of St. Dominic, which rightly claims this great teacher for its own glory, the statutes of the Benedictines, the Carmelites, the Augustinians, the Society of Jesus, and many others, all testify that they are bound by this law.

And here how pleasantly one's thoughts fly back to those celebrated schools and academies which flourished of old in Europe, to Paris, Salamanca, Alcala, to Douay, Toulouse, and Louvain, to Padua and Bologna, to Naples and Coimbra, and to many another! All know how the fame of these seats of learning grew with their years, and that their judgment, often asked in matters of grave moment, held great weight everywhere. And we know how in those great homes of human wisdom, as in his own kingdom, Thomas reigned supreme; and that the minds of all, of teachers as well as of taught, rested in wonderful harmony under the shield and authority of the Angelic Doctor.

But, furthermore, Our predecessors in the Roman pontificate have celebrated the wisdom of Thomas Aquinas by exceptional tributes of praise and the most ample testimonials. Clement VI in the Bull *In Ordine,* Nicholas V in his Brief to the Friars of the Order of Preachers, 1451, Benedict XIII in the Bull *Pretiosus,* and others bear witness that the universal Church borrows lustre from his admirable teaching; while St. Pius V declares in the Bull *Mirabilis* that heresies, confounded and convicted by the same teaching, were dissipated, and the whole world daily freed from fatal errors; others, such as Clement XII in the Bull *Verbo Dei,* affirm that most fruitful bessings have spread abroad from his writings over the whole Church, and that he is worthy of the honor which is bestowed on the greatest doctors of the Church, on Gregory and Ambrose, Augustine and Jerome; while others have not hesitated to propose

St. Thomas for the exemplar and master of the academies and great lyceums, whom they may follow with unfaltering feet. On which point the words of Blessed Urban V to the Academy of Toulouse are worthy of recall: "It is our will, which we hereby enjoin upon you, that ye follow the teaching of Blessed Thomas as the true and Catholic doctrine, and that ye labor with all your force to profit by the same." [34] Innocent XII in the Letter in the form of a Brief addressed on the 6th February, 1694, to the University of Louvain, followed the example of Urban in the case of the University of Louvain, and Benedict XIV in the Letter in the form of a Brief addressed on the 26th August, 1752, to the Dionysian College of Granada; while to these judgments of great Pontiffs on Thomas Aquinas comes the crowning testimony of Innocent VI.: "His teaching above that of others, the canons alone excepted, enjoys such an elegance of phraseology, a method of statement, a truth of proposition, that those who hold to it are never found swerving from the path of truth, and he who dare assail it will always be suspected of error." [35]

The oecumenical councils also, where blossoms the flower of all earthly wisdom, have always been careful to hold Thomas Aquinas in singular honor. In the councils of Lyons, Vienne, Florence, and the Vatican one might almost say that Thomas took part and presided over the deliberations and decrees of the Fathers, contending against the errors of the Greeks, of heretics and rationalists, with invincible force and with the happiest results. But the chief and special glory of Thomas, one which he has shared with none of the Catholic doctors, is that the Fathers of Trent made it part of the order of the conclave to lay upon the altar, together with the code of sacred Scripture and the decrees of the Supreme Pontiffs, the *Summa* of Thomas Aquinas, whence to seek counsel, reason, and inspiration.

A last triumph was reserved for this incomparable man—namely, to compel the homage, praise, and admiration of even the very enemies of the Catholic name. For it has come to light that there were not lacking among the leaders of heretical sects some who openly declared that, if the teaching of Thomas Aquinas were only taken away, they could easily battle with all Catholic teachers, gain

[34] *Const.* 5a. dat. die 3 Aug. 1368 ad Concell. Univ. Tolo.
[35] *Serm. de S. Thoma.*

the victory, and abolish the Church.[36] A vain hope indeed, but no vain testimony.

Therefore, Venerable Brethren, as often as We contemplate the good, the force, and the singular advantages to be derived from this system of philosophy which Our Fathers so dearly loved, We think it hazardous that its special honor should not always and everywhere remain, especially when it is established that daily experience, and the judgment of the greatest men, and, to crown all, the voice of the Church, have favored the scholastic philosophy. Moreover, to the old teaching a novel system of philosophy has succeeded here and there, in which We fail to perceive those desirable and wholesome fruits which the Church and civil society itself would prefer. For it pleased the struggling innovators of the sixteenth century to philosophize without any respect for faith, the power of inventing in accordance with his own pleasure and bent being asked and given in turn by each one. Hence it was natural that systems of philosophy multiplied beyond measure, and conclusions differing and clashing one with another arose even about those matters which are the most important in human knowledge. From a mass of conclusions men often come to wavering and doubt; and who knows not how easily the mind slips from doubt to error? But as men are apt to follow the lead given them, this new pursuit seems to have caught the souls of certain Catholic philosophers, who, throwing aside the patrimony of ancient wisdom, chose rather to build up a new edifice than to strengthen and complete the old by aid of the new—ill advisedly, in sooth, and not without detriment to the sciences. For a multiform system of this kind, which depends on the authority and choice of any professor, has a foundation open to change, and consequently gives us a philosophy not firm and stable and robust like that of old, but tottering and feeble. And if perchance it sometimes finds itself scarcely equal to sustain the shock of its foes, it should recognize that the cause and the blame lie in itself. In saying this We have no intention of discountenancing the learned and able men who bring their industry and erudition, and, what is more, the wealth of new discoveries, to the service of philosophy; for, of course, We understand that this tends to the development of learning. But one should be very careful lest all or his chief labor be

[36] Bucer.

exhausted in these pursuits and in mere erudition. And the same thing is true of sacred theology, which, indeed, may be assisted and illustrated by all kinds of erudition, though it is absolutely necessary to approach it in the grave manner of the scholastics, in order that, the forces of revelation and reason being united in it, it may continue to be "the invincible bulwark of the faith." [37]

With wise forethought, therefore, not a few of the advocates of philosophical studies, when turning their minds recently to the practical reform of philosophy, aimed and aim at restoring the renowned teaching of Thomas Aquinas and winning it back to its ancient beauty.

We have learned with great joy that many members of your order, Venerable Brethren, have taken this plan to heart; and while We earnestly commend their efforts, We exhort them to hold fast to their purpose, and remind each and all of you that Our first and most cherished idea is that you should all furnish a generous and copious supply to studious youth of those crystal rills of wisdom flowing in a never-ending and fertilizing stream from the fountainhead of the Angelic Doctor.

Many are the reasons why We are so desirous of this. In the first place, then, since in the tempest that is on us the Christian faith is being constantly assailed by the machinations and craft of a certain false wisdom, all youths, but especially those who are the growing hope of the Church, should be nourished on the strong and robust food of doctrine, that so, mighty in strength and armed at all points, they may become habituated to advance the cause of religion with force and judgment, *being ready always,* according to the apostolic counsel, *to satisfy every one that asketh you a reason of that hope which is in you,*[38] and that they may be able to exhort in sound doctrine and to convince the gainsayers.[39] Many of those who, with minds alienated from the faith, hate Catholic institutions, claim reason as their sole mistress and guide. Now, We think that, apart from the supernatural help of God, nothing is better calculated to heal those minds and to bring them into favor with the Catholic faith than the solid doctrine of the Fathers and the scholastics, who so clearly and forcibly demonstrate the firm foundations of the faith, its divine origin, its certain truth, the arguments that sustain

[37] Sixtus V, Bulla *Triumphantis.*   [38] *I. Peter* iii, 15.   [39] *Tit.* i, 5.

it, the benefits it has conferred on the human race, and its perfect accord with reason, in a manner to satisfy completely minds open to persuasion, however unwilling and repugnant.

Domestic and civil society even, which, as all see, is exposed to great danger from this plague of perverse opinions, would certainly enjoy a far more peaceful and secure existence if a more wholesome doctrine were taught in the academies and schools—one more in conformity with the teaching of the Church, such as is contained in the works of Thomas Aquinas.

For the teachings of Thomas on the true meaning of liberty, which at this time is running into license, on the divine origin of all authority, on laws and their force, on the paternal and just rule of princes, on obedience to the higher powers, on mutual charity one towards another—on all of these and kindred subjects have very great and invincible force to overturn those principles of the new order which are well known to be dangerous to the peaceful order of things and to public safety. In short, all studies ought to find hope of advancement and promise of assistance in this restoration of philosophic discipline which We have proposed. The arts were wont to draw from philosophy, as from a wise mistress, sound judgment and right method, and from it also their spirit as from the common fount of life. When philosophy stood stainless in honor and wise in judgment, then, as facts and constant experience showed, the liberal arts flourished as never before or since; but, neglected and almost blotted out, they lay prone since philosophy began to lean to error and join hands with folly. Nor will the physical sciences, which are now in such great repute, and by the renown of so many inventions draw such universal admiration to themselves, suffer detriment but find very great assistance in the re-establishment of the ancient philosophy. For the investigation of facts and the contemplation of nature is not alone sufficient for their profitable exercise and advance; but when facts have been established it is necessary to rise and apply ourselves to the study of the nature of corporeal things, to inquire into the laws which govern them and the principles whence their order and varied unity and mutual attraction in diversity arise. To such investigations it is wonderful what force and light and aid the scholastic philosophy, if judiciously taught, would bring.

And here it is well to note that Our philosophy can only by the grossest injustice be accused of being opposed to the advance and development of natural science. For when the Scholastics, following the opinion of the holy Fathers, always held in anthropology that the human intelligence is led to the knowledge of things without body and matter only by things sensible, they readily understood that nothing was of greater use to the philosopher than diligently to search into the mysteries of nature and to be devoted with assiduous patience to the study of physical things. And this they confirmed by their own example; for St. Thomas, Blessed Albertus Magnus, and other leaders of the scholastics were never so wholly rapt in the study of philosophy as not to give large attention to the knowledge of natural things; and, indeed, the number of their sayings and writings on these subjects, which recent professors approve of and admit to harmonize with truth, is by no means small. Moreover, in this very age many illustrious professors of the physical sciences openly testify that between certain and accepted conclusions of modern physics and the philosophic principles of the schools there is no conflict worthy of the name.

While, therefore, We hold that every word of wisdom, every useful thing by whomsoever discovered or planned, ought to be received with a willing and grateful mind, We exhort you, Venerable Brethren, in all earnestness to restore the golden wisdom of St. Thomas, and to spread it far and wide for the defence and beauty of the Catholic faith, for the good of society, and for the advantage of all the sciences. The wisdom of St. Thomas, We say; for if anything is taken up with too great subtlety by the Scholastic doctors, or too carelessly stated—if there be anything that ill agrees with the discoveries of a later age, or, in a word, improbable in whatever way, it does not enter Our mind to propose that for imitation to Our age. Let carefully selected teachers endeavor to implant the doctrine of Thomas Aquinas in the minds of students, and set forth clearly his solidity and excellence over others. Let the academies already founded or to be founded by you illustrate and defend this doctrine, and use it for the refutation of prevailing errors. But, lest the false for the true or the corrupt for the pure be drunk in, be ye watchful that the doctrine of Thomas be drawn from his own fountains, or at least from those rivulets which, derived from the very fount, have thus far flowed, according to the established agreement of learned men, pure and clear; be careful to guard the minds of youth from those which are said to flow thence, but in reality are gathered from strange and unwholesome streams.

But well do We know that vain will be Our efforts unless, Venerable Brethren, He helps Our common cause Who, in the words of divine Scripture, is called the God of all knowledge; [40] by which we are also admonished that *every best gift and every perfect gift is from above, coming down from the Father of lights;* [41] and again: *If any of you want wisdom, let him ask of God, who giveth to all men abundantly, and upbraideth not: and it shall be given him.* [42]

Therefore in this also let us follow the example of the Angelic Doctor, who never gave himself to reading or writing without first begging the blessing of God, who modestly confessed that whatever he knew he had acquired not so much by his own study and labor as by the divine gift; and therefore let us all, in humble and united prayer, beseech God to send forth the spirit of knowledge and of understanding to the children of the Church, and open their senses for the understanding of wisdom. And that we may receive fuller fruits of the divine goodness, offer up to God the most efficacious patronage of the Blessed Virgin Mary, who is called the seat of wisdom; having at the same time as advocates St. Joseph, the most chaste spouse of the Virgin, and Peter and Paul, the chiefs of the apostles, whose truth renewed the earth, which had fallen under the impure blight of error, filling it with the light of heavenly wisdom.

In fine, relying on the divine assistance and confiding in your pastoral zeal, We bestow on all of you, Venerable Brethren, on all the clergy and the flocks committed to your charge, the apostolic benediction as a pledge of heavenly gifts and a token of Our special esteem.

[40] *I Kings* ii, 3.   [41] Jas. i. 17.   [42] Jas. i. 5.

POPE PIUS XI

Encyclical Letter

ON THE RECONSTRUCTION
of the SOCIAL ORDER

(*Quadragesimo Anno*)

> Then only will it be possible to unite all in harmonious
> striving for the common good, when all sections of so-
> ciety have the intimate conviction that they are members
> of a single family and children of the same Heavenly
> Father, and further that they are "one body in Christ
> and every one members one of another" *(Rom. xii, 5).*

ORTY YEARS HAVE ELAPSED SINCE THE INCOMPA-
rable Encyclical of Leo XIII of happy memory,
Rerum Novarum, first saw the light. The whole
Catholic world gratefully recalls the event, and
prepares to celebrate it with befitting solemnity.
The way for this remarkable document of pas-
toral solicitude, it is true, had been in a measure prepared by other
pronouncements of Our Predecessor. His letters on The Foundation
of Human Society, The Family and the Holy Sacrament of Matrimony; [1] On the Origin of Civil Power; [2] and its proper coordination
with the Church; [3] on the Belief and Duties of Christian Citizens, [4]

[1] Encycl. *Arcanum,* February 10, 1880.
[2] Encycl. *Diuturnum,* June 29, 1881.
[3] Encycl. *Immortale Dei,* November 1, 1885.
[4] Encycl. *Sapientiae Christianae,* January 10, 1890.

Against the Tenets of Socialism; [5] and the False Notions of Human Liberty; [6] these and others of the kind had unmistakably revealed the mind of Leo XIII. *Rerum Novarum,* however, stood out in this, that it laid down for all mankind unerring rules for the right solution of the difficult problem of human solidarity, called the social question, at the very time when such guidance was most opportune and necessary.

Occasion

Towards the close of the Nineteenth Century the new economic methods and the new development of industry had sprung into being in almost all civilized nations, and had made such headway that human society appeared more and more divided into two classes. The first, small in numbers, enjoyed practically all the comforts so plentifully supplied by modern invention. The second class, comprising the immense multitude of workingmen, was made up of those who, oppressed by dire poverty, struggled in vain to escape from the straits which encompassed them.

This state of things was quite satisfactory to the wealthy, who looked upon it as the consequence of inevitable and natural economic laws, and who, therefore, were content to abandon to charity alone the full care of relieving the unfortunate, as though it were the task of charity to make amends for the open violation of justice, a violation not merely tolerated, but sanctioned at times by legislators. On the other hand, the working classes, victims of these harsh conditions, submitted to them with extreme reluctance, and became more and more unwilling to bear the galling yoke. Some, carried away by the heat of evil counsels, went so far as to seek the disruption of the whole social fabric. Others, whom a solid Christian training restrained from such misguided excesses, convinced themselves nevertheless that there was much in all this that needed a radical and speedy reform.

Such also was the opinion of many Catholics, priests and laymen, who with admirable charity had long devoted themselves to relieving the undeserved misery of the laboring classes, and who could not persuade themselves that so radical and unjust a dis-

[5] Encycl. *Quod Apostolici Muneris,* December 28, 1878.
[6] Encycl. *Libertas,* June 20, 1888.

tinction in the distribution of temporal goods was quite in harmony with the designs of an all-wise Creator.

They therefore sought in all sincerity a remedy against the lamentable disorder already existing in society, and a firm barrier against worse dangers to come. But such is the infirmity of even the best minds, that these men either found themselves repelled as dangerous innovators or opposed by fellow workers in the same cause, who held views different from theirs, and thus wavering in uncertainty, they did not, under the circumstances, know which way to turn.

This grave conflict of opinions was accompanied by discussions not always of a peaceful nature. The eyes of all, as often in the past, turned towards the Chair of Peter, that sacred repository of all truth whence words of salvation are dispensed to the whole world. To the feet of Christ's Vicar on Earth were seen to flock, in unprecedented numbers, sociological students, employers, the very workingmen themselves, begging with one voice that at last a safe road might be pointed out to them. Long did the prudent Pontiff consider the matter before God, seeking the advice of the most experienced counsellors available, and carefully weighing the reason for and against. At last, "urged by the responsibility of the apostolic office" [7] and lest by keeping silence he should seem to neglect his duty,[8] he decided in virtue of the divine *Magisterium* committed to him, to address himself, to the Universal Church of Christ, nay, to the whole human race. On May 15, 1891, therefore, the long-desired message was given to the world. Undaunted by the difficulty of the undertaking or by the weight of years, with unbending courage, the venerable Pontiff taught mankind new methods of approach to social problems.

You know, Venerable Brethren and Beloved Children, you know full well the admirable teaching which has made the Encyclical *Rerum Novarum* forever memorable. In this document the Supreme Shepherd, grieving for the misery and wretchedness pressing unjustly on such a large proportion of mankind, boldly took in his own hands the cause of workingmen, surrendered, isolated and helpless, to the hard-heartedness of employers and the greed of unchecked competition.[9] He sought help neither from Liberalism nor

[7] Encycl. *Rerum Novarum*, ¶ 1.   [8] *Ibid.*, ¶ 13.   [9] *Ibid.*, ¶ 2.

Socialism. The former had already shown its utter impotence to find a right solution of the social question, while the latter would have exposed human society to still graver dangers by offering a remedy much more disastrous than the evil it designed to cure. The Sovereign Pontiff approached the subject in the exercise of his manifest rights, deeply conscious that he was the chief guardian of religion and the chief dispenser of all that closely appertains to it, for the question at issue was one to which no solution could be found apart from the intervention of religion and of the Church.[10] Basing his doctrine solely upon the unchangeable principles drawn from right reason and divine revelation, he indicated and proclaimed with confidence and as one having power,[11] the relative rights and mutual duties of the rich and of the poor, of capital and of labor,[12] and at the same time the part that was to be taken by the Church, by the state and by the persons immediately concerned.

Nor was the Apostolic voice raised in vain. It was listened to with genuine admiration and greeted with profound sympathy not only by the loyal children of the Church, but by many also who had wandered far from the truth and from the unity of faith; nay more, by well-nigh every one who, either as private student or as legislator, was thereafter interested in social and economic questions. With particular enthusiasm was the Pontifical Letter welcomed by Christian workingmen, who felt themselves vindicated and defended by the highest authority on earth, and by all those devoted men whose concern it had long been to better the conditions of labor, and who heretofore had found nothing but general indifference, not to say unfriendly suspicion, or even open hostility. All these men have ever deservedly held the Encyclical in the highest esteem, to the extent of solemnizing its memory in various ways year after year throughout the world in token of gratitude.

Despite this widespread agreement, however, some minds were not a little disturbed, with the result that the noble and exalted teaching of Leo XIII, quite novel to worldly ears, was looked upon with suspicion by some, even amongst Catholics, and gave offense to others. For it boldly attacked and overthrew the idols of Liberalism, swept aside inveterate prejudices, and was so far and so unexpectedly in advance of its time, that the slow of heart ridiculed

[10] *Ibid.,* ¶ 13.   [11] *Matt.* vii, 29.   [12] Encycl. *Rerum Novarum,* ¶ 1.

the study of the new social philosophy, and the timid feared to scale its lofty heights. Nor were there wanting those who, while professing their admiration for this message of light, regarded it as a Utopian ideal, desirable rather than attainable in practice.

The Scope of the Present Encyclical

And now that the solemn commemoration of the fortieth anniversary of *Rerum Novarum* is being enthusiastically celebrated in every country, but particularly in the Holy City, to which Catholic workingmen are gathering from all sides, We deem it opportune, Venerable Brethren and Beloved Children, first, to recall the great benefits which this Encyclical has brought to the Catholic Church and to the world at large; secondly, to vindicate the social and economic doctrine of so great a master against certain doubts which have arisen, and to develop more fully some of its points; finally, after arraigning modern economics and examining the nature of Socialism, to expose the root of the present social disorder, and to point out the only salutary cure, a reform of Christian morals. Such are the three topics to the treatment of which the present Letter is dedicated.

Benefits Due to Encyclical

Beginning, then, with the topic We have mentioned first, We cannot refrain from paying to Almighty God the tribute of Our earnest gratitude for the benefits which have come from the Encyclical of Leo XIII. For We remember the counsel of St. Ambrose: "No duty is more urgent than that of returning thanks." [13] Were We to enumerate these benefits even in a cursory way, it would be necessary to recall almost the whole social history of the past forty years. We may summarize them conveniently under three heads, corresponding to the three forms of intervention for which Our Predecessor pleaded in order to bring about his great work of reconstruction.

What Was Done by the Church

In the first place, Leo himself clearly stated what could be expected from the Church. "The Church insists, on the authority of

[13] St. Ambrose, on the Passing of His Brother Satyrus, Book 1, Chapter 44.

the Gospel, upon those teachings whereby the conflict can be brought to an end, or rendered, at least, far less bitter. The Church uses her efforts not only to enlighten the mind, but to direct by her precepts the life and conduct of each and all. The Church improves and betters the condition of the workingman by means of numerous organizations." [14]

In Doctrinal Matters

This mighty power for good the Church did not suffer to remain unprofitably stored away, but drew upon it freely in the cause of a peace that was so universally desired. Time and again the social and economic doctrine of the Encyclical *Rerum Novarum* was proclaimed and emphasized in spoken and written word by Leo XIII himself and by his successors, who were ever careful to adapt it to the changing conditions of the times, and who never relaxed their paternal solicitude and pastoral constancy, particularly in defense of the poor and of the weak.[15] With like zeal and erudition did numerous Bishops of the Catholic world interpret and comment upon this doctrine, and apply it, according to the mind and instructions of the Holy See, to the special circumstances of the various nations.[16]

It is not surprising, therefore, that under the teaching and guidance of the Church, many learned priests and laymen earnestly devoted themselves to the problem of elaborating social and economic science in accordance with the conditions of our age, for the chief purpose of adapting to modern needs the unchanging and unchangeable doctrine of the Church.

Under the guidance and in the light of Leo's Encyclical was thus evolved a truly Christian social science, which continues to be fostered and enriched daily by the tireless labors of those picked men whom We have named the auxiliaries of the Church. They do not

---

[14] Encycl. *Rerum Novarum*, ¶ 13.

[15] Leo XIII, Litt. Apost. *Praeclara*, June 20, 1894; Encycl. *Graves De communi*, January 18, 1901; Pius X, Motu Proprio *De Actione Populari Christiana*, December 8, 1903; Benedict XV, Encycl. *Ad. Beatissimi*, November 1, 1914; Pius XI, Encycl. *Ubi Arcano*, December 23, 1922; Encycl. *Rite Expiatis*, April 30, 1926.

[16] Cf. *La Hiérarchie Catholique et le Probleme Social Depuis L'Encyclique Rerum Novarum*, 1891-1931, pp. xvi, 335; *Union Internationale d'Etudes Sociales Fondée à Malines, en 1920, Sous La Présidence du Card. Mercier*, Paris, "Editions Spes," 1931.

allow it to remain hidden in learned obscurity, but bring it forth into the full view of public life, as is clearly shown by the valuable and well-frequented courses founded in Catholic universities, academies and seminaries, by social congresses and weeks held at frequent intervals and with gratifying success, by study circles, by sound and timely publications spread far and wide.

Nor were these the only blessings which followed from the Encyclical. The doctrine of *Rerum Novarum* began little by little to penetrate among those also who, being outside Catholic unity, do not recognize the authority of the Church; and thus Catholic principles of sociology gradually became part of the intellectual heritage of the whole human race. Thus, too, We rejoice that the Catholic truths, proclaimed so vigorously by Our illustrious Predecessor, are advanced and advocated not merely in non-Catholic books and journals, but frequently also in legislative assemblies and in courts of justice.

Moreover, when after the great war the rulers of the leading nations wished to restore peace by an entire reform of social conditions, and among other measures drew up principles to regulate the just rights of labor, many of their conclusions agreed so perfectly with the principles and warnings of Leo XIII as to seem expressly deduced from them. The Encyclical *Rerum Novarum* has become in truth a memorable document to which may well be applied the words of Isaias, *A standard set up unto the nations.*[17]

In Practical Application

In the meantime, study and investigation caused Pope Leo's teaching to become widely known throughout the world, and steps were taken to apply it to practical use. In the first place in a spirit of active beneficence, every effort was made to lift up a class of men, who, owing to the expansion of modern industry, had enormously increased in numbers, but whose rightful position in society had not yet been determined, and who in consequence were the objects of much neglect and contempt.

These were the workingmen. In addition, therefore, to their other heavy pastoral duties, the secular and regular clergy, under

[17] *Isa.* xi, 12.

the guidance of the Bishops began at once the work of popular education and culture to the immense advantage of souls.

This constant endeavor to imbue the minds of the workingmen with the Christian spirit did much to awaken in them at the same time a sense of their true dignity. By keeping clearly before their mind the rights and duties of their position, it rendered them capable of legitimate genuine progress, and of becoming leaders of their fellows.

From that time onward, the resources of life were provided for in larger measure and more securely. In answer to the appeal of the Pontiff, works of beneficence and charity began to multiply, under the direction of the Church. And frequently under the guidance of her priests, there sprang up further an ever increasing number of new institutions, by which workingmen, craftsmen, husbandmen, wage-earners of every class could give and receive mutual assistance and support.

What Was Done by Civil Authority

With regard to the civil power, Leo XIII boldly passed beyond the restrictions imposed by Liberalism, and fearlessly proclaimed the doctrine that the civil power is more than the mere guardian of law and order, and that it must strive with all zeal "to make sure that the laws and institutions, the general character and administration of the commonwealth, should be such as of themselves to realize public well-being and private prosperity." [18] It is true, indeed, that a just freedom of action should be left to individual citizens and families: but this principle is only valid as long as the common good is secure and no injustice is entailed. The duty of rulers is to protect the community and its various elements; in protecting the rights of individuals they must have special regard for the infirm and needy. "For the richer class have many ways of shielding themselves and stand less in need of help from the state, whereas the mass of the poor have no resources of their own to fall back upon and must chiefly depend upon the assistance of the state. And for this reason wage-earners, since they mostly belong to that class, should be especially cared for and protected by the government." [19]

---

[18] Encycl. *Rerum Novarum*, ¶ 26.　　　[19] Encycl. *Rerum Novarum*, ¶ 29.

We do not, of course, deny that even before the Encyclical of Leo, some rulers had provided for the more urgent needs of the working classes, and had checked the more flagrant acts of injustice perpetrated against them. But after the Apostolic Voice had sounded from the Chair of Peter throughout the world, the leaders of the nations became at last more fully conscious of their obligations, and set to work seriously to promote a broader social policy.

In fact, the Encyclical *Rerum Novarum* completely overthrew those tottering tenets of Liberalism which had long hampered effective interference by the government. It prevailed upon the peoples themselves to develop their social policy more intensely and on truer lines, and encouraged the élite among Catholics to give such efficacious help and assistance to rulers of the state that in legislative assemblies they were not infrequently the foremost advocates of the new policy. Furthermore, not a few recent laws dealing with social questions were originally proposed to the suffrages of the people's representatives by ecclesiastics thoroughly imbued with Leo's teaching, who afterwards with watchful care promoted and fostered their execution.

As a result of these steady and tireless efforts, there has arisen a new branch of jurisprudence unknown to earlier times, whose aim is the energetic defense of those sacred rights of the workingman which proceed from his dignity as a man and as a Christian. These laws concern the soul, the health, the strength, the housing, workshops, wages, dangerous employments, in a word, all that concerns the wage-earners, with particular regard to women and children. Even though these regulations do not agree always and in every detail with the recommendations of Pope Leo, it is none the less certain that much which they contain is strongly suggestive of *Rerum Novarum,* to which in large measure must be attributed the improved condition of the workingmen.

What Was Done by the Parties Concerned

In the last place, the wise Pontiff pointed out that employers and workmen may of themselves effect much in the matter We are treating, by means of such organizations as afford opportune aid to those who are in distress and which draw the two classes more closely together.[20] Among these he attributed prime importance to societies consisting either of workingmen alone, or of workingmen and employers together. He devotes much space to describing and commending these societies and expounds with remarkable prudence their nature, reason and opportunities, their rights, duties and laws.

The lesson was well timed. For at that period rulers of not a few nations were deeply infected with Liberalism and regarded such unions of workingmen with disfavor, if not with open hostility. While readily recognizing and patronizing similar corporations amongst other classes, with criminal injustice they denied the innate right of forming associations to those who needed them most for self-protection against oppression by the more powerful. There were even Catholics who viewed with suspicion the efforts of the laboring classes to form such unions, as if they reflected the spirit of Socialistic or revolutionary agitators.

Workingmen's Unions

Worthy of all praise, therefore, are the directions authoritatively promulgated by Leo XIII, which served to break down this opposition and dispel these suspicions. They have a still higher distinction, however, that of encouraging Christian workingmen to form unions according to their several trades, and of teaching them how to do it. Many were thus confirmed in the path of duty, in spite of the vehement attractions of Socialist organizations, which claimed to be the sole defenders and champions of the lowly and the oppressed.

The Encyclical *Rerum Novarum* declared most appropriately that "these workingmen's associations should be organized and governed so as to furnish the best and most suitable means for attempting what is aimed at, that is to say, for helping each member to better his condition to the utmost in body, soul and property"; yet that it is clear "that they must pay special and chief attention to the duties of religion and morality, and that social betterment should have this chiefly in view." For "the foundation of social laws being thus laid in religion, it is not hard to establish

[20] Encycl. *Rerum Novarum*, ¶ 36.

the relations of members one to another, in order that they may live together in concord and achieve prosperity." [21]

Eager to carry out to the full the program of Leo XIII, the clergy and many of the laity devoted themselves everywhere with admirable zeal to the creation of such unions, which in turn became instrumental in building up a body of truly Christian workingmen. These happily combined the successful plying of their trade with deep religious convictions; they learned to defend their temporal rights and interests energetically and efficiently, retaining at the same time a due respect for justice and a sincere desire to collaborate with other classes. Thus they prepared the way for a Christian renewal of the whole social life. These counsels of Leo XIII were reduced to practice differently in different places. In some countries one and the same association included within its scope all the ends and purposes proposed by him. In others, according as circumstances seemed to counsel or demand, a division of function developed, and various associations were founded. Of these some undertook the protection of the rights and legitimate interests of their members in the hiring of their labor; others had as their object the provision of mutual help in economic matters; while others, still, were exclusively concerned with religion and pursuits of a similar kind. The latter method was chiefly used wherever the laws of the country, or peculiar economic conditions, or the lamentable dissension of minds and hearts so prevalent in modern society, or the necessity of uniting forces to combat the growing ranks of revolutionaries, made it impossible for Catholics to form Catholic unions. Under such circumstances, they seem to have no choice but to enroll themselves in neutral trade unions. These, however, should always respect justice and equity, and leave to their Catholic members full freedom to follow the dictates of their conscience and to obey the precepts of the Church. It belongs to the Bishops to permit Catholic workingmen to join these unions, where they judge that circumstances render it necessary and there appears no danger for religion, observing however the rules and precautions recommended by Our Predecessor of saintly memory, Pius X.[22]

[21] Encycl. *Rerum Novarum*, ¶ 42, 43.
[22] Encycl. *Singulari Quadam*, September 24, 1912.

Among these precautions the first and most important is that, side by side with these trade unions, there must always be associations which aim at giving their members a thoroughly religious and moral training, that these in turn may impart to the labor unions to which they belong the upright spirit which should direct their entire conduct. Thus will these unions exert a beneficent influence far beyond the ranks of their own members.

It must be set to the credit of the Encyclical that these unions of workingmen have everywhere so flourished, that in our days, though unfortunately still inferior in number to the organizations of Socialists and Communists, they already muster an imposing body of wage-earners able to maintain successfully, both in national and international assemblies, the rights and legitimate demands of Catholic laborers, and to assert the saving principles on which Christian society is based.

Organizations Among Other Classes

There is the further fact that the doctrine concerning the innate right of forming unions, which Leo XIII treated so learnedly and defended so bravely, began to find ready application to corporations other than those of workingmen. It would seem, therefore, that the Encyclical is in no small measure responsible for the gratifying increase and spread of associations amongst farmers and others of the humbler classes. These excellent organizations, with others of a similar kind, happily combine economic advantages with mental culture.

Associations of Employers

Associations of employers and captains of industry, which Our Predecessor so earnestly pleaded for, did not meet with the same success; they are, We regret to say, still few in number. The reason for this must not be entirely attributed to want of good will, but to other and far more serious obstacles, whose nature and gravity we know and appreciate to the full. There are, however, well founded hopes that these obstacles also will shortly be removed. We hail even now with deep joy of soul certain experiments, far from negligible, which have been made in this regard, for the future.[23]

"Rerum Novarum" Magna Charta of Social Order

These beneficent results of Leo's Encyclical, Venerable Brethren and Beloved Children, which We have here suggested rather than described, are so many and so great as to prove beyond question that this immortal document exhibits more than a beautiful, a merely imaginary picture of human society.

We would rather say that Our illustrious Predecessor drew from the Gospel as from a living and life-giving source doctrines capable, if not of settling at once, at least of considerably mitigating the fatal internal strife which rends the human family. That the good seed sown with a lavish hand forty years ago fell in part on good ground is shown by the rich harvest which by God's favor the Church of Christ and the whole human race have reaped unto salvation. It would not be rash to say that during the long years of its usefulness Leo's Encyclical has proved itself the Magna Charta on which all Christian activities in social matters are ultimately based.

Nevertheless, there are some who seem to attach little importance to his Encyclical and to the present anniversary celebration. These men either slander a doctrine of which they are entirely ignorant, or if not unacquainted with this teaching, they betray their failure to understand it, or else if they understand it they lay themselves open to the charge of base injustice and ingratitude.

In the course of these years, however, doubts have arisen concerning the correct interpretation of certain passages of the Encyclical or their inferences, and these doubts have led to controversies even among Catholics, not always of a peaceful character. On the other hand, the new needs of our age and the changed conditions of society have rendered necessary a more precise application and amplification of Leo's doctrine. We, therefore, gladly seize this opportunity of answering their doubts, so far as in Us lies, and of satisfying the demands of the present day. This We do in virtue of Our Apostolic office by which We are a debtor to all.[24]

[23] See Letter of the S. Congregation of the Council to the Bishop of Lille, June 5, 1929. [24] *Rom.* i, 14.

The Authority of the Church in Social and Economic Spheres

But before proceeding to discuss these problems We lay down the principle long since clearly established by Leo XIII that it is Our right and Our duty to deal authoritatively with social and economic problems.[25] It is not of course for the Church to lead men to transient and perishable happiness only, but to that which is eternal. Indeed the Church believes that it would be wrong for her to interfere without just cause in such earthly concerns; [26] but she never can relinquish her God-given task of interposing her authority, not indeed in technical matters, for which she has neither the equipment nor the mission, but in all those that have a bearing on moral conduct. For the deposit of truth entrusted to Us by God, and Our weighty office of propagating, interpreting and urging in season and out of season the entire moral law, demand that both social and economic questions be brought within Our supreme jurisdiction, in so far as they refer to moral issues.

For, though economic science and moral discipline are guided each by its own principles in its own sphere, it is false that the two orders are so distinct and alien that the former in no way depends on the latter. The so-called laws of economics, derived from the nature of earthly goods and from the qualities of the human body and soul, determine what aims are unattainable or attainable in economic matters and what means are thereby necessary, while reason itself clearly deduces from the nature of things and from the individual and social character of man, what is the end and object of the whole economic order assigned by God the Creator.

For it is the moral law alone which commands us to seek in all our conduct our supreme and final end, and to strive directly in our specific actions for those ends which nature, or rather, the Author of Nature, has established for them, duly subordinating the particular to the general. If this law be faithfully obeyed, the result will be that particular economic aims, whether of society as a body or of individuals, will be intimately linked with the universal teleological order, and as a consequence we shall be led by progressive stages to the final end of all, God Himself, our highest and lasting good.

[25] Encycl. *Rerum Novarum*, ¶ 13.
[26] Encycl. *Ubi Arcano*, December 23, 1922.

The Right of Property

Descending now to details, We commence with ownership, or the right of property. You are aware, Venerable Brethren and Beloved Children, how strenuously Our Predecessor of happy memory defended the right of property against the teachings of the Socialists of his time, showing that the abolition of private ownership would prove to be not beneficial, but grievously harmful to the working classes. Yet, since there are some who falsely and unjustly accuse the Supreme Pontiff and the Church as upholding, both then and now, the wealthier classes against the proletariat, and since controversy has arisen among Catholics as to the true sense of Pope Leo's teaching, We have thought it well to defend from calumny the Leonine doctrine in this matter, which is also the Catholic doctrine, and to safeguard it against false interpretations.

Its Individual and Social Character

First, let it be made clear beyond all doubt that neither Leo XIII, nor those theologians who have taught under the guidance and direction of the Church, have ever denied or called in question the twofold aspect of ownership, which is individual or social accordingly as it regards individuals or concerns the common good. Their unanimous contention has always been that the right to own private property has been given to man by nature or rather by the Creator Himself, not only in order that individuals may be able to provide for their own needs and those of their families, but also that by means of it, the goods which the Creator has destined for the human race may truly serve this purpose. Now these ends cannot be secured unless some definite and stable order is maintained.

There is, therefore, a double danger to be avoided. On the one hand, if the social and public aspect of ownership be denied or minimized, the logical consequence is Individualism, as it is called; on the other hand, the rejection or diminution of its private and individual character necessarily leads to some form of Collectivism. To disregard these dangers would be to rush headlong into the quicksands of Modernism with its moral, juridical and social order, which We condemned in the Encyclical Letter issued at the beginning of Our Pontificate.[27]

Let this be noted particularly by those seekers after novelties who launch against the Church the odious calumny that she has allowed a pagan concept of ownership to creep into the teachings of her theologians and that another concept must be substituted, which in their astounding ignorance they call Christian.

The Obligations of Ownership

That We may keep within bounds the controversies which have arisen concerning ownership and the duties attaching to it, We reassert in the first place the fundamental principle laid down by Leo XIII, that the right of property must be distinguished from its use.[28] It belongs to what is called commutative justice faithfully to respect the possessions of others, not encroaching on the rights of another and thus exceeding the rights of ownership. The putting of one's own possessions to proper use, however, does not fall under this form of justice, but under certain other virtues, and therefore it is "a duty not enforced by courts of justice." [29] Hence it is false to contend that the right of ownership and its proper use are bounded by the same limits; and it is even less true that the very misuse or even the non-use of ownership destroys or forfeits the right itself.

Most helpful therefore and worthy of all praise are the efforts of those who, in a spirit of harmony and with due regard for the traditions of the Church, seek to determine the precise nature of these duties and to define the boundaries imposed by the requirements of social life upon the right of ownership itself or upon its use. On the contrary, it is a grievous error so to weaken the individual character of ownership as actually to destroy it.

The Power of the State

It follows from the twofold character of ownership, which We have termed individual and social, that men must take into account

[27] Encycl. *Ubi Arcano*, December 23, 1922.
[28] Encycl. *Rerum Novarum*, ¶ 19.   [29] Encycl. *Rerum Novarum*, ¶ 19.

in this matter not only their own advantage but also the common good. To define in detail these duties, when the need occurs and when the natural law does not do so, is the function of the government. Provided that the natural and divine law be observed, the public authority, in view of the common good, may specify more accurately what is licit and what is illicit for property owners in the use of their possessions. Moreover, Leo XIII had wisely taught that "the defining of private possession has been left by God to man's industry and to the laws of individual peoples." [30]

History proves that the right of ownership, like other elements of social life, is not absolutely rigid, and this doctrine We Ourselves have given utterance to on a previous occasion in the following terms: "How varied are the forms which the right of property has assumed! First, the primitive form used amongst rude and savage peoples, which still exists in certain localities even in our own day; then, that of the patriarchal age; later came various tyrannical types (We use the word in its classical meaning); finally, the feudal and monarchic systems down to the varieties of more recent times." [31]

"It is plain, however, that the state may not discharge this duty in an arbitrary manner. Man's natural right of possessing and transmitting property by inheritance must be kept intact and cannot be taken away by the state from man.[32] Hence, the domestic household is antecedent, as well in idea as in fact, to the gathering of men into a community." [33]

The prudent Pontiff had already declared it unlawful for the state to exhaust the means of individuals by crushing taxes and tributes: "The right to possess private property is derived from nature, not from man; and the state has by no means the right to abolish it, but only to control its use and bring it into harmony with the interests of the public good." [34]

However, when civil authority adjusts ownership to meet the needs of the public good it acts not as an enemy, but as the friend of private owners; for thus it effectively prevents the possession of private property, intended by Nature's Author in His Wisdom for

[30] Encycl. *Rerum Novarum*, ¶ 7.   [31] Allocution to the A. C. I., May 16, 1926.
[32] Encycl. *Rerum Novarum*, ¶ 6.   [33] Encycl. *Rerum Novarum*, ¶ 10.
[34] Encycl. *Rerum Novarum*, ¶ 35.

the sustaining of human life, from creating intolerable burdens and so rushing to its own destruction. It does not therefore abolish, but protects private ownership, and, far from weakening the right of private property, it gives it new strength.

Obligations Regarding Superfluous Income

At the same time a man's superfluous income is not left entirely to his own discretion. We speak of that portion of his income which he does not need in order to live as becomes his station. On the contrary, the grave obligations of charity, beneficence and liberality which rest upon the wealthy are constantly insisted upon in telling words by Holy Scripture and the Fathers of the Church.

However, the investment of superfluous income in searching favorable opportunities for employment, provided the labor employed produces results which are really useful is to be considered, according to the teaching of the Angelic Doctor [35] an act of real liberality particularly appropriate to the needs of our time.

Titles in Acquiring Ownership

The original acquisition of property takes place by first occupation and by industry, or, as it is called, specification. This is the universal teaching of tradition and the doctrine of Our Predecessor, despite unreasonable assertions to the contrary, and no wrong is done to any man by the occupation of goods unclaimed and which belong to nobody. The only form of labor, however, which gives the workingman a title to its fruits is that which a man exercises as his own master, and by which some new form or new value is produced.

Capital and Labor

Altogether different is the labor one man hires out to another, and which is expended on the property of another. To it apply appositely the words of Leo XIII: "It is only by the labor of workingmen that states grow rich." [36] Is it not indeed apparent that the huge possessions which constitute human wealth are begotten by

[35] St. Thomas, *Sum. Theol.*, II-II, q. 134.   [36] Encycl. *Rerum Novarum*, ¶ 27.

and flow from the hands of the workingman, toiling either unaided or with the assistance of tools and machinery which wonderfully intensify his efficiency?

Universal experience teaches us that no nation has ever yet risen from want and poverty to a better and loftier station without the unremitting toil of all its citizens, both employers and employed. But it is no less self-evident that these ceaseless labors would have remained ineffective, indeed could never have been attempted, had not God, the Creator of all things, in His goodness bestowed in the first instance the wealth and resources of nature, its treasures and its powers. For what else is work but the application of one's forces of soul and body to these gifts of nature for the development of one's powers by their means?

Now the natural law, or rather, God's Will manifested by it, demands that right order be observed in the application of natural resources to human need; and this order consists in everything having its proper owner. Hence it follows that unless a man apply his labor to his own property, an alliance must be formed between his toil and his neighbor's property, for each is helpless without the other. This was what Leo XIII had in mind when he wrote: "Capital cannot do without labor, nor labor without capital." [37] It is therefore entirely false to ascribe the results of their combined efforts to either party alone; and it is flagrantly unjust that either should deny the efficacy of the other and seize all the profits.

Unjust Claims of Capital

Capital, however, was long able to appropriate to itself excessive advantages; it claimed all the products and profits and left to the laborer the barest minimum necessary to repair his strength and to ensure the continuation of his class. For by an inexorable economic law, it was held, all accumulation of riches must fall to the share of the wealthy, while the workingman must remain perpetually in indigence or reduced to the minimum needed for existence. It is true that the actual state of things was not always and everywhere as deplorable as the Liberalistic tenets of the so-called Manchester School might lead us to conclude; but it cannot be

[37] Encycl. *Rerum Novarum*, ¶ 15.

denied that a steady drift of economic and social tendencies was in this direction. These false opinions and specious axioms were vehemently attacked, as was to be expected, and by others also than merely those whom such principles deprived of their innate right to better their condition.

Unjust Claims of Labor

The cause of the harassed workingman was espoused by the intellectuals, as they are called, who set up in opposition to this fictitious law another equally false moral principle: that all products and profits, excepting those required to repair and replace invested capital, belong by every right to the workingman. This error, more subtle than that of the Socialists who hold that all means of production should be transferred to the state, or, as they term it, socialized, is for that reason more dangerous and apt to deceive the unwary. It is an alluring poison, consumed with avidity by many not deceived by open Socialism.

Principle of Just Distribution

To prevent erroneous doctrines of this kind from blocking the path of justice and peace, the advocates of these opinions should have hearkened to the wise words of Our Predecessor: "The earth, even though apportioned amongst private owners, ceases not thereby to minister to the needs of all." [38] This teaching We Ourselves have reaffirmed above when We wrote that the division of goods which is effected by private ownership is ordained by nature itself and has for its purpose that created things may minister to man's needs in orderly and stable fashion. These principles must be constantly borne in mind if we would not wander from the path of truth.

Now, not every kind of distribution of wealth and property amongst men is such that it can at all, and still less can adequately, attain the end intended by God. Wealth, therefore, which is constantly being augmented by social and economic progress, must be so distributed amongst the various individuals and classes of society

[38] Encycl. *Rerum Novarum*, ¶ 7.

that the common good of all, of which Leo XIII spoke, be thereby promoted. In other words, the good of the whole community must be safeguarded. By these principles of social justice one class is forbidden to exclude the other from a share in the profits. This sacred law is violated by an irresponsible wealthy class who, in the excess of their good fortune, deem it a just state of things that they should receive everything and the laborer nothing; it is violated also by a propertyless wage-earning class who demand for themselves all the fruits of production, as being the work of their hands. Such men, vehemently incensed against the violation of justice by capitalists, go too far in vindicating the one right of which they are conscious; they attack and seek to abolish all forms of ownership and all profits not obtained by labor, whatever be their nature or significance in human society, for the sole reason that they are not acquired by toil. In this connection it must be noted that the appeal made by some to the words of the Apostle: *If any man will not work, neither let him eat,*[39] is as inept as it is unfounded. The Apostle is here passing judgment on those who refuse to work though they could and ought to do so; he admonishes us to use diligently our time and our powers of body and mind, and not to become burdensome to others as long as we are able to provide for ourselves. In no sense does he teach that labor is the sole title which gives a right to a living or to profits.[40]

Each class, then, must receive its due share, and the distribution of created goods must be brought into conformity with the demands of the common good and social justice, for every sincere observer is conscious that the vast differences between the few who hold excessive wealth and the many who live in destitution constitute a grave evil in modern society.

The Uplifting of the Proletariat

This is the aim which Our Predecessor urged as the necessary object of Our efforts: the uplifting of the proletariat. It calls for more emphatic assertion and more insistent repetition on the present occasion because these salutary injunctions of the Pontiff have not infrequently been forgotten, deliberately ignored, or deemed

---

[39] *II Thess.* iii, 10.   [40] *II Thess.* iii, 8, 10.

impracticable, though they were both feasible and imperative. They
have lost none of their force or wisdom for our own age, even
though the horrible condition of the days of Leo XIII is less prevalent today. The condition of the workingman has indeed been
improved and rendered more equitable in many respects, particularly in the larger and more civilized states, where the laboring
class can no longer be said to be universally in misery and want.
But after modern machinery and modern industry had progressed
with astonishing speed and taken possession of many newly colo-
nized countries no less than of the ancient civilizations of the Far
East, the number of the dispossessed laboring masses, whose groans
mount to Heaven from these lands, increased beyond all measure.

Moreover, there is the immense army of hired rural laborers,
whose condition is depressed in the extreme, and who have no hope
of ever obtaining a share in the land.[41] These, too, unless efficacious remedies be applied, will remain perpetually sunk in the
proletarian condition.

It is true that there is a formal difference between pauperism and
proletarianism. Nevertheless, the immense number of propertyless
wage-earners on the one hand, and the superabundant riches of the
fortunate few on the other, is an unanswerable argument that the
earthly goods so abundantly produced in this age of industrialism
are far from rightly distributed and equitably shared among the
various classes of men.

Proletarian Conditions to be Overcome by Wage-Earner Ownership

Every effort, therefore, must be made that at least in future a
just share only of the fruits of production be permitted to accumu-
late in the hands of the wealthy, and that an ample sufficiency be
supplied to the workingmen. The purpose is not that these become slack at their work, for man is born to labor as the bird to
fly, but that by thrift they may increase their possessions and by
the prudent management of the same may be enabled to bear the
family burden with greater ease and security, being freed from that
hand-to-mouth uncertainty which is the lot of the proletarian. Thus
they will not only be in a position to support life's changing for-

41 Encycl. *Rerum Novarum,* ¶ 35.

tunes, but will also have the reassuring confidence that when their lives are ended, some little provision will remain for those whom they leave behind them.

These ideas were not merely suggested, but stated in frank and open terms by Our Predecessor. We emphasize them with renewed insistence in this present Encyclical; for unless serious attempts be made, with all energy and without delay to put them into practice, let nobody persuade himself that the peace and tranquillity of human society can be effectively defended against the forces of revolution!

A Just Wage

This program cannot, however, be realized unless the property-less wage-earner be placed in such circumstances that by skill and thrift he can acquire a certain moderate ownership, as was already declared by Us, following the footsteps of Our Predecessor. But how can he ever save money, except from his wages and by living sparingly, who has nothing but his labor by which to obtain food and the necessities of life? Let Us turn, therefore, to the question of wages, which Leo XIII held to be "of great importance," [42] stating and explaining where necessary its principles and precepts.

Wage Contract Not Essentially Unjust

And first of all, those who hold that the wage contract is essentially unjust, and that in its place must be introduced the contract of partnership, are certainly in error. They do a grave injury to Our Predecessor, whose Encyclical not only admits this contract, but devotes much space to its determination according to the principles of justice.

In the present state of human society, however, We deem it advisable that the wage contract should, when possible, be modified somewhat by a contract of partnership, as is already being tried in various ways to the no small gain both of the wage-earners and of the employers. In this way wage-earners are made sharers in some sort in the ownership, or the management, or the profits.

In estimating a just wage, not one consideration alone but many

[42] Encycl. *Rerum Novarum,* ¶ 34.

must be taken into account. According to the wise words of Leo XIII: "Before deciding whether wages are fair, many things have to be considered." [43]

In this way he refuted the irresponsible view of certain writers who declare that this momentous question can easily be solved by the application of a single principle, and that not even a true one.

Entirely false is the principle, widely propagated today, that the worth of labor and therefore the equitable return to be made for it, should equal the worth of its net result. Thus the right to the full product of his toil is claimed for the wage-earner. How erroneous this is appears from what We have written above concerning capital and labor.

Individual and Social Character of Labor

The obvious truth is that in labor, especially hired labor, as in ownership, there is a social as well as a personal or individual aspect to be considered. For unless human society forms a truly social and organic body; unless labor be protected in the social and juridical order; unless the various forms of human endeavor, dependent one upon the other, are united in mutual harmony and mutual support; unless, above all, brains, capital and labor combine together for common effort, man's toil cannot produce due fruit. Hence, if the social and individual character of labor be overlooked, it can be neither equitably appraised nor properly recompensed according to strict justice.

From this double aspect, growing out of the very notion of human labor, follow important conclusions for the regulation and fixing of wages.

Support of the Workingman and His Family

In the first place, the wage paid to the workingman must be sufficient for the support of himself and of his family.[44] It is right indeed that the rest of the family contribute according to their power towards the common maintenance, as in the rural home or in the

[43] Encycl. *Rerum Novarum,* ¶ 17.
[44] Encycl. *Casti Connubii,* December 31, 1930.

families of many artisans and small shopkeepers. But it is wrong to abuse the tender years of children or the weakness of woman. Mothers will above all devote their work to the home and the things connected with it; intolerable, and to be opposed with all Our strength, is the abuse whereby mothers of families, because of the insufficiency of the father's salary, are forced to engage in gainful occupations outside the domestic walls to the neglect of their own proper cares and duties, particularly the education of their children.

Every effort must therefore be made that fathers of families receive a wage sufficient to meet adequately ordinary domestic needs. If in the present state of society this is not always feasible, social justice demands that reforms be introduced without delay which will guarantee every adult workingman just such a wage. In this connection We might utter a word of praise for various systems devised and attempted in practice, by which an increased wage is paid in view of increased family burdens, and a special provision is made for special needs.

The State of Business

The condition of any particular business and of its owner must also come into question in settling the scale of wages; for it is unjust to demand wages so high that an employer cannot pay them without ruin, and without consequent distress amongst the working people themselves. If the business make smaller profit on account of bad management, want of enterprise or out-of-date methods, this is not a just reason for reducing the workingmen's wages. If, however, the business does not make enough money to pay the workman a just wage, either because it is overwhelmed with unjust burdens, or because it is compelled to sell its products at an unjustly low price, those who thus injure it are guilty of grievous wrong; for it is they who deprive the workingmen of the just wage, and force them to accept lower terms.

Let employers, therefore, and employed join in their plans and efforts to overcome all difficulties and obstacles, and let them be aided in this wholesome endeavor by the wise measures of the public authority. In the last extreme, counsel must be taken whether the business can continue, or whether some other provision should be made for the workers. The guiding spirit in this crucial decision should be one of mutual understanding and Christian harmony between employers and workers.

The Exigencies of the Common Good

The exigencies of the common good finally must be regulated with a view to the economic welfare of the whole people. We have already shown how conducive it is to the common good that wage-earners of all kinds be enabled, by economizing that portion of their wages which remains after necessary expenses have been met, to attain to the possession of a certain modest fortune. Another point, however, of no less importance must not be overlooked, in these days especially, namely, that opportunities for work be provided for those who are willing and able to work. This depends in large measure upon the scale of wages, which multiplies opportunities for work as long as it remains within proper limits, and reduces them if allowed to pass these limits. All are aware that a scale of wages too low, no less than a scale excessively high, causes unemployment. Now unemployment, particularly if widespread and of long duration, as We have been forced to experience it during Our Pontificate, is a dreadful scourge; it causes misery and temptation to the laborer, ruins the prosperity of nations, and endangers public order, peace and tranquillity the world over. To lower or raise wages unduly, with a view to private profit, and with no consideration for the common good, is contrary to social justice which demands that by union of effort and good will such a scale of wages be set up, if possible, as to offer to the greatest number opportunities of employment and of securing for themselves suitable means of livelihood.

A reasonable relationship between different wages here enters into consideration. Intimately connected with this is a reasonable relationship between the prices obtained for the products of the various economic groups, agrarian, industrial, etc. Where this harmonious proportion is kept, man's various economic activities combine and unite into one single organism and become members of a common body, lending each other mutual help and service. For then only will the economic and social organism be soundly established and attain its end, when it secures for all and each those goods which the wealth and resources of nature, technical achievement, and the social organization of economic affairs can give. These goods should be sufficient to supply all needs and an honest livelihood, and to uplift men to that higher level of prosperity and culture which, provided it be used with prudence, is not only no hindrance but is of singular help to virtue.[45]

The Reconstruction of the Social Order

What We have written thus far regarding a right distribution of property and a just scale of wages is concerned directly with the individual, and deals only indirectly with the social order. To this latter, however, Our Predecessor, Leo XIII, devoted special thought and care in his efforts to reconstruct and perfect it according to the principles of sound philosophy and the sublime precepts of the Gospel.[46]

A happy beginning has here been made. But in order that what has been well begun may be rendered stable, that what has not yet been accomplished may now be achieved, and that still richer and brighter blessings may descend upon mankind, two things are particularly necessary: the reform of the social order and the correction of morals.

When We speak of the reform of the social order it is principally the state We have in mind. Not indeed that all salvation is to be hoped for from its intervention, but because on account of the evil of Individualism, as We called it, things have come to such a pass that the highly developed social life which once flourished in a variety of prosperous institutions organically linked with each other, has been damaged and all but ruined, leaving thus virtually only individuals and the state. Social life lost entirely its organic form. The state, which now was encumbered with all the burdens once borne by associations rendered extinct by it, was in consequence submerged and overwhelmed by an infinity of affairs and duties.

It is indeed true, as history clearly proves, that owing to the change in social conditions, much that was formerly done by small

[45] Cf. St. Thomas, *De Regimine Principum*, 1, 15; Encycl. *Rerum Novarum*, ¶ 27.
[46] Encycl. *Rerum Novarum*, ¶ 16.

bodies can nowadays be accomplished only by large corporations. None the less, just as it is wrong to withdraw from the individual and commit to the community at large what private enterprise and industry can accomplish, so, too, it is an injustice, a grave evil and a disturbance of right order for a larger and higher organization to arrogate to itself functions which can be performed efficiently by smaller and lower bodies. This is a fundamental principle of social philosophy, unshaken and unchangeable, and it retains its full truth today. Of its very nature the true aim of all social activity should be to help individual members of the social body, but never to destroy or absorb them.

The state should leave to these smaller groups the settlement of business of minor importance. It will thus carry out with greater freedom, power and success the tasks belonging to it, because it alone can effectively accomplish these, directing, watching, stimulating and restraining, as circumstances suggest or necessity demands. Let those in power, therefore, be convinced that the more faithfully this principle be followed, and a graded hierarchical order exist between the various subsidiary organizations, the more excellent will be both the authority and the efficiency of the social organization as a whole and the happier and more prosperous the condition of the state.

Harmony Between Ranks in Society

Now this is the primary duty of the state and of all good citizens; to abolish conflict between classes with divergent interests, and thus foster and promote harmony between the various ranks of society.

The aim of social legislation must therefore be the reestablishment of vocational groups. Society today still remains in a strained and therefore unstable and uncertain state, being founded on classes with contradictory interests and hence opposed to each other, and consequently prone to enmity and strife. Labor, indeed, as has been well said by Our Predecessor in his Encyclical, is not a mere chattel, since the human dignity of the workingman must be recognized in it, and consequently it cannot be bought and sold like any piece of merchandise. None the less the demand and supply of labor divides men on the labor market into two classes, as into two camps, and the bargaining between these parties transforms this labor market into an arena where the two armies are engaged in combat. To this grave disorder which is leading society to ruin a remedy must evidently be applied as speedily as possible. But there cannot be question of any perfect cure, except this opposition be done away with, and well ordered members of the social body come into being anew, vocational groups namely, binding men together not according to the position they occupy in the labor market, but according to the diverse functions which they exercise in society. For as nature induces those who dwell in close proximity to unite into municipalities, so those who practice the same trade or profession, economic or otherwise, combine into vocational groups. These groups, in a true sense autonomous, are considered by man to be, if not essential to civil society, at least its natural and spontaneous development.

Order, as the Angelic Doctor well defines, is unity arising from the apt arrangement of a plurality of objects; hence, true and genuine social order demands various members of society, joined together by a common bond.[47] Such a bond of union is provided on the one hand by the common effort of employers and employees of one and the same group joining forces to produce goods or give service; on the other hand, by the common good which all groups should unite to promote, each in its own sphere, with friendly harmony. Now this union will become powerful and efficacious in proportion to the fidelity with which the individuals and the groups strive to discharge their professional duties and to excel in them.

From this it is easy to conclude that in these associations the common interest of the whole group must predominate: and among these interests the most important is the directing of the activities of the group to the common good. Regarding cases in which interests of employers and employees call for special care and protection against opposing interests, separate deliberation will take place in their respective assemblies and separate votes will be taken as the matter may require.

It is hardly necessary to note that what Leo XIII taught concerning the form of political government can, in due measure, be applied also to vocational groups. Here, too, men may choose what-

[47] St. Thomas, *Cont. Gent.* iii, 71; cf. *Sum. Theol.*, I, q. 65, a. 2.

ever form they please, provided that both justice and the common good be taken into account.[48]

Just as the citizens of the same municipality are wont to form associations with diverse aims, which various individuals are free to join or not, similarly, those who are engaged in the same trade or profession will form free associations among themselves, for purposes connected with their occupations. Our Predecessor explained clearly and lucidly the nature of free associations. We are content, therefore, to emphasize this one point: not only is man free to institute these unions which are of a private character, but he has the right to adopt such organization and such rules as may best conduce to the attainment of their respective objects.[49] The same liberty must be claimed for the founding of associations which extend beyond the limits of a single trade. Let those free associations which already flourish and produce salutary fruits make it the goal of their endeavors, in accordance with Christian social doctrine, to prepare the way and to do their part towards the realization of that ideal type of vocational groups which We have mentioned above.

The Restoration of the True Guiding Principle of Economics

Still another aim must be kept in view. Just as the unity of human society cannot be built upon class warfare, so the proper ordering of economic affairs cannot be left to free competition alone. From this source have proceeded in the past all the errors of the "Individualistic" school. This school, ignorant or forgetful of the social and moral aspects of economic matters, teaches that the state should refrain in theory and practice from interfering therein, because these possess in free competition and open markets a principle of self-direction better able to control them than any created intellect. Free competition, however, though within certain limits just and productive of good results, cannot be the ruling principle of the economic world. This has been abundantly proved by the consequences that have followed from the free rein given to these dangerous individualistic ideals. It is therefore very necessary that economic affairs be once more subjected to and governed by a true

[48] Encycl. *Immortale Dei,* November 1, 1885.
[49] Encycl. *Rerum Novarum,* ¶ 42.

..nd effective guiding principle. Still less can this function be exercised by the economic supremacy which within recent times has taken the place of free competition: for this is a headstrong and vehement power, which, if it is to prove beneficial to mankind, needs to be curbed strongly and ruled with prudence. It cannot, however, be curbed and governed by itself. More lofty and noble principles must therefore be sought in order to control this supremacy sternly and uncompromisingly: to wit, social justice and social charity.

To that end all the institutions of public and social life must be imbued with the spirit of justice, and this justice must above all be truly operative. It must build up a juridical and social order able to pervade all economic activity. Social charity should be, as it were, the soul of this order and the duty of the state will be to protect and defend it effectively. This task it will perform the more readily if it free itself from those burdens which, as we have already declared, are not properly its own.

Further, it would be well if the various nations in common counsel and endeavor strove to promote a healthy economic cooperation by prudent pacts and institutions, since in economic matters they are largely dependent one upon the other, and need one another's help.

If then the members of the social body be thus reformed, and if the true directive principle of social and economic activity be thus reestablished, it will be possible to say, in a sense, of this body what the Apostle said of the Mystical Body of Christ: *The whole body being compacted and fitly joined together, by what every joint supplieth, according to the operation in the measure of every part, maketh increase of the body, unto the edifying of itself in charity.*[50]

Within recent times, as all are aware, a special syndical and corporative organization has been inaugurated which, in view of the subject of the present Encyclical, demands of Us some mention and opportune comment.

The state here grants legal recognition to the syndicate or union, and thereby confers on it some of the features of a monopoly, for in virtue of this recognition, it alone can represent respectively

[50] *Ephes.* iv, 16.

workingmen and employers, and it alone can conclude labor contracts and labor agreements. Affiliation to the syndicate is optional for everyone; but in this sense only can the syndical organization be said to be free, since the contribution to the union and other special taxes are obligatory for all who belong to a given branch, whether workingmen or employers, and the labor contracts drawn up by the legal syndicate are likewise obligatory. It is true that it has been authoritatively declared that the legal syndicate does not exclude the existence of unrecognized trade associations.

The corporations are composed of representatives of the unions of workingmen and employers of the same trade or profession, and as true and genuine organs and institutions of the state they direct and coordinate the activities of the unions in all matters of common interest. Strikes and lock-outs are forbidden. If the contending parties cannot come to an agreement, public authority intervenes.

Little reflection is required to perceive the advantage of the institution thus summarily described; peaceful collaboration of the classes, repression of Socialist organizations and efforts, the moderating influence of a special ministry.

But in order to overlook nothing in a matter of such importance, and in the light of the general principles stated above, as well as of that which We are now about to formulate, We feel bound to add that to Our knowledge there are some who fear that the state is substituting itself in the place of private initiative, instead of limiting itself to necessary and sufficient help and assistance. It is feared that the new syndical and corporative institution possesses an excessively bureaucratic and political character, and that, notwithstanding the general advantages referred to above, it risks serving particular political aims rather than contributing to the initiation of a better social order.

We believe that to attain this last named lofty purpose for the true and permanent advantage of the commonwealth, there is need before and above all else of the blessing of God, and, in the second place, of the cooperation of all men of good will. We believe, moreover, as a necessary consequence, that the end intended will be the more certainly attained the greater the contribution furnished by men of technical, commercial and social competence, and, more still, by Catholic principles and their application. We look for this contribution, not to Catholic Action which has no intention of displaying any strictly syndical or political activities, but to Our sons, whom Catholic Action imbues with these principles and trains for the Apostolate under the guidance and direction of the Church, of the Church We say, which in the above mentioned sphere, as in all others where moral questions are discussed and regulated, cannot forget or neglect its mandate as custodian and teacher given it by God.

However, all that We have taught about reconstructing and perfecting the social order will be of no avail without a reform of manners. Of this, history affords the clearest evidence. At one period there existed a social order which, though by no means perfect in every respect, corresponded nevertheless in a certain measure to right reason according to the needs and conditions of the times. That this order has long since perished is not due to the fact that it was incapable of development and adaptation to changing needs and circumstances, but rather to the wrong-doing of men. Men were hardened in excessive self-love and refused to extend that order, as was their duty, to the increasing numbers of the people; or else, deceived by the attractions of false liberty and other errors, they grew impatient of every restraint and endeavored to throw off all authority.

It remains for Us then to turn Our attention to the actual condition of the economic order and to its bitterest adversary and accuser: We mean Socialism. On these We shall pronounce a frank and just sentence; shall examine more closely the root of the present grave evils, and shall indicate the first and most necessary remedy, which lies in a reform of morals.

Changes Since Leo XIII

Since the time of Leo XIII important changes have taken place both in economic conditions and in regard to Socialism. In the first place, it is obvious to all that the entire economic scene has greatly changed. You are aware, Venerable Brethren and Beloved Children, that Our Predecessor, of happy memory, had chiefly in mind that economic régime in which were provided by different people the capital and labor jointly needed for production. He described it in a happy phrase: "Capital cannot do without labor." [51]

Leo XIII's whole endeavor was to adjust this economic régime to the standards of true order; whence it follows that the system itself is not to be condemned. And surely it is not vicious of its very nature; but it violates right order whenever capital so employs the working or wage-earning classes as to divert business and economic activity entirely to its own arbitrary will and advantage without any regard to the human dignity of the workers, the social character of economic life, social justice and the common good.

It is true that even today these economic conditions do not everywhere exist exclusively, for there is another economic system which still embraces a very large and influential group of men. There are for instance the agricultural classes, who form the larger portion of the human family and who find in their occupation the means of obtaining honestly and justly what is needful for their maintenance. The system, too, has its difficulties and problems, of which Our Predecessor spoke repeatedly in his Encyclical, and to which We Ourselves have more than once referred in the present Letter.

But it is the capitalist economic régime that, with the world-wide diffusion of industry, has penetrated everywhere, particularly since the publication of Leo XIII's Encyclical. It has invaded and pervaded the economic and social sphere even of those who live outside its ambit, influencing them, and, as it were, intimately affecting them by its advantages, inconveniences and vices.

When We turn Our attention, therefore, to the changes which this capitalistic economic order has undergone since the days of Leo XIII, We have regard to the interests, not of those only who live in countries where "capital" and industry prevail, but of the whole human race.

Domination Has Followed From Free Competition

In the first place, then, it is patent that in our days not alone is wealth accumulated, but immense power and despotic economic domination is concentrated in the hands of a few, and that those

51 Encycl. *Rerum Novarum,* ¶ 15.

few are frequently not the owners, but only the trustees and directors of invested funds, who administer them at their good pleasure.

This power becomes particularly irresistible when exercised by those who, because they hold and control money, are able also to govern credit, and determine its allotment, for that reason supplying, so to speak, the life-blood to the entire economic body, and grasping, as it were, in their hands the very soul of production, so that no one dare breathe against their will.

This accumulation of power, the characteristic note of the modern economic order, is a natural result of limitless free competition which permits the survival of those only who are the strongest, which often means those who fight most relentlessly, who pay least heed to the dictates of conscience.

This concentration of power has led to a threefold struggle for domination. First, there is the struggle for dictatorship in the economic sphere itself; then, the fierce battle to acquire control of the state, so that its resources and authority may be abused in the economic struggles. Finally, the clash between states themselves.

This latter arises from two causes:—Because the nations apply their power and political influence, regardless of circumstances, to promote the economic advantages of their citizens; and because, *vice versa,* economic forces and economic domination are used to decide political controversies between peoples.

Disastrous Consequences

You assuredly know, Venerable Brethren and Beloved Children, and you lament the ultimate consequences of this Individualistic spirit in economic affairs. Free competition is dead; economic dictatorship has taken its place.

Unbridled ambition for domination has succeeded the desire for gain; the whole economic life has become hard, cruel and relentless in a ghastly measure. Furthermore, the intermingling and scandalous confusing of the duties and offices of civil authority and of economics has produced crying evils and has gone so far as to degrade the majesty of the state. The state which should be the supreme arbiter, ruling in kingly fashion far above all party contention, intent only upon justice and the common good, has become instead a slave, bound over to the service of human passion and greed. As regards the relations of peoples among themselves, a double stream has issued forth from this one fountainhead: on the one hand, economic nationalism or even economic imperialism; on the other, a not less noxious and detestable internationalism or international imperialism in financial affairs, which holds that where a man's fortune is, there is his country.

The remedies for these great evils We have exposed in the second part of the present Encyclical, where We explicitly dwelt upon their doctrinal aspect. It will, therefore, be sufficient to recall them briefly here. Since the present economic régime is based mainly upon capital and labor, it follows that the principles of right reason and Christian social philosophy regarding capital, labor and their mutual cooperation must be accepted in theory and reduced to practice. In the first place, due consideration must be had for the double character, individual and social, of capital and labor, in order that the dangers of Individualism and of Collectivism be avoided. The mutual relations between capital and labor must be determined according to the laws of the strictest justice, called commutative justice, supported however by Christian charity. Free competition and still more economic domination must be kept within just and definite limits, and must be brought under the effective control of the public authority, in matters appertaining to this latter's competence. The public institutions of the nations must be such as to make the whole of human society conform to the common good, *i. e.,* to the standard of social justice. If this is done, the economic system, that most important branch of social life, will necessarily be restored to sanity and right order.

Changes in Socialism

Since the days of Leo XIII, Socialism too, the great enemy with which his battles were waged, has undergone profound changes, no less than economics. At that time Socialism could fairly be termed a single system, which defended certain definite and mutually coherent doctrines. Nowadays it has in the main become divided into two opposing and often bitterly hostile camps, neither of which, however, has abandoned the principle peculiar to Socialism, namely, opposition to the Christian Faith.

The More Violent Section, Communism

One section of Socialism has undergone approximately the same change through which, as We have described, the capitalistic economic régime has passed; it has degenerated into Communism. Communism teaches and pursues a twofold aim: Merciless class warfare and complete abolition of private ownership; and this it does, not in secret and by hidden methods, but openly, frankly, and by every means, even the most violent. To obtain these ends, Communists shrink from nothing and fear nothing; and when they have attained power it is unbelievable, indeed it seems portentous, how cruel and inhuman they show themselves to be. Evidence for this is the ghastly destruction and ruin with which they have laid waste immense tracts of Eastern Europe and Asia, while their antagonism and open hostility to Holy Church and to God Himself are, alas! but too well known and proved by their deeds. We do not think it necessary to warn upright and faithful children of the Church against the impious and nefarious character of Communism. But We cannot contemplate without sorrow the heedlessness of those who seem to make light of these imminent dangers and with stolid indifference allow the propagation far and wide of those doctrines which seek by violence and bloodshed the destruction of all society. Even more severely must be condemned the foolhardiness of those who neglect to remove or modify such conditions as exasperate the minds of the people, and so prepare the way for the overthrow and ruin of the social order.

More Moderate Section

The other section, which has retained the name of Socialism, is much less radical in its views. Not only does it condemn recourse to physical force; it even mitigates and moderates to some extent class warfare and the abolition of private property. It does not reject them entirely. It would seem as if Socialism were afraid of its own principles and of the conclusion drawn therefrom by the

Communists, and in consequence were drifting towards the truth which Christian tradition has always held in respect; for it cannot be denied that its programs often strikingly approach the just demands of Christian social reformers.

It recedes somewhat from class war and the extinction of ownership.

Class war, provided it abstains from enmities and mutual hatred, is changing gradually to an honest discussion of differences, based upon the desire of social justice. If this is by no means the blessed social peace which we all long for, it can be and must be an approach towards the mutual cooperation of vocational groups. The war declared against private ownership has also abated more and more. In such a way that nowadays it is not really the possession of the means of production which is attacked but that type of social rulership, which, in violation of all justice, has been seized and usurped by the owners of wealth. This rulership in fact belongs, not to the individual owners, but to the state.

If these changes continue, it may well come about that gradually the tenets of mitigated Socialism will no longer be different from the program of those who seek to reform human society according to Christian principles.

For it is rightly contended that certain forms of property must be reserved to the state, since they carry with them an opportunity of domination too great to be left to private individuals without injury to the community at large.

Just demands and desires of this kind contain nothing opposed to Christian truth, nor are they in any sense peculiar to Socialism. Those therefore who look for nothing else have no reason for becoming Socialists.

The Possibility of a Middle Course

It must not be imagined however that all the Socialist sects or factions which are not Communist have in fact or in theory uniformly returned to this reasonable position. For the most part they do not reject class warfare and the abolition of property, but merely are more moderate in regard to them. Now, when false principles are thus mitigated and in some sense waived, the question arises, or is unwarrantably proposed in certain quarters, whether the principles of Christian truth also could not be somewhat moderated and attenuated, so as to meet Socialism, as it were, halfway upon common ground. Some are engaged by the empty hope of gaining in this way the Socialists to our cause. But such hopes are vain. Those who wish to be apostles amongst the Socialists should preach the Christian truth whole and entire, openly and sincerely, without any connivance with error. If they wish in truth to be heralds of the Gospel, let their endeavor be to convince Socialists that their demands, in so far as they are just, are defended much more cogently by the principles of Christian faith, and are promoted much more efficaciously by the power of Christian charity.

But what if, in questions of class war and private ownership, Socialism were to become so mitigated and amended, that nothing reprehensible could any longer be found in it? Would it by that very fact have laid aside its character of hostility to the Christian religion? This is a question which holds many minds in suspense; and many are the Catholics who, realizing clearly that Christian principles can never be either sacrificed or minimized, seem to be raising their eyes towards the Holy See, and earnestly beseeching Us to decide whether or not this form of Socialism has retracted so far its false doctrines that it can now be accepted without the loss of any Christian principle, and be baptized into the Church. In Our fatherly solicitude We desire to satisfy these petitions, and We pronounce as follows: whether Socialism be considered as a doctrine, or as a historical fact, or as a movement, if it really remain Socialism, it cannot be brought into harmony with the dogmas of the Catholic Church, even after it has yielded to truth and justice in the points We have mentioned; the reason being that it conceives human society in a way utterly alien to Christian truth.

Socialism Conceives Society and Social Character of Men Foreign to Christian Truth

According to Christian doctrine, Man, endowed with a social nature, is placed here on earth in order that he may spend his life in society, and under an authority ordained by God, that he may develop and evolve to the full all his faculties to the praise and glory of his Creator; and that, by fulfilling faithfully the duties of his station, he may attain to temporal and eternal happiness. Socialism, on the contrary, entirely ignorant of or unconcerned about this sublime end both of individuals and of society, affirms that living in community was instituted merely for the sake of advantages which it brings to mankind.

Goods are produced more efficiently by a suitable distribution of labor than by the scattered efforts of individuals. Hence the Socialists argue that economic production, of which they see only the material side, must necessarily be carried on collectively, and that because of this necessity men must surrender and submit themselves wholly to society with a view to the production of wealth. Indeed, the possession of the greatest possible amount of temporal goods is esteemed so highly, that man's higher goods, not excepting liberty, must, they claim, be subordinated and even sacrificed to the exigencies of efficient production. They affirm that the loss of human dignity, which results from these socialized methods of production, will be easily compensated for by the abundance of goods produced in common and accruing to the individual who can turn them at his will to the comforts and culture of life. Society, therefore, as the Socialist conceives it, is, on the one hand, impossible and unthinkable without the use of compulsion of the most excessive kind: on the other, it fosters a false liberty, since in such a scheme no place is found for true social authority, which is not based on temporal and material advantages, but descends from God alone, the Creator and Last End of all things.[52]

Catholic and Socialist Are Contradictory Terms

If, like all errors, Socialism contains a certain element of truth (and this the Sovereign Pontiffs have never denied), it is nevertheless founded upon a doctrine of human society peculiarly its own, which is opposed to true Christianity. "Religious Socialism," "Christian Socialism" are expressions implying a contradiction in terms. No one can be at the same time a sincere Catholic and a true Socialist.

[52] Encycl. *Diuturnum Illud,* June 29, 1881.

Cultural Socialism

All that We have thus far laid down and established by Our sovereign authority bears application also to a certain new Socialist phenomenon, hitherto little known, but nowadays common to many sections of Socialism. Its main aim is the formation of minds and manners. Under the appearance of friendship, it attracts little children in particular and attaches them to itself, though its activity extends to all the people, to make of them convinced Socialists, upon whom to build society modeled on Socialistic principles.

In Our Encyclical Letter *Divini Illius Magistri*,[53] We have expounded at length the true principles on which Christian education rests and the end which it pursues. The contradiction between these and the actions and aims of cultural Socialism is so clear and evident as to require no comment. Nevertheless, the formidable dangers which this form of Socialism brings in its train seem to be ignored or underestimated by those who are little concerned to resist it with strength and zeal, as the gravity of the situation demands.

It is a duty of Our pastoral office to warn these men of the grave danger which threatens. Let us bear in mind that the parent of this cultural Socialism was Liberalism, and that its offspring will be Bolshevism.

Catholic Deserters to Socialism

This being so, you can understand, Venerable Brethren and Beloved Children, with what grief We perceive, in certain countries particularly, not a few of Our children, who, while still preserving, as We are convinced, their true faith and good will, have deserted the camp of the Church and passed over to the ranks of Socialism. Some openly boast of its name and profess Socialistic doctrines; others, either through indifference or even almost in spite of themselves, join associations which, in theory or in fact, are Socialist.

In Our paternal solicitude, therefore, We have meditated and sought to understand what can have been the reason of their going so far astray; and We seem to hear what many of them allege in excuse: the Church and those professing attachment to the Church favor the rich and neglect workingmen and have no care for them:

[53] Encycl. *Divini Illius Magistri,* December 31, 1929.

they were obliged therefore in their own interest to open the Socialist ranks.

What a lamentable fact, Venerable Brethren and Beloved Children, that there have been, and that there are even now some who, while professing the Catholic Faith, are well-nigh unmindful of that sublime law of justice and charity which binds us not only to give each man his due, but to succor our brethren as Christ Our Lord Himself: worse still, that there are those who out of greed for gain do not shame to oppress the workingman. Indeed there are some who can abuse religion itself, cloaking their own unjust imposition under its name, that they may protect themselves against the clearly just demands of their employees.

We shall never desist from gravely censuring such conduct. Such men are the cause that the Church, without deserving it, may have the appearance and be accused of taking sides with the wealthy, and of being little moved by the needs and sufferings of the disinherited. That these appearances and these accusations are undeserved and unjust, the whole history of the Church clearly shows. The very Encyclical, the anniversary of which We are celebrating, affords the clearest evidences that these calumnies and contumelies have been most unfairly passed upon the Church and upon her teaching.

The Invitation to Return

But We are far indeed from being exasperated by these injustices or dejected by Our pastoral sorrow. We have no wish to drive away or repel Our children who have been so unhappily deceived, and who are wandering so far from the paths of truth and salvation. On the contrary, We invite them with all possible solicitude to return to the maternal bosom of the Church. God grant that they listen to Our voice. God grant that whence they set out, thither they may return, to their father's house: that where their true practice, their true place is, there they may remain, amongst the ranks of those who, zealously following the directions promulgated by Leo XIII and solemnly repeated by Ourselves, unremittingly endeavor to reform society according to the mind of the Church on a firm basis of social justice and social charity. Let it be their firm persuasion that nowhere, even on earth, can they find an ampler happiness than in company with Him, Who being rich became poor for our sakes. That through His poverty we might become rich:[54] Who was poor and in labors from His youth:[55] Who invites to Himself all who labor and are burdened that He may refresh them bounteously in the love of His heart:[56] Who, in fine, without any respect for persons, will require more of him to whom more has been given.[57]

Cites Moral Renovation

However, if We examine matters diligently and thoroughly, We shall perceive clearly that this longed-for social reconstruction must be preceded by a profound renewal of the Christian spirit, from which multitudes engaged in industry in every country have unhappily departed. Otherwise, all Our endeavors will be futile, and Our social edifice will be built, not upon a rock, but upon shifting sand.[58]

We have passed in review, Venerable Brethren and Beloved Children, the state of the modern economic world, and have found it suffering from the greatest evils. We have investigated anew Socialism and Communism, and have found them, even in their mitigated forms, far removed from the precepts of the Gospel.

"And if society is to be healed now"—We use the words of Our Predecessor—"in no way can it be healed save by a return to Christian life and Christian institutions," [59] for Christianity alone can apply an efficacious remedy for the excessive solicitude for transitory things, which is the origin of all vices. When men are fascinated and completely absorbed in the things of the world, it alone can draw away their attention and raise it to Heaven. And who will deny that this remedy is not urgently needed by society?

The Chief Disorder of the Modern World: The Ruin of Souls

For most men are affected almost exclusively by temporal upheavals, disasters and ruins. Yet if we view things with Christian

---

[54] *II Cor.* viii, 8.   [55] Cf. *Ps.* lxxxvii, 16.   [56] Cf. *Matt.* xi, 28.
[57] *Luke* xii, 48.   [58] *Matt.* vii, 24, 27.   [59] Encycl. *Rerum Novarum,* ¶ 22.

eyes, and we should, what are they all in comparison with the ruin of souls?

Nevertheless, it may be said with all truth that nowadays the conditions of social and economic life are such that vast multitudes of men can only with great difficulty pay attention to that one thing necessary, namely, their eternal salvation.

Constituted pastor and protector of these innumerable sheep by the Prince of Pastors Who redeemed them by His Blood, We can scarcely restrain Our tears when We reflect upon the dangers which threaten them. Our pastoral office, moreover, reminds Us to search constantly, with paternal solicitude, for means of coming to their assistance, appealing to the unwearying zeal of others who are bound to this cause by justice and charity. For what will it profit men that a more prudent distribution and use of riches make it possible for them to gain even the whole world, if thereby they suffer the loss of their own souls? [60] What will it profit to teach them sound principles in economics, if they permit themselves to be so swept away by selfishness, by unbridled and sordid greed, that *hearing the Commandments of the Lord, they do all things contrary?* [61]

The Cause of Loss of Souls

The fundamental cause of this defection from the Christian law in social and economic matters, and of the apostasy of many workingmen from the Catholic Faith which has resulted from it, is the disorderly affection of the soul, a sad consequence of original sin, the source of these and of all other evils. By original sin the marvelous harmony of man's faculties has been so deranged that now he is easily led astray by low desires, and strongly tempted to prefer the transient goods of this world to the lasting goods of Heaven.

Hence comes that unquenchable thirst for riches and temporal possessions, which at all times has impelled men to break the law of God and trample on the rights of their neighbors; but the condition of the economic world today lays more snares than ever for human frailty. For the uncertainty of economic conditions and of the whole economic régime demands the keenest and most unceasing straining of energy on the part of those engaged therein; and as

60 Cf. *Matt.* xvi, 26.   61 Cf. *Judges* ii, 17.

a result, some have become so hardened against the stings of conscience as to hold all means good which enable them to increase their profits, and to safeguard against sudden changes of fortune the wealth amassed by unremitting toil. Easy returns, which an open market offers to any one, lead many to interest themselves in trade and exchange, their one aim being to make clear profits with the least labor. By their unchecked speculation prices are raised and lowered out of mere greed for gain, making void all the most prudent calculations for manufacturers.

The regulations legally enacted for corporations, with their divided responsibility and limited liability, have given occasion to abominable abuses. The greatly weakened accountability makes little impression, as is evident, upon the conscience. The worst injustices and frauds take place beneath the obscurity of the common name of a corporative firm. Boards of directors proceed in their unconscionable methods even to the violation of their trust in regard to those whose savings they administer. In the last place must still be mentioned the unscrupulous but well-calculated speculation of men who, without seeking to answer real needs, appeal to the lowest human passions. These are aroused in order to turn their satisfaction into gain.

A stern insistence on the moral law, enforced with vigor by civil authority, could have dispelled or perhaps averted these enormous evils. This, however, was too often lamentably wanting. For at the time when the new social order was beginning, the doctrines of Rationalism had already taken firm hold of large numbers, and an economic science alien to the true moral law had soon arisen, whence it followed that free rein was given to human avarice.

As a result, a much greater number than ever before, solely concerned with adding to their wealth by any means whatsoever, sought their own selfish interests above all things; they had no scruple in committing the gravest injustices against others.

Those who first entered upon this broad way which leads to destruction,[62] easily found many imitators of their iniquity because of their manifest success, their extravagant display of wealth, their derision of the scruples of more delicate consciences and the crushing of more cautious competitors

[62] Cf. *Matt.* vii, 13.

With the leaders of business abandoning the true path, it is not surprising that in every country multitudes of workingmen, too, sank in the same morass: all the more so, because very many employers treated their workmen as mere tools, without any concern for the welfare of their souls, indeed, without the slightest thought of higher interests. The mind shudders if we consider the frightful perils to which the morals of workers (of boys and young men particularly), and the virtue of girls and women are exposed in modern factories; if we recall how the present economic régime and above all the disgraceful housing conditions prove obstacles to the family tie and family life; if we remember the insuperable difficulties placed in the way of a proper observance of the holy days.

How universally has the true Christian spirit become impaired, which formerly produced such lofty sentiments even in uncultured and illiterate men! In its stead, man's one solicitude is to obtain his daily bread in any way he can. And so bodily labor, which was decreed by Providence for the good of man's body and soul even after original sin, has everywhere been changed into an instrument of strange perversion: for dead matter leaves the factory ennobled and transformed, where men are corrupted and degraded.

The Remedies

Economic life must be inspired by Christian principles. For this pitiable ruin of souls, which if it continue, will frustrate all efforts to reform society,[63] there can be no other remedy than a frank and sincere return to the teaching of the Gospel. Men must observe anew the precepts of Him Who alone has the words of eternal life, words which, even though Heaven and earth be changed, shall not pass away.[64]

All those versed in social matters demand a rationalization of economic life which will introduce sound and true order. But this order, which We Ourselves desire and make every effort to promote, will necessarily be quite faulty and imperfect, unless all man's activities harmoniously unite to imitate and, as far as is humanly possible, attain the marvelous unity of the divine plan. This is the perfect order which the Church preaches, with intense earnestness,

63 Cf. *Jo.* vi, 69.   64 Cf. *Matt.* xxiv, 35.

and which right reason demands: which places God as the first and supreme end of all created activity, and regards all created goods as mere instruments under God, to be used only in so far as they help towards the attainment of our supreme end.

Nor is it to be imagined that remunerative occupations are thereby belittled or deemed less consonant with human dignity. On the contrary, we are taught to recognize and reverence in them the manifest will of God the Creator, Who placed man upon earth to work it and use it in various ways in order to supply his needs. Those who are engaged in production are not forbidden to increase their fortunes in a lawful and just manner: indeed it is just that he who renders service to society and develops its wealth should himself have his proportionate share of the increased public riches, provided always that he respects the laws of God and the rights of his neighbor, and uses his property in accord with faith and right reason. If these principles be observed by all, everywhere and at all times, not merely the production and acquisition of goods, but also the use of wealth, now so often uncontrolled, will within a short time be brought back again to the standards of equity and just distribution.

Mere sordid selfishness, which is the disgrace and the great crime of the present age, will be opposed in very deed by the kindly and forcible law of Christian moderation, whereby man is commanded to seek first the Kingdom of God and His Justice, confiding in God's liberality and definite promise that temporal goods also, as far as he has need of them, will be added unto him.[65]

The Law of Charity Must Operate

Now, in effecting this reform, charity *which is the bond of perfection,*[66] must play a leading part. How completely deceived are those inconsiderate reformers, who zealous only for commutative justice, proudly disdain the help of charity. Charity cannot take the place of justice unfairly withheld, but, even though a state of things be pictured in which every man receives at last all that is his due, a wide field will nevertheless remain open for charity. For, justice alone, even though most faithfully observed, can remove in-

[65] Cf. *Matt.* vi, 33.   [66] *Coloss.* iii, 14.

deed the cause of social strife, but can never bring about a union of hearts and minds. Yet this union, binding men together, is the main principle of stability in all institutions, no matter how perfect they may seem, which aim at establishing social peace and promoting mutual aid. In its absence, as repeated experience proves, the wisest regulations come to nothing. Then only will it be possible to unite all in harmonious striving for the common good, when all sections of society have the intimate conviction that they are members of a single family and children of the same Heavenly Father, and further, that they are *one body in Christ and everyone members one of another,*[67] then the rich and others in power will change their former negligence of their poorer brethren into solicitous and effective regard;[68] will listen with kindly feeling to their just complaints, and will readily forgive them the faults and mistakes they possibly make. Workingmen, too, will lay aside all feelings of hatred or envy, which the instigators of social strife arouse so skilfully. Not only will they cease to feel weary of the position assigned them by Divine Providence in human society; they will become proud of it, well aware that every man by doing his duty is working usefully and honorably for the common good, and is following in the footsteps of Him, Who, being in the form of God, chose to become a Carpenter among men, and to be known as the Son of a Carpenter.

A Difficult Task

Because of this new diffusion throughout the world of the Gospel spirit, which is a spirit of Christian moderation and of universal charity, We confidently look forward to that complete and much desired renewal of human society, and to "the Peace of Christ in the Kingdom of Christ," to which We firmly resolved at the very beginning of Our Pontificate to devote all Our care and all Our pastoral solicitude.[69] You, Venerable Brethren, who by ordinance of the Holy Spirit rule with Us the Church of God,[70] are laboring strenuously and with admirable zeal in all parts of the world, not exclusive of the sacred Missions among the pagans, towards this same end of capital importance and necessity today. Receive your

[67] *Rom.* xii, 5. [68] *Phil.* ii, 6. [69] Encycl. *Ubi Arcano,* December 23, 1922.
[70] Cf. *Acts* xx, 28.

well-deserved meed of praise; and with you all those, of the clergy
and laity, whom We rejoice to see daily taking part in this great
work and affording valuable help; Our beloved sons devoted to
Catholic Action, who with extraordinary zeal aid Us in the solution
of social problems, in so far as the Church in virtue of her divine
institution has the right and the duty to concern herself with them.
With repeated insistence We exhort all these in the Lord to spare
no labor and be overcome by no difficulty, but daily more to take
courage and be valiant.[71]

The task We propose to them is truly difficult, for well do We
know that many are the obstacles to be overcome on either side,
whether amongst the higher classes of society or the lower. Still,
let them not lose heart, nor in any way allow themselves to be
diverted by any art from their purpose. To face stern combats is
the part of a Christian: and to endure labor is the lot of those, who,
as good soldiers of Christ,[72] follow closely in His footsteps.

Relying therefore solely on the assistance of Him Who "will
have all men be saved," [73] let us devote all our energies to helping
those unhappy souls who are turned away from God; let us withdraw them from the temporal cares in which they are too much
involved, and teach them to aspire with confidence to things that
are eternal. At times, indeed, this will be easier to accomplish than
appears at first sight: for if in the depths of even the most abandoned hearts lurk, like sparks beneath the ashes, spiritual forces of
unexpected strength—a clear testimony of a "naturally Christian
soul"—how much more then must these abide in the hearts of the
many who largely through ignorance and unfavorable surroundings
have wandered into error!

For the rest, the associations of the workingmen themselves
provide glad signs of coming social reconstruction. To the great
joy of Our heart We discern amongst them dense masses of young
workers who listen readily to the call of divine grace and strive
with splendid zeal to win their fellows to Christ. No less praise is
due to those leaders of workingmen's organizations who, sacrificing
their own interests, and anxious only for the good of their companions, strive with prudence to bring their just demands into harmony
with the prosperity of their entire vocational group, nor by any

[71] Cf. *Deut.* xxxi, 7.   [72] *II Tim.* ii, 3.   [73] *I Tim.* ii, 4.

obstacle or misgiving do they permit themselves to be deterred from this noble task. Further, many young men, destined soon by reason of their talents or their wealth to hold distinguished places in the foremost ranks of society, are studying social problems with growing earnestness. These youths encourage the fairest hopes that they will devote themselves wholly to social reforms.

The Course to be Followed

Present circumstances, therefore, Venerable Brethren and Beloved Children, indicate clearly the course to be followed. Nowadays, as more than once in the history of the Church, we are confronted with a world which in large measure has almost fallen back into paganism. In order to bring back to Christ these whole classes of men who have denied Him, we must gather and train from amongst their very ranks auxiliary soldiers of the Church, men who know their mentality and their aspirations, and who with kindly fraternal charity will be able to win their hearts. Undoubtedly the first and immediate apostles of the workingmen must themselves be workingmen, while the apostles of the industrial and commercial world should themselves be employers and merchants. It is your chief duty, Venerable Brethren, and that of your clergy, to seek diligently, to select prudently, and train fittingly these lay apostles, amongst workingmen and amongst employers.

No easy task is here imposed upon the clergy, wherefore all candidates for the sacred priesthood must be adequately prepared to meet it by intense study of social matters. It is particularly necessary, however, that they whom you specially select and devote to this work show themselves endowed with a keen sense of justice ready to oppose with real manly constancy unjust claims and unjust actions; that they avoid every extreme with consummate prudence and discretion; above all, that they be thoroughly imbued with the charity of Christ, which alone has power to incline men's hearts and wills firmly and gently to the laws of equity and justice. This course, already productive of success in the past, we must follow now with alacrity.

Further, We earnestly exhort in the Lord the beloved sons who are chosen for this task, to devote themselves whole-heartedly to

the formation of the men entrusted to them. In the execution of
this most priestly and apostolic work, let them make opportune use
of the powerful resources of Christian training, by instructing
youth, by founding Christian associations, by forming study circles
on Christian lines.

Above all, let them hold in high esteem and employ with diligence for the benefit of their disciples the spiritual exercises, a most
precious means of personal and of social reform, as We said in Our
Encyclical *Mens Nostra.* These exercises We declared in express
terms to be most useful for the laity in general and especially for
workingmen, and We warmly recommend them; for in that school
of the spirit not only are excellent Christians formed, but real
apostles of every state of life are trained and enkindled with the
fire of the heart of Christ. From that school they will go forth, as
the Apostles from the Cenacle in Jerusalem, strong in faith, unconquerable in steadfastness under trials, aflame with zeal, eager only
for the spread in every way of the Kingdom of Christ.

And in truth, the world has nowadays sore need of valiant soldiers of Christ, who strain every thew and sinew to preserve the
human family from the dire havoc which would befall it were the
teachings of the Gospel to be flouted, and a social order permitted
to prevail which spurns no less the laws of nature than those of
God. For herself the Church of Christ, built upon the solid rock,
has nothing to fear, for she knows that the Gates of Hell shall not
prevail against her:[74] and the experience of centuries has taught
her that storms, even the most violent, pass, leaving her stronger
and triumphantly victorious. But her maternal bosom cannot but
be stirred at the thought of the countless ills which tempests of the
world occasion to so many thousands; at the thought, above all, of
the immense spiritual evils which ensue, entailing the eternal ruin
of so many souls redeemed by the Blood of Christ. No stone, then,
must be left unturned to avert these grave misfortunes from human
society.

Towards this one aim we must bend all Our effort and endeavor,
supported by assiduous and fervent prayers to God. For, with the
assistance of Divine Grace, the destiny of the human family lies in
Our hands.

74 *Matt.* xvi. 18.

Intimate Union and Harmony between All Good Men

Let us not permit, Venerable Brethren and Beloved Children, the children of this world to seem wiser in their generation than we, who by God's goodness are Children of Light.[75] We see these men cunningly select and train resolute disciples, who spread their false doctrines daily more widely amongst men of every station and of every clime.

And when it becomes a question of attacking more vehemently the Church of Christ, we see them lay aside their internal quarrels, link up harmoniously into a single battle-line, and strive with united forces towards this common aim.

No one indeed is unaware of the many and splendid works in the social and economic field, as well as in education and religion, laboriously set in motion with indefatigable zeal by Catholics. But this admirable and self-sacrificing activity not unfrequently loses some of its effectiveness by being directed into too many different channels. Let, then, all men of good will stand united. Let all those who, under the pastors of the Church, wish to fight this good and peaceful fight of Christ, as far as talents, powers and station allow, strive to play their part in the Christian renewal of human society, which Leo XIII inaugurated in his immortal Encyclical *Rerum Novarum*. Let them seek, not themselves and the things that are their own, but the things that are Jesus Christ's.[76] Let them not urge their own ideas with undue persistence, but be ready to abandon them, however admirable, should the greater common good seem to require it: that in all and above all Christ may reign and rule, to Whom be honor and glory and power forever and ever.[77]

That this happy result may be attained, Venerable Brethren and Beloved Children, We impart to you all members of the great Catholic family entrusted to Our care, but with special affection of Our heart to artisans and other workingmen engaged in manual labor, by Divine Providence committed to Us in a particular manner, and to Christian employers and masters, with paternal affection, the Apostolic Benediction.

Given at Rome, at Saint Peter's, the fifteenth day of May, in the year 1931, the tenth of Our Pontificate.

[75] *Luke* xvi. 8.   [76] *Phil.* ii, 21.   [77] *Apoc.* v, 13.

POPE PIUS XII

Encyclical Letter
ON *the* MYSTICAL BODY
of CHRIST
(*Mystici Corporis Christi*)

It is Christ Who lives in the Church, Who teaches,
governs and sanctifies through Her.

INTRODUCTION

E FIRST LEARNED OF THE MYSTICAL BODY OF
Christ, which is the Church,[1] from the lips of the
Redeemer Himself. Illustrating, as it does, the
grand and inestimable privilege of our intimate
union with a Head so exalted, this doctrine is
certainly calculated by its sublime dignity to draw
all spiritual-minded men to deep and serious study, and to give
them in the truths which it unfolds to the mind a strong incentive
to such virtuous conduct as is conformable to its lessons. This is why
We have thought it fitting to speak with you on this subject through
this Encyclical Letter, examining and explaining above all what
concerns the Church Militant. The surpassing magnificence of the
argument attracts Us; the circumstances of the present hour urge
Us on.

For We intend to speak of the riches hidden in a Church, which
Christ hath purchased with His own blood,[2] and whose members

[1] *Coloss.* i, 24.   [2] *Acts* xx, 28.

glory in a thorn-crowned Head. Striking proof is this, that the greatest glory and exaltation are born only of sufferings, and hence that we should rejoice if we partake of the sufferings of Christ, that when His glory shall be revealed we may also be glad with exceeding joy.[3]

Like Its Divine Founder

And a first observation to be made is, that the society established by the Redeemer of the human race is not unlike its divine Founder Who was persecuted, calumniated and tortured by those very men whom He had undertaken to save. We do not deny, rather from a heart filled with gratitude to God We admit that even in our turbulent times there are many who though outside the fold of Jesus Christ look to the Church as the only haven of salvation; but neither are We unaware that the Church of God not only is ridiculed and hated disdainfully and maliciously by those who shut their eyes to the light of Christian wisdom and pitiably return to the teachings and customs and practices of ancient paganism; but even by many Christians, who are allured by specious error or caught in the meshes of the world's corruption, it is not understood, is neglected and even at times looked upon as an irksome nuisance. There is reason then, Venerable Brothers, why in obedience to the voice of Our conscience and in answer to many prayers, We should give honor before the eyes of all to the beauty, the grandeur, the glory of Mother Church. To her after God We owe everything.

And one may hope that these, Our instructions and exhortations, will be all the more helpful to the faithful in the circumstances of today. For we know that if all the painful calamities of this turbulent period, that cruelly torture almost countless men, are accepted as from God's hands with calm and submissive spirit, they naturally lift souls above the passing things of earth to those of heaven that abide forever, and stimulate a certain unsuspected thirst and keen desire for spiritual things. Thus, with the added grace of the Divine Spirit, men are moved and, one might say, compelled to be more thoughtful in seeking the Kingdom of God. The more men are withdrawn from the vanities of this world and from an inordinate love of temporal things, certainly the more likely it is that they will

[3] *I Peter* iv, 13.

perceive the light of heavenly mysteries. But the vanity and emptiness of earthly riches are more manifest today than perhaps at any
other period, when kingdoms and States are crumbling, when huge
piles of goods and all kinds of wealth are sunk in the measureless
depths of the sea, and cities, towns and fertile fields are strewn with
massive ruins and defiled with the blood of brothers.

For Those Outside the Church

Moreover We trust that the following exposition of the doctrine
of the Mystical Body of Christ will be acceptable and useful to
those, also, who are without the fold of the Church. This confidence
is based not only on the fact that their good will towards the Church
seems to grow from day to day, but also because, while before their
eyes today nation rises up against nation, kingdom against kingdom,
and discord is sown everywhere and the seeds of envy and hatred,
if they turn their gaze to the Church, if they contemplate her
divinely-given unity—by which all men of every race are united to
Christ in the bond of brotherhood—they will be forced to admire
this fellowship in charity, and with the guidance and assistance of
divine grace will long to share in the same union and charity.

There is a special reason, too, a supremely happy reason, that
brings this mystery to Our mind and with it a deep sense of joy.
During the year that has passed since the twenty-fifth anniversary
of Our Episcopal consecration, We have had the great consolation
of witnessing something that has made the image of the Mystical
Body of Jesus Christ stand out most clearly before the whole world.
Though a deadly and long war has pitilessly broken the bond of
brotherly union between nations, We have seen Our children in
Christ, in whatever part of the world they happened to be, with one
heart and one affection lift up their souls to the common Father,
Who carrying in His own heart the cares and fears of all, is guiding
the bark of the Catholic Church in the teeth of a raging tempest.
This is a testimony to the marvelous union existing among Christians; but it also proves that, as Our paternal love embraces all
peoples, whatever their nationality and race, so Catholics the world
over, though their countries have drawn the sword against each
other, look up to the Vicar of Jesus Christ as to the loving Father

of them all, who with unswerving impartiality and unsullied judgment rising above the conflicting gales of human passions, speaks truth and justice and charity and with all His power defends them.

We have been no less consoled to know that with ready generosity a fund has been created for the erection of a church in Rome to be dedicated to Our saintly predecessor and patron, Eugene I. As this temple, to be built through the gracious gifts of all the faithful, will be a lasting memorial of this happy event, so We desire to offer this Encyclical Letter in testimony of Our gratitude. It tells of those living stones which rest upon the living cornerstone, which is Christ, and are built together into a holy temple, far surpassing any temple built by hands, into a habitation of God in the spirit.[4]

Solicitude for Souls

But the chief reason for Our present exposition of this sublime doctrine is Our solicitude for the souls entrusted to Us. Much indeed has been written on this subject; and We know that many today are turning with greater zest to a study which delights and nourishes Christian piety. This, it would seem, is chiefly because a revived interest in the sacred liturgy, the more widely spread custom of receiving Holy Communion and the more fervent devotion to the Sacred Heart of Jesus practiced today have brought many souls to a deeper consideration of the unsearchable riches of Christ which are preserved in the Church. Add to this, that recent documents on Catholic Action by drawing closer the bonds of union between Christians and between them and the ecclesiastical hierarchy and especially the Roman Pontiff, have undoubtedly helped not a little to place this truth in its proper light. Nevertheless, while We can derive legitimate joy from all this, We must confess that grave errors in regard to this doctrine are being spread among those outside the true Church, and that among the faithful, too, inaccurate or thoroughly false ideas are entering which turn minds aside from the straight path of truth.

For while there still survives a false *rationalism,* which ridicules anything that transcends and defies the power of human genius, and it is accompanied by a cognant error, *popular naturalism* they

[4] *Ephes.* ii, 21-22; *I Peter* ii, 5.

call it, which sees and wants to see in the Church nothing but a juridical and social union; there is on the other hand a false *mysticism* creeping in, which in its attempt to eliminate the immovable frontier that separates creatures from their Creator garbles the Sacred Scriptures.

As a result of these conflicting and mutually antagonistic schools of thought some through empty fear look upon so profound a doctrine as something dangerous and so they fight shy of it as of the beautiful but forbidden fruit of Paradise. It is not so. Mysteries revealed by God cannot be harmful to men; nor should they remain as treasures hidden in a field, useless. They have been given from on high precisely to help the spiritual progress of those who study them in a spirit of piety. For, as the Vatican Council teaches, "reason illumined by faith, if it seeks earnestly, piously and wisely, does attain, under God, to a certain knowledge and a most helpful knowledge of mysteries, by considering their analogy with what it knows naturally, and their mutual relations and their common relation with man's last end," although, as the same holy Synod observes, reason even thus illumined "is never made capable of understanding these mysteries as it does those truths which form its proper object." [5]

After pondering all this long and seriously before God We consider it part of Our pastoral duty to explain to the entire flock of Christ through this Encyclical Letter the doctrine of the Mystical Body of Christ and of the union of this Body of the faithful with the divine Redeemer; and then from this consoling doctrine to point certain lessons, that will make a deeper study of this mystery bear yet richer fruits of perfection and holiness. Our purpose is to throw an added ray of glory on to the supreme beauty of the Church; to bring out into fuller light the exalted supernatural nobility of the faithful who in the Body of Christ are united with their Head; and finally to exclude definitely the many errors current in this matter.

[5] *Sessio* III: *Const. de Fide Cath.*, c. 4.

FIRST PART

THE CHURCH, MYSTICAL BODY OF CHRIST

When one reflects on this doctrine, one recalls immediately the words of the Apostle: *Where sin abounded, grace did more abound!* [6] All know that the father of the whole human race was constituted by God in a state so exalted that he was to hand on to his posterity together with earthly existence the heavenly life of divine grace. But after the unhappy fall of Adam, the universal progeny of mankind, infected by a hereditary stain, lost their sharing of the divine nature, and We were all children of wrath. [7] But God, all merciful, *so loved the world as to give His only-begotten Son;* [8] and the Word of the Eternal Father through this same divine love assumed human nature from the race of Adam—but an innocent and spotless nature it was—so that He, as a new Adam, might be the source whence the grace of the Holy Spirit should flow unto all the children of the first parent. Through the sin of the first man they had been excluded from adoption into the children of God: through the Word Incarnate made brothers according to the flesh of the only-begotten Son of God, they would receive the power to become the sons of God. [9]

As He hung upon the Cross, Jesus Christ not only avenged the justice of the Eternal Father that had been flouted, but He also won for us, His brothers, an unending flow of graces. It was possible for Him personally, immediately to impart these graces to men; but He wished to do so only through a visible Church that would be formed by the union of men, and thus through that Church every man would perform a work of collaboration with Him in dispensing the graces of Redemption. The Word of God willed to make use of our nature, when in excruciating agony He would redeem mankind; in much the same way throughout the centuries He makes use of the Church that the work begun might endure.

If we would define and describe this true Church of Jesus Christ —which is the One, Holy, Catholic, Apostolic, Roman Church— we shall find no expression more noble, more sublime or more

[6] *Rom.* v, 20.   [7] *II Peter* i, 4; *Ephes.* ii, 3.   [8] *Jo.* iii, 16.   [9] *Jo.* i, 12.

divine than the phrase which calls it "the Mystical Body of Jesus Christ." This title is derived from and is, as it were, the fair flower of the repeated teaching of Sacred Scripture and the Holy Fathers.

The Church, a Body

That the Church is a body is frequently asserted in Sacred Scripture. *Christ,* says the Apostle, *is the Head of the Body of the Church.*[10] If the Church is a body, it must be an unbroken unity according to those words of Paul: *Though many we are one body in Christ.*[11] But it is not enough that the Body of the Church be an unbroken unity; it must also be something definite and perceptible to the senses, as Our predecessor of happy memory, Leo XIII, in his Encyclical, *Satis cognitum,* asserts: "The Church is visible because she is a Body." Hence they err in a matter of divine truth, who imagine the Church to be invisible, intangible, a something merely "pneumatological," as they say, by which many Christian communities, though they differ from each other in their profession of faith, are united by a bond that eludes the senses.

But a body calls also for a multiplicity of members, which are linked together in such a way as to help one another. And as in our mortal composite being when one member suffers, all other members share its pain, and the healthy members come to the assistance of those ailing; so in the Church the individual members do not live for themselves alone, but also help their fellows, and all work in mutual collaboration for their common comfort and for the more perfect building up of the whole Body.

Again, as in nature a body is not formed by any haphazard grouping of members but must be constituted of organs, that is members that have not the same function and are arranged in due order; so for this reason above all the Church is called a body, that it is constituted by the coalescence of structurally united parts, and that it has a variety of members reciprocally dependent. It is thus the Apostle describes the Church when he writes: *As in one body we have many members, but all the members have not the same office: so we being many are one body in Christ, and everyone members one of another.*[12]

[10] *Coloss.* i, 18.   [11] *Rom.* xii, 5.   [12] *Rom.* xii, 4.

Pope Pius XII

Not Only Those in Orders

One must not think, however, that this ordered or "organic" structure of the Body of the Church contains only hierarchical elements and with them is complete; or, as an opposite opinion holds, that it is composed only of those who enjoy charismatic gifts—though members gifted with miraculous powers will never be lacking in the Church. That those who exercise sacred power in this Body are its first and chief members, must be maintained uncompromisingly. It is through them, commissioned by the Divine Redeemer Himself, that Christ's apostolate as teacher, king, priest, is to endure. At the same time, when the Fathers of the Church sing the praises of this Mystical Body of Christ, with its ministries, its variety of ranks, its offices, its conditions, its order, its duties, they are thinking not only of those who have received sacred orders, but of all those, too, who following the evangelical counsels pass their lives either actively among men or in the silence of the cloister, or who aim at combining the active and contemplative life according to their Institute. They are thinking of those who though living in the world consecrate themselves whole-heartedly to spiritual or corporal works of mercy; as well as those who live in the state of holy matrimony. Indeed let this be clearly understood, especially in these our days: the fathers and mothers of families, and those who are spiritual parents through Baptism, and in particular those members of the laity who assist the ecclesiastical hierarchy in spreading the Kingdom of the Divine Redeemer, occupy an honorable, even though often lowly place in the Christian community. Under the impulse of God and with His help they can reach the peak of holiness; and such holiness, Jesus Christ has promised, will never be wanting to the Church.

Now we see how the human body is given its own means to provide for its own life, health and growth and for the same of all its members. Similarly the Saviour of mankind out of His infinite goodness has provided in a marvelous way for His Mystical Body, endowing it with the sacraments; so that by so many consecutive graduated graces, as it were, its members should be supported from the cradle to life's last breath, and that the social needs of the Church might also be generously provided for. As all know, through the waters of Baptism those who are born into this world, being dead in sin, are not only born again and made members of the Church, but being stamped with a spiritual seal, they become capable and fit to receive the other sacraments. By the chrism of Confirmation, the faithful are given added strength to protect and defend the Church, their mother, and the faith she has given them. In the Sacrament of Penance a saving medicine is offered to the Church's members who have fallen into sin, not only to provide for their own health, but to remove from other members of the Mystical Body all danger of contagion or rather to afford them the tonic of virtuous example.

Nor is that enough; for in the Holy Eucharist the faithful are nourished and grow strong at the same table, and in a divine, ineffable way are brought into union with each other and with the divine Head of the whole Body. Finally, like a devoted mother the Church is at the bedside of those who are sick unto death; and if it be not always God's will that by the sacred anointing of the sick she restore health to this mortal body, yet she does minister supernatural medicine for wounded souls, and sends new citizens on to heaven to enjoy forever the happiness of God—new advocates assigned to her.

Social Needs Provided For

For the social needs of the Church Christ has provided in a particular way by two sacraments which He instituted. Through Matrimony, when the contracting parties are ministers of grace to each other, provision is made for the external and properly regulated increase of Christian society and, what is of greater importance, for the correct religious education of the offspring, without which this Mystical Body would be in grave danger. Through Holy Orders men are set aside and consecrated to God, to offer in sacrifice the eucharistic Victim, to feed the flock of the faithful with the Bread of Angels and the food of doctrine, to guide them in the way of God's commandments and counsels, to strengthen them with all the other supernatural helps.

Here it is pertinent to remark that just as at the beginning of time God gave man's body the most extraordinary power to subject all creatures to himself and to increase and multiply and fill the earth, so at the beginning of the Christian era He gave the Church those means that were needed to overcome dangers without number and to fill not only the whole world but the realms of heaven as well.

Only those are really to be included as members of the Church who have been baptized and profess the true faith and who have not unhappily withdrawn from Body-unity or for grave faults been excluded by legitimate authority. *For in one Spirit,* says the Apostle, *were we all baptized into one Body, whether Jews or Gentiles, whether bond or free.*[13] As therefore in the true Christian community there is only one Body, one Spirit, one Lord and one Baptism, so there can be only one faith.[14] And so if a man refuse to hear the Church, let him be considered—so the Lord commands— as a heathen and a publican. It follows that those who are divided in faith or government cannot be living in one body such as this, and cannot be living the life of its one divine Spirit.[15]

One must not imagine that the Body of the Church, just because it bears the name of Christ, is made up during the days of its earthly pilgrimage only of members conspicuous for their holiness, or consists only of the group of those whom God has predestined to eternal happiness. It is the Saviour's infinite mercy that allows place in His Mystical Body here for those whom He did not exclude from the banquet of old. For not every sin, however grave and enormous it be, is such as to sever a man automatically from the Body of the Church, as does schism or heresy or apostasy. Men may lose charity and divine grace through sin and so become incapable of supernatural merit, and yet not be deprived of all life, if they hold on to faith and Christian hope, and, illumined from above they are spurred on by the strong promptings of the Holy Spirit to salutary fear and by God are moved to prayer and penance for their sins.

Let everyone then abhor sin, which defiles the members, of our Redeemer; but if anyone unhappily falls and his obstinacy has not made him unworthy of communion with the faithful, let him be received with all affection and let eager charity see in him a weak member of Jesus Christ. For, as the Bishop of Hippo remarks, it is better "to be cured within the Church's community than to be cut

[13] *I Cor.* xii, 13.   [14] *Ephes.* iv, 5.   [15] *Matt.* xviii, 17.

off from its body as incurable members." "No reason to despair of the health of whatever is still part of the body; once it has been cut off, it can be neither cured nor healed." [16]

The Church, the Body of Christ

In the course of the present study, Venerable Brothers, We have thus far seen that the Church has been so constituted that it may be likened to a body. We must now explain clearly and precisely why it is to be called not merely a body, but the Body of Jesus Christ. This follows from the fact that our Lord is the Founder, the Head, the Support and the Saviour of this Mystical Body.

Christ, Founder of the Body

As we set out briefly to expound in what sense Christ founded His social Body, the following thought of Our predecessor of happy memory, Leo XIII, occurs to Us at once: "The Church which, already conceived, came forth from the side of the second Adam in His sleep on the Cross, first showed herself before the eyes of men on the great day of Pentecost." [17] For the divine Redeemer began the building of the mystical temple of the Church when by His preaching He announced His precepts; He completed it when He hung glorified on the Cross; and He manifested and proclaimed it when He sent the Holy Ghost as Paraclete in visible form on His disciples.[18]

For while fulfilling His office as preacher, He chose Apostles, sending them as He had been sent by the Father, namely, as teachers, rulers, instruments of holiness in the assembly of the believers; He appointed their chief and His Vicar on Earth; He made known to them all things whatsoever He had heard from His Father; He also established Baptism by which those who should believe would be incorporated in the Body of the Church; and finally, when He came to the close of His life, at the Last Supper He instituted the wonderful Sacrifice and Sacrament of the Eucharist.

[16] St. Augustine, *Epist.* CLVII, 3, 22 (PL 33, 686); *Serm.* CXXXVII (PL 38, 754). [17] Encycl. *Divinum Illud.*
[18] *Jo.* xvii, 18; *Matt.* xvi, 18-19; *Jo.* xv, 15; xvii, 8, 14; iii, 5.

That He completed His work on the gibbet of the Cross is the unanimous teaching of the Holy Fathers, who assert that the Church was born from the side of our Saviour on the Cross like a new Eve, mother of all the living. "And it is now," says the great Ambrose, speaking of the pierced side of Christ, "that it is built, it is now that it is formed, it is now that it is . . . molded, it is now that it is created. . . . Now it is that arises a spiritual house for a holy priesthood." [19] One who reverently considers this venerable teaching will easily discover the reasons on which it is based.

Old Law Replaced

And first of all, by the death of our Redeemer, the New Testament took the place of the Old Law which had been abolished; then the Law of Christ together with its mysteries, laws, institutions and sacred rites was ratified for the whole world in the Blood of Jesus Christ. For, while our divine Saviour was preaching in a restricted area—He was not sent but to the sheep that were lost of the house of Israel—the Law and the Gospel were together in force; but on the gibbet of His death Jesus made void the Law with its decrees, fastened the handwriting of the Old Testament to the Cross, establishing the New Testament in His Blood, shed for the whole human race.[20] "To such an extent, then," says St. Leo the Great, speaking of the Cross of our Lord, "was there effected a transfer from the Law to the Gospel, from the Synagogue to the Church, from many sacrifices to one Victim, that, as our Lord expired, that mystical veil which shut off the innermost part of the temple and its sacred secret from the main temple was rent violently from top to bottom." [21]

On the Cross, then, the Old Law died, soon to be buried and to be a bearer of death, in order to give way to the New Testament, of which Christ had chosen the Apostles as qualified ministers; and it is by the power of the Cross that our Saviour, although He had been constituted the Head of the whole human family in the womb of the Blessed Virgin, exercises fully the office itself of Head in His

[19] *In Lucam* II, 8 (PL 15, 1585).
[20] *Ephes.* ii, 15; *Coloss.* ii, 14; *Matt.* xxvi, 28; *I Cor.* xi, 25.
[21] *Serm.* LXVIII, 3 (PL 54, 374).

Church. "For it was through His triumph on the Cross," according to the teaching of the Angelic and Common Doctor, "that He won power and dominion over the Gentiles"; [22] by that same victory He increased that immense treasury of graces, which, as He reigns in glory in heaven, He lavishes continuously on His mortal members; it was by His Blood shed on the Cross that God's anger was removed, and that all the heavenly gifts, especially the spiritual graces of the New and Eternal Testament, could then flow from the fountains of our Saviour for the salvation of men, of the faithful first of all; it was on the tree of the Cross, finally, that He entered into possession of His Church, that is, all the members of His Mystical Body; for they would not have been united to this Mystical Body through the waters of Baptism except by the salutary virtue of the Cross, by which they had been already brought under the complete sway of Christ.

Effects of the Passion

But if our Saviour, by His death, became in the full and complete sense of the word the Head of the Church, it was likewise through His blood that the Church was endowed with that fullest communication of the Holy Spirit, through which, from the time when the Son of Man was lifted up and glorified on the gibbet by His sufferings, she is divinely illumined. For then, as Augustine notes,[22] with the rending of the veil of the temple it happened that the dew of the Paraclete's gifts, which heretofore had descended only on the fleece, that is, on the people of Israel, fell copiously and abundantly (while the fleece remained dry and deserted) on the whole earth, that is, on the Catholic Church, which is confined by no boundaries of race or territory. Just as at the first moment of the Incarnation, the Son of the Eternal Father adorned with the fullness of the Holy Spirit the human nature which was substantially united to Him, that it might be a fitting instrument of the Divinity in the sanguinary task of the Redemption, so at the hour of His precious death He wished that His Church should be enriched with the abundant gifts of the Paraclete in order that in dispensing the divine fruits of the Redemption it might be for the Incarnate Word a powerful instrument that would certainly never fail. For the ju-

[22] *Sum. Theol.* III, q. 42, a. 1.   [23] *De Pecc. Orig.*, XXV, 29 (PL 44, 400).

ridical mission of the Church, and the power to teach, govern and administer the sacraments derive their supernatural efficacy and force for the building up of the Body of Christ from the fact that Jesus Christ, hanging on the Cross, opened up to His Church the fountain of divine graces, which protect it from ever teaching men false doctrine, and enable it to rule them for their soul's salvation through supernaturally enlightened pastors and to bestow on them abundant heavenly graces.

If we closely consider all these mysteries of the Cross, those words of the Apostles are no longer obscure for us, in which he teaches the Ephesians that Christ by His blood made the Jews and the Gentiles one, *breaking down the middle wall of partition . . . in His flesh* by which the two peoples were divided; and that He had made the Old Law void *that He might make the two in Himself into one new man,* that is the Church, and might reconcile both to God by the Cross.[24]

The Church which He founded by His Blood, He strengthened on the day of Pentecost by a special power, given from heaven. For, having solemnly installed in his exalted office him whom He had already nominated as His Vicar, He had ascended into heaven; and sitting now at the right hand of the Father He wished to make known and proclaim His Spouse through the visible coming of the Holy Spirit with the sound of a mighty wind and tongues of fire. For just as He Himself, when He began to preach, was made known by His Eternal Father through the Holy Spirit descending and remaining on Him; so likewise, as the Apostles were about to enter upon their office of preaching, Christ our Lord sent the Holy Spirit down from heaven, to touch them with tongues of fire and to point out as by the finger of God the supernatural mission and supernatural office of the Church.

Christ, Head of the Body

That this Mystical Body, which is the Church, should be called Christ's, is proved, in the second place, from the fact that He must be universally acknowledged as its actual Head. *He,* as St. Paul says, *is the Head of the Body, the Church.*[25] He is the Head from

[24] *Ephes.* ii, 14-16. [25] *Coloss.* i, 18.

Whom the whole body, perfectly organized, *groweth and maketh increase unto the edifying of itself*.[26]

You are aware, Venerable Brothers, of the brilliant language used by the masters of Scholastic Theology, and chiefly by the Angelic and Common Doctor, when treating this question; and you know that the reasons advanced by Aquinas are a faithful reflection of the mind and writings of the Holy Fathers, who after all merely repeated and commented on the inspired word of Sacred Scripture.

However for the good of all We wish to touch this point briefly. And first of all it is clear that the Son of God and of the Blessed Virgin is to be called the Head of the Church for His singular preeminence. For the Head is in the highest place. But who is in higher place than Christ, God, Who as the Word of the Eternal Father must be acknowledged to be the *first born of every creature*? [27] Who has reached more lofty heights than Christ, Man, who, though born of the Immaculate Virgin, is the true and natural Son of God, and thanks to His miraculous and glorious resurrection, a resurrection triumphant over death, has become the *first born of the dead*? [28] Who finally has been so exalted as He, Who as *the one Mediator of God and men* [29] has in a most marvelous manner linked earth to heaven, Who, raised on the Cross as on a throne of mercy, has drawn all things, to Himself, Who as the Son of Man, chosen from among countless, is the object of God's love beyond all men, all angels and all creation?

Because Christ is so exalted, He alone by every right rules and governs the Church; and herein is yet another reason why He must be likened to a head. As the head is the "royal citadel" of the body—to use the words of Ambrose [30]—and all the members, over which it is placed for their good, are naturally guided by it as being endowed with superior powers, so the Divine Redeemer holds the helm of the universal state of Christians, and directs its course. And as a government of human society means merely this, to lead men to the end proposed by means that are expedient, just and helpful, it is easy to see how our Saviour, model and ideal of good shepherds, performs all these functions in a most striking way.

[26] *Ephes.* iv, 16; *Coloss.* ii, 19.   [27] *Coloss.* i, 15.
[28] *Coloss.* i, 18; *Apoc.* i, 5.   [29] *I Tim.* ii, 5.
[30] *Hexaem.*, VI, 55 (PL 4, 265).

Triple Power Conferred

For while still on earth, He instructed Us by precept, counsel and warning in words that shall never pass away, and will be spirit and life to all men of all times. Moreover He conferred a triple power on His Apostles and their successors, to teach, to govern, to lead men to holiness. This triple power, defined by special ordinances, by rights and obligations, He made the fundamental law of the whole Church.

But our Divine Saviour governs and guides His community also directly and personally. For it is He Who reigns within the minds and hearts of men and bends and subjects to His purpose their wills even when rebellious. *The heart of the King is in the hand of the Lord; whithersoever He will, He shall turn it.*[31] By this interior guidance the *Shepherd and Bishop of our souls* [32] not only watches over individuals, but exercises His providence over the universal Church as well, whether by enlightening and giving courage to the Church's rulers for the loyal and effective performance of their respective duties, or by singling out from the body of the Church— especially when times are grave—men and women of conspicuous holiness, who may point the way for the rest of Christendom to the perfecting of His Mystical Body. Besides, from heaven Christ never ceases to look down with extraordinary love on His unspotted Spouse so sorely tried in her earthly exile; and when He sees her in danger, either Himself or through the ministry of His Angels, or through her whom we hail the Help of Christians, and other heavenly advocates, takes her out of the tempestuous sea, and in calm and tranquil waters comforts her with the peace *which surpasseth all understanding.*[33]

But we must not think that He rules only in a hidden or extraordinary way. On the contrary, our Divine Redeemer also governs His Mystical Body in a visible way and ordinarily through His Vicar on earth. You know, Venerable Brothers, that after He had ruled the "little flock" Himself during His mortal pilgrimage, when about to leave this world and return to the Father, Christ our Lord entrusted to the chief of the Apostles the visible government of the entire community He had founded. He was all wise; and

[31] *Prov.* xxi, 1.   [32] *I Peter* ii, 25.   [33] *Phil.* iv, 7.

in no wise could He leave without a visible head the body of the Church He had founded as a human society.

Nor against this may one argue, that the primacy of jurisdiction established in the Church gives such a Mystical Body two heads. For Peter in virtue of his Primacy is only Christ's Vicar; so that there is only one chief Head of this Body, namely, Christ. He never ceases personally to guide the Church by an unseen hand, though at the same time He rules it externally, visibly through him who is His representative on earth. After His glorious Ascension into heaven, this Church rested not on Him alone, but on Peter, too, its visible foundation stone. That Christ and His Vicar constitute one only Head is the solemn teaching of Our Predecessor of immortal memory, Boniface VIII, in the Apostolic Letters *Unam Sanctum;* and his successors have never ceased to repeat the same.

Path of Dangerous Error

They, therefore, walk the path of dangerous error who believe that they can accept Christ as the Head of the Church, while they reject genuine loyalty to His Vicar on earth. They have taken away the visible head, broken the visible bonds of unity, and they leave the Mystical Body of the Redeemer in such obscurity and so maimed, that those who are seeking the haven of eternal salvation cannot see it and cannot find it.

What We have thus far said of the universal Church must be understood also of the individual Christian communities, whether Eastern or Latin, which go to make up the one Catholic Church. For they, too, are ruled by Christ Jesus through the voice of their own respective Bishops. Bishops, then, must be considered as the nobler members of the universal Church, for they are linked in an altogether special way to the Divine Head of the whole Body and so are rightly called *principal parts of the members of the Lord;* [34] what is more, as far as one's own diocese is concerned, they each and all as true Shepherds feed the flocks entrusted to them and rule them in the name of Christ. Yet in exercising this office they are not altogether independent, but are duly subordinate to the authority of the Roman Pontiff; and although their jurisdiction is inherent

[34] St. Gregory the Great, *Moralia,* XIV, 35, 43: (PL 75, 1062).

in their office, yet they receive it directly from the same Supreme Pontiff. Hence, they should be revered by the faithful as divinely appointed successors of the Apostles. To Bishops, more than to the rulers of this world, even those in supreme authority, should be applied the sentence: *Touch not my anointed ones!* [35] For Bishops have been anointed with the chrism of the Holy Spirit.

That is why We are deeply pained when We hear that not a few of Our Brother Bishops are being attacked and persecuted not only in their own person, but—what is more cruel and heart-rending for them—in the faithful committed to their care, in those who share their apostolic labor, even in the Virgins consecrated to God; and all this, just because they are *a pattern of the flock from the heart*,[36] and conserve, with justifiable energy and loyalty, the sacred "deposit of faith" confided to them, just because they insist on the sacred laws that have been engraved by God on the souls of men, and, after the example of the Supreme Shepherd, defend their flock against ravenous wolves. Such an offense We consider as committed against Our own person, and We repeat the magnificent words of Our Predecessor of immortal memory, Gregory the Great: "Our honor is the united strength of Our Brothers; and We are truly honored, when due honor is given to each and every one."

Requires Body's Help

Because Christ the Head holds such an eminent position, one must not think that He does not require the Body's help. What Paul said of the human organism is to be applied likewise to this Mystical Body: *The head cannot say to the feet: I have no need of you*. It is manifestly clear that the faithful need the help of the Divine Redeemer, for He has said: *Without Me you can do nothing*,[37] and in the teaching of the Apostle, every advance of this Body towards its perfection derives from Christ the Head. Yet this, too, must be held, marvelous though it appears: Christ requires His members. First, the person of Jesus Christ is borne by the Supreme Pontiff, who in turn must call on others to share much of his solicitude lest he be overwhelmed by the burden of his pastoral office, and must be helped daily by the Church praying. Moreover, our

---

[35] *I Paral.* xvi, 22; *Ps.* civ, 15.   [36] *I Peter* v, 3.   [37] *I Cor.* xii, 21; *Jo.* xv, 5.

Saviour does not rule the Church directly in a visible manner, and so in carrying out the work of Redemption He wishes to be helped by the members of His Body. This is not because He is indigent and weak, but rather because He has so willed it for the greater glory of His unspotted Spouse. Dying on the Cross He left to His Church the immense treasury of the Redemption; towards this she contributed nothing. But when those graces come to be distributed, not only does He share this task of sanctification with His Church, but He wants it in a way to be due to her action. Deep mystery this, subject of inexhaustible meditation; that the salvation of many depends on the prayers and voluntary penances which the members of the Mystical Body of Jesus Christ offer for this intention and on the assistance of pastors of souls and of the faithful, especially of fathers and mothers of families, which they must offer to our divine Saviour as though they were His associates.

To the reasons thus far adduced to show that Christ the Lord should be called the Head of the society which is His Body three others may be added here. They are closely related to one another.

We begin with the similarity which We see existing between Head and Body, in that they have the same nature. Our human nature is inferior to angelic nature; and yet, be it observed, through God's goodness it has risen above angelic nature: "For Christ," as Aquinas says, "is Head of the angels; for even in His humanity He is superior to angels. Even as man He illumines the angelic intellect and influences the angelic will. But in respect to similarity of nature Christ is not Head of the angels, because He did not take hold of the angels—to quote the Apostle—but of the seed of Abraham." [38] And Christ not only took our nature, He became one of our flesh and blood with a frail body that could suffer and die.

But *if the Word emptied Himself, taking the form of a slave,*[39] it was that He might make His brothers in the flesh partakers of the divine nature,[40] in this earthly exile through sanctifying grace, in heaven through the joys of eternal bliss. The reason why the only-begotten Son of the Eternal Father wished to be a Son of Man, was that we might be made conformed to the image of the Son of God and be renewed according to the image of Him Who created us. Let those then who glory in the name of Christian all look to

[38] St. Thomas, *In Epist. ad Ephes.,* I, lect. 8.   [39] *Phil.* ii, 7.   [40] *II Peter* i, 4.

our Divine Saviour as the most exalted and most perfect exemplar of all virtues; but then let them also, by careful avoidance of sin and assiduous practice of virtue, bear witness by their conduct to His teaching and His life, so that when God appears they may be like unto Him and see Him as He is.[41]

Resemblance to Christ

The whole Body of the Church, no less than the individual members, should bear resemblance to Christ. Such is His will. And We see that realized when following in the footsteps of her Founder she teaches, she governs and offers the Divine Sacrifice. Embracing the evangelical counsels she reflects the Redeemer's poverty, obedience and virginal purity. Enriched with institutes of many different kinds as with so many precious jewels, she points out Christ deep in prayer on the mountain, or preaching to the people or healing the sick and wounded and bringing sinners back to the path of virtue, or in a word doing good to everyone. What wonder then if, while she walks this earth, she be persecuted like Christ, hounded and weighed down with sorrows.

Christ must be acknowledged Head of the Church for this reason too, that, as supernatural gifts have found their supreme fullness and perfection in Him, it is from this fullness that His Mystical Body receives. It is an observation made by a number of Fathers, that as the head of our mortal body is the seat of all the senses, while the other parts of our organism have only the sense of touch, so all the powers that are found in Christian society, all the gifts, all the extraordinary graces, all attain their utmost perfection in the Head, Christ. *In Him it hath well pleased the Father that all fullness should dwell.*[42] He is gifted with those supernatural powers that accompany the hypostatic union. Is not the Holy Spirit dwelling in Him with a fullness of grace, than which no greater can be imagined? To Him has been given *power over all flesh; all the treasures of wisdom and knowledge are in Him,* abundantly.[43] The knowledge, which is called "vision," He possesses with such clarity and comprehensiveness that it surpasses similar celestial knowledge

---

[41] *I John* iii, 2.   [42] *Coloss.* i, 19.   [43] *Jo.* xvii, 2; *Coloss.* ii, 3.

found in all the saints of heaven. So full of grace and truth is He, that of His inexhaustible fullness we have all received.[44]

These words of the disciple, whom Jesus loved, lead us to the last reason why Christ our Lord should be declared in a very particular way Head of His Mystical Body. In us the nerves reach from the head to all parts of the body and give them the power to feel and move; in like manner our Saviour communicates power to His Church so that the things of God are understood more clearly and more eagerly desired by the faithful. From Him shines into the Body of the Church whatever light illumines supernaturally the minds of those who believe, from Him every grace to make them holy, as He is holy.

Christ enlightens His whole Church. This is evident from almost numberless passages from the Sacred Scriptures and holy Fathers. *No man hath seen God at any time: the only-begotten Son Who is in the bosom of the Father, He hath declared Him.* Come a teacher from God to give testimony to the truth, He shed such light upon the nascent apostolic Church that the chief of the Apostles exclaimed: *Lord, to whom shall we go? Thou hast the words of eternal life.*[45] From heaven He assisted the evangelists in such a way that as members of Christ they wrote what they had learnt at the dictation, as it were, of the Head. And for us today, who still linger on in this earthly exile, He is the author of faith as in our heavenly house he will be its finisher. It is He Who grants the light of faith to believers; it is He Who from His divine riches imparts the supernatural gifts of knowledge, understanding, and wisdom to the pastors and teachers and above all to His Vicar on earth, so that they may faithfully preserve the treasury of faith, defend it, and with reverence and devotion explain and protect it. It is He Who, though unseen, presides at the Church's Councils and guides them.

Holiness From Christ

Holiness begins from Christ; by Christ it is effected. For no act conducive to salvation can be performed unless it proceeds from Him as its supernatural cause. *Without Me, He says, you can do nothing.*[46] If we grieve and do penance for our sins, if with filial

---

[44] *Jo.* i, 14-16.   [45] *Jo.* i, 18; iii, 2; xviii, 37; vi, 68.   [46] *Jo.* xv, 5.

fear and hope we turn again to God, it is because He is leading us. Grace and glory flow from His unfathomed fullness. Our Saviour is continually pouring out His gifts of counsel, fortitude, fear and piety, especially on the leading members of His Body, so that the whole Body may grow daily more and more in spotless holiness. When the Sacraments of the Church are administered by external rite, it is He Who produces their effects in souls. He nourishes the redeemed with His own flesh and blood, and thus calms the soul's turbulent passions; He gives increase of grace and is preparing future glory for souls and bodies.

All these treasures of His divine goodness He is said to disburse to the members of His Mystical Body, not merely because He, Who is the Eucharistic Victim on earth and the glorified Victim in Heaven, lets His wounds and prayers plead our cause before the Eternal Father, but because He selects, He determines, He distributes every single grace to every single person *according to the measure of the giving of Christ*.[47] Hence it follows that from our Lord as from a fountain-head *the whole body compacted and fitly joined by which every joint supplieth, according to the operation in the measure of every part, maketh increase of the body unto the edifying of itself in charity*.[48]

Christ, Support of the Body

The thoughts which We have expounded, briefly and succinctly tracing the manner in which Christ our Lord wishes that His abundant graces should flow from His fullness into the Church, in order that it should become most like Himself, help not a little to clarify the third reason why the social Body of the Church should be honored by the name of Christ: that reason lies in the fact that our Saviour Himself sustains in a divine manner the society which He founded.

As Bellarmine notes with acumen and accuracy,[49] this naming of the Body of Christ is not to be explained solely by the fact that Christ must be called the Head of His Mystical Body, but also by the fact that He so sustains the Church, and so in a certain sense

[47] *Ephes.* iv, 7.   [48] *Ephes.* iv, 16.
[49] St. Robert Bellarmine, *De Rom. Pont.* I, 9.

lives in the Church, that it is as it were another Christ. The doctor of the Gentiles in his letter to the Corinthians affirms this when, without further qualification, he called the Church "Christ," following no doubt the example of his Master Who called out to him from on high, when he was attacking the Church: *Saul, Saul, why persecutest thou Me?* [50] Indeed, if we are to believe Gregory of Nyssa, the Church is often called "Christ" by the Apostle; and you are conversant, Venerable Brothers, with that phrase of Augustine: *Christ preaches Christ.*[51]

But this noble title of the Church must not be so taken as if that ineffable bond, by which the Son of God assumed a definite human nature, belongs to the universal Church; but it consists in this, that our Saviour shares His most personal prerogatives with the Church in such a way that she may portray in her whole life, both external and interior, a most faithful image of Christ. For in virtue of the juridical mission by which our divine Redeemer sent His Apostles into the world, as He had been sent by the Father, it is He Who through the Church baptizes, teaches, rules, looses, binds, offers, sacrifices.

But in virtue of that higher, interior and wholly sublime communication, with which We dealt when We described the manner in which the Head influences the members, Christ our Lord brings the Church to live His own supernatural life, by His divine power permeates His whole Body and nourishes and sustains each of the members according to the place which they occupy in the Body, very much as the vine nourishes and makes fruitful the branches which are joined to it.

Principle of Life, Power

If we examine closely this divine principle of life and power given by Christ, in so far as it constitutes the very source of every gift and created grace, we easily see that it is nothing else than the Holy Spirit, the Paraclete who proceeds from the Father and the Son, and Who is called in a special way the *Spirit of Christ* or the *Spirit of the Son.*[52] For it was by His breath of grace and truth that

[50] *I Cor.* xii, 12; *Acts* ix, 4.
[51] St. Gregory of Nyssa, *De Vita Moysis* (PG 44, 385); St. Augustine, *Serm.* CCCLIV, 1 (PL 39, 1563).　　[52] *Rom.* viii, 9; *II Cor.* iii, 17; *Gal.* iv, 6.

the Son made beautiful His soul in the immaculate womb of the Blessed Virgin; this Spirit delights to dwell in the dear soul of our Redeemer as in His most cherished shrine; this Spirit Christ merited for us on the Cross by shedding His own blood; this Spirit He bestowed on the Church for the remission of sins, when He breathed on the Apostles; and while Christ alone received this Spirit without measure, to the members of the Mystical Body He is imparted only according to the measure of the giving of Christ, from Christ's own fullness.[53] But after Christ's glorification on the Cross, His Spirit is communicated to the Church in an abundant outpouring, so that she, and her single members may become daily more and more like to our Saviour. It is the Spirit of Christ that has made us adopted sons of God in order that one day *we all beholding the glory of the Lord with open face may be transformed into the same image from glory to glory.*[54]

To this Spirit of Christ, too, as to an invisible principle, is to be ascribed the fact that all the parts of the Body are joined one with the other and with their exalted Head; for He is entire in the Head, entire in the Body and entire in each of the members. To the members He is present and assists them in proportion to their various tasks and offices and the greater or less grade of spiritual health which they enjoy. It is He Who through His heavenly grace is the principle of every supernatural act in all the parts of the Body. It is He Who while He is personally present and divinely active in all the members, also acts in the inferior members through the ministry of the higher members. Finally, while with His grace He provides for the constant growth of the Church, He yet refuses to dwell with sanctifying grace in members that are wholly severed from the Body. This presence and activity of the Spirit of Jesus Christ is tersely and vigorously described by Our predecessor of immortal memory Leo XIII in his Encyclical Letter *Divinum Illud* in these words: "Let it suffice to say that, as Christ is the Head of the Church, so is the Holy Spirit her soul."

If that vital principle by which the whole community of Christians is sustained by its Founder, be considered now not in itself, but in its created effects, it consists in those heavenly gifts which our Redeemer together with His Spirit bestows on the Church and

---

[53] *Jo.* xx, 22; iii, 34; *Ephes.* i, 8; iv, 7.   [54] *II Cor.* iii, 18; *Rom.* viii, 14-17.

which He and His Spirit, from Whom come supernatural light and holiness, make operative in the Church. The Church, then, no less than each of her holy members can make this thought of the Apostle her own: *And I live, now not I; but Christ liveth in me.*[55]

Christ, Saviour of the Body

The account which We have given you of the "Mystic Head" would indeed remain incomplete, if We were not at least briefly to touch on this thought of the same Apostle: *Christ is the Head of the Church; He is the saviour of His Body.*[56] For in these words we have the last reason why the Body of the Church is given the name of Christ. Christ is, namely, the divine Saviour of this Body. The Samaritans were right in proclaiming Him *Saviour of the world;* [57] indeed He is most certainly to be called the *Saviour of all men,* even though We must add, with Paul: *especially of the faithful.*[58] Before all others, that is, He has purchased with His blood His members, who constitute the Church. But since We have already treated this subject clearly enough when treating of the Church's birth on the Cross, of Christ as the source of light and principle of sanctity, and of Christ as Support of His Mystical Body, there is no reason why We should explain it further; but rather let us all, giving perpetual thanks to God, meditate on it with a humble and attentive mind. For what our Lord, hanging on the Cross, began, He does not cease to continue always and uninterruptedly amid the joys of heaven: "Our Head," says St. Augustine, "intercedes for us: some members He is receiving, others He is chastising, others cleansing, others consoling, others creating, others calling, others recalling, others correcting, others renewing." [59] But to us it has been granted to collaborate with Christ in this work of salvation, "from one and through one saved and saving." [60]

The Church, the "Mystical" Body of Christ

And now, Venerable Brothers, We come to that part of Our explanation, in which We desire to make clear that the Body of Christ,

---

[55] *Gal.* ii, 20. [56] *Ephes.* v. 23. [57] *Jo.* iv, 42. [58] *I Tim.* iv, 10.
[59] *Enarr. in Ps.,* LXXXV, 5 (PL 38, 1085).
[60] Clement of Alexandria, *Strom.,* VII, 2 (PG 9, 413).

which is the Church, should be called mystical. This word, used by many early writers, has the sanction of numerous Pontifical documents. There are several reasons why it should be used; for by it we may distinguish the Body of the Church, which is a society whose Head and Ruler is Christ, from His physical Body, which born of the Virgin Mother of God now sits at the right hand of the Father and rests hidden under the Eucharistic veil; as well as from any ordinary body in the natural order, whether physical or moral. This latter distinction is of greater importance in view of modern errors.

In a natural body the principle of unity so unites the parts, that each lacks its own individual subsistence; on the contrary in the Mystical Body that mutual union, though intrinsic, links the members by a bond which leaves to each intact his own personality. Besides, if we examine the relation existing between the several members and between the members and the head, in every physical, living body all the different members are ultimately destined to the good of the whole alone; while every moral association of men, if we look to its ultimate usefulness, is in the end directed to the advancement of all and of every single member. For they are persons. And so—to return to our theme—as the Son of the Eternal Father came down from heaven for the salvation of us all, He likewise established the Body of the Church and enriched it with the divine Spirit to assure immortal souls attaining their happiness, according to the words of the Apostle: *All things are yours; but you are Christ's; and Christ is God's.*[61] For the Church exists both for the good of the faithful, and to give glory to God and Jesus Christ Whom He sent.

Differences Not Slight

But if we compare a Mystical Body to a moral body, here again we must notice that the difference between them is not slight; rather it is very considerable and very important. In the moral body, the principle of union is nothing more than the common end, and the common co-operation of all under authority for the attainment of that end; whereas in the Mystical Body, of which We are speaking, this collaboration is supplemented by a distinct internal principle, which exists effectively in the whole and in each of its parts, and

[61] *I Cor.* iii, 23.

whose excellence is such, that of itself it is vastly superior to whatever bonds of union may be found in a physical or moral body. This is something, as We said above, not of the natural but of the supernatural order. Essentially it is something infinite, uncreated: the Spirit of God, Who, as the Angelic Doctor says, "numerically one and the same, fills and unifies the whole Church." [62]

Hence, this word in its correct signification gives us to understand that the Church, a perfect society of its kind, is not made up of merely moral and juridical elements and principles. It is far superior to all other human societies; it surpasses them as grace surpasses nature, as things immortal are above all those that perish. Such human societies, and in the first place Civil Society, are by no means to be despised or belittled. But the Church in its entirety is not found within this natural order, any more than the whole of man is encompassed within the organism of our mortal body. The juridical principles, on which also the Church rests and is established, derive from the divine constitution given to it by Christ, and contribute to attaining its supernatural end; but what lifts the society of Christians far, far above the whole natural order is the Spirit of our Redeemer Who until the end of time penetrates every part of the Church's being and is active within it.

He is the source of every grace and every gift and every miraculous power. Just as our composite mortal body, for all its being a marvelous work of the Creator, falls short of the eminent dignity of our soul, so the social structure of the Christian community, though eloquent of its divine Architect's wisdom, remains still something inferior, when compared to the spiritual gifts which give it beauty and life and to their divine source.

From what We have thus far written and explained, Venerable Brothers, it is clear, We think, how grievously they err who arbitrarily picture the Church as something hidden and invisible, as do they also who look upon it as a mere human institution with a certain disciplinary code and external ritual, but lacking power to communicate supernatural life. No; the Mystical Body of Christ is like Christ the Head and Exemplar of the Church; "Who is not complete, if only His visible human nature is considered, or if only His divine, invisible nature . . . but He is one through the union of

[62] St. Thomas, *De Veritate*, xxix, 4.

both and one in both . . ." [63] Thus the Word of God took unto Himself a human nature liable to sufferings, so that He might consecrate in His blood the visible society founded by Him and "lead man back to things invisible under a visible rule." [64]

Imaginary "Church"

For this reason We deplore and condemn the pernicious error of those who conjure up from their fancies an imaginary Church, a kind of Society that finds its origin and growth in charity, to which they somewhat contemptuously oppose another, which they call juridical. But this distinction, which they introduce, is baseless.

For they fail to understand that the same reason that led our divine Redeemer to give to the community of men He founded the constitution of a society, perfect of its kind, containing all the juridical and social elements, namely that He might perpetuate on earth the saving work of Redemption, was also the reason why He wished to be enriched with the heavenly gifts of the Consoling Spirit. The Eternal Father indeed wished it to be the *kingdom of the Son of His predilection;* [65] but it was to be a real kingdom, in which all believers would make the obeisance of their intellect and will, and humbly and obediently model themselves on Him, Who for our sake *was made obedient unto death.*[66] There can, then, be no real opposition or conflict between the invisible mission of the Holy Spirit and the juridical commission of Ruler and Teacher received from Christ. Like body and soul in us, they complement and perfect each other, and have their source in our one Redeemer, Who not only said, as He breathed on the Apostles: *Receive ye the Holy Spirit,* but also clearly commanded: *As the Father hath sent Me, so I send you;* and again: *He who heareth you, heareth Me.*[67]

And if at times there appears in the Church something that points to the weakness of our human nature, put it down not to the juridical constitution, but rather to that regrettable inclination to evil found in everyone, which its divine Founder permits even at times in the most exalted members of His Mystical Body, for the

[63] Pope Leo XIII, *Satis Cognitum.*   [64] St. Thomas, *ibid.,* ad 3.
[65] *Coloss.* i, 13.   [66] *Phil.* ii, 8.   [67] *Jo.* xx, 21-22; *Luke* x, 16.

purpose of testing the virtue of flocks and Shepherds, and that all may increase the merit of their Christian faith. For, as We said above, Christ did not wish to exclude sinners from His Church; hence if some members of the Church are spiritually ill, that is no reason why we should lessen our love for the Church, but rather a reason why we should increase our devotion to her members. Oh, the loving Mother is spotless in the Sacraments, by which she gives birth to her children and nourishes them, she is spotless in the faith, which she has preserved inviolate always, in her sacred laws imposed on all, in the evangelical counsels which she recommends, in those heavenly gifts and extraordinary graces through which, with inexhaustible fecundity, she generates hosts of martyrs, virgins and confessors!

But it cannot be laid to her charge if some members fall weak or wounded. In their name she prays to God daily: "Forgive us our trespasses"; and with the brave heart of a mother turns at once to nurse them back to spiritual health. When therefore we call the Body of Jesus Christ "mystical" we hear a solemn warning in the very significance of the word. It is a warning that echoes these words of St. Leo: "Recognize, O Christian, your dignity, and being made a sharer of the divine nature go not back to your former worthlessness along the way of unseemly conduct. Keep in mind of what Head and of what Body you are a member." [68]

SECOND PART

THE UNION OF THE FAITHFUL WITH CHRIST

Here, Venerable Brothers, We wish to speak in a particular way of Our union with Christ in the Body of the Church. St. Augustine has justly remarked that this union is something sublime, mysterious and divine; [69] but for that very reason it often happens that many misunderstand it and explain it incorrectly. It is at once evident that this union is very close. In Sacred Scripture it is likened to the pure

[68] *Serm.* XXI, 3 (PL 54, 192-193).
[69] *Contra Faustum*, XXI, 8 (PL 42, 392).

union of man and wife, and is compared with the vital union of branch and vine, and with the cohesion found in our body. Even more, it is represented as being so close that the Apostle says: *He (Christ) is Head of the Body of the Church*,[70] and the unbroken tradition of the Father from the earliest times teaches that the divine Redeemer and the society which is His Body form but one mystical person, that is to say, to quote Augustine, the whole Christ.[71] Our Saviour Himself, in His high-priestly prayer, has gone so far as to liken this union with that marvelous oneness by which the Son is in the Father and the Father in the Son.[72]

Our union in and with Christ is first evident from the fact that, since Christ wishes His Christian community to be a Body which is a perfect society, its members must be united because they all work together towards a single end. The nobler this end, towards which they work together, and the diviner the motive which actuates this collaboration, the higher no doubt will be the form of union. Now the end in question is supremely exalted: the continuous sanctifying of the members of the Body for the glory of God and of the Lamb, that was slain.[73] The motive is altogether divine: not only the will of the Eternal Father and the earnest wish of our Saviour, but the interior inspiration and impulse of the Holy Spirit in our minds and hearts. For if not even the smallest act conducive to salvation can be performed except in the Holy Spirit, how can unnumbered multitudes of every people and every race work together harmoniously for the supreme glory of the Triune God, except in the power of Him Who proceeds from Father and Son in one eternal act of love?

Now since this social Body of Christ has been designed by its Founder to be visible, this co-operation of all its members must also be externally manifest through their profession of the same faith, and their sharing the same sacred rites, through participation in the same sacrifice and practical observance of the same laws. Above all, everyone must be able to see the Supreme Head, who gives effective direction to what all are doing in a mutually helpful way towards attaining the desired end, that is, the Vicar on earth of Jesus Christ. As the Divine Redeemer sent a Paraclete, the Spirit of Truth, who in His name should govern the Church in an invisible way, sim-

70 *Coloss.* i, 18.   71 *Enarr. in Ps.,* XVII, 51; XC, II, 1 (PL 36, 154; 37, 1159).
72 *Jo.* xvii, 21-23.   73 *Apoc.* v, 12-13.

ilarly He commissioned Peter and his Successors to be His personal representatives on earth and to assume the visible government of the Christian community.

Faith, Hope, Charity

These juridical bonds far surpass those of any other human society, however exalted; and yet another principle of union must be added to them in those three virtues, which link us so closely to each other and to God: Christian faith, hope and charity.

One Lord, one faith, writes the Apostle: [74] the faith, that is, by which we hold fast to God, and to Him Whom He has sent, Jesus Christ. The beloved Apostle tells us how close this faith binds us to God; *Whosoever shall confess that Jesus is the Son of God, God abideth in him, and he in God.*[75] This Christian faith binds us no less closely with each other and with our Divine Head. For all we who believe, *having the same spirit of faith,*[76] are illuminated by the same light of Christ, are nourished by the same food of Christ, live under the jurisdiction and teaching authority of Christ. If the same spirit of faith breathes in all, we all are living the same life *in the faith of the Son of God, Who loved us and delivered Himself for us.*[77] And once Christ, our Head, through an ardent faith enters into us and dwells within our hearts, He becomes the *Author and finisher* of our faith.[78]

As by faith on this earth we hold fast to God as the Author of truth, so Christian hope leads us to long for Him as the fount of blessedness, *looking for the blessed hope and coming of the glory of the great Lord.*[79] It is because of this united desire of the heavenly Kingdom, whence our refusal to accept a permanent home here, our seeking for one beyond and our yearning for the glory on high, that the Apostle of the Gentiles did not hesitate to write: *One Body and one Spirit, as you are called in one hope of your calling,* and to assert that Christ in us is our hope of glory.[80]

But if the bonds of faith and hope, which bind us to our Redeemer in His Mystical Body are weighty and important, those of

---

[74] *Ephes.* iv, 5; cf. *Jo.* xvii, 3.   [75] *I John* iv, 15.   [76] *II Cor.* iv, 13.
[77] *Gal.* ii, 20.   [78] *Ephes.* iii, 17; *Heb.* xii, 2.   [79] *Titus* ii, 13.
[80] *Ephes.* iv, 4; *Coloss.* i, 27.

charity surely are no less so. Even in the natural order the love of friendship is something supremely noble. What then shall we say of that supernatural love, which God pours into our souls? *God is charity and who abides in charity, abides in God and God in him.*[81] The effect of this charity—such would seem to be God's law—is to force Him to enter into our loving hearts to return love for love: *if anyone love Me . . . My Father, too, will love him, and we shall come to Him and make our abode with Him.*[82] Charity, then, more than any other virtue binds us closely to Christ. On fire with this flame from heaven, how many children of the Church have rejoiced to suffer insults for Him, and to face and overcome the hardest trials, though it cost their lives and the shedding of their blood. For that reason our Divine Saviour earnestly exhorts us in these words: *Remain in My love.* And as charity, if it find no outward expression and effectiveness in good work, is something jejune and altogether empty, He added at once: *If you keep My commandments, you will remain in My love; as I also have kept My Father's commandments and remain in His love.*[83]

Love of Neighbor

Corresponding to this love of God and of Christ there must be love of the neighbor. How can we claim to love the divine Redeemer, if we hate those whom He has redeemed with His precious blood, so that He might make them members of His Mystical Body? For that reason the beloved disciple warns us: *If any man say: I love God, and hateth his brother, he is a liar. For he that loveth not his brother whom he seeth, how can he love God Whom he seeth not? And this commandment we have from God, that he who loveth God love also his brother.*[84] Rather one should say that the more we become "members one of another," "mutually one of another," the closer we shall be united with God, with Christ; as on the other hand the more ardent the love that binds us to God and our divine Head, the closer we shall be united to each other in the bonds of charity.

Now the only-begotten Son of God embraced us in His infinite knowledge and undying love even before the world began. To give

[81] *I John* iv, 16.   [82] *Jo.* xiv, 23.   [83] *Jo.* xv, 9-10.   [84] *I John* iv, 20-21.

visible, and exquisitely beautiful expression to this love, He took unto Himself in hypostatic union our nature: whence—as Maximus of Turin with a certain unaffected simplicity remarks—"in Christ our own flesh loves us." [85]

But the knowledge and love of our divine Redeemer, of which we were the object from the first moment of His Incarnation, are more than any human intellect or heart can hope to grasp. For hardly was He conceived in the womb of the Mother of God, when He began to enjoy the vision of the blessed, and in that vision all the members of His Mystical Body were continually and unceasingly present and He embraced them with His redeeming love. O marvelous condescension of divine love for us! O inestimable disposition of limitless charity! In the Crib, on the Cross, in the unending glory of the Father, Christ has all the members of the Church present before Him and united to Him in a clearer and more loving way than a mother loves her little one clasped to her breast, than anyone knows and loves himself.

You will readily understand from all this, Venerable Brothers, why Paul the Apostle so often writes that Christ is in us and we in Christ. In proof of which there is this other more subtle reason. Christ is in us through His Spirit, whom He gives to us, and through whom He acts within us in such a way that all divine activity of the Holy Spirit within our souls must also be attributed to Christ. *If a man have not the spirit of Christ, he is none of His,* says the Apostle, *but if Christ be in you . . . the spirit liveth because of justification.*[86]

Communication of the Spirit

This communication of the Spirit of Christ is the channel through which flow into all the members of the Church those gifts, powers and extraordinary graces found superabundantly in the Head as in their source, and they are perfected day by day in these members according to the office they may hold in the Mystical Body of Jesus Christ. Thus the Church becomes, as it were, the filling out and complement of the Redeemer, while Christ in a sense attains through the Church a fullness in all things. Here we touch

[85] *Serm.* XXIX (PL 57, 194).   [86] *Rom.* viii, 9-10.

the reason why to the mind of Augustine the Mystical Head, which is Christ, and the Church, which on this earth as another Christ bears His person, constitute one new man, in whom heaven and earth are yoked together in perpetuating the Cross's work of salvation: by Christ we mean the Head and the Body, the whole Christ.

We are well aware that many a veil shrouds this profound truth of our union with the divine Redeemer, and in particular of the Holy Spirit's dwelling within our souls, and impedes our power to understand and explain it. This mystery is enveloped in a darkness, rising out of the mental limitations of those who seek to grasp it. But We know, too, that well-directed and earnest study of this doctrine and the clash of diverse opinions and their discussion, provided love of truth and due submission to the Church be the arbiter, will open rich and bright vistas, whose light will help to progress in kindred sacred sciences. Hence We do not censure those who in various ways and with diverse reasonings strain every effort to understand and to clarify the mystery of this our marvelous union with Christ. But let all agree uncompromisingly on this, if they would not err from truth and from the orthodox teaching of the Church: to reject every kind of mystic union, by which the faithful would in any way pass beyond the sphere of creatures and rashly enter the divine even to the extent of one single attribute of the eternal Godhead being predicted of them as their own. And besides let all hold this as certain truth, that all these activities are common to the most Blessed Trinity, in so far as they have God as supreme efficient cause.

Let it be observed also that one is treating here of a hidden mystery, which in this earthly exile can never be fully disclosed and grasped, and expressed in human language. The Divine Persons are said to be indwelling in as much as They are present to intellectual creatures in a way that lies beyond human comprehension, and are known and loved by them in a purely supernatural manner alone within the deepest sanctuary of the soul. If we approach at least a little towards perceiving this truth, let us not neglect the method recommended by the Vatican Council in similar cases. Seeking light so as to discern at least partially the hidden things of God, the

Council finds it in comparing these mysteries one with the other and with the last end towards which they point.

Eucharistic Sacrifice

It seems to Us that something would be lacking to what We have thus far proposed concerning this close union of the Mystical Body of Jesus Christ with its Head, if We did not add here a few words on the Holy Eucharist, wherein this union during this mortal life reaches, as it were, a climax.

Through the Eucharistic Sacrifice Christ our Lord wished to give special evidence to the faithful of our union among ourselves and with our divine Head, marvelous as it is and beyond all praise. For here the sacred ministers act in the person not only of our Saviour but of the whole Mystical Body and of everyone of the faithful. In this act of sacrifice through the hands of the priest, whose word alone has brought the Immaculate Lamb to be present on the altar, the faithful themselves with one desire and one prayer offer It to the Eternal Father,—the most acceptable victim of praise and pro-pitiation for the Church's universal needs. And just as the divine Redeemer, dying on the Cross, offered Himself as Head of the whole human race to the Eternal Father, so *in this pure oblation* [87] He offers not only Himself as Head of the Church to the heavenly Father, but in Himself His mystical members as well. He embraces them all, even the weak and ailing ones, in the tenderest love of His Heart.

The Sacrament of the Eucharist is itself a striking image of the Church's unity, if we consider how in the bread to be consecrated many grains go to form one substance; and in it the very Author of supernatural grace is given to us, so that through Him we may receive the Spirit of charity, in which we are bidden to live now not our life but the life of Christ, and in all the members of His social Body to love the Redeemer Himself.

If in the sad and anxious days through which we are passing there are many who cling so firmly to Christ the Lord hidden beneath the Eucharistic veils that neither tribulation nor distress nor famine nor nakedness nor danger nor persecution nor the sword can

[87] *Mal.* i, 11.

separate them from His love,[88] then undoubtedly Holy Communion, which once again in God's providence is much more frequented even from the days of early childhood, may become a source of the courage that makes heroes out of Christians.

+⁺+

THIRD PART

PASTORAL EXHORTATION

1. Errors Touching the Spiritual Life

False "Mysticism"

If the faithful, Venerable Brothers, in a spirit of sincere piety understand what has been written here and hold to it, it will be easier for them to escape the errors which arise from an irresponsible investigation of this difficult matter, such as some have made, and which are noised abroad not without seriously endangering the Catholic faith and disturbing the peace of souls. For some there are who neglect the fact that the Apostle Paul has used metaphorical language in speaking of this doctrine, and failing to distingush the physical from the social Body of Christ as they should, out of their fancy draw some deformed kind of unity. They want the divine Redeemer and the members of the Church to coalesce into one physical person and, while they bestow divine attributes on man, they make Christ our Lord subject to error and to human inclination to evil. Catholic faith and the writings of the Holy Fathers reject such false teaching as impious and sacrilegious; to the mind of the Apostle of the Gentiles it is equally abhorrent. He brings Christ and His Mystical Body into a marvelously intimate union, it is true; but he distinguishes one from the other as Bridegroom and Bride.[89]

False "Quietism"

Just as false and dangerous is the error of those who try to deduce from the mysterious union of all with Christ a certain un-

[88] *Ephes.* v, 22-23.   [89] *Ephes.* v, 22-23.

healthy quietism. They would attribute the whole spiritual life of Christians and their progress in virtue exclusively to the action of the divine Spirit, setting aside and neglecting the corresponding work and collaboration which we must contribute to this action. No one of course can deny that the Holy Spirit of Jesus Christ is the one source of whatever supernatural power enters into the Church and its members. For *the Lord will give grace and glory,* as the Psalmist says.[90]

But that men should continue consistently in their good works, that they advance generously in grace and virtue, that they strive earnestly to reach the heights of Christian perfection and at the same time do their best to stimulate others to gain the same goal, —all this the Spirit from above does not wish to bring about, unless men contribute their daily share of zealous activity. "For not on those who sleep but on the diligent," says St. Ambrose, "divine favors are conferred." [91] In our mortal body the members are strengthened and grow through continued exercise; much more so is this true in the social Body of Jesus Christ, in which each member retains his own personal freedom, responsibility and principles of conduct. For that reason he who said: *I live, now not I, but Christ liveth in me,* did not at the same time hesitate to aver: *His* (God's) *grace in me has not been void, but I have labored more abundantly than all they: yet not I, but the grace of God with me.*[92] It is perfectly clear, therefore, that these false doctrines distort the mystery which we are considering and make it contribute not to the spiritual advancement of the faithful but to their tragic ruin.

Frequent Confession

The same result would follow from the opinions of those who assert that little importance should be given to the frequent confession of venial sins. Of far greater importance, they say, is that general confession which the Spouse of Christ surrounded by her children in the Lord makes each day by the mouth of the priest as he approaches the altar. It is true indeed, Venerable Brothers, that venial sins may be expiated in many ways which are to be highly

[90] *Ps.* lxxxiii, 12.   [91] *Expos. Evang. sec. Lucam,* IV, 49 (PL 15, 1626).
[92] *Gal.* ii, 20; *I Cor.* xv, 10.

commended. But to hasten daily progress along the path of virtue We wish the pious practice of frequent confession to be earnestly advocated. Not without the inspiration of the Holy Spirit was this practice introduced into the Church. By it genuine self-knowledge is increased, Christian humility grows, bad habits are corrected, spiritual neglect and tepidity are countered, the conscience is purified, the will strengthened, a salutary self-control is attained and grace is increased in virtue of the sacrament itself. Let those, therefore, among the young clergy who make light of or weaken the esteem of frequent confession realize that what they are doing is foreign to the Spirit of Christ, and disastrous for the Mystical Body of our Saviour.

Prayer, Public and Private

There are others who deny any impetratory power to our prayers, and would spread abroad the idea that prayers offered to God in private should not be considered worth very much. Public prayers, they say, prayers that are made in the name of the Church, are those which really count, as they come from the Mystical Body of Jesus Christ. Such an opinion is false; for the Divine Redeemer maintains closest union not only with His Church, which is His loved Spouse, but also with each and every faithful soul in it, and He longs to speak with them heart to heart, especially after Holy Communion. It is true that public prayers, prayers, that is, that are offered by Mother Church, because of the dignity of the Spouse of Christ, excel any other kind of prayer; but no prayer, even the most private, lacks its own dignity and power, and all prayer is immensely helpful to the Mystical Body.

In that Body, thanks to the Communion of Saints, no good can be done, no virtue practiced by individual members without its contributing something also to the salvation of all. Similarly, just because a man is a member of this Body, he is not forbidden to ask for himself particular favors even for this life, provided he is always resigned to the Divine Will. The members do not lose their own personality, and remain subject to their own individual needs. Moreover the common practice of the Saints as well as ecclesiastical documents demonstrate how highly everyone should esteem mental prayer.

Prayers to Christ

Finally some would have it, that our prayers should not be directed to the person of Jesus Christ, but rather to God, or to the Eternal Father through Christ, since our Saviour, as Head of His Mystical Body, is only *mediator of God and men*.[93] But that, too, not only is opposed to the mind of the Church and to Christian usage but is false. For to speak exactly, Christ is Head of the universal Church, as He exists at once in both His natures. Moreover He Himself has solemnly stated: *If you shall ask Me anything in My name, that I will do*.[94] Though it is true especially in the Eucharistic Sacrifice—in which Christ, at once priest and victim, exercises in an extraordinary way the office of conciliator—that prayers are very often directed to the Eternal Father through the only-begotten Son; nevertheless it occurs, not seldom even in this sacrifice, that prayers to the divine Redeemer also are used. For, after all, every Christian must know full well that the man Christ Jesus is also the Son of God and God Himself.

And so when the Church Militant is offering its adoration and prayers to the unspotted Lamb and the sacred Victim, her voice comes to us as an echo of the triumphant Church's chorus, singing without end: *To Him that sitteth on the throne and to the Lamb, benediction and honor and glory and power for ever and ever*.[95]

II. Exhortation to Love the Church

Venerable Brothers, in explaining this mystery that surrounds the hidden union of us all with Christ, We have thus far as Teacher of the universal Church illumined the mind with the light of truth. Our pastoral office now demands that We add a stimulus for the heart to love this Mystical Body with a burning love that will enkindle not only thoughts and words but also deeds. Followers of the Old Law sang of their earthly homeland: *If I shall forget thee, O Jerusalem, let my right hand be forgotten; let my tongue cleave to my jaws, if I do not remember thee, if I make not Jerusalem the beginning of my joy*.[96] How much greater then is the sense of glory and exultant joy that should fill our hearts, who dwell in a City

---

[93] *I Tim.* ii, 5.   [94] *Jo.* xiv, 14. Cf. St. Thomas, *De Veritate,* xxix, 4.
[95] *Apoc.* v, 13.   [96] *Ps.* cxxxvi, 5-6.

built on the holy mountain of living and chosen stones, *Jesus Christ Himself being the chief corner-stone.*[97]

For nothing more glorious, nothing nobler, nothing surely more ennobling can be imagined than to belong to the Holy, Catholic, Apostolic, and Roman Church. In that Church we become members of one Body that deserves all veneration, are guided by one supremely eminent Head; in it we are filled with one divine Spirit; in it we are nourished during our earthly exile with one doctrine and one Bread of Angels, until at last we enter into the one, unending blessedness of heaven.

But one may be deceived by the angel of darkness who assumes the appearance of an angel of light. Lest this happen, let this be the supreme law of our love: to love the Spouse of Christ as Christ wished her to be and as He purchased her with His blood. Hence not only should we cherish the sacraments with which Holy Mother Church sustains our life, the solemn ceremonies she offers for our solace and our joy, the sacred chant and liturgy by which she lifts our souls up to heaven, but the sacramentals too and all those exercises of piety which she uses to console the hearts of the faithful and gently to imbue them with the Spirit of Christ. It behooves us as sons to recompense her for this motherly goodness to us; but it is also our duty to respect the authority which she has received from Christ, and with which she brings unto captivity our understanding unto the obedience of Christ.[98]

Thus we are commanded to obey her laws and her moral precepts, often hard enough to our fallen nature; through self-imposed mortification to bring this rebellious body to submission; at times we are warned to abstain even from harmless pleasures. Nor is it enough to love this Mystical Body for the glory of its divine Head and its celestial dowry. Our zealous love must follow it even as it appears in this mortal flesh of ours, made up, that is, of weak, human elements, although at times they are little fitted to the place of dignity which they occupy in this venerable Body.

See Christ in the Church

That such a love, solidly grounded and undivided, may abide and increase in our souls, we must accustom ourselves to see Christ

[97] *Ephes.* ii, 20; *I Peter* ii, 4-5.   [98] *II Cor.* x, 5.

in the Church. It is Christ Who lives in the Church, Who teaches, governs and sanctifies through her. It is Christ, too, Who manifests Himself differently in different members of His society.

Once the faithful try to live in this spirit of conscious faith, they will not only pay due honor and reverence to the superior members of this Mystical Body, especially those who according to Christ's mandate will have to render an account of our souls,[99] but they will take to their hearts those members who are the object of our Saviour's special love: the weak, the mean, the wounded and the sick, who are in need of natural or supernatural assistance; children whose innocence is so easily exposed to danger these days and whose little hearts are as wax to be moulded; and finally the poor, in helping whom we touch, as it were, through His supreme mercy the very person of Jesus Christ.

For as the Apostle with good reason admonishes us: *Much more those that seem to be the more feeble members of the Body, are more necessary, and such as we think to be the less honorable members of the Body, about these we put more abundant honor.*[100] Conscious of the obligations of Our high office, We deem it necessary to reiterate this grave statement today, when to Our profound grief We see the bodily-deformed, the insane and those suffering from hereditary disease at times deprived of their lives, as though they were a useless burden to society. And this procedure is hailed by some as a new discovery of human progress, and as something that is altogether justified by the common good. Yet what sane man does not recognize that this not only violates the natural and divine law written in the heart of every man, but flies in the face of every sensibility of civilized humanity? The blood of these victims, all the dearer to our Redeemer because deserving of greater pity, *cries to God from the earth.*[101]

If we would forestall the gradual weakening of that sincere love which makes us see our Saviour in the Church and its members, then we should look to Jesus Himself as the perfect model of love for the Church.

And first of all let Us imitate the breadth of His love. One only is the Spouse of Christ, the Church; but the love of the divine Spouse is so vast that it embraces in His Spouse the whole human

---

[99] *Heb.* xiii. 17.   [100] *I Cor.* xii, 22-23.   [101] *Gen.* iv, 10.

race without exception. Men may be separated by nationality and race, but our Saviour poured out His Blood to reconcile all men to God through the Cross, and to bid them all unite in one Body. Genuine love of the Church therefore is not satisfied with our being within this Body members one of another, mutually careful one for another, rejoicing with him who glories, suffering with him who suffers; we must also recognize as brothers of Christ according to the flesh, destined together with us to eternal salvation, those others who have not yet joined us in the body of the Church.[102]

There are some unfortunately, today especially, who proudly boast of enmity, of hate and spite as something that elevates and honors the dignity of man and his power. Let us, however, follow on after our King of peace, the while we gaze with sorrow on the pernicious consequences of that teaching. He has taught us not only to have love for those of a different nation and a different race, but to love even our enemies.[103] While Our heart overflows with the sweetness of the Apostle's teaching We chant with him the length, the width, the height, the depth of the charity of Christ, which neither diversity of race or culture, neither the wasteless tracts of ocean, nor wars, be their cause just or unjust, can ever weaken or destroy.[104]

Supernatural Charity

In this gravest of hours, Venerable Brothers, when bodies are wracked with pain and souls with grief, every man must rise to this supernatural charity, so that by the combined efforts of all good men—We have in mind especially those who are active in any kind of relief organization—the gigantic needs of mankind, spiritual and corporal, may be alleviated. Let pity and mercy try to outdo themselves. Thus the devoted generosity and the inexhaustible resourcefulness of the Mystical Body of Jesus Christ are seen in the beauty of their perfection in every quarter of the world.

The vastness of Christ's love for the Church is equalled by its constant activity. With the same charity let us show our devoted, active love for Christ's Mystical Body. Now from the moment of His Incarnation, when He laid the first foundations of the Church,

---

[102] *Rom.* xii, 5; *I Cor.* xii, 25-26.   [103] *Luke* vi, 27-35; *Matt.* v, 44-48.
[104] *Ephes.* iii, 18.

down to His last mortal breath, our Redeemer never ceased for an instant, though He was the Son of God, to labor unto weariness for the establishing and strengthening of the Church, whether in giving us the bright example of His Holiness, or preaching, or conversing, or gathering and instructing disciples.

And so We desire that all who claim the Church as their mother, should seriously consider that not only the sacred ministers and those who have consecrated themselves to God in religious life, but the other members as well of the Mystical Body of Jesus Christ have the obligation of working hard and constantly for the upbuilding and increase of this Body. We wish this to be remembered especially by members of Catholic Action who assist the bishops and priests in their apostolic labors—and to their praise be it said that they do remember—and also by those associates of pious unions who contribute their work to the same end. Everyone is witness to the high seriousness and extraordinary importance of their energetic zeal especially in present circumstances.

In this connection We cannot pass over in silence the fathers and mothers of families, to whom our Saviour has entrusted the most delicate members of His Mystical Body. We plead with them for the love of Christ and the Church to give the greatest possible care to the children confided to them, and to look to protecting them from the multiplicity of snares into which they can fall so easily today.

Christ Prayed for the Church

Our Redeemer showed His burning love for the Church particularly by praying for her to the heavenly Father. To recall but a few instances: everyone knows, Venerable Brothers, that just before the crucifixion He prayed repeatedly for Peter, for the other Apostles, for all who through the preaching of the divine Gospel would believe in Him.[105] Imitating this example of Christ, let us pray each day to the Lord of the harvest to send laborers into His harvest. Let our united prayer rise daily to heaven for all the members of the Mystical Body of Jesus Christ, first for the Bishops who are responsible in a particular way for their respective dioceses, then for the priests and religious men and women who have been called

---

[105] *Luke* xxii, 32; *Jo.* xvii, 9-23.

to the service of God, and are protecting, increasing, advancing the Kingdom of the divine Redeemer at home and in the foreign missions.

Let no member of this revered Body be forgotten in this common prayer; let there be a special memento for those who are burdened with the sorrows and afflictions of this earthly habitation and for the departed souls in Purgatory. They, too, will be included who are being instructed in Christian doctrine, so that they may be able to receive baptism without delay.

And oh how earnestly We desire that the immense charity of these common prayers embrace those also who not yet perceiving the light of the Gospel's truth are still without the Church's safe fold, or for the regrettable conflict of faith and unity are separated from us, who though unworthy bear the person of Jesus Christ on earth. Let us then re-echo that divine prayer of our Saviour to the heavenly Father: *That they all may be one, as Thou Father in Me and I in Thee, that they also may be one in Us; that the world may believe that Thou hast sent Me.*[106]

As you know, Venerable Brothers, from the very beginning of Our Pontificate We have committed to the protection and guidance of heaven those who do not belong to the visible organization of the Catholic Church, solemnly declaring that after the example of the Good Shepherd We desire nothing more ardently than that they may have life and have it more abundantly.[107] Calling on the prayers of the whole Church We wish to repeat this solemn declaration in this Encyclical Letter in which We have retold the praises of the *great and glorious Body of Christ*.[108] From a heart overflowing with love We ask each and every one of them to be quick and ready to follow the interior movements of grace, and to look to withdrawing from that state in which they cannot be sure of their salvation. For even though unsuspectingly they are related to the Mystical Body of the Redeemer in desire and resolution, they still remain deprived of so many precious gifts and helps from heaven, which one can enjoy only in the Catholic Church.

May they then enter into Catholic unity, and united with us in the organic oneness of the Body of Jesus Christ may they hasten

---

[106] *Jo.* xvii, 21.   [107] Encycl. *Summi Pontificatus.*
[108] Irenaeus, *Adv. Haer.* iv, 33, 7 (PG 7, 1076).

to the one Head in the society of glorious love. With persevering prayer to the Spirit of love and truth We wait for them with open arms to return, not to a stranger's house, but to their own, their Father's house.

Wholly Free Submission

While We want this unceasing prayer to rise to God from the whole Mystical Body in common, that all the straying sheep may hasten to enter the one fold of Jesus Christ, yet We recognize that this step must come of their own free will; for no one believes unless he wills to believe. Hence they are most certainly not genuine Christians who against their belief are forced to go into a Church, to approach the altar and to receive the Sacraments.[109] The "faith without which it is impossible to please God" is a wholly free "submission of intellect and will." [110]

Therefore, whenever it happens, despite the invariable teaching of this Apostolic See, that anyone against his will is compelled to embrace the Catholic faith, Our sense of duty demands that We condemn the act. Men must be effectively drawn to the truth by the Father of light through the Spirit of His beloved Son, because endowed as they are with a free will they can misuse their freedom under the impulse of mental doubts and base desires. Unfortunately many are still walking far from the Catholic truth, not willing to follow the suggestions of divine grace; and the reason is, that not only they but the faithful too fail to intensify their prayers to God for this intention. Again and again We beg all who really love the Church, after the example of the divine Redeemer, to have constant recourse to that prayer.

And it is something more than commendable, in the present crisis above all, it is imperative that fervent prayers rise to God for kings and princes and for all those who govern the nations and are thus in a position by their protecting power to help the Church, so that, the conflict ended, wearied man may see *peace, the work of justice* [111] emerge under the gentle breeze of divine charity from out these dread, tempestuous seas, and Holy Mother Church, *may lead a quiet and peaceable life in all piety and chastity.*[112] We must plead

[109] St. Augustine, *In Joann. Evang.,* Tr. XXVI, 2 (PL 30, 1607).
[110] *Heb.* xi, 6; Conc. Vat. *Const. De Fide Cath.,* cap. 3.
[111] *Isa.* xxxii, 17.   [112] *I Tim.* ii, 5.

with God to grant that the rulers of peoples may love wisdom, so that this severe judgment of the Holy Spirit may never fall on them: *Because being ministers of His kingdom you have not judged rightly nor kept the law of justice, nor walked according to the will of God; horribly and speedily will He appear to you; for most severe judgment shall be for them that bear rule. For to him that is little, mercy is granted, but the mighty shall be mightily tormented. For God will not except any man's person, neither will He stand in awe of any man's greatness; for He made the little and the great, and He hath equally care of all. But a greater punishment is ready for the more mighty. To you, therefore, O kings, are these my words, that you may learn wisdom and not fall from it.*[113]

Christ Suffered for the Church

Christ proved His love for His spotless Bride not only by His tireless labors and constant prayers, but by His sorrows and His sufferings, gladly, lovingly endured for her sake. *Having loved His own . . . He loved them unto the end.*[114] It was only with His Blood that He purchased the Church.[115] Let us then not be unwilling to follow in the blood-stained footsteps of our King. The security of our salvation demands it: *For if we have been planted together in the likeness of His death, we shall be also in the likeness of His resurrection,* and *if we be dead with Him, we shall also live with Him.*[116] Our zealous love for the Church demands it, and our brotherly love for the souls she brings forth to Christ. For although our Saviour's cruel passion and death merited for His Church an infinite treasure of graces, God's inscrutable providence has decreed that these abundant graces should not be granted us all at once; and the amount of grace to be given depends in no small part also on our good deeds. They draw to the souls of men this ready flow of heavenly gifts granted by God.

These heavenly gifts will surely flow more abundantly if we not only pray fervently to God, especially by participating devoutly every day if possible in the Eucharistic Sacrifice, if we not only try to relieve the distress of the needy by works of Christian charity,

[113] *Wis.* vi, 4-10.   [114] *Jo.* xiii, 1.   [115] *Acts* xx, 28.
[116] *Rom.* vi, 5; *II Tim.* ii, 11.

but if we also set our hearts on eternal treasures rather than the passing things of this world, restrain this mortal body by voluntary mortification, denying it what is forbidden, forcing it to do what is hard and distasteful, and finally humbly accept as from God's hands the burdens and sorrows of this present life. Thus, according to the Apostle, *we shall fill up those things that are wanting of the sufferings of Christ, in our flesh, for His Body, which is the Church.*[117]

As We write these words, there passes before Our eyes, alas, an almost endless throng of unfortunates for whom We mourn and weep; sick, poor, mutilated, widows, orphans, and many not infrequently languishing even unto death for their own bitter afflictions or those of their dear ones. From a father's heart We appeal to all who from whatever cause are plunged into grief, to lift their eyes in confidence to heaven, and to offer their sorrows to Him Who will one day reward them abundantly. Let them remember that their sufferings are not in vain, but will be to their great gain and that of the Church, if for this purpose they but take courage and bear them with patience. To make this intention more efficacious, the daily use of the offering made by the members of the Apostleship of Prayer will contribute very, very much; and We welcome this occasion to recommend that Association highly, as one which is most pleasing to God.

There never was a time, Venerable Brothers, when the salvation of souls did not impose on all the duty of associating their sufferings with the torments of our divine Redeemer. But today that duty is clearer than ever when a gigantic conflict has set almost the whole world on fire, and leaves in its wake so much death, so much misery, so much sorrow. Today imposes with particular stress on everyone the duty to flee the vices and blandishments of the world, and to renounce the unrestrained pleasures of the body and that worldly frivolity and vanity which contribute nothing to the Christian formation of the soul, nothing towards gaining heaven. Rather let those words of Our immortal predecessor Leo the Great be deeply engraven in our minds, that Baptism has made us flesh of the Crucified One; and that beautiful prayer of St. Ambrose: "Carry me,

[117] *Coloss.* i, 24.

Christ, on the Cross, which is salvation to the wanderers, sole rest for the wearied, wherein alone is life for those who die." [118]

Before concluding, Venerable Brothers, We cannot but plead with all, to love holy Mother Church with a devoted and active love. Let us pray every day to the Eternal Father for her safety and for her happy and large increase. For this intention let us offer to Him our works and our sufferings, if the salvation of the whole human family, bought by divine Blood, is really dear to our hearts. And while the skies are heavy with storm clouds and untold dangers menace all human society and the Church herself, let us commit ourselves and all that we have to the Father of mercies with the prayer: "Look down, we beseech Thee, Lord, on this Thy family, for which our Lord Jesus Christ did not hesitate to be betrayed into the hands of evil men and to undergo the torture of the Cross."

CONCLUSION

Venerable Brothers, may the Virgin Mother of God grant the prayers of Our paternal heart—and they are yours too—and obtain for all a true love of the Church. Her sinless soul was filled with the divine Spirit of Jesus Christ more than all other created souls; and "in the name of the whole human race," she gave her consent for a "spiritual marriage between the Son of God and human nature." [119] Within her virginal womb Christ our Lord already bore the exalted title of Head of the Church; in a marvelous birth she brought Him forth as source of all supernatural life, and presented Him, new born, as Prophet, King and Priest to those who were the first come of Jews and Gentiles to adore Him. Her only Son, yielding to a mother's prayer in *Cana of Galilee,* performed the miracle by which *His disciples believed in Him*.[120] Free from all sin, original and personal, always most intimately united with her Son, as another Eve she offered Him on Golgotha to the Eternal Father for all the children of Adam sin-stained by his fall, and her mother's rights and mother's love were included in the holocaust.

Thus she who corporally was the mother of our Head, through

[118] St. Leo the Great, *Serm.* LXIII, 6; LXVI, 3 (PL 64, 357; 366); St. Ambrose *In Ps. CXVIII,* XXIII, 30 (PL 15, 1521).
[119] St. Thomas, *Sum. Theol.,* III, q. 30, a. 1.   [120] *Io.* ii, 11.

the added title of pain and glory became spiritually the mother of all His members. She it was who through her powerful prayers obtained the grace that the Spirit of our divine Redeemer, already given to the Church on the Cross, should be bestowed through miraculous gifts on the newly founded Hierarchy on Pentecost. Bearing with courage and confidence the tremendous burden of her sorrows and desolation, truly the Queen of Martyrs, she more than all the faithful *filled up those things that are wanting of the suffering of Christ . . . for His Body, which is the Church;* [121] and she continued to show for the Mystical Body of Christ, born from the pierced Heart of the Saviour, the same mother's care and ardent love, with which she clasped the Infant Jesus to her warm and nourishing breast.

May she, then, most holy mother of all Christ's members, to Whose Immaculate Heart We have trustingly consecrated all men, her body and soul refulgent with the glory of heaven where she reigns with her Son—may she never cease to beg from Him that a continuous, copious flow of graces may pass from its glorious Head into all the members of the Mystical Body. May she throw about the Church today, as in times gone by, the mantle of her protection and obtain from God that now at last the Church and all mankind may enjoy more peaceful days.

With full confidence in this hope, from an overflowing heart We impart to you all, Venerable Brothers, and to the flocks confided to your care, as a promise of heavenly graces and a token of Our special affection, the Apostolic Benediction.

Given at Rome, at St. Peter's, June 29th, the Feast of the Holy Apostles Peter and Paul, 1943, the fifth of Our Pontificate.

[121] *Coloss.* i, 24.

PAUL CLAUDEL

THE SATIN SLIPPER

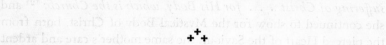

Lord, it is not so easy to escape You!

PAUL CLAUDEL, lawyer, much-traveled diplomat, renowned Catholic poet and playwright, was born in 1868 and experienced an extraordinary conversion in the Cathedral of Notre-Dame in Paris in 1886. He has served as French Minister to Brazil, Denmark, Japan, the United States (1927-1933) and Belgium. It is impossible to give the titles of all his works. Of his plays, perhaps *The Tidings Brought to Mary* (1910) and *The Satin Slipper* (1924) are best known to English readers.

The Satin Slipper is a vast and bewilderingly complicated play, set in sixteenth-century Spain. Its bare theme is as old as St. Augustine: *even sin serves.* In the opening scene, the Jesuit lashed to a ship's mast prays for his brother Rodrigo. He prays that if Rodrigo cannot go to God by the straight and the simple way, he may at least go to Him by indirect and laborious paths. So it happened. And Dona Prouheze, married to one man and loving another, offers her slipper to the Virgin and prays that, should she set out upon a sinful road, she might do so with a limping foot. The dream of Prouheze, what is it but a moment when God straightened one more crooked line in her journey to Him?

SELECTIONS

First Day, *Scene I* (in part)
First Day, *Scene V* (in part)
Third Day, *Scene VIII* (complete)

THE FIRST DAY

Scene I

THE JESUIT FATHER: Lord, I thank You for having fastened me so! And, sometimes, I have chanced to find Your commandments painful. And my will, at sight of Your rule, Perplexed, restive.
But, today, it is not possible to be closer bound to You than I am, and, verify each limb as I will, there is not one that can withdraw from You ever so little.

True, also, I am fastened to the cross, but my cross is no longer fast to anything. 'Tis floating on the sea,

The free sea, away to that point where the limit of the known sky melts

And is equally distant from this old world, which I have left,

And from the other world the new.

All has breathed its last around me.

All has been consumed upon this narrow altar, laden with the bodies of my sisters one upon other; doubtless the vintage could not come to pass without some disorder,

But everything, after a little stir, is gone back again into the great paternal peace.

Even though I think myself forsaken, I have but to await the return of that unfailing power beneath, which takes me down and lifts me up with it, as if for the moment I were one with the rapture of the great deep.

Lo! this oncoming wave, the last of them, is carrying me off.

I take over to my use all this unseen work which God has made with a word, and with which I am inmostly amalgamated within His holy will, having given up my own,

All this past which with the future weaves one untearable web, this sea which has been put at my disposal,

The breeze breathing from those two friendly worlds, which I feel upon my face by turns with its surcease, and beyond them in the sky those great unquestionable constellations,—

I take them all to my service for benison upon this land so longed-for, which my heart surmised back there in the night!

Blessings upon her, like that of Abel the shepherd, in the midst of her floods and forests! May war and dissension pass her by, may Islam never sully her shores, nor that still worse plague which is heresy!

I have given myself to God, and now the day of rest and relaxation is come and I can yield myself to these bonds which fasten me.

They speak of sacrifice, when every choice one makes is but a matter of almost imperceptible movement like a turn of the hand.

In sooth, it is only evil that demands effort, since it is against reality to sunder oneself from those great constant forces which on every side engage and make us their own.

And now, behold the last prayer of this Mass which already in the midst of death I am celebrating by the means of my poor self: my God, I pray You for my brother Rodrigo! My God, I entreat You for my son Rodrigo!

I have no other child, Oh my God, and well he knows that he shall have no other brother.

You see how first he enlisted in my footsteps under the standard which bears Your monogram, and doubtless, now that he has left Your novitiate, he thinks he is turning his back on You,

His business, as he thinks, not being to stand and wait but to conquer and possess

All he can—as if there were anything that did not belong to You and as if he could be otherwhere than where You are.

But Lord, it is not so easy to escape You, and, if he goes not to You by what he has of light, let him go to You by what he has of darkness; and if not by what he has of straight, may he go to You by what he has of indirection: and if not by what he has of simple, let him go by what in him is manifold and laborious and entangled,

And if he desire evil, let it be such evil as be compatible only with good,

And if he desire disorder, such disorder as shall involve the rending and the overthrow of those walls about him which bar him from salvation,

I mean him and that multitude with him which he is darkly implicating. For he is of those who cannot be saved except in saving all that mass which takes its impress in their wake.

Even by now You have taught him longing, but he does not yet suspect what it is to be desired.

Teach him that not You alone can be far away. Clog him by the weight of this other lovely being which lacks him and is calling him across the space between.

Make him a wounded man apart, for that once in this life he has seen the face of an angel!

Fill these lovers with such longing as shall involve, in the deprivation of each other's presence through the daily play of circumstance,

Their primal integrity, and their very essences as God conceived them both, long since in imperishable kinship;

And what He shall try to say on earth in wretchedness I am at hand in heaven to construe.

THE FIRST DAY

Scene V

(DON BALTHAZAR *holds the mule's head and* DONA PROUHEZE *climbs up on the saddle; taking off her shoe she puts the satin thing between the hands of the Virgin.*)

DONA PROUHEZE: Virgin, patron and mother of this house, protectress and surety of this man whose heart lies open to you more than to me, and companion of his long loneliness,

If not for my sake then at least for his, since this bond between him and me has not been my doing but your intervening will:

Keep me from being to this house whose door you guard, O mighty extern, a cause of corruption:

Keep me from being false to this name which you have given me to bear, and from ceasing to be honourable in the eyes of them that love me.

I cannot say that I understand this man whom you picked out for me, but you I understand, who are his mother and mine.

See, while there is yet time, holding my heart in one hand and my shoe in the other,

I give myself over to you! Virgin mother, I give you my shoe, Virgin mother, keep in your hand my luckless little foot!

I warn you that presently I shall see you no longer and that I am about to set everything going against you!

But when I try to rush on evil let it be with limping foot! The barrier that you have set up,

When I want to cross it, be it with a crippled wing!

I have done so much as I could; keep you my poor little shoe,

Keep it against your heart, tremendous Mother of mine!

THE THIRD DAY

Scene VIII

DONA PROUHEZE *asleep*, THE GUARDIAN ANGEL

DONA PROUHEZE: I have found the lost bead! A single bead. But with a bead missing the bond of the prayer is undone.

I have found my missing number. This little transparent pebble. I hold it hard in my hand. This hoarded tear, this unalterable diamond. This pearl unmatched.

Water found at last.

This drop of water that the rich man coveted from Lazarus' finger tip, and which is the hundredfold of all things. This hope within me, the seed of the day to be.

(On the screen at the back of the stage appears first dim, then better defined, a bluish image of the terrestrial globe.)

But did I say that I held this drop of water? 'Tis I am held in it.

Someone has put it into my hand, this pearl unmatched, this essential bead without which the whole rosary of the heavens would be undone!

The earth saying *Ave Maria.*

How small she is among all the cities of Judah! So small, tiny, so little among so many lights.

So little, that no eye without a guide could find Bethlehem. And yet, the Son of God desired no other woman to be born of there, 'tis because of her that all the rest was made.

(The globe turns slightly and now nothing is seen by the ocean.)

I am thirsty!

I know that my beloved is beyond the sea. Rodrigo!

I know we both are drinking of the same cup, 'tis the common horizon of our banishment.

It is that I see every morning come up sparkling in the rising sun,

And when I have drained it, from me in the darkness he receives it in his turn.

(The globe turns again and there is seen on the horizon on the edge of the curve the long sinuous line of the Isthmus of Panama, behind which the waters of a new ocean begin to shine.)

Between the two seas, the western horizon,

There where the barrier is thinner, between those two sundered masses of a continent,

There is where you have planted yourself, there is the gate given you to open.

(Again the ocean only.)

The sea! The untrammelled sea!

(There is seen the shadow of a hand behind the luminous screen sweeping the whole expanse.)

THE VOICE OF RODRIGO: *behind the screen.* Prouheze!

DONA PROUHEZE: Rodrigo! 'Tis me! I am there, I hear, I have heard.

THE VOICE OF RODRIGO: *lower, almost imperceptible.* Prouheze!

DONA PROUHEZE: Why hold me back on this threshold almost crossed? Why try to forbid me that gate which thou thyself hast opened?

Why hinder them coming to take me to the other side of that sunken barrier, 'tis not the sea in the mist, 'tis the army of God, in countless movement, coming to meet me.

The boundary between this sea and that other, two seas which seek to mingle their waters, through the intervening bulwark, did you then think it so strong?

Not stronger than what this woman's heart long since set up against thee!

Let me begin my penance in the lap of those eternal joys! Let me be the drop of water uniting them with thy heart. Let me have no more body that I may have no more bounds to thy desire! Let me have no more face that I may go right through to thy heart!

Do not hold up on this half-open threshold, this half-broken woman!

(She hearkens.)

I hear nothing now.

(The globe on the screen turns again. On the horizon is seen the group of the Japanese islands.)

What are those islands over there, like motionless clouds, which by their shape, their strongholds, their hollows, their gorges, seem like musical instruments for a mysterious concert, instruments at once gathered together and kept asunder?

I hear the sea endlessly breaking on those eternal shores!

Near a stake planted in the sand I see a stone staircase going up.

The clouds, slow to part, the curtain of the rain,

Hardly allow me at times to make out inky mountains, a waterfall with sombre trees, the fold of dark forests on which suddenly opens a revealing ray!

To the moon's torch answers the glare of subterranean fires, and the drum beneath a thatched roof joins with the shrilling flute.

Then, what mean at times these clouds of flowers-covering all? The inestimable gold of that annual consummation before the snow comes down?

Above the mountains, among forests, there is a great white angel looking at the sea.

(The great island of Japan slowly comes to life and takes the form of one of those guards in sombre armour that may be seen at Nara.)

THE GUARDIAN ANGEL: Do you recognize me?

DONA PROUHEZE: I do not know. I see only an uncertain shape, like a shadow in the fog.

THE GUARDIAN ANGEL: It is I. I was there. I have never left you,
Your Guardian Angel. Do you really think that you were far from me until now? There was continuity between us. You were touching me.

Thus, when autumn comes how warm it is still! The air is blue, the swallow everywhere finds abundant provender,

And yet how does she know it? The autumn is come, nothing will hinder her departure, she must, she goes, braving the sea.

She is not troubled about direction.

In like manner, in a conversation, one who is all caught up and possessed by the conversation,

If he hear a violin somewhere, or simply two or three times in succession those taps one gives on a piece of wood,

Bit by bit he holds his tongue, he is interrupted, he is elsewhere, as they say, he is hearkening.

You yourself, tell me, is it really true that you have never felt in the depth of yourself, between the heart and the liver, that dull thud, that sharp pull-up, that urgent touch?

DONA PROUHEZE: Too well I know them.

THE GUARDIAN ANGEL: It was my hook in the very midst of you and I was paying out the line like a patient angler. Look at it twined about my wrist. There are only a few lengths left.

DONA PROUHEZE: It is true, then, that I am going to die?

THE GUARDIAN ANGEL: And who knows if you are not dead already, otherwise whence would come to you that indifference to place, that helpless inertia?

So near the frontier, who knows from which side I can send you, back or forward at my playful will?

DONA PROUHEZE: Where am I and where are you?

THE GUARDIAN ANGEL: Together and apart. Far away and with you.

But to bring you to the inwardness of this union of time with no time, of distance with no space, of movement with a different movement, I would need that music which your ears as yet cannot endure.

Where, you say, is perfume? *Where,* you will say, is sound? Between the perfume and the sound what is the common frontier! They exist together. And I exist with you.

Listen to my being. Yield to the persuasion of those waters gradually unbinding you. Give up this earth which you think solid and is but chained down.

A frail mixture, at every second thrilled with being as well as not being.

DONA PROUHEZE: Ah, when you speak again I feel in the depths of me the fishing line, the pull of that straightforward longing against the surge, of which I have so often known the ebb and flow.

THE GUARDIAN ANGEL: The angler brings his catch from the river to the land, but my trade is to bring to those waters where I dwell the fish that is native to them.

DONA PROUHEZE: How shall I get there with this dense body?

THE GUARDIAN ANGEL: You must leave it behind a little while.

DONA PROUHEZE: Then how shall I do without it?

THE GUARDIAN ANGEL: Is it not now a little late to ask me that?

DONA PROUHEZE: Myself that corpse I see down there forsaken on the sand, is that it?

THE GUARDIAN ANGEL: Try if you can again fit yourself into it.

DONA PROUHEZE: Wax does not take a print more accurately, a vessel the water, than I fill this body in all its parts; is it filling or understanding? Bereaved henceforward

Of this fellowship that should give it life, powerless to lend it my lips.

The body, am I within it or without it? I live it simultaneously as I see it. Every movement of its life I live together in a single stroke.

Ah, poor Dona Prouheze, what pity you move in me, I see, I understand all!

THE GUARDIAN ANGEL: Is she alone?

DONA PROUHEZE: No, through her I make out another shadow—of a man, walking in the night.

THE GUARDIAN ANGEL: Look closer. What do you see?

DONA PROUHEZE: Rodrigo, I am thine.

THE GUARDIAN ANGEL: Again the line in my hand has unrolled.

DONA PROUHEZE: Rodrigo, I am thine.

THE GUARDIAN ANGEL: He hears, he stops, he listens. Silence, a faint rustle in the palm-trees, a soul in Purgatory going up to Heaven,

An enormous cloud-bank hanging in the stilled air, a wavering sun, lighting up innumerable surges, a sun clearly not the sun of day, the moon on Oceania!

And again, like a captive beast worried by the gadfly, I see him between the two walls taking up his furious race, that bitter beat of his.

Will he never stop? Ah, what a hopeless road he has already trodden between those two walls!

DONA PROUHEZE: I know it. Day and night I hear those steps continually.

THE GUARDIAN ANGEL: Are you glad that he suffers?

DONA PROUHEZE: Hold, dour angler! Do not pull the line so! Yes, I am glad that he is suffering for me.

THE GUARDIAN ANGEL: Do you think it was for you that he was created and sent into the world?

DONA PROUHEZE: Yes! Yes! Yes, I believe from the bottom of my heart that it is for me he was created and sent into the world.

THE GUARDIAN ANGEL: Are you great enough for a man's soul?

DONA PROUHEZE: Yes, I am great enough for him.

THE GUARDIAN ANGEL: Is that the way you answer me on the threshold of death?

DONA PROUHEZE: Brother, kill this poor creature quickly and do not let her be so foolish any more.

THE GUARDIAN ANGEL: What keeps you from going to him?

DONA PROUHEZE: This line holds me back.

THE GUARDIAN ANGEL: So that if I let you go . . .

DONA PROUHEZE: Ah, then no more a fish, 'tis a bird that you would see take wing! Thought is not so prompt, the arrow does not cleave the air so fast,
   As, away beyond the sea, I should be that laughing, sobbing bride in his arms!

THE GUARDIAN ANGEL: Have you never learned that 'tis the heart that must obey, and not the will materially held back by an obstacle?

DONA PROUHEZE: I obey as I am able.

THE GUARDIAN ANGEL: Then 'tis time for me to pull the line.

DONA PROUHEZE: But I can pull so hard against that it will break.

THE GUARDIAN ANGEL: What would you say if I ask you to choose between God and Rodrigo?

DONA PROUHEZE: You are too clever an angler.

THE GUARDIAN ANGEL: Why too clever?

DONA PROUHEZE: To let the question be heard before the answer is ready. Where would be the angler's art?

THE GUARDIAN ANGEL: Still if I put the question?

DONA PROUHEZE: I am deaf! I am deaf! A deaf fish, I am deaf and have not heard.

THE GUARDIAN ANGEL: By why this Rodrigo my enemy, who holds me up, why did I not strike him? 'Tis not the line alone that my hand can manage, but the trident.

DONA PROUHEZE: And I will hold him so close in my arms that you will never see him.

THE GUARDIAN ANGEL: You only do him ill.

DONA PROUHEZE: But every night he tells me something else.

THE GUARDIAN ANGEL: What does he say?

DONA PROUHEZE: That is a secret between us.

THE GUARDIAN ANGEL: Your tears are enough to reveal it.

DONA PROUHEZE: I am Hagar in the desert! Without hands, without eyes, there is someone that has foregathered with me, bitterly, in the desert!
  'Tis desire that grasps despair! 'Tis Africa, above the sea, wedding the poisonous lands of Mexico.

THE GUARDIAN ANGEL: Sister, we must learn to fare towards happier climes.

DONA PROUHEZE: What my hand each night swears to him 'tis not in my power to belie.

THE GUARDIAN ANGEL: So the fish thinks itself wiser than the fisherman. He labours and fights it out without more ado, not knowing that every somersault of his delights the old fellow in the reeds
  Who holds him and will not let him get away.

DONA PROUHEZE: Why do you play him cruelly and if you do not bring him to land why not give him his freedom?

THE GUARDIAN ANGEL: But how if you were not only a catch for me but a bait?

DONA PROUHEZE: Rodrigo, is it with me you want to catch him?

THE GUARDIAN ANGEL: That man of pride! There was no other way to get him to understand his neighbour, to get inside his skin;
  There was no other way to get him to understand the dependence, the necessity and the need of another on him,
  The law upon him of that being, different for no other reason save that it exists.

DONA PROUHEZE: Oh! And so 'twas lawful, that love of creatures for each other, 'tis true then that God is not jealous? Man in woman's arms . . .

THE GUARDIAN ANGEL: How should He be jealous of what He has made, and how should He make anything that does not serve Him?

DONA PROUHEZE: Man in woman's arms forgets God.

THE GUARDIAN ANGEL: Is it forgetting Him to be with Him? Is it away from Him to be bound up in the mystery of His creation,
    Crossing again for a moment into Eden by the gate of humiliation and death?

DONA PROUHEZE: Love without the sacrament, is it not sin?

THE GUARDIAN ANGEL: Even sin! Sin also serves.

DONA PROUHEZE: So it was good that he loved me?

THE GUARDIAN ANGEL: It was good that you taught him longing.

DONA PROUHEZE: Longing for an illusion? For a shadow that evermore escapes him?

THE GUARDIAN ANGEL: Desire is for what is, illusion is what is not. Desire through and by illusion
    Is of what is, by and through what is not.

DONA PROUHEZE: But I am not an illusion, I exist! The good that I alone can give him exists.

THE GUARDIAN ANGEL: That is why it must give him the good and nowise the evil.

DONA PROUHEZE: But, cruelly dragged by you, I can give him nothing at all.

THE GUARDIAN ANGEL: Would you give him evil?

DONA PROUHEZE: Yes, sooner than stay barren and unfruitful like this, what you call evil.

THE GUARDIAN ANGEL: Evil is that which does not exist.

DONA PROUHEZE: Let us then unite our double non-existence.

THE GUARDIAN ANGEL: Prouheze my sister, the child of God exists.

DONA PROUHEZE: But what use existing if I do not exist for Rodrigo?

THE GUARDIAN ANGEL: How should Prouheze ever exist otherwise than for Rodrigo when 'tis by him that she exists?

DONA PROUHEZE: Brother, I do not understand you.

THE GUARDIAN ANGEL: 'Tis in him that you were necessary.

DONA PROUHEZE: Oh sweet word to hear! Let me say it after you. What, was I necessary to him?

THE GUARDIAN ANGEL: No, not that ugly and ill-favored creature at the end of my line, not that sorry fish.

DONA PROUHEZE: Which then?

THE GUARDIAN ANGEL: Prouheze my sister, that child of God in light whom I do hail. That Prouheze the angels see, 'tis to her he looks without knowing it, 'tis her you have to make, to give to him.

DONA PROUHEZE: And 'twill be the same Prouheze?

THE GUARDIAN ANGEL: A Prouheze for ever, whom death does not destroy.

DONA PROUHEZE: Always lovely?

THE GUARDIAN ANGEL: A Prouheze always lovely.

DONA PROUHEZE: Will he love me for ever?

THE GUARDIAN ANGEL: What makes you so beautiful cannot die, what makes him love you cannot die.

DONA PROUHEZE: I shall be his for ever in soul and in body?

THE GUARDIAN ANGEL: We must leave the body behind some little while.

DONA PROUHEZE: What, he will never know the taste of me?

THE GUARDIAN ANGEL: It is the soul that makes the body.

DONA PROUHEZE: How, then, has she made it mortal?

THE GUARDIAN ANGEL: Sin has made it mortal.

DONA PROUHEZE: 'Twas fine to be a woman for his sake.

THE GUARDIAN ANGEL: And I will make you into a star.

DONA PROUHEZE: A star, that is the name he calls me always in the night and my heart thrilled to its depths to hear it.

THE GUARDIAN ANGEL: Have you not then been always like a star for him?

DONA PROUHEZE: Far apart!

THE GUARDIAN ANGEL: Guiding star.

DONA PROUHEZE: Behold, 'tis quenching on the road.

THE GUARDIAN ANGEL: I will rekindle it in the sky.

DONA PROUHEZE: How shall I shine, blind that I am?

THE GUARDIAN ANGEL: God will breathe upon you.

DONA PROUHEZE: I am only a brand beneath the ashes.

THE GUARDIAN ANGEL: But I will make of you a star flaming in the breath of the Holy Spirit.

DONA PROUHEZE: Farewell! then, here below! Farewell, farewell, my best beloved! Rodrigo! Rodrigo! Over there, farewell for ever.

THE GUARDIAN ANGEL: Why farewell? Why over there? When you will be nearer to him than you are now? Bound up beyond the veil with that cause which makes him live.

DONA PROUHEZE: He is seeking and will not find me any more.

THE GUARDIAN ANGEL: How should he find you outside when you are nowhere else but within his heart, himself?

DONA PROUHEZE: You say true, I shall really be there?

THE GUARDIAN ANGEL: This hook deep-bedded in his heart.

DONA PROUHEZE: Shall he always desire me?

THE GUARDIAN ANGEL: For some, the understanding is enough. This the spirit that speaks purely to the spirit.

But for others, the flesh also must be gradually evangelised and converted. And what flesh can speak to man more powerfully than that of woman?

Now he can no longer desire you without at the same time desiring where you are.

DONA PROUHEZE: But will heaven ever be so desirable to him as I?

THE GUARDIAN ANGEL, *making as if to pull the line*: For such a silly word you shall be punished here and now.

DONA PROUHEZE, *crying out*: Ah, brother, let this moment still endure.

THE GUARDIAN ANGEL: Hail dear-beloved sister! Welcome, Prouheze, to the flame!

Do you know them now, those waters where I willed to guide you?

DONA PROUHEZE: Ah, I have not enough! More! More! Give it back to me at last then, that water I was baptized in!

THE GUARDIAN ANGEL: Behold it laving and entering into thee on all sides.

DONA PROUHEZE: It bathes me and I cannot taste it! It is a ray that pierces, it is a sword that sunders, it is a red-hot iron dreadfully pressed on that very nerve of life, it is the bubbling of the spring that seizes on all my constituent parts, to dissolve and recompose them, it is the nothingness I drown in every moment, and God upon my lips reviving me. And beyond all delights, ah, is the pitiless drain of thirst, that horror of dreadful thirst that lays me open crucified!

THE GUARDIAN ANGEL: Do you ask me to bring you back to the bygone life?

DONA PROUHEZE: No, no do not separate me any more for ever from these desired flames! I must give up to their melting and devouring this frightful shell. I must bring my bonds to the fire to be burnt! I must hug it to the destruction of all my horrid sheathing, all that God did not make, all this rigid bristling wood of illusions and sin, this idol, this abominable doll that I built up in the place of the living image of God, whose seal my flesh bore printed!

THE GUARDIAN ANGEL: And this Rodrigo, where do you think you can be useful to him, here below

   Or now in this place that you know?

DONA PROUHEZE: Ah, leave me here! Ah, do not draw me out yet! And, while in that dark place he finishes his course, let me burn myself out for him like a candle at Mary's feet.

   And let him feel on his forehead from time to time a drop of this glowing oil.

THE GUARDIAN ANGEL: 'Tis enough. The time is not yet wholly come for you to cross the sacred frontier.

DONA PROUHEZE: Ah, 'tis like a bier that you lay me down on, see my limbs again take on the sheath of narrowness and weight, once more upon me the yoke of the finite and the accidental!

THE GUARDIAN ANGEL: 'Tis now but for a little time.

DONA PROUHEZE: Those two beings who from far apart without ever touching keep each other in balance as the opposite plates of a scale,

   Now that one has shifted his place will the position of the other not be changed thereby?

THE GUARDIAN ANGEL: 'Tis true. What you weigh in heaven we must put him on a different scale ere he can feel it.

   He must complete his narrow orbit on this little globe in imitation of those huge distances in the sky which we are going to give you unmoving, to annihilate.

DONA PROUHEZE: He asked but a drop of water and do you, brother, help me to give him the ocean.

THE GUARDIAN ANGEL: Is he not waiting for it on the other side of that mystic horizon which was so long

   The Horizon of bygone mankind? Those waters that you so craved, are they not making ready to cure you of earth?

The passage he has opened will not he be the first to go through?

Across that supreme barrier from one pole to the other, already half eaten away in its middle by the setting sun,

Across the New World, he is on the march to find again the eternal.

DONA PROUHEZE: At the ocean's other end there are Isles awaiting him,

Those mysterious isles at the end of the world whence I saw you rise,

How draw him thither—now that you no longer have my body for bait?

THE GUARDIAN ANGEL: No longer your body, but your reflection on the bitter waters of banishment, on exile's moving waters unceasingly fading and reforming.

DONA PROUHEZE: Now I see your face, ah, how severe and threatening it is!

THE GUARDIAN ANGEL: You shall know another face later on, this one goes with this place of justice and of penance.

DONA PROUHEZE: Is it penance he is going to, he also?

THE GUARDIAN ANGEL: The straightforward ways of God, his time is come to begin to tread them.

DONA PROUHEZE: Is it I shall have to open him the approach?

THE GUARDIAN ANGEL: What he desires cannot be at once in heaven and on earth.

DONA PROUHEZE: What are you waiting for, to let me die?

THE GUARDIAN ANGEL: I am waiting for your consent.

DONA PROUHEZE: I consent, I have consented.

THE GUARDIAN ANGEL: But how can you consent to give me what is not yours?

DONA PROUHEZE: Is my soul no longer mine?

THE GUARDIAN ANGEL: Have you not given it to Rodrigo in the night?

DONA PROUHEZE:　Then you must tell him to bring it back to me.

THE GUARDIAN ANGEL:　'Tis from him that you must get leave.

DONA PROUHEZE:　Leave me, my beloved, let me go!
Let me become a star.

THE GUARDIAN ANGEL:　This death that will make a star of you; do you consent to receive it at his hand?

DONA PROUHEZE:　Ah, I thank God! Come, dear Rodrigo! I am ready! Over this thing which is thine uplift thy slaughtering hand! Sacrifice chattel to thine own! To die, to die by thee, is sweet!

THE GUARDIAN ANGEL:　Now I have no more to say to you except farewell until we meet! I have finished my task with you! Until we meet, darling sister, in the everlasting light!

DONA PROUHEZE:　Do not leave me yet, eagle of God, take me for a moment in thy claws, lift me up while I count one! The finished round of our two existences, let me see it!

The road he is to follow, let me wind it round my arms so that he may not take one step without me, and that I be at the end of it and that it guide him towards me.

—What is that stone you are showing me in your hand?

THE GUARDIAN ANGEL:　The rock on which presently his ship will founder. He escapes alone, his head white with the foam, he lands in this unknown country.

But what matters the shipwreck, he is landed. It was not a matter of discovering a new world but of finding again the old one which was lost.

He has laid upon it the impress of his foot and of his hand, he has finished the enterprise of Columbus, he has carried out the promise of Columbus.

For what Columbus promised to the King of Spain was not a new district of the universe, 'twas the reunion of the earth, 'twas the embassy towards those peoples that you felt close behind you, 'twas the trampling of man's feet in the land behind the morning, it was the highway of the sun!

He has got back to the beginning of all things by the way of the rising sun.

See him linking up those darkling expectant peoples, those allotments beyond the dawn of day where imprisoned multitudes are trampling!

(The globe has turned, showing the whole continent of Asia, then India as far as China.)

Think you that God has given up his creation to chance? Think you that the shape of this earth which he has made is void of meaning?

While you are going to Purgatory he also upon earth is going to reconnoitre that image of Purgatory.

He also, the barrier once crossed,

That double purse, America, after he has taken it in his hand and thrown it away, that two-fold breast presented in your afternoon hour to your material greed,

He joins up with the other world as before, having taken it in rear.

Here they suffer and wait. And, behind that partition, as high as the sky, above, below, begins the other slope, the world from which he comes, the Church Militant.

He is going to survey those kneeling populations, those enclosed and dense-packed regions which are looking not for a way out, but for their centre.

One in the shape of a triangle and the other of a circle,

And the other is those torn islands endlessly tormented with storm and fire.

India hangs done to a turn in scorching vapour, China for ever in that inmost laboratory where water turns to mud, tramples down that slime mingled with her own scourings.

And the third is tearing herself with rage.

Such are those peoples groaning and awaiting, facing towards the rising sun.

'Tis to them he is sent as ambassador.

He bears with him enough sin to understand their darkness.

God has shown him joy enough for him to understand their despair.

That nothingness on whose brink they have sat so long, that Void made by the absence of Being, played upon by the reflex of heaven, he had to bring them God to make them understand it quite.

It is not Rodrigo that is bringing God, but he must come so that the lack of God in which those multitudes are lying may be looked into.

Oh Mary, Queen of Heaven, round whom unrolls the whole chaplet of the skies, have pity on those waiting people!

(He goes back into the earth which shrinks and becomes no bigger than a pin's head. The whole screen is filled with sparkling sky across which looms a gigantic image of the Immaculate Conception.)

HILAIRE BELLOC

THE RESTORATION *of* PROPERTY

(from *An Essay on the Restoration of Property*)

+‡+

> It is our business to restore economic freedom through
> the restoration of the only institution under which it
> flourishes, which institution is Property.

BORN near Paris (1870), of French and English parents, Belloc went to Oxford in 1895 and later became a member of Parliament (1906-1910). His talents have been many. Historian, biographer, essayist, formidable controversialist, and poet, Belloc has been the great champion of the Catholic basis of European civilization. Though he has had a high disdain for the trappings of scholarship, yet this disdain is born of the massive historical knowledge that he commands. Among his dozens of books we may note *The Path to Rome* (1902), *The Servile State* (1915), *Europe and the Faith* (1920), *Survivals and New Arrivals* (1927), *How the Reformation Happened* (1928).

Belloc is a passionate critic of capitalism, and an uncompromising defender of private property. The following essay is one of the distinctive pieces of his economic writing.

AN, TO LIVE, MUST TRANSFORM HIS ENVIRON-
ment from a state in which it is less to a state in
which it is more useful to himself. This process
is called "The Production of Wealth".

Moreover, if a man is to live conformably to
his nature, there must be available for his consumption a certain amount of wealth, in a certain variety, for a
certain unit of time. For instance, in our society, he must have so
much bread, so much meat, so much of a number of different foods
every day, so much beer or wine or spirits (or, if he be too weak
to consume these) so much tea or coffee or what not; a sufficient
amount of somewhat complicated clothing, all to last over such
and such an amount of time; and a sufficiency of fuel, housing and
all the rest of it, also to last a certain time.

Now this transformation of environment called "The Production
of Wealth" is obviously only possible through the use of the instruments of production. A family can only live conformably to
its human nature (that is, without undue suffering) in a given
civilization on condition that it receive securely and constantly so
much of this varied wealth for its consumption. But the wealth can
only come into existence through the manipulating of natural forces
by certain instruments; and there must also be an existing store of
food and clothing and housing and the rest of it so that human
beings may carry on during the process of production. These stores
of wealth, these instruments and these natural forces are the *Means
of Production.*

It is obvious that whoever controls the means of production controls the supply of wealth. If, therefore, the means for the production of that wealth which a family needs are in the control of
others than the family, the family will be dependent upon those
others; it will not be economically free.

The family is ideally free when it fully controls all the means
necessary for the production of such wealth as it should consume
for normal living.

But such an ideal is inhuman and, therefore, not to be fixedly
attained, because man is a social animal. It is not impossible of
achievement for a short time, and has been briefly achieved when-

ever a lonely settler has fixed himself with his family and his stores in an isolated spot. But such complete economic freedom for each family cannot be permanent, because the family increases and divides into further numerous families, forming a larger community. Moreover, even were the isolated free family to endure, it would fall below the requirements of human nature, its isolation stunting and degrading it. For men cannot fulfil themselves save through a diversity of interests and ideas. Multiplicity is essential to life, and man to be truly human must be social.

Society being necessary to man, there arise in the economic field these two limitations to economic freedom:—

First, Difference of Occupation: Each in a society will concentrate upon what he has the best opportunity for producing and, by exchanging his surplus of it for that which another has the best opportunity of producing, will increase the wealth of all: or what comes to the same thing, lessen the burden of labour for all. Thus men live more happily in an agricultural village if there be a miller to grind the wheat instead of every family grinding it under its own roof, a cobbler to mend and make the boots—and so on.

Second, a Principle of Unity: There must exist in some form the State. A sufficiently large unit for the development of the arts and the better complexities of life must be organised. Its power must be appealed to for the satisfaction of justice, the prevention of internal disorder and for the arrangement of defence against external aggression. In general the State must exercise some restraint upon the ideal economic freedom of the family or freedom itself cannot be guaranteed.

But, while difference of occupation restricts the ideal independence of the family, it does not destroy freedom until one or another differentiated (and necessary) occupation can withhold its necessary function and thus impose its will. If the miller can refuse to supply flour to the rest, who have lost their instruments and aptitude for grinding wheat, he will be their master. So with the unifying authority of the State. If the State can cut off livelihood from the family it is their master, and freedom has disappeared.

Therefore there is a test of the limit after which such restriction of freedom is hostile to our aims and that test lies in the power of the family to re-act against that which limits its freedom. There must be a human relation between the family and those forces which, whether through the division of labour or the action of the State, restrict the family's liberty of choice in action. The family must have not only power to complain against arbitrary control external to it, but power to make its complaint effective.

It has been found in practice (that is, it is discoverable through history) that economic freedom thus somewhat limited satisfies the nature of man, and at the basis of it is the control of the means of production by the family unit. For though the family exchange its surplus, or even all its production, for the surplus of others, yet it retains its freedom, so long as the social structure, made up of families similarly free, exercises its effect through customs and laws consonant to its spirit: the guild; a jealous watch against, and destruction of, monopoly; the safeguarding of inheritance, especially the inheritance of small patrimonies. The freehold miller, in such a society as was ours not so long ago, though he had no arable or pasture, was a free man. The yeoman, though he got his flour from the miller, was a free man.

The name for a control of the Means of Production is "Property." When that control is exercised severally by individual units we call it "Private Property" to distinguish it from property vested in public bodies. When so great a number of families in the State possess Private Property in a sufficient amount as to give its colour to the whole, we speak of "widely distributed property."

It has been found in practice, and the truth is witnessed to by the instincts in all of us, that such widely distributed property as a condition of freedom is necessary to the normal satisfaction of human nature. In its absence general culture ultimately fails and so certainly does citizenship. The cells of the body politic are atrophied and the mass of men have not even, at last, an opinion of their own, but are moulded by the few who retain ownership of land and endowments and reserves. So essential is property to full life, though it is debatable whether a full life is to be aimed at. There may be some who dislike freedom for themselves. There are certainly many who dislike it for others. But, at any rate, freedom involves property.

Today in England, and to a less degree in many other countries, widespread property has been lost. Ownership is not a general feature of our society, determining its character. On the contrary, absence of ownership, dependence on a precarious wage at the will of others is the general feature of our society and determines its character.

The family does not possess that freedom which is necessary for its full moral health and that of the State of which it is the unit. Hence our society has fallen into the diseased condition known as "Industrial Capitalism." In this state the control of the Means of Production is vested in a comparatively small number; consequently economic freedom has ceased to be the note, giving its tone to society.

"Capitalism" does not mean a state of society in which capital has been accumulated, its accumulation protected, and itself put to use in producing wealth. Capital so accumulated, protected and used *must* exist in any human society whatsoever, including, of course, a Communist one. Nor does "Capitalism" mean a state of society in which capital is owned as private property by the citizens. On the contrary, such a society of free owners is the opposite of Capitalism as the word is here used. I use the term "Capitalism" here to mean a state of society in which a minority control the means of production, leaving the mass of the citizens dispossessed. Such a dispossessed body of citizens is called a "Proletariat."

Industrial Capitalism has in its present phase other grave evils attached to it besides the loss of freedom, for the twin evils of Insecurity and Insufficiency are attached to it. The main body of citizens, the Proletariat, are not sufficiently clothed, housed and fed, and even their insufficient supply is unstable. They live in a perpetual anxiety.

Now those two evils of insecurity and insufficiency might be eliminated and yet economic freedom be absent from the mass of society.

There are two ways in which they could be eliminated without the restoration of freedom:—

The first way is through that which I have called elsewhere "The Servile State." [1] In this form of society the minority controlling the means of production supports all the vast majority of the dispossessed, even those whom it does not use in exploitation, and thus

1 In my book *The Servile State,* published by Messrs. Constable and Co.

forms a stable society though one from which freedom is eliminated. That is the direction in which we are drifting today. The
capitalists keep men alive by exploiting them at a wage, and when
they cannot do this, still keep them alive in idleness by some small
subsidy.

The second way is Communism—of its nature unstable but prac-
ticable at a heavy strain though, presumably, for only a comparatively short space of time. Under this second system the means of
production are controlled by the officers of the State, who are the
masters of all the workers (slaves of the State), and the wealth
produced is distributed, at the discretion of the State officials,
among the families, or, if an attempt be made to abolish even the
family, then among the individuals of the community.

There is a third form of society, and it is the only one in which
sufficiency and security can be combined with freedom, and that
form is *a society in which property is well distributed and so large
a proportion of the families in the State severally* OWN *and therefore control the means of production as to determine the general
tone of society*; making it neither Capitalist nor Communist, but
Proprietary. If, then, we regard economic freedom as a good, our
object must be thus to restore property. We must seek political and
economic reforms which shall tend to distribute property more and
more widely until the owners of sufficient Means of Production
(land or capital or both) are numerous enough to determine the
character of society.

But is economic freedom a good?

Unless we regard it as a good the search for methods by which
property may be restored is futile or harmful. Indeed, as we shall
see in a moment, unless a sufficient number of our fellow-citizens
feel with a sufficient degree of intensity that economic freedom is
a good, economic freedom (that is, well-divided Property) can
never be restored.

So it behoves us at the outset to consider this question, whether
or no economic freedom be a good.

Economic freedom can only be a good if it fulfils some need
in our nature.

Now there is discoverable in man, Freewill. His actions are of
moral value to him if they are undertaken upon his own initiative;

not if they are undertaken under compulsion. Therefore the use of choice is necessary to human dignity. A man deprived of choice is by that the less a man, and this we all show through the repugnance excited in us by unauthorized restraint and subjection, through coercion rather than authority, to another's will. We cannot do good, or even evil, unless we do it freely; and if we admit the idea of good at all in human society, freedom must be its accompaniment.

Next, economic freedom is a good because man's actions are multiple, both his desires and his creative faculties; but it is only in possession of economic freedom that this multiplicity can be effective. Deprived of economic freedom the units of society, the family and in some degree the individual, lack the power to express that diversity which is life. In the absence of economic freedom there must weigh upon any human society a dead and mechanical uniformity, increasingly leaden, and heavy, and stifling, in proportion to the absence of freedom.

To all this two answers may be given by those who dread the restoration of property, or those who regard it as impossible.

First, it may be said that men do have economic freedom under State ownership. Secondly, it may be said that economic freedom, though a good, is of no moment in comparison with material satisfaction.

As to the first answer: It has been widely said in the recent past that economic freedom can exist without the institution of property, because, under a Communist system, men own though they own corporately; they can dispose of their own lives, though such disposition be indirect and through delegates. This false argument is born of the dying Parliamentary theory in politics; it proceeds from the false statement which deceived three generations of Europe, from the French Revolution to our own day, that corporate action may be identified with individual action. So men speak of their so-called political "Representatives" as having been "chosen" by themselves. But in experienced reality there is no such thing as this imagined permanent corporate action through delegation. On some very simple and universal point, which all understand, in which all are interested and on which all feel strongly, the desire of the bulk of the people may be expressed for a brief moment by delegation.

Men voting under strong emotion on one single clear issue, may instruct others to carry out their wishes; but the innumerable acts of choice and expression which make up human life can never work through a system of delegation. Even in the comparatively simple field of mere political action, delegation destroys freedom. Parliaments have everywhere proved irreconcilable with democracy. They are not the people. They are oligarchies, and those oligarchies are corrupt because they pretend to a false character and to be, or to mirror, the nation. They are in reality, and can only be, cliques of professional politicians; unless, indeed, they are drawn from an aristocratic class which the community reveres. For class government, the product of the aristocratic spirit, is the condition of oligarchies working successfully and therefore of a reasonably efficient Parliament. Such an instrument is not to be found save in the hands of the governing class.

If this be true of mere politics it is obviously true of that millioned affair, our daily lives. Ownership by delegation is a contradiction in terms.

When men say, for instance (by a false metaphor), that each member of the public should feel himself an owner of public property—such as a Town Park—and should therefore respect it as his own, they are saying something which all our experience proves to be completely false. No man feels of public property that it is his own; no man will treat it with the care or the affection of a thing which is his own; still less can a man express himself through the use of a thing which is not his own, but shared in common with a mass of other men.

As to the second answer: It is said by many to-day that the satisfaction of man's immediate material necessities is on a different and infinitely more important plane than the satisfaction of his need for freedom. Economic freedom, if indeed it be a good at all, is (they say) a good of a much lesser sort, intangible, and something which men can well do without; therefore, since the enjoyment of it imperils the obtaining of material necessities, it must give way to that much greater good: a secure sufficiency of livelihood.

There is in this reply a measure of truth which gives it all its strength. It is half-true; but the falsehood attached to the half truth vitiates the whole statement.

Where urgent material necessities are unsatisfied they must be satisfied first. Shipwrecked men on a raft at sea must live, exceptionally, under Communism. The dispossessed in a capitalist society must at least be kept alive. But it is not true that, such exceptional remedies for an unnatural evil having been used, we must go on to destroy the good of economic freedom for the advantage of enjoying greater material wealth.

This last argument is one of the many which we find in common to those who defend the Capitalist system and those who defend the Communist system; for Socialism and Capitalism are twin successive products of the same false philosophy.

The defenders of Capitalism tell us that it may have destroyed men's economic freedom; under Capitalism a man can less and less choose what he wants nor express his personality and character in the arts; but at least Capitalism has given him in far greater numbers a far greater mass of material goods than he had before it arose. The Communist goes one better. He says, "Yes; and under *my* system, by suppressing economic freedom altogether we shall give him yet more material goods, and we shall see that everybody gets them in almost unlimited amount."

If it were indeed true that economic freedom could not coexist with a great deal of production, and still less with a sufficient distribution, it would still be worth while for those of our temper to sacrifice some portion of the material good, and even more worth while to permit inequality in distribution, for the sake of the economic freedom. But the truth is, as we shall see later on, that the supposed conflict between freedom and abundance, between freedom and a general enjoyment of that abundance, is an illusion born of Capitalism. It is an illusion which arises from the fact that the men who cherish it have so lived under a capitalist system all their lives that they can conceive of no alternative save a further development of it into Communism.

There remains indeed one unanswerable reply or objection. It is that of the man who says, "This or that, which economic freedom endangers, is a greater good in my eyes than is such freedom." For instance, he may think the military glory of the State a greater good; or magnificence on the part of the few a greater good. To such an objection we can only reply that our tastes differ and that we prefer freedom.

Economic freedom is in our eyes a good. It is among the highest of temporal goods because it is necessary to the highest life of society through the dignity of man and through the multiplicity of his action, in which multiplicity is life. Through well-divided property alone can the units of society react upon the State. Through it alone can a public opinion flourish. Only where the bulk of the cells are healthy can the whole organism thrive. It is therefore our business to restore economic freedom through the restoration of the only institution under which it flourishes, which institution is Property. The problem before us is, how to restore Property so that it shall be, as it was not so long ago, a general institution.

Three provisos must be kept clearly in mind before we approach the problem and attempt its practical solution.

The first Proviso is that in the restoration of property we are not attempting, and could never reach, a mechanical perfection. We are only attempting to change the general tone of society and restore property as a commonly present, not a universal, institution.

The second Proviso is that we cannot even begin such a reform unless there is a favourable state of mind present in society, a desire to own property, sufficient to support and maintain the movement and to nourish institutions which will make it permanent.

The third Proviso is that in this attempt to restore Economic Freedom, the powers of the State must be invoked.

The first Proviso is, I say, that, unlike the Servile State and unlike the Communist State, the Proprietary State does not present an ideal solution. There can be no perfection about it; it must remain incomplete: nor could there be a better proof that the attempt is a human one, consonant to human nature.

To establish the Servile State one has but to follow certain lines which lead rapidly to an ideal conclusion, a society where *all* men, the few Capitalists and the mass of the proletariat are *all* securely nourished—the latter on a wage, or, lacking this, a subsidy in idleness. The same is true with regard to the Communist State: a society where *all* men are securely nourished as slaves of the government. A simple formula and its exact application will, in each case, produce the ideal society envisaged.

In the first case all that is needed to produce the complete Servile State is a series of laws whereby every family—or every individual, if the family be eliminated—shall receive at least so much wealth as will maintain a certain standard of comfort and leisure; this minimum being provided for the dispossessed out of the stores controlled by the possessors. It will be distributed either in the form of wages, that is, the granting to the dispossessed by the possessors of some portion of the wealth which the dispossessed are producing by leave of the possessors; *or,* in the case of those who cannot be so employed, of relief during their enforced idleness.

This is the simple ideal of society to which we, in modern England, are advancing with great rapidity; indeed we have almost reached it.

The Possessors alone remain to enjoy economic freedom, the dispossessed—the very great majority—are deprived of it; but there is already at least security of *some* revenue for nearly all, and there can, with proper organization, be sufficiency for all as well. The only good lost to the masses, if it be a good, is freedom. For in such a state of society (the Servile State) the determining note is lack of freedom: the determining mass of society have no experience of economic liberty. The master class directs and is free: but society thinks and acts in terms of wage-earners. The masses are kept alive, they are taught by a subsidy in childhood, treated by a subsidy in illness, and maintained by a subsidy in old age, widowhood and incapacity from accident. Soon no one of them may be suffering either hunger or cold or lack of any plain material necessity consonant to the type of civilization in which they live. But their activities are at the mercy of their masters.

Under the Communist scheme the matter is simpler still. It being made an offence for any man to own, all right to the use of accumulation by a family or an individual being destroyed, and all right of inheritance being also destroyed, the whole produce of the community is available for distribution to all. And Economic Freedom has disappeared for all through the action of a very few and simple but absolute coercive laws.

The formulae of the two schemes have been put in the past very well by the late Mr. Orage, in words which appeared some 20 or

30 years ago in "The New Age." I have not the exact phrases by me, but their sense is as follows:—

"Imagine a condition of affairs in which one machine is capable of producing all that society requires. Let that machine (and the natural forces) be under the control of one man. He is then the Capitalist of an ideally perfect Industrial Capitalist System. He will employ directly in industry as many men as may be required to work the machine. They will receive sustenance in the form of wages. He will also employ sundry other men, not directly in producing wealth with the machine, but ministering to his enjoyment; they may paint for him, print books for him, act plays for him, supply his domestic wants, and so forth. The rest will be unemployed. But as society would never be stable if the rest were to be condemned to death by starvation, laws will appear which demand by taxation, or customs will appear which demand by voluntary organization, so much of the produce of the machine as is necessary to support the unemployed. But these will not have the determining of what they are to receive, for they are not possessors. Their subsistence is doled out to them without their having discretion in the matter. And that is the Servile State. Or imagine the machine, and the material forces to which it is to be applied, controlled, not by one possessor, the Capitalist, but by the officers of the community, who shall at their discretion employ or dole out to each from the production of the machine; *then* you have the Communist State."

But the Proprietary State, the state of society such as our ancestors enjoyed, in which property is well distributed, does not admit of this simplicity, nor, being human, of this mechanical perfection. Property being a personal and human institution, normal to man, will always be, and must be, diversified. There is no advantage moral or social in land and capital being exactly distributed and there is no possibility of their being universally distributed. It would suffice for the health of the State by the Restoration of Property if, at the end of the reforming process, so many families were found possessed of property (in a sufficient amount) to give their tone to the State; just as to-day the wage-earner and salary-earner, the proletarians of every grade, give *their* proletarian tone to the State. The proletarians to-day vary in the degree of their dispossession, some have only the clothes they stand in, others a little furniture as well, others some further small insufficient accumulation—a few shares or a mortgaged house or what not—but the note which they strike, the character which they impress upon society, is that of a wage-earning State rapidly turning into a Servile State.

But whereas the Servile State to which we are now tending can be complete, the Proprietary (or Distributist) State neither can, nor should be, complete; for it cannot of its nature be mechanical. There will be many comparatively poor, and some comparatively rich. There will presumably be some proportion of dispossessed. But Property, and its accompaniment, Economic Freedom, will be the mark of society as a whole.

The second Proviso, that we can do nothing unless there is a state of mind favourable to us, may seem to make the whole effort futile. The state of society in which we are now living in England has largely forgotten what property is. Men talk in terms of employment and wages. When they talk of ownership the word calls up in their minds the ownership of large property by a few. Whether there remains to-day in England a desire for economic freedom (that is, for property) sufficient to nourish the beginnings of a change, nothing but experiment can decide. Increase of revenue, not ownership, is the object of most men. Ownership is certainly not the object of *most* men; if it were, there would have been successful protest long ago against the wage-earning system.

As we all know, there was some confused protest at the beginning of the Industrial Revolution and throughout its earlier stages; there was violence used to try and prevent the enclosure of the commons and there were riots against the new machines. But that was a long time ago. Take the process as a whole, from the first step, the great confiscation of corporate property in the XVI Century, through the Statute of Frauds in the XVII Century, when a mass of small yeomen were dispossessed, follow it on to the mid XIX Century, and you do not find at any stage a clear determination to maintain well-divided property, nor even a widespread instinct in its favour. It was because such a spirit was lacking that Capitalism came upon us. In countries where that spirit was present, though Capitalism has also taken root there, it has never flourished in the same way, it has always been handicapped.

But though the appetite for private property has weakened,

though it is not present as yet in the mass of the wage-earning population, its relics may *possibly* prove, if the first experiments can be undertaken, sufficiently alive to leaven the whole body of society gradually. It *may* be possible to "re-plant" property even in England, just as one can re-afforest wind-swept poor ground by taking advantage of exceptional patches, establishing the new growth there, sheltering its beginnings, and leaving it to propagate itself when it shall have sufficient strength. Only, what we must not trust to is the mere machinery of reform. Of its nature property is the product of a human desire: we can help on that desire to achieve its fulfilment, but we cannot create it. We cannot make owners by merely giving men something to own. And, I repeat, whether there be sufficient desire for property left upon which we can work, only experience can decide.

The third Proviso, that we must call in the State to help us, should present no difficulties save to minds misled by the false categories of the XIX Century—by such terms as "Individualism," for instance, which never did or could correspond to any reality.

The evil from which we are suffering to-day is not the evil of State-interference but the evil of the loss of Freedom. State interference may have for its effect a loss of Freedom and certainly usually has for its object the loss of Freedom; but it always may be, and very often must be, invoked for the very purpose of restoring Freedom. There must be laws to protect property not only against direct rapine but against dissolution through the exaggeration of competition. There must be State sanction for the powers of the Guild, for the process of Inheritance, for the restriction of undue burdens. There must be some official machinery for fostering the propagation of small property just as there is official machinery to-day fostering the destruction of small, widespread property by large owners: and the effort at restoring property will certainly fail if it is hampered by any superstition against the use of force as the handmaid of justice. All the powers of the State have been invoked by Capitalism to restore servile conditions; we shall not react against servile conditions unless we avail ourselves of the same methods.

GILBERT KEITH CHESTERTON

THE WORLD INSIDE OUT

(from *The Catholic Church and Conversion*)

> Paganism was the largest thing in the world and Christianity was larger; and everything else has been comparatively small.

BRILLIANT is a word that must be used in writing of Chesterton. His paradoxes literally dazzle the reader by their extraordinary obviousness, their depth, and their unanswerableness. Chesterton was born in 1874 in Kensington, turned to writing early in his life and entered the Church in 1922. He died in 1936. *Heretics* was written in 1905; *The Man Who Was Thursday* in 1908; *Orthodoxy* in 1908; *The Flying Inn* in 1914; *The Everlasting Man* in 1925; *The Autobiography* in 1936. Chesterton has all the nobility of a plumed knight defending his lady, the Church, with a loyalty whose fierceness is surpassed only by the innocence of his heart. His poetry has a sonorous quality, full of gallantry and flying banners. His insight is remarkable, as can be seen from his biography of St. Thomas Aquinas. The following selection is taken from the autobiographical *The Catholic Church and Conversion* (1926).

HE FIRST FALLACY ABOUT THE CATHOLIC
Church is the idea that it is a church. I mean
that it is a church in the sense in which the Non-
conformist newspapers talk about The Churches.
I do not intend any expression of contempt about
The Churches; nor is it an expression of con-
tempt to say that it would be more convenient to call them the sects.
This is true in a much deeper and more sympathetic sense than may
at first appear; but to begin with, it is certainly true in a perfectly
plain and historical sense, which has nothing to do with sympathy
at all. Thus, for instance, I have much more sympathy for small
nationalities than I have for small sects. But it is simply a historical
fact that the Roman Empire was the Empire and that it was not a
small nationality. And it is simply a historical fact that the Roman
Church is the Church and is not a sect. Nor is there anything narrow or unreasonable in saying that the Church is the Church. It may
be a good thing that the Roman Empire broke up into nations; but
it certainly was not one of the nations into which it broke up. And
even a person who thinks it fortunate that the Church broke up into
sects ought to be able to distinguish between the little things he
likes and the big thing he has broken. As a matter of fact, in the
case of things so large, so unique and so creative of the culture
about them as were the Roman Empire and the Roman Church, it
is not controversial but simply correct to confine the one word to
the one example. Everybody who originally used the word "Empire"
used it of that Empire; everybody who used the word "Ecclesia"
used it of that Ecclesia. There may have been similar things in other
places, but they could not be called by the same name for the simple
reason that they were not named in the same language. We know
what we mean by a Roman Emperor; we can if we like talk of a
Chinese Emperor, just as we can if we like take a particular sort of
a Mandarin and say he is equivalent to a Marquis. But we never
can be certain that he is exactly equivalent; for the thing we are
thinking about is peculiar to our own history and in that sense
stands alone. Now in that, if in no other sense, the Catholic Church
stands alone. It does not merely belong to a class of Christian
churches. It does not merely belong to a class of human religions.

Considered quite coldly and impartially, as by a man from the moon, it is much more *sui generis* than that. It is, if the critic chooses to think so, the ruin of an attempt at a Universal Religion which was bound to fail. But calling the wreckers to break up a ship does not turn the ship into one of its own timbers; and cutting Poland up into three pieces does not make Poland the same as Posen.

But in a much more profound and philosophical sense this notion that the Church is one of the sects is the great fallacy of the whole affair. It is a matter more psychological and more difficult to describe. But it is perhaps the most sensational of the silent upheavals or reversals in the mind that constitute the revolution called conversion. Every man conceives himself as moving about in a cosmos of some kind; and the man of the days of my youth walked about in a kind of vast and airy Crystal Palace in which there were exhibits set side by side. The cosmos, being made of glass and iron, was partly transparent and partly colourless; anyhow, there was something negative about it; arching over all our heads, a roof as remote as a sky, it seemed to be impartial and impersonal. Our attention was fixed on the exhibits, which were all carefully ticketed and arranged in rows; for it was the age of science. Here stood all the religions in a row—the churches or sects or whatever we called them; and towards the end of the row there was a particularly dingy and dismal one, with a pointed roof half fallen in and pointed windows most broken with stones by passers-by; and we were told that this particular exhibit was the Roman Catholic Church. Some of us were sorry for it and even fancied it had been rather badly used; most of us regarded it as dirty and disreputable; a few of us even pointed out that many details in the ruin were artistically beautiful or architecturally important. But most people preferred to deal at other and more business-like booths; at the Quaker shop of Peace and Plenty or the Salvation Army store where the showman beat the big drum outside. Now conversion consists very largely, on its intellectual side, in the discovery that all that picture of equal creeds inside an indifferent cosmos is quite false. It is not a question of comparing the merits and defects of the Quaker meeting-house set beside the Catholic cathedral. It is the Quaker meeting-house that is inside the Catholic cathedral; it is the Catholic cathedral that covers everything like the vault of the Crystal Palace; and it is when we look up at the vast distant dome covering all the exhibits that we trace the Gothic roof and the pointed windows. In other words, Quakerism is but a temporary form of Quietism which has arisen technically outside the Church as the Quietism of Fénelon appeared technically inside the Church. But both were in themselves temporary and would have, like Fénelon, sooner or later to return to the Church in order to live. The principle of life in all these variations of Protestantism, in so far as it is not a principle of death, consists of what remained in them of Catholic Christendom; and to Catholic Christendom they have always returned to be recharged with vitality. I know that this will sound like a statement to be challenged; but it is true. The return of Catholic ideas to the separated parts of Christendom was often indeed indirect. But though the influence came through many centres, it always came from one. It came through the Romantic Movement, a glimpse of the mere picturesqueness of mediævalism; but it is something more than an accident that Romances, like Romance languages, are named after Rome. Or it came through the instinctive reaction of old-fashioned people like Johnson or Scott or Cobbett, wishing to save old elements that had originally been Catholic against a progress that was merely Capitalist. But it led them to denounce that Capitalist progress and become, like Cobbett, practical foes of Protestantism without being practising followers of Catholicism. Or it came from the Pre-Raphaelites or the opening of continental art and culture by Matthew Arnold and Morris and Ruskin and the rest. But examine the actual make-up of the mind of a good Quaker or Congregational minister at this moment, and compare it with the mind of such a dissenter in the Little Bethel before such culture came. And you will see how much of his health and happiness he owes to Ruskin and what Ruskin owed to Giotto; to Morris and what Morris owed to Chaucer; to fine scholars of his own school like Philip Wicksteed, and what they owe to Dante and St. Thomas. Such a man will still sometimes talk of the Middle Ages as the Dark Ages. But the Dark Ages have improved the wallpaper on his wall and the dress on his wife and all the whole dingy and vulgar life which he lived in the days of Stiggins and Brother Tadger. For he also is a Christian and lives only by the life of Christendom.

It is not easy to express this enormous inversion which I have here tried to suggest in the image of a world turned inside out. I mean that the thing which had been stared at as a small something swells out and swallows everything. Christendom is in the literal sense a continent. We come to feel that it contains everything, even the things in revolt against itself. But it is perhaps the most towering intellectual transformation of all and the one that it is hardest to undo even for the sake of argument. It is almost impossible even in imagination to reverse that reversal. Another way of putting it is to say that we have come to regard all these historical figures as characters in Catholic history, even if they are not Catholics. And in a certain sense, the historical as distinct from the theological sense, they never do cease to be Catholic. They are not people who have really created something entirely new, until they actually pass the border of reason and create more or less crazy nightmares. But nightmares do not last; and most of them even now are in various stages of waking up. Protestants are Catholics gone wrong; that is what is really meant by saying they are Christians. Sometimes they have gone very wrong; but not often have they gone right ahead with their own particular wrong. Thus a Calvinist is a Catholic obsessed with the Catholic idea of the sovereignty of God. But when he makes it mean that God wishes particular people to be damned, we may say with all restraint that he has become a rather morbid Catholic. In point of fact he is a diseased Catholic; and the disease left to itself would be death or madness. But, as a matter of fact, the disease did not last long, and is itself now practically dead. But every step he takes back towards humanity is a step back towards Catholicism. Thus a Quaker is a Catholic obsessed with the Catholic idea of gentle simplicity and truth. But when he made it mean that it is a lie to say "you" and an act of idolatry to take off your hat to a lady, it is not too much to say that whether or not he had a hat off, he certainly had a tile loose. But as a matter of fact he himself found it necessary to dispense with the eccentricity (and the hat) and to leave the straight road that would have led him to a lunatic asylum. Only, every step he takes back towards common sense is a step back towards Catholicism. In so far as he was right he was a Catholic; and in so far as he was wrong he has not himself been able to remain a Protestant.

To us, therefore, it is henceforth impossible to think of the Quaker as a figure at the beginning of a new Quaker history or the Calvinist as the founder of a new Calvinistic world. It is quite obvious to us that they are simply characters in our own Catholic history, only characters who caused a great deal of trouble by trying to do something that we could do better and that they did not really do at all. Now some may suppose that this can be maintained of the older sects like Calvinists and Quakers, but cannot be maintained of modern movements like those of Socialists or Spiritualists. But they will be quite wrong. The covering or continental character of the Church applies just as much to modern manias as to the old religious manias; it applies quite as much to Materialists or Spiritualists as to Puritans. In all of them you find that some Catholic dogma is, first, taken for granted; then exaggerated into an error; and then generally reacted against and rejected as an error, bringing the individual in question a few steps back again on the homeward road. And this is almost always the mark of such a heretic; that while he will wildly question any other Catholic dogma, he never dreams of questioning his own favourite Catholic dogma and does not even seem to know that it could be questioned. It never occurred to the Calvinist that anybody might use his liberty to deny or limit the divine omnipotence, or to the Quaker that anyone could question the supremacy of simplicity. That is exactly the situation of the Socialist. Bolshevism and every shade of any such theory of brotherhood is based upon one unfathomably mystical Catholic dogma; the equality of men. The Communists stake everything on the equality of men, as the Calvinists staked everything on the omnipotence of God. They ride it to death as the others rode their dogma to death, turning their horse into a nightmare. But it never seems to occur to them that some people do not believe in the Catholic dogma of the mystical equality of men. Yet there are many, even among Christians, who are so heretical as to question it. The Socialists get into a great tangle when they try to apply it; they compromise with their own ideals; they modify their own doctrine; and so find themselves, like the Quakers and the Calvinists, after all their extreme extravagances, a day's march nearer Rome.

In short, the story of these sects is not one of straight lines strik-

ing outwards and onwards, though if it were they would all be
striking in different directions. It is a pattern of curves continually
returning into the continent and common life of their and our civilisation; and the summary of that civilisation and central sanity is
the philosophy of the Catholic Church. To us, Spiritualists are men
studying the existence of spirits, in a brief and blinding oblivion of
the existence of evil spirits. They are, as it were, people just educated enough to have heard of ghosts but not educated enough to
have heard of witches. If the evil spirits succeed in stopping their
education and stunting their minds, they may of course go on for
ever repeating silly messages from Plato and doggerel verses from
Milton. But if they do go a step or two further, instead of marking
time on the borderland, their next step will be to learn what the
Church could have taught. To us, Christian Scientists are simply
people with one idea, which they have never learnt to balance and
combine with all the other ideas. That is why the wealthy business
man so often becomes a Christian Scientist. He is not used to ideas
and one idea goes to his head, like one glass of wine to a starving
man. But the Catholic Church is used to living with ideas and
walks among all those very dangerous wild beasts with the poise
and the lifted head of a lion-tamer. The Christian Scientist can go
on monotonously repeating his one idea and remain a Christian
Scientist. But if ever he really goes on to any other ideas, he will
be so much the nearer to being a Catholic.

When the convert has once seen the world like that, with one
balance of ideas and a number of other ideas that have left it and
lost their balance, he does not in fact experience any of the inconveniences that he might reasonably have feared before that silent
but stunning revolution. He is not worried by being told that there
is something in Spiritualism or something in Christian Science. He
knows there is something in everything. But he is moved by the
more impressive fact that he finds everything in something. And he
is quite sure that if these investigators really are looking for everything, and not merely looking for anything, they will be more and
more likely to look for it in the same place. In that sense he is far
less worried about them than he was when he thought that one or
other of them might be the only person having any sort of communication with the higher mysteries and obviously rather capable

of making a mess of it. He is no more likely to be overawed by the fact that Mrs. Eddy achieved spiritual healing or Mr. Home achieved bodily levitation than a fully dressed gentleman in Bond Street would be overawed by the top-hat on the head of a naked savage. A top-hat may be a good hat but it is a bad costume. And a magnetic trick may be a sufficient sensation but it is a very insufficient philosophy. He is no more envious of a Bolshevist for making a revolution than of a beaver for making a dam; for he knows his own civilisation can make things on a pattern not quite so simple or so monotonous. But he believes this of his civilisation and his religion and not merely of himself. There is nothing supercilious about his attitude; because he is well aware that he has only scratched the surface of the spiritual estate that is now open to him. In other words, the convert does not in the least abandon investigation or even adventure. He does not think he knows everything, nor has he lost curiosity about the things he does not know. But experience has taught him that he will find nearly everything somewhere inside that estate and that a very large number of people are finding next to nothing outside it. For the estate is not only a formal garden or an ordered farm; there is plenty of hunting and fishing on it, and, as the phrase goes, very good sport.

For this is one of the very queerest of the common delusions about what happens to the convert. In some muddled way people have confused the natural remarks of converts, about having found moral peace, with some idea of their having found mental rest, in the sense of mental inaction. They might as well say that a man who has completely recovered his health, after an attack of palsy or St. Vitus' dance, signalises his healthy state by sitting absolutely still like a stone. Recovering his health means recovering his power of moving in the right way as distinct from the wrong way; but he will probably move a great deal more than before. To become a Catholic is not to leave off thinking, but to learn how to think. It is so in exactly the same sense in which to recover from palsy is not to leave off moving but to learn how to move. The Catholic convert has for the first time a starting-point for straight and strenuous thinking. He has for the first time a way of testing the truth in any question that he raises. As the world goes, especially at present, it is the other people, the heathen and the heretics, who seem to have every virtue except the power of connected thought. There was indeed a brief period when a small minority did some hard thinking on the heathen or heretical side. It barely lasted from the time of Voltaire to the time of Huxley. It has now entirely disappeared. What is now called free thought is valued, not because it is free thought, but because it is freedom from thought; because it is free thoughtlessness.

Nothing is more amusing to the convert, when his conversion has been complete for some time, than to hear the speculations about when or whether he will repent of the conversion; when he will be sick of it, how long he will stand it, at what stage of his external exasperation he will start up and say he can bear it no more. For all this is founded on that optical illusion about the outside and the inside which I have tried to sketch in this chapter. The outsiders, stand by and see, or think they see, the convert entering with bowed head a sort of small temple which they are convinced is fitted up inside like a prison, if not a torture-chamber. But all they really know about it is that he has passed through a door. They do not know that he has not gone into the inner darkness, but out into the broad daylight. It is he who is, in the beautiful and beatific sense of the word, an outsider. He does not want to go into a larger room, because he does not know of any larger room to go into. He knows of a large number of much smaller rooms, each of which is labelled as being very large; but he is quite sure he would be cramped in any of them. Each of them professes to be a complete cosmos or scheme of all things; but then so does the cosmos of the Clapham Sect or the Clapton Agapomene. Each of them is supposed to be domed with the sky or painted inside with all the stars. But each of these cosmic systems or machines seems to him much smaller and even much simpler than the broad and balanced universe in which he lives. One of them is labelled Agnostic; but he knows by experience that it has not really even the freedom of ignorance. It is a wheel that must always go round without a single jolt of miraculous interruption—a circle that must not be squared by any higher mathematics of mysticism; a machine that must be scoured as clean of all spirits as if it were the avowed machine of materialism. In living in a world with two orders, the supernatural and the natural, the convert feels he is living in a larger world and does not feel any temptation to crawl back into a smaller one. One of them is labelled Theosophical or Buddhistic; but he knows by experience that it is only the same sort of wearisome wheel used for spiritual things instead of material things. Living in a world where he is free to do anything, even to go to the devil, he does not see why he should tie himself to the wheel of a mere destiny. One of them is labelled Humanitarian; but he knows that such humanitarians have really far less experience of humanity. He knows that they are thinking almost entirely of men as they are at this moment in modern cities, and have nothing like the huge human interest of what began by being preached to legionaries in Palestine and is still being preached to peasants in China. So clear is this perception that I have sometimes put it to myself, as something between a melancholy meditation and a joke. Where *should* I go now, if I did leave the Catholic Church? I certainly would not go to any of those little social sects which only express one idea at a time, because that idea happens to be fashionable at the moment. The best I could hope for would be to wander away into the woods and become, *not* a Pantheist (for that is also a limitation and a bore) but rather a pagan, in the mood to cry out that some particular mountain peak or flowering fruit tree was sacred and a thing to be worshipped. That at least would be beginning all over again; but it would bring me back to the same problem in the end. If it was reasonable to have a sacred tree it was not unreasonable to have a sacred crucifix; and if the god was to be found on one peak he may as reasonably be found under one spire. To find a new religion is sooner or later to have found one; and why should I have been discontented with the one I had found? Especially, as I said in the first words of this essay, when it is the one old religion which seems capable of remaining new.

I know very well that if I went upon that journey I should either despair or return; and that none of the trees would ever be a substitute for the real sacred tree. Paganism is better than pantheism, for paganism is free to imagine divinities, while pantheism is forced to pretend, in a priggish way, that all things are equally divine. But I should not imagine any divinity that was sufficiently divine. I seem to know that weary return through the woodlands; for I think in some symbolic fashion I have walked that road before. For as I have tried to confess here without excessive egotism, I think I am the sort of man who came to Christ from Pan and Dionysus and not from Luther or Laud; that the conversion I understand is that of the pagan and not the Puritan; and upon that antique conversion is founded the whole world that we know. It is a transformation far more vast and tremendous than anything that has been meant for many years past, at least in England and America, by a sectarian controversy or a doctrinal division. On the height of that ancient empire and that international experience, humanity had a vision. It has not had another; but only quarrels about that one. Paganism was the largest thing in the world and Christianity was larger; and everything else has been comparatively small.

+ +

CHRISTOPHER DAWSON

THE FAILURE *of* LIBERALISM

(from *The Judgment of The Nations*)

+⁺+

> At the roots of the development of Western freedom
> and Western democracy there lies the mediaeval idea
> that men possess rights even against the state and that
> society is not a totalitarian political unit but a com-
> munity made up of a complex variety of social organ-
> isms, each possessing an autonomous life and its own
> free institutions.

CHRISTOPHER DAWSON was born in 1889, he graduated from
Oxford in 1912 and entered the Church in 1914. He has been a
diagnostician of society in the grand manner. His perspective is
all time, and, to his wise learning and deep meditation on the roots
of civilization, he has added the spiritual insight of his Faith. His
books have a remarkable lucidity of exposition. Among them are
The Age of the Gods (1928), *Progress and Religion* (1929),
The Making of Europe (1932), *Enquiries into Religion and
Culture* (1933), *The Judgment of the Nations* (1942). In the
footsteps of St. Augustine, he could write that "the world mission
of Christianity is based on its conception of a spiritual society which
transcends all states and cultures and is the final goal of humanity." [1]
As a historian, Dawson has been a Christian humanist, con-

[1] *The Judgment of the Nations* (New York: Sheed and Ward, 1942), p. 220.

cerned to teach his contemporaries, both Catholic and non-Catholic, the pillars of a living culture. These are the religious and spiritual character of human history as well as the political and economic needs of man's temporal life. The desecularization of the modern world has been his constant plea. In the following essay, written during the last war, he urges not only that we save man from totalitarianism, but also that we rediscover the ancient dignity and freedom of man, and dedicate ourselves to them.

URING THE LAST TWENTY YEARS WE HAVE seen the collapse of constitutional government throughout Europe, and with it the loss of personal freedom and economic freedom and intellectual freedom—in fact all the liberties which the nineteenth century believed had been won or were being won as a permanent possession for humanity. Are we to believe that these liberties were a sham and proved their worthlessness as soon as they were won? Or were they so bound up with the social and economic circumstances of the last century that they were necessarily transcended by the new developments of the twentieth-century culture? Or finally have they been betrayed by the liberals themselves? And is their defeat due to lack of faith in principles that are eternally valid?

There is something to be said for each of these explanations which one may describe respectively as Fascist, Marxist, and Democratic. The collapse of constitutional government and the renaissance of despotism are far too real and too momentous to be explained superficially. They amount to a change in the whole spirit of our civilization which could not have occurred unless the process of disintegration had been a far-reaching and many-sided one.

The failure to recognize this on the part of Liberals during the last two or three generations is largely responsible for the gravity of the present situation. Before we can look forward to the future, we must recognize the mistakes of the past and understand the real nature of the forces that are transforming the modern world.

The great obstacle that stands in the way of this clarification of the issues is the confusion of thought which has created such misunderstanding of the true nature of liberalism alike among its supporters and its opponents. It is essential to define our terms; for there is no word—not even democracy—that has been used so loosely to cover such a variety of divergent elements. The term conservatism is so closely associated with party politics that it does not give occasion to anything like the same degree of confusion, whereas liberalism has always had an ideological character that carries it far beyond the field of politics. For example when Professor Laski writes the history of the Rise of European Liberalism he is writing the history of a philosophy or a *Weltanschauung,* and the whole history of Liberalism as an English political movement lies outside the scope of his book which, I think, ends with the French Revolution. Hence we must distinguish between liberalism as a political party, liberalism as an ideology, and liberalism as a tradition.

The roots of the liberal *tradition* lie so deep in English and American history that they are almost inseparable, while the liberal *ideology* owes almost as much to France as it does to England. Liberalism as a *party name,* on the other hand, had its origins in Spain and had spread throughout the greater part of Europe and South America before being officially adopted in this country. Used in this sense liberalism is of course limited to a particular political and social environment. In fact there are as many liberalisms as there are liberal parties so that what is liberalism in one country may be conservatism in another and revolution in a third. Thus in England political liberalism in the narrower sense took shape in the middle decades of the nineteenth century under the leadership of Cobden and Bright and Gladstone in close relation with the Free Trade movement and with Protestant nonconformity. The identification of economic interest and religious idealism which resulted from the combination of these two influences may seem naive to the modern post-Marxian age, but it was the very essence of the movement. When, for example, Cobden wrote, "We advocate nothing but what is agreeable to the highest behests of Christianity—to buy in the cheapest market and to sell in the dearest," he was both completely sincere and entirely representative of the spirit of utilitarian pietism which inspired English liberalism in its classical period.

French liberalism, on the other hand, had a far more intellectual and doctrinaire character. It was in the main the creation of the philosophers and men and women of letters who were in opposition to Napoleon and whom he described in Fascist style as "Twelve or fifteen metaphysicians who ought to be thrown into the water." Thus French liberalism from the first had a far more vivid sense of the danger of despotism than English and since it had seen France pass from the despotism of the *ancien regime* to the revolutionary totalitarianism of the Jacobins and then to the military dictatorship of Napoleon, it realized that this danger was not confined to one political extreme. Hence the great French liberals like Benjamin Constant, Maine de Biran, Royer-Collard and de Tocqueville are in a sense more modern and certainly more conscious of the fundamental issues of politics than the English liberals who were their successors in time. Nevertheless they were better philosophers than politicians. They lacked the firmly established tradition of political and social liberty which England possessed, and consequently they built too high for their foundation so that again and again the whole political edifice crumbled under the shock of revolution.

In the case of the third country I have mentioned, Spain, liberalism was even farther removed from the political and cultural traditions of the nation than it was in France. Spanish liberalism was an imported product which at certain periods enjoyed all the popularity that a foreign fashion in ideas often acquires. And for the same reason it aroused the native fanaticism of the Spanish character against it. And this situation was rendered even more acute by the identification of the old order in Spain with the Church and by the theocratic character which the Spanish monarchy had acquired by its relation to the Inquisition. Thus in Spain and in South America alike liberalism was forced into the position of a rival religion and this identification of liberalism with anti-clericalism has not only had a permanent effect on Spanish history but has had its repercussion on Catholics elsewhere, above all in Southern Italy where the origins of liberalism were associated with the Spanish movement, as opposed to Lombardy and Tuscany where Italian liberalism had a much closer affinity to the French type.

I have made this brief survey of some of the main types of European liberalism, because it is useless to discuss liberalism in the abstract unless one bears in mind the concrete social and historical background of the different forms of liberalism. In England, for example, when the doctrine of *laissez faire* and the cult of economic individualism became discredited there was a tendency for liberalism to become an abstract ideal somewhat insecurely attached to a party machine. And when the machine broke down, as it did in most countries long before the rise of Fascism, this abstract idealism provided no solid basis for any new political activity.

Are we to conclude as Dr. Mannheim does in his *Man and Society* that "from the wreckage of Liberalism nothing can be saved but its values"? It would certainly be the case if we regard Liberalism as inseparable from the old economic individualism or explain it, as Professor Laski does, as "the by-product of the effort of the middle classes to win their place in the sun." But the liberal ideology is much more than that and the tradition out of which that ideology arose is greater still. For this tradition has been central to Western civilization and in spite of the defeats and disillusions of the last thirty years it is still a living force in the world today. I admit that liberalism is not an altogether satisfactory name to give it, for it means narrowing it down to one particular manifestation of it. On the other hand the term democracy which is in general use today is in some respects even less satisfactory, since equalitarian democracy can so easily be used (and has in fact so often been used) as the instrument of mass despotism which is diametrically opposed to the liberal principle, alike in its narrower and its more universal sense.

For it is freedom and not equality that has been the inspiration of Western culture and the whole history of Western man has been a long quest for freedom. Western civilization has never been a geographical or racial unity. It was born on the shores of the Aegean between the barbarism of continental Europe and the civilized despotism of Asia and that new world of tiny city states which was the source of a new way of living and new conceptions of law and citizenship. But this freedom was no lawless individualism like that of the barbarian. It was the fruit of an intensive effort of social discipline and organization. As Herodotus says in the speech that he puts into the mouth of the exiled Spartan king at the Persian court, "For though the Greeks are freemen they are not free in every respect. Law is the master they own, and this master they fear more than thy subjects fear thee."

This new conception of life was put to the test in the great war in which the free Greek cities withstood the mass attack of Asiatic despotism and emerged triumphant. And in the following centuries the Hellenic world proved for the first time and for all time what the human spirit was capable of when it was set free from slavery to the rule of force. How this tradition of Western civilization survived the decline of the city state and the loss of its political freedom has always been the greatest of historical problems. The answer of the old school of liberal historians was that it did not survive:—that the light of classical civilization was extinguished in the night of the Dark Ages and was reborn miraculously at the Renaissance which was the starting point of the new period of progress and enlightenment. The other view which I myself hold is that the ancient world saved its soul by its conversion to Christianity and that the tradition of its culture lived on in Western Christendom. The loss of political freedom in the ancient world was in fact counterbalanced by the revelation of a new spiritual freedom; so when the earthly city was enslaved men acquired faith in the existence of a spiritual city "which is free and the mother of us all." And as the first epoch in the history of freedom is marked by the rise of the free Greek cities and their struggle with Persia, the second is marked by the rise of the Christian Church and its struggle with the Roman Empire which had lost the ideals of citizenship and political freedom and was rapidly becoming a vast servile state like those of the ancient East. The battle was fought out under the shadow of the executioners' rods and axes in praetoria and amphitheatres and concentration camps from Germany to Africa and from Spain to Armenia, and its heroes were the martyrs—Martyrum candidatus exercitus. Henceforward wherever the Christian faith was preached not only in Europe but from one end of the world to the other, from Japan and Annam to Canada, the names of the men who bore witness with their blood to truth and spiritual freedom

have been held in honour and it is only today with the rise of the
new totalitarian challenge to Christian values that the principle of
martyrdom and *the honour of the martyrs* has been called in question.

The dynamic force of this spiritual ideal put new life into the
dying civilization of the ancient world and gave Latin Christendom
the power to incorporate the northern barbarians in the new syn-
thesis of Western medieval civilization. Here again the principle of
freedom was central to the new cultural development, hard as it
may be for the modern democrat to recognize anything in common
between his ideals and those of the Catholic feudal world. Nevertheless the old liberals realized it half consciously by their idealiza-
tion of Magna Charta and of the medieval communal and constitutional movement. It is true that what the Middle Ages called
liberties were very different from the liberty of the Declaration of
Independence and still more from that of the French Revolution.
Nevertheless, at the roots of the development of Western freedom
and Western democracy there lies the medieval idea that men possess rights even against the state and that society is not a totalitarian
political unit but a community made up of a complex variety of
social organisms, each possessing an autonomous life and its own
free institutions.

It was in England in the seventeenth century that the Christian
ideal of spiritual freedom and the medieval tradition of political
liberties came together to produce the new liberal ideology which
was the main inspiration of Western civilization for more than two
centuries and out of which political liberalism in the strict sense
finally developed. The failure of liberalism in the course of the last
century has been due above all to the failure of the liberal parties
to give adequate expression to this ideology and to the still deeper
social tradition that lies behind it. The liberal movement in the
wider sense transformed the world by an immense liberation of
human energies, but liberalism in the narrower sense proved incapable of guiding the forces that it released. It became a negative
and defensive creed which from the socialist standpoint represented
nothing more than class interest. Nevertheless the socialist criticism
of liberalism was at least in its early form a product of liberal ideology. It was the extension to a wider class of the ideal which had

been at first limited to the politically conscious minority. The fundamental appeal of socialism lay in its assertion of real social rights against abstract political ones. It is a recall to the same principle which had inspired the forerunners of English liberalism and which was stated so admirably by one of the spokesmen of Cromwell's army when he declared "The poorest he that is in England hath a life to live as the richest he." [2]

This assertion of the right of every man to live a full human life is the essence of socialism, and thus, so far from being in opposition to the liberal tradition it is an extension of that tradition from the sphere of law and politics to economics and culture. Yet it is impossible to ignore the existence of an anti-liberal element in socialism which has contributed more than any other single factor to the breakdown of freedom in the modern world. For continental socialism, as represented above all by Karl Marx, is responsible not only for the discrediting of the liberal ideology but for the totalitarian challenge to liberty under the shadow of which we are living today. The revolutionary dictatorship of the proletariat, the use of the power of the state as a weapon to destroy every social element which is opposed to the interests of the dominant class, the substitution of the mass for the individual as the centre of all cultural and moral values—all these principles which lie at the root of the totalitarian state are derived from Marxism and revolutionary socialism. For when once the liberal tradition has been abandoned, the rival forces of totalitarianism rapidly lose their ideological masks and become merely different ways of doing the same thing: that thing being the destruction of freedom and the sacrifice of human life—whether it is the life of rich or poor, bourgeois or proletarian—to the cult of mass power.

Is it possible on the one hand to recover the human and liberal values in socialism from the totalitarian forces that have overcome them and on the other hand to free the liberal tradition itself from its association with the narrow economic individualism of the last century? These are the questions that we have to solve, if Democracy is to adapt itself to the changed world of the mid-twentieth century as well as or better than the totalitarian ideologies. The latter, after all, spring from a different soil from ours. They are

[2] Col. Rainborough speaking against Ireton at Putney, Oct. 29, 1647.

systems by which societies that have been disciplined for centuries by the traditions of theocratic autocracy or military monarchy have adapted themselves to the new world. Such societies can be revolutionized by a determined minority more easily and rapidly than any democratic society. But that is a source of weakness as well as of strength. The imposing facade of totalitarian unity may conceal the internal weakness of the structure or impose a strain which its social foundations are incapable of supporting.

Moreover the external successes of such movements do nothing to diminish the dangers that confront the modern state as soon as it abandons the political traditions that have hitherto guided Western civilization. The terrifying thing is not the revolutionary violence of the first years of the Russian Revolution or the putsch of 1933 in Germany. It is not the reign of the secret police and the cruelty and treachery that accompany it. It is that there is no limit to the regressive movement: that in a few years a society can pass from a high revolutionary idealism to a state of organized inhumanity which plans the liquidation of classes, the transplantation of populations and the destruction of whole peoples as ruthlessly as the ancient Assyrians or the medieval Tartars. This new barbarism is, in fact, worse than that of the past in that it is inspired not by the naive cruelty of a simple warrior society but by the perverted science of a corrupt civilization.

But though this barbarism is already upon us, it is largely unconscious and involuntary, and it is not welcomed or openly approved even by those peoples which have contributed most to its onset. Hence the democratic nations in their resistance to this progress to the abyss can rely not only on the support of those who are still faithful to the spiritual traditions of Western civilization, but also to some extent on the secret sympathy of the totalitarian peoples themselves.

The idea of freedom is practically universal, and there is no people, however lacking in political capacity or experience, that is entirely insensitive to its appeal. Where they differ is in the quality of the freedom that they prize most highly and in their power of achieving it against the hostile forces of nature and circumstance. Human life has always been bound by the ultimate necessities of labour and conflict and death, so that many men in every age have been forced to surrender all the other liberties they prize for the bare right to live at all. The essence of civilization consists in the limitation of this empire of necessity and the widening of the sphere of freedom, but in the past there has been so much inequality in the distribution of social gains as to give some colour to Rousseau's criticism of civilization. It was only in the nineteenth century that the advance of science and the growth of man's control over nature made it possible to push back the frontiers of necessity to a point which would have seemed incredible to the thinkers of the past, so that freedom and the opportunity to live the good life need no longer be the privilege of a minority but could become the birthright of every human being.

But the liberal optimism which inspired the nineteenth century expansion of democracy has ended in disillusionment. The new forces that have been generated by science and industry are so gigantic that they seem to dwarf humanity and require giants to control them. Hence the conflict we see today between a liberalism which abandoned the traditional social control in an access of premature optimism and the new collectivism which sacrifices political and social liberty to the ideal of a total organization of society in the interest of efficiency and mass power.

The old liberalism with all its shortcomings had its roots deep in the soil of Western and Christian culture. As Madame de Stael once wrote, "In France liberty is ancient, it is despotism that is modern." But the new collectivism is out of line with the whole Western development. It has more community with the oriental monarchies—with Persia and Assyria and Egypt, with the spirit that inspired the building of the Pyramids and the Great Wall of China.

It is easy to understand the appeal of this spirit to a people like the Russians who have been moulded for centuries by the theocratic ideals of Orthodoxy and Czarism. It is even possible to reconcile it with one side of the German and Central European tradition. But for Western civilization as a whole the victory of such a spirit means death, because it is the denial and destruction of the spiritual principles by which the West has lived. The great tradition of Western civilization has endured so long and survived so many crises that we may believe it is too strong to be destroyed by the new totalitarian enemy. But it cannot be saved by economic and military means alone. As I have said, the crisis would never have arisen if the spiritual forces of Western culture had not been divided and disintegrated. Thus the need transcends politics and demands nothing less than a spiritual re-orientation of Western society and a recall to the essential values which it must preserve at all costs in spite of the revolutionary changes which have destroyed the economic foundations of the old liberal individualism. It is an immense task which demands the co-operation of all the living forces in our culture, in a sustained effort of social and intellectual reorganization. In this work, it seems to me, liberalism occupies a key position, because it is the only political force in Europe which is identified with the cause of freedom and which cannot abandon that cause without ceasing to exist. Socialism, Conservatism and Nationalism are none of them immune to totalitarian influences, whether by propaganda or by a power of internal assimilation. They can assume totalitarian forms without a conscious betrayal of their principles. Even Democracy does not stand in a very firm position since it is always easy for a mass dictatorship to use democratic slogans, especially at the present moment when the leaders of the attack on freedom are not hereditary monarchs or aristocrats but demagogues in the strict sense—perhaps the greatest demagogues that the world has ever known.

But though it is impossible to exaggerate the value of the liberal tradition in Western culture and the importance of a liberal renaissance it is useless to look for a solution to the revival of the old liberal parties and their recapture of power by the old political methods. The whole situation has changed so fundamentally that we are today faced by the problems that lie outside the scope of politics in the old sense. The new style of totalitarian party dictatorships against which we are fighting attempts to solve these problems and that is the reason for its power. But it does so by a brutal simplification of the issues which sacrifices all the higher values of culture for the sake of immediate material success. It is an attempt to find a short essential cut, and like most such attempts it has only succeeded in losing the way. The task is to bring Western civilization back to the right road. But this cannot be accomplished by the old programmes or political coalitions. It can only be done by the free co-operation of all those who recognize their inherence in the common spiritual tradition of Western civilization and the necessity of creating an organic communion between the scattered and disorganized elements of freedom which still exist though they are politically divided and almost powerless. Such an ideal may seem vague and utopian, but history shows that though permanent elements in a culture like the liberal tradition in Europe may be temporarily submerged or forcibly suppressed they inevitably reassert themselves sooner or later often in a new and unexpected way. The essential thing is to adjust our thought to the new conditions; to see what is living and what is dead in the Western tradition; and to realize that the immense new powers that man has acquired during the last half century can be used in the service of freedom just as easily as they have been used to destroy it.

SIGRID UNDSET

THE CROSS

(from *Kristin Lavransdatter*)

+ + +

A handmaiden of God had she been—a wayward, unruly servant, oftenest an eye-servant in her prayers and faithless in her heart, slothful and neglectful, impatient under correction, but little constant in her deeds —yet had He held her fast in His service, and under the glittering golden ring a mark had been set secretly upon her, showing that she was His handmaid, owned by the Lord and King who was now coming, borne by the priest's anointed hands, to give her freedom and salvation—

SIGRID UNDSET was born in Kallundborg, Denmark, in 1882 of a Norwegian father and Danish mother. She was educated in Oslo, Norway, where her father, a noted professor of archaeology, had moved his family. Until the German invasion of Norway, she lived and wrote in Lillehammer. She fled the Nazis, lost a son in the war, and traveled halfway around the world to the United States. She returned to Norway in 1945, to a Norway that she prayed would be swept clean of the evil forces that had engulfed it. In 1928 Madame Undset entered the Catholic Church, and also received a highly coveted literary award, the Nobel prize. One must go back to Dostoievsky to find a novelist of her stature. In addition to *Kristin Lavransdatter,* she is the author of such other novels as *Ida Elizabeth* (1932), *The Faithful Wife* (1936), *Madame Dorthea* (1939). *Kristin Lavransdatter* was originally published (in Oslo) in 1920-1922.

Kristin Lavransdatter is a trilogy (*The Bridal Wreath, The Mistress of Husaby, The Cross*) set in late mediaeval Norway. The story, so rich in the understanding of human nature, is the life of Kristin, and the theme, like that of Claudel's *The Satin Slipper,* concerns the growth of Kristin as a handmaid of God. Evil is in the world, Claudel has written, as the slave of grace. The life of Kristin, of which we see the end in the accompanying selection, embodies that lesson.

PART THREE

CHAPTER V

 O AT LAST SHE WAS AT HER JOURNEY'S END. Kristin Lavransdatter sat resting on a haycock by the wayside below Sionsborg. There was sunshine and a blowing wind; the part of the meadow that was not yet mown waved red and silky bright with seeding grass. Nowhere but in the Trondheim country were the meadows red like this. Below the slope she could see a glimpse of the fjord, dark blue and flecked with foam; fresh white sea spray dashed up against the bluffs, as far as she could see along the strand below the forest-clad Byness.

Kristin drew a deep breath. After all, 'twas good to be here again; good, though 'twas strange as well to know that she should never go from here any more. The grey-clad sisters out at Rein followed the same rule, Saint Bernard's rule, as the brothers at Tautra. When she rose at cock-crow and went to the church, she would know that now Naakkve and Björgulf too were going to their places in the monk's choir. Thus, after all, she would come to live out her old age with certain of her sons—although not in the fashion she had thought.

She drew off her shoes and stockings and washed her feet in the beck. Into Nidaros she would walk barefoot.

Behind her on the path up the castle hill some boys were playing noisily—they were hard at work below the barbican, trying to find a way into the tumble-down work. When they grew ware of her, they fell to calling down foul words at her, laughing and hooting the while. She made as if she did not hear, till a little imp—eight years old the boy might have been—came rolling down the steep sward and almost bumped into her, shrieking out some ugly words he had picked up in wantonness from the older boys. Kristin turned towards him and said smiling:

"No need to shriek so to let me know you for a troll imp, for I see you have the rolling-breeches [1] on you—"

When the boys marked that the woman answered, they came bounding down, the whole pack. But they fell silent and abashed when they saw 'twas an ageing woman in pilgrim's garb, and that she chid them not for their bad words, but sat looking at them with great, clear, calm eyes and a stealthy little smile on her lips. She had a lean, round face with broad forehead and small rounded chin; she was sunburnt and much wrinkled under the eyes, but after all she looked not so exceeding old.

So the boldest of the boys took to talking and asking questions to hide the sheepishness of the troop. Kristin felt she could have laughed—these boys seemed so like her own rascals, the twins, when they were small, though she prayed to God that *hers* had never been so foul-mouthed. These seemed to be children of common folk in the town.

And when the moment came that she had longed for all through her journey, when she stood below the cross on Feginsbrekka and looked down on Nidaros, it came not so that she could collect her thoughts for prayer or meditation. All the bells of the town burst forth at that moment to ring to Vespers, and the boys all talked together, wanting to point out all that was before her—

Tautra she could not see, for a squall of wind, with mist and scudding showers, was sweeping over the fjord beneath Frosta.

[1] In the popular tales trolls are sometimes equipped with "rolling-breeches" (*trille-brok*)—breeches which enable them to lie down and roll rapidly after prey, or from their pursuers.

In the midst of the flock of boys she took the steep path that led down the Steinberg heights—and now cow-bells clinked and herdsmen whooped around them—the cows were bound homewards from the town pastures. At the gate in the town wall across the Nidareid, Kristin and her young attendants had to wait while the cattle were driven through—herdsmen hallooed, shouted, and cursed, oxen butted, cows were crowded and crushed together, and the boys named the owners of this bull or that as they passed. And when they were through the port and were passing towards the town lanes, Kristin had more than enough ado to pick her way with her naked feet amid the cow-dung on the poached-up track.

Some of the boys followed her unbidden even into Christ's Church. And as she stood in the dim forest of pillars and gazed towards the lights and the gilding of the choir, the boys plucked ever at the stranger-woman's gown, and would fain have shown her all such things as most draw children's eyes—from the patches of coloured sunlight falling through the rose-window among the arches, and the tombstones on the floor, to the canopies of costly stuffs above the altars. Kristin was given no peace to collect her thoughts—but each word the boys said wakened the dull yearning in her heart—for her sons first and foremost, but for the manor too, the houses, the outhouses, the cattle—for the toil and the sway of motherhood.

She had still that loathness to be known again of any who had been her friends or Erlend's in days gone by. They were wont ever to be in their town houses at festival tide and to have guests living with them—she shrank at the thought of meeting a company of them. Ulf Haldorssön she must seek out, for, as her bailiff, he had charge of the shares she still had in some farms north of the fells and meant now to give in payment for her commons in the Rein cloister. But 'twas like he would have with him now his kinsfolk from the farm at Skaun; so she must wait. But she had heard that a man who had served among Erlend's men-at-arms in the days he was Warden had his dwelling in a small yard out on Bratören; he worked with the dolphin- and porpoise-fishers on the fjord, and kept a lodging for seafarers.

When she came thither she was told that all the houses were overfull already; but then came the man himself, Aamunde, and knew her straightway. 'Twas strange to hear him cry out her old name:

"Now I ween—is't not Erlend Nikulaussön's lady of Husaby—all hail, Kristin—how can it be that you are come hither to my house?"

He was full glad that she would be content with such shelter as he could give her for the night, and he promised he would sail her out to Tautra himself, the day after the festival.

Till far on in the night she sat out in the courtyard talking with their one-time house-carl, and it moved her deeply when she marked that they that had been Erlend's men still loved their young chieftain's memory and held it in high honour—again and again Aamunde spoke of him as "young." From Ulf Haldorssön they knew of his hapless death, and Aamunde said, never did he meet any of his old fellows of Husaby days but they drank to the memory of their gallant master—and twice some of them had put their money together and had masses said for him on his death-day. Aamunde asked much after Erlend's sons, and Kristin too asked of old acquaintance. 'Twas midnight ere she got to bed by the side of Aamunde's wife—naught would serve him at first but that they both should give up their bed to her, and at last she was fain to accept with thanks of his proffer that at least she should take his place.

Next day was Olav's Wake. From early morning Kristin walked about the shore by the river mouth, looking at the bustle on the wharves. Her heart beat faster when she saw the Lord Abbot of Tautra step ashore—but the monks who were with him were all elder men.

Long ere nones folk were streaming towards Christ's Church, bearing or holding up their sick and cripples, so that they might come near the shrine when it was borne out in procession next day after High Mass.

As Kristin came up through the booths set up by the fence round the churchyard—they sold, for the most, meat and drink, wax-candles, and mats woven of rush or birch twigs to lay beneath one on the church floor—she stumbled upon the folk from Andabu, and Kristin took the child while the young wife got herself a draught of ale. At that moment came the procession of English pilgrims with songs and banners and lighted tapers; in the press and crush, as they made their way through the throng of folk by the booths, she lost the Andabu folk and could not find them again.

For long she wandered hither and thither on the outskirts of the crowd, lulling the shrieking child. When she laid its face against her neck and would have comforted it with caresses, it mouthed about and sucked at her skin; she saw that it was athirst, and she knew not what to do. It seemed vain to seek for the mother; she must go down into the streets and ask where she could get it milk. But when she came out on to Upper Langstræte and would have gone northward, there was again a great press of folk—from the south came a train of knights, and at the same time the men-at-arms from the palace marched into the space betwixt the church and the Crossed-friars' House. Kristin was thrust aside into the nearest lane; but here, too, folk were hurrying to the church ahorse and afoot, and the press grew so great that at length she had to take refuge up on a stone dyke.

The air above her was full of the noise of bells—the cathedral chimes ringing out *nona hora*. The child stopped shrieking at the sound—it looked up at the sky, and a gleam of understanding showed in its dull eyes—it smiled a little. Touched with pity, the mother of other children bent and kissed the poor little creature. Then she saw that she was sitting on the stone wall around the garden of the Nikulaus house, their old town mansion.

—Well should she know the stone-built chimney rising through the turf roof—the back of their hall-house. Close by her stood the houses of the spital whose right to share the garden with them had roused Erlend's wrath.

She pressed the stranger-woman's child to her breast, kissed it and kissed it. Then someone touched her knee—

—A monk in the white gown and black cowl of the preaching brothers. She looked down into a pale yellow, furrowed, old man's face—a long, narrow, in-fallen mouth, two deeply sunken, amber eyes.

"Can it be—is it you yourself, Kristin Lavransdatter?" The monk laid his crossed arms upon the dyke and buried his face in them. "Are you here?"

"Gunnulf!" At that he moved his head so that it touched her knee where she sat: "Deem you 'tis so strange that I am here—?" Then she called to mind that she was sitting on the garden wall of this house that had been his first and her own afterwards, and thought, 'twas strange indeed.

"But what child is this you have on your knee—sure, this cannot be Gaute's son?"

"No—" At the thought of little Erlend's healthy, sweet face, and strong, well-made body, she pressed the poor little stranger-child to her, overcome with pity: " 'Tis the child of a woman that crossed the fells along with me."

—But then there dawned upon her what Andres Simonssön had seen in his childish wisdom. Filled with reverence, she gazed on the pitiful creature that lay upon her lap.

But now it wept again, and before aught else she had to ask the monk if he could tell her where she could get milk for the child. Gunnulf led her eastward round the church to the House of the Preaching Friars, and got her a bowl of milk. While Kristin was feeding her foster-child, they talked together, but their talk went but haltingly.

"So long a time has gone by, and so much has befallen since last we met," she said sorrowfully. "And heavy to bear for you, too, the tidings must have been—the tidings of your brother?"

"God be merciful to his poor soul," whispered Brother Gunnulf in a shaken voice.

Only when she asked about her sons at Tautra did Gunnulf speak something more freely. With great gladness had the convent welcomed these two novices, come of the best kindreds in the land. Nikulaus seemed to have such excellent gifts of mind and made such strides in learning and godliness that the abbot must needs call to mind his noble forefather, the Church's well-gifted champion, Bishop Nikulaus Arnessön. That was in the first days. But a while after the brothers had taken the cowl, Nikulaus had misbehaved him grievously, and had wrought much trouble in the cloister. Gunnulf knew not the causes of the trouble fully—*one* was that Abbot Johannes would not suffer that young brothers should be ordained priests before they were full thirty years old, and he would not depart from this rule for Nikulaus' behoof. And as the reverend father deemed that Nikulaus read and pondered more than sorted with his measure of spiritual ripeness, and that he was breaking down his health with pious exercises, he thought fit to send him to one of the cloister's cattle-farms on Inderö, to work there, under some of the elder monks, at the planting of an apple orchard. Then, 'twas said, Nikulaus had broken out into flat disobedience to the abbot's behests, had charged his brethren with having wasted the cloister's goods in high living, with sluggishness in the worship of God, and with looseness in their talk. The matter, said Gunnulf, was kept, for the most part, within the convent walls, as was but reason; but 'twas said, too, that he had defied the brother whom the abbot appointed to chasten him. For some time he had lain in the penitentiary cell, Gunnulf knew, but since then he had humbled him, when the abbot threatened to part him from Brother Björgulf, and to send one of them to Munkabu—'twas like it had been the blind brother that egged him on. But on this threat Nikulaus had grown meek and contrite.

" 'Tis their father's nature that is in them," said Gunnulf bitterly. "None could look that my brother's sons should find it easy to learn obedience, or that they should show steadfastness in the godly life——"

" 'Tis as like to be their heritage from their mother," answered Kristin, sorrowfully. "Disobedience was the chief of my sins, Gunnulf—and I too was unsteadfast. All the days of my life have I longed both to go the right way and to follow my own wildered paths as well——"

"Erlend's wildered paths, mean you?" said the monk, darkly. " 'Twas not once only that my brother lured you astray, Kristin; I trow he lured you astray each day you lived with him. Such forgetfulness he wrought in you that you remembered not, when you thought thoughts you yourself blushed at, that you could not hide the thoughts of your heart from an all-knowing God——"

Kristin gazed before her.

"Now I know not, Gunnulf, if you are right in this—I wot not that I have forgotten at any time that God saw into my heart—all the greater, belike, is my sin. And, moreover, 'tis not so, as you deem perchance, that I had most need to blush for my immodest wantonness and for my weakness—rather must I feel shame that my thoughts of my husband were many a time more bitter than the poison of serpents. But like enough it must needs have come to this —'twas you who once said to me, that they who have loved one another with the fieriest desire come in the end to be as two vipers biting each other's tails.

"But it has been my comfort in these years, Gunnulf, as often as I thought how 'twas Erlend's lot to go before God's judgment-seat unhouseled and unholpen, struck down with wrath in his heart and blood upon his hands—that *he* did not grow to be—what you said, and what I became. He bore in mind anger, and wrong done him, as little as he bore aught else in mind—Gunnulf, he was so fair and he looked so peaceful when I had laid his body out—I wot that the all-knowing God knows that Erlend never bore a grudge to any man, for any cause—"

The brother gazed at her with wide-opened eyes. Then he nodded.

After a while the monk asked:

"Know you that Eiliv Serkssön is priest and counsellor to the nuns out at Rein?"

"No?" said Kristin, beaming with gladness.

"I deemed 'twas therefore you had chosen to enter there," said Gunnulf. Soon after, he said that he must go back to his cloister.

The first nocturn was begun already when Kristin came into the church. In the nave and about all the altars there was a throng of folk, but one of the vergers, who saw that she bore a most sickly child in her arms, pushed her forward through the press till she came right in front among the many cripples and sick folk in sorest need, who were gathered in the middle of the church under the great dome and in full view of the choir.

Many hundred lights burned in the church—the church servants took the pilgrims' tapers and fixed them upon the little hillock-shaped towers studded with spikes, that were set up all down the nave and aisles. As the light of day died out behind the many-coloured panes of glass, the church grew warm with the smell of the burning wax, and ere long it was filled, too, with the sour stench from the rags of the sick folk and the poor.

When the song of the choir soared under the vaulting, and the organ pealed, and the noise of flutes, drums, and stringed instruments resounded, Kristin understood why it might be that the church was called a ship—in the mighty house of stone all these folk seemed to be on board a vessel, and the singing was like the noise of the sea whereon it was upborne. Ever and anon it came to rest, as when the billows are stilled, and a single man's voice bore the lesson out over the listening throng.

The close-packed faces grew paler and more weary as the wake-night wore on. Scarce one went out between the services, not at least of those who had places midway of the church. Between the nocturns they dozed or prayed. The child slept well-nigh the whole night—once or twice Kristin had to lull it a little, or give it milk from a wooden flask that Gunnulf had gotten for her from the cloister.

The meeting with Erlend's brother had stirred her strangely—the more so that every step of the road hither had brought her nearer and nearer home to the memory of the dead man. She had *thought* little on him in these last years, while her work for her growing sons gave her little time for memory of her own fate—none the less the thought of him had been ever, as it were, close behind her, only that she had not had the time to turn her towards it. Now she seemed to see her soul as it had been in these years; it had lived as folk live on a manor through the busy summer half-year, when they move out of the great hall and bide in the store-house loft. All day long they go to and fro past the winter hall, never thinking of going in thither, though they have but to lay their hand on a latch and push open a door. And when at last some day they have an errand thither, the house has grown strange and almost solemn, because of the air of loneliness and quiet that has come to it—

But while she was speaking with him who was the last living witness of the interplay 'twixt seed-time and harvest in her life with the dead man, it seemed to her that she had come to look out over her life in a new way: as when a man comes up on a height above his native place where he has never climbed before, and looks down from it into his own dale. He knows each farm and fence, each thicket, the gully of each beck; but he seems to see for the first time how these things all lie on the face of the land. And seeing things in this new way, she had found all at once words that swept away both her bitterness against Erlend and her terrors for his soul, borne off by sudden death. Ill-will he had never borne to any; she saw it now, and God had seen it always.

So at last she was come so far that she deemed she could look on her own life as from the uppermost step of a glen. Now did her road lead down into the darkling valley, but ere she took that road she had been given grace to understand that, in the loneliness of the cloister and at the gates of death, there waited for her one who had ever beheld the life of mankind as men's parishes look, seen from the mountain brow. He had seen the sin and sorrow, the love and hate, in the hearts of men, as one sees the rich manors and the humble cots, the teeming cornfields and the abandoned wastes, all borne on the bosom of the same country-side. And He had descended; His feet had trodden the peopled lands, and stood in palaces and in huts; He had gathered up the sorrows and the sins of rich and poor, and lifted them aloft with Him upon a cross. Not my happiness and my pride, but my sin and my sorrow, O my sweet Lord—She looked up where the crucifix stood, uplifted high over the triumphal arch.

—While the morning sun lit up the high-set coloured panes deep among the pillars of the choir, and a glory, as of red and brown and green and blue gems, dimmed the light from the tapers on the altar and from the golden shrine behind, Kristin listened to the last vigil—the matins. She knew that the lessons in this service told of God's healing miracles through the power vouchsafed to his faithful knight King Olav Haraldsson. She lifted the sick stranger-child up towards the choir, and prayed for it.

But she was so icy chill from her long vigil in the cold of the church that her teeth chattered; and she felt faint from fasting. The smell of the many folk, and the sickening fumes of the sick and the beggars, mingled with the smoke of the wax-candles and sank down in a heavy, strangely greasy and clammy cloud upon the people kneeling on the stone floor, cold in the cold morning. But a fat, kind, cheerful countrywoman who had sat dozing a little against the foot of the pillar just behind them, with a bearskin below her and another over her lame legs, awoke now and drew

Kristin's weary head down upon her wide lap: "Rest a little now, sister—you have need of it, I trow—"

Kristin slept in the strange woman's lap, and dreamed:

She stepped over the threshold of the old hearth-room house at home. She was young and unwed, for she saw her own uncovered thick brown plaits hanging forward over her shoulders. She was in company with Erlend, for he was even now drawing him upright, after going through the doorway before her.

By the hearth her father was sitting, binding arrow-heads on the shafts—he had his lap full of bunches of sinew string, and on either side of him on the bench lay piles of arrow-heads and sharpened shafts. Just as they stepped in, he bent him forward over the heap of embers and made to take up the little three-legged metal cup that he ever used to melt resin in. But swiftly he caught back his hand, shook it in the air, and then he stuck his burnt finger-tips into his mouth and sucked them, while he turned his head towards her and Erlend, and looked up at them with a wrinkled brow and a smile about his lips—

Then she awoke, her face wet with tears.

She kneeled through the High Mass, when the Archbishop himself served the holy rite before the high altar. The clouds of incense rolled through the echoing church, where many-coloured sunlight was mingled now with the wax tapers' shining; the fresh, spicy scent of the frankincense spread abroad and overcame the smell of poverty and sickness. With a heart that seemed bursting with ruth for the flock of the infirm and the needy in whose midst God had set her, she prayed in a rush of sisterly tenderness for all who were poor as she, and who suffered as she herself had suffered—

—"I will arise and go to my father—"

CHAPTER VI

THE CONVENT stood on a rising ground near the fjord, so that, with most winds, the roll of the surf on the beach drowned the soughing of the pine woods that covered great part of the ridge's slopes, north and west, and hid the sea from sight.

Kristin had seen the church tower above the trees when she sailed by with Erlend, but the pilgrimage out to the nunnery that his forefather had founded, which Erlend had sometimes said they must make, had never come about. She had never landed at Rein Cloister before she came to make it her abiding-place.

She had thought that the life here would be like that she knew at the nunneries in Oslo or at Bakke, but here much was otherwise than there, and 'twas far more quiet. Here the sisters were truly dead to the world. Lady Ragnhild, the abbess, made it her boast that 'twas five years since she had been in to the market town, and as long since some of her nuns had set foot outside the bounds of the cloister.

There were no children here to be nurtured, and, at the time Kristin came to Rein, there were no novices either; so long was it since any young maid had sought to be taken into the sisterhood, that 'twas six winters already since the last, Sister Borghild Marcellina, had taken the veil. Youngest in age was Sister Turid, but she had been sent hither in her seventh year by her father's father, who was priest of Clement's Church, an exceeding strict and earnest man, and the child had had a shrivelled hand from birth and was besides something of a cripple, so she had donned the habit as soon as she reached the age for it. Now she was thirty years old, and sadly frail, but she had a lovesome face, and from the first day she came to the cloister Kristin took great joy in serving her, for she deemed that Sister Turid minded her of her own little sister Ulvhild, who died so young.

Sira Eiliv said that low birth should assuredly not stand in the way of any maids who were minded to come hither to serve God. Nevertheless, so it had been that, ever since the convent had been set up, few but the daughters or widows of mighty and high-born men of the Trondheim country entered there. But during the evil and restless days that had been in the realm since King Haakon Haalegg, of blessed memory, died, piety seemed to have fallen away greatly amongst the great nobles—now 'twas the daughters of townsmen and well-to-do farmers for the most part who turned their thoughts to a convent life. And they betook them rather to Bakke, where many of them had been nurtured in godliness and womanly handicrafts, and where the sisters for the most were come of homely people—there, too, the rule was not so strict, and the cloister lay not so far removed from the highway.

Howbeit, 'twas not often that Kristin had the chance to speak with Sira Eiliv, and she soon saw that the priest's duties and his footing in the cloister were both toilsome and ticklish. Though Rein was a rich cloister and the sisterhood scarce numbered half as many nuns as the foundation might well have fed, yet its money affairs were in great disorder, and it was hard put to it to meet its outgoings. The last three abbesses had been more pious than worldly-wise; none the less they and their convent had fought, with tooth and claw, to make good their freedom from the Archbishop's obedience—so far did they go in this that they would not even take counsel proffered in fatherly goodwill. And the brethren of their order from Tautra and Munkabu, chosen to be priests of the convent church, had ever been old men, that no colour might be given to evil speaking, and their guidance of the cloister's worldly weal had been none too skilful. When King Skule built the fair stone church and gave his udal manor to the cloister, the houses were first built of wood; and they had burnt down thirty winters agone. Lady Audhild, who was abbess then, began the building of them up again in stone; much was done in her time for the betterment of the church, and the goodly convent hall was built. She had journeyed also to the general chapter at the mother house of the order, Tart [2] in Burgundy, and from that journey she had brought back the noble ivory tower that stood in the choir near the high altar—a fitting tabernacle for God's body, the church's greatest adornment and the nuns' pride and darling treasure. Lady Audhild left behind her the fairest renown for piety and worth, but her unskilful conduct of the building works, and her unwise dealings with the convent lands, had wrought mischief to the cloister's welfare and the later abbesses had not had the skill to repair the ill.

How it had come about that Sira Eiliv was sent thither as priest and counsellor, Kristin never learned; but so much she understood, that from the first the abbess and the sisters had met him, as a secular, with misliking and mistrust; and so 'twas Sira Eiliv's task at Rein to be the nuns' priest and spiritual guide, to set the husbandry of the estates on its feet again, and bring order into the

[2] Now Tart l'Abbaye, in the Côte d'Or department, near Citeaux, the cradle of the Cistercian order. Tart was the mother house of all the Scandinavian Cistercian nunneries.

convent's money affairs, while deferring to the abbess's overhead-ship, the sisters' right of self-governance, and the right of the abbot at Tautra to oversee all, and keeping friends with the other priest at the church, a monk from Tautra. His age and his name for un-stained purity of walk and conversation, humble fear of God, and skill both of the canon law and of the law of the land, stood him in good stead, but he had to walk most warily in all his goings. Together with the other priest and the church servants, he dwelt in a little house lying north-east from the cloister. 'Twas there, too, that the monks lodged who came out from Tautra on divers occa-sions. Kristin knew that, if she lived so long, some time, when Nikulaus had come to be ordained priest, she should hear her eldest son say Mass in the convent church.

Kristin Lavransdatter had been received at first as a commoner.[3] But after she had taken a vow of chastity and obedience to the abbess and the sisterhood, before Lady Ragnhild and the sisters, in presence of Sira Eiliv and two monks from Tautra, and, in token that she forwent all rights over worldly goods, had put her seal into Sira Eiliv's hands to be broken in pieces, she was given leave to wear a garb like to the sisters', but without the scapular; a grey-white woollen robe, white head-linen and black veil. The intent was that, after some time had gone by, she should seek to be re-ceived into the sisterhood as a professed nun.

But 'twas still a hard matter for her not to think overmuch on what had been. To read aloud during meal-times in the refectory, Sira Eiliv had written out in the Norse tongue a book of the life of Christ, made by the general of the Minorites, the most learned and godly doctor Bonaventura. And while Kristin listened to it, and her eyes filled with tears as she thought how blessed they must be who could love Christ and His mother, pains and afflictions, poverty and humility, in such wise as was there written—yet all the time she could not but remember the day at Husaby when

---

[3] The "proventsfolk" (*Commoners*) were what in modern times would be called boarders—laymen and women, chiefly elderly people, who were boarded and lodged by the convent on payment. Both monasteries and nunneries had such boarders, and as, in both cases, the boarders were of both sexes (in spite of the orders of the bishops to the contrary), they were lodged in houses outside the convent gates.

Gunnulf and Sira Eiliv had shown her the Latin book from which this was taken. 'Twas a thick little book, written upon parchment so thin and shining white that she had never believed calfskin could be wrought so fine; and there were the fairest pictures and capital letters in it, the colours glowing like jewels against the gold. And while she looked, Gunnulf spoke laughingly, and Sira Eiliv gave assent with his quiet smile—of how the buying of this book left them so penniless, they had to sell their clothes and get them meat along with the alms-folk in a cloister, till they came to know that some Norse churchmen were come to Paris, and made shift to raise a loan from them.

When, after matins, the sisters went back to the dormitory, Kristin would tarry behind in the church. On summer mornings 'twas sweet and delightsome to her there—but in winter it was bitterly cold, and she was fearful in the dark among all the tombstones, even though she kept her eyes bent fixedly on the little lamp that burned always before the ivory tower with the host in it. But, winter or summer, while she tarried in her corner of the nuns' choir, she thought of how Naakkve and Björgulf were now watching and praying for their father's soul; and that 'twas Nikulaus who had begged her to join with them in these prayers and penitential psalms each morning after matins.

Ever, ever she saw before her those two, as she had seen them that grey day of rain she went out to the monks' cloister: when Nikulaus stood before her in the parlour of a sudden, marvellous tall and strange in the grey-white monk's habit, with his hands thrust under the scapular, her son, and yet so changed. 'Twas most of all his likeness to his father that moved her so deeply—'twas as though she saw Erlend in monk's garb.

Whilst they sat talking together, and he had her tell him of all that had befallen at the manor since he took his way from home, she was waiting, waiting. At length she asked fearfully if Björgulf would not come soon.

"I know not, mother," answered her son. A little after he said: "For Björgulf it has been a hard struggle to bow beneath his cross and serve God—And it seemed to affright him when he heard that you were here—lest too many thoughts should be called up again—"

Thereafter she sat on, deathly sad, gazing at Nikulaus while he talked. He was much sunburned in the face, and his hands were worn with toil—he said, with a little smile, now had he had to learn after all how to guide a plough and work with scythe and sickle. In the hostel that night she could not sleep, and she hasted to the church when the bell rang to matins. But the monks stood so that there were but few whose faces she could see, and her sons were not amongst these.

But next day she walked in the garden with a lay brother who worked there, and he showed her the many rare plants and trees it was renowned for. While they so walked, the clouds broke, the sun came forth, and with it the scent of celery and onion and thyme, and the clumps of yellow lilies and blue columbines that decked the corners of the beds glittered with great raindrops. And then came her sons; they came forth, both of them, from the little arched door of the stone house. And Kristin deemed that she had a fore-taste of the joy of Paradise when she saw the two tall brothers in light-hued raiment come down towards her on the path beneath the apple trees.

Yet they spoke not much together; Björgulf was silent well-nigh all the time. He had become a giant in frame, now he was full-grown. And it seemed as though in the long time they had been sundered her sight had grown keener—now, for the first time, she understood to the full what the battle was that this son of hers had fought, that doubtless he was still fighting, while he grew so great and strong of limb, while his inward sight waxed keen, and he felt his eyesight grow dim—

Once he asked after his foster-mother, Frida Styrkaarsdatter. Kristin told him that she was wed.

"God bless her," said the monk. "She was a good woman—to me she was a good and faithful foster-mother."

"Ay, methinks almost she was more a mother to you than was I," said Kristin, sadly. "Little must you have marked of the mother's heart in me, when you were tried so sorely in your youth."

Björgulf answered low:

"I thank God, none the less, that the enemy was never suffered to bow me to such unmanliness as to try the mother's heart in you —though I felt it, of a truth—but I saw that you bore too heavy a burden already—and after God 'twas Nikulaus here who saved me, those times I was like to fall into the Tempter's power—"

No more was said of this, nor of whether they were happy in the cloister, nor of how 'twas said they had done amiss and brought disgrace upon themselves. But it seemed to give them great joy when they heard 'twas their mother's purpose to take the veil in Rein convent.

When, after this hour of prayer, Kristin went back through the dormitory and saw the sisters sleeping two and two on sacks of straw in the beds, clad in the habits which they never put off, she thought how much unlike she must be to these women, who from their youth up had done naught but serve their Maker. The world was a master whom 'twas not easy to fly, when once one had yielded to its dominion. Ay, and in sooth she had not fled the world—she had been cast out, as a hard master drives a worn-out servant from his door—and now she had been taken in here, as a merciful lord takes in an old serving-maid and of his mercy gives her a little work, while he shelters and feeds the worn-out, friendless old creature—

From the nuns' sleeping-house a covered way led to the weaving-house. There Kristin now sat alone, and spun. The nuns of Rein were famed for their linen, and those days in summer and autumn, when all the sisters and lay sisters went to work in the flax-fields, were like feast days in the cloister; but most of all the day the plants were pulled. The nuns were busied in most of their working-hours with making ready the flax, spinning the thread, weaving the linen, and making vestments from it. Here were none who copied or adorned books, as the sisters in Oslo under Lady Groa Guttorms-datter had done with such great skill, nor did they practise much the craft of broidering with silk and gold thread.

In a while she would hear with joy the sounds of the wakening farm-yard. The lay sisters went to the kitchen-house to make ready the food for the serving-folk; the nuns touched not meat nor drink till after the Mass of the day, saving when they were sick. When the bell rang for primes, Kristin went to the sick-ward, if any lay there, to take the place of Sister Agata or of whichever other nun was there. Sister Turid, poor soul, lay there often.

Soon, now, she might begin to look forward to the morning meal, which followed after the third hour of prayer and the Mass for the cloister's serving-folk. Each day alike Kristin took joy in this comely and solemn repast. The refectory was timber-built, but a fair hall notwithstanding, and there all the women in the cloister ate together—the nuns at the upper board, where the abbess sat in the high-seat, and where the three old dames who were commoners like herself had also seats—and the lay sisters further down. When the prayer was ended, the meat and drink borne in, and all sat eating and drinking in silence, with still, seemly behaviour, while often one of the sisters read aloud from a book, Kristin would think that, could folk in the world without but take their meals in such goodly wise, they might well come to see more clearly that food and drink are gifts from God, and they would begrudge them less to their fellow-Christians, and think less on scraping together for their own and their children's behoof. But she herself had felt quite otherwise, when she spread her board for a flock of wild, riotous men, amid laughter and uproar, while the dogs snuffed about beneath the board, or thrust up their noses and got a meat bone or a thwack, as the mood of the boys might chance to be.

Travellers seldom came hither. At times a vessel with folk from the nobles' seats around would put in when sailing down or up the fjord, and men and their wives, with children and young folk, would go up to Rein to greet a kinswoman among the sisters. Then there were the bailiffs from the cloister's farms and fisheries, and a messenger from Tautra now and then. At the feast-tides that were kept with greatest state—Mary Virgin's Mass days, Corpus Christi, and the day of Saint Andrew the Apostle—folk sought the nuns' church from the parishes on both sides the fjord, but otherwise 'twas but those of the cloister's tenants and work-folk who dwelt nearest that came thither to the Masses. They took up but little room in the great church.

Then there were the poor—the alms-folk who had their doles of ale and meat at fixed times under rich folk's testaments, in requital of yearly masses for the donors' souls—and who, besides, drifted up to Rein well-nigh daily, sat by the kitchen-house wall and ate, and when the nuns came out into the courtyard made up to them to talk of their sorrows and troubles. Sick folks, cripples, and lepers wandered out and in—there were many here who suffered from leprosy, but 'twas ever so in the sea parishes, said Lady Ragnhild. Tenants came to crave abatements in their rents or grace time for their payments, and these had ever much to tell of hardships and adversity. The more wretched and hapless these folk were, the more open and unashamed they were in telling the sisters of their condition, though most often they blamed others for their ill-fortune, and had pious words ever on their lips. 'Twas not strange that the nuns' talk at recreation and in the weaving-house ran much on these folks' lives—nay, Sister Turid avowed to Kristin that when the nuns met in convent to take counsel together concerning bargains and the like, the talk would often wander, and turn to gossip about the folk who were mixed in the matters in hand. Kristin marked, by what the sisters said, that they knew little of what they talked of, save what they had heard from the folks themselves or from the lay servants who had been out into the parish. They were passing easy of belief, whether their underlings praised themselves or spoke ill of their neighbours—and she thought with anger of all the times she had heard godless lay folk, ay, even a beggar monk like Brother Arngrim, cry down the nunneries for dens of scandal, and tax the sisters with greedy swallowing of waif rumours and immodest gossip. The very folk who came hither and dinned Lady Ragnhild's ears, or any of the sisters' they could get speech of, full of idle talk, would be the first to blame the nuns for talking among themselves of the tidings that reached them from the world they had renounced. It seemed to her 'twas the same with the talk of the convent ladies' luxurious living—it came from folk's mouths who had many a time had both morning bite and breakfast at the sisters' hands, while these servants of God watched, prayed and laboured fasting, ere they all met for their first solemn meal in the refectory.

So Kristin served the nuns with loving reverence in the time that must go by before she might make profession. A good nun she could never be, she thought; she had scattered abroad all too much what gift she might have had for meditation and piety—but she would be as meek and as steadfast as God would give her grace to be. 'Twas now well on in the summer of the year 1349; she had dwelt in the Rein convent two years, and ere Yule-tide came she was to take the veil. And the glad tidings came to her that, for her dedication, both her sons would come out thither in Abbot Johannes' train. Brother Björgulf had said, when he heard of his mother's purpose:

"Now is my dream like to come true—I have dreamed twice this year that before Yule we should both see her—though *wholly* as it appeared in my dream it cannot be, for in my dream I *saw* her."

Brother Nikulaus, too, had been overjoyed. But at the same time she heard other tidings of him that were not so good. He had sorely mishandled certain farmers up the fjord near Steinker—they were at odds with the cloister over some fishing-rights, and when the monks came upon them one night while they were busy breaking up the cloister's salmon weir, brother Nikulaus had hurt one man grievously and flung another into the river and therewithal had sinned heinously in the matter of cursing and swearing.

CHAPTER VII

A FEW days after, Kristin went to the pine woods with some of the nuns and lay sisters, to gather moss for green dye. This moss is somewhat hard to come by, growing most on wind-fallen trees and dry branches. So the women soon scattered through the woods, and lost one another from sight in the fog.

For some days now this unwonted weather had held—windless, with a thick mist, that showed a strange leaden blue out over the sea and away against the hill-sides, when now and again it thinned so much that the eye caught glimpses of the country round. Between-whiles it thickened to a drizzling rain; then again it lightened so much that a whitish patch showed where the sun hung amid the towering mists. But there brooded ever a strange, heavy warmth, as of a bath-house, that was unwonted down here by the fjord, in especial at this time of the year—'twas two days before Nativitas Mariæ [4]—so that all folk talked of the weather and marvelled what it might betoken.

Kristin sweated in the lifeless, damp heat, and the thought of this tidings that she had heard of Naakkve weighed upon her

[4] 8th September.

breast. She was come down to the skirts of the wood, to the log fence by the path up from the sea, and, as she stood there scraping moss from the fence, Sira Eiliv came riding homewards through the fog. He stopped his horse and said some words of the weather, and so they fell in talk. Then she asked the priest if he knew aught of this matter of Naakkve—though she knew 'twas in vain, for Sira Eiliv ever made as though he had no knowledge of the inside affairs of the Tautra cloister.

"I trow, Kristin, you need have no fear that 'twill hinder his coming hither in the winter, this mischance," said the priest. " 'Tis that you feared, belike?"

" 'Tis more than that, Sira Eiliv. I fear me Naakkve never was meant to be a monk."

"Think you that you dare judge of such things?" asked the priest, bending his brows. He lighted down from his horse, bound it to a fence log, and leaned over the fence, gazing fixedly and searchingly at the woman. Kristin said:

"I fear 'tis hard for Naakkve to bow beneath the rule of the order—and he was so young when he withdrew him from the world, he knew not what he forwent, and knew not his own mind. All that befell in his young days—the loss of his father's heritage, the sight of the discord 'twixt his father and mother, that ended in Erlend's death—so wrought in him that he lost all heart to live in the world. But I could never mark that it made him godly—"

"You could not?—It may well have been as hard for Nikulaus as for many another good monk to bow him beneath the order's rule; hot of mood is he, and a young man—too young, maybe, to have understood, ere he turned his back on the world, that the world is as hard a taskmaster as any other lord, and in the end a tyrant without mercy. Of that, I ween, you yourself can judge, sister—

"And if so it be that Naakkve entered into the cloister more for his brother's sake than from love for his Maker—none the less I believe not that God will let it go unrequited that he took up the cross for his brother's sake. God's mother Mary, whom I know that Naakkve honoured and loved from his boyhood up, will surely show him clearly one day, that her son came hither to this earthly home to be his brother and bear the cross for him—

"—Nay—" The horse whinnied, with its nose against the priest's breast; he caressed it, while he said, half 'to himself: "From his childhood up my Nikulaus had a wondrous gift of loving and of suffering—I deem that he should be right well fitted for a monk.

"But you, Kristin," he said, turning to the woman, "you should have seen so much now, methinks, that you might trust in God Almighty with a surer trust. Have you not yet understood that He bears up every soul so long as the soul lets not go its hold on Him? Think you, woman, child that you still are in your old age, that 'tis God punishing the sin, when you must reap sorrow and humiliation because you followed your lusts and your overweening pride over paths that God has forbidden His children to tread? Would you say that *you* had punished your children if they scalded their hands when they took up the boiling kettle you had forbidden them to touch, or if the slippery ice broke under them that you had warned them not to go upon? Have you not understood, when the brittle ice broke beneath you—that you were drawn under each time you let go God's hand, and you were saved from out the deep each time you called on Him? Was not the love that bound you and your father in the flesh together, even when you defied him and set your wilfulness against his will, was it not a comfort and a solace none the less when you had to reap the fruits of your disobedience to him?

"Have you not understood yet, sister, that God has helped you each time you prayed, though you prayed half-heartedly and with feigning, and helped you much beyond what you prayed for? You loved God as you loved your father, not so hotly as you loved your own will, yet none the less so that you ever sorrowed much when you forsook Him—and therefore His mercy towards you suffered good to grow, amidst the evil harvest you must needs reap from the seed of your stubborn will—

"Your sons—two of them He took to Himself while they were innocent little children; for them you need never fear. And the others have turned out well—even if they have not turned out as *you* would have had them. Doubtless Lavrans deemed the like of you—

"And your husband, Kristin—God be merciful to his soul—I wot you have blamed him in your heart early and late for his reckless unwisdom. Yet meseems it had been much harder for a proud woman to remember that Erlend Nikulaussön led you with him through shame and deceit and blood-guiltiness, if you had seen but *once* that the man could do aught with cold contrivance. And almost I believe, too, 'twas because you were steadfast in anger and hardness as in love, that you were able to hold Erlend fast so long as you both lived—with him 'twas out of sight, out of mind, with all things else but you. God help Erlend; I fear me he never had the wit to know true repentance for his sins—yet did your husband repent and sorrow truly for his deeds wherein he sinned against you. That lesson, we may dare to trust, has profited Erlend now that he is dead."

Kristin stood still and silent; neither did Sira Eiliv say any more. He loosed the reins, gave her a "Peace be with you," mounted his horse, and rode away.

When, a little after, she came back to the cloister, Sister Ingrid met her at the door with word that one of her sons was come to greet her—Skule he called himself; he was at the parlour gateway.

He was sitting talking with his boat-folk—he sprang up when his mother came to the door. Ah, she knew her own by the quick nimbleness—the small head, borne high above broad shoulders, the long-limbed, slender form. Beaming with joy she went towards him—but she stopped suddenly and caught her breath at the sight of his face—oh, who had done this to her fair son—?

His upper-lip showed as though kneaded out thin—a blow must have crushed it, and afterwards it had grown together flat and long and misshapen, barred with a network of white scars; it had left his mouth twisted awry, fixed in what seemed a sneering grimace—and the bone of his nose had been broken and had set again crooked. He lisped a little when he spoke—he wanted one front tooth, and another was blue-black and dead.

Skule reddened under his mother's gaze: "I trow you know me not, mother?" He laughed a little, and passed a finger over his lip —'twas not sure whether he pointed to his blemish, or whether 'twas but a chance movement.

"So long parted, I trow, we have not been, my son, that your mother should not know you again," Kristin answered calmly, with an untroubled smile.

Skule Erlendssön was come two days before with a light sloop from Björgvin, with letters from Bjarne Erlingssön for the Archbishop and the Treasurer of Nidaros. Later in the day, mother and son walked in the garden beneath the ash trees, and, now that they were alone, he gave his mother the news of his brothers:

Lavrans was in Iceland still.—His mother knew not even that he had gone thither! Ay, said Skule, he had met his youngest brother in Oslo the winter before at the gathering of the nobles; he was with Jammælt Halvardssön. But, as she knew, the boy had ever had a longing to come abroad and look about him in the world, and so he took service with the Bishop of Skaalholt and sailed away—

Ay, he himself had gone in Sir Bjarne's train to Sweden, and thereafter to the war in Russia. His mother shook her head gently —she had known naught of *that* either! Skule had liked the life, he said, laughing—it had given him his chance to greet the old friends his father spoke so much of—Karelians, Ingrians, Russians. No, that brave scar of honour was not won in war—he laughed a little —ay, 'twas in a fight; the fellow that gave it him would never have need now to beg his bread. More of it, or of the war, Skule seemed to have little mind to tell. Now he was captain of Sir Bjarne's horsemen at Björgvin, and the knight had promised to get back for him some of the manors his father had owned in Orkladal, that were now under the Crown—but Kristin saw that Skule's great, steel-gray eyes took on a strange, dark look as he said this.

"You deem you cannot put much faith in such a promise?" asked his mother.

"No, no." Skule shook his head. "The deeds are even now being drawn. Sir Bjarne has kept all he promised when I took service with him—calls me kinsman and friend. Almost I have the like place in his household that Ulf had at home with us"—he laughed; and the laugh became his marred face ill.

But he was the comeliest of men in bodily form, now that he was full-grown—he wore garments of a new-fashioned cut, tight hose and a small close-fitting *kothardi* that barely reached to the middle of his thigh and was buttoned with small brass buttons all down the front—it showed up in well-nigh unseemly wise his body's supple strength. He looked as though he went about in his undergarments, thought the mother. But his forehead and his comely eyes were not changed.

"You look as though something were weighing on you, Skule," the mother ventured.

"No, no, no." 'Twas but the weather, he said, shaking himself. There was a strange red-brown glow in the fog as the hidden sun went down. The church stood out above the garden tree-tops, strange and dark, melting into the dull red mist. They had had to row the whole fjord, from the very mouth, 'twas so calm, said Skule. Then again he shifted a little in his clothes, and began to speak once more of his brothers.

He had been on an errand south in the land for Sir Bjarne this spring, so he could give her fresh tidings of Ivar and Gaute, for he had ridden up overland and made his way across the fells from Vaagaa home to the west country. All was well with Ivar; they had two little sons at Rognheim, Erlend and Gamal, comely children. "But at Jörundgaard I chanced upon a christening-ale—and Jofrid and Gaute deemed, as you were dead to the world now, they might name the little maid after you; Jofrid is so proud that you are her mother-in-law—ay, you laugh, but, now that you are not to dwell under one roof, be sure Jofrid knows well it has a brave sound when she talks of 'my mother-in-law, Kristin Lavransdatter.' But I gave Kristin Gautesdatter my best finger-ring, for she has such winsome eyes; almost I deem she will be like you—"

Kristin smiled sadly:

"Soon will you bring me to think, my Skule, that my sons deem me as great and good as old folk are wont to be, once they are beneath the sod."

"Speak not so, mother," said the man, with a strange vehemence. Then he laughed a little: "You wot well that all we brothers, ever since we were breeched, deemed you were the bravest and most high-minded of women—though you clinched us full tightly under your wings many a time, and we flapped back, maybe, somewhat hard again ere we scaped from the nest—

"—But it has proved, sure enough, that you were right in deeming Gaute the one of us brothers that was born to be a chieftain," said he, laughing loud.

"No need to mock me for that now, Skule," said Kristin—and Skule saw that his mother flushed with a young, tender red. At that he laughed all the more:

" 'Tis true, my mother—Gaute Erlendssön of Jörundgaard is grown a mighty man in the northern dales. This theft of his bride brought him such renown"—Skule laughed loudly, with the laughter that so ill became his ravaged mouth. "They sing a ballad of it; ay, they sing now that he took the maid with iron and with steel, and he fought her kinsmen three livelong days on the mountain— and the feast that Sir Sigurd held at Sundbu, and whereat he made peace betwixt the kinsmen with silver and with gold, for that too Gaute gets all the honour in the ballad—and it seems to make no matter that 'tis all a lie; Gaute rules the whole parish and somewhat beyond—and Jofrid rules Gaute—"

Kristin shook her head, with her little sad smile. But she grew young of face as she gazed on Skule. Now seemed it to her that *he* was most like his father—after all, the young warrior with the ravaged face had the most of Erlend's gallant mettle—and that he had so early had to take his fate into his own hands had given him a cool firmness of spirit that filled his mother's heart with a strange security. With Sira Eiliv's words of the day before in mind, she saw all at once—fearful as she had been for her headstrong sons, and hard as she had often laid hand upon them by reason of her dread—yet had she been much less content with her children had they been meek and unmanly.

Then she asked again and again of her grandson, little Erlend— but him had Skule given small heed to, it seemed—ay, he was strong and comely, and was wont to have his way at all times.

The uncanny glow in the fog, as of clotted blood, faded away; the dark was falling. The church's bells began to ring; Kristin and her son rose. Then Skule took her hand:

"Mother," he said in a low voice. "Mind you that I once lifted my hand against you? I threw a bat at you in anger, and it struck you on the brow—mind you of it? Mother, while we two are all alone, tell me that you have forgiven me!"

Kristin drew a long breath—ay, she remembered. She had bidden the twins go on an errand up to the sæter—but when she came out into the courtyard the horse was there, grazing, with the pack-saddle on its back, and her sons running about and playing at ball. When she chid them angrily for this, Skule flung the bat from him in a towering rage—But she remembered best what came after—How, as she went about after, one eye quite closed by the swelling of the lid—the brothers looked at her and at Skule, and shrank from him as though he were a leper—though Naakkve had beaten him mercilessly first. And Skule wandered away, and sat boiling with defiance and shame under a hard, scornful mien. But when in the evening she was standing putting off her clothes in the dark, he stole up to her—said nothing, but took her hand and kissed it. And, when she touched his shoulder, he cast his arms about her neck and pressed his cheek to hers—his was cool and soft and still a little rounded; she felt 'twas a child's cheek still—he was but a child, after all, this headstrong, fiery youth—

"That have I, Skule—so fully, that God alone knows, for I cannot tell you, how fully I have forgiven it you, my son!"

A moment she stood with her hand on his shoulder. Then he grasped her wrists, gripped them so tight that she winced with pain—and the next moment he flung his arms about her with the same passionate, fearful, bashful tenderness as that other time.

"My son—what ails you?" whispered the mother, in fear.

She felt in the dark that the man shook his head. Then he let her go, and together they went upward to the church.

During the Mass Kristin called to mind that she had forgotten to bring in blind Lady Aasa's cloak, from where they had sat together on the bench outside the priest's door that morning. After the service she went round to fetch it.

Under the archway stood Sira Eiliv, lanthorn in hand, and Skule. "He died as we came alongside the wharf," she heard Skule say, in a strangely wild, despairing voice.

"Who?"

Both men started violently when they saw her.

"One of my ship-folk," said Skule, low.

Kristin looked from one to the other. At the sight of their blank, strained faces in the lanthorn's glimmer she broke unwittingly into a little cry of fear. The priest set his teeth in his under-lip—she saw that his chin quivered a little.

" 'Twere best, my son, you should tell your mother. Better that we all make us ready to bear it, if 'tis God's will this folk too shall be awaked by so hard a—" But Skule uttered a kind of groan and said no word; and on that the priest spoke: "Pestilence has come to Björgvin, Kristin—The great and deathly sickness that we have heard say is laying waste the lands in the world around—"

"The black death—?" whispered Kristin.

"It boots not to try to tell you how things were in Björgvin when I sailed from there," said Skule. "None can think it that has not seen it. At first Sir Bjarne took the hardest measures to quench the fire where it broke out, away in the houses around Jons cloister; he would have cut off the whole Nordnes from the town with a chain of his men-at-arms, though the monks of the Michael cloister threatened him with the Church's ban—There came an English ship that had the pest aboard, and he would not suffer them to unload the lading or to leave the ship; every man on the sloop died, and then he had her scuttled. But some of the wares had already been brought to land, and some of the burghers smuggled more ashore one night—and the friars of the Jons church stood to it that the dying must have ghostly comfort—Then folk began to die throughout all the town, so 'twas bootless, we saw—Now is there not a living soul in the city save the bearers of the dead—all flee the town that can, but the pest goes with them—"

"O Jesus Christus!"

"Mother—mind you the last time 'twas lemming-year at home in Sil? The throngs that rolled along all the roads and paths—mind you how they lay and died in every bush, and rotted, and poisoned every runnel with stench and festering foulness—?" He clenched his fists; his mother shuddered:

"Lord, have mercy on us all—Praise be to God and Mary Virgin that you were sent hither even now, my Skule—"

The man ground his teeth together in the dark:

"So said we too, my men and I, the morning we hoisted sail and stood down Vägen out to sea. When we were come north to Moldö Sound, the first fell sick. We bound stones to his feet and a cross upon his breast when he was dead, vowed a mass for his soul when we came to Nidaros, and cast his body into the sea—God forgive us. We put in to shore with the next two and got them help for their souls, and Christian burial—for 'tis bootless to flee from fate. The fourth died as we pulled into the river, and the fifth last night—"

"Is it needful that you go back to the town?" asked his mother a little later. "Can you not bide here?"

Skule shook his head, with a joyless laugh:

"—Oh, soon, methinks, 'twill matter naught where one is. Useless to be afeared—a man in dread is half dead. But would that I were as old as you are, Mother!"

"None knows what they are spared who die young," said his mother, low.

"Be still, mother! Think on the time when you yourself were three-and-twenty winters old—would you have missed the years you have lived since then—?"

Fourteen days later Kristin saw for the first time one sick of the plague. Rumour that the pest was raging in Nidaros and spreading through the country-side had come to Rissa—how, 'twas not easy to understand, for folk kept their houses, and every man fled to the woods or thickets if he saw an unknown wayfarer on the road; none would open his door to stranger-folk.

But one morning two fishers came up to the cloister bearing a man between them in a sail; when at daybreak they came down to their boat, they had found a strange bark at the wharf, and in its bottom lay this man, senseless—he had found strength to make his boat fast, but not to get out of it to land. The man had been born in a house owned by the cloister, but his kindred had all left the country-side.

The dying man lay on the wet sail in the midst of the grass-grown courtyard; the fishermen stood afar off talking with Sira Eiliv. The lay sisters and serving-women had fled into the houses, but the nuns stood in a cluster at the door of the convent hall—a throng of startled, trembling, despairing old women.

Then Lady Ragnhild stepped forth. She was a little, thin old woman, with a broad, flat face and a little round, red nose like a button; her great, light-brown eyes were red-rimmed, and always watered a little.

"In nomine patris et filii et spiritus sancti," she said in a clear voice, then gulped once. "Bear him into the guest-house——"

And Sister Agata, the eldest of the nuns, elbowed her way through the throng and, unbidden, went with the abbess and the men who bore the sick man.

Kristin went in thither late at night with a remedy she had made ready in the pantry, and Sister Agata asked if she durst bide there and tend the fire.

She deemed herself she should have been hardened—well used as she was to births and deaths, she had seen worse sights than this—she strove to think of all the worst that she had seen—The plague-stricken man sat upright, for he was like to choke with the bloody spittle that he brought up at each coughing-fit—Sister Agata had slung him up in a band passed across his lean, yellow, red-haired chest, and his head hung forward; his face was leaden grey-blue, and fit on fit of shivering shook him. But Sister Agata sat calmly saying over her prayers, and, when the cough took him, she rose, put one arm about his head, and held a cup below his mouth. The sick man roared loud in his agony, rolled his eyes fearfully, and at length thrust a black tongue far out of his gullet, while his lamentable cries died away in pitiful groaning. The nun emptied out the cup into the fire—and while Kristin threw on more juniper, and the wet branches first filled the room with a stinging, yellow smoke, and then burst hissing into flame, she saw Sister Agata settle the cushions and pillows under the sick man's back and arm-pits, wipe his face and cracked brown lips with vinegar-water, and draw the fouled coverlid up about his body. 'Twould soon be over and done, she said to Kristin—he was cold already; at first he had been hot as fire—but Sira Eiliv had prepared him already for his going. Then she sat her down beside him, thrust the calamus root into its place in her cheek with her tongue, and fell again to prayer.

Kristin strove to overcome the fearful horror that she felt. She had seen folk die a harder death—But 'twas in vain—this was the plague, a chastisement from the Lord for all mankind's secret hardness of heart, of which He alone had knowledge. She felt as if she were rocked giddily on a sea, where all the bitter and angry thoughts she had ever thought towered up like one huge wave amid a thousand, and broke in helpless woe and lamentation. Lord, help us, for we perish—

Sira Eiliv came in late in the night. He chid Sister Agata sharply that she had not followed his counsel to bind a linen cloth dipped in vinegar over her mouth and nose. She mumbled testily that 'twas of no avail—but both she and Kristin had now to do as he bade them.

The priest's quietude and steadfastness put some measure of courage into Kristin—or awoke a feeling of shame—she ventured out of the juniper smoke and began to help Sister Agata. A choking stench came from the sick man, that the smoke availed not to deaden—filth, blood, sour sweat, and a noisome smell from his throat. She thought of Skule's words about the lemming swarm; once more there came upon her the awful longing to fly, though she knew there was no place whither one could flee from this. But when once she had taken heart of grace and touched the dying man, the worst was over; and she helped as well as she might until he had breathed his last. He was black in the face already when he died.

The nuns walked in procession, with the holy relics, crosses, and burning tapers, round the church and the cloister hill, and all in the parish who could walk or crawl went with them. But, not many days after, a woman died near by at Strömmen—and then the deadly sickness broke out at a stroke on every hand throughout the country-side.

Death and horror and direst need seemed to bear away the land and its folk into a timeless world—'twas not more than a few weeks that were gone by, if one were to reckon the days, and already it seemed as if the world that had been, ere pestilence and death stalked naked through the land, was fading from folk's memories, as a sea-coast sinks when one stands out to sea before a rushing wind. 'Twas as though no human soul could keep in memory that once life and the daily round of work had seemed sure and near, death far away—or had the power to conceive that so it would be again—if so be all men did not die. But "Belike, we shall all die," said the men who came to the cloister with their motherless little ones; some said it with dull, hard faces, some with weeping

and lamentations; they said it when they fetched a priest to the dying, they said it when they bore the corpses to the parish church
down the hill and to the graveyard by the cloister chapel. Often the
bearers themselves must dig the grave—Sira Eiliv had set the lay
serving-men—such as were left—to work at saving and garnering
the corn from the cloister's fields; and wheresoever he went in the
parish he admonished the folk to get their crops housed, and to help
one another to care for the cattle, that so they might not perish in
the dearth the plague was like to leave behind when it had spent
its rage.

The nuns in the cloister met the visitation at first with a kind of
bewildered calm. They settled them down for good in the convent
hall, kept a fire blazing night and day in the great masoned fire-
place, slept there, and there took their food. Sira Eiliv counselled
that great fires should be kept up in the courts and in all the houses
where there were fireplaces; but the sisters were afraid of fire—they
had heard so many tales from the oldest sisters of the burning of
the convent thirty years before. Meal-times and working-hours were
kept no longer, and the divers offices of the sisters could not be
kept apart, by reason of the many children who came from without,
praying for food and help. Sick folk were brought in—these for
the most were well-to-do folk who could pay for a grave-stead in
the cloister and for masses for their souls, or the poorest and lone-
liest of the poor who could get no help at home. Those of a middle
station lay and died in their own houses. On some manors every
human being died. But amid all this the nuns had as yet made shift
to keep up the hours of prayer.

The first of the nuns who fell sick was Sister Inga, a woman
of Kristin's age, near fifty years; but none the less was she so
afeared of death that 'twas horrible to see and hear her. The shivering fit came upon her in the church during Mass, and she crept
on hands and knees, shaking and with chattering teeth, praying
and beseeching God and Mary Virgin for her life—Before long
she lay in a burning fever, groaning, and sweating blood from all
her body. Kirstin's heart shuddered within her—doubtless she,
too, would be as wretchedly afraid as this when her time came.
'Twas not alone that death was sure—'twas the awful horror that
clung about death from pestilence.

Then Lady Ragnhild herself fell sick. Kristin had wondered a little that this woman had been chosen to an abbess's high office —she was a quiet, somewhat peevish old woman, unlearned, and, it seemed, lacking any great gifts of the spirit—but, when death laid his hand upon her, she showed she was in truth a bride of Christ. Her the sickness smote with boils—she would not suffer even her spiritual daughters to bare her old body, but under one of her arms the swelling grew at last as big as an apple, and under her chin too boils broke out and waxed huge and blood-red, and at last turned black; she suffered unbearable pains from them, and burned with fever; but as oft as her mind was clear, she lay there a pattern of holy patience, sighing to God for forgiveness of her sins, and praying in fair and heartfelt words for her cloister and her daughters, for all sick and sorrowful, and for the salvation of all souls who now must part from hence. Even Sira Eiliv wept, when he had given her the viaticum—and *his* steadfastness as well as his unwearied zeal in the midst of all this misery had been a thing to wonder at. Lady Ragnhild had many times already given her soul into God's keeping and prayed Him to take the nuns into His ward—and then at last the boils on her body began to burst. But this proved a turning towards life, not death—and after, too, folk deemed they saw that those whom the sickness smote with boils were sometimes healed, but those to whom it came with a bloody vomit, died every one.

It seemed as though the nuns took new courage from the abbess's steadfastness, and from the having seen one stricken with the pest who yet did not die. They had now to milk and tend the byres themselves, to make ready their own food, and themselves fetch home juniper and fresh pine branches to burn for cleansing smoke—each one had to do what came to her hand. They cared for the sick as best they could, and doled out remedies—theriac and calamus root had given out; they dealt round ginger, pepper, saffron and vinegar to ward off the poison; and milk and meat— the bread gave out and they baked at night—the spices gave out, and folk must needs chew juniper-berries and pine-needles against the infection. One by one the sisters drooped and died; passing-bells rang from the cloister church and the parish church early and late in the heavy air; for the strange, uncanny mist still lay upon the land; there seemed to be a secret privity 'twixt the fog and the deadly sickness. Sometimes it turned to a frosty fog and sifted down in small ice-needles and a half-frozen drizzle, and the land grew white with rime—then came mild weather and mist again. Folk deemed it a sign of evil omen that the sea-fowl, that else were wont to flock in thousands along the creek that runs inland from the fjord and lies like a river between the low stretches of meadow, but widens to a salt-water lake north of Rein cloister —that they suddenly vanished, and in their stead came ravens in countless numbers—on every stone by the water-side the black birds sat amidst the fog, making their hideous croaking; while flocks of crows, so huge that none before had seen the like, settled on all the woods and groves, and flew with ugly screechings over the stricken land.

Now and again Kristin thought of her own—the sons who were scattered so far and wide, the grandchildren she should never see —little Erlend's golden head wavered before her sight. But they were grown to seem far off and pale to her. Almost it seemed as though all mankind in this time of need were alike near to each other and alike far apart. And then she had her hands full all day long—it stood her in good stead now that she was used to all kinds of work. While she sat milking, she would find beside her suddenly little starving children she had never before set her eyes on, and she would scarce remember to ask whence they were or how things were with them at home; she would give them food and lead them to the shelter of the chapter-hall, or some other place where a fire was burning, then stow them away in a bed in the dormitory.

She marked, with a kind of wonder, that in this time of calamity, when more than ever there was need that all should be vigilant in prayer, she scarce ever found time to meditate or to pray. She would fling her down in the church before the tabernacle when she found a vacant moment, but naught came of it but wordless sighs, and Paternosters and Aves uttered by rote. She herself knew not that the nun-like ways and bearing she had fallen into in these two years were dropping from her more and more, and that she was growing ever liker to the housewife of the old days—as the flock of nuns dwindled, the round of cloister duties fell into disar-

ray, and the abbess still lay abed, weak and with half-palsied tongue
—and the work grew more and more for the few that were left to
do it.

One day she learned by chance that Skule was still in Nidaros—
his ship-folk were dead or fled away, and he had not been able to
get new folk. He was whole yet, but he had plunged into wild
living, as had many young men in this desperate pass. For him who
was afraid, death was sure, they said, and so they deadened thought
with drink and riot, gambled and danced and wantoned with
women. Even honourable burghers' wives and young maids of the
best kindreds ran from their homes in this evil time; in company
with the women of the bordels they caroused in the inns and tav-
erns amongst the wildered men. God forgive them, thought the
mother—but 'twas as though her heart were too weary to sorrow
much for these things.

But in the country-side too, for sure, there was enough of sin
and distraction. They heard little of it at the cloister, for there
they had no time for much talk. But Sira Eiliv, who went about
everywhere, without rest or respite, to the sick and dying, said one
day to Kristin that the folk's souls stood in yet direr need than
their bodies.

There came an evening when they were sitting round the chim-
ney-place in the convent hall—the little flock of folk that were left
alive in Rein cloister. Four nuns and two lay sisters, an old stable-
man and a half-grown boy, two bedeswomen and some children,
huddled together round the fire. On the high-seat bench, where a
great crucifix gleamed in the dusk on the light-hued wall, lay the
abbess, and Sister Kristin and Sister Turid sat at her hands and feet.

It was nine days since the last death among the sisters, and five
days since any had died in the cloister or the nearer houses. The
pestilence seemed to be lessening throughout the parish, too, said
Sira Eiliv. And for the first time for near three months something
like a gleam of peace and hope and comfort fell upon the silent and
weary folk that sat together there. Old Sister Torunn Marta let
her rosary sink upon her lap, and took the hand of the little girl
who stood at her knee:

"What can it be she means? Ay, child, now seems it as we should see that never for long does God's mother, Mary, turn away her loving-kindness from her children."

"Nay, 'tis not Mary Virgin, Sister Torunn, 'tis Hel.[5] She will go from out this parish, with both rake and broom, when they offer up a man without blemish at the graveyard gate—to-morrow she'll be far away—"

"What means she?" asked the nun again, uneasily. "Fie upon you, Magnhild; what ugly heathenish talk is this? 'Twere fit you should taste the birch—"

"Tell us what it is, Magnhild—have no fear"—Sister Kristin was standing behind them; she asked the question breathlessly. She had remembered—she had heard in her youth from Lady Aashild —of dreadful, unnamably sinful devices that the devil tempts desperate men to practise—

The children had been down in the grove by the parish church in the falling dusk, and some of the boys had strayed through the wood to a turf hut that stood there, and had eavesdropped and heard some men in it laying plans. It seemed from what they heard that these men had laid hold on a little boy, Tore, the son of Steinunn, that lived by the strand, and to-night they were to offer him up to the pest-ogress, Hel. The children talked eagerly, proud that the grown-up folk were paying heed to what they said. They seemed not to think of pitying the hapless Tore—maybe because he was somewhat of an outcast. He wandered about the parish begging, but never came to the cloister, and if Sira Eiliv or any sent by the abbess sought out his mother, she ran away, or she kept a stubborn silence, whether they spoke lovingly or harshly to her. She had lived in the stews of Nidaros for ten years, but then a sickness took hold on her, and left her of so ill a favour that at last she could not win her livelihood so as she had used her to do; so she had forsaken the town for the Rein parish, and now dwelt in a hut down by the strand. It still befell at times that a chance beggar or some such stroller would take lodging with her for a while. Who was father to her boy she herself knew not.

[5] In Norse folk-lore the plague was personified as a hideous old woman carrying a rake and a broom. Where she used the rake, some part of the population survived; where she used the broom, she swept the country-side of every living soul. It would be natural, in the fourteenth century, for the popular imagination to identify her with Hel, the death goddess of the old mythology.

"We must go thither," said Kristin. "Here we cannot sit, I trow, while christened souls sell themselves to the devil at our very doors."

The nuns whimpered in fear. These were the worst men in the parish; rough, ungodly fellows; and uttermost need and despair must have turned them now into very devils. Had Sira Eiliv only been at home, they moaned. In this time of trial the priest had so won their trust, that they deemed he could do all things—

Kristin wrung her hands:

"Even if I must go alone—my mother, have I your leave to go thither?"

The abbess gripped her by the arm so hard that she cried out. The old, tongue-tied woman got upon her feet; by signs she made them understand that they should dress her to go out, and called for her golden cross, the badge of her office, and her staff. Then she took Kristin by the arm—for she was the youngest and strongest of the women. All the nuns stood up and followed.

Through the door of the little room 'twixt the chapter-hall and the choir of the church they went forth into the raw, cold winter night. Lady Ragnhild's teeth began to chatter and her whole frame to shiver—she still sweated without cease by reason of her sickness, and the pest-boil sores were not fully healed, so that it must have wrought her great agony to walk. But she muttered angrily and shook her head when the sisters prayed her to turn, clung the harder to Kristin's arm, and plodded, shaking with cold, on before them through the garden. As their eyes grew used to the darkness, the women made out the dim sheen of the withered leaves strewn on the path beneath their feet, and the faint light from the clouded sky above the naked tree-tops. Cold waterdrops dripped from the branches, and puffs of wind went by with a faint soughing sound. The roll of the waves on the strand behind the high ground came to them in dull, heavy sighs.

At the bottom of the garden was a little wicket—the sisters shuddered when the bolt, fast rusted in its socket, shrieked as Kristin withdrew it by main force. Then they crept onward through the grove down towards the parish church. Now they could see dimly the black-tarred mass, darker against the darkness; and against the opening in the clouds above the low hills beyond the lake they saw the roof-top, and the ridge turret with its beasts' heads and cross over all.

Ay—there were folk in the graveyard—they felt rather than saw or heard it. And now a faint gleam of light was to be seen low down, as of a lanthorn set upon the ground. Close by it the darkness seemed moving.

The nuns pressed together, moaning almost soundlessly amid whispered prayers, went a few steps, halted and listened, and went on again. They were well-nigh come to the graveyard gate. Then they heard from out of the dark a thin child-voice crying:

"Oh, oh, my bannock; you've thrown dirt on it!"

Kristin let go the abbess's arm, and ran forward through the churchyard gate. She pushed aside some dark shapes of men's backs, stumbled over heaps of upturned earth, and then was at the edge of the open grave. She went down on her knees, bent over, and lifted up the little boy who stood at the bottom, still whimpering because the dirt had spoiled the good bannock he had been given for staying quietly down there.

The men stood there frighted from their wits—ready to fly—some stamped about on the same spot—Kristin saw their feet in the light from the lanthorn on the ground. Then one, she made sure, would have sprung at her—at the same moment the grey-white nuns' dresses came into sight—and the knot of men hung wavering—

Kristin had the boy in her arms still; he was crying for his bannock; so she set him down, took the bread, and brushed it clean:

"There, eat it—your bannock is as good as ever now—And now go home, you men"—the shaking of her voice forced her to stop a little. "Go home and thank God you were saved from the doing of a deed 'twere hard to atone." She was speaking now as a mistress speaks to her serving-folk, mildly, but as if it could not cross her mind that they would not obey. Unwittingly some of the men turned towards the gate.

Then one of them shrieked:

"Stay a little—see you not our lives at the least are forfeit—mayhap all we own—now that these full-fed monks' whores have stuck their noses into this! Never must they come away from here to spread the tidings of it—"

Not a man moved—but Sister Agnes broke into a shrill shriek, and cried in a wailing voice:

"O sweet Jesus, my bridegroom—I thank Thee that Thou sufferest Thy handmaidens to die for the glory of Thy name—!"

Lady Ragnhild pushed her roughly behind her, tottered forward, and took up the lanthorn from the ground—no one moved a hand to hinder her. When she lifted it up, the gold cross on her breast shone out. She stood propped on her staff, and slowly turned the light upon the ring about her, nodding a little at each man she looked on. Then she made a sign to Kristin to speak. Kristin said:

"Go home peaceably and quietly, dear brothers—be sure that the reverend mother and these good sisters will be as merciful as their duty to God and the honour of His Church will suffer. But stand aside now, that we may come forth with this child—and thereafter let each man go his way."

The men stood wavering. Then one shrieked out as though in direst need:

"Is't not better that *one* be offered up than that we should all perish—? This child here who is owned by none—"

"Christ owns him. 'Twere better we should perish one and all than to hurt one of His little ones—"

But the man who had spoken first shouted again:

"Hold your tongue—no more such-like words, or I cram them back down your throat with this"—he shook his knife in the air. "Go you home, go to your beds and pray your priest to comfort you, and say naught of this—or I tell you, in Satan's name, you shall learn 'twas the worst thing you ever did to put your fingers into our affairs—"

"You need not to cry so loud for him you named to hear you, Arntor—be sure he is not far from here," said Kristin calmly, and some of the men seemed affrighted, and pressed unwittingly nearer to the abbess, who stood holding the lanthorn. "The worst had been, both for us and for you, had we sat quiet at home while you went about to make you a dwelling-place in hottest hell."

But the man Arntor swore and raved. Kristin knew that he hated the nuns; for his father had been forced to pledge his farm to them when he had to pay amends for man-slaying and incest with his wife's cousin. Now he went on casting up at the sisters all the Enemy's most hateful lies, charging them with sins so black and unnatural that only the devil himself could prompt a man to think such thoughts.

The poor nuns bowed them terrified and weeping under the hail of his taunts, but they stood fast around their old mother, and she held the lanthorn high, throwing the light upon the man, and looking him calmly in the face while he raved.

But anger flamed up in Kristin like new-kindled fire:

"Silence! Have you lost your wits, or has God smitten you with blindness? Should we dare to murmur under His chastisement—we who have seen His consecrated brides go forth to meet the sword that has been drawn by reason of the world's sins? They watched and prayed while we sinned and each day forgot our Maker—shut them from the world within the citadel of prayer while we scoured the world around, driven by greed of great and small possessions, of our own lusts and our own wrath. But they came forth to us when the angel of death was sent out amongst us—gathered in the sick and the defenceless and the hungry—twelve of our sisters have died in this plague—that you all know—not one turned aside, and not one gave over praying for us all in sisterly love, till the tongue dried in their mouths and their life's blood ebbed away—"

"Bravely speak you of yourself and your like—"

"*I* am *your* like," she cried, beside herself with anger; "I am not one of these holy sisters—I am one of you—"

"You have grown full humble, woman," said Arntor, scornfully; "you are frighted, I mark well. A little more and you will be fain to call her—the mother to this boy—your like."

"That must God judge—He died both for her and for me, and He knows us both.—Where is she—Steinunn?"

"Go down to her hut; you will find her there sure enough," answered Arntor.

"Ay, truly someone must send word to the poor woman that we have her boy," said Kristin to the nuns. "We must go out to her to-morrow."

Arntor gave a jeering laugh, but another man cried, uneasily:

"No, no—She is dead," he said to Kristin. " 'Tis fourteen days since Bjarne left her and barred the door. She lay in the death-throes then—"

"She lay in—" Kristin gazed at the men, horror-struck. "Was there none to fetch a priest to her—? Is the—body—lying there—and no one has had so much compassion on her as to bring her to hallowed ground—and her child you would have—?"

At the sight of the woman's horror, 'twas as though the men went clean beside themselves with fear and shame; all were shouting at once; a voice louder than all the rest rang out:

"Fetch her yourself, sister!"

"Ay! Which of you will go with me?"

None answered. Arntor cried:

"You will have to go alone, I trow."

"To-morrow—as soon as 'tis light—we will fetch her, Arntor —I myself will buy her a resting-place and masses for her soul—"

"Go thither now, go to-night—then will I believe you nuns are choke-full of holiness and pureness—"

Arntor had stuck his head forward close to hers. Kristin drove her clenched fist into his face, with a single loud sob of rage and horror—

Lady Ragnhild went forward and placed herself at Kristin's side; she strove to bring forth some words. The nuns cried out that to-morrow the dead woman should be brought to her grave. But the devil seemed to have turned Arntor's brain; he went on shrieking:

"Go now—then will we believe on God's mercy—"

Kristin drew herself up, white and stiff:

"I will go."

She lifted the child and gave it into Sister Torunn's arms, pushed the men aside, and ran quickly, stumbling over grass tussocks and heaps of earth, towards the gate, while the nuns followed wailing, and Sister Agnes cried out that she would go with her. The abbess shook her clenched hands towards Kristin, beckoning her to stop; but she seemed quite beside herself and gave no heed—

Suddenly there was a great commotion in the dark over by the graveyard gate—next moment Sira Eiliv's voice asked: who was holding Thing here? He came forward into the glimmer of the lanthorn—they saw that he bore an axe in his hand. The nuns flocked around him; the men made shift to steal away in the dark, but in the gateway they were met by a man bearing a drawn sword in his hand. There was some turmoil and the clash of arms, and Sira Eiliv shouted towards the gate: woe to any who broke the churchyard peace. Kristin heard one say 'twas the strong smith from Credo Lane—the moment after, a tall, broad-shouldered, white-haired man appeared at her side—'twas Ulf Haldorssön.

The priest handed him the axe—he had borrowed it from Ulf —and took the boy Tore from the nun, while he said:

" 'Tis past midnight already—none the less 'twere best you all came with me to the church; I must get to the bottom of these doings this very night."

None had any thought but to obey. But, when they were come out on to the road, one of the light-grey women's forms stepped aside from the throng and turned off by the path through the wood. The priest called out, bidding her come on with the others. Kristin's voice answered from the darkness—she was some way along the track already:

"I cannot come, Sira Eiliv, till I have kept my promise—"

The priest and some others sprang after her. She was standing leaning against the fence when Sira Eiliv came up with her. He held up the lanthorn—she was fearfully white of face, but, when he looked into her eyes, he saw that she was not gone mad, as at first he had feared.

"Come home, Kristin," he said. "To-morrow we will go thither with you, some men—I myself will go with you—"

"I have given my word. I cannot go home, Sira Eiliv, till I have done that which I vowed to do."

The priest stood silent a little. Then he said in a low voice:

"Mayhap you are right. Go then, sister, in God's name."

Like a shadow, Kristin melted away into the darkness, which swallowed up her grey form.

When Ulf Haldorssön came up by her side, she said—she spoke by snatches, vehemently: "Go back—I asked not you to come with me—"

Ulf laughed low:

"Kristin, my lady—you have not learnt yet, I see, that some things can be done without your asking or bidding—nor, though you have seen it many a time, I ween—that you cannot alway carry through alone all that you take upon you. But this burden of yours *I* will help you to carry."

The pine woods sighed above them, and the boom of the rollers away on the strand came stronger or more faint as the gusts of wind rose or died away. They walked in pitch darkness. After a while Ulf said:

"—I have borne you company before, Kristin, when you went out at night—methought 'twere but fitting I should go with you this time too—"

She breathed hard and heavily in the dark. Once she stumbled over somewhat, and Ulf caught her. After that he took her hand and led her. In a while the man heard that she was weeping as she went, and he asked her why she wept.

"I weep to think how good and faithful you have been to us, Ulf, all our days. What can I say—? I know well enough 'twas most for Erlend's sake, but almost I believe, kinsman—all our days you have judged of me more kindly than you had a right to, after what you first saw of my doings."

"I loved you, Kristin—no less than him." He was silent. Kristin felt that he was strongly stirred. Then he said:

"Therefore meseemed 'twas a hard errand when I sailed out hither to-day—I came to bring you such tidings as I myself deemed it hard to utter. God strengthen you, Kristin!"

"Is it Skule?" asked Kristin softly in a little. "Skule is dead?"

"No; Skule was well when I spoke with him yesterday—and now not many are dying in the town. But I had news from Tautra this morning—" He heard her sign heavily once, but she said naught. A little after he said:

"'Tis ten days now since they died. There are but four brothers left alive in the cloister, and the island is all but swept clean of folk."

They were come now where the wood ended. Over the flat stretch of land in front the roaring of the sea and the wind came to meet them. One spot out in the dark shone white—the surf in a little bay, by a steep, light-hued sand-hill.

"She dwells there," said Kristin. Ulf felt that long, convulsive shudders went through her frame. He gripped her hand hard:

"You took this on yourself. Remember that, and lose not your wits now."

Kristin said, in a strangely thin, clear voice, that the blast caught and bore away:

"Now will Björgulf's dream come true—I trust in God's and Mary's grace."

Ulf tried to see her face—but 'twas too dark. They were walking on the strand—in some places 'twas so narrow under the bluffs that now and then a wave washed right up to their feet. They tramped forward over tangled heaps of seaweed and great stones. After a while they were ware of a dark hump in against the sandy bank.

"Stay here," said Ulf, shortly. He went forward and thrust against the door—then she heard him hew at the withy bands and thrust at the door again. Then she was ware that the door had fallen inwards, and he had gone in through the black hole.

'Twas not a night of heavy storm. But it was so dark that Kristin could see naught save the little flashes of foam that came and vanished the same instant on the lifting sea, and the shining of the waves breaking along the shores of the bay—and against the sand-dune she could make out that black hump. And it seemed to her that she was standing in a cavern of night, and that 'twas the fore-court of death. The roll of breaking waves and the hiss of their waters ebbing among the stones of the beach kept time with the blood-waves surging through her, though all the time 'twas as though her body must shiver in pieces, as a vessel of wood falls apart in staves—her breast ached as if something would burst it in sunder from within; her head felt hollow and empty and as 'twere rifted, and the unceasing wind wrapped her round and swept clean through her. She felt, with a strange listlessness, that she herself had surely caught the sickness now—but 'twas as though she looked that the darkness should be riven by a great light that would drown the roar of the sea with its thunder, and that in the horror of this she should perish. She drew up her hood, blown back from her head by the wind, wrapped the black nun's cloak close about her, and stood with her hands crossed beneath it—but it came not into her thought to pray; 'twas as though her soul had more than enough to do to work a way forth from its mansion trembling to its fall, and as though it tore at her breast with every breath.

She saw a light flare up within the hut. A little after, Ulf Haldorssön called out to her: "You must come hither and hold the light for me, Kristin"—he was standing in the doorway—as she came, he reached her a torch of some tarred wood.

A choking stench from the corpse met her, though the hut was so draughty and the door was gone. With staring eyes and mouth half open—and she felt her jaws and lips grow stiff the while and wooden—she looked round for the dead. But there was naught to see but a long bundle lying in the corner on the earthen floor, wrapped in Ulf's cloak.

He had torn loose some long planks from somewhere and laid the door upon them. Cursing his unhandy tools, he made notches and holes with his light axe and dagger, and strove to lash the door fast to the boards. Once or twice he looked up at her swiftly, and each time his dark, grey-bearded face grew more hard set.

"I marvel much how you had thought to get through this piece of work alone," he said as he wrought—then glanced up at her— but the stiff, death-like face in the red gleam of the tar brand was set and unmoved as ever—'twas the face of a dead woman or of one distraught. "Can you tell me that, Kristin?" he laughed harshly —but still 'twas of no avail. "Methinks now were the time for you to say a prayer."

Stiff and lifeless as ever, she began to speak:

"*Pater noster qui es in cœlis. Adveniat regnum tuum. Fiat voluntas tua sicut in cœlo et in terra—*" Then she came to a stop.

Ulf looked at her. Then he took up the prayer:

"*Panem nostrum quotidianum da nobis hodie—*" Swiftly and firmly he said the Lord's prayer to the end, went over and made the sign of the cross over the bundle—swiftly and firmly he took it up and bore it to the bier that he had fashioned.

"Go you in front," he said. "Maybe 'tis somewhat heavier, but you will smell the stench less there. Throw away the torch—we can see more surely without it—and see you miss not your footing, Kristin—for I had liefer not have to take a hold of this poor body any more."

The struggling pain in her breast seemed to rise in revolt when she got the bier poles set upon her shoulders; her chest *would* not bear up the weight. But she set her teeth hard. So long as they went along the strand, where the wind blew strong, but little of the corpse smell came to her.

"Here I must draw it up first, I trow, and the bier after," said Ulf, when they were come to the steep slope they had climbed down.

"We can go a little farther on," said Kristin; " 'tis there they come down with the seaweed sleighs—there 'tis not steep."

She spoke calmly, the man heard, and as in her right mind. And a fit of sweating and trembling took him, now it was over—he had deemed she must lose her wits that night.

They struggled forward along the sandy track that led across the flat towards the pine wood. The wind swept in freely here, but yet 'twas not as it had been down on the strand, and, as they drew farther and farther away from the roar of the beach, she felt it as a homefaring from the horror of utter darkness. Beside their path the ground showed lighter—'twas a cornfield that there had been none to reap. The scent of it, and the sight of the beaten-down straw, welcomed her home again—and her eyes filled with tears of sisterly pity—out of her own desolate terror and woe she was coming home to fellowship with the living and the dead.

At times, when the wind was right behind, the fearful carrion stench enwrapped her wholly, but yet 'twas not so awful as when she stood in the hut—for the night was full of fresh, wet, cold, cleansing streams of air.

And much stronger than the feeling that she bore a thing of dread upon the bier behind her, was the thought that Ulf Haldorssön was there, guarding her back against the black and living horror they were leaving behind—and whose roar sounded fainter and more faint.

When they were come to the edge of the pine woods they were ware of lights: "They are coming to meet us," said Ulf.

Soon after, they were met by a whole throng of men bearing pine-root torches, a couple of lanthorns and a bier covered with a pall—Sira Eiliv was with them, and Kristin saw with wonder that in the troop were many of the men who had been that same night in the churchyard, and that many of them were weeping.

When they lifted the burthen from her shoulders she was like to fall. Sira Eiliv would have caught a hold of her, but she said quickly:

"Touch me not—come not near me—I have the pest myself; I feel it—"

But none the less Sira Eiliv stayed her up with a hand below her arm:

"Then be of good cheer, woman, remembering that our Lord has said: 'Inasmuch as ye have done it unto one of the least of these My brethren or sisters, ye have done it unto Me.'"

Kristin gazed at the priest. Then she looked across to where the men were shifting the body from the stretcher that Ulf had fashioned to the bier they had brought. Ulf's cloak slipped aside a little—the point of a worn-out shoe stuck out, dark wet in the light of the torches.

Kristin went across, kneeled between the poles of the bier, and kissed the shoe:

"God be gracious to you, sister—God give your soul joy in His light—God look in His mercy on us here in our darkness—"

Then it seemed to her as 'twere life itself that tore its way from out of her—a grinding, inconceivable pain, as though something within her, rooted fast in every outermost fibre of her limbs, were riven loose. All that was within her breast was torn out—she felt her throat full of it, her mouth filled with blood that tasted of salt and foul copper—next moment her whole dress in front was a glistening wet blackness—Jesus! is there so much blood in an old woman? she thought.

Ulf Haldorssön lifted her in his arms and bore her away.

At the gate of the cloister the nuns, bearing lighted candles, came to meet the train of men. Already Kristin scarce had her full senses, but she felt that she was half borne, half helped, through the door, and was ware of the whitewashed, vaulted room, filled with the flickering light of yellow candle flames and red pine torches, and of the tramp of feet rolling like a sea—but to the dying woman the light was like the shimmer of her own dying life-flame, and the footfalls on the flags as the rushing of the rivers of death rising up to meet her.

Then the candlelight spread out into a wider space—she was once again under the open, murky sky—in the courtyard—the flickering light played upon a grey stone wall with heavy buttresses and high, tall windows—the church. She was borne in someone's arms—'twas Ulf again—but now he seemed to take on for her the semblance of all who had ever borne her up. When she laid her arms about his neck and pressed her cheek against his stubbly throat, 'twas as though she were a child again with her father, but also as though she were clasping a child to her own bosom—And behind his dark head there were red lights, and they seemed like the glow of the fire that nourishes all love.

—A little later she opened her eyes, and her mind was clear and calm. She was sitting, propped up, in a bed in the dormitory; a nun with a linen band over her lower face stood bending over her; she marked the smell of vinegar. 'Twas Sister Agnes, she knew by her eyes and the little red wart she had on her forehead. And now 'twas day—clear, grey light was sifting into the room from the little glass window.

She had no great pain now—she was but wet through with sweat, woefully worn and weary, and her breast stung and smarted when she breathed. Greedily she drank down a soothing drink that Sister Agnes held to her mouth. But she was cold—

Kristin lay back on the pillows, and now she remembered all that had befallen the night before. The wild dream fantasies were wholly gone—her wits must have wandered a little, she understood—but 'twas good that she had got this thing done, had saved the little boy, and hindered these poor folk from burdening their souls with such a hideous deed. She knew she had need to be overjoyed—that *she* had been given grace to do this thing just before she was to die—and yet she could not rejoice as 'twas meet she should; 'twas more a quiet content she felt, as when she lay in her bed at home at Jörundgaard, tired out after a day's work well done. And she must thank Ulf too—

She had spoken his name, and he must have been sitting hidden away by the door, and have heard her, for here he came across the room and stood before her bed. She reached out her hand to him, and he took and pressed it in a firm clasp.

Suddenly the dying woman grew restless; her hands fumbled under the folds of linen about her throat.

"What is it, Kristin?" asked Ulf.

"The cross," she whispered, and painfully drew forth her father's gilded cross. It had come to her mind that yesterday she had promised to make a gift for the soul's weal of that poor Steinunn. She had not remembered then that she had no possessions on earth any more. She owned naught that she could give, saving the cross she had had of her father—and then her bridal ring. She wore that on her finger still.

She drew it off and gazed at it. It lay heavy in her hand; 'twas pure gold, set with great red stones. Erlend—she thought—and it came upon her now 'twere liker she should give this away—she knew not wherefore, but it seemed that she ought. She shut her eyes in pain and held it out to Ulf:

"To whom would you give this?" he asked, low, and as she did not answer: "Mean you I should give it to Skule—?"

Kristin shook her head, her eyes tight closed.

"Steinunn—I promised—masses for her—"

She opened her eyes, and sought with them the ring where it lay in the smith's dusky palm. And her tears burst forth in a swift stream, for it seemed to her that never before had she understood to the full what it betokened. The life that ring had wed her to, that she had complained against, had murmured at, had raged at and defied—none the less she had loved it so, joyed in it so, both in good days and evil, that not one day had there been when 'twould not have seemed hard to give it back to God, nor one grief that she could have forgone without regret—

Ulf and the nun changed some words that she could not hear, and he went from the room. Kristin would have lifted her hand to dry her eyes, but she could not—the hand lay moveless on her breast. And now the pain within was sore; her hand felt so heavy, and it seemed as though the ring were on her finger still. Her head began to grow unclear again—she *must* see if 'twere true that the ring was gone, that she had not only dreamed she had given it away —And now too she began to grow uncertain—all that had befallen last night: the child in the grave; the black sea with its swift little flashing waves; the corpse she had borne—she knew not whether she had dreamed it all or had been awake. And she had no strength to open her eyes.

"Sister," said the nun, "you must not sleep now—Ulf is gone to fetch a priest for you."

Kristin woke up fully again with a start, and fixed her eyes upon her hand. The gold ring was gone, that was sure enough—but there was a white, worn mark where it had been on her middle finger. It showed forth quite clearly on the rough brown flesh—like a scar of thin, white skin—she deemed she could make out two round spots on either side where the rubies had been, and somewhat like a little mark, an M, where the middle plate of gold had been pierced with the first letter of Mary Virgin's holy name.

And the last clear thought that formed in her brain was that she should die ere this mark had time to vanish—and she was glad. It seemed to her to be a mystery that she could not fathom, but which she knew most surely none the less, that God had held her fast in a covenant made for her without her knowledge by a love poured out upon her richly—and in despite of her self-will, in despite of her heavy, earthbound spirit, somewhat of this love had become *part* of her, had wrought in her like sunlight in the earth, had brought forth increase which not even the hottest flames of fleshly love nor its wildest bursts of wrath could lay waste wholly. A handmaiden of God had she been—a wayward, unruly servant, oftenest an eye-servant in her prayers and faithless in her heart, slothful and neglectful, impatient under correction, but little constant in her deeds—yet had he held her fast in his service, and under the glittering golden ring a mark had been set secretly upon her, showing that she was His handmaid, owned by the Lord and King who was now coming, borne by the priest's anointed hands, to give her freedom and salvation—

Soon after Sira Eiliv had given her the last oil and viaticum, Kristin Lavransdatter again lost the knowledge of all around. She lay in the sway of sore fits of blood-vomiting and burning fever, and the priest, who stayed by her, told the nuns that 'twas like to go quickly with her.

—Once or twice the dying woman came so far to herself that she knew this or the other face—Sira Eiliv's, the sister's—Lady

Ragnhild herself was there once, and Ulf too she saw. She strove to show she knew them, and that she felt 'twas good they should be by her and wished her well. But to those who stood around it seemed as she were but fighting with her hands in the throes of death.

Once she saw Munan's face—her little son peeped in at her through a half-open door. Then he drew back his head, and the mother lay gazing at the door—if perchance the boy might peep out again. But instead came Lady Ragnhild and wiped her face with a wet cloth; and that too was good—Then all things were lost in a dark red mist, and a roar, that first grew fearsomely; but then it died away little by little, and the red mist grew thinner and lighter, and at last 'twas like a fair morning mist ere the sun breaks through, and all sound ceased, and she knew that now she was dying—

Sira Eiliv and Ulf Haldorssön went out together from the room of death. In the doorway out to the cloister yard they stopped short—

Snow had fallen. None had marked it, of them who had sat by the woman while she fought with death. The white gleam from the steep church roof over against the two men was strangely dazzling; the tower shone white against the ash-grey sky. The snow lay so fine and white on all the window-mouldings, and all buttresses and jutting points, against the church's walls of grey hewn stone. And 'twas as though the two men lingered because they were loath to break with their footprints the thin coverlid of new-fallen snow.

They drank in the air. After the noisome smell that ever fills the sick-room of one pest-stricken, it tasted sweet—cool, and as it were a little thin and empty; but it seemed as though this snow-fall must have washed the air clean of all poison and pestilence—'twas as good as fresh spring water.

The bell in the tower began to ring again—the two looked up to where it swung behind the belfry bars. Small grains of snow loosened from the tower roof as it shook, rolled down, and grew to little balls—leaving spots where the black of the shingles showed through.

"This snow will scarce lie," said Ulf.

"No, 'twill melt, belike, before evening," answered the priest. There were pale golden rifts in the clouds, and a faint gleam of sunshine fell, as it were provingly, across the snow.

The men stood still. Then Ulf Haldorssön said low:

"I am thinking, Sira Eiliv—I will give some land to the church here—and a beaker of Lavrans Björgulfssön's that she gave me—to found a mass for her—and my foster-sons—and for him, Erlend, my kinsman—"

The priest answered as low, without looking at the man:

"—Meseems, too, you might think you had need to show your thankfulness to Him who led you hither yestereven—you may be well content, I trow, that 'twas granted you to help her through this night."

"Ay, 'twas that I thought of," said Ulf Haldorssön. Then he laughed a little: "And now could I well-nigh repent me, priest, that I have been so meek a man—towards her!"

"Bootless to waste time in such vain regrets," answered the priest.

"What mean you—?"

"I mean, 'tis but a man's sins that it boots him to repent," said the priest.

"Why so?"

"For that none is good saving God only. And we can do no good save of Him. So it boots not to repent a good deed, Ulf, for the good you have done cannot be undone; though all the hills should crash in ruin, yet would it stand—"

"Ay, ay. These be things I understand not, my Sira. I am weary—"

"Ay—and hungry too you may well be—you must come with me to the kitchen-house, Ulf," said the priest.

"Thanks, but I have no stomach to meat," said Ulf Haldorssön.

"None the less must you go with me and eat," said Sira Eiliv—he laid his hand on Ulf's sleeve and led him along with him. They went out into the courtyard and down towards the kitchen-house. Unwittingly, both men trod as lightly and charily as they could upon the new-fallen snow.

ETIENNE GILSON

ST. THOMAS AQUINAS

> The central intuition which governs the whole philo-
> sophical and theological undertaking of Saint Thomas
> is that it is impossible to do justice to God without
> doing justice to nature, and that doing justice to nature
> is, at the same time, the surest way of doing justice
> to God.

A HISTORIAN whose scholarship has been recognized by universities all over the world, Etienne Gilson (1884-   ) is at once an
erudite historian and an uncompromising philosopher. His honorary
degrees and awards are many and impressive, surpassed only by
the extraordinary number of his publications during the last forty
years. He has been elected to the Collège de France (1932) and,
more recently, to the French Academy (1947). Since 1929, except
for the war years, he has divided his time between Paris and
Toronto, where he helped to found the Institute of Mediaeval
Studies, and where he continues to serve as professor and director
of studies. During 1946-48 he was a member of the French Senate.

He has written books on St. Augustine, St. Bernard, St. Bonaventure, St. Thomas Aquinas, Descartes; he is the author of a
monumental history of mediaeval philosophy. His *Spirit of Mediaeval Philosophy* (1932) and *The Unity of Philosophical Experience*
(1937) have been particularly noted for the sweep of their vision
and judgment.

Gilson embarked upon the study of St. Thomas as a historian; but years of contact with the Angelic Doctor have turned the historian into a defender of the perennial wisdom of the thirteenth-century Dominican friar who stemmed the philosophical invasion of the Arabs, even as, centuries before, Charles Martel had stopped them on the field of battle.

HEN THE BRITISH ACADEMY INVITED ME TO GIVE a lecture on a master mind, the suggestion was made that Saint Thomas Aquinas be selected as a special subject. I felt equally inclined to accept the honour and to yield to the suggestion; for indeed there never was in my mind the slightest hesitation as to the full right of Saint Thomas to be called a master mind, nor was it until, having accepted the invitation, I tried to put my ideas in order, that I became aware of an unforeseen difficulty. That Saint Thomas Aquinas was a master mind, I knew, but what it was to be a master mind, I certainly did not know.

Now a poet, or even a literary critic, would be fully justified in lecturing on Shakespeare, for instance, without going to the trouble of defining what a master mind is. Whatever it may be, we are sure that Shakespeare was that, and it is enough for us to read him, in order to *feel* that he was a mind great among the greatest. But where we deal with a philosopher, the problem is different. He is not great by his aptness to impart pleasure through the perception of sense or the play of imagination, but by his power to disclose truth to our intellect: a truth which, heretofore, had remained hidden from it. And because the greatness of a philosopher lies in the order of understanding, we cannot even feel that he was a master mind, unless we first understand it.

In the case of Saint Thomas perhaps the simplest way to grasp the meaning of his work is to define the main problem his contemporaries had to solve, and to see how he solved it. Now nobody who is at all acquainted with modern history would question the fact that the Renaissance, for instance, or the eighteenth century, has been influential in shaping our modern civilization. Comparatively few people, on the contrary, are aware of that other fact, that the Middle Ages have been at least as effective in making us what we are, that is to say, in predetermining what are to-day our usual ways of acting, of feeling, and of thinking. Strangely enough, we would rather feel inclined to hold the opposite view, that to be modern means the contrary of being medieval. What is the truth about it?

In the first years of the eighth century, European civilization found itself in a very critical condition. We all remember that in earlier times Europe had been invaded by Arabian armies, and that after being defeated in 732 by Charles Martel near the French town of Poitiers, those armies had retreated towards Spain. The first historian I consulted upon the significance of that victory expresses himself thus: "It must remain one of the great events of the history of the world, as upon its issue depended whether Christian civilization should continue or Mohammedanism prevail throughout Europe." And that statement is undoubtedly correct. What Europe would be to-day if Charles Martel had lost the battle, I am not prepared to say; but one thing is certain, namely, that it would be something very different from what it actually is. An armed occupation of our countries by the troops of Abd-er-Rahman, had it lasted but two or three centuries, would have brought Spain, France, and eventually Great Britain under the sway of Mohammedan art, Mohammedan philosophy, and Mohammedan religion. Instead of belonging to countries where the usual ways of feeling, thinking, and acting have been moulded by the protracted influence of Christianity, we should today be the heirs of an essentially Mohammedan civilization. Not only our own history, but even that of our invaders themselves would have been changed. Those Mohammedan countries which are at present awakening to the value of Western civilization would not now find us to teach them, together with many useless or harmful things, the few useful lesssons they can learn from us. Without prophesying, even in regard to a past event, it is not an improbable supposition that an Arabian victory in 732 would have tremendously altered the course of European civilization.

It is even more than a mere supposition, since, despite Charles

Martel's victory and the final triumph of the Spanish kings, that same change very nearly came about. After the armed conflict had subsided on the battle-fields, another one burst out within the minds—a conflict upon whose issue, exactly as in the case of the first one, depended whether Europe should be Islamized or whether Christian civilization should prevail. The Arabian princes had not merely subjected Europe to a military occupation, they had brought with them their artists, their poets, their philosophers, and their theologians; established libraries, founded schools, and taught there, among many other things, a metaphysics technically far ahead of that which European scholars, up to that time, had been able to produce. Even after their final defeat by the Spanish kings, the Arabs gave to the world perhaps the greatest of their philosophers, since Averroes was born in Spain, taught and wrote, died and was buried in Spain, leaving behind him, though the spokesman of a defeated race, a work powerful enough to conquer its conquerors.

When the writings of Avicenna were translated into Latin in the twelfth century, and those of Averroes in the thirteenth, the Arabian peril became again as threatening as it had been at the time of Charles Martel. But where was the Charles Martel who would stop that second invasion? More than one tried it, and partly accomplished it, and partly failed. William of Auvergne in France; in England, Robert Grosseteste, Alexander of Hales, Roger Bacon, Adam of Marsh; Albertus Magnus in Germany; Saint Bonaventura and Matthew of Aquasparta in Italy, all of them engaged the fight or gallantly came to the rescue; let us add that all of them were helpful in preparing the victory, but one only had the glory of winning it, and his name was Thomas Aquinas.

It is but true to say that if Charles Martel and the Spanish kings had not won their victories on the battle-fields, Saint Thomas would never have had the opportunity of fighting his own battle; but it remains equally true to say that if he had not fought that battle, and won it, the work of those great soldiers would have been undone, their achievements brought to nothing. In every one of his main works, in practically all the countless lectures he delivered in Naples or in Paris, before students coming from all parts of civilized Europe to hear him, he bore the tremendous task of rescuing European civilization from the Mohammedan peril. When his forces left him, Thomas laid down his pen, and looking at the unfinished *Summa Theologica,* he said to his friend, brother Reginald: "It is to me as straw." And what else indeed could even the deepest treatise about God possibly be? But of that straw European civilization was going to make its bed.

What was Arabian philosophy? It was essentially a mixture of Greek neoplatonism and Mohammedan religious feeling. A detailed examination of those doctrines would undoubtedly bring to light many discrepancies, between their methods as well as their conclusions. The doctrine of Plotinus, for instance, which, through the so-called *Theology of Aristotle,* became the source of the whole movement, was not identical with that of Alkindi and Alfarabi; Algazel not infrequently disagrees with Avicenna, and, as a rule, Averroes disagrees with them both. Behind their oppositions, however, there remained a fundamental agreement on some essential principles, a likeness of purpose, a spiritual affinity.

In their doctrines, as in that of Plotinus, the First Principle is an eternal, necessary, self-thinking substance, whose contemplation is at the same time beatitude. As such, the First is by definition the One, but he contains within himself, as consequences are virtually included in the unity of their principle, all that which is intelligible. Such had already been the God of Aristotle, eternally living a life of self-contemplation, while a world which he has not created, and whose existence he does not even know, eternally revolves its spheres in a ceaseless effort to imitate the perfection of its cause. To pass from the Aristotelian conception of the world to that of Plotinus and his Arabian followers, we have but to suppose that the virtual multiplicity which is implied in the perfect unity of the divine contemplation, instead of remaining in that state of non-differentiation, actualizes itself, so to speak, outside of him. While God thinks, the world is. And yet God himself is not involved in the adventures of those things, which flow from his own perfection. A father of all that is, he does not even know that he has children; much more fittingly than to a father, he might be compared to a source, which ceaselessly pours forth its water, but does not know that it gives rise to a stream, to whose existence and course it remains indifferent.

Besides, how could such a world have adventures? It has not
even got a history! It has not been created in time by the conscious
decision of a divine will, but eternally and necessarily flows from
its cause. And not only the existence of things, but their essence,
and their very order of succession are necessary. After God comes
the first Intelligence from which emanates a second one, then the
soul and the body of the first heaven moved by that second Intelligence; then the third Intelligence with the soul and body of the
second heaven, and so on, until we come to the last and lowest of
these Intelligences, which eternally radiates its forms upon the matter and the souls of this sublunary world. Nothing there to suggest
the progressive unfolding of some history: the world eternally
expresses, under the form of a necessary deduction, a thought
which, in God, is an eternal and simple intuition.

In a world where necessity reigns supreme, what can be the particular lot of man? Man is body and soul, and his soul is endowed
with the strange power, not only to animate its body, which even
the soul of an animal or of a plant is able to do, but to acquire intellectual knowledge which resembles that of the separate Intelligences. Human nature is therefore a composite one; it lies on the
border line between the intelligible world and that of material substances; but since matter is the principle of individuation, we can
safely rule that our intellectual knowledges do not belong to us
as individuals. True enough, they are in us, but they cannot possibly
come from us as individuals, and for this reason did Avicenna decide that a separate Intelligence was the common active intellect of
all mankind. As an individual, each of us has nothing but a possible
intellect, which is enlightened from above and receives from the
universal active intellect a ready-made truth, provided only he be
fittingly prepared to receive it. But Averroes went still farther, and
on very good grounds. If intellectual knowledge cannot be caused
by an individual as such, one does not see why an individual as
such could even receive it. Hence the Averroistic doctrine of the
unity of the possible intellect. As an individual, every man is but
a fleeting thing, whose only function it is to represent, for a very
short time, the species to which it belongs; he does not know; he
does not even think; rather should we say that, while he lives, he is
being "thought in" by a separate Intelligence, having nothing of his

own but glimpses, or, more accurately, flashings of the eternal truth.

Now to the simple faith of a Christian such a world was both a scandal and an absurdity. Many centuries ago Saint Augustine had clearly shown that if God begets the Word, he did not beget the world: he created it. Having created it, and ever keeping it in being by a free decision of his will, he cannot ignore its existence, but rather leads it by the foreknowing and beneficent care of his providence towards its appointed end. In a world where five sparrows are sold for two farthings *and not one of them is forgotten before God,* how could we believe that individuals as such are of no importance? Even the very hairs of our head are numbered, and we are *of more value than many sparrows* (*Luke* xii, 6-7). Has not every one of us been known and foreseen by God from eternity? And not only foreseen, but singled out by his will among an infinity of other possible beings, that might have existed, and yet have not existed, do not exist, nor ever will? Nor is this all. Individually created and protected by God, man has been individually redeemed, that is to say: re-created by him. And at what a price! *I have given this one drop of my blood for thee.* In a world where each individual soul has received from Christ such a promise, how could man question the value of his own individuality?

We cannot then be surprised at the violence of the Christian reaction which followed the discovery of those Arabian philosophies. Christianity itself was at stake, and, with it, the future of Christian civilization. But if it was easy enough to show that the positions of Avicenna and Averroes were religiously wrong, it was much more difficult to prove that the contrary position was philosophically true. William of Auvergne, Alexander of Hales, Roger Bacon, Albertus Magnus, Bonaventura, all of them wanted to make clear that man is a complete substance in his own right, endowed with an immortal soul and an intellect of his own. But how could they prove it? Behind Avicenna and Averroes was Plotinus; and the same Plotinus was, as surely, behind every one of the Christian thinkers to whom they could apply for help. Saint Augustine had borrowed from him the elements of his own philosophy; Pseudo-Dionysius had done the same, and as to Scotus Eriugena, he had twice borrowed from Plotinus, through Augustine and through Pseudo-Dionysius. All they could do, therefore, was to borrow from their common adversary the very weapons they were trying to turn against him. Their position was very weak; the contest being ultimately Plotinus versus Plotinus, Plotinus had to win. He won, at least until Aquinas realized that something was wrong in such an attitude and changed it.

His master stroke was to go straight to the root of the difficulty. All Christian thinkers around him would agree that the world had been created by God, and yet they described it as if it had been begotten by a Greek God. The problem was therefore: What is the Christian God? What is it for him to create? What is it for things to be created? When Plotinus had tried to find a name for God such as he conceived him, the best he had been able to propose was: "He who is what he ought to have been" (that is to say: if, by an impossible supposition, he had not been); or again: "He who is what he had to be." Such a God is so completely determined by his very perfection that, as he could not be other than he is, so also he could not have done anything different from what he did. Not so with the Christian God of Saint Thomas. His name is not: "I am who I had to be," but, as He Himself once revealed to Moses: *I am that I am*. The God of St. Thomas is essentially Being in its absolute infinity; and because he is existence itself, he can give it to others, that is to say, he can create. But creation is not a natural process, it is a voluntary act, and since their causes are different in nature, a created world must needs be different from a begotten world. The Greek God naturally begets an order of necessary things; the Christian God, since he creates, must therefore have created an order of active, and, eventually, of free causes, each of which bears witness to the infinite generosity of its author.

Such is precisely the world of Saint Thomas Aquinas. It is a world of created causes, and since they are created they cannot create, but being causes they must be endowed with an efficiency of their own.

This conclusion is not only important in itself, it leads us to the central point where the true meaning of Thomism appears in full. Some critics have rejected its conclusions, on the ground that, being a theologian, Saint Thomas was bound to mix together philosophy and theology, nature and grace. They charge him with having done precisely what he always admonished his contemporaries not to do, namely, forgetting that if there were no nature, there would be no grace: *gratia praesupponit naturam*. At the same time, other critics (either Protestants as Luther, or Catholics as Malebranche) accuse him of having been so blindly indulgent to nature as to forget the fundamental principle of Christian theology. As a matter of fact, they reproach him with having lost sight of Christianity itself; a mistake which, excusable in a pagan philosopher, becomes a crime in a theologian whose proper function it is to maintain that nature depends upon God in all its operations.

Thus, while his first critics are blaming Aquinas for not having done what in reality he always did against the Augustinians, the others blame him for not having done what likewise he always did against the Averroists. Perhaps it is because he always tried to do justice to what was true on both sides; and this could not possibly be done except by refusing to grant what on both sides was wrong. He had therefore to go his own solitary way, which he is still doing among us, an object of aversion to the positivists, who suspect his theology, and to the fideists, who utterly dislike his reliance on philosophy. A dislike indeed which, in some cases, would be more fittingly described as hatred.

It may be the very nature of Thomism that makes those opposite reactions unavoidable. Saint Thomas thinks it quite right to maintain the existence and autonomy of a natural order; there must be a nature since there was a creation: but it is wrong to forget that, if it were not for the will of God, there would be no nature. In fact, nature depends upon God, both in its existence and in its operations. On the other hand, it would be just as wrong to extoll the rights of God at the expense of nature, since, in the long run, God's own glory would have to pay for it. If God wanted to produce by himself all that which we call natural effects, why should he have created a universe of things that seem to be causes, and are not? Would it be a wise thing to create useless beings, and to keep in existence such a monster as powerless causes would be, that is to say: causes that are not able to produce any effect? Far from being a credit to God, such a world would be an insult to the divine wisdom: *repugnat igitur prædicta positio divinae sapientiae*.

We should not therefore follow those Augustinians in their effort to depreciate the natural order. They try to prove that God is

Etienne Gilson

great by proving the smallness of his creation. It is bad apologetics. If we really want to prove that God is great, let us remember that our best chance to discover some proofs of his greatness is to look for them in the very structure of his creation. The effect of a good cause is always good; the effect of the most perfect of all causes must needs be excellent and represent, in a recognizable way, the perfection of its cause. Now what did God do when he created the world? An act of infinite generosity. He imparted to creatures, as far as created beings could receive it, something of his own perfection. Made after the likeness of such a cause, the world should then exhibit at least some elementary traces of the infinite generosity of its creator. This is what it does through causality. God, Saint Thomas says, "has imparted His own goodness to created things in such a way that each of them could transmit to the others what it had itself received. Consequently those who withdraw from things their own operations, do wrong to the goodness of God: *detrahere ergo actiones proprias rebus est divinæ bonitati derogare*" (*Cont. Gent.* iii. 69).

The central intuition which governs the whole philosophical and theological undertaking of Saint Thomas is, therefore, that it is impossible to do justice to God without doing justice to nature, and that doing justice to nature is, at the same time, the surest way of doing justice to God. When Saint Thomas says that, unless there be an order of really efficient causes, there can be no science, because there can be nothing left for the human mind to know, he certainly shows his desire to lay for science the most solid foundation possible: *et sic subtrahitur nobis ominis cognito scientiae naturalis* (*ibid*). And yet the same mental intuition which provides so solid a foundation for the sciences, provides, at the same time, the surest foundation for theology. As a man is known by what he does, so also is God; his creation is his natural revelation. Unless we know things, we shall never be able to know God; unless we know God, we are liable to be mistaken about the true nature of things. Had Averroes been more of a theologian, he would have been a better philosopher; let us add, with all due deference to him, that, great as he may be, if Augustine had been a better philosopher, he would have been a still greater theologian than he is. A perfect harmony between the demands of reason and those of the most exacting religious feeling, such is the secret of Saint Thomas. For the whole truth is indeed a whole, and it is as a whole that we must keep it, or lose it.

We are now in a better position to understand why the same theologian who never tired of extolling the glory of God was the first philosopher to discover, if not the dignity of human nature, at least the true nature of its dignity. His first move was to show how unreasonable it is to admit that God has created man as a rational being, without granting him those mental powers without which he could not possibly know. This was, in his age, a very bold step. Against the disciples of Avicenna and of Averroes, it implied the recognition of an individual intellect in every man; against the Augustinians, it led to the admission that since every man had an intellect of his own, he should be considered as the responsible maker of his own truth. This was precisely what the greatest among those Augustinians refused to admit, which only shows, I might say in an aside, that if hell is paved with good intentions, some ways to heaven may be paved with wrong means. Saint Bonaventura was busy with proving that God is the immediate cause of our true knowledge, the master who dwells and teaches within, the sun that shines upon the human intellect; in short, the true light that enlightens every man that comes into this world. Roger Bacon would rather say that all knowledge is a divine revelation; all knowledge —that is to say, not only theology, but also science and philosophy, which had formerly been taught by God to the Patriarchs and Prophets, forgotten by men, and have now to be recovered by them, under the guidance of Christian Wisdom. Even the immediate master of Saint Thomas, Saint Albertus Magnus, was convinced that all true knowledge, including that which bears on the natural order, is in us a special grace of God, for which we are indebted to the Holy Ghost.

It was the more difficult for Saint Thomas to question such doctrines, as they seemed to be inseparable from the deepest of all Christian feelings: that of the radical subordination of all things to God. But no less Christian and much more philosophically true was going to be the answer of Saint Thomas. Since every cause, in a created world, must be able to produce its own effects, and thereby to communicate to others what perfection it has itself received, the principle should first apply to the noblest of all created causes in this terrestrial world: the human intellect. We do not receive a ready-made truth from God, we make it, after gathering its elements from things: "Hence it is made manifest, that the knowledge of things in us is not caused through participation or through the influx of some actually intelligible forms subsisting in their own right, as the Platonists, and some others who followed them, averred, but the intellect comes by them from sensible things, by the intermediary of the senses" (*Comp. Theol.* i, chap. 83). True, the light by which we can abstract from things our concepts, and make them into necessary judgments, comes to us from God. Like Saint Augustine, Thomas can repeat with Saint John, that the Word is the true light that enlighteneth every man that cometh into this world; but it means to him that God has created in every one of us a natural light, namely reason itself, which is in us both a participation of, and a resemblance to, the divine light. God has created us capable of knowing; he maintains our being together with our intellect and its natural light, and in this sense it is true to say that we are indebted to him for every one of our intellectual operations, but that natural light, being a gift to us, becomes truly ours.

It now remains to be seen if Saint Thomas could win on that ground without losing on another. According to Aristotle and Averroes, men are individualized by their bodies, and such was their reason for refusing to grant every individual an intellect of his own. Being immaterial by definition, how could an intellect be at the same time individual? Hence their lack of appreciation of the value of individual human beings. Perhaps Averroes was wrong; at least, he was consistently wrong. Now it is a fact that Saint Thomas attempted to maintain the principle without granting the conclusion. He repeatedly says that matter is the principle of individuation, while adding not only that each intellect is individual, but that each individual is a permanent and stable being, endowed with a value of his own, quite distinct from that of the species to which he belongs. How can such contradictory statements be reconciled?

By showing that they really involve no contradictions. First of all, it is true that men are individualized by their bodies, but the human body truly deserves to be called such only while the soul animates and imparts life into it; it is a body because the soul actually confers upon it the being it possesses. Rather than saying: the soul is individualized by its body, let us say that our intellect builds up the individual body which it needs in order to actualize itself as a concrete individual being. Man is not a body *plus* a soul, but the union of both; and as he could not in this life have an intellect if he had not a body, so also he could not have a body if he had not an intellect. In such an intimate union neither of the integral parts can be conceived without the other, but it is the intellect, not the body, that gives to the whole its actual existence, its very being.

And there is more. Man is an individual by his body, but he is more than an individual, he is a person. Precisely because the form of his body is an intellect, the relation of soul and body is very different in man from what it is in any other animated being. Animals, even trees, are individuals, and they are such by their bodies, it being impossible that the matter of a certain animal body, or of a tree, should be at the same time numerically the same as that of another animal or another tree. But in their case the force that builds up those bodies spends its whole strength in producing them. In the case of man the living principle, before being an organic principle, is an intellect. It is, in fact, an intellect that builds to itself a body, because it needs it for its own intellectual operations. No concepts without sensations, no sensations without a body; here is why the human intellect *has* a body and *is* a soul. Such being the case, there is in man something far above the animating powers of his soul; an intellect which is an original principle of knowledge and of self-determination. Each of us is not only numerically distinct from the others, he is something that is unique in himself, an irreducible value, for which no other possible substitute could be conceived. What the old poet, William Dunbar, once said of your city:

O London, thou art of townes a per se!

can be said with much more truth of every one of us. In fact, if London is a *per se*, is it not because, as a human body is but the external manifestation of a personal life, this great city of yours shows forth something of the countless personal efforts which gave it its peculiar and even unique appearance? *Persona, per se*

una; wrong though it be, the etymology is very deep and better
than a good one. Person is not merely individual, it is *singular,*
as having properties or characters not shared by any other member
of the same species. For this reason, as Thomas Aquinas says, personality is the highest degree of reality: *Persona significat id quod
est perfectissimum in natura (Sum. Theol.* I, 29, 3).

Here, again, we are invited to witness the wonderful unity of his
philosophical discoveries and of his Christian feeling. The founding of modern personalism by Aquinas was both a complete declaration of the rights of man and a full acknowledgement of the
infinite generosity of the Christian God. When God said: *Let us
make man to our image, and likeness (Gen.* i, 26), he gave us to
understand that man has been established by him in a dignity than
which no higher can be found in nature. Man alone is endowed
with an intellect, which is the very root of his free will. A knowing
being and a free being, God could appoint him his vicar upon
earth, trust him with the management of that great frame in which
all things are contained. Below God, there was no room left for a
vice-creator, but there still was room for a vice-providence, and this
is exactly what man is. A providence to himself, since through his
knowledge and free will he is the responsible author of his own
destiny; but a providence to the rest of the world as well, since God
has given him *dominion . . . over the whole earth (Gen.* i, 26).
Nor was this merely a permission, it was a formal injunction: *Increase and multiply, and fill the earth, and subdue it (Gen.* i, 28).
God has therefore deliberately chosen to rely on man for the conduct of the world. *What is man, that Thou are mindful of him?*
To the question of the Psalmist (viii, 5), Aquinas readily answers
with Saint Paul: *Dei sumus adjutores;* we are the fellow-helpers of
God *(I Cor.* iii, 9); or else, with Pseudo-Dionysius: *Omnium
divinius est Dei cooperatorem fieri:* of all things the most divine is
to become the fellow-worker of God *(Coel. Hier.* c. iii).

Nothing could lead us farther from the fatalism of the Mohammedan world, or from the necessity of the Greek world. The world
of Saint Thomas is a truly Christian world, and such too is the
world in which, knowing it or not, we are still living to-day.

Whatever our philosophers and sociologists may choose to say
about it, we still believe that every man is a person in his own right,

invited by nature to decide what kind of a man he is going to be, and to shape his own self in his own way. We are constantly moulding ourselves, as an artist ceaselessly busies himself in completing his work, and always postpones giving it the final touch. As an artist, too, we sometimes make it better, and sometimes make it worse; what our final success will be we never know for sure until the last instant has arrived. Even then it is not for us to pass judgment on the ultimate value of our work: God alone can do it. The only thing we are sure of is that, good or bad, our life will then appear what we ourselves made it to be. No man is self-created, but, in the last resort, every man is a self-made man.

This human creed of ours we certainly would not hold today if, instead of Avicenna and Averroes, Saint Thomas had not become, directly or indirectly, the master of our minds; and better than anybody else, he still can prevent the civilization for which we are so largely indebted to him from becoming a total wreck. He had taught us that, as a person, man deserves to be considered by other men as an end in himself, never as a means to their own ends; by forgetting what a person is, we have come to deal with men as if they were naught but individuals. Now a society in which every individual is allowed to consider his own individuality as an ultimate value, seldom fails to bring about the triumph of selfishness and the systematic oppression of the weak. The so-called Liberalism of the previous generation was but a flattering name for that monster: a human society, not of persons, but of individuals. Against such a Liberalism the brutal reaction of the so-called "totalitarian State" was, if not justified, at least almost necessarily required. Its exponents have clearly seen that if men are nothing but individuals, they should not be allowed to form a society; they are a herd, and should be driven accordingly. But the totalitarian State is wrong when it forgets in its turn that if it is well founded in submitting the individuals to the exigencies of the common good, it has no jurisdiction whatsoever over persons. The State can tell us what to do, or what not to do, for the common good; it has no right to tell us what to think. If we do not want to be endlessly tossed between these two forms of the same mistake, the best thing for us to do is to steer the middle course of Thomas Aquinas: the middle course, not of some compromise, but of the hard and rigid truth between two errors.

If we were again to follow Aquinas, we should not indulge in any kind of individualism, because, as individuals, we are parts of a whole, and the common good of the whole is above the private interests of its members. But we would not either allow the State, that new Separate Substance which does not always act as an Intelligence, to forget that there is in every one of us something that is even above the State: a person, higher than which there is nothing but God. Assuredly, the man who first stated in their fullness those ever timely principles was more than a master mind; he was, and still remains, the master whose proper mission it is to uphold among us, against all adverse forces, the supremacy of the mind.

JACQUES MARITAIN

WHO IS MY NEIGHBOUR?
(from *Ransoming the Time*)

> We hold that every man of good faith and right will,
> provided he does not sin against the light and does
> not refuse the grace interiorly offered to him, belongs,
> as we put it, to the Soul of the Church, or, in other
> words, is invisibly and by the motion of his heart a
> member of the visible Church and partakes of her life,
> which is eternal life.

JACQUES MARITAIN (1882-   ) became a Catholic in 1905. From the first publication of his book on Bergson (1913) until, in the midst of his duties as French Ambassador to the Holy See, he published his *Existence and the Existent* (1948), he has been a flaming center of Thomism in the modern world. He has loved truth with the passionate and anxious fidelity characteristic of great men; he has been devoted to the cause of the human person, his dignity and his liberty, with a love which is nothing short of heroic. His philosophy, while remaining fully autonomous, has been open to the light of faith and the warmth of charity, to the experience and lessons of the past as well as to the needs and problems of the present. Yet the present in which Maritain lives is not a narrow *now*: it is a present in which, being turned toward God and toward his fellow man in God, he sees the world of time bathed in the mysterious splendors of eternity.

He has been a prolific writer. Of his many books mention must be made of a veritable philosophical *summa, The Degrees of Knowing* (1932); *Integral Humanism* (1936); *Science and Wisdom* (1935); *Ransoming the Time* (1941). He has left few aspects of the modern world and its problems untouched. His many controversies show how little he lives in the clouds inhabited by so many philosophers. The following essay, one of the most magnificent that Maritain has written, is an enduring statement of the foundations of human solidarity.

THE PROBLEM I SHOULD LIKE TO CONSIDER IN this chapter is a very difficult one, but it is of vital importance. I think that there is a decided advantage for us in courageously facing this problem, and becoming aware of its reality, even if we are unable to do much more. The question is to determine whether the diversity of religious creeds, an evident historical fact, is an insurmountable obstacle to human co-operation.

Surely it is a paradox that despite the state of religious division in which mankind lives, good fellowship, brotherly intercourse and a spirit of union can be established between men in the earthly commonwealth, while each of them is bound to his God and is attached with all his heart to his faith in Him and to the form of worship he renders Him. But man himself is a paradox. And more astonishing still appears the "exceeding great love" of Him who loved us first and whose very predilections work for the welfare of all.

Nothing in history, indeed, goes to show that religious feeling or religious ideas have been particularly successful in pacifying men. Religious differences seem rather to have fed and sharpened their conflicts. And yet, if it is true that human society must bring together in the service of the same terrestrial common good men belonging to different spiritual families, how can the peace of that temporal society be lastingly assured if first in the domain that matters most to the human being—in the spiritual and religious domain itself—relationships of mutual respect and mutual under-standing cannot be established? I prefer the word fellowship to "tolerance," for it connotes something positive—positive and elementary—in human relationships. It conjures up the image of travelling companions, who meet here below by chance and journey through life—however fundamental their differences may be—good humouredly, in cordial solidarity and human agreement. Well, then, for the reasons I have just mentioned, the problem of good fellowship between the members of the various religious families sems to me to be a cardinal one for the new age of civilization, the rough outlines of which are beginning to take shape in our present night. I should like to quote in this connection the words pro-nounced by Pope Pius XII at his coronation: "Our thoughts go out also in this solemn moment to all those who are outside the Church and who, we should like to think, will rejoice to learn that the Pope prays to Almighty God for them also and wishes them every possible good."

A deliberate attempt to bring closer together the believers of the various religious families is something relatively new. On a solemn occasion, Pope Pius XI called upon all men of good will to such an attempt. No doubt this attempt is partly due to the im-minent dangers, to the spiritual evils threatening us: open atheism publicly warring against God, or pseudo-theism seeking to turn the living God into some protecting genius for the State or some demon of the race. If that is so, we must admit that it is a stern lesson for believers. Was it needful that God permit the frightful degradation of mankind that we are witnessing today, so many per-secutions and so much suffering, to teach those who believe in Him to go down into the real depth of their own hearts, even into those mysterious regions where we more or less faintly hear the hand of the God of love knocking at our bolted doors?

Let me say immediately that this attempt at rapprochement might easily be misunderstood. I shall therefore begin by clearing the ground of any possible sources of misunderstanding. Such a rap-prochement obviously cannot be effectuated at the cost of straining fidelity, or of any yielding in dogmatic integrity, or of any lessening of what is due to truth. Nor is there any question whatever either of agreeing upon I know not what common minimum of truth or of subjecting each one's convictions to a common index of doubt. On the contrary, such a coming together is only conceivable if we assume that each gives the maximum of fidelity to the light that is shown to him. Furthermore, it obviously can only be pure, and therefore valid and efficacious, if it is free from any *arrière-pensée* of a temporal nature and from even the shadow of a tendency to subordinate religion to the defense of any earthly interest or acquired advantage.

I am sure that everyone is agreed on these negative conditions I have just enumerated. But one aspect of the paradox I mentioned at the outset is that, as soon as we pass on to positive considerations, each one sees the very justification and the very reason for being of this good fellowship between believers of different religious families mirrored in his own particular outlook and in his own world of thought. And these outlooks are irreducibly heterogeneous, these worlds of thought never exactly meet. Until the day of eternity comes, their dimensions can have no common measure. There is no use closing one's eyes to this fact, which simply bears witness to the internal coherence of the systems of signs, built up in accordance with different principles, on which human minds depend for their cognitive life. Fundamental notions such as that of the absolute oneness of God have not the same meaning for a Jew as for a Christian; nor has the notion of the divine transcendence and incommunicability the same meaning for a Christian as for a Moslem; nor the notions of person, of freedom, grace, revelation, incarnation, of nature and the supernatural, the same meaning for the Orient as for the Occident. And the "non-violence" of the Indian is not the same as Christian "charity." No doubt it is the privilege of the human intelligence to understand other languages than the one it itself uses. It is none the less true that if, instead of being men, we were patterns of Pure Ideas, our nature would be to devour each other in order to absorb into our own world of thought whatever other such worlds might hold of truth.

But it happens that we are men, each containing within himself the ontological mystery of personality and freedom; in each of us the abyss of holiness of the Supreme Being is present with His universal presence, and He asks to dwell there as in His temple, by manner of a gift of Himself to us. Well, each one must speak in accordance with his outlook. I suppose there are readers of this book who do not share my own creed. I shall try to tell them as briefly, but also as frankly and as precisely as possible—and this frankness is itself one of the characteristics of mutual confidence— how the paradox of fellowship I am at present examining can be solved for me, a Catholic, from the point of view of a philosophy which takes into account the data of Christian theology. I do not apologize for this excursion into the field of theology, it is required by the subject I am discussing.

The Catholic doctrine concerning the status of non-Catholics before God

IT IS well known that, according to the Catholic Faith, God, after having spoken in various and imperfect ways through the prophets, spoke once and for all, in a perfect and final manner, through His own uncreated Word, who took flesh in the womb of a virgin of Israel in order to die for mankind. And that the deposit of this revelation of the Word of God was confided to a living and visible body, made up both of just men and of sinners, but specially assisted by the Spirit of God in its mission of truth and salvation. Thus authority plays a most important part for Catholics. But apart from dogmas and their connected truths and apart from the discipline of salvation, freedom plays a big part also, and the diversity of opinions in human affairs is far greater in the Catholic Church than is generally realized by those not in it. I know that the teaching of the Church can deal with every matter connected with faith; but in being integrally mindful of this teaching, I can still disagree most sharply with other Catholics about political or social matters: democracy, trade unionism, the late war in Spain or the second World War, as well as about philosophical or historical questions. This is because it is only to the purity and integrity of the Word of God that the faithful are bound as such; the teaching authority of the Church intends of itself only to safeguard this living deposit of truth, just as the disciplinary authority of the Church has no other object than to enable the faithful to live by that truth. It is to the First Truth in person, speaking to my heart, that I adhere by means of the statements of dogma that bring the revelation to all. As a

Catholic and by my Catholic Faith, I am bound in conscience to
no human, theological or philosophical opinion, however well
founded it may be, and still less to any judgments on contingent or
worldly matters, or to any temporal power. Nor am I bound to
any particular form of culture or civilization, and still less of race
or blood. I am bound uniquely to what is universality itself and
superuniversality: to the Divine, to the words and precepts of Him
who said, *I am the Truth, I who speak to you.*

That in brief is how the Catholic outlook appears to me. Catholic
theology teaches that it is upon our love, as Saint John of the Cross
says, that we shall be judged; in other words, that salvation and
eternal life depend on charity. It teaches that charity presupposes
faith and has its root in faith, in other words, in truth divinely revealed. It teaches that *explicit* faith in Christ, illuminating the human mind regarding the inmost secrets of divine truth and life, is
not only the requisite means for souls to attain the highest degree
of conformity with God and divine union, and a prerequisite for
peoples to achieve a firm position of general morality and perfectly
human civilization, but that that faith is also the response of reverence justly due to God's gift, inclining His glory toward us. Explicit
faith in revealed truth, therefore, is the first duty of everyone who
is not incapable of hearing through his ears and in his heart the
word of God. But Catholic theology adds that faith together with
grace are offered to all souls, even if they are unable to know the
truth explicitly in its integrity. If those souls are in good faith and
do not refuse the internal grace offered to them, they have *implicit*
faith in Christ and accept implicitly the entire divinely revealed
truth, even if they only believe, having no clearer light, that God
exists and saves those who seek Him.[1] (And God knows much
better than do they themselves whether they believe that.)

If, therefore, Catholics hold that there is no salvation outside the
Church, you can see that this maxim can shock only those who
understand it wrongly and who are ignorant of what is commonly
taught concerning the "soul of the Church." All it means to us is
that there is no salvation outside the Truth, which, explicitly or
implicitly, is freely offered to all. And does that not seem fully in
harmony with the nature of man and his essential dignity? Surely

[1] Cf. *Heb.* xi, 6.

if there were salvation outside the Truth, I should not want such a salvation, for I prefer the Truth to my own joy and freedom; or rather I know that only the Truth can give me real joy and set me free.

We believe that there is no salvation outside the Truth, and the fact that all men do not explicitly know the Truth, the fact of religious division, far from being a good in itself, is a mark of the distress of our condition. But we also hold, as I have just explained, that the Truth speaks to every man's heart; and God alone knows who those are, in whatever part of the world they may be born and whether or not they live under the régime of His publicly revealed word, who truly and efficaciously hear His interior and secret word. We believe that there is no salvation outside Christ, but we also believe that Christ died for all men and that the possibility of believing in Him—either explicitly or implicitly—is offered to all. We believe that there is no salvation outside the Mystical Body of Christ, but we also believe that those who visibly belong to that Body by confessing the faith and by the sacraments, and are thus designated to continue in time the work of redemption and receive more generous effusions of the vehicles of grace, are not its only members. We hold that every man of good faith and right will, provided he does not sin against the light and does not refuse the grace interiorly offered to him, belongs, as we put it, to the Soul of the Church, or, in other words, is invisibly and by the motion of his heart a member of the visible Church and partakes of her life, which is eternal life. And no man, withal, whether Christian or non-Christian, can know whether he is worthy of love or of hatred.

Catholics are sometimes reproached with speaking to others in a domineering or patronizing manner. Human weakness being what it is, that may well be the case with some. Yet in reality, their position is far from being a comfortable one. They are twice wounded, with the wounds of their faults and with the requirements of their God. Not only does their reason show them that other religions can also transmit to mankind many great truths, although in their eyes incomplete or mixed—and on occasion, if it is a question of certain techniques of natural spirituality or of psycho-physical mastery of self—certain truths which the Gospel did not take pains to teach. But what is more important still, they see that, through the very

supernatural truth which they have received—not as a monopoly
but as something to give to others—men belonging to other spiritual families, even poor idolaters, can, if they are of good faith
and if their hearts are pure, live better than some members of their
own religious family. And who would not lose heart, if he were
not helped by grace! The tree bends, says Saint Thomas Aquinas,
under the fullness of its fruit. The Church rejoices over the testimony she is required to give, and the Christian rejoices in her.
She knows that it is a bounden duty to acknowledge the holy reality
of privileges received. For the divine freedom gives as it pleases to
whomever it pleases. But, as Saint Paul puts it, it is in a fragile
vessel that each faithful soul contains grace. That he should have
on his pitiable human shoulders some measure of the burden of
divine truth in no way justifies the believer in being supercilious
or patronizing; rather he feels inclined to excuse himself and to
ask forgiveness of every passer-by. *Euntes ibant et flebant;* going,
they went and wept. I know well that there are men—and it is perhaps to make up for their little practical faith—who despise others
and ceaselessly repeat: we believers, we respectable people, we
Christians, we Catholics, at times even we "born" Catholics, as if
they were not born sinners like everyone else. They never suspect
that, by thus placing their pride in evidence of their religion, they
make those who see them want to blaspheme the Almighty.

The basis of good fellowship among men of different creeds,
considered on the spiritual level

TO RETURN to the question of the fellowship of believers. I think
it is clear what the basis of such a fellowship is in the Catholic outlook. This basis is not of the order of the intellect and of ideas, but
of the heart and of love. It is friendship, natural friendship, but
first and foremost mutual love in God and for God. Love does not
go out to essences nor to qualities nor to ideas, but to persons; and
it is the mystery of persons and of the divine presence within them
which is here in play. This fellowship, then, is not a fellowship of
beliefs, but the fellowship of men who believe.

The conviction each of us has, rightly or wrongly, regarding the
limitations, deficiencies, errors of others does not prevent friendship

between minds. In such a fraternal dialogue, there must be a kind
of forgiveness and remission, not with regard to ideas—ideas deserve no forgiveness if they are false—but with regard to the condition of him who travels the road at our side. Every believer knows
very well that all men will be judged—both himself and all others.
But neither he nor another is God, able to pass judgment. And
what each one is before God, neither the one nor the other knows.
Here the "Judge not" of the Gospels applies with its full force.
We can render judgment concerning ideas, truths or errors; good
or bad actions; character, temperament, and what appears to us
of a man's interior disposition. But we are utterly forbidden to
judge the innermost heart, that inaccessible center where the person day after day weaves his own fate and ties the bonds binding
him to God. When it comes to that, there is only one thing to do,
and that is to trust in God. And that is precisely what love for our
neighbour prompts us to do.

There are some people who do not like that word, "love." It
embarrasses them, because it has become hackneyed, and because we
hear it as well from lips that have gone to rot, or from hearts that
worship themselves. God is not so squeamish. The Apostle John
tells us that God is self-subsisting Love.

There is only one proper and fitting way through which peace
and union can come to men, and that is through love: first, love
springing from nature for beings—for those poor beings who have
the same essence as we have ourselves, and the same sufferings, and
the same natural dignity. But that love is not enough, for the roots
of strife are too strong for it. There must be a love of higher origin,
immediately divine, which Christian theology calls supernatural, a
love in God and for God, which both strengthens in their proper
sphere our various inclinations toward one another in the natural
order, and also transcends them to infinity. Charity is very different
from that simple human benevolence which philosophers praise,
which is noble indeed in itself, yet inefficacious in the end. Charity
alone, as Bergson observed in his great book, *The Two Sources of
Morality and Religion,* can open the heart to the love of *all men,*
because, coming from God who first loves us, charity desires for
all men the same divine good, the same eternal life, as it does for

ourselves, and it sees in all human beings the summoned of God,
streaming, as it were, with the mysteries of His mercy and the
prevenient gifts of His goodness.

I should like to dwell a moment on the inner law and the privileges of this friendship of charity, as regards precisely the relations
between believers of different religious denominations (as well as
between believers and non-believers). I have already made it sufficiently clear that it is wrong to say that such a friendship *transcends dogma* or exists *in spite of* the dogmas of faith. Such a view
is inadmissible for all those who believe that the word of God is as
absolute as His unity or His transcendence. I know very well that if
I lost my faith in the least article of revealed truth, I should lose
my soul. A mutual love which would be bought at the price of faith,
which would base itself on some form of syncretism or eclecticism,
or which, recalling Lessing's parable of the three rings, would
say: "I love him who does not have my faith because, after all, I
am not sure that my faith is the true faith and that it bears the
device of the true ring," in so saying would reduce faith to a mere
historic inheritance and seal it with the seal of agnosticism and
relativity. Such a love, for anyone who believes he has heard the
word of God, would amount to putting man above God.

That love which is charity, on the contrary, goes first to God, and
then to all men, because the more men are loved in God and for
God, the more they are loved themselves and in themselves. Moreover this love is born in faith and necessarily presupposes faith,
at least the implicit faith I mentioned earlier. And it remains within
faith, while at the same time reaching out to those who have not
the same faith. That is the very characteristic of love; wherever our
love goes, it carries with it our faith.

Nor does the friendship of charity merely make us recognize the
existence of others—although as a matter of fact here is something
already difficult enough for men, and something which includes
everything essential. Not only does it make us recognize that another exists, and not as an accident of the empirical world, but as
a human being who exists before God, and has the right to exist.
While remaining within the faith, the friendship of charity helps
us to recognize whatever beliefs other than our own include of truth

and of dignity, of human and divine values. It makes us respect them, urges us on ever to seek in them everything that is stamped with the mark of man's original greatness and of the prevenient care and generosity of God. It helps us to come to a mutual understanding of one another. It is not supradogmatic; it is suprasubjective. It does not make us go beyond our faith, but beyond ourselves. In other words it helps us to purify our faith of the shell of egotism and subjectivity in which we instinctively tend to enclose it. And it also inevitably carries with it a sort of heart-rending, attached, as is the heart, at once to the truth we love and to the neighbour who is ignorant of that truth. This condition is even associated with what is called the "ecumenical" bringing together of divided Christians; how much more is it associated with the labour of bringing into mutual comprehension believers of every denomination.

I distrust any friendship between believers of all denominations which is not accompanied, as it were, by a kind of compunction or soul's sorrow—which would be easy and comfortable; just as I distrust any universalism which claims to unite in one and the same service of God, and in one and the same transcendental piety—as in some World's Fair Temple—all forms of belief and all forms of worship. The duty of being faithful to the light, and of always following it to the extent that one sees it, is a duty which cannot be evaded. In other words the problem of conversion, for anyone who feels the spur of God, and to the extent that he is pricked by it, cannot be cast aside, any more than can be cast aside the obligation of the apostolate. And by the same token I also distrust a friendship between believers of the same denomination which is, as it were, easy and comfortable, because in that case charity would be reserved to their fellow-worshippers, there would be a universalism which would limit love to brothers in the same faith, a proselytism which would love another man only in order to convert him and only in so far as he is capable of conversion, a Christianity which would be the Christianity of *good* people as against *bad* people, and which would confuse the order of charity with what a great spiritual writer of the seventeenth century called a policeforce order.

The co-operation of men of different creeds, considered at the temporal level

IT FOLLOWS from what I have said that from the Catholic point of view (which is mine) a rapprochement between believers of diverse religious denominations can be accomplished, on the religious and spiritual level itself, only by and in friendship and charity, by and in the pure spirituality and freedom of love. It cannot in any way involve any less intangible, more definite, more visible communion, expressed in the order of the speculative and practical intellect by some community of symbol or of sacred ritual. But on the level of the temporal and profane life (and that is indeed quite another level) it is proper that the effort toward union should express itself in common activities, should be *signed* by a more or less close co-operation for concrete and definite purposes, whether it be a question of the common good of the political community to which we all respectively belong, or of the common good of temporal civilization as a whole.

No doubt in that field it is not as believers but rather as members of a given fatherland, as men bound together by customs, traditions, interests and particular outlooks of a fleshly community, or as men having in common a given concrete historical ideal, that believers belonging to different religions are called upon to do a common work. But even in that common temporal task, ethical and spiritual values are involved, which concern the believer as such. And in that common temporal task itself, the mutual good will and fellowship I have been discussing remain factors of primary importance (I say primary; I do not say sufficient) for the pacification of men. In this sphere of temporal and political life, the most suitable phrase is not the phrase *love of charity,* but rather *civic friendship,* which is a virtue of the natural order, that must, however, be leavened by charity. It is a great pity that in an agonized world, men who believe in the supernatural, enchained as they are by so many sociological prejudices, should be so slow to broaden their hearts and to co-operate boldly in order to save from the inheritance of their fellows the elementary values of threatened humanity. From the English *Blue Book* anyone may learn about the atrocities and abominations committed in Nazi concentration camps, which blaspheme the image of God in the human person. But why were these things, that the British Government had known very well for many years, published only when war had already broken out? Anyone may also discover for himself the similar degradation of the human person practiced in Soviet prisons and concentration camps or during the persecution of the Kulaks. If a true feeling for justice and friendship had, at the appropriate time, brought into play the firm intervention of free peoples against such indignities—not by war, but by normal political or economic pressure and for aims purely and truly disinterested—in place of their seeking business accommodations with butchers, maybe the world could have avoided today's dreadful convulsions.

It is impossible to exaggerate the vital importance, so little understood by the sectarian liberalism of the nineteenth century and by the paganism of the present, of the spirit of friendship in human society. Perhaps by force of contrast the extreme sufferings and the terrible conflicts that men are undergoing today will at least have the effect of awakening in a goodly number of them a feeling for friendship and co-operation.

The cruel anomaly with which we are concerned here lies in the fact that historically, as I have pointed out, religion seems to have done as much to divide men and sharpen their conflicts as it has to pacify them. This anomaly is linked with what is deepest in man's nature. If man is not drawn above himself toward eternal values, he becomes less than human; and when he makes use of these eternal values for the sake of his own world of weakness and sin, he uses them to feed and strengthen, and to hallow his passions and malice. To this contradictory situation there is only one key; that key is charity. Religion, like everything great and noble and demanding within us, increases the tension in mankind; and together with the tension, suffering; and with the suffering, spiritual effort; and with the spiritual effort, joy. *Tantum relligio potuit suadere malorum* (So much evil could religion precipitate) said Lucretius of old in a formula after all amphibological. He should have added, and how necessary also is it to the very breath of humanity! And what great good it has been able to call forth, what hopes and virtues it has been able to inspire! Nothing that has been done through the substance of the centuries has been lastingly useful to human beings without religion, at least without religion in its purest forms.

It is not religion that helps to divide men and sharpen their conflicts; it is the distress of our human condition and the interior strife in our hearts. And without religion we should certainly be far worse than we are. We see today how, when man rejects the sacred traditions of humanity and aspires either to free himself from religion by atheism, or to pervert religion by deifying his own sinful blood through a kind of racist pseudo-theism or para-theism, the darkest forms of fanaticism then spread throughout the world. Only by a deeper and purer religious life, only by charity, is it possible to surmount the state of conflict and opposition produced by the impact of religion upon human weakness. To bring to an end all fanaticism and all pharisaism will require, I believe, the whole of human history. But it is the task of the religious conscience itself to overcome these evils. It alone is capable of doing so. It is the religious conscience which, by spiritualizing itself in suffering, must gradually rid itself and the world of the leaven of the pharisees and the fanaticism of the sectarians.

I believe that when we think of all these things, we better perceive the dramatic greatness of our time. As has often been pointed out, a certain unification of the world is taking place on the subhuman level of matter and technique, whereas on the human level itself, the most savage conflicts come into being. In an apocalyptic upheaval, which imperils the very foundations of life, the advent of men to a new age of civilization is thus being prepared, which doubtless will indicate not only an historical transformation of great importance, for good as well as for evil, in the forms of consciousness and culture, but also the coming of a higher state of unity and integration. In the meantime—and it is this which lies at the root of our unhappiness—technical progress has outstripped the mind, matter has gone faster than spirit. And that leaves to those who would hope—I am among them—only one hope: hope in a heroic effect of spiritualization thanks to which all progress in the material and technical order—a progress we must utilize, not condemn— can at last serve to effect a real progress in the emancipation of the human being.

All this is to say that the world itself is serving men an awful summons, and this summons is primarily addressed to those who are believers. The future will be good neither for the world nor for religion unless those who believe understand what is first and foremost required of them. If those very men who wear the insignia of the spirit allow their souls to become subject to those forces of destruction which desperately set evil against evil, and if they enlist religion—even, as some may say, in its own interest—in any undertaking whatever of domination and violence, I think that the disaster for civilization will be irreparable. What is required of believers at the outset and before everything else, even in the struggles of this world, with all the harsh means they imply, is not to dominate but to serve. It is to preserve among men confidence in good will, in the spirit of co-operation, in justice, in goodness, in pity for the weak and the outcast, in human dignity and in the power of truth. These are big words, but it is not enough to let them remain words; they must be made flesh in our lives. If we speak the truth without *doing it,* we run the risk of leading men to regard truth as an imposture. It has been said again and again in recent times, and rightly, that the believer is specially called upon to confess his God in social and temporal life, in the hard work of men. Many things which he accepts today in the earthly state of his fellows and in the conditions of human societies, will appear later to be as little worthy of acceptance as now appears to us the slavery of antiquity. The tragedy of unemployment, the tragedy of the refugee and the émigré, the tragedy of war, are symptoms of a deep disorder which we must work tirelessly to remedy.

Undoubtedly the world needs bread. It is horrible to think that there are so many millions of men on this earth who cannot satisfy their hunger. But what the world needs also and above all are the words that come from the mouth of God, words of active truth, of effective and fertile truth; it needs—I do not say solely or exclusively, but I do say primarily—the contemplation of the saints, their love and activity. And from us who are not saints it needs that in the patient insignificant acts of our everyday life, and in our social and political activities, each of us should faithfully witness, according as his state of life permits, the love of God for all beings and the respect due to the image of God in each human creature.

The analogical similarities in basic principles and ideas required for the co-operation of men of different creeds in the temporal order

THERE is still one question about which, in conclusion, I should like to say something. In the first part of this chapter, I emphasized the fact that religious division creates for believers of different denominations a fundamental plurality of points of view, and I drew attention to the illusion of seeking for the basis and purpose of good fellowship in a common minimum of doctrinal identity— a common minimum which would be seen gradually to shrink to nothing while we discussed it, like the wild ass's skin in Balzac's story.

Yet on the other hand I have just said that this fellowship, based on friendship and charity, should extend, on the level of temporal civilization, to common action (doubtless not free from a certain amount of inevitable opposition and conflict); that it should extend real cooperation for the good of temporal society. But how can such common action be possible without common principles, without a certain basic community of doctrine?

Before passing to more concrete considerations, I shall first answer this question in my own philosophical language. We are all bound together by a more primitive and fundamental unity than any unity of thought and doctrine: we all have the same human nature and, considered in their extra-mental reality, the same primordial tendencies. That sameness of nature is not sufficient to ensure community of action, since we act as thinking beings and not simply by natural instinct. But it subtends the very exercise of our thought. And the nature we hold in common is a rational nature, subject intellectually to the attraction of the same fundamental objects; this unity of nature lies at the deepest foundation of what similarities our principles of action may have, however diverse they may be in other respects. Now, in order to do the same terrestrial work and pursue the same temporal goal, there must be a *certain community* of principles and doctrine. But there need not necessarily be—however desirable and obviously more effective this might be in itself—a strict and pure and simple *identity* of doctrine. It is sufficient that the various principles and doctrines between themselves should have some unity and community of similarity or proportion or, in the technical sense of the word, of *analogy,* with regard to the practical end proposed. Besides, this practical end in itself, although subordinated to a higher end, belongs to the natural order. And no doubt it will be conceived differently according to each one's particular outlook; but in its existential reality it will be placed outside each one's particular conception. Considered thus, in real existence, it will in a measure fall short of, and, at the same time, give actual reality to, each one's particular conceptions.

Therefore, men with different religious convictions will be able not only to collaborate in working out a technique, in putting out a fire, in succouring a man who is starving or sick, in resisting aggression. All that is obvious. But—and this is the problem that concerns us here—if there really is that "analogical" likeness I have just mentioned between their principles, they can also cooperate—at least as regards the primary values of existence in this world —in a constructive action involving the right ordering of the life of temporal society and earthly civilization and the moral values inherent therein. I acknowledge this possibility at the same time— and the two things are not incompatible—as I realize even more keenly my personal conviction that a complete doctrine, based on all principles of Catholic teaching, is alone capable of supplying an entirely true solution for the problems of civilization.

I shall give an example of what I mean from the field I know best, namely Western Christianity, and an example which relates to the religious life itself. The practical problems connected with the relationship between the spiritual and the temporal, and their practical solutions, are so much alike for the Orthodox Church in the Soviet Union, for the Catholic Church and Protestant communities in Germany, that the experience and testimony of believers belonging to these different Christian families are, with their sufferings, a kind of common property. Another example can be drawn from the practical convergence which appears today, in connection with questions of civilization and the defense of the human person, between speculative outlooks as incompatible as Karl Barth's and my own. A Thomist and a Barthian will always clash in theology and philosophy; they can work together within human society.

But we must be even more precise. I have said that the basis of fellowship between believers of different spiritual families is friendship and the love of charity. I now add that it is the implications of love itself that supply us with the guiding idea we need and that make manifest for us the "analogical" likeness of practical thought I referred to earlier.

It is obvious in fact that, if I am right in what I have said, the primary and fundamental likeness between us is the acknowledgment of the fundamental and primordial ethical value of the law of brotherly love, however much this law may have different theological and metaphysical connotations for us, according to the religion or school of thought to which we belong. For the Christian it corresponds to and raises to divine levels a fundamental though terribly thwarted tendency of our nature. It is the second commandment, which forms but one with the first: the commandment to love our neighbour as ourselves. "I feel," wrote Gandhi in a note on the *Satyagraha* in 1920, "that nations cannot be one in reality, nor can their activities be conducive to the common good of the whole humanity, unless there is this definite recognition and acceptance of the law of the family in national and international affairs, in other words, on the political platform. Nations can be called civilized, only to the extent that they obey this law." [2] That, I also believe, is the truth.

Now this very law of brotherly friendship in practice has many implications. The first truth it implies, and which underlies all the rest, is that our existence is directed towards God and that, in accordance with the first commandment, we must love God above everything. How indeed can the law of love have *absolute* value, transcending all the conflicts and discords which flourish among men, unless all men, whatever their race or colour, their class, their nation, their social conditions, their natural shortcomings, receive from an Absolute above the world the bond creating between them a more fundamental and far-reaching communion than all their diversities, and unless they are created to love first and foremost this Absolute in which all things live and move and have their being? We see only too readily that, in the great contemporary

[2] Report of the Commissioners appointed by the Punjab Subcommittee of the Indian National Congress, 1920, Vol. I, Chap. 4.

movements in which God is in practice denied, whether by virtue of an atheism that refuses to admit His existence or by virtue of a pseudo-theism that blasphemes His nature, love and charity are alike rejected as weaknesses and as the worst enemies either of the State or of the Revolution. The theorists of these movements make that abundantly clear in their writings.

The second implication is on the one hand the holiness of truth and on the other hand the eminent value of good will. If man can bend the truth to his own desires, will he not also want to bend other men in like manner? Those who despise charity are also those who think that truth depends, not on *what is,* but on what at each moment serves most effectively their party, their greed, or their hate. And those who despise charity also despise good will. The word to them seems pale and dangerously liberal. They forget—at any rate the Christians among them—that the word has its origin in the Gospels. It is true enough that good will is not sufficient, and that men who mistake that will which is good will for that willingness which is weakness cheat people. But good will is necessary and of primary necessity. It is useful in everything. Real, authentic good will indicates the sacred mystery which spells salvation for men and which makes it possible to say of a man that he is purely and simply good. It enables men to go out of themselves to meet their neighbours halfway. That is why the pharisees and the fanatics, walled up in their whited sepulchres, wherein they would like to enclose the whole world, are not only suspicious of good will; they detest the very idea.

The third implication contained in fraternal amity is the dignity of the human person with the rights it implies and the realities on which it is based. I refer to the spirituality of the human soul and its eternal destiny. In the text from which I have already quoted, Gandhi also pointed out that, "It [*Satyagraha*] is called also soul-force, because a definite recognition of the soul within is a necessity, if a *Satyagrahi* is to believe that death does not mean cessation of the struggle, but a culmination." I as a Christian know very well on what my faith in the immortality of the soul and the dignity of the human person is based. I read in the Gospels: *What doth it profit a man if he gain the whole world and lose his own soul?* I read also that the hairs on each of our heads are counted, and that the

angels who see the face of the Father watch over each of the children of men, who are equal in that dignity, and that we must love
our enemies. And I read the story of the man who went down from
Jerusalem to Jericho and whom robbers left half-dead by the road-
side. A Samaritan, in other words a foreigner, with whom the Jews
did not mix and whose religious beliefs were different from theirs,
recognized his neighbour in that man by having pity on him;
whereas a doctor of the law and a priest, going on their way with
closed hearts, by so doing excluded themselves from neighbourship
with men. The mysterious words of Christ on this matter mean that
it is up to us really to become the neighbour of any man, by loving
him and having pity on him. It is not community of race, of class,
or of nation; it is the love of charity that makes us what we ought
to be, members of the family of God, of the only community where
each person, drawn out from his fundamental loneliness, truly communicates with others and truly makes them his brothers, by giving
himself to them and in a certain sense dying for them. Nothing
that has ever been said points out more profoundly the mystery and
dignity of the human person. Who is my neighbour? The man of
my blood? Of my party? The man who does me good? No. It is
the man to whom I show mercy, the man to whom is transmitted
through me the universal gift and love of God, who makes the rain
from heaven fall upon both the good and the wicked.

The existence of God, the sanctity of truth, the value and necessity of good will, the dignity of the person, the spirituality and
immortality of the soul: these, and all the other implications bound
up with them which I shall not mention here, correspond to spontaneous perceptions of our reason and to primary tendencies of our
nature; but they are not understood in an identical and univocal way
by believers in the various religions of humanity. Thus Christianity
and Buddhism have different conceptions of the human person; the
survival of the soul has a different meaning for those who believe
in personal immortality and in the resurrection of the body and
those who believe in transmigration; the sanctity of truth appears
in a different light according to the fashion in which both revelation and human reason are conceived; the value of good will has
different connotations for the Catholic who believes in sanctifying
grace, for the Orthodox who believes in the sanctifying uncreated

Spirit but not in created grace, for the Protestant who believes that the merits of Christ are imputed to an essentially corrupt nature, for the Israelite who believes in the Law, for the Moslem who believes in salvation by the mere profession of Islamic faith; and this difference is still greater as between these religious groups and the religious groups who believe in Karma. As regards the existence of God itself, I do not think that Buddhism rejects, as is often stated, the existence of God, nor that it is in reality an atheistic religion. I believe that this apparent atheism comes from the fact that Buddhism has developed historically as a kind of mystical destruction of the Brahmanic affirmation, so that the Buddhist ascesis and Nirvana are, as it were, like a vast apophatic or negative theology, standing alone in emptiness. But this example does serve to cast light on the extent to which the idea of God may differ among believers of the various religions. It should be added that those who believe that they are non-believers may, in their practical lives, by choosing as the aim of their activity the authentic moral good, choose God, and may do so by virtue of God's grace, without their knowing God in a consciously and conceptually formulated manner.

All this goes to show that there is nothing *univocal* between the various paths travelled by men, and that practical good fellowship is not based on a common minimum of doctrinal identity. In a certain sense, *less* than a common minimum is to be found there, since ultimately no notion appears to be univocally common to all the different religious outlooks. Yet in another sense there is much *more* than a common minimum, since among those who, belonging to different religious families, allow the spirit of love to enter into them, the implications of brotherly love create, for the principles of the practical reason and of action and as regards terrestrial civilization, a community of similitude and *analogy* which corresponds on the one hand to the fundamental unity of our rational nature and is, on the other hand, not merely concerned with a minimum number of points of doctrine, but penetrates the whole gamut of practical notions and of the principles of action of each one. The coming together of such men to co-operate for the good of human society is not based upon an equivocation. It is based upon "analogical" likeness as between the practical principles, motions, and progressions implied in their common acceptance of the law of love, and corresponding to the primary inclinations of human nature.

And why should I, a Christian, according to whose faith a single Name has been given to men through whom they can be saved, even in the temporal order, why should I disguise the fact that this community of analogy itself supposes a *primum analogatum* purely and simply true; and that implicitly and ultimately everything which is authentic love, working in the world for the reconciliation of men and the common good of their life here below, tends, under forms more or less perfect, more or less pure, toward Christ, who is known to some, unknown to others?

In this philosophical attempt to solve a difficult problem, I have spoken in accordance with my faith, and I hope that I have said nothing which might offend the conscience of any of my readers. I shall be glad if I have succeeded in outlining with sufficient clarity what are, from my point of view, the foundations of mutual fellowship and understanding between believers of different religious families and of a constructive co-operation between them for the good of civilization. The good of civilization is also the good of the human person, the recognition of his rights and of his dignity, based ultimately on the fact that he is the image of God. Let no one deceive himself; the cause of religion and the cause of the human person are closely linked. They have the same enemies. The time has passed when a rationalism fatal to reason, which has prepared the way for all our misfortunes, could claim to defend the person and his autonomy *against* religion. Both against atheistic materialism and against an irrationalism drunk with inflicting domination and humiliation, an irrationalism which perverts the genuine instincts of human nature and makes of the political State a supreme idol and a Moloch, religion is the best defender of the person and of his freedom.

And finally if I am asked what I believe to be the reason for God's having permitted the religious divisions in mankind, and those heresies which "must be," according to Saint Paul—I should answer: For the education of mankind, and in order to prepare the way for final religious unity. Because on the one hand it is something above human powers to maintain purity and strength in the collective virtues of any natural community, unless it be within the particular hereditary bias of this earthly, sociologically closed social group. And on the other hand the common life of the Church, the Kingdom of God, is that of a spiritual, supernatural, supra-racial, supra-national, supra-earthly community, open to all humanity as it is open to Deity and divine and deifying blood. Much suffering and many purifications throughout human history are necessary to extricate us from any restriction and adulteration of spiritual unity brought about by fleshly unities.

On the day when all the faithful could live with men of other creeds in perfect justice, love and understanding, and at the same time keep the true faith perfectly whole and pure, on that day men would not need actually to practice these virtues toward people of other creeds, because infidelity and religious division would on such a day have vanished from the face of the earth.

ETIENNE GILSON

MEDIEVAL UNIVERSALISM
and *its* PRESENT VALUE

Not to know the middle ages, from which it has come,
is for all Western thought not to know itself.

THE following essay is a lecture delivered by Gilson at the Harvard
Tercentenary Celebration in 1936. As a moralist of history no less
than as an eminent historian, Gilson presents to his contemporaries
the mediaeval ideal of reason and liberty as a lesson to heed in an
irrational world.

HE AIM AND PURPOSE OF THE COMMUNICATION IS
to describe a certain aspect of medieval thought
and medieval culture that can be rightly considered
as typical of that period, and whose lasting value
is so high that everything should be done in order
to revive it under some form suitable to our own
times. I am thereby alluding to the deeply-rooted medieval conviction that though the various expressions of truth unavoidably
bear the mark of their local origins, truth itself, both in the speculative and in the practical order, is not true for a certain civilization,
nor for a certain nation, but belongs to mankind as a whole. In short,
truth is universal in its own right.

Commonplace as it may be, such a statement would certainly not be allowed to pass unchallenged by some historians, especially in the field of medieval philosophy. They would rather favor the contrary view, that before anything else, medieval civilization was the work of a new race, whose specific qualities were for the first time expressing themselves in theology, philosophy, literature, and fine arts. These historians do not always agree on the exact nature of the message brought by that new race to the medieval world, but they seldom think of questioning its existence. For instance, in his famous *Geschichte und System der mittelalterlichen Weltanschauung,*[1] Heinrich von Eicken has suggested that the German genius had brought to the Middle Ages a hitherto unknown feeling for the value of individualism. According to a more recent philosopher and historian, Dr. H. E. Lauer, things were slightly more complicated. What strikes him as typical of medieval culture is the outstanding part that was played by France in its development. All that was of really vital importance in medieval thought and art, Dr. Lauer says, first originated in France: scholastic theology, scholastic philosophy, poetry, polyphonic music, and Gothic architecture. If we were now to ask him why French philosophers and artists were the first to create new forms of thought and new artistic styles, his answer would be that the French were but a particular branch of the German stock which, being slightly more precocious than the rest, were naturally the first to express the fundamental tendencies of the German race—not individualism, nor a mystical feeling for the unspeakable depths of reality, but something quite different, which Dr. Lauer calls a *Bewusstseinseelenanlage.* Instead of being characterized, as had been the Greeks, by exceptionally brilliant dispositions for intellectual creation, the Germans had an exceptionally fine feeling for moral conscience and its many problems. Let us then suppose that the French were the first among the Germans to develop that disposition, and it will become clear that nobody but they could have created the medieval forms of theology, philosophy, literature, and art.[2]

Such generalizations are always impressive. It is very tempting

[1] Stuttgart, 1887; edition of Berlin, 1917, p. 168.
[2] H. E. Lauer, *Die Volkseelen Europas, Grundzüge einer Völkerpsychologie auf Geisteswissenschaftlicher Basis* (Vienna, 1936), pp. 54-58.

to reduce an enormous amount of various facts to a single cause, yet as soon as we try to reconcile facts with their supposed cause, there usually arise a few difficulties. Even granting that there are such things as races, and that races are characterized by some psychological features scientifically describable, the problem of finding out what psychological features are typical of such and such a race would raise huge difficulties. For instance, without questioning the intellectual ability of the Greeks, it is rather hard to think that Socrates, Plato, Aristotle, the Stoics, and the Epicureans had no special feeling for the nature and exigencies of moral conscience. As to the medieval Germans, I would not at all deny their exceptional ability to deal with moral and religious problems, but it is difficult to forget that they were greatly helped in realizing the importance of such problems by their knowledge of the Old and New Testaments, that is to say, of the two books that are a complete expression of the moral and religious feeling of the Jewish people. As to the French, their own case would raise an incredible number of similar difficulties. We are asked by Dr. Lauer to consider them as an exceptionally precocious branch of the German stock; but the founder of medieval philosophy in France, Peter Abelard, was born a few miles from Nantes, in Brittany, and we know certainly that he never ascribed his philosophical genius to some exceptional qualities proper to the German race. He used to call himself a *Brito,* that is to say, in Abelard's own words, one of those men who are thus called because they are brutes: "Brito dictus est quasi brutus." In spite of some honorable exceptions, the fact remains that "what the man who coined the name *Brito* had in mind, when he copied it from the word brute, was that the better part of the Britons are fools." [3]

Of course, it could be objected that Abelard, though a brilliant exception, was but an exception. Let us therefore grant Dr. Lauer that there was in the Middle Ages such a thing as a distinct French nation, that it was a distinct branch of some common German stock, most generously endowed by nature with a special feeling for ethical problems and so precocious that it was able to do pioneering work in that field. After all, if the French really created scholastic philosophy and scholastic theology, to say nothing of the rest, there should

3 Cf. Ch. de Rémusat, *Vie d'Abélard* (Paris, 1855), I, 3.

be some reason for it. The only question now is: did they actually do it? And, for that matter, did any particular race, people or nation do anything of that kind, between the ninth and fifteenth centuries? Strangely enough, not one of those who have resorted to the most brilliant explanations for the spiritual supremacy of the French during the Middle Ages has even dreamt of questioning the fact under discussion. Everything goes in their theories as if a so brilliantly and perfectly explained fact had lost all rights not to exist. Yet, its existence is an important question and, as it seems, the first one to be asked.

That during the Middle Ages the center of philosophical and theological studies was situated in Paris, is an unquestionable fact. A medieval chronicler once wrote that just as Germany had the Empire, and Rome the Pope, Paris had the University. But the very wording of that striking formula clearly shows that the problem at stake has nothing to do with the particular interests of a nation or of a race. What we today call Europe was then considered as a loose, but real, moral entity, endowed with a unity of its own, ruled by a common temporal power, a common spiritual power, and quickened by a common intellectual and moral life. It is enough to consider the intellectual activity of the Parisian scholars at the time when their newly founded University reigned supreme in the fields of philosophy and theology, to realize the non-national and non-racial character of medieval thought.

Who was the first professor of international repute to teach in Paris? Alexander of Hales, *Doctor irrefragabilis,* born about 1170-1180 at Hales, in the county of Gloucester; he was an Englishman. Immediately after him came Albertus Magnus, *Doctor universalis*; born in Lauingen, in 1206-1207, Albertus was a German. The most famous among his contemporaries was the Franciscan saint, Bonaventura, *Doctor Seraphicus;* born in Bagnorea, in 1221, Bonaventura was an Italian. During the same years when that Italian was residing in the Franciscan convent of Paris, another Franciscan was writing there his main works; born in England around 1210-1216, Roger Bacon, the *Doctor mirabilis,* was not a Frenchman. As to the most illustrious among those professors, Thomas Aquinas, the Angelic doctor, born in 1225 at Roccasecca, near Aquino: he was an Italian. His most dangerous opponent, Siger of Brabant, whose name is honorably mentioned by Dante in the *Divine Comedy,* was what we would today call a Belgian. Saint Thomas' rival in acuteness of mind and metaphysical genius, Duns Scotus, was born about 1265, at Littledean, near Dumfries. Although some of his fellow countrymen might more willingly forgive me for calling him a Frenchman than an Englishman, the fact remains that the Subtle Doctor was Scotch—and very much so, at least if what an old commentator says is true, that one of the main reasons why William of Ockham always contradicted Duns Scotus was that the one was an Englishman while the other was a Scotchman, people who seldom agree (*qui raro concordant*). In point of fact, there is not a single European nation, including Great Britain, Italy, and Germany, to which France is not indebted for part at least of her intellectual and moral formation. This is a debt which, I hope, shall never be forgotten. If, as I honestly believe, I have not overlooked a single important Parisian doctor in the thirteenth century, the question how many Frenchmen were there among them can easily be answered: not a single one. Such is the fact, and were we tempted to call it an astounding fact, our very surprise would be a sufficient indication that we have lost the medieval feeling for the universal character of true learning and that the Middle Ages still have something to teach us on that point.

As a matter of fact, there was nothing to surprise a medieval scholar in what seemed to him a perfectly normal situation. In the first place, no medieval professor would have considered himself as representing the particular truth of a chosen people, trusted by God and nature with the mission of teaching it to the rest of the world. On the other hand, if he went to Paris as a student, and often stayed there as a professor, it was not because of some exceptional precocity of the French genius. Like everybody else, he knew full well that Paris was an exceptional and, in a way, a unique place of learning. Schools were there the like of which could not be found in any other part of the world, but neither in the mind of an Englishman, of an Italian, of a German, nor of a Frenchman, were those schools a French affair. They were in France, as the Empire was in Germany and the Papacy in Rome, but neither the Empire, nor the Papacy, nor the University was a local institution. True enough, the question why they were there rather than somewhere else could still be asked; it often was, and in the case of the University it received an answer which I beg to relate, for it is both historically and philosophically significant.

In the first chapter of the famous Chronicle of St. Gall, its anonymous author tells us how two Irishmen, who had crossed the Channel on an English boat, once landed on the French coast and arrived at a small town on market day. As was to be expected, those foreigners soon found themselves surrounded by people who wanted to know what sort of goods they had come to sell. The answer was that they had brought nothing with them but wisdom and that their intention was not to sell it, but to give it free to anybody who might care for it. The only reward they were asking for such a gift was a shelter and some food, so that they could teach and live. No sooner had the mighty Emperor Charlemagne been informed of their arrival than he summoned the two scholars to his court. To one of them, Clemens of Ireland, he assigned France as a permanent residence. As to the other one, whose name was Albinus, he was directed to Italy, with the special mission of teaching there all those who might choose to study under his direction.

I am quite ready to grant that the Chronicle of St. Gall is not a model of historical accuracy. In point of fact, the man whom it calls Albinus was not Irish, but English; again, he was not sent to Italy by Charlemagne, but was simply met by the great emperor while he was journeying back from Italy to England; last but not least, the old Chronicler does not seem to realize that the Albinus whom he has described as arriving from England at the end of his first chapter is the same whom he is about to describe as leaving England at the beginning of his second chapter. The main point however is not there. What I am now concerned with is much less the historical reliability of that ancient Chronicle than the general meaning ascribed by its author to the epoch-making events which he relates. What he says on that point at least is perfectly clear: "When Albinus, who was English by birth, heard it said that the most pious King Charles so graciously welcomed all learned men, he boarded a ship and went to him. Now, that Albinus was a disciple of the most learned Bede, and his knowledge of Holy Writ far excelled that of any other man in modern times. For those reasons did King Charles always keep him at his own court until the end of his life, save only during such periods when he was making war. The King felt always proud to be called his pupil, and he himself always called Albinus his own master. He gave him the Abbey of St. Martin, near the city of Tours, so that he could stay there during the King's absences, and teach those who crowded there from all sides in order to hear him." Then comes the final and highly significant statement of the old Chronicler: "Albinus' teaching bore such fruit, that the modern Gauls, or French (*moderni Galli, seu Franci*) now stand the equals of the ancient Romans and Athenians" (*antiquis Romanis et Atheniensibus aequarentur*).[4]

This was of course a naïve exaggeration, but the very enthusiasm by which it was dictated is in itself an instructive fact. Besides, there remains in the old monk's historical tale a solid nucleus of truth. There really was an Englishman who called himself Albinus and whose real name was Alcuin. He had been born around the year 735, the son of noble parents, in the neighborhood of York. Trusted by Charlemagne with the special mission of organizing schools and spreading learning in a then practically wild country, Alcuin so well fulfilled the most ambitious expectations of his master that, at his death, France had already become in Europe a universal center of learning. It is hardly exaggerating to say that, without Alcuin's missionary work, the birth of the thirteenth century University of Paris could not be fully explained; but what is especially interesting for us in that story is something else. It is the fact that, in the eyes of a foreign observer, France had become the main European center of studies, not at all because the French genius had created learning, but merely because, through an Englishman, she had received it from the Greeks. That modest interpretation of facts was never questioned by anybody during the course of the Middle Ages. The French poet Chrétien de Troyes repeated it, in particularly eloquent and moving terms, at the beginning of his rhymed novel *Cligès,* as if it were an obvious and universally recognized truth. We find it quoted again in the *Speculum* of Vincent of Beauvais and in the Great Chronicles of the Kingdom of France. As Chrétien de Troyes had said, what an honor, but at the same time what a responsibility! Having fallen heir to Greek and Latin learning, those men felt that

[4] *Sangallensis Monachi De Gestis Caroli Magni,* lib. I, cap. 1, 2 (PL 98, 1371-1373).

it was their solemn duty to keep it, to foster it, and when such would be the will of God, to pass it in due time to other nations, just as they themselves had once received it. They certainly felt proud of having been selected by God for such a mission, but to the best of my knowledge not a single one ever claimed the privilege of having created out of nothing a new truth and a new culture, either for himself or for his own country.

Unless we see it in the light of that intimate conviction, such an extraordinary institution as the thirteenth-century University of Paris ceases to be an intelligible fact. The slightest pretension, on the part of any nation, to be the independent source of a merely local truth would have made life unbearable to that crowd of Englishmen, Germans, Italians, Belgians, Spaniards, Danes, Swedes, and so on, who were teaching and working together in Paris. Seen from afar, and quite especially from our own times, a university of that type seems so incredible a phenomenon that many historians have tried to account for it by a certain lack of national feeling in the members of the University. I cannot help thinking that there is something wrong in that explanation. Those men were not different from us by reason of something we have, and which they did not have, but rather by something they had and which unfortunately we have lost.

When the English humanist, John of Salisbury, went to France in 1166, his personal reactions to that new environment were most distinctly English. His letters show that he was quite disturbed by the fact that, though he was there on a secret mission, practically everything related to it seemed to be already known in France. Those French, he writes to Thomas of Canterbury, must have very clever spies, be they English or French, for the most private things that have been said in our own deliberations are known by them in the smallest details. The Count of Soissons, for instance, talks about it as though he had personally attended all the meetings. Yet, as soon as that Englishman arrived at Paris and saw its schools, that stupendous sight brought his indignation to an end. "When," John says, "I first descried that ladder of Jacob whose top reached up to heaven, and it was as a way for the Angels of God ascending and descending on it, I felt compelled to confess at the sight of their joyful intercourse that truly the Lord was in that place, and I did not know it. And the famous poetic saying then occurred to my mind: *Felix exilium, cui locus iste datur!*" [5]

What can be said of such great scholars as John of Salisbury was no less true of common students. As everybody knows, each of them belonged to a definite group that was called a "nation," and those so-called nations were not overfond of each other. There was a good deal of national rivalry between them. As Jacques de Vitry tells us: "They wrangled and disputed not merely about their various sects or about some discussions, but the differences between the countries also caused dissensions, hatreds, and virulent animosities among them, and they impudently uttered all kinds of affronts and insults against one another." They affirmed that the English were drunkards, and had tails; the sons of France proud, effeminate, and carefully adorned like women; they also said that the Germans were furious and obscene in their feasts, and so on, until at last, reaching the end of his long catalogue of various abuses, Jacques de Vitry coldly concludes: "After such insults, from words they often came to blows." [6] Since, in spite of their national feelings, those students and masters succeeded in living and working together, there must have been in their minds some other ideal, high and strong enough to hold in check national pride. What was it?

It was, before anything else, a religious ideal. Some historians have attempted to describe medieval Europe as endowed with a political unity of its own. It is partly true, and partly an illusion. In a way the Holy Roman Empire always remained a more or less abstract myth; it was a dream that never came fully true, except, perhaps, much later, in the books of its historians. In the same way, it would be just as correct to say that even medieval Christendom never quite succeeded in becoming a concrete and tangible reality. Christendom, that is to say a universal society of all Christians, tied together, even in the temporal order, by the bonds of their common faith and common charity; men thinking, feeling, and behaving as true Christians should do, loving and helping each other as true children of the same Father who is in heaven—all those

[5] Heinrich Denifle and Emile Chatelain, *Chartularium Universitatis Parisiensis,* I (Paris, 1889), 17-18.
[6] As translated by D. C. Munro in *The Mediaeval Student* (Philadelphia, 1895), p. 19; also quoted by C. H. Haskins in *The Rise of Universities* (New York, 1923), pp. 25-26.

magnificent virtues were perhaps not much more common in medieval societies than they are now. The main difference between our medieval ancestors and ourselves does not lie there, it rather rests with their belief in the absolute value of those virtues. The best among them were fully convinced that there was an order of absolute religious truth, of absolute ethical goodness, of absolute political and social justice, to which differences had to submit and by which they had to be judged. In other words, besides being members of various political and racial groups, those men felt themselves both members of the same Church and fellow citizens in a temporal community whose frontiers were the same as those of Christian faith itself. Irrespective of their various countries, two Christians were always able to meet on the same metaphysical and moral grounds, with the result that no national considerations could ever be allowed to interfere with such questions. Religious life being the same for all, there was no reason why John of Salisbury should not have been appointed as a bishop of Chartres; and why indeed should French people have been appointed as professors at the University of Paris, since better men coming from foreign countries were at hand? They were not asked by the University to teach what was French, but what was true. Thus did it come to pass that, viewing themselves as members of the same spiritual family, using a common language to impart to others the same fundamental truth, those medieval scholars succeeded in living and working together for about three centuries, and so long as they did, there was in the world, together with a vivid feeling for the universal character of truth, some sort at least of Occidental unity.

Is it now possible for us to recover it? I feel inclined to think so, at least to some extent and under certain conditions, the first of those conditions being not to dream of the Middle Ages as of some lost paradise, or a golden age, to which it would be our imperative duty to go back as fast as possible. For better or worse, we are now living in the twentieth century, and the only thing for us to do is to make the best of it. The disruption of medieval Europe into national groups, attended by the growth of more and more nationalized educational institutions, has been, as far as we can judge, a practically unavoidable fact. Let it be added that the multiplication of national centers of culture, first in Europe and later in

America, cannot be considered as in itself an evil. On the contrary, much good has occurred in the past, and much more will no doubt follow in the future, from the fact that many human groups, working in different conditions and developing different mental habits, are co-operating in the same effort for the advancement of learning. Let us therefore quietly accept our own times, with the firm conviction that just as much good can be done today as at any time in the past, provided only that we have the will and find the way to do it.

A second illusion to be set aside is that the present lack of religious unity unavoidably condemns the modern world to live in a state of complete dispersion, both in the moral and in the intellectual order. It is true that the Middle Ages were powerfully helped by their faith in the unquestionable validity of the Christian truth; medieval unity, in so far at least as it was a reality, was essentially the unity of the common faith. Yet it was at the same time something else, which, closely related to it and even rooted in it, was nevertheless distinct from it. When Alcuin died, on the 19th of May, 806, his long-cherished dream was already beginning to materialize; to use his own words, a new Athens had been erected in Frankland, "nay a more excellent Athens . . . which, being ennobled by the mastership of Christ our Lord, would surpass all the wisdom and learning of the Academy." With a remarkable insight, Alcuin had soon perceived that religious unity could not live, and still less quicken political bodies from within, unless it found in them, already established by literary and scientific culture, some sort of natural unity. As he himself once said, in the new Athens the seven liberal arts would be there to support the seven gifts of the Holy Ghost.

The whole intellectual history of the Middle Ages was to justify Alcuin's own position on the question. In those times the central problem that spiritual authorities had to solve was, how to universalize Christian faith? A very hard problem indeed, for they were in charge of the Catholic Church, and catholic means universal; but faith is not universal in its own right because, strictly speaking, it cannot be logically or experimentally proved. The acute feeling of that difficulty can be rightly considered as the psychological origin of the extraordinary development of philosophical culture in the Middle Ages. Since faith could not possibly be proved by reason, the only hope of universalizing it was to make it at least acceptable to reason. Hence the remarkable emphasis laid by medieval theologians on the rational aspect of religious truth, as well as on the universal character of rational truth itself. To most of them the necessary foundation for solid theological studies was logic; to some of them, it was mathematics and experimental science as it was known in their own times; but all of them were of one mind on the fundamental principle, that since there was a philosophical, moral, and scientific truth, it could not but be one and the same for all races and all nations. In short, coupled with their belief in the universal character of religious faith, there was in those scholars an equally strong belief in the universal character of rational truth.

This part at least of their ideal could be fruitfully upheld and, if need be, revived in our own days. The problem of religious unity essentially belongs to the theologians, but the problem of philosophical unity is in itself an essentially philosophical problem, and unless philosophers tackle it, somebody else will solve it for them, and probably against them. This indeed is a point in which each and every one of us should feel vitally interested; culture and learning themselves are at stake, and with them the very freedom of the mind which is their only conceivable source. Whether we like it or not, the sad fact is that after losing our common faith, our common philosophy, and our common art, we are in great danger of losing even our common science and of exchanging it for state-controlled dogmas.

Such a development was to be expected. A good many years ago, at a meeting of the Société Française de Philosophie where the notion of Democracy was under discussion, the French philosopher Jules Lachelier made the casual remark that the only conceivable form of democracy was theocracy and, he added, that very kind of theocracy which William Penn had once established in the forests of Pennsylvania.

Both Lachelier and Penn were no doubt alluding to the Book of Judges (xxi, 25), where it is written: *In those days there was no king in Israel, but everyone did that which seemed right to himself.* Strangely enough, the Book adds, those free men grew weary of their freedom, and as Samuel himself was getting old, they went to him and said to him: *Make us a king, to judge us, as all nations have.* And the word was displeasing in the eyes of Samuel; for he had been a good judge; he had always enforced the law of the Lord, but he was afraid lest, by some fault of his, he had induced the people of Israel to reject that law. The Lord knew his thoughts, and He said to him, *Hearken to the voice of the people in all that they say to thee. For they have not rejected* thee, *but* me, *that I should not reign over them.*[7] Yet, before granting the Jewish people what they wanted, God clearly told them what the right of the king was going to be: *He will take your sons, and put them in his chariots, and will make them his horsemen, and his running footmen to run before his chariots. And he will appoint of them . . . to plough his fields, and to reap his corn and to make him arms and chariots. Your daughters he will also take to make him ointments, and to be his cooks. Moreover, he will take the tenth of your corn, to give his servants.*[8] We have seen all those things, and worse; but since men have declined to be ruled by God, and now that there is nobody to arbitrate between them and the state, who is going to judge the king?

It thus appears that despite its paradoxical appearance, Lachelier's statement was fundamentally sound, in this at least, that as soon as men refuse to be ruled directly by God, they condemn themselves to be ruled directly by man; and if they decline to receive from God the leading principles of their moral and social conduct, they are bound to accept them from the king, or from the state, or from their race, or from their own social class. In all cases, there will be a state-decreed philosophical, moral, historical, and even scientific, truth, just as tyrannical in its pretensions, and much more effective in its oppressions of individual conscience, than any state religion may have ever been in the past.

Against the encroachments of the totalitarian state in its various forms, our only conceivable protection, humanly speaking at least, is in a powerful revival of the medieval feeling for the universal character of truth. I say feeling, because it is a natural temptation for every one of us to coin a truth of his own, made after his own image and likeness, so that its contemplation may give us at the

[7] *I Samuel* viii, 7.   [8] *Ibid.*, 11-15.

same time the selfish pleasure of self-contemplation. We have so often thought, and written, and taught our students that the *discovery* of truth is a personal affair, that we have come either to think, or to make them believe, that truth itself is a personal affair. Yet the most commonplace truth is infinitely better than a whole system of the most original errors. Now, perhaps, is for us the time to remind ourselves and to teach others the old Greek principle, that unity is better than multiplicity. Not uniformity, which is the mere lack of diversity, but unity, that is to say, the rational ordering of a manifold reality. Do we believe that truth is one? Are we convinced that truth consists in finding out an order where there is one as in nature and putting it where there is none, or not enough of it, as in moral, social, and political life? Upon our answer to that first question hangs the future of the mind and of what is left of its liberty.

Should we answer it in the affirmative, it would then become necessary for us to go a few steps farther. If it is our honest conviction that truth is one, it will be our absolute duty to stick to rationalism as the only sound form of philosophy. Humanly and naturally speaking, there is no unifying force above reason. It could even be said that, absolutely speaking, it really is the only unifying force. What is rationally true is universally true, for the only thing that lies behind truth is reality itself, which is the same for all. Not so with feeling, be it moral, social, or national feeling; not so with intuition, be it the highest form of aesthetic or metaphysical intuition; and still less than with anything else with the will, its passions, desires or interests of any kind. Every time philosophy yields to the temptation of giving up reason as an organizing power, it regularly brings about the triumph of those obscure forces whose self-assertion is the only possible justification. Deep intuition is always my own intuition; good taste is always my own taste; sacred feelings are my own feelings, and, in the long run, lawful interests are always my own interests. Where those forces do not serve individual selfishness, they serve the still more tyrannical selfishness of social and national groups. The only thing in the natural order that is unconditionally and unreservedly neither mine nor yours, but ours, is reason. But what is the proper use of reason?

Medieval philosophers would answer that it consists in using it according to its own nature, which is to judge things according to what they are. Every sound rationalism is at the same time a realism. In spite of their many differences, all varieties of idealism agree precisely in this, that nature is determined by the laws of the human mind. Medieval realism, on the contrary, always stood firm on the Greek platform, that the human mind is right when it conforms to reality. In other words, medieval rationalism, taken in its purest forms, always went hand in hand with some sort of realism. Now it is a fact that ever since the seventeenth century realism has been considered by most philosophers as a naïve and antiquated philosophical position. Until the realistic reaction that has recently taken place, particularly in England and in the United States, Scholasticism remained the only upholder of a seemingly lost cause. We are now beginning to realize what vital interests were at stake, in the most concrete order of reality, behind those academical discussions. When it is pursued to its ultimate conclusions, a rationalism of the idealistic type always considers itself as justified in prescribing what reality ought to be. As he rejects all material and external criteria of what is true or false, the idealist usually ends in establishing what is his own individual truth as a universally valid dogma. Reason itself then becomes the very reverse of what it should be; instead of a unifying force it acts as a principle of intellectual and social division.

It is a common experience to every one of us that we are easily satisfied with our own ideas. We are strong on building theories, or a general interpretation of an enormous number of facts, on the knowledge of a very small number of facts. And once our convictions have been formed we stick to them, in spite of all that other people, equally satisfied with their own convictions, may say to the contrary. What does this mean, if not that we are naturally, normally, the prisoners of our own convictions? What is true of our everyday convictions is equally true of philosophy and of science. By deciding that the human mind is free to prescribe its own law to things, idealism has, under pretence of liberating the human mind from those things, enslaved the human mind to itself. This is the reason why we are today confronted with several scientific interpretations of the world, each of which is equally dogmatic in itself and contradictory to the others. As to philosophy, it is strictly true to say that today each philosopher has his own system, and that far from being disturbed at the idea that his system is not accepted by anybody else, he rather rejoices in it. If he were satisfied with accepting as true what everybody else holds to be true, he would not consider himself as original; nor would he be considered as such by the others. As a rule, modern philosophers disagree; it is their dignity, or rather, it is their very essence, because they are idealists, while the only thing which can reconcile different human minds is the recognition of an independent reality upon the existence and nature of which they can agree. True, in the thirteenth century, as in our days, there were many doctrinal oppositions, and many philosophical divergences, but, at the same time, there was a common agreement on a certain number of fundamental doctrines, because all philosophers admitted the existence of an order of things and tried to express it. As the things were the same for all of them, what they could say about things was at least comparable, and what all of them were saying represented at least an effort to express the same reality. Today, the effort of an idealist has no other object than to express his mind, and as all our professors of philosophy in all the colleges and all the universities where idealism is prevailing are teaching their students to express their own minds, to describe, not the world as it is, but the world as they see it, the result is that we have as many philosophies as we have minds; rather, the result is that we have so many philosophies and so few minds.

For indeed, what is a mind that feeds upon itself? It is empty. As St. Thomas Aquinas used to say, the human mind is made to say that that which is, is; and that which is not, is not. Thus centered upon things, the mind feeds upon them, by assimilating them and conforming its own thoughts to their nature. When our knowing power is filled up with things, it is a mind, and then it can express itself, because it is. But it cannot do it unless it first gathers within itself that knowledge which it finds only in the external world. This is the reason why, when a professor of philosophy asks his students to evolve, each of them, an original conception of the world, he forgets that the only real originality for a human mind is not to describe things as it sees them, but as they are, and that unless a man believes that his mind is regulated by things, he will never have anything true to say.

Let us therefore frankly state that we are realists; that we do not care for a system of philosophy so personal that nobody save ourselves would be ready to accept it. The true freedom of mind is to yield to the teaching of facts; to reject our own preconceived ideas every time somebody else is able to show us that they are wrong; in short, mental liberty consists in a complete liberation from our personal prejudices and in our complete submission to reality. This is the true spirit of scholastic realism. And besides, it is Christian. The Gospel does not ask us to say: "It seems to me, hence it is"; or, "I do not think so, hence it is not so"; but, "Est, est; non, non: that which is, is; that which is not, is not." Either we shall be free from things, and slaves to our minds, or free from our minds because submitted to things. Realism always was and still remains the source of our personal liberty. Let us add that, for the same reason, it remains the only guarantee of our social liberty.

For it is a last and all-important feature of medieval philosophy that its rationalism was not only a realism, but a personalism as well. Just like trees and any kind of living things, men are individualized and distinct from each other by their bodies. Such is the metaphysical reason why, grounded as it is on matter, individualism is always a source of divisions and oppositions. When men consider themselves as mere individuals, then so-called Liberalism is bound to prevail, until political disorders and social injustice make it unavoidable for the State to become totalitarian. Individualism always breeds tyranny, but personalism always breeds liberty, for a group of individuals is but a herd, whereas a group of persons is a people. Just as they are individuals by their bodies, men are persons by their intellects. Now it is a remarkable character of intellectual knowledge, at least as medieval philosophers understood it, that it is in us both strictly personal and wholly universal. As a rational being, every one of us is a person, that is to say an original source of true knowledge and of free determinations. Yet, precisely because and in so far as our knowledge is rational, it is universal in its own right. Human reasons and human wills are bound to agree, to the full extent that every one of them keeps faith with its own nature, which is to be rational. Our only hope is therefore in a widely spread revival of the Greek and medieval principle, that truth, morality, social justice, and beauty are necessary and universal in their own right. Should philosophers, scientists, artists make up their minds to teach that principle and if necessary to preach it in time and out of time, it would become known again that there is a spiritual order of realities whose absolute right it is to judge even the State, and eventually to free us from its oppression.

Rationalism, realism, personalism, such were the philosophical foundations of medieval universalism, such also are today the philosophical conditions for its revival. No nations, no races, no learned bodies have anything to lose by favoring such an attitude; never was the French influence more warmly welcomed or more universally felt than in the thirteenth century, when it exerted itself through that strange University of Paris, where not a single one of the most famous professors was French. This is one of the most useful lessons we can still learn from the Middle Ages, and one that should remain before our minds as a safeguard against the worst kind of slavery to which mankind is now being submitted by totalitarian states—mental slavery. In the conviction that there is nothing in the world above universal truth lies the very root of intellectual and social liberty.

BIBLIOGRAPHY

*(Contains simply the sources of the selections used in
the present volume)*

St. Ignatius of Antioch, *To the Romans* (trans. by Gerald G. Walsh, S.J.,
in *The Apostolic Fathers,* New York: Cima Publishing Co., 1947,
pp. 107-112).

St. Basil the Great, *Address to Young Men on Reading Greek Literature*
(trans. by R. J. Deferrari and M. R. P. McGuire, in *St. Basil: The
Letters,* ed. R. J. Deferrari, vol. IV [The Loeb Classical Library,
Cambridge, Mass.: Harvard University Press, 1934], pp. 378-435).

St. John Chrysostom, *On Charity to the Poor* (taken from *The Homilies
of St. John Chrysostom on the Epistle of St. Paul the Apostle to the
Romans,* Hom. XIV [in part], trans. by J. B. Morris, Oxford:
J. H. Parker, 1841, pp. 255-262).

St. Augustine, *The Confessions* (Books VIII, 6.13-X, 42.70, revised
translation by E. D. Pusey, *The Confessions of St. Augustine,* Oxford: J. H. Parker, 1838, pp. 142-223).

St. Augustine, *The City of God* (Book XIX, trans. by Marcus Dods
[*The Works of Aurelius Augustine,* vol. II, *The City of God,* trans.
by George Wilson, Marcus Dods and J. J. Smith, vol. II, Edinburgh:
T. & T. Clark, 1872, pp. 293-344]).

Boethius, *The Consolation of Philosophy* (Books IV-V, trans. by "I. T.,"
revised by H. F. Stewart [The Loeb Classical Library, London:
William Heinemann, 1918, reprinted 1926], pp. 299-411).

St. Anselm of Canterbury, *The Proslogion* (Latin text edited by F. S.
Schmitt, O.S.B. [Florilegium Patristicum, XXIX, Bonn: Peter
Hanstein, 1931], newly translated into English by A. C. Pegis).

St. Bernard of Clairvaux, *On the Necessity of Loving God* (trans. by T. L. Connolly, S.J., under the title *On the Love of God*, New York: Spiritual Book Associates, 1935, pp. 3-65; with some revisions by A. C. Pegis).

Anonymous, *Jesu Dulcis Memoria* (trans. by E. Caswall, *Lyra Catholica*, London—New York, 1884, pp. 56-59).

St. Bonaventure, *The Ascent of the Mind to God* (Prologue and Chapters V-VII [*D.S.S. Bonaventurae . . . Opera Omnia*, 10 vols., Quaracchi: Ex Typographia Collegii S. Bonaventurae, 1882-1902, vol. V, 1891, pp. 295-296, 308-313], newly translated into English by A. C. Pegis).

St. Thomas Aquinas, *Summa Contra Gentiles* (Book I, chapters 2-8; III, 25, 37, 48; IV, 54 [S. Thomae Aquinatis *Summa Contra Gentiles,* Romae: Apud Sedem Commissionis Leoninae, 1934], newly translated into English by A. C. Pegis).

Dante Alighieri, *The Paradiso* (*The Divine Comedy of Dante Alighieri,* the Carlyle-Wicksteed translation, New York: The Modern Library, 1932, pp. 407-594).

Francis Petrarch, *Letter to Denis of Borgo-San Sepolcro* (*Familiarium Rerum* IV, 1 [ed. V. Rossi *Le Familiari* I, Florence, 1933, pp. 153-161], newly translated into English by J. Reginald O'Donnell, C.S.B.).

François Villon, *The Ballade to Our Lady* (trans. by Dante Gabriel Rossetti [*The Collected Works of Dante Gabriel Rossetti,* vol. II, London: Ellis and Elvy, 1890, pp. 463-464]).

Geoffrey Chaucer, *The Parson's Tale* (Part I, from *The Canterbury Tales,* ed. W. W. Skeat, Oxford Press, 1912, reprinted 1947, pp. 674-684).

Thomas à Kempis, *The Imitation of Christ* (Book II, trans. by Richard Whitford and edited by E. J. Klein, New York: Harper and Brothers, 1941, pp. 59-89).

St. Thomas More, *The Four Last Things: Death* (*The English Works of Sir Thomas More,* edited by W. E. Campbell and A. W. Reid, London: Eyre & Spottiswoode, 1931, vol. I, pp. 459-476).

Desiderius Erasmus, *The Paraclesis* (*Desiderii Erasmi Roterdami Opera Omnia,* vol. V [Leyden, 1704], pp. 137-148, translated into English by J. Reginald O'Donnell, C.S.B.).

St. Teresa of Avila, *The Interior Castle* (Seventh Mansion, trans. by E. A. Peers, *The Complete Works of St. Teresa of Avila,* 3 vols., New York: Sheed and Ward, 1946, vol. III, pp. 329-351).

St. John of the Cross, *The Ascent of Mount Carmel* (Book I, chapters 1-13, trans. by David Lewis, *The Complete Works of St. John of the Cross,* London: Longman, 1864, vol. I, pp. 1-51).

St. Robert Bellarmine, *On the Ascent of the Mind to God* (The Thirteenth Step [*V. C. Roberti Bellarmini Politiani, S.J., Opera Omnia,* ed. J. Fèvre, 11 vols., Paris: L. Vivès, 1870-1876, vol. VIII, 1875, pp. 295b-303a], trans. by Peter W. Nash, S.J.).

Blaise Pascal, *Pensées* (Selections [Blaise Pascal, *Pensées et Opuscules,* ed. by Léon Brunschvicg, Paris: Lib. Hachette, 9th ed., 1920], newly translated into English by Alexander J. Denomy, C.S.B.).

John Henry Cardinal Newman, *Apologia Pro Vita Sua* (Part VII [*Apologia Pro Vita Sua: Being a Reply to a Pamphlet entitled* "What, then, does Dr. Newman Mean?," by John Henry Newman, London: Longman, Green, Longman, Roberts and Green, 1864, pp. 375-430]). The original title of Part VII was: "General Answer to Mr. Kingsley." The pamphlet referred to in the title is, of course, Kingsley's notorious tract. The text of Part VII of the *Apologia* herein printed contains the corrections and changes made by Newman in 1865.

Charles Péguy, *A Vision of Prayer* (trans. by Ann and Julian Green, *Charles Péguy: Basic Verities,* New York: Pantheon Books Inc., 1943, pp. 254-273).

Pope Leo XIII, *On the Restoration of Christian Philosophy (The Catholic World,* vol. XXX, October, 1879, pp. 111-131).

Pope Pius XI, *On Reconstructing the Social Order* (Romae: Typis Polyglottis Vaticanis, 1931); reprinted: *On the Reconstruction of the Social Order* (New York: Paulist Press, 1939).

Pope Pius XII, *On the Mystical Body of Christ* (New York: Paulist Press, 1943).

Paul Claudel, *The Satin Slipper* (First Day, Scenes I & V; Third Day, Scene VIII; trans. by John O'Connor, London: Sheed and Ward, 1931, pp. 1-3, 23, 165-180).

Hilaire Belloc, "The Restoration of Property" (taken from *An Essay on the Restoration of Property,* London: The Distributist League, 1936, pp. 7-21).

G. K. Chesterton, "The World Inside Out" (taken from *The Catholic Church and Conversion,* New York: The Macmillan Co., 1926, pp. 75-90).

Christopher Dawson, "The Failure of Liberalism" (taken from *The Judgment of the Nations,* New York: Sheed and Ward, 1942, pp. 57-72).

Sigrid Undset, *The Cross* (taken from *Kristin Lavransdatter,* III, *The Cross,* iii, 5 [trans. by Charles Archer, New York: Alfred A. Knopf, 1945, pp. 998-1047]).

Etienne Gilson, *St. Thomas Aquinas* (Master Mind Lecture, delivered before the British Academy in 1935, and published in the *Proceedings of the British Academy,* vol. XXI, Oxford Press, 1935).

Jacques Maritain, "Who is my Neighbour?" (taken from *Ransoming the Time,* New York: Charles Scribner's Sons, 1941, pp. 115-140).

Etienne Gilson, *Medieval Universalism and Its Present Value* (from *Independence, Convergence, and Borrowing in Institutions, Thought and Art,* Harvard Tercentenary Publications, Cambridge, Mass.: Harvard University Press, 1937, pp. 194-215).

The Best of the World's Best Books
COMPLETE LIST OF TITLES IN
THE MODERN LIBRARY
A series of handsome, cloth-bound books, formerly available only in expensive editions.

MISCELLANEOUS